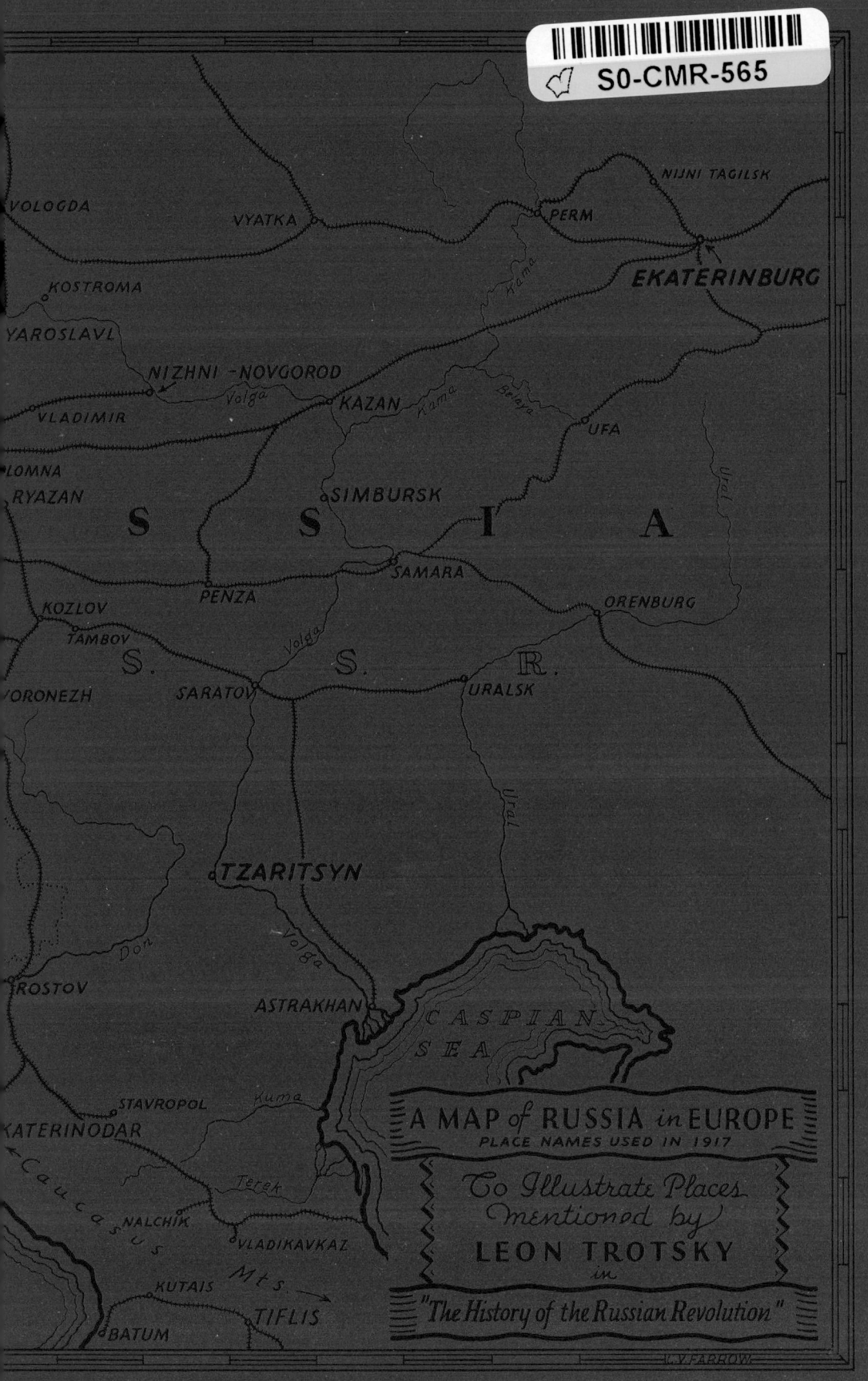

VOLOGDA

VYATKA

NIJNI TAGILSK

PERM

KOSTROMA

EKATERINBURG

YAROSLAVL

NIZHNI -NOVGOROD

Volga

KAZAN

Kama

UFA

VLADIMIR

Kama

Belaya

Ural

LOMNA

RYAZAN

S   S   I   A

SIMBURSK

SAMARA

KOZLOV

PENZA

ORENBURG

TAMBOV

Volga

S.   S.   R.

VORONEZH

SARATOV

URALSK

Ural

TZARITSYN

Don

Volga

ROSTOV

ASTRAKHAN

CASPIAN

SEA

STAVROPOL

Kuma

KATERINODAR

A MAP of RUSSIA in EUROPE

PLACE NAMES USED IN 1917

Caucasus

Terek

To Illustrate Places

Mentioned by

NALCHIK

LEON TROTSKY

VLADIKAVKAZ

in

KUTAIS

Mts

TIFLIS

"The History of the Russian Revolution"

BATUM

L. V. FARROW

LEON TROTSKY

THE HISTORY
OF THE
RUSSIAN
REVOLUTION

Three Volumes in One

1. THE OVERTHROW OF TZARISM

2. THE ATTEMPTED COUNTER-REVOLUTION

3. THE TRIUMPH OF THE SOVIETS

TRANSLATED FROM THE RUSSIAN BY
MAX EASTMAN

SIMON AND SCHUSTER · NEW YORK
1936

CONTENTS

VOLUME ONE

The Overthrow of Tzarism

CONTENTS

VOLUME TWO

The Attempted Counter-Revolution

CONTENTS

VOLUME THREE

The Triumph of the Soviets

vii

A NOTE ABOUT THE AUTHOR

THIS is the first time the scientific history of a great event has been written by a man who played a dominant part in it. It is the first time a revolution was ever retraced and explained by one of its leaders. As the author has chosen to write the book objectively, speaking of himself in the third person, and not dwelling upon his own acts or experiences except as they are recorded by others, it seems fair to give the reader some preliminary glimpse of him and the part he played.

In the Complete Works of Lenin, the first great publishing enterprise undertaken by the Russian Soviet Government after the revolution, there was included a brief biographical sketch of all the important revolutionists mentioned by Lenin. This glossary was prepared by the official historians of the Bolshevik Party under the editorship of Kamenev, one of the leading members of its Central Committee. The paragraph dealing with Leon Trotsky reads as follows:

L. D. Trotsky was born in 1881 (1879—*Ed.*) Organized workmen's circles in Nikolaev, was exiled to Siberia in 1898, soon escaped and going abroad collaborated on *Iskra* (the paper edited by Lenin and others in London—Ed.). He attended the Second Congress of the Party as a delegate from the Siberian Union. After the split in the Party, he joined the Mensheviks. Before the Revolution of 1905 he advanced his own unique and now especially celebrated theory of Permanent Revolution, asserting that the bourgeois revolution of 1905 would pass over directly into a Socialist revolution, which would prove the first of a series of national revolutions. He defended this theory in the paper *Nachalo*, the central organ of the Menshevik faction, published in Petersburg from November to December, 1905. After the arrest of Khrystalev-Nosar, Trotsky was elected president of the first Petersburg Soviet of

Workers' Deputies. Arrested together with its executive committee on December 3, 1905, and exiled for life to the penal colony at Obdersk, he escaped on the way there and went abroad. Trotsky chose Vienna for his residence and there published a popular workers' paper, *Pravda,* for distribution in Russia. He broke with the Mensheviks and attempted to form an extra-party group. . . . From the beginning of the imperialist war he took a clear internationalist position, taking part in the publication of *Nashe Slovo* in Paris, and adhering to the platform of Zimmerwald. Expelled from France, he went to the United States. Returning from there after the February Revolution, he was arrested by the British and freed only at the demand of the Provisional Government, acting under compulsion from the Petersburg Soviet. In Petersburg he joined the organization of the *Mezhrayontsi,* together with which he entered the Bolshevik Party at the Sixth Congress in July, 1917, in Petersburg. After the July Days he was arrested by the government of Kerensky and indicted "for leading an insurrection," but was soon liberated on the insistence of the Petersburg proletariat. After the Petersburg Soviet went Bolshevik he was elected its president, and in that capacity organized and led the insurrection of October 25. He has been a permanent member of the Central Committee of the Russian Communist Party since 1917 and a member of the Soviet of People's Commissars, as People's Commissar of Foreign Affairs until the signing of the peace of Brest-Litovsk, and then as People's Commissar of War."

In this brief outline the three high points in Trotsky's life are indicated in the statement that he became president of the St. Petersburg Soviet in 1905, that is, the leader—in so far as there was one—of the first Russian revolution; that he "organized and led the insurrection of October, 1917,"—which means that under Lenin's political leadership, Lenin himself being in hiding, he commanded the forces in the Bolshevik revolution, about which this book is essentially written; and in the statement that he became People's Commissar of War in the Soviet government. This means that he organized the defense of the new workers' republic, creating the Red Army and conducting a war against the counter-revolutionary forces, backed up with ammunition and supplies by all the great powers of the world— a war which was fought on fourteen different fronts with a battle-line 7,000 miles long and which was carried to victory under his leadership. The degree of Trotsky's independent power as supreme commander during this civil war is indicated in the fact that Lenin, the head of the Bolshevik party and the government, gave him a blank paper endorsing with his signature any order or command which Trotsky saw fit to write upon it.

A comment upon each of these three high points in Trotsky's life from those in a position to judge, will be more useful than anything we can say. Lunacharsky, another eminent Bolshevik, who became Commissar of Education in the first Soviet government, wrote as follows about Trotsky's work in the revolution of 1905: "Trotsky's popularity among the Petersburg proletariat up to the time of his arrest was very great, and it increased as a result of his extraordinarily picturesque and heroic conduct in court. I ought to say that Trotsky, of all the social democratic leaders of 1905 and 1906, undoubtedly showed himself, in spite of his youth, the most thoroughly prepared; least of all, he wore the imprint of a certain emigrant narrowness, which, as I have said, impeded even Lenin at that time; he more than any other realized what a broad struggle for sovereignty really is. And he came out of the revolution with the greatest gain in popularity. Neither Lenin nor Martov made any essential gain. Plekhanov lost much in consequence of his semi-Kadet tendencies. Trotsky from that time stood in the front rank. . . ."

This statement will show how fantastic is the newspaper legend that Trotsky leaped from an obscure position as a tailor in the Bronx to the leadership of the Russian revolution. Trotsky came to New York, after being exiled from Switzerland, France and Spain as a dangerous agitator against the imperialist war, was welcomed by the Slavic laboring population here as the hero of their past revolution, an inevitable leader in the revolution to come. He addressed immense mass-meetings, one of them that many Americans remember in the Hippodrome, and earned his living as an editor of the Russian revolutionary daily, *Novy Mir*.

As to the second great achievement of Trotsky's life, the organization and leadership of the insurrection of October, 1917, it is hardly necessary to introduce comments, for the facts are known to the whole world. The reader will be interested, however, in the following tribute to Trotsky's leadership from one who subsequently became his bitter political enemy. Writing on "The Role of the Most Eminent Party Leaders" (in *Pravda* No. 241) Josef Stalin confirmed the official account of Trotsky's role in October in the following words: "All the work of practical organization of the insurrection was conducted under the immediate leadership of the President of the Petrograd Soviet, Comrade Trotsky. It is possible to declare with certainty that the swift passing of the garrison to the side of the Soviet, and the bold execution of the work of the Military Revolutionary Committee, the party owes principally and first of all to Comrade Trotsky."

The third great achievement of Trotsky's life, his organization and command of the Red Army in the Civil War, is also so well known as to need no comment. There is, however, a passage in the memoirs of Maxim Gorky in which he records Lenin's own tribute to Trotsky's achievement in the military sphere. In a conversation between Gorky and Lenin, the question of some rumored discord between Lenin and Trotsky came up, and Lenin exclaimed: "They lie a lot it seems, an awful lot about me and Trotsky!" And then, striking his fist on the table: "Show me another man who could organize almost a model army in a single year!"

We believe that this present work, "The History of the Russian Revolution," will take its place in the record of Trotsky's life with his youthful prowess in the Revolution of 1905, his organization and leadership of the insurrection of October, his creation and victorious command of the Red Army, as one of the supreme achievements of this versatile and powerful mind and will.

In this book Trotsky has given character sketches of the other eminent men in the Russian Revolution, but he has naturally omitted to give such a sketch of himself. To supply this defect we offer the reader the following additional excerpts from the study of Trotsky written by A. V. Lunacharsky, the Soviet Commissar of Education— the study from which we have already quoted a paragraph. It was published in Moscow in 1923 in a little volume called *Revolutionary Silhouettes.*

"I first met Trotsky in 1905, after the event of January. He came to Geneva, I have forgotten whence, and was to speak with me at a big meeting called to discuss that tragedy. Trotsky was then unusually elegant, in distinction from all of us, and very beautiful. That elegance of his, and especially a kind of careless, high-and-mighty manner of talking with no-matter-who, struck me very unpleasantly. I looked with great disapproval on that dude, who swung his leg over his knee, and dashed off with a pencil an outline of the impromptu speech he was going to make at the meeting. But Trotsky spoke mighty well. . . .

"I met him very little in the revolution of 1905. He held himself apart not only from us, but from the Mensheviks. His work was mainly in the Soviet of Workers' Deputies. . . .

"I remember how somebody said in the presence of Lenin: 'Khrystalev's star has fallen, and the strong man in the Soviet now is Trotsky.' Lenin somewhat darkened for a minute, and then said: 'Well, Trotsky has won that with his tireless and fine work. . . .'

"A tremendous imperiousness and a kind of inability or unwillingness to be at all caressing and attentive to people, an absence of that charm which always surrounded Lenin, condemned Trotsky to a certain loneliness. Remember that even some of his personal friends (I speak, of course, only of the political sphere) afterward became his sworn enemies. . . .

"For work in political groups Trotsky seemed little fitted, but in the ocean of historic events, where such personal features lose their importance, only his favorable side came to the front. . . .

"I always considered Trotsky a big man. Yes, and who could doubt it? In Paris (during the War) he had already mightily grown up in my eyes as a statesman, and thereafter he grew continually— whether because I knew him better, and he could better show the whole measure of his strength on the wider field that history offered him, or because the actual experience of the Revolution and its problems enlarged him and increased the spread of his wings.

"The agitational work of the spring of 1917 does not belong to the task of these silhouettes, but I ought to say that, under the influence of its enormous scope and blinding success, many people near to Trotsky were even inclined to see in him the genuine first leader of the Russian Revolution. Thus M. C. Uritsky, who regarded Trotsky

xiii

with immense respect, said once to me, and, it seems, Manuilsky: 'You see, the great revolution is come, and no matter how intelligent Lenin is, he begins to dim a little beside the genius of Trotsky.' That evaluation proved incorrect, not because it exaggerated the endowment and power of Trotsky, but because at that time the dimensions of the political genius of Lenin were not yet clear. . . .

"The chief external endowments of Trotsky are his oratorical gift and his talent as a writer. I consider Trotsky probably the greatest orator of our times. I have heard in my day all the great parliamentary and popular orators of Socialism, and very many of the famous orators of the bourgeois world, and I should have difficulty in naming any of them, except Jaurès, whom I might place beside Trotsky.

"Effective presence, beautiful broad gesture, mighty rhythm of speech, loud, absolutely tireless voice, wonderful compactness, literariness of phrase, wealth of imagery, scorching irony, flowing pathos, and an absolutely extraordinary logic, really steel-like in its clarity—those are the qualities of Trotsky's speech. He can speak epigrammatically, shoot a few remarkably well-aimed arrows, and he can pronounce such majestic political discourses as I have heard elsewhere only from Jaurès. I have seen Trotsky talk for two and a half to three hours to an absolutely silent audience, standing on their feet, and listening as though bewitched to an enormous political treatise. . . .

"As to Trotsky's inner structure as a leader, as I said, he was, on the small scale of party organization, unapt and unskilful. He was impeded here by the extreme definiteness of the outlines of his personality.

"Trotsky is prickly, imperative. Only in his relations with Lenin after their union, he showed always a touching and tender yieldingness. With the modesty characteristic of truly great men, he recognized Lenin's priority.

"As a political man of wisdom, Trotsky stands on the same height that he does as an orator. And how could it be otherwise? The most skilful orator whose speech is not illumined with thought is nothing but an idle virtuoso, and all his oratory is a tinkling cymbal. That love of which the Apostle Paul speaks may not be necessary to the orator; he may be full of hate, but thought is absolutely necessary. . . .

"It is often said of Trotsky that he is personally ambitious. That is of course pure nonsense. I remember one very significant phrase spoken by Trotsky at the time when Chernov accepted a place in the Government: 'What contemptible ambitiousness—to abandon his historic position for a portfolio!' In that you have the whole of Trotsky. There is not a drop of vanity in him. . . .

"Lenin also is not the least bit ambitious. I believe that Lenin never looks at himself, never glances in the mirror of history, never even thinks of what posterity will say of him—simply does his work. He does his work imperiously, not because power is sweet to him, but because he is sure that he is right, and cannot endure to have anybody spoil his work. His love of power grows out of his tremendous sureness and the correctness of his principles, and, if you please, out of an inability (very useful in a political leader) to see from the point of view of his opponent. . . .

"In distinction from him, Trotsky often looks at himself. Trotsky treasures his historic role, and would undoubtedly be ready to make any personal sacrifice, not by any means excluding the sacrifice of his life, in order to remain in the memory of mankind with the halo of a genuine revolutionary leader. His love of power has the same character as Lenin's, with the difference that he is oftener capable of making mistakes, not possessing the almost infallible instinct of Lenin, and that, being a man of choleric temperament he is capable, although only temporarily, of being blinded by passion, while Lenin, equable and always master of himself, hardly ever even gets into a fit of irritation.

"You must not think, however, that the second great leader of the Russian Revolution yields in all respects to his colleague; there are points in which Trotsky indubitably excells him: he is more brilliant, he is more clear, he is more motile. Lenin is perfectly fitted for sitting in the president's chair of the Soviet of People's Commissars, and guiding with genius the world revolution, but obviously he could not handle the titanic task which Trotsky took upon his shoulders, those lightning trips from place to place, those magnificent speeches, fanfares of instantaneous commands, that role of continual electrifier now at one point and now another of the weakening army. There is not a man on earth who could replace Trotsky there.

"When a really great revolution comes, a great people always find for every part a suitable actor, and one of the signs of the greatness of our revolution is that the Communist Party advanced from its midst, or adopted from other parties and strongly implanted in its body, so many able people suited to this and that governmental function.

"Most of all suited to their parts are the two strongest of the strong—Lenin and Trotsky."

M. E.

PREFACE

DURING the first two months of 1917 Russia was still a
Romanov monarchy. Eight months later the Bolsheviks
stood at the helm. They were little known to anybody
when the year began, and their leaders were still under indictment for state treason when they came to power. You will
not find another such sharp turn in history—especially if you
remember that it involves a nation of 150 million people. It
is clear that the events of 1917, whatever you think of them,
deserve study.

The history of a revolution, like every other history, ought
first of all to tell what happened and how. That, however,
is little enough. From the very telling it ought to become
clear why it happened thus and not otherwise. Events can
neither be regarded as a series of adventures, nor strung on the
thread of some preconceived moral. They must obey their
own laws. The discovery of these laws is the author's task.

The most indubitable feature of a revolution is the direct
interference of the masses in historic events. In ordinary times
the state, be it monarchical or democratic, elevates itself above
the nation, and history is made by specialists in that line of
business—kings, ministers, bureaucrats, parliamentarians, journalists. But at those crucial moments when the old order becomes no longer endurable to the masses, they break over the
barriers excluding them from the political arena, sweep aside
their traditional representatives, and create by their own interference the initial groundwork for a new régime. Whether this
is good or bad we leave to the judgment of moralists. We ourselves will take the facts as they are given by the objective course
of development. The history of a revolution is for us first of
all a history of the forcible entrance of the masses into the realm
of rulership over their own destiny.

In a society that is seized by revolution classes are in conflict. It is perfectly clear, however, that the changes intro-

duced between the beginning and the end of a revolution in the economic bases of the society and its social substratum of classes, are not sufficient to explain the course of the revolution itself, which can overthrow in a short interval age-old institutions, create new ones, and again overthrow them. The dynamic of revolutionary events is *directly* determined by swift, intense and passionate changes in the psychology of classes which have already formed themselves before the revolution.

The point is that society does not change its institutions as need arises, the way a mechanic changes his instruments. On the contrary, society actually takes the institutions which hang upon it as given once for all. For decades the oppositional criticism is nothing more than a safety valve for mass dissatisfaction, a condition of the stability of the social structure. Such in principle, for example, was the significance acquired by the social-democratic criticism. Entirely exceptional conditions, independent of the will of persons or parties, are necessary in order to tear off from discontent the fetters of conservatism, and bring the masses to insurrection.

The swift changes of mass views and moods in an epoch of revolution thus derive, not from the flexibility and mobility of man's mind, but just the opposite, from its deep conservatism. The chronic lag of ideas and relations behind new objective conditions, right up to the moment when the latter crash over people in the form of a catastrophe, is what creates in a period of revolution that leaping movement of ideas and passions which seems to the police mind a mere result of the activities of "demagogues."

The masses go into a revolution not with a prepared plan of social reconstruction, but with a sharp feeling that they cannot endure the old régime. Only the guiding layers of a class have a political program, and even this still requires the test of events, and the approval of the masses. The fundamental political process of the revolution thus consists in the gradual comprehension by a class of the problems arising from the social crisis—the active orientation of the masses by a method of successive approximations. The different stages of a revolutionary process, certified by a change of parties in which the more extreme always supersedes the less, express the growing pressure to the left of the masses—so long as the swing of the movement does not run into objective obstacles. When it does, there begins a reaction: disappointments of the different layers of the revolutionary class, growth of indifferentism, and therewith a strengthening of the position of the counter-revolutionary forces. Such, at least, is the general outline of the old revolutions.

Only on the basis of a study of political processes in the masses themselves, can we understand the rôle of parties and leaders, whom we least of all are inclined to ignore. They constitute not an independent, but nevertheless a very important, element in the process. Without a guiding organization the energy of the masses would dissipate like steam not enclosed in a piston-box. But nevertheless what moves things is not the piston or the box, but the steam.

The difficulties which stand in the way of studying the changes of mass consciousness in a revolutionary epoch are quite obvious. The oppressed classes make history in the factories, in the barracks, in the villages, on the streets of the cities. Moreover, they are least of all accustomed to write things down. Periods of high tension in social passions leave little room for contemplation and reflection. All the muses—even the plebeian muse of journalism, in spite of her sturdy hips—have hard sledding in times of revolution. Still the historian's situation is by no means hopeless. The records are incomplete, scattered, accidental. But in the light of the events themselves these fragments often permit a guess as to the direction and rhythm of the hidden process. For better or worse, a revolutionary party bases its tactics upon a calculation of the changes of mass consciousness. The historic course of Bolshevism demonstrates that such a calculation, at least in its rough features, can be made. If it can be made by a revolutionary leader in the whirlpool of the struggle, why not by the historian afterwards?

However, the processes taking place in the consciousness of the masses are not unrelated and independent. No matter how the idealists and eclectics rage, consciousness is nevertheless determined by conditions. In the historic conditions which formed

Russia, her economy, her classes, her State, in the action upon
her of other states, we ought to be able to find the premises
both of the February revolution and of the October revolution
which replaced it. Since the greatest enigma is the fact that a
backward country was the *first* to place the proletariat in power,
it behooves us to seek the solution of that enigma in the *peculiarities* of that backward country—that is, in its differences
from other countries.

The historic peculiarities of Russia and their relative weight
will be characterized by us in the early chapters of this book,
which give a short outline of the development of Russian society
and its inner forces. We venture to hope that the inevitable
schematism of these chapters will not repel the reader. In the
further development of the book he will meet these same forces
in living action.

This work will not rely in any degree upon personal recollections. The circumstance that the author was a participant in
the events does not free him from the obligation to base his exposition upon strictly verified documents. The author speaks
of himself, in so far as that is demanded by the course of events,
in the third person. And that is not a mere literary form: the
subjective tone, inevitable in autobiographies or memoirs, is not
permissible in a work of history.

However, the fact that the author did participate in the
struggle naturally makes easier his understanding, not only of
the psychology of the forces in action, both individual and collective, but also of the inner connection of events. This advantage will give positive results only if one condition is observed:
that he does not rely upon the testimony of his own memory
either in trivial details or in important matters, either in questions of fact or questions of motive and mood. The author believes that in so far as in him lies he has fulfilled this condition.

There remains the question of the political position of the
author, who stands as a historian upon the same viewpoint upon
which he stood as a participant in the events. The reader, of
course, is not obliged to share the political views of the author,
which the latter on his side has no reason to conceal. But the
reader does have the right to demand that a historical work

should not be the defense of a political position, but an internally well-founded portrayal of the actual process of the revolution. A historical work only then completely fulfills its mission when events unfold upon its pages in their full natural necessity.

For this, is it necessary to have the so-called historian's "impartiality"? Nobody has yet clearly explained what this impartiality consists of. The often quoted words of Clemenceau that it is necessary to take a revolution "en bloc," as a whole—are at the best a clever evasion. How can you take as a whole a thing whose essence consists in a split? Clemenceau's aphorism was dictated partly by shame for his too resolute ancestors, partly by embarrassment before their shades.

One of the reactionary and therefore fashionable historians of contemporary France, L. Madelin, slandering in his drawing-room fashion the great revolution—that is, the birth of his own nation—asserts that "the historian ought to stand upon the wall of a threatened city and behold at the same time the besiegers and the besieged": only in this way, it seems, can he achieve a "conciliatory justice." However, the words of Madelin himself testify that if he climbs out on the wall dividing the two camps, it is only in the character of a reconnoiterer for the reaction. It is well that he is concerned only with war camps of the past: in a time of revolution standing on the wall involves great danger. Moreover, in times of alarm the priests of "conciliatory justice" are usually found sitting on the inside of four walls waiting to see which side will win.

The serious and critical reader will not want a treacherous impartiality, which offers him a cup of conciliation with a well-settled poison of reactionary hate at the bottom, but a scientific conscientiousness, which for its sympathies and antipathies—open and undisguised—seeks support in an honest study of the facts, a determination of their real connections, an exposure of the causal laws of their movement. That is the only possible historic objectivism, and moreover it is amply sufficient, for it is verified and attested not by the good intentions of the historian, for which only he himself can vouch, but by the natural laws revealed by him of the historic process itself.

THE sources of this book are innumerable periodical publications, newspapers and journals, memoirs, reports, and other material, partly in manuscript, but the greater part published by the Institute of the History of the Revolution in Moscow and Leningrad. We have considered it superfluous to make reference in the text to particular publications, since that would only bother the reader. Among the books which have the character of collective historical works we have particularly used the two-volume *Essays on the History of the October Revolution* (Moscow-Leningrad, 1927). Written by different authors, the various parts of this book are unequal in value, but they contain at any rate abundant factual material.

The dates in our book are everywhere indicated according to the old style—that is, they are 13 days behind the international and the present Soviet calendar. The author felt obliged to use the calendar which was in use at the time of the revolution. It would have been no labor of course to translate the dates into the new style. But this operation in removing one difficulty would have created others more essential. The overthrow of the monarchy has gone into history as the February revolution; according to the Western calendar, however, it occurred in March. The armed demonstration against the imperialist policy of the Provisional Government has gone into history under the name of the "April Days," whereas according to the Western calendar it happened in May. Not to mention other intervening events and dates, we remark only that the October revolution happened according to European reckoning in November. The calendar itself, we see, is tinted by the events, and the historian cannot handle revolutionary chronology by mere arithmetic. The reader will be kind enough to remember that before overthrowing the Byzantine calendar, the revolution had to overthrow the institutions that clung to it.

L. TROTSKY

Prinkipo
November 14, 1930

VOLUME ONE

The Overthrow of Tzarism

Chapter I

PECULIARITIES OF RUSSIA'S DEVELOPMENT

THE fundamental and most stable feature of Russian history is the slow tempo of her development, with the economic backwardness, primitiveness of social forms and low level of culture resulting from it.

The population of this gigantic and austere plain, open to eastern winds and Asiatic migrations, was condemned by nature itself to a long backwardness. The struggle with nomads lasted almost up to the end of the seventeenth century; the struggle with winds, bringing winter cold and summer drought, continues still. Agriculture, the basis of the whole development, advanced by extensive methods. In the north they cut down and burned up the forests, in the south they ravished the virgin steppes. The conquest of nature went wide and not deep.

While the western barbarians settled in the ruins of Roman culture, where many an old stone lay ready as building material, the Slavs in the East found no inheritance upon their desolate plain: their predecessors had been on even a lower level of culture than they. The western European peoples, soon finding their natural boundaries, created those economic and cultural clusters, the commercial cities. The population of the eastern plain, at the first sign of crowding, would go deeper into the forest or spread out over the steppe. The more aggressive and enterprising elements of the peasantry in the west became burghers, craftsmen, merchants. The more active and bold in the east became, some of them, traders, but most of them Cossacks, frontiersmen, pioneers. The process of social differentiation, intensive in the west, was delayed in the east and diluted by the process of expansion. "The Tzar of Muscovia, although a Christian, rules a lazy-minded people," wrote Vico, a contemporary of Peter I. That "lazy" mind of the Muscovites was a reflection of the slow tempo of economic development, the formlessness of class relations, the meagerness of inner history.

The ancient civilizations of Egypt, India and China had a character self-sufficient enough, and they had time enough at their disposal, to bring their social relations, in spite of low productive powers, almost to the same detailed completion to which their craftsmen brought the products of their craft. Russia stood not only geographically, but also socially and historically, between Europe and Asia. She was marked off from the European West, but also from the Asiatic East, approaching at different periods and in different features now one, now the other. The East gave her the Tartar yoke, which entered as an important element into the structure of the Russian state. The West was a still more threatening foe—but at the same time a teacher. Russia was unable to settle in the forms of the East because she was continually having to adapt herself to military and economic pressure from the West. The existence of feudal relations in Russia, denied by former historians, may be considered unconditionally established by later investigation. Furthermore, the fundamental elements of Russian feudalism were the same as in the West. But the mere fact that the existence of the feudal epoch had to be established by means of extended scientific arguments sufficiently testifies to the incompleteness of Russian feudalism, its formlessness, its poverty of cultural monuments.

A backward country assimilates the material and intellectual conquests of the advanced countries. But this does not mean that it follows them slavishly, reproduces all the stages of their past. The theory of the repetition of historic cycles—Vico and his more recent followers—rests upon an observation of the orbits of old pre-capitalistic cultures, and in part upon the first experiments of capitalist development. A certain repetition of cultural stages in ever new settlements was in fact bound up with the provincial and episodic character of that whole process. Capitalism means, however, an overcoming of those conditions. It prepares and in a certain sense realizes the universality and permanence of man's development. By this a repetition of the forms of development by different nations is ruled out. Although compelled to follow after the advanced countries, a backward country does not take things in the same order. The privilege of historic backwardness—and such a privilege exists—permits, or rather compels, the adoption of whatever is ready in advance of any specified date, skipping a whole series of intermediate stages. Savages throw away their bows and arrows for rifles all at once, without traveling the road which lay between those two weapons in the past. The European colonists in America did not begin history all over again from the beginning. The fact that Germany and the United States have now economically outstripped England was made possible by the very backwardness of their capitalist development. On the other hand, the conservative anarchy in the British coal industry—as also in the heads of MacDonald and his friends—is a paying-up for the past when England played too long the rôle of capitalist pathfinder. The development of historically backward nations leads necessarily to a peculiar combination of different stages in the historic process. Their development as a whole acquires a planless, complex, combined character.

The possibility of skipping over intermediate steps is of course by no means absolute. Its degree is determined in the long run by the economic and cultural capacities of the country. The backward nation, moreover, not infrequently debases the achievements borrowed from outside in the process of adapting them to its own more primitive culture. In this the very process of assimilation acquires a self-contradictory character. Thus the introduction of certain elements of Western technique and training, above all military and industrial, under Peter I, led to a strengthening of serfdom as the fundamental form of labor organization. European armament and European loans—both indubitable products of a higher culture—led to a strengthening of tzarism, which delayed in its turn the development of the country.

The laws of history have nothing in common with a pedantic schematism. Unevenness, the most general law of the historic process, reveals itself most sharply and complexly in the destiny of the backward countries. Under the whip of external necessity their backward culture is compelled to make leaps. From the universal law of unevenness thus derives another law which, for the lack of a better name, we may call the law of *combined development*—by which we mean a drawing together of the different stages of the journey, a combining of separate steps, an amalgam of archaic with more contemporary forms. Without this law, to be taken of course in its whole material content, it is impossible to understand the history of Russia, and indeed of any country of the second, third or tenth cultural class.

Under pressure from richer Europe the Russian State swallowed up a far greater relative part of the people's wealth than in the West, and thereby not only condemned the people to a twofold poverty, but also weakened the foundations of the possessing classes. Being at the same time in need of support from the latter, it forced and regimented their growth. As a result the bureaucratized privileged classes never rose to their full height, and the Russian state thus still more approached an Asiatic despotism. The Byzantine autocratism, officially adopted by the Muscovite tzars at the beginning of the sixteenth century, subdued the feudal Boyars with the help of the nobility, and then gained the subjection of the nobility by making the peasantry their slaves, and upon this foundation created the St. Petersburg imperial absolutism. The backwardness of the whole process is sufficiently indicated in the fact that serfdom, born at the end of the sixteenth century, took form in the seventeenth, flowered in the eighteenth, and was juridically annulled only in 1861.

The clergy, following after the nobility, played no small rôle in the formation of the tzarist autocracy, but nevertheless a servile rôle. The church never rose in Russia to that commanding height which it attained in the Catholic West; it was satisfied with the rôle of spiritual servant of the autocracy, and counted this a recompense for its humility. The bishops and metropolitans enjoyed authority merely as deputies of the temporal power. The patriarchs were changed along with the tzars. In the Petersburg period the dependence of the church upon the state became still more servile. Two hundred thousand priests and monks were in all essentials a part of the bureaucracy, a sort of police of the gospel. In return for this the monopoly of the orthodox clergy in matters of faith, land and income was defended by a more regular kind of police.

Slavophilism, the messianism of backwardness, has based its philosophy upon the assumption that the Russian people and their church are democratic through and through, whereas official Russia is a German bureaucracy imposed upon them by Peter the Great. Marx remarked upon this theme: "In the same way the Teutonic jackasses blamed the despotism of Frederick the Second upon the French, as though backward slaves were not always in need of civilized slaves to train them." This brief comment completely finishes off not only the old philosophy of the Slavophiles, but also the latest revelations of the "Racists."

The meagerness not only of Russian feudalism, but of all the old Russian history, finds its most depressing expression in the absence of real medieval cities as centers of commerce and craft. Handicraft did not succeed in Russia in separating itself from agriculture, but preserved its character of home industry. The old Russian cities were commercial, administrative, military and manorial—centers of consumption, consequently, not of production. Even Novgorod, similar to Hansa and not subdued by the Tartars, was only a commercial, and not an industrial city. True, the distribution of the peasant industries over various districts created a demand for trade mediation on a large scale. But nomad traders could not possibly occupy that place in social life which belonged in the West to the craft-guild and merchant-industrial petty and middle bourgeoisie, inseparably bound up with its peasant environment. The chief roads of Russian trade, moreover, led across the border, thus from time immemorial giving the leadership to foreign commercial capital, and imparting a semi-colonial character to the whole process, in which the Russian trader was a mediator between the Western cities and the Russian villages. This kind of economic relation developed further during the epoch of Russian capitalism and found its extreme expression in the imperialist war.

The insignificance of the Russian cities, which more than anything else promoted the development of an Asiatic state, also made impossible a Reformation—that is, a replacement of

7

the feudal-bureaucratic orthodoxy by some sort of modernized kind of Christianity adapted to the demands of a bourgeois society. The struggle against the state church did not go farther than the creation of peasant sects, the faction of the Old Believers being the most powerful among them.

Fifteen years before the great French revolution there developed in Russia a movement of the Cossacks, peasants and worker-serfs of the Urals, known as the Pugachev Rebellion. What was lacking to this menacing popular uprising in order to convert it into a revolution? A Third Estate. Without the industrial democracy of the cities a peasant war could not develop into a revolution, just as the peasant sects could not rise to the height of a Reformation. The result of the Pugachev Rebellion was just the opposite—a strengthening of bureaucratic absolutism as the guardian of the interests of the nobility, a guardian which had again justified itself in the hour of danger.

The Europeanization of the country, formally begun in the time of Peter, became during the following century more and more a demand of the ruling class itself, the nobility. In 1825 the aristocratic intelligentsia, generalizing this demand politically, went to the point of a military conspiracy to limit the powers of the autocracy. Thus, under pressure from the European bourgeois development, the progressive nobility attempted to take the place of the lacking Third Estate. But nevertheless they wished to combine their liberal régime with the security of their own caste domination, and therefore feared most of all to arouse the peasantry. It is thus not surprising that the conspiracy remained a mere attempt on the part of a brilliant but isolated officer caste which gave up the sponge almost without a struggle. Such was the significance of the Dekabrist uprising.

The landlords who owned factories were the first among their caste to favor replacing serfdom by wage labor. The growing export of Russian grain gave an impulse in the same direction. In 1861 the noble bureaucracy, relying upon the liberal landlords, carried out its peasant reform. The impotent bourgeois liberalism during this operation played the rôle of humble chorus. It is needless to remark that tzarism solved the fundamental problem of Russia, the agrarian problem, in a

8

more niggardly and thieving fashion than that in which the Prussian monarchy during the next decade was to solve the fundamental problem of Germany, its national consolidation. The solution of the problems of one class by another is one of those combined methods natural to backward countries.

The law of combined development reveals itself most indubitably, however, in the history and character of Russian industry. Arising late, Russian industry did not repeat the development of the advanced countries, but inserted itself into this development, adapting their latest achievements to its own backwardness. Just as the economic evolution of Russia as a whole skipped over the epoch of craft-guilds and manufacture, so also the separate branches of industry made a series of special leaps over technical productive stages that had been measured in the West by decades. Thanks to this, Russian industry developed at certain periods with extraordinary speed. Between the first revolution and the war, industrial production in Russia approximately doubled. This has seemed to certain Russian historians a sufficient basis for concluding that "we must abandon the legend of backwardness and slow growth."[1] In reality the possibility of this swift growth was determined by that very backwardness which, alas, continued not only up to the moment of liquidation of the old Russia, but as her legacy up to the present day.

The basic criterion of the economic level of a nation is the productivity of labor, which in its turn depends upon the relative weight of the industries in the general economy of the country. On the eve of the war, when tzarist Russia had attained the highest point of its prosperity, the national income per capita was 8 to 10 times less than in the United States—a fact which is not surprising when you consider that 4/5 of the self-supporting population of Russia was occupied with agriculture, while in the United States, for every one engaged in agriculture, 2½ were engaged in industry. We must add that for every one hundred square kilometers of land, Russia had, on the eve of the war, 0.4 kilometers of railroads, Germany 11.7, Austria-Hungary 7. Other comparative coefficients are of the same type.

[1] The assertion is made by Professor M. N. Pokrovsky. See Appendix I.

But it is just in the sphere of economy, as we have said, that the law of combined development most forcibly emerges. At the same time that peasant land-cultivation as a whole remained, right up to the revolution, at the level of the seventeenth century, Russian industry in its technique and capitalist structure stood at the level of the advanced countries, and in certain respects even outstripped them. Small enterprises, involving less than 100 workers, employed in the United States, in 1914, 35 per cent of the total of industrial workers, but in Russia only 17.8 per cent. The two countries had an approximately identical relative quantity of enterprises involving 100 to 1000 workers. But the giant enterprises, above 1000 workers each, employed in the United States 17.8 per cent of the workers and in Russia 41.4 per cent! For the most important industrial districts the latter percentage is still higher: for the Petrograd district 44.4 per cent, for the Moscow district even 57.3 per cent. We get a like result if we compare Russian with British or German industry. This fact—first established by the author in 1908—hardly accords with the banal idea of the economic backwardness of Russia. However, it does not disprove this backwardness, but dialectically completes it.

The confluence of industrial with bank capital was also accomplished in Russia with a completeness you might not find in any other country. But the subjection of the industries to the banks meant, for the same reasons, their subjection to the western European money market. Heavy industry (metal, coal, oil) was almost wholly under the control of foreign finance capital, which had created for itself an auxiliary and intermediate system of banks in Russia. Light industry was following the same road. Foreigners owned in general about 40 per cent of all the stock capital of Russia, but in the leading branches of industry that percentage was still higher. We can say without exaggeration that the controlling shares of stock in the Russian banks, plants and factories were to be found abroad, the amount held in England, France and Belgium being almost double that in Germany.

The social character of the Russian bourgeoisie and its political physiognomy were determined by the condition of origin

sion openly disputed the power with the monarchy. However, all the revolutionary forces were then going into action for the first time, lacking experience and confidence. The liberals demonstratively backed away from the revolution exactly at the moment when it became clear that to shake tzarism would not be enough, it must be overthrown. This sharp break of the bourgeoisie with the people, in which the bourgeoisie carried with it considerable circles of the democratic intelligentsia, made it easier for the monarchy to differentiate within the army, separating out the loyal units, and to make a bloody settlement with the workers and peasants. Although with a few broken ribs, tzarism came out of the experience of 1905 alive and strong enough.

What changes in the correlation of forces were introduced by the eleven years' historical development dividing the prologue from the drama? Tzarism during this period came into still sharper conflict with the demands of historic development. The bourgeoisie became economically more powerful, but as we have seen its power rested on a higher concentration of industry and an increased predominance of foreign capital. Impressed by the lessons of 1905, the bourgeoisie had become more conservative and suspicious. The relative weight of the petty and middle bourgeoisie, insignificant before, had fallen still lower. The democratic intelligentsia generally speaking had no firm social support whatever. It could have a transitional political influence, but could play no independent rôle: its dependence upon bourgeois liberalism had grown enormously. In these circumstances only the youthful proletariat could give the peasantry a program, a banner and leadership. The gigantic tasks thus presented to the proletariat gave rise to an urgent necessity for a special revolutionary organization capable of quickly getting hold of the popular masses and making them ready for revolutionary action under the leadership of the workers. Thus the soviets of 1905 developed gigantically in 1917. That the soviets, we may remark here, are not a mere child of the historic backwardness of Russia, but a product of her combined development, is indicated by the fact that the proletariat of the most industrial country, Germany, at the time of its revolutionary

13

high point—1918 to 1919—could find no other form of organization.

The revolution of 1917 still had as its immediate task the overthrow of the bureaucratic monarchy, but in distinction from the older bourgeois revolutions, the decisive force now was a new class formed on the basis of a concentrated industry, and armed with new organizations, new methods of struggle. The law of combined development here emerges in its extreme expression: starting with the overthrow of a decayed medieval structure, the revolution in the course of a few months placed the proletariat and the Communist Party in power.

In its initial task the Russian revolution was thus a democratic revolution. But it posed the problem of political democracy in a new way. While the workers were covering the whole country with soviets, including in them the soldiers and part of the peasantry, the bourgeoisie still continued to dicker—shall we summon or not summon a Constituent Assembly? In the course of our exposition this question will rise before us in full completeness. Here we wish only to mark the place of the soviets in the historic succession of revolutionary ideas and forms.

In the middle of the seventeenth century the bourgeois revolution in England developed under the guise of a religious reformation. A struggle for the right to pray according to one's own prayer book was identified with the struggle against the king, the aristocracy, the princes of the church, and Rome. The Presbyterians and Puritans were deeply convinced that they were placing their earthly interests under the unshakable protection of the divine Providence. The goals for which the new classes were struggling commingled inseparably in their consciousness with texts from the Bible and the forms of churchly ritual. Emigrants carried with them across the ocean this tradition sealed with blood. Hence the extraordinary virility of the Anglo-Saxon interpretation of Christianity. We see even today how the minister "socialists" of Great Britain back up their cowardice with these same magic texts with which the people of the seventeenth century sought to justify their courage.

14

In France, which stepped across the Reformation, the Catholic Church survived as a state institution until the revolution, which found its expression and justification for the tasks of the bourgeois society, not in texts from the Bible, but in the abstractions of democracy. Whatever the hatred of the present rulers of France for Jacobinism, the fact is that only thanks to the austere labor of Robespierre are they still able to cover their conservative rulership with those formulas with the help of which the old society was exploded.

Each of the great revolutions marked off a new stage of the bourgeois society, and new forms of consciousness for its classes. Just as France stepped over the Reformation, so Russia stepped over the formal democracy. The Russian revolutionary party, which was to place its stamp upon a whole epoch, sought an expression for the tasks of the revolution neither in the Bible nor in that secularized Christianity called "pure" democracy, but in the material relations of the social classes. The soviet system gave to these relations their simplest, most undisguised and transparent expression. The rule of the toilers has for the first time been realized in the soviet system, which, whatever its immediate historic vicissitudes, has penetrated as irrevocably into the consciousness of the masses as did in its day the system of the Reformation or of pure democracy.

PROLETARIANS OR RUSH AS DEVELOPMENT

CHAPTER II

TZARIST RUSSIA IN THE WAR

RUSSIA'S participation in the war was self-contradictory both in motives and in aims. That bloody struggle was waged essentially for world domination. In this sense it was beyond Russia's scope. The war aims of Russia herself (the Turkish Straits, Galicia, Armenia) were provincial in character, and to be decided only incidentally according to the degree in which they answered the interests of the principal contestants.

At the same time Russia, as one of the great powers, could not help participating in the scramble of the advanced capitalist countries, just as in the preceding epoch she could not help introducing shops, factories, railroads, rapid-fire guns and airplanes. The not infrequent disputes among Russian historians of the newest school as to how far Russia was ripe for present-day imperialist policies often fall into mere scholasticism, because they look upon Russia in the international arena as isolated, as an independent factor, whereas she was but one link in a system.

India participated in the war both essentially and formally as a colony of England. The participation of China, though in a formal sense "voluntary," was in reality the interference of a slave in the fight of his masters. The participation of Russia falls somewhere halfway between the participation of France and that of China. Russia paid in this way for her right to be an ally of advanced countries, to import capital and pay interest on it—that is, essentially, for her right to be a privileged colony of her allies—but at the same time for her right to oppress and rob Turkey, Persia, Galicia, and in general the countries weaker and more backward than herself. The twofold imperialism of the Russian bourgeoisie had basically the character of an agency for other mightier world powers.

The Chinese compradors are the classic type of the national

bourgeoisie, a kind of mediating agency between foreign finance capital and the economy of their own country. In the world hierarchy of the powers, Russia occupied before the war a considerably higher position than China. What position she would have occupied after the war, if there had been no revolution, is a different question. But the Russian autocracy on the one hand, the Russian bourgeoisie on the other, contained features of compradorism, ever more and more clearly expressed. They lived and nourished themselves upon their connections with foreign imperialism, served it, and without its support could not have survived. To be sure, they did not survive in the long run even with its support. The semi-comprador Russian bourgeoisie had world-imperialistic interests in the same sense in which an agent working on percentages lives by the interests of his employer.

The instrument of war is the army. Inasmuch as every army is considered unconquerable in the national mythology, the ruling classes of Russia saw no reason for making an exception of the army of the tzar. In reality, however, this army was a serious force only against semi-barbaric peoples, small neighbors and disintegrating states; on the European arena it could act only as part of a coalition; in the matter of defense it could fulfill its task only by the help of the vastness of spaces, the sparsity of population, and the impassability of the roads. The virtuoso of this army of serfs had been Suvorov. The French revolution in breaking open the doors to the new society and the new military art, had pronounced a death-sentence on the Suvorov type of army. The semi-annulment of serfdom and the introduction of universal military service had modernized the army only as far as it had the country—that is, it introduced into the army all the contradictions proper to a nation which still has its bourgeois revolution to accomplish. It is true that the tzar's army was constructed and armed upon Western models; but this was more form than essence. There was no correspondence between the cultural level of the peasant-soldier and modern military technique. In the commanding staff, the ignorance, light-mindedness, and thievery of the ruling classes found their expression. Industry and transport continually re-

17

vealed their bankruptcy before the concentrated demands of wartime. Although appropriately armed, as it seemed, on the first day of the war, the troops soon turned out to have neither weapons nor even shoes. In the Russo-Japanese war the tzarist army had shown what it was worth. In the epoch of counter-revolution the monarchy, with the aid of the Duma, had filled up the military stores and put many new patches on the army, especially upon its reputation for invincibility. In 1914 came a new and far heavier test.

In the matter of military supplies and finances, Russia at war suddenly finds herself in slavish dependence upon her allies. This is merely a military expression of her general dependence upon advanced capitalist countries. But help from the Allies does not save the situation. The lack of munitions, the small number of factories for their production, the sparseness of railroad lines for their transportation, soon translated the backwardness of Russia into the familiar language of defeat—which served to remind the Russian national liberals that their ancestors had not accomplished the bourgeois revolution and that the descendants, therefore, owed a debt to history.

The first days of war were the first days of disgrace. After a series of partial catastrophes, in the spring of 1915 came the general retreat. The generals took out their own criminal incapacity on the peaceful population. Enormous tracts of land were violently laid waste. Clouds of human locusts were driven to the rear with whips. The external rout was completed with an internal one.

In answer to alarmed questions from his colleagues as to the situation at the front, the War Minister Polivanov answered in these words: "I place my trust in the impenetrable spaces, impassable mud, and the mercy of Saint Nicholas Mirlikisky, Protector of Holy Russia" (Session of August 4, 1915). A week later General Ruszky confessed to the same ministers: "The present-day demands of military technique are beyond us. At any rate we can't keep up with the Germans." That was not the mood of a moment. Officer Stankevich reports the words of an engineer of the corps: "It is hopeless to fight with the Germans, for we are in no condition to do anything; even the new methods of fighting become the causes of our failure." There is a cloud of such testimony. The one thing the Russian generals did with a flourish was to drag human meat out of the country. Beef and pork are handled with incomparably more economy. Gray staff-nonentities, like Yanushkevich under Nikolai Nikolaievich, and Alexeiev under the tzar, would stop up all cracks with new mobilizations, and comfort themselves and the Allies with columns of figures when columns of fighters were wanted. About fifteen million men were mobilized, and they brimmed the depots, barracks, points of transit, crowded, stamped, stepped on each other's feet, getting harsh and cursing. If these human masses were an imaginary magnitude for the front, for the rear they were a very real factor of destruction. About five and a half million were counted as killed, wounded and captured. The number of deserters kept growing. Already in July 1915 the ministers chanted: "Poor Russia! Even her army, which in past ages filled the world with the thunder of its victories . . . Even her army turns out to consist only of cowards and deserters."

The ministers themselves, with a gallows joke at the "bravery in retreat" of their generals, wasted hours in those days discussing such problems as whether to remove or not to remove the bones of the saints from Kiev. The tsar submitted that it was not necessary, since "the Germans would not risk touching them, and if they did touch them, so much the worse for the Germans." But the Synod had already started to remove them. "When we leave," they said, "we will take with us what is most precious." This happened not in the epoch of the Crusades, but in the twentieth century when the news of the Russian defeats came over the wireless.

The Russian successes against Austria-Hungary had their roots rather in Austria-Hungary than in Russia. The disintegrating Hapsburg monarchy had long ago hung out a sign for an undertaker, not demanding any high qualifications of him. In the past Russia had been successful against inwardly decomposing states like Turkey, Poland, Persia. The southwestern front of the Russian army, facing Austria, celebrated immense victories which made it very different from the other fronts. Here

19

there emerged a few generals, who to be sure demonstrated no military gifts, but were at least thoroughly imbued with the fatalism of steadily-beaten commanders. From this milieu there arose subsequently several white "heroes" of the civil war.

Everybody was looking for someone upon whom to lay the blame. They accused the Jews wholesale of espionage. They set upon people with German names. The staff of the Grand Duke Nikolai Nikolaievich gave orders to shoot a colonel of gendarmes, Myasoyedov, as a German spy, which he obviously was not. They arrested Sukhomlinov, the War Minister, an empty and slovenly man, accusing him—possibly not without foundation—of treason. The British Minister of Foreign Affairs, Grey, said to the president of the Russian Parliamentary Delegation: Your government is very bold if it dares in time of war indict its War Minister for treason. The staff and the Duma accused the court of Germanophilism. All of them together envied the Allies and hated them. The French command spared its army by putting in Russian soldiers. England warmed up slowly. In the drawing-rooms of Petrograd and the headquarters at the front they gently joked: "England has sworn to fight to the last drop of blood . . . of the Russian soldier." These jokes seeped down and reached the trenches. "Everything for the war!" said the ministers, deputies, generals, journalists. "Yes," the soldier began to think in the trenches, "they are all ready to fight to the last drop . . . of my blood."

The Russian army lost in the whole war more men than any army which ever participated in a national war—approximately two and a half million killed, or forty per cent of all the losses of the Entente. In the first months the soldiers fell under shell fire unthinkingly or thinking little; but from day to day they gathered experience—bitter experience of the lower ranks who are ignorantly commanded. They measured the confusion of the generals by the number of purposeless maneuvers on soleless shoes, the number of dinners not eaten. From the bloody mash of people and things emerged a generalized word: "the mess," which in the soldiers jargon was replaced by a still juicier term.

The swiftest of all to disintegrate was the peasant infantry.

As a general rule, the artillery with its high percentage of industrial workers, is distinguished by an incomparably greater hospitality to revolutionary ideas: this was clearly evident in 1905. If in 1917, on the contrary, the artillery showed more conservatism than the infantry, the cause lies in the fact that through the infantry divisions, as through a sieve, there passed ever new and less and less trained human masses. The artillery, moreover, suffering infinitely fewer losses, retained its original *cadres*. The same thing was observed in other specialized troops. But in the long run the artillery yielded too. During the retreat from Galicia a secret order was issued by the commander-in-chief: flog the soldiers for desertion and other crimes. The soldier Pireiko relates: "They began to flog soldiers for the most trivial offenses; for example, for a few hours' absence without leave. And sometimes they flogged them in order to rouse their fighting spirit." As early as September 17, 1915, Kuropatkin wrote, citing Guchkov: "The lower orders began the war with enthusiasm; but now they are weary, and with the continual retreats have lost faith in a victory." At about the same time the Minister of the Interior spoke of the presence in Moscow of 30,000 convalescent soldiers: "That's a wild crowd of libertines knowing no discipline, rough-housing, getting into fights with the police (not long ago a policeman was killed by soldiers), rescuing arrested men, etc. Undoubtedly, in case of disorders this entire horde will take the side of the mob." The same soldier, Pireiko, writes: "Everyone, to the last man, was interested in nothing but peace . . . Who should win and what kind of peace it would be, that was of small interest to the army. It wanted peace at any cost, for it was weary of war."

An observant woman, Feodorchenko, serving as sister of mercy, listened to the conversations of the soldiers, almost to their thoughts, and cleverly wrote them down on scattered slips of paper. The little book thus produced, *The People at War*, permits us to look in that laboratory where bombs, barbed-wire entanglements, suffocating gases, and the baseness of those in power, had been fashioning for long months the consciousness of several million Russian peasants, and where along with human bones age-old prejudices were cracking. In many of the self-

21

made aphorisms of the soldiers appear already the slogans of the coming civil war.

General Ruszky complained in December 1916 that Riga was the misfortune of the northern front. This is a "nest of propaganda, and so is Dvinsk." General Brussilov confirmed this: From the Riga district troops arrive demoralized; soldiers refuse to attack. They lifted one company commander on the points of their bayonets. It was necessary to shoot several men, etc., etc. "The ground for the final disintegration of the army was prepared long before the revolution," concedes Rodzianko, who was in close association with the officers and visited the front.

The revolutionary elements, scattered at first, were drowned in the army almost without a trace, but with the growth of the general discontent they rose to the surface. The sending of striking workers to the front as a punishment increased the ranks of the agitators and the retreat gave them a favorable audience. "The army in the rear and especially at the front," reports a secret service agent, "is full of elements of which some are capable of becoming active forces of insurrection, and others may merely refuse to engage in punitive activities." The Gendarme Administration of the Petrograd province declares in October 1916, on the basis of a report made by a representative of the Land Union, that "the mood in the army is alarming, the relation between officers and soldiers is extremely tense, even bloody encounters are taking place. Deserters are to be met everywhere by the thousands. Everyone who comes near the army must carry away a complete and convincing impression of the utter moral disintegration of the troops." Out of caution the report adds that although much in these communications seems hardly probable, nevertheless it must be believed, since many physicians returning from the active army have made reports to the same effect. The mood of the rear corresponded to that of the front. At a conference of the Kadet party in October 1916, a majority of the delegates remarked upon the apathy and lack of faith in the victorious outcome of the war "in all layers of the population, but especially in the villages and among the city poor." On October 30, 1916, the director of the Police Department wrote, in a summary of his report, of "the weariness of war to be observed everywhere, and the longing for a swift peace, regardless of the conditions upon which it is concluded." In a few months all these gentlemen—deputies, police, generals and land representatives, physicians and former gendarmes—will nevertheless assert that the revolution killed patriotism in the army, and that the Bolsheviks snatched a sure victory out of their hands.

*

THE place of coryphées, in the chorus of military patriotism, undoubtedly belonged to the Constitutional Democrats (Kadets). Having already in 1905 broken its dubious ties with the revolution, liberalism at the beginning of the counter-revolutionary period had raised the banner of imperialism. One thing flowed from another: once it proved impossible to purge the country of the feudal rubbish in order to assure to the bourgeoisie a dominant position, it remained to form a union with the monarchy and the nobility in order to assure to capital the best position in the world market. If it is true that the world catastrophe was prepared in various quarters, so that it arrived to a certain degree unexpectedly even to its most responsible organizers, it is equally indubitable that Russian liberalism, as the inspirer of the foreign policy of the monarchy, did not occupy the last place in its preparation. The war of 1914 was quite rightly greeted by the leaders of the Russian bourgeoisie as their war. In a solemn session of the State Duma on July 26, 1914, the president of the Kadet faction announced: "We will make no conditions or demands. We will simply throw in the scales our firm determination to conquer the enemy." In Russia, too, national unity became the official doctrine. During a patriotic manifestation in Moscow the master of ceremonies, Count Benkendorff, cried to the diplomats: "Look! There is your revolution which they were prophesying in Berlin!" "A similar thought," explained the French minister Paléologue, "was evidently in the minds of all." People considered it their duty to nourish and propagate illusions in a situation which, it would seem, absolutely forbade illusions.

23

They did not wait long for sobering lessons. Very soon after the beginning of the war one of the more expansive Kadets, a lawyer and landlord, Rodichev, exclaimed at a session of the Central Committee of his party: "Do you really think we can conquer with those fools?" Events proved that it was not possible to conquer with fools. Liberalism, having more than half lost faith in the victory, tried to employ the momentum of the war in order to carry out a purgation of the camarilla and compel the monarchy to a compromise. The chief implement towards this end was to accuse the court party of Germanophilism and of preparing a separate peace.

In the spring of 1915, while the weaponless soldiers were retreating along the whole front, it was decided in governmental circles, not without pressure from the Allies, to recruit the initiative of private industry for work in behalf of the army. The Special Conference called for this end included, along with bureaucrats, the more influential industrialists. The Land and City unions which had arisen at the beginning of the war, and the Military-Industrial Committees created in the spring of 1915, became the points of support of the bourgeoisie in the struggle for victory and for power. The State Duma, backed by these organizations, was induced to intercede more confidently between the bourgeoisie and the monarchy.

These broad political perspectives did not, however, distract attention from the important problems of the day. Out of the Special Conference as out of a central reservoir tens of hundreds of millions, mounting up to billions, flowed down through distributing canals, abundantly irrigating the industries and incidentally nourishing numberless appetites. In the State Duma and in the press a few of the war profits for 1914 and 1915 were published. The Moscow textile company of the Riabushinskys showed a net profit of 75 per cent; the Tver Company, 111 per cent; the copper-works of Kolchugin netted over 12 million on a basic capital of 10 million. In this sector patriotic virtue was rewarded generously, and moreover immediately.

Speculation of all kinds and gambling on the market went to the point of paroxysm. Enormous fortunes arose out of the bloody foam. The lack of bread and fuel in the capital did not prevent the court jeweler Faberget from boasting that he had never before done such a flourishing business. Lady-in-waiting Vyrubova says that in no other season were such gowns to be seen as in the winter of 1915-16, and never were so many diamonds purchased. The night clubs were brimful of heroes of the rear, legal deserters, and simply respectable people too old for the front but sufficiently young for the joys of life. The grand dukes were not among the last to enjoy this feast in times of plague. Nobody had any fear of spending too much. A continual shower of gold fell from above. "Society" held out its hands and pockets, aristocratic ladies spread their skirts high, everybody splashed about in the bloody mud—bankers, heads of the commissariat, industrialists, ballerinas of the tzar and the grand dukes, orthodox prelates, ladies-in-waiting, liberal deputies, generals of the front and rear, radical lawyers, illustrious mandarins of both sexes, innumerable nephews, and more particularly nieces. All came running to grab and gobble, in fear lest the blessed rain should stop. And all rejected with indignation the shameful idea of a premature peace.

Common gains, external defeats, and internal dangers, drew together the parties of the ruling classes. The Duma, divided on the eve of the war, achieved in 1915 its patriotic oppositional majority which received the name of "Progressive Bloc." The official aim of this bloc was of course declared to be "a satisfaction of the needs created by the war." On the left the social-democrats and Trudoviks did not enter the bloc; on the right the notorious Black Hundred groups. All the other factions of the Duma—the Kadets, Progressives, three groups of Octobrists, the Center and a part of the Nationalists, entered the bloc or adhered to it—as also the national groups: Poles, Lithuanians, Mussulmans, Jews, etc. In order not to frighten the tzar with the formula of a responsible ministry, the bloc demanded "a united government composed of men enjoying the confidence of the country." The Minister of the Interior, Prince Sherbatov, at that time characterized the bloc as a temporary "union called forth by the danger of social revolution." It required no great penetration to realize this. Miliukov, the leader of the Kadets, and thus also of the oppositional bloc, said at a conference of his party: "We are treading a volcano. . . . The tension has reached its extreme limit. . . . A carelessly dropped match will be enough to start a terrible conflagration. . . . Whatever the government—whether good or bad—a strong government is needed now more than ever before."

The hope that the tzar, under the burden of defeat, would grant concessions, was so great that in the liberal press there appeared in August the slate of a proposed "Cabinet of confidence" with the president of the Duma, Rodzianko, as premier (according to another version, the president of the Land Union, Prince Lvov, was indicated for that office), Guchkov as Minister of the Interior, Miliukov, Foreign Minister, etc. A majority of these men who here nominated themselves for a union with the tzar against the revolution, turned up a year later as members of the "Revolutionary Government." History has permitted herself such antics more than once. This time the joke was at least a brief one.

A majority of the ministers of Goremykin's cabinet were no less frightened than the Kadets by the course things were taking, and therefore inclined towards an agreement with the Progressive Bloc. "A government which has not behind it the confidence of the supreme ruler, nor the army, nor the cities, nor the zemstvos, nor the nobles, nor the merchants, nor the workers, not only cannot function, but cannot even exist—the thing is obviously absurd." In these words, Prince Sherbatov in August 1915 appraised the government in which he himself was Minister of the Interior. "If you only arrange the scene properly and offer a loophole," said the Foreign Minister Sazonov, "the Kadets will be the first to propose a compromise. Miliukov is the greatest possible bourgeois and fears a social revolution above everything. Besides, a majority of the Kadets are trembling for their own capital." Miliukov on his side considered that the Progressive Bloc "would have to give in somewhat." Both sides were ready to bargain, and everything seemed thoroughly oiled. But on August 29 the Premier, Goremykin, a bureaucrat weighed down with years and honors, an old cynic playing politics between two games of *grand-patience* and defending himself against all complaints by remarking that the war is "not my business," journeyed out to the tzar at headquarters and returned with the information that all and everybody should remain in their places, except the rambunctious Duma, which was to be dissolved on the 3rd of September. The reading of the tzar's order dissolving the Duma was heard without a single word of protest: the deputies gave a "hurrah" for the tzar, and dispersed.

How did the tzar's government, supported according to its own confession by nobody at all, survive for over a year and a half after that? A temporary success of the Russian troops undoubtedly exerted its influence and this was reënforced by the good golden rain. The successes at the front soon ceased, to be sure, but the profits at the rear continued. However, the chief cause of the successful propping up of the monarchy for twelve months before its fall, was to be found in a sharp division in the popular discontent. The chief of the Moscow Secret Service Department reported a rightward tendency of the bourgeoisie under the influence of "a fear of possible revolutionary excesses after the war." During the war, we note, a revolution was still considered impossible. The industrialists were alarmed, over and above that, by "a coquetting of certain leaders of the Military Industrial Committee with the proletariat." The general conclusion of this colonel of gendarmes, Martynov—in whom a professional reading of Marxist literature had left some traces—announced as the cause of a certain improvement in the political situation "the steadily growing differentiation of social classes concealing a sharp contradiction in their interests, a contradiction felt especially keenly in the times we are living through."

The dissolution of the Duma in September 1915 was a direct challenge to the bourgeoisie, not to the workers. But while the liberals were dispersing with cries of "Hurrah!"—to be sure, not very enthusiastic cries—the workers of Petrograd and Moscow responded with strikes of protest. That cooled off the liberals still more. They feared worst of all the intrusion of an uninvited third party in their family discussion with the monarchy. But what further step was to be taken? Accompanied by a

slight growl from the left wing, liberalism cast its vote for a
well-tried recipe: to stand exclusively on legal grounds, and
render the bureaucracy "as it were, unnecessary" in the course
of a mere fulfillment of our patriotic functions. The ministerial slate at any rate would have to be laid aside for a time.

The situation in those days was getting worse automatically.
In May 1916 the Duma was again convoked, but nobody knew
exactly what for. The Duma, in any case, had no intention of
summoning a revolution, and aside from that there was nothing
for it to say. "At that session"—Rodzianko remembers—"the
proceedings were languid; the deputies attended irregularly.
. . . The continual struggle seemed fruitless, the government
would listen to nothing, irregularities were increasing, and the
country was headed for ruin." In the bourgeoisie's fear of
revolution and its impotence without revolution, the monarchy
found, during the year 1916, a simulacrum of social support.

By autumn the situation was still worse. The hopelessless
of the war had become evident to all. The indignation of the
popular masses threatened any moment to flow over the brim.
While attacking the court party as before for Germanophilism,
the liberals now deemed it necessary to feel out the chances of
peace themselves, preparing their own future. Only in this way
can you explain the negotiations of one of the leaders of the
Progressive Bloc, the deputy Protopopov, with the German
diplomat, Warburg, in Stockholm in the autumn of 1916. The
Duma delegation, making friendly visits to the French and
English, could easily convince itself in Paris and London that
the dear Allies intended in the course of the war to squeeze
all the live juice out of Russia, in order after the victory to
make this backward country their chief field of economic exploitation. A defeated Russia in tow to a victorious Entente
would have meant a colonial Russia. The Russian possessing
classes had no other course but to try to free themselves from
the too close embraces of the Entente, and find an independent
road to peace, making use of the antagonism of the two more
powerful camps. The meeting of the Duma deputy with the
German diplomat, as a first step on this road, was both a threat
in the direction of the Allies with a view to gaining concessions,

and a feeling out of the actual possibilities of rapprochement with Germany. Protopopov was acting in agreement not only with the tzarist diplomats—the meeting occurred in the presence of the Russian ambassador in Sweden—but also with the whole delegation of the State Duma. Incidentally the liberals by means of this reconnoiter were pursuing a not unimportant domestic goal. "Rely on us"—they were hinting to the tzar— "and we will make you a separate peace better and more reliable than Stürmer [1] can." According to Protopopov's scheme—that is, the scheme of his backers—the Russian government was to inform the Allies "several months in advance" that she would be compelled to end the war, and that if the Allies refused to institute peace negotiations, Russia would have to conclude a separate peace with Germany. In his confession written after the revolution, Protopopov speaks as of something which goes without saying of the fact that "all reasonable people in Russia, among them probably all the leaders of the party of 'the People's Freedom' (Kadets), were convinced that Russia was unable to continue the war."

The tzar, to whom Protopopov upon his return reported his journey and negotiations, treated the idea of a separate peace with complete sympathy. He merely did not see the necessity of drawing the liberals into the business. The fact that Protopopov himself was included incidentally in the staff of the court camarilla, having broken with the Progressive Bloc, is explained by the personal character of this fop, who had fallen in love, according to his own words, with the tzar and the tzarina—and at the same time, we may add, with an expected portfolio as Minister of the Interior. But this episode of Protopopov's treason to liberalism does not alter the general content of the liberal foreign policy—a mixture of greed, cowardice and treachery.

The Duma again assembled on November 1. The tension in the country had become unbearable. Decisive steps were expected of the Duma. It was necessary to do something, or at the very least say something. The Progressive Bloc found itself again compelled to resort to parliamentary exposures. Count-

[1] Prime Minister from January to November 1916. [Trans.]

29

ing over from the tribune the chief steps taken by the government, Miliukov asked after each one: "Was this stupidity or treason?" High notes were sounded also by other deputies. The government was almost without defenders. It answered in its usual way: the speeches of the Duma orators were forbidden publication. The speeches therefore circulated by the million. There was not a government department, not only in the rear but at the front, where the forbidden speeches were not transcribed—frequently with additions corresponding to the temperament of the transcriber. The reverberation of the debate of November 1 was such that terror seized the very authors of the arraignment.

A group of extreme rights, sturdy bureaucrats inspired by Durnovo, who had put down the revolution of 1905, took that moment to present to the tzar a proposed program. The eye of these experienced officials, trained in a serious police school, saw not badly and pretty far, and if their prescription was no good, it is only because no medicine existed for the sickness of the old régime. The authors of the program speak against any concessions whatever to the bourgeois opposition, not because the liberals want to go too far, as think the vulgar Black Hundreds—upon whom these official reactionaries look with some scorn—no, the trouble is that the liberals are "so weak, so disunited and, to speak frankly, so mediocre, that their triumph would be as brief as it would be unstable." The weakness of the principal opposition party, the "Constitutional Democrats" (Kadets), is indicated, they point out, by its very name. It is called democratic, when it is in essence bourgeois. Although to a considerable degree a party of liberal landlords, it has signed a program of compulsory land redemption. "Without these trumps from a deck not their own"—write these secret counselors, using the images to which they are accustomed— "the Kadets are nothing more than a numerous association of liberal lawyers, professors and officials of various departments— nothing more." A revolutionist, they point out, is a different thing. They accompany their recognition of the significance of the revolutionary parties with a grinding of teeth: "The danger and strength of these parties lies in the fact that they have

30

an idea, they have money (!), they have a crowd ready and well organized." The revolutionary parties "can count on the sympathy of an overwhelming majority of the peasantry, which will follow the proletariat the very moment the revolutionary leaders point a finger to other people's land." What would a responsible ministry yield in these circumstances? "A complete and final destruction of the right parties, a gradual swallowing of the intermediate parties—the Center, the Liberal-Conservatives, the Octobrists and the Progressives of the Kadet party—which at the beginning would have a decisive importance. But the same fate would menace the Kadets . . . and afterwards would come the revolutionary mob, the Commune, destruction of the dynasty, pogroms of the possessing classes, and finally the peasant-brigand." It is impossible to deny that the police anger here rises to a certain kind of historic vision.

The positive part of their program was not new, but consistent: a government of ruthless partisans of the autocracy; abolition of the Duma; martial law in both capitals; preparation of forces for putting down a rebellion. This program did in its essentials become the basis of the government policy of the last pre-revolutionary months. But its success presupposed a power which Durnovo had had in his hands in the winter of 1905, but which by the autumn of 1917 no longer existed. The monarchy tried, therefore, to strangle the country stealthily and in sections. Ministers were shifted upon the principle of "our people"—meaning those unconditionally devoted to the tzar and tzarina. But these "our people"—especially the renegade Protopopov—were insignificant and pitiful. The Duma was not abolished, but again dissolved. The declaration of martial law in Petrograd was saved for a moment when the revolution had already triumphed. And the military forces prepared for putting down the rebellion were themselves seized by rebellion. All this became evident after two or three months.

Liberalism in those days was making its last efforts to save the situation. All the organizations of the enfranchised bourgeoisie supported the November speeches of the Duma opposition with a series of new declarations. The most impudent of these was the resolution of the Union of Cities on December 9: "Irresponsible criminals, fanatics, are preparing for Russia's defeat, shame and slavery." The State Duma was urged "not to disperse until the formation of a responsible government is attained." Even the State Council, organ of the bureaucracy and of the vast properties, expressed itself in favor of calling to power people who enjoyed the confidence of the country. A similar intercession was made by a session of the united nobility: even the moss-covered stones cried out. But nothing was changed. The monarchy would not let the last shreds of power slip out of its hands.

The last session of the last Duma was convoked, after waverings and delays, on February 14, 1917. Only two weeks remained before the coming of revolution. Demonstrations were expected. In the Kadet organ *Rech*, alongside an announcement by the chief of the Petrograd Military District, General Khabalov, forbidding demonstrations, was printed a letter from Miliukov warning the workers against "dangerous and bad counsel" issuing from "dark sources." In spite of strikes, the opening of the Duma was sufficiently peaceful. Pretending that the question of power no longer interested it, the Duma occupied itself with a critical, but still strictly business question: food supplies. The mood was languid, as Rodzianko subsequently remembered: "We felt the impotence of the Duma, weariness of a futile struggle." Miliukov kept repeating that the Progressive Bloc "will act with words and with words only." Such was the Duma that entered the whirlpool of the February revolution.

CHAPTER III

THE PROLETARIAT AND THE PEASANTRY

THE Russian proletariat learned its first steps in the political circumstances created by a despotic state. Strikes forbidden by law, underground circles, illegal proclamations, street demonstrations, encounters with the police and with troops—such was the school created by the combination of a swiftly developing capitalism with an absolutism slowly surrendering its positions. The concentration of the workers in colossal enterprises, the intense character of governmental persecution, and finally the impulsiveness of a young and fresh proletariat, brought it about that the political strike, so rare in western Europe, became in Russia the fundamental method of struggle. The figures of strikes from the beginning of the present century are a most impressive index of the political history of Russia. With every desire not to burden our text with figures, we cannot refrain from introducing a table of political strikes in Russia for the period 1903 to 1917. The figures, reduced to their simplest expression, relate only to enterprises undergoing factory inspection. The railroads, mining industries, mechanical and small enterprises in general, to say nothing of agriculture, for various reasons do not enter into the count. But the changes in the strike curve in the different periods emerge no less clearly for this.

We have before us a curve—the only one of its kind—of the political temperature of a nation carrying in its womb a great revolution. In a backward country with a small proletariat—for in all the enterprises undergoing factory inspection there were only about 1½ million workers in 1905, about 2 million in 1917—the strike movement attains such dimensions as it never knew before anywhere in the world. With the weakness of the petty bourgeois democracy, the scatteredness and political blindness of the peasant movement, the revolu-

33

tionary strike of the workers becomes the battering ram which the awakening nation directs against the walls of absolutism. Participants in political strikes in 1905 numbering 1,843,000—workers participating in several strikes are here, of course counted twice—that number alone would permit us to put our finger on the revolutionary year in our table, if we knew nothing else about the Russian political calendar.

Year	Number in thousands of participants in political strikes
1903	87*
1904	25*
1905	1,843
1906	651
1907	540
1908	93
1909	8
1910	4
1911	8
1912	550
1913	502
1914 (first half)	1,059
1915	156
1916	310
1917 (January-February)	575

* The figures for 1903 and 1904 refer to all strikes, the economic undoubtedly predominating.

For 1904, the first year of the Russo-Japanese war, the factory inspection indicates in all only 25,000 strikers. In 1905, political and economic strikes together involved 2,863,000 men —115 times more than in the previous year. This remarkable fact by itself would suggest the thought that a proletariat, impelled by the course of events to improvise such unheard-of revolutionary activities, must at whatever cost produce from its depths an organization corresponding to the dimensions of the struggle and the colossal tasks. This organization was the soviets—brought into being by the first revolution, and made the instrument of the general strike and the struggle for power.

Beaten in the December uprising of 1905, the proletariat

during the next two years makes heroic efforts to defend a part of the conquered positions. These years, as our strike figures show, still belong directly to the revolution, but they are the years of ebb. The four following years (1908-11) emerge in our mirror of strike statistics as the years of victorious counter-revolution. An industrial crisis coincident with this still further exhausts the proletariat, already bled white. The depth of the fall is symmetrical with the height of the rise. National convulsions find their reflection in these simple figures.

The industrial boom beginning in 1910 lifted the workers to their feet, and gave a new impulse to their energy. The figures for 1912-14 almost repeat those for 1905-07, but in the opposite order: not from above downwards, but from below up. On a new and higher historical basis—there are more workers now, and they have more experience—a new revolutionary offensive begins. The first half-year of 1914 clearly approaches in the number of political strikes the culminating point of the year of the first revolution. But war breaks out and sharply interrupts this process. The first war months are marked by political inertness in the working class, but already in the spring of 1915 the numbness begins to pass. A new cycle of political strikes opens, a cycle which in February 1917 will culminate in the insurrection of soldiers and workers.

The sharp ebbs and flows of the mass struggle had left the Russian proletariat after a few years almost unrecognizable. Factories which two or three years ago would strike unanimously over some single arbitrary police action, today have completely lost their revolutionary color, and accept the most monstrous crimes of the authorities without resistance. Great defeats discourage people for a long time. The consciously revolutionary elements lose their power over the masses. Prejudices and superstitions not yet burnt out come back to life. Gray immigrants from the village during these times dilute the workers' ranks. Sceptics ironically shake their heads. So it was in the years 1907-11. But molecular processes in the masses are healing the psychological wounds of defeat. A new turn of events, or an underlying economic impulse, opens a new political cycle. The revolutionary elements again find their audience. The struggle reopens on a higher level.

In order to understand the two chief tendencies in the Russian working class, it is important to have in mind that Menshevism finally took shape in the years of ebb and reaction. It relied chiefly upon a thin layer of workers who had broken with the revolution. Whereas Bolshevism, cruelly shattered in the period of the reaction, began to rise swiftly on the crest of a new revolutionary tide in the years before the war. "The most energetic and audacious element, ready for tireless struggle, for resistance and continual organization, is that element, those organizations, and those people who are concentrated around Lenin." In these words the Police Department estimated the work of the Bolsheviks during the years preceding the war.

In July 1914, while the diplomats were driving the last nail into the cross designed for the crucifixion of Europe, Petrograd was boiling like a revolutionary cauldron. The President of the French Republic, Poincaré, had to lay his wreath on the tomb of Alexander III amid the last echoes of a street fight and the first murmurs of a patriotic demonstration.

Would the mass offensive of 1912-14 have led directly to an overthrow of tzarism if the war had not broken out? It is hardly possible to answer that question with certainty. The process would inexorably have led to a revolution, but through what stages would the revolution in those circumstances have had to go? Would it not have experienced another defeat? How much time would have been needed by the workers in order to arouse the peasantry and win the army? In all these directions only guesses are possible. The war, at any rate, gave the process at first a backward movement, but only to accelerate it more powerfully in the next period and guarantee its overwhelming victory.

At the first sound of the drum the revolutionary movement died down. The more active layers of the workers were mobilized. The revolutionary elements were thrown from the factories to the front. Severe penalties were imposed for striking. The workers' press was swept away. Trade unions were strangled. Hundreds of thousands of women, boys, peasants, poured into the workshops. The war—combined with the wreck of the International—greatly disoriented the workers politically, and made it possible for the factory administration, then just lifting its head, to speak patriotically in the name of the factories, carrying with it a considerable part of the workers, and compelling the more bold and resolute to keep still and wait. The revolutionary ideas were barely kept glowing in small and hushed circles. In the factories in those days nobody dared to call himself "Bolshevik" for fear not only of arrest, but of a beating from the backward workers.

The Bolshevik faction in the Duma, weak in its personnel, had not risen at the outbreak of the war to the height of its task. Along with the Menshevik deputies, it introduced a declaration in which it promised "to defend the cultural weal of the people against all attacks wheresoever originating." The Duma underlined with applause this yielding of a position. Not one of the Russian organizations or groups of the party took the openly defeatist position which Lenin came out for abroad. The percentage of patriots among the Bolsheviks, however, was insignificant. In contrast to the Narodniks [1] and Mensheviks, the Bolsheviks began in 1914 to develop among the masses a printed and oral agitation against the war. The Duma deputies soon recovered their poise and renewed their revolutionary work— about which the authorities were very closely informed, thanks to a highly developed system of provocation. It is sufficient to remark that out of seven members of the Petersburg committee of the party, three, on the eve of the war, were in the employ of the Secret Service. Thus tzarism played blind man's buff with the revolution. In November the Bolshevik deputies were arrested. There began a general smash-up of the party throughout the country. In February 1915 the case of the Duma faction was called in the courts. The deputies conducted themselves cautiously. Kamenev, theoretical instigator of the faction, stood apart from the defeatist position of Lenin; so did

[1] *Narodnik* is a general name for those non-Marxians who had originally hoped to accomplish the regeneration of Russia by "going to the people (*narod*)," and out of whom developed the Social Revolutionary party. The Mensheviks were the right, or so-called "moderate," wing of the Marxian or Social Democratic party, whom Lenin abandoned in 1903. [Trans.]

37

Petrovsky, the present president of the Central Committee in the Ukraine. The Police Department remarked with satisfaction that the severe sentences dealt out to the deputies did not evoke any movement of protest among the workers.

It seemed as though the war had produced a new working class. To a considerable extent this was the fact: in Petrograd the personnel of the workers had been renewed almost forty per cent. The revolutionary succession had been abruptly broken. All that existed before the war, including the Duma faction of the Bolsheviks, had suddenly retired to the background and almost disappeared in oblivion. But under cover of this quietness and patriotism—and to some extent even monarchism—the moods of a new explosion were gradually accumulating in the masses.

In August 1915 the tzarist ministers were telling each other that the workers "are everywhere hunting out treason, betrayal and sabotage in behalf of the Germans, and are enthusiastic in the search for those guilty of our unsuccesses at the front." It is true that in that period the awakening mass-criticism—in part sincerely and in part for the sake of defensive coloration—often adopted the standpoint of "defense of the fatherland." But that idea was only a point of departure. The discontent of the workers was digging a deeper and deeper course, silencing the masters, the Black Hundred workers, the servants of the administration, permitting the worker-Bolsheviks to raise their heads.

From criticism the masses pass over to action. Their indignation finds expression first of all in food disturbances, sometimes rising to the height of local riots. Women, old men and boys, in the market or on the open square, feel bolder and more independent than the workers on military duty in the factories. In Moscow in May the movement turns into a pogrom of Germans, although the participants in this are chiefly the scum of the town armed under police protection. Nevertheless, the very possibility of such a pogrom in industrial Moscow proves that the workers are not yet sufficiently awakened to impose their slogans and their discipline upon the disturbed small-town people. These food disorders, spreading over the whole country, broke the war hypnosis and laid the road to strikes.

The inflow of raw labor power to the factories and the greedy scramble for war-profits, brought everywhere a lowering of the conditions of labor, and gave rise to the crudest methods of exploitation. The rise in the cost of living automatically lowered wages. Economic strikes were the inevitable mass reflection—stormy in proportion as they had been delayed. The strikes were accompanied by meetings, adoption of political resolutions, scrimmages with the police, not infrequently by shots and casualties.

The struggle arose chiefly in the central textile district. On June 5 the police fire a volley at the weavers in Kostroma: 4 killed, 9 wounded. On August 10 the troops fire on the Ivanovo-Voznesensk workers: 16 killed, 30 wounded. In the movement of the textile workers some soldiers of a local battalion are involved. Protest strikes in various parts of the country give answer to the shootings at Ivanovo-Voznesensk. Parallel to this goes the economic struggle. The textile workers often march in the front rank.

In comparison with the first half of 1914 this movement, as regards strength of pressure and clarity of slogans, represents a big step backward. This is not surprising, since raw masses are to a large extent being drawn into the struggle, and there has been a complete disintegration of the guiding layer of the workers. Nevertheless even in these first strikes of the war the approach of great battles can be heard. The Minister of Justice, Khvostov, said on the 16th of August: "If there are at present no armed demonstrations of the workers, it is only because they have as yet no organization." Goremykin expressed himself more concisely: "The trouble among the workers' leaders is that they have no organization, since it was broken up by the arrest of the five members of the Duma." The Minister of the Interior added: "We must not amnesty the members of the Duma (Bolsheviks)—they are the organizing center of the movement in its most dangerous form." These people at least made no mistake as to who was the real enemy.

While the ministry, even at the moment of its greatest dismay and readiness for liberal concessions, deemed it necessary as before to pound the workers' revolution on the head—i.e. on the Bolsheviks—the big bourgeoisie was trying to fix up a co-operation with the Mensheviks. Frightened by the scope of the strike movement, the liberal industrialists made an attempt to impose patriotic discipline upon the workers by including their elected representatives in the staff of the Military Industrial Committees. The Minister of the Interior complained that it was very difficult to oppose this scheme, fathered by Guchkov. "The whole enterprise," he said, "is being carried out under a patriotic flag, and in the interests of the defense." We must remark, however, that even the police avoided arresting the social-patriots, seeing in them a side partner in the struggle against strikes and revolutionary "excesses." It was indeed upon their too great confidence in the strength of patriotic socialism, that the Secret Service based their conviction that no insurrection would occur while the war lasted.

In the elections to the Military-Industrial Committees the defensists, headed by an energetic metal worker, Gvozdev—we shall meet him later as Minister of Labor in the Coalition Government of the revolution—turned out to be a minority. They enjoyed the support, however, not only of the liberal bourgeoisie, but of the bureaucracy, in getting the better of those who, led by the Bolsheviks, wished to boycott the committees. They succeeded in imposing a representation in these organs of industrial patriotism upon the Petersburg proletariat. The position of the Mensheviks was clearly expressed in a speech one of their representatives later made to the industrialists in the Committee: "You ought to demand that the existing bureaucratic power retire from the scene, yielding its place to you as the inheritors of the present social structure." This young political friendship was growing by leaps and bounds. After the revolution it will bring forth its ripe fruit.

The war produced a dreadful desolation in the underground movement. After the arrest of the Duma faction the Bolsheviks had no centralized party organization at all. The local committees had an episodic existence, and often had no connections with the workers districts. Only scattered groups, circles

40

and solitary individuals did anything. However, the reviving strike movement gave them some spirit and some strength in the factories. They gradually began to find each other and build up the district connections. The underground work revived. In the Police Department they wrote later: "Ever since the beginning of the war, the Leninists, who have behind them in Russia an overwhelming majority of the underground social-democratic organizations, have in their larger centers (such as Petrograd, Moscow, Kharkov, Kiev, Tula, Kostroma, Vladimir Province, Samara) been issuing in considerable numbers revolutionary appeals with a demand to stop the war, overthrow the existing government, and found a republic. And this work has had its palpable result in workers' strikes and disorders."

The traditional anniversary of the march of the workers to the Winter Palace, which had passed almost unnoticed the year before, produces a widespread strike on January 9, 1916. The strike movement doubles during this year. Encounters with the police accompany every big and prolonged strike. In contact with the troops, the workers conduct themselves with demonstrative friendliness, and the Secret Police more than once notice this alarming fact.

The war industries swelled out, devouring all resources around them and undermining their own foundation. The peace-time branches of production began to die away. In spite of all plannings, nothing came of the regulation of industry. The bureaucracy, incapable of taking this business in hand against the opposition of the powerful Military-Industrial Committees, at the same time refused to turn over the regulating rôle to the bourgeoisie. The chaos increased. Skilled workers were replaced by unskilled. The coal mines, shops and factories of Poland were soon lost. In the course of the first year of the war a fifth part of the industrial strength of the country was cut off. As much as 50 per cent of production went to supply the needs of the army and the war—including about 75 per cent of the textile production of the country. The overloaded transport proved incapable of supplying factories with the necessary quantity of fuel and raw material. The war not only swallowed up the whole current national income, but seriously began to cut into the basic capital of the country.

The industrialists grew less and less willing to grant anything to the workers, and the government, as usual, answered every strike with severe repressions. All this pushed the minds of the workers from the particular to the general, from economics to politics: "We must all strike at once." Thus arose the idea of the general strike. The process of radicalization of the masses is most convincingly reflected in the strike statistics. In 1915, two and a half times fewer workers participated in political strikes than in economic conflicts. In 1916, twice as few. In the first months of 1917, political strikes involved six times as many workers as economic. The rôle of Petrograd is portrayed in one figure: 72 per cent of the political strikers during the years of the war fall to her lot!

Many of the old beliefs are burned up in the fires of this struggle. The Secret Service reports, "with pain," that if they should react according to the dictates of the law to "every instance of insolence and open insult to His Majesty, the number of trials under Article 103 would reach an unheard-of figure." Nevertheless the consciousness of the masses is far behind their action. The terrible pressure of the war and the national ruin is accelerating the process of struggle to such a degree that broad masses of the workers, right up to the very revolution, have not freed themselves from many opinions and prejudices brought with them from the village or from the petty bourgeois family-circle in the town. This fact will set its stamp on the first stage of the February revolution.

By the end of 1916 prices are rising by leaps and bounds. To the inflation and the breakdown of transport, there is added an actual lack of goods. The demands of the population have been cut down by this time to one-half. The curve of the workers' movement rises sharply. In October the struggle enters its decisive phase, uniting all forms of discontent in one. Petrograd draws back for the February leap. A wave of meetings runs through the factories. The topics: food supplies, high cost of living, war, government. Bolshevik leaflets are distributed; political strikes begin; improvised demonstrations occur at factory gates; cases of fraternization between certain factories and the soldiers are observed; a stormy protest-strike flares up over the trial of the revolutionary sailors of the Baltic Fleet. The French ambassador calls Premier Stürmer's attention to the fact, become known to him, that some soldiers have shot at the police. Stürmer quiets the ambassador: "The repressions will be ruthless." In November a good-sized group of workers on military duty are removed from the Petrograd factories and sent to the front. The year ends in storm and thunder.

Comparing the situation with that in 1905, the director of the Police Department, Vassiliev, reaches a very uncomforting conclusion: "The mood of opposition has gone very far—far beyond anything to be seen in the broad masses during the above-mentioned period of disturbance." Vassiliev rests no hope in the garrison; even the police officers are not entirely reliable. The Intelligence Department reports a revival of the slogan of the general strike, the danger of a resurrection of the terror. Soldiers and officers arriving from the front say of the present situation: "What is there to wait for?—Why don't you take and bump off such-and-such a scoundrel? If we were here, we wouldn't waste much time thinking," etc. Shliapnikov, a member of the Bolshevik Central Committee, himself a former metal worker, describes how nervous the workers were in those days: "Sometimes a whistle would be enough, or any kind of noise—the workers would take it for a signal to stop the factory." This detail is equally remarkable both as a political symptom and as a psychological fact: the revolution is there in the nerves before it comes out on the street.

The provinces are passing through the same stages, only more slowly. The growth in massiveness of the movement and in fighting spirit shifts the center of gravity from the textile to the metal-workers, from economic strikes to political, from the provinces to Petrograd. The first two months of 1917 show 575,000 political strikers, the lion's share of them in the capital. In spite of new raids carried out by the police on the eve of January 9, 150,000 workers went on strike in the capital on that anniversary of blood. The mood was tense. The metal-workers were in the lead. The workers all felt that no re-

treat was possible. In every factory an active nucleus was forming, oftenest around the Bolsheviks. Strikes and meetings went
on continuously throughout the first two weeks of February.
On the 8th, at the Putilov factory, the police received "a hail of
slag and old iron." On the 14th, the day the Duma opened,
about 90,000 were on strike in Petrograd. Several plants also
stopped work in Moscow. On the 16th, the authorities decided
to introduce bread cards in Petrograd. This novelty rasped the
nerves. On the 19th, a mass of people gathered around the
food shops, especially women, all demanding bread. A day later
bakeries were sacked in several parts of the city. These were
the heat lightnings of the revolution, coming in a few days.

*

THE Russian proletariat found its revolutionary audacity not
only in itself. Its very position as minority of the nation suggests that it could not have given its struggle a sufficient scope—
certainly not enough to take its place at the head of the state—if
it had not found a mighty support in the thick of the people.
Such a support was guaranteed to it by the agrarian problem.

The belated half-liberation of the peasants in 1861 had
found agricultural industry almost on the same level as two
hundred years before. The preservation of the old area of
communal land—somewhat filched from during the reform—
together with the archaic methods of land culture, automatically
sharpened a crisis caused by the rural excess population, which
was at the same time a crisis in the three-field system. The peasantry felt still more caught in a trap because the process was not
taking place in the seventeenth but in the nineteenth century—
that is, in the conditions of an advanced money economy which
made demands upon the wooden plow that could only be met by
a tractor. Here too we see a drawing together of separate stages
of the historic process, and as a result an extreme sharpening of
contradictions. The learned agronomes and economists had been
preaching that the old area with rational cultivation would be
amply sufficient—that is to say, they proposed to the peasant to
make a jump to a higher level of technique and culture without

44

disturbing the landlord, the bailiff, or the tzar. But no economic régime, least of all an agricultural régime, the most tardy of all, has ever disappeared before exhausting all its possibilities. Before feeling compelled to pass over to a more intensive economic culture, the peasant had to make a last attempt to broaden his three fields. This could obviously be achieved only at the expense of non-peasant lands. Choking in the narrowness of his land area, under the smarting whip of the treasury and the market, the muzhik was inexorably forced to attempt to get rid of the landlord once for all.

On the eve of the first revolution the whole stretch of arable land within the limits of European Russia was estimated at 280 million dessiatins.[1] The communal allotments constituted about 140 million. The crown lands, above 5 million. Church and monastery lands, about 2½ million. Of the privately owned land, 70 million dessiatins belonged to the 30,000 great landlords, each of whom owned above 500 dessiatins. This 70 million was about what would have belonged to 10 million peasant families. These land statistics constitute the finished program of a peasant war.

The landlords were not settled with in the first revolution. Not all the peasants rose. The movement in the country did not coincide with that in the cities. The peasant army wavered, and finally supplied sufficient forces for putting down the workers. As soon as the Semenovsky Guard regiment had settled with the Moscow insurrection, the monarchy abandoned all thought of cutting down the landed estates, as also its own autocratic rights.

However, the defeated revolution did not pass without leaving traces in the village. The government abolished the old land redemption payments and opened the way to a broader colonization of Siberia. The frightened landlords not only made considerable concessions in the matter of rentals, but also began a large-scale selling of their landed estates. These fruits of the revolution were enjoyed by the better-off peasants, who were able to rent and buy the landlords' land.

However, the broadest gates were opened for the emerging

[1] A dessiatin is 2.702 English acres. [Trans.]

45

of capitalist farmers from the peasant class by the law of November 9, 1906, the chief reform introduced by the victorious counter-revolution. Giving the right even to a small minority of the peasants of any commune, against the will of the majority, to cut out from the communal land a section to be owned independently, the law of November 9 constituted an explosive capitalist shell directed against the commune. The president of the Council of Ministers, Stolypin, described the essence of this governmental policy towards the peasants as "banking on the strong ones." This meant: encourage the upper circles of the peasantry to get hold of the communal land by buying up these "liberated" sections, and convert these new capitalist farmers into a support for the existing régime. It was easier to propose such a task, however, than to achieve it. In this attempt to substitute the kulak [1] problem for the peasant problem, the counter-revolution was destined to break its neck.

By January 1, 1916, 2½ million home-owners had made good their personal possession of 17 million dessiatins. Two more million home-owners were demanding the allotment to them of 14 million dessiatins. This looked like a colossal success for the reform. But the majority of the homesteads were completely incapable of sustaining life, and represented only material for natural selection. At that time when the more backward landlords and small peasants were selling on a large scale—the former their estates, the latter their bits of land—there emerged in the capacity of principal purchaser a new peasant bourgeoisie. Agriculture entered upon a state of indubitable capitalist boom. The export of agricultural products from Russia rose between 1908 and 1912 from 1 billion roubles to 1½ billion. This meant that broad masses of the peasantry had been proletarianized, and the upper circles of the village were throwing on the market more and more grain.

To replace the compulsory communal ties of the peasantry, there developed very swiftly a voluntary coöperation, which succeeded in penetrating quite deeply into the peasant masses in the course of a few years, and immediately became a subject

---

[1] *Kulak,* the Russian word for fist, is a nick-name for rich peasants—"land-grabbers," as we might say. [Trans.]

of liberal and democratic idealization. Real power in the co-operatives belonged, however, only to the rich peasants, whose interests in the last analysis they served. The Narodnik intelligentsia, by concentrating its chief forces in peasant coöperation, finally succeeded in shifting its love for the people on to good solid bourgeois rails. In this way was prepared, partially at least, the political bloc of the "anti-capitalist" party of the Social Revolutionaries with the Kadets, the capitalist party *par excellence*.

Liberalism, although preserving the appearance of opposition to the agrarian policy of the reaction, nevertheless looked with great hopes upon this capitalist destruction of the communes. "In the country a very powerful petty bourgeoisie is arising," wrote the liberal Prince Troubetskoy, "in its whole make and essence alien alike to the ideals of the united nobility and to the socialist dreams."

But this admirable medal had its other side. There was arising from the destroyed communes not only a "very powerful bourgeoisie," but also its antithesis. The number of peasants selling tracts of land they could not live on had risen by the beginning of the war to a million, which means no less than five million souls added to the proletarian population. A sufficiently explosive material was also supplied by the millions of peasant-paupers to whom nothing remained but to hang on to their hungry allotments. In consequence those contradictions kept reproducing themselves among the peasants which had so early undermined the development of bourgeois society as a whole in Russia. The new rural bourgeoisie which was to create a support for the old and more powerful proprietors, turned out to be as hostilely opposed to the fundamental masses of the peasantry as the old proprietors had been to the people as a whole. Before it could become a support to the existing order, this peasant bourgeoisie had need of some order of its own wherewith to cling to its conquered positions. In these circumstances it is no wonder that the agrarian problem continued a sharp one in all the State Dumas. Everyone felt that the last word had not yet been spoken. The peasant deputy Petrichenko once declared from the tribune of the Duma: "No matter how long you debate you won't create a new planet—that means that you will have to give us the land." This peasant was neither a Bolshevik, nor a Social Revolutionary. On the contrary, he was a Right deputy, a monarchist.

The agrarian movement, having, like the strike movement of the workers, died down toward the end of 1907, partially revives in 1908, and grows stronger during the following years. The struggle, to be sure, is transferred to a considerable degree within the commune: that is just what the reaction had figured on politically. There are not infrequent armed conflicts among peasants during the division of the communal land. But the struggle against the landlord also does not disappear. The peasants are more frequently setting fire to the landlord's manors, harvests, haystacks, seizing on the way also those individual tracts which had been cut off against the will of the communal peasants.

The war found the peasantry in this condition. The government carried away from the country about 10 million workers and about 2 million horses. The weak homesteads grew still weaker. The number of peasants who could not sow their fields increased. But in the second year of the war the middle peasants also began to go under. Peasant hostility toward the war sharpened from month to month. In October 1916, the Petrograd Gendarme Administration reported that in the villages they had already ceased to believe in the success of the war—the report being based on the words of insurance agents, teachers, traders, etc. "All are waiting and impatiently demanding: When will this cursed war finally end?" And that is not all: "Political questions are being talked about everywhere and resolutions adopted directed against the landlords and merchants. Nuclei of various organizations are being formed. . . . As yet there is no uniting center, but there is reason to suppose that the peasants will unite by way of the coöperatives which are daily growing throughout all Russia." There is some exaggeration here. In some things the gendarme has run ahead a little, but the fundamentals are indubitably correct.

The possessing classes could not but foresee that the village was going to present its bill. But they drove away these black thoughts, hoping to wriggle out of it somehow. On this theme the inquisitive French ambassador Paléologue had a chat during the war days with the former Minister of Agriculture Krivo-shein, the former Premier Kokovtsev, the great landlord Count Bobrinsky, the President of the State Duma Rodzianko, the great industrialist Putilov, and other distinguished people. Here is what was unveiled before him in this conversation: In order to carry into action a radical land reform it would require the work of a standing army of 300,000 surveyors for no less than fifteen years; but during this time the number of homesteads would increase to 30 million, and consequently all these pre-liminary calculations by the time they were made would prove invalid. To introduce a land reform thus seemed in the eyes of these landlords, officials and bankers something like squaring the circle. It is hardly necessary to say that a like mathematical scrupulousness was completely alien to the peasant. He thought that first of all the thing to do was to smoke out the landlord, and then see.

If the village nevertheless remained comparatively peaceful during the war, that was because its active forces were at the front. The soldiers did not forget about the land—whenever at least they were not thinking about death—and in the trenches the muzhik's thoughts about the future were saturated with the smell of powder. But all the same the peasantry, even after learning to handle firearms, could never of its own force have achieved the agrarian democratic revolution—that is, its own revolution. It had to have leadership. For the first time in world history the peasant was destined to find a leader in the person of the worker. In that lies the fundamental, and you may say the whole, difference between the Russian revolution and all those preceding it.

In England serfdom had disappeared in actual fact by the end of the fourteenth century—that is, two centuries before it arose in Russia, and four and a half centuries before it was abol-ished. The expropriation of the landed property of the peasants dragged along in England through one Reformation and two revolutions to the nineteenth century. The capitalist develop-ment, not forced from the outside, thus had sufficient time to

49

liquidate the independent peasant long before the proletariat awoke to political life.

In France the struggle with royal absolutism, the aristocracy, and the princes of the church, compelled the bourgeoisie in various of its layers, and in several installments, to achieve a radical agrarian revolution at the beginning of the eighteenth century. For long after that an independent peasantry constituted the support of the bourgeois order, and in 1871 it helped the bourgeoisie put down the Paris Commune.

In Germany the bourgeoisie proved incapable of a revolutionary solution of the agrarian problem, and in 1848 betrayed the peasants to the landlords, just as Luther some three centuries before in the peasant wars had betrayed them to the princes. On the other hand, the German proletariat was still too weak in the middle of the nineteenth century to take the leadership of the peasantry. As a result the capitalist development of Germany got sufficient time, although not so long a period as in England, to subordinate agriculture, as it emerged from the uncompleted bourgeois revolution, to its own interests.

The peasant reform of 1861 was carried out in Russia by an aristocratic and bureaucratic monarchy under pressure of the demands of a bourgeois society, but with the bourgeoisie completely powerless politically. The character of this peasant emancipation was such that the forced capitalistic transformation of the country inevitably converted the agrarian problem into a problem of revolution. The Russian bourgeois dreamed of an agrarian evolution on the French plan, or the Danish, or the American—anything you want, only not the Russian. He neglected, however, to supply himself in good season with a French history or an American social structure. The democratic intelligentsia, notwithstanding its revolutionary past, took its stand in the decisive hour with the liberal bourgeoisie and the landlord, and not with the revolutionary village. In these circumstances only the working class could stand at the head of the peasant revolution.

The law of combined development of backward countries —in the sense of a peculiar mixture of backward elements with the most modern factors—here rises before us in its most finished form, and offers a key to the fundamental riddle of the Russian revolution. If the agrarian problem, as a heritage from the barbarism of the old Russian history, had been solved by the bourgeoisie, if it could have been solved by them, the Russian proletariat could not possibly have come to power in 1917. In order to realize the Soviet state, there was required a drawing together and mutual penetration of two factors belonging to completely different historic species: a peasant war—that is, a movement characteristic of the dawn of bourgeois development—and a proletarian insurrection, the movement signalizing its decline. That is the essence of 1917.

CHAPTER IV

THE TZAR AND THE TZARINA

THIS book will concern itself least of all with those unrelated psychological researches which are now so often substituted for social and historical analysis. Foremost in our field of vision will stand the great, moving forces of history, which are super-personal in character. Monarchy is one of them. But all these forces operate through people. And monarchy is by its very principle bound up with the personal. This in itself justifies an interest in the personality of that monarch whom the process of social development brought face to face with a revolution. Moreover, we hope to show in what follows, partially at least, just where in a personality the strictly personal ends—often much sooner than we think—and how frequently the "distinguishing traits" of a person are merely individual scratches made by a higher law of development.

Nicholas II inherited from his ancestors not only a giant empire, but also a revolution. And they did not bequeath him one quality which would have made him capable of governing an empire or even a province or a county. To that historic flood which was rolling its billows each one closer to the gates of his palace, the last Romanov opposed only a dumb indifference. It seemed as though between his consciousness and his epoch there stood some transparent but absolutely impenetrable medium.

People surrounding the tzar often recalled after the revolution that in the most tragic moments of his reign—at the time of the surrender of Port Arthur and the sinking of the fleet at Tsu-shima, and ten years later at the time of the retreat of the Russian troops from Galicia, and then two years later during the days preceding his abdication when all those around him were depressed, alarmed, shaken—Nicholas alone preserved his tranquillity. He would inquire as usual how many versts he had covered in his journeys about Russia, would recall episodes

52

of hunting expeditions in the past, anecdotes of official meetings, would interest himself generally in the little rubbish of the day's doings, while thunders roared over him and lightnings flashed. "What is this?" asked one of his attendant generals, "a gigantic, almost unbelievable self-restraint, the product of breeding, of a belief in the divine predetermination of events? Or is it inadequate consciousness?" The answer is more than half included in the question. The so-called "breeding" of the tzar, his ability to control himself in the most extraordinary circumstances, cannot be explained by a mere external training; its essence was an inner indifference, a poverty of spiritual forces, a weakness of the impulses of the will. That mask of indifference which was called breeding in certain circles, was a natural part of Nicholas at birth.

The tzar's diary is the best of all testimony. From day to day and from year to year drags along upon its pages the depressing record of spiritual emptiness. "Walked long and killed two crows. Drank tea by daylight." Promenades on foot, rides in a boat. And then again crows, and again tea. All on the very borderline of physiology. Recollections of church ceremonies are jotted down in the same tone as a drinking party.

In the days preceding the opening of the State Duma, when the whole country was shaking with convulsions, Nicholas wrote: "April 14. Took a walk in a thin shirt and took up paddling again. Had tea in the balcony. Stana dined and took a ride with us. Read." Not a word as to the subject of his reading. Some sentimental English romance? Or a report from the Police Department? "April 15: Accepted Witte's resignation. Marie and Dmitri to dinner. Drove them home to the palace."

On the day of the decision to dissolve the Duma, when the court as well as the liberal circles were going through a paroxysm of fright, the tzar wrote in his diary: "July 7. Friday. Very busy morning. Half hour late to breakfast with the officers. . . . A storm came up and it was very muggy. We walked together. Received Goremykin. Signed a decree dissolving the Duma! Dined with Olga and Petia. Read all evening." An exclamation point after the coming dissolution of the Duma is the highest expression of his emotions. The deputies of the dispersed Duma summoned the people to refuse to pay taxes. A series of military uprisings followed: in Sveaborg, Kronstadt, on ships, in army units. The revolutionary terror against high officials was renewed on an unheard-of scale. The tzar writes: "July 9. Sunday. It has happened! The Duma was closed today. At breakfast after Mass long faces were noticeable among many. . . . The weather was fine. On our walk we met Uncle Misha who came over yesterday from Gatchina. Was quietly busy until dinner and all evening. Went paddling in a canoe." It was in a canoe he went paddling—that is told. But with what he was busy all evening is not indicated. So it was always.

And further in those same fatal days: "July 14. Got dressed and rode a bicycle to the bathing beach and bathed enjoyably in the sea." "July 15. Bathed twice. It was very hot. Only us two at dinner. A storm passed over." "July 19. Bathed in the morning. Received at the farm. Uncle Vladimir and Chagin lunched with us." An insurrection and explosions of dynamite are barely touched upon with a single phrase, "Pretty doings!"—astonishing in its imperturbable indifference, which never rose to conscious cynicism.

"At 9:30 in the morning we rode out to the Caspian regiment . . . walked for a long time. The weather was wonderful. Bathed in the sea. After tea received Lvov and Guchkov." Not a word of the fact that this unexpected reception of the two liberals was brought about by the attempt of Stolypin to include opposition leaders in his ministry. Prince Lvov, the future head of the Provisional Government, said of that reception at the time: "I expected to see the sovereign stricken with grief, but instead of that there came out to meet me a jolly, sprightly fellow in a raspberry-colored shirt." The tzar's outlook was not broader than that of a minor police official—with this difference, that the latter would have a better knowledge of reality and be less burdened with superstitions. The sole paper which Nicholas read for years, and from which he derived his ideas, was a weekly published on state revenue by Prince Meshchersky, a vile, bribed journalist of the reactionary bureaucratic clique, despised even in his own circle. The tzar kept his outlook unchanged through two wars and two revolutions. Between his consciousness and events stood always that impenetrable medium—indifference. Nicholas was called, not without foundation, a fatalist. It is only necessary to add that his fatalism was the exact opposite of an active belief in his "star." Nicholas indeed considered himself unlucky. His fatalism was only a form of passive self-defense against historic evolution, and went hand in hand with an arbitrariness, trivial in psychological motivation, but monstrous in its consequences.

"I wish it and therefore it must be—" writes Count Witte. "That motto appeared in all the activities of this weak ruler, who only through weakness did all the things which characterized his reign—a wholesale shedding of more or less innocent blood, for the most part without aim."

Nicholas is sometimes compared with his half-crazy great-great-grandfather Paul, who was strangled by a camarilla acting in agreement with his own son, Alexander "the Blessed." These two Romanovs were actually alike in their distrust of everybody due to a distrust of themselves, their touchiness as of omnipotent nobodies, their feeling of abnegation, their consciousness, as you might say, of being crowned pariahs. But Paul was incomparably more colorful; there was an element of fancy in his rantings, however irresponsible. In his descendant everything was dim; there was not one sharp trait.

Nicholas was not only unstable, but treacherous. Flatterers called him a charmer, bewitcher, because of his gentle way with the courtiers. But the tzar reserved his special caresses for just those officials whom he had decided to dismiss. Charmed beyond measure at a reception, the minister would go home and find a letter requesting his resignation. That was a kind of revenge on the tzar's part for his own nonentity.

Nicholas recoiled in hostility before everything gifted and significant. He felt at ease only among completely mediocre and brainless people, saintly fakers, holy men, to whom he did not have to look up. He had his *amour propre*—indeed it was rather keen. But it was not active, not possessed of a grain of initiative, enviously defensive. He selected his ministers on a principle of continual deterioration. Men of brain and character he summoned only in extreme situations when there was no other way out, just as we call in a surgeon to save our lives. It was so with Witte, and afterwards with Stolypin. The tzar treated both with ill-concealed hostility. As soon as the crisis had passed, he hastened to part with these counselors who were too tall for him. This selection operated so systematically that the president of the last Duma, Rodzianko, on the 7th of January 1917, with the revolution already knocking at the doors, ventured to say to the tzar: "Your Majesty, there is not one reliable or honest man left around you; all the best men have been removed or have retired. There remain only those of ill repute."

All the efforts of the liberal bourgeoisie to find a common language with the court came to nothing. The tireless and noisy Rodzianko tried to shake up the tzar with his reports, but in vain. The latter gave no answer either to argument or to impudence, but quietly made ready to dissolve the Duma. Grand Duke Dmitri, a former favorite of the tzar, and future accomplice in the murder of Rasputin, complained to his colleague, Prince Yussupov, that the tzar at headquarters was becoming every day more indifferent to everything around him. In Dmitri's opinion the tzar was being fed some kind of dope which had a benumbing action upon his spiritual faculties. "Rumors went round," writes the liberal historian Miliukov, "that this condition of mental and moral apathy was sustained in the tzar by an increased use of alcohol." This was all fancy or exaggeration. The tzar had no need of narcotics: the fatal "dope" was in his blood. Its symptoms merely seemed especially striking on the background of those great events of war and domestic crisis which led up to the revolution. Rasputin, who was a psychologist, said briefly of the tzar that he "lacked insides."

This dim, equable and "well-bred" man was cruel—not with the active cruelty of Ivan the Terrible or of Peter, in the pursuit of historic aims—What had Nicholas the Second in common with them?—but with the cowardly cruelty of the late born, frightened at his own doom. At the very dawn of his reign

Nicholas praised the Phanagoritsy regiment as "fine fellows" for shooting down workers. He always "read with satisfaction" how they flogged with whips the bob-haired girl-students, or cracked the heads of defenseless people during Jewish pogroms. This crowned black sheep gravitated with all his soul to the very dregs of society, the Black Hundred hooligans. He not only paid them generously from the state treasury, but loved to chat with them about their exploits, and would pardon them when they accidentally got mixed up in the murder of an opposition deputy. Witte, who stood at the head of the government during the putting down of the first revolution, has written in his memoirs: "When news of the useless cruel antics of the chiefs of these detachments reached the sovereign, they met with his approval, or in any case his defense." In answer to the demand of the governor-general of the Baltic States that he stop a certain lieutenant-captain, Richter, who was "executing on his own authority and without trial non-resistant persons," the tzar wrote on the report: "Ah, what a fine fellow!" Such encouragements are innumerable. This "charmer," without will, without aim, without imagination, was more awful than all the tyrants of ancient and modern history.

The tzar was mightily under the influence of the tzarina, an influence which increased with the years and the difficulties. Together they constituted a kind of unit—and that combination shows already to what an extent the personal, under pressure of circumstances, is supplemented by the group. But first we must speak of the tzarina herself.

Maurice Paléologue, the French ambassador at Petrograd during the war, a refined psychologist for French academicians and janitresses, offers a meticulously licked portrait of the last tzarina: "Moral restlessness, a chronic sadness, infinite longing, intermittent ups and downs of strength, anguishing thoughts of the invisible other world, superstitions—are not all these traits, so clearly apparent in the personality of the empress, the characteristic traits of the Russian people?" Strange as it may seem, there is in this saccharine lie just a grain of truth. The Russian satirist Saltykov, with some justification, called the ministers and governors from among the Baltic barons "Germans with a Russian soul." It is indubitable that aliens, in no way connected with the people, developed the most pure culture of the "genuine Russian" administrator.

But why did the people repay with such open hatred a tzarina who, in the words of Paléologue, had so completely assimilated their soul? The answer is simple. In order to justify her new situation, this German woman adopted with a kind of cold fury all the traditions and nuances of Russian medievalism, the most meager and crude of all medievalisms, in that very period when the people were making mighty efforts to free themselves from it. This Hessian princess was literally possessed by the demon of autocracy. Having risen from her rural corner to the heights of Byzantine despotism, she would not for anything take a step down. In the orthodox religion she found a mysticism and a magic adapted to her new lot. She believed the more inflexibly in her vocation, the more naked became the foulness of the old régime. With a strong character and a gift for dry and hard exaltations, the tzarina supplemented the weak-willed tzar, ruling over him.

On March 17, 1916, a year before the revolution, when the tortured country was already writhing in the grip of defeat and ruin, the tzarina wrote to her husband at military headquarters: "You must not give indulgences, a responsible ministry, etc. . . . or anything that *they* want. This must be your war and your peace, and the honor yours and our fatherland's, and not by any means the Duma's. They have not the right to say a single word in these matters." This was at any rate a thoroughgoing program. And it was in just this way that she always had the whip hand over the continually vacillating tzar.

After Nicholas' departure to the army in the capacity of fictitious commander-in-chief, the tzarina began openly to take charge of internal affairs. The ministers came to her with reports as to a regent. She entered into a conspiracy with a small camarilla against the Duma, against the ministers, against the staff-generals, against the whole world—to some extent indeed against the tzar. On December 6, 1916, the tzarina wrote to the tzar: ". . . Once you have said that you want to keep Protopopov, how does he (Premier Trepov) go against you? Bring down your fist on the table. Don't yield. Be the boss. Obey your firm little wife and our Friend. Believe in us." Again three days later: "You know you are right. Carry your head high. Command Trepov to work with him. . . . Strike your fist on the table." Those phrases sound as though they were made up, but they are taken from authentic letters. Besides, you cannot make up things like that.

On December 13 the tzarina suggests to the tzar: "Anything but this responsible ministry about which everybody has gone crazy. Everything is getting quiet and better, but people want to feel your hand. How long they have been saying to me, for whole years, the same thing: 'Russia loves to feel the whip.' That is *their* nature!" This orthodox Hessian, with a Windsor upbringing and a Byzantine crown on her head, not only "incarnates" the Russian soul, but also organically despises it. *Their* nature demands the whip—writes the Russian tzarina to the Russian tzar about the Russian people, just two months and a half before the monarchy tips over into the abyss.

In contrast to her force of character, the intellectual force of the tzarina is not higher, but rather lower than her husband's. Even more than he, she craves the society of simpletons. The close and long-lasting friendship of the tzar and tzarina with their lady-in-waiting Vyrubova gives a measure of the spiritual stature of this autocratic pair. Vyrubova has described herself as a fool, and this is not modesty. Witte, to whom one cannot deny an accurate eye, characterized her as "a most commonplace, stupid, Petersburg young lady, homely as a bubble in the biscuit dough." In the society of this person, with whom elderly officials, ambassadors and financiers obsequiously flirted, and who had just enough brains not to forget about her own pockets, the tzar and tzarina would pass many hours, consulting her about affairs, corresponding with her and about her. She was more influential than the State Duma, and even than the ministry.

But Vyrubova herself was only an instrument of "The Friend," whose authority superseded all three. ". . . This is my *private* opinion," writes the tzarina to the tzar, "I will find out what our Friend thinks." The opinion of the "Friend" is not private, it decides. ". . . I am firm," insists the tzarina a few weeks later, "but listen to me, *i.e. this means* our Friend, and trust us in everything. . . . I suffer for you as for a gentle soft-hearted child—who needs guidance, but listens to bad counselors, while a man sent by God is telling him what he should do."

The Friend sent by God was Gregory Rasputin.

". . . . The prayers and the help of our Friend—then all will be well."

"If we did not have Him, all would have been over long ago. I am absolutely convinced of that."

Throughout the whole reign of Nicholas and Alexandra soothsayers and hysterics were imported for the court not only from all over Russia, but from other countries. Special official purveyors arose, who would gather around the momentary oracle, forming a powerful Upper Chamber attached to the monarch. There was no lack of bigoted old women with the title of countess, nor of functionaries weary of doing nothing, nor of financiers who had entire ministries in their hire. With a jealous eye on the unchartered competition of mesmerists and sorcerers, the high priesthood of the Orthodox Church would hasten to pry their way into the holy of holies of the intrigue. Witte called this ruling circle, against which he himself twice stubbed his toe, "the leprous court camarilla."

The more isolated the dynasty became, and the more unsheltered the autocrat felt, the more he needed some help from the other world. Certain savages, in order to bring good weather, wave in the air a shingle on a string. The tzar and tzarina used shingles for the greatest variety of purposes. In the tzar's train there was a whole chapel full of large and small images, and all sorts of fetiches, which were brought to bear, first against the Japanese, then against the German artillery.

The level of the court circle really had not changed much from generation to generation. Under Alexander II, called the "Liberator," the grand dukes had sincerely believed in house spirits and witches. Under Alexander III it was no better, only quieter. The "leprous camarilla" had existed always, changing only its personnel and its method. Nicholas II did not create, but inherited from his ancestors, this court atmosphere of savage medievalism. But the country during these same decades had been changing, its problems growing more complex, its culture rising to a higher level. The court circle was thus left far behind.

Although the monarchy did under compulsion make concessions to the new forces, nevertheless inwardly it completely failed to become modernized. On the contrary it withdrew into itself. Its spirit of medievalism thickened under the pressure of hostility and fear, until it acquired the character of a disgusting nightmare overhanging the country.

Towards November 1905—that is, at the most critical moment of the first revolution—the tzar writes in his diary: "We got acquainted with a man of God, Gregory, from the Tobolsk province." That was Rasputin—a Siberian peasant with a bald scar on his head, the result of a beating for horse-stealing. Put forward at an appropriate moment, this "Man of God" soon found official helpers—or rather they found him—and thus was formed a new ruling circle which got a firm hold of the tzarina, and through her of the tzar.

From the winter of 1913-14 it was openly said in Petersburg society that all high appointments, posts and contracts depended upon the Rasputin clique. The "Elder" himself gradually turned into a state institution. He was carefully guarded, and no less carefully sought after by the competing ministers. Spies of the Police Department kept a diary of his life by hours, and did not fail to report how on a visit to his home village of Pokrovsky he got into a drunken and bloody fight with his own father on the street. On the same day that this happened—September 9, 1915—Rasputin sent two friendly telegrams, one to Tzarskoe Selo to the tzarina, the other to headquarters to the tzar. In epic language the police spies registered from day to day the revels of the Friend. "He returned today 5 o'clock in the morning completely drunk." "On the night of the 25-26th the actress V. spent the night with Rasputin." "He arrived with Princess D. (the wife of a gentleman of the bedchamber of the Tzar's court) at the Hotel Astoria." . . . And right beside this: "Came home from Tzarskoe Selo about 11 o'clock in

the evening." "Rasputin came home with Princess Sh— very
drunk and together they went out immediately." In the morning or evening of the following day a trip to Tzarskoe Selo. To
a sympathetic question from the spy as to why the Elder was
thoughtful, the answer came: "Can't decide whether to convoke
the Duma or not." And then again: "He came home at 5
in the morning pretty drunk." Thus for months and years
the melody was played on three keys: "Pretty drunk," "Very
drunk," and "Completely drunk." These communications of
state importance were brought together and countersigned by
the general of gendarmes, Gorbachev.

The bloom of Rasputin's influence lasted six years, the last
years of the monarchy. "His life in Petrograd," says Prince
Yussupov, who participated to some extent in that life, and afterward killed Rasputin, "became a continual revel, the drunken
debauch of a galley slave who had come into an unexpected
fortune." "I had at my disposition," wrote the president of
the Duma, Rodzianko, "a whole mass of letters from mothers
whose daughters had been dishonored by this insolent rake."
Nevertheless the Petrograd metropolitan, Pitirim, owed his position to Rasputin, as also the almost illiterate Archbishop Var-
nava. The Procuror of the Holy Synod, Sabler, was long sustained by Rasputin; and Premier Kokovtsev was removed at
his wish, having refused to receive the "Elder." Rasputin appointed Stürmer President of the Council of Ministers, Protopopov Minister of the Interior, the new Procuror of the Synod,
Raev, and many others. The ambassador of the French Republic, Paléologue, sought an interview with Rasputin, embraced
him and cried, *"Voilà, un véritable illuminé!"* hoping in this
way to win the heart of the tzarina to the cause of France. The
Jew Simanovich, financial agent of the "Elder," himself under
the eye of the Secret Police as a night club gambler and usurer
—introduced into the Ministry of Justice through Rasputin the
completely dishonest creature Dobrovolsky.

"Keep by you the little list," writes the tzarina to the tzar,
in regard to new appointments. "Our friend has asked that
you talk all this over with Protopopov." Two days later: "Our
friend says that Stürmer may remain a few days longer as

President of the Council of Ministers." And again: "Protopopov venerates our friend and will be blessed."

On one of those days when the police spies were counting
up the number of bottles and women, the tzarina grieved in a
letter to the tzar: "They accuse Rasputin of kissing women, etc.
Read the apostles; they kissed everybody as a form of greeting."
This reference to the apostles would hardly convince the police
spies. In another letter the tzarina goes still farther. "During
vespers I thought so much about our friend," she writes, "how
the Scribes and Pharisees are persecuting Christ pretending that
they are so perfect . . . yes, in truth no man is a prophet in
his own country."

The comparison of Rasputin and Christ was customary in
that circle, and by no means accidental. The alarm of the
royal couple before the menacing forces of history was too
sharp to be satisfied with an impersonal God and the futile
shadow of a Biblical Christ. They needed a second coming of
"the Son of Man." In Rasputin the rejected and agonizing
monarchy found a Christ in its own image.

"If there had been no Rasputin," said Senator Tagantsev, a
man of the old régime, "it would have been necessary to invent
one." There is a good deal more in these words than their author imagined. If by the word *hooliganism* we understand the
extreme expression of those anti-social parasite elements at the
bottom of society, we may define Rasputinism as a crowned
hooliganism at its very top.

CHAPTER V

THE IDEA OF A PALACE REVOLUTION

WHY did not the ruling classes, who were trying to save themselves from a revolution, attempt to get rid of the tzar and his circle? They wanted to, but they did not dare. They lacked both resolution and belief in their cause. The idea of a palace revolution was in the air up to the very moment when it was swallowed up in a state revolution. We must pause upon this in order to get a clearer idea of the inter-relations, just before the explosion, of the monarchy, the upper circles of the nobility, the bureaucracy and the bourgeoisie.

The possessing classes were completely monarchist, by virtue of interests, habits and cowardice. But they wanted a monarchy without Rasputin. The monarchy answered them: Take me as I am. In response to demands for a decent ministry, the tzarina sent to the tzar at headquarters an apple from the hands of Rasputin, urging that he eat it in order to strengthen his will. "Remember," she adjured, "that even Monsieur Philippe (a French charlatan-hypnotist) said that you must not grant a constitution, as that would mean ruin to you and Russia. . . ." "Be Peter the Great, Ivan the Terrible, Emperor Paul—crush them all under your feet!"

What a disgusting mixture of fright, superstition and malicious alienation from the country! To be sure, it might seem that on the summits the tzar's family could not be quite alone. Rasputin indeed was always surrounded with a galaxy of grand ladies, and in general shamanism flourishes in an aristocracy. But this mysticism of fear does not unite people, it divides them. Each saves himself in his own way. Many aristocratic houses have their competing saints. Even on the summits of Petrograd society the tzar's family was surrounded as though plague-stricken, with a quarantine of distrust and hostility. Lady-in-waiting Vyrubova remembers: "I was aware and felt deeply in all those around us a malice toward those whom I revered, and I felt that this malice would assume terrible dimensions."

Against the purple background of the war, with the roar of underground tremors clearly audible, the privileged did not for one moment renounce the joys of life; on the contrary, they devoured them greedily. Yet more and more often a skeleton would appear at their banquets and shake the little bones of his fingers. It began to seem to them that all their misery lay in the disgusting character of "Alix," in the treacherous weakness of the tzar, in that greedy fool Vyrubova, and in the Siberian Christ with a scar on his skull. Waves of unendurable foreboding swept over the ruling class, contracting it with spasms from the periphery to the center, and more and more isolating the hated upper circle at Tzarskoe Selo. Vyrubova has pretty clearly expressed the feelings of the upper circle at that time in her, generally speaking, very lying reminiscences: ". . . For the hundredth time I asked myself what has happened to Petrograd society. Are they all spiritually sick, or have they contracted some epidemic which rages in war time? It is hard to understand, but the fact is, all were in an abnormally excited condition." To the number of those out of their heads belonged the whole copious family of the Romanovs, the whole greedy, insolent and universally hated pack of grand dukes and grand duchesses. Frightened to death, they were trying to wriggle out of the ring narrowing around them. They kowtowed to the critical aristocracy, gossiped about the royal pair, and egged on both each other and all those around them. The august uncles addressed the tzar with letters of advice in which between the lines of respect was to be heard a snarl and a grinding of teeth.

Protopopov, some time after the October revolution, colorfully if not very learnedly characterized the mood of the upper circles: "Even the very highest classes became *frondeurs* before the revolution; in the grand salons and clubs the policy of the government received harsh and unfriendly criticism. The relations which had been formed in the tzar's family were analyzed and talked over. Little anecdotes were passed around about the head of the state. Verses were composed. Many grand dukes openly attended these meetings, and their presence gave a special authority in the eyes of the public to tales that were caricatures and to malicious exaggerations. A sense of the danger of this sport did not awaken till the last moment."

These rumors about the court camarilla were especially sharpened by the accusation of Germanophilism and even of direct connections with the enemy. The noisy and not very deep Rodzianko definitely stated: "The connection and the analogy of aspirations is so logically obvious that I at least have no doubt of the coöperation of the German Staff and the Rasputin circle: nobody can doubt it." The bare reference to a "logical" obviousness greatly weakens the categorical tone of this testimony. No evidence of a connection between the Rasputinists and the German Staff was discovered after the revolution. It was otherwise with the so-called "Germanophilism." This was not a question, of course, of the national sympathies and antipathies of the German tzarina, Premier Stürmer, Countess Kleinmichel, Minister of the Court Count Frederiks, and other gentlemen with German names. The cynical memoirs of the old *intriguante* Kleinmichel demonstrate with remarkable clearness how a supernational character distinguished the aristocratic summits of all the countries of Europe, bound together as they were by ties of birth, inheritance, scorn for all those beneath them, and last but not least, cosmopolitan adultery in ancient castles, at fashionable watering places, and in the courts of Europe. Considerably more real were the organic antipathies of the court household to the obsequious lawyers of the French Republic, and the sympathy of the reactionaries—whether bearing Teuton or Slavic family names—for the genuine Russian soul of the Berlin régime which had so often impressed them with its waxed mustachios, its sergeant-major manner and self-confident stupidity.

But that was not the decisive factor. The danger arose from the very logic of the situation, for the court could not help seeking salvation in a separate peace, and this the more insistently the more dangerous the situation became. Liberalism in the person of its leaders was trying, as we shall see, to reserve for itself the chance of making a separate peace in connection with the prospect of its own coming to power. But for just this reason it carried on a furious chauvinist agitation, deceiving the people and terrorizing the court. The camarilla did not dare show its real face prematurely in so ticklish a matter, and was even compelled to counterfeit the general patriotic tone, at the same time feeling out the ground for a separate peace.

General Kurlov, a former chief of police belonging to the Rasputin camarilla, denies, of course, in his reminiscences any German connection or sympathies on the part of his protector, but immediately adds: "We cannot blame Stürmer for his opinion that the war with Germany was the greatest possible misfortune for Russia and that it had no serious political justification." It is hardly possible to forget that while holding this interesting opinion Stürmer was the head of the government of a country waging war against Germany. The last tzarist Minister of the Interior, Protopopov, just before he entered the government, had been conducting negotiations in Stockholm with the German diplomat Warburg and had reported them to the tzar. Rasputin himself, according to the same Kurlov, "considered the war with Germany a colossal misfortune for Russia." And finally the empress wrote to the tzar on April 5, 1916: ". . . They dare not say that He has anything in common with the Germans. He is good and magnanimous toward all, like Christ. No matter to what religion a man may belong: that is the way a good Christian ought to be." To be sure, this good Christian who was almost always intoxicated might quite possibly have been made up to, not only by sharpers, usurers and aristocratic procuresses, but by actual spies of the enemy. "Connections" of this kind are not inconceivable. But the oppositional patriots posed the matter more directly and broadly: they directly accused the tzarina of treason. In his memoirs, written considerably later, General Denikin testifies: "In the army there was loud talk, unconstrained both in time and place, as to the insistent demands of the empress for a separate peace, her treachery in the matter of Field-Marshal Kitchener, of whose journey she was supposed to have told the Germans, etc. . . . This circumstance played a colossal rôle in determining the mood of the army in its attitude to the dynasty and the revolution." The same Denikin relates how after the revolution General Alexeiev, to a direct question about the treason of the empress, answered, "vaguely and reluctantly," that in going over the papers they had found in the possession of the tzarina a chart with a detailed designation of troops on the whole front, and that upon him, Alexeiev, this had produced a depressing effect. "Not another word," significantly adds Denikin. "He changed the subject." Whether the tzarina had the mysterious chart or not, the luck- less generals were obviously not unwilling to shoulder off upon her the responsibility for their own defeat. The accusation of treason against the court undoubtedly crept through the army chiefly from above downward—starting with that incapable staff.

But if the tzarina herself, to whom the tzar submitted in everything, was betraying to Wilhelm the military secrets and even the heads of the Allied chieftains, what remained but to make an end of the royal pair? And since the head of the army and of the anti-German party was the Grand Duke Nikolai Nikolaievich, was he not as a matter of duty chosen for the rôle of supreme patron of a palace revolution? That was the reason why the tzar, upon the insistence of Rasputin and the tzarina, removed the grand duke and took the chief command into his own hands. But the tzarina was afraid even of a meeting be- tween the nephew and the uncle in turning over the command. "Sweetheart, try to be cautious," she writes to the tzar at head- quarters, "and don't let Nikolasha catch you in any kind of promises or anything else—remember that Gregory saved you from him and from his bad people . . . remember in the name of Russia what they wanted to do, oust you (this is not gossip— Orloff had all the papers ready), and put me in a monastery."

The tzar's brother Michael said to Rodzianko: "The whole family knows how harmful Alexandra Feodorovna is. Nothing but traitors surround her and my brother. All honest people have left. But what's to be done in such a situation?" That is it exactly: what is to be done?

The Grand Duchess Maria Pavlovna insisted in the presence of her sons that Rodzianko should take the initiative in "remov- ing the tzarina." Rodzianko suggested that they consider the conversation as not having taken place, as otherwise in loyalty to his oath he should be obliged to report to the tzar that the grand duchess had suggested to the President of the Duma that he destroy the tzarina. Thus the ready-witted Lord Chamberlain reduced the question of murdering the tzarina to a pleasantry of the drawing room.

At times the ministry itself came into sharp opposition to the tzar. As early as 1915, a year and a half before the revolution, at the sittings of the government, talk went on openly which even now seems unbelievable. The War Minister Polivanov: "Only a policy of conciliation toward society can save the situation. The present shaky dykes will not avert a catastrophe." The Minister of Marine Grigorovich: "It's no secret that the army does not trust us and is awaiting a change." The Minister of Foreign Affairs Sazonov: "The popularity of the tzar and his authority in the eyes of the popular mass is considerably shaken." The Minister of the Interior Prince Sherbatov: "All of us together are unfit for governing Russia in the situation that is forming. . . . We must have either a dictatorship or a conciliatory policy" (Session of August 21, 1915). Neither of these measures could now be of help; neither was now attainable. The tzar could not make up his mind to a dictatorship; he rejected a conciliatory policy, and did not accept the resignation of the ministers who considered themselves unfit. The high official who kept the record makes a short commentary upon these ministerial speeches: evidently we shall have to hang from a lamp-post.

With such feelings prevailing it is no wonder that even in bureaucratic circles they talked of the necessity of a palace uprising as the sole means of preventing the advancing revolution. "If I had shut my eyes," remembers one of the participants of these conversations, "I might have thought that I was in the company of desperate revolutionists."

A colonel of gendarmes making a special investigation of the army in the south of Russia painted a dark picture in his report: Thanks to propaganda chiefly relating to the Germanophilism of the empress and the tzar, the army is prepared for the idea of a palace revolution. "Conversations to this effect are openly carried on in officers' meetings and have not met the necessary opposition on the part of the high command." Protopopov on his part testifies that "a considerable number of people in the high commanding staff sympathized with the idea of a coup d'état: certain individuals were in touch with and under the influence of the chief leaders of the so-called Progressive Bloc."

The subsequently notorious Admiral Kolchak testified before the Soviet Investigation Commission after his troops were routed by the Red Army that he had connections with many oppositional members of the Duma whose speeches he welcomed, since "his attitude to the powers existing before the revolution was adverse." As to the plan for a palace revolution, however, Kolchak was not informed.

After the murder of Rasputin and the subsequent banishment of grand dukes, high society talked still louder of the necessity of a palace revolution. Prince Yussupov tells how when the Grand Duke Dmitry was arrested at the palace the officers of several regiments came up and proposed plans for decisive action, "to which he, of course, could not agree."

The Allied diplomats—in any case, the British ambassador—were considered accessories to the plot. The latter, doubtless upon the initiative of the Russian liberals, made an attempt in January 1917 to influence Nicholas, having secured the preliminary sanction of his government. Nicholas attentively and politely listened to the ambassador, thanked him, and—spoke of other matters. Protopopov reported to Nicholas the relations between Buchanan and the chief leaders of the Progressive Bloc, and suggested that the British Ambassador be placed under observation. Nicholas did not seem to approve of the proposal, finding the watching of an ambassador "inconsistent with international tradition." Meanwhile Kurlov has no hesitation in stating that "the Intelligence Service remarks daily the relations between the leader of the Kadet Party Miliukov and the British Ambassador." International traditions, then, had not stood in the way at all. But their transgression helped little: even so, a palace conspiracy was never discovered.

Did it in reality exist? There is nothing to prove this. It

was a little too broad, that "conspiracy." It included too many and too various circles to *be* a conspiracy. It merely hung in the air as a mood of the upper circles of Petrograd society, as a confused idea of salvation, or a slogan of despair. But it did not thicken down to the point of becoming a practical plan.

The upper nobility in the eighteenth century had more than once introduced practical corrections into the succession by imprisoning or strangling inconvenient emperors: this operation was carried out for the last time on Paul in 1801. It is impossible to say, therefore, that a palace revolution would have transgressed the traditions of the Russian monarchy. On the contrary, it had been a steady element in those traditions. But the aristocracy had long ceased to feel strong at heart. It surrendered the honor of strangling the tzar and the tzarina to the bourgeoisie. But the leaders of the latter showed little more resolution.

Since the revolution references have been made more than once to the liberal capitalists Guchkov and Tereshchenko, and to General Krymov who was close to them, as the nucleus of the conspirators. Guchkov and Tereshchenko themselves have confirmed this, but indefinitely. The former volunteer in the army of the Boers against England, the duelist Guchkov, a liberal with spurs, must have seemed to "social opinion" in a general way the most suitable figure for a conspiracy. Surely not the wordy Professor Miliukov! Guchkov undoubtedly recurred more than once in his thoughts to the short and sharp blow in which one regiment of the guard would replace and forestall the revolution. Witte in his memoirs had already told on Guchkov, whom he hated, as an admirer of the Young Turk methods of disposing of an inconvenient sultan. But Guchkov, having never succeeded in his youth in displaying his young Turkish audacity, had had time to grow much older. And more important, this henchman of Stolypin could not help but see the difference between Russian conditions and the old Turkish conditions, could not fail to ask himself: Will not the palace revolution, instead of a means for preventing a real revolution, turn out to be the last jar that loosens the avalanche? May not the cure prove more ruinous than the disease?

71

In the literature devoted to the February revolution the preparation of a palace revolution is spoken of as a firmly established fact. Miliukov puts it thus: "Its realization was already on the way in February." Denikin transfers its realization to March. Both mention a "plan" to stop the tzar's train in transit, demand an abdication, and in case of refusal, which was considered inevitable, carry out a "physical removal" of the tzar. Miliukov adds that, foreseeing a possible revolution, the heads of the Progressive Bloc, who did not participate in the plot, and were not "accurately" informed of its preparation, talked over in a narrow circle how best to make use of the coup d'état in case of success. Certain Marxian investigations of recent years also take on faith the story of the practical preparation of a coup d'état. By that example we may learn how easily and firmly legends win a place in historical science.

As chief evidence of the plot they not infrequently advance a certain colorful tale of Rodzianko, which testifies to the very fact that there was no plot. In January 1917 General Krymov arrived from the front and complained before members of the Duma that things could not continue longer as they were: "If you decide upon this extreme measure (replacement of the tzar) we will support you." *If* you decide! The Octobrist Shidlovsky angrily exclaimed: "There is no need to pity or spare him when he is ruining Russia." In the noisy argument these real or imaginary words of Brussilov are also reported: "If it is necessary to choose between the tzar and Russia, I side with Russia." *If* it is necessary! The young millionaire Tereshchenko spoke as an inflexible tzaricide. The Kadet Shingarev spoke: "The General is right, an overturn is necessary . . . *but who will resolve upon it?*" That is just the question: who will resolve upon it? Such is the essence of the testimony of Rodzianko, who himself spoke against an overturn. In the course of the few following weeks the plan apparently did not move forward an inch. They conversed about stopping the tzar's train, but it is quite unknown who was to carry out that operation.

Russian liberalism, when it was younger, had supported the revolutionary terrorists with money and sympathy in the hope that they would drive the monarchy into its arms with their bombs. None of those respected gentlemen was accustomed to risk his own head. But all the same the chief rôle was played not by personal but by class fear: Things are bad now—they reasoned—but they might get worse. In any case, if Guchkov, Tereshchenko and Krymov had seriously moved toward a coup d'état—that is, practically prepared it, mobilizing the necessary forces and means—that would have been established definitely and accurately after the revolution. For the participants, especially the active young men of whom not a few would have been needed, would have had no reason to keep mum about the "almost" accomplished deed. After February this would only have assured them a career. However, there were no revelations. It is quite obvious that the affair never went any farther with Krymov and Guchkov than patriotic sighs over wine and cigars. The light-minded *frondeurs* of the aristocracy, like the heavy-weight oppositionists of the plutocracy, could not find the heart to amend by action the course of an unpropitious providence.

In May 1917 one of the most eloquent and empty liberals, Maklakov, will cry out at a private conference of that Duma which the revolution will sweep away along with the monarchy: "If posterity curses this revolution they will curse us for having been unable to prevent it in time with a revolution from above!" Still later, when he is already in exile, Kerensky, following Maklakov, will lament: "Yes, enfranchised Russia was too slow with its timely coup d'état from above (of which they talked so much, and for which they prepared [?] so much)—she was too slow to forestall the spontaneous explosion of the state."

These two exclamations complete the picture of how, even after the revolution had unleashed its inconquerable forces, educated nincompoops continued to think that it could have been forestalled by a "timely" change of dynastic figure-heads.

＊

THE determination was lacking for a "big" palace revolution. But out of it there arose a plan for a small one. The liberal conspirators did not dare to remove the chief actor of the monarchy, but the grand dukes decided to remove its prompter. In the murder of Rasputin they saw the last means of saving the dynasty.

Prince Yussupov, who was married to a Romanov, drew into the affair the Grand Duke Dmitry Pavlovich and the monarchist deputy Purishkevich. They also tried to involve the liberal Maklakov, obviously to give the murder an "all-national" character. The celebrated lawyer wisely declined, supplying the conspirators however with poison—a rather stylistic distinction! The conspirators judged, not without foundation, that a Romanov automobile would facilitate the removal of the body after the murder. The grand ducal coat-of-arms had found its use at last. The rest was carried out in the manner of a moving picture scenario designed for people of bad taste. On the night of the 16-17th of December, Rasputin, coaxed in to a little party, was murdered in Yussupov's maisonette.

The ruling classes, with the exception of a narrow camarilla and the mystic worshipers, greeted the murder of Rasputin as an act of salvation. The grand duke, placed under house arrest, his hands, according to the tzar's expression, stained with the blood of a muzhik,—although a Christ, still a muzhik!—was visited with sympathy by all the members of the imperial household then in Petersburg. The tzarina's own sister, widow of the Grand Duke Sergei, telegraphed that she was praying for the murderers and calling down blessings on their patriotic act. The newspapers, until they were forbidden to mention Rasputin, printed estatic articles. In the theaters people tried to demonstrate in honor of the murderers. Passers-by congratulated one another in the streets. "In private houses, in officers' meetings, in restaurants," relates Prince Yussupov, "they drank to our health; the workers in the factories cried *Hurrah* for us." We may well concede that the workers did not grieve when they learned of the murder of Rasputin, but their cries of Hurrah! had nothing in common with the hope for a rebirth of the dynasty. The Rasputin camarilla dropped out of sight and waited. They buried Rasputin in secrecy from the whole world—the tzar, the tzarina, the tzar's daughters and Vyrubova. Around the body of the Holy Friend, the former horse thief murdered by grand dukes, the tzar's family must have seemed outcast even to themselves. However, even after he was buried Rasputin did not find peace. Later on, when Nicholas and Alexandra Romanov were under house arrest, the soldiers of Tzarskoe Selo dug up the grave and opened the coffin. At the head of the murdered man lay an icon with the signatures: Alexandra, Olga, Tatiana, Maria, Anastasia, Ania. The Provisional Government for some reason sent an emissary to bring the body to Petrograd. A crowd resisted, and the emissary was compelled to burn the body on the spot.

After the murder of its "Friend" the monarchy survived in all ten weeks. But this short space of time was still its own. Rasputin was no longer, but his shadow continued to rule. Contrary to all the expectations of the conspirators, the royal pair began after the murder to promote with special determination the most scorned members of the Rasputin clique. In revenge for Rasputin, a notorious scoundrel was named Minister of Justice. A number of grand dukes were banished from the capital. It was rumored that Protopopov took up spiritualism, calling up the ghost of Rasputin. The noose of hopelessness was drawing tighter.

The murder of Rasputin played a colossal rôle, but a very different one from that upon which its perpetrators and inspirers had counted. It did not weaken the crisis, but sharpened it. People talked of the murder everywhere: in the palaces, in the staffs, at the factories, and in the peasant's huts. The inference drew itself: even the grand dukes have no other recourse against the leprous camarilla except poison and the revolver. The poet Blok wrote of the murder of Rasputin: "The bullet which killed him reached the very heart of the ruling dynasty."

*

ROBESPIERRE once reminded the Legislative Assembly that the opposition of the nobility, by weakening the monarchy, had roused the bourgeoisie, and after them the popular masses. Robespierre gave warning at the same time that in the rest of Europe the revolution could not develop so swiftly as in France, for the privileged classes of other countries, taught by the experience of the French nobility, would not take the revolutionary initiative. In giving this admirable analysis, Robespierre was mistaken only in his assumption that with its oppositional recklessness the French nobility had given a lesson once for all to other countries. Russia proved again, both in 1905 and yet more in 1917, that a revolution directed against an autocratic and half-feudal régime, and consequently against a nobility, meets in its first step an unsystematic and inconsistent but nevertheless very real coöperation not only from the rank and file nobility, but also from its most privileged upper circles, including here even members of the dynasty. This remarkable historic phenomenon may seem to contradict the class theory of society, but in reality it contradicts only its vulgar interpretation.

A revolution breaks out when all the antagonisms of a society have reached their highest tension. But this makes the situation unbearable even for the classes of the old society—that is, those who are doomed to break up. Although I do not want to give a biological analogy more weight than it deserves, it is worth remarking that the natural act of birth becomes at a certain moment equally unavoidable both for the maternal organism and for the offspring. The opposition put up by the privileged classes expresses the incompatibility of their traditional social position with the demands of the further existence of society. Everything seems to slip out of the hands of the ruling bureaucracy. The aristocracy finding itself in the focus of a general hostility lays the blame upon the bureaucracy, the latter blames the aristocracy, and then together, or separately, they direct their discontent against the monarchical summit of their power.

Prince Sherbatov, summoned into the ministry for a time from his service in the hereditary institutions of the nobility, said: "Both Samarin and I are former heads of the nobility in our provinces. Up till now nobody has ever considered us as Lefts and we do not consider ourselves so. But we can neither of us understand a situation in a state where the monarch and his government find themselves in radical disagreement with all reasonable (we are not talking here of revolutionary intrigue) society—with the nobility, the merchants, the cities, the zemstvos, and even the army. If those above do not want to listen to our opinion, it is our duty to withdraw."

The nobility sees the cause of all its misfortunes in the fact that the monarchy is blind or has lost its reason. The privileged caste cannot believe that no policy whatever is possible which would reconcile the old society with the new. In other words, the nobility cannot accept its own doom and converts its death-weariness into opposition against the most sacred power of the old régime, that is, the monarchy. The sharpness and irresponsibility of the aristocratic opposition is explained by history's having made spoiled children of the upper circles of the nobility, and by the unbearableness to them of their own fears in face of revolution. The unsystematic and inconsistent character of the noble discontent is explained by the fact that it is the opposition of a class which has no future. But as a lamp before it goes out flares up with a bright although smoky light, so the nobility before disappearing gives out an oppositional flash, which performs a mighty service for its mortal enemy. Such is the dialectic of this process, which is not only consistent with the class theory of society, but can only by this theory be explained.

CHAPTER VI

THE DEATH AGONY OF THE MONARCHY

THE dynasty fell by shaking, like rotten fruit, before the revolution even had time to approach its first problems. Our portrayal of the old ruling class would remain incomplete if we did not try to show how the monarchy met the hour of its fall.

The tzar was at headquarters at Moghilev, having gone there not because he was needed, but in flight from the Petrograd disorders. The court chronicler, General Dubensky, with the tzar at headquarters, noted in his diary: "A quiet life begins here. Everything will remain as before. Nothing will come of his (the tzar's) presence. Only accidental external causes will change anything. . . ." On February 24, the tzarina wrote Nicholas at headquarters, in English as always: "I hope that Duma man Kedrinsky (she means Kerensky) will be hung for his horrible speeches—it is necessary (war time law) and it will be an example. All are thirsting and beseeching that you show your firmness." On February 25, a telegram came from the Minister of War that strikes were occurring in the capital, disorders beginning among the workers, but measures had been taken and there was nothing serious. In a word: "It isn't the first time, and won't be the last!"

The tzarina, who had always taught the tzar not to yield, here too tried to remain firm. On the 26th, with an obvious desire to hold up the shaky courage of Nicholas, she telegraphs him: "It is calm in the city." But in her evening telegram she has to confess: "Things are not going at all well in the city." In a letter she says: "You must say to the workers that they must not declare strikes, if they do, they will be sent to the front as a punishment. There is no need at all of shooting. Only order is needed, and not to let them cross the bridges." Yes, only a little thing is needed, *only* order! But the chief thing is not to admit the workers into the city—let them choke in the raging impotence of their suburbs.

On the morning of the 27th, General Ivanov moves from the front with the Battalion of St. George, entrusted with dictatorial powers—which he is to make public, however, only upon occupying Tzarskoe Selo. "It would be hard to imagine a more unsuitable person," General Denikin will recall later, himself having taken a turn at military dictatorship, "a flabby old man, meagerly grasping the political situation, possessing neither strength, nor energy, nor will, nor austerity." The choice fell upon Ivanov through memories of the first revolution. Eleven years before that he had subdued Kronstadt. But those years had left their traces; the subduers had grown flabby, the subdued, strong. The northern and western fronts were ordered to get ready troops for the march on Petrograd; evidently everybody thought there was plenty of time ahead. Ivanov himself assumed that the affair would be ended soon and successfully; he even remembered to send out an adjutant to buy provisions in Moghilev for his friends in Petrograd.

On the morning of February 27, Rodzianko sent the tzar a new telegram, which ended with the words: "The last hour has come when the fate of the fatherland and the dynasty is being decided." The tzar said to his Minister of the Court, Frederiks: "Again that fat-bellied Rodzianko has written me a lot of nonsense, which I won't even bother to answer." But no. It was not nonsense. He will have to answer.

About noon of the 27th, headquarters received a report from Khabalov of the mutiny of the Pavlovsky, Volynsky, Litovsky and Preobrazhensky regiments, and the necessity of sending reliable troops from the front. An hour later from the War Ministry came a most reassuring telegram: "The disorders which began this morning in certain military units are being firmly and energetically put down by companies and battalions loyal to their duty. . . . I am firmly convinced of an early restoration of tranquillity." However, a little after seven in the evening, the same minister, Belyaev, is reporting that "We are not succeeding in putting down the military rebellion with the few detachments that remain loyal to their duty," and requesting a speedy despatch of really reliable troops—and that too in sufficient numbers "for simultaneous activity in different parts of the city."

The Council of Ministers deemed this a suitable day to remove from their midst the presumed cause of all misfortunes—the half-crazy Minister of the Interior Protopopov. At the same time General Khabalov issued an edict—prepared in secrecy from the government—declaring Petrograd, on His Majesty's orders, under martial law. So here too was an attempt to mix hot with cold—hardly intentional, however, and anyway of no use. They did not even succeed in pasting up the declaration of martial law through the city: the burgomaster, Balka, could find neither paste nor brushes. Nothing would stick together for those functionaries any longer; they already belonged to the kingdom of shades.

The principal shade of the last tzarist ministry was the seventy-year old Prince Golytsin, who had formerly conducted some sort of eleemosynary institutions of the tzarina, and had been advanced by her to the post of head of the government in a period of war and revolution. When friends asked this "good-natured Russian squire, this old weakling"—as the liberal Baron Nolde described him—why he accepted such a troublesome position, Golytsin answered: "So as to have one more pleasant recollection." This aim, at any rate, he did not achieve. How the last tzarist government felt in those hours is attested by Rodzianko in the following tale: With the first news of the movement of a crowd toward the Mariinsky Palace, where the Ministry was in session, all the lights in the building were immediately put out. (The government wanted only one thing—that the revolution should not notice it.) The rumor, however, proved false; the attack did not take place; and when the lights were turned on, one of the members of the tzarist government was found "to his own surprise" under the table. What kind of recollections he was accumulating there has not been established.

But Rodzianko's own feelings apparently were not at their highest point. After a long but vain hunt for the government by telephone, the President of the Duma tries again to ring up Prince Golytsin. The latter answers him: "I beg you not to come to me with anything further, I have resigned." Hearing this news, Rodzianko, according to his loyal secretary, sank heavily in an armchair and covered his face with both hands. . . . "My God, how horrible! . . . Without a government . . . Anarchy . . . Blood . . ." and softly wept. At the expiring of the senile ghost of the tzarist power Rodzianko felt unhappy, desolate, orphaned. How far he was at that moment from the thought that tomorrow he would have to "head" a revolution!

The telephone answer of Golytsin is explained by the fact that on the evening of the 27th the Council of Ministers had definitely acknowledged itself incapable of handling the situation, and proposed to the tzar to place at the head of the government a man enjoying general confidence. The tzar answered Golytsin: "In regard to changes in the personal staff in the present circumstances, I consider that inadmissible. Nicholas." Just what circumstances was he waiting for? At the same time the tzar demanded that they adopt "the most decisive measures" for putting down the rebellion. That was easier said than done.

On the next day, the 28th, even the untamable tzarina at last loses heart. "Concessions are necessary," she telegraphs Nicholas. "The strikes continue; many troops have gone over to the side of the revolution. Alix."

It required an insurrection of the whole guard, the entire garrison, to compel this Hessian zealot of autocracy to agree that "concessions are necessary." Now the tzar also begins to suspect that the "fat-bellied Rodzianko" had not telegraphed nonsense. Nicholas decides to join his family. It is possible that he is a little gently pushed from behind by the generals of the staff, too, who are not feeling quite comfortable.

The tzar's train traveled at first without mishap. Local chiefs and governors came out as usual to meet him. Far from the revolutionary whirlpool, in his accustomed royal car, surrounded by the usual suite, the tzar apparently again lost a sense of the close coming crisis. At three o'clock on the 28th, when the events had already settled his fate, he sent a telegram to the tzarina from Vyazma: "Wonderful weather. Hope you are well and calm. Many troops sent from the front. With tender love. Niki." Instead of the concessions, upon which even the tzarina is insisting, the tenderly loving tzar is sending troops from the front. But in spite of that "wonderful weather," in just a few hours the tzar will stand face to face with the revolutionary storm. His train went as far as the Visher station. The railroad workers would not let it go farther: "The bridge is damaged." Most likely this pretext was invented by the courtiers themselves in order to soften the situation. Nicholas tried to make his way, or they tried to get him through, by way of Bologoe on the Nikolaevsk railroad; but here too the workers would not let the train pass. This was far more palpable than all the Petrograd telegrams. The tzar had broken away from headquarters, and could not make his way to the capital. With its simple railroad "pawns" the revolution had cried "check" to the king!

The court historian Dubensky, who accompanied the tzar in his train, writes in his diary: "Everybody realizes that this midnight turn at Visher is a historical night . . . To me it is perfectly clear that the question of a constitution is settled; it will surely be introduced. . . . Everybody is saying that it is only necessary to strike a bargain with them, with the members of the Provisional Government." Facing a lowered semaphore, behind which mortal danger is thickening, Count Frederiks, Prince Dolgoruky, Count Leuchtenberg, all of them, all those high lords, are now for a constitution. They no longer think of struggling. It is only necessary to strike a bargain, that is, try to fool them again as in 1905.

While the train was wandering and finding no road, the tzarina was sending the tzar telegram after telegram, appealing to him to return as soon as possible. But her telegrams came back to her from the office with the inscription in blue pencil: "Whereabouts of the addressee unknown." The telegraph clerks were unable to locate the Russian tzar.

The regiments marched with music and banners to the Tauride Palace. A company of the Guards marched under the command of Cyril Vladimirovich, who had quite suddenly, according to Countess Kleinmichel, developed a revolutionary streak. The sentries disappeared. The intimates were abandoning the palace. "Everybody was saving himself who could," relates Vyrubova. Bands of revolutionary soldiers wandered about the palace and with eager curiosity looked over everything. Before they had decided up above what should be done, the lower ranks were converting the palace of the tzar into a museum.

The tzar—his location unknown—turns back to Pskov, to the headquarters of the northern front, commanded by the old General Ruszky. In the tzar's suite one suggestion follows another. The tzar procrastinates. He is still reckoning in days and weeks, while the revolution is keeping its count in minutes.

The poet Blok characterized the tzar during the last months of the monarchy as follows: "Stubborn, but without will; nervous, but insensitive to everything; distrustful of people, taut and cautious in speech, he was no longer master of himself. He had ceased to understand the situation, and did not take one clearly conscious step, but gave himself over completely into the hands of those whom he himself had placed in power." And how much these traits of tautness and lack of will, cautiousness and distrust, were to increase during the last days of February and first days of March!

Nicholas finally decided to send—and nevertheless evidently did not send—a telegram to the hated Rodzianko stating that for the salvation of the fatherland he appointed him to form a new ministry, reserving, however, the ministries of foreign affairs, war and marine for himself. The tzar still hoped to bargain with "them": the "many troops," after all, were on their way to Petrograd.

General Ivanov actually arrived without hindrance at Tzarskoe Selo: evidently the railroad workers did not care to come in conflict with the Battalion of St. George. The general confessed later that he had three or four times found it necessary on the march to use fatherly influence with the lower ranks, who were impudent to him: he made them get down on their knees. Immediately upon the arrival of the "dictator" in Tsarskoe Selo, the local authorities informed him that an encounter between the Battalion of St. George and the troops would mean danger to the tzar's family. They were simply afraid for themselves, and advised the dictator to go back without detraining.

General Ivanov telegraphed to the other "dictator," Khabalov, in Petrograd ten questions, to which he received succinct answers: We will quote them in full, for they deserve it:

Ivanov's questions:

Khabalov's replies:

1. How many troops are in order and how many are misbehaving?

1. I have at my disposal in the Admiralty building four companies of the Guard, five squadrons of cavalry and Cossacks, and two batteries; the rest of the troops have gone over to the revolutionists, or by agreement with them are remaining neutral. Soldiers are wandering through the town singly or in bands disarming officers.

2. Which railroad stations are guarded?

2. All the stations are in the hands of the revolutionists and strictly guarded by them.

3. In what parts of the city is order preserved?

3. The whole city is in the hands of the revolutionists. The telephone is not working, there is no communication between different parts of the city.

4. What authorities are governing the different parts of the city?

4. I cannot answer this question.

5. Are all the ministries functioning properly?

5. The ministers have been arrested by the revolutionists.

6. What police forces are at your disposal at the present moment?

6. None whatever.

84

Ivanov's questions:	*Khabalov's replies:*
7. What technical and supply institutions of the War Department are now in your control?	7. I have none.
8. What quantity of provisions is at your disposal?	8. There are no provisions at my disposal. In the city on February 5 there were 5,600,000 poods of flour in store.
9. Have many weapons, artillery and military stores fallen into the hands of the mutineers?	9. All the artillery establishments are in the hands of the revolutionists.
10. What military forces and staffs are in your control?	10. The chief of the Staff of the District is in my personal control. With the other district administrations I have no connections.

Having received this unequivocal illumination as to the situation, General Ivanov "agreed" to turn back his echelon without detraining to the station "Dno." [1] "Thus," concludes one of the chief personages of the staff, General Lukomsky, "nothing came of the expedition of General Ivanov with dictatorial powers but a public disgrace."

That disgrace, incidentally, was a very quiet one, sinking unnoticed in the billowing events. The dictator, we may suppose, delivered the provisions to his friends in Petrograd, and had a long chat with the tzarina. She referred to her self-sacrificing work in the hospitals, and complained of the ingratitude of the army and the people.

During this time news was arriving at Pskov by way of Moghilev, blacker and blacker. His Majesty's own bodyguard, in which every soldier was known by name and coddled by the royal family, turned up at the State Duma asking permission to arrest those officers who had refused to take part in the insurrec-

---

[1] The name of this station is also the Russian word meaning "bottom." [Trans.]

tion. Vice-Admiral Kurosh reported that he found it impossible to take any measures to put down the insurrection at Kronstadt, since he could not vouch for the loyalty of a single detachment. Admiral Nepenin telegraphed that the Baltic Fleet had recognized the Provisional Committee of the State Duma. The Moscow commander-in-chief, Mrozovsky, telegraphed: "A majority of the troops have gone over with artillery to the revolutionists. The whole town is therefore in their hands. The burgomaster and his aide have left the city hall." *Have left* means that they fled.

All this was communicated to the tzar on the evening of March 1. Deep into the night they coaxed and argued about a responsible ministry. Finally, at two o'clock in the morning the tzar gave his consent, and those around him drew a sigh of relief. Since they took it for granted that this would settle the problem of the revolution, an order was issued at the same time that the troops which had been sent to Petrograd to put down the insurrection should return to the front. Ruszky hurried at dawn to convey the good news to Rodzianko. But the tzar's clock was way behind. Rodzianko in the Tauride Palace, already buried under a pile of democrats, socialists, soldiers, workers' deputies, replied to Ruszky: "Your proposal is not enough; it is now a question of the dynasty itself. . . . Everywhere the troops are taking the side of the Duma, and the people are demanding an abdication in favor of the Heir with Mikhail Alexandrovich as regent." Of course the troops never thought of demanding either the Heir or Mikhail Alexandrovich. Rodzianko merely attributed to the troops and the people that slogan upon which the Duma was still hoping to stop the revolution. But in either case the tzar's concession had come too late: "The anarchy has reached such proportions that I (Rodzianko) was this night compelled to appoint a Provisional Government. Unfortunately, the edict has come too late. . . ." These majestic words bear witness that the President of the Duma had succeeded in drying the tears shed over Golytsin. The tzar read the conversation between Rodzianko and Ruszky, and hesitated, read it over again, and decided to wait. But now the military chiefs had begun to sound the alarm: the matter concerned them too a little!

General Alexeiev carried out during the hours of that night a sort of plebiscite among the commanders-in-chief at the fronts. It is a good thing present-day revolutions are accomplished with the help of the telegraph, so that the very first impulses and reactions of those in power are preserved to history on the tape. The conversations of the tzarist field-marshals on the night of March 1-2 are an incomparable human document. Should the tzar abdicate or not? The commander-in-chief of the western front, General Evert, consented to give his opinion only after Generals Ruszky and Brussilov had expressed themselves. The commander-in-chief of the Roumanian front, General Sakharov, demanded that before he express himself the conclusions of all the other commanders-in-chief should be communicated to him. After long delays this valiant chieftain announced that his warm love for the monarch would not permit his soul to reconcile itself with an acceptance of the "base suggestion"; nevertheless, "with sobs" he advised the tzar to abdicate in order to avoid "still viler pretensions." Adjutant-General Evert quite reasonably explained the necessity for capitulation: "I am taking all measures to prevent information as to the present situation in the capital from penetrating the army, in order to protect it against indubitable disturbances. No means exist for putting down the revolution in the capitals." Grand Duke Nikolai Nikolaievich on the Caucasian front beseeched the tzar on bended knee to adopt the "supermeasure" and renounce the throne. A similar prayer came from Generals Alexeiev and Brussilov and Admiral Nepenin. Ruszky spoke orally to the same effect. The generals respectfully presented seven revolver barrels to the temple of the adored monarch. Fearing to let slip the moment for reconciliation with the new power, and no less fearing their own troops, these military chieftains, accustomed as they were to surrendering positions, gave the tzar and the High Commander-in-Chief a quite unanimous counsel: Retire without fighting. This was no longer distant Petrograd against which, as it seemed, one might send troops; this was the front from which the troops had to be borrowed.

Having listened to this suggestively circumstanced report, the tzar decided to abdicate the throne which he no longer possessed. A telegram to Rodzianko suitable to the occasion was drawn up; "There is no sacrifice that I would not make in the name of the real welfare and salvation of my native mother Russia. Thus I am ready to abdicate the throne in favor of my son, and in order that he may remain with me until he is of age, under the regency of my brother, Mikhail Alexandrovich. Nicholas." This telegram too, however, was not despatched, for news came from the capital of the departure for Pskov of the deputies Guchkov and Shulgin. This offered a new pretext to postpone the decision. The tzar ordered the telegram returned to him. He obviously dreaded to sell too cheap, and still hoped for comforting news—or more accurately, hoped for a miracle. Nicholas received the two deputies at twelve o'clock midnight March 2-3. The miracle did not come, and it was impossible to evade longer. The tzar unexpectedly announced that he could not part with his son—what vague hopes were then wandering in his head?—and signed an abdication in favor of his brother. At the same time edicts to the Senate were signed, naming Prince Lvov President of the Council of Ministers, and Nikolai Nikolaievich Supreme Commander-in-Chief. The family suspicions of the tzarina seemed to have been justified: the hated "Nikolasha" came back to power along with the conspirators. Guchkov apparently seriously believed that the revolution would accept the Most August War Chief. The latter also accepted his appointment in good faith. He even tried for a few days to give some kind of orders and make appeals for the fulfillment of patriotic duty. However the revolution painlessly removed him.

In order to preserve the appearance of a free act, the abdication was dated three o'clock in the afternoon, on the pretense that the original decision of the tzar to abdicate had taken place at that hour. But as a matter of fact that afternoon's "decision," which gave the scepter to his son and not to his brother, had been taken back in anticipation of a more favorable turn of the wheel. Of that, however, nobody spoke out loud. The tzar made a last effort to save his face before the hated deputies, who upon their part permitted this falsification of a historic act—this deceiving of the people. The monarchy retired from the scene preserving its usual style; and its successors also remained true to themselves. They probably even regarded their connivance as the magnanimity of a conqueror to the conquered.

Departing a little from the phlegmatic style of his diary, Nicholas writes on March 2: "This morning Ruszky came and read me a long conversation over the wire with Rodzianko. According to his words the situation in Petrograd is such that a ministry of the members of the State Duma will be powerless to do anything, for it is being opposed by the social-democratic party in the person of a workers' committee. My abdication is necessary. Ruszky transmitted this conversation to Alexeiev at headquarters and to all the commanders-in-chief. Answers arrived at 12:30. To save Russia and keep the army at the front, I decided upon this step. I agreed, and they sent from headquarters the text of an abdication. In the evening came Guchkov and Shulgin from Petrograd, with whom I talked it over and gave them the document amended and signed. At 1 o'clock in the morning I left Pskov with heavy feelings; around me treason, cowardice, deceit."

The bitterness of Nicholas was, we must confess, not without foundation. It was only as short a time ago as February 28, that General Alexeiev had telegraphed to all the commanders-in-chief at the front: "Upon us all lies a sacred duty before the sovereign and the fatherland to preserve loyalty to oath and duty in the troops of the active army." Two days later Alexeiev appealed to these same commanders-in-chief to violate their "loyalty to oath and duty." In all the commanding staff there was not found one man to take action in behalf of his tzar. They all hastened to transfer to the ship of the revolution, firmly expecting to find comfortable cabins there. Generals and admirals one and all removed the tzarist braid and put on the red ribbon. There was news subsequently of one single righteous soul, some commander of a corps, who died of heart failure taking the new oath. But it is not established that his heart failed through injured monarchist feelings, and not through other causes. The civil officials naturally were not obliged to show more courage than the military—each one was saving himself as he could.

But the clock of the monarchy decidedly did not coincide with the revolutionary clocks. At dawn of March 3, Ruszky was again summoned to the direct wire from the capital: Rodzianko and Prince Lvov were demanding that he hold up the tzar's abdication, which had again proved too late. The installation of Alexei,—said the new authorities evasively—might perhaps be accepted—by whom?—but the installation of Mikhail was absolutely unacceptable. Ruszky with some venom expressed his regret that the deputies of the Duma who had arrived the night before had not been sufficiently informed as to the aims and purposes of their journey. But here too the deputies had their justification. "Unexpectedly to us all there broke out such a soldiers' rebellion as I never saw the like of," explained the Lord Chamberlain to Ruszky, as though he had done nothing all his life but watch soldiers' rebellions. "To proclaim Mikhail emperor would pour oil on the fire and there would begin a ruthless extermination of everything that can be exterminated." How it whirls and shakes and bends and contorts them all!

The generals silently swallowed this new "vile pretension" of the revolution. Alexeiev alone slightly relieved his spirit in a telegraphic bulletin to the commanders-in-chief: "The left parties and the workers' deputies are exercising a powerful pressure upon the President of the Duma, and there is no frankness or sincerity in the communications of Rodzianko." The only thing lacking to the generals in those hours was sincerity!

But at this point the tzar again changed his mind. Arriving in Moghilev from Pskov, he handed to his former chief-of-staff, Alexeiev, for transmission to Petrograd, a sheet of paper with his consent to the handing over of the scepter to his son. Evidently he found this combination in the long run more promising. Alexeiev, according to Denikin's story, went away with the telegram and . . . did not send it. He thought that those two manifestoes which had already been published to the army and the country were enough. The discord arose from the fact that not only the tzar and his counselors, but also the Duma liberals, were thinking more slowly than the revolution.

Before his final departure from Moghilev on March 8, the tzar, already under formal arrest, wrote an appeal to the troops ending with these words: "Whoever thinks now of peace, whoever desires it, that man is a traitor to the fatherland, its betrayer." This was in the nature of a prompted attempt to snatch out of the hands of liberalism the accusation of Germanophilism. The attempt had no result: they did not even dare publish the appeal.

Thus ended a reign which had been a continuous chain of ill luck, failure, misfortune, and evildoing, from the Khodynka catastrophe during the coronation, through the shooting of strikers and revolting peasants, the Russo-Japanese war, the frightful putting-down of the revolution of 1905, the innumerable executions, punitive expeditions and national pogroms —and ending with the insane and contemptible participation of Russia in the insane and contemptible world war.

Upon arriving at Tzarskoe Selo, where he and his family were confined in the palace, the tzar, according to Vyrubova, softly said: "There is no justice among men." But those very words irrefutably testify that historic justice, though it comes late, does exist.

✻

THE similarity of the last Romanov couple to the French royal pair of the epoch of the Great Revolution is very obvious. It has already been remarked in literature, but only in passing and without drawing inferences. Nevertheless it is not at all accidental, as appears at the first glance, but offers valuable material for an inference.

Although separated from each other by five quarter centuries, the tzar and the king were at certain moments like two actors playing the same rôle. A passive, patient, but vindictive treachery was the distinctive trait of both—with this difference, that in Louis it was disguised with a dubious kindliness, in Nicholas with affability. They both make the impression of people who are overburdened by their job, but at the same time unwilling to give up even a part of those rights of which they are unable to make any use. The diaries of both, similar in style or lack of style, reveal the same depressing spiritual emptiness.

The Austrian woman and the Hessian German form also a striking symmetry. Both queens stand above their kings, not only in physical but also in moral growth. Marie Antoinette was less pious than Alexandra Feodorovna, and unlike the latter was passionately fond of pleasures. But both alike scorned the people, could not endure the thought of concessions, alike mistrusted the courage of their husbands, looking down upon them —Antoinette with a shade of contempt, Alexandra with pity.

When the authors of memoirs, approaching the Petersburg court of their day, assure us that Nicholas II, had he been a private individual, would have left a good memory behind him, they merely reproduce the long-ago stereotyped remarks about Louis XVI, not enriching in the least our knowledge either of history or of human nature.

We have already seen how Prince Lvov became indignant when, at the height of the tragic events of the first revolution, instead of a depressed tzar, he found before him a *"jolly, sprightly little man* in a raspberry colored shirt." Without knowing it, the prince merely repeated the comment of Gouverneur Morris writing in Washington in 1790 about Louis: "What will you have from a creature who, situated as he is, eats and drinks and sleeps well, and laughs and is as merry a grig as lives?"

When Alexandra Feodorovna, three months before the fall of the monarchy, prophesies: "All is coming out for the best, the dreams of our Friend mean so much!", she merely repeats Marie Antoinette, who one month before the overthrow of the royal power wrote: "I feel a liveliness of spirit, and something tells me that we shall soon be happy and safe." They both see rainbow dreams as they drown.

Certain elements of similarity of course are accidental, and have the interest only of historic anecdotes. Infinitely more important are those traits of character which have been grafted, or more directly imposed, on a person by the mighty force of conditions, and which throw a sharp light on the interrelation of personality and the objective factors of history.

"He did not know how to wish: that was his chief trait of character," says a reactionary French historian of Louis. Those words might have been written of Nicholas: neither of them knew how to wish, but both knew how to not wish. But what really could be "wished" by the last representatives of a hopelessly lost historic cause? "Usually he listened, smiled, and rarely decided upon anything. His first word was usually *No*." Of whom is that written? Again of Capet. But if this is so, the manners of Nicholas were an absolute plagiarism. They both go toward the abyss "with the crown pushed down over their eyes." But would it after all be easier to go to an abyss, which you cannot escape anyway, with your eyes open? What difference would it have made, as a matter of fact, if they had pushed the crown way back on their heads?

Some professional psychologist ought to draw up an anthology of the parallel expressions of Nicholas and Louis, Alexandra and Antoinette, and their courtiers. There would be no lack of material, and the result would be a highly instructive historic testimony in favor of the materialist psychology. Similar (of course, far from identical) irritations in similar conditions call out similar reflexes; the more powerful the irritation, the sooner it overcomes personal peculiarities. To a tickle, people react differently, but to a red-hot iron, alike. As a steam-hammer converts a sphere and a cube alike into sheet metal, so under the blow of too great and inexorable events resistances are smashed and the boundaries of "individuality" lost.

Louis and Nicholas were the last-born of a dynasty that had lived tumultuously. The well-known equability of them both, their tranquillity and "gaiety" in difficult moments, were the well-bred expression of a meagerness of inner powers, a weakness of the nervous discharge, poverty of spiritual resources. Moral castrates, they were absolutely deprived of imagination and creative force. They had just enough brains to feel their own triviality, and they cherished an envious hostility toward everything gifted and significant. It fell to them both to rule a country in conditions of deep inner crisis and popular revolutionary awakening. Both of them fought off the intrusion of new ideas, and the tide of hostile forces. Indecisiveness, hypocrisy, and lying were in both cases the expression, not so much of personal weakness, as of the complete impossibility of holding fast to their hereditary positions.

And how was it with their wives? Alexandra, even more than Antoinette, was lifted to the very heights of the dreams of a princess, especially such a rural one as this Hessian, by her marriage with the unlimited despot of a powerful country. Both of them were filled to the brim with the consciousness of their high mission: Antoinette more frivolously, Alexandra in a spirit of Protestant bigotry translated into the Slavonic language of the Russian Church. An unlucky reign and a growing discontent of the people ruthlessly destroyed the fantastic world which these two enterprising but nevertheless chickenlike heads had built for themselves. Hence the growing bitterness, the gnawing hostility to an alien people that would not bow before them; the hatred toward ministers who wanted to give even a little consideration to that hostile world, to the country; hence their alienation even from their own court, and their continued irritation against a husband who had not fulfilled the expectations aroused by him as a bridegroom.

Historians and biographers of the psychological tendency not infrequently seek and find something purely personal and accidental where great historical forces are refracted through a personality. This is the same fault of vision as that of the courtiers who considered the last Russian tzar born "unlucky." He himself believed that he was born under an unlucky star. In reality his ill-luck flowed from the contradictions between those old aims which he inherited from his ancestors and the new historic conditions in which he was placed. When the ancients said that Jupiter first makes mad those whom he wishes to destroy, they summed up in superstitious form a profound historic observation. In the saying of Goethe about reason becoming nonsense—"*Vernunft wird Unsinn*"—this same thought is expressed about the impersonal Jupiter of the historical dialectic, which withdraws "reason" from historic institutions that have outlived themselves and condemns their defenders to failure.

The scripts for the rôles of Romanov and Capet were prescribed by the general development of the historic drama; only the nuances of interpretation fell to the lot of the actors. The ill-luck of Nicholas, as of Louis, had its roots not in his personal horoscope, but in the historical horoscope of the bureaucratic-caste monarchy. They were both, chiefly and above all, the last-born offspring of absolutism. Their moral insignificance, deriving from their dynastic epigonism, gave the latter an especially malignant character.

You might object: if Alexander III had drunk less he might have lived a good deal longer, the revolution would have run into a very different make of tzar, and no parallel with Louis XVI would have been possible. Such an objection, however, does not refute in the least what has been said above. We do not at all pretend to deny the significance of the personal in the mechanics of the historic process, nor the significance in the personal of the accidental. We only demand that a historic personality, with all its peculiarities, should not be taken as a bare list of psychological traits, but as a living reality grown out of definite social conditions and reacting upon them. As a rose does not lose its fragrance because the natural scientist points out upon what ingredients of soil and atmosphere it is nourished, so an exposure of the social roots of a personality does not remove from it either its aroma or its foul smell.

The consideration advanced above about a possible longer life of Alexander III is capable of illuming this very problem from another side. Let us assume that this Alexander III had not become mixed up in 1904 in a war with Japan. This would have delayed the first revolution. For how long? It is possible that the "revolution of 1905"—that is, the first test of strength, the first breach in the system of absolutism—would have been a mere introduction to the second, republican, and the third, proletarian revolution. Upon this question more or less interesting guesses are possible, but it is indubitable in any case that the revolution did not result from the character of Nicholas II, and that Alexander III would not have solved its problem. It is enough to remember that nowhere and never was the transition from the feudal to the bourgeois régime made without

95

violent disturbances. We saw this only yesterday in China; today we observe it again in India. The most we can say is that this or that policy of the monarchy, this or that personality of the monarch, might have hastened or postponed the revolution, and placed a certain imprint on its external course.

With what angry and impotent stubbornness tzarism tried to defend itself in those last months, weeks and days, when its game was hopelessly lost! If Nicholas himself lacked the will, the lack was made up by the tzarina. Rasputin was an instrument of the action of a clique which rabidly fought for self-preservation. Even on this narrow scale the personality of the tzar merges in a group which represents the coagulum of the past and its last convulsion. The "policy" of the upper circles at Tzarskoe Selo, face-to-face with the revolution, were but the reflexes of a poisoned and weak beast of prey. If you chase a wolf over the steppe in an automobile, the beast gives out at last and lies down impotent. But attempt to put a collar on him, and he will try to tear you to pieces, or at least wound you. And indeed what else can he do in the circumstances?

The liberals imagined there was something else he might do. Instead of coming to an agreement with the enfranchised bourgeoisie in good season, and thus preventing the revolution—such is liberalism's act of accusation against the last tzar—Nicholas stubbornly shrank from concessions, and even in the last days when already under the knife of destiny, when every minute was to be counted, still kept on procrastinating, bargaining with fate, and letting slip the last possibilities. This all sounds convincing. But how unfortunate that liberalism, knowing so accurately how to save the monarchy, did not know how to save itself!

It would be absurd to maintain that tzarism never and in no circumstances made concessions. It made them when they were demanded by the necessity of self-preservation. After the Crimean defeat, Alexander II carried out the semi-liberation of the peasants and a series of liberal reforms in the sphere of land administration, courts, press, educational institutions, etc. The tzar himself expressed the guiding thought of this reformation: to free the peasants from *above* lest they free themselves

96

from *below*. Under the drive of the first revolution Nicholas II granted a semi-constitution. Stolypin scrapped the peasant communes in order to broaden the arena of the capitalist forces. For tzarism, however, all these reforms had a meaning only in so far as the partial concession preserved the whole—that is, the foundations of a caste society and the monarchy itself. When the consequences of the reform began to splash over those boundaries the monarchy inevitably beat a retreat. Alexander II in the second half of his reign stole back the reforms of the first half. Alexander III went still farther on the road of counter-reform. Nicholas II in October 1905 retreated before the revolution, and then afterward dissolved the Dumas created by it, and as soon as the revolution grew weak, made his coup d'état. Throughout three-quarters of a century—if we begin with the reform of Alexander II—there developed a struggle of historic forces, now underground, now in the open, far transcending the personal qualities of the separate tzars, and accomplishing the overthrow of the monarchy. Only within the historic framework of this process can you find a place for individual tzars, their characters, their "biographies."

Even the most despotic of autocrats is but little similar to a "free" individuality laying its arbitrary imprint upon events. He is always the crowned agent of the privileged classes which are forming society in their own image. When these classes have not yet fulfilled their mission, then the monarchy is strong and self-confident. Then it has in its hands a reliable apparatus of power and an unlimited choice of executives—because the more gifted people have not yet gone over into the hostile camp. Then the monarch, either personally, or through the mediation of a powerful favorite, may become the agent of a great and progressive historic task. It is quite otherwise when the sun of the old society is finally declining to the west. The privileged classes are now changed from organizers of the national life into a parasitic growth; having lost their guiding function, they lose the consciousness of their mission and all confidence in their powers. Their dissatisfaction with themselves becomes a dissatisfaction with the monarchy; the dynasty becomes isolated; the circle of people loyal to the death narrows down;

their level sinks lower; meanwhile the dangers grow; new forces are pushing up; the monarchy loses its capacity for any kind of creative initiative; it defends itself, it strikes back, it retreats; its activities acquire the automatism of mere reflexes. The semi-Asiatic despotism of the Romanovs did not escape this fate.

If you take the tzarism in its agony, in a vertical section, so to speak, Nicholas is the axis of a clique which has its roots in the hopelessly condemned past. In a horizontal section of the historic monarchy, Nicholas is the last link in a dynastic chain. His nearest ancestors, who also in their day were merged in a family, caste and bureaucratic collectivity—only a broader one —tried out various measures and methods of government in order to protect the old social régime against the fate advancing upon it. But nevertheless they passed on to Nicholas a chaotic empire already carrying the matured revolution in its womb. If he had any choice left, it was only between different roads to ruin.

Liberalism was dreaming of a monarchy on the British plan. But was parliamentarism born on the Thames by a peaceful evolution? Was it the fruit of the "free" foresight of a single monarch? No, it was deposited as the result of a struggle that lasted for ages, and in which one of the kings left his head at the crossroads.

The historic-psychological contrast mentioned above between the Romanovs and the Capets can, by the way, be aptly extended to the British royal pair of the epoch of the first revolution. Charles I revealed fundamentally the same combination of traits with which memoirists and historians have endowed Louis XVI and Nicholas II. "Charles, therefore, remained passive," writes Montague, "yielded where he could not resist, betrayed how unwillingly he did so, and reaped no popularity, no confidence." "He was not a stupid man," says another historian of Charles Stuart, "but he lacked firmness of character. . . . His evil fate was his wife, Henrietta, a French-woman, sister of Louis XIII, saturated even more than Charles with the idea of absolutism." We will not detail the characteristics of this third—chronologically first—royal pair to be crushed by a national revolution. We will merely observe that in England the hatred was concentrated above all on the queen, as a Frenchwoman and a papist, whom they accused of plotting with Rome, secret connections with the Irish rebels, and intrigues at the French court.

But England had, at any rate, ages at her disposal. She was the pioneer of bourgeois civilization; she was not under the yoke of other nations, but on the contrary held them more and more under her yoke. She exploited the whole world. This softened the inner contradictions, accumulated conservatism, promoted an abundance and stability of fatty deposits in the form of a parasitic caste, in the form of a squirarchy, a monarchy, House of Lords, and the state church. Thanks to this exclusive historic privilege of development possessed by bourgeois England, conservatism combined with elasticity passed over from her institutions into her moral fiber. Various continental Philistines, like the Russian professor Miliukov, or the Austro-Marxist Otto Bauer, have not to this day ceased going into ecstasies over this fact. But exactly at the present moment, when England, hard pressed throughout the world, is squandering the last resources of her former privileged position, her conservatism is losing its elasticity, and even in the person of the Laborites is turning into stark reactionism. In the face of the Indian revolution the "socialist" MacDonald will find no other methods but those with which Nicholas II opposed the Russian revolution. Only a blind man could fail to see that Great Britain is headed for gigantic revolutionary earthquake shocks, in which the last fragments of her conservatism, her world domination, her present state machine, will go down without a trace. MacDonald is preparing these shocks no less successfully than did Nicholas II in his time, and no less blindly. So here too, as we see, is no poor illustration of the problem of the rôle of the "free" personality in history.

But how could Russia with her belated development, coming along at the tail end of the European nations, with her meager economic foundation underfoot, how could she develop an "elastic conservatism" of social forms—and develop it for the special benefit of professorial liberalism and its leftward shadow, reformist socialism? Russia was too far behind. And when world imperialism once took her in its grip, she had to pass through her political history in too brief a course. If Nicholas had gone to meet liberalism and replaced Stürmer with Miliukov, the development of events would have differed a little in form, but not in substance. Indeed it was just in this way that Louis behaved in the second stage of the revolution, summoning the Gironde to power: this did not save Louis himself from the guillotine, nor after him the Gironde. The accumulating social contradictions were bound to break through to the surface, and breaking through to carry out their work of purgation. Before the pressure of the popular masses, who had at last brought out into the open arena their misfortunes, their pains, indignations, passions, hopes, illusions and aims, the high-up combinations of the monarchy with liberalism had only an episodic significance. They could exert, to be sure, an influence on the order of events, maybe upon the number of actions, but not at all upon the development of the drama nor its momentous climax.

Chapter VII.

FIVE DAYS

(february 23-27, 1917)

THE 23d of February was International Woman's Day. The social-democratic circles had intended to mark this day in a general manner: by meetings, speeches, leaflets. It had not occurred to anyone that it might become the first day of the revolution. Not a single organization called for strikes on that day. What is more, even a Bolshevik organization, and a most militant one—the Vyborg borough-committee, all workers—was opposing strikes. The temper of the masses, according to Kayurov, one of the leaders in the workers' district, was very tense; any strike would threaten to turn into an open fight. But since the committee thought the time unripe for militant action—the party not strong enough and the workers having too few contacts with the soldiers—they decided not to call for strikes but to prepare for revolutionary action at some indefinite time in the future. Such was the course followed by the committee on the eve of the 23rd of February, and everyone seemed to accept it. On the following morning, however, in spite of all directives, the women textile workers in several factories went on strike, and sent delegates to the metal workers with an appeal for support. "With reluctance," writes Kayurov, "the Bolsheviks agreed to this, and they were followed by the workers—Mensheviks and Social Revolutionaries. But once there is a mass strike, one must call everybody into the streets and take the lead." Such was Kayurov's decision, and the Vyborg committee had to agree to it. "The idea of going into the streets had long been ripening among the workers; only at that moment nobody imagined where it would lead." Let us keep in mind this testimony of a participant, important for understanding the mechanics of the events.

101

It was taken for granted that in case of a demonstration the soldiers would be brought out into the streets against the workers. What would that lead to? This was war time; the authorities were in no mood for joking. On the other hand, a "reserve" soldier in war time is nothing like an old soldier of the regular army. Is he really so formidable? In revolutionary circles they had discussed this much, but rather abstractly. For no one, positively no one—we can assert this categorically upon the basis of all the data—then thought that February 23 was to mark the beginning of a decisive drive against absolutism. The talk was of a demonstration which had indefinite, but in any case limited, perspectives.

Thus the fact is that the February revolution was begun from below, overcoming the resistance of its own revolutionary organizations, the initiative being taken of their own accord by the most oppressed and downtrodden part of the proletariat —the women textile workers, among them no doubt many soldiers' wives. The overgrown bread-lines had provided the last stimulus. About 90,000 workers, men and women, were on strike that day. The fighting mood expressed itself in demonstrations, meetings, encounters with the police. The movement began in the Vyborg district with its large industrial establishments; thence it crossed over to the Petersburg side. There were no strikes or demonstrations elsewhere, according to the testimony of the secret police. On that day detachments of troops were called in to assist the police—evidently not many of them —but there were no encounters with them. A mass of women, not all of them workers, flocked to the municipal duma demanding bread. It was like demanding milk from a he-goat. Red banners appeared in different parts of the city, and inscriptions on them showed that the workers wanted bread, but neither autocracy nor war. Woman's Day passed successfully, with enthusiasm and without victims. But what it concealed in itself, no one had guessed even by nightfall.

On the following day the movement not only fails to diminish, but doubles. About one-half of the industrial workers of Petrograd are on strike on the 24th of February. The workers come to the factories in the morning; instead of going to work they hold meetings; then begin processions toward the center. New districts and new groups of the population are drawn into the movement. The slogan "Bread!" is crowded out or obscured by louder slogans: "Down with autocracy!" "Down with the war!" Continuous demonstrations on the Nevsky [1]— first compact masses of workmen singing revolutionary songs, later a motley crowd of city folk interspersed with the blue caps of students. "The promenading crowd was sympathetically disposed toward us, and soldiers in some of the war-hospitals greeted us by waving whatever was at hand." How many clearly realized what was being ushered in by this sympathetic waving from sick soldiers to demonstrating workers? But the Cossacks constantly, though without ferocity, kept charging the crowd. Their horses were covered with foam. The mass of demonstrators would part to let them through, and close up again. There was no fear in the crowd. "The Cossacks promise not to shoot," passed from mouth to mouth. Apparently some of the workers had talks with individual Cossacks. Later, however, cursing, half-drunken dragoons appeared on the scene. They plunged into the crowd, began to strike at heads with their lances. The demonstrators summoned all their strength and stood fast, "They won't shoot." And in fact they didn't.

A liberal senator was looking at the dead street-cars—or was that on the following day and his memory failed him?—some of them with broken windows, some tipped over on the tracks, and was recalling the July days of 1914 on the eve of the war. "It seemed that the old attempt was being renewed." The senator's eyes did not deceive him; the continuity is clear. History was picking up the ends of the revolutionary threads broken by the war, and tying them in a knot.

Throughout the entire day, crowds of people poured from one part of the city to another. They were persistently dispelled by the police, stopped and crowded back by cavalry detachments and occasionally by infantry. Along with shouts of "Down with the police!" was heard oftener and oftener a "Hurrah!" addressed to the Cossacks. That was significant. Toward the

---

[1] Nevsky Prospect, the main avenue of the city. [Trans.]

police the crowd showed ferocious hatred. They routed the mounted police with whistles, stones, and pieces of ice. In a totally different way the workers approached the soldiers. Around the barracks, sentinels, patrols and lines of soldiers, stood groups of working men and women exchanging friendly words with the army men. This was a new stage, due to the growth of the strike and the personal meeting of the worker with the army. Such a stage is inevitable in every revolution. But it always seems new, and does in fact occur differently every time: those who have read and written about it do not recognize the thing when they see it.

In the State Duma that day they were telling how an enormous mass of people had flooded Znamensky Square and all Nevsky Prospect and the adjoining streets, and that a totally unprecedented phenomenon was observed: the Cossacks and the regiments with bands were being greeted by revolutionary and not patriotic crowds with shouts of "Hurrah!" To the question, "What does it all mean?" the first person accosted in the crowd answered the deputy: "A policeman struck a woman with a knout; the Cossacks stepped in and drove away the police." Whether it happened in this way or another, will never be verified. But the crowd believed that it was so, that this was possible. The belief had not fallen out of the sky; it arose from previous experience, and was therefore to become an earnest of victory.

The workers at the Erikson, one of the foremost mills in the Vyborg district, after a morning meeting came out on the Sampsonievsky Prospect, a whole mass, 2,500 of them, and in a narrow place ran into the Cossacks. Cutting their way with the breasts of their horses, the officers first charged through the crowd. Behind them, filling the whole width of the Prospect, galloped the Cossacks. Decisive moment! But the horsemen, cautiously, in a long ribbon, rode through the corridor just made by the officers. "Some of them smiled," Kayurov recalls, "and one of them gave the workers a good wink." This wink was not without meaning. The workers were emboldened with a friendly, not hostile, kind of assurance, and slightly infected the Cossacks with it. The one who winked found imitators. In spite of renewed efforts from the officers, the Cossacks, without openly breaking discipline, failed to force the crowd to disperse, but flowed through it in streams. This was repeated three or four times and brought the two sides even closer together. Individual Cossacks began to reply to the workers' questions and even to enter into momentary conversations with them. Of discipline there remained but a thin transparent shell that threatened to break through any second. The officers hastened to separate their patrol from the workers, and, abandoning the idea of dispersing them, lined the Cossacks out across the street as a barrier to prevent the demonstrators from getting to the center. But even this did not help: standing stock-still in perfect discipline, the Cossacks did not hinder the workers from "diving" under their horses. The revolution does not choose its paths: it made its first steps toward victory under the belly of a Cossack's horse. A remarkable incident! And remarkable the eye of its narrator—an eye which took an impression of every bend in the process. No wonder, for the narrator was a leader; he was at the head of over two thousand men. The eye of a commander watching for enemy whips and bullets looks sharp.

It seems that the break in the army first appeared among the Cossacks, those age-old subduers and punishers. This does not mean, however, that the Cossacks were more revolutionary than others. On the contrary, these solid property owners, riding their own horses, highly valuing their Cossack peculiarities, scorning the plain peasants, mistrustful of the workers, had many elements of conservatism. But just for this reason the changes caused by the war were more sharply noticeable in them. Besides, they were always being pulled around, sent everywhere, driven against the people, kept in suspense—and they were the first to be put to the test. They were sick of it, and wanted to go home. Therefore they winked: "Do it, boys, if you know how—we won't bother you!" All these things, however, were merely very significant symptoms. The army was still the army, it was bound with discipline, and the threads were in the hands of the monarchy. The worker mass was unarmed. The leaders had not yet thought of the decisive crisis.

On the calendar of the Council of Ministers that day there

stood, among other questions, the question of disorders in the capital. Strikes? Demonstrations? This isn't the first time. Everything is provided for. Directions have been issued. Return to the order of business.

And what were the directions? In spite of the fact that on the 23rd and 24th twenty-eight policemen were beaten up—persuasive exactness about the number!—the military commander of the district, General Khabalov, almost a dictator, did not resort to shooting. Not from kind-heartedness: everything was provided for and marked down in advance, even the time for the shooting.

The revolution caught them unawares only with regard to the exact moment. Generally speaking, both sides, the revolutionary and the governmental, were carefully preparing for it, had been preparing for years, had always been preparing. As for the Bolsheviks, all their activity since 1905 was nothing but preparation for a second revolution. And the activities of the government, an enormous share of them, were preparations to put down the new revolution. In the fall of 1916 this part of the government's work had assumed an aspect of particularly careful planning. A commission under Khabalov's chairmanship had completed by the middle of January 1917 a very exact plan for crushing a new insurrection. The city was divided into six police districts, which in turn were subdivided into rayons. The commander of the reserve guard units, General Chebykin, was placed at the head of all the armed forces. Regiments were assigned to different rayons. In each of the six police districts, the police, the gendarmes and the troops were united under the command of special staff officers. The Cossack cavalry was at the disposal of Chebykin himself for larger-scale operations. The order of action was planned as follows: first the police act alone, then the Cossacks appear on the scene with whips, and only in case of real necessity the troops go into action with rifles and machine guns. It was this very plan, developed out of the experience of 1905, that was put into operation in the February days. The difficulty lay not in lack of foresight, nor defects of the plan itself, but in the human material. Here the whole thing threatened to hang fire.

Formally the plan was based on the entire garrison, which comprised one hundred and fifty thousand soldiers, but in reality only some ten thousand came into the count. Besides the policemen, numbering three and a half thousand, a firm hope was placed in the military training schools. This is explained by the makeup of the Petrograd garrison which at that time, consisted almost exclusively of reserve units, primarily of the fourteen reserve battalions attached to the regiments of the Guard which were then at the front. In addition to that, the garrison comprised one reserve infantry regiment, a reserve bicycle battalion, a reserve armored car division, small units of sappers and artillerymen and two regiments of Don Cossacks. That was a great many—it was too many. The swollen reserve units were made up of a human mass which had either escaped training almost entirely, or succeeded in getting free of it. But for that matter, substantially the same thing was true of the entire army.

Khabalov meticulously adhered to the plan he had worked out. On the first day, the 23rd, the police operated alone. On the 24th, for the most part the cavalry was led into the streets, but only to work with whip and lance. The use of infantry and firearms was to depend on the further development of events. But events came thick and fast.

On the 25th, the strike spread wider. According to the government's figures, 240,000 workers participated that day. The most backward layers are following up the vanguard. Already a good number of small establishments are on strike. The street-cars are at a stand. Business concerns are closed. In the course of the day students of the higher schools join the strike. By noon tens of thousands of people pour to the Kazan cathedral and the surrounding streets. Attempts are made to organize street meetings; a series of armed encounters with the police occurs. Orators address the crowds around the Alexander III monument. The mounted police open fire. A speaker falls wounded. Shots from the crowd kill a police inspector, wound the chief of police and several other policemen. Bottles, petards and hand grenades are thrown at the gendarmes. The war has taught this art. The soldiers show indifference, at times hostility, to the police. It spreads excitedly through the crowd that

107

when the police opened fire by the Alexander III monument, the Cossacks let go a volley at the horse "Pharaohs" (such was the nickname of the police) and the latter had to gallop off. This apparently was not a legend circulated for self-encouragement, since the incident, although in different versions, is confirmed from several sources.

A worker-Bolshevik, Kayurov, one of the authentic leaders in those days, relates how at one place, within sight of a detachment of Cossacks, the demonstrators scattered under the whips of the mounted police, and how he, Kayurov, and several workers with him, instead of following the fugitives, took off their caps and approached the Cossacks with the words: "Brothers— Cossacks, help the workers in a struggle for their peaceable demands; you see how the Pharaohs treat us, hungry workers. Help us!" This consciously humble manner, those caps in their hands—what an accurate psychological calculation! Inimitable gesture! The whole history of street fights and revolutionary victories swarms with such improvisations. But they are drowned without a trace in the abyss of great events—the shell remains to the historian, the generalization. "The Cossacks glanced at each other in some special way," Kayurov continues, "and we were hardly out of the way before they rushed into the fight." And a few minutes later, near the station gate, the crowd were tossing in their arms a Cossack who before their eyes had slaughtered a police inspector with his saber.

Soon the police disappear altogether—that is, begin to act secretly. Then the soldiers appear—bayonets lowered. Anxiously the workers ask them: "Comrades, you haven't come to help the police?" A rude "Move along!" for answer. Another attempt ends the same way. The soldiers are sullen. A worm is gnawing them, and they cannot stand it when a question hits the very center of the pain.

Meanwhile disarmament of the Pharaohs becomes a universal slogan. The police are fierce, implacable, hated and hating foes. To win them over is out of the question. Beat them up and kill them. It is different with the soldiers: the crowd makes every effort to avoid hostile encounters with them; on the contrary, seeks ways to dispose them in its favor, convince, attract, fraternize, merge them in itself. In spite of the auspicious rumors about the Cossacks, perhaps slightly exaggerated, the crowd's attitude toward the mounted men remains cautious. A horseman sits high above the crowd; his soul is separated from the soul of the demonstrator by the four legs of his beast. A figure at which one must gaze from below always seems more significant, more threatening. The infantry are beside one on the pavement—closer, more accessible. The masses try to get near them, look into their eyes, surround them with their hot breath. A great rôle is played by women workers in the relation between workers and soldiers. They go up to the cordons more boldly than men, take hold of the rifles, beseech, almost command: "Put down your bayonets—join us." The soldiers are excited, ashamed, exchange anxious glances, waver; someone makes up his mind first, and the bayonets rise guiltily above the shoulders of the advancing crowd. The barrier is opened, a joyous and grateful "Hurrah!" shakes the air. The soldiers are surrounded. Everywhere arguments, reproaches, appeals— the revolution makes another forward step.

Nicholas from headquarters sent Khabalov a telegraphic command to put an end to the disorders "tomorrow." The tzar's will fell in with the next step in Khabalov's "plan," and the telegram served merely as an extra stimulus. Tomorrow the troops will say their say. Isn't it too late? You can't tell yet. The question is posed, but far from answered. The indulgence of the Cossacks, the wavering of certain infantry lines—these are but much-promising episodes repeated by the thousand-voiced echo of the sensitive street. Enough to inspire the revolutionary crowd, but too little for victory. Especially since there are episodes of an opposite kind. In the afternoon a detachment of dragoons, supposedly in response to revolver shots from the crowd, first opened fire on the demonstrators near Gostinny Dvor. According to Khabalov's report to headquarters three were killed and ten wounded. A serious warning! At the same time Khabalov issued a threat that all workers registered in the draft would be sent to the front if they did not go to work before the 28th. The general issued a three-day ultimatum—that is, he gave the revolution more time than it needed to overthrow Khabalov and the monarchy into the bargain. But that will become known only after the victory. On the evening of the 25th nobody guessed what the next day had in its womb.

Let us try to get a clearer idea of the inner logic of the movement. On February 23, under the flag of "Woman's Day," began the long-ripe and long-withheld uprising of the Petrograd working masses. The first step of the insurrection was the strike. In the course of three days it broadened and became practically general. This alone gave assurance to the masses and carried them forward. Becoming more and more aggressive, the strike merged with the demonstrations, which were bringing the revolutionary mass face to face with the troops. This raised the problem as a whole to the higher level where things are solved by force of arms. The first days brought a number of individual successes, but these were more symptomatic than substantial.

A revolutionary uprising that spreads over a number of days can develop victoriously only in case it ascends step by step, and scores one success after another. A pause in its growth is dangerous; a prolonged marking of time, fatal. But even successes by themselves are not enough; the masses must know about them in time, and have time to understand their value. It is possible to let slip a victory at the very moment when it is within arm's reach. This has happened in history.

The first three days were days of uninterrupted increase in the extent and acuteness of the strife. But for this very reason the movement had arrived at a level where mere symptomatic successes were not enough. The entire active mass of the people had come out on the streets. It was settling accounts with the police successfully and easily. In the last two days the troops had been drawn into the events—on the second day, cavalry, on the third, the infantry too. They barred the way, pushed and crowded back the masses, sometimes connived with them, but almost never resorted to firearms. Those in command were slow to change their plan, partly because they underestimated what was happening—the faulty vision of the reaction supplemented that of the leaders of the revolution—partly because they lacked confidence in the troops. But exactly on the third day, the force of the developing struggle, as well as the tzar's command, made it necessary for the government to send the troops into action in dead earnest. The workers understood this, especially their advance ranks; the dragoons had already done some shooting the day before. Both sides now faced the issue unequivocally.

On the night of the 26th about a hundred people were arrested in different parts of the city—people belonging to various revolutionary organizations, and among them five members of the Petrograd Committee of the Bolsheviks. This also meant that the government was taking the offensive. What will happen today? In what mood will the workers wake up after yesterday's shooting? And most important: what will the troops say? The sun of February 26 came up in a fog of uncertainty and acute anxiety.

In view of the arrest of the Petrograd Committee, the guidance of the entire work in the city fell into the hands of the Vyborg rayon. Maybe this was just as well. The upper leadership in the party was hopelessly slow. Only on the morning of the 25th, the Bureau of the Bolshevik Central Committee at last decided to issue a handbill calling for an all-Russian general strike. At the moment of issue, if indeed it ever did issue, the general strike in Petrograd was facing an armed uprising. The leaders were watching the movement from above; they hesitated, they lagged—in other words, they did not lead. They dragged after the movement.

The nearer one comes to the factories, the greater the decisiveness. Today however, the 26th, there is anxiety even in the rayons. Hungry, tired, chilled, with a mighty historic responsibility upon their shoulders, the Vyborg leaders gather outside the city limits, amid vegetable gardens, to exchange impressions of the day and plan the course . . . of what? Of a new demonstration? But where will an unarmed demonstration lead, now the government has decided to go the limit? This question bores into their minds. "One thing seems evident: the insurrection is dissolving." Here we recognize the voice of Kayurov, already familiar to us, and at first it seems hardly his voice. The barometer falls so low before the storm.

111

In the hours when hesitation seized even those revolutionists closest to the mass, the movement itself had gone much
farther than its participants realized. Even the day before,
towards evening of the 25th, the Vyborg side was wholly in the
hands of the insurrection. The police stations were wrecked, individual officers had been killed, and the majority had fled. The
city headquarters had completely lost contact with the greater
part of the capital. On the morning of the 26th it became evident that not only the Vyborg side, but also Peski almost up to
Liteiny Prospect, was in control of the insurrection. At least
so the police reports defined the situation. And it was true in
a sense, although the revolutionists could hardly realize it: the
police in so many cases abandoned their lairs before there was
any threat from the workers. But even aside from that, ridding
the factory districts of the police could not have decisive significance in the eyes of the workers: the troops had not yet said
their final word. The uprising is "dissolving," thought the boldest of the bold. Meanwhile it was only beginning to develop.

The 26th of February fell on a Sunday; the factories were
closed, and this prevented measuring the strength of the mass
pressure in terms of the extent of the strike. Moreover the
workers could not assemble in the factories, as they had done
on the preceding days, and that hindered the demonstrations.
In the morning the Nevsky was quiet. In those hours the tzarina
telegraphed the tzar: "The city is calm."

But this calmness does not last long. The workers gradually concentrate, and move from all suburbs to the center.
They are stopped at the bridges. They flock across the ice: it
is only February and the Neva is one solid bridge of ice. The
firing at their crowds on the ice is not enough to stop them.
They find the city transformed. Posses, cordons, horse-patrols
everywhere. The approaches to the Nevsky are especially well
guarded. Every now and then shots ring out from ambush.
The number of killed and wounded grows. Ambulances dart
here and there. You cannot always tell who is shooting and
where the shots come from. One thing is certain: after their
cruel lesson, the police have decided not to expose themselves
again. They shoot from windows, through balcony doors, from

behind columns, from attics. Hypotheses are formed, which easily become legends. They say that in order to intimidate the demonstrators, many soldiers are disguised in police uniforms. They say that Protopopov has placed numerous machine-gun nests in the garrets of houses. A commission created after the revolution did not discover such nests, but this does not mean that there were none. However, the police on this day occupy a subordinate place. The troops come decisively into action. They are given strict orders to shoot, and the soldiers, mostly training squads—that is, non-commissioned officers' regimental schools—do shoot. According to the official figures, on this day about forty are killed and as many wounded, not counting those led or carried away by the crowd. The struggle arrives at a decisive stage. Will the mass ebb before the lead and flow back to its suburbs? No, it does not ebb. It is bound to have its own.

Bureaucratic, bourgeois, liberal Petersburg was in a fright. On that day Rodzianko, the President of the State Duma, demanded that reliable troops be sent from the front; later he "reconsidered" and recommended to the War Minister Belyaev that the crowds be dispersed, not with lead, but with cold water out of a fire-hose. Belyaev, having consulted General Khabalov, answered that a dowse of water would produce precisely the opposite effect "because it excites." Thus in the liberal and bureaucratic upper circles they discussed the relative advantages of hot and cold douches for the people in revolt. Police reports for that day testify that the fire-hose was inadequate: "In the course of the disorders it was observed as a general phenomenon, that the rioting mobs showed extreme defiance towards the military patrols, at whom, when asked to disperse, they threw stones and lumps of ice dug up from the street. When preliminary shots were fired into the air, the crowd not only did not disperse but answered these volleys with laughter. Only when loaded cartridges were fired into the very midst of the crowd, was it found possible to disperse the mob, the participants in which, however, would most of them hide in the yards of near-by houses, and as soon as the shooting stopped come out again into the street." This police report shows that

113

the temperature of the masses had risen very high. To be sure, it is hardly probable that the crowd would have begun of itself to bombard the troops—even the training squads—with stones and ice: that would too much contradict the psychology of the insurrectionary masses, and the wise strategy they had shown with regard to the army. For the sake of supplementary justification for mass murders, the colors in the report are not exactly what they were, and are not laid on the way they were, in actual fact. But the essentials are reported truly and with remarkable vividness: the masses will no longer retreat, they resist with optimistic brilliance, they stay on the street even after murderous volleys, they cling, not to their lives, but to the pavement, to stones, to pieces of ice. The crowd is not only bitter, but audacious. This is because, in spite of the shooting, it keeps its faith in the army. It counts on victory and intends to have it at any cost.

The pressure of the workers upon the army is increasing—countering the pressure from the side of the authorities. The Petrograd garrison comes into the focus of events. The expectant period, which has lasted almost three days, during which it was possible for the main mass of the garrison to keep up friendly neutrality toward the insurrection, has come to an end. "Shoot the enemy!" the monarchy commands. "Don't shoot your brothers and sisters!" cry the workers. And not only that: "Come with us!" Thus in the streets and squares, by the bridges, at the barrack-gates, is waged a ceaseless struggle—now dramatic, now unnoticeable—but always a desperate struggle, for the heart of the soldier. In this struggle, in these sharp contacts between working men and women and the soldiers, under the steady crackling of rifles and machine guns, the fate of the government, of the war, of the country, is being decided.

The shooting of demonstrators increased the uncertainty among the leaders. The very scale of the movement began to seem dangerous. Even at the meeting of the Vyborg committee the evening of the 26th—that is, twelve hours before the victory—arose discussions as to whether it was not time to end the strike. This may seem astonishing. But remember, it is far easier to recognize victory the day after, than the day before. Besides, moods change frequently under the impact of events and the news of them. Discouragement quickly gives way to a flow of enthusiasm. Kayurovs and Chugurins have plenty of personal courage, but at moments a feeling of responsibility for the masses clutches them. Among the rank-and-file workers there were fewer oscillations. Reports about their moods were made to the authorities by a well-informed agent in the Bolshevik organization, Shurkanov. "Since the army units have not opposed the crowd," wrote this provocateur, "and in individual cases have even taken measures paralyzing the initiative of the police officers, the masses have got a sense of impunity, and now, after two days of unobstructed walking the streets, when the revolutionary circles have advanced the slogans 'Down with war' and 'Down with the autocracy!', the people have become convinced that the revolution has begun, that success is with the masses, that the authorities are powerless to suppress the movement because the troops are with it, that a decisive victory is near, since the troops will soon openly join the side of the revolutionary forces, that the movement begun will not subside, but will ceaselessly grow to a complete victory and a state revolution." A characterization remarkable for compactness and clarity! The report is a most valuable historic document. This did not, of course, prevent the victorious workers from executing its author.

These provocateurs, whose number was enormous, especially in Petrograd, feared, more than anyone else did, the victory of the revolution. They followed a policy of their own: in the Bolshevik conferences Shurkanov defended the most extreme actions; in his reports to the secret police he suggested the necessity of a decisive resort to firearms. It is possible that with this aim, Shurkanov tried even to exaggerate the aggressive confidence of the workers. But in the main he was right: events would soon confirm his judgment.

The leaders in both camps guessed and vacillated, for not one of them could estimate *a priori* the relation of forces. External indications ceased absolutely to serve as a measure. Indeed one of the chief features of a revolutionary crisis consists in this sharp contradiction between the present consciousness and the old forms of social relationship. A new relation of forces was mysteriously implanting itself in the consciousness of the workers and soldiers. It was precisely the government's offensive, called forth by the previous offensive of the revolutionary masses, which transformed the new relation of forces from a potential to an active state. The worker looked thirstily and commandingly into the eyes of the soldier, and the soldier anxiously and diffidently looked away. This meant that, in a way, the soldier could no longer answer for himself. The worker approached the soldier more boldly. The soldier sullenly, but without hostility—guiltily rather—refused to answer. Or sometimes—now more and more often—he answered with pretended severity in order to conceal how anxiously his heart was beating in his breast. Thus the change was accomplished. The soldier was clearly shaking off his soldiery. In doing so he could not immediately recognize himself. The authorities said that the revolution intoxicated the soldier. To the soldier it seemed, on the contrary, that he was sobering up from the opium of the barracks. Thus the decisive day was prepared—the 27th of February.

However, on the eve of that day an incident occurred which in spite of its episodic nature paints with a new color all the events of the 26th. Towards evening the fourth company of the Pavlovsky regiment of the Imperial Guard mutinied. In the written report of a police inspector the cause of the mutiny is categorically stated: "Indignation against the training squad of the same regiment which, while on duty in the Nevsky, fired on the crowd." Who informed the fourth company of this? A record has been accidentally preserved. About two o'clock in the afternoon, a handful of workers ran up to the barracks of the Pavlovsky regiment. Interrupting each other, they told about a shooting on the Nevsky. "Tell your comrades that the Pavlovtsi, too, are shooting at us—we saw soldiers in your uniform on the Nevsky." That was a burning reproach, a flaming appeal. "All looked distressed and pale." The seed fell not upon the rock. By six o'clock the fourth company had left the barracks without permission under the command of a non-

commissioned officer—Who was he? His name is drowned forever among hundreds and thousands of equally heroic names—
and marched to the Nevsky to recall its training squad. This
was not a mere soldiers' mutiny over wormy meat; it was an act
of high revolutionary initiative. On their way down, the company had an encounter with a detachment of mounted police.
The soldiers opened fire. One policeman and one horse were
killed; another policeman and another horse were wounded.
The further path of the mutineers in the hurricane of the streets
is unknown. The company returned to the barracks and aroused
the entire regiment. But their arms had been hidden. According to some sources, they nevertheless got hold of thirty rifles.
They were soon surrounded by the Preobrazhentsi. Nineteen
Pavlovtsi were arrested and imprisoned in the fortress; the rest
surrendered. According to other information, the officers on
that evening found twenty-one soldiers with rifles missing. A
dangerous leak! These twenty-one soldiers would be seeking
allies and defenders all night long. Only the victory of the
revolution could save them. The workers would surely learn
from them what had happened. This was not a bad omen for
tomorrow's battles.

Nabokov, one of the most prominent liberal leaders, whose
truthful memoirs seem at times to be the very diary of his party
and of his class, was returning home from a visit at one o'clock
in the morning along the dark and watchful streets. He was
"perturbed and filled with dark forebodings." It is possible that
at one of the crossings he met a fugitive Pavlovetz. Both hurried past: they had nothing to say to each other. In the workers'
quarters and the barracks some kept watch or conferred, others
slept the half-sleep of the bivouac, or dreamed feverishly about
tomorrow. Here the fugitive Pavlovetz found shelter.

*

How scant are the records of the mass fighting in the February
days—scant even in comparison with the slim records of the
October fights. In October the party directed the insurrection
from day to day; in its articles, proclamations, and reports, at

117

least the external continuity of the struggle is recorded. Not so in February. The masses had almost no leadership from above. The newspapers were silenced by the strike. Without a look back, the masses made their own history. To reconstruct a living picture of the things that happened in the streets, is almost unthinkable. It would be well if we could recreate at least the general continuity and inner order of events.

The government, which had not yet lost hold of the machinery of power, observed the events on the whole even less ably than the left parties, which, as we know, were far from brilliant in this direction. After the "successful" shootings of the 26th, the ministers took heart for an instant. At dawn of the 27th Protopopov reassuringly reported that, according to information received, "part of the workers intend to return to work." But the workers never thought of going back to the shops. Yesterday's shootings and failures had not discouraged the masses. How explain this? Apparently the losses were out-balanced by certain gains. Pouring through the streets, colliding with the enemy, pulling at the arms of soldiers, crawling under horses' bellies, attacking, scattering, leaving their corpses on the crossings, grabbing a few firearms, spreading the news, catching at rumors, the insurrectionary mass becomes a collective entity with numberless eyes, ears and antennæ. At night, returning home from the arena of struggle to the workers' quarter, it goes over the impressions of the day, and sifting away what is petty and accidental, casts its own thoughtful balance. On the night of the 27th, this balance was practically identical with the report made to the authorities by the provocateur, Shurkanov.

In the morning the workers streamed again to the factories, and in open meetings resolved to continue the struggle. Especially resolute, as always, were the Vyborgtsi. But in other districts too these morning meetings were enthusiastic. To continue the struggle! But what would that mean today? The general strike had issued in revolutionary demonstrations by immense crowds, and the demonstrations had led to a collision with the troops. To continue the struggle today would mean to summon an armed insurrection. But nobody had formulated this summons. It had grown irresistibly out of the events, but it was never placed on the order of the day by a revolutionary party.

The art of revolutionary leadership in its most critical moments consists nine-tenths in knowing how to sense the mood of the masses—just as Kayurov detected the movement of the Cossack's eyebrow, though on a larger scale. An unexcelled ability to detect the mood of the masses was Lenin's great power. But Lenin was not in Petrograd. The legal and semi-legal "socialistic" staffs, Kerensky, Cheidze, Skobelev, and all those who circled around them, pronounced warnings and opposed the movement. But even the central Bolshevik staff, composed of Shliapnikov, Zalutsky and Molotov was amazing in its helplessness and lack of initiative. In fact, the districts and barracks were left to themselves. The first proclamation to the army was released only on the 26th by one of the Social Democratic organizations close to the Bolsheviks. This proclamation, rather hesitant in character —not even containing an appeal to come over to the people—was distributed throughout all the city districts on the morning of the 27th. "However," testifies Yurenev, the leader of this organization, "the tempo of the revolutionary events was such that our slogans were already lagging behind it. By the time the leaflets had penetrated into the thick of the troops, the latter had already come over." As for the Bolshevik center— Shliapnikov, at the demand of Chugurin, one of the best worker-leaders of the February days, finally wrote an appeal to the soldiers on the morning of the 27th. Was it ever published? At best it might have come in at the finish. It could not possibly have influenced the events of February 27. We must lay it down as a general rule for those days that the higher the leaders, the further they lagged behind.

But the insurrection, not yet so named by anyone, took its own place on the order of the day. All the thoughts of the workers were concentrated on the army. "Don't you think we can get them started?" Today haphazard agitation would no longer do. The Vyborg section staged a meeting near the barracks of the Moscow regiment. The enterprise proved a failure. Is it difficult for some officer or sergeant-major to work the handle of a machine gun? The workers were scattered by a

119

cruel fire. A similar attempt was made at the barracks of a Reserve regiment. And there too: officers with machine guns interfered between the workers and soldiers. The leaders of the workers fumed, looked for firearms, demanded them from the party. And the answer was: "The soldiers have the firearms, go get them." That they knew themselves. But how to get them? Isn't everything going to collapse all at once today? Thus came on the critical point of the struggle. Either the machine gun will wipe out the insurrection, or the insurrection will capture the machine gun.

In his recollections, Shliapnikov, the chief figure in the Petrograd center of the Bolsheviks, tells how he refused the demands of the workers for firearms—or even revolvers—sending them to the barracks to get them. He wished in this way to avoid bloody clashes between workers and soldiers, staking everything on agitation—that is, on the conquest of the soldiers by work and example. We know of no other testimony which confirms or refutes this statement of a prominent leader of those days—a statement which testifies to sidestepping rather than foresight. It would be simpler to confess that the leaders had no firearms.

There is no doubt that the fate of every revolution at a certain point is decided by a break in the disposition of the army. Against a numerous, disciplined, well-armed and ably led military force, unarmed or almost unarmed masses of the people cannot possibly gain a victory. But no deep national crisis can fail to affect the army to some extent. Thus along with the conditions of a truly popular revolution there develops a possibility —not, of course, a guarantee—of its victory. However, the going over of the army to the insurrection does not happen of itself, nor as a result of mere agitation. The army is heterogeneous, and its antagonistic elements are held together by the terror of discipline. On the very eve of the decisive hour, the revolutionary soldiers do not know how much power they have, or what influence they can exert. The working masses, of course, are also heterogeneous. But they have immeasurably more opportunity for testing their ranks in the process of preparation for the decisive encounter. Strikes, meetings, demonstrations, are not only acts in the struggle, but also measures of its force. The whole mass does not participate in the strike. Not all the strikers are ready to fight. In the sharpest moments the most daring appear in the streets. The hesitant, the tired, the conservative, sit at home. Here a revolutionary selection takes place of itself; people are sifted through the sieve of events. It is otherwise with the army. The revolutionary soldiers—sympathetic, wavering or antagonistic—are all tied together by a compulsory discipline whose threads are held, up to the last moment, in the officer's fist. The soldiers are told off daily into first and second files, but how are they to be divided into rebellious and obedient?

The psychological moment when the soldiers go over to the revolution is prepared by a long molecular process, which, like other processes of nature, has its point of climax. But how determine this point? A military unit may be wholly prepared to join the people, but may not receive the needed stimulus. The revolutionary leadership does not yet believe in the possibility of having the army on its side, and lets slip the victory. After this ripened but unrealized mutiny, a reaction may seize the army. The soldiers lose the hope which flared in their breasts; they bend their necks again to the yoke of discipline, and in a new encounter with the workers, especially at a distance, will stand opposed to the insurrection. In this process there are many elements imponderable or difficult to weigh, many cross-currents, collective suggestions and autosuggestions. But out of this complicated web of material and psychic forces one conclusion emerges with irrefutable clarity: the more the soldiers in their mass are convinced that the rebels are really rebelling—that this is not a demonstration after which they will have to go back to the barracks and report, that this is a struggle to the death, that the people may win if they join them, and that this winning will not only guarantee impunity, but alleviate the lot of all—the more they realize this, the more willing they are to turn aside their bayonets, or go over with them to the people. In other words, the revolutionists can create a break in the soldiers' mood only if they themselves are actually ready to seize the victory at any price whatever, even the price of blood. And this highest determination never can, or will, remain unarmed.

The critical hour of contact between the pushing crowd and

the soldiers who bar their way has its critical minute. That is when the gray barrier has not yet given way, still holds together shoulder to shoulder, but already wavers, and the officer, gathering his last strength of will, gives the command: "Fire!" The cry of the crowd, the yell of terror and threat, drowns the command, but not wholly. The rifles waver. The crowd pushes. Then the officer points the barrel of his revolver at the most suspicious soldier. From the decisive minute now stands out the decisive second. The death of the boldest soldier, to whom the others have involuntarily looked for guidance, a shot into the crowd by a corporal from the dead man's rifle, and the barrier closes, the guns go off of themselves, scattering the crowd into the alleys and backyards. But how many times since 1905 it has happened otherwise! At the critical moment, when the officer is ready to pull the trigger, a shot from the crowd—which has its Kayurovs and Chugurins—forestalls him. This decides not only the fate of the street skirmish, but perhaps the whole day, or the whole insurrection.

The task which Shliapnikov set himself of protecting the workers from hostile clashes with the troops by not giving firearms to the insurrectionists, could not in any case be carried out. Before it came to these clashes with the troops, innumerable clashes had occurred with the police. The street fighting began with the disarming of the hated Pharaohs, their revolvers passing into the hands of the rebels. The revolver by itself is a weak, almost toy-like weapon against the muskets, rifles, machine guns and cannon of the enemy. But are these weapons genuinely in the hands of the enemy? To settle this question the workers demanded arms. It was a psychological question. But even in an insurrection psychic processes are inseparable from material ones. The way to the soldier's rifle leads through the revolver taken from the Pharaoh.

The feelings of the soldiers in those hours were less active than those of the workers, but not less deep. Let us recall again that the garrison consisted mainly of reserve battalions many thousand strong, destined to fill up the ranks of those at the front. These men, most of them fathers of families, had the prospect of going to the trenches when the war was lost and the country ruined. They did not want war, they wanted to go home to their farms. They knew well enough what was going on at court, and had not the slightest feeling of attachment to the monarchy. They did not want to fight with the Germans, and still less with the Petrograd workers. They hated the ruling class of the capital, who had been having a good time during the war. Among them were workers with a revolutionary past, who knew how to give a generalized expression to all these moods.

To bring the soldiers from a deep but as yet hidden revolutionary discontent to overt mutinous action—or, at least, first to a mutinous refusal to act—that was the task. On the third day of the struggle the soldiers totally ceased to be able to maintain a benevolent neutrality toward the insurrection. Only accidental fragments of what happened in those hours along the line of contact between workers and soldiers have come down to us. We heard how yesterday the workers complained passionately to the Pavlovsky regiment about the behavior of its training squad. Such scenes, conversations, reproaches, appeals, were occurring in every corner of the city. The soldiers had no more time for hesitation. They were compelled to shoot yesterday, and they would be again today. The workers will not surrender or retreat; under fire they are still holding their own. And with them their women—wives, mothers, sisters, sweethearts. Yes, and this is the very hour they had so often whispered about: "If only we could all get together. . . ." And in the moment of supreme agony, in the unbearable fear of the coming day, the choking hatred of those who are imposing upon them the executioner's rôle, there ring out in the barrack room the first voices of open indignation, and in those voices—to be forever nameless—the whole army with relief and rapture recognizes itself. Thus dawned upon the earth the day of destruction of the Romanov monarchy.

At a morning conference in the home of the indefatigable Kayurov, where over forty shop and factory representatives had assembled, a majority spoke for continuing the movement. A majority, but not all. Too bad we cannot establish what majority, but in those hours there was no time for records. Anyway, the decision was belated. The meeting was interrupted by the intoxicating news of the soldiers' insurrection and the opening of the jails. Shurkanov kissed all those present. A kiss of Judas, but not, fortunately, to be followed by a crucifixion.

One after another, from early morning, the Reserve Guard battalions mutinied before they were led out of the barracks, continuing what the 4th Company of the Pavlovsky regiment had begun the day before. In the documents, records, memoirs, this grandiose event of human history has left but a pale, dim imprint. The oppressed masses, even when they rise to the very heights of creative action, tell little of themselves and write less. And the overpowering rapture of the victory later erases memory's work. Let us take up what records there are.

The soldiers of the Volynsky regiment were the first to revolt. As early as seven o'clock in the morning a battalion commander disturbed Khabalov with a telephone call and this threatening news: the training squad—that is, the unit especially relied on to put down the insurrection—had refused to march out, its commander was killed, or had shot himself in front of the troops. The latter version, by the way, was soon rejected. Having burned their bridges behind them, the Volintzi hastened to broaden the base of the insurrection. In that lay their only salvation. They rushed into the neighboring barracks of the Litovsky and Preobrazhensky regiments "calling out" the soldiers, as strikers go from factory to factory calling out the workers. Some time after, Khabalov received a report that the Volynsky regiment had not only refused to surrender their rifles when ordered by the general, but together with the Litovsky and Preobrazhensky regiments—and what is even more alarming, "having joined the workers"—had wrecked the barracks of the political police. This meant that yesterday's experiment of the Pavlovtsi had not been in vain: the insurrection had found leaders, and at the same time a plan of action.

In the early hours of the 27th, the workers thought the solution of the problem of the insurrection infinitely more distant than it really was. It would be truer to say that they saw the problem as almost entirely ahead of them, when it was really nine-tenths behind. The revolutionary pressure of the workers

124

on the barracks fell in with the existing revolutionary movement of the soldiers to the streets. During the day these two mighty currents united to wash out clean and carry away the walls, the roof, and later the whole groundwork of the old structure.

Chugurin was among the first to appear at the Bolshevik headquarters, a rifle in his hands, a cartridge belt over his shoulder, "all spattered up, but beaming and triumphant." Why shouldn't he beam? Soldiers with rifles in their hands are coming over to us! In some places the workers had succeeded in uniting with the soldiers, penetrating the barracks and receiving rifles and cartridges. The Vyborgtsi,[1] together with the most daring of the soldiers, outlined a plan of action: seize the police stations where the armed police have entrenched themselves; disarm all policemen; free the workers held in the police stations, and the political prisoners in the jails; rout the government troops in the city proper; unite with the still inactive troops and with the workers of other districts.

The Moscow regiment joined the uprising not without inner struggle. Amazing that there was so little struggle among the regiments. The monarchist command impotently fell away from the soldier mass, and either hid in the cracks or hastened to change its colors. "At two o'clock," remembers Korolev, a worker from the "Arsenal" factory, "when the Moscow regiment marched out, we armed ourselves. . . . We took a revolver and rifle apiece, picked out a group of soldiers who came up (some of them asked us to take command and tell them what to do), and set out for Tikhvinskaia street to shoot up the police station." The workers, it seems, did not have a moment's trouble telling the soldiers "what to do."

One after another came the joyful reports of victories. Our own armored cars have appeared! With red flags flying, they are spreading terror through the districts to all who have not yet submitted. Now it will no longer be necessary to crawl under the belly of a Cossack's horse. The revolution is standing up to its full height.

Toward noon Petrograd again became the field of military

---

[1] *Vyborgtsi* means the men of the Vyborg district—the workers—just as *Pavlovtsi* means men of the Pavlovsky regiment. In the singular, *Pavlovets*. [Trans.]

action; rifles and machine guns rang out everywhere. It was not easy to tell who was shooting or where. One thing was clear: the past and the future were exchanging shots. There was much casual firing; young boys were shooting off revolvers unexpectedly acquired. The arsenal was wrecked. "They say that several tens of thousands of Brownings alone were carried off." From the burning buildings of the District Court and the police stations pillars of smoke rolled to the sky. At some points clashes and skirmishes thickened into real battles. On Sampsonievsky boulevard the workers came up to a barrack occupied by the bicycle men, some of whom crowded into the gate. "Why don't you get on the move, comrades?" The soldiers smiled— "not a good smile," one of the participants testifies—and remained silent, while the officers rudely commanded the workers to move on. The bicyclists, along with the cavalry, proved to be the most conservative part of the army in the February, as in the October revolution. A crowd of workers and revolutionary soldiers soon gathered round the fence. "We must pull out the suspicious battalion!" Someone reported that the armored cars had been sent for; perhaps there was no other way of getting these bicyclists, who had set up the machine guns. But it is hard for a crowd to wait; it is anxiously impatient, and quite right in its impatience. Shots rang out from both sides. But the board fence stood in the way, dividing the soldiers from the revolution. The attackers decided to break down the fence. They broke down part of it and set fire to the rest. About twenty barracks came into view. The bicyclists were concentrated in two or three of them. The empty barracks were set fire to at once. Six years later Kayurov would recall: "The flaming barracks and the wreckage of the fence around them, the fire of machine guns and rifles, the excited faces of the besiegers, a truck load of armed revolutionists dashing up, and finally an armored car arriving with its gleaming gun-mouths, made a memorable and magnificent picture." This was the old tzarist, feudal, priestly, police Russia burning down, barracks and fences and all, expiring in fire and smoke, spewing out its soul with the hiccough of machine-gun shots. No wonder Kayurov, and tens, hundreds, thousands of Kayurovs, rejoiced! The arriving armored car fired several shells at the barrack where the bicyclists and officers were barricaded. The commander was killed. The officers, tearing off their epaulets and other insignia, fled through the vegetable gardens adjoining the barracks; the rest gave themselves up. This was probably the biggest encounter of the day.

The military revolt had meanwhile become epidemic. Only those did not mutiny that day who did not get around to it. Toward evening the Semenovsky regiment joined in, a regiment notorious for its brutal putting down of the Moscow uprising of 1905. Eleven years had not passed in vain. Together with the chasseurs, the Semenovtsi late at night "called out" the Izmailovtsi, whom the command were holding locked up in their barracks. This regiment, which on December 3, 1905 had surrounded and arrested the first Petrograd soviet, was even now considered one of the most backward.

The tzarist garrison of the capital, numbering 150,000 soldiers, was dwindling, melting, disappearing. By night it no longer existed.

After the morning's news of the revolt of the regiments, Khabalov still tried to offer resistance, sending against the revolution a composite regiment of about a thousand men with the most drastic orders. But the fate of that regiment has become quite a mystery. "Something impossible begins to happen on that day," the incomparable Khabalov relates after the revolution, ". . . the regiment starts, starts under a brave, a resolute officer (meaning Colonel Kutyepov), but . . . there are no results." Companies sent after that regiment also vanished, leaving no trace. The general began to draw up reserves on Palace Square, "but there were no cartridges and nowhere to get them." This is taken from Khabalov's authentic testimony before the Commission of Inquiry of the Provisional Government. What became of the punitive regiments? It is not hard to guess that as soon as they marched out they were drowned in the insurrection. Workers, women, youths, rebel soldiers, swarmed around Khabalov's troops on all sides, either considering the regiment their own or striving to make it so, and did not let them move any way but with the multitude. To fight with this thick-swarming, inexhaustible, all-penetrating mass, which now feared nothing, was as easy as to fence in dough.

Together with reports of more and more military revolts, came demands for reliable troops to put down the rebels, to defend the telephone building, the Litovsky Castle, the Marinsky Palace, and other even more sacred places. Khabalov demanded by telephone that loyal troops be sent from Kronstadt, but the commandant replied that he himself feared for the fortress. Khabalov did not yet know that the insurrection had spread to the neighboring garrisons. The general attempted, or pretended to attempt, to convert the Winter Palace into a redoubt, but the plan was immediately abandoned as unrealizable, and the last handful of "loyal" troops was transferred to the Admiralty. Here at last the dictator occupied himself with a most important and urgent business: he printed for publication the last two governmental decrees: on the retirement of Protopopov "owing to illness," and on the state of siege in Petrograd. With the latter he really had to hurry, for several hours later Khabalov's army lifted the "siege" and departed from the Admiralty for their homes. It was due only to ignorance that the revolution had not already on the evening of the 27th arrested this formidably empowered but not at all formidable general. This was done without any complications the next day.

Can it be that that was the whole resistance put up by the redoubtable Russian Empire in the face of mortal danger? Yes, that was about all—in spite of its great experience in crushing the people and its meticulously elaborated plans. When they came to themselves later, the monarchists explained the ease of the February victory of the people by the peculiar character of the Petrograd garrison. But the whole further course of the revolution refutes this explanation. True, at the beginning of the fatal year, the camarilla had already suggested to the tzar the advisability of renovating the garrison. The tzar had easily allowed himself to be persuaded that the cavalry of the Guard, considered especially loyal, "had been under fire long enough" and had earned a rest in its Petrograd barracks. However, after respectful representations from the front, the tzar agreed that four regiments of the cavalry Guard should be replaced by three crews of the naval Guard. According to Protopopov's version, this replacement was made by the command without the tzar's consent, and with treacherous design: ". . . The sailors are recruited from among the workers and constitute the most revolutionary element of the forces." But this is sheer nonsense. The highest officers of the Guard, and particularly the cavalry, were simply cutting out too good a career for themselves at the front to want to come back. Besides that, they must have thought with some dread of the punitive functions to be allotted to them. In these they would be at the head of troops totally different after their experience at the front from what they used to be on the parade grounds of the capital. As events at the front soon proved, the horse Guard at this time no longer differed from the rest of the cavalry, and the naval Guard, which was transferred to the capital, did not play an active part in the February revolution. The whole truth is that the fabric of the régime had completely decayed; there was not a live thread left.

During the 27th of February the crowd liberated without bloodshed from the many jails of the capital, all political prisoners—among them the patriotic group of the Military and Industrial Committee, which had been arrested on the 26th of January, and the members of the Petrograd Committee of the Bolsheviks, seized by Khabalov forty hours earlier. A political division occurred immediately outside the prison gates. The Menshevik-patriots set out for the Duma, where functions and places were to be assigned; the Bolsheviks marched to the districts, to the workers and soldiers, to finish with them the conquest of the capital. The enemy must have no time to breathe. A revolution, more than any other enterprise, has to be carried through to the end.

It is impossible to say who thought of leading the mutinous troops to the Tauride Palace. This political line of march was dictated by the whole situation. Naturally all the elements of radicalism not bound up with the masses gravitated toward the Tauride Palace as the center of oppositional information. Quite probably these elements, having experienced on the 27th a sudden injection of vital force, became the guides of the mutinous soldiers. This was an honorable rôle and now hardly a dangerous one. In view of its location, Potemkin's palace was well fitted to be the center of the revolution. The Tauride park is separated by just one street from the whole military community, containing the barracks of the Guard and a series of military institutions. It is true that for many years this part of the city was considered both by the government and the revolutionists to be the military stronghold of the monarchy. And so it was. But now everything had changed. The soldiers' rebellion had begun in the Guard sector. The mutinous troops had only to cross the street in order to reach the park of the Tauride Palace, which in turn was only one block from the Neva River. And beyond the Neva lies the Vyborg district, the very cauldron of the revolution. The workers need only cross Alexander's Bridge, or if that is up, walk over the ice of the river, to reach the Guards' barracks or the Tauride Palace. Thus the heterogeneous, and in its origins contradictory, northeast triangle of Petrograd—the Guards, Potemkin's palace, and the giant factories—closely interlocked—became the field of action of the revolution.

In the Tauride Palace various centers are already created, or at least sketched out—among them the field staff of the insurrection. It has no very serious character. The revolutionary officers—that is, those officers who had somehow or other, even though by mistake, got connected with the revolution in the past, but who have safely slept through the insurrection—hasten after the victory to call attention to themselves, or upon summons from others arrive "to serve the revolution." They survey the situation with profound thought and pessimistically shake their heads. These tumultuous crowds of soldiers, often unarmed, are totally unfit for battle. No artillery, no machine guns, no communications, no commanders. One strong regiment is all the enemy needs! To be sure, just now the revolutionary crowds prevent any planned maneuvers in the streets. But the workers will go home for the night, the residents will quiet down, the town will be emptied. If Khabalov were to strike with a strong regiment at the barracks, he might become master of the situation. This idea, by the way, will meet us in different versions throughout all the stages of the revolution. "Give me a strong regiment," gallant colonels will more than once exclaim to their friends, "and in two seconds I will clean up all this mess!" And some of them, as we shall see, will make the attempt. But they will all have to repeat Khabalov's words: "The regiment starts, starts under a brave officer, but . . . there are no results."

Yes, and how could there be results? The most reliable of all possible forces had been the police and the gendarmes, and the training squads of certain regiments. But these proved as pitiful before the assault of the real masses as the Battalion of St. George and the officers' training schools were to prove eight months later in October. Where could the monarchy get that salvation regiment, ready and able to enter a prolonged and desperate duel with a city of two million? The revolution seems defenseless to these verbally so enterprising colonels, because it is still terrifically chaotic. Everywhere aimless movements, conflicting currents, whirlpools of people, individuals astounded as though suddenly gone deaf, unfastened trench coats, gesticulating students, soldiers without rifles, rifles without soldiers, boys firing into the air, a thousand-voiced tumult, hurricanes of wild rumor, false alarms, false rejoicings. Enough, you would think, to lift a sword over all that chaos, and it would scatter apart and leave never a trace. But that is a crude error of vision. It is only a seeming chaos. Beneath it is proceeding an irresistible crystallization of the masses around new axes. These innumerable crowds have not yet clearly defined what they want, but they are saturated with an acid hatred of what they do not want. Behind them is an irreparable historic avalanche. There is no way back. Even if there were someone to scatter them, they would be gathering again in an hour, and the second flood would be more furious and bloodier than the first. After the February days the atmosphere of Petrograd becomes so red hot that every hostile military detachment arriving in that mighty forge, or even coming near to it, scorched by its breath, is transformed, loses confidence, becomes paralyzed, and throws itself upon the mercy of the victor without a struggle. Tomorrow General Ivanov, sent from the front by the tzar with a battalion of the Knights of St. George, will find this out. In five months the same fate will befall General Kornilov, and in eight months it will happen to Kerensky.

On the streets in the preceding days the Cossacks had seemed the most open to persuasion; it was because they were the most abused. But when it came to the actual insurrection, the cavalry once more justified its conservative reputation and lagged behind the infantry. On the 27th, it was still preserving the appearance of watchful neutrality. Though Khabalov no longer relied upon it, the revolution still feared it.

The fortress of Peter and Paul, which stands on an island in the Neva opposite the Winter Palace and the palaces of the grand dukes, remained a puzzle. Behind its walls the garrison of the fortress was, or seemed to be, a little world completely shielded from outside influences. The fortress had no permanent artillery—except for that antiquated cannon which daily announced the noon hour to Petrograd. But today field guns are set up on the walls and aimed at the bridge. What are they getting ready for? The Tauride staff has worried all night what to do about the fortress, and in the fortress they were worrying— what will the revolution do with us? By morning the puzzle is solved: "On condition that officers remain inviolable," the fortress will surrender to the Tauride Palace. Having analyzed the situation—not so difficult a thing to do—the officers of the fort hastened to forestall the inevitable march of events.

Towards evening of the 27th, a stream of soldiers, workers, students and miscellaneous people flows toward the Tauride Palace. Here they hope to find those who know everything—to get information and instructions. From all sides ammunition is being carried by armfuls into the palace, and deposited in a room that has been converted into an arsenal. At nightfall, the revolutionary staff settles down to work. It sends out detachments to guard the railway stations, and despatches reconnoitering squads wherever danger lurks. The soldiers carry out eagerly and without a murmur, although very unsystematically, the orders of the new authorities. But they always demand a written order. The initiative in this probably came from the fragments of the military staff which had remained with the troops, or from the military clerks. But they were right; it is necessary to bring order immediately into the chaos. The staff, as well as the new-born Soviet, had as yet no seals. The revolution has still to fit itself out with the implements of bureaucratic management. In time this will be done—alas, too well.

The revolution begins a search for enemies. Arrests are made all over the city—"arbitrarily," as the Liberals will say reproachfully later. But the whole revolution is arbitrary. Streams of people are brought into the Tauride under arrest—such people as the Chairman of the State Council, ministers, policemen, secret service men, the "pro-German" countess, whole broods of gendarme officers. Several statesmen, such as Proto-popov, will come of their own volition to be arrested: it is safer so. "The walls of the chamber, which had resounded to hymns in praise of absolutism, now heard but sobbing and sighs," the countess will subsequently relate. "An arrested general sank down exhausted on a near-by chair. Several members of the Duma kindly offered me a cup of tea. Shaken to the depths of his soul, the general was saying excitedly: 'Countess, we are witnessing the death of a great country.' "

Meanwhile, the great country, which had no intention of dying, marched by these people of the past, stamping its boots, clanging the butts of its rifles, rending the air with its shouts and stepping all over their feet. A revolution is always dis-tinguished by impoliteness, probably because the ruling classes did not take the trouble in good season to teach the people fine manners.

The Tauride became the temporary field headquarters, gov-ernmental center, arsenal, and prison-fortress of the revolution, which had not yet wiped the blood and sweat from its face. Into this whirlpool some enterprising enemies also made their way. A disguised captain of gendarmes was accidentally dis-covered taking down notes in a corner—not for history, but for the court-martials. The soldiers and workers wanted to end him right there. But people from the "staff" interfered, and easily led the gendarme out of the crowd. The revolution was then still good-natured—trustful and kind-hearted. It will become ruthless only after a long series of treasons, deceits and bloody trials.

The first night of the triumphant revolution was full of alarms. The improvised commissars of the railway terminals and other points, most of them chosen haphazard from the intelligentsia through personal connection, upstarts and chance acquaintances of the revolution—non-commissioned officers, especially of worker origin, would have been more useful—got nervous, saw danger on all sides, nagged the soldiers and ceaselessly telephoned to the Tauride asking for reënforcements. But in the Tauride too they were nervous. They were telephoning. They were sending out reënforcements which for the most part did not arrive. "Those who receive orders," said a member of the Tauride night staff, "do not execute them; those who act, act without orders."

The workers' districts act without orders. The Revolutionary chiefs who have led out their factories, seized the police stations, "called out" the soldiers and wrecked the strongholds of the counter-revolution, do not hurry to the Tauride Palace, to the staffs, to the administrative centers. On the contrary, they jerk their heads in that direction with irony and distrust: "Those brave boys are getting in early to divide the game they didn't kill—before it's even killed." Worker-Bolsheviks, as well as the best workers of the other Left parties, spend their days on the streets, their nights in the district headquarters, keeping in touch with the barracks and preparing tomorrow's work. On the first night of victory they continue, and they enlarge, the same work they have been at for the whole five days and nights. They are the young bones of the revolution, still soft, as all revolutions are in the first days.

On the 27th, Nabokov, already known to us as a member of the Kadet center, and at that time working—a legalized deserter—at General Headquarters, went to his office as usual and stayed until three o'clock, knowing nothing of the events. Toward evening shots were heard on the Morskaia. Nabokov listened to them from his apartment. Armored cars dashed along, individual soldiers and sailors ran past, sidling along the wall. The respected liberal observed them from the side windows of his vestibule. "The telephone continued to function, and my friends, I remember, kept me in touch with what was going on during the day. At the usual time we went to bed." This man will soon become one of the inspirators of the revolutionary (!) Provisional Government, occupying the position of General Administrator. Tomorrow an unknown old man will approach him on the street—a bookkeeper, perhaps, or a teacher —bow low and remove his hat, and say to him: "Thank you for all that you have done for the people." Nabokov, with modest pride, will relate the incident himself.

CHAPTER VIII

WHO LED THE FEBRUARY INSURRECTION?

LAWYERS and journalists belonging to the classes damaged by the revolution wasted a good deal of ink subsequently trying to prove that what happened in February was essentially a petticoat rebellion, backed up afterwards by a soldiers' mutiny and given out for a revolution. Louis XVI in his day also tried to think that the capture of the Bastille was a rebellion, but they respectfully explained to him that it was a revolution. Those who lose by a revolution are rarely inclined to call it by its real name. For that name, in spite of the efforts of spiteful reactionaries, is surrounded in the historic memory of mankind with a halo of liberation from all shackles and all prejudices. The privileged classes of every age, as also their lackeys, have always tried to declare the revolution which overthrew them, in contrast to past revolutions, a mutiny, a riot, a revolt of the rabble. Classes which have outlived themselves are not distinguished by originality.

Soon after the 27th of February attempts were also made to liken the revolution to the military coup d'état of the Young Turks, of which, as we know, they had been dreaming not a little in the upper circles of the Russian bourgeoisie. This comparison, was so hopeless however, that it was seriously opposed even in one of the bourgeois papers. Tugan-Baranovsky, an economist who had studied Marx in his youth, a Russian variety of Sombart, wrote on March 10 in the *Birzhevoe Vedomosti:*

"The Turkish revolution consisted in a victorious uprising of the army, prepared and carried out by the leaders of the army; the soldiers were merely obedient executives of the plans of their officers. But the regiments of the Guard which on February 27 overthrew the Russian throne, came without their officers . . . Not the army but the workers began the insurrection; not the generals but the soldiers came to the State Duma. The

136

soldiers supported the workers not because they were obediently fulfilling the commands of their officers, but because . . . they felt themselves blood brothers of the workers as a class composed of toilers like themselves. The peasants and the workers—those are the two social classes which made the Russian revolution."

These words require neither correction, nor supplement. The further development of the revolution sufficiently confirmed and reënforced their meaning. In Petrograd the last day of February was the first day after the victory: a day of raptures, embraces, joyful tears, voluble outpourings; but at the same time a day of final blows at the enemy. Shots were still crackling in the streets. It was said that Protopopov's Pharaohs, not informed of the people's victory, were still shooting from the roofs. From below they were firing into attics, false windows and belfries where the armed phantoms of tzarism might still be lurking. About four o'clock they occupied the Admiralty where the last remnants of what was formerly the state power had taken refuge. Revolutionary organizations and improvised groups were making arrests throughout the town. The Schlüsselburg hard-labor prison was taken without a shot. More and more regiments were joining the revolution, both in the capital and in the environs.

The overturn in Moscow was only an echo of the insurrection in Petrograd. The same moods among the workers and soldiers, but less clearly expressed. A slightly more leftward tendency among the bourgeoisie. A still greater weakness among the revolutionary organizations than in Petrograd. When the events began on the Neva, the Moscow radical intelligentsia called a conference on the question what to do, and came to no conclusion. Only on the 27th of February strikes began in the shops and factories of Moscow, and then demonstrations. The officers told the soldiers in the barracks that a rabble was rioting in the streets and they must be put down. "But by this time," relates the soldier Shishilin, "the soldiers understood the word rabble in the opposite sense." Towards two o'clock there arrived at the building of the city duma many soldiers of various regiments inquiring how to join the revolution. On the next day the strikes increased. Crowds flowed toward the

137

duma with flags. A soldier of an automobile company, Muralov, an old Bolshevik, an agriculturist, a good-natured and courageous giant, brought to the duma the first complete and disciplined military detachment, which occupied the wireless station and other points. Eight months later Muralov will be in command of the troops of the Moscow military district.

The prisons were opened. The same Muralov was driving an automobile truck filled with freed political prisoners: a police officer with his hand at his vizor asked the revolutionist whether it was advisable to let out the Jews also. Dzerzhinsky, just liberated from a hard labor prison and without changing his prison dress, spoke in the duma building where a soviet of deputies was already formed. The artillerist Dorofeev relates how on March 1 workers from the Siou candy factory came with banners to the barracks of an artillery brigade to fraternize with the soldiers, and how many could not contain their joy, and wept. There were cases of sniping in the town, but in general neither armed encounters nor casualties: Petrograd answered for Moscow.

In a series of provincial cities the movement began only on March 1, after the revolution was already achieved even in Moscow. In Tver the workers went from their work to the barracks in a procession and having mixed with the soldiers marched through the streets of the city. At that time they were still singing the "Marseillaise," not the "International." In Nizhni-Novgorod thousands of workers gathered round the city duma building, which in a majority of the cities played the rôle of the Tauride Palace. After a speech from the mayor the workers marched off with red banners to free the politicals from the jails. By evening, eighteen out of the twenty-one military divisions of the garrison had voluntarily come over to the revolution. In Samara and Saratov meetings were held, soviets of workers' deputies organized. In Kharkov the chief of police, having gone to the railroad station and got news of the revolution, stood up in his carriage before an excited crowd and, lifting his hat, shouted at the top of his lungs: "Long live the revolution. Hurrah!" The news came to Ekaterinoslav from Kharkov. At the head of the demonstration strode the assistant chief of police carrying in his hand a long saber as in the grand parades on saints' days. When it became finally clear that the monarchy could not rise, they began cautiously to remove the tzar's portraits from the government institutions and hide them in the attics. Anecdotes about this, both authentic and imaginary, were much passed around in liberal circles, where they had not yet lost a taste for the jocular tone when speaking of the revolution. The workers, and the soldier barracks as well, took the events in a very different way. As to a series of other provincial cities (Pskov, Orel, Rybinsk, Penza, Kazan, Tzaritsyn, and others), the *Chronicle* remarks under date of March 2: "News came of the uprising and the population joined the revolution." This description, notwithstanding its summary character, tells with fundamental truth what happened.

News of the revolution trickled into the villages from the near-by cities, partly through the authorities, but chiefly through the markets, the workers, the soldiers on furlough. The villages accepted the revolution more slowly and less enthusiastically than the cities, but felt it no less deeply. For them it was bound up with the question of war and land.

It would be no exaggeration to say that Petrograd achieved the February revolution. The rest of the country adhered to it. There was no struggle anywhere except in Petrograd. There were not to be found anywhere in the country any groups of the population, any parties, institutions, or military units which were ready to put up a fight for the old régime. This shows how ill-founded was the belated talk of the reactionaries to the effect that if there had been cavalry of the Guard in the Petersburg garrison, or if Ivanov had brought a reliable brigade from the front, the fate of the monarchy would have been different. Neither at the front nor at the rear was there a brigade or regiment to be found which was prepared to do battle for Nicholas II.

The revolution was carried out upon the initiative and by the strength of one city, constituting approximately about 1/75 of the population of the country. You may say, if you will, that this most gigantic democratic act was achieved in a most undemocratic manner. The whole country was placed before a *fait accompli*. The fact that a Constituent Assembly was in prospect does not alter the matter, for the dates and methods of convoking this national representation were determined by institutions which issued from the victorious insurrection of Petrograd. This casts a sharp light on the question of the function of democratic forms in general, and in a revolutionary epoch in particular. Revolutions have always struck such blows at the judicial fetichism of the popular will, and the blows have been more ruthless the deeper, bolder and more democratic the revolutions.

It is often said, especially in regard to the great French revolution, that the extreme centralization of a monarchy subsequently permits the revolutionary capital to think and act for the whole country. That explanation is superficial. If revolutions reveal a centralizing tendency, this is not in imitation of overthrown monarchies, but in consequence of irresistible demands of the new society, which cannot reconcile itself to particularism. If the capital plays as dominating a rôle in a revolution as though it concentrated in itself the will of the nation, that is simply because the capital expresses most clearly and thoroughly the fundamental tendencies of the new society. The provinces accept the steps taken by the capital as their own intentions already materialized. In the initiatory rôle of the centers there is no violation of democracy, but rather its dynamic realization. However, the rhythm of this dynamic has never in great revolutions coincided with the rhythm of formal representative democracy. The provinces adhere to the activity of the center, but belatedly. With the swift development of events characteristic of a revolution this produces sharp crises in revolutionary parliamentarism, which cannot be resolved by the methods of democracy. In all genuine revolutions the national representation has invariably come into conflict with the dynamic force of the revolution, whose principal seat has been the capital. It was so in the seventeenth century in England, in the eighteenth in France, in the twentieth in Russia. The rôle of the capital is determined not by the tradition of a bureaucratic centralism, but by the situation of the leading revolutionary class, whose vanguard is naturally concentrated

140

in the chief city: this is equally true for the bourgeoisie and the proletariat.

When the February victory was fully confirmed, they began to count up the victims. In Petrograd they counted 1443 killed and wounded, 869 of them soldiers, and 60 of these officers. By comparison with the victims of any battle in the Great Slaughter these figures are suggestively tiny. The liberal press declared the February revolution bloodless. In the days of general salubrity and mutual amnesty of the patriotic parties, nobody took the trouble to establish the truth. Albert Thomas, a friend of everything victorious, even a victorious insurrection, wrote at that time about the "sunniest, most holiday-like, most bloodless Russian revolution." To be sure, he was hopeful that this revolution would remain at the disposal of the French Bourse. But after all Thomas did not invent this habit. On the 27th of June 1789, Mirabeau exclaimed: "How fortunate that this great revolution will succeed without evil-doing and without tears! . . . History has too long been telling us only of the actions of beasts of prey. . . . We may well hope that we are beginning the history of human beings." When all the three estates were united in the National Assembly the ancestors of Albert Thomas wrote: "The revolution is ended. It has not cost a drop of blood." We must acknowledge, however, that at that period blood had really not yet flowed. Not so in the February days. Nevertheless the legend of a bloodless revolution stubbornly persisted, answering the need of the liberal bourgeois to make things look as though the power had come to him of its own accord.

Although the February revolution was far from bloodless, still one cannot but be amazed at the insignificant number of victims, not only at the moment of revolution but still more in the first period after it. This revolution, we must remember, was a paying-back for oppression, persecution, taunts, vile blows, suffered by the masses of the Russian people throughout the ages! The sailors and soldiers did in some places, to be sure, take summary revenge upon the most contemptible torturers in the person of their officers, but the number of these acts of settlement was at first insignificant in comparison with the number of the old bloody insults. The masses shook off their good-naturedness only a good while later, when they were convinced that the ruling classes wanted to drag everything back and appropriate to themselves a revolution not achieved by them, just as they had always appropriated the good things of life not produced by themselves.

*

TUGAN-BARANOVSKY is right when he says that the February revolution was accomplished by workers and peasants—the latter in the person of the soldiers. But there still remains the great question: Who led the revolution? Who raised the workers to their feet? Who brought the soldiers into the streets? After the victory these questions became a subject of party conflict. They were solved most simply by the universal formula: Nobody led the revolution, it happened of itself. The theory of "spontaneousness" fell in most opportunely with the minds not only of all those gentlemen who had yesterday been peacefully governing, judging, convicting, defending, trading, or commanding, and today were hastening to make up to the revolution, but also of many professional politicians and former revolutionists, who having slept through the revolution wished to think that in this they were not different from all the rest.

In his curious *History of the Russian Disorders,* General Denikin, former commander of the White Army, says of the 27th of February: "On that decisive day there were no leaders, there were only the elements. In their threatening current there were then visible neither aims, nor plans, nor slogans." The learned historian Miliukov delves no deeper than this general with a passion for letters. Before the revolution the liberal leader had declared every thought of revolution a suggestion of the German Staff. But the situation was more complicated after a revolution which had brought the liberals to power. Miliukov's task was now not to dishonor the revolution with a Hohenzollern origin, but on the contrary to withhold the honor of its initiation from revolutionists. Liberalism therefore has whole-heartedly fathered the theory of a spontaneous

142

and impersonal revolution. Miliukov sympathetically cites the semi-liberal, semi-socialist Stankevich, a university instructor who became Political Commissar at the headquarters of the Supreme Command: "The masses moved of themselves, obeying some unaccountable inner summons . . ." writes Stankevich of the February days. "With what slogans did the soldiers come out? Who led them when they conquered Petrograd, when they burned the District Court? Not a political idea, not a revolutionary slogan, not a conspiracy, and not a revolt, but a spontaneous movement suddenly consuming the entire old power to the last remnant." Spontaneousness here acquires an almost mystic character.

This same Stankevich offers a piece of testimony in the highest degree valuable: "At the end of January, I happened in a very intimate circle to meet with Kerensky. . . . To the possibility of a popular uprising they all took a definitely negative position, fearing lest a popular mass movement once aroused might get into an extreme leftward channel and this would create vast difficulties in the conduct of the war." The views of Kerensky's circle in nowise essentially differed from those of the Kadets. The initiative certainly did not come from there.

"The revolution fell like thunder out of the sky," says the president of the Social Revolutionary Party, Zenzinov. "Let us be frank: it arrived joyfully unexpected for us too, revolutionists who had worked for it through long years and waited for it always."

It was not much better with the Mensheviks. One of the journalists of the bourgeois emigration tells about his meeting in a tramcar on February 21 with Skobelev, a future minister of the revolutionary government: "This Social Democrat, one of the leaders of the movement, told me that the disorders had the character of plundering which it was necessary to put down. This did not prevent Skobelev from asserting a month later that he and his friends had made the revolution." The colors here are probably laid on a little thick, but fundamentally the position of the legal Social Democrats, the Mensheviks, is conveyed accurately enough.

Finally, one of the most recent leaders of the left wing of

143

the Social Revolutionaries, Mstislavsky, who subsequently went over to the Bolsheviks, says of the February uprising: "The revolution caught us, the party people of those days, like the foolish virgins of the Bible, napping." It does not matter how much they resembled virgins, but it is true they were all fast asleep.

How was it with the Bolsheviks? This we have in part already seen. The principal leaders of the underground Bolshevik organization were at that time three men: the former workers Shliapnikov and Zalutsky, and the former student Molotov. Shliapnikov, having lived for some time abroad and in close association with Lenin, was in a political sense the most mature and active of these three who constituted the Bureau of the Central Committee. However, Shliapnikov's own memoirs best of all confirm the fact that the events were too much for the trio. Up to the very last hour these leaders thought that it was a question of a revolutionary manifestation, one among many, and not at all of an armed insurrection. Our friend Kayurov, one of the leaders of the Vyborg section, asserts categorically: "Absolutely no guiding initiative from the party centers was felt . . . the Petrograd Committee had been arrested and the representative of the Central Committee, Comrade Shliapnikov, was unable to give any directives for the coming day."

The weakness of the underground organizations was a direct result of police raids, which had given exceptional results amid the patriotic moods at the beginning of the war. Every organization, the revolutionary included, has a tendency to fall behind its social basis. The underground organization of the Bolsheviks at the beginning of 1917 had not yet recovered from its oppressed and scattered condition, whereas in the masses the patriotic hysteria had been abruptly replaced by revolutionary indignation.

In order to get a clear conception of the situation in the sphere of revolutionary leadership it is necessary to remember that the most authoritative revolutionists, the leaders of the left parties, were abroad and, some of them, in prison and exile. The more dangerous a party was to the old régime, the more cruelly beheaded it appeared at the moment of revolution. The Narodniks had a Duma faction headed by the non-party radical Kerensky. The official leader of the Social-Revolutionaries, Chernov, was abroad. The Mensheviks had a party faction in the Duma headed by Cheidze and Skobelev; Martov was abroad; Dan and Tseretelli, in exile. A considerable number of socialistic intellectuals with a revolutionary past were grouped around these left factions—Narodnik and Menshevik. This constituted a kind of political staff, but one which was capable of coming to the front only after the victory. The Bolsheviks had no Duma faction: their five worker-deputies, in whom the tzarist government had seen the organizing center of the revolution, had been arrested during the first few months of the war. Lenin was abroad, Zinoviev with him; Kamenev was in exile; in exile also, the then little known practical leaders: Sverdlov, Rykov, Stalin. The Polish social-democrat, Dzerzhinsky, who did not yet belong to the Bolsheviks, was at hard labor. The leaders accidentally present, for the very reason that they had been accustomed to act under unconditionally authoritative supervisors, did not consider themselves and were not considered by others capable of playing a guiding rôle in revolutionary events.

But if the Bolshevik Party could not guarantee the insurrection an authoritative leadership, there is no use talking of other organizations. This fact has strengthened the current conviction as to the spontaneous character of the February revolution. Nevertheless the conviction is deeply mistaken, or at least meaningless.

The struggle in the capital lasted not an hour, or two hours, but five days. The leaders tried to hold it back; the masses answered with increased pressure and marched forward. They had against them the old state, behind whose traditional façade a mighty power was still assumed to exist, the liberal bourgeoisie with the State Duma, the Land and City Unions, the military-industrial organizations, academies, universities, a highly developed press, and finally the two strong socialist parties who put up a patriotic resistance to the assault from below. In the party of the Bolsheviks the insurrection had its nearest organization, but a headless organization with a scattered staff and with weak illegal nuclei. And nevertheless the revolution, which nobody in those days was expecting, unfolded, and just when it seemed from above as though the movement was already dying down, with an abrupt revival, a mighty convulsion, it seized the victory.

Whence came this unexampled force of aggression and self-restraint? It is not enough to refer to bitter feelings. Bitterness alone is little. The Petersburg workers, no matter how diluted during the war years with human raw material, had in their past a great revolutionary experience. In their aggression and self-restraint, in the absence of leadership and in the face of opposition from above, was revealed a vitally well-founded, although not always expressed, estimate of forces and a strategic calculation of their own.

On the eve of the war the revolutionary layers of the workers had been following the Bolsheviks, and leading the masses after them. With the beginning of the war the situation had sharply changed: conservative groups lifted their heads, dragging after them a considerable part of the class. The revolutionary elements found themselves isolated, and quieted down. In the course of the war the situation began to change, at first slowly, but after the defeats faster and more radically. An active discontent seized the whole working class. To be sure, it was to an extent patriotically colored, but it had nothing in common with the calculating and cowardly patriotism of the possessing classes, who were postponing all domestic questions until after the victory. The war itself, its victims, its horror, its shame, brought not only the old, but also the new layers of workers into conflict with the tzarist régime. It did this with a new incisiveness and led them to the conclusion: we can no longer endure it. The conclusion was universal; it welded the masses together and gave them a mighty dynamic force.

The army had swollen, drawing into itself millions of workers and peasants. Every individual had his own people among the troops: a son, a husband, a brother, a relative. The army was no longer insulated, as before the war, from the people. One met with soldiers now far oftener; saw them off to the front, lived with them when they came home on leave, chatted

146

with them on the streets and in the tramways about the front, visited them in the hospitals. The workers' districts, the barracks, the front, and to an extent the villages too, became communicating vessels. The workers would know what the soldiers were thinking and feeling. They had innumerable conversations about the war, about the people who were getting rich out of the war, about the generals, government, tzar and tzarina. The soldier would say about the war: To hell with it! And the worker would answer about the government: To hell with it! The soldier would say: Why then do you sit still here in the center? The worker would answer: We can't do anything with bare hands; we stubbed our toe against the army in 1905. The soldier would reflect: What if we should all start at once! The worker: That's it, all at once! Conversations of this kind before the war were conspirative and carried on by twos; now they were going on everywhere, on every occasion, and almost openly, at least in the workers' districts.

The tzar's intelligence service every once in a while took its soundings very successfully. Two weeks before the revolution a spy, who signed himself with the name Krestianinov, reported a conversation in a tramcar traversing the workers' suburb. The soldier was telling how in his regiment eight men were under hard labor because last autumn they refused to shoot at the workers of the Nobel factory, but shot at the police instead. The conversation went on quite openly, since in the workers' districts the police and the spies preferred to remain unnoticed. " 'We'll get even with them,' the soldier concluded." The report reads further: "A skilled worker answered him: 'For that it is necessary to organize so that all will be like one.' The soldier answered: 'Don't you worry, we've been organized a long time. . . . They've drunk enough blood. Men are suffering in the trenches and here they are fattening their bellies!' . . . No special disturbance occurred. February 10, 1917. Krestianinov." Incomparable spy's epic. "No special disturbance occurred." They will occur, and that soon: this tramway conversation signalizes their inexorable approach.

The spontaneousness of the insurrection Mstislavsky illustrates with a curious example: When the "Union of Officers of

147

February 27," formed just after the revolution, tried to determine with a questionnaire who first led out the Volynsky regiment, they received seven answers naming seven initiators of this decisive action. It is very likely, we may add, that a part of the initiative really did belong to several soldiers, nor is it impossible that the chief initiator fell in the street fighting, carrying his name with him into oblivion. But that does not diminish the historic importance of his nameless initiative. Still more important is another side of the matter which will carry us beyond the walls of the barrack room. The insurrection of the battalions of the Guard, flaring up a complete surprise to the liberal and legal socialist circles, was no surprise at all to the workers. Without the insurrection of the workers the Volynsky regiment would not have gone into the street. That street encounter of the workers with the Cossacks, which a lawyer observed from his window and which he communicated by telephone to the deputy, was to them both an episode in an impersonal process: a factory locust stumbled against a locust from the barracks. But it did not seem that way to the Cossack who had dared wink to the worker, nor to the worker who instantly decided that the Cossack had "winked in a friendly manner." The molecular interpenetration of the army with the people was going on continuously. The workers watched the temperature of the army and instantly sensed its approach to the critical mark. Exactly this was what gave such inconquerable force to the assault of the masses, confident of victory.

Here we must introduce the pointed remark of a liberal official trying to summarize his February observations: "It is customary to say that the movement began spontaneously, the soldiers themselves went into the street. I cannot at all agree with this. After all, what does the word 'spontaneously' mean? . . . Spontaneous conception is still more out of place in sociology than in natural science. Owing to the fact that none of the revolutionary leaders with a name was able to hang his label on the movement, it becomes not impersonal but merely nameless." This formulation of the question, incomparably more serious than Miliukov's references to German agents and

Russian spontaneousness, belongs to a former Procuror who met the revolution in the position of a tzarist senator. It is quite possible that his experience in the courts permitted Zavadsky to realize that a revolutionary insurrection cannot arise either at the command of foreign agents, or in the manner of an impersonal process of nature.

The same author relates two incidents which permitted him to look as through a keyhole into the laboratory of the revolutionary process. On Friday, February 24, when nobody in the upper circles as yet expected a revolution in the near future, a tramcar in which the senator was riding turned off quite unexpectedly, with such a jar that the windows rattled and one was broken, from the Liteiny into a side street, and there stopped. The conductor told everybody to get off: "The car isn't going any farther." The passengers objected, scolded, but got off. "I can still see the face of that unanswering conductor: angrily resolute, a sort of wolf look." The movement of the tramways stopped everywhere as far as the eye could see. That resolute conductor, in whom the liberal official could already catch a glimpse of the "wolf look," must have been dominated by a high sense of duty in order all by himself to stop a car containing officials on the streets of imperial Petersburg in time of war. It was just such conductors who stopped the car of the monarchy and with practically the same words—this car does not go any farther!—and who ushered out the bureaucracy, making no distinction in the rush of business between a general of gendarmes and a liberal senator. The conductor on the Liteiny boulevard was a conscious factor of history. It had been necessary to educate him in advance.

During the burning of the District Court a liberal jurist from the circle of that same senator started to express in the street his regret that a roomful of judicial decisions and notarial archives was perishing. An elderly man of somber aspect dressed as a worker angrily objected: "We will be able to divide the houses and the lands ourselves, and without your archives." Probably the episode is rounded out in a literary manner. But there were plenty of elderly workers like that in the crowd, capable of making the necessary retort. They them-

149

selves had nothing to do with burning the District Court: why burn it? But at least you could not frighten them with "excesses" of this kind. They were arming the masses with the necessary ideas not only against the tzarist police, but against liberal jurists who feared most of all lest there should burn up in the fire of the revolution the notarial deeds of property. Those nameless, austere statesmen of the factory and street did not fall out of the sky: they had to be educated.

In registering the events of the last days of February the Secret Service also remarked that the movement was "spontaneous," that is, had no planned leadership from above; but they immediately added: "with the generally propagandized condition of the proletariat." This appraisal hits the bull's-eye: the professionals of the struggle with the revolution, before entering the cells vacated by the revolutionists, took a much closer view of what was happening than the leaders of liberalism.

The mystic doctrine of spontaneousness explains nothing. In order correctly to appraise the situation and determine the moment for a blow at the enemy, it was necessary that the masses or their guiding layers should make their examination of historical events and have their criteria for estimating them. In other words, it was necessary that there should be not masses in the abstract, but masses of Petrograd workers and Russian workers in general, who had passed through the revolution of 1905, through the Moscow insurrection of December 1905, shattered against the Semenovsky Regiment of the Guard. It was necessary that throughout this mass should be scattered workers who had thought over the experience of 1905, criticized the constitutional illusions of the liberals and Mensheviks, assimilated the perspectives of the revolution, meditated hundreds of times about the question of the army, watched attentively what was going on in its midst—workers capable of making revolutionary inferences from what they observed and communicating them to others. And finally, it was necessary that there should be in the troops of the garrison itself progressive soldiers, seized, or at least touched, in the past by revolutionary propaganda.

In every factory, in each guild, in each company, in each tavern, in the military hospital, at the transfer stations, even in the depopulated villages, the molecular work of revolutionary thought was in progress. Everywhere were to be found the interpreters of events, chiefly from among the workers, from whom one inquired, "What's the news?" and from whom one awaited the needed words. These leaders had often been left to themselves, had nourished themselves upon fragments of revolutionary generalizations arriving in their hands by various routes, had studied out by themselves between the lines of the liberal papers what they needed. Their class instinct was refined by a political criterion, and though they did not think all their ideas through to the end, nevertheless their thought ceaselessly and stubbornly worked its way in a single direction. Elements of experience, criticism, initiative, self-sacrifice, seeped down through the mass and created, invisibly to a superficial glance but no less decisively, an inner mechanics of the revolutionary movement as a conscious process. To the smug politicians of liberalism and tamed socialism everything that happens among masses is customarily represented as an instinctive process, no matter whether they are dealing with an anthill or a beehive. In reality the thought which was drilling through the thick of the working class was far bolder, more penetrating, more conscious, than those little ideas by which the educated classes live. Moreover, this thought was more scientific: not only because it was to a considerable degree fertilized with the methods of Marxism, but still more because it was ever nourishing itself on the living experience of the masses which were soon to take their place on the revolutionary arena. Thoughts are scientific if they correspond to an objective process and make it possible to influence that process and guide it. Were these qualities possessed in the slightest degree by the ideas of those government circles who were inspired by the Apocalypse and believed in the dreams of Rasputin? Or maybe the ideas of the liberals were scientifically grounded, who hoped that a backward Russia, having joined the scrimmage of the capitalist giants, might win at one and the same time victory and parliamentarism? Or maybe the intellectual life of those circles

151

of the intelligentsia was scientific, who slavishly adapted themselves to this liberalism, senile since childhood, protecting their
imaginary independence the while with long-dead metaphors?
In truth here was a kingdom of spiritual inertness, specters, superstition and fictions, a kingdom, if you will, of "spontaneousness." But have we not in that case a right to turn this liberal
philosophy of the February revolution exactly upside down?
Yes, we have a right to say: At the same time that the official
society, all that many-storied superstructure of ruling classes,
layers, groups, parties and cliques, lived from day to day by
inertia and automatism, nourishing themselves with the relics
of worn-out ideas, deaf to the inexorable demands of evolution,
flattering themselves with phantoms and foreseeing nothing—
at the same time, in the working masses there was taking place
an independent and deep process of growth, not only of hatred
for the rulers, but of critical understanding of their impotence,
an accumulation of experience and creative consciousness which
the revolutionary insurrection and its victory only completed.

To the question, Who led the February revolution? we can
then answer definitely enough: Conscious and tempered workers
educated for the most part by the party of Lenin. But we
must here immediately add: This leadership proved sufficient
to guarantee the victory of the insurrection, but it was not
adequate to transfer immediately into the hands of the proletarian vanguard the leadership of the revolution.

CHAPTER IX

THE PARADOX OF THE FEBRUARY REVOLUTION

THE insurrection triumphed. But to whom did it hand over the power snatched from the monarchy? We come here to the central problem of the February revolution: Why and how did the power turn up in the hands of the liberal bourgeoisie?

In Duma circles and in bourgeois "society" no significance was attributed to the agitation beginning the 23rd of February. The liberal deputies and patriotic journalists were assembling in drawing rooms as before, talking over the questions of Trieste and Fiume, and again confirming Russia's need of the Dardanelles. When the decree dissolving the Duma was already signed, a Duma commission was still hastily considering the question of turning over the food problem to the city administration. Less than twelve hours before the insurrection of the battalions of the Guard, the Society for Slavic Reciprocity was peacefully listening to its annual report. "Only when I had returned home on foot from that meeting," remembers one of the deputies, "I was struck by some sort of awesome silence and emptiness in the usually lively streets." That awesome emptiness was forming around the old ruling classes and already oppressing the hearts of their future inheritors.

By the 26th the seriousness of the movement had become clear both to the government and to the liberals. On that day negotiations about a compromise were going on between the tzar's ministers and members of the Duma, negotiations from which even subsequently the liberals never lifted the curtain. Protopopov states in his testimony that the leaders of the Duma bloc demanded as formerly the naming of new ministers from among people enjoying social confidence: "This measure perhaps will pacify the people." But the 26th created, as we know,

153

a certain stoppage in the development of the revolution, and for a brief moment the government felt firmer. When Rodzianko called on Golytsin to persuade him to resign, the Premier pointed in answer to a portfolio on his desk in which lay the completed edict dissolving the Duma, with the signature of Nicholas but without a date. Golytsin put in the date. How could the government decide upon such a step at the moment of growing pressure from the revolution? Upon this question the ruling bureaucrats long ago arrived at a firm conviction. "Whether we have a bloc or not, it is all the same to the workers' movement. We can handle that movement by other means, and up till now the Ministry of the Interior has managed to deal with it." Thus Goremykin had spoken in August 1915. On the other hand, the bureaucracy believed that the Duma, in case of its dissolution, would not venture upon any bold step. Again in August 1915, in discussing the question of dissolving a discontented Duma, the Minister of the Interior, Prince Sherbatov, had said: "The Duma will hardly venture upon direct disobedience. The vast majority are after all cowards and are trembling for their hides." The prince expressed himself none too nicely, but in the long run correctly. In its struggle with the liberal opposition, then, the bureaucracy felt plenty of firm ground under its feet.

On the morning of the 27th, the Deputies, alarmed at the mounting events, assembled at a regular session. The majority learned only here that the Duma had been dissolved. The news seemed the more surprising as on the very day before they had been carrying on peace negotiations with the ministers. "And nevertheless," writes Rodzianko with pride, "the Duma submitted to the law, still hoping to find a way out of the tangled situation, and passed no resolution that it would not disperse, or that it would illegally continue its sessions." The deputies gathered at a private conference in which they made confessions of impotence to each other. The moderate liberal Shidlovsky subsequently remembered, not without a malicious pleasure, a proposal made by an extreme left Kadet, Nekrasov, a future colleague of Kerensky, "to establish a military dictatorship, handing over the whole power to a popular general."

At that time a practical attempt at salvation was undertaken by the leaders of the Progressive Bloc, not present at this private conference of the Duma. Having summoned the Grand Duke. Mikhail to Petrograd, they proposed to him to take upon himself the dictatorship, to "impel" the personal staff of the government to resign, and to demand of the tzar by direct wire that he "grant" a responsible ministry. In those hours, when the uprising of the first Guard regiments was beginning, the liberal bourgeoisie were making a last effort to put down the insurrection with the help of a dynastic dictator, and at the same time at the expense of the revolution to enter into an agreement with the monarchy. "The hesitation of the grand duke," complains Rodzianko, "contributed to the letting slip of the favorable moment."

How easily a radical intelligentsia believes whatever it wants to, is testified by a non-party socialist, Sukhanov, who begins in this period to play a certain political rôle in the Tauride Palace. "They told me the fundamental political news of those morning hours of that unforgettable day," he relates in his extensive memoirs: "The decree dissolving the State Duma had been promulgated, and the Duma had answered with a refusal to disperse, electing a Provisional Committee." This is written by a man who hardly ever left the Tauride Palace, and was there continually buttonholing his deputy friends. Miliukov in his history of the revolution, following Rodzianko, categorically declares: "There was adopted after a series of hot speeches a resolution not to leave Petrograd, but no resolution that the State Duma should as an institution 'not disperse,' as the legend runs." "Not to disperse" would have meant to take upon themselves, however belatedly, a certain initiative. "Not to leave Petrograd" meant to wash their hands of the matter and wait to see which way the course of events would turn. The credulousness of Sukhanov has, by the way, mitigating circumstances. The rumor that the Duma had adopted a revolutionary resolution not to submit to the tzar's decree was slipped in hurriedly by the Duma journalists in their information bulletin, the only paper published at that time owing to the general strike. Since the insurrection triumphed during that day the deputies were in no hurry to correct this mistake, being quite willing to sustain the illusions of their "left" friends. They did not in fact undertake to establish the facts of the matter until they were out of the country. The episode seems secondary, but it is full of meaning. The revolutionary rôle of the Duma on the 27th of February was a complete myth, born of the political credulity of the radical intelligentsia delighted and frightened by the revolution, distrusting the ability of the masses to carry the business through, and eager to lean as quickly as possible toward the enfranchised bourgeoisie.

In the memoirs of the deputies belonging to the Duma majority, there is preserved by good luck a story of how the Duma did meet the revolution. According to the account of Prince Mansyrev, one of the right Kadets, among the deputies who assembled in great numbers on the morning of the 27th there were no members of the præsidium, no leaders of parties, nor heads of the Progressive Bloc: they already knew of the dissolution and the insurrection and had preferred as long as possible to refrain from showing their heads. Moreover, at just that time they were, it seems, negotiating with Mikhail about the dictatorship. "A general consternation and bewilderment prevailed in the Duma," says Mansyrev. "Even lively conversations ceased, and in their place were heard sighs and brief ejaculations like 'It's come,' or indeed frank expressions of fear for life." Thus speaks a very moderate deputy who sighed the loudest of all. At two o'clock in the afternoon, when the leaders had found themselves obliged to appear in the Duma, the secretary of the præsidium brought in the joyful but ill-founded news: "The disorders will soon be put down, because measures have been taken." It is possible that by "measures" was meant the negotiations for a dictatorship, but the Duma was downcast and awaited a decisive word from the leader of the Progressive Bloc. "We cannot adopt any decision at the present moment," Miliukov announced, "because the extent of the disorders is unknown to us; likewise it is unknown upon which side a majority of the local troops, workers and social organizations will take their stand. It is necessary to gather accurate information about this, and then will be time enough to judge the situation. At present it is too soon." At two o'clock in the afternoon of February 27 it is still for liberalism "too soon"! "Gather information" means wash your own hands and await the outcome of the struggle. But Miliukov had not ended his speech—which, by the way, he began with a view to ending in nothing—when Kerensky came running into the hall in high excitement: An enormous crowd of people and soldiers is coming to the Tauride Palace, he announces, and intends to demand of the Duma that it seize the power in its hands! The radical deputy knows accurately just what the enormous crowd of people is going to demand. In reality it is Kerensky himself who first demands that the power shall be seized by a Duma which is still hoping in its soul that the insurrection may yet be put down. Kerensky's announcement is met with "general bewilderment and dismayed looks." He has however not finished speaking when a frightened Duma attendant, rushing in, interrupts him: the advanced detachment of the soldiers has already reached the Palace, a detachment of sentries stopped them at the entrance, the chief of the sentries, it seems, was heavily wounded. A minute later it transpires that the soldiers have entered the Palace. It will be declared later in speeches and articles that the soldiers came to greet the Duma and swear loyalty to it, but right now everything is in mortal panic. The water is up to their necks. The leaders whisper together. We must get a breathing space. Rodzianko hastily introduces a proposal, suggested to him by somebody, that they form a Provisional Committee. Affirmative cries. But they all want to get out of there as quickly as possible. No time for voting. The president, no less frightened than the others, proposes that they turn over the formation of the committee to the council of elders. Again affirmative cries from the few still remaining in the hall. The majority have already vanished. Such was the first reaction of the Duma, dissolved by the tzar, to the victory of the insurrection.

At that time the revolution was creating in the same building, only in a less showy part of it, another institution. The revolutionary leaders did not have to invent it; the experience of the *Soviets* of 1905 was forever chiseled into the consciousness of the workers. At every lift of the movement, even in war time, the idea of soviets was almost automatically reborn. And although the appraisal of the rôle of the soviets was different among Bolsheviks and Mensheviks—the Social Revolutionaries had in general no stable appraisals—the form of organization itself stood clear of all debate. The Mensheviks liberated from prison, members of the Military-Industrial Committee, meeting in the Tauride Palace with leaders of the Trade Union and Coöperative movements, likewise of the right wing, and with the Menshevik deputies of the Duma, Cheidze and Skobelev, straightway formed a "Provisional Executive Committee of the Soviet of Workers' Deputies," which in the course of the day was filled out principally with former revolutionists who had lost connection with the masses but still preserved their "names." This Executive Committee, including also Bolsheviks in its staff, summoned the workers to elect deputies at once. The first session was appointed for the same evening in the Tauride Palace. It actually met at nine o'clock and ratified the staff of the Executive Committee, supplementing it with official representatives from all the socialist parties. But not here lay the significance of this first meeting of representatives of the victorious proletariat of the capital. Delegates from the mutinied regiments made speeches of greeting at this meeting. Among their number were completely gray soldiers, shellshocked as it were by the insurrection, and still hardly in control of their tongues. But they were just the ones who found the words which no orator could find. That was one of the most moving scenes of the revolution, now first feeling its power, feeling the unnumbered masses it has aroused, the colossal tasks, the pride in success, the joyful failing of the heart at the thought of the morrow which is to be still more beautiful than today. The revolution still has no ritual, the streets are in smoke, the masses have not yet learned the new songs. The meeting flows on without order, without shores, like a river at flood. The Soviet chokes in its own enthusiasm. The revolution is mighty but still naïve, with a child's naïveness.

At this first session it was decided to unite the garrison with the workers in a general Soviet of Workers' and Soldiers'

Deputies. Who first proposed this resolution? It probably arose from various, or rather from all sides, as an echo of that fraternization of workers and soldiers which had this day decided the fate of the revolution. From the moment of its formation the Soviet, in the person of its Executive Committee, begins to function as a sovereign. It elects a temporary food commission and places it in charge of the mutineers and of the garrison in general. It organizes parallel with itself a Provisional revolutionary staff—everything was called provisional in those days—of which we have already spoken above. In order to remove financial resources from the hands of the officials of the old power, the Soviet decides to occupy the State Bank, the Treasury, the Mint and the Printing Office with a revolutionary guard. The tasks and functions of the Soviet grow unceasingly under pressure from the masses. The revolution finds here its indubitable center. The workers, the soldiers, and soon also the peasants, will from now on turn only to the Soviet. In their eyes the Soviet becomes the focus of all hopes and all authority, an incarnation of the revolution itself. But representatives of the possessing classes will also seek in the Soviet, with whatever grindings of teeth, protection and counsel in the resolving of conflicts.

However, even in those very first days of victory, when the new power of the revolution was forming itself with fabulous speed and inconquerable strength, those socialists who stood at the head of the Soviet were already looking around with alarm to see if they could find a real "boss." They took it for granted that the power ought to pass to the bourgeoisie. Here the chief political knot of the new régime is tied: one of its threads leads into the chamber of the Executive Committee of workers and soldiers, the other into the central headquarters of the bourgeois parties.

The Council of the Elders at three o'clock in the afternoon, when the victory was already fully assured in the capital, elected a "Provisional Committee of Members of the Duma" made up from the parties of the Progressive Bloc with the addition of Cheidze and Kerensky. Cheidze declined, Kerensky wigglewaggled. The designation prudently indicated that it was not

159

a question of an official committee of the State Duma, but a private committee of a conference of members of the Duma. The leaders of the Progressive Bloc thought to the very end of but one thing: how to avoid responsibility and not tie their own hands. The task of the committee was defined with meticulous equivocation: "The restoration of order and conducting of negotiations with institutions and persons." Not a word as to the kind of order which those gentlemen intended to restore, nor with what institutions they intended to negotiate. They were not yet openly reaching out their hands toward the bear's hide: what if he is not killed but only badly wounded? Only at eleven o'clock in the evening of the 27th, when, as Miliukov acknowledged, "the whole scope of the revolutionary movement had become clear, did the Provisional Committee decide upon a further step, and take in its hands the power which had fallen from the hands of the government." Imperceptibly the new institution changed from a committee of the members of the Duma to a committee of the Duma itself. There is no better means of preserving the state juridical succession than forgery. But Miliukov remains silent about the chief thing: the leaders of the Executive Committee of the Soviet, created during that day, had already appeared before the Provisional Committee and insistently demanded that it take the power into its hands. This friendly push had its effect. Miliukov subsequently explained the decision of the Duma Committee by saying that the government was supposed to be sending loyal troops against the insurrectionists, "and on the streets of the capital it threatened to come to actual battle." In reality the government was already without troops, the revolution was wholly in the past. Rodzianko subsequently wrote that in case they had declined the power, "the Duma would have been arrested and killed off to the last man by the mutinied troops, and the power would have gone immediately to the Bolsheviks." That is, of course, an inept exaggeration, wholly in the character of the respected Lord Chamberlain; but it unmistakably reflects the feelings of the Duma, which regarded the transfer of power to itself as an act of political rape.

With such feelings the decision was not easily arrived at.

Rodzianko especially stormed and vacillated, putting a question to the others: "What will this be? Is it a rebellion or not a rebellion?" The monarchist deputy Shulgin answered him, according to his own report: "There is no rebellion in this at all; take the power as a loyal subject . . . If the ministers have run away somebody has got to take their place . . . There may be two results: Everything quiets down—the sovereign names a new government, we turn over the power to him. Or it doesn't quiet down. In that case if we don't take the power, others will take it, those who have already elected some sort of scoundrels in the factories. . . ." We need not take offense at the low-class abuse directed by the reactionary gentleman toward the workers: the revolution had just firmly stepped on the tails of all these gentlemen. The moral is clear: if the monarchy wins, we are with it; if the revolution wins, we will try to plunder it.

The conference lasted long. The democratic leaders were anxiously waiting for a decision. Finally, Miliukov came out of the office of Rodzianko. He wore a solemn expression. Approaching the Soviet delegation Miliukov announced: "The decision is reached, we will take the power. . . ." "I did not inquire whom he meant by *we*," relates Sukhanov with rapture, "I asked nothing further, but I felt with all my being, as they say, a new situation. I felt that the ship of the revolution, tossed in the squall of those hours by the complete caprice of the elements, had put up a sail, acquired stability and regularity in its movements amid the terrible storm and the rocking." What a high-flying formula for a prosaic recognition of the slavish dependence of the petty bourgeois democracy upon capitalistic liberalism! And what a deadly mistake in political perspective. The handing over of power to the liberals not only will not give stability to the ship of state, but, on the contrary, will become from that moment a source of headlessness of the revolution, enormous chaos, embitterment of the masses, collapse of the front, and in the future extreme bitterness of the civil war.

*

161

IF YOU look only backward, to past ages, the transfer of power to the bourgeoisie seems sufficiently regular: in all past revolutions those who fought on the barricades were workers, apprentices, in part students, and the soldiers came over to their side. But afterwards the solid bourgeoisie, having cautiously watched the barricades through their windows, gathered up the power. But the February revolution of 1917 was distinguished from former revolutions by the incomparably higher social character and political level of the revolutionary class, by the hostile distrust of the insurrectionists toward the liberal bourgeoisie, and the consequent formation at the very moment of victory of a new organ of revolutionary power, the Soviet, based upon the armed strength of the masses. In these circumstances the transfer of power to a politically isolated and unarmed bourgeoisie demands explanation.

First of all, we must examine more closely the correlation of forces which resulted from the revolution. Was not the Soviet democracy compelled by the objective situation to renounce the power in favor of the big bourgeoisie? The bourgeoisie itself did not think so. We have already seen that it not only did not expect power from the revolution, but on the contrary foresaw in it a mortal danger to its whole social situation. "The moderate parties not only did not desire a revolution," writes Rodzianko, "but were simply afraid of it. In particular the Party of the People's Freedom, 'the Kadets,' as a party standing at the left wing of the moderate group, and therefore having more than the rest a point of contact with the revolutionary parties of the country, was more worried by the advancing catastrophe than all the rest." The experience of 1905 had too significantly hinted to the liberals that a victory of the workers and peasants might prove no less dangerous to the bourgeoisie than to the monarchy. It would seem that the course of the February insurrection had only confirmed this foresight. However formless in many respects may have been the political ideas of the revolutionary masses in those days, the dividing line between the toilers and the bourgeoisie was at any rate implacably drawn.

Instructor Stankevich who was close to liberal circles—a

friend, not an enemy of the Progressive Bloc—characterizes in
the following way the mood of those circles on the second day
after the overturn which they had not succeeded in preventing:
"Officially they celebrated, eulogized the revolution, cried 'Hurrah!' to the fighters for freedom, decorated themselves with red
ribbons and marched under red banners. . . But in their souls,
in their conversations tête-à-tête, they were horrified, they shuddered, they felt themselves captives in the hands of hostile elements traveling an unknown road. Unforgettable is the figure
of Rodzianko, that portly lord and imposing personage, when,
preserving a majestic dignity but with an expression of deep
suffering despair frozen on his pale face, he made his way
through a crowd of dishevelled soldiers in the corridor of the
Tauride Palace. Officially it was recorded: The soldiers have
come to support the Duma in its struggle with the government.
But actually the Duma had been abolished from the very first
day. And the same expression was on the faces of all the members of the Provisional Committee of the Duma and those circles
which surrounded it. They say that the representatives of the
Progressive Bloc in their own homes wept with impotent despair."

This living testimony is more precious than any sociological
research into the correlation of forces. According to his own
tale, Rodzianko trembled with impotent indignation when he
saw unknown soldiers, "at whose orders is not recorded" arresting
the officials of the old régime and bringing them to the Duma.
The Lord Chamberlain turned out to be something in the nature of a jailer in relation to people, with whom he had, to be
sure, his differences, but who nevertheless remained people of
his own circle. Shocked by this "arbitrary" action, Rodzianko
invited the arrested Minister Sheglovitov into his office, but
the soldiers brusquely refused to turn over to him the hated
official. "When I tried to show my authority," relates Rodzianko, "the soldiers surrounded their captive and with the
most challenging and insolent expression pointed to their rifles,
after which without more ado they led Sheglovitov away I
know not where." Would it be possible to confirm more ab-

solutely Stankevich's assertion that the regiments supposedly coming to support the Duma, in reality abolished it?

That the power was from the very first moment in the hands of the Soviet—upon that question the Duma members less than anybody else could cherish any illusion. The Octobrist deputy Shidlovsky, one of the leaders of the Progressive Bloc, relates how, "The Soviet seized all the Post and Telegraph bureaus, the wireless, all the Petrograd railroad stations, all the printing establishments, so that without its permission it was impossible to send a telegram, to leave Petrograd, or to print an appeal." In this unequivocal characterization of the correlation of forces, it is necessary to introduce one slight correction: the "seizure" by the Soviet of the telegraph, railroad stations, printing establishments, etc., meant merely that the workers and clerks in those enterprises refused to submit to anybody but the Soviet.

The plaint of Shidlovsky is admirably illustrated by an incident which occurred at the very height of the negotiations about the power between the leaders of the Soviet and the Duma. Their joint session was interrupted by an urgent communication from Pskov, where after his railroad wanderings the tzar had now come to a stand, stating that they wanted Rodzianko on the direct wire. The all-powerful President of the Duma declared that he would not go to the telegraph office alone. "Let some of these messieurs soldiers' and workers' deputies give me a bodyguard or go with me, otherwise I will be arrested there in the telegraph office. Look here, you've got the power and the sovereignty," he continued excitedly, "you can, of course, arrest me . . . maybe you are going to arrest us all, how do we know?" This happened on the 1st of March, less than twenty-four hours after the power was "taken over" by the Provisional Committee with Rodzianko at its head.

How did it happen then that in such a situation the liberals turned out to be in power? How and by whom were they authorized to form a government as the result of a revolution which they had dreaded, which they resisted, which they tried to put down, which was accomplished by masses completely hostile to them, and accomplished with such audacity and decisiveness that the Soviet of Workers and Soldiers arising from the insurrection became the natural, and by all unequivocally recognized, master of the situation?

Let us listen now to the other side, to those who surrendered the power. "The people did not gravitate toward the State Duma," writes Sukhanov of the February days, "they were not interested in it, and never thought of making it either politically or technically the center of the movement." This acknowledgment is the more remarkable in that its author will soon devote all his force to getting the power handed over to a committee of the State Duma. "Miliukov perfectly understood," says Sukhanov further, speaking of the negotiations of March 1, "that the Executive Committee was in a perfect position either to give the power to the bourgeois government, or not give it." Could it be more categorically expressed? Could a political situation be clearer? And nevertheless Sukhanov, in direct contradiction to the situation and to himself, immediately adds: "The power destined to replace tzarism must be only a bourgeois power . . . we must steer our course by this principle. Otherwise the uprising will not succeed and the revolution will collapse." The revolution will collapse without Rodzianko!

The problem of the living relations of social forces is here replaced by an *a priori* scheme and a conventional terminology: and this is the very essence of the doctrinairism of the intelligentsia. But we shall see later that this doctrinairism was by no means Platonic: it fulfilled a very real political function, although with blindfolded eyes.

We have quoted Sukhanov for a reason. In that first period the inspirer of the Executive Committee was not its president, Cheidze, an honest and limited provincial, but this very Sukhanov, a man, generally speaking, totally unsuited for revolutionary leadership. Semi-Narodnik, semi-Marxist, a conscientious observer rather than a statesman, a journalist rather than a revolutionist, a rationalizer rather than a journalist—he was capable of standing by a revolutionary conception only up to the time when it was necessary to carry it into action. A passive internationalist during the war, he decided on the very first day of the revolution that it was necessary just as quickly as possible to toss the power and the war over to the bourgeoisie. As a theorist—that is, at least in his feeling of the need that things should be reasoned out, if not in his ability to fulfill it— he stood above all the then members of the Executive Committee. But his chief strength lay in his ability to translate into a language of doctrinairism the organic traits of all that many-colored and yet nevertheless homogeneous brotherhood: distrust of their own powers, fear of the masses, and a heartily respectful attitude toward the bourgeoisie. Lenin described Sukhanov as one of the best representatives of the petty bourgeoisie, and that is the most flattering thing that can be said of him.

Only in this connection it must not be forgotten that the question is here of a new capitalist type of petty bourgeoisie, of industrial, commercial and bank clerks, the functionaries of capital on one side, and the workers' bureaucracy on the other —that is of that *new middle caste,* in whose name the well-known German social democrat Edward Bernstein undertook at the end of the last century a revision of the revolutionary conceptions of Marx. In order to answer the question how a revolution of workers and peasants came to surrender the power to the bourgeoisie, it is necessary to introduce into the political chain an intermediate link: the petty bourgeois democrats and socialists of the Sukhanov type, journalists and politicians of the new middle caste, who had taught the masses that the bourgeoisie is an enemy, but themselves feared more than anything else to release the masses from the control of that enemy. The contradiction between the character of the revolution and the character of the power that issued from it, is explained by the contradictory character of this new petty bourgeois partition-wall between the revolutionary masses and the capitalist bourgeoisie. In the course of further events the political rôle of this petty bourgeois democracy of the new type will fully open before us. For the time being we will limit ourselves to a few words.

A minority of the revolutionary class actually participates in the insurrection, but the strength of that minority lies in the support, or at least sympathy, of the majority. The active and militant minority inevitably puts forward under fire from the enemy its more revolutionary and self-sacrificing element. It is thus natural that in the February fights the worker-Bolsheviks occupied the leading place. But the situation changes the moment the victory is won and its political fortification begins. The elections to the organs and institutions of the victorious revolution attract and challenge infinitely broader masses than those who battled with arms in their hands. This is true not only of general democratic institutions like the city dumas and zemstvos, or later on, the Constituent Assembly, but also of class institutions, like the Soviet of Workers' Deputies. An overwhelming majority of the workers, Menshevik, Social Revolutionary and non-party, supported the Bolsheviks at the moment of direct grapple with tzarism. But only a small minority of the workers understood that the Bolsheviks were different from other socialist parties. At the same time, however, all the workers drew a sharp line between themselves and the bourgeoisie. This fact determined the political situation after the victory. The workers elected socialists, that is, those who were not only against the monarchy, but against the bourgeoisie. In doing this they made almost no distinction between the three socialist parties. And since the Mensheviks and Social Revolutionaries comprised infinitely larger ranks of the intelligentsia—who came pouring in from all sides—and thus got into their hands immediately an immense staff of agitators, the elections, even in shops and factories, gave them an enormous majority. An impulse in the same direction, but an incomparably stronger one, came from the awakening army. On the fifth day of the insurrection the Petrograd garrison followed the workers. After the victory it found itself summoned to hold elections for the Soviet. The soldiers trustfully elected those who had been for the revolution against monarchist officers, and who knew. how to say this out loud: these were volunteers, clerks, assistant-surgeons, young war-time officers from the intelligentsia, petty military officials—that is, the lowest layers of that *new middle caste*. All of them almost to the last man inscribed themselves, beginning in March, in the party of the Social Revolutionaries, which with its intellectual formlessness perfectly expressed their intermediate social situation and their limited political outlook.

167

The representation of the garrison thus turned out to be incomparably more moderate and bourgeois than the soldier masses. But the latter were not conscious of this difference: it would reveal itself to them only during the experience of the coming months. The workers, on their part, were trying to cling as closely as possible to the soldiers, in order to strengthen their blood-bought union and more permanently arm the revolution. And since the spokesmen of the army were predominantly half-baked Social Revolutionaries, this fact could not help raising the authority of that party along with its ally, the Mensheviks, in the eyes of the workers themselves. Thus resulted the predominance in the soviets of the two Compromise parties. It is sufficient to remark that even in the soviet of the Vyborg district the leading rôle in those first times belonged to the worker-Mensheviks. Bolshevism in that period was still only simmering in the depths of the revolution. Thus the official Bolsheviks, even in the Petrograd Soviet, represented an insignificant minority, who had moreover none too clearly defined its tasks.

Thus arose the paradox of the February revolution. The power was in the hands of the democratic socialists. It had not been seized by them accidentally by way of a Blanquist coup; no, it was openly delivered to them by the victorious masses of the people. Those masses not only did not trust or support the bourgeoisie, but they did not even distinguish them from the nobility and the bureaucracy. They put their weapons at the disposal only of the soviets. Meanwhile the socialists, having so easily arrived at the head of the soviets, were worrying about only one question: Will the bourgeoisie, politically isolated, hated by the masses and hostile through and through to the revolution, consent to accept the power from our hands? Its consent must be won at any cost. And since obviously a bourgeoisie cannot renounce its bourgeois program, we, the "socialists," will have to renounce ours: we will have to keep still about the monarchy, the war, the land, if only the bourgeoisie will accept the gift of power. In carrying out this operation, the "socialists," as though to ridicule themselves, continued to designate the bourgeoisie no otherwise than as their class enemy. In the ceremonial forms of their worship was thus introduced an act of arrant blasphemy. A class struggle carried to its conclusion is a struggle for state power. The fundamental character of a revolution lies in its carrying the class struggle to its conclusion. A revolution is a direct struggle for power. Nevertheless, our "socialists" are not worried about getting the power away from the class enemy who does not possess it, and could not with his own forces seize it, but, just the opposite, with forcing this power upon him at any cost. Is not this indeed a paradox? It seems all the more striking, because the experience of the German revolution of 1918 did not then exist, and humanity had not yet witnessed a colossal and still more successful operation of this same type carried out by the "new middle caste" led by the German social democracy.

How did the Compromisers explain their conduct? One explanation had a doctrinaire character: Since the revolution is bourgeois, the socialists must not compromise themselves with the power—let the bourgeoisie answer for itself. This sounded very implacable. In reality, however, the petty bourgeoisie disguised with this false implacability its obsequiousness before the power of wealth, education, enfranchised citizenship. The right of the big bourgeoisie to power, the petty bourgeois acknowledged as a right of primogeniture, independent of the correlation of forces. Fundamentally we had here the same almost instinctive movement which has compelled the small merchant or teacher to step aside respectfully in the stations or theaters to let a Rothschild pass. Doctrinaire arguments served as a compensation for the consciousness of a personal insignificance. In only two months, when it became evident that the bourgeoisie was totally unable with its own force to keep the power thus delivered to it, the Compromisers had no difficulty in tossing away their "socialistic" prejudices and entering a coalition ministry—not in order to crowd out the bourgeoisie but, on the contrary, in order to save it—not against its will but, on the contrary, at its invitation, which sounded almost like a command. Indeed, the bourgeoisie threatened the democrats, if they refused, to let the power drop on their heads.

The second argument for refusing the power, although no

more serious in essence, had a more practical appearance. Our friend Sukhanov made the most of the "scatteredness" of democratic Russia: "The democrats had at that time no stable or influential organizations, party, professional or municipal." That sounds almost like a joke! Not a word about the soviets of workers' and soldiers' deputies from this socialist who is acting in the name of the soviets. As a matter of fact, thanks to the tradition of 1905, the soviets sprang up as though from under the earth, and immediately became incomparably more powerful than all the other organizations which later tried to compete with them (the municipalities, the coöperatives, and in part the trade unions). As for the peasantry, a class by its very nature scattered, thanks to the war and revolution it was exactly at that moment organized as never before. The war had assembled the peasants into an army, and the revolution had given the army a political character! No fewer than eight million peasants were united in companies and squadrons, which had immediately created their revolutionary representation and could through it at any moment be brought to their feet by a telephone call. Is this at all similar to "scatteredness"?

You may say, to be sure, that at the moment of deciding the question of power, the democracy did not know what would be the attitude of the army at the front. We will not raise the question whether there was the slightest basis for fearing or hoping that the soldiers at the front, worn out with the war, would want to support the imperialist bourgeoisie. It is sufficient to remark that this question was fully decided during the next two or three days, which the Compromisers passed in the backstage preparation of a bourgeois government. "The revolution was successfully achieved by the 3rd of March," concedes Sukhanov. In spite of the adherence of the whole army to the soviets, the leaders of the latter continued with all their strength to push away the power: they feared it the more, the more completely it became concentrated in their hands.

But why? How could those democrats, "socialists," directly supported by such human masses as no democracy in history ever had behind it—masses, moreover, with a considerable experience, disciplined and armed, and organized in soviets—how could that all-powerful and apparently inconquerable democracy fear the power? This apparently intricate enigma is explained by the fact that the democracy did not trust its own support, feared those very masses, did not believe in the stability of their confidence in itself, and worst of all dreaded what they called "anarchy," that is, that having seized the power, they might along with the power prove a mere plaything of the so-called unbridled elements. In other words, the democracy felt that it was not called to be the leader of the people at the moment of its revolutionary uprising, but the left wing of a bourgeois order, its feeler stretched out toward the masses. It called itself, and even deemed itself "socialistic," in order to disguise not only from the masses, but from itself too, its actual rôle: without this self-inebriation it could not have fulfilled this rôle. This is the solution of the fundamental paradox of the February revolution.

On the evening of March 1, representatives of the Executive Committee, Cheidze, Steklov, Sukhanov and others, appeared at a meeting of the Duma Committee, in order to discuss the conditions upon which the soviets would support the new government. The program of the democrats flatly ignored the question of war, republic, land, eight-hour day, and confined itself to one single demand: to give the left parties freedom of agitation. An example of disinterestedness for all peoples and ages! Socialists, having all the power in their hands, and upon whom alone it depended whether freedom of agitation should be given to others or not, handed over the power to their "class enemy" upon the condition that the latter should promise them . . . freedom of agitation! Rodzianko was afraid to go to the telegraph office and said to Cheidze and Sukhanov: "You have the power, you can arrest us all." Cheidze and Sukhanov answered him: "Take the power, but don't arrest us for propaganda." When you study the negotiations of the Compromisers with the liberals, and in general all the incidents of the interrelation of the left and right wings at the Tauride Palace in those days, it seems as though upon that gigantic stage upon which the historic drama of a people is developing, a group of provincial actors, availing themselves of a vacant corner and a pause, were playing out a cheap quick-change vaudeville act.

The leaders of the bourgeoisie, we must do them justice, never expected anything of the kind. They would surely have less dreaded the revolution if they had counted upon this kind of politics from its leaders. To be sure, they would have miscalculated even in that case, but at least together with the latter. Fearing, nevertheless, that the bourgeoisie might not agree to take the power on the proposed conditions, Sukhanov delivered a threatening ultimatum: "Either we or nobody can control the elements . . . there is but one way out—agree to our terms." In other words: accept the program, which is your program; for this we promise to subdue for you the masses who gave us the power. Poor subduers of the elements!

Miliukov was astonished. "He did not try to conceal," remembers Sukhanov, "his satisfaction and his agreeable astonishment." When the Soviet delegates, to make it sound more important, added that their conditions were "final," Miliukov even became expansive and patted them on the head with the remark: "Yes, I was listening and I was thinking how far forward our workers' movement has progressed since the days of 1905 . . ." In the same tone of the good-natured crocodile the Hohenzollern diplomat at Brest-Litovsk conversed with the delegates of the Ukranian Rada, complimenting them upon their statesman-like maturity just before swallowing them up. If the Soviet democracy was not swallowed up by the bourgeoisie, it was not Miliukov's fault, and no thanks to Sukhanov. The bourgeoisie received the power behind the backs of the people. It had no support in the toiling classes. But along with the power it received a simulacrum of support second hand. The Mensheviks and Social Revolutionaries, lifted aloft by the masses, delivered as if from themselves a testimonial of confidence to the bourgeoisie. If you look at this operation of formal democracy in cross-section you have a picture of a twofold election, in which the Mensheviks and Social Revolutionaries play the technical rôle of a middle link, that is, Kadet electors. If you take the question politically, it must be conceded that the Compromisers betrayed the confidence of the masses by calling to power those against whom they themselves were elected. And finally from a deeper, more social point of view, the question presents itself thus: the petty bourgeois parties, having in everyday circumstances shown an extraordinary pretentiousness and satisfaction with themselves, as soon as they were raised by a revolution to the heights of power, were frightened by their own inadequacy and hastened to surrender the helm to representatives of capital. In this act of prostration is immediately revealed the terrible shakiness of the new middle caste and its humiliating dependence upon the big bourgeoisie. Realizing or only feeling that the power in their hands would not last long anyway, that they would soon have to surrender it either to the right or the left, the democrats decided that it was better to give it today to the solid liberals than tomorrow to the extreme representatives of the proletariat. But in this view also, the rôle of the Compromisers, in spite of its social conditioning, does not cease to be a treachery to the masses.

In giving their confidence to the socialists the workers and soldiers found themselves, quite unexpectedly, expropriated politically. They were bewildered, alarmed, but did not immediately find a way out. Their own betrayers deafened them from above with arguments to which they had no ready answer, but which conflicted with all their feelings and intentions. The revolutionary tendencies of the masses, even at the moment of the February revolution, did not at all coincide with the Compromise tendencies of the petty bourgeois parties. The proletariat and the peasantry voted for the Mensheviks and the Social Revolutionaries not as compromisers, but as opponents of the tzar, the capitalists and the landowners. But in voting for them they created a partition-wall between themselves and their own aims. They could not now move forward at all without bumping into this wall erected by themselves, and knocking it over. Such was the striking *quid pro quo* comprised in the class relations as they were uncovered by the February revolution.

*

TO THIS fundamental paradox a supplementary one was immediately added. The liberals agreed to take the power from the hands of the socialists only on condition that the monarchy should agree to take it from their hands. During the time when Guchkov, with the monarchist Shulgin, already known to us, was traveling out to Pskov to save the dynasty, the problem of a constitutional monarchy was at the center of negotiation between the two committees in the Tauride Palace. Miliukov was trying to convince the democrats who had come to him with the power in the palms of their hands, that the Romanovs could now no longer be dangerous, that Nicholas, to be sure, would have to be removed, but that the tzarevich Alexei, with Mikhail as regent, could fully guarantee the welfare of the country: "The one is a sick child, the other an utterly stupid man." We will add also a characterization which the liberal monarchist Shidlovsky gave of the candidate for tzar: "Mikhail Alexandrovich has tried every way possible to avoid interfering in any affairs of state, devoting himself whole-heartedly to horse-racing." A striking recommendation, especially if it were repeated before the masses. After the flight of Louis XVI to Varennes, Danton proclaimed in the Jacobin Club that once a man is weak-minded he can no longer be king. The Russian liberals thought on the contrary that the weak-mindedness of a monarch would serve as the best possible decoration for a constitutional régime. However, this was a random argument calculated to impress the mentality of the "left" simpletons—a little too crude, however, even for them. It was suggested to broad circles of the liberal Philistines that Mikhail was an "Anglomaniac"—without making clear whether in the matter of horse-racing or parliamentarism. But the main argument was that they needed a "customary symbol of power." Otherwise the people would imagine that anarchy had come.

The democrats listened, were politely surprised and tried to persuade them . . . to declare a republic? No. Only not to decide the question in advance. The third point of the Executive Committee's conditions read: "The Provisional Government shall not undertake any steps which would define in advance the future form of government." Miliukov made of the question of the monarchy an ultimatum. The democrats were in despair. But here the masses came to their help. At the meetings in the Tauride Palace absolutely nobody, not only among the workers, but among the soldiers, wanted a tzar, and there was no means of imposing one upon them. Nevertheless, Miliukov tried to swim against the current, and to save the throne and dynasty over the heads of his left allies. In his history of the revolution he himself cautiously remarks that towards the end of the 2nd of March the excitement produced by his announcement of the Regency of Mikhail "had considerably increased." Rodzianko far more colorfully paints the effect upon the masses produced by this monarchist maneuver of the liberals. The moment he arrived from Pskov with the tzar's abdication in favor of Mikhail, Guchkov upon the demand of the workers went from the station to the railroad shops to tell what had happened, and having read the act of abdication he concluded: "Long live the Emperor Mikhail!" The result was unexpected. The orator was, according to Rodzianko, immediately arrested by the workers, and even apparently threatened with execution. "He was liberated with great difficulty, with the help of a sentry company of the nearest regiment." Rodzianko, as always, exaggerates a little, but the essence of the matter is correctly stated. The country had so radically vomited up the monarchy that it could not ever crawl down the people's throat again. The revolutionary masses did not permit even the thought of a new tzar.

Facing such a situation the members of the Provisional Committee sidled away from Mikhail one after another—not decisively, but "until the Constituent Assembly" and then we shall see. Only Miliukov and Guchkov stood out for monarchy to the end, continuing to make it a condition of their entering the cabinet. What to do? The democrats thought that without Miliukov it was impossible to create a bourgeois government, and without a bourgeois government to save the revolution. Bickerings and persuasions went on without end. At a morning conference on March 3, a conviction of the necessity of "persuading the grand duke to abdicate"—they considered him tzar then, after all!—seemed to gain the upper hand completely in the Provisional Committee. The left Kadet Nekrasov even drew up a text of the abdication. But since Miliukov stubbornly refused to yield, a decision was finally reached after further passionate quarrels: "Both sides shall present before the grand duke their opinions and without further argument leave the decision to the grand duke himself." Thus an "utterly stupid man," to whom his older brother overthrown by the insurrection had tried, in conflict even with the dynastic statute, to slip the throne, unexpectedly became the super-umpire on the question of the state structure of the revolutionary country. However improbable it may seem, a betting competition had arisen over the fate of the state. In order to induce the duke to tear himself away from the stables for the throne, Miliukov assured him that there was an excellent possibility of collecting outside of Petrograd a military force to defend his rights. In other words, having barely received the power from the hands of the socialists, Miliukov advanced a plan for a monarchist coup d'état. At the end of the speeches for and against, of which there were not a few, the grand duke requested time for reflection. Inviting Rodzianko into another room Mikhail flatly asked him: Would the new authorities guarantee him only the crown, or also his head? The incomparable Lord Chamberlain answered that he could only promise the monarch in case of need to die with him. This did not at all satisfy the candidate. Coming out to the deputies after an embrace with Rodzianko, Mikhail Romanov "pretty firmly" declared that he would decline the lofty but risky position offered to him. Here Kerensky, who personified in these negotiations the conscience of the democracy, ecstatically jumped up from his chair with the words: "Your Highness, you are a noble man!"—and swore that from that time on he would proclaim this everywhere. "Kerensky's grandiloquence," comments Miliukov drily, "harmonized badly with the prose of the decision just taken." It is impossible to disagree. The text of this interlude truly left no place for pathos. To our comparison with a vaudeville played in the corner of an ancient amphitheater, it is necessary to add that the stage was divided by screens into two halves: in one the revolutionists were begging the liberals to save the revolution, in the other the liberals were begging the monarchy to save liberalism.

The representatives of the Executive Committee were sincerely perplexed as to why such a cultured and farsighted man as Miliukov should be obstinate about some old monarchy, and even be ready to renounce the power if he could not get a Romanov thrown in. Miliukov's monarchism, however, was neither doctrinaire, nor romantic; on the contrary, it was a result of the naked calculation of the frightened property-owners. In its nakedness indeed lay its hopeless weakness. Miliukov the historian, might, it is true, cite the example of the leader of the French revolutionary bourgeoisie, Mirabeau, who also in his day strove to reconcile the revolution with the king. There too at the bottom it was the fear of the property owners for their property: the more prudent policy was to disguise it with the monarchy, just as the monarchy had disguised itself with the church. But in 1789 the tradition of kingly power in France had still a universal popular recognition, to say nothing of the fact that all surrounding Europe was monarchist. In clinging to the king the French bourgeoisie was still on common ground with the people—at least in the sense that it was using against the people their own prejudices. The situation was wholly different in Russia in 1917. Aside from the shipwreck of the monarchist régime in various other countries of the world, the Russian monarchy itself had been irremediably damaged already in 1905. After the 9th of January, Father Gapon had cursed the tzar and his "serpent offspring." The Soviet of Workers' Deputies of 1905 had stood openly for a republic. The monarchist feelings of the peasantry, upon which the monarchy itself had long counted, and with references to which the bourgeoisie camouflaged its own monarchism, simply did not exist. The militant counter-revolution which arose later, beginning with Kornilov, although hypocritically, nevertheless all the more demonstratively, disavowed the tzarist power—so little was left of the monarchist roots in the people. But that same revolution of 1905, which mortally wounded the monarchy, had undermined forever the unstable republican tendencies of the "advanced" bourgeoisie. In contradicting each

177

other, these two processes supplemented each other. Feeling in the first hours of the February revolution that it was drowning, the bourgeoisie grabbed at a straw. It needed the monarchy, not because that was a faith common to it and the people; on the contrary, the bourgeoisie had nothing left to set against the faith of the people but a crowned phantom. The "educated" classes of Russia entered the arena of the revolution not as the announcers of a rational state, but as defenders of medieval institutions. Having no support either in the people or in themselves, they sought it above themselves. Archimedes undertook to move the earth if they would give him a point of support. Miliukov was looking for a point of support in order to prevent the overthrow of the landlord's earth.[1] He felt in this operation much nearer to the calloused Russian generals and the hierarchs of the orthodox church, than to these tame democrats who were worried about nothing but the approval of the liberals. Not being in a position to break the revolution, Miliukov firmly decided to outwit it. He was ready to swallow a great deal: civil liberty for soldiers, democratic municipalities, Constituent Assembly, but on one condition: that they should give him an Archimedian point of support in the form of monarchy. He intended gradually and step by step to make the monarchy the axis of a group of generals, a patched-up bureaucracy, princes of the church, property owners, all those who were dissatisfied with the revolution, and starting with a "symbol," to create gradually a real monarchist bridle for the masses as soon as the latter should get tired of the revolution. If only he could gain time. Another leader of the Kadet Party, Nabokov, explained later what a capital advantage would have been gained if Mikhail had consented to take the throne: "The fatal question of convoking a Constituent Assembly in war time would have been removed." We must bear those words in mind. The conflict about the date of the Constituent Assembly occupied a great place between February and October, during which time the Kadets categorically denied their intention to delay the summoning of the people's representatives, while insistently and stubbornly carrying out a policy of post-

[1] In Russian, the words *earth* and *land* are the same. [Trans.]

ponement in fact. Alas, they had only themselves to rely on in this effort: the monarchist camouflage they never got. After the desertion of Mikhail, Miliukov had not even a straw to grab.

Chapter X

THE NEW POWER

THE belated Russian bourgeoisie, separated from the people,
bound up much more closely with foreign finance capital
than with its own toiling masses, hostile to the revolution
which had triumphed, could not in its own name find a single
justification for its pretense to power. And yet some justification was necessary, for the revolution was subjecting to a ruthless examination not only inherited rights but new claims. Least
of all capable of presenting convincing arguments to the masses
was the President of the Provisional Committee, Rodzianko,
who arrived at the head of the revolutionary nation during the
first days of the uprising.

A page in the court of Alexander II, an officer of the Cavalier Guard, head of the nobles of his province, Lord Chamberlain under Nicholas II, a monarchist through and through, a
rich landlord and agrarian administrator, a member of the
Octobrist Party, a deputy in the State Duma, Rodzianko was
finally elected its president. This happened after the resignation of Guchkov, who was hated by the court as a "Young
Turk." The Duma hoped that through the mediation of the
Lord Chamberlain it would find easier access to the heart of
the monarch. Rodzianko did what he could: sincerely enough
assured the tzar of his loyalty to the dynasty, begged the honor
of being presented to the Heir Apparent, and introduced himself to the latter as "the biggest and fattest man in Russia." In
spite of all his Byzantine clowning, the Lord Chamberlain did
not win over the tzar to the constitution, and the tzarina briefly
referred to Rodzianko in her letters as a scoundrel. During the
war the President of the Duma undoubtedly gave the tzar not
a few unpleasant moments, cornering him when making personal reports and filling his ears with prolix exhortations, patriotic criticisms and gloomy forebodings. Rasputin considered

Rodzianko a personal enemy. Kurlov, who was close to the court gang, speaks of Rodzianko's "insolence combined with obvious limitations." Witte spoke in better terms, although condescendingly, of the President of the Duma: "Not a stupid man, rather sensible; but still Rodzianko's chief talent lies not in his mind but his voice—he has an excellent bass." At first Rodzianko tried to put down the revolution with the help of the fire-hose; he wept when he found out that the government of Count Golytsin had abandoned its post; declined with terror the power which the socialists offered him; afterwards decided to take it, but only in order as a loyal subject to restore the lost property as soon as possible to the monarch. It wasn't Rodzianko's fault if that opportunity never arrived. However the revolution—with the help of the socialists—did offer the Lord Chamberlain a grand opportunity to exercise his thunderous bass before the revolting troops. As early as the 27th of February this retired Captain of the Guard said to a cavalier regiment which had come to the Tauride Palace: "Christian warriors, hearken to my counsel. I am an old man; I will not deceive you—obey your officers—they will not teach you evil, and will act in full agreement with the State Duma. Long live holy Russia!" Such a revolution as that would have been agreeable to all the Guard officers, but the soldiers couldn't help wondering what was the use making such a revolution. Rodzianko feared the soldiers, feared the workers, considered Cheidze and other left deputies German agents, and while he stood at the head of the revolution kept looking around every few minutes to see whether the Soviet was going to arrest him.

The figure of Rodzianko was a little funny, but by no means accidental. This Lord Chamberlain with an excellent bass personified the union of the two ruling classes of Russia, the landlords and the bourgeoisie, with the progressive priesthood adhering to them. Rodzianko himself was very pious and expert in hymn singing—and the liberal bourgeoisie, whatever its attitude towards Greek orthodoxy, considered a union with the church just as necessary to law and order as a union with the monarchy. The venerable monarchist, having received the power from the hands of conspirators, rebels and tyrannicides, wore a haunted expression in those days. And the other members of the Provisional committee felt but little better. Some of them never appeared at the Tauride Palace at all, considering that the situation had not yet sufficiently defined itself. The wisest of them sneaked on tiptoe round the blaze of the revolution, choking from the smoke, and saying to themselves: let it burn down to the coals, then we'll try to cook up something. Although it agreed to accept the power, the Committee did not immediately decide to form a ministry. "Awaiting the proper moment for the formation of a government"—as Miliukov expresses it—the Committee confined itself to the naming of commissars from the membership of the Duma to the principal governmental departments. That left them a chance to retreat.

To the Ministry of the Interior they delegated the deputy Karaulov, insignificant but rather less cowardly than the others, and he issued on March 1 an order for the arrest of all police officials, public, secret and political. This ferocious revolutionary gesture was purely platonic in character, for the police were already being arrested and the jails were their only refuge from massacre. It was some time later that the reaction began to regard this demonstrative act of Karaulov as the beginning of all their troubles.

As commander of Petrograd, they appointed Colonel Engelhardt, an officer of the Cavalier Guard, owner of a racing stud and vast landed properties. Instead of arresting the "dictator" Ivanov, sent from the front to pacify the capital, Engelhardt put at his disposition a reactionary officer in the capacity of chief of staff. It was all a matter between friends.

To the Ministry of Justice they delegated a bright light of the Moscow liberal bar, the eloquent and empty Maklakov, who began by giving the reactionary bureaucrats to understand that he did not want to accept the ministry as a favor from the revolution, and "glancing around at a messenger boy who had just come in," said in French: *"Le danger est à gauche."* The workers and soldiers did not have to understand French in order to recognize in all these gentlemen their mortal enemies.

Rodzianko's reverberations at the head of the Committee

did not last very long. His candidacy for president of the revolution faded away of itself. The mediator between the monarchy and the property owners was too obviously useless as a mediator between the property owners and the revolution. But he did not disappear from the scene. He stubbornly attempted to revive the Duma as a counter-weight to the Soviet, and invariably appears in the center of all attempts to solidify the capitalist-landlord counter-revolution. We shall hear of him again.

On the 1st of March the Provisional Committee undertook the formation of a ministry, appointing to it those men whom the Duma had been recommending to the tzar since 1915 as enjoying the confidence of the country. They were big landlords and industrialists, opposition deputies in the Duma, leaders of the Progressive Bloc. The fact is that, with one single exception, the revolution accomplished by workers and soldiers found no reflection whatever in the staff of the revolutionary government. The exception was Kerensky. The distance from Rodzianko to Kerensky appeared officially to represent the whole gamut of the February revolution.

Kerensky entered the government somewhat in the character of a plenipotentiary ambassador. His connection with the revolution, however, was that of a provincial lawyer who had defended political cases. Kerensky was not a revolutionist; he merely hung around the revolution. Arriving in the fourth Duma thanks to his legal position, Kerensky became the president of a gray and characterless faction, the Trudoviks, anemic fruit of a cross-breeding between liberalism and Narodnikism. He had no theoretical preparation, no political schooling, no ability to think, no political will. The place of these qualities was occupied by a nimble susceptibility, an inflammable temperament, and that kind of eloquence which operates neither upon mind or will, but upon the nerves. His speeches in the Duma, couched in a spirit of declamatory radicalism which had no lack of occasions, gave Kerensky, if not popularity, at least a certain notoriety. During the war Kerensky, a patriot, had looked with the liberals upon the very idea of revolution as ruinous. He acknowledged the revolution only after it had come and catching him up by his pseudo-popularity lifted him aloft. The revolution naturally identified itself for him with the new power. The Executive Committee decided, however, that it was a bourgeois revolution and the power should belong to the bourgeoisie. This formula seemed false to Kerensky, if only because it slammed the doors of the ministry in his face. Kerensky was quite rightly convinced that his socialism would not trouble the bourgeois revolution, nor would the bourgeois revolution do any damage to his socialism. The Provisional Committee of the Duma decided to try to draw this radical deputy away from the Soviet, and achieved it with no difficulty by offering him the portfolio of Justice, which had already been refused by Maklakov. Kerensky buttonholed his friends in the *couloirs*, and asked: Shall I take it or not? His friends had no doubt whatever that he would take it. Sukhanov, who was very friendly toward Kerensky at that period, attributes to him in his subsequent memoirs, "a confidence in some mission of his own . . . and an enormous vexation with those who had not yet found out about that mission." In the long run his friends, and Sukhanov among them, advised Kerensky to take the portfolio: We will be safer this way—we will have our own man to tell us what is going on among those foxy liberals. But while pushing Kerensky *sub rosa* toward that sin to which he himself aspired with all his heart, the leaders of the Executive Committee refused him their official sanction. As Sukhanov reminded Kerensky, the Executive Committee had already expressed itself against its members' entering the government, and to raise the question again in the Soviet would be "not without danger," for the Soviet might simply answer: "The power ought to belong to the soviet democracy." Those are the very words of Sukhanov himself, an unbelievable mixture of naïveté and cynicism. The inspirer of this whole governmental mystification thus openly acknowledges that, as early as the 2nd of March, the Petrograd Soviet was in a mood for the *formal* seizure of that power which had belonged to it *in fact* since the evening of February 27—that only behind the backs of the workers and soldiers, without their knowledge, and against their actual will, had the socialist leaders been able to expropriate this power for the benefit of the bourgeoisie. In Sukhanov's account this deal between the democrats and the liberals acquires all the necessary juridical marks of a crime against the revolution, a veritable secret conspiracy against the sovereignty and rights of the people.

Discussing Kerensky's impatience, the leaders of the Executive Committee whispered that it would be embarrassing for the socialists to take back from the members of the Duma a small piece of the power when they had only just handed the whole thing over to them. Better let Kerensky do it on his own responsibility. Truly those gentlemen had an infallible instinct for finding in every situation the most false and tangled-up solution possible. But Kerensky did not want to enter the government in the business suit of a radical deputy; he wanted to wear the cloak of a plenipotentiary of the triumphant revolution. In order to avoid obstacles, he did not appeal for sanction either to that party of which he professed himself a member, nor to the Executive Committee of which he was one of the vice presidents. Without warning the leaders, he appeared at a plenary session of the Soviet—chaotic meetings in those days—requested the floor for a special announcement, and in a speech which some describe as incoherent, others as hysterical—in which, to be sure, there is no contradiction—demanded the personal confidence of the deputies, and spoke of his general readiness to die for the revolution, and his more immediate readiness to take the portfolio of Minister of Justice. He had only to mention the necessity of complete political amnesty and a prosecution of the tzar's officials, in order to win tumultuous applause from that inexperienced and leaderless assembly. "This farce," Shliapnikov remembers, "produced in many a deep indignation and disgust for Kerensky." But nobody opposed him. Having turned over the power to the bourgeoisie, the socialists, as we have heard, wanted to avoid raising that question before the masses. There was no vote. Kerensky decided to interpret the applause as a vote of confidence. In a way he was right. The Soviet was undoubtedly in favor of socialists entering the ministry, seeing in that a step toward the liquidation of the bourgeois government with which it had

185

not for a moment reconciled itself. At any rate, Kerensky, flouting the official doctrine of the sovereignty, accepted on March 2 the post of Minister of Justice. "He was highly pleased with his appointment," the Octobrist Shidlovsky relates, "and I distinctly remember him in the chambers of the Provisional Committee, lying in an armchair, telling us heatedly upon what an unattainably high pedestal he was going to place justice in Russia." He demonstrated this some months later in his prosecution of the Bolsheviks.

The Menshevik Cheidze, upon whom the liberals—guided by a too simple calculation and an international tradition—wanted in a hard moment to unload the Ministry of Labor, categorically refused, and remained President of the Soviet. Although less brilliant than Kerensky, Cheidze was made of more serious material.

The axis of the Provisional Government, although not formally its head, was Miliukov, the indubitable leader of the Kadet Party. "Miliukov was incomparably above his colleagues in the cabinet," wrote the Kadet Nabokov, after he had broken with Miliukov, "as an intellectual force, as a man of enormous, almost inexhaustible knowledge and wide intelligence." Sukhanov, while blaming Miliukov personally for the wreck of Russian liberalism, nevertheless wrote: "Miliukov was then the central figure, the soul and brain of all the bourgeois political circles. . . . Without him there would have been no bourgeois policy in the first period of the revolution." In spite of their slightly exalted tone, these reports truly indicate the superiority of Miliukov to the other political men of the Russian bourgeoisie. His strength lay, and his weakness too, in this: he expressed more fully and elegantly than others in the language of politics the fate of the Russian bourgeoisie—the fact that it was caught historically in a blind alley. The Mensheviks wept because Miliukov ruined liberalism, but it would be truer to say that liberalism ruined Miliukov.

In spite of his Neo-Slavism warmed over for imperialistic purposes, Miliukov always remained a bourgeois "Westerner." The goal of his party was always the triumph in Russia of European civilization. But the farther he went, the more he feared those revolutionary paths upon which the Western peoples were traveling. His "Westernism" therefore reduced itself to an impotent envy of the West.

The English and French bourgeoisie created a new society in their own image. The Germans came later, and they were compelled to live for a long time on the pale gruel of philosophy. The Germans invented the phrase "speculative world," which does not exist in English or French. While these nations were creating a new world the Germans were thinking one up. But the German bourgeoisie, although poor in political activity, created the classical philosophy, and that is no small achievement. Russia came much later. To be sure, she translated the German phrase "speculative world" into Russian, and that with several variations, but this only the more clearly exposed both her political impotence and her deadly philosophical poverty. She imported ideas as well as machines, establishing high tariffs for the latter, and for the former a quarantine of fear. To these characteristics of his class Miliukov was called to give a political expression.

A former Moscow professor of history, author of significant scholarly works, founder of the Kadet Party—a union of the liberal landlords and the left intelligentsia—Miliukov was completely free from that insufferable, half-aristocratic and half-intellectual political dilettantism which is proper to the majority of Russian liberal men of politics. Miliukov took his profession very seriously and that alone distinguished him.

Before 1905, the Russian liberals were customarily embarrassed about being liberal. A tinge of Narodnikism, and later of Marxism, long served them as a defensive coloration. This rather shallow, shamefaced capitulation to socialism on the part of wide bourgeois circles, among them a number of young industrialists, expressed the lack of self-confidence of a class which appeared soon enough to concentrate millions in its hands, but too late to stand at the head of the nation. The bearded fathers, wealthy peasants and shopkeepers, had piled up their money, thinking nothing of their social rôle. Their sons graduated from the university in the period of pre-revolutionary intellectual ferment, and when they tried to find their place in society, they were in no hurry to adopt the banner of liberalism, already worn out in advanced countries, patched and half faded. For a period of time they gave a part of their souls, and even a part of their incomes, to the revolutionists. This is especially true of the representatives of the liberal professions. A very considerable number of them passed through a stage of socialistic sympathy in their youth. Professor Miliukov never had these measles. He was organically bourgeois and not ashamed of it.

It is true that at the time of the first revolution, Miliukov did not wholly renounce the idea of utilizing the revolutionary masses—with the help of tame and well-trained socialist parties. Witte relates that when he was forming his constitutional cabinet in October 1905, and appealed to the Kadets to "cut off their revolutionary tail," the answer was that they could no more get along without the armed forces of the revolution than Witte could without the army. In the essence of the matter, this was a bluff even then: in order to raise their own price, the Kadets tried to frighten Witte with the masses whom they themselves feared. It was precisely the experience of 1905 which convinced Miliukov that, no matter how strong the liberal sympathies of the socialist groups of the intelligentsia might be, the genuine forces of the revolution, the masses, would never give up their weapons to the bourgeoisie, and would be the more dangerous the better armed they were. When he declared openly that the red flag is a red rag, Miliukov ended to everybody's relief a romance which in reality nobody had seriously begun. The isolation of the so-called intelligentsia from the people has been one of the traditional themes of Russian journalism—and by "intelligentsia" the liberals, in contrast with the socialists, mean all the "educated," that is, possessing, classes. Ever since that isolation proved such a calamity to the liberals in the first revolution, the ideologues of the "educated" classes have lived in a kind of perpetual expectation of the judgment day. One of the liberal writers, a philosopher not restrained by the exigencies of politics, has expressed this fear of the masses with an ecstatic force which reminds us of the epileptic reactionism of Dostoyevsky: "Whatever we stand for, we must not dream of uniting with the people—we must fear them more than all

188

the persecutions of the government, and we must give thanks to the government which alone protects us with its prisons and bayonets from the ferocity of the people." With such political feelings, could the liberals possibly dream of leading a revolutionary nation? Miliukov's whole policy is marked with a stamp of hopelessness. At the moment of national crisis his party thinks about dodging the blow, not dealing it.

As a writer, Miliukov is heavy, prolix and wearisome. He has the same quality as an orator. Decorativeness is unnatural to him. That might have been an advantage, if the niggardly policies of Miliukov had not so obviously needed a disguise—or if they had had, at least, an objective disguise in the shape of a great tradition. There was not even a little tradition. The official policy in France—quintessence of bourgeois perfidy and egotism—has two mighty allies: tradition and rhetoric. Each promoting the other, they surround with a defensive covering any bourgeois politician, even such a prosaic clerk of the big proprietors as Poincaré. It is not Miliukov's fault if he had no glorious ancestors, and if he was compelled to conduct a policy of bourgeois egotism on the borders of Europe and Asia.

"Along with a sympathy for Kerensky," we read in the memoirs of the Social Revolutionary, Sokolov, "one felt from the beginning an immense and unconcealed, and yet rather strange, antipathy for Miliukov. I did not understand, and do not now, why that respectable social reformer was so unpopular." If the Philistines had understood the cause of their admiration for Kerensky and their distaste for Miliukov, they would have ceased to be Philistines. The everyday bourgeois did not like Miliukov, because Miliukov too prosaically and soberly, without adornment, expressed the political essence of the Russian bourgeoisie. Beholding himself in the Miliukov mirror, the bourgeois saw that he was gray, self-interested and cowardly; and, as so often happens, he took offense at the mirror.

On his side, observing the displeased grimaces of the liberal bourgeois, Miliukov quietly and confidently remarked: "The everyday man is a fool." He pronounced these words without

189

irritation, almost caressingly, as though to say: He does not understand me today, but never mind, he will understand later. Miliukov was deeply confident that the bourgeoisie would not betray him, that it would obey the logic of the situation and follow, for it had no other way to go. And in reality, after the February revolution all the bourgeois parties, even those to the right, followed the Kadet leader, abusing and even cursing him.

It was very different with the democratic politicians of a socialist coloring, men of the type of Sukhanov. This was no ordinary Philistine, but on the contrary a professional man-of-politics, sufficiently expert in his small trade. He could never look intelligent, because one saw too plainly the continual contrast between what he wanted, and what he arrived at. But he intellectualized and blundered and bored. In order to lead him after you, it was necessary to deceive him by acknowledging his genuine independence, even accusing him of being self-willed, excessively given to command. That flattered him and reconciled him to the rôle of helper. It was in conversation with just these socialistic highbrows that Miliukov tossed out that phrase: "The everyday man is a fool." This was delicate flattery: "Only you and I are intelligent." As a matter of fact, at that very moment Miliukov was hooking a ring in the noses of his democratic friends. By that ring they were subsequently led out of the way.

His personal unpopularity prevented Miliukov from standing at the head of the government. He took the Ministry of Foreign Affairs, which had been his specialty in the Duma.

The War Minister of the revolution was the big Moscow industrialist, Guchkov, already known to us—in his youth a liberal with an adventurous temperament, but afterward, in the period of the defeat of the first revolution, the trusted man of the big bourgeoisie under Stolypin. The dissolution of the two first Dumas, dominated by the Kadets, led to the governmental overturn of the 3rd of June 1907, which changed the election law to the benefit of the party of Guchkov. It became the leader of the two subsequent Dumas and continued so right up to the day of the revolution. In Kiev in 1911, at

the unveiling of a monument to Stolypin who was killed by
a terrorist, Guchkov, in placing a wreath, bowed silently down
to the ground: a gesture in the name of his class. In the Duma,
Guchkov dedicated himself chiefly to the question of "military
might," and in preparing for war walked hand-in-hand with
Miliukov. In the position of President of the Central Military-
Industrial Committee, Guchkov united the industrialists under
the banner of a patriotic opposition—not however preventing
the leaders of the Progressive Bloc, including Rodzianko, from
getting a rake-off on military contracts. For revolutionary
recommendation there was attached to Guchkov's name that
semi-legend about the plot of a palace revolution. A former
chief of police asserted, moreover, that Guchkov "had permitted
himself in private conversations about the monarch to employ
an epithet insulting in the highest degree." That was very
likely true, but in that Guchkov was no exception. The pious
tzarina hated Guchkov, lavished crude abuse upon him in her
letters, and expressed the hope that he would hang "on a high
tree." But the tzarina had many others in view for this same
high position. Somehow, at any rate, this man who bowed to
the earth in honor of the hangman of the first revolution became the War Minister of the second.

The Minister of Agriculture was the Kadet Shingarev, a
provincial doctor who had subsequently become a deputy in the
Duma. His close associates in the party considered him an
honest mediocrity or, as Nabokov expressed it, "a Russian provincial intellectual, designed on a small-town or county, rather
than a national, scale." The indefinite radicalism of his early
years had long washed away, and the chief anxiety of Shingarev
was to demonstrate his statesmanlike maturity to the possessing
classes. Although the old Kadet program spoke of the "confiscation with just indemnity of the landed estates," none of the
property owners took this program seriously—especially now in
the years of the war inflation. And Shingarev made it his chief
task to delay the decision of the agrarian problem, deluding
the peasants with the mirage of a Constituent Assembly which
the Kadets did not want to summon. On the land question

191

and the question of war, the February revolution was destined to break its neck. Shingarev helped all he could.

The portfolio of Finance was given to a young man named Tereshchenko. "Where did they get him?" everybody was inquiring with bewilderment in the Tauride Palace. The well-informed explained that this was an owner of sugar factories, estates, forests, and other innumerable properties, worth some eighty million roubles in gold, president of the Military-Industrial Committee of Kiev, possessed of a good French pronunciation, and on top of it all a connoisseur of the ballet. And they added—more importantly—that as the favorite of Guchkov, Tereshchenko had almost taken part in the great conspiracy which was to have overthrown Nicholas II. The revolution which prevented that conspiracy was of great help to Tereshchenko.

In the course of those five February days when the revolutionary fight was being waged in the cold streets of the capital, there flitted before us several times like a shadow the figure of a liberal of noble family, the son of a former tzarist minister, Nabokov—almost symbolic in his self-satisfied correctness and dry egotism. Nabokov passed the decisive days of the insurrection within the four walls of the chancellery, or his home, "in dull and anxious expectancy." He now became General Administrator of the Provisional Government, actually a minister without portfolio. In his Berlin exile where he was finally killed by the stray bullet of a White Guard, he left memoirs of the Provisional Government which are not without interest. Let us place that to his credit.

But we have forgotten to mention the Prime Minister—whom, by the way, in the most serious moments of his brief term everybody forgot. On March 2, in recommending the new government to a meeting at the Tauride Palace, Miliukov described Prince Lvov as "the incarnation of the Russian social consciousness so persecuted by the tzarist régime." Later, in his history of the revolution, Miliukov prudently remarks that at the head of the government was placed Prince Lvov, "personally little known to the majority of the Provisional Committee." The historian here tries to relieve the politician of responsibility for

192

this choice. As a matter of fact, the prince had long been a member of the Kadet Party, belonging to its right wing. After the dissolution of the first Duma, at that famous meeting of the deputies at Vyborg which addressed the population with the ritual of offended liberalism: "Refuse to pay the taxes!" Prince Lvov attended but did not sign the appeal. Nabokov relates that immediately upon his arrival at Vyborg the prince fell sick, and his sickness was "attributed to the emotional condition in which he found himself." The prince was evidently not built for revolutionary excitement. This moderate prince, owing to a political indifference that looked like broadmindedness, tolerated in the organizations which he administered a large number of left intellectuals, former revolutionists, socialistic patriots, and draft-dodgers. They worked just as well as the bureaucrats, did not graft, and moreover created for the prince a simulacrum of popularity. A prince, a rich man, and a liberal—that was very impressive to the average bourgeois. For that reason Prince Lvov was marked for the premiership even under the tzar. To sum it all up in a word, the head of the government of the February revolution was an illustrious but notoriously empty spot. Rodzianko would at least have been more colorful.

The legendary history of the Russian state begins with a tale in the *Chronicle* to the effect that delegates of the Slavic tribes went to the Scandinavian princes with the request: "Come and rule and be princes over us." The pitiable representatives of the social democracy transformed this historic legend into a fact—not in the ninth but in the twentieth century, and with this difference, that they did not address themselves to princes over the sea, but to their own home princes. Thus as a result of a victorious insurrection of workers and soldiers, there appeared at the helm of government a handful of the very richest landlords and industrialists, remarkable for less than nothing, political dilettantes without a program—and at the head of them a prince with a strong dislike for excitement.

The composition of the new government was greeted with satisfaction in the Allied embassies, in the bourgeois and bureaucratic salons, and in the broader circles of the middle, and part

of the petty, bourgeoisie. Prince Lvov, Octobrist Guchkov, Kadet Miliukov—those names sounded reassuring. The name of
Kerensky perhaps caused some eyebrows to rise among the
Allies, but they were not badly frightened. The more farseeing understood: after all, there is a revolution in the country;
with such a steady wheel-horse as Miliukov, a mettlesome team-
mate can only be helpful. Thus the French ambassador Paléologue, a great lover of Russian metaphors, must have expressed it.

Among the workers and soldiers the composition of the government created an immediate feeling of hostility, or at the
best a dumb bewilderment. The name of Miliukov or Guchkov
did not evoke one voice of greeting in either factory or
barrack. There exists no little testimony to this. Officer Msti-
slavisky reports the sullen alarm of his soldiers at the news that
the power had passed from tzar to prince: Is that worth shedding blood for? Stankevich, one of Kerensky's intimate circle,
made the rounds of his sapper battalion, company by company,
recommending the new government, which he himself considered the best possible and of which he spoke with great enthusiasm. "But I felt a coolness in the audience." Only when
the officer mentioned Kerensky did the soldiers "kindle with sincere satisfaction." By that time the bourgeois social opinion of
the capital had already converted Kerensky into the central hero
of the revolution. The soldiers even more than the workers
desired to see in Kerensky a counterpoise to the bourgeois government, and only wondered why he was there alone. Kerensky
was not a counterpoise, however, but a finishing touch, a screen,
a decoration. He was defending the same interests as Miliukov,
but with magnesium flashlights.

What was the real constitution of the country after the inauguration of the new power?

The monarchist reaction was hiding in the cracks. With
the very first ebb of the wave, property owners of all kinds and
tendencies gathered around the banner of the Kadet Party,
which had suddenly become the only non-socialist party—and
at the same time the extreme right party—in the open arena.

The masses went over in droves to the socialists, whom they

identified with the Soviet. Not only the workers and soldiers of the enormous garrisons in the rear, but all the many-colored small people of the towns—mechanics, street peddlers, petty officials, cab-drivers, janitors, servants of all kinds—feeling alien to the Provisional Government and its bureaus, were seeking a closer and more accessible authority. In continually increasing numbers, peasant delegates were appearing at the Tauride Palace. The masses poured into the Soviet as though into the triumphal gates of the revolution. All that remained outside the boundaries of the Soviet seemed to fall away from the revolution, seemed somehow to belong to a different world. And so it was in reality. Beyond the boundaries of the Soviet remained the world of the property owner, in which all colors mingled now in one grayish-pink defensive tint.

Not all the toiling masses chose the Soviet; not all awakened at once; not every layer of the oppressed dared instantly believe that the revolution concerned them. In the consciousness of many only an undiscriminating hope was stirring. But all the active elements of the masses poured into the Soviet, and activity prevails in times of revolution. Moreover, since mass activity was growing from day to day, the basis of the Soviet was continually broadening. It was the sole genuine basis of the revolution.

In the Tauride Palace there were two halves: the Duma and the Soviet. The Executive Committee was at first crowded into some narrow secretarial chambers, through which flowed an uninterrupted human flood. The deputies of the Duma tried to feel like proprietors in their sumptuous chambers. But the barriers were soon swept away by the overflow of the revolution. In spite of all the indecisiveness of its leaders, the Soviet spread out irresistibly, and the Duma was crowded away into the back yard. The new correlation of forces broke its path everywhere.

Deputies in the Tauride Palace, officers in their regiments, commanders in the staffs, directors and managers in factories, on the railroads, in the telegraph offices, landlords or managers of estates—all felt themselves during those first days of the revolution to be under the suspicious and tireless scrutiny of the masses. In the eyes of those masses the Soviet was an organized expression of their distrust of all who had oppressed them. Typesetters would jealously follow the text of the articles which they had set up, railroad workers would anxiously and vigilantly watch over the military trains, telegraphers would become absorbed in rereading the texts of telegrams, soldiers would glance around suspiciously every time their officer made a move, workers would dismiss from the factory an overseer belonging to the Black Hundreds and take in under observation a liberal manager. The Duma from the first hours of the revolution, and the Provisional Government from its first days, became reservoirs into which flowed a continuous stream of complaints and objections from the upper layers of society, their protests against "excesses," their woeful comments and dark forebodings.

"Without the bourgeoisie we cannot manage the state apparatus," reasoned the socialistic petty bourgeois, timidly looking up at the official buildings where the skeleton of the old government looked out with empty eyes. The problem was solved by setting some sort of a liberal head on the institution which the revolution had beheaded. The new ministers entered into the tzarist bureaus, took possession of the apparatus of typewriters, telephones, couriers, stenographers and clerks, and found out from day to day that the machine was running empty.

Kerensky subsequently related how the Provisional Government "took the power in its hands on the third day of all-Russian anarchy, when throughout the whole extent of the Russian land there existed not only no governmental power, but literally not one policeman." The soviets of workers and soldiers deputies standing at the head of millions of people, counted for nothing: that of course was merely one element of the anarchy. The orphaned condition of the country is summed up for Kerensky in the disappearance of policemen. In that confession of faith of the most leftward of the ministers, you have the key to the whole policy of the government.

The place of the governors of provinces was occupied, on the order of Prince Lvov, by the presidents of the provincial zemstvos, who differed but little from their predecessors. Often enough they were feudal landlords who regarded even the governors as Jacobins. At the head of the counties stood the presidents of the county zemstvos. Under the new name of "commissars" the population recognized their old enemies. "New Presbyter is but Old Priest writ large," as Milton once said of the cowardly Presbyterian reformation. The provincial and district commissars took possession of the typewriters, correspondence, and clerks of the governors and chiefs of police, only to find out that they had inherited no real power. Real life both in the provinces and in the counties concentrated around the Soviet. A two-power system thus reigned from top to bottom. But in the provinces the Soviet leaders, those same Social Revolutionaries and Mensheviks, were a little simpler and by no means everywhere renounced that power which the whole situation was imposing upon them. As a result of this, the activity of the provincial commissars consisted mainly of submitting complaints as to the complete impossibility of fulfilling the duties of their office.

Two days after the formation of the liberal ministry the bourgeoisie were feeling that they had not acquired the power, but lost it. In spite of all the fantastic caprices of the Rasputin clique before the revolution, its real power had been limited. The influence of the bourgeoisie upon the government had been enormous. The very participation of Russia in the war was more the work of the bourgeoisie than the monarchy. But the main thing was that the tzarist government had guaranteed to the property owners their factories, land, banks, houses, newspapers; it was consequently upon the most vital questions *their* government. The February revolution changed the situation in two contrary directions: it solemnly handed over to the bourgeoisie the external attributes of power, but at the same time it took from them that share in the actual rulership which they had enjoyed before the revolution. The former employees of the zemstvos where Prince Lvov was the boss, and of the Military-Industrial Committee where Guchkov was in command, became today, under the name of Social Revolutionaries and Mensheviks, lords of the situation in the country and on the front, in the city and in the village. They appointed Lvov and Guchkov to the ministry, and laid down the conditions of their work as though they were hiring stewards.

On the other hand, the Executive Committee, having created a bourgeois government, could not make up its mind like the Bible God to call the creation good. On the contrary, it made great haste to increase the distance between itself and the work of its hands, and announced that it intended to support the new power only in so far as it should truly serve the democratic revolution. The Provisional Government very well knew that it could not survive an hour without the support of the official democracy. But this support was promised only as a reward for good behavior—that is, for fulfilling tasks alien to it, and which the democracy itself had just declined to fulfill. The government never knew within what limits it might dare to reveal its semi-contraband sovereignty. The leaders of the Executive Committee could not always advise it, because it was hard for them to guess just where some dissatisfaction would break out in their own midst, expressing the dissatisfaction of the masses. The bourgeoisie pretended that the socialists were deceiving them. The socialists in their turn were afraid that the liberals, with their premature demands, would stir up the masses and complicate a situation difficult enough as it was. *"In so far as"*—that equivocal formula laid its imprint on the whole pre-October period. It became the juridical formulation of the inner lie contained in the hybrid régime of the February revolution.

To bring pressure upon the government, the Executive Committee elected a special commission which it politely but ludicrously named "Contact Commission." The organization of the revolutionary power was thus based upon the principle of mutual persuasion. The mystic writer Merezhkovsky could find a precedent for such a régime only in the Old Testament: the kings of Israel had their prophets. But the prophets of the Bible, like the prophets of the last Romanov, used at least to receive suggestions directly from heaven, and the kings did not dare to contradict. In that way a single sovereignty was assured. It was quite different with the prophets of the Soviet: they prophesied only under the stimulus of their own limited intelligence. The liberal ministers moreover believed that nothing good could come out of the Soviet. Cheidze, Skobelev, Sukhanov and others would run to the government and garrulously try to persuade it to make some concession; the ministers would object; the delegates would return to the Executive Committee, try to influence it with the authority of the government; again get into contact with the ministers; and so begin over again from the beginning. This complicated mill-wheel never did any grinding.

In the Contact Commission everybody complained. Guchkov especially wept over the disorders in the army caused by the connivances of the Soviet. At times the War Minister of the revolution "in the literal sense of the word . . . poured out tears, or at least earnestly wiped his eyes with his handkerchief." He was quite right in thinking that to dry the tears of the anointed is one of the functions of a prophet.

On the ninth of March General Alexeiev, the Chief of Staff, telegraphed the War Minister: "The German yoke is near if only we indulge the Soviet." Guchkov answered him tearfully: "The government, alas, has no real power; the troops, the railroads, the post and telegraph are in the hands of the Soviet. The simple fact is that the Provisional Government exists only so long as the Soviet permits it."

Week followed week, but the situation did not improve in the least. Early in April when the Provisional Government sent deputies of the Duma to the front, it directed them, gritting its teeth, not to reveal any disagreements with the delegates of the Soviet. Throughout the whole journey the liberal deputies felt as though they were under convoy, but they also knew that without this, notwithstanding their lofty credentials, they not only could not approach the soldiers, but they could not even find seats in the trains. That prosaic detail in the memoirs of Prince Mansyrev excellently supplements Guchkov's correspondence with the staff as to the essence of the February constitution. One of the reactionary wits pretty well characterized the situation thus: "The old government is in prison, and the new one under house arrest."

But did the Provisional Government have no other support

but this equivocal one of the Soviet leaders? What had become
of the possessing classes? The question is a fundamental one.
United by their past with the monarchy, the possessing classes
had hastened to group themselves around a new axis after the
revolution. On the 2nd of March, the Council of Trade and
Industry, representing the united capital of the whole country,
saluted the act of the State Duma, and declared itself "wholly
at the disposition" of its Committee.

The zemstvos and the town dumas adopted the same course.
On March 10, even the Council of the United Nobility, the
mainstay of the throne, summoned all the people of Russia in
a language of eloquent cowardice "to unite around the Provisional Government as now the sole lawful power in Russia."
Almost at the same time the institutions and organs of the possessing classes began to denounce the dual power, and to lay
the blame for the disorders upon the Soviet—at first cautiously,
but then bolder and bolder. The employers were soon followed
by the clerks, the united liberal professions, the government
employees. From the army came telegrams, addresses and resolutions of the same character—manufactured in the staff. The
liberal press opened a campaign "for a single sovereignty," which
in the coming months acquired the character of a hurricane
of fire around the heads of the Soviet. All these things together looked exceedingly impressive. The ·enormous number of institutions, well-known names, resolutions, articles, the
decisiveness of tone—it had an indubitable effect upon the sug-
gestible heads of the Committee. And yet there was no serious
force behind this threatening parade of the propertied classes.
How about the force of property? said the petty bourgeois
socialists, answering the Bolsheviks. Property is a relation among
people. It represents an enormous power so long as it is universally recognized and supported by that system of compulsion
called Law and the State. But the very essence of the present
situation was that the old state had suddenly collapsed, and the
entire old system of rights had been called in question by the
masses. In the factories the workers were more and more regarding themselves as the proprietors, and the bosses as uninvited guests. Still less assured were the feelings of the landlords

in the provinces, face to face with those surly vengeful muzhiks, and far from that governmental power in whose existence they did for a time, owing to their distance from the capital, believe. The property-holders, deprived of the possibility of using their property, or protecting it, ceased to be real property-holders and became badly frightened Philistines who could not give any support to the government for the simple reason that they needed support themselves. They soon began to curse the government for its weakness, but they were only cursing their own fate.

In those days the joint activity of the Executive Committee and the ministry seemed to have for its goal to demonstrate that the art of government in time of revolution consists in a garrulous waste of time. With the liberals this was a consciously adopted plan. It was their firm conviction that all measures demanded postponement except one: the oath of loyalty to the Entente.

Miliukov acquainted his colleagues with the secret treaties. Kerensky let them in one ear and out the other. Apparently only the Procuror of the Holy Synod, a certain Lvov, rich in surprises, a namesake of the Premier but not a prince, went into a storm of indignation and even called the treaties "brigandage and swindle"—which undoubtedly provoked a condescending smile from Miliukov ("The everyday man is a fool") and a quiet proposal to return to the order of business. The official Declaration of the government promised to summon a Constituent Assembly at the earliest possible date—which date, however, was intentionally not stated. Nothing was said about the form of government: they still hoped to return to the lost paradise of monarchy. But the real meat of the Declaration lay in its promise to carry the war through to victory, and "unswervingly carry out the agreements made with our Allies." So far as concerned the most threatening problems of the people's existence, the revolution had apparently been achieved only in order to make the announcement: everything remains as before. Since the democrats attributed an almost mystic importance to recognition by the Entente—a small trader amounts to nothing until the bank recognizes his credit—the

Executive Committee swallowed in silence the imperialist declaration of March 6.

"Not one official organ of the democracy," grieves Sukhanov a year later, "publicly reacted to the Declaration of the Provisional Government, which disgraced our revolution at its very birth in the eyes of democratic Europe."

At last, on the 8th of March, there issued from the ministerial laboratory a Decree of Amnesty. By that time the doors of the prisons had been opened by the people throughout the whole country, political exiles were returning in a solid stream with meetings, hurrahs, military speeches, flowers. The decree sounded like a belated echo from the government buildings. On the twelfth they announced the abolition of the death penalty. Four months later it was restored in the army. Kerensky promised to elevate justice to unheard-of heights. In a moment of heat he actually did carry out a resolution of the Executive Committee introducing representatives of the workers and soldiers as members of the courts of justice. That was the sole measure in which could be felt the heartbeat of the revolution, and it raised the hair on the heads of the eunuchs of justice. But the matter stopped right there. Lawyer Demianov, an important officer in the ministry under Kerensky, and also a "socialist," decided to adopt the principle of leaving all former officials at their posts. To quote his own words: "The policies of a revolutionary government ought never to offend anybody unnecessarily." That was, at bottom, the guiding principle of the whole Provisional Government, which feared most of all to offend anybody from the circles of the possessing classes, or even the tzarist bureaucracy. Not only the judges, but even the prosecutors of the tzarist régime remained at their posts. To be sure, the masses might be offended. But that was the Soviet's business: the masses did not enter into the field of vision of the government.

The sole thing in the nature of a fresh stream was brought in by the above-mentioned temperamental Procuror, Lvov, who gave an official report on the "idiots and scoundrels" sitting in the Holy Synod. The ministers listened to his juicy characterizations with some alarm, but the synod continued a state institution, and Greek Orthodoxy the state religion. Even the membership of the Synod remained unchanged. A revolution ought not to quarrel with anybody!

The members of the State Council—faithful servants of two or three emperors—continued to sit, or at least to draw their salaries. And this fact soon acquired a symbolic significance. Factories and barracks noisily protested. The Executive Committee worried about it. The government spent two sessions debating the question of the fate and salaries of the members of the State Council, and could not arrive at a decision. Why disturb these respectable people, among whom, by the way, we have many good friends?

The Rasputin ministers were still in prison, but the Provisional Government hastened to vote them a pension. This sounded like mockery, or a voice from another world. But the government did not want to offend its predecessors even though they were locked up in jail.

The senators continued to drowse in their embroidered jackets, and when a left senator, Sokolov, newly appointed by Kerensky, dared to appear in a black frock coat, they quietly removed him from the hall. These tzarist legislators were not afraid to offend the February revolution, once convinced that its government had no teeth.

Karl Marx saw the cause of the failure of the March revolution in Germany in the fact that it "reformed only the very highest political circles, leaving untouched all the layers beneath them—the old bureaucracy, the old army, the old judges, born and brought up and grown old in the service of absolutism." Socialists of the type of Kerensky were seeking salvation exactly where Marx saw the cause of failure. And the Menshevik Marxists were with Kerensky, not Marx.

The sole sphere in which the government showed initiative and revolutionary tempo, was that of legislation on stock holdings. Here the decree of reform was issued on the 17th of March. National and religious limitations were annulled only three days later. There were quite a few people on the staff

203

of the government, you see, who had suffered under the old régime, if at all, only from a lack of business in stocks.

The workers were impatiently demanding an eight-hour day. The government pretended to be deaf in both ears. Besides it is war time, and all ought to sacrifice themselves for the good of the Fatherland. Moreover that is the Soviet's business: let them pacify the workers.

Still more threatening was the land question. Here it was really necessary to do something. Spurred on by the prophets, the Minister of Agriculture, Shingarev, ordered the formation of local land committees—prudently refraining, however, from defining their tasks and functions. The peasants had an idea that these committees ought to give them the land. The landlords thought the committees ought to protect their property. From the very start the muzhik's noose, more ruthless than all others, was tightening round the neck of the February régime.

Agreeably to the official doctrine, all those problems which had caused the revolution were postponed to the Constituent Assembly. How could you expect these irreproachable democrats to anticipate the national will, when they had not even succeeded in seating Mikhail Romanov astride of it? The preparation of a national representation was approached in those days with such bureaucratic heaviness and deliberate procrastination that the Constituent Assembly itself became a mirage. Only on the 25th of March, almost a month after the insurrection—a month of revolution!—the government decided to call a lumbering Special Conference for the purpose of working out an election law. But the conference never opened. Miliukov in his *History of the Revolution*—which is false from beginning to end—confusedly states that as a result of various difficulties "the work of the Special Conference was not begun under the first government." The difficulties were inherent in the constitution of the conference and in its function. The whole idea was to postpone the Constituent Assembly until better times: until victory, until peace, or until the Calends of Kornilov.

The Russian bourgeoisie, which appeared in the world too late, mortally hated the revolution. But its hatred had no strength. It had to bide its time and maneuver. Being unable to overthrow and strangle the revolution, the bourgeoisie counted on starving it out.

CHAPTER XI

DUAL POWER

WHAT constitutes the essence of a dual power?[1] We must pause upon this question, for an illumination of it has never appeared in historic literature. And yet this dual power is a distinct condition of social crisis, by no means peculiar to the Russian revolution of 1917, although there most clearly marked out.

Antagonistic classes exist in society everywhere, and a class deprived of power inevitably strives to some extent to swerve the governmental course in its favor. This does not as yet mean, however, that two or more powers are ruling in society. The character of a political structure is directly determined by the relation of the oppressed classes to the ruling class. A single government, the necessary condition of stability in any régime, is preserved so long as the ruling class succeeds in putting over its economic and political forms upon the whole of society as the only forms possible.

The simultaneous dominion of the German Junkers and the bourgeoisie—whether in the Hohenzollern form or the republic —is not a double government, no matter how sharp at times may be the conflict between the two participating powers. They have a common social basis, therefore their clash does not threaten to split the state apparatus. The two-power régime arises only out of irreconcilable class conflicts—is possible, therefore, only in a revolutionary epoch, and constitutes one of its fundamental elements.

The political mechanism of revolution consists of the trans-

[1] *Dual power* is the phrase settled upon in communist literature as an English rendering of *dvoevlastie*. The term is untranslatable both because of its form—twin-powerdom—and because the stem, *vlast*, means *sovereignty* as well as *power*. *Vlast* is also used as an equivalent of *government*, and in the plural corresponds to our phrase *the authorities*. In view of this, I have employed some other terms besides *dual power*: *double sovereignty, two-power régime*, etc. [Trans.]

206

fer of power from one class to another. The forcible over-turn is usually accomplished in a brief time. But no historic class lifts itself from a subject position to a position of ruler-ship suddenly in one night, even though a night of revolution. It must already on the eve of the revolution have assumed a very independent attitude towards the official ruling class; more-over, it must have focussed upon itself the hopes of intermediate classes and layers, dissatisfied with the existing state of affairs, but not capable of playing an independent rôle. The historic preparation of a revolution brings about, in the pre-revolution-ary period, a situation in which the class which is called to realize the new social system, although not yet master of the country, has actually concentrated in its hands a significant share of the state power, while the official apparatus of the government is still in the hands of the old lords. That is the initial dual power in every revolution.

But that is not its only form. If the new class, placed in power by a revolution which it did not want, is in essence an already old, historically belated, class; if it was already worn out before it was officially crowned; if on coming to power it encounters an antagonist already sufficiently mature and reach-ing out its hand toward the helm of state; then instead of one unstable two-power equilibrium, the political revolution pro-duces another, still less stable. To overcome the "anarchy" of this twofold sovereignty becomes at every new step the task of the revolution—or the counter-revolution.

This double sovereignty does not presuppose—generally speaking, indeed, it excludes—the possibility of a division of the power into two equal halves, or indeed any formal equilibrium of forces whatever. It is not a constitutional, but a revolu-tionary fact. It implies that a destruction of the social equi-librium has already split the state superstructure. It arises where the hostile classes are already each relying upon essen-tially incompatible governmental organizations—the one out-lived, the other in process of formation—which jostle against each other at every step in the sphere of government. The amount of power which falls to each of these struggling classes in such a situation, is determined by the correlation of forces in the course of the struggle.

By its very nature such a state of affairs cannot be stable. Society needs a concentration of power, and in the person of the ruling class—or, in the situation we are discussing, the two half-ruling classes—irresistibly strives to get it. The splitting of sovereignty foretells nothing less than a civil war. But before the competing classes and parties will go to that extreme—especially in case they dread the interference of a third force—they may feel compelled for quite a long time to endure, and even to sanction, a two-power system. This system will nevertheless inevitably explode. Civil war gives to this double sovereignty its most visible, because territorial, expression. Each of the powers, having created its own fortified drill ground, fights for possession of the rest of the territory, which often has to endure the double sovereignty in the form of successive invasions by the two fighting powers, until one of them decisively installs itself.

The English revolution of the seventeenth century, exactly because it was a great revolution shattering the nation to the bottom, affords a clear example of this alternating dual power, with sharp transitions in the form of civil war.

At first the royal power, resting upon the privileged classes or the upper circles of these classes—the aristocrats and bishops, —is opposed by the bourgeoisie and the circles of the squirarchy that are close to it. The government of the bourgeoisie is the Presbyterian Parliament supported by the City of London. The protracted conflict between these two régimes is finally settled in open civil war. The two governmental centers—London and Oxford—create their own armies. Here the dual power takes a territorial form, although, as always in civil war, the boundaries are very shifting. Parliament conquers. The king is captured and awaits his fate.

It would seem that the conditions are now created for the single rule of the Presbyterian bourgeoisie. But before the royal power could be broken, the parliamentary army has converted itself into an independent political force. It has concentrated in its ranks the Independents, the pious and resolute petty bour-

geoisie, the craftsmen and farmers. This army powerfully in-
terferes in the social life, not merely as an armed force, but as
a Praetorian Guard, and as the political representative of a new
class opposing the prosperous and rich bourgeoisie. Corre-
spondingly the army creates a new state organ rising above the
military command: a council of soldiers' and officers' deputies
("agitators"). A new period of double sovereignty has thus
arrived: that of the Presbyterian Parliament and the Independents' army. This leads to open conflicts. The bourgeoisie
proves powerless to oppose with its own army the "model army"
of Cromwell—that is, the armed plebeians. The conflict ends
with a purgation of the Presbyterian Parliament by the sword
of the Independents. There remains but the rump of a parliament; the dictatorship of Cromwell is established. The
lower ranks of the army, under the leadership of the Levellers—
the extreme left wing of the revolution—try to oppose to the
rule of the upper military levels, the patricians of the army,
their own veritably plebeian régime. But this new two-power
system does not succeed in developing: the Levellers, the lowest
depths of the petty bourgeoisie, have not yet, nor can have,
their own historic path. Cromwell soon settles accounts with
his enemies. A new political equilibrium, and still by no means
a stable one, is established for a period of years.

In the great French revolution, the Constituent Assembly,
the backbone of which was the upper levels of the Third Estate,
concentrated the power in its hands—without however fully
annulling the prerogatives of the king. The period of the
Constituent Assembly is a clearly-marked period of dual power,
which ends with the flight of the king to Varennes, and is formally liquidated with the founding of the Republic.

The first French constitution (1791), based upon the fiction
of a complete independence of the legislative and executive
powers, in reality concealed from the people, or tried to conceal, a double sovereignty: that of the bourgeoisie, firmly entrenched in the National Assembly after the capture by the
people of the Bastille, and that of the old monarchy still relying
upon the upper circles of the priesthood, the clergy, the bureaucracy, and the military, to say nothing of their hopes of

foreign intervention. In this self-contradictory régime lay the germs of its inevitable destruction. A way out could be found only in the abolition of bourgeois representation by the powers of European reaction, or in the guillotine for the king and the monarchy. Paris and Coblenz must measure their forces.

But before it comes to war and the guillotine, the Paris Commune enters the scene—supported by the lowest city layers of the Third Estate—and with increasing boldness contests the power with the official representatives of the national bourgeoisie. A new double sovereignty is thus inaugurated, the first manifestation of which we observe as early as 1790, when the big and medium bourgeoisie is still firmly seated in the administration and in the municipalities. How striking is the picture —and how vilely it has been slandered!—of the efforts of the plebeian levels to raise themselves up out of the social cellars and catacombs, and stand forth in that forbidden arena where people in wigs and silk breeches are settling the fate of the nation. It seemed as though the very foundation of society, tramped underfoot by the cultured bourgeoisie, was stirring and coming to life. Human heads lifted themselves above the solid mass, horny hands stretched aloft, hoarse but courageous voices shouted! The districts of Paris, bastards of the revolution, began to live a life of their own. They were recognized— it was impossible not to recognize them!—and transformed into sections. But they kept continually breaking the boundaries of legality and receiving a current of fresh blood from below, opening their ranks in spite of the law to those with no rights, the destitute Sansculottes. At the same time the rural municipalities were becoming a screen for a peasant uprising against that bourgeois legality which was defending the feudal property system. Thus from under the second nation arises a third.

The Parisian sections at first stood opposed to the Commune, which was still dominated by the respectable bourgeoisie. In the bold outbreak of August 10, 1792, the sections gained control of the Commune. From then on the revolutionary Commune opposed the Legislative Assembly, and subsequently the Convention, which failed to keep up with the problems and progress of the revolution—registering its events, but not performing them—because it did not possess the energy, audacity and unanimity of that new class which had raised itself up from the depths of the Parisian districts and found support in the most backward villages. As the sections gained control of the Commune, so the Commune, by way of a new insurrection, gained control of the Convention. Each of the stages was characterized by a sharply marked double sovereignty, each wing of which was trying to establish a single and strong government—the right by a defensive struggle, the left by an offensive. Thus, characteristically—for both revolutions and counter-revolutions—the demand for a dictatorship results from the intolerable contradictions of the double sovereignty. The transition from one of its forms to the other is accomplished through civil war. The great stages of a revolution—that is, the passing of power to new classes or layers—do not at all coincide in this process with the succession of representative institutions, which march along after the dynamic of the revolution like a belated shadow. In the long run, to be sure, the revolutionary dictatorship of the Sansculottes unites with the dictatorship of the Convention. But with what Convention? A Convention purged of the Girondists, who yesterday ruled it with the hand of the Terror—a Convention abridged and adapted to the dominion of new social forces. Thus by the steps of the dual power the French revolution rises in the course of four years to its culmination. After the 9th Thermidor it begins—again by the steps of the dual power—to descend. And again civil war precedes every downward step, just as before it had accompanied every rise. In this way the new society seeks a new equilibrium of forces.

The Russian bourgeoisie, fighting with and coöperating with the Rasputin bureaucracy, had enormously strengthened its political position during the war. Exploiting the defeat of tzarism, it had concentrated in its hands, by means of the Country and Town unions and the Military-Industrial Committees, a great power. It had at its independent disposition enormous state resources, and was in the essence of the matter a parallel government. During the war the tzar's ministers complained that Prince Lvov was furnishing supplies to the

211

army, feeding it, medicating it, even establishing barber shops for the soldiers. "We must either put an end to this, or give the whole power into his hands," said Minister Krivoshein in 1915. He never imagined that a year and a half later Lvov would receive "the whole power"—only not from the tzar, but from the hands of Kerensky, Cheidze and Sukhanov. But on the second day after he received it, there began a new double sovereignty: alongside of yesterday's liberal half-government—today formally legalized—there arose an unofficial, but so much the more actual government of the toiling masses in the form of the soviets. From that moment the Russian revolution began to grow up into an event of world-historic significance.

What, then, is the peculiarity of this dual power as it appeared in the February revolution? In the events of the seventeenth and eighteenth centuries, the dual power was in each case a natural stage in a struggle imposed upon its participants by a temporary correlation of forces, and each side strove to replace the dual power with its own single power. In the revolution of 1917, we see the official democracy consciously and intentionally creating a two-power system, dodging with all its might the transfer of power into its own hands. The double sovereignty is created, or so it seems at a glance, not as a result of a struggle of classes for power, but as the result of a voluntary "yielding" of power by one class to another. In so far as the Russian "democracy" sought for an escape from the two-power régime, it could find one only in its own removal from power. It is just this that we have called the paradox of the February revolution.

A certain analogy can be found in 1848, in the conduct of the German bourgeoisie with relation to the monarchy. But the analogy is not complete. The German bourgeoisie did try earnestly to divide the power with the monarchy on the basis of an agreement. But the bourgeoisie neither had the full power in its hands, nor by any means gave it over wholly to the monarchy. "The Prussian bourgeoisie nominally possessed the power, it did not for a moment doubt that the forces of the old government would place themselves unreservedly at its disposition and convert themselves into loyal adherents of its own omnipotence" (Marx and Engels).

The Russian democracy of 1917, having captured the power from the very moment of insurrection, tried not only to divide it with the bourgeoisie, but to give the state over to the bourgeoisie absolutely. This means, if you please, that in the first quarter of the twentieth century the official Russian democracy had succeeded in decaying politically more completely than the German liberal bourgeoisie of the nineteenth century. And that is entirely according to the laws of history, for it is merely the reverse aspect of the upgrowth in those same decades of the proletariat, which now occupied the place of the craftsmen of Cromwell and the Sansculottes of Robespierre.

If you look deeper, the twofold rule of the Provisional Government and the Executive Committee had the character of a mere reflection. Only the proletariat could advance a claim to the new power. Relying distrustfully upon the workers and soldiers, the Compromisers were compelled to continue the double bookkeeping—of the kings and the prophets. The twofold government of the liberals and the democrats only reflected the still concealed double sovereignty of the bourgeoisie and the proletariat. When the Bolsheviks displace the Compromisers at the head of the Soviet—and this will happen within a few months—then that concealed double sovereignty will come to the surface, and this will be the eve of the October revolution. Until that moment the revolution will live in a world of political reflections. Refracted through the rationalizations of the socialist intelligentsia, the double sovereignty, from being a stage in the class struggle, became a regulative principle. It was just for this reason that it occupied the center of all theoretical discussions. Every thing has its uses: the mirror-like character of the February double government has enabled us better to understand those epochs in history when the same thing appears as a full-blooded episode in a struggle between two régimes. The feeble and reflected light of the moon makes possible important conclusions about the sunlight.

In the immeasurably greater maturity of the Russian proletariat in comparison with the town masses of the older revolutions, lies the basic peculiarity of the Russian revolution. This led first to the paradox of a half-spectral double government, and afterwards prevented the real one from being resolved in favor of the bourgeoisie. For the question stood thus: Either the bourgeoisie will actually dominate the old state apparatus, altering it a little for its purposes, in which case the soviets will come to nothing; or the soviets will form the foundation of a new state, liquidating not only the old governmental apparatus, but also the dominion of those classes which it served. The Mensheviks and the Social Revolutionaries were steering toward the first solution, the Bolsheviks toward the second. The oppressed classes, who, as Marat observed, did not possess in the past the knowledge, or skill, or leadership to carry through what they had begun, were armed in the Russian revolution of the twentieth century with all three. The Bolsheviks were victorious.

A year after their victory the same situation was repeated in Germany, with a different correlation of forces. The social democracy was steering for the establishment of a democratic government of the bourgeoisie and the liquidation of the soviets. Luxemburg and Liebknecht steered toward the dictatorship of the soviets. The Social Democrats won. Hilferding and Kautsky in Germany, Max Adler in Austria, proposed that they should "combine" democracy with the soviet system, including the workers' soviets in the constitution. That would have meant making potential or open civil war a constituent part of the state régime. It would be impossible to imagine a more curious Utopia. Its sole justification on German soil is perhaps an old tradition: the Württemberg democrats of '48 wanted a republic with a duke at the head.

Does this phenomenon of the dual power—heretofore not sufficiently appreciated—contradict the Marxian theory of the state, which regards government as an executive committee of the ruling class? This is just the same as asking: Does the fluctuation of prices under the influence of supply and demand contradict the labor theory of value? Does the self-sacrifice of a female protecting her offspring refute the theory of a struggle for existence? No, in these phenomena we have a more complicated combination of the same laws. If the state is an organization of class rule, and a revolution is the overthrow of the ruling class, then the transfer of power from the one class to the other must necessarily create self-contradictory state conditions, and first of all in the form of the dual power. The relation of class forces is not a mathematical quantity permitting *a priori* computations. When the old régime is thrown out of equilibrium, a new correlation of forces can be established only as the result of a trial by battle. That is revolution.

It may seem as though this theoretical inquiry has led us away from the events of 1917. In reality it leads right into the heart of them. It was precisely around this problem of twofold power that the dramatic struggle of parties and classes turned. Only from a theoretical height is it possible to observe it fully and correctly understand it.

CHAPTER XII

THE EXECUTIVE COMMITTEE

THE organization created on February 27 in the Tauride Palace, and called "Executive Committee of The Soviet of Workers' Deputies," had little really in common with its name. The Soviet of Workers' Deputies of 1905, the originator of the system, rose out of a general strike. It directly represented the masses in struggle. The leaders of the strike became the deputies of the Soviet; the selection of its membership was carried out under fire; its Executive Committee was elected by the Soviet for the further prosecution of the struggle. It was this Executive Committee which placed on the order of the day the armed insurrection.

The February revolution, thanks to the revolt of the troops, was victorious before the workers had created a soviet. The Executive Committee was self-constituted, in advance of the Soviet and independently of the factories and regiments, after the victory of the revolution.

We have here the classic initiative of the radicals—standing aside from the revolutionary struggle, but getting ready to harvest its fruit. The real leaders of the workers had not yet left the streets. They were disarming some, arming others, making sure of the victory. The more far-sighted among them were alarmed by the news that in the Tauride Palace some kind of a soviet of workers' deputies had come into being. Just as in the autumn of 1916 the liberal bourgeoisie, in expectation of a palace revolution which somebody was supposed to put through, had got ready a reserve government to impose upon the new tzar in case it succeeded, so the radical intelligentsia got ready its reserve sub-government at the moment of the February victory. Inasmuch as they had been, at least in the past, adherents of the workers' movement and inclined to cover themselves with its tradition, they now named their offspring

Executive Committee of the Soviet. That was one of those half-intentional falsifications with which all history is filled, especially the history of popular revolutions. In a revolutionary turn of events involving a break in the succession, those "educated" classes who have now to learn to wield the power, gladly seize hold of any names and symbols connected with the heroic memories of the masses. And words not infrequently conceal the essence of things—especially when this is demanded by the interests of influential groups. The immense authority of the Executive Committee from the very day of its birth rested upon its seeming continuance of the Soviet of 1905. This Committee, ratified by the first chaotic meeting of the Soviet, thereafter exerted a decisive influence both upon the membership of the Soviet and upon its policy. This influence was the more conservative, in that the natural selection of revolutionary representatives which is guaranteed by the red-hot atmosphere of a struggle no longer existed. The insurrection was already in the past. All were drunk with victory, were planning how to get comfortable on the new basis, were relaxing their souls, partly also their heads. It required months of new conflicts and struggles in new circumstances, with the consequent reshuffling of personnel, in order that the soviets, from being organs for consecrating the victory, should become organs of struggle and preparation for a new insurrection. We emphasize this aspect of the matter because it has until now been left completely in the shade.

However, not only the conditions in which the Executive Committee and the Soviet arose determined their moderate and compromising character. Deeper and more enduring causes were operating in the same direction.

There were over 150,000 soldiers in Petrograd. There were at least four times as many working men and women of all categories. Nevertheless for every two worker-delegates in the Soviet, there were five soldiers. The rules of representation were extremely elastic, and they were always stretched to the advantage of the soldiers. Whereas the workers elected only one delegate for every thousand, the most petty military unit

217

would frequently send two. The grey army cloth became the general ground-tone of the Soviet.

But by no means all even of the civilians were selected by workers. No small number of people got into the Soviet by individual invitation, through pull, or simply thanks to their own penetrative ability. Radical lawyers, physicians, students, journalists, representing various problematical groups—or most often representing their own ambition. This obviously distorted character of the Soviet was even welcomed by the leaders, who were not a bit sorry to dilute the too concentrated essence of factory and barrack with the lukewarm water of cultivated Philistia. Many of these accidental crashers-in, seekers of adventure, self-appointed Messiahs, and professional bunk shooters, for a long time crowded out with their authoritative elbows the silent workers and irresolute soldiers.

And if this was so in Petrograd, it is not hard to imagine how it looked in the provinces, where the victory came wholly without struggle. The whole country was swarming with soldiers. The garrisons at Kiev, Helsingfors, Tiflis, were as numerous as that in Petrograd; in Saratov, Samara, Tambov, Omsk, there were 70,000 to 80,000 soldiers; in Yaroslavl, Ekaterinoslav, Ekaterinburg 60,000; in a whole series of other cities, 50,000, 40,000 and 30,000. The soviet representation was differently organized in different localities, but everywhere it put the troops in a privileged position. Politically this was caused by the workers themselves, who wanted to go as far as possible to meet the soldiers. The soviet leaders were equally eager to go to meet the officers. Besides the considerable number of lieutenants and ensigns at first elected by the soldiers themselves, a special representation was often given, particularly in the provinces, to the commanding staff. As a result the military had in many soviets an absolutely overwhelming majority. The soldier masses, who had not yet had time to acquire a political physiognomy, nevertheless determined through their representatives the physiognomy of the soviets.

In every representative system there is a certain lack of correspondence. It was especially great on the second day of the revolution. The deputies of the politically helpless soldiers often turned out in those early days to be people completely alien to the soldiers and to the revolution—all sorts of intellectuals and semi-intellectuals who had been hiding in the rear barracks and consequently came out as extreme patriots. Thus was created a divergence between the mood of the barracks and the mood of the soviet. Officer Stankevich, whom the soldiers of his battalion had received back sullenly and distrustfully after the revolution, made a successful speech in the soldiers' section on the delicate question of discipline. Why, he asked, is the mood of the Soviet gentler and more agreeable than that of the battalions? This naïve perplexity testifies once more how hard it is for the real feelings of the lower ranks to find a path to the top.

Nevertheless, as early as March 3, meetings of soldiers and workers began to demand that the Soviet depose forthwith the Provisional Government of the liberal bourgeoisie, and take the power in its own hands. Here again the initiative belonged to the Vyborg district. And could there be, indeed, a demand more intelligible and nearer to the hearts of the masses? But this agitation was soon broken off, not only because the Defensists sharply opposed it; worse than that, the majority leadership had already in the first half of March bowed down in real fact to the two-power régime. And anyway, aside from the Bolsheviks, there was no one to bring up squarely the question of power. The Vyborg leaders had to back down. The Petrograd workers, however, did not for one moment give their confidence to the new government, nor consider it their own. They did listen keenly, though, to the soldiers and try not to oppose them too sharply. The soldiers, on the other hand, just learning the first syllables of political life, although as shrewd peasants they would not trust any master who happened along, nevertheless intently listened to their representatives, who in turn lent a respectful ear to the authoritative leaders of the Executive Committee; and these latter did nothing but listen with alarm to the pulse of the liberal bourgeoisie. Upon this system of universal listening from the bottom toward the top everything rested—for the time being.

However, the mood from below had to break out on the

surface. The question of power, artificially sidetracked, kept pushing up anew, although in disguised form. "The soldiers don't know whom to listen to," complained the districts and the provinces, expressing in this way to the Executive Committee their dissatisfaction with the divided sovereignty. Delegations from the Baltic and Black Sea fleets announced on the 16th of March that they were ready to recognize the Provisional Government in so far as it went hand in hand with the Executive Committee; in other words, they did not intend to recognize it at all. As time goes on, this note sounds louder and louder. "The army and the population should submit only to the directions of the Soviet," resolves the 172nd Reserve Regiment, and then immediately formulates the contrary theorem: "Those directions of the Provisional Government which conflict with the decision of the Soviet are not to be obeyed." With a mixed feeling of satisfaction and anxiety the Executive Committee sanctioned this situation; with grinding teeth the government endured it. There was nothing else for either of them to do.

Already early in March, soviets were coming into being in all the principal towns and industrial centers. From these they spread in the next few weeks throughout the country. They began to arrive in the villages only in April and May; at first it was practically the army alone which spoke in the name of the peasants.

The Executive Committee of the Petrograd Soviet actually acquired a state significance. The other soviets guided themselves by the capital, one after the other adopting resolutions of conditional support to the Provisional Government. Although in the first months the relations between the Petrograd and provincial soviets worked themselves out smoothly, and without conflict or serious disagreement, nevertheless the necessity of a state organization was obvious in the whole situation. A month after the overthrow of the autocracy a first conference of soviets was summoned—incomplete and one-sided in its membership. Although, out of 185 organizations represented, two-thirds were provincial soviets, these were for the most part soldiers' soviets. Together with the representatives of the front organizations, these military delegates—for the most part officers—were in an overwhelming majority. Speeches resounded about war to complete victory, and outcries resounded against the Bolsheviks, notwithstanding their more than moderate behavior. The conference filled out the Petrograd Executive Committee with sixteen conservative provincials, thus legitimizing its state character.

That strengthened the right wing still more. From now on they frightened the malcontents by alluding to the provinces. The resolution on regulating the membership of the Petrograd Soviet—adopted March 14—was hardly carried out at all. It is not the local soviet that decides, but the All-Russian Executive Committee. The official leaders thus occupied an almost unassailable position. The most important decisions were made by the Executive Committee, or rather by its ruling nucleus, after a preliminary agreement with the nucleus of the government. The Soviet remained on one side. They treated it like a meeting: "Not there, not in general meetings, is the policy wrought out; all these 'plenary sessions' had decidedly no practical importance" (Sukhanov). These complacent rulers of destiny thought that in entrusting the leadership to them the soviets had essentially completed their task. The future will soon show them that this is not so. The masses are long-suffering, but they are not clay out of which you can fashion anything you want to. Moreover, in a revolutionary epoch they learn fast. In that lies the power of a revolution.

*

IN order better to understand the further development of events, it is necessary to pause upon the character of the two parties which from the very beginning formed a close political bloc, dominating in the soviets, in the democratic municipalties, in the congresses of the so-called revolutionary democracy, and even carrying their steadily dwindling majority to the Constituent Assembly, which became the last reflection of their former power, like the glow on a hilltop illumined by a sun already set.

If the Russian bourgeoisie appeared in the world too late to be democratic, the Russian democracy for the same reason wanted to consider itself socialistic. The democratic ideology had been hopelessly played out in the course of the nineteenth century. A radical intelligentsia standing on the edge of the twentieth, if it wanted to find a path to the masses, had need of a socialist coloring. This is the general historic cause which gave rise to those two intermediate parties: Menshevik and Social Revolutionary. Each of them, however, had its own genealogy and its own ideology.

The views of the Mensheviks were built up on a Marxian basis. In consequence of that same historical belatedness of Russia, Marxism had there become at first not so much a criticism of capitalist society as an argument for the inevitability of the bourgeois development of the country. History cleverly made use of the emasculated theory of proletarian revolution, in order with its help to Europeanize, in the bourgeois sense, wide circles of the moldy "Narodnik" intelligentsia. In this process a very important rôle fell to the Mensheviks. Constituting the left wing of the bourgeois intelligentsia, they put the bourgeoisie in touch with the more moderate upper layers of the workers, those with a tendency towards legal activity around the Duma and in the trade unions.

The Social Revolutionaries, on the contrary, struggled theoretically against Marxism—although sometimes surrendering to it. They considered themselves a party which realized the union of the intelligentsia, the workers and the peasants—under the leadership, it goes without saying, of the Critical Reason. In the economic sphere their ideas were an indigestible mess of various historical accumulations, reflecting the contradictory life-conditions of the peasantry in a country rapidly becoming capitalistic. The coming revolution presented itself to the Social Revolutionaries as neither bourgeois nor socialistic, but "democratic": they substituted a political formula for a social content. They thus laid out for themselves a course half-way between the bourgeoisie and the proletariat, and consequently a position of arbiter between them. After February it might seem as though the Social Revolutionaries did actually approach this position.

From the time of the first revolution they had had their roots in the peasantry. In the first months of 1917, the whole rural intelligentsia adopted for its own the traditional formula of the Narodniks: "Land and Freedom." In contrast to the Mensheviks who remained always a party of the cities, the Social Revolutionaries had found, it seemed, an amazingly powerful support in the country. More than that, they dominated even in the cities: in the soviets through the soldiers' sections, and in the first democratic municipalities where they had an absolute majority of the votes. The power of this party seemed unlimited. In reality it was a political aberration. A party for whom everybody votes except that minority who know what they are voting for, is no more a party, than the tongue in which babies of all countries babble is a national language. The Social Revolutionary Party came forward as a solemn designation for everything in the February revolution that was immature, unformulated and confused. Everybody who had not inherited from the pre-revolutionary past sufficient reasons to vote for the Kadets or the Bolsheviks, voted for the Social Revolutionaries. But the Kadets stood inside a closed circle of property owners; and the Bolsheviks were still few, misunderstood, and even terrifying. To vote for the Social Revolutionaries meant to vote for the revolution in general, and involved no further obligation. In the city it meant the desire of the soldiers to associate themselves with a party that stood for the peasants, the desire of the backward part of the workers to stand close to the soldiers, the desire of the small townspeople not to break away from the soldiers and the peasants. In those days the Social Revolutionary membership-card was a temporary ticket of admission to the institutions of the revolution, and this ticket remained valid until it was replaced by another card of a more serious character. It has been truly said of this great party, which took in all and everybody, that it was only a grandiose zero.

From the time of the first revolution, the Mensheviks had inferred the necessity of a union with the liberals from the

223

bourgeois character of the revolution. And they valued this union higher than coöperation with the peasantry, whom they considered an unsafe ally. The Bolsheviks, on the contrary, had founded their view of the revolution on a union of the proletariat with the peasantry against the liberal bourgeoisie. As an actual fact we see in the February revolution an opposite grouping—the Mensheviks and Social Revolutionaries come out in a close union, completed by their common bloc with the liberal bourgeoisie. The Bolsheviks, on the official political field, are completely isolated.

This apparently inexplicable fact is in reality wholly in accord with the laws of things. The Social Revolutionaries were not by any means a peasant party, notwithstanding the wholesale sympathy for their slogans in the villages. The central nucleus of the party—what actually defined its policies and created ministers and bureaucrats from its midst—was far more closely associated with the liberal and radical circles of the cities than with the masses of the peasants in revolt. This ruling nucleus—monstrously swelled by the careerist flood of Social Revolutionaries of the March vintage—was frightened to death by the spread of the peasant movement under Social Revolutionary slogans. These freshly baked "Narodniks" wished the peasants all good things, of course, but did not want the red cock to crow. And the horror of the Social Revolutionaries before the peasant revolt was paralleled by the horror of the Mensheviks before the assault of the proletariat. In its entirety this democratic fright was a reflection of the very real danger to the possessing classes caused by a movement of the oppressed, a danger which united them in a single camp, the bourgeois-landlord reaction. The bloc of the Social Revolutionaries with the government of landlord Lvov signalized their break with the agrarian revolution, just as the bloc of the Mensheviks with industrialists and bankers of the type of Guchkov, Tereshchenko and Konovalov, meant their break with the proletarian movement. In these circumstances the union of Mensheviks and Social Revolutionaries meant not a coöperation of proletariat with peasants, but a coalition of those parties which had broken with the proletariat and the peasants respectively, for the sake of a bloc with the possessing classes.

From what has been said it is clear that the socialism of the two democratic parties was a fiction. But this is far from saying that their democratism was real. It is a bloodless sort of democratism that requires a socialistic disguise. The Russian proletariat had waged its struggle for democracy in irreconcilable antagonism to the liberal bourgeoisie. The democratic parties therefore, in entering a bloc with the liberal bourgeoisie, had inevitably to enter into conflict with the proletariat. Such were the social roots of the cruel struggle to come between Compromisers and Bolsheviks.

If you reduce the above outlined processes to their naked class mechanism—of which of course the participants, and even the leaders, of the two compromise parties were not thoroughly conscious—you get approximately the following distribution of historic functions: The liberal bourgeoisie was already unable to win over the masses. Therefore it feared a revolution. But a revolution was necessary for the bourgeois development. From the enfranchised bourgeoisie two groups split off, consisting of sons and younger brothers. One of these groups went to the workers, the other to the peasants. They tried to attach these workers and peasants to themselves, sincerely and hotly demonstrating that they were socialists and hostile to the bourgeoisie. In this way they actually gained a considerable influence over the people. But very soon the effect of their ideas outstripped the original intention. The bourgeoisie sensed a mortal danger and sounded the alarm. Both the groups which had split off from it, the Mensheviks and the Social Revolutionaries, eagerly responded to the summons from the head of the family. Hastily patching up the old disagreements they all stood shoulder to shoulder, abandoned the masses, and rushed to the rescue of bourgeois society.

The Social Revolutionaries made a feeble and flabby impression even in comparison with the Mensheviks. To the Bolsheviks at all important moments they seemed merely third-rate Kadets. To the Kadets they seemed third-rate Bolsheviks. (The second-rate position was occupied, in both cases, by the

Mensheviks.) Their unstable support and the formlessness of their ideology were reflected in their personnel: on all the Social Revolutionary leaders lay the imprint of unfinishedness, superficiality and sentimental unreliability. We may say without any exaggeration that the rank-and-file Bolshevik revealed more political acumen, more understanding of the relations between classes, than the most celebrated Social Revolutionary leaders.

Having no stable criteria, the Social Revolutionaries showed a tendency toward moral imperatives. It is hardly necessary to add that these moral pretentions did not in the least hinder them from employing in big politics those petty knaveries so characteristic of intermediate parties lacking a stable support, a clear doctrine, and a genuine moral axis.

In the Menshevik-Social Revolutionary bloc the dominant place belonged to the Mensheviks, in spite of the weight of numbers on the side of the Social Revolutionaries. In this distribution of forces was expressed in a way the hegemony of the town over the country, the predominance of the city over the rural petty bourgeoisie, and finally the intellectual superiority of a "Marxist" intelligentsia over an intelligentsia which stood by the simon-pure Russian sociology, and prided itself on the meagerness of the old Russian history.

In the first weeks after the revolution not one of the left parties, as we know, had its actual headquarters in the capital. The generally recognized leaders of the socialist parties were abroad. The secondary leaders were on their way to the center from the Far East. This created a mood of prudence and watchful waiting among the temporary leaders, which drew them closer together. Not one of the guiding groups in those weeks thought anything through to the end. The struggle of parties in the Soviet was extremely peaceable in character. It was a question, almost, of mere nuances within one and the same "revolutionary democracy." It is true that with the arrival of Tseretelli from exile (March 19) the Soviet leadership took a rather sharp turn toward the right—toward direct responsibility for the government and the war. But the Bolsheviks also toward the middle of March, under the influence of Kamenev and Stalin who had arrived from exile, swung sharply to the right, so that the distance between the Soviet majority and its left opposition had become by the beginning of April even less than it was at the beginning of March. The real differentiation began a little later. It is possible to set the exact date: April 4, the day after the arrival of Lenin in Petrograd.

The Menshevik Party had a number of distinguished figures at the head of its different tendencies, but not one revolutionary leader. Its extreme right wing, led by the old teachers of the Russian social democracy—Plekhanov, Zassulich, Deutsch—had taken a patriotic position even under the autocracy. On the very eve of the February revolution, Plekhanov, who had so pitifully outlived himself, wrote in an American newspaper that strikes and other forms of working-class struggle in Russia would now be a crime. The broader circles of old Mensheviks—among their number such figures as Martov, Dan, Tseretelli—had inscribed themselves in the camp of Zimmerwald and refused to accept responsibility for the war. But this internationalism of the left Mensheviks, as also of the left Social Revolutionaries, concealed in the majority of cases a mere democratic oppositionism. The February revolution reconciled a majority of those Zimmerwaldists [1] to the war, which from now on they discovered to be a struggle in defense of the revolution. The most decisive in this matter was Tseretelli, who carried Dan and the others along with him. Martov, whom the war had found in France, and who arrived from abroad only on May 9, could not help seeing that his former party associates had after the February revolution arrived at the same position occupied by Guesde, Sembat and others at the beginning of 1914, when they took upon themselves the defense of a bourgeois republic against German absolutism. Standing at the head of the left wing of the Mensheviks, which did not rise to any serious rôle in the revolution, Martov remained in opposition to the policy of Tseretelli and Dan—at the same time opposing a rapprochement between the left Mensheviks and the Bolsheviks.

[1] This term is applied to those who attended the conference of anti-war socialists held in Zimmerwald in 1915, or adhered to its program. The conference reassembled the following year at Kienthal. [Trans.]

Tseretelli spoke in the name of official Menshevism and had an indubitable majority—pre-revolutionary patriots having found it easy to unite with these patriots of the February vintage. Plekhanov, however, had his own group, completely chauvinist and standing outside the party and outside the Soviet. Martov's faction, which did not quit the party, had no paper of its own and no policy of its own. As always at times of great historic action, Martov floundered hopelessly and swung in the air. In 1917, as in 1905, the revolution hardly noticed this unusually able man.

The president of the Menshevik faction of the Duma, Cheidze, became almost automatically the president of the Petrograd Soviet, and afterwards of its Executive Committee. He tried to consecrate to the duties of his office all the resources of his conscientiousness, concealing his perpetual lack of confidence in himself under an ingenuous jocularity. He carried the ineradicable imprint of his province. Mountainous Georgia, the land of sun, vineyards, peasants and petty princes, with a small percentage of workers, produced a very wide stratum of left intellectuals, flexible, temperamental, but the vast majority of them not rising above the petty bourgeois outlook. Georgia sent Mensheviks as deputies to all four Dumas, and in all four factions her deputies played the rôle of leaders. Georgia became the Gironde of the Russian revolution. But whereas the Girondists of the eighteenth century were accused of federalism, the Girondists of Georgia, although at first defending a single and indivisible Russia, ended in separatism.

The most distinguished figure produced by the Georgian Gironde was undoubtedly the former deputy of the second Duma, Tseretelli, who immediately on his arrival from exile took the leadership, not only of the Mensheviks, but of the whole Soviet majority. Not a theoretician and not even a journalist, but a distinguished orator, Tseretelli remained a radical of the southern French type. In conditions of ordinary parliamentary routine he would have been a fish in water. But he was born into a revolutionary epoch, and had poisoned himself in youth with a dose of Marxism. At any rate, of all the Mensheviks, Tseretelli revealed in the events of the revolution

228

the widest horizon and the desire to pursue a consistent policy. For this reason he, more than any other, helped on with the destruction of the February régime. Cheidze wholly submitted to Tseretelli, although at moments he was frightened by that doctrinaire straightforwardness which caused the revolutionary hard-labor convict of yesterday to unite with the conservative representatives of the bourgeoisie.

The Menshevik Skobelev, indebted for his new popularity to his position as deputy in the last Duma, conveyed—and not only on account of his youthful appearance—the impression of a student playing the rôle of statesman on a homemade stage. Skobelev specialized in putting down "excesses," quieting local conflicts, and in general caulking up the cracks of the two-power régime—until he was included, in the unlucky rôle of Minister of Labor, in the Coalition government of May.

A most influential figure among the Mensheviks was Dan, an old party worker, always considered the second figure after Martov. If Menshevism in general was nourished upon the flesh, blood, tradition, and spirit of the German social democracy of the period of decline, Dan actually seemed to be a member of the German party administration—an Ebert on a smaller scale. Ebert, the German Dan, successfully carried out in Germany a year later that policy which Dan, the Russian Ebert, had failed to carry out in Russia. The cause of the difference however was not in the men, but in the conditions.

If the first violin in the orchestra of the Soviet majority was Tseretelli, the piercing clarinet was played by Lieber—with all his lung power and blood in his eyes. This was a Menshevik from the Jewish workers' union (The Bund), with a long revolutionary past, very sincere, very temperamental, very eloquent, very limited, and passionately desirous of showing himself an inflexible patriot and iron statesman. Lieber was literally beside himself with hatred of Bolsheviks.

We may close the phalanx of Menshevik leaders with the former ultra-left Bolshevik, Voitinsky, a prominent participant in the first revolution, who had served at hard labor, and who broke with his party in March on grounds of patriotism. After joining the Mensheviks, Voitinsky became, as was to be expected, a professional Bolshevik-eater. He lacked only Lieber's temperament in order to equal him in baiting his former party comrades.

The general staff of the Narodniks was equally heterogeneous, but far less significant and bright. The so-called Popular Socialists, the extreme right flank, were led by the old emigrant Chaikovsky, who equaled Plekhanov in military chauvinism but lacked his talent and his past. Alongside him stood the old woman Breshko-Breshkovskaia, whom the Social Revolutionaries called the "grandmother of the Russian Revolution," but who zealously forced herself as godmother on the Russian counter-revolution. The superannuated anarchist Kropotkin, who had had a weakness ever since youth for the Narodniks, made use of the war to disavow everything he had been teaching for almost half a century. This denouncer of the state supported the Entente, and if he denounced the dual power in Russia, it was not in the name of anarchy, but in the name of a single power of the bourgeoisie. However, these old people played mostly a decorative rôle—although later on in the war against the Bolsheviks Chaikovsky headed one of the White governments financed by Churchill.

The first place among the Social Revolutionaries—far in advance of the others, though not in the party but above it—was occupied by Kerensky, a man without any party past whatever. We shall meet often again this providential figure, whose strength in the two-power period lay in his combining the weaknesses of liberalism with the weaknesses of the democracy. His formal entrance into the Social Revolutionary Party did not destroy Kerensky's scornful attitude toward parties in general: he considered himself the directly chosen one of the nation. But after all, the Social Revolutionary Party had ceased by that time to be a party, and become a grandiose and indeed national zero. In Kerensky this party found an adequate leader.

The future Minister of Agriculture, and afterwards President of the Constituent Assembly, Chernov, was indubitably the most representative figure of the old Social Revolutionary Party, and by no accident was considered its inspirator, theoretician and leader. A well-read rather than educated man, with a considerable but unintegrated learning, Chernov always had at his disposition a boundless assortment of appropriate quotations, which for a long time caught the imagination of the Russian youth without teaching them much. There was only one single question which this many-worded leader could not answer: Whom was he leading and whither? The eclectic formulas of Chernov, ornamented with moralisms and verses, united for a time a most variegated public who at all critical moments pulled in different directions. No wonder Chernov complacently contrasted his methods of forming a party with Lenin's "sectarianism."

Chernov arrived from abroad five days after Lenin: England after some hesitation had passed him. To the numerous greetings of the Soviet, the leader of its biggest party answered with its longest speech—a speech about which Sukhanov, himself a half Social Revolutionary, comments as follows: "Not only I, but many other Social Revolutionary party patriots wrinkled our brows and shook our heads, because he chanted so unpleasantly and minced and rolled his eyes—yes, and talked endlessly and without aim or purpose." All the further activity of Chernov in the revolution developed in tune with this first speech. After some attempts to oppose Kerensky and Tseretelli from the left, finding himself pressed on all sides, Chernov surrendered without a struggle, purged himself of his emigrant Zimmerwaldism, took a seat in the Contact Commission, and later also in the coalition government. Everything he did was inappropriate. He decided therefore to evade all issues. Abstaining from the vote became for him a form of political life. His authority melted away from April to October, faster even than the ranks of his party. With all the differences between Chernov and Kerensky, who hated each other, they were both completely rooted in the pre-revolutionary past —in the old flabby Russian society, in that thin-blooded and pretentious intelligentsia, burning with a desire to teach the masses of the people, to be their guardian and benefactor, but completely incapable of listening to them, understanding them, and learning from them. And without learning from the masses there can be no revolutionary statesmanship.

Avksentiev, who was raised by his party to the highest revolutionary posts—president of the Executive Committee of the Peasants' Deputies, Minister of the Interior, President of the Pre-Parliament—was the complete caricature of a statesman. A charming teacher of language in a ladies' seminary in Orel—that is really all you can say about him, although, to be sure, his political activity turned out far more pernicious than his personality.

A large rôle was played—although mostly behind the scenes —in the Social Revolutionary faction, and in the ruling nucleus of the Soviet, by Gotz. A terrorist of well-known revolutionary family, Gotz was less pretentious and more business-like than his closest political friends. But in his character as a so-called "practical," he limited himself to kitchen matters, leaving the big questions to others. It is necessary to add that he was neither orator nor writer, and that his chief resource was his personal authority bought with years of imprisonment at hard labor.

We have named essentially all who can be named among the ruling circle of the Narodniks. Below them are completely accidental figures like Filipovsky, whose arrival at the very height of the February Olympus nobody ever could explain: the deciding factor would seem to have been his naval officer's uniform.

Alongside the official leaders of the two ruling parties in the Executive Committee, there were quite a few "wild ones," solitaries, participants of the past movement at its various stages, people who had withdrawn from the struggle long before the uprising, and now, after a hasty return under the banner of the victorious revolution, were in no hurry to adopt the yoke of any party. On all fundamental questions the "wild ones" followed the line of the Soviet majority. For the first few days they played even a leading rôle, but in proportion as the official leaders began to arrive from exile and from abroad, these non-party men retired to a secondary place. Politics began to take form, and party allegiance entered into its rights.

Enemies of the Executive Committee in the reactionary camp made a great point of the "preponderance" in it of non-

Russians: Jews, Georgians, Letts, Poles, and so forth. Although by comparison with the whole membership of the Executive Committee the non-Russian elements were not very numerous, it is nevertheless true that they occupied a very prominent place in the præsidium, in the various committees, among the orators, etc. Since the intelligentsia of the oppressed nationalities —concentrated as they were for the most part in cities—had flowed copiously into the revolutionary ranks, it is not surprising that among the old generation of revolutionaries the number of non-Russians was especially large. Their experience, although not always of a high quality, made them irreplaceable when it came to inaugurating new social forms. The attempt, however, to explain the policy of the soviets and the course of the whole revolution by an alleged "predominance" of non-Russians is pure nonsense. Nationalism in this case again reveals its scorn for the real nation—that is, the people—representing them in the period of their great national awakening as a mere block of wood in alien and accidental hands. But why and how did the non-Russians acquire such miracle-working power over the native millions? As a matter of fact, at a moment of deep historic change, the bulk of a nation always presses into its service those elements which were yesterday most oppressed, and therefore are most ready to give expression to the new tasks. It is not that aliens lead the revolution, but that the revolution makes use of the aliens. It has been so even in great reforms introduced from above. The policy of Peter I did not cease to be national when, swinging out of the old tracks, it impressed into its service non-Russians and foreigners. The master of some German suburb, or some Dutch skipper, would express far better at that period the demands of the national development of Russia, than Russian priests dragged in long ago by the Greeks, or Moscow Boyars, who also complained of foreign predominance, although themselves descended from those alien tribes who created the Russian state. In any case, the non-Russian intelligentsia of 1917 were distributed among the same parties as the one hundred per cent Russians, suffered from the same vices, made the same mistakes—and moreover the non-Russians among the Mensheviks and Social

Revolutionaries displayed a most particular zeal for the defense and unity of Russia.

Such was the Executive Committee, the highest organ of the democracy. Two parties which had lost their illusions but preserved their prejudices, with a staff of leaders who were incapable of passing from word to deed, arrived at the head of a revolution called to break the fetters of a century and lay the foundations of a new society. The whole activity of the Compromisers became one long chain of painful contradictions, exhausting the masses and leading to the convulsions of civil war.

The workers, soldiers and peasants took events seriously. They thought that the soviets which they had created ought to undertake immediately to remove those evils which had caused the revolution. They all ran to the Soviet. Everybody brought his pains there. And who was without pains? They demanded decisions, hoped for help, awaited justice, insisted upon indemnification. Solicitors, complainers, petitioners, exposers, all came assuming that at last they had replaced a hostile power with their own. The people believe in the Soviet, the people are armed, therefore the Soviet is the sovereign power. That was the way they understood it. And were they not indeed right? An uninterrupted flood of soldiers, workers, soldiers' wives, small traders, clerks, mothers, fathers, kept opening and shutting the doors, sought, questioned, wept, demanded, compelled action—sometimes even indicating what action—and converted the Soviet in very truth into a revolutionary government. "That was not at all in the interest, or at least did not at all enter into the plans, of the Soviet itself," complains our friend Sukhanov, who of course struggled with all his might against this process. But with what success did he struggle? Alas, he is soon compelled to acknowledge that "the Soviet apparatus began involuntarily, automatically, against the will of the Soviet, to crowd out the official governmental machine, which was grinding more and more without grain." What did the doctrinaires of capitulation do—the mechanics of this empty grinding? "It became necessary to reconcile oneself and take up the separate functions of administration,"

Sukhanov sadly confesses, "at the same time preserving the fiction that the Marinsky Palace was performing them." That is what those people were busy with in a shattered country caught in the flames of war and revolution—protecting with masquerade measures the prestige of a government which the people had organically ejected. The revolution may die, but long live the fiction! And all the while the power which they had driven out of the door, kept crawling back through the window, catching them every time unawares and making them look cheap or ludicrous.

On the night of the 28th of February, the Executive Committee closed up the monarchist press and established a licensing system for newspapers. Protests were heard, those shouting the loudest who had been accustomed to stop the mouths of others. After a few days the Committee had to take up again the problem of a free press: to permit or not to permit the publication of reactionary papers? Disagreements arose. Doctrinaires of the type of Sukhanov stood for absolute freedom of the press. Cheidze at first disagreed: how can we leave weapons at the uncontrolled disposition of our mortal enemies? It occurred to nobody, by the way, to turn over the whole question to the decision of the government. Anyway, that would have been useless; the typographical workers took orders only from the Soviet. On March 5 the Executive Committee confirmed this fact as follows: "The right press is closed and the issue of new papers will depend upon the decision of the Soviet." But as early as the 10th, under pressure from bourgeois circles, that resolution was annulled. "They took only three days to come to their senses," exults Sukhanov. Ill-founded exultation! The press does not stand above society; the conditions of its existence during a revolution reflect the progress of the revolution itself. When the latter assumes, or may assume, the character of a civil war, not one of the warring camps will permit the existence of a hostile press within the sphere of its influence—no more than it will let escape from its control the arsenals, the railroads, the printing establishments. In a revolutionary struggle the press is only one kind of weapon. The right to speech is certainly not higher than the right to life. A revolution takes the latter too into its hands. We may lay this down as a law: Revolutionary governments are the more liberal, the more tolerant, the more "magnanimous" to the reaction, the shallower their program, the more they are bound up with the past, the more conservative their rôle. And the converse: the more gigantic their tasks and the greater the number of vested rights and interests they are to destroy, the more concentrated will be the revolutionary power, the more naked its dictatorship. Whether this is a good thing or bad, it is by these roads that humanity has thus far moved forward. The Soviet was right when it wanted to retain control of the press. Why did it so easily give this up? Because in general it was refusing to make a serious fight. It remained silent about peace, about the land, even about a republic. Having turned over the power to the conservative bourgeoisie, it had neither a reason for fearing the right press, nor a possibility of struggling against it. The government, on the other hand, began after a few months, with the support of the Soviet, to suppress ruthlessly the left press. The Bolshevik papers were shut down one after another.

On March 7 in Moscow, Kerensky declaimed: "Nicholas II is in my hands. I will never be the Marat of the Russian revolution. Nicholas II is to go under my personal supervision to England. . . ." Ladies threw flowers; students applauded. But the depths bestirred themselves. Not one serious revolution yet—not one that had something to lose—has let the deposed monarch escape over the border. From the workers and soldiers came continuous demands: arrest the Romanovs. The Executive Committee sensed the fact that there could be no joking here. It was decided that the Soviet must take into its own hands the question of the Romanovs: the government was thus openly proclaimed undeserving of confidence. The Executive Committee gave an order to all railroads not to let Romanov through. That was why the tzar's train got lost in the tracks. One of the members of the Executive Committee, the worker Gvosdev, a right Menshevik, was commissioned to arrest Nicholas. Kerensky was disavowed—and along with him the government. But instead of resigning it submitted in silence. On March 9 Cheidze reported to the Executive Committee that the government had "renounced" the thought of sending Nicholas to England. The tzar's family was put under arrest in the Winter Palace.

Thus the Executive Committee stole the power from under its own pillow. But from the front the demand became more and more insistent: transfer the former tzar to the Peter and Paul fortress.

Revolutions have always involved a reshuffling of property, not only by legislative means, but also by mass seizure. No agrarian revolution in history has ever proceeded otherwise: legal reforms always trail behind the red cock. In the towns, forcible seizures have played a smaller rôle: bourgeois revolutions have not had the task of uprooting bourgeois property relations. But there has never been any revolution, it seems, in which the masses have not appropriated for social purposes the buildings which formerly belonged to the enemies of the people. Immediately after the February revolution the parties came out from underground, trade unions arose, continuous meetings were held, there were soviets in every district; for all these things quarters were needed. Organizations seized the uninhabited summer homes of the tzarist ministers, or the vacant palaces of the tzar's ballerinas. The victims complained, or else the government interfered on its own initiative. But since the expropriators really possessed the sovereign power—the official power being a ghost—it became necessary for the Prosecuting Attorney to appeal in the long run to that same Executive Committee to restore the ravished rights of a certain ballerina, whose none too complicated functions had been so highly paid for by the members of the dynasty out of the people's wealth. The Contact Commission of course was brought into operation; the ministers held sittings; the Bureau of the Executive Committee conferred; delegations were sent to the expropriators—and the affair dragged on for months.

Sukhanov relates that as a "Left" he had nothing against the most radical legislative invasions of the rights of property, but on the other hand he was a "bitter opponent of all forcible seizures." With ruses like this the unhappy "Lefts" have always covered up their bankruptcy. A genuinely revolutionary government might unquestionably have reduced these chaotic seizures to a minimum by a timely decree on the requisition of quarters. But the left Compromisers had turned over the power to the fanatics of property, in order afterwards carefully to preach to the masses—under an open sky—a respect for revolutionary legality. The climate of Petrograd is not favorable to Platonism.

The bread-lines had given the last stimulus to the revolution. They also proved the first threat to the new régime. At the very first session of the Soviet a food commission had been created. The government bothered little about feeding the capital. It would not have been averse to holding it down with hunger. The task lay on the Soviet. It had at its disposition economists and statisticians with some practical experience, people who had served formerly in the economic and administrative organs of the bourgeoisie. They were in most cases Mensheviks of the right wing, like Grohman and Cherevanin, or former Bolsheviks like Bazarov and Avilov, who had moved far to the right. But they had hardly approached the problem of feeding the capital, when they found themselves compelled by the whole situation to apply extremely radical measures to control speculation and organize a market. In a series of sessions of the Soviet a whole system of measures of "military socialism" was adopted, including the declaring of all grain stores public property, the establishment of a definite price for bread, to accord with similar prices for industrial products, state control of industry, a regulated exchange of goods with the peasants. The leaders of the Executive Committee looked at each other in alarm; not knowing what else to propose, however, they supported these radical resolutions. The members of the Contact Commission afterward communicated them, in some embarrassment, to the government. The government promised to examine them. But Prince Lvov, and Guchkov, and Konovalov had not the least desire to control, requisition, or otherwise cut down on themselves and their friends. All the economic measures of the Soviet went to pieces against the passive resistance of the state apparatus—except in so far as they were carried out independently by local soviets. The sole practical measure carried through by the Petrograd Soviet in the matter of food supply was the limitation of the consumer to a strict ration: a pound and a half of bread for people engaged in physical labor, a pound for the rest. To be sure, this limitation introduced almost no change into the natural food budget of the population of the capital: you can live on a pound, or a pound and a half. The misery of daily undernourishment was still ahead. For a period of years—not months, but years—the revolution will have to take in its belt tighter and tighter on a shrinking stomach. It will weather the ordeal. At present what troubles it is not hunger but doubt, indefiniteness, uncertainty of tomorrow. Economic difficulties that have been multiplied by thirty-two months of war, are knocking at the doors and windows of the new régime. The breakdown of transport, the lack of various kinds of raw materials, the exhaustion of a considerable part of the equipment, alarming inflation, dislocation of trade, all these things demand bold and immediate measures. But while approaching these problems economically, the Compromisers made the solution of them impossible politically. Every economic problem they encountered turned into a condemnation of the dual power; every decision they had to sign burned their fingers unbearably.

The eight-hour working day was the great test of strength and mutual relations. The insurrection had conquered, but the general strike continued. The workers seriously assumed that a change in the régime ought to introduce changes into their lives. This caused instant alarm to the new rulers, both liberal and socialist. The patriotic parties and newspapers adopted the cry: "Soldiers to the barracks, workers to the shops!" "Does that mean that everything is going to remain the same?" asks the worker. "For the time being," answer the Mensheviks, embarrassed. But the workers understand: If there isn't a change right now, there never will be.

The bourgeoisie left the task of settling things with the workers to the socialists. Referring to the fact that the victory already won "has sufficiently guaranteed the position of the working class in its revolutionary struggle"—to be sure, have not the liberal landlords come into power?—the Executive Committee designated March 5 as the date for resuming work in the Petrograd district. Workers to the shops! Such is the iron-clad egotism of the educated classes, liberals and socialists alike. Those people believed that millions of workers and soldiers lifted to the heights of insurrection by the inconquerable pressure of discontent and hope, would after their victory tamely submit to the old conditions of life. From reading historical works, they had got the impression that it happened this way in previous revolutions. But no, even in the past it has never been so. If the workers have been driven back into their former stalls, it has been only in a roundabout way, after a whole series of defeats and deceptions. Marat was keenly aware of this cruel social perversion of political revolutions. For that reason he is so well slandered by the official historians. "A revolution is accomplished and sustained only by the lowest classes of society," he wrote a month before the revolution of August 10, 1792, "by all the disinherited, whom the shameless rich treat as *canaille,* and whom the Romans with their usual cynicism once named proletarians." And what will the revolution give to the disinherited? "Winning a certain success at the beginning, the movement is finally conquered; it always lacks knowledge, skill, means, weapons, leaders and a definite plan of action; it remains defenseless in the face of conspirators possessed of experience, adroitness and craft." Is it any wonder that Kerensky did not want to be the Marat of the Russian revolution?

One of the former captains of Russian industry, V. Auerbach, relates with indignation how "the revolution was understood by the lower orders as something in the nature of an Easter carnival: servants, for example, disappeared for whole days, promenaded in red ribbons, took rides in automobiles, came home in the morning only long enough to wash up and again went out for fun." It is remarkable that in trying to demonstrate the demoralizing effect of a revolution, this accuser describes the conduct of a servant in exactly those terms which —with the exception, to be sure, of the red ribbon—most perfectly reproduce the daily life of the bourgeois lady-patrician. Yes, a revolution is interpreted by the oppressed as a holiday—

or the eve of a holiday—and the first impulse of the household drudge aroused by it is to loosen the yoke of the day-by-day humiliating, anguishing, ineluctable slavery. The working class as a whole could not, and did not intend to, comfort themselves with mere red ribbons as a symbol of victory—a victory won for others. There was agitation in the factories of Petrograd. A considerable number of shops openly refused to submit to the resolution of the Soviet. The workers were of course ready to return to the shops, for that was necessary—but upon what terms? They demanded the eight-hour day. The Mensheviks answered by alluding to 1905 when the workers tried to introduce the eight-hour day by forcible methods and were defeated. "A struggle on two fronts—against the reaction and against the capitalist—is too much for the proletariat." That was the central idea of the Mensheviks. They recognized in a general way the inevitability of a break in the future with the bourgeoisie. But this purely theoretical recognition did not bind them to anything. They considered that it was wrong to force the break. And since the bourgeoisie is driven into alliance with the reaction not by heated phrases from orators and journalists, but by the independent activity of the toiling classes, the Mensheviks tried with all their power to oppose this activity —to oppose the economic struggle of the workers and peasants. "For the working class," they taught, "social questions are not now of the first importance. Its present task is to achieve political freedom." But just what this speculative freedom consisted of, the workers could not understand. They wanted in the first place a little freedom for their muscles and nerves. And so they brought pressure on their bosses. By the irony of fate it was exactly on the 10th of March, when the Mensheviks were explaining that the eight-hour day is not a current issue, that the Manufacturers' Association—which had already been obliged to enter into official relations with the Soviet—announced its readiness to introduce the eight-hour day and permit the organization of factory and shop committees. The industrialists were more farseeing than the democratic strategists of the Soviet. And no wonder: these employers came face to face with the workers, and the workers in no less than half of the Petrograd plants—among them a majority of the biggest ones—were already leaving the shops in a body after eight hours of work. They themselves took what the Soviet and the government refused them. When the liberal press unctuously compared this gesture of the Russian industrialists of March 10, 1917 with that of the French nobility of August 4, 1789, they were far nearer the historic truth than they themselves imagined: like the feudalists of the end of the eighteenth century, the Russian capitalists acted under the club of necessity, hoping by this temporary concession to make sure of getting back in the future what they had lost. One of the Kadet publicists, breaking through the official lie, frankly acknowledged this: "Unfortunately for the Mensheviks, the Bolsheviks had already by means of terror compelled the Manufacturers' Association to agree to an immediate introduction of the eight-hour day." In what this terror consisted we already know. Worker-Bolsheviks indubitably occupied the front ranks in the movement, and here as in the decisive days of February an overwhelming majority of the workers followed them.

The Soviet, led by Mensheviks, recorded with mixed feelings this gigantic victory gained essentially against its opposition. The disgraced leaders were compelled, however, to make a still further step forward; they had to propose to the Provisional Government the promulgation in advance of the Constituent Assembly of an eight-hour law for all Russia. The government, however, in agreement with the manufacturers, resisted. Hoping for better days, they refused to fulfill this demand—presented to them, to be sure, without any particular insistence.

In the Moscow region the same struggle arose, but it lasted longer. Here too the soviet in spite of the resistance of the workers demanded a return to work. In one of the biggest factories a resolution against calling off the strike received 7000 votes against 6. Other factories reacted in much the same way. On the 10th of March the soviet again proclaimed the duty of returning immediately to the shops. Although work began after that in a majority of shops, there developed almost everywhere a struggle for the shortening of the working day. The workers corrected their leaders by direct action. After a long resistance the Moscow Soviet was obliged on the 21st of March to introduce the eight-hour day by its own act. The industrialists immediately submitted. In the provinces the same struggle was carried over into April. Almost everywhere the soviets at first refrained and resisted, and afterwards under pressure from the workers entered into negotiations with the manufacturers. And where the latter did not accede, the soviets were obliged independently to decree the eight-hour day. What a breach in the system!

The government stood aside on purpose. In those days, a furious campaign was opening under liberal leadership against the workers. In order to subdue them it was decided to turn the soldiers against them. To shorten the working day means, you see, to weaken the front. How can anybody think only of himself in war time? Are they counting the hours in the trenches? . . . When the possessing classes make a start on the road of demagogism, they stop at nothing. The agitation assumed a frenzied character, and was soon carried into the trenches. The soldier Pireiko in his reminiscences of the front confesses that this agitation—carried on chiefly by half-baked socialists among the officers—was not without success. "But the great weakness of the official staff in their effort to turn the soldiers against the workers lay in the fact that they were officers. It was too fresh in the mind of every soldier what his officer had been to him in the past." This baiting of the workers was most bitter, however, in the capital. The industrialists along with the Kadet staff found unlimited means and opportunities for agitation in the garrison. "Towards the end of March," says Sukhanov, "you could see at all street crossings, in the tramways, and in every public place, workers and soldiers locked together in a furious verbal battle." Even physical fights occurred. The workers understood the maneuver and skillfully warded it off. For this it was only necessary to tell the truth—to cite the figures of war profits, to show the soldiers the factories and shops with the roar of machines, the hell fires of the furnaces, their perpetual front where victims are innumerable. On the initiative of the workers there began regular visits by the troops of the garrison to the factories, and especially to those working on munitions. The soldiers looked and listened. The workers demonstrated and explained. These visits would end in triumphant fraternization. The socialist papers printed innumerable resolutions of the military units as to their indestructible solidarity with the workers. By the middle of April the very topic of the conflict had disappeared from the newspapers. The bourgeois press was silent. Thus after their economic victory, the workers won a political and moral victory.

The events connected with this struggle for the eight-hour day had an immense significance for the whole future development of the revolution. The workers had gained a few free hours a week for reading, for meetings, and also for practice with the rifle, which became a regular routine from the moment of the creation of the workers' militia. Moreover, after this clear lesson, the workers began to watch the Soviet leadership more closely. The authority of the Mensheviks suffered a serious drop. The Bolsheviks grew stronger in the factories, and partly too in the barracks. The soldier became more attentive, thoughtful, cautious: he understood that somebody was stalking him. The treacherous design of the demagogues turned against its own inspirers. Instead of alienation and hostility, they got a closer welding together of workers and soldiers.

The government, in spite of the idyll of "Contact," hated the Soviet, hated its leaders and their guardianship. It revealed this upon the very first occasion. Since the Soviet was fulfilling purely governmental functions, and this moreover at the request of the government itself whenever it became necessary to subdue the masses, the Executive Committee requested the payment of a small subsidy for expenses. The government refused, and in spite of the repeated insistence of the Soviet, stood pat: it could not pay out the resources of the state to a "private organization." The Soviet swallowed it. The budget of the Soviet lay on the workers, who never tired of taking up collections for the needs of the revolution. In those days both sides, the liberals and the socialists, kept up the decorum of a complete mutual friendliness. At the All-Russian Conference of Soviets the existence of the dual power was declared a fiction.

Kerensky assured the delegates from the army that between the government and the soviets there was a complete unity of problems and aims. The dual power was no less zealously denied by Tseretelli, Dan and other Soviet pillars. With the help of these lies, they tried to reënforce a régime which was founded on lies.

However, the régime tottered from the very first weeks. The leaders were tireless in the matter of organizational combinations. They tried to bring to bear all sorts of accidental representative bodies against the masses—the soldiers against the workers, the new dumas, zemstvos and coöperatives against the soviets, the provinces against the capital, and finally the officers against the people.

The soviet form does not contain any mystic power. It is by no means free from the faults of every representative system—unavoidable so long as that system is unavoidable. But its strength lies in that it reduces all these faults to a minimum.

We may confidently assert—and the events will soon prove it—that any other representative system, atomizing the masses, would have expressed their actual will in the revolution incomparably less effectively, and with far greater delay. Of all the forms of revolutionary representation, the soviet is the most flexible, immediate and transparent. But still it is only a form. It cannot give more than the masses are capable of putting into it at a given moment. Beyond that, it can only assist the masses in understanding the mistakes they have made and correcting them. In this function of the soviets lay one of the most important guarantees of the development of the revolution.

What was the political plan of the Executive Committee? You could hardly say that any one of the leaders had a plan thoroughly thought out. Sukhanov subsequently asserted that, according to his plan, the power was turned over to the bourgeoisie only for a short time, in order that the democracy, having strengthened itself, might the more surely take it back. However, this construction—naïve enough in any case—was obviously retrospective. At least it was never formulated by anybody at the time. Under the leadership of Tseretelli, the vacillations of the Executive Committee, if they were not put an end to, were at least organized into a system. Tseretelli openly announced that without a firm bourgeois power the revolution would inevitably fail. The democracy must limit itself to bringing pressure on the liberal bourgeoisie, beware of pushing it over by some incautious step into the camp of the reaction, and conversely, support it in so far as it backs up the conquests of the revolution. In the long run that half-minded régime would have ended in a bourgeois republic with the socialists as a parliamentary opposition.

The main difficulty for the leaders was not so much to find a general plan, as a current program of action. The Compromisers had promised the masses to get from the bourgeoisie by way of "pressure" a democratic policy, foreign and domestic. It is indubitable that under pressure from the popular mass, ruling classes have more than once in history made concessions. But "pressure" means, in the last analysis, a threat to crowd the ruling class out of the power and occupy its place. Just this weapon however was not in the hands of the democracy. They had themselves voluntarily given over the power to the bourgeoisie. At moments of conflict the democracy did not threaten to seize the power, but on the contrary the bourgeoisie frightened them with the idea of giving it back. Thus the chief lever in the mechanics of pressure was in the hands of the bourgeoisie. This explains how, in spite of its complete impotence, the government succeeded in resisting every somewhat serious undertaking of the Soviet leaders.

By the middle of April, even the Executive Committee had proven too broad an organ for the political mysteries of the ruling nucleus, who had turned their faces completely toward the liberals. A "bureau" was therefore appointed, consisting exclusively of right defensists. From now on big politics was carried on in its own small circle. Everything seemed nicely and permanently settled. Tseretelli dominated in the Soviet without limit. Kerensky was riding higher and higher. But exactly at that moment appeared clearly the first alarming signs from below—from the masses. "It is amazing," writes Stankevich, who was close to the circle of Kerensky, "that at the very moment when this committee was formed, when responsibility for the work was assumed by a bureau selected only from defensist parties, exactly at this moment they let slip from their hands the leadership of the masses—the masses moved away from them." Not at all amazing, but quite in accord with the laws of things.

CHAPTER XIII

THE ARMY AND THE WAR

IN the months preceding the revolution discipline in the army was already badly shaken. You can pick up plenty of officers' complaints from those days: soldiers disrespectful to the command; their treatment of horses, of military property, even of weapons, indescribably bad; disorders in the military trains. It was not equally serious everywhere. But everywhere it was going in the same direction—toward ruin.

To this was now added the shock of revolution. The uprising of the Petrograd garrison took place not only without officers, but against them. In the critical hours the command simply hid its head. Deputy-Octobrist Shidlovsky conversed on the 27th of February with the officers of the Preobrazhensky regiment—obviously in order to feel out their attitude to the Duma—but found among these aristocrat-cavaliers a total ignorance of what was happening, perhaps a half-hypocritical ignorance, for they were all frightened monarchists.

"What was my surprise," says Shidlovsky, "when the very next morning I saw the whole Preobrazhensky regiment marching down the street in military formation led by a band, their order perfect and without a single officer!" To be sure, a few companies arrived at the Tauride with their officers—more accurately, they brought their officers with them. But the officers felt that in this triumphal march they occupied the position of captives. Countess Kleinmichel, observing these scenes while under arrest, says plainly: "The officers looked like sheep led to the slaughter."

The February uprising did not create the split between soldiers and officers but merely brought it to the surface. In the minds of the soldiers the insurrection against the monarchy was primarily an insurrection against the commanding staff. "From the morning of the 28th of February," says the Kadet Nabokov, then wearing an officer's uniform, "it was dangerous to go out, because they had begun to rip off the officers' epaulets." That is how the first day of the new régime looked in the garrison.

The first care of the Executive Committee was to reconcile soldiers with officers. That meant nothing but to subordinate the troops to their former command. The return of the officers to their regiments was supposed, according to Sukhanov, to protect the army against "universal anarchy or the dictatorship of the dark and disintegrated rank-and-file." These revolutionists, just like the liberals, were afraid of the soldiers, not of the officers. The workers on the other hand, along with the "dark" rank-and-file, saw every possible danger exactly in the ranks of those brilliant officers. The reconciliation therefore proved temporary.

Stankevich describes in these words the mental attitude of the soldiers to the officers who returned to them after the uprising: "The soldiers, breaking discipline and leaving their barracks, not only without officers, but in many cases against their officers and even after killing them at their posts, had achieved, it turned out, a great deed of liberation. If it was a great deed, and if the officers themselves now affirm this, then why didn't they lead the soldiers into the streets? That would have been easier and less dangerous. Now, after the victory, they associate themselves with this deed. But how sincerely and for how long?" These words are the more instructive that the author himself was one of those "left" officers to whom it did not occur to lead his soldiers into the streets.

On the morning of the 28th, on Sampsonievsky Prospect, the commander of an engineers' division was explaining to his soldiers that "the government which everybody hated is overthrown," a new one is formed with Prince Lvov at the head—therefore it is necessary to obey officers as before. "And now I ask all to return to their places in the barracks." A few soldiers cried: "Glad to try." [1] The majority merely looked bewildered: "Is that all?"

The scene was observed accidentally by Kayurov. It jarred

---

[1] "Glad to try, your excellency," was the customary reply to an order in the old army.

him. "Permit me a word, Mr. Commander." . . . And without waiting for permission, Kayurov put this question: "Has the workers' blood been flowing in the streets of Petrograd for three days merely to exchange one landlord for another?" Here Kayurov took the bull by the horns. His question summarized the whole struggle of the coming months. The antagonism between soldier and officer was a refraction of the hostility between peasant and landlord.

The officers in the provinces, having evidently got their instructions in good season, explained the events all in the same way: "His Majesty has exceeded his strength in his efforts for the good of the country, and has been compelled to hand over the burden of government to his brother." The reply was plain on the faces of the soldiers, complains an officer in a far corner of the Crimea: "Nicholas or Mikhail—it's all the same to us." When, however, this same officer was compelled next morning to communicate the news of the revolutionary victory, the soldiers, he tells us, were transformed. Their questions, gestures, glances, testified to the "prolonged and resolute work which somebody had been doing on those dark and cloudy brains, totally unaccustomed to think." What a gulf between the officer, whose brain accommodates itself without effort to the latest telegram from Petrograd, and those soldiers who are, however stiffly, nevertheless honestly, defining their attitude to the events, independently weighing them in their calloused palms!

The high command, although formally recognizing the revolution, decided not to let it through to the front. The chief of staff ordered the commander-in-chief of all the fronts, in case revolutionary delegations arrived in his territory—delegations which General Alexeiev called "gangs" for short—to arrest them immediately and turn them over to court-martial. The next day the same general, in the name of "His Highness," the Grand Duke Nikolai Nikolaievich, demanded of the government "an end of all that is now happening in the rear of the army"—in other words, an end of the revolution.

The command delayed informing the active army about the revolution as long as possible, not so much through loyalty to the monarchy as through fear of the revolution. On several fronts they established a veritable quarantine: stopped all letters from Petrograd, and held up newcomers. In that way the old régime stole a few extra days from eternity. The news of the revolution rolled up to the line of battle not before the 5th or 6th of March—and in what form? About the same as above: "The grand duke is appointed commander-in-chief; the tzar has abdicated in the name of the Fatherland; everything else as usual." In many trenches, perhaps even in the majority, the news of the revolution came from the Germans before it got there from Petrograd. Could there have been any doubt among the soldiers that the whole command was in a conspiracy to conceal the truth? And could those same soldiers trust those same officers to the extent of two cents, when a couple of days later they pinned on a red ribbon?

The chief of staff of the Black Sea fleet tells us that the news of the events in Petrograd at first made no marked impression on the soldiers. But when the first socialist papers arrived from the capital, "in the wink of an eye the mood changed, meetings began, criminal agitators crawled out of their cracks." The admiral simply did not understand what was happening before his eyes. The newspapers did not create this change of mood. They merely scattered the doubt of the soldiers as to the depth of the revolution, and permitted them to reveal their true feelings without fear of reprisals from the staff. The political physiognomy of the Black Sea staff, his own among them, is characterized by the same author in a single phrase: "The majority of the officers of the fleet thought that without the tzar the Fatherland would perish." The democrats also thought that the Fatherland would perish—unless they brought back bright lights of this kind to the "dark" sailors!

The commanding staff of the army and fleet soon divided into two groups. One group tried to stay in their places, tuning in on the revolution, registering as Social Revolutionaries. Later a part of them even tried to crawl into the Bolshevik camp. The other group strutted a while and tried to oppose the new order, but soon broke out in some sharp conflict and were swept away by the soldier flood. Such groupings are so natural that they have been repeated in all revolutions. The irreconcilable officers of the French monarchy, those who in the words of one of them "fought as long as they could," suffered less over the disobedience of the soldiers than over the knuckling under of their noble colleagues. In the long run the majority of the old command were pushed out or suppressed, and only a small part reëducated and assimilated. In a more dramatic form the officers shared the fate of those classes from which they were recruited.

An army is always a copy of the society it serves—with this difference, that it gives social relations a concentrated character, carrying both their positive and negative features to an extreme. It is no accident that the war did not create one single distinguished military name in Russia. The high command was sufficiently characterized by one of its own members: "Much adventurism, much ignorance, much egotism, intrigue, careerism, greed, mediocrity and lack of foresight"— writes General Zalessky—"and very little knowledge, talent or desire to risk life, or even comfort and health." Nikolai Nikolaievich, the first commander-in-chief, was distinguished only by his high stature and august rudeness. General Alexeiev, a gray mediocrity, the oldest military clerk of the army, won out through mere perseverence. Kornilov was a bold young commander whom even his admirers regarded as a bit simple; Kerensky's War Minister, Verkhovsky, later described him as the lion heart with the brain of a sheep. Brussilov and Admiral Kolchak a little excelled the others in culture, if you will, but in nothing else. Denikin was not without character, but for the rest, a perfectly ordinary army general who had read five or six books. And after these came the Yudeniches, the Dragomirovs, the Lukomskies, speaking French or not speaking it, drinking moderately or drinking hard, but amounting to absolutely nothing.

To be sure, not only feudal, but also bourgeois and democratic Russia had its representatives in the officers' corps. The war poured into the ranks of the army tens of thousands of petty bourgeois youths in the capacity of officers, military clerks, doctors, engineers. These circles, standing almost solid for war to complete victory, felt the necessity of some broad measures of reform, but submitted in the long run to the reactionary command. Under the tzar they submitted through fear, and after the revolution through conviction—just as the democracy in the rear submitted to the bourgeoisie. The conciliatory wing of the officers shared subsequently the unhappy fate of the conciliatory parties—with this difference, that at the front the situation developed a thousand times more sharply. In the Executive Committee you could hold on for a long time with ambiguities; in the face of the soldiers it was not so easy.

The ill-will and friction between the democratic and aristocratic officers, incapable of reviving the army, only introduced a further element of decomposition. The physiognomy of the army was determined by the old Russia, and this physiognomy was completely feudal. The officers still considered the best soldier to be a humble and unthinking peasant lad, in whom no consciousness of human personality had yet awakened. Such was the "national" tradition of the Russian army—the Suvorov tradition—resting upon primitive agriculture, serfdom and the village commune. In the eighteenth century Suvorov was still creating miracles out of this material. Leo Tolstoy, with a baronial love, idealized in his Platon-Karatayev the old type of Russian soldier, unmurmuringly submitting to nature, tyranny and death (*War and Peace*). The French revolution, initiating the magnificent triumph of individualism in all spheres of human activity, put an end to the military art of Suvorov. Throughout the nineteenth century, and the twentieth too—throughout the whole period between the French and Russian revolutions—the tzar's army was continually defeated because it was a feudal army. Having been formed on that "national" basis, the commanding staff was distinguished by a scorn for the personality of the soldier, a spirit of passive Mandarinism, an ignorance of its own trade, a complete absence of heroic principles, and an exceptional disposition toward petty larceny. The authority of the officers rested upon the exterior signs of superiority, the ritual of caste, the system of suppression, and even a special caste language—contemptible idiom of slavery—

in which the soldier was supposed to converse with his officer.[1] Accepting the revolution in words and swearing fealty to the Provisional Government, the tzar's marshals simply shouldered off their own sins on the fallen dynasty. They graciously consented to allow Nicholas II to be declared scapegoat for the whole past. But farther than that, not a step! How could they understand that the moral essence of the revolution lay in the spiritualization of that human mass upon whose inertness all their good fortune had rested? Denikin, appointed to command the front, announced at Minsk: "I accept the revolution wholly and irrevocably. But to revolutionize the army and bring demagogism into it, I consider ruinous to the country." A classic formula of the dull-wittedness of major-generals! As for the rank-and-file generals, to quote Zalessky, they made but one demand: "Only keep your hands off us—that is all we care about!" However, the revolution could not keep its hands off them. Belonging to the privileged classes, they stood to win nothing, but they could lose much. They were threatened with the loss not only of officer privileges, but also of landed property. Covering themselves with loyalty to the Provisional Government, the reactionary officers waged so much the more bitter a campaign against the soviets. And when they were convinced that the revolution was penetrating irresistibly into the soldier mass, and even into their home estates, they regarded this as a monstrous treachery on the part of Kerensky, Miliukov, even Rodzianko—to say nothing of the Bolsheviks.

The life conditions of the fleet even more than the army nourished the live seeds of civil war. The life of the sailors in their steel bunkers, locked up there by force for a period of years, was not much different even in the matter of food from that of galley slaves. Right beside them the officers, mostly from privileged circles and having voluntarily chosen naval service as their calling, were identifying the Fatherland with the tzar, the tzar with themselves, and regarding the sailor as the least valuable part of the battleship. Two alien and tight-shut

[1] "Just so," "in no wise," and "I cannot know," instead of "yes," "no," and "I don't know" are translations of the examples given by the author of this idiom. [Trans.]

worlds thus live in close contact, and never out of each other's sight. The ships of the fleet have their base in the industrial seaport towns with their great population of workers needed for building and repairing. Moreover, on the ships themselves, in the engineering and machine corps, there is no small number of qualified workers. Those are the conditions which convert the fleet into a revolutionary mine. In the revolutions and military uprisings of all countries the sailors have been the most explosive material; they have almost always at the first opportunity drastically settled accounts with their officers. The Russian sailors were no exception.

In Kronstadt the revolution was accompanied by an outbreak of bloody vengeance against the officers, who attempted, as though in horror at their own past, to conceal the revolution from the sailors. One of the first victims to fall was Admiral Viren, who enjoyed a well-earned hatred. A number of the commanding staff were arrested by the sailors. Those who remained free were deprived of arms.

In Helsingfors and Sveaborg, Admiral Nepenin did not admit the news of the insurrection in Petrograd until the night of March 4, threatening the soldiers and sailors meanwhile with acts of repression. So much the more ferocious was the insurrection of these soldiers and sailors. It lasted all night and all day. Many officers were arrested. The most hateful were shoved under the ice. "Judging by Skobelev's account of the conduct of the officers of the fleet and the Helsingfors authorities," writes Sukhanov, who is by no means indulgent to the "dark rank-and-file," "it is a wonder these excesses were so few."

But in the land forces too there were bloody encounters, several waves of them. At first this was an act of vengeance for the past, for the contemptible striking of soldiers. There was no lack of memories that burned like ulcers. In 1915 disciplinary punishment by flogging had been officially introduced into the tzar's army. The officers flogged soldiers upon their own authority—soldiers who were often the fathers of families. But it was not always a question of the past. At the All-Russian Conference of Soviets, a delegate speaking for the army stated that as early as the 15th or 17th of March an order had been issued introducing corporal punishment in the active army. A deputy of the Duma, returning from the front, reported that the Cossacks said to him, in the absence of officers: "Here, you say, is the order. [Evidently the famous Order Number 1, of which we will speak further.] We got it yesterday, and yet today an officer soaked me on the jaw." The Bolsheviks went out to try to restrain the soldiers from excesses as often as the Conciliators. But bloody acts of retribution were as inevitable as the recoil of a gun. The liberals had no other ground for calling the February revolution bloodless except that it gave them the power.

Some of the officers managed to stir up bitter conflicts about the red ribbons, which were in the eyes of the soldiers a symbol of the break with the past. The commander of the Sumsky regiment got killed in this way. Another commander, having ordered newly arrived reëforcements to remove their ribbons, was arrested by the soldiers and locked up in the guard house. A number of encounters also resulted from the tzar's portraits, not yet removed from the official quarters. Was this out of loyalty to the monarchy? In a majority of cases it was mere lack of confidence in the revolution, an act of personal insurance. But the soldiers were not wrong in seeing the ghost of the old régime lurking behind those portraits.

It was not thought-out measures from above, but spasmodic movements from below, which established the new régime in the army. The disciplininary power of the officers was neither annulled nor limited. It merely fell away of itself during the first weeks of March. "It was clear," said the chief of the Black Sea staff, "that if an officer attempted to impose disciplinary punishment upon a soldier, the power did not exist to get it executed." In that you have one of the sure signs of a genuinely popular revolution.

With the falling away of their disciplinary power, the practical bankruptcy of the staff of officers was laid bare. Stankevich, who possessed both a gift of observation and an interest in military affairs, gives a withering account in this respect of the commanding staff. The drilling still went on according to the old rules, he tells us, totally out of relation to the demands of the war. "Such exercises were merely a test of the patience and obedience of the soldiers." The officers, of course, tried to lay the blame for this, their own bankruptcy, upon the revolution.

Although they were quick with cruel reprisals, the soldiers were also inclined to childlike trustfulness and self-forgetful acts of gratitude. For a short time the deputy Filonenko, a priest and a liberal, seemed to the soldiers at the front a standard-bearer of the idea of freedom, a shepherd of the revolution. The old churchly ideas united in funny ways with the new faith. The soldiers carried this priest on their hands, raised him above their heads, carefully seated him in his sleigh. And he afterward, choking with rapture, reported to the Duma: "We could not finish our farewells. They kissed our hands and feet." This deputy thought that the Duma had an immense authority in the army. What had authority in the army was the revolution. And it was the revolution that threw this blinding reflection on various accidental figures.

The symbolic cleansing carried out by Guchkov in the upper circles of the army—the removal of a few score of generals—gave no satisfaction to the soldiers, and at the same time created a state of uncertainty among the high officers. Each one was afraid that he would lose his place. The majority swam with the current, spoke softly and clenched their fists in their pockets. It was still worse with the middle and lower officers, who came face to face with the soldiers. Here there was no governmental cleansing at all. Seeking a legal method, the soldiers of one artillery battery wrote to the Executive Committee and the State Duma about their commander: "Brothers, we humbly request you to remove our domestic enemy, Vanchekhaza." Receiving no answer to such petitions, the soldiers would employ what means they had: disobedience, crowding out, even arrest. Only after that the command would wake up, remove the arrested or assaulted officer, sometimes trying to punish the soldiers, but oftener leaving them unpunished in order to avoid complicating things. This created an intolerable situation for the officers, and yet gave no clear definition to the situation of the soldiers.

Even many fighting officers, those who seriously cared about the fate of the army, insisted upon the necessity of a general clean-up of the commanding staff. Without that, they said, it is useless to think of reviving the fighting ability of the troops. The soldiers presented to the deputies of the Duma no less convincing arguments. Formerly, they said, when they had a grievance, they had to complain to the officers, who ordinarily paid no attention to their complaint. And what were they to do now? The officers were the same—the fate of their complaints would be the same. "It was very difficult to answer that question," a deputy confesses. But nevertheless that question contained the whole fate of the army and foreordained its future.

It would be a mistake to represent the state of affairs in the army as homogeneous throughout the country in all kinds of troops and all regiments. The variation was very considerable. While the sailors of the Baltic fleet responded to the first news of the revolution by killing officers, right beside them in the garrison at Helsingfors the officers were occupying a leading position in the soldiers' soviet by the beginning of April, and here an imposing general was speaking at celebrations in the name of the Social Revolutionaries. There were many such contrasts between hate and trustfulness. But nevertheless the army was like a system of communicating vessels, and the political mood of the soldiers and sailors gravitated towards a single level.

Discipline was maintained somehow while the soldiers were counting on a quick and decisive change. "But when the soldiers saw," to quote a delegate from the front, "that everything remained as before—the same oppression, slavery, ignorance, the same insults—an agitation began." Nature, who was not thoughtful enough to arm the majority of men with rhinoceros skin, also endowed the soldier with a nervous system. Revolutions serve to remind us from time to time of this carelessness on the part of nature.

In the rear as well as at the front, accidental pretexts easily led to conflicts. The soldiers were given the right to attend theaters, meetings, concerts, etc., "equally with all citizens." Many soldiers interpreted this as a right to attend theaters free. The ministry explained that "freedom" was to be understood in a speculative sense. But a people in insurrection has never shown any inclination towards Platonism or Kantianism.

The worn-out tissue of discipline broke through in various ways at different times, in different garrisons, and in different regiments. A commander would often think that everything had gone well in his regiment until certain newspapers appeared, or until the arrival of some outside agitator. It was all really the work of deep inexorable forces.

The liberal deputy Yanushkevich came back from the front with a generalization—that the disorganization is worst of all in the "green" troops composed of muzhiks. "In the more revolutionary regiments the soldiers are getting along very well with the officers." As a matter of fact discipline rested for the most part on two foundations: the privileged cavalry made up of well-off peasants, and the artillery or technical branch in general with a high percentage of workers and intellectuals. The land-owning Cossacks held out longest of all, dreading an agrarian revolution in which the majority of them would lose and not gain. More than once after the revolution individual Cossack divisions carried out punitive operations, but in general all these differences were merely in the date and tempo of disintegration.

The blind struggle had its ebbs and flows. The officers would try to adapt themselves; the soldiers would again begin to bide their time. But during this temporary relief, during these days and weeks of truce, the social hatred which was decomposing the army of the old régime would become more and more intense. Oftener and oftener it would flash out in a kind of heat lightning. In Moscow, in one of the amphitheaters, a meeting of invalids was called, soldiers and officers together. An orator-cripple began to cast aspersions on the officers. A noise of protest arose, a stamping of shoes, canes, crutches. "And how long ago were you, Mr. Officer, insulting the soldiers with lashes and fists?" These wounded, shell-shocked, mutilated people stood like two walls, one facing the other. Crippled soldiers against crippled officers, the majority against the minority, crutches against crutches. That nightmare scene in the amphitheater foreshadowed the ferocity of the coming civil war.

*

ABOVE all these fluctuations and contradictions in the army and in the country, one eternal question was hanging, summed up in the short word, war. From the Baltic to the Black Sea, from the Black Sea to the Caspian and beyond into the depths of Persia, on an immeasurable front, stood sixty-eight corps of infantry and nine of cavalry. What should happen to them further? What was to be done with the war?

In the matter of military supplies the army had been considerably strengthened before the revolution. Domestic production for its needs had increased, and likewise the importation of war material through Murmansk and Archangel—especially artillery from the Allies. Rifles, cannon, cartridges, were on hand in incomparably greater quantities than during the first years of the war. New infantry divisions were in process of organization. The engineering corps had been enlarged. On this ground a number of the unhappy military chieftains attempted later to prove that Russia had stood on the eve of victory, and that only the revolution had prevented it. Twelve years before, Kuropatkin and Linevich had asserted with as good a foundation that Witte prevented them from cleaning up the Japanese. In reality Russia was farther from victory in 1917 than at any other time. Along with the increase in ammunition there appeared in the army toward the end of 1916 an extreme lack of food supplies. Typhus and scurvy took more victims than the fighting. The breakdown of transport alone canceled all strategy involving large-scale regroupings of the military mass. Moreover an extreme lack of horses often condemned the artillery to inaction. But the chief trouble was not even here; it was the moral condition of the army that was hopeless. You might describe it by saying that the army as an army no longer existed. Defeats, retreats, and the rottenness of the ruling group had utterly undermined the troops. You could no more correct that with administrative measures, than you could change the nervous system of the country. The soldier now looked at a heap of cartridges with the same disgust that he would at a pile of wormy meat; the whole thing seemed to him unnecessary and good for nothing; a deceit and a thievery. And his officer could say nothing convincing to him, couldn't even make up his mind to crack him on the jaw. The officer himself felt deceived by the higher command, and moreover not infrequently ashamed before the soldiers for his own superiors. The army was incurably sick. It was still capable of speaking its word in the revolution, but so far as making war was concerned, it did not exist. Nobody believed in the success of the war, the officers as little as the soldiers. Nobody wanted to fight any more, neither the army nor the people.

To be sure, in the high chancelleries, where a special kind of life is lived, they were still chattering, through mere inertia, about great operations, about the spring offensive, the capture of the Dardanelles. In the Crimea they even got ready a big army for this latter purpose. It stood in the bulletins that the best element of the army had been designated for the siege. They sent the regiments of the guard from Petrograd. However, according to the account of an officer who began drilling them on the 25th of February—two days before the revolution—these reënforcements turned out to be indescribably bad. Not the slightest desire to fight was to be seen in those imperturbable blue, hazel and gray eyes. . . . "All their thoughts and their aspirations were for one thing only—peace."

There is no lack of such testimony. The revolution merely brought to the surface what already existed. The slogan "Down with the war!" became for that reason one of the chief slogans of the February days. It came from demonstrations of women, from the workers of the Vyborg quarter, from the regiments of the Guard. Early in March when deputies from the Duma made a tour of the front, the soldiers, especially the older ones, would continually ask them: "What are they saying about the land?" The deputies answered evasively that the land question would be decided by the Constituent Assembly. But here would sound out a voice betraying the hidden thought of everybody: "Well, as for the land, if I'm not here, you know, I won't need it." Such was the original soldier program of revolution: first peace, and then the land.

Toward the end of March at the All-Russian Conference of Soviets, where there was a good deal of patriotic bragging, one of the delegates representing the soldiers in the trenches reported very sincerely how the front received the news of the revolution: "All the soldiers said, 'Thank God! Maybe now we will have peace!'" The trenches instructed the delegate to tell the conference: "We are ready to lay down our lives for freedom, but just the same, Comrades, we want an end of the war." That was the living voice of reality—especially the latter half of it. We will wait a while if we have to, but you up there at the top, hurry along with the peace.

The tzar's troops in France—in a completely unnatural atmosphere—being moved by the same feelings, passed through the same stages of disintegration. "When we heard that the tzar had abdicated," an illiterate middle-aged peasant soldier explained to his officer, "we all thought it meant that the war was over. . . . The tzar sent us to war, and what is the use of freedom if I have got to rot in the trenches again?" That was the genuine soldier philosophy of the revolution—not brought in from the outside. No agitator could think up those simple and convincing words.

The liberals and the half-liberal socialists tried afterwards to represent the revolution as a patriotic uprising. On the 2nd of March, Miliukov explained to the French journalists: "The Russian revolution was made in order to remove the obstacles on Russia's road to victory." Here hypocrisy goes hand-in-hand with self-deceit—the hyprocrisy somewhat the larger of the two. The candid reactionaries saw things clearer. Von Struve, a German Pan-Slavist, a Lutheran Greek Orthodox, and a Marxian monarchist, better defined the actual sources of the revolution, although in the language of reactionary hatred. "In so far as the popular, and especially the soldier, masses took part in the revolution, it was not a patriotic explosion, but a riotous self-demobilization, and was directed straight against a prolongation of the War. That is, it was made in order to stop the War."

Along with a true thought, those words contain also a slander. The riotous demobilization was growing as a matter of fact right out of the war. The revolution did not create, but on the contrary checked it. Deserting, extraordinarily frequent on the eve of the revolution, was very infrequent in the first weeks after. The army was waiting. In the hope that the revolution would give peace, the soldier did not refuse to put a shoulder under the front: Otherwise, he thought, the new government won't be able to conclude a peace.

"The soldiers are definitely expressing the opinion," reports the chief of the Grenadier Division on the 23rd of March, "that we can only defend ourselves and not attack." Military reports and political speeches repeat this thought in various forms. Ensign Krylenko, an old revolutionist and a future commander-in-chief under the Bolsheviks, testified that for the soldier the war question was settled in those days with this formula: "Support the front, but don't join the offensive." In a more solemn but wholly sincere language, that meant: defend freedom.

"We mustn't stick our bayonets in the ground!" Under the influence of obscure and contradictory moods the soldiers in those days frequently refused even to listen to the Bolsheviks. They thought perhaps, impressed by certain unskillful speeches, that the Bolsheviks were not concerned with the defense of the revolution and might prevent the government from concluding peace. The social patriotic papers and agitators more and more cultivated this idea among the soldiers. But even though sometimes preventing the Bolsheviks from speaking, the soldiers from the very first days decisively rejected the idea of an offensive. To the politicians of the capital this seemed some kind of a misunderstanding which could be removed with appropriate pressure. The agitation for war reached extraordinary heights. The bourgeois press in millions of issues portrayed the problems of the revolution in the light of "War to complete victory." The Compromisers hummed the same tune—at first under their breath, then more boldly. The influence of the Bolsheviks, very weak in the army at the moment of the revolution, became even weaker when thousands of workers who had been banished to the front for striking left its ranks. The desire for peace thus found no open and clear expression exactly where it was most intense. This situation made it possible for the commanders and commissars, who were looking round for comforting illusions, to deceive themselves about the actual state of affairs. In the articles and speeches of those times it is frequently asserted that the soldiers declined the offensive because they did not correctly understand the formula "without annexations or indemnities." The Compromisers spared no effort to explain that defensive warfare permits taking the offensive, and sometimes even requires it. As though that scholastic question were at issue! An offensive meant reopening the war. A waiting support of the front meant armistice. The soldiers' theory and practice of defensive warfare was a form of silent, and later indeed of quite open, agreement with the Germans: "Don't touch us and we won't touch you." More than that the army had nothing to give to the war.

The soldiers were still less open to warlike persuasions because, under the form of preparation for an offensive, reactionary officers were obviously trying to get the reins in their hands. In the soldiers' conversation appeared the phrase: "Bayonet for the Germans, butt for the inside enemy." The bayonet, however, had here a defensive significance. The soldiers in the trenches never thought of the Dardanelles. The desire for peace was a mighty underground current which must soon break out on the surface.

Although he did not deny that negative signs were "to be observed" in the army, Miliukov tried for a long time after the revolution to assert that the army was capable of fulfilling the tasks laid out for it by the Entente. "The Bolshevik propaganda," he writes in his character of historian, "by no means immediately reached the front. For the first month or month-and-a-half after the revolution the army remained healthy." He approaches the whole question at the level of propaganda, as though that exhausts the historic process. Under the form of a belated struggle against Bolsheviks, to whom he attributes veritably mystic powers, Miliukov carries on his struggle against facts. We have already seen how the army looked in reality. Let us see how the commanders themselves appraised its fighting capacity in the first weeks, and even days, after the revolution.

On March 6 the commander-in-chief of the northern front, General Ruszky, informs the Executive Committee that a complete insubordination of the soldiers is beginning, popular personalities must be sent to the front in order to introduce some sort of tranquillity into the army.

The chief of the staff of the Black Sea fleet says in his memoirs: "From the first days of the revolution it was clear to me that it was impossible to wage war, and that the war was lost." Kolchak, according to him, was of the same opinion, and if he remained at his post as commander at the front, it was merely to defend the staff officers against violence.

Count Ignatiev, who occupied a high command in the Imperial Guard, wrote to Nabokov in March: "You must clearly understand that the war is finished, that we can't and won't fight any longer. Intelligent people ought to be thinking up a way to liquidate the war painlessly, otherwise there will be a catastrophe. . . ." Guchkov told Nabokov at the same time that he was receiving such letters by the thousand. Certain superficially more hopeful reports, rare enough in any case, were mostly contradicted by their own supplementary explanations. "The desire of the troops for victory remains," says the commander of the 2nd Army, Danilov. "In some regiments it is even stronger." But just here he adds: "Discipline has fallen off. . . . It would be well to postpone offensive action until the situation quiets down (say one to three months)." And then an unexpected supplement: "Only 50 per cent of the reënforcements are arriving. If they continue to melt away in the future, and are equally undisciplined, we cannot count on the success of the offensive."

"Our Division is fully capable of defensive action," reports the valiant commander of the 51st Infantry Division, and immediately adds: "It is necessary to rescue the army from the influence of the Soldiers' and Workers' Deputies." That, however, was not so easy to do.

The chief of the 182nd Division reports to the commander of the corps: "With every day misunderstandings are increasing, essentially about trifles, but ominous in their character. The soldiers are increasingly nervous, and the officers still more so."

This is so far only scattered testimony, although there is much of it. But on the 18th of March there was held at staff headquarters a conference of high officers on the condition of the army. The conclusion of the central organs of command was unanimous: "It will be impossible to send troops to the front in sufficient numbers to replace the losses, for there is unrest among all the reserves. The army is sick. It will probably take two or three months to adjust the relations between officers and soldiers." The generals did not understand that the disease could only progress. For the present they observed a decline of spirits among the officers, agitation among the troops, and a considerable tendency to desert. "The fighting capacity of the army is lowered, and it is difficult at present to rely on the possibility of an advance." Conclusion: "It is now impossible to carry into execution the active operations indicated for the spring."

In the weeks following, the situation continues to get worse and similar testimony is endlessly multiplied. Late in March the commander of the 5th Army, General Dragomirov, wrote to General Ruszky: "The fighting spirit has declined. Not only is there no desire among the soldiers to take the offensive, but even a simple stubbornness on the defensive has decreased to a degree threatening the success of the war. . . . Politics, which has spread through all the layers of the army, has made the whole military mass desire only one thing—to end the war and go home."

General Lukomsky, one of the pillars of the reactionary staff, dissatisfied with the new order, took over the command of a corps and found, as he tells us, that discipline remained only in the artillery and engineering division in which there were many officers and soldiers of the regular army. "As for the three infantry divisions, they were all on the road to complete disintegration."

Deserting, which had decreased after the revolution under the influence of hope, increased again under the influence of disappointment. In one week, from the 1st to the 7th of April, according to the report of General Alexeiev, approximately 8,000 soldiers deserted from the northern and western fronts. "I read with the utmost astonishment," he wrote to Guchkov, "the irresponsible reports as to the 'excellent' temper of the army. What is the use? It will not deceive the Germans, and for us it is a fatal self-deception."

So far, it is well to note, there is hardly a reference to the Bolsheviks. The majority of officers had hardly learned that strange name. When they raised the question of the causes of the army's disintegration, it was newspapers, agitators, soviets, "politics" in general—in a word, the February revolution.

You still could find individual officer-optimists who hoped that everything would turn out all right. There were still more who intentionally shut their eyes to the facts, in order not to cause unpleasantness to the new government. On the other hand a considerable number, especially of the highest officers, consciously exaggerated the signs of disintegration in order to get from the government some decisive action, which they themselves, however, were not quite ready to call by name. But the fundamental picture is indubitable. Finding the army sick, the revolution clothed the inexorable process of its decline in political forms which became more cruelly definite from week to week. The revolution carried to its logical end not only the passionate thirst for peace, but also the hostility of the soldier mass to the commanding staff and to the ruling classes in general.

In the middle of April, Alexeiev made a personal report to the government on the mood of the army, in which he evidently did not hesitate to lay on colors. "I well remember," writes Nabokov, "what a feeling of awe and hopelessness seized me." We may assume that Miliukov was present during that report, which must have occurred in the first six weeks after the revolution. More likely indeed it was he who had summoned Alexeiev with the desire of frightening his colleagues, and through their mediation, his friends the socialists.

Guchkov actually had a conversation after that with the

representatives of the Executive Committee. "A ruinous fraternization has begun," he complained. "Cases of direct insubordination are reported. Orders are talked over in army organizations and at general meetings before being carried out. In such and such regiments they wouldn't even hear of active operations. When people are hoping that peace will come tomorrow—" Guchkov added, wisely enough—"you can't expect them to give up their lives today." From this the War Minister drew the conclusion: "We must stop talking out loud about peace." But since the revolution was just what had taught people to say out loud what they were formerly thinking in silence, this meant stop the revolution.

The soldier, of course, from the very first day of the war, did not want either to die or to fight. But he did not want this just the way an artillery horse does not want to drag a heavy gun through the mud. Like the horse, he never thought that he might get rid of the load they had hitched to him. There was no connection between his will and the events of the war. The revolution showed him that connection. For millions of soldiers the revolution meant the right to a personal life, and first of all the right to life in general, the right to protect their lives from bullets and shells, and by the same token their faces from the officers' fists. In this sense it was said above, that the fundamental psychological process taking place in the army was the awakening of personality. In this volcanic eruption of individualism, which often took anarchistic forms, the educated classes saw only treachery to the nation. But as a matter of fact in the stormy speeches of the soldiers, in their intemperate protests, even in their bloody excesses, a nation was merely beginning to form itself out of impersonal prehistoric raw material. This flood of mass individualism, so hateful to the bourgeoisie, was due to the very character of the February revolution, to the fact that it was a *bourgeois* revolution.

But that was not its only content, either. For besides the peasant and his soldier son, the worker took part in this revolution. The worker had long ago felt himself a personality, and he entered into the war not only with hatred of it, but also with the thought of struggling against it. The revolution meant for him not only the naked fact of conquering, but also the partial triumph of his ideas. The overthrow of the monarchy was for him only a first step, and he did not pause on it but hastened toward other goals. The whole question for him was, how much farther would the soldier and peasant go with him? . . . What good is the land to me if I won't be there? asked the soldier. What good is freedom to me, he repeated after the worker before the closed doors of the theater, if the keys to freedom are in the hand of the master? Thus across the immeasurable chaos of the February revolution, the steely gleams of October were already visible.

CHAPTER XIV

THE RULING GROUP AND THE WAR

WHAT did the Provisional Government and the Executive Committee intend to do with this war and this army?

First of all it is necessary to understand the policy of the liberal bourgeoisie, since they played the leading rôle. In external appearance the war policy of liberalism remained aggressive-patriotic, annexationist, irreconcilable. In reality it was self-contradictory, treacherous, and rapidly becoming defeatist.

"Even if there had been no revolution," wrote Rodzianko later, "the war would have been lost just the same, and in all probability a separate peace signed." Rodzianko's views were not distinguished by independence, and for that reason ably typify the average opinions of liberally conservative circles. The mutiny of the battalions of the Guard foretold to the possessing classes not victory abroad but defeat at home. The liberals were the less able to deceive themselves about this, because they had foreseen, and to the best of their ability struggled against, this danger. The unexpected revolutionary optimism of Miliukov —declaring the revolution a step towards victory—was in reality the last resort of desperation. The question of war and peace had almost ceased for the liberals to be an independent question. They felt that they would not be able to use the revolution for the purposes of war, and so much the more imperative became their other task: to use the war against the revolution.

Problems concerning the international situation of Russia after the war, debts and new loans, the capital market and the sales market, of course still confronted the leaders of the Russian bourgeoisie; but these questions did not directly determine their policy. The concern of the moment was not to secure advantageous international conditions for bourgeois

Russia, but to save the bourgeois régime itself, even at the price of Russia's further enfeeblement. "First we must recover," said this heavily wounded class. "After that we will put things in order." But to recover meant to put down the revolution.

To keep up the war hypnosis and the mood of chauvinism was the only possible way the bourgeoisie could maintain their hold upon the masses—especially upon the army—against the so-called "deepeners" of the revolution. The problem was to sell to the people an old war which had been inherited from tzarism, with all its former aims and allies, as a new war in defense of the conquests and hopes of the revolution. That would be something of an achievement. But how achieve it? The liberals firmly expected to direct against the revolution that whole organization of patriotic social opinion which they had been using yesterday against the Rasputin clique. Since they had failed to save the monarchy, the highest court of appeal against the people, so much the more must they hold fast to the Allies. In time of war at any rate, the Entente was a far more powerful court of appeal than their own monarchy could be.

A prolongation of war would justify them in preserving the old military bureaucratic apparatus, postponing the Constituent Assembly, subordinating the revolutionary country to the front —that is, to the commanding staff acting in unison with the liberal bourgeoise. All domestic questions, especially the agrarian, and all social legislation, were to be postponed until the end of the war—which in turn was to be postponed until a victory in which the liberals did not believe. A war to exhaust the enemy was thus converted into a war to exhaust the revolution. This was not perhaps a completed plan, thought-up in advance and talked over in official meetings. But that was unnecessary. The plan flowed inevitably from the whole preceding policy of liberalism and the situation created by the revolution.

Compelled to choose the path of war, Miliukov could not of course refuse in advance to participate in the division of the booty. The Allied hopes of victory remained very real, and indeed with the entrance of America into the war had grown immensely stronger. To be sure, the Entente was one thing and Russia another. The leaders of the Russian bourgeoisie had learned during the war that, in view of the economic and military weakness of Russia, a victory of the Entente over the Central Empires would also mean a victory over Russia. For whatever might happen, Russia could only come out of the war broken and weakened. But the liberal imperialists quite consciously decided to close their eyes to this prospect. There was really nothing else for them to do. Guchkov frankly stated to his circle that only a miracle could save Russia, and that his program as War Minister was to hope for a miracle. For domestic purposes Miliukov needed the myth of victory. It does not matter how much he himself believed in it. At any rate, he stubbornly asserted that Constantinople must be ours. In this he acted with his usual cynicism. On the 20th of March this Russian Minister of Foreign Affairs tried to persuade the Allied ambassadors to betray Serbia in order by this means to purchase the treason of Bulgaria to the Central Empires. The French ambassador wrinkled his nose. Miliukov, however, insisted upon the "necessity of abandoning sentimental considerations in this matter"—abandoning at the same time that Neo-Slavism which he had been preaching ever since the defeat of the first revolution. Engels was right when he wrote to Bernstein as early as 1882: "What does all this Russian Pan-Slavic charlatanism amount to? The seizure of Constantinople and nothing more."

The charge of being Germanophile, even of being bribed by the Germans—directed yesterday against a court camarilla—was now directed with venom against the revolution. Bolder, louder, more insolent day by day, this note resounded in the speeches and articles of the Kadet Party. Before capturing the Turkish waters, liberalism was going to dirty the springs and poison the wells of the revolution.

By no means all the liberal leaders took an irreconcilable position, at least immediately after the revolution, on the question of war. Many were still in the pre-revolutionary mood, contemplating the prospect of a separate peace. Certain leading Kadets told about this afterwards with complete frankness. Nabokov, according to his own confession, was already talking with members of the government about a separate peace on the

7th of March. Several members of the Kadet center tried collectively to demonstrate to their leaders the impossibility of continuing the war. "Miliukov with his usual cold precision explained," says Baron Nolde, "that the aims of the war must be achieved." General Alexeiev, at that time drawing near to the Kadet Party, joined his voice with Miliukov's, asserting that "the army could be revived." That staff organizer of calamities apparently felt called to revive it.

A good many of the liberals and democrats, a little more naïve, misunderstood Miliukov's course, and thought him a very knight of loyalty to the Allies, the Don Quixote of the Entente. What nonsense! After the Bolsheviks seized the power, Miliukov did not hesitate one second to hurry down to Kiev, then occupied by the Germans, and offer his services to the Hohenzollern government—which, to be sure, was in no hurry to accept them. Miliukov's immediate goal in this was to secure for the purpose of his struggle with the Bolsheviks that same German gold with whose specter he had earlier tried to befoul the revolution. Miliukov's appeal to Germany in 1918 seemed to many liberals just as incomprehensible as his program of shattering Germany in the first months of 1917. But these were merely two sides of the same medal. In preparing to betray the Allies—as formerly he tried to betray Serbia—Miliukov did not betray himself nor his class. He was pursuing the same policy, and it was not his fault if it didn't look nice. In feeling out under tzarism the path to a separate peace in order to avoid revolution; in demanding war to complete victory in order to stop the February revolution when it came; in seeking an alliance with the Hohenzollerns in order to overthrow the October revolution—in all this Miliukov remained true to the interests of the possessing classes. If he did not succeed in helping them, but only butted his head each time into a new wall, that is merely because his patrons were in a blind alley. What Miliukov especially needed in the first days after the uprising was an enemy attack, a good German crack over the skull for the revolution. Unfortunately for him, March and April were inauspicious from a climatic point of view for large operations on the Russian front. And more important, the Germans, whose own situation was getting more and more difficult, decided after some hesitation to leave the Russian revolution to its own inner course. General Lisingen alone showed some private initiative at the Stokhod, the 20th and 21st of March. His success simultaneously frightened the German, and delighted the Russian governments. The staff, with the same shamelessness with which under the tzar it had exaggerated every trivial success, now exaggerated this defeat on the Stokhod. And the liberal press took up the cry. They described examples of weakness, panic, and loss in the Russian troops with the same gusto with which they had formerly described war-prisoners and trophies. The bourgeoisie and the general staff had quite plainly gone over to the defeatist position. But Lisingen was stopped by his superior officers, and the front again stood stock-still in spring mud and expectation.

The device of using the war against the revolution had a chance of success only if the intermediate parties, whom the popular masses followed, agreed to play the part of transmitting mechanism for this liberal policy. Liberalism was not in a position to unite the idea of war with the idea of revolution; only yesterday it had been preaching that a revolution would be ruinous to the war. This task must be turned over to the democrats. But of course the "secret" must not be revealed to them. They must not be initiated into the scheme, but taken with a hook. The best way to take them was through their prejudices, their vanity, their high opinion of their own statesmanlike intelligence, their fear of anarchy, their superstitious bowing down to the bourgoisie.

In the first days the socialists—for brevity we will use this name for both Mensheviks and Social Revolutionaries—did not know what to do with the war. Cheidze heaved a sigh: "We have been talking against war all the time—how can I now advocate continuing the war?" On March 10 the Executive Committee voted to send a greeting to Franz Mehring.[1] With this little gesture, the left wing tried to quiet its not very active socialist conscience. Upon the war itself the Soviet continued to say nothing. The leaders were afraid they might stir up a conflict

---

[1] A German revolutionary socialist. [Trans.]

with the Provisional Government on this subject, and darken those honeymoon weeks of "contact." They were no less afraid of a split in their own ranks. They had both defenders of the Fatherland and Zimmerwaldists among them. Each of these groups over-estimated their differences. Wide circles of the revolutionary intelligentsia had undergone a deep bourgeois metamorphosis during the war. Patriotism, open or disguised, had united the intelligentsia with the ruling classes, drawing them away from the masses. The banner of Zimmerwald with which the left wing had covered themselves did not bind them to anything much, and it did permit them to keep hidden their patriotic solidarity with the Rasputin clique. But now the Romanov régime was overthrown. Russia had become a democratic country. Her freedom, dancing in all colors, stood out sharply on the background of well-policed Europe with her military dictatorships. "Must we not defend our revolution against the Hohenzollern?" exclaimed both the old and the new patriots at the head of the Executive Committee. Zimmerwaldists of the type of Sukhanov and Steklov diffidently pointed out that the war remained imperialist, that the liberals were insisting that the revolution guarantee the annexations agreed on under the tzar. "How can I now advocate continuing the war?" says the worried Cheidze. But since these Zimmerwaldists were themselves the initiators of the transfer of power to the liberals, their objection to the liberal policy merely hung in the air. After some weeks of wavering and obstruction the first part of Miliukov's plan was, with the help of Tseretelli, decided in a satisfactory manner: these half-hearted democrats calling themselves socialists were hitched up in the war harness, and under the whip of the liberals tried with all their tiny strength to guarantee victory—the victory of the Entente over Russia and of America over Europe!

The chief function of the Compromisers was to short circuit the revolutionary energy of the masses into patriotic wires. They tried on the one hand to revive the fighting capacity of the army—that was difficult. They tried on the other hand to induce the governments of the Entente to renounce their prospective robberies—that was ludicrous. In both efforts they

275

passed from illusion to disappointment, from error to humiliation. Let us note the first signposts on this road.

In the brief hours of his grandeur, Rodzianko succeeded in publishing an order for the immediate return of the soldiers to their barracks, and their subordination to the officers. The indignation this caused in the garrison compelled the Soviet to dedicate one of its first sessions to the question of the future of the soldier. In the heated atmosphere of those hours, in the chaos of those sessions like mass meetings, and at the direct dictation of the soldiers whom the absent leaders could not restrain, there was born the famous "Order No. 1"—the single worthy document of the February revolution, a charter of the freedom of the revolutionary army. Its bold paragraphs, giving the soldiers an organizational mode of entry to the new highway, declare: that elective committees shall be formed in all military regiments; soldiers' deputies shall be elected to the Soviet; in all political acts the soldiers shall submit to the Soviet and its committees; weapons shall be in the control of the regimental and battalion committees, and shall "in no case be given up to the officer"; on duty, the severest military discipline—off duty, complete citizens' rights; saluting off duty and titling of officers, is abolished; uncivil treatment of soldiers is forbidden, and particularly addressing them as *thou*. . . . Such were the inferences drawn by the Petrograd soldiers from their participation in the revolution. Could they have been other? Nobody dared to oppose them. During the preparation of this "order" the leaders of the Soviet were distracted by more lofty business —they were conducting negotiations with the liberals. That gave them an alibi later when they had to justify themselves before the bourgeoisie and the commanding staff. Simultaneously with "Order No. 1," the Executive Committee—having hastily pulled itself together—sent to the printer, by way of antidote, an appeal to the soldiers, which, under the pretext of condemning lynch law for officers, demanded the soldiers' subordination to the old commanding staff. The typesetters simply refused to set up this document. Its democratic authors were beside themselves with indignation: where are we headed for? It would be a mistake to imagine, however, that the typesetters

were longing for bloody reprisals upon officers. The demand
for subordination to the tzarist commanding staff on the second
day after the revolution, seemed to them to be merely opening the door to the counter-revolution. Of course the typesetters exceeded their rights. But they did not feel themselves
to be only typesetters. It was a question, in their opinion, of
the life of the revolution.

In those first days, when both the soldiers and the workers
were intensely excited about the future of the officers who had
returned to their troops, the Mezhrayontsi, a Social Democratic
organization close to the Bolsheviks, formulated this sore question with revolutionary audacity. "In order that the aristocrats and officers shall not deceive you," said their appeal to the
soldiers, "choose your own platoon, company and regiment commanders, accept only those officers whom you know to be
friends of the people." And what happened? This proclamation, which adequately met the situation, was immediately confiscated by the Executive Committee, and Cheidze in his speech
called it an act of provocateurs. The democrats, you see, were
not in the least embarrassed about limiting the freedom of the
press when it came to dealing blows to the left. Fortunately
their own freedom was sufficiently limited, for the workers and
soldiers, although supporting the Executive Committee as their
highest organ, at all important moments corrected the policy
of the leadership by direct interference. Before two days
passed, the Executive Committee was trying by means of "Order No. 2" to annul the first order, limiting its application to
the Petrograd military district. In vain. "Order No. 1" was
indestructible—it had not invented anything, but merely affirmed and strengthened what had already come to pass both in
the rear and at the front, and was demanding recognition. Even
liberal deputies, when face to face with the soldiers, defended
themselves against questions and reproaches by referring to
"Order No. 1." But in the sphere of Big Politics, that audacious order became the chief argument of the bourgeoisie against
the Soviet. From that time on, the beaten generals discovered
in "Order No. 1" the chief obstacle which had prevented them
from crushing the German armies. Its origin was even traced

to Germany! The Compromisers never ceased to apologize for what they had done, and bewildered the soldiers by trying to take away with their right hand what their left hand had let slip.

Meanwhile in the Soviet the majority of rank-and-file deputies were already demanding the election of officers. The democrats got excited. Finding no better argument, Sukhanov tried to frighten the deputies with the idea that the bourgeoisie, to whom they had turned over the power, would not go this far. The democrats frankly hid behind Guchkov's back. In their scheme, the liberals occupied the same place which the monarchy was to have occupied in the scheme of the liberals. "As I was returning from the tribune to my place," Sukhanov relates, "I ran into a soldier who blocked my path, and shaking his fist in my face, angrily shouted something about 'gentlemen who have never been in a soldier's skin.'" After this "excess" our democrat, completely losing his equilibrium, ran to find Kerensky, and only with the latter's help was "the question somehow smoothed over." Those people did nothing all the time but smooth questions over.

For two weeks they succeeded in pretending that they had not noticed the war. At last, however, a further postponement became impossible. On the 14th of March, the Executive Committee introduced into the Soviet the project of a manifesto written by Sukhanov and addressed to "the people of the whole world." The liberal press soon named this document—which united the right and left Compromisers—"Order No. 1 in the sphere of foreign policy." But this flattering appraisal was just as false as the document to which it referred. "Order No. 1" had been the honest answer of the lower ranks themselves to the questions raised before the army by the revolution. The manifesto of March 14 was the treacherous answer of the upper ranks to the questions honestly presented to them by soldiers and workers.

The manifesto of course expressed a desire for peace, and moreover a democratic peace without annexations or indemnities. But long before the February revolution, the Western imperialists had learned to make use of that same phraseology. It was exactly in the name of a durable, honorable, "democratic" peace, that Wilson was getting ready just at that moment to go into the war. The pious Mr. Asquith had given to Parliament a learned classification of annexations, from which it could be unmistakably inferred that all those annexations were to be condemned as immoral which conflicted with the interests of Great Britain. As for French diplomacy, its very essence consisted in giving the most liberating possible aspect to the greediness of the shopkeeper and moneylender. The Soviet document, to which one cannot deny a rather simple sincerity of motive, dropped with fatal perfection into the well-worn rut of official French hypocrisy. The manifesto promised "firmly to defend our own freedom" against foreign militarism. The French social patriots had been occupied with just that business ever since August 1914. "The hour has come for the people to take into their own hands the decision about war and peace," declares this manifesto, whose authors, in the name of the Russian people, had just turned over the decision of that question to the big bourgeoisie. The workers of Germany and Austria-Hungary were summoned by the manifesto, "to refuse to serve as an instrument of conquest and spoliation in the hands of kings, landlords and bankers!" Those words are the quintessence of a lie—for the leaders of the Soviet had no intention of breaking off their own alliance with the kings of Great Britain and Belgium, with the emperor of Japan, with the landlords and bankers of their own and all the countries of the Entente. While turning over the leadership of foreign policy to Miliukov, who had been scheming not long before to convert East Prussia into a Russian province, the leaders of the Soviet summoned the German and Austro-Hungarian workers to follow the lead of the Russian revolution. Their theatrical condemnation of slaughter altered nothing: the Pope himself was doing that. With the help of magniloquent phrases directed against the shadows of bankers, landlords and kings, these Compromisers were converting the February revolution into an instrument in the hands of real kings, landlords and bankers. In his telegram of salutation to the Provisional Government, Lloyd George had appraised the revolution as a proof that "the present war is in its foundations a struggle for popular government and freedom." The manifesto of March 14 associated itself with Lloyd George "in its foundations," and gave invaluable aid to the war propaganda in America. Miliukov's paper was a thousand times right when it declared that "the manifesto, although it began with so typical a note of pacifism, developed an ideology essentially common to us and to all our allies." If the Russian liberals nevertheless at times fiercely attacked the manifesto, and the French censorship would not let it through, that was merely due to a fear of the interpretation which would be given it by revolutionary but still trustful masses. Although written by Zimmerwaldists, the manifesto signalized the victory of the patriotic wing. The local soviets understood the signal. They pronounced the slogan "war against war" unpermissible. Even in the Urals and in Kostroma, where the Bolsheviks were strong, the patriotic manifesto received unanimous approval. No wonder, when in the Petrograd Soviet itself the Bolsheviks offered no resistance to this false document.

After a few weeks it became necessary to make partial payments on bills of exchange. The Provisional Government issued a war loan, of course called "liberty loan." Tseretelli explained that since the government "as a whole and in general" was fulfilling its obligations, the democracy ought to support the loan. In the Executive Committee the opposition captured more than a third of the votes. But at the plenum of the Soviet (April 22) only 112 votes were cast against the loan out of almost 2,000. From this the conclusion is sometimes drawn that the Executive Committee was further to the left than the Soviet. But that is not true. The Soviet was merely more honest than the Executive Committee: if the war is in defense of the revolution, then you must give money for the war, you must support the loan. The Executive Committee was not more revolutionary, but more evasive. It lived on ambiguities and reservations. It supported the government set up by itself only "as a whole and in general," and took the responsibility for the war "in so far as." These petty trickeries are alien to the masses. Soldiers cannot fight "in so far as," nor die "as a whole and in general."

In order to reënforce the victory of statesmanly thinking

over wild talk, General Alexeiev—who had been intending on March 5 to shoot all "gangs" of propagandists—was on April 1 officially placed at the head of the armed forces. From then on everything was in order. The inspirer of the tzarist foreign policy, Miliukov, was Minister of Foreign Affairs; the leader of the army under the tzar, Alexeiev, had become commander-in-chief of the revolution. The succession was fully reëstablished.

At the same time, however, the Soviet leaders felt compelled by the logic of the situation to unravel the loops of the net they were weaving. The official democracy mortally feared those officers whom they tolerated and supported. They could not help opposing to them their own authority, trying to find support for it among the rank-and-file soldiers and make it as independent of the officers as possible. At the session of March 6, the Executive Committee considered it advisable to install its own commissars in all regiments and all military institutions. Thus was created a threefold bond between the soldier and the Soviet: the regiments sent their representatives to the Soviet; the Executive Committee sent its commissars to the regiments; and finally at the head of each regiment stood an elective committee, constituting a sort of lower nucleus of the Soviet.

One of the principal duties of the commissars was to keep watch over the political reliability of the staff and commanding officers. "The democratic régime outdid in this respect the autocratic," says Denikin with indignation. And he boasts how cleverly his staff intercepted and handed over to him the cipher-correspondence of the commissars with Petrograd. To watch over monarchists and feudal lords—what could be more outrageous! To steal the correspondence of commissars with the government is, of course, a different matter. But however things stood in the field of morals, the internal situation in the ruling apparatus of the army at that time is perfectly clear: each side was afraid of the other and watching the other with hostility; they were united only by their common fear of the soldier. Even the generals and admirals, whatever further hopes and plans they may have had, saw clearly that without a democratic smoke-screen things would go badly with them. The resolutions on committees in the fleet were drawn up by Kolchak. He counted on strangling the committees in the future. But since it was impossible for the present to take a single step without them, Kolchak interceded with the staff to get them confirmed. Similarly General Markov, one of the future White chieftains, sent to the ministry early in April a plan for the institution of commissars to keep watch over the loyalty of the commanding staff. Thus the "age-old laws of the army"—that is, the traditions of military bureaucratism—went to pieces like straws under the pressure of the revolution.

The soldiers approached the committees from the opposite angle, and united around them against the commanding staff. And although the committees did defend officers against the soldiers, this was only within certain limits. The situation of an officer who came into conflict with the committee became unbearable. Thus was created the unwritten right of the soldiers to remove their commanders. On the western front by the month of July, according to Denikin, sixty of the old officers ranking from commander of a corps to commander of a regiment, had gone. Similar removals had occurred within the regiments.

At that time a meticulous secretarial work was going on in the War Ministry, in the Executive Committee, in the Contact Sessions, aiming to create "reasonable" relations in the army, raise the authority of the officers, and reduce the army committees to a secondary and mainly economic rôle. But while the high-up leaders were thus cleaning away the shadow of the revolution with the shadow of a broom, the committees were actually developing into a powerful system ascending toward the Petrograd Executive Committee and strengthening its organizational control over the army. The Executive Committee used this control, however, chiefly in order, through the commissars and committees, to drag the army once more into the war. More and more the soldiers found themselves pondering the question: how does it come about that committees elected by us so often say, not what we think, but what our officers want of us?

The trenches are more and more frequently sending deputies to the capital to find out how things stand. From the beginning of April this movement of the soldiers from the front becomes continual. Every day mass conversations are going on in the Tauride. Arriving soldiers are stirring their heavy brains, trying to find their way among the mysteries of the politics of an Executive Committee which cannot give a clear answer to any single question. The army is ponderously moving over to a Soviet position—but only in order the more clearly to convince itself of the bankruptcy of the Soviet leadership.

The liberals, not daring to oppose the Soviet openly, nevertheless tried to carry on a struggle for the control of the army. Chauvinism, of course, must serve as their political bond with the soldiers. The Kadet minister Shingarev, in one of the conferences with the trench delegates, defended the order of Guchkov against "unnecessary indulgence" towards war-prisoners, and spoke of "German ferocity." His remarks did not meet with the slightest sympathy. The conference decisively expressed itself in favor of relieving the conditions of the prisoners of war. These were the same men whom the liberals had so casually accused of excesses and ferocities. But the gray men from the front had their own criterion. They considered it permissible to take vengeance on an officer for insulting soldiers, but it seemed contemptible to them to avenge on a captive German soldier the real or imagined ferocity of Ludendorff. The Eternal Standards of Morality remained, alas, quite foreign to those rough and lousy muzhiks.

Out of the attempt of the bourgeoisie to get control of the army there arose a contest—which, however, never came to anything—between the liberals and the Compromisers. It was at a congress of delegates from the western front on the 7th-10th of April. This first congress of one of the fronts was to be a decisive political test of the army, and both sides sent to Minsk their best forces. From the Soviet: Tseretelli, Cheidze, Skobelev, Gvozdev. From the bourgeoisie: Rodzianko himself, the Kadet, Demosthenes Rodichev, and others. An intense feeling reigned in the crowded hall of the Minsk theater, and spread in ripples throughout the town. The reports of the delegates painted a picture of the real state of affairs. Fraternization was going on along the whole front; the soldiers were taking the initiative more and more boldly; the commanding staff could not even think of repressive measures. What could the liberals say here? Faced by this passionate audience, they at once gave up the idea of opposing their own resolutions to those of the Soviet. They confined themselves to a patriotic note in their speeches of greeting, and soon erased themselves entirely. The battle was won by the democrats without a struggle. Their task was not to lead the masses against the bourgeoisie, but to hold them back. The slogan of peace—equivocally woven in with war for the defense of the revolution, in the spirit of the manifesto of March 14—ruled the congress. The Soviet resolution on the war was adopted by 610 votes against 8, with 46 abstaining. The last hope of the liberals, that of opposing the front to the rear, the army to the Soviet, went up in smoke. But the democratic leaders returned from the congress more frightened than inspired by their victory. They had seen the ghosts raised by the revolution and they felt unable to cope with them.

Chapter XV

THE BOLSHEVIKS AND LENIN

ON the 3rd of April Lenin arrived in Petrograd from abroad. Only from that moment does the Bolshevik Party begin to speak out loud, and, what is more important, with its own voice.

For Bolshevism the first months of the revolution had been a period of bewilderment and vacillation. In the "manifesto" of the Bolshevik Central Committee, drawn up just after the victory of the insurrection, we read that "the workers of the shops and factories, and likewise the mutinied troops, must immediately elect their representatives to the Provisional Revolutionary Government." The manifesto was printed in the official organ of the Soviet without comment or objection, as though the question were a purely academic one. But the leading Bolsheviks themselves also regarded their slogans as purely demonstrative. They behaved not like representatives of a proletarian party preparing an independent struggle for power, but like the left wing of a democracy, which, having announced its principles, intended for an indefinite time to play the part of loyal opposition.

Sukhanov asserts that at the sitting of the Executive Committee on March 1 the central question at issue was merely as to the conditions of the handing over of power. Against the thing itself—the formation of a bourgeois government—not one voice was raised, notwithstanding that out of 39 members of the Executive Committee, 11 were Bolsheviks or their adherents, and moreover three members of the Bolshevik center, Zalutsky, Shliapnikov and Molotov, were present at the sitting.

In the Soviet on the next day, according to the report of Shliapnikov himself, out of 400 deputies present, only 19 voted against the transfer of power to the bourgeoisie—and this although there were already 40 in the Bolshevik faction. The

voting itself passed off in a purely formal parliamentary manner, without any clear counter-proposition from the Bolsheviks, without conflict, and without any agitation whatever in
the Bolshevik press.

On the 4th of March the Bureau of the Bolshevik Central
Committee adopted a resolution on the counter-revolutionary
character of the Provisional Government, and the necessity of
steering a course towards the democratic dictatorship of the proletariat and the peasantry. The Petrograd committee, rightly
regarding this resolution as academic—since it gave no directives for today's action—approached the problem from the
opposite angle. "Taking cognizance of the resolution on the
Provisional Government adopted by the Soviet," it announces
that "it will not oppose the power of the Provisional Government in so far as," etc. . . . In essence this was the position
of the Mensheviks and Social Revolutionaries—only moved back
to the second line trenches. This openly opportunist resolution of the Petrograd Committee contradicted only in a formal
way the resolution of the Central Committee, whose academic
character had meant nothing politically but putting up with an
accomplished fact.

This readiness to submit silently, or with reservations, to
the government of the bourgeoisie did not have by any means
the entire sympathy of the party. The Bolshevik workers met
the Provisional Government from the first as a hostile rampart
unexpectedly grown up in their path. The Vyborg Committee held meetings of thousands of workers and soldiers, which
almost unanimously adopted resolutions on the necessity for a
seizure of power by the soviets. An active participant in this
agitation, Dingelstedt, testifies: "There was not one meeting,
not one workers' meeting, which would have voted down such
a resolution from us if there had only been somebody to present
it." The Mensheviks and Social Revolutionaries were afraid in
those first days to appear openly before audiences of workers
and soldiers with their formulation of the question of power.
A resolution of the Vyborg workers, in view of its popularity,
was printed and pasted up as a placard. But the Petrograd Com-

286

mittee put an absolute ban upon this resolution, and the Vyborg workers were compelled to submit.

On the question of the social content of the revolution and the prospects of its development, the position of the Bolshevik leadership was no less cloudy. Shliapnikov recalls: "We agreed with the Mensheviks that we were passing through the period of the breakdown of feudal relations, and that in their place would appear all kinds of 'freedoms' proper to bourgeois relations." *Pravda* said in its first number: "The fundamental problem is to establish a democratic republic." In an instruction to the workers' deputies, the Moscow Committee announced: "The proletariat aims to achieve freedom for the struggle for socialism, its ultimate goal." This traditional reference to the "ultimate goal" sufficiently emphasizes the historic distance from socialism. Farther than this nobody ventured. The fear to go beyond the boundaries of a democratic revolution dictated a policy of waiting, of accommodation, and of actual retreat before the Compromisers.

It is easy to imagine how heavily this political characterlessness of the center influenced the provinces. We will confine ourselves to the testimony of one of the Saratov organizations: "Our party after taking an active part in the insurrection has evidently lost its influence with the masses, and this has been caught up by the Mensheviks and Social Revolutionaries. Nobody knew what the slogans of the Bolsheviks were. . . . It was a very unpleasant picture."

The left Bolsheviks, especially the workers, tried with all their force to break through this quarantine. But they did not know how to refute the premise about the bourgeois character of the revolution and the danger of an isolation of the proletariat. They submitted, gritting their teeth, to the directions of the leaders. There were various conflicting currents in Bolshevism from the very first day, but no one of them carried its thoughts through to the end. *Pravda* reflected this cloudy and unstable intellectual state of the party, and did not bring any unity into it. The situation became still more complicated toward the middle of March, after the arrival from exile of

Kamenev and Stalin, who abruptly turned the helm of official party policy to the right.

Although a Bolshevik almost from the very birth of Bolshevism, Kamenev had always stood on the right flank of the party. Not without theoretical foundations or political instinct, and with a large experience of factional struggle in Russia and a store of political observations made in Western Europe, Kamenev grasped better than most Bolsheviks the general ideas of Lenin, but he grasped them only in order to give them the mildest possible interpretation in practice. You could not expect from him either independence of judgment or initiative in action. A distinguished propagandist, orator, journalist, not brilliant but thoughtful, Kamenev was especially valuable for negotiations with other parties and reconnoiters in other social circles—although from such excursions he always brought back with him a bit of some mood alien to the party. These characteristics of Kamenev were so obvious that almost nobody ever misjudged him as a political figure. Sukhanov remarks in him an absence of "sharp corners." "It is always necessary to lead him on a tow-line," he says. "He may resist a little, but not strongly." Stankevich writes to the same effect: Kamenev's attitude to his enemies "was so gentle that it seemed as though he himself were ashamed of the irreconcilableness of his position; in the committee he was certainly not an enemy but merely an opposition." There is little to add to that.

Stalin was a totally different type of Bolshevik, both in his psychological makeup and in the character of his party work: a strong, but theoretically and politically primitive, organizer. Whereas Kamenev as a publicist stayed for many years abroad with Lenin, where stood the theoretical forge of the party, Stalin as a so-called "practical," without theoretical viewpoint, without broad political interests, and without a knowledge of foreign languages, was inseparable from the Russian soil. Such party workers appeared abroad only on short visits to receive instructions, discuss their further problems, and return again to Russia. Stalin was distinguished among the practicals for energy, persistence, and inventiveness in the matter of moves behind the scenes. Where Kamenev as a natural result of his character felt "embarrassed" by the practical conclusions of Bolshevism, Stalin on the contrary was inclined to defend the practical conclusions which he adopted without any mitigation whatever, uniting insistence with rudeness.

Notwithstanding their opposite characters, it was no accident that Kamenev and Stalin occupied a common position at the beginning of the revolution: they supplemented each other. A revolutionary conception without a revolutionary will is like a watch with a broken spring. Kamenev was always behind the time—or rather beneath the tasks—of the revolution. But the absence of a broad political conception condemns the most willful revolutionist to indecisiveness in the presence of vast and complicated events. Stalin, the empiric, was open to alien influences not on the side of will but on the side of intellect. Thus it was that this publicist without decision, and this organizer without intellectual horizon, carried Bolshevism in March 1917 to the very boundaries of Menshevism. Stalin proved even less capable than Kamenev of developing an independent position in the Executive Committee, which he entered as a representative of the party. There is to be found in its reports and its press not one proposal, announcement, or protest, in which Stalin expressed the Bolshevik point of view in opposition to the fawning of the "democracy" at the feet of liberalism. Sukhanov says in his *Notes of the Revolution:* "Among the Bolsheviks, besides Kamenev, there appeared in the Executive Committee in those days Stalin. . . . During the time of his modest activity in the Executive Committee he gave me the impression—and not only me—of a gray spot which would sometimes give out a dim and inconsequential light. There is really nothing more to be said about him." Although Sukhanov obviously underestimates Stalin as a whole, he nevertheless correctly describes his political characterlessness in the Executive Committee of the Compromisers.

On the 14th of March the manifesto "to the people of the whole world," interpreting the victory of the February revolution in the interests of the Entente, and signifying the triumph of a new republican social patriotism of the French stamp, was adopted by the Soviet *unanimously.* That meant a considerable success for Kamenev and Stalin, but one evidently attained without much struggle. *Pravda* spoke of it as a "conscious compromise between different tendencies represented in the Soviet." It is necessary to add that this compromise involved a direct break with the tendency of Lenin, which was not represented in the Soviet at all.

Kamenev, a member of the emigrant editorial staff of the central organ, Stalin, a member of the Central Committee, and Muranov, a deputy in the Duma who had also returned from Siberia, removed the old editors of *Pravda*, who had occupied a too "left" position, and on the 15th of March, relying on their somewhat problematical rights, took the paper into their own hands. In the program announcement of the new editorship, it was declared that the Bolsheviks would decisively support the Provisional Government "in so far as it struggles against reaction or counter-revolution." The new editors expressed themselves no less categorically upon the question of war: While the German army obeys its emperor, the Russian soldier must "stand firmly at his post answering bullet with bullet and shell with shell." "Our slogan is not the meaningless 'down with war.' Our slogan is pressure upon the Provisional Government with the aim of compelling it . . . to make an attempt to induce all the warring countries to open immediate negotiations . . . and until then every man remains at his fighting post!" Both the idea and its formulation are those of the defensists. This program of pressure upon an imperialist government with the aim of "inducing" it to adopt a peace-loving form of activity, was the program of Kautsky in Germany, Jean Longuet in France, MacDonald in England. It was anything but the program of Lenin, who was calling for the overthrow of imperialist rule. Defending itself against the patriotic press, *Pravda* went even farther: "All 'defeatism,'" it said, "or rather what an undiscriminating press protected by the tzar's censorship has branded with that name, died at the moment when the first revolutionary regiment appeared on the streets of Petrograd." This was a direct abandonment of Lenin. "Defeatism" was not invented by a hostile press under the protection of a censorship, it was proclaimed by Lenin in the formula: "The defeat

of Russia is the lesser evil." The appearance of the first revolutionary regiment, and even the overthrow of the monarchy,
did not alter the imperialist character of the war. "The day of
the first issue of the transformed *Pravda*," says Shliapnikov,
"was a day of rejoicing for the defensists. The whole Tauride
Palace, from the business men in the committee of the State
Duma to the very heart of the revolutionary democracy, the
Executive Committee, was brimful of one piece of news: the
victory of the moderate and reasonable Bolsheviks over the ex-
tremists. In the Executive Committee itself they met us with
venomous smiles. . . . When that number of *Pravda* was received in the factories it produced a complete bewilderment
among the members of the party and its sympathizers, and a
sarcastic satisfaction among its enemies. . . . The indignation
in the party locals was enormous, and when the proletarians
found out that *Pravda* had been seized by three former editors
arriving from Siberia they demanded their expulsion from the
party." *Pravda* was soon compelled to print a sharp protest
from the Vyborg district: "If the paper does not want to lose
the confidence of the workers, it must and will bring the light
of revolutionary consciousness, no matter how painful it may
be, to the bourgeois owls." These protests from below compelled the editors to become more cautious in their expressions,
but did not change their policy. Even the first article of Lenin
which got there from abroad passed by the minds of the editors.
They were steering a rightward course all along the line. "In
our agitation," writes Dingelstedt, a representative of the left
wing, "we had to take up the principle of the dual power . . .
and demonstrate the inevitability of this roundabout road to
that same worker and soldier mass which during two weeks of
intensive political life had been educated in a wholly different
understanding of its tasks."

The policy of the party throughout the whole country
naturally followed that of *Pravda*. In many soviets resolutions
about fundamental problems were now adopted unanimously:
the Bolsheviks simply bowed down to the Soviet majority. At
a conference of the soviets of the Moscow region the Bolsheviks
joined in the resolution of the social patriots on the war. And

finally at the All-Russian Conference of the representatives of 82 soviets at the end of March and the beginning of April, the Bolsheviks voted for the official resolution on the question of power, which was defended by Dan. This extraordinary political rapprochement with the Mensheviks caused a widespread tendency towards unification. In the provinces the Bolsheviks and Mensheviks entered into united organizations. The Kamenev-Stalin faction was steadily converting itself into a left flank of the so-called revolutionary democracy, and was taking part in the mechanics of parliamentary "pressure" in the *couloirs* upon the bourgeoisie, supplementing this with a similar pressure upon the democracy.

*

THE part of the Central Committee which lived abroad and the Central Organ, *The Social Democrat,* had been the spiritual center of the party. Lenin, with Zinoviev as assistant, had conducted the whole work of leadership. The most responsible secretarial duties were fulfilled by Lenin's wife, Krupskaia. In the practical work this small center relied upon the support of a few score of Bolshevik emigrants. During the war their isolation from Russia became the more unbearable as the military police of the Entente drew its circle tighter and tighter. The revolutionary explosion they had so long and tensely awaited caught them unawares. England categorically refused to the emigrant internationalists, of whom she had kept a careful list, a visa to Russia. Lenin was raging in his Zurich cage, seeking a way out. Among a hundred plans that were talked over, one was to travel on the passport of a deaf-and-dumb Scandinavian. At the same time Lenin did not miss any chance to make his voice heard from Switzerland. On March 6 he telegraphed through Stockholm to Petrograd: "Our tactic; absolute lack of confidence; no support to the new government; suspect Kerensky especially; arming of proletariat the sole guarantee; immediate elections to the Petrograd Duma; no rapprochement with other parties." In this directive, only the suggestion about elections to the Duma instead of the Soviet, had an episodic character and soon dropped out of sight. The other points, expressed with telegraphic incisiveness, fully indicate the general direction of the policy to be pursued. At the same time Lenin begins to send to *Pravda* his *Letters from Afar* which, although based upon fragments of foreign information constitute a finished analysis of the revolutionary situation. The news in the foreign papers soon enabled him to conclude that the Provisional Government, with the direct assistance not only of Kerensky but of Cheidze, was not unsuccessfully deceiving the workers, giving out the imperialist war for a war of defense. On the 17th of March, through friends in Stockholm, he wrote a letter filled with alarm. "Our party would disgrace itself for ever, kill itself politically, if it took part in such deceit. . . . I would choose an immediate split with no matter whom in our party, rather than surrender to social patriotism. . . ." After this apparently impersonal threat—having definite people in mind however—Lenin adjures: "Kamenev must understand that a world historic responsibility rests upon him." Kamenev is named here because it is a question of political principle. If Lenin had had a practical militant problem in mind, he would have been more likely to mention Stalin. But in just those hours when Lenin was striving to communicate the tensity of his will to Petrograd across smoking Europe, Kamenev with the coöperation of Stalin was turning sharply toward social patriotism.

Various schemes—disguises, false whiskers, foreign or false passports—were cast aside one after the other as impossible. And meanwhile the idea of traveling through Germany became more and more concrete. This plan frightened the majority of emigrants—and not only those who were patriotic, either. Martov and the other Mensheviks could not make up their minds to adopt the bold action of Lenin, and continued to knock in vain on the doors of the Entente. Later on even many of the Bolsheviks repented of their journey through Germany, in view of the difficulties caused by the "sealed train" in the sphere of agitation. From the beginning Lenin never shut his eyes to those future difficulties. Krupskaia wrote not long before the departure from Zurich: "Of course the patriots will raise an outcry in Russia, but for that we must be prepared." The question stood as follows: either stay in Switzerland or travel through Germany. There was no other choice. Could Lenin have hesitated for a moment? Just one month later Martov, Axelrod and the others had to follow in his steps.

In the organization of this unusual trip through hostile territory in war time, the fundamental traits of Lenin as a statesman expressed themselves—boldness of conception and meticulous carefulness in its fulfillment. Inside that great revolutionist there dwelt a pedantic notary—one who knew his function, however, and drew up his paper at the moment when it might help in the overthrow of all such notarial acts for ever. The conditions of the journey through Germany were worked out with extraordinary care in this unique international treaty between the editorial staff of a revolutionary paper and the empire of the Hohenzollerns. Lenin demanded complete extraterritoriality during the transit: no supervision of the personnel of the passengers, their passports or baggage. No single person should have the right to enter the train throughout the journey. (Hence the legend of the "sealed" train.) On their part, the emigrant group agreed to insist upon the release from Russia of a corresponding number of German and Austro-Hungarian civil prisoners.

At the same time a joint declaration was drawn up with several foreign revolutionists. "The Russian internationalists who are now going to Russia in order to serve there the cause of the revolution, will help us arouse the proletariat of other countries, especially of Germany and Austria, against their governments." So speaks the protocol signed by Loriot and Gilbeaux from France, Paul Levy from Germany, Platten from Switzerland, by Swedish left deputies and others. On those conditions and with those precautions, thirty Russian emigrants left Switzerland at the end of March. A rather explosive trainload even among the loads of those war days!

In his farewell letter to the Swiss workers Lenin reminded them of the declaration of the central organ of the Bolsheviks in the autumn of 1915: If the revolution brings to power in Russia a republican government which wants to continue the imperialist war, the Bolsheviks will be against the defense of the republican Fatherland. Such a situation has now arisen. "Our slogan is no support to the government of Guchkov-Miliukov." With those words Lenin now entered the territory of the revolution.

However, the members of the Provisional Government did not see any ground for alarm. Nabokov writes: "At one of the March sessions of the Provisional Government, during a recess, in a long conversation about the increasing propaganda of the Bolsheviks, Kerensky exclaimed with his usual hysterical giggle: 'Just you wait, Lenin himself is coming, then the real thing will begin!'" Kerensky was right. The real thing would begin only then. However the ministers, according to Nabokov, were not greatly disturbed: "The very fact of his having appealed to Germany will so undermine the authority of Lenin that we need not fear him." As was to be expected, the ministers were exceedingly perspicacious.

Friendly disciples went to meet Lenin in Finland. "We had hardly got into the car and sat down," writes Raskolnikov, a young naval officer and a Bolshevik, "when Vladimir Ilych flung at Kamenev: 'What's this you're writing in *Pravda?* We saw several numbers and gave it to you good and proper." Such was their meeting after a separation of several years. But even so it was a friendly meeting.

The Petrograd Committee, with the coöperation of the military organization, mobilized several thousand workers and soldiers for a triumphal welcome to Lenin. A friendly armored car division detailed all their cars to meet him. The committee decided to go to the station with the armored cars. The revolution had already created a partiality for that type of monster, so useful to have on your side in the streets of a city.

The description of the official meeting which took place in the so-called "Tzar's Room" of the Finland station, constitutes a very lively page in the many-volumed and rather faded memoirs of Sukhanov. "Lenin walked, or rather ran, into the Tzar's Room in a round hat, his face chilled, and a luxurious bouquet in his arms. Hurrying to the middle of the room, he stopped still in front of Cheidze as though he had run into a completely unexpected obstacle. And here Cheidze, not abandoning his previous melancholy look, pronounced the following 'speech of greeting,' carefully preserving not only the spirit and letter, but also the tone of voice of a moral instructor: 'Comrade Lenin, in the name of the Petrograd Soviet and the whole revolution, we welcome you to Russia . . . *but* we consider that the chief task of the revolutionary democracy at present is to defend our revolution against every kind of attack both from within and from without. . . . We hope that you will join us in striving towards this goal.' Cheidze ceased. I was dismayed with the unexpectedness of it. But Lenin, it seemed, knew well how to deal with all that. He stood there looking as though what was happening did not concern him in the least, glanced from one side to the other, looked over the surrounding public, and even examined the ceiling of the 'Tzar's Room' while rearranging his bouquet (which harmonized rather badly with his whole figure), and finally, having turned completely away from the delegates of the Executive Committee, 'answered' thus: 'Dear comrades, soldiers, sailors and workers, I am happy to greet in you the victorious Russian revolution, to greet you as the advance guard of the international proletarian army. . . . The hour is not far when, at the summons of our comrade Karl Liebknecht, the people will turn their weapons against their capitalist exploiters. . . . The Russian revolution achieved by you has opened a new epoch. Long live the world-wide socialist revolution!' "

Sukhanov is right—the bouquet harmonized badly with the figure of Lenin, and doubtless hindered and embarrassed him with its inappropriateness to the austere background of events. In general, as it happens, Lenin did not like flowers in a bouquet. But doubtless he was far more embarrassed by that official and hypocritical Sunday school greeting in the parade room of a station. Cheidze was better than his speech of greeting. He was a little timid of Lenin. But they undoubtedly had told him that it was necessary to pull up on the "sectarian" from the very beginning. To supplement Cheidze's speech, which had demonstrated the pitiable level of the leadership, a young naval commander, speaking in the name of the sailors, was brilliant enough to express the hope that Lenin might become a member of the Provisional Government. Thus the February revolution, garrulous and flabby and still rather stupid, greeted the man who had arrived with a resolute determination to set it straight both in thought and in will. Those first impressions, multiplying tenfold the alarm which he had brought with him, produced a feeling of protest in Lenin which it was difficult to restrain. How much more satisfactory to roll up his sleeves! Appealing from Cheidze to the sailors and workers, from the defense of the Fatherland to international revolution, from the Provisional Government to Liebknecht, Lenin merely gave a short rehearsal there at the station of his whole future policy.

And nevertheless that clumsy revolution instantly and heartily took its leader into its bosom. The soldiers demanded that Lenin climb up on one of the armored cars, and he had to obey. The oncoming night made the procession especially impressive. The lights on the other armored cars being dimmed, the night was stabbed by the sharp beam from the projector of the machine on which Lenin rode. It sliced out from the darkness of the street sections of excited workers, soldiers, sailors—the same ones who had achieved the great revolution and then let the power slip through their fingers. The band ceased playing every so often, in order to let Lenin repeat or vary his speech before new listeners. "That triumphal march was brilliant," says Sukhanov, "and even somewhat symbolic."

In the palace of Kshesinskaia, Bolshevik headquarters in the satin nest of a court ballerina—that combination must have amused Lenin's always lively irony—greetings began again. This was too much. Lenin endured the flood of eugolistic speeches like an impatient pedestrian waiting in a doorway for the rain to stop. He felt the sincere joyfulness at his arrival, but was bothered by its verboseness. The very tone of the official greetings seemed to him imitative, affected—in a word borrowed from the petty bourgeois democracy, declamatory, sentimental and false. He saw that the revolution, before having even defined its problems and tasks, had already created its tiresome etiquette. He smiled a good-natured reproach, looked at his watch, and from time to time doubtless gave an unrestrained yawn. The echo of the last greeting had not died away, when this unusual guest let loose upon that audience a cataract of passionate thought which at times sounded almost like a lashing. At that period the stenographic art was not yet open to Bolshevism. Nobody made notes. All were too absorbed in what was happening. The speeches have not been preserved. There remain only general impressions in the memoirs of the listeners. And these have been edited by the lapse of time; rapture has been added to them, and fright washed away. The fundamental impression made by Lenin's speech even among those nearest to him was one of fright. All the accepted formulas, which with innumerable repetition had acquired in the course of a month a seemingly unshakable permanence, were exploded one after another before the eyes of that audience. The short Leninist reply at the station, tossed out over the head of the startled Cheidze, was here developed into a two-hour speech addressed directly to the Petrograd cadres of Bolshevism.

The non-party socialist, Sukhanov, was accidentally present at this meeting as a guest—admitted by the good-natured Kamenev, although Lenin was intolerant of such indulgences. Thanks to this we have a description made by an outsider— half-hostile and half-ecstatic—of the first meeting of Lenin with the Petersburg Bolsheviks.

"I will never forget that thunderlike speech, startling and amazing not only to me, a heretic accidentally dropped in, but also to the faithful, all of them. I assert that nobody there had expected anything of the kind. It seemed as if all the elements and the spirit of universal destruction had risen from their lairs, knowing neither barriers nor doubts nor personal difficulties nor personal considerations, to hover through the banquet chambers of Kshesinskaia above the heads of the bewitched disciples."

Personal considerations and difficulties—to Sukhanov that meant for the most part the editorial waverings of the *Novy Zhizn* circle having tea with Maxim Gorky. Lenin's considerations went deeper. Not the elements were hovering in that banquet hall, but human thoughts—and they were not embarrassed by the elements, but were trying to understand in order to control them. But never mind—the impression is clearly conveyed.

"On the journey here with my comrades," said Lenin, according to Sukhanov's report—"I was expecting they would take us directly from the station to Peter and Paul. We are far from that, it seems. But let us not give up the hope that it will happen, that we shall not escape it."

For the others at that time the development of the revolution was identical with a strengthening of the democracy; for Lenin the nearest prospect led straight to the Peter and Paul prison-fortress. It seemed a sinister joke. But Lenin was not joking, nor was the revolution joking.

"He swept aside legislative agrarian reform," complains Sukhanov, "along with all the rest of the policies of the Soviet. He spoke for an organized seizure of the land by the peasants, not anticipating . . . any governmental power at all."

" 'We don't need any parliamentary republic. We don't need any bourgeois democracy. We don't need any government except the Soviet of workers', soldiers', and farmhands' deputies!' "

At the same time Lenin sharply separated himself from the Soviet majority, tossing them over into the camp of the enemy. "That alone was enough in those days to make his listeners dizzy!"

"Only the Zimmerwald Left stands guard over the proletarian interests and the world revolution"—thus Sukhanov reports, with indignation, the thoughts of Lenin. "The rest are the same old opportunists, speaking pretty words but in reality betraying the cause of socialism and the worker masses."

Raskolnikov supplements Sukhanov: "He decisively assailed the tactics pursued before his arrival by the ruling party groups and by individual comrades. The most responsible party workers were here. But for them too the words of Ilych were a veritable revelation. They laid down a Rubicon between the tactics of yesterday and today." That Rubicon, as we shall see, was not laid down at once.

There was no discussion of the speech. All were too much

astounded, and each wanted a chance to collect his thoughts. "I came out on the street," concludes Sukhanov, "feeling as though on that night I had been flogged over the head with a flail. Only one thing was clear: There was no place for me, a non-party man, beside Lenin!"

Indeed not!

The next day Lenin presented to the party a short written exposition of his views, which under the name of *Theses of April 4* has become one of the most important documents of the revolution. The theses expressed simple thoughts in simple words comprehensible to all: The republic which has issued from the February revolution is not our republic, and the war which it is now waging is not our war. The task of the Bolsheviks is to overthrow the imperialist government. But this government rests upon the support of the Social Revolutionaries and Mensheviks, who in turn are supported by the trustfulness of the masses of the people. We are in the minority. In these circumstances there can be no talk of violence from our side. We must teach the masses not to trust the Compromisers and defensists. "We must patiently explain." The success of this policy, dictated by the whole existing situation, is assured, and it will bring us to the dictatorship of the proletariat, and so beyond the boundaries of the bourgeois régime. We will break absolutely with capital, publish its secret treaties, and summon the workers of the whole world to cast loose from the bourgeoisie and put an end to the war. We are beginning the international revolution. Only its success will confirm our success, and guarantee a transition to the socialist régime.

These theses of Lenin were published in his own name and his only. The central institutions of the party met them with a hostility softened only by bewilderment. Nobody—not one organization, group or individual—affixed his signature to them. Even Zinoviev, arriving with Lenin from abroad, where for ten years his ideas had been forming under the immediate and daily influence of Lenin, silently stepped aside. Nor was this sidestepping a surprise to the teacher, who knew his closest disciple all too well.

Where Kamenev was a propagandist popularizer, Zinoviev

was an agitator, and indeed, to quote an expression of Lenin, "nothing but an agitator." He has not, in the first place, a sufficient sense of responsibility to be a leader. But not only that. Lacking inner discipline, his mind is completely incapable of theoretical work, and his thoughts dissolve into the formless intuitions of the agitator. Thanks to an exceptionally quick scent, he can catch out of the air whatever formulas are necessary to him—those which will exercise the most effective influence on the masses. Both as journalist and orator he remains an agitator, with only this difference—that in his articles you usually see his weaker side, and in oral speech his stronger. Although far more bold and unbridled in agitation than any other Bolshevik, Zinoviev is even less capable than Kamenev of revolutionary initiative. He is, like all demagogues, indecisive. Passing from the arena of factional debate to that of direct mass fighting, Zinoviev almost involuntarily separated from his teacher.

*

THERE have been plenty of attempts of late years to prove that the April party crisis was a passing and almost accidental confusion. They all go to pieces at first contact with the facts.[1]

What we already know of the activity of the party in March reveals the deepest possible contradiction between Lenin and the Petersburg leadership. This contradiction reached its highest intensity exactly at the moment of Lenin's arrival. Simultaneously with the All-Russian Conference of representatives of 82 soviets, where Kamenev and Stalin voted for the resolution on sovereignty introduced by the Social Revolutionaries and Mensheviks, there took place in Petrograd a party conference of Bolsheviks assembled from all over Russia. This conference, at the very end of which Lenin arrived, has an exceptional interest for anyone wishing to characterize the mood and opinions of the party and all its upper layers as they issued from the war.

---

[1] In the big collected volume issued under the editorship of Professor Pokrovsky, *Essays on the History of the October Revolution* (vol. II, Moscow, 1927) an apologetic work is devoted to the "April Confusion" by a certain Bayevsky, which for its unceremonious treatment of facts and documents might be called cynical, were it not childishly impotent.

A reading of the reports, to this day unpublished, frequently produces a feeling of amazement: is it possible that a party represented by these delegates will after seven months seize the power with an iron hand? A month had already passed since the uprising—a long period for a revolution, as also for a war. Nevertheless opinions were not defined in the party even on the most basic questions of the revolution. Extreme patriots such as Voitinsky, Eliava, and others, participated in the conference alongside of those who considered themselves internationalists. The percentage of outspoken patriots, incomparably less than among the Mensheviks, was nevertheless considerable. The conference as a whole did not decide the question whether to break with its own patriots or unite with the patriots of Menshevism. In an interval between sessions of the Bolshevik conference there was held a united session of Bolsheviks and Mensheviks—delegates to the Soviet conference—to consider the war question. The most furious Menshevik-patriot, Lieber, announced at this session: "We must do away with the old division between Bolshevik and Menshevik, and speak only of our attitude toward the war." The Bolshevik, Voitinsky, hastened to proclaim his readiness to put his signature to every word of Lieber. All of them together, Bolsheviks and Mensheviks, patriots and internationalists, were seeking a common formula for their attitude to the war.

The views of the Bolshevik conference undoubtedly found their most adequate expression in the report of Stalin on relations with the Provisional Government. It is necessary to introduce here the central thought of this speech, which, like the reports as a whole, is not yet published. "The power has been divided between two organs of which neither one possesses full power. There is debate and struggle between them, and there ought to be. The rôles have been divided. The Soviet has in fact taken the initiative in the revolutionary transformation; the Soviet is the revolutionary leader of the insurrectionary people; an organ controlling the Provisional Government. And the Provisional Government has in fact taken the rôle of fortifier of the conquests of the revolutionary people. The Soviet mobilizes the forces, and controls. The Provisional Government, balking and confused, takes the rôle of fortifier of those conquests of the people, which they have already seized as a fact. This situation has disadvantageous, but also advantageous sides. It is not to our advantage at present to force events, hastening the process of repelling the bourgeois layers, who will in the future inevitably withdraw from us."

Transcending class distinctions, the speaker portrays the relation between the bourgeoisie and the proletariat as a mere division of labor. The workers and soldiers achieve the revolution, Guchkov and Miliukov "fortify" it. We recognize here the traditional conception of the Mensheviks, incorrectly modeled after the events of 1789. This superintendent's approach to the historical process is exactly characteristic of the leaders of Menshevism, this handing out of instructions to various classes and then patronizingly criticizing their fulfillment. The idea that it is disadvantageous to hasten the withdrawal of the bourgeoisie from the revolution, has always been the guiding principle of the whole policy of the Mensheviks. In action this means blunting and weakening the movement of the masses in order not to frighten away the liberal allies. And finally, Stalin's conclusion as to the Provisional Government is wholly in accord with the equivocal formula of the Compromisers: "In so far as the Provisional Government fortifies the steps of the revolution, in so far we must support it, but in so far as it is counter-revolutionary, support to the Provisional Government is not permissible."

Stalin's report was made on March 29. On the next day the official spokesman of the Soviet conference, the non-party social democrat Steklov, defending the same conditional support to the Provisional Government, in the ardor of his eloquence painted such a picture of the activity of the "fortifiers" of the revolution—opposition to social reforms, leaning towards monarchy, protection of counter-revolutionary forces, appetite for annexation—that the Bolshevik conference recoiled in alarm from this formula of support. The right Bolshevik Nogin declared: "The speech of Steklov has introduced one new thought: it is clear that we ought not now to talk about support, but about resistance." Skrypnik also arrived at the conclusion that since the speech of Steklov "many things have changed, there can be no more talk of supporting the government. There is a conspiracy of the Provisional Government against the people and the revolution." Stalin, who a day before had been painting an idealistic picture of the "division of labor" between the government and the Soviet, felt obliged to eliminate this point about supporting the government. The short and superficial discussion turned about the question whether to support the Provisional Government "in so far as," or only to support the revolutionary activities of the Provisional Government. The delegate from Saratov, Vassiliev, not untruthfully declared: "We all have the same attitude to the Provisional Government." Krestinsky formulated the situation even more clearly: "As to practical action there is no disagreement between Stalin and Voitinsky." Notwithstanding the fact that Voitinsky went over to the Mensheviks immediately after the conference, Krestinsky was not very wrong. Although he eliminated the open mention of support, Stalin did not eliminate support. The only one who attempted to formulate the question in principle was Krassikov, one of those old Bolsheviks who had withdrawn from the party for a series of years, but now, weighed down with life's experience, was trying to return to its ranks. Krassikov did not hesitate to seize the bull by the horns. Is this then a dictatorship of the proletariat you are about to inaugurate? he asked ironically. But the conference passed over his irony, and along with it passed over this question as one not deserving attention. The resolution of the conference summoned the revolutionary democracy to urge the Provisional Government toward "a most energetic struggle for the complete liquidation of the old régime"—that is, gave the proletarian party the rôle of governess of the bourgeoisie.

The next day they considered the proposal of Tseretelli for a union of Bolsheviks and Mensheviks. Stalin was wholly in favor of the proposal: "We must do it. It is necessary to define our proposal for a basis of union; union is possible on the basis of Zimmerwald-Kienthal." Molotov, who had been removed from the editorship of *Pravda* by Kamenev and Stalin because of the too radical line of the paper, spoke in opposition: Tseretelli wants to unite heterogeneous elements, he himself calls himself a Zimmerwaldist; a union on that basis is wrong. But Stalin stuck to his guns: "There is no use running ahead and trying to forestall disagreements. There is no party life without disagreements. We will live down petty disagreements within the party." The whole struggle which Lenin had been carrying on during the war years against social patriotism and its pacifist disguise, was thus casually swept aside. In September 1916 Lenin had written through Shliapnikov to Petrograd with special insistence: "Conciliationism and consolidation is the worst thing for the workers' party in Russia, not only idiotism, but ruin to the party. . . . We can rely only on those who have understood the whole deceit involved in the idea of unity and the whole necessity of a split with that brotherhood (Cheidze & Co.) in Russia." This warning was not understood. Disagreements with Tseretelli, the leader of the ruling Soviet bloc, seemed to Stalin petty disagreements, which could be "lived down" within a common party. This furnishes the best criterion for an appraisal of the views held by Stalin at that time.

On April 4, Lenin appeared at the party conference. His speech, developing his "theses," passed over the work of the conference like the wet sponge of a teacher erasing what had been written on the blackboard by a confused pupil.

"Why didn't you seize the power?" asked Lenin. At the Soviet conference not long before that, Steklov had confusedly explained the reasons for abstaining from the power: the revolution is bourgeois—it is the first stage—the war, etc. "That's nonsense," Lenin said. "The reason is that the proletariat was not sufficiently conscious and not sufficiently organized. That we have to acknowledge. The material force was in the hands of the proletariat, but the bourgeoisie was conscious and ready. That is the monstrous fact. But it is necessary to acknowledge it frankly, and say to the people straight out that we did not seize the power because we were unorganized and not conscious."

From the plane of pseudo-objectivism, behind which the political capitulators were hiding, Lenin shifted the whole question to the subjective plane. The proletariat did not seize the power in February because the Bolshevik Party was not equal to its objective task, and could not prevent the Compromisers from expropriating the popular masses politically for the benefit of the bourgeoisie.

The day before that, lawyer Krassikov had said challengingly: "If we think that the time has now come to realize the dictatorship of the proletariat, then we ought to pose the question that way. We unquestionably have the physical force for a seizure of power." The chairman at that time deprived Krassikov of the floor on the ground that practical problems were under discussion, and the question of dictatorship was out of order. But Lenin thought that, as the sole practical question, the question of preparing the dictatorship of the proletariat was exactly in order. "The peculiarity of the present moment in Russia," he said in his theses, "consists in the transition from the first stage of the revolution, which gave the power to the bourgeoisie on account of the inadequate consciousness and organization of the proletariat, to its second stage which must give the power to the proletariat and the poor layers of the peasantry." The conference, following the lead of *Pravda*, had limited the task of the revolution to a democratic transformation to be realized through the Constituent Assembly. As against this, Lenin declared that "life and the revolution will push the Constituent Assembly into the background. A dictatorship of the proletariat exists, but nobody knows what to do with it."

The delegates exchanged glances. They whispered to each other that Ilych had stayed too long abroad, had not had time to look around and familiarize himself with things. But the speech of Stalin on the ingenious division of labor between the government and the Soviet, sank out of sight once and forever. Stalin himself remained silent. From now on he will have to be silent for a long time. Kamenev alone will man the defenses.

Lenin had already given warning in letters from Geneva that he was ready to break with anybody who made concessions on the question of war, chauvinism and compromise with the bourgeoisie. Now, face to face with the leading circles of the party, he opens an attack all along the line. But at the beginning he does not name a single Bolshevik by name. If he has need of a living model of equivocation and half-wayness, he points his finger at the non-party men, or at Steklov or Cheidze. That was the customary method of Lenin: not to nail anybody down to his position too soon, to give the prudent a chance to withdraw from the battle in good season and thus weaken at once the future ranks of his open enemies. Kamenev and Stalin had thought that in participating in the war after February, the soldiers and workers were defending the revolution. Lenin thinks that, as before, the soldier and the worker take part in the war as the conscripted slaves of capital. "Even our Bolsheviks," he says, narrowing the circle around his antagonists, "show confidence in the government. Only the fumes of the revolution can explain that. That is the death of socialism. . . . If that's your position, our ways part. I prefer to remain in the minority." That was not a mere oratorical threat; it was a clear path thought through to the end.

Although naming neither Kamenev nor Stalin, Lenin was obliged to name the paper: "*Pravda* demands of the government that it renounce annexation. To demand from the government of the capitalists that it renounce annexation is nonsense, flagrant mockery." Restrained indignation here breaks out with a high note. But the orator immediately takes himself in hand: he wants to say no less than is necessary, but also no more. Incidentally and in passing, Lenin gives incomparable rules for revolutionary statesmanship: "When the masses announce that they do not want conquests, I believe them. When Guchkov and Lvov say they do not want conquests, they are deceivers! When a worker says that he wants the defense of the country, what speaks in him is the instinct of the oppressed." This criterion, to call it by its right name, seems simple as life itself. But the difficulty is to call it by its right name in time.

On the question of the appeal of the Soviet "to the people of the whole world"—which caused the liberal paper *Rech* at one time to declare that the theme of pacifism is developing among us into an ideology common to the Allies—Lenin expressed himself more clearly and succinctly: "What is peculiar to Russia is the gigantically swift transition from wild violence to the most delicate deceit."

"This appeal," wrote Stalin concerning the manifesto, "if it reaches the broad masses (of the West), will undoubtedly recall hundreds and thousands of workers to the forgotten slogan 'Proletarians of all Countries Unite!' "

"The appeal of the Soviet," objects Lenin, "—there isn't a word in it imbued with class consciousness. There is nothing to it but phrases." This document, the pride of the home-grown Zimmerwaldists, is in Lenin's eyes merely one of the weapons of "the most delicate deceit."

Up to Lenin's arrival *Pravda* had never even mentioned the Zimmerwald left. Speaking of the International, it never indicated which International. Lenin called this "the Kautsky-anism of *Pravda*." "In Zimmerwald and Kienthal," he declared at a party conference, "the Centrists predominated. . . . We declare that we created a left and broke with the center. . . . The left Zimmerwald tendency exists in all the countries of the world. The masses ought to realize that socialism has split throughout the world. . . ."

Three days before that Stalin had announced at that same conference his readiness to live down differences with Tseretelli on the basis of Zimmerwald-Kienthal—that is, on the basis of Kautskyanism. "I hear that in Russia there is a trend toward consolidation," said Lenin. "Consolidation with the defensists —that is betrayal of socialism. I think it would be better to stand alone like Liebknecht—one against a hundred and ten." The accusation of betrayal of socialism—for the present still without naming names—is not here merely a strong word; it fully expresses the attitude of Lenin toward those Bolsheviks who were extending a finger to the social patriots. In oppo-sition to Stalin who thought it was possible to unite with the Mensheviks, Lenin thought it was unpermissible to share with them any longer the name of Social Democrat. "Personally and speaking for myself alone," he said, "I propose that we change the name of the party, that we call it the Communist Party." "Personally and speaking for myself alone"—that means that nobody, not one of the members of the conference, agreed to that symbolic gesture of ultimate break with the Second International.

"You are afraid to go back on your old memories?" says the orator to the embarrassed, bewildered and partly indignant delegates. But the time has come "to change our linen; we've got to take off the dirty shirt and put on clean." And he again insists: "Don't hang on to an old word which is rotten through and through. Have the will to build a new party . . . and all the oppressed will come to you."

Before the enormity of the task not yet begun, and the intellectual confusion in his own ranks, a sharp thought of the precious time foolishly wasted in meetings, greetings, ritual resolutions, wrests a cry from the orator: "Have done with greetings and resolutions! It's time to get down to business. We must proceed to practical sober work!"

An hour later Lenin was compelled to repeat his speech at the previously designated joint session of the Bolsheviks and Mensheviks, where it sounded to a majority of the listeners like something between mockery and delirium. The more condescending shrugged their shoulders: This man evidently fell down from the moon; hardly off the steps of the Finland station after a ten-year absence he starts preaching the seizure of power by the proletariat. The less good-natured among the patriots made references to the sealed train. Stankevich testifies that Lenin's speech greatly delighted his enemies: "A man who talks that kind of stupidity is not dangerous. It's a good thing he has come. Now he is in plain sight. . . . Now he will refute himself."

Nevertheless, with all its boldness of revolutionary grasp, its inflexible determination to break even with his former longtime colleagues and comrades-in-arms, if they proved unable to march with the revolution, the speech of Lenin—every part balanced against the rest—was filled with deep realism and an infallible feeling for the masses. Exactly for this reason, it seemed to the democrats a fantastic skimming of the surface.

The Bolsheviks are a tiny minority in the Soviet, and Lenin dreams of seizing the power; isn't that pure adventurism? There was not a shadow of adventurism in Lenin's statement of the problem. He did not for a moment close his eyes to the existence of "honest" defensist moods in the broad masses. He did not intend either to lose himself in the masses or to act behind their backs. "We are not charlatans"—he throws this in the eyes of future objections and accusations—"we must base ourselves only upon the consciousness of the masses. Even if it is necessary to remain in a minority—so be it. It is a good thing to give up for a time the position of leadership; we must not be afraid to remain in the minority." Do not fear to remain in a minority—even a minority of one, like Liebknecht's one against a hundred and ten—such was the leit-motif of his speech.

"The real government is the Soviet of workers' deputies. . . . In the Soviet our party is the minority. . . . What can we do? All we can do is to explain patiently, insistently, systematically the error of their tactics. So long as we are in the minority, we will carry on the work of criticism, in order to free the masses from deceit. We do not want the masses to believe us just on our say so; we are not charlatans. We want the masses to be freed by experience from their mistakes." Don't be afraid to remain in the minority! Not forever, but for a time. The hour of Bolshevism will strike. "Our line will prove right. . . . All the oppressed will come to us, because the war will bring them to us. They have no other way out."

"At the joint conference," relates Sukhanov, "Lenin was the living incarnation of a split. . . . I remember Bogdanov (a prominent Menshevik) sitting two steps away from the orator's tribune. 'Why, that is raving,' he interrupted Lenin, 'that is the raving of a lunatic. . . . You ought to be ashamed to applaud such spouting,' he cried, turning to the audience, white in the face with rage and scorn. 'You disgrace yourselves, Marxists!'"

A former member of the Bolshevik Central Committee, Goldenberg, at that time a non-party man, appraised Lenin's theses in these withering words: "For many years the place of Bakunin has remained vacant in the Russian revolution, now it is occupied by Lenin."

"His program at that time was met not so much with indignation," relates the Social Revolutionary Zenzinov, "as with ridicule. It seemed to everybody so absurd and fantastic."

On the evening of the same day, in the *couloirs* of the Contact Commission, two socialists were talking with Miliukov, and the conversation touched on Lenin. Skobelev estimated him as "a man completely played out, standing apart from the movement." Sukhanov was of the same mind, and added that "Lenin is to such a degree inacceptable to everybody that he is no longer dangerous even to my companion Miliukov here."

The distribution of rôles in this conversation, however, was exactly according to Lenin's formula: the socialists were protecting the peace of mind of the liberal from the trouble which Bolshevism might cause him.

Rumors even arrived in the ears of the British ambassador that Lenin had been declared a bad Marxist. "Among the newly arrived anarchists," wrote Buchanan, "was Lenin, who came through in a sealed train from Germany. He made his first public appearance at a meeting of the Social Democratic Party and was badly received."

The most condescending of all toward Lenin in those days was no other than Kerensky, who in a circle of members of the Provisional Government unexpectedly stated that he must go to see Lenin, and explained in answer to their bewildered questions: "Well, he is living in a completely isolated atmosphere, he knows nothing, sees everything through the glasses of his fanaticism. There is no one around him who might help him orient himself a little in what is going on." Thus testifies Nabokov. But Kerensky never found the time to orient Lenin in what was going on.

The April theses of Lenin not only evoked the bewildered indignation of his opponents and enemies. They repelled a number of old Bolsheviks into the Menshevik camp—or into that intermediate group which found shelter around Gorky's paper. This leakage had no serious political significance. Infinitely more important was the impression which Lenin's position made on the whole leading group of the party. "In the first days after his arrival," writes Sukhanov, "his complete isolation among all his conscious party comrades cannot be doubted in the least." "Even his party comrades, the Bolsheviks," confirms the Social Revolutionary Zenzinov, "at that time turned away in embarrassment from him." The authors of these comments were meeting the leading Bolsheviks every day in the Executive Committee, and had first-hand evidence of what they said.

But there is no lack of similar testimony from among the ranks of the Bolsheviks. "When the theses of Lenin appeared," wrote Tsikhon, softening the colors as much as possible, as do a majority of the old Bolsheviks when they stumble on the February revolution, "there was felt in our party a certain wavering. Many of the comrades argued that Lenin showed a syndicalist deviation, that he was out of touch with Russia, that he was not taking into consideration the given moment," etc. One of the prominent Bolshevik leaders in the provinces, Lebedev, writes: "On Lenin's arrival in Russia, his agitation, at first not wholly intelligible to us Bolsheviks, but regarded as Utopian and explainable by his long removal from Russian life, was gradually absorbed by us, and entered, as you might say, into our flesh and blood."

Zalezhski, a member of the Petrograd Committee and one of the organizers of the welcome to Lenin, expresses it more frankly: "Lenin's theses produced the impression of an exploding bomb." Zalezhski fully confirms the complete isolation of Lenin after that so warm and impressive welcome. "On that day (April 4) Comrade Lenin could not find open sympathizers even in our own ranks."

Still more important, however, is the evidence of *Pravda*. On April 8, after the publication of the theses—when time enough had passed to make explanations and reach a mutual understanding—the editors of *Pravda* wrote: "As for the general scheme of Comrade Lenin, it seems to us unacceptable in that it starts from the assumption that the bourgeois-democratic revolution is ended, and counts upon an immediate transformation of this revolution into a socialist revolution." The central organ of the party thus openly announced before the working class and its enemies a split with the generally recognized leader of the party upon the central question of the revolution for which the Bolshevik ranks had been getting ready during a long period of years. That alone is sufficient to show the depth of the April crisis in the party, due to the clash of two irreconcilable lines of thought and action. Until it surmounted this crisis the revolution could not go forward.

313

Chapter XVI

REARMING THE PARTY

HOW explain Lenin's extraordinary isolation at the beginning of April? How in general could such a situation arise, and how was the rearming of the Bolshevik staff accomplished?

From the year 1905 the Bolshevik Party had waged a struggle against the autocracy under the slogan "Democratic Dictatorship of the Proletariat and the Peasantry." This slogan, as well as its theoretical background, derives from Lenin. In opposition to the Mensheviks, whose theoretician, Plekhanov, stubbornly opposed the "mistaken idea of the possibility of accomplishing a bourgeois revolution without the bourgeoisie," Lenin considered that the Russian bourgeoisie was already incapable of leading its own revolution. Only the proletariat and peasantry in close union could carry through a democratic revolution against the monarchy and the landlords. The victory of this union, according to Lenin, should inaugurate a democratic dictatorship, which was not only not identical with the dictatorship of the proletariat, but was in sharp contrast to it, for its problem was not the creation of a socialist society, nor even the creation of forms of transition to such a society, but merely a ruthless cleansing of the Augean stables of medievalism. The goal of the revolutionary struggle was fully described in three militant slogans: Democratic Republic, Confiscation of the Landed Estates, Eight-Hour Working Day—colloquially called the three whales of Bolshevism, by analogy with those whales upon which according to an old popular fable the earth reposes.

The question of the possibility of a democratic dictatorship of the proletariat and peasantry hinged upon the question of the ability of the peasantry to accomplish their own revolution —that is, to put forward a new government capable of liquidating the monarchy and the landed nobility. To be sure, the slogan of democratic dictatorship assumed also a participation in the revolutionary government of workers' representatives. But this participation was limited in advance by the rôle attributed to the proletariat as ally on the left in solving the problems of the peasant revolution. The popular and even officially recognized idea of the *hegemony* of the proletariat in the democratic revolution could not, consequently, mean anything more than that the workers' party would help the peasantry with a political weapon from its arsenal, suggest to them the best means and methods for liquidating the feudal society, and show them how to apply these means and methods. In any case, to speak of the leading rôle of the proletariat in the bourgeois revolution did not at all signify that the proletariat would use the peasant uprising in order with its support to place upon the order of the day its own historic task—that is, the direct transition to a socialist society. The hegemony of the proletariat in the democratic revolution was sharply distinguished from the dictatorship of the proletariat, and polemically contrasted against it. The Bolshevik Party had been educated in these ideas ever since the spring of 1905.

The actual course of the February revolution disrupted this accustomed schema of Bolshevism. It is true that the revolution was accomplished by a union of the workers and peasants. The fact that the peasants functioned chiefly in the guise of soldiers did not alter this. The behavior of the peasant army of tzarism would have had decisive import even if the revolution had developed in peace times. So much the more natural if in war time these millions of armed men at first completely concealed the peasantry. After the victory of the insurrection the workers and soldiers were bosses of the situation. In that sense it would seem possible to say that a democratic dictatorship of the workers and peasants had been established. But as a matter of fact, the February overturn led to a bourgeois government, in which the power of the possessing classes was limited by the not yet fully realized sovereignty of the workers' and soldiers' soviets. All the cards were mixed. Instead of a revolutionary dictatorship—*i.e.* the most concentrated power—there was established the flabby régime of the dual power, in which the feeble energy of the ruling classes was wasted in overcoming inner conflicts. Nobody had foreseen this régime. And indeed one cannot demand from a prognosis that it indicate not only the fundamental tendencies of development, but also accidental conjunctions. "Who ever made a great revolution knowing beforehand how to carry it through to the end?" asked Lenin later. "Where could you get such knowledge? It is not to be found in books. There are no such books. Our decisions could only be born out of the experience of the masses."

But human thought is conservative, and the thought of revolutionists is at times especially so. The Bolshevik staff in Russia continued to stand by the old formula and regarded the February revolution, notwithstanding its obvious establishment of two incompatible régimes, merely as the first stage of a bourgeois revolution. At the end of March Rykov sent to *Pravda* from Siberia, in the name of the Social Democrats, a telegram of greeting to the victory of the "national revolution," whose problem was "the winning of political liberty." All the leading Bolsheviks—not one exception is known to us—considered that the democratic dictatorship still lay in the future. After the Provisional Government of the bourgeoisie "exhausts itself," then a democratic dictatorship of the workers and peasants will be established as the forerunner of the bourgeois parliamentary régime. This was a completely erroneous perspective. The régime which issued from the February revolution not only was not preparing a democratic dictatorship, but was a living and exhaustive proof of the fact that such a dictatorship was impossible. That the compromising democracy did not *accidentally*, through the light-mindedness of Kerensky and the limited intelligence of Cheidze, hand over the power to the liberals, is demonstrated by the fact that throughout the eight months following, it struggled with all its force to preserve the bourgeois government. It repressed the workers, peasants and soldiers, and on the 25th of October it fell fighting at its post as ally and defender of the bourgeoisie. Moreover it was clear enough from the beginning, when the democracy, with gigantic tasks before it and the unlimited support of the masses, voluntarily renounced the power, that this was not due to political principles or prejudices, but to the hopelessness of the situation of the petty bourgeoisie in the capitalist society—especially in a period of war and revolution, when the fundamental life-problems of countries, peoples and classes are under decision. In handing Miliukov the scepter, the petty bourgeoisie said: "No, I am not equal to these tasks."

The peasantry, lifting on its shoulders the conciliatory democracy, contains in itself in a rudimentary form all the classes of bourgeois society. Along with the petty bourgeoisie of the cities—which in Russia, however, never played a serious rôle —it constitutes that protoplasm out of which new classes have been differentiated in the past, and continue to be differentiated in the present. The peasantry always has two faces, one turned towards the proletariat, the other toward the bourgeoisie. But the intermediary, compromising position of "peasant" parties like the Social Revolutionaries, can be maintained only in conditions of comparative political stagnation; in a revolutionary epoch the moment inevitably comes when the petty bourgeoisie is compelled to choose. The Social Revolutionaries and Mensheviks made their choice from the first moment. They destroyed the "democratic dictatorship" in embryo, in order to prevent it from becoming a bridge to the dictatorship of the proletariat. But they thus opened a road to the latter—only a different road, not through them, but against them.

The further development of the revolution must obviously proceed from new facts, not old schemas. Through their representatives the masses were drawn, partly against their will, partly without their consciousness, into the mechanics of the two-power régime. They now had to pass through this in order to learn by experience that it could not give them either peace or land. To recoil from the two-power régime henceforward meant for the masses to break with the Social Revolutionaries and the Mensheviks. But it is quite evident that a political turning of the workers and soldiers toward the Bolsheviks, having knocked over the whole two-power construction, could now no longer mean anything but the establishment of a dictatorship of the proletariat resting upon a union of the workers and peasants. In case the popular mass had been defeated, only a military dictatorship of capital could have risen on the ruins of the Bolshevik Party. "The democratic dictatorship" was impossible in either case. In looking toward it, the Bolsheviks had actually to turn their faces toward a phantom of the past. It was in this position that Lenin found them when he arrived with his inflexible determination to bring the party out on a new road.

Lenin himself, to be sure, did not replace the formula of democratic dictatorship by any other formula, even conditional or hypothetical, until the very beginning of the February revolution. Was he correct in this? We think not. What happened in the party after the revolution revealed all too alarmingly the belatedness of that rearming—which moreover in the given situation no one but Lenin himself could have carried through. He had prepared himself for that. He had heated his steel white hot and retempered it in the fires of the war. In his eyes the general prospect of the historic process had changed; the shock of the war had sharply advanced the possible date of a socialist revolution in the West. While remaining for Lenin still democratic, the Russian revolution was to give the stimulus to a socialist revolution in Europe, which should then drag belated Russia into its whirlpool. Such was Lenin's general conception when he left Zurich. The letter to the Swiss workers which we have already quoted says: "Russia is a peasant country, one of the most backward of European countries. Here socialism cannot immediately conquer, but the peasant character of the country, with enormous tracts of land remaining intact in the hands of the nobility, can, on the basis of the experience of 1905, give enormous scope to a bourgeois-democratic revolution in Russia, and make our revolution a prologue to the world-wide socialist revolution, a step leading to it." In this sense Lenin now first wrote that the Russian proletariat *will begin* the socialist revolution.

Such was the connecting link between the old position of Bolshevism, which limited the revolution to democratic aims, and the new position which Lenin first presented to the party in his theses of April 4. This new prospect of an immediate tran-

sition to the dictatorship of the proletariat seemed completely
unexpected, contradictory to tradition, and indeed simply would
not fit into the mind. Here it is necessary to remember that up
to the outbreak of the February revolution and for a time after,
Trotskyism did not mean the idea that it was impossible to build
a socialist society within the national boundaries of Russia
(which "possibility" was never expressed by anybody up to 1924
and hardly came into anybody's head). Trotskyism meant the
idea that the Russian proletariat might win the power in advance of the Western proletariat, and that in that case it could
not confine itself within the limits of a democratic dictatorship,
but would be compelled to undertake the initial socialist measures. It is not surprising, then, that the April theses of Lenin
were condemned as Trotskyist.

The counter-arguments of the old Bolsheviks developed
along several lines. The principal quarrel was about the question whether the bourgeois-democratic revolution was finished.
Inasmuch as the agrarian revolution was not yet complete, the
opponents of Lenin justly asserted that the democratic revolution as a whole was not finished, and hence, they concluded,
there is no place for a dictatorship of the proletariat, even
though the social conditions of Russia render it possible in general at a more or less proximate date. It was in this way that
the editors of *Pravda* posed the question in the passage we have
already cited. Later on, in the April conference, Kamenev repeated this: "Lenin is wrong when he says that the bourgeois
democratic revolution is finished. . . . The classical relics of
feudalism, the landed estates, are not yet liquidated. . . . The
state is not transformed into a democratic society. . . . It is
early to say that the bourgeois democracy has exhausted all its
possibilities."

"The democratic dictatorship is our foundation stone"—
this was Tomsky's argument—"We ought to organize the power
of the proletariat and the peasants, and we ought to distinguish
this from the Commune, since that means the power of the
proletariat alone."

Rykov seconded him: "Gigantic revolutionary tasks stand

before us, but the fulfillment of these tasks does not carry us beyond the framework of the bourgeois régime."

Lenin saw, of course, as clearly as his opponents that the democratic revolution was not finished, that, on the contrary, without really beginning it had already begun to drop into the past. But from this very fact it resulted that only the rulership of a new class could carry it through to the end, and that this could be achieved no otherwise but by drawing the masses out from under the influence of the Mensheviks and Social Revolutionaries—that is to say, from the indirect influence of the liberal bourgeoisie. The connection of those parties with the workers, and especially with the soldiers, was based on the idea of defense—"defense of the country" or "defense of the revolution." Lenin, therefore, demanded an irreconcilable opposition to all shades of social patriotism. Separate the party from the backward masses, in order afterwards to free those masses from their backwardness. "We must abandon the old Bolshevism," he kept repeating. "We must make a sharp division between the line of the petty bourgeoisie and the wage worker."

At a superficial glance it might seem that the age-old enemies had exchanged weapons. The Mensheviks and Social Revolutionaries now represented a majority of the workers and soldiers, and seemed to have realized that political union of the proletariat and peasantry which Bolshevism had always been advocating against the Mensheviks. Lenin was demanding that the proletarian vanguard break away from this union. In reality, however, both sides remained true to themselves. The Mensheviks, as always, saw their mission in supporting the liberal bourgeoisie. Their union with the Social Revolutionaries was only a means of broadening and strengthening this support. On the contrary, the break of the proletarian vanguard with the petty bourgeois bloc meant the preparation of a union of the workers and peasants under the leadership of the Bolshevik Party—that is, the dictatorship of the proletariat.

Another argument against Lenin was derived from the backwardness of Russia. A government of the working class inevitably means a transition to socialism, but economically and culturally Russia is not ripe for this. We must carry through the democratic revolution. Only a socialist revolution in the West can justify a dictatorship of the proletariat here. This was Rykov's argument at the April conference. That the cultural-economic condition of Russia in itself was inadequate for the construction of a socialist society was mere a-b-c to Lenin. But societies are not so rational in building that the dates for proletarian dictatorships arrive exactly at that moment when the economic and cultural conditions are ripe for socialism. If humanity evolved as systematically as that, there would be no need for dictatorship, nor indeed for revolutions in general. Living historic societies are inharmonious through and through, and the more so the more delayed their development. The fact that in a backward country like Russia the bourgeoisie had decayed before the complete victory of the bourgeois régime, and that there was nobody but the proletariat to replace it in the position of national leadership, was an expression of this inharmony. The economic backwardness of Russia does not relieve the working class of the obligation to fulfill its allotted task, but merely surrounds this task with extraordinary difficulties. To Rykov, who kept repeating that socialism must come from countries with a more developed industry, Lenin gave a simple but sufficient answer: "You can't say who will begin and who finish."

*

In 1921, when the party—still far from bureaucratic ossification —was appraising its past as freely as it prepared its future, one of the older Bolsheviks, Olminsky, who had played a leading part in the party press in all stages of its development, raised the question: How explain the fact that the February revolution found the party on the opportunist path, and what permittted it thereafter to turn so sharply to the path of October? The author correctly found the source of the party's going astray in March in the fact that it held on too long to the "democratic dictatorship." "The coming revolution must be only a bourgeois revolution. . . . That was," says Olminsky, "an obligatory premise for every member of the party, the official opinion of the party, its continual and unchanging slogan right up to the February revolution of 1917, and even some time after." In illustration Olminsky might have referred to the fact that *Pravda,* even before Stalin and Kamenev—that is under the "left" editorship, which included Olminsky himself—declared on March 7, as though mentioning something that goes without saying: "Of course there is no question among us of the downfall of the rule of capital, but only of the downfall of the rule of autocracy and feudalism." From this too short aim resulted the March captivity of the party to the bourgeois democracy. "Whence then the October revolution?" asks the same author. "How did it happen that the party, from its leaders to its rank-and-file members, so suddenly renounced everything that it had regarded as fixed truth for almost two decades?"

Sukhanov, speaking as an enemy, raises the question differently. "How did Lenin manage to outwit and conquer his Bolsheviks?" It is true that Lenin's victory within the party was not only complete, but was won in a very short time. The party enemies indulged on this theme in a good deal of irony as to the personal régime in the Bolshevik Party. Sukhanov himself answers the question he had raised wholly in the heroic spirit: "Lenin, the genius, was a historic authority—that is one side of it. The other is that there was nobody and nothing in the party besides Lenin. A few great generals without Lenin amounted to as little as a few gigantic planets without the sun (I here omit Trotsky who was not then within the ranks of the Order)." These curious lines attempt to explain the influence of Lenin by his influentialness, as the capacity of opium to produce sleep is explained by its soporific powers. Such an explanation does not, of course, get us forward very far.

Lenin's actual influence in the party was indubitably very great, but it was by no means unlimited. It was still subject to appeal even later, after October, when his authority had grown extraordinarily because the party had measured his power with the yardstick of world events. So much the more insufficient are these mere personal references to his authority in

April 1917, when the whole ruling group of the party had already taken up a position contradictory to that of Lenin.

Olminsky comes much nearer to answering the question when he argues that, in spite of its formula of bourgeois democratic revolution, the party had in its whole policy toward the bourgeoisie and the democracy, been for a long time actually preparing to lead the proletariat in a direct struggle for power. "We (or at least many of us)"—says Olminsky—"were unconsciously steering a course toward proletarian revolution, although thinking we were steering a course toward a bourgeois-democratic revolution. In other words we were preparing the October revolution while thinking we were preparing the February." An extremely valuable generalization, and at the same time the testimony of an irreproachable witness!

In the theoretical education of the revolutionary party there had been an element of contradiction, which had found its expression in the equivocal formula "democratic dictatorship" of the proletariat and peasantry. Speaking on the report of Lenin to the conference, a woman delegate expressed the thought of Olminsky still more simply: "The prognosis made by the Bolsheviks proved wrong, but their tactics were right."

In his April theses which seemed so paradoxical, Lenin was relying against the old formula upon the living tradition of the party—its irreconcilable attitude to the ruling classes and its hostility to all half-way measures—whereas the "old Bolsheviks" were opposing a still fresh although already outdated memory to the concrete development of the class struggle. But Lenin had a too strong support prepared by the whole historic struggle of the Bolsheviks against the Mensheviks. Here it is suitable to remember that the official Social Democratic program was still at that time common to the Bolsheviks and the Mensheviks, that the practical tasks of the democratic revolution looked the same on paper to both parties. But they were by no means so in action. The worker-Bolsheviks immediately after the revolution took the initiative in the struggle for the eight-hour day; the Mensheviks declared this demand untimely. The Bolsheviks took the lead in arresting the tzarist officials; the Mensheviks opposed "excesses." The Bolsheviks energetically undertook the

creation of a workers' militia; the Mensheviks delayed the arming of the workers, not wishing to quarrel with the bourgeoisie.
Although not yet overstepping the bounds of bourgeois democracy, the Bolsheviks acted, or strove to act—however confused
by their leadership—like uncompromising revolutionists. The
Mensheviks sacrificed their democratic program at every step
in the interests of a coalition with the liberals. In the complete
absence of democratic allies, Kamenev and Stalin inevitably hung
in the air.

This April conflict between Lenin and the general staff of
the party was not the only one of its kind. Throughout the
whole history of Bolshevism, with the exception of some episodes
which in essence only confirm the rule, all the leaders of the
party at all the most important moments stood to the *right* of
Lenin. This was not an accident. Lenin became the unqualified
leader of the most revolutionary party in the world's history,
because his thought and will were really equal to the demands
of the gigantic revolutionary possibilities of the country and the
epoch. Others fell short by an inch or two, and often more.

Almost the whole ruling circle of the Bolshevik Party for
months and even years before the revolution had been outside
the active work. Many had carried away into jails and exile
the oppressive recollections of the first months of the war, and
had lived through the wreck of the International in solitude
or in small groups. Although in the ranks of the party they
had manifested a sufficient receptivity to those thoughts of
revolution which had attracted them to Bolshevism, in isolation
they were not strong enough to resist the pressure of the surrounding milieu and make an independent Marxist appraisal
of events. The enormous shift of opinion in the masses during
the two and a half years of war had remained almost outside
their field of vision. Nevertheless the revolution had not only
dragged them out of their isolation, but immediately placed
them, thanks to their prestige, in a commanding position in the
party. They were often much closer in mood to the "Zimmerwald" intelligentsia than to the revolutionary workers in
the factories.

The "Old Bolsheviks"—who pretentiously emphasized this

appellation in April 1917—were condemned to defeat because
they were defending exactly that element of the party tradition
which had not passed the historic test. "I belong to the old
Bolshevik Leninists," said Kalinin, for instance, at the Petrograd conference of April 14, "and I consider that the old Leninism has not by any means proved good-for-nothing in the
present peculiar moment, and I am astonished at the declaration
of Comrade Lenin that the old Bolsheviks have become an obstacle at the present moment." Lenin had to listen to many
such offended voices in those days. However, in breaking with
the traditional formula of the party, Lenin did not in the least
cease to be a "Leninist." He threw off the worn-out shell of
Bolshevism in order to summon its nucleus to a new life.

Against the old Bolsheviks Lenin found support in another
layer of the party, already tempered, but more fresh and more
closely united with the masses. In the February revolution, as
we know, the worker-Bolsheviks played the decisive rôle. They
thought it self-evident that that class which had won the victory
should seize the power. These same workers protested stormily
against the course of Kamenev and Stalin, and the Vyborg district even threatened the "leaders" with expulsion from the
party. The same thing was to be observed in the provinces.
Almost everywhere there were left Bolsheviks accused of maxi-
malism, even of anarchism. These worker-revolutionists only
lacked the theoretical resources to defend their position. But
they were ready to respond to the first clear call. It was on
this stratum of workers, decisively risen to their feet during the
upward years of 1912-14, that Lenin was now banking. Already
at the beginning of the war, when the government dealt the
party a heavy blow by arresting the Bolshevik faction of the
Duma, Lenin, speaking of the further revolutionary work, had
demanded the education by the party, of "thousands of class-
conscious workers, from among whom in spite of all difficulties a
new staff of leaders will arise."

Although separated from these workers by two war fronts,
and almost without communication, Lenin had never lost touch
with them. "Let the war, jails, Siberia, hard labor, shatter

them twice, ten times, you cannot destroy that stratum. It is alive. It is imbued with revolutionism and anti-chauvinism."

In his mind Lenin had been living through the events along with these worker-Bolsheviks, making with them the necessary inferences—only broader and more boldly than they. In his struggle with the indecisiveness of the staff and the broad officer layer of the party, Lenin confidently relied on its under-officer layer which better reflected the rank-and-file worker-Bolshevik.

The temporary strength of the social-patriots, and the hidden weakness of the opportunist wing of the Bolsheviks, lay in the fact that the former were basing themselves on the temporary prejudices and illusions of the masses, and the latter were conforming themselves to these temporary prejudices and illusions. The chief strength of Lenin lay in his understanding the inner logic of the movement, and guiding his policy by it. He did not impose his plan on the masses; he helped the masses to recognize and realize their own plan. When Lenin reduced all the problems of the revolution to one—"patiently explain" —that meant that it was necessary to bring the consciousness of the masses into correspondence with that situation into which the historic process had driven them. The worker or the soldier, disappointed with the policy of the Compromisers, had to be brought over to the position of Lenin and not left lingering in the intermediate stage of Kamenev and Stalin.

Once the Leninist formulas were issued, they shed a new light for the Bolsheviks upon the experience of the past months and of every new day. In the broad party mass a quick differentiation took place—leftward and leftward, toward the theses of Lenin. "District after district adhered to them," says Zalezhsky, "and by the time of the all-Russian party conference on April 24, the Petersburg organization as a whole was in favor of the theses."

The struggle for the rearming of the Bolshevik ranks, begun on the evening of April 3, was essentially finished by the end of the month.[1] The party conference, which met in Petrograd

[1] On the very day when Lenin arrived in Petrograd, on the other side of the Atlantic Ocean, at Halifax, the British Naval Police removed from the Norwegian steamer *Christianiafjord* five emigrants returning from New York to Russia: Trotsky,

April 24-29, cast the balance of March, a month of opportunist vacillations, and of April, a month of sharp crisis. By that time the party had grown greatly, both quantitatively and in a political sense. The 149 delegates represented 79,000 party members, of whom 15,000 lived in Petrograd. For a party that had been illegal yesterday, and was today anti-patriotic, that was an impressive number, and Lenin several times called attention to it with satisfaction. The political physiognomy of the conference was immediately defined by the election of a præsidium of five members. It did not include either Kamenev or Stalin, the chief culprits of the March misfortune.

Although for the party as a whole the debated questions were already firmly decided, many of the leaders, still clinging to the past, continued at this conference in opposition, or semi-opposition, to Lenin. Stalin remained silent and waited. Dzerzhinsky, in the name of "many," who "did not agree in principle with the theses of the spokesman," demanded that a dissenting report be heard from "the comrades who have along with us experienced the revolution in a practical way." This was an evident thrust at the emigrant character of the Leninist theses. Kamenev did actually make a dissenting report in defense of the bourgeois democratic dictatorship. Rykov, Tomsky, Kalinin, tried to stand more or less by their March positions. Kalinin continued to advocate a coalition with the Mensheviks in the interests of the struggle with liberalism. The prominent Moscow party worker, Smidovich, hotly complained in his speech that "every time we speak they raise against us a certain bogey in the form of the theses of Comrade Lenin." Earlier,

---

Chudnovsky, Melnichansky, Mukhin, Fishelev and Romanchenko. These men succeeded in reaching Petrograd only on the 4th of May, when the political rearming of the Bolshevik party was, at least in outline, completed. We do not, therefore, consider it permissible to introduce into the text of our recital an exposition of the views of the revolution expounded by Trotsky in a Russian daily paper issued in New York. Since however an acquaintance with these views will promote the reader's understanding of the further groupings of the party, and especially the intellectual struggle on the eve of October, we consider it expedient to place this information at the end of the book, in Appendix No. 2. The reader who does not find himself interested in studying the theoretic preparation for the October revolution can tranquilly ignore this Appendix.

when the Moscow members were voting for the resolutions of the Mensheviks, life had been a good deal more peaceful.

As a pupil of Rosa Luxemburg, Dzerzhinsky spoke against the right of nations to self-determination, accusing Lenin of protecting separatist tendencies which weakened the Russian proletariat. To Lenin's answering accusation of giving support to Great-Russian chauvinism, Dzerzhinsky answered: "I can reproach him (Lenin) with standing at the point of view of the Polish, Ukrainian and other chauvinists." This dialogue is not without a political piquancy: the Great-Russian Lenin accuses the Pole, Dzerzhinsky, of Great-Russian chauvinism directed against the Poles, and is accused by the latter of Polish chauvinism. Politically Lenin was in the right in this quarrel. His policy on nationalities entered as a most important constitutent element into the October revolution.

The opposition was obviously on the wane. It did not muster more than seven votes on the questions under debate. There was, however, one curious and sharp exception, touching the international relations of the party. At the very end of the conference, in the evening session of April 29, Zinoviev introduced in the name of his commission a resolution: "To take part in the international conference of Zimmerwaldists designated for May 18 (at Stockholm)." The report says: "Adopted by all votes against one." That one was Lenin. He demanded a break with Zimmerwald, where the majority had been decisively with the German Independents and neutral pacifists of the type of the Swiss, Grimm. But for the Russian circles of the party, Zimmerwald had during the war become almost identified with Bolshevism. The delegates were not yet ready to give up the name of Social Democrat or break with Zimmerwald, which remained moreover in their eyes a bond with the masses of the Second International.

Lenin tried at least to limit participation in the coming conference to an attendance for informational purposes. Zinoviev spoke against him. Lenin's proposal was rejected. He then voted against the resolution as a whole. Nobody supported him. That was the last splash of the "March" tendency —a clinging to yesterday's position, a fear of "isolation." The

Stockholm Conference, however, was never held—a result of those same inner diseases of Zimmerwald, which had led Lenin to break with it. His unanimously rejected policy of boycott was thus realized in fact.

The abruptness of the turn in the policy of the party was obvious to all. Schmidt, a worker-Bolshevik, afterward People's Commissar of Labor, said at the April conference: "Lenin gave a different direction to the character of the work." According to Raskolnikov,—writing, to be sure, several years later, —Lenin in April 1917 "carried out an October revolution in the consciousness of the party leaders. . . . The tactic of our party is not a single straight line, but makes after the arrival of Lenin a sharp jump to the left." The old Bolshevik, Ludmila Stahl, more directly and also more accurately appraised the change: "All the comrades before the arrival of Lenin were wandering in the dark," she said, at the city conference on the 14th of April. "We knew only the formulas of 1905. Seeing the independent creative work of the people, we could not teach them. . . . Our comrades could only limit themselves to getting ready for the Constituent Assembly by parliamentary means, and took no account of the possibility of going farther. In accepting the slogans of Lenin we are now doing what life itself suggests to us. We need not fear the Commune, and say that we already have a workers' government; the Commune of Paris was not only a workers', but also a petty bourgeois government." It is possible to agree with Sukhanov that the rearming of the army "was the chief and fundamental victory of Lenin, completed by the first days of May." Sukhanov, it is true, thought that Lenin in this operation substituted an anarchist for a Marxist weapon.

It remains to ask—and this is no unimportant question, although easier to ask than answer: How would the revolution have developed if Lenin had not reached Russia in April 1917? If our exposition demonstrates and proves anything at all, we hope it proves that Lenin was not a demiurge of the revolutionary process, that he merely entered into a chain of objective historic forces. But he was a great link in that chain. The dictatorship of the proletariat was to be inferred from the whole

329

situation, but it had still to be established. It could not be
established without a party. The party could fulfill its mission
only after understanding it. For that Lenin was needed.
Until his arrival, not one of the Bolshevik leaders dared to
make a diagnosis of the revolution. The leadership of Kamenev
and Stalin was tossed by the course of events to the right, to
the Social Patriots: between Lenin and Menshevism the revolution left no place for intermediate positions. Inner struggle
in the Bolshevik Party was absolutely unavoidable. Lenin's
arrival merely hastened the process. His personal influence
shortened the crisis. Is it possible, however, to say confidently
that the party without him would have found its road? We
would by no means make bold to say that. The factor of
time is decisive here, and it is difficult in retrospect to tell
time historically. Dialectic materialism at any rate has nothing
in common with fatalism. Without Lenin the crisis, which
the opportunist leadership was inevitably bound to produce,
would have assumed an extraordinarily sharp and protracted
character. The conditions of war and revolution, however,
would not allow the party a long period for fulfilling its mission. Thus it is by no means excluded that a disoriented and
split party might have let slip the revolutionary opportunity
for many years. The rôle of personality arises before us here
on a truly gigantic scale. It is necessary only to understand
that rôle correctly, taking personality as a link in the historic
chain.

The "sudden" arrival of Lenin from abroad after a long
absence, the furious cry raised by the press around his name,
his clash with all the leaders of his own party and his quick
victory over them—in a word, the external envelope of circumstance—make easy in this case a mechanical contrasting of
the person, the hero, the genius, against the objective conditions,
the mass, the party. In reality, such a contrast is completely
one-sided. Lenin was not an accidental element in the historic
development, but a product of the whole past of Russian history.
He was embedded in it with deepest roots. Along with the
vanguard of the workers, he had lived through their struggle
in the course of the preceding quarter century. The "accident"

was not his interference in the events, but rather that little straw with which Lloyd George tried to block his path. Lenin did not oppose the party from outside, but was himself its most complete expression. In educating it he had educated himself in it. His divergence from the ruling circles of the Bolsheviks meant the struggle of the future of the party against its past. If Lenin had not been artificially separated from the party by the conditions of emigration and war, the external mechanics of the crisis would not have been so dramatic, and would not have overshadowed to such a degree the inner continuity of the party development. From the extraordinary significance which Lenin's arrival received, it should only be inferred that leaders are not accidentally created, that they are gradually chosen out and trained up in the course of decades, that they cannot be capriciously replaced, that their mechanical exclusion from the struggle gives the party a living wound, and in many cases may paralyze it for a long period.

331

Chapter XVII

THE "APRIL DAYS"

ON the 23rd of March the United States entered the war. On that day Petrograd was burying the victims of the February revolution. The funeral procession—in its mood a procession triumphant with the joy of life—was a mighty concluding chord in the symphony of the five days. Everybody went to the funeral: both those who had fought side by side with the victims, and those who had held them back from battle, very likely also those who killed them— and above all, those who had stood aside from the fighting. Along with workers, soldiers and the small city people here were students, ministers, ambassadors, the solid bourgeois, journalists, orators, leaders of all the parties. The red coffins carried on the shoulders of workers and soldiers streamed in from the workers' districts to Mars Field. When the coffins were lowered into the grave there sounded from Peter and Paul fortress the first funeral salute, startling the innumerable masses of the people. That cannon had a new sound: our cannon, our salute. The Vyborg section carried fifty-one red coffins. That was only a part of the victims it was proud of. In the procession of the Vyborg workers, the most compact of all, numerous Bolshevik banners were to be seen, but they floated peacefully beside other banners. On Mars Field itself there stood only the members of the government, of the Soviet, and the State Duma—already dead but stubbornly evading its own funeral. All day long no less than 800,000 people filed past the grave with bands and banners. And although, according to preliminary reckonings by the highest military authorities, a human mass of that size could not possibly pass a given point without the most appalling chaos and fatal whirlpools, nevertheless the demonstration was carried out in complete order— a thing to be observed generally in revolutionary processions,

332

dominated as they are by a satisfying consciousness of a great deed achieved, combined with a hope that everything will grow better and better in the future. It was only this feeling that kept order, for organization was still weak, inexperienced and unconfident of itself. The very fact of the funeral was, it would seem, a sufficient refutation of the myth of a bloodless revolution. But nevertheless the mood prevailing at the funeral recreated to some extent the atmosphere of those first days when the legend was born.

Twenty-five days later—during which time the soviets had gained much experience and self-confidence—occurred the May 1 celebration. (May 1 according to the Western calendar— April 18 old style). All the cities of Russia were drowned in meetings and demonstrations. Not only the industrial enterprises, but the state, city and rural public institutions were closed. In Moghilev, the headquarters of the General Staff, the Cavaliers of St. George marched at the head of the procession. The members of the staff—unremoved tzarist generals—marched under May 1 banners. The holiday of proletarian anti-militarism blended with revolution-tinted manifestations of patriotism. The different strata of the population contributed their own quality to the holiday, but all flowed together into a whole, very loosely held together and partly false, but on the whole majestic. In both capitals and in the industrial centers the workers dominated the celebration, and amid them the strong nuclei of Bolshevism stood out distinctly with banners, placards, speeches and shouts. Across the immense façade of the Mariin-sky Palace, the refuge of the Provisional Government, was stretched a bold red streamer with the words: "Long Live the Third International!" The authorities, not yet rid of their administrative shyness, could not make up their mind to remove this disagreeable and alarming streamer. Everybody, it seemed, was celebrating. So far as it could, the army at the front celebrated. News came of meetings, speeches, banners and revolutionary songs in the trenches, and there were responses from the German side.

The war had not yet come to an end; on the contrary it had only widened its circle. A whole continent had recently

—on the very day of the funeral of the martyrs—joined the war and given it a new scope. Yet meanwhile throughout Russia, side by side with soldiers, war-prisoners were taking part in the processions under the same banners, sometimes singing the same song in different languages. In this immeasurable rejoicing, obliterating like a spring flood the delineations of classes, parties and ideas, that common demonstration of Russian soldiers with Austro-German war-prisoners was a vivid hope-giving fact which made it possible to believe that the revolution, in spite of all, did carry within itself the foundation of a better world.

Like the March funeral, the 1st of May celebration passed off without clashes or casualties as an "all-national festival." However, an attentive ear might have caught already among the ranks of the workers and soldiers impatient and even threatening notes. It was becoming harder and harder to live. Prices had risen alarmingly; the workers were demanding a minimum wage; the bosses were resisting; the number of conflicts in the factories was continually growing; the food situation was getting worse; bread rations were being cut down; cereal cards had been introduced; dissatisfaction in the garrison had grown. The district staff, making ready to bridle the soldiers, was removing the more revolutionary units from Petrograd. At a general assembly of the garrison on April 17 the soldiers, sensing these hostile designs, had raised the question of putting a stop to the removal of troops. That demand will continue to arise in the future, taking a more and more decisive form with every new crisis of the revolution. But the root of all evils was the war, of which no end was to be seen. When will the revolution bring peace? What are Kerensky and Tseretelli waiting for? The masses were listening more and more attentively to the Bolsheviks, glancing at them obliquely, waitingly, some with half-hostility, others already with trust. Underneath the triumphal discipline of the demonstration the mood was tense. There was ferment in the masses.

However, nobody—not even the authors of the streamer on the Marinsky Palace—imagined that the very next two or three days would ruthlessly tear off the envelope of national unity from the revolution. The menacing event whose inevitability many foresaw, but which no one expected so soon, was suddenly upon them. The stimulus was given by the foreign policy of the Provisional Government, *i.e.*, the problem of war. No other than Miliukov touched the match to the fuse.

The history of that match and fuse is as follows: On the day of America's entry into the war, the Minister of Foreign Affairs of the Provisional Government, greatly encouraged, developed his program before the journalists: seizure of Constantinople, seizure of Armenia, division of Austria and Turkey, seizure of Northern Persia, and over and above all this, the right of nations to self-determination. "In all his speeches"— thus the historian Miliukov explains Miliukov the minister— "he decisively emphasized the pacifist aims of the war of liberation, but always presented them in close union with the national problems and interests of Russia." This interview disquieted the listeners. "When will the foreign policy of the Provisional Government cleanse itself of hypocrisy?" stormed the Menshevik paper. "Why does not the Provisional Government demand from the Allied governments an open and decisive renunciation of annexations?" What these people considered hypocrisy, was the frank language of the predatory. In a pacifist disguise of such appetites they were quite ready to see a liberation from all hypocrisy. Frightened by the stirring of the democracy, Kerensky hastened to announce through the press bureau: "Miliukov's program is merely his personal opinion." That the author of this personal opinion happened to be the Minister of Foreign Affairs was, if you please, a mere accident.

Tseretelli, who had a talent for solving every question with a commonplace, began to insist on the necessity of a governmental announcement that for Russia the war was exclusively one of defense. The resistance of Miliukov and to some extent of Guchkov was broken, and on March 27 the government gave birth to a declaration to the effect that "the goal of free Russia is not domination over other peoples, nor depriving them of their national heritage, nor violent seizure of alien territory," but "nevertheless complete observance of the obligations undertaken to our Allies." Thus the kings and the prophets of the two-power system proclaimed their intention to enter into the Kingdom of Heaven in union with patricides and adulterers. Those gentlemen, besides everything else that they lacked, lacked a sense of humor. That declaration of March 27 was welcomed not only by the entire Compromisers' press, but even by the *Pravda* of Kamenev and Stalin, which said in its leading editorial four days before Lenin's arrival: "The Provisional Government has clearly and definitely announced before the whole people that the aim of Russia is not the domination of other nations," etc., etc. The English press immediately and with satisfaction interpreted Russia's renunciation of annexations as her renunciation of Constantinople, by no means intending of course to extend this formula of renunciation to herself. The Russian ambassador in London sounded the alarm, and demanded an explanation from Moscow to the effect that "the principle of peace without annexations is to be applied by Russia not unconditionally, but in so far as it does not oppose our vital interests." But that, of course, was exactly the formula of Miliukov: "We promise not to rob anybody whom we don't need to." Paris, in contrast to London, not only supported Miliukov but urged him on, suggesting through Paléologue the necessity of a more vigorous policy toward the Soviet.

The French Premier, Ribot, out of patience with the terrible red tape at Petrograd, asked London and Rome: "Whether they did not consider it necessary to demand of the Provisional Government that they put an end to all equivocation." London answered that it would be wise "to give the French and English socialists, who had been sent to Russia, time to influence their colleagues."

The sending of allied socialists into Russia had been undertaken on the initiative of the Russian Staff—that is, the old tzarist generals. "We counted upon him," wrote Ribot of Albert Thomas, "to give a certain firmness to the decisions of the Provisional Government." Miliukov complained, however, that Thomas associated too closely with the leaders of the Soviet. Ribot answered that Thomas "is sincerely striving" to support the point of view of Miliukov, but nevertheless promised to urge his ambassador to a more active support.

The declaration of March 27, although totally empty, disquieted the Allies, who saw in it a concession to the Soviet. From London came threats of a loss of faith "in the military power of Russia." Paléologue complained of "the timidity and indefiniteness" of the declaration. But that was just what Miliukov needed. In the hope of help from the Allies, Miliukov had embarked on a big game, far exceeding his resources. His fundamental idea was to use the war against the revolution, and the first task upon this road was to demoralize the democracy. But the Compromisers had begun just in the first days of April to reveal an increasing nervousness and fussiness upon questions of foreign policy, for upon these questions the lower classes were unceasingly pressing them. The government needed a loan. But the masses, with all their defensism, were ready to defend a peace loan but not a war loan. It was necessary to give them at least a peep at the prospect of peace.

Developing his policy of salvation by commonplaces, Tseretelli proposed that they demand from the Provisional Government that it despatch a note to the Allies similar to the domestic declaration of March 27. In return for this, the Executive Committee would undertake to carry through the Soviet a vote for the "Liberty Loan." Miliukov agreed to the exchange—the note for the loan—but decided to make a double use of the bargain. Under the guise of interpreting the declaration, his note disavowed it. It urged that the peace-loving phrases of the government should not give anyone "the slightest reason to think that the revolution which had occurred entailed a weakening of the rôle of Russia in the common struggle of the Allies. Quite the contrary—the universal desire to carry the world war through to a decisive victory had only been strengthened." The note further expressed confidence that the victors "will find a means to attain those *guarantees* and *sanctions*, which are necessary for the prevention of new bloody conflicts in the future." That word about "guarantees and sanctions," introduced at the insistence of Thomas, meant nothing less in the thieves' jargon of diplomacy, especially French, than annexations and indemnities. On the day of the May 1 celebration Miliukov telegraphed his note, composed at the dictation of Allied diplomats, to the governments of the Entente. And only after this was it sent to the Executive Committee, and simultaneously to the newspapers. The government had ignored the Contact Commission, and the leaders of the Executive Committee found themselves in the position of everyday citizens. Even had the Compromisers found in the note nothing they had not heard from Miliukov before, they could not help seeing in this a premeditated hostile act. The note disarmed them before the masses, and demanded from them a direct choice between Bolshevism and imperialism. Was not this in fact Miliukov's purpose? Everything points in that direction, and suggests indeed that his design went even farther. Already in March Miliukov had been trying with all his might to resurrect that ill-fated plan for the seizure of the Dardanelles by a Russian raid, and had carried on many conversations with General Alexeiev, urging him to carry out the operation—which would in Miliukov's calculations place the democracy with its protest against annexations before an accomplished fact. Miliukov's note of April 18 was a similar raid upon the ill-defended coastlines of the democracy. The two acts—military and political—supplemented each other, and in case of success would have justified each other. Generally speaking, one does not condemn a victor. But Miliukov was not destined to be a victor. Two to three hundred thousand troops were needed for the raid, and the plan fell through because of a mere detail: the refusal of the soldiers. They agreed to defend the revolution, but not to take the offensive. Miliukov's attempt upon the Dardanelles came to nothing, and that broke down all his further plans. But it must be confessed that they were not badly worked out—provided he won.

On April 17 there took place in Petrograd the patriotic nightmare demonstration of the war invalids. An enormous number of wounded from the hospitals of the capital, legless, armless, bandaged, advanced upon the Tauride Palace. Those who could not walk were carried in automobile trucks. Their banners read: "War to the end." That was a demonstration of

ing that the revolution should not acknowledge that their sacrifice had been in vain. But the Kadet Party stood behind the
demonstration, or rather Miliukov stood behind it, getting ready
his great blow for the following day.

At a special night session of the 19th, the Executive Committee discussed the note sent the day before to the Allied governments. "After the first reading," relates Stankevich, "it was
unanimously and without debate acknowledged by all that this
was not at all what the Committee had expected." But responsibility for the note had been assumed by the government
as a whole, including Kerensky. Consequently, it was necessary first of all to save the government. Tseretelli began to
"decode" the note, which had never been coded, and to discover
in it more and more merits. Skobelev profoundly reasoned that
in general it is impossible to demand "a complete coincidence
of the aims of the democracy with that of the government." The wise men harried themselves until dawn, but
found no solution. They dispersed in the morning only to meet
again after a few hours. Apparently they were counting upon
time to heal all wounds.

In the morning the note appeared in all the papers. *Rech*
commented upon it in a spirit of carefully prepared provocation. The socialist press expressed itself with great excitement.
The Menshevik *Rabochaia Gazeta*, not yet having succeeded like
Tseretelli and Skobelev in freeing itself from the vapors of the
night's indignation, wrote that the Provisional Government had
published "a document which is a mockery of the democracy,"
and demanded from the Soviet decisive measures "to prevent its
disastrous consequences." The growing pressure of the Bolsheviks was very clearly felt in those phrases.

The Executive Committee resumed its sitting, but only in
order once more to convince itself of its incapacity to arrive at
a solution. It resolved to summon a special plenary session of
the Soviet "for purposes of information"—in reality for the
purpose of feeling out the amount of dissatisfaction in the lower
ranks, and to gain time for its own vacillations. In the mean-

time all kinds of contact sessions were suggested with the aim of bringing the whole agitation to nothing.

But amid all this ritual diddling of the double sovereignty, a third power unexpectedly intervened. The masses came out into the streets with arms in their hands. Among the bayonets of the soldiers glimmered the letters on a streamer: "Down with Miliukov!" On other streamers Guchkov figured in the same way. In these indignant processions it was hard to recognize the demonstrators of May 1.

Historians call this movement "spontaneous" in the conditional sense that no party took the initiative in it. The immediate summons to the streets was given by a certain Linde, who therewith inscribed his name in the history of the revolution. "Scholar, mathematician, philosopher," Linde was a non-party man—*for* the revolution with all his heart and earnestly desirous that it should fulfill its promise. Miliukov's note and the comments of *Rech* had aroused him. "Taking counsel with no one," says his biographer, "he acted at once, went straight to the Finland regiment, assembled its committee and proposed that they march immediately as a whole regiment to the Marinsky Palace . . . Linde's proposal was accepted, and at three o'clock in the afternoon a significant demonstration of the Finlanders was marching through the streets of Petrograd with challenging placards." After the Finland regiment came the soldiers of the 180th Reserve, the Moscow regiment, the Pavlovsky, the Keksgolmsky, the sailors of the 2nd Baltic fleet—25,000 or 30,000 men in all, and all armed. The commotion spread to the workers' district; work stopped and whole factories came out into the streets after the soldiers.

"The majority of the soldiers did not know why they had come," affirms Miliukov, as though he had asked them. "Besides the troops, boy workers took part in the demonstration, loudly(!) proclaiming that they were paid ten to fifteen roubles for doing it." The source of this money is also clear: "The idea of removing the two ministers (Miliukov and Guchkov) was directly inspired from Germany." Miliukov offered this profound explanation not in the heat of the April struggle, but three years after the October events had abundantly demonstrated to him that nobody had to pay a high wage for the people's hatred of Miliukov.

The unexpected sharpness of the April demonstration is explained by the directness of the mass reaction to deceit from above. "Until the government achieves peace, it is necessary to be on our guard." That was spoken without enthusiasm, but with conviction. It had been assumed that, up above, everything was being done to bring peace. The Bolsheviks, to be sure, were asserting that the government wanted the war prolonged for the sake of robberies. But could that be possible? How about Kerensky? We have known the Soviet leaders since February. They were the first to come to us in the barracks. They are for peace. Moreover, Lenin came straight from Berlin, whereas Tseretelli was at hard labor. We must be patient. . . . Meanwhile the progressive factories and regiments were more and more firmly adopting the Bolshevik slogans of a peace policy: publication of the secret treaties; break with the plans of conquest of the Entente; open proposal of immediate peace to all warring countries. The note of April 18 fell among these complex and wavering moods. How can this be? They are not for peace up there after all, but for the old war aims? All our patience and waiting for nothing? Down with . . . but down with whom? Can the Bolsheviks be right? Hardly. But what about this note? It means that somebody is selling our hides, all right, to the tzar's allies. From a simple comparison of the press of the Kadets and the Compromisers, it could be inferred that Miliukov, betraying the general confidence, was intending to carry on a policy of conquest in company with Lloyd George and Ribot. And yet Kerensky had declared that the attempt upon Constantinople was "the personal opinion of Miliukov." . . . That was how this movement flared up.

But it was not homogeneous. Certain hot-headed elements among the revolutionists greatly overestimated the volume and political maturity of the movement, because it had broken out so sharply and suddenly. The Bolsheviks developed an energetic campaign among the troops and in the factories. They supplemented the demand to "remove Miliukov," which was,

so to speak, a program-minimum of the movement, with placards against the Provisional Government as a whole. But different elements understood this differently: some as slogans of
propaganda, others as the task of the day. The slogan carried
into the streets by the armed soldiers and sailors: "Down with
the Provisional Government!" inevitably introduced into the
demonstration a strain of armed insurrection. Considerable
groups of workers and soldiers were quite ready to shake down
the Provisional Government right then and there. They made
an attempt to enter the Mariinsky Palace, occupy its exits, and
arrest the ministers. Skobelev was delegated to rescue the ministers, and he fulfilled his mission the more successfully in that
the Mariinsky Palace happened to be unoccupied.

In consequence of Guchkov's illness, the government had
met that day in his private apartment. But it was not this accident which saved the ministers from arrest; they were not
seriously threatened. That army of 25,000 to 30,000 soldiers,
which had come into the streets for a struggle with the pro-
longers of the war, was plenty enough to do away with a far
solider government than that headed by Prince Lvov, but the
demonstrators had not set themselves this goal. All they really
intended was to show their fist at the window, so that these
high gentlemen should cease sharpening their teeth for Constantinople and get busy as they should about the question of
peace. In this way the soldiers hoped to help Kerensky and
Tseretelli against Miliukov.

General Kornilov attended that sitting of the government,
reported the armed demonstrations which were taking place,
and declared that as the commander of the troops of the Petrograd military district he had at his disposition sufficient forces
to put down the disturbance with a mailed fist: he merely
awaited the command. Kolchak, who happened accidentally to
be present, related afterwards, at the trial which preceded his
execution, that Prince Lvov and Kerensky spoke against the
attempt to put down the demonstration with military force.
Miliukov did not express himself directly, but summed up the
situation by saying that the honorable ministers might of course
reason as they wished, but their decision would not prevent

their removal to prison. There is no doubt whatever that Kornilov was acting in agreement with the Kadet center.

The Compromise leaders had no difficulty in persuading the soldier demonstrators to withdraw from the square before the Marinsky Palace, and even go back to their barracks. The commotion which had overflowed the city, however, did not recede to its banks. Crowds gathered, meetings assembled, they wrangled at street corners, the crowds in the tramways divided into partisans and opponents of Miliukov. On the Nevsky and adjoining streets, bourgeois orators waged an agitation against Lenin—sent from Germany to overthrow the great patriot Miliukov. In the suburbs and workers' districts the Bolsheviks tried to extend the indignation aroused against the note and its author to the government as a whole.

At seven in the evening the plenum of the Soviet assembled. The leaders did not know what to say to that audience, quivering with tense passion. Cheidze explained to them at great length that after the session there was to be a meeting with the Provisional Government. Chernov tried to scare them with the approach of civil war. Feodorov, the metal worker, a member of the Central Committee of the Bolsheviks, replied that the civil war was already here, that what the soviets ought to do was to rely upon it and seize the power in their hands. "Those were new and at that time terrible words," writes Sukhanov. "They hit the very center of the prevailing mood and received a response such as the Bolsheviks had never met in the Soviet before, and did not meet for a long time after."

The pivot of the conference, however, was an unexpected speech by Kerensky's favorite, the liberal socialist, Stankevich: "Comrades," he asked, "why should we take any 'action' at all? Against whom marshal our forces? The sole power that exists is you and the masses which stand behind you. . . . Look there! It is now five minutes to seven."—(Stankevich pointed his finger to the clock on the wall, and the whole assembly turned in that direction)—"Resolve that the Provisional Government does not exist, that it has resigned. We will communicate this by telephone, and in five minutes it will surrender its authority. Why all this talk about violence, demonstrations, civil war?"

343

Loud applause. Elated shouts. The orator wanted to frighten the soviets with an extreme inference from the existing situation, but frightened himself with the effect of his own speech. That unexpected truth about the power of the Soviet lifted the assembly above the wretched puttering of its leaders, whose main occupation was to prevent the Soviet from arriving at any decision. "Who will take the place of the government?" An orator replied to the applause. "We? But our hands tremble. . . ." That was an incomparable characterization of the Compromisers—high and mighty leaders with trembling hands.

Prime Minister Lvov, as though to supplement Stankevich from the other side, made the next day the following announcement: "Up till now the Provisional Government has received unwavering support from the ruling organ of the Soviet. For the last two weeks . . . the government has been under suspicion. In these circumstances . . . it is best for the Provisional Government to withdraw." We see again what was the real constitution of the February revolution!

The meeting of the Executive Committee with the Provisional Government took place in the Marinsky Palace. Prince Lvov in an introductory speech regretted the campaign undertaken by the socialist circles against the government, and half offendedly, half threateningly, spoke of resignation. The ministers described in turn the difficulties which they had assisted with all their might to accumulate. Miliukov, turning his back to all this "contact" oratory, spoke from the balcony to a Kadet demonstration. "Seeing those placards with the inscription 'Down with Miliukov!' . . . I did not fear for Miliukov, I feared for Russia." Thus the historian Miliukov reports the modest words which the minister Miliukov pronounced before the crowds assembled in the square. Tseretelli demanded from the government a new note. Chernov found a brilliant solution, proposing that Miliukov go over to the Ministry of Public Education. Constantinople as a topic in geography would at any rate be less dangerous than as a topic in diplomacy. Miliukov, however, categorically refused both to return to science, and to write a new note. The leaders of the Soviet did not need much persuasion, and agreed to an "explanation" of the old note. It remained to find a few phrases whose falsity should be sufficiently oiled over with democraticness, and the situation might be considered saved—and with it Miliukov's portfolio.

But the restless third power would not be quiet. The 21st of April brought a new wave of commotion, more powerful than yesterday's. Today the Petrograd Committee of the Bolsheviks had called for the demonstration. In spite of the counter-agitation of the Mensheviks and Social Revolutionaries, immense masses of workers advanced to the center from the Vyborg side, and later too from other districts. The Executive Committee sent to meet the demonstrators their most authoritative pacifiers with Cheidze at the head. But the workers firmly intended to speak their word—and they had a word to speak. A well-known liberal journalist described in *Rech* this demonstration of workers on the Nevsky: "About a hundred armed men marched in front; after them solid phalanxes of unarmed men and women, a thousand strong. Living chains on both sides. Songs. Their faces amazed me. All those thousands had but one face, the stunned ecstatic face of the early Christian monks. Implacable, pitiless, ready for murder, inquisition and death." The liberal journalist had looked the workers' revolution in the eye, and felt for a second its intense determination. How little those phalanxes resembled Miliukov's "boy-workers" hired by Ludendorff at fifteen roubles a day!

Today as yesterday the demonstrators did not come out to overthrow the government, although a majority of them, we may guess, had already seriously thought about this problem, and a part were ready even today to carry the demonstration far beyond the bounds of the majority mood. Cheidze asked the demonstration to turn round and go back to its districts. But the leaders sternly answered that the workers themselves knew what to do. This was a new note—and Cheidze would have to get used to it in the course of the next few weeks.

While the Compromisers were persuading and hushing up, the Kadets were challenging and inflaming. In spite of the fact that Kornilov had not yesterday been authorized to employ firearms, he not only had not abandoned the plan, but on the

345

contrary was all this day from early morning getting ready to oppose the demonstrators with cavalry and artillery. Firmly counting on the boldness of the generals, the Kadets had issued a special handbill summoning their partisans to the streets, clearly intending to carry matters to the point of a decisive conflict. Although failing of his raid on the Dardanelles coast-line, Miliukov continued his general offensive, with Kornilov in the capacity of advance guard and the Entente as heavy reserves. The note despatched behind the back of the Soviet, and the editorial in *Rech*, were to serve the liberal Chancellor of the February revolution in the rôle of the Ems despatch. "All who stand for Russia and her freedom must unite round the Provisional Government and support it." Thus read the appeal of the Kadet Central Committee, inviting all good citizens into the street for the struggle against the advocates of immediate peace.

The Nevsky, the chief artery of the bourgeoisie, was converted into a solid Kadet meeting. A considerable demonstration headed by the members of the Kadet Central Committee marched to the Mariinsky Palace. Everywhere could be seen brand-new placards, fresh from the sign-painters: "Full Confidence to the Provisional Government!" "Long Live Miliukov!" The ministers looked like guests of honor. They had their own "people," and this the more noticeably since emissaries of the Soviet were doing their utmost to help them, dispersing revolutionary meetings, steering workers' and soldiers' demonstrations toward the suburbs, and restraining the barracks and factories from going out. Under the flag of defense of the government, the first open and broad mobilization of counter-revolutionary forces took place. In the center of the town appeared trucks with armed officers, cadets and students. The Cavaliers of St. George were sent out. The gilded youth organized a mock trial on the Nevsky, establishing on the spot the existence both of Leninists and of "German spies." There were skirmishes and casualties. The first bloody encounter began, according to reports, with an attempt of officers to snatch from the workers a banner with a slogan against the Provisional Government. The encounters became more and more fierce; shots were interchanged, and towards afternoon they became almost continuous. Nobody knew exactly who was shooting or why, but there were already victims of this disorderly shooting, partly malicious, partly the result of panic. The temperature was reaching red heat.

No, that day was not in the least like a manifestation of national unity. Two worlds stood face to face. The patriotic columns called into the streets against the workers and soldiers by the Kadet Party consisted exclusively of the bourgeois layers of the population—officers, officials, intelligentsia. Two human floods—one for Constantinople, one for Peace—had issued from different parts of the town. Different in social composition, not a bit similar in external appearance, and with hostile inscriptions on their placards, as they clashed together they brought into play fists, clubs, and even firearms.

The unexpected news reached the Executive Committee that Kornilov was moving cannon into the Palace Square. Was this independent initiative on the part of the commander? The character and further career of Kornilov testify that somebody was always leading that brave general by the nose—a function fulfilled on this occasion by the Kadet leaders. It was only because they counted on the interference of Kornilov, and in order to make this interference necessary, that they had summoned their masses into the street. One of the younger historians has correctly remarked that Kornilov's attempt to draw away the military schools to Palace Square coincided, not with the moment of real or pretended necessity to defend the Marinsky Palace from a hostile crowd, but with the moment of highest pitch of the Kadet manifestation.

The Miliukov-Kornilov plan went to pieces, however, and very ignominiously. However naïve the leaders of the Executive Committee may have been, they could not fail to understand that their own heads were in question. Even before the first news of bloody encounters on the Nevsky, the Executive Committee had sent to all the military units of Petersburg and its environs telegraphic instructions not to leave the barracks without orders from the Soviet—not one detachment to the streets of the capital. Now, when the intentions of Kornilov became evident, the Executive Committee, contradicting all its solemn declarations, put both hands to the helm, not only demanding of the commander that he immediately send back the troops, but also commissioning Skobelev and Filipovsky to send back those which had come out in the name of the Soviet. "Except upon a summons from the Executive Committee in these alarming days, do not come out on the streets with arms in your hands. *To the Executive Committee alone belongs the right to command you.*" Thereafter every order for the despatch of troops had, besides the customary formalities, to be issued on an official paper of the Soviet and countersigned by no less than two persons authorized for this purpose. It seemed that the Soviet had unequivocally interpreted Kornilov's act as an attempt on the part of the counter-revolution to create a civil war. But, although by its order it reduced to nothing the commandership of the district, the Executive Committee never thought of removing Kornilov himself. How could one think of violating the prerogatives of the government? "Their hands trembled." The young régime was wrapped up in fictions like a patient in pillows and compresses. From the point of view of the correlation of forces, most instructive is the fact that not only the military units, but also the officers' schools, even before receiving the order of Cheidze, refused to go out without the sanction of the Soviet. These unpleasantnesses, not foreseen by the Kadets, dropping upon them one after another, were inevitable consequences of the fact that the Russian bourgeoisie up to the time of the national revolution had been an anti-national class. That could be concealed for a short time by the dual power, but could not be corrected.

The April crisis apparently was coming to nothing. The Executive Committee had succeeded in holding back the masses on the threshold of the dual power. On its side, the grateful government explained that by "guarantees" and "sanctions" was to be understood world courts, limitation of armaments and all admirable things. The Executive Committee hastily seized upon these terminological concessions, and by a majority of 34 against 19 voted the matter adjusted. In order to quiet their alarmed ranks, the majority also adopted the following resolution: Our control of the activities of the Provisional Government must be strengthened; without previously informing the Executive Committee no important political steps must be taken; the diplomatic personnel must be radically changed. The double sovereignty which had existed in fact was thus translated into the juridical language of a constitution. But this changed nothing in the nature of things. The left wing could not even secure from the compromising majority the resignation of Miliukov. Everything must remain as before. Over the Provisional Government hung the far more effective control of the Entente, which the Executive Committee did not dare to touch.

On the evening of the 21st the Petrograd Soviet cast up its balance. Tseretelli reported on the fresh victory of the wise leadership, which had put an end to all false interpretations of the note of March 27. Kamenev, in the name of the Bolsheviks, proposed the formation of a purely soviet government. Kollantai, a popular revolutionist who had come over during the war from the Mensheviks to the Bolsheviks, proposed a referendum throughout all the districts of Petrograd and its environs on the desirability of this provisional government or another. But these proposals hardly entered into the consciousness of the Soviet: the question, it seemed, was adjusted. The solacing resolution of the Executive Committee was adopted by an enormous majority against 13. To be sure, a majority of the Bolshevik deputies were then still in their factories, on the streets, or attending demonstrations. But nevertheless it remains indubitable that in the central mass of the Soviet there was not any move to the side of the Bolsheviks.

The Soviet directed all to refrain for two days from any street demonstrations. This resolution was adopted unanimously. Nobody had a shadow of doubt that all would submit to the decision. And as a fact the workers, the soldiers, the bourgeois youth, the Vyborg side, the Nevsky Prospect— no one at all dared to disobey the order of the Soviet. Tranquillity was attained without any forcible measures whatever. The Soviet had only to feel itself master of the situation and it would have been so in fact.

Into the editorial offices of the left papers in those days

poured many scores of factory and regimental resolutions demanding the immediate resignation of Miliukov, and sometimes of the whole Provisional Government. And not only Petrograd surged up. In Moscow too the workers abandoned the shops, and the soldiers issued from the barracks, filling the streets with stormy protests. Telegrams poured in to the Executive Committee from scores of local soviets, opposing the policy of Miliukov and promising full support to the Soviet. The same voices came from the front. But all was to remain as before.

"During April 21," asserted Miliukov later, "a mood favorable to the government again took possession of the streets." He evidently had in mind those streets which he had an opportunity to view from the balcony after the majority of the workers and soldiers had gone home. As an actual fact, the government had been completely shown up. There was no serious force behind it. We have just heard this from the lips of Stankevich and Prince Lvov himself. What did Kornilov's assurance that he had sufficient forces to put down the rebels mean? Nothing whatever except the extreme light-mindedness of the respected general. This light-mindedness will reach its highest bloom in August, when the conspirator Kornilov will deploy against Petrograd a non-existent army. The trouble was that Kornilov was still trying to judge the troops by the commanding staff. The officers, a majority of them, were indubitably with him—that is, they were ready, under the pretext of defending the Provisional Government, to smash the ribs of the Soviet. The soldiers stood for the Soviet, being very much farther to the left than the Soviet itself. But inasmuch as the Soviet stood for the Provisional Government, it happened that Kornilov was able to bring out in its defense Soviet soldiers commanded by reactionary officers. Thanks to the two-power régime, they were all playing hide and seek with one another. However, the leaders of the Soviet had hardly issued the command to the troops not to leave their barracks, when Kornilov found himself hanging in the air along with the whole Provisional Government.

And yet the government did not fall. The masses who had

made the attack were totally unready to carry it through to the end. The Compromise leaders were thus still able to try to turn back the February régime to its original position. Having forgotten, or desiring to make others forget, that the Executive Committee had been openly compelled in opposition to the "legally constituted" authorities to lay its hands on the army, the *Izvestia* of the Soviet complained on April 22: "The Soviet did not aspire to seize the power in its own hands, but nevertheless upon many banners carried by the partisans of the Soviet there were inscriptions demanding the overthrow of the government and the transfer of all power to the Soviet." . . . Is it not indeed exasperating that the workers and soldiers had tried to tempt the Compromisers with power—that is, had seriously imagined these gentlemen capable of making a revolutionary use of it?

No, the Social Revolutionaries and Mensheviks did not want the power. As we saw, the Bolshevik resolution demanding the transfer of power to the soviets, mustered in the Petrograd Soviet an insignificant number of votes. In Moscow the vote of "no confidence" in the Provisional Government, introduced by the Bolsheviks on April 22, mustered only 74 votes out of many hundreds. To be sure the Helsingfors Soviet, notwithstanding its domination by Social Revolutionaries and Mensheviks, adopted on that same day an extraordinarily bold resolution for those times, offering the Petrograd Soviet its armed assistance in removing the "imperialist Provisional Government." But that resolution, adopted under direct pressure from the sailors, was an exception. By an overwhelming majority, the Soviet deputies, representing those masses who had been but yesterday so near to an armed insurrection against the Provisional Government, stood pat on the two-power system. What does this signify?

This crying contradiction between the decisiveness of the mass offensive and the half-heartedness of its political reflection was not accidental. In a revolutionary epoch the oppressed masses turn more easily and quickly to direct action, than they learn to give their desires and demands a formal expression through their own representatives. The more abstract the sys-

351

tem of representation, the more it lags behind the rhythm of those events which determine the activity of the masses. A Soviet representation, the least abstract of all, has immeasurable advantages in revolutionary conditions: it is sufficient to remember that the democratic Dumas, elected according to the their own regulations of April 17, hampered by nothing and by nobody, proved absolutely powerless to compete with the soviets. But with all the advantages of their organic connection with the factories and regiments—that is, with the active masses—the soviets are nevertheless representative organs, and are therefore not free from the qualifications and distortions of parliamentarism. The contradiction inherent in representation, even of the soviet form, lies in the fact that it is on the one hand necessary to the action of the masses, but on the other hand easily becomes a conservative obstacle to it. The practical way out of this contradiction is to renew the representation continually. But this operation, nowhere very simple, must in a revolution be the result of direct action and therefore lag behind such action. At any rate, on the day after the April semi-insurrection, or more accurately, quarter-insurrection— the semi-insurrection will occur in July—the same deputies were sitting in the Soviet as on the day before. Arriving once more in their accustomed seats they voted for the motions of their accustomed leaders.

But this by no means signifies that the April storm had passed without effect on the Soviet, on the entire February system, and still more on the masses themselves. That giant interference of the workers and soldiers in political events, although not yet carried through to the end, altered the political scene, gave impulse to the general movement of the revolution, accelerated inevitable regroupings, and forced the parlor and backstage politicians to forget their plans of yesterday and adapt their action to new sets of circumstances.

When the Compromisers had liquidated this flare-up of civil war, and thought that everything was coming back to its old position, the government crisis was only just beginning. The liberals did not want to rule any longer without a direct participation of socialists in the government. The socialists on their part, forced by the logic of the two-power system to agree to this condition, demanded an unequivocal repudiation of the Dardanelles program, and this inevitably led to the downfall of Miliukov. On May 2, Miliukov found himself compelled to leave the ranks of the government. The slogan of the demonstration of April 20 was thus realized within the space of twelve days, and against the will of the Soviet leaders.

But delays and procrastinations succeeded only in accentuating more strongly the impotence of the rulers. Miliukov, attempting with the aid of his general to make a sharp break in the correlation of forces, had popped out of the government with a noise like a cork. The smashing general found himself obliged to resign. The ministers did not look a bit like guests of honor any more. The government implored the Soviet to agree to a coalition. All this because the masses were pressing on the long end of the lever.

This does not mean, however, that the Compromising parties were coming nearer to the workers and soldiers. On the contrary, the April events by suggesting what unexpected surprises lie hidden in the masses, impelled the democratic leaders still further toward the right, toward a closer union with the bourgeoisie. From that time on the patriotic course definitely predominates. The majority of the Executive Committee becomes more united. Formless radicals like Sukhanov, Steklov, etc., who had but recently inspired the policies of the Soviet, and had made attempts to save something at least of the traditions of socialism, are pushed aside. Tseretelli takes a firm, conservative and patriotic position, an accommodation of Miliukov's policies to the representative organ of the laboring masses.

The conduct of the Bolshevik Party during the April days was not uniform. Events had caught the party unprepared. The internal crisis was just being wound up, and busy preparations were going on for the party conference. Impressed by the keen excitement in the workers' districts some Bolsheviks expressed themselves in favor of overthrowing the Provisional Government. The Petrograd Committee, which on March 5 had been still passing resolutions of qualified confidence in the Provisional Government, wavered. It was decided to hold a demonstration on the 21st, though its purpose was still insufficiently defined. A part of the Petrograd Committee were bringing the workers and soldiers into the streets with the intention—not very clear, to be sure—of attempting, so to speak incidentally, to overthrow the Provisional Government. Individual left elements standing outside the party acted in the same direction. There was apparently also an anarchist element —not numerous but bustling. The military quarters were approached by individual persons demanding armored cars or general reënforcements, now for the arrest of the Provisional Government, now for street fighting with the enemy. An armored car division close to the Bolsheviks declared, however, that they would give no machines to anyone except by order of the Executive Committee.

The Kadets did their best to place the blame for the bloody encounters on the Bolsheviks. But a special committee of the Soviet established beyond a doubt that the shooting had started, not in the streets, but from doorways and windows. The newspapers published an announcement from the Public Prosecutor: "The shooting was done by the scum of the population for the purpose of arousing disorders and disturbances—always useful to the criminal elements."

The hostility of the ruling Soviet parties to the Bolsheviks had not yet reached that intensity which two months later, in July, completely eclipsed both reason and conscience. The Department of Justice, although it had kept its old staff, was standing at attention before the revolution, and in April had not yet permitted itself to apply to the extreme left the methods of the tzar's secret service. Along this line too Miliukov's attack was repelled without difficulty.

The party Central Committee pulled up on the left wing Bolsheviks, and declared on April 21 that they considered the Soviet's veto of demonstrations perfectly in order, and to be submitted to unconditionally. "The motto 'Down with the Provisional Government' is incorrect at present," stated the resolution of the Central Committee, "because without a solid (that is, conscious and organized) majority of the people on the side of the revolutionary proletariat, such a motto is either an empty phrase, or leads to attempts of an adventurous character." This resolution declared the task of the moment to be criticism, propaganda, and winning of the majority in the soviets, as the groundwork for capturing the power. In this their opponents saw either the retreat of frightened leaders, or a sly maneuver. We already know the fundamental position of Lenin on the question of power; he was now teaching the party to apply the "April theses" on the basis of actual experience.

Three weeks before this, Kamenev had declared that he was "happy" to vote with the Mensheviks and Social Revolutionaries for a joint resolution on the Provisional Government, and Stalin had been developing his theory of a division of labor between Kadets and Bolsheviks. How far those days and those theories were gone into the past! Only after the lesson of the April days, Stalin at last came out against the theory of benevolent "control" over the Provisional Government, cautiously retreating from his own previous position. But this maneuver passed unnoticed.

In what consisted the element of adventurism in the policy of certain parts of the party? asked Lenin at a conference which opened right after the menacing days. It consisted in the attempt to employ violence where there was not yet, or no longer, any place for revolutionary violence. "You can overthrow one who is known to the people as a tyrant; but there are no tyrants now; the cannon and rifles are in the hands of the soldiers, not the capitalists. The capitalists are not prevailing with violence, but deceit, and you can't talk now about violence —it's mere nonsense. . . . We gave the slogan of peaceful demonstration. We wanted only to make a peaceful reconnoiter of the enemy's strength, not to give battle. But the Petrograd Committee aimed a wee bit too far to the left. . . . Along with the correct slogan, 'Long Live the Soviets!' they gave a wrong one, 'Down with the Provisional Government!' A moment of action is no time to aim 'a wee bit too far to the left.' We look upon that as the greatest crime, disorganization."

What lies underneath the dramatic events of a revolution? Shifts in the correlation of class forces. What causes these shifts? For the most part oscillations of the intermediary classes, the peasantry, the petty bourgeoisie, the army. There is a gigantic amplitude of oscillation between Kadet imperialism and Bolshevism. These oscillations go simultaneously in two opposite directions. The political representatives of the petty bourgeoisie, their chiefs, the compromising leaders, gravitate farther and farther to the right, toward the bourgeoisie. The oppressed masses, on the other hand, will each time take a sharper and more daring swing to the left. In protesting against the adventurism shown by the leaders of the Petrograd organization, Lenin made this exception: if the intermediate masses had swung toward our side seriously, deeply, steadily, we would not have hesitated one minute to oust the government from the Marinsky Palace. But this has not yet happened. The April crisis, bursting into the street, was "not the first and not the last swing of the petty bourgeois and semi-proletarian masses." Our task is still for the time being to "patiently explain"—to prepare the next swing of the masses to our side, a deeper and more conscious one.

As for the proletariat, its movement to the side of the Bolsheviks assumed during April a clearly expressed character. Workers came to the party committees asking how to transfer their names from the Menshevik Party to the Bolshevik. At the factories they began insistently to question the deputies about foreign policy, the war, the two-power system, the food question; and as a result of these examinations Menshevik and Social Revolutionary delegates were more and more frequently replaced by Bolsheviks. The sharp turn began in the district soviets, as these were closer to the factories. In the soviets of the Vyborg side, Vasiliev Island, Narva district, the Bolsheviks seemed suddenly and unexpectedly to find themselves toward the end of April in a majority. This was a fact of the greatest significance, but the Executive Committee leaders, busy with high politics, looked with disdain upon the fussing of the Bolsheviks in the workers' districts. However, the districts began to press on the center more and more perceptibly. In the factories, without orders from the Petrograd Committee, an energetic and successful campaign was carried on for the re-election of representatives to the municipal soviet of workers' deputies. Sukhanov estimates that at the beginning of May the Bolsheviks had behind them a third of the Petrograd proletariat. Not less, certainly—and the most active third besides. The March formlessness had disappeared; political lines were sharpening; the "fantastic" theses of Lenin were taking flesh in the Petrograd workers' districts.

Every step forward of the revolution was evoked or compelled by direct intervention of the masses—in most cases utterly unexpected by the Soviet parties. After the February uprising, when the workers and soldiers overthrew the monarchy without anyone's permission, the leaders of the Executive Committee considered the rôle of the masses fulfilled. But they were fatally wrong. The masses had no intention of getting off the stage. Already in the beginning of March, during the campaign for the eight-hour day, the workers wrested this concession from capital in spite of the efforts of Mensheviks and Social Revolutionaries to hold them back. The Soviet was forced to record a victory obtained without it and against it. The April demonstration was a second correction of the same kind. Every mass action, regardless of its immediate aim, is a warning addressed to the leadership. This warning is at first mild in character, but becomes more and more resolute. By July it has become a threat. In October we have the final act.

In all critical moments the masses intervene "spontaneously" —in other words, obeying only their own inferences drawn from political experience, and their as yet officially unrecognized leaders. Assimilating this or that premise from the talk of agitators, the masses on their own volition translate its conclusions into the language of action. The Bolsheviks, as a party, were not yet leading the campaign for the eight-hour day. The Bolsheviks did not summon the masses to the April demonstration. The Bolsheviks will not call the armed masses into the streets at the beginning of July. Only in October will the party finally fall in step and march out at the head of the masses, not for a demonstration, but for a revolution.

357

Chapter XVIII

THE FIRST COALITION

ALL official theories, declarations and advertisements to the
contrary notwithstanding, the power belonged to the
Provisional Government on paper only. The revolution,
paying no attention to the resistance of the so-called democracy,
was striding along, lifting up new masses of the people, strengthening the soviets, and to a limited extent even arming
the workers. The local commissars of the government and the
"social committees" created under them, in which representatives of bourgeois organizations usually predominated, were
quite naturally and without effort crowded out by the soviets.
In certain cases, when these agents of the central power tried
to resist, sharp conflicts arose. The commissars accused the local
soviets of refusing to recognize the central government. The
bourgeois press began to cry out that Cronstadt, Schlüsselburg
or Tzaritsyn had seceded from Russia and become independent
republics. The local soviets protested against this nonsense.
The ministers got excited. The governmental socialists hastened
to these places, persuading, threatening, justifying themselves
before the bourgeoisie. But all this did not change the correlation of forces. The fatefulness of the processes undermining the two-power system could be seen in the fact that these
processes were developing, although at different tempos, all
over the country. From organs for controlling the government
the soviets were becoming organs of administration. They
would not accommodate themselves to any theory of the division
of powers, but kept interfering in the administration of the
army, in economic conflicts, questions of food and transport,
even in the courts of justice. The soviets under pressure from
the workers decreed the eight-hour day, removed reactionary
executives, ousted the more intolerable commissars of the Provisional Government, conducted searches and arrests, sup-

pressed hostile newspapers. Under the influence of continually increasing food difficulties and a goods famine, the provincial soviets undertook to fix prices, forbid export from the provinces, and requisition provisions. Nevertheless at the head of the soviets everywhere stood the Social Revolutionaries and Mensheviks who rejected with indignation the Bolshevik slogan, "Power to the Soviets!"

Especially instructive in this connection is the activity of the soviet in Tiflis, the very heart of the Menshevik *Gironde*, which gave the February revolution such leaders as Tseretelli and Cheidze, and sheltered them afterwards when they had hopelessly squandered themselves in Petrograd. The Tiflis Soviet, led by Jordania—afterwards head of independent Georgia —found itself compelled at every step to trample on the principles of the Menshevik Party in control of it, and act as a sovereign power. This soviet confiscated a private printing establishment for its own uses, made arrests, took charge of investigations and trials for political offenses, established a bread ration, and fixed the prices of food and the necessaries of life. That contrast between official doctrine and real life, manifest from the very first day, only continued to grow throughout March and April.

In Petrograd a certain decorum at least was observed—although not always, as we have seen. The April days, however, had unequivocally lifted the curtain on the impotence of the Provisional Government, showing that it had no serious support whatever in the capital. In the last ten days of April the government was flickering and going out. "Kerensky stated with anguish that the government was already non-existent, that it did not work but merely discussed its condition" (Stankevich). You might say in general about this government, that up to the days of October in hard moments it was always undergoing a crisis, and in the intervals between crises it was merely existing. Continually "discussing its condition," it found no time for business.

From the crisis created by the April rehearsal of future events, three outcomes were theoretically possible. The power might have gone over wholly to the bourgeoisie; that could have been achieved only through civil war; Miliukov made the attempt, but failed. The power should have gone over wholly to the soviets; this could have been accomplished without any civil war whatever, merely by raising of hands—merely by wishing it. But the Compromisers did not want to wish it, and the masses still preserved their faith in the Compromisers, although it was badly cracked. Thus both of the fundamental ways out—the bourgeois and the proletarian—were closed. There remained a third possibility, the confused, weak-hearted, cowardly half-road of compromise. The name of that road was Coalition.

At the end of the April days the socialists had no thought of a coalition. In general those people never foresaw anything. By the resolution of April 21 the Executive Committee had officially converted the double sovereignty from a fact into a constitutional principle. But here again the owl of wisdom made her flight too late: this juridical consecration of the March form of double sovereignty—the kings and the prophets—was carried out just at the moment when this form had already been exploded by the action of the masses. The socialists tried to close their eyes to this. Miliukov relates that when the question of a coalition was raised from the government side, Tseretelli said: "What good will it do you if we enter your cabinet? We will be compelled, in case you are stubborn, to withdraw from the ministry with a loud bang." Tseretelli was trying to frighten the liberals with his future "bang." As always in the fundamentals of their policies, the Mensheviks were appealing to the interests of the bourgeoisie themselves. But the water was up to their necks. Kerensky frightened the Executive Committee: "The government is at present in an impossibly difficult situation: the rumors of its resignation are no political by-play." At the same time there was pressure from the bourgeois circles. The Moscow city duma passed a resolution in favor of coalition. On April 26, when the ground was sufficiently prepared, the Provisional Government announced in a special appeal the necessity of bringing in to the governmental work "those active creative forces of the country which have not yet participated in it." The question was thus presented point-blank.

The feeling against coalition was nevertheless pretty strong. At the end of April the following soviets declared themselves against the participation of socialists in the government: Moscow, Tiflis, Odessa, Ekaterinburg, Nizhni-Novgorod, Tver and others. Their motives were very clearly expressed by one of the Menshevik leaders in Moscow: If the socialists enter the government, there will be nobody to lead the movement of the masses "in a definite channel." But it was difficult to convey this idea to the workers and soldiers against whom it was directed. The masses, in so far as they were not yet for the Bolsheviks, stood solid for the entrance of socialists into the government. If it is a good thing to have Kerensky as a minister, then so much the better six Kerenskys. The masses did not know that this was called coalition with the bourgeoisie, and that the bourgeoisie wanted to use these socialists as a cover for their activities against the people. A coalition looked different from the barracks and from the Marinsky Palace. The masses wanted to use the socialists to crowd out the bourgeoisie from the government. Thus two forces tending in opposite directions united for a moment in one.

In Petrograd a series of military units, among them an armored car division friendly to the Bolsheviks, declared in favor of coalition government. The provinces voted for the coalition by an overwhelming majority. The coalition tendency prevailed among the Social Revolutionaries; they only feared to go into the government without the Mensheviks. And finally, the army was in favor of coalition. One of its delegates later—at the June congress of the soviets—expressed not at all badly the attitude of the front toward the question of power: "We thought that the groan which arose from the army when it learned that the socialists would not enter the ministry to work with people whom they did not trust, while the whole army was compelled to go on dying with people whom it did not trust, must have been heard in Petrograd."

The war was the deciding factor in this question, as in others. The socialists had at first intended to sit out the war,

361

as also the sovereignty, and wait. But the war would not wait. The Allies would not wait. The front did not want to wait any longer. Right in the middle of the governmental crisis came delegates from the front and put up to their leaders in the Executive Committee the question: Are we going to fight or not? Which meant: Do you assume the responsibility for the war or not? There was no dodging that question. The Entente was posing the same question in the language of a half-threat.

The April offensive on the west European front cost the Allies heavily and gave no results. A wavering was felt in the French army under the influence of the Russian revolution and of the failure of its own offensive from which so much had been hoped. The army, in the words of Marshal Pétain, "was bending in our hands." To stop this threatening process the French Government had need of a Russian offensive—and until that at least a firm promise of one. Aside from the material relief to be gained, it was necessary as quickly as possible to snatch the halo of peace from the Russian revolution, poison the hope in the hearts of the French soldiers, compromise the revolution by associating it with the crimes of the Entente, trample the banner of the Russian workers' and soldiers' insurrection in the blood and mud of the imperialist slaughter.

In order to attain this high aim, all possible levers were brought into play. Among these levers not the last place was occupied by the patriotic socialists of the Entente. The most experienced of them were sent into revolutionary Russia. They arrived armed to the teeth with obsequious consciences and boneless talk. "The foreign social-patriots," writes Sukhanov, "were received with open arms in the Marinsky Palace, Branting, Cachin, O'Grady, De Brouckère, and others felt at home there and formed a united front with our ministers against the Soviet." It must be conceded that even the Compromisers' Soviet was often ill at ease with those gentlemen.

The Allied socialists made the rounds of the fronts. "General Alexeiev," wrote Vandervelde, "did everything in his power in order that our efforts should be applied to the same end as were those undertaken a little earlier by delegations of sailors from the Black Sea, by Kerensky, Albert Thomas—that is to complete what he called the moral preparation of the offensive." The President of the Second International and the former chief of staff of Nicholas the Second thus found a common language in their struggle for the glorious ideals of democracy. Renaudel, one of the leaders of French socialism, was able to cry out with relief: "Now we can talk without blushing of the war for justice." It was three years before humanity learned that those people had something to blush about.

On the 1st of May the Executive Committee, having passed through all the stages of vacillation known to nature, decided by a majority of 41 votes against 18, with 3 abstaining, to enter into a coalition government. Only the Bolsheviks and a small group of Menshevik-Internationalists voted against it.

It is not without interest that the victim of this closer rapprochement was the recognized leader of the bourgeoisie, Miliukov. "I did not go out, they put me out," said Miliukov later. Guchkov had withdrawn already on April 30, refusing to sign the "Declaration of the Rights of the Soldier." How dark it was in those day in the hearts of the liberals is evident from the fact that the Central Committee of the Kadet Party decided, in order to save the Coalition, not to insist upon Miliukov's remaining in the government. "The party betrayed its leader," writes the right Kadet, Isgoyev. The party, however, had no great choice. The same Isgoyev remarks quite correctly: "At the end of April the Kadet Party was smashed to pieces; morally it had received a blow from which it would never recover."

But on the question of Miliukov the Entente was to have the last word. England was entirely willing that the Dardanelles patriot should be replaced by a more temperate "democrat." Henderson, who was in Petrograd with authorization to replace Buchanan as ambassador in case of need, learning of the state of affairs, deemed this change unnecessary. As a fact, Buchanan was exactly in the right place, for he was a resolute opponent of annexations in so far as they did not coincide with the appetites of Great Britain. "If Russia has no need of Constantinople," he whispered tenderly to Tereshchenko, "the sooner she announces this, the better." France at first supported Miliukov, but here Thomas played his rôle, coming out after Buchanan and the Soviet leaders against Miliukov. Thus that politician, hated by the masses, was abandoned by the Allies, by the democrats, and lastly by his own party.

Miliukov really did not deserve such cruel punishment—at least not from these hands. But the Coalition demanded a purification sacrifice. They pictured Miliukov to the masses as that evil spirit who had been darkening the universal triumphant procession towards democratic peace. In cutting off Miliukov, the Coalition purified itself at one stroke from the sins of imperialism. The staff of the Coalition Government, and its program, were approved by the Petrograd Soviet on May 5. The Bolsheviks mustered 100 votes against it. "The meeting warmly greeted the orator-ministers," Miliukov ironically tells of this meeting. "It greeted with the same stormy applause, however, 'the old leader of the first revolution' Trotsky, who had arrived the day before from America, and who sharply condemned the entrance of socialists into the ministry, asserting that the 'double sovereignty' is not destroyed, but 'merely transferred into the ministry,' and that the real single power which will 'save' Russia will arrive only when 'the next step is taken, the transfer of power into the hands of the workers' and soldiers' deputies'; then will begin 'a new epoch, an epoch of blood and iron, but not in a struggle of nation against nation, but of the suffering and oppressed class against the ruling classes.'" Such is Miliukov's rendering. In his conclusion Trotsky formulated three rules for the policy of the masses—"three revolutionary articles of faith: do not trust the bourgeoisie; control the leaders; rely only on your own force." Speaking of this speech, Sukhanov remarks: "He evidently did not expect any sympathy for his words." And in truth the orator left the hall amid far less applause than had greeted his entrance. Sukhanov, very sensitive to what is going on in the *couloirs* of the intelligentsia, adds: "Although Trotsky did not belong to the Bolshevik Party, rumors were already going around to the effect that he was worse than Lenin.'"

The socialists appropriated six portfolios out of fifteen. They wanted to be in the minority. Even after deciding openly to enter the government, they continued to play this game of give-away. Prince Lvov remained Premier; Kerensky became Minister of War and Marine; Chernov, Minister of Agriculture. Miliukov's place as Minister of Foreign Affairs was taken by Tereshchenko, a connoisseur of the ballet who had become the confidential man at one and the same time of Kerensky and Buchanan. They all three agreed in thinking that Russia could get along exceptionally well without Constantinople. At the head of the Department of Justice stood an insignificant law-yer, Pereverzev, who subsequently acquired a passing glory in connection with the July incident of the Bolsheviks. Tseretelli limited himself to the portfolio of Posts and Telegraphs in order to keep his time for the Executive Committee. Skobelev, be-coming Minister of Labor, promised in the heat of the excite-ment to cut down the profits of the capitalists one hundred per cent. That phrase soon acquired wings. For the sake of sym-metry the Ministry of Trade and Industry was given to a great Moscow industrialist, Konovalov. He brought along with him certain notables from the Moscow Stock Exchange who received important government posts. After two weeks, by the way, Konovalov resigned as a protest against the "anarchy" in public economy. Skobelev, even before two weeks, had renounced his attack on profits, and was busying himself with the struggle against anarchy—quelling strikes, summoning the workers to self-restraint. The Declaration of the new government con-sisted, as is to be expected of all coalitions, of commonplaces. It referred to an active foreign policy in the cause of peace, a solution of the food question, and a getting ready to solve the land question. All this was mere talk. The single serious point —at least from the standpoint of intention—was the one about the preparation of the army "for defensive and offensive ac-tivity to prevent the possible defeat of Russia and her Allies." In this was essentially summed up the whole meaning of the Coalition, which was created as the last play of the Entente in Russia.

"The Coalition Government in Russia," wrote Buchanan,

"is for us the last, and almost the only, hope for salvation of the military situation on that front." Thus behind the platforms, speeches, compromises and votes of the liberal and democratic leaders of the February revolution, stood an imperialist stage director in the person of the Entente. Being obliged hastily to enter the government in the name of the interests of the Entente front, which was hostile to the revolution, the socialists took upon themselves about a third of the power and the whole war.

The new Minister of Foreign Affairs had to delay publishing for two weeks the answers of the Allied governments to the declaration of March 27, in order to work out certain stylistic changes which would disguise their polemic against the Declaration of the Coalition Cabinet. That "active foreign policy in the cause of peace" expressed itself thereafter in Tereshchenko's zealously editing the texts of the diplomatic telegrams drawn up for him by old-régime clerks. Crossing out "claims" he would write "the demands of justice"; in place of "safeguarding the interests" he would write "for the good of the peoples." Miliukov, with a slight grinding of teeth, said of his successor: "The Allied diplomats knew that the 'democratic' terminology of his despatches was a reluctant concession to the demands of the moment, and treated it with indulgence."

Thomas and the newly arrived Vandervelde did not sit with folded arms. They zealously interpreted the "good of the peoples" in correspondence with the needs of the Entente, and manipulated with a fair success the simpletons of the Executive Committee. "Skobelev and Chernov," reported Vandervelde, "are energetically protesting against all thoughts of premature peace." No wonder Ribot, relying on such assistants, felt able to announce to the French Parliament on May 9, that he intended to make a satisfactory reply to Tereshchenko "without giving up anything."

No, the real masters of the situation were not intending to give up anything that was lying around loose. It was just in those days that Italy announced the independence of Albania, and immediately placed her under Italy's protectorate. That was not a bad object lesson. The Provisional Government had an idea of protesting—not so much in the name of democracy, as because of the destruction of "equilibrium in the Balkans." But impotence compelled it for the time to bite its tongue.

The only new thing in the foreign policy of the Coalition was its hasty rapprochement with America. This young friendship offered three not unimportant advantages: the United States was not so compromised with military depravities as France and England; the transatlantic republic opened before Russia broad prospects in the matter of loans and military supplies; finally, the diplomacy of Wilson—a mixture of knavery with democratic piety—fell in admirably with the stylistic needs of the Provisional Government. In sending the Root mission to Russia, Wilson addressed the Provisional Government with one of his parish letters in which he declared: "No people must be forced under sovereignty under which it does not wish to live." The aims of the war were defined by the American President not too definitely, but beguilingly: ". . . to secure the future peace of the world and the future welfare and happiness of its people." What could be better? Tereshchenko and Tseretelli needed only that: fresh credits and the commonplaces of pacifism. With the help of the first, and under cover of the second, they could make ready for the offensive which the Shylock on the Seine was demanding with a furious shaking of all his promissory notes.

On the 11th of May, Kerensky went to the front to open his agitation in favor of an offensive. "A wave of enthusiasm is growing and spreading in the army," reported the new War Minister to the Provisional Government, choking with the enthusiasm of his own speeches. On May 14, Kerensky issued a command to the army: "You will go where your leaders conduct you," and in order to adorn this well-known and not very attractive prospect for the soldier, he added: "You will carry on the points of your bayonets—peace." On May 22, the cautious General Alexeiev, a man of no parts in any case, was removed, and replaced in the position of commander-in-chief by the more flexible and enterprising Brussilov. The democrats with all their power were preparing the offensive—the grand catastrophe, that is, of the February revolution.

*

THE Soviet was the organ of the workers and soldiers—and soldiers here means peasants. The Provisional Government was the organ of the bourgeoisie. The Contact Commission was the organ of compromise. The Coalition simplified this mechanism by converting the Provisional Government itself into a contact commission. But the double sovereignty was not in the least done away with. Whether Tseretelli was a member of the Contact Commission or Minister of Posts—that did not decide anything. There were in the country two incompatible state organizations: the hierarchy of old and new officials appointed from above crowned by the Provisional Government, and the system of elective soviets reaching down to the most remote companies at the front. These two state systems rested upon different classes, which as yet were only getting ready to settle their historic accounts. In entering the Coalition, the Compromisers counted on a peaceful and gradual dissolution of the soviet system. They imagined that the power of the soviets, concentrated in their persons, would now flow over into the official government. Kerensky categorically assured Buchanan that "the soviets will die a natural death." This hope soon became the official doctrine of the Compromise leaders. According to their thought, the center of gravity ought to be transferred from the local soviets to the new organs of self-government. The place of the Central Committee should be occupied by the Constituent Assembly. The Coalition Government was in this way to become a bridge to the bourgeois parliamentary republic.

The trouble was that the revolution did not want to, and could not, travel along this road. The fate of the new city dumas had given unequivocal warning in this sense. These dumas had been elected upon the widest possible franchise basis. The soldiers voted equally with the civil population, women equally with men. Four parties took part in the struggle.

Novoye Vremya, the old official sheet of the tzarist government, one of the most dishonest newspapers in the world—and that is saying something—summoned the Rights, the nationalists, the Octobrists, to vote for the Kadets. But when the political impotence of the possessing classes became fully evident, the majority of the bourgeois papers adopted the slogan: "Vote for anybody you please, only not the Bolsheviks!" In all the dumas and zemstvos the Kadets were the right wing, the Bolsheviks a growing left minority. The majority, immense as usual, belonged to the Social Revolutionaries and Mensheviks.

It would seem as if these new dumas, which differed from the soviets by a broader representation, ought to have enjoyed great authority. Moreover as socio-juridical institutions, the dumas had the immense advantage of official governmental support. The militia, the food supplies, the municipal transport, popular education, all were officially in the hands of the duma. The soviet as a "private" institution had neither budget nor rights. And nevertheless the power remained with the soviets. The dumas turned out to be in the essence of the matter municipal commissions of the soviets. This rivalry of the soviet system with formal democracy was the more striking in its outcome, in that it took place under the leadership of those same parties, Social Revolutionaries and Mensheviks, who, ruling in the dumas and the soviets alike, were profoundly convinced that the soviets ought to give way to the dumas, and themselves did their best to promote the process. The explanation of this remarkable phenomenon—about which there was very little speculation in the whirlpool of the actual events—is simple: municipal governments, like any other institutions of democracy, can function only on the basis of firmly established social relations—that is, a definite property system. The essence of revolution, however, is that it calls in question this, the very basis of all bases. And its question can be answered only by an open revolutionary test of the correlation of forces. The soviets, in spite of the quality of their leadership, were the fighting organizations of the oppressed classes, who had consciously or half-consciously united to transform the bases of the social structure. The municipal governments gave equal representation to all classes of the population, reduced to the abstraction of citizenship, and behaved in the revolutionary situation very much like a diplomatic conference expressing itself in qualified and hypocritical language while the hostile camps represented by it are feverishly preparing for battle. In the everyday of the revolution the municipal governments dragged out a half-fictitious existence. But at critical moments, when the interference of the masses was defining the further direction of events, these governments simply exploded in the air, their constituent elements appearing on different sides of a barricade. It was sufficient to contrast the parallel rôles of the soviets and the municipal governments from May to October, in order to foresee the fate of the Constituent Assembly.

The Coalition Government was in no hurry to summon that Constituent Assembly. The liberals being, notwithstanding the democratic arithmetic, a majority in the government, were in no haste to become in the Constituent Assembly a feeble right wing such as they were in the new dumas. The special conference on the convocation of a Constituent Assembly began work only at the end of May—three months after the revolution. The liberal jurists divided every hair into sixteen parts, shook up in their alembics all the different kinds of democratic sediment, bickered endlessly about the elective rights of the army, whether or not it would be necessary to give votes to the deserters, numbering millions, and to the members of the tzar's family, numbering tens. As to the date of the assembly, as little was said as possible. To raise this question was considered in the conference a breach of etiquette such as only Bolsheviks would commit.

Weeks passed, but in spite of the hopes and prophecies of the Compromisers the soviets did not die out. At times, lulled and confused by their leaders, they did fall into semi-prostration, but the first signal of danger would bring them to their feet, and reveal to the eyes of all that they were the real masters of the situation. While attempting to sabotage the soviets, Social Revolutionaries and Mensheviks were obliged in every important incident to recognize their priority. This was ex-

370

pressed among other things by the fact that the best forces of both parties were concentrated in the soviets. To the municipal governments and the zemstvos they appointed people of the second rank, technicians and administrators. The same thing was to be observed among the Bolsheviks. The Kadets alone, not having access to the soviets, concentrated their best forces in those institutions of self-government. But that hopeless bourgeois minority was not able to convert them into a real support.

Thus nobody considered the municipal governments their own institutions. The sharpening antagonism between worker and boss, soldier and officer, peasant and landlord, could not be openly brought up for discussion in the municipal bodies or zemstvos, as was done in their own circles by the soviets on the one side, and by "private" meetings of the State Duma and all kinds of conferences of the "enfranchised" politicians on the other. One can talk over petty details with an enemy, but not matters of life and death.

If you accept the Marxian formula according to which a government is a committee of the ruling class, then you must admit that the genuine "committees" of the classes struggling for power were to be found outside the Coalition Government. As regards the soviets, represented in the government as a minority, that was perfectly obvious. But it was no less true of the bourgeois majority. The liberals were totally unable to discuss in a serious and businesslike way in the presence of socialists the questions of most moment to the bourgeoisie. The crowding out of Miliukov, the acknowledged and indubitable leader of the bourgeoisie, around whom a staff of property owners had united, had a symbolic character, completely revealing the fact that the government was in every sense of the word eccentric. Life revolved around two axes, one of which was to the left and one to the right of the Mariinsky Palace.

Not daring to say what they thought in the staff of the government, the ministers lived in an atmosphere of conventions created by themselves. The double sovereignty concealed by a coalition became a school of two-mindedness, two-heartedness and every possible kind of duplicity. The Coalition Government in the course of the next six months lived through a whole series of crises, reconstructions and reshufflings, but its fundamental features, impotence and hypocrisy, survived to the day of its death.

Chapter XIX

THE OFFENSIVE

IN the army as in the country there was a continual political regrouping of forces, the lower ranks moving to the left, the upper to the right. Just as the Executive Committee was becoming an instrument of the Entente for taming the revolution, the soldiers' committees, having arisen to represent the soldiers against the commanding staff, were being converted into assistants of the commanding staff against the soldiers.

The membership of these committees was variegated. There were not a few patriots who sincerely identified the war with the revolution, courageously joined an offensive imposed from above, and laid down their heads in an alien cause. Beside them stood the heroes of the phrase, regimental and divisional Kerenskys. Finally, there were not a few petty cheats and chairwarmers who got into the committees to keep out of the trenches, always on a hunt for privileges. Every mass movement, especially in its first stages, inevitably raises up on its crest all these human varieties. But the compromise period was especially rich in such loud talkers and chameleons. People form programs but programs also form people. The school of "contact" politics becomes in a revolution a school of trickery and intrigue.

The two-power régime made it impossible to create a military force. The Kadets were hated by the mass of the people, and were compelled in the army to retitle themselves Social Revolutionaries. The democracy could not resurrect the army for the same reason that it could not take over the power. The one was inseparable from the other. As a curiosity, which nevertheless very clearly illumines the situation, Sukhanov remarks that the Provisional Government did not organize a single parade for the soldiers in Petrograd. The liberals and generals did not want the soviets to participate in their parade, but perfectly well understood that without the soviets a parade was impossible. The higher officers were clinging closer and closer to the Kadets, biding the time when more reactionary parties might lift their heads. The petty bourgeois intelligentsia could give the army a considerable number of lower officers, as they had done under tzarism, but they could not create a commanding corps in their own image, for they had no image of their own. As the whole further course of the revolution showed, it was only possible either to take the commanding corps as it was from the nobility and the bourgeoisie, as the Whites did, or bring forward and train up a new one on the basis of proletarian recruiting, as did the Bolsheviks. The petty bourgeois democracy could do neither one thing nor the other. All they could do was to persuade, plead, and deceive everybody, and when nothing came of it, turn over the power in despair to the reactionary officers, and let them teach the people the correct revolutionary ideas.

One after the other the ulcers of the old society broke out and destroyed the organism of the army. The problem of nationality in all its forms—and Russia is rich in nationalities —went deeper and deeper into the soldier mass, which was made up less than half of Great Russians. National antagonisms intercrossed and interwove in all directions with class antagonisms. The policy of the government in the sphere of nationalities, as in all others, was vacillating, confused, and therefore seemed doubly treacherous. Certain generals flirted with national formations such as the "Mussulman Corps with French discipline" on the Rumanian front. These new national units did as a rule prove the most sturdy of the old army, for they were formed under a new idea and a new banner. This national cement however did not last long. Class struggles soon broke it up. But the very process of these national formations, threatening to affect half the army, reduced it to a fluid condition, decomposing the old units before it succeeded in welding the new. Thus misfortune came from all sides.

Miliukov writes in his history that the army was ruined by "the conflict between 'revolutionary' ideas and normal military discipline, between 'democratization of the army' and the 'preservation of its fighting power' "—in which statement, by "normal" discipline is to be understood that which existed under tzarism. A historian ought to know, it would seem, that every great revolution brings ruin to the old army, a result of the clash, not of abstract disciplinary principles, but of living classes. A revolution not only permits strict discipline in an army, but creates it. However, this discipline cannot be established by representatives of the class which the revolution has overthrown.

"Surely, the fact is evident," wrote one wise German to another on September 26, 1851, "that a disorganized army and a complete breakdown of discipline has been the condition as well as the result of every victorious revolution." The whole history of humanity proves this simple and indubitable law. But along with the liberals, the Russian socialists—with the experience of 1905 behind them—did not understand this, although they called the two Germans, one of whom was Frederick Engels and the other Karl Marx, their teachers. The Mensheviks seriously believed that the army after making a revolution would continue the war under the old command. And those people called the Bolsheviks utopians!

General Brussilov at a conference at headquarters in the beginning of May succinctly characterized the condition of the commanding staff: 15 to 20 per cent had adapted themselves to the new order through conviction; a part of the officers were beginning to flirt with the soldiers and incite them against the commanding staff; but the majority, about 75 per cent, could not adapt themselves, were offended, were hiding in their shells, and did not know what to do. The overwhelming mass of the officers were, in addition, good-for-nothing from a purely military point of view.

At a conference with the generals, Kerensky and Skobelev zealously apologized for the revolution, which, alas, "was continuing" and must be taken into consideration. To this the Black Hundred general Gurko answered the ministers moralizingly: "You say the revolution is continuing. Listen to us. Stop the revolution, and let us, the military, do our duty to the end." Kerensky went to meet the generals with all his heart—until one of them, the valorous Kornilov, almost strangled him in his embraces.

Compromisism in a time of revolution is a policy of feverish scurrying back and forth between classes. Kerensky was the incarnation of scurrying back and forth. Placed at the head of an army, an institution unthinkable without a clear and concise régime, Kerensky became the immediate instrument of its disintegration. Denikin publishes a curious list of changes of personnel in the high commanding staff—changes which missed the mark, although nobody really knew, and least of all Kerensky, where the mark was. Alexeiev dismissed the commander-in-chief at the front, Ruszky, and the army commander Radko-Dmitriev, for weakness and indulgence to the committees. Brussilov removed for the same reason the panic-stricken Yudenich. Kerensky dismissed Alexeiev himself and the commanders-in-chief at the front, Gurko and Dragomirov, for resisting democratization of the army. On the same grounds Brussilov removed General Kaledin, and was himself subsequently relieved for excessive indulgence to the committees. Kornilov left the command of the Petrograd district through inability to get along with the democracy. This did not prevent his appointment to the front, and subsequently to the supreme command. Denikin was removed from the post of chief of staff under Alexeiev for his obviously feudal administration, but was soon after named commander-in-chief of the western front. This game of leap-frog, showing that the people at the top did not know what they wanted, gradually extending downward to the companies, hastened the breakdown of the army.

While demanding that soldiers obey the officers, the commissars themselves did not trust them. At the very height of the offensive, at a meeting of the soviet at headquarters in Moghilev, one of the members of the soviet declared in the presence of Kerensky and Brussilov: "Eighty-eight per cent of the officers of the staff are giving rise by their activities to a danger of counter-revolutionary manifestations." This was no secret to the soldiers. They had had plenty of time to get acquainted with their officers before the revolution.

Throughout May the reports of the commanding staff from top to bottom consist of variations on one single theme: "The attitude to the offensive is in general adverse, and especially in the infantry." Sometimes they add: "A little better in the cavalry and hearty enough in the artillery."

At the end of May when the troops were already marshaled for the offensive, the commissar with the 7th Army telegraphed to Kerensky: "In the 12th Division, the 48th Regiment has gone out in full force. The 45th and 46th Regiments, with only half of the front-line companies. The 47th refuses to go out. Of the regiments of the 13th Division, the 50th came out almost in full force. The 51st promises to come out tomorrow, the 49th did not come out as ordered, and the 52nd refused to come out and arrested all its officers." The same picture was to be observed almost everywhere. To the report of the commissar, the government answered: "Disband the 45th, 46th, 47th and 52nd regiments, court-martial those who incited the officers and soldiers to disobedience." That sounded terrible, but did not frighten anybody. The soldiers who did not want to fight were not afraid either of disbandment or of court-martial. In deploying the soldiers it was often necessary to send one detachment against another. The instrument of repression would most often be the Cossacks, as under the tzar. But they were now led by socialists: it was a question, you see, of defending the revolution.

On June 4, less than two weeks before the beginning of the offensive, the chief of the headquarters staff reported: "The northern front is still in a ferment, fraternization continues, the infantry is opposed to the offensive. . . . On the western front the situation is indefinite. . . . On the southwestern a certain improvement of mood is noticeable. . . . On the Rumanian no special improvement is observable, the infantry does not want to advance."

On June 11, 1917, the commander of the 61st Regiment writes: "The officers and I have nothing left to do but save ourselves, because there has arrived from Petrograd a soldier of the 5th Company, a Leninist. . . . Many of the best soldiers and officers have already fled." The appearance in the regiment of one Leninist was enough to start the officers running away. It is clear that the arriving soldier played the part of the first crystal in a saturate solution. However, we must not think that the talk here is necessarily of a Bolshevik. In those days the commanding staff called every soldier a Leninist who raised his voice more boldly than others against the offensive. Many of those "Leninists" still sincerely believed that Lenin had been sent by Wilhelm. The commander of the 61st Regiment tried to frighten his soldiers with punishment at the hands of the government. One of the soldiers answered: "We overthrew the former government, we'll kick out Kerensky." That was new talk. They were nourished on Bolshevik agitation, but went far beyond it.

From the Black Sea fleet, which was under the leadership of Social Revolutionaries and was considered by contrast to the Kronstadt sailors a bulwark of patriotism, a special delegation of 300 men was sent out through the country at the end of April with a brisk student, Batkin, dressed up as a sailor, at the head. There was a good deal of the masquerade in that delegation but there was also a more sincere impulse. The delegation was selling to the country the idea of war to victory. But with every week the listeners became more hostile. And just as these Black Sea sailors were beginning to lower the tone of their pro-war sermons, a Baltic delegation arrived in Sebastopol to preach peace. The Northerners had more success in the south than the Southerners in the north. Under the influence of the Kronstadt sailors, the Sebastopol sailors undertook on June 8 to disarm the commanding staff and arrest their worst-hated officers.

At a meeting of the soviet Congress on June 9, Trotsky asked how it could happen that "in that model Black Sea fleet which had sent patriotic deputations throughout the country, in that nest of organized patriotism, an explosion of this nature could occur at such a critical moment? What does this prove?" He received no answer.

The headless and brainless condition of the army tortured everybody—soldiers, commanders and committeemen. To them all the need of some way out became unbearable. To the chiefs

it seemed that the offensive would overcome this reign of bed-
lam and bring definiteness. And to a certain extent this was
true. While Tseretelli and Chernov expressed themselves in
Petrograd in favor of the offensive with all the careful modula-
tions of the democratic rhetoric, the committeemen at the front
had to wage a campaign hand-in-hand with the officers against
the new régime in the army—a régime incompatible with war,
but without which the revolution was unthinkable. The results of the change were soon visible. "With every day that
passed, the members of the committee were noticeably moving
to the right," recounts one of the naval officers, "but at the
same time there was an obvious decline in their authority among
the soldiers and sailors." It happens, however, that soldiers and
sailors are just what is needed for a war.

Brussilov, with Kerensky's approval, undertook the formation of shock battalions of volunteers, thus frankly acknowledging the incapacity of the army to fight. All sorts of elements immediately attached themselves to this enterprise—for
the most part adventurers like Captain Muraviev, who subsequently, after the October revolution, swung round to the left
Social Revolutionaries, and then after a stormy and in its way
brilliant career, betrayed the Soviet power, and died of a bullet
shot, either from a Bolshevik or from his own hand. It is
needless to say that the counter-revolutionary officers greedily
seized upon the shock battalion idea as a legal way of mustering
their own forces. The idea got almost no response, however,
in the soldier mass. Some women in search of adventure created a woman's battalion of "Black Death Hussars." One of
these battalions became Kerensky's last armed force in the defense of the Winter Palace in October. But all this gave very
little help to the cause of crushing German militarism—as the
task was described.

The offensive promised by the staff to the Allies for early
spring had been postponed from week to week. But now the
Entente firmly refused to accept any further postponements.
In pressing for an immediate offensive the Allies did not mince
methods. Along with the pathetic adjurations of Vandervelde,
they employed the threat to stop sending military supplies. The

Italian consul-general in Moscow announced to the press—not the Italian, but the Russian press—that in case of a separate peace on the part of Russia, the Allies would give Japan a free hand in Siberia. The liberal papers—not the Rome, but the Moscow papers—printed these insolent threats with patriotic rapture, making them apply not to a separate peace, but to a delayed offensive. In other respects the Allies did not stand upon ceremony: for instance, they sent artillery that was known to be damaged. Thirty-five per cent of the weapons received from abroad did not survive two weeks of moderate shooting. England was shutting down on credits; but then America, the new benefactor, without the knowledge of England, offered the Provisional Government on the security of the new offensive a credit of $75,000,000. Although supporting the demands of the Allies by waging a frantic agitation for the offensive, the Russian bourgeoisie withheld its own confidence from the offensive by refusing to subscribe the Liberty loan. The overthrown monarchy utilized this incident to remind the public of its existence. In a declaration in the name of the Provisional Government, Romanov expressed a desire to subscribe to the loan, but added: "The extent of the subscription will depend on the question whether the treasury supplies money to support the members of the tzar's family." All this was read by the army, which knew very well that the majority of the Provisional Government, as also a majority of the upper officers, were still hoping for a restoration. Justice demands the observation that in the Allied camp not all agreed with Vandervelde, Thomas and Cachin in pushing the Russian army over the precipice. There were warning voices. "The Russian army is nothing but a façade," said General Pétain, "it will fall to pieces if it makes a move." The American mission, for another example, expressed the same view. But other considerations prevailed. It was necessary to take the heart out of the revolution. "The German-Russian fraternization," explained Painlevé later, "had caused such ravages that to leave the Russian army inactive would mean to risk its rapid disintegration." The political preparation for the offensive was at first carried on by Kerensky and Tseretelli, in secrecy even from their closest colleagues.

In the days when these half-consecrated leaders were still continuing to spout about the defense of the revolution, Tseretelli was more and more firmly insisting on the necessity that the army make ready for active service. The longest to resist—that is, the coyest—was Chernov. At a meeting of the Provisional Government on May 17, the "rural minister," as he called himself, was asked with heat whether it was true that he had expressed himself at a certain meeting on the subject of the offensive without the necessary sympathy. It transpired that Chernov answered as follows: "The offensive does not concern me, a man of politics; that is a question for the strategists at the front." Those people were playing hide-and-seek with the war, as with the revolution. But only for the time being.

The preparation for the offensive was accompanied, of course, by a redoubled struggle against the Bolsheviks. They were being accused now oftener and oftener of working for a separate peace. The possibility that a separate peace would be the only way out, was evident in the whole situation—the weakness and exhaustion of Russia in comparison with the other warring countries. But nobody had yet measured the strength of the new factor, revolution. The Bolsheviks believed that the prospect of a separate peace could be avoided only in case the force and authority of revolution were boldly and conclusively set against the war. For this was needed first of all a break with our own bourgeoisie. On June 9, Lenin announced at the congress of the soviets: "When they say that we are striving for a separate peace, that is not true. We say: No separate peace, not with any capitalists, and least of all with the Russian capitalists. But the Provisional Government has made a separate peace with the Russian capitalists. Down with that separate peace!" "Applause," remarks the report. That was the applause of a small minority at the congress, and for that reason especially fervent.

In the Executive Committee some still lacked decision, others wanted to hide behind the more authoritative institutions. At the last moment it was resolved to bring to Kerensky's attention the undesirability of giving the order for the offensive before the question had been decided upon by the soviet congress. A declaration introduced at the very first session of the congress by the Bolshevik faction had stated: "An offensive can only utterly disorganize the army, bringing one part into antagonism with the other, and the Congress should either immediately oppose this counter-revolutionary onslaught, or else frankly assume the whole responsibility for this policy."

The decision of the soviet congress in favor of the offensive was merely a democratic formality. Everything was already prepared. The artillery had for a long time been aimed at the enemy's positions. On June 16, in an order to the army and the fleet, Kerensky, referring to the commander-in-chief as "our leader fanned by the wings of victory," demonstrated the necessity of "an immediate and decisive blow," and concluded with the words: "I command you—forward!" In an article written on the eve of the offensive, commenting on the declaration of the Bolshevik faction at the soviet congress, Trotsky wrote: "The policy of the government completely undermines the possibility of successful military action . . . The material premises for an offensive are extremely unfavorable. The organization of supplies for the army reflects the general economic collapse, against which a government constituted like the present one cannot undertake a single radical measure. The spiritual premises of the offensive are still more unfavorable. The government . . . has exposed before the army . . . its incapacity to determine Russia's policy independently of the will of the imperialist Allies. No result is possible but the progressive breakdown of the army. . . . The mass desertions . . . are ceasing in the present conditions to be the result of depraved individual wills, and are becoming an expression of the complete incapacity of the government to weld the revolutionary army with an inward unity of purpose. . . ." Pointing out further that the government could not make up its mind "to an immediate annulment of landlordship—that is, to the sole measure which would convince the most backward peasant that this revolution is his revolution," the article concluded: "In such material and spiritual conditions an offensive must inevitably have the character of an adventure."

The commanding staff was almost unanimous in thinking that the offensive, hopeless from a military point of view, was dictated by political considerations. Denikin after making the rounds of his front reported to Brussilov: "I haven't the slightest belief in the success of the offensive." A supplementary element of hopelessness was introduced by the good-for-nothingness of the commanding staff itself. Stankevich, an officer and a patriot, testifies that the technical dispositions of things made victory impossible regardless of the morale of the troops: "The offensive was organized in a manner beneath criticism." A delegation of officers came to the leaders of the Kadet Party with the president of the officers' union, the Kadet Novosiltsev, at its head, and warned them that the offensive was doomed to failure, and would mean only the extermination of the best units. The higher powers waved away these warnings with general phrases: "A last spark of hope remains," said the chief of the headquarters staff, the reactionary general Lukomsky, "that perhaps a beginning of successful battles will change the psychology of the masses, and the officers will be able to seize the reins that have been torn from their hands." That was their main purpose—to get hold of those reins.

The chief blow was to be delivered, according to a plan worked out long before, by the forces of the southwestern front in the direction of Lvov; the work of the northern and western fronts was to help this operation. The advance was to have begun simultaneously on all fronts. It was soon evident that this plan was far beyond the powers of the command. They decided to start off one front after the other, beginning with those of secondary importance. But that too proved impossible. "Then the supreme command," says Denikin, "decided to give up all idea of planned strategy, and had to allow the fronts to begin operations whenever they were ready." All was left to the will of Providence. Only the icons of the tzarina were lacking. They tried to replace them with the icons of democracy. Kerensky traveled everywhere, appealing and pronouncing benedictions. The offensive began: June 16 on the southwestern front, July 7 on the western, 8th on the northern, 9th on the Rumanian. The advance of the last three fronts was in reality fictitious, coinciding with the beginning of the collapse of the principal one, the southwestern.

Kerensky reported to the Provisional Government: "Today is the great triumph of the revolution. On June 18 the Russian revolutionary army with colossal enthusiasm assumed the offensive." "The long expected advance has arrived," wrote the Kadet organ *Rech,* "which has at one stroke restored the Russian revolution to its best days." On the 19th the old man Plekhanov declaimed to a patriotic manifestation: "Citizens, if I ask you what day this is, you will say 'Monday.' But that is a mistake. Today is the resurrection day.[1] Resurrection of our country and of the whole world. Russia, having thrown off the yoke of tzarism, has decided to throw off the yokes of the enemy." Tseretelli said on the same day at the soviet congress: "A new page is opening in the history of the great Russian revolution. The success of our revolutionary army ought to be welcomed not only by the Russian democracy, but . . . by all those who are really striving to fight against imperialism." The patriotic democracy had opened all its taps. The newspapers meanwhile carried joyful news: "The Paris Bourse greets the Russian offensive with a rise in all Russian securities." Those socialists were trying to estimate the stability of the revolution by the stock-ticker. But history teaches that bourses feel better the worse it goes with revolutions.

The workers and the garrison of the capital were not for one minute infected by this wave of artificially warmed-over patriotism. Its sole arena was the Nevsky Prospect. "We went out on the Nevsky," relates the soldier Chinenov in his memoirs, "and tried to agitate against the offensive. Some of the bourgeois took after us with their umbrellas. . . . We grabbed them and dragged them into the barracks . . . and told them that tomorrow they would be sent to the front." That was a preliminary symptom of the advancing explosion of civil war. The July days were drawing near.

On the 21st of June a machine gun regiment in Petrograd resolved in general meeting: "In the future we will send forces to the front only when the war shall have a revolutionary character." In answer to the threat of disbandment, the regi-

[1] The Russian word for Sunday is "Resurrection."

ment answered that it would not hesitate to disband "the Provisional Government and the other organizations which support it." Here again, a threatening note far in advance of the Bolshevik agitation. The *Chronicle* of the Revolution remarks under date of June 23: "Detachments of the 2nd Army have occupied the first and second line trenches of the enemy. . . ." And right beside this: "At the Baranovsky factory (6000 men) there were reëlections to the Petrograd Soviet. In place of three Social Revolutionaries, three Bolsheviks were elected."

By the end of the month the physiognomy of the Petrograd Soviet had already considerably changed. It is true that on June 20 the Soviet adopted a resolution of greeting to the advancing army. But with what majority?—472 votes against 271, with 39 abstaining. That is a totally new correlation of forces, something we have not seen before. The Bolsheviks, together with the left groups of Mensheviks and Social Revolutionaries, constitute already two-fifths of the Soviet. This means that in the factories and barracks the opponents of the offensive are already an indubitable majority.

The Vyborg district soviet adopted a resolution on June 24 every word of which strikes like a heavy hammer: "We . . . protest against the adventure of the Provisional Government, which is conducting an offensive for the old robber treaties . . . and we lay the whole responsibility for this policy on the Provisional Government and the Menshevik and Social Revolutionary parties supporting it." Having been pushed out after the February insurrection into the back-yard, the Vyborg district was now confidently advancing to the leading position. The Bolsheviks already completely dominated the Vyborg Soviet.

Everything now depended upon the fate of the offensive —that is, upon the trench soldiers. What changes had the offensive made in the consciousness of those who were supposed to carry it through? They had been irrepressibly longing for peace. But the rulers had succeeded to a certain degree—at least among a part of the soldiers and for a short time—in converting this very longing into a readiness to advance.

After the revolution the soldiers had expected from the new power a swift conclusion of peace, and had been ready until then to defend the front. The peace did not come. The soldiers resorted to attempts at fraternization with the Germans and Austrians, partly under the influence of Bolshevik agitation, but chiefly seeking their own road to peace. But a drive had been opened against fraternization from all sides. And moreover it was discovered that the German soldiers were still far from casting off obedience to their officers. Fraternization, not having led to peace, dwindled rapidly.

There was on the front at that time a *de facto* armistice. The Germans availed themselves of it for a wholesale transfer of troops to the western front. The Russian soldiers noticed how the enemy trenches were emptied, machine guns removed, cannon carted away. Upon this rested the plan of the "moral preparation for the offensive." It was systematically suggested to the soldiers that the enemy was completely weakened, that he had no force left, that America was pressing upon him from the west, and that we had only to give a small push on our side, and the enemy front would crumple and we would have peace. The authorities did not believe this for a single minute, but they calculated that once having put its hand to the war machine, the army would not be able to let go.

Having failed of their goal, both through the diplomacy of the Provisional Government and through fraternization, a part of the soldiers undoubtedly inclined to this third scheme: to give that push which would make the war crumble into dust. One of the front delegates to the congress reported exactly in this way the mood of the soldiers: "At present we have before us a thinned out German front; there are at present no cannon; and if we advance and overthrow the enemy then we will be close to the wished-for peace."

The enemy at first actually did seem extremely weak, and retired without accepting the battle, which incidentally the attackers were not able to give. But instead of crumbling, the enemy regrouped and concentrated his forces. Penetrating a few score kilometers inland, the Russian soldiers discovered a picture sufficiently familiar to them in the experience of the preceding years: the enemy was waiting for them in new and reënforced positions. Here it became evident that although the soldiers had agreed to give a push in the direction of peace, they were not in the least desirous of war. Having been dragged into it by a combination of force, moral pressure, and most of all deceit, they so much the more indignantly turned back.

"After an artillery fire unprecedented on the Russian side in its intensity and power," says the Russian historian of the World War, General Zayonchkovsky, "the troops occupied the enemy positions almost without loss and did not wish to go any farther. There began a steady desertion and withdrawal of whole units from their positions." A Ukrainian leader, Doroshenko, former commissar of the Provisional Government in Galicia, tells how after the seizure of the cities Galich and Kalush: "In Kalush there immediately occurred a frightful pogrom of the local population—but only of Ukrainians and Jews, they did not touch Poles. Some experienced hand guided the pogrom, pointing out with special care the local Ukrainian cultural and educational institutions." The pogrom was participated in by "the better class of troops, the least depraved by the revolution"—those carefully picked for the offensive. But what still more clearly shows its face in this affair is the leadership of the offensive—the old tzarist commanders, experienced organizers of pogroms.

On July 9 the committees and commissars of the 11th Army telegraphed the government: "A German attack begun on July 6 against the 11th Army front is developing into an overwhelming catastrophe. . . . In the morale of the troops, only recently induced to move by the heroic efforts of a minority, a sharp and ruinous break has occurred. The aggressive flare-up is rapidly exhausting itself. The majority of the troops are now in a state of increasing disintegration. There is nothing left of authority or obedience. Persuasions and arguments have lost their force. They are answered with threats and sometimes with death."

The commander-in-chief of the southwestern front, with the agreement of the commissars and committees, gave an order to shoot those running away. On June 12 the commander-in-chief of the western front, Denikin, returned to his headquarters, as he says, "with despair in my heart, and with a clear consciousness of the complete collapse of the last flickering hope for . . . a miracle."

The soldiers did not want to fight. The rear troops, to whom the weakened units turned for replacements after occupying the enemy trenches, answered: "What did you advance for anyway? Who told you to? It's time to end the war, not attack." The commander of the 1st Siberian Corps, considered one of the best commanders, reported how at nightfall the soldiers began to abandon the unattacked first line in crowds and whole companies. "I understood that we, the officers, were powerless to alter the elemental psychology of the soldier masses, and I sobbed bitterly and long." One of the companies refused even to toss a leaflet to the enemy announcing the capture of Galich, until a soldier could be found who could translate the German text into Russian. In that is expressed the utter lack of confidence of the soldier mass in its ruling staff, both the old one and the new February one. A century of taunts and violence had burst to the surface like a volcano. The soldiers felt themselves again deceived. The offensive had not led to peace but war. The soldiers did not want war. And they were right. Patriots hiding in the rear were branding the soldiers as slackers and baiting them. But the soldiers were right. They were guided by a true national instinct, refracted through the consciousness of men oppressed, deceived, tortured, raised up by a revolutionary hope and again thrown back into the bloody mash. The soldiers were right. A prolongation of the war could give the Russian people nothing but new victims, humiliation, disasters—nothing but an increase of domestic and foreign slavery.

The patriotic press of 1917—not only the Kadet but also the socialist press—was tireless in contrasting the Russian soldiers, cowards and deserters, with the heroic battalions of the great French revolution. This testifies not only to a failure to understand the dialectic of a revolutionary process, but also to a crude ignorance of history.

The remarkable warriors of the French revolution and empire frequently began their careers as breakers of discipline, disorganizers—Miliukov would say, as Bolsheviks. The future

Marshal Davout spent many months of 1789-90 as Lieutenant d'Avout destroying the "normal" discipline in the garrison of Hesdin, driving out the commanding staff. Throughout France up to the middle of 1790 a complete disintegration of the whole army was taking place. The soldiers of the Vincennes regiment compelled their officers to eat with them. The fleet drove out their officers. Twenty regiments did various deeds of violence upon their officers. At Nancy three regiments locked their highest officers in prison. Beginning with 1790 the leaders of the French revolution never tire of repeating on the subject of soldier excesses: "The executive power is guilty, because it has not removed officers hostile to the revolution." It is remarkable that both Mirabeau and Robespierre spoke in favor of dismissing the entire old corps of officers. The former was trying the more quickly to establish a firm discipline, the latter wanted to disarm the counter-revolution. But both understood that the old army could not survive.

To be sure, the Russian revolution, in contrast with the French, took place in a time of war. But you cannot infer from this an exception to the historic law noted by Engels. On the contrary, conditions of prolonged and unsuccessful war could only hasten and sharpen the process of revolutionary disintegration of the army. That miserable and criminal offensive of the democrats did the rest. The soldiers were now saying, to the last man: "Enough of bloodshed! What good are land and freedom if we are not here?" When enlightened pacifists try to abolish war by rationalistic arguments they are merely ridiculous, but when the armed masses themselves bring weapons of reason into action against a war, that means that the war is about over.

THE PEASANTRY

THE subsoil of the revolution was the agrarian problem. In the antique land system, born directly out of serfdom, in the traditional power of the landlord, the close ties between landlord, local administration and caste zemstvo, lay the roots of the most barbarous features of Russian life which had their crown in the Rasputin monarchy. The muzhik, age-old support of orientalism, proved also its first victim.

In the first weeks after the February revolution, the village remained almost inert. Those of the most active age were at the front. The elderly generation left at home too well remembered how revolutions end in punitive expeditions. The village was silent, and therefore the city was silent about the village. But the specter of a peasant war hung over the nests of the landlords from the first March days. Out of the most aristocratic—that is, backward and reactionary—provinces a cry for help was heard almost before the real danger appeared. The liberals sensitively reflected the fright of the landlords. The Compromisers reflected the mood of the liberals. "It would be dangerous," rationalizes the left radical, Sukhanov, just after the revolution, "to force the agrarian problem in the next few weeks; and moreover there is not the slightest need of it." As we know, Sukhanov likewise thought it would be dangerous to force the question of peace, or of the eight-hour day. To hide from difficulties is simpler. Moreover, the landlords were afraid a shake-up of land relations would reflect itself harmfully upon the spring sowing and the provisioning of the cities. The Executive Committee sent telegrams to the localities recommending that they should not "become absorbed in the agrarian question to the neglect of food supplies to the cities."

In many regions the landlords, frightened by the revolution, abstained from the spring sowing. With a heavy food crisis throughout the country, those empty fields themselves seemed to cry for a new owner. The peasantry stirred dimly. Hoping little from the new power, the landlords hastened to dispose of their properties. The kulaks began zealously to buy up these estates, figuring that as peasants they would escape forcible expropriation. Many of these land sales were notoriously fictitious. It was assumed that private holdings below a certain norm would be spared; in view of this, the landlords artificially divided their property into small allotments, creating dummy owners. Not infrequently the lands were transferred to foreigners, citizens of the allied or neutral countries. Kulak speculation and landlord trickery threatened to leave nothing of the public land by the time the Constituent Assembly was convoked.

The villages saw these maneuvers. Hence their demand: stop all land sales by decree. Peasant delegates kept pouring into the cities to the new authorities seeking land and justice. It happened to the ministers more than once, after their exalted debates and ovations, to run into the gray figures of peasant deputies at the doorway. Sukhanov tells how one of these delegates with tears in his eyes beseeched the citizen minister to promulgate a law protecting the land from being sold off. He was impatiently interrupted by Kerensky, excited and pale: "I said it would be done, and that means it will be . . . and you needn't look at me with those suspicious eyes." Sukhanov, who was present at this scene, adds: "I report this verbatim. And Kerensky was right: the muzhik did look with suspicious eyes at the eminent people's minister and leader." In this short dialogue between a peasant who is still asking but no longer trusting, and the radical minister gesturing away the peasant's distrust, is contained the inevitability of the February régime's collapse.

The act creating land committees as organs of preparation for agrarian reform was published by the first Minister of Agriculture, the Kadet Shingarev. The main land committee, presided over by the liberal bureaucratic professor, Postnikov, consisted chiefly of Narodniks who feared more than anything else to appear less moderate than their president. Local land committees were established in the provinces, counties and rural districts. Whereas the Soviets, which took hold rather slowly in the villages, were considered private organizations, these committees had a governmental character. But the more indefinite their functions were according to the act, the harder it was for them to resist the pressure of the peasants. The lower a committee stood in the general hierarchy—the nearer, that is, to the land—the sooner it became an instrument of the peasant movement.

Toward the end of March there began to flow into the capital the first alarming tidings of the peasants' entrance upon the scene. The Novgorod commissar telegraphed of disorders caused by a certain corporal Panasiuk, of "unwarranted arrests of land-lords," etc. In Tambov province a crowd of peasants, with certain furloughed soldiers at their head, had sacked a landlord's estate. The first communications were doubtless exaggerated. The landlords certainly magnified these conflicts in their complaints, running ahead of the actual events. But one thing is beyond doubt; namely, that the leading rôle in the peasant movement was played by the soldier, who brought home from the front and from the city barracks a spirit of initiative.

One of the district land committees of Kharkov province decided, on April 5, to conduct a search for weapons among the landowners. That already smacks of the coming civil war. A disturbance arising in Skopinsky county, Riazan province, is explained by the commissar as due to a decree of the executive committee of a neighboring county establishing compulsory rental to the peasants of the landlords' lands. "The agitation of students in favor of tranquillity until the Constituent Assembly, has had no success." Thus we learn that the "students," who had summoned the peasants in the first revolution to a campaign of terror, such being the tactic of the Social Revolutionaries at that time, were now, in 1917, preaching lawfulness and tranquillity—to be sure, without success.

The commissar of Simbirsk province draws the picture of a more developed peasant movement: The district and village committees—of which something will be said later—are arresting the landlords, banishing them from the province, calling out the workers from the landlords' fields, seizing the land, establishing arbitrary rentals. "The delegates sent by the Executive Committee are taking their stand on the side of the peasants." At the same time there begins a movement of the communal peasants against the individual landowners—against the strong peasants, that is, who had detached themselves and taken up individual holdings on the basis of Stolypin's law of November 9, 1906. "The situation in the provinces menaces the sowing of the fields." As early as April, the Simbirsk province commissar can see no way out but immediately to declare the land national property, the terms on which it is to be used to be defined later by the Constituent Assembly.

From Kashir county, just outside Moscow, come complaints that the executive committee is inciting the population to the seizure without indemnity of the church, monastery and landlords' estates. In Kursk province the peasants are removing the war-prisoners from work on the estates, and even locking them up in the local jail. After the peasant congresses, the peasants in the Penza province, inclining to a literal interpretation of the Social Revolutionary resolution on land and freedom, begin to violate a recently concluded contract with the landlords. At the same time they make an assault on the new organs of power. "Upon the organization of the district and county executive committees in March, the intelligentsia composed the majority of their staffs, but afterwards"—reports the commissar of Penza—"voices began to be heard against the intelligentsia, and by the middle of April the staff of the committees everywhere was exclusively composed of peasants whose tendency on the land question was clearly lawless." A group of landlords of the neighboring Kazan province complains to the Provisional Government of the impossibility of carrying on their business, because the peasants are calling off their workers, stealing seed, in many localities carrying off the movables of the estate, not permitting the landlord to cut wood in his own forest, threatening him with violence and death. "There are no courts; everybody does as he wishes; sensible people are terrorized." The Kazan landlords already know who is guilty of this anarchy: "The instructions of the

Provisional Government are unknown in the village, but Bolshevik leaflets are widely distributed." However, there was no lack of instructions from the Provisional Government. In a telegram of March 20, Prince Lvov proposed to the commissars to create district committees as organs of the local power, recommending that they should draw into the work of these committees "the local landowners and all the intellectual forces of the village." It was proposed to organize the whole state structure in the manner of a system of chambers of conciliation. The commissars, however, were soon weeping about the crowding out of the "intellectual forces." The muzhik obviously did not trust his county and district Kerenskys.

On April 3, Prince Lvov's substitute, Prince Yurussov—the Ministry of the Interior was adorned, we see, with lofty titles—recommends that no arbitrary acts shall be permitted, and especially "the freedom of every proprietor to dispose of his own land"—sweetest of all freedoms—shall be defended. Ten days later Prince Lvov himself considers it necessary to do something, and recommends to the commissars "to put a stop to every manifestation of violence and robbery with the whole power of the law." Again two days later, Prince Yurussov instructs the provincial commissars "to take measures for the protection of the stud farms from lawless acts, explaining to the peasants . . . and so forth." On April 18, Prince Yurussov is troubled because the war-prisoners working for the landlords are beginning to present immoderate demands, and instructs the commissars to penalize these insolent fellows on the basis of the authority formerly enjoyed by the tzar's governors. Circulars, instructions, telegraphic directions pour down from above in a continual shower. On May 12 Prince Lvov enumerates in a new telegram the unlawful activities which are "unceasing throughout the country": arbitrary arrests, searches; removals from office, from management of estates, from administration of factories and shops; wrecking of properties; pillage, insubordination, hooliganism; acts of violence against official personages; imposition of taxes upon the population; inciting one part of the population against another, etc., etc. "All such forms of activity must be recognized as clearly unlawful and in certain cases even anarchistic. . . ." The characterization is not very clear, but the conclusion is: "That the most decisive measures must be taken." The provincial commissars resolutely issued orders to the counties, the counties brought pressure to bear on the district committees, and all of them together revealed their impotence in the face of the muzhiks.

Almost everywhere the nearest military detachments had a hand in the business. Oftenest indeed they took the initiative. The movement assumed widely different forms, according to local conditions and the sharpness of the struggle. In Siberia, where there were no landlords, the peasants took possession of the church and monastery lands. In other parts of the country, too, the clergy had a hard time. In the pious province of Smolensk, under the influence of soldiers arriving from the fronts, the priests and the monks were arrested. Local organizations were often compelled to go farther than they wanted to, merely to prevent the peasants from taking incomparably more radical steps. Early in May a county executive committee of Samara province appointed a social trustee over the property of Count Orlov-Davidov, thus protecting it from the peasants. Since the decree promised by Kerensky forbidding the sale of lands never did appear, the peasants began to stop these sales in their own way, preventing surveys of the land. Confiscation of the landlords' weapons, even their hunting weapons, was spreading wider and wider. The peasants of Minsk province, complains the commissar, "take the resolutions of a peasant congress for law." Yes, and how could they take them otherwise? Those congresses were the sole real power in the localities. Thus is revealed the vast dissonance between the Social Revolutionary intelligentsia drowning in words, and the peasantry demanding action.

Towards the end of May the far steppes of Asia billowed up. The Kirghiz, from whom the tzardom used to take away their best lands for the benefit of its servants, arose now against the landlords, suggesting that they hand over at once the stolen goods. "This view is gaining ground in the steppes," reported the Akmolinsk commissar. At the opposite end of the country, in Lifland province, a county executive committee sent a commission to investigate the sacking of the property of Baron Stahl von Holstein. The commission declared the disorders insignificant and the presence of the baron in the county undesirable for the public tranquillity, and proposed: To forward him along with the baroness to Petrograd and place them at the disposal of the Provisional Government. Thus arose one of the innumerable conflicts between the local and the central powers, between the Social Revolutionaries down below and the Social Revolutionaries on top.

A report of May 27 from Pavlograd county in Ekaterinoslav province paints an almost idyllic picture of law and order: The members of the land committee are explaining to the population all misunderstandings and thus "preventing any kind of excess." Alas, this idyll will last but a few weeks. The head of one of the Kostroma monasteries bitterly complained at the end of May against a requisition by the peasants of a third of his horned cattle. The reverend monk should have been more meek: he will soon bid farewell to the other two-thirds.

In Kursk province there began a persecution of the individual settlers who had refused to return to the commune. In the hour of its great land revolution, its "Black Division," the peasantry wanted to act as a single whole. Inner distinctions might prove an obstacle; the commune must stand forth as one man. The fight for the landlord's land was therefore accompanied by acts of violence against the separate farmer—the land individualist.

On the last day of May, a soldier, Samoilov, was arrested in Perm province for inciting to non-payment of land taxes. Soldier Samoilov will soon be arresting others. During a religious procession in one of the villages in Kharkov province, a peasant Grichenko chopped down with an axe before the eyes of the entire village the revered icon of St. Nicholas. Thus all kinds of protests arise and express themselves in action. An anonymous naval officer and landlord, in his Notes of a White Guard, gives an interesting picture of the evolution of the village in the first months of the revolution. To all offices "almost everywhere they elected at first men from the bourgeois layers.

Everybody was striving for but one thing—to maintain order."
The peasants, to be sure, made demands for the land, but during
the first two or three months without violence. You could
hear everywhere such phrases as "We do not want to rob, we
want to get it by agreement," etc. In these reassuring af-
firmations the ear of the lieutenant caught a note of "concealed
threat." And in truth, although the peasantry in the first
period did not resort to violence, still in relation to the so-called
intellectual forces "they immediately began to reveal their dis-
respect." This half-waiting attitude continued, according to the
White Guard, until May or June, "after which a sharp change
was to be observed—a tendency appeared to quarrel with the
provisional regulations, to put things through to suit themselves." In other words, the peasants gave the February revolution approximately three months' grace on the promissory
notes of the Social Revolutionaries, after which they began to
collect in their own way.

A soldier, Chinenov, who had joined the Bolsheviks, made
two trips from Moscow after the revolution to his home in
Orel. In May the Social Revolutionaries were dominant in
the district. The muzhiks in many localities were still paying
rent to the landlords. Chinenov organized a Bolshevik nucleus
of soldiers, peasant farmhands and poor peasants. The nucleus
advocated the cessation of rent payments and a distribution
of land among the landless. They immediately registered the
landlords' meadow lands, divided them among the villages, and
mowed them. "The Social Revolutionaries sitting in the district
committees cried out against the illegality of our act, but did
not renounce their own share of the hay." As the village
representatives would give up their offices through fear of
responsibility, the peasants would select new ones who were
more resolute. The latter were by no means always Bolsheviks.
By direct pressure the peasants were producing a split in the
Social Revolutionary Party, dividing the revolutionary elements
from the functionaries and careerists. Having mowed the
manorial hay, the muzhiks turned to the fallow land and began
to divide it for the fall sowing. The Bolshevik nucleus decided to look over the manorial granaries and send the reserves

397

of grain to the hungering capital. The resolution of the nucleus was carried out because it coincided with the mood of the peasants. Chinenov brought with him to his homeland some Bolshevik literature, a thing nobody had ever heard of until he arrived. "The local intelligentsia and the Social Revolutionaries," he said, "spread a rumor that I was bringing with me a great deal of German gold and that I would bribe the peasants." The same processes developed on a small as on a large scale. The districts had their Miliukovs, their Kerensky's, and . . . their Lenins.

In Smolensk province the influence of the Social Revolutionaries began to grow after the Provincial Congress of peasant deputies, which declared itself, as was to be expected, for a transfer of land to the people. The peasants swallowed this decision whole, but in distinction from their leaders they swallowed it in earnest. Thenceforward the number of Social Revolutionaries in the villages increased continuously. "Anyone who had been in the Social Revolutionary faction at any congress," relates one of the local party workers, "considered himself either a Social Revolutionary, or something very much like it." In the county seat there were two regiments, also under the influence of the Social Revolutionaries. The district land committee began to plow the landlord's land and mow his meadows. The provincial commissar, a Social Revolutionary, Efimov, issued threatening orders. The village was bewildered. Why, didn't this same commissar tell us that the peasants themselves are now the government and that only he who works the land can benefit by it? But as a matter of fact at the direction of this Social Revolutionary commissar, Efimov, 16 district land committees out of 17, in Yelnin county alone, were brought to trial in the coming months for seizing the landlords' land. Thus, in its own way, the romance between the Narodnik intelligentsia and the people drew to its dénouement. In the whole county there were not more than three or four Bolsheviks. Their influence grew quickly, however, crowding out or splitting the Social Revolutionaries.

An All-Russian Peasant Congress was convoked in Petrograd at the beginning of May. The representation was largely upper crust, and in many cases accidental. If the workers' and soldiers' congresses continually lagged behind the course of events and the political evolution of the masses, it is needless to say how far the representation of a scattered peasantry lagged behind the actual mood of the Russian villages. As delegates there appeared, on the one hand, Narodnik intellectuals of the extreme right, associated with the peasantry chiefly through commercial coöperatives or the reminiscences of childhood. The genuine "people," on the other hand, were represented by the better-off upper strata of the villages, kulaks, shopkeepers, peasant coöperators. The Social Revolutionaries dominated this congress absolutely, and moreover in the person of their extreme right wing. At times, however, even they paused in fright before the reeking mixture of land greed and political "blackhundred-ism" which exuded from some of the deputies. In regard to the landlord problem an extremely radical position was formulated at this congress: "Conversion of all land into national property for equal working use, without any indemnity." To be sure, the kulak understood equality only in the sense of his equality with the landlord, not at all in the sense of his equality with the hired hands. However, this little misunderstanding between the fictitious socialism of the Narodniks and the agrarian democratism of the muzhiks would come out in the open only in the future.

The Minister of Agriculture, Chernov, burning with a desire to present an Easter egg to the Peasant Congress, vainly busied himself with the project of a decree forbidding land sales. The Minister of Justice, Pereverzev, also counting himself something of a Social Revolutionary, issued instructions during the very days of the congress that in the various localities no obstacles should be put in the way of land sales. On this subject the peasant deputies raised a noise. But the matter did not move forward a step. The Provisional Government of Prince Lvov would not agree to lay a hand on the landlords' estates. The socialists did not want to lay a hand on the Provisional Government. And least of all was the staff of the congress capable of finding a way out of the contradiction between its appetite for land and its reactionism.

On the 20th of May, Lenin spoke at the Peasant Congress.

It seemed, says Sukhanov, as though Lenin had landed in a pit of crocodiles. "However, the little muzhiks listened attentively and very likely not without sympathy, although they did not dare show it." The same thing was repeated in the soldiers' section, which was extremely hostile to the Bolsheviks. In the style of the Social Revolutionaries and Mensheviks, Sukhanov tries to give Lenin's tactics on the land question an anarchist tint. This is not so far from the attitude of Prince Lvov, who was always inclined to regard infringements of landlord rights as anarchist activities. According to this logic, the revolution as a whole is equivalent to anarchy. In reality Lenin's way of posing the question was far deeper than it seemed to his critics. The instruments of the agrarian revolution, and primarily of the seizure of the landed estates, were to be the soviets of peasants' deputies with the land committees subject to them. In Lenin's eyes these soviets were the organs of a future state power, and that too a most concentrated power—namely, the revolutionary dictatorship. This is certainly far from anarchism, from the theory and practice of non-government. Lenin said on April 28: "We favor an immediate transfer of the land to the peasants, with the highest degree of organization possible. We are absolutely against anarchist seizures." Why, then, are we unwilling to await the Constituent Assembly? For this reason: "The important thing for us is revolutionary initiative; the laws should be the result of it. If you wait until the law is written, and do not yourselves develop revolutionary energy, you will get neither law nor land." Are not these simple words the voice of all revolutions?

After a month's sitting, the Peasant Congress elected as a permanent institution an executive committee composed of two hundred sturdy village petty bourgeois and Narodniks of the professorial or trader type, adorning them at the summit with the decorative figures of Breshkovskaia, Chaikovsky, Vera Figner and Kerensky. As president they elected the Social Revolutionary, Avksentiev, a man made for provincial banquets, but not for a peasant war.

Henceforward the more important questions were taken up at joint sessions of the two executive committees, that of the worker-soldiers and that of the peasants. This combination entailed a great strengthening of the right wing which blended directly with the Kadets. In all cases where it was necessary to bring pressure against the workers, come down on the heads of the Bolsheviks, or threaten the independent Kronstadt republic with whips and scorpions, the two hundred hands, or rather the two hundred fists, of the peasant executive committee would be lifted like a wall. Those people were fully in accord with Miliukov, that it was necessary to "make an end" of the Bolsheviks. But in regard to the landed estates, they had the views not of liberals, but of muzhiks, and this brought them into opposition with the bourgeoisie and the Provincial Government. The Peasant Congress had not had time to disperse, when complaints began to arrive that its resolutions were being taken seriously in the localities and that peasants were going about the business of appropriating the land and equipment of the landlords. It was simply impossible to hammer into those stubborn peasant skulls the difference between words and deeds.

The Social Revolutionaries, frightened, sounded the retreat. At the beginning of June, at their Moscow congress, they solemnly condemned all arbitrary seizures of land: we must wait for the Constituent Assembly. But their resolution proved impotent, not only to stop, but even to weaken the agrarian movement. The matter was further greatly complicated by the fact that in the Social Revolutionary party itself there was no small number of elements actually ready to go the limit with the muzhiks against the landlords. These left Social Revolutionaries, not yet having made up their minds to break openly with the party, helped the muzhiks get around the law, or at least interpret it in their own fashion.

In Kazan province, where the peasant movement assumed especially stormy proportions, the left wing of the Social Revolutionaries defined itself sooner than in other places. At their head stood Kalegaev, subsequently Commissar of Agriculture in the Soviet Government during the bloc between the Bolsheviks and the Social Revolutionaries. From the middle of May there began in Kazan province a systematic transfer of land to the district committees. This measure was adopted most boldly of all in Spassk county, where a Bolshevik stood at the head of the peasant organizations. The provincial authorities complained to the center about the agrarian agitation carried on by Bolsheviks coming from Kronstadt, and added that the pious nun Tamara was arrested for "making objections."

From the province of Vorenezh the commissar reported on June 2: "Incidents of lawbreaking and illegal activity in the province are growing more numerous every day, especially in the agrarian matter." In Penza province also, the seizures of land were becoming more insistent. One of the district land committees in Kaluga province deprived the monastery of half of its meadow lands, and upon the complaint of the abbot the county committee resolved: that the meadows should be taken as a whole. It is not often that the higher institution proves more radical than the lower. In Penza province an abbess, Maria, weeps over the seizure of the nunnery's land: "The local authorities are powerless."

In Viatka province the peasants closed up the property of the Skoropadskys, the family of the future Ukrainian hetman, and "until the decision of the question of landed property" resolved that nobody should touch the forests, and that the income from the property should be paid into the public treasury. In a series of other localities the land committees not only lowered the rent five or six times, but directed that it should not be paid to the landlords, but placed at the disposal of the committees until the question should be settled by the Constituent Assembly. This was not a lawyer's but a muzhik's way—that is, a serious way—of postponing the question about land reforms until the Constituent Assembly. In Saratov province the peasants who only yesterday forbade the landlords to cut down the forests have today begun to fell the trees themselves. Oftener and oftener the peasants are seizing the church and monastery lands, especially where there are few landlords. In Lifland, the Lettish farm workers, along with soldiers of the Lettish Battalion, undertake an organized seizure of the baronial lands.

The lumber kings from Vitebsk province cry loudly that the measures adopted by the land committees are destroying the lumber industry and preventing them from supplying the needs of the front. Those no less disinterested patriots, the landlords of the Poltava province, grieve over the fact that agrarian disorders are making it impossible for them to supply provisions for the army. Finally a congress of horse breeders in Moscow gives warning that peasant seizures are threatening with gigantic misfortunes the studs of the Fatherland. In those days the Procuror of the Holy Synod, the same one who called the members of that sacred institution "idiots and scoundrels," complains to the government that in Kazan province the peasants are taking away from the monks not only lands and cattle, but also the flour necessary for the holy bread. In Petrograd province, two steps from the capital, the peasants drive the lessee out of a property and begin to run it themselves. The wide-awake Prince Yurussov again telegraphs on June 2 to the four winds: "In spite of a series of demands from me . . . etc., etc. . . . I again ask you to take the most decisive measures." The prince only forgets to say what measures.

In those times, when a gigantic job of tearing up the deepest roots of medievalism and serfdom was under way throughout the whole country, the Minister of Agriculture, Chernov, was gathering in his chancelleries materials for the Constituent Assembly. He intended to introduce the reform no otherwise than on the basis of the most accurate agricultural data and statistics of all possible kinds, and therefore kept urging the peasants with the sweetest of voices to wait until his exercises were finished. This did not, however, prevent the landlords from kicking out the "Rural Minister" long before he had completed his sacramental tables.

*

On the basis of the archives of the Provisional Government, young investigators have concluded that in March the agrarian movement had arisen with more or less strength in only 34 counties. In April, it had seized 174 counties; in May, 236; in June, 280; in July, 325. These figures, however, do not give a complete picture of the actual growth of the movement, because in each county the struggle assumed from month to month a more and more stubborn and broad mass character.

In that first period, from March to July, the peasants in their overwhelming majority are still refraining from direct acts of violence against the landlords, and from open seizures of the land. Yakovlev, the leader of the above-mentioned investigations, now People's Commissar of Agriculture of the Soviet Union, explains the comparatively peaceful tactics of the peasants by their trustfulness toward the bourgeoisie. This explanation must be declared invalid. To say nothing of the continual suspiciousness of the muzhik toward the city, the authorities and cultivated society, a government headed by Prince Lvov could not possibly dispose the peasants to trustfulness. If the peasants during this first period hardly ever resort to measures of open violence, and are still trying to give their activities the form of legal or semi-legal pressure, this is explained by their very distrustfulness of the government, combined with an insufficient trust in their own powers. The peasants are only pacing the take-off, feeling out the ground, measuring the resistance of the enemy—bringing pressure upon the landlords from all directions. "We do not want to rob," they recite, "we want to do everything nicely." They are not appropriating the meadow, but only cutting the hay. They are only compelling the landlords to rent them the land, but are themselves establishing the price. Or with a similar compulsion they are "buying" the land—but at a price designated by themselves. All these legal coverings, none too convincing to the landlord or the liberal jurists, are dictated in reality by a concealed but deep distrust of the government. "You won't get it by being good," says the muzhik to himself, "and force is dangerous—let's try foxiness." He would prefer, of course, to expropriate the landlord with his own consent.

"Throughout all these months," insists Yakovlev, "there prevails a wholly unique method of 'peaceful' struggle with the landlord, a thing never before seen in history, a result of the peasants' trust in the bourgeoisie and the government of the bourgeoisie." These methods here declared to have been never before seen in history, are in reality the typical and inevitable methods historically obligatory throughout the entire planet in the initial stages of a peasant war. The attempt to disguise its first rebel steps with legality, both sacred and secular, has from time immemorial characterized the struggle of every revolutionary class, before it has gathered sufficient strength and confidence to break the umbilical cord which bound it to the old society. This is more completely true of the peasantry than of any other class, for even in its best periods the peasantry advances in semi-darkness, looking upon its city friends with distrustful eyes. It has good reasons for this. The friends of an agrarian movement in its first steps are the agents of the liberal and radical bourgeoisie. And while promoting a part of the peasant demands, these friends are nevertheless alarmed for the fate of bourgeois property rights, and therefore try their best to lead the peasant uprising on to the rails of bourgeois legality.

Long before the revolution, other factors operate in the same direction. From the milieu of the nobility itself there arise preachers of conciliation. Leo Tolstoy looked deeper into the soul of the muzhik than anybody else. His philosophy of non-resistance to evil by violence was a generalization of the first stages of the muzhik revolution. Tolstoy dreamed of a day when it would all come to pass "without robbery, by mutual consent." He built up a religious foundation under this tactic in the form of a purified Christianity. Mahatma Gandhi is now fulfilling the same mission in India, only in a more practical form. If we go backward from the present day we shall have no difficulty in finding similar "never before seen in history" phenomena in all sorts of religious, national, philosophical and political disguises, beginning with Biblical times and still earlier.

The peculiarity of the peasant uprising of 1917 lay only in the fact that the agents of bourgeois legality were people who called themselves socialists, and also revolutionists. But it was not they who determined the character of the peasant movement and its rhythm. The peasants followed the Social Revolutionaries only in so far as they could secure from them adequate formulas for a settlement with the landlord. At the same time the Social Revolutionaries served them in the capacity of a juridical disguise: this was, after all, the party of Kerensky, Minister of Justice and afterwards War Minister, and of Chernov, Minister of Agriculture. The delay in the promulgation of the necessary decrees would be explained by the district and county Social Revolutionaries as due to the resistance of the landlords and liberals. They would assure the peasants that "our people" in the government are doing their very best. To this of course the muzhik had no answer. But not suffering in the least from that precious "trustfulness," he deemed it necessary to help "our people" from below, and he did this so thoroughly that "our people" up above soon began to feel their very joints cracking.

The weakness of the Bolsheviks in relation to the peasantry was temporary, and due to the fact that the Bolsheviks did not share the peasant illusions. The village could come to Bolshevism only through experience and disappointment. The strength of the Bolsheviks lay in the fact that on the agrarian question, as on others, they were free of the divergence between word and deed.

General sociological considerations could not yield an *a priori* decision as to whether the peasantry as a whole were capable of rising against the landlords or not. The strengthening of capitalist tendencies in agriculture during the period between the two revolutions, the dividing off of a layer of wealthy farmers from the primitive commune, the extraordinary growth of rural coöperation administered by well-off and rich peasants—all this made it impossible to say with certainty which of two tendencies would weigh the most in the revolution: the agrarian caste antagonism between the peasantry and the nobility, or the class antagonism within the peasantry itself.

Lenin upon his arrival took a very cautious position upon this question. "The agrarian movement," he said on April 14, "is only a prophecy, not a fact. . . . We must be prepared for a union of the peasantry with the bourgeoisie." That was not a thought accidentally tossed off. On the contrary, Lenin insistently repeated it in many connections. At a party conference on April 24, he said attacking the "old Bolsheviks" who had accused him of underestimating the peasantry: "It is not permissible for a proletarian party to rest its hopes at this time on a community of interest with the peasantry. We are struggling to bring the peasantry over to our side, but they now stand— to a certain degree consciously—on the side of the capitalists."

This demonstrates among other things how far Lenin was from that theory of an eternal harmony of interest between proletariat and peasantry subsequently attributed to him by the epigones. While admitting the possibility that the peasantry, as a caste, might act as a revolutionary factor, Lenin nevertheless was getting ready in April for a less favorable variant; namely, a stable bloc of the landlords, bourgeoisie and broad layers of the peasantry. "To try to attract the peasant now," he said, "means to throw ourselves on the mercy of Miliukov." Hence the conclusion: "Transfer the center of gravity to the soviets of farm-hand deputies."

But the more favorable variant was realized. The agrarian movement from being a prophecy became a fact, revealing for a brief moment, but with extraordinary force, the superiority of the caste ties of the peasantry over the capitalistic antagonisms. The soviets of farm-hand deputies attained significance only in a few localities, chiefly the Baltic provinces. The land committees, on the contrary, became the instruments of the whole peasantry, who with their heavy-handed pressure converted them from chambers of conciliation into weapons of agrarian revolution.

This fact that the peasantry as a whole found it possible once more—for the last time in their history—to act as a revolutionary factor, testifies at once to the weakness of capitalist relations in the country and to their strength. The bourgeois economy had not yet by any means sucked up the land relations of medieval serfdom. At the same time the capitalist development had gone so far that it had made the old forms of landed property equally unbearable for all layers of the village. The interweaving of landlord and peasant property—quite often consciously arranged in such a way as to convert the landlord's rights into a trap for the whole commune—the frightful striped ownership of the village land, and finally the very recent antagonism between the land commune and the individualist owners—all this together created an unbearable tangle of land relationships from which it was impossible to escape by way of half-hearted legislative measures. Moreover, the peasants felt it more deeply than any agrarian theoreticians could. The experience of life handed down through a series of generations led them all to the same conclusion: we must bury both hereditary and acquired rights in the land, erase all boundary marks, and hand over the land, purged of historic deposits, to those who work it. This was the meaning of the muzhik's aphorism: the land is no man's, the land is God's. And in this same spirit the peasantry interpreted the Social Revolutionary program: *socialization of the land*. All Narodnik theories to the contrary notwithstanding, there was not in this one grain of socialism. The most audacious of agrarian revolutions has never yet by itself overstepped the bounds of the bourgeois régime. That socialization which was to guarantee to each toiler his "right to the land," was with the preservation of unrestricted market relations, an utter utopia. Menshevism criticized this utopia from the liberal-bourgeois point of view. Bolshevism, on the other hand, exposed the progressive democratic tendency which was finding in these theories of the Social Revolutionaries a utopian expression. This exposure of the genuine historic meaning of the Russian agrarian movement was one of the greatest services of Lenin.

Miliukov wrote that for him, "as a sociologist and investigator of Russian historic evolution"—that is, a man surveying the course of events from a height—"Lenin and Trotsky are leading a movement far nearer to Pugatchev and Razin, to Bolotnikov—to the eighteenth and seventeenth centuries of our history—than to the last word in European anarcho-syndicalism." That dole of truth which is contained in this assertion of the liberal sociologist—leaving aside his reference to "anarcho-syndicalism" which was dragged in here for some unknown reason—militates not against the Bolsheviks, but rather against the Russian bourgeoisie, their belatedness and political insignificance. The Bolsheviks are not to blame that those colossal peasant movements of past ages did not lead to a democratization of social relations in Russia—without cities to lead them it was unattainable!—nor are the Bolsheviks to blame that the so-called liberation of the peasants in 1861 was carried out in such a way as to involve stealing of the communal land, enslavement of the peasant to the state, and complete preservation of the caste sys-

THE PEASANTRY

tem. One thing is true: the Bolsheviks were obliged to carry through in the first quarter of the twentieth century that which was not carried through—or not even undertaken at all—in the seventeenth, eighteenth and nineteenth centuries. Before taking up their own great task, they had to clear the ground of the historic rubbish of the old ruling classes and the old ages. We may add that the Bolsheviks at least fulfilled this preliminary task most conscientiously. This Miliukov will now hardly venture to deny.

409

Chapter XXI

SHIFTS IN THE MASSES

IN the fourth month of its existence the February régime was already choking from its own contradictions. June had begun with the all-Russian congress of the soviets, whose task was to create a political cover for the advance on the front. The beginning of the advance coincided in Petrograd with a gigantic demonstration of workers and soldiers organized by the Compromisers against the Bolsheviks, but which turned out to be a Bolshevik demonstration against the Compromisers. The growing indignation of the masses led after two weeks to another demonstration, which broke out without any summons from above, led to bloody encounters, and has gone into history under the name of "the July days." Taking place exactly half-way between the February and the October revolutions, the July semi-insurrection closes the former and constitutes a kind of dress rehearsal for the latter. We shall end this volume on the threshold of the July days, but before passing over to those events whose arena in June was Petrograd, it is necessary to have a glance at certain processes which were taking place in the masses.

To a certain liberal who had affirmed at the beginning of May that the more the government moves to the left, the more the country moves to the right—meaning by "country," of course, "the possessing classes"—Lenin replied: "the 'country' of workers and poorer and poorest peasants, I assure you, citizen, is a thousand times farther to the left than the Chernovs and Tseretellis, and a hundred times farther than we. Live a little and you will see." Lenin estimated that the workers and peasants were "a hundred times" farther to the left than the Bolsheviks. This may seem a little unfounded: the workers and soldiers were still supporting the Compromisers, and the majority of them were on their guard against the Bolsheviks. But

410

Lenin was delving deeper. The social interests of the masses, their hatred and their hope, were still only seeking a mode of expression. The policy of the Compromisers had been for them a first stage. The masses were immeasurably to the left of the Chernovs and Tseretellis, but were themselves still unconscious of their radicalism. Lenin was right in asserting that the masses were to the left of the Bolsheviks, for the party in its immense majority had not yet realized the mightiness of the revolutionary passions that were simmering in the depths of the awakening people. The indignation of the masses was nourished by the dragging-out of the war, the economic ruin and the malicious inactivity of the government.

The measureless European-Asiatic plain had become a country only thanks to railroads. The war struck them most heavily of all. Transport was steadily breaking down; the number of disabled locomotives on certain roads had reached 50 per cent. At headquarters learned engineers read reports to the effect that no later than in six months the railroad transport would be in a state of complete paralysis. In these calculations there was a certain amount of conscious spreading of panic. But the breakdown of transport had really reached threatening dimensions. It had created tie-ups on the roads, intensified the disturbance of commodity exchange, and augmented the high cost of living.

The food situation in the cities was becoming worse and worse. The agrarian movement had established its center in 43 provinces. The flow of grain to the army and the towns was dangerously dwindling. In the more fertile regions, to be sure, there were still tens and hundreds of millions of poods of surplus grain, but the purchasing operations at a fixed price gave extremely unsatisfactory results: and moreover it was difficult to deliver the ready grain to the centers owing to the breakdown of transport. From the autumn of 1916 on, an average of about one half of the expected provision trains arrived at the front. Petrograd, Moscow and other industrial centers received no more than 10 per cent of what they needed. They had almost no reserves. The standard of living of the city masses oscillated between undernourishment and hunger. The arrival

411

of the Coalition Government was signalized with a democratic order forbidding the baking of white bread. It will be several years after that before the "French roll" will again appear in the capital. There was not enough butter. In June the consumption of sugar was cut down by definite rationing for the whole country.

The mechanism of the market, broken by the war, had not been replaced by that state regulation to which the advanced capitalist governments had been compelled to resort, and which alone permitted Germany to hold on through four years of war.

Threatening symptoms of economic collapse appeared at every step. The fall in productivity in the factories was caused, aside from the breakdown of transport, by the wearing out of equipment, the lack of raw materials and supplies, the flux of personnel, bad financing, and finally the universal uncertainty. The principal plants were still working for the war. Orders had been distributed for two or three years ahead. Meantime the workers were unwilling to believe that the war would continue. The newspapers were publishing appalling figures of war profits. The cost of living was rising. The workers were awaiting a change. The technical and administrative personnels of the factories were uniting in unions and advancing their demands. In this sphere the Mensheviks and Social Revolutionaries dominated. The régime of the factories was disintegrating. All joints were weakening. The prospects of the war and of the national economy were becoming misty, and property rights unreliable. Profits were falling off, dangers growing, the bosses losing their taste for production under the conditions created by the revolution. The bourgeoisie as a whole was entering upon a policy of economic defeatism. Temporary losses and deficits due to economic paralysis were in their eyes the overhead expenses of a struggle with the revolution which threatened the foundations of "culture." At the same time the virtuous press was accusing the workers from day to day of maliciously sabotaging industry, stealing raw materials, unnecessarily burning up fuel in order to produce stoppages. The falsity of these accusations exceeded all bounds, and since this was the press of a party which actually stood at the head of the Coalition power, the indignation of the workers naturally transferred itself to the Provisional Government.

The industrialists had not forgotten the experience of 1905 when a correctly organized lockout actively supported by the government had not only broken up the struggle of the workers for an eight-hour day, but also had rendered the monarchy an invaluable service in the matter of wiping out the revolution. The question of a lockout was now again brought up for discussion at a Council of the Congresses of Industry and Trade— thus innocently they named the fighting organ of trustified and syndicated capital. One of the leaders of industry, the engineer Auerbach, explained later in his memoirs why the idea of a lockout was rejected: "This would have looked like a blow at the rear of the army . . . The consequences of such a step, *in the absence of governmental support,* looked to the majority very dark." The whole misfortune lay in the absence of a "real" government. The Provisional Government was paralyzed by the Soviet; the reasonable leaders of the Soviet were paralyzed by the masses; the workers in the factories were armed; moreover, almost every factory had in the neighborhood a friendly regiment or battalion. In these circumstances these gentlemen-industrialists considered a lockout "odious in its national aspect." But they did not by any means renounce the idea of an offensive, but merely adapted it to existing circumstances, giving it not a simultaneous, but a creeping character. According to the diplomatic expression of Auerbach, the industrialists "finally came to the conclusion that an object lesson would be given by life itself, in the form of an inevitable gradual closing of the factories, so to speak, one at a time—a thing which soon did actually occur." In other words, renouncing a demonstrative lockout as involving "an enormous responsibility," this Council of the United Industries recommended to its members to close up the enterprises one at a time, seeking out a respectable pretext.

This plan of a creeping lockout was carried out with remarkable system. Leaders of capital like the Kadet Kutler, a former minister in the cabinet of Witte, read significant reports about the breakdown of industry, laying the blame not on the three years of war, but on the three months of revolution.

413

"In the course of two or three weeks," prophesied the impatient newspaper *Rech,* "the shops and factories will begin to shut down one after another." A threat was here dressed up in the form of a prophecy. Engineers, professors, journalists started a campaign in both the general and the specialized press, in which a bridling of the workers was presented as the fundamental condition of salvation. The minister-industrialist Konovalov had declared on the 17th of May, just before his demonstrative withdrawal from the government: "If there does not soon come a sobering up of cloudy heads . . . we will witness a stoppage of tens and hundreds of plants."

In the middle of June a Congress of Trade and Industry demands of the Provisional Government "a radical break with the system of developing the revolution." We have already heard this demand made by the generals: "Stop the Revolution." But the industrialists make it more concise: "The source of evil is not only in the Bolsheviks, but also in the socialist parties. Only a firm iron hand can save Russia."

Having prepared the political setting, the industrialists passed from words to deeds. In the course of March and April, 129 small plants involving 9,000 workers were shut down; in May, 108 with a like number of workers; in June, 125 plants with 38,000 workers were shut down; in July, 206 plants threw out on the streets 48,000 workers. The lockout developed in a geometric progression. But that was only a beginning. Textile Moscow got into motion after Petrograd, and the provinces after Moscow. The manufacturers would refer to an absence of fuel, raw materials, accessories, credits. The factory committees would interfere in the matter and in many cases indubitably establish the fact of a malicious dislocation of industry with the goal of bringing pressure on the workers, or holding up the government for subsidies. Especially impudent were the foreign capitalists acting through the mediation of their embassies. In several cases the sabotage was so obvious that as a result of the exposures of the shop committees the industrialists found themselves compelled to reopen the factories, thus laying bare one contradiction after another. The revolution soon arrived at the chief of them all: that between the social character of industry and the private ownership of its tools and equipment. In the interests of victory over the workers, the entrepreneur closes the factory as though it were a question of a mere snuff-box, and not an enterprise necessary to the life of the whole nation.

The banks, having successfully boycotted the Liberty Loan, took a militant attitude against fiscal encroachments on big capital. In a letter addressed to the Ministry of Finance the bankers "prophesied" a flow of capital abroad and a transfer of papers to the safes in case of radical financial reforms. In other words the banker-patriots threatened a financial lockout to complete the industrial one. The government hastened to accede: after all, the organizers of this sabotage were respected people who had been compelled as the result of the war and the revolution to risk their capital, and not any old Kronstadt sailors who risked nothing but their heads.

The Executive Committee could not fail to understand that the responsibility for the economic fate of the country, especially since the open association of the socialists in the government, would lie in the eyes of the masses upon the ruling Soviet majority. The economic department of the Executive Committee had worked out a broad program of state regulation of the economic life. Under pressure of the threatening situation, the proposals of very moderate economists had proved much more radical than their authors. "For many branches of industry," read this program, "the time is ripe for a state trade monopoly (bread, meat, salt, leather); for others, the conditions are ripe for the formation of regulating state trusts (coal, oil, metals, sugar, paper); and finally, for almost all branches of industry contemporary conditions demand a regulative participation of the state in the distribution of raw materials and finished products, and also in the fixation of prices . . . Simultaneously with this it is necessary to place under control . . . all credit institutions."

On May 16, the Executive Committee with its bewildered political leadership adopted the proposals of the economists almost without debate, and backed them up with a unique warning addressed to the government: It should take upon itself "the task of a planned organization of the national industry and labor," calling to memory that in consequence of the non-fulfillment of this task "the old régime fell and it had been necessary to reorganize the Provisional Government." In order to pump up their courage the Compromisers were scaring themselves.

"The program is excellent," wrote Lenin, "both the control and the governmentalizing of the trusts, also the struggle with speculation, and liability for labor. . . . It is necessary to recognize this program of 'frightful' Bolshevism, for no other program and no other way out of the actually threatening terrible collapse can be found. . . ." However, the whole question was: Who was to carry out this excellent program? Would it be the Coalition? The answer was given immediately. The day after the adoption by the Executive Committee of the economic program, the Minister of Trade and Industry, Konovalov, resigned and slammed the door behind him. He was temporarily replaced by the engineer Palchinsky, a no less loyal but more energetic representative of big capital. The minister-socialists did not even dare seriously propose the program of the Executive Committee to their liberal colleagues. Chernov, you remember, was vainly trying to get the government to adopt a veto on land sales. In answer to its growing difficulties, the government, on its side, brought forward a program of unloading Petrograd, that is, transferring shops and factories into the depths of the country. This program was motivated both by military considerations—the danger that the Germans might seize the capital—and by economic: Petrograd was too far from the sources of fuel and raw materials. This unloading would have meant the liquidation of the Petrograd industries for a series of months and years. The political aim was to scatter throughout the whole country the vanguard of the working class. Parallel with this the military power brought forward one pretext after another for deporting from Petrograd the revolutionary military units.

Palchinsky tried with all his might to convince the workers' section of the Soviet of the advantages of an unloading. To accomplish this task against the will of the workers was impossible. But the workers would not agree. The unloading scheme got forward as little as the regulation of industry. The breakdown was going deeper. Prices were rising. The silent lockout was broadening, and therewith unemployment. The government was marking time. Miliukov wrote later: "The ministry was simply swimming with the current, and the current was running in the Bolshevik channel." Yes, the current was running in the Bolshevik channel.

*

THE proletariat was the chief motive force of the revolution. At the same time the revolution was giving shape to the proletariat. And the proletariat was badly in need of this.

We have observed the decisive rôle of the Petrograd workers in the February days. The most militant positions were occupied by the Bolsheviks. Immediately after the overturn, however, the Bolsheviks retired into the background. The Compromise parties advanced to the front of the political stage. They turned over the power to the liberal bourgeoisie. Patriotism was the countersign of this bloc. Its assault was so strong that at least one half of the leaders of the Bolshevik Party capitulated to it. With Lenin's arrival the course of the party changed abruptly, and thereafter its influence grew swiftly. In the armed April demonstration the front ranks of the workers and soldiers were already trying to break the chain of the Compromisers. But after a first effort they fell back. The Compromisers remained at the helm.

Later on, after the October revolution, a good deal was written to the effect that the Bolsheviks owed their victory to the peasant army, tired of the war. That is a very superficial explanation. The opposite statement would be nearer to the truth: If the Compromisers got a dominant position in the February revolution, it is thanks most of all to the unusual place occupied in the life of the country by a peasant army. If the revolution had developed in peace time, the leading rôle of the proletariat would have had from the beginning a far more sharply expressed character. Without the war the revolutionary victory would have come later, and if you do not count the victims of the war, would have been paid for at a higher price. But it would not have left a place for an inundation of compromising and patriotic moods. At any rate, the Russian Marxists who had prophesied long before these events a conquest of power by the proletariat in the course of the bourgeois revolution, did not take for their starting point the temporary moods of a peasant army, but the class structure of the Russian society. That prophecy was wholly confirmed. But the fundamental correlation of classes was refracted through the war and temporarily shifted by the pressure of the army—that is, by an organization of declassed and armed peasants. It was just this artificial social formation which so extraordinarily strengthened the hold of the petty bourgeois compromise policy, and made possible an eight-months' period of experiments, weakening to the country and the revolution.

However, the question as to the roots of compromisism is not exhausted by reference to the peasant army. In the proletariat itself, in its make-up, its political level, we must seek supplementary causes for the temporary entrenchment of the Mensheviks and Social Revolutionaries. The war brought vast changes in the constitution and mood of the working class. If the preceding years had been a time of revolutionary afflux, the war sharply broke off that process. The mobilization was thought out and conducted not only from a military, but still more from a police viewpoint. The government made haste to clean out from the industrial districts the more active and restless groups of workers. We may consider it established that the mobilization of the first months of war tore away from the industries as many as 40 per cent of the workers, chiefly the skilled workers. Their absence, having a very damaging effect on the course of production, called out hot protests from the industrialists in proportion to their high profits from the war industries. A further destruction of the workers' cadres was thus stopped. The workers indispensable to the industries remained in the capacity of men on military duty. The breaches effected by the mobilization were made up by immigrants from the villages, small-town people, badly qualified workers, women, boys. The percentage of women in industry rose from 32 to 40 per cent.

The process of renewal and dilution of the proletariat reached its extreme dimensions in the capital. For the years of the war, 1914-17, the number of workers in large enterprises, those hiring more than 500, almost doubled in the Petrograd province. In consequence of the liquidation of plants and factories in Poland, and especially in the Baltic states, and still more in consequence of the general growth of the war industries, there were concentrated in Petrograd by 1917 about 400,000 workers in plants and factories. Out of these, 335,000 were in the one hundred and forty giant plants. The more militant elements of the Petrograd proletariat played no small part at the front in giving form to the revolutionary moods of the army. But those yesterday's immigrants from the villages who replaced them, often well-to-do peasants and shopkeepers hiding from the front, women and boys, were far more submissive than the ranking workers. To this we must add that the qualified workers who found themselves in the position of men on military duty—and of these there were hundreds of thousands—observed an extraordinary caution through fear of being thrown over to the front. Such was the social basis of the patriotic mood, which had prevailed with a part of the workers even under the tzar.

But there was no stability in this patriotism. The merciless military and police repression, the redoubled exploitation, defeats at the front, and industrial breakdown, pushed the workers into the struggle. Strikes during the war were predominantly economic in character, however, and distinguished by far more moderation than before the war. The weakening of the class was increased by the weakening of its party. After the arrest and exile of the Bolshevik Duma deputies, there was carried out with the help of a previously prepared hierarchy of provocateurs a general smash-up of the Bolshevik organizations, from which the party did not recover until the February revolution. During 1915 and 1916 the diluted working class had to go through an elementary school of struggle before the partial economic strikes and demonstrations of hungry women could in February 1917 fuse in a general strike, and draw the army into an insurrection.

419

The Petrograd proletariat thus entered the February revolution not only in a heterogeneous condition, not yet having amalgamated its constituent parts, but with a lowered political level even of its advanced layers. In the provinces it was still worse. It was this revival of political illiteracy and semi-illiteracy in the proletariat, caused by the war, which created the second condition necessary for the temporary dominance of the Compromise parties.

A revolution teaches and teaches fast. In that lies its strength. Every week brings something new to the masses. Every two months creates an epoch. At the end of February, the insurrection. At the end of April, a demonstration of the armed workers and soldiers in Petrograd. At the beginning of July, a new assault, far broader in scope and under more resolute slogans. At the end of August, Kornilov's attempt at an overthrow beaten off by the masses. At the end of October, conquest of power by the Bolsheviks. Under these events, so striking in their rhythm, molecular processes were taking place, welding the heterogeneous parts of the working class into one political whole. In this again the chief rôle was played by the strike.

Frightened by the lightning of revolution striking in the midst of their bacchanalia of war profits, the industrialists made concessions in the first weeks to the workers. The Petrograd factory owners even agreed, with qualifications and exceptions, to the eight-hour day. But that did not quiet things, since the standard of living continually sank. In May the Executive Committee was obliged to concede that with the increasing cost of living the situation of the workers "borders for many categories upon chronic starvation." The mood in the workers' districts was becoming more and more nervous and tense. What depressed them most of all was the absence of prospects. The masses are capable of enduring the heaviest deprivations when they understand what for, but the new régime was more and more revealing itself to them as a mere camouflage of the old relations against which they had revolted in February. This they would not endure.

The strikes were especially stormy among the more backward and exploited groups of workers. Laundry workers, dyers, coopers, trade and industrial clerks, structural workers, bronze workers, unskilled workers, shoemakers, paper-box makers, sausage makers, furniture workers, were striking, layer after layer, throughout the month of June. The metal-workers were beginning, on the contrary, to play a restraining rôle. To the advanced workers it was becoming more and more clear that individual economic strikes in the conditions of war, breakdown and inflation could not bring a serious improvement, that there must be some change in the very foundations. The lockout not only made the workers favorable to the demand for the control of industry, but even pushed them toward the thought of the necessity of taking the factories into the hands of the state. This inference seemed the more natural in that the majority of private factories were working for the war, and that alongside them were state enterprises of the same type. Already in the summer of 1917 delegations began to arrive in the capital from the far ends of Russia, delegations of workers and clerks, with a plea that the factories should be taken over by the treasury, since the shareholders had stopped financing them. But the government would not hear of this; consequently it was necessary to change the government. The Compromisers opposed this. The workers began to shift their front against the Compromisers. The Putilov factory with its 40,000 workers was a stronghold of the Social Revolutionaries during the first months of the revolution. But its garrison did not long defend it against Bolsheviks. At the head of the Bolshevik attack most often was to be seen Volodarsky, a tailor in the past. A Jew who had spent some years in America and spoke English well, Volodarsky was a magnificent mass orator, logical, ingenious and bold. His American intonation gave a unique expressiveness to his resonant voice, ringing out concisely at meetings of many thousands. "From the moment of his arrival in the Narva district," says the worker Minichev, "the ground in the Putilov factory began to slip under the feet of the Social Revolutionary gentlemen, and in the course of something like two months the Putilov workers had gone over to the Bolsheviks."

The growth of strikes, and of the class struggle in general, almost automatically raised the influence of the Bolsheviks. In all cases where it was a question of life-interests the workers became convinced that the Bolsheviks had no ulterior motives, that they were concealing nothing, and that you could rely on them. In the hours of conflict all the workers tended toward the Bolsheviks, the non-party workers, the Social Revolutionaries, the Mensheviks. This is explained by the fact that the factory and shop committees, waging a struggle for the life of their factories against the sabotage of the administration and the proprietors, went over to the Bolsheviks much sooner than the Soviet. At a conference of the factory and shop committees of Petrograd and its environs at the beginning of June, the Bolshevik resolution won 335 out of 421 votes. This fact went by utterly unnoticed in the big newspapers. Nevertheless it meant that in the fundamental questions of economic life the Petrograd proletariat, not yet having broken with the Compromisers, had nevertheless as a fact gone over to the Bolsheviks.

At the June conference of trade unions it became known that in Petrograd there were over 50 unions with no less than 250,000 members. The metal workers' union numbered about 100,000 workers; its membership had doubled in the course of the one month of May. The influence of the Bolsheviks in the union had grown still more swiftly.

All the by-elections to the soviets showed a victory for the Bolsheviks. By the 1st of June in the Moscow Soviet there were already 206 Bolsheviks against 176 Mensheviks and 110 Social Revolutionaries. The same shifts occurred in the provinces, only more slowly. The membership of the party was growing steadily. At the end of April the Petrograd organization had 15,000 members. By the end of June, over 32,000.

The workers' section of the Petrograd Soviet had at that time already a Bolshevik majority. But at a joint session of both sections the soldier delegates overweighed the Bolsheviks. *Pravda* was more and more insistently demanding general elections: "The 500,000 Petrograd workers have four times fewer delegates in the Soviet than the 150,000 soldiers of the Petrograd garrison."

At the June congress of the Soviets Lenin demanded serious

measures of struggle against lockouts, plunderings and organized disruption of economic life on the part of the industrialists and bankers. "Publish the profits of the capitalist gentlemen, arrest fifty or a hundred of the biggest millionaires. It will be enough to hold them for a few weeks, even on such privileged terms as Nicholas Romanov is held, with the simple aim of compelling them to reveal the threads, the tricky manipulations, the filth, and selfishness, which even under the new government are costing our country millions." To the Soviet leaders Lenin's proposal seemed monstrous. "You imagine that you can alter the laws of economic life by acts of violence against individual capitalists?" The circumstance that these industrialists were dictating the laws by way of a conspiracy against the nation was considered a part of the due order of things. Kerensky, who came down on Lenin with thunderous indignation, did not hesitate a month later to arrest many thousands of workers who differed with the industrialists in their understanding of the "laws of economic life."

The bond between economics and politics was being revealed. The state, accustomed to appear in the quality of a mystic principle, was operating now oftener and oftener in its most primitive form, that is, in the form of detachments of armed men. The workers in various parts of the country were subjecting the bosses who refused to make concessions or even negotiate, now to enforced appearance before the soviet, now to house arrest. It is no wonder that the workers' militia became an object of special hatred to the possessing classes.

The initial decision of the Executive Committee to arm ten per cent of the workers had not been carried out. But the workers succeeded in arming partially just the same, and moreover the more active elements got into the ranks of the militia. The leadership of the workers' militia was concentrated in the hands of the factory committees, and the leadership of the factory committees was coming over more and more into the hands of the Bolsheviks. A worker of the Moscow factory, Postavshchik, relates: "On the 1st of June as soon as the new Factory Committee was elected with a Bolshevik majority . . . a detachment of eighty men was formed, which in the absence of

423

weapons drilled with sticks, under the leadership of an old soldier, Comrade Levakov."

The press accused the militia of acts of violence, requisitions, and illegal arrests. It is indubitable that the militia did employ violence: it was created exactly for that. Its crime consisted, however, in resorting to violence in dealing with representatives of that class which was not accustomed to be the object of violence and did not want to get accustomed to it.

In the Putilov factory, which played the leading rôle in the struggle for higher wages, a conference assembled on the 23rd of June, in which participated representatives of the Central Council of Factory and Shop Committees, the Central Bureau of the Trade Unions and 73 plants. Under the influence of the Bolsheviks the conference recognized that the strike of a factory under the given conditions might entail an "unorganized political struggle of the Petrograd workers," and therefore proposed to the Putilov workers to "restrain their legitimate indignation" and prepare their forces for a general attack.

On the eve of that important conference the Bolshevik faction had warned the Executive Committee: "A mass of 40,000 . . . may any day strike and come into the street. It would already have done so if our party had not restrained it. And moreover there is no guarantee that in the future we can restrain it. But a coming out of the Putilov men—there can be no doubt of it—will inevitably bring after it an action of the majority of the workers and soldiers."

The leaders of the Executive Committee judged these warnings to be demagogy, or else simply let them go in one ear and out the other, preserving their tranquillity. They themselves had almost ceased to visit the factories and barracks, since they had succeeded in making themselves odious in the eyes of the soldiers and workers. Only the Bolsheviks enjoyed sufficient authority to make it possible for them to restrain the workers and soldiers from scattered action. But the impatience of the masses was already sometimes directed even against the Bolsheviks.

Anarchists appeared in the factories and in the fleet. As always in the face of great events and great masses, they exposed their organic bankruptcy. They found it the more easy to reject the state power in that they completely failed to understand the significance of the soviets as organs of a new state. Moreover, stunned by the revolution, they most often simply kept mum on the subject of the state. They revealed their bankruptcy for the most part by encouraging petty flare-ups. The economic blind alley and the growing embitterment of the Petrograd workers gave certain points of support to the anarchists. Incapable of seriously appraising the correlation of forces on a national scale, ready to regard every little impulse from below as the last stroke of salvation, they sometimes accused the Bolsheviks of irresolution and even of compromisism. But beyond grumbling they usually did not go. The response of the masses to the action of the anarchists sometimes served the Bolsheviks as a gauge of the steam pressure of the revolution.

*

The sailors who had met Lenin at the Finland station declared two weeks later, under patriotic pressure from all sides: "If we had known . . . by what ways he came to us, instead of rapturous cries of hurrah! we would have made heard our indignant shouts: 'Down with you! Back to the country you came through.'" The soldiers' soviets in the Crimea threatened one after another to prevent with armed fists Lenin's entry into that patriotic peninsula, where he had no idea of going. The Volynsky regiment, the coryphée of February 27, in the heat of the moment even resolved to arrest Lenin, so that the Executive Committee found itself obliged to take its own measures against such an event. Moods of this kind had not finally dissipated up to the June offensive, and they flared up sharply again after the July days. At the same time in the most far-away garrisons and the most remote parts of the front the soldiers were speaking more and more boldly in the language of Bolshevism, often enough never guessing it. The Bolsheviks in the regiments were only single individuals, but the Bolshevik slogans were penetrating deeper and deeper. They seemed to be coming up spontaneously in all parts of the country. Liberal observers saw nothing in this but ignorance and chaos. *Rech* wrote: "Our Fatherland is veritably turning into a sort of madhouse, where those possessed are in action and command, and people who have not yet lost their reason stand aside in fright and cling along the walls." In exactly these words the "moderates" have poured out their souls in all revolutions. The Compromisers' press comforted itself that the soldiers in spite of all misunderstanding did not want to have anything to do with the Bolsheviks. Meanwhile the unconscious Bolshevism of the mass, reflecting the logic of evolution, was constituting the inconquerable power of the Lenin party.

The soldier Pireiko relates how at the elections at the front to the congress of soviets, after a three-day debate, only Social Revolutionaries were elected. But right after that, notwithstanding the protest of the leaders, the soldiers adopted a resolution in favor of taking the land from the landlords without waiting for the Constituent Assembly. "In general on questions which the soldiers understood, they were inclined farther to the left than the most extreme of extreme Bolsheviks." That is what Lenin had in mind when he said that the masses "are a hundred times to the left of us."

A clerk in a motor-cycle shop somewhere in the Tauride province tells how not infrequently after reading the bourgeois papers, the soldiers would abuse some sort of unknown creatures called Bolsheviks, and then immediately take up the discussion of the necessity of stopping the war, seizing the land from the landlords, etc. These were those same patriots who swore not to let Lenin into the Crimea. The soldiers in the gigantic rear garrisons were chafing. A vast accumulation of idle people impatiently awaiting a change in their fate created a nervous condition which expressed itself in a continuous readiness to bring their discontent out into the street, in wholesale tramway rides and an epidemical chewing of sunflower seeds. The soldier with his trench-coat thrown over his shoulders, with a seed-shell on his lip, became the most hated image to the bourgeois press. This man whom in war time they had crudely flattered, naming him no less than hero—which did not prevent their flogging this hero at the front—he whom after the February revolution they had lifted aloft as a liberator, became suddenly a thug, a traitor, a gunman, a German agent. Really, there was no vileness that the patriotic press would not attribute to the Russian soldiers and sailors.

All the Executive Committee did was to justify itself, struggle with anarchy, abate excesses, distribute frightened questionnaires and moral instructions. The president of the soviet in Tzaritsyn—that city was considered a nest of anarcho-Bolshevism—to a questionnaire from the center as to the state of affairs, answered with a clean-cut phrase: "The more the garrison goes to the left, the more the everyday man goes to the right." You can extend this formula from Tzaritsyn to the whole country. The soldier is moving to the left, the bourgeois to the right.

Every soldier who expressed a little more boldly than the rest what they were all feeling, was so persistently shouted at from above as a Bolshevik that he was obliged in the long run to believe it. From peace and land the soldiers' thoughts began to pass over to the question of power. Responsiveness to the scattered slogans of Bolshevism changed into a conscious sympathy for the Bolshevik Party. In the Volynsky regiment, which in April had intended to arrest Lenin, the mood shifted in the course of two months in favor of the Bolsheviks. The same in the Egersky and Litovsky regiments. The Lettish sharpshooters had been brought into being by the autocracy in order to use for the ends of war the hatred of parceled-out peasants and farm-hands against the Baltic barons. These regiments fought magnificently. But that spirit of class hatred on which the monarchy thought to rely, found a road of its own. The Lettish sharpshooters were among the first to break with the monarchy, and afterwards with the Compromisers. As early as May 17, the representatives of eight Lettish regiments almost unanimously adhered to the Bolshevik slogan: "All Power to the Soviets." In the further course of the revolution they will play a mighty rôle.

An unknown soldier writes from the front: "Today, June 13, we had a little meeting at headquarters, and they talked of Lenin and Kerensky. The soldiers for the most part were for

Lenin, but the officers said that Lenin was very 'bourgui.' "
After the collapse of the offensive Kerensky's name became
utterly hateful to the army.

On June 21 the military students in Peterhof marched
through the streets with banners and placards: "Down with the
Spies," "Long Live Kerensky and Brussilov." It was Brussilov,
of course, that the military students themselves stood for. Soldiers of the 4th Battalion attacked the military students and
roughhoused them, scattering the demonstration. The placard
in honor of Kerensky was what provoked the most hatred.

The June demonstration greatly accelerated the political
evolution of the army. The popularity of the Bolsheviks, the
only party which had raised its voice in advance against the
offensive, began to grow with extraordinary speed. It is true
that the Bolshevik papers only with great difficulty found access
to the army. Their circulation was extremely small in comparison with the liberal press and the patriotic press in general.
"There is not even one of your papers to be seen anywhere,"
writes to Moscow a clumsy soldier's hand, "and we only make
use of the rumor of your papers. They sprinkle us here with
free bourgeois papers, carrying them along the front in whole
bales." But it was just these patriotic papers which gave
the Bolsheviks an incomparable popularity. Every case of protest from the oppressed, of land seizure, of accounts squared
with the hated officers, these papers attributed to Bolsheviks.
The soldiers concluded that the Bolsheviks are a righteous folk.

The commissar of the 12th Army reports to Kerensky at the
beginning of July as to the mood of the soldiers: "Everything
is in the long run blamed on the bourgeois ministers and the
Soviet, which has sold out to the bourgeoisie. But in general
in the immense mass is an opaque darkness; I am unhappy to
report that even the newspapers are but little read lately; complete distrust of the printed word: 'They write pretty,' 'They
are good at the tall talk.' " In the first months the reports of
the patriotic commissars were ordinarily a hymn to the revolutionary army, its consciousness, its discipline. Then, after four
months of uninterrupted disappointments, when the army had

lost confidence in the government orators and journalists, these same commissars discovered in it nothing but opaque darkness.

The more the garrison moves to the left, the more the every-day man moves to the right. Stimulated by the offensive, counter-revolutionary unions sprang up in Petrograd like mush-rooms after rain. They gave themselves names, one more resonant than the other: Union of the Honor of the Fatherland, Union of Military Duty, Battalion of Freedom, Organization of the Spirit, etc. These admirable signboards concealed the am-bitions and attempts of the nobility, the officers, the officialdom, the bureaucracy, the bourgeoisie. Some of these organizations, such as the Military League, the Union of the Cavaliers of St. George, or the Volunteers' Division, were the finished nuclei of a military plot. Coming forward as flaming patriots, these knights of "honor" and "the spirit" not only found easy access to the Allied Missions, but even at times received governmental subsidies, a thing which had in its day been refused to the Soviet as a "private organization." One of the offshoots of the family of the newspaper magnate Suvorin undertook the publication in those days of a *Little Newspaper,* which as an organ of "in-dependent socialism" advocated an iron dictatorship, advancing Admiral Kolchak as its candidate. The more solid press, with-out as yet quite dotting its i's, tried in every way to create a popularity for Kolchak. The further career of the admiral tes-tifies that already in the summer of 1917 there was a broad plan connected with his name, and that there were influential circles behind Suvorin's back.

In obedience to a simple tactical calculation, the reaction, aside from certain individual explosions, pretended that it was directing its blows only against Leninists. The word "Bolshe-vik" became a synonym for satanic origin. Just as before the revolution the tzarist commanders had put the responsibility for all misfortunes, including their own stupidity, upon German spies and more particularly upon "Yids," so now, after the col-lapse of the June offensive, the blame for failure and defeat was unceasingly laid upon Bolsheviks. In this matter democrats such as Kerensky and Tseretelli were almost in nowise distin-

429

guished, not only from liberals like Miliukov, but from outspoken feudalists like General Denikin.

As always happens when contradictions are intensified to the limit but the moment of explosion has not yet come, the grouping of political forces revealed itself more frankly and clearly not on fundamental questions, but on accidental side issues. One of the lightning rods for the diversion of political passions in those days was Kronstadt. That old fortress which was to have been a loyal sentry at the sea gates of the imperial capital, had in the past more than once lifted the banner of revolt. In spite of ruthless vengeances, the flame of rebellion never went out in Kronstadt. It flared up threateningly after the revolution. The name of this naval fortress soon became on the pages of the patriotic press a synonym of the worst aspect of the revolution, a synonym of Bolshevism. In reality, the Kronstadt Soviet was not yet Bolshevik. It contained in May 107 Bolsheviks, 112 Social Revolutionaries, 30 Mensheviks, and 97 non-party men. But these were Kronstadt Social Revolutionaries and Kronstadt non-party men, living under high pressure: a majority of them on important questions followed the Bolsheviks.

In the political sphere the Kronstadt sailors were not inclined either toward maneuvering or toward diplomacy. They had their own rule: no sooner said than done. It is no wonder that in relation to a phantom government they tended toward an extremely simplified method of action. On May 13 the soviet resolved: "The sole power in Kronstadt is the Soviet of Workers' and Soldiers' Deputies." The removal of the government commissar, the Kadet Pepelyaev, who occupied the position of fifth wheel in a wagon, passed off in the fortress totally unnoticed. Model order was maintained. Card playing in the city was forbidden. All brothels were closed, and their inmates deported. Under threat of "confiscation of property and banishment to the front," the soviet forbade drunkenness in the streets. The threat was more than once carried into action.

Tempered in the terrible régime of the tzarist fleet and the naval fortress, accustomed to stern work, to sacrifices, but also to fury, these sailors, now when the curtain of the new life was beginning to rise before them, a life in which they felt them-

SHIFTS IN THE MASSES

selves to be the coming masters, tightened all their sinews in order to prove themselves worthy of the revolution. They thirstily threw themselves upon both friends and enemies in Petrograd and almost dragged them by force to Kronstadt, in order to show them what revolutionary seamen are in action. Such moral tension could not of course last forever, but it lasted a long time. The Kronstadt sailors became a kind of fighting crusaders of the revolution. But what revolution? Not that, in any case, which was incarnated in the minister Tseretelli and his commissar Pepelyaev. Kronstadt stood there as a herald of the advancing second revolution. For that reason it was hated by all those for whom the first revolution had been more than enough.

The peaceful and unnoticed removal of Pepelyaev was portrayed in the press of the existing order almost as an armed insurrection against the unity of the state. The government complained to the Soviet. The Soviet immediately appointed a delegation to exert influence. The machine of the double sovereignty came into action with a creak. On May 24 the Kronstadt Soviet, with Tseretelli and Skobelev present, agreed, upon the insistence of the Bolsheviks, to acknowledge that in prolonging its struggle for the power of the soviets, it was practically obliged to submit to the power of the Provisional Government until the power of the soviets was established throughout the land. However, the next day, under pressure from the sailors, indignant at this submissiveness, the Soviet announced that the ministers had received only an "explanation" of the point of view of Kronstadt which remained unchanged. This was clearly a tactical mistake, but one behind which nothing was concealed except revolutionary ambition.

It was decided up above to make use of this lucky chance to give the Kronstadters a lesson, making them pay at the same time for their previous sins. The prosecutor, of course, was Tseretelli. With heartbreaking references to his prison days Tseretelli thundered especially against the Kronstadters for holding eighty officers behind the fortress bars. All the virtuous press backed him up. However, even the Compromisist, that is, the ministerial, papers had to acknowledge that it was a

431

question of "direct embezzlement" and of "men who carried fist rule to a point of horror." "The sailor witnesses"—according to *Izvestia,* the official paper of Tseretelli himself "testify to the putting down (by the arrested officers) of the insurrection of 1906, to mass shootings, to barges filled with the corpses of men executed and drowned in the sea, and to other horrors. . . . They tell of these things quite simply as of everyday events."

The Kronstadters stubbornly refused to give up the arrestees to the government, to whom the hangmen and the peculators of noble birth were incomparably nearer than were those tortured sailors of 1906 and other years. It was no accident that the Minister of Justice, Pereverzev, whom Sukhanov mildly describes as "one of the most suspicious figures in the Coalition Government," systematically liberated from the Peter and Paul fortress the vilest agents of the tzarist political police. The democratic upstarts were above all striving to compel the reactionary bureaucracy to acknowledge their nobleness.

To Tseretelli's indictment the Kronstadters answered in their appeal: "The officers, gendarmes and police arrested by us in the days of the revolution have themselves declared to representatives of the government that they have nothing to complain of in the treatment they have received from the prison management. It is true that the prison buildings of Kronstadt are horrible, but those are the same prisons which were built by tzarism for us. We haven't any others. And if we keep the enemies of the people in those prisons it is not out of vengeance, but from considerations of revolutionary self-preservation."

On the 27th of May the Petrograd Soviet tried the Kronstadters. Appearing in their defense, Trotsky warned Tseretelli that in case of danger "when a counter-revolutionary general tries to throw a noose around the neck of the revolution, the Kadets will soap the rope, and the Kronstadt sailors will come to fight and die with us." This warning came true three months later with unexpected literalness: when General Kornilov raised his revolt and led troops against the capital, Kerensky, Tseretelli and Skobelev summoned the Kronstadt sailors to defend the Winter Palace. But what of that? In June the democratic gentlemen were defending law and order against anarchy, and no arguments or prophecies had weight with them. By a majority of 580 votes against 162, with 74 abstaining, Tseretelli carried through the Petrograd Soviet a resolution denouncing the "apostasy" of "anarchist" Kronstadt from the revolutionary democracy. No sooner had the impatiently awaited news reached the Marinsky Palace that this bull of excommunication had been adopted than the government immediately cut off telephone communication for private people between the capital and the fortress in order to prevent the Bolshevik center from influencing the Kronstadters, ordered all the training ships to leave the Kronstadt waters, and demanded of its soviet "unconditional submission." The congress of peasant deputies sitting at that time threatened to "refuse foodstuffs to Kronstadt." The reaction standing behind the back of the Compromisers sought a decisive and, to the extent possible, a bloody settlement.

"The reckless step of the Kronstadt Soviet," writes one of the young historians, Yugov, "might have brought undesirable consequences. It was necessary to find a suitable way to get out of the situation created. With this aim Trotsky went to Kronstadt, where he addressed the soviet and wrote a declaration which was adopted by the soviet and afterwards carried—unanimously—by Trotsky at a meeting on Yakorny Square." Preserving their position in principle, the Kronstadters yielded upon the practical issue.

The peaceful settlement of the conflict left the bourgeois press completely beside themselves: There is anarchy in the fortress; the Kronstadters are printing their own money—fantastic specimens of it were reproduced in the papers—they are plundering state property, the women are nationalized, robberies and drunken orgies are in progress. The sailors, so proud of their austere order, doubled their horny fists on reading these papers which in millions of copies were distributing slanders against them throughout all Russia.

Having got the Kronstadt officers in their hands the judicial institutions of Pereverzev freed them one after another. It would be very instructive to find out how many of them subsequently participated in the civil war, and how many sailors, soldiers, workers and peasants were shot and hung by them.

Unfortunately, we are not here in a position to carry out this instructive census.

The authority of the government was saved. But the sailors soon got satisfaction for the indignities suffered. From all corners of the country there began to arrive resolutions of greeting to Red Kronstadt: from individual left soviets, from factories, regiments, mass-meetings. The first machine-gun regiment demonstrated in solid ranks on the streets of Petrograd its respect for the Kronstadters "for their firm attitude of non-confidence in the Provisional Government."

Kronstadt was getting ready, however, to take a more significant revenge. The baiting of the bourgeois press had made it a factor of all-national importance. "Fortifying itself in Kronstadt," writes Miliukov, "Bolshevism with the help of suitably trained agitators threw out widely over Russia a net of propaganda. Kronstadt emissaries were sent also to the front, where they undermined discipline, and to the rear, into the villages, where they incited to the sacking of estates. The Kronstadt Soviet gave these emissaries special mandates: 'N.N. has been sent to his province to be present with the right of a deciding vote in the county, district and village committees, and also to speak at meetings and call meetings at his own discretion wherever he wants to,' with 'the right to bear arms, with unhindered and free transportation on all railroads and steamships.' And therewith 'the inviolability of the person of the said agitator is guaranteed by the Soviet of the City of Kronstadt.'"

In exposing the undermining work of the Baltic sailors Miliukov only forgets to explain how and why, notwithstanding the presence of learned authorities, institutions and newspapers, solitary sailors armed with this strange mandate of the Kronstadt Soviet traveled all over the country without hindrance, found food and lodging everywhere, were admitted to all popular meetings, everywhere attentively listened to, and left the imprint of a sailor's hand on the events of history. The historian in the service of liberal politics does not ask himself this simple question. But the Kronstadt miracle was thinkable only because the sailors far more deeply expressed the demands of historic evolution than the very intelligent professors. The semi-literate mandate was, to speak in the language of Hegel, real because it was reasonable, whereas the subjectively most intelligent plans were spectral because the reason of history was not even camping in them for the night.

*

THE soviets lagged behind the shop committees. The shop committees lagged behind the masses. The soldiers lagged behind the workers. Still more the provinces lagged behind the capital. Such is the inevitable dynamic of a revolutionary process, which creates thousands of contradictions only in order accidentally and in passing, as though in play, to resolve them and immediately create new ones. The party also lagged behind the revolutionary dynamic—an organization which has the least right to lag, especially in a time of revolution. In such workers' centers as Ekaterinburg, Perm, Tula, Nizhni-Novgorod, Sormovo, Kolomna, Yuzovka, the Bolsheviks separated from the Mensheviks only at the end of May. In Odessa, Nikolaev, Elisavetgrad, Poltava and other points in the Ukraine, the Bolsheviks did not have independent organizations even in the middle of June. In Baku, Zlatöust, Bezhetsk, Kostroma, the Bolsheviks divided from the Mensheviks only toward the end of June. These facts cannot but seem surprising when you take into consideration that within four months the Bolsheviks are going to seize the power. How far the party during the war had fallen behind the molecular process in the masses, and how far the March leadership of Kamenev and Stalin lagged behind the gigantic historic tasks! The most revolutionary party which human history until this time had ever known was nevertheless caught unawares by the events of history. It reconstructed itself in the fires, and straightened out its ranks under the onslaught, of events. The masses at the turning point were "a hundred times" to the left of the extreme left party. The growth of the Bolshevik influence, which took place with the force of a natural historical process, reveals its own contradiction upon a closer examination, its zigzags, its ebbs and flows. The masses are not homogeneous, and moreover they learn to handle the fire of revolution only

435

by burning their hands and jumping away. The Bolsheviks could only accelerate the process of education of the masses. They patiently explained. And history this time did not take advantage of their patience.

While the Bolsheviks were resolutely winning the shops, factories and regiments, the elections to the democratic dumas gave an enormous and apparently growing advantage to the Compromisers. This was one of the sharpest and most enigmatical contradictions of the revolution. To be sure, the duma of the Vyborg district, which was purely proletarian, prided itself upon its Bolshevik majority. But that was an exception. In the city elections of Moscow in June, the Social Revolutionaries got more than 60 per cent of the votes. They themselves were astonished at this figure, for they could not but feel that their influence was swiftly dwindling. In the effort to understand the mutual relation between the real development of the revolution and its reflection in the mirrors of democracy, the Moscow elections have an extraordinary interest. The vast layers of workers and soldiers were already hastily shaking off their Compromisist illusions. Meanwhile, the broadest layers of the small town people were also beginning to stir. For these scattered masses the democratic elections offered almost the first, and in any case one of the very rare opportunities to show themselves politically. While the worker, yesterday's Menshevik or Social Revolutionary, gave his vote to the Bolshevik Party and drew the soldier along with him, the cabman, the delivery-man, the janitor, the market woman, the shopkeeper, his assistant, the teacher, in performing so heroic a deed as giving their vote to the Social Revolutionaries, for the first time emerged from political non-existence. The petty bourgeois layers belatedly voted for Kerensky because he personified in their eyes the February revolution, which had only today seeped down to them. With its 60 per cent Social Revolutionary majority the Moscow Duma glowed with the last flare of a dying luminary. It was so also with all the other organs of democratic self-administration. Having barely arrived, they were already stricken with the impotence of belatedness. That meant that the course of the revolution depended upon the workers and soldiers, and not upon that human dust which had been kicked up and was dancing in the whirlwind of the revolution.

Such is the deep and at the same time simple dialectic of the revolutionary awakening of the oppressed classes. The most dangerous of the aberrations of the revolution arises when the mechanical accountant of democracy balances in one column yesterday, today and tomorrow, and thereby impels the formal democrats to look for the head of the revolution where in reality is to be found its very heavy tail. Lenin taught his party to distinguish head from tail.

CHAPTER XXII

THE SOVIET CONGRESS AND THE JUNE
DEMONSTRATION

THE first congress of the soviets, which sanctioned the offensive for Kerensky, assembled in Petrograd on June 3 in the building of the Cadet Corps. There were 820 delegates with a vote and 268 with a voice. They represented 305 local soviets, 53 district and regional organizations at the front, the rear institutions of the army, and a few peasant organizations. The right to a vote was accorded to soviets containing not less than 25,000 men. Soviets containing from 10,-000 to 25,000 had a voice. On the basis of this rule—by the way, none too strictly observed—we may assume that over 20,-000,000 people stood behind the soviets. Out of 777 delegates giving information as to their party allegiance, 285 were Social Revolutionaries, 248 Mensheviks, 105 Bolsheviks; a few belonged to less important groups. The left wing—the Bolsheviks, and the Internationalists adhering to them—constituted less than a fifth of the delegates. The congress consisted for the most part of people who had registered as socialists in March but got tired of the revolution by June. Petrograd must have seemed to them a town gone mad.

The congress began by ratifying the banishment of Grimm, an unhappy Swiss socialist who had been trying to save the Russian revolution and the German social democracy by means of back-stage negotiations with the Hohenzollern diplomats. The demand of the left wing that they take up immediately the question of the coming offensive was rejected by an overwhelming majority. The Bolsheviks looked like a tiny group. But on that very day and perhaps hour, a conference of the factory and shop committees of Petrograd adopted, also with an overwhelming majority, a resolution that only a government of soviets could save the country.

438

The Compromisers, no matter how nearsighted they were, could not help seeing what was happening around them every day. In the session of June 4 the Bolshevik-hater, Lieber, evidently under the influence of the provincials, denounced the good-for-nothing commissars of the government to whom the power had not been surrendered in the provinces. "A whole series of functions of the governmental organs have as a result gone over into the hands of the soviets, even when the soviets did not want them." Those people had to complain to somebody even against themselves.

One of the delegates, a school teacher, complained to the congress that after four months of revolution there had not been the slightest change in the sphere of education. All of the old teachers, inspectors, directors, overseers of districts, many of them former members of the Black Hundreds, all of the old school programs, reactionary textbooks, even the old assistant ministers, remained peacefully at their posts. Only the tzar's portraits had been removed to the attics, and these might any day be stuck back in their places.

The congress could not make up its mind to lift a hand against the State Duma, or against the State Council. Its timidity before the reaction was covered up by the Menshevik orator Bogdanov with the remark that the Duma and the Soviet are "dead and non-existent organizations anyway." Martov, with his polemical wit, answered: "Bogdanov proposes that we should declare the Duma dead but not make any attempt upon its life."

The congress, in spite of its solid government majority, proceeded in an atmosphere of alarm and uncertainty. Patriotism had grown rather damp and gave out only lazy flashes. It was obvious that the masses were dissatisfied, and the Bolsheviks were immeasurably stronger throughout the country, and especially in the capital, than at the congress. Reduced to its elements, the quarrel between the Bolsheviks and the Compromisers invariably revolved around the question: With whom shall the democrats side, the imperialists or the workers? The shadow of the Entente stood over the congress. The question of the offensive was predetermined; the democrats had nothing to do but accede.

"At this critical moment," preached Tseretelli, "not one social force ought to be thrown out of the scales, so long as it may be useful to the cause of the people." Such was the justification for a coalition with the bourgeoisie. Seeing that the proletariat, the army, and the peasantry were upsetting their plans at every step, the democrats had to open a war against the people under guise of a war against the Bolsheviks. Thus Tseretelli had declared the Kronstadt sailors apostates in order not to throw out of his scales the Kadet Pepelyaev. The coalition was ratified by a majority of 543 votes against 126, with 52 abstaining.

The work of this enormous and flabby assembly in the Cadet Corps was distinguished by grandeur in the matter of declarations, and conservative stinginess in practical tasks. This laid on all its decisions a stamp of hopelessness and hypocrisy. The congress recognized the right of all Russian nationalities to self-determination, but gave the key to this problematic right not to the oppressed nations themselves, but to a future Constituent Assembly, in which the Compromisers hoped to be in a majority and capitulate before the imperialists, exactly as they had done in the government.

The congress refused to pass a decree on the eight-hour day. Tseretelli explained this side-stepping by the difficulty of reconciling the interests of the different layers of the population. As though any single great deed in history were ever accomplished by "reconciling interests," and not by the victory of progressive interests over reactionary!

Grohman, a Soviet economist, introduced toward the end of the congress his inevitable resolution: as to the oncoming economic catastrophe and the necessity of governmental regulation. The congress adopted this ritual resolution, but only so that everything might remain as before.

"Having deported Grimm," wrote Trotsky, on the 7th of June, "the congress returned to the order of the day. But capitalistic profits remain as before inviolable for Skobelev and his colleagues. The food crisis is getting sharper every hour. In the diplomatic sphere the government is taking blow after blow. And finally this so hysterically proclaimed offensive is obviously getting ready to come down on the nation, a monstrous adventure.

"We should be willing to watch peacefully the sanctified activities of the ministers—Lvov-Tereshchenko-Tseretelli—for a number of months. We need time for our own preparations. But the underground mole digs too fast. With the help of the 'socialist' ministers the problem of power may rise before the members of this congress a great deal sooner than any of us imagine."

Trying to shield themselves from the masses with a higher authority, the leaders dragged the congress into all current conflicts, pitilessly compromising it in the eyes of the Petrograd workers and soldiers. The most resounding episode of this kind was the incident about the summer home of Durnovo, an old tzarist bureaucrat who had made himself famous as Minister of the Interior by putting down the revolution of 1905. The vacant home of this hated, and moreover dirty-handed, bureaucrat was seized by workers' organizations on the Vyborg side —chiefly because of the enormous gardens which became a favorite playground for children. The bourgeois press represented the place as a lair of pogromists and hold-up men—the Kronstadt of the Vyborg district. No one took the trouble to find out what the facts were.. The government, carefully avoiding all important questions, undertook with fresh passion to rescue this house. They demanded sanction for the heroic undertaking from the Executive Committee, and Tseretelli of course did not refuse. The Procuror gave an order to evict the group of anarchists from the place in twenty-four hours. Learning about the military activities in preparation, the workers sounded the alarm. The anarchists on their side threatened armed resistance. Twenty-eight factories proclaimed a protest strike. The Executive Committee issued a proclamation accusing the Vyborg workers of aiding the counter-revolution. After all these preliminaries a representative of justice and the militia penetrated into the lions' den. They found complete order reigning; the house was occupied by a number of workers' educational organizations. They were compelled to withdraw in shame. This history had, however, a further development.

441

On the 9th of June a bomb was exploded at the congress: in the morning's edition of *Pravda* appeared an appeal for a demonstration on the following day. Cheidze, who knew how to get scared, and was therefore inclined to scare others, announced in a voice from the tomb: "If measures are not taken by the congress, tomorrow will be fatal." The delegates lifted their heads in alarm.

The idea of a show-down between the Petrograd workers and soldiers and the congress was suggested by the whole situation. The masses were urging on the Bolsheviks. The garrison especially was seething—fearing that in connection with the offensive they would be distributed among the regiments and scattered along the front. To this was united a bitter dissatisfaction with the "Declaration of the Rights of the Soldier," which had been a big backward step in comparison with "Order No. 1," and with the régime actually established in the army. The initiative for the demonstration came from the military organization of the Bolsheviks. Its leaders asserted, and quite rightly as events showed, that if the party did not take the leadership upon itself, the soldiers themselves would go into the streets. That sharp turn in the mood of the masses, however, could not be easily apprehended, and hence there was a certain vacillation in the ranks of the Bolsheviks themselves. Volodarsky was not sure that the workers would come out on the street. There was fear, too, as to the possible character of the demonstration. Representatives of the military organization declared that the soldiers, fearing attacks and reprisals, would not go out without weapons. "What will come out of the demonstration?" asked the prudent Tomsky, and demanded supplementary deliberations. Stalin thought that "the fermentation among the soldiers is a fact; among the workers there is no such definite mood," but nevertheless judged it necessary to show resistance to the government. Kalinin, always more inclined to avoid than welcome a battle, spoke emphatically against the demonstration, referring to the absence of any clear motive, especially among the workers: "The demonstration will be purely artificial." On June 8, at a conference with the representatives of the workers' sections, after a series of preliminary votes, 131 hands against 6 were finally raised for the demonstration, with 22 abstaining.

The work of preparation was carried on up to the last moment secretly, in order not to permit the Social Revolutionaries and Mensheviks to start a counter-agitation. That legitimate measure of caution was afterwards interpreted as evidence of a military conspiracy. The Central Council of Factory and Shop Committees joined in the decision to organize the demonstration. "Upon the insistence of Trotsky and against the objection of Lunacharsky," writes Yugov, "the Committee of the Mezhrayontzi decided to join the demonstration." Preparations were carried on with boiling energy.

The manifestation was to raise the banner of "Power to the Soviets." The fighting slogan ran: "Down with the Ten Minister-Capitalists!" That was the simplest possible expression for a break-up of the coalition with the bourgeoisie. The procession was to march to the Cadet Corps where the congress was sitting. This was to emphasize that the question was not of overthrowing the government, but of bringing pressure on the Soviet leaders.

To be sure, other ideas were expressed at the preliminary conferences of the Bolsheviks. For instance, Smilga, then a young member of the Central Committee, proposed that they should not "hesitate to seize the Post Office, telegraph, and arsenal, if events developed to the point of a clash." Another participant in the conference, a member of the Petrograd Committee, Latsis, comments in his diary upon the rejection of Smilga's proposal: "I cannot reconcile myself . . . I arrange with comrades Semashko and Rakhia to be fully armed in case of necessity and seize the railroad terminals, arsenals, banks, post and telegraph offices, with the help of a machine-gun regiment." Semashko was the officer of a machine-gun regiment, Rakhia, a worker, one of the militant Bolsheviks.

The existence of such moods is easily understandable. The whole course of the party was toward a seizure of power, and the question was merely of appraising the present situation. An obvious break in favor of the Bolsheviks was taking place in Petrograd, but in the provinces the same process was going slower. Moreover the front needed the lesson of an advance before it could shake off its distrust of the Bolsheviks. Lenin therefore stood firm on his April position: "Patiently explain."

Sukhanov in his *Notes* describes the plan of the demonstration of June 10, as a direct device of Lenin for seizing the power "if the situation proves favorable." As a matter of fact, only individual Bolsheviks tried to put the matter this way, aiming according to the ironic expression of Lenin, "just a wee bit too far to the left." Strangely enough, Sukhanov does not even try to compare his arbitrary guesses with the political line of Lenin expressed in innumerable speeches and articles.[1]

The Bureau of the Executive Committee immediately presented the Bolsheviks with a demand to call off the demonstration. On what grounds? Only the state power, obviously, could formally forbid a demonstration; but the state power did not dare think of it. How could the Soviet, itself a "private organization," led by a bloc composed of two political parties, prevent a third party from demonstrating? The Bolshevik Central Committee refused to accede to the demand, but decided to emphasize more sharply the peaceful character of the demonstration. On the 9th of June, a Bolshevik proclamation was pasted up in the workers' districts. "We are free citizens, we have the right to protest, and we ought to use this right before it is too late. The right to a peaceful demonstration is ours."

The Compromisers carried the question before the congress. It was at that moment that Cheidze pronounced his words about the fatal outcome, and that it would be necessary for the congress to sit all night. A member of the præsidium, Gegechkori, also one of the sons of the Gironde, concluded his speech with a rude cry in the direction of the Bolsheviks: "Take your dirty hands off a glorious cause!" They did not give the Bolsheviks time, though it was demanded, to take up the question in a meeting of their faction. The congress passed a resolution forbidding all demonstrations for three days. Besides being an act of violence with relation to the Bolsheviks, this was an act

[1] Further details about this in Appendix 3.

444

of usurpation with relation to the government. The soviets continued to steal the power from under their own pillow.

Miliukov was speaking at this time at a Cossack conference, and called the Bolsheviks "the chief enemies of the Russian revolution." Its chief friend, he allowed them to infer, was Miliukov himself, who just before February had agreed to accept defeat from the Germans rather than revolution from the Russian people. To a question from the Cossacks as to the attitude toward Leninists, Miliukov answered: "It's time to make an end of these people." The leader of the bourgeoisie was in too great a hurry. However, he really could not afford to waste time.

Meanwhile meetings were being held in factories and regiments, adopting resolutions to go into the streets the next day with the slogan "All Power to the Soviets." Under the noise of the soviet and Cossack congresses, the fact passed unnoticed that 37 Bolsheviks were elected to the duma of the Vyborg district, only 22 from the Social Revolutionary-Menshevik bloc, and 4 Kadets.

Confronted with the categorical resolution of the congress —and moreover with a mysterious reference to a threatening blow from the right—the Bolsheviks decided to reconsider the question. They wanted a peaceful demonstration, not an insurrection, and they could not have any motive for converting a forbidden demonstration into a half-insurrection. On its side the præsidium of the congress decided to take measures. Several hundred delegates were grouped in tens and sent out to the workers' districts and the barracks to prevent the demonstration. They were to meet in the morning at the Tauride Palace and compare notes. The executive committee of the peasant deputies joined in this expedition, appointing 70 from its membership.

Thus, in however unexpected a manner, the Bolsheviks achieved their goal. The delegates of the congress found themselves obliged to get acquainted with the workers and soldiers of the capital. If the mountain was not allowed to come to the prophet, the prophet at least went to the mountain. The meeting proved instructive in the highest degree. In the *Izvestia* of the Moscow Soviet, a Menshevik correspondent paints the following picture: "All night long, without a wink of sleep,

445

a majority of the congress, more than 500 members, dividing themselves into tens, traveled through the factories and shops and military units of Petrograd, urging everybody to stay away from the demonstration. . . . The congress had no authority in a good many of the factories and shops, and also in several regiments of the garrison. . . . The members were frequently met in a far from friendly manner, sometimes hostilely, and quite often they were sent away with insults." This official Soviet organ does not exaggerate in the least. On the contrary, it gives a very much softened picture of this nocturnal meeting of two different worlds.

The Petrograd masses at least left no doubt among the delegates as to who was able henceforth to summon a demonstration, or to call it off. The workers of the Putilov factory agreed to paste up the declaration of the congress against the demonstration only after they learned from *Pravda* that it did not contradict the resolution of the Bolsheviks. The first machine gun regiment—which played the leading rôle in the garrison, as did the Putilov factory among the workers—after hearing the speeches of Cheidze and Avksentiev representing the two executive committees, adopted the following resolution: "In agreement with the Central Committee of the Bolsheviks and their military organization, the regiment postpones its action."

This brigade of pacifiers arrived at the Tauride Palace after their sleepless night in a condition of complete demoralization. They had assumed that the authority of the congress was inviolable, but had run into a stone wall of distrust and hostility. "The masses are thick with Bolsheviks." "The attitude to the Mensheviks and Social Revolutionaries is hostile." "They trust only *Pravda.*" "In some places they shouted: 'We are not your comrades.'" One after another the delegates reported how, although they had called off the battle, they were defeated.

The masses submitted to the decision of the Bolsheviks, but not without protest and indignation. In certain factories they adopted resolutions of censure of the Central Committee. The more fiery members of the party in the sections tore up their membership cards. That was a serious warning.

The Compromisers had motivated their three-day veto of

446

demonstrations by references to a monarchist plot, which hoped
to avail itself of the action of the Bolsheviks; they mentioned
the participation in it of a part of the Cossack congress and
the approach to Petrograd of counter-revolutionary troops. It
is not surprising if after calling off the demonstration the
Bolsheviks demanded an explanation as to this conspiracy. In
place of an answer the leaders of the congress accused the Bolsheviks themselves of a conspiracy. They found this happy
way out of the situation.

It must be acknowledged that on the night of June 10 the
Compromisers did discover a conspiracy, and one which shook
them badly—a conspiracy of the masses with the Bolsheviks
against the Compromisers. However, the submission of the
Bolsheviks to the resolution of the congress encouraged them
and permitted their panic to turn into madness. The Mem-
sheviks and Social Revolutionaries decided to show an iron
energy. On the 10th of June the Menshevik paper wrote:
"It is time to brand the Leninists as traitors and betrayers of
the revolution." A representative of the Executive Committee
appeared at the Cossack congress and requested them to support
the Soviet against the Bolsheviks. He was answered by the
chairman, the ataman of the Urals, Dutov: "We, Cossacks, will
never go against the Soviet." Against the Bolsheviks the reactionaries were ready to go hand in hand even with the Soviet
—in order the better to strangle it later on.

On June 11 there assembles a formidable court of justice:
the Executive Committee, members of the præsidium of the
congress, leaders of the factions—in all about a hundred men.
Tseretelli as usual appears in the rôle of prosecutor. Choking
with rage, he demands deadly measures, and scornfully waves
away Dan, who is always ready to bait the Bolsheviks, but
still not quite ready to destroy them. "What the Bolsheviks
are now doing is not ideological propaganda, but a conspiracy.
. . . The Bolsheviks must excuse us. Now we are going to
adopt different methods of struggle. . . . *We have got to disarm the Bolsheviks.* We cannot leave in their hands those two
great technical instruments which they have possessed up to
now. We cannot leave machine guns and rifles in their hands.

We will not tolerate conspiracies." That was a new note. What did it mean exactly to disarm the Bolsheviks? Sukhanov writes on this subject: "The Bolsheviks really did not have any special stores of weapons. All the weapons were actually in the hands of soldiers and workers, the immense mass of whom were following the Bolsheviks. Disarming the Bolsheviks could mean only disarming the proletariat. More than that, it meant disarming the troops."

In other words, that classic moment of the revolution had arrived when the bourgeois democracy, upon the demand of the reaction, undertakes to disarm the workers who had guaranteed the revolutionary victory. These democratic gentlemen, among whom were well-read people, had invariably given their sympathy to the disarmed, not to the disarmers—so long as it was a question of reading old books. But when this question presented itself in reality, they did not recognize it. The mere fact that Tseretelli, a revolutionist, a man who had spent years at hard labor, a Zimmerwaldist of yesterday, was undertaking to disarm the workers, had some difficulty in making its way into people's heads. The hall was stunned into silence. The provincial delegates nevertheless felt that someone was pushing them into an abyss. One of the officers went into hysterics.

No less pale than Tseretelli, Kamenev rose in his seat and cried out with a dignity the strength of which was felt by the audience: "Mr. Minister, if you are not merely talking into the wind, you have no right to confine yourself to speech. Arrest me, and try me for conspiracy against the revolution." The Bolsheviks left the hall with a protest, refusing to participate in this mockery of their own party. The tenseness in the hall became almost unbearable. Lieber hastened to the aid of Tseretelli. Restrained rage was replaced by hysterical fury. Lieber called for ruthless measures. "If you want to win the masses who follow the Bolsheviks, then break with Bolshevism." But he was heard without sympathy, even with a half-hostility.

Impressionable as always, Lunacharsky immediately tried to find a common ground with the majority: Although the Bolsheviks had assured him that they had in mind only a peaceful demonstration, nevertheless his own experience had convinced him that "it was a mistake to organize a demonstration;" however, we must not sharpen the conflicts. Without pacifying his enemies, Lunacharsky irritated his friends.

"We are not fighting with the left tendency," said Dan jesuitically—he was the most experienced, but also most futile of the leaders of the swamp. "We are fighting with the counter-revolution. It is not our fault if behind your shoulders stand the agents of Germany." The reference to Germans was merely a substitute for an argument. Of course these gentlemen could not point to any agents of Germany.

Tseretelli wanted to deal a blow; Dan merely wanted to show his fist. In its helplessness the Executive Committee sided with Dan. The resolution offered to the congress next day had the character of an exceptional law against Bolsheviks, but without immediate practical inferences.

"You can have no doubt after the visit of your delegates to the factories and regiments," said a declaration addressed to the congress in writing by the Bolsheviks, "that if the demonstration did not take place, it was not because of your veto, but because our party called it off. . . . The fiction of a military conspiracy was created by the members of the Provisional Government in order to carry out the disarming of the proletariat of Petrograd and the disbanding of the Petrograd garrison. . . . Even if the state power went over wholly into the hands of the Soviet—which we advocate—and the Soviet tried to put fetters upon our agitation, that would not make us passively submit; we should go to meet imprisonment and other punishments in the name of the idea of international socialism which separates us from you."

The Soviet majority and the Soviet minority confronted each other breast to breast three days as though for a decisive battle. But both sides stepped back at the last moment. The Bolsheviks gave up the demonstration. The Compromisers abandoned the idea of disarming the workers.

Tseretelli remained in the minority among his own people. But nevertheless from his point of view he was right. The policy of union with the bourgeoisie had arrived at a point where it became necessary to paralyze the masses who were

449

not reconciled to the coalition. To carry the Compromise policy through to a successful end—that is, to the establishment of a parliamentary rule of the bourgeoisie—demanded the disarming of the workers and soldiers. But Tseretelli was not only right. He was besides that powerless. Neither the soldiers nor the workers would have voluntarily given up their arms. It would have been necessary to employ force against them. But Tseretelli was already without forces. He could procure them, if at all, only from the hands of the reaction. But they, in case of a successful crushing of the Bolsheviks, would have immediately taken up the job of crushing the Compromise soviets, and would not have failed to remind Tseretelli that he was a former hard-labor convict and nothing more. However, the further course of events will show that even the reaction did not have forces enough for this.

Politically Tseretelli grounded his argument for fighting the Bolsheviks upon the assertion that they were separating the proletariat from the peasantry. Martov answered him: Tseretelli does not get his guiding ideas "from the depth of the peasantry. A group of right Kadets, a group of capitalists, a group of landlords, a group of imperialists, the bourgeoisie of the West"—these are the ones who are demanding the disarmament of the workers and soldiers. Martov was right: the possessing classes have more than once in history hidden their pretensions behind the backs of a peasantry.

From the moment of publication of Lenin's April theses, a reference to the danger of isolating the proletariat from the peasants became the principal argument of all those who wanted to drag the revolution backward. It was no accident that Lenin compared Tseretelli to the "old Bolsheviks."

In one of his works of the year 1917, Trotsky wrote on this theme: "The isolation of our party from the Social Revolutionaries and Mensheviks, even its extreme isolation, even by way of solitary confinement, would still in no case mean the isolation of the proletariat from the oppressed peasantry and the oppressed city masses. On the contrary, a sharp demarcation of the policy of the revolutionary proletariat from the treacherous apostacy of the present leaders of the Soviet, can alone bring a saving political differentiation into the peasant millions, draw away the poor peasants from the traitorous leadership of the aggressive Social Revolutionary type of mu-zhik, and convert the socialist proletariat into genuine leaders of the national plebeian revolution."

But Tseretelli's totally false argument remained alive. On the eve of the October revolution it reappeared with redoubled force as the argument of many "old Bolsheviks" against the uprising. Several years later when the intellectual reaction against October began, Tseretelli's formula became the chief theoretical weapon of the school of the epigones.

*

At the same session of the congress which condemned the Bol-sheviks in their absence, a representative of the Mensheviks unexpectedly moved to appoint for the following Sunday, the 18th of June, a manifestation of workers and soldiers in Petro-grad and other important cities, in order to demonstrate to the enemy the unity and strength of the democracy. The motion was carried, although not without bewilderment. Something over a month later Miliukov fairly well explained this un-expected turn on the part of the Compromisers: "In delivering Kadet speeches at the congress of the soviets, in disorgan-izing the armed demonstration of June 10. . . the minister-socialists felt that they had gone too far in our direction, that the ground was slipping under their feet. They got frightened and backed away abruptly toward the Bolsheviks." The decision to hold a demonstration on June 18 was, of course, not a step in the direction of the Bolsheviks, but an attempt to turn toward the masses as against the Bolsheviks. Their nocturnal experience with the workers and soldiers had caused a certain amount of trepidation among the heads of the soviets. Thus, for instance, in direct opposition to what had been in mind at the beginning of the congress, they hastily produced in the name of the government a resolution calling for the abolition of the State Duma and the summoning of a Con-stituent Assembly for the 30th of September. The slogans of the demonstration were chosen with this same idea of not causing any irritation to the masses: "Universal Peace," "Immediate Convocation of a Constituent Assembly," "Democratic Republic." Not a word either about the offensive or the coalition. Lenin asked in *Pravda*: "And what has become of 'Complete Confidence to the Provisional Government,' gentlemen? . . . Why does your tongue stick in your throat?" This irony was accurately to the point: the Compromisers did not dare demand of the masses confidence in that government of which they themselves were members.

The Soviet delegates, having a second time made the rounds of the workers' districts and the barracks, gave wholly encouraging reports on the eve of the demonstration to the Executive Committee. Tseretelli, to whom these communications restored his equilibrium and inclination toward complacent sermonizing, addressed some remarks to the Bolsheviks: "Now we shall have an open and honest review of the revolutionary forces. . . . Now we shall see whom the majority is following, you or us." The Bolsheviks had accepted the challenge even before it was so incautiously formulated. "We shall join the demonstration on the 18th," wrote *Pravda*, "in order to struggle for those aims for which we had intended to demonstrate on the 10th."

The line of march—evidently in memory of the funeral procession of three months before, which had been, at least superficially, a gigantic manifestation of the unity of the democracy —again led to Mars Field and the grave of the February martyrs. But aside from the line of march nothing whatever was reminiscent of those earlier days. About 400,000 people paraded, considerably less than at the funeral: absent from the Soviet demonstration were not only the bourgeoisie with whom the soviets were in coalition, but also the radical intelligentsia, which had occupied so prominent a place in the former parades of the democracy. Few but the factories and barracks marched.

The delegates of the congress, assembled on Mars Field, read and counted the placards. The first Bolshevik slogans were met half-laughingly—Tseretelli had so confidently thrown down his challenge the day before. But these same slogans were repeated

again and again. "Down with the Ten Minister-Capitalists!"
"Down with the Offensive!" "All Power to the Soviets!" The
ironical smiles froze, and then gradually disappeared. Bolshevik banners floated everywhere. The delegates stopped counting the uncomfortable totals. The triumph of the Bolsheviks
was too obvious. "Here and there," writes Sukhanov, "the chain
of Bolshevik banners and columns would be broken by specifical-
ly Social Revolutionary or official Soviet slogans. But these
were drowned in the mass. Soviet officialdom was recounting
the next day 'how fiercely here and there the crowd tore up
banners bearing the slogan 'Confidence to the Provisional Government.' " There is obvious exaggeration in this. Only three
small groups carried placards in honor of the Provisional Government: the circle of Plekhanov, a Cossack detachment, and a
handful of Jewish intellectuals who belonged to the Bund. This
threefold combination, which gave the impression with its variegated membership of a political curio, seemed to have set itself
the task of publicly exhibiting the impotence of the régime.
Under the hostile cries of the crowd the Plekhanovites and the
Bund lowered their placards. The Cossacks were stubborn, and
their banners were literally torn from them by the demonstrators, and destroyed. "The stream which had been flowing quietly
along until then," writes *Izvestia,* "turned into a veritable river
at the flood, just at the point of overflowing its banks." That
was the Vyborg section, all under the banners of the Bolsheviks.
"Down with the Ten Minister-Capitalists!" One of the factories
carried a placard: "The right to Life is Higher than the rights
of Private Property." This slogan had not been suggested by
the party.

Dismayed provincials were looking everywhere for their
leaders. The latter lowered their eyes or simply went into hiding.
The Bolsheviks went after the provincials. Does this look like
a gang of conspirators? The delegates agreed that it did not.
"In Petrograd you are the power," they conceded in a totally
different tone from that in which they had spoken at the official sessions, "but not in the provinces, not at the front. Petrograd cannot go against the whole country." That's all right,

answered the Bolsheviks, your turn will soon come—the same slogans will be raised.

"During this demonstration," wrote the old man Plekhanov, "I stood on Mars Field beside Cheidze; I saw in his face that he was not deceiving himself in the least about the significance of the astonishing number of placards demanding the overthrow of the capitalist ministers. It was emphasized as though intentionally by the veritably imperious commands with which some of the Leninists addressed him as they passed by like people celebrating a holiday." The Bolsheviks certainly had ground for a holiday feeling. "Judging by the placards and slogans of the demonstrators," wrote Gorky's paper, "the Sunday demonstration revealed the complete triumph of Bolshevism among the Petersburg proletariat." It was a great victory, and moreover it was won on the arena and with the weapons chosen by the enemy. While sanctioning the offensive, recognizing the coalition, and condemning the Bolsheviks, the soviet congress had called the masses on its own initiative into the streets. They came with the announcement: We don't want either offensive or coalition; we are for Bolshevism. Such was the political meaning of the demonstration. No wonder the papers of the Mensheviks, who had initiated the demonstration, asked themselves mournfully the next day: Who suggested that unhappy idea?

Of course not all the workers and soldiers in the capital took part in the demonstration, and not all the demonstrators were Bolsheviks. But by this time not one of them wanted a coalition. Those workers who still remained hostile to Bolshevism did not know what to oppose to it. Their hostility was thus converted into a watchful neutrality. Under the Bolshevik slogans marched no small number of Mensheviks and Social Revolutionaries who had not yet broken with their party, but had already lost faith in its slogans.

The demonstration of June 18 made an enormous impression on its own participants. The masses saw that the Bolsheviks had become a power, and the vacillating were drawn to them. In Moscow, Kiev, Kharkov, Ekaterinoslav, and many other provincial towns the demonstrations revealed an immense growth of the influence of the Bolsheviks. Everywhere the same slogans were advanced, and they struck at the very heart of the February régime. It was impossible not to draw conclusions. It seemed as though the Compromisers had nowhere to go. But the offensive helped them at the very last moment. On the 19th of June, there was a patriotic demonstration on the Nevsky under the leadership of Kadets, and with a portrait of Kerensky. In the words of Miliukov, "It was so different from what happened on the same street the day before that there mingled with the feeling of triumph an involuntary feeling of uneasiness." Legitimate feeling! But the Compromisers gave a sigh of relief. Their thoughts immediately soared above both demonstrations in the form of a democratic synthesis. Those people were fated to drain the cup of illusion and humiliation to the dregs.

In the April days two simultaneous demonstrations, one revolutionary and the other patriotic, had gone to meet each other, and their clash resulted in casualties. The hostile demonstrations of the 18th and 19th of June followed one after the other. There was no direct clash then. But a clash was not to be avoided. It had only been postponed for two weeks.

The anarchists, not knowing how else to show their independence, availed themselves of the demonstration of June 18 for an attack on the Vyborg prisons. The prisoners, a majority of them criminal, were liberated without a fight and without casualties—and not from one prison, but from several simultaneously. It seems obvious that the attack had not caught the administration unawares—that the administration had gladly gone half-way to meet actual and pretended anarchists. That whole enigmatical episode had nothing whatever to do with the demonstration. But the patriotic press linked them together. The Bolsheviks proposed to the congress of soviets a strict investigation of the manner in which 460 criminals had been let loose from various prisons. However, the Compromisers could not permit themselves this luxury: they were afraid they would run into men higher up in the administration and their own allies in a political bloc. Moreover, they had no desire to defend their own demonstration against malicious slanders.

The Minister of Justice, Pereverzev—who had disgraced himself a few days before in connection with the summer house of Durnovo—decided to have vengeance, and under the pretext of a search for escaped convicts made a new raid on the place. The anarchists resisted; one of them was killed, and the house wrecked. The workers of the Vyborg side, considering the house their own, sounded the alarm. Several factories quit work; the alarm spread to other sections and even to the barracks.

The last days of June pass in a continual commotion. A machine gun regiment prepares for an immediate attack on the Provisional Government. Workers from the striking factories make the rounds of the regiments calling them into the streets. Bearded peasants in soldiers' coats, many of them gray-haired, pass in processions of protest along the pavements: these middle-aged peasants are demanding that they be discharged for work in the fields. The Bolsheviks are carrying on an agitation against going into the streets: The demonstration of the 18th has said all that can be said; in order to produce a change, demonstrating is not enough; and yet the hour of revolution has not yet struck. On the 22nd of June, the Bolshevik press appeals to the garrison: "Do not trust any summons to action in the street delivered in the name of the Military Organization." Delegates are arriving from the front with complaints of violence and punishments. Threats to reorganize the unsubmissive regiments pour oil on the fire. "In many regiments the soldiers are sleeping with weapons in their hands," says a declaration of the Bolsheviks to the Executive Committee. Patriotic demonstrations, often armed, lead to street fights. These are small discharges of the accumulated electricity. Neither side directly intends to attack: the reaction is too weak, the revolution is not yet fully confident of its power. But the streets of the town seem paved with explosive material. A battle hovers in the air. The Bolshevik press explains and restrains. The patriotic press gives away its fright with an unbridled baiting of Bolsheviks. On the 25th, Lenin writes: "This universal wild cry of spite and rage against the Bolsheviks is the common complaint of Kadets,

Social Revolutionaries and Mensheviks against their own flabbiness. They are in a majority. They are the government. They are all together in a bloc. And they see that nothing comes of it. What can they do but rage against the Bolsheviks?"

CONCLUSION

IN the first pages of this work we tried to show how deeply the October revolution was rooted in the social relations of Russia. Our analysis, far from having been accommodated *ex post facto* to the achieved events, was on the contrary made by us long before the revolution—indeed before its prologue of 1905.

In the further pages we tried to see how the social forces of Russia revealed themselves in the events of the revolution. We recorded the activity of the political parties in their interrelations with the classes. The sympathies and antipathies of the author may be set aside. A historic exposition has a right to demand that its objectivity be recognized if, resting upon accurately established facts, it reproduces their inner connection on the basis of the real development of social relations. The inner causal order of the process thus coming to life becomes itself the best proof of the objectivity of the exposition.

The events of the February revolution passing before the reader have confirmed our theoretical prognosis—for the time being by one half at least—through a method of successive elimination. Before the proletariat came to power all the other variants of the political development were subjected to the test of life and thrown aside as worthless.

The government of the liberal bourgeoisie with Kerensky as a democratic hostage, proved a total failure. The "April days" were the first candid warning addressed by the October to the February revolution. The bourgeois Provisional Government was replaced after this by a Coalition whose fruitlessness was revealed on every day of its existence. In the June demonstration summoned by the Executive Committee on its own initiative, although perhaps not quite voluntarily, the February revolution tried to measure strength with the October and suffered a cruel defeat. The defeat was the more fatal in that it occurred in the Petrograd arena, and at the hands of those same workers and soldiers who had achieved the February revolution and turned it over to the rest of the country. The June demonstration proved that the workers and soldiers of Petrograd were on their way to a new revolution whose aims were inscribed on their banners. Unmistakable signs testified that all the rest of the country, although with an inevitable delay, would catch up with Petrograd. Thus by the end of its fourth month the February revolution had already exhausted itself politically. The Compromisers had lost the confidence of the soldiers and workers. A conflict between the leading soviet parties and the soviet masses now became inevitable. After the manifestation of June 18, which was a peaceful test of the correlation of forces of the two revolutions, the contradiction between them must inevitably take an open and violent form.

Thus arose the "July days." Two weeks after the demonstration which had been organized from above, the same workers and soldiers went out into the street on their own initiative and demanded of the Central Executive Committee that it seize the power. The Compromisers flatly refused. The July days led to street encounters and casualties, and ended with the dispersion of the Bolsheviks who were declared responsible for the bankruptcy of the February régime. That resolution which Tseretelli had introduced on June 11 and which was then voted down—to declare the Bolsheviks beyond the law and disarm them—was carried out in full at the beginning of July. The Bolshevik papers were shut down; the Bolshevik military units were dissolved. The workers were disarmed. The leaders of the party were declared hirelings of the German Staff. One of them went into hiding, the others were locked up in jail.

But just this "victory" of the Compromisers over the Bolsheviks completely revealed the impotence of the democracy. Against the workers and soldiers the democrats were compelled to employ notoriously counter-revolutionary units, hostile not only to the Bolsheviks, but also to the Soviet: the Executive Committee already had no troops of its own.

The liberals drew from this the correct conclusion, which Miliukov formulated in the form of an alternative: Kornilov or

Lenin? The revolution actually left no more room for the empire of the golden mean. The counter-revolution was saying to itself: now or never. The supreme commander-in-chief, Kornilov, raised a rebellion against the revolution under the guise of a campaign against the Bolsheviks. Just as all forms of the legal opposition before the revolution had adopted the camouflage of patriotism—that is, the necessities of the struggle against the Germans—so now all forms of legal counter-revolution adopted as camouflage the necessities of the struggle against the Bolsheviks. Kornilov had the support of the possessing classes and their party, the Kadets. This did not hinder, but rather promoted, the result that the troops deployed against Petrograd by Kornilov were defeated without a fight, capitulated without an encounter, went up in vapor like a drop falling on a hot stove-lid. Thus the attempt at a revolution *from the right* was made, and moreover by a man standing at the head of the army. The correlation of forces between the possessing classes and the people was tested in action. In the choice between Kornilov and Lenin, Kornilov fell like a rotten fruit, although Lenin was still at that time compelled to remain in deep hiding.

What variant after that still remained unused, untried, untested? The variant of Bolshevism. Actually after the Kornilov attempt and its inglorious collapse, the masses stormily and decisively swung over to the Bolsheviks. The October revolution advanced with a physical necessity. In distinction from the February revolution, which has been called bloodless although it cost Petrograd a considerable number of victims, the October revolution was actually achieved in the capital without bloodshed. Have we not the right to ask: What further demonstration could be given of the deep natural inevitability of the October revolution? Is it not clear that this revolution can seem the fruit of adventurism and demagogy only to those whom it damaged at the most sensitive point, the pocketbook? The bloody struggle breaks out only after the conquest of power by the Bolshevik soviets when the overthrown classes, with material support from the governments of the Entente, make desperate efforts to get back what they have lost. Then

CONCLUSION

come the years of civil war. The Red Army is created, the
hungry country is put under the régime of military communism
and converted into a Spartan war camp. The October revolution step by step lays down its road, beats back all enemies,
passes over to the solution of its industrial problems, heals the
heaviest wounds of the imperialist and civil war, and achieves
gigantic successes in the sphere of the development of industry.
There arise before it, however, new difficulties flowing from
its isolated position with mighty capitalistic lands surrounding
it. That belatedness of development which had brought the
Russian proletariat to power, has imposed upon that power
tasks which in their essence cannot be fully achieved within the
framework of an isolated state. The fate of that state is thus
wholly bound up with the further course of world history.

This first volume, dedicated to the February revolution,
shows how and why that revolution was bound to come to nothing. The second and third volumes will show how the October
revolution triumphed.

461

APPENDIX I

(To the Chapter *Peculiarities of Russia's Development*)

THE question of the peculiarities of Russia's historic development, and, bound up therewith, the question of its future destinies, lay at the bottom of all the debates and groupings of the Russian intelligentsia throughout almost the whole of the nineteenth century. Slavophilism and westernism resolved this question in opposite ways but with similar dogmatism. They were replaced by the theories of the Narodniks and Marxism. Before the Narodnik theory conclusively faded out under the influence of bourgeois liberalism, it long and stubbornly defended the idea of a completely unique course of development for Russia, a detour around capitalism. In this sense the Narodniks continued the Slavophile tradition, purging it however of monarchist-churchly-Pan-Slavic elements, and giving it a revolutionary-democratic character.

In the essence of the matter the Slavophile conception, with all its reactionary fantasticness, and also Narodnikism, with all its democratic illusions, were by no means mere speculations, but rested upon indubitable and moreover deep peculiarities of Russia's development, understood one-sidedly however and incorrectly evaluated. In its struggle with Narodnikism, Russian Marxism, demonstrating the identity of the laws of development for all countries, not infrequently fell into a dogmatic mechanization discovering a tendency to pour out the baby with the bath. This tendency is revealed especially sharply in many of the works of the well-known Professor Pokrovsky.

In 1922 Pokrovsky came down upon the historic conception of the author which lies at the basis of the theory of Permanent Revolution. We consider it useful, at least for readers interesting themselves not only in the dramatic course of events but also in revolutionary doctrine, to adduce here the more essential excerpts from our answers to Professor Pokrovsky published in two issues of the central organ of the Bolshevik Party, *Pravda*, July 1 and 2, 1922:

Concerning the Peculiarities of Russia's Historic Development

Pokrovsky has published an article dedicated to my book: *1905*, which demonstrates—negatively, alas!—what a complex matter it is to *apply* methods of historic materialism to living human history, and what a rubber-stamp affair is often made out of history even by such deeply erudite people as Pokrovsky. The book which Pokrovsky criticizes was directly called out by a desire to establish historically and justify theoretically the slogan of the conquest of power by the proletariat, as against the slogan of a bourgeois democratic republic, and also that of a democratic government of the proletariat and the peasantry. . . . This line of thought produced a very great theoretic indignation on the part of no small number of Marxists, indeed an overwhelming majority of them. Those who expressed this indignation were not only Mensheviks, but also Kamenev and Rozhkov (a Bolshevik-historian). Their point of view in broad outlines was as follows: The political rule of the bourgeoisie must precede the political rule of the proletariat; the bourgeois democratic republic must be a prolonged historic schooling for the proletariat; the attempt to jump over this stage is adventurism; if the working class in the West has not yet conquered the power, how can the Russian proletariat set itself this task? etc., etc. From the point of view of this pseudo-Marxism, which confines itself to historical mechanisms, formal analogies, converting historic epochs into a logical succession of inflexible social categories (feudalism, capitalism, socialism, autocracy, bourgeois republic, dictatorship of the proletariat)—from this point of view the slogan of the conquest of power by the working class in Russia must have seemed a monstrous departure from Marxism. However, a serious empirical evaluation of the social forces as they stood in 1903-05 powerfully suggested the entire viability of a struggle for a conquest of power by the working class. Is this a peculiarity, or is it not? Does it assume profound peculiarities in the whole historical development or does it not? How does it come that such a task arose before the proletariat of Russia—that is, the most backward (with Pokrovsky's permission) country of Europe?

And in what consists the backwardness of Russia? Merely in the fact that Russia is belatedly repeating the history of the western European countries? But in that case would it be possible to talk of a conquest of power by the Russian proletariat? This conquest, however (we permit ourselves to remember), was actually made. Where lies the essence of all this? In that the indubitable and irrefutable belatedness of Russia's development under influence and pressure of the higher culture from the West, results not in a simple repetition of the West European historic process, but in the creation of profound *peculiarities* demanding independent study.

This deep uniqueness in our political situation, which led to the victorious October revolution before the beginning of the revolution in Europe, had its roots in the peculiar correlation of forces among the different classes and the state power. When Pokrovsky and Rozhkov quarreled with the Narodniks or liberals, demonstrating that the organization and policy of tzarism was determined by the economic development and the interests of the possessing classes, they were fundamentally right. But when Pokrovsky tries to repeat this against me, he simply hits the wrong mark.

The result of our belated historic development, in the conditions of the imperialist encirclement, was that our bourgeoisie did not have time to push out tzarism before the proletariat had become an independent revolutionary force.

But for Pokrovsky the very question which constitutes for us the central theme of the investigation, does not exist.

Pokrovsky writes: "To portray the Moscow Russ of the sixteenth century on a background of general European relations of that time is an extremely alluring enterprise. There is no better way to refute the prejudices prevailing until now even in Marxist circles about the 'primitiveness' of those economic foundations upon which the Russian autocracy arose." And further: "To present this autocracy in its real historic connections, as one of the aspects of commercial-capitalist Europe . . . that is an undertaking not only of extraordinary interest to the historian, but also of extraordinary educational importance for the reading public: there is no more radical way of putting an end to the legend of 'peculiarities' of the Russian historic process." Pokrovsky, as we see, flatly denies the primitiveness and backwardness of our economic development, and therewith relegates the peculiarities of the Russian historic process to the sphere of legend. And the whole trouble in that Pokrovsky is completely hypnotized by the comparatively broad development of trade noticed by him and also by Rozhkov in sixteenth century Russia. It is hard to understand how Pokrovsky could make such a mistake. You might indeed imagine that trade is the basis of economic life and its infallible measuring rod. The German economist Karl Bücher twenty years ago tried to find in trade (the path between the producer and the consumer) a criterion of the whole economic development. Struve, of course, hastened to transport this "discovery" into the Russian economic "science." At that time the theory of Bücher met a perfectly natural opposition from the Marxists. We find the criteria of economic development in production—in technique and the social organization of labor—and the path followed by

465

the product from the producer to the consumer we regard as a secondary phenomenon, whose roots are to be found in that same production.

The large scope, at least in a spatial sense, of Russian trade in the sixteenth century—however paradoxical from the standpoint of the Bücher-Struve criterion—is explained exactly by the extraordinary primitiveness of Russian economy. The West European city was a craft-guild and trade-league city; our cities were above all administrative, military, consequently consuming and not producing, centers. The craft-guild culture of the West formed itself on a relatively high level of economic development when all the fundamental processes of the manufacturing industries had been distinguished from agriculture, had been converted into independent crafts, had created their own organizations, their own focuses—the cities—and at first a limited (belonging to local districts), but nevertheless stable, market. At the basis of the medieval European city therefore lay a comparatively high differentiation of industry, giving rise to regular interrelations between the city center and its agricultural periphery. Our economic backwardness, on the other hand, found its expression in the fact that craft, not yet separated from agriculture, preserved the form of home industry. Here we were nearer to India than to Europe, just as our medieval cities were nearer to the Asiatic than the European type, and as our autocracy, standing between the European absolutism and the Asiatic despotism, in many features approached the latter.

With the boundlessness of our spaces and the sparseness of the population (also a sufficiently objective sign, it would seem, of backwardness) the exchange of products presupposed a mediating rôle of trade-capital on the broadest scale. This scale was possible exactly because the West stood at a far higher level of development, had its own innumerable demands, sent out its merchants and its goods, and therewith stimulated our trade turnover with its extremely primitive, and in a certain measure barbarian, economic basis. Not to see this immense peculiarity of our historic development means not to see our whole history.

My Siberian boss (I spent two months entering poods and arshines in his ledger), Jacob Andreievich Chernykh—this was not in the sixteenth century, but at the very beginning of the twentieth—enjoyed an almost unlimited rulership within the limits of Kirensky county, thanks to his trade operations. Jacob Andreievich bought up furs from the Tunghuz and bought in the parish contributions in kind from the priests of more remote districts, imported calico from the Irbitsk and Nizhni-Novgorod market, and above all supplied vodka. (In the Irkutsk province at that epoch the monopoly had not yet been introduced.) Jacob Andreievich was illiterate, but a millionaire (according to the value of the decimal in those days, not now). His "dictatorship," as the representative of trade capital, was indubitable. He even always talked of "my little Tunghuzi." The city of Kirensk, like Verkholensk and Nizhni-Ilimsk, was a residence of sheriffs and magistrates, kulaks in hierarchical dependence one upon another, all kinds of officials, and a few wretched artisans. An organized handicraft as the basis of city economic life I did not find there, neither guilds, nor guild holidays, nor trade leagues, although Jacob Andreievich counted himself a member of the "second League." Really this live bit of Siberian reality carries us far deeper into an understanding of the historic peculiarities of Russia's development than what Pokrovsky says on this subject. That is a fact. The trade operations of Jacob Andreievich extended from the midstream of the Lena and its eastern tributaries to Nizhni-Novgorod and even Moscow. Few trades of Continental Europe can mark off such distances on their maps. However, this trade dictator—this "king of clubs," in the language of the Siberian farmers—was the most finished and convincing incarnation of our industrial backwardness, barbarism, primitiveness, sparseness of population, scatteredness of peasant towns and villages, impassable country roads, creating around the counties, districts and villages in the spring and autumn floods a two-months' swampy blockade, of our universal illiteracy, etc., etc. And Chernykh had risen to his commercial importance on the basis of the Siberian (mid-Lensky) barbarism, because the West—"Rassea," "Moskva"—was exerting pressure, and was taking Siberia in tow, creating a combination of nomad economic primitiveness with alarm clocks from Warsaw.

The guild craft was the basis of the medieval city culture, which radiated also into the village. Medieval science, scholasticism, religious reformation, grew out of a craft-guild soil. We did not have these things. Of course the embryo symptoms, the signs, can be found, but in the West these things were not signs but powerful cultural economic formations with a craft-guild basis. Upon this basis stood the medieval European city, and upon this it grew and entered into conflict with the church and the feudal lords, and brought into play against the lords the hand of the monarchy. That same city created the technical premises for standing armies in the shape of firearms.

Where were our craft-guild cities even in a remote degree similar to the western cities? Where was their struggle with the feudal lords?

And was the foundation for the development of the Russian autocracy laid by a struggle of the industrial-commercial city with the feudal lord? By the very nature of our cities we had no such struggle, just as we had no Reformation. Is this a peculiarity or is not it?

Our handicraft remained at the stage of home industry—that is, did not split off from peasant agriculture. Our Reformation remained at the stage of the peasant sect, because it found no leadership from the cities. Primitiveness and backwardness here cry to the heavens. . . .

Tzarism arose as an independent state organization (again only relatively independent within the limits of the struggle of living historic forces on an economic foundation), not thanks to a struggle of powerful feudal cities with powerful lords, but in spite of the complete industrial feebleness of our cities and thanks to the feebleness of our feudal lords.

Poland in her social structure stood between Russia and the West, just as Russia stood between Asia and Europe. The Polish cities knew already much more of guild craft than ours did, but they did not succeed in rising high enough to help the kingly power break the barons. The state power remained in the immediate hands of the nobility. The result: complete impotence of the state and its disintegration.

What has been said of tzarism relates also to capital and the proletariat. I cannot understand why Pokrovsky directs his rage only against my first chapter dealing with tzarism. Russian capitalism did not develop from handicraft through manufacture to the factory, because European capital, at first in the trade form and afterwards in the finance and industrial form, poured down on us during that period when Russian handicraft had not in the mass divided itself from agriculture. Hence the appearance among us of the most modern capitalist industry in an environment of economic primitiveness: the Belgian or American factory, and round about it settlements, villages of wood and straw, burning up every year, etc. The most primitive beginnings and the latest European endings. Hence the mighty rôle of West European capital in Russian industry; hence the political weakness of the Russian bourgeoisie; hence the ease with which we settled accounts with the Russian bourgeoisie; hence our further difficulties when the European bourgeoisie interfered.

And our proletariat? Did it pass through the school of the medieval apprentice brotherhoods? Has it the ancient tradition of the guilds? Nothing of the kind. It was thrown into the factory cauldron snatched directly from the plow. Hence the absence of conservative tradition, absence of caste in the proletariat itself, revolutionary freshness; hence—along with other causes—October, the first workers' government in the world. But hence also illiteracy, backwardness, absence of organizational habits, absence of system in labor, of cultural and technical education. All these minuses in our cultural economic structure we are feeling at every step.

The Russian state encountered the military organization of Western nations standing on a higher political and cultural level. Thus Russian capital in its first step ran into the far more developed and powerful capital of the West and fell under its leadership. Thus the Russian working class in its first steps also found ready weapons worked out by the experience of the West European proletariat; the Marxian theory, the trade union, the political party. Whoever explains the character and policy of the autocracy merely by the interests of the Russian possessing classes forgets that besides the more backward, poorer and more ignorant exploiters in Russia, there were the richer and more powerful exploiters in Europe. The possessing classes of Russia had to encounter the possessing classes of Europe, hostile or semi-hostile. This encounter was mediated through a state organization. Such an organization was the autocracy. The whole structure and history of the autocracy would have been different if it had not been for the European cities, European gunpowder (for we did not invent it), if it had not been for the European stock markets.

In the last epoch of its existence the autocracy was not only an organ of the possessing classes of Russia, but also of the organization of European stock markets for the exploitation of Russia. This double rôle again gave it a very considerable independence. A sharp expression of this is the fact that the French Bourse made a loan for the support of the autocracy in 1905 against the will of the party of the Russian bourgeoisie.

Tzarism was shattered in the imperialist war. And why? Because it had under it a too low-grade productive foundation (*"primitiveness"*). In military-technical matters tzarism tried to fall in line with more perfected models. It was every way assisted in this by the more rich and cultured Allies. Thanks to this fact tzarism had at its disposal the most finished weapons of war, but it had not, and could not have, the capacity to reproduce these weapons and transport them (and the human masses also) on railroads and waterways with sufficient speed. In other words, tzarism was defending the interests of the ruling classes of Russia in the international struggle, while relying upon a more primitive economic basis than her enemies and allies.

Tzarism exploited this basis during the war mercilessly—devoured, that is to say, a far greater percentage of the national wealth and the national income than her mighty enemies and allies. This fact finds its confirmation on the one hand in the system of war debts, on the other in the complete ruin of Russia. . . .

All these circumstances, which immediately predetermined the October revolution, the victory of the proletariat and its future difficulties, remain totally unexplained by the commonplaces of Pokrovsky.

APPENDIX II

(To the Chapter *Rearming of the Party*)

IN a New York daily paper, *Novy Mir,* published for the Russian workers in America, the author of this book attempted an analysis and a prognosis of the development of the revolution on the basis of the scant information supplied by the American press. "The inner history of the developing events," wrote the author on March 6, 1917 (old style), "is known to us only in fragments and hints which have crept into the official despatches." The series of articles devoted to the revolution begins on February 27 and breaks off on March 14 with the departure of the author from New York. We reproduce below a series of excerpts from these articles in chronological order, which will give an idea of the views of the revolution with which the author arrived in Russia on May 4.

FEBRUARY 27:

"The disorganized, compromised, disintegrated government at the top, the army shaken to the depths, the discontent, uncertainty and fear among the ruling classes, deep bitterness in the popular masses, the numerically developed proletariat tempered in the fire of events—all this gives us the right to say that we are witnessing the beginning of the second Russian revolution. Let us hope that many of us will be participants in it."

MARCH 3:

"The Rodziankos and Miliukovs have begun talking too soon about law and order; not tomorrow will tranquillity descend on billowing Russia. Stratum after stratum now, the country will arise—all the oppressed, destitute, robbed by tzarism and the ruling classes—throughout the whole measureless space of the whole Russian prison of the people. The Petrograd events are only beginning. At the head of the popular masses the Russian revolutionary proletariat will fulfill its historic task: it will drive out the monarchical and aristocratic reaction from all its refuges, and stretch out its hand to the proletariat of Germany and all Europe. For it is necessary to liquidate not only tzarism, but also the war."

471

"Now the second wave of the revolution will roll over the heads of the Rodziankos and Miliukovs, busy with their attempts to restore order and come to terms with monarchy. From its own depths the revolution will produce its government, a revolutionary organ of the people marching to victory. Both the chief battles and the chief sacrifices are in the future, and only after them will come complete and genuine victory."

MARCH 4:

"The long-restrained discontent of the masses has broken to the surface so late, on the 32nd month of the war, not because there stood before the masses a police bulwark, very much shaken during the war, but because all the liberal institutions and organs including their social-patriotic hangers-on, have exercised an enormous political pressure upon the less conscious layers of the workers, suggesting to them the necessity of 'patriotic' discipline and order."

"Now only (after the victory of the insurrection) came the turn of the Duma. The tzar tried at the last moment to disperse it. And it would have submissively dispersed 'following the precedent of former years,' if it had been able to. But the capitals were already in the control of the revolutionary people, that same people who, against the will of the liberal bourgeoisie, come out into the street to fight. The army was with the people. And if the bourgeoisie had not made an attempt to organize their power, a revolutionary government would have issued from the midst of the insurrectionary worker masses. That Duma of June 3 would never have ventured to snatch the power from the hands of tzarism, but it could not help making use of the created interregnum: the monarchy had temporarily disappeared from the face of the earth and a revolutionary power was not yet created."

MARCH 6:

"An open conflict between the forces of revolution at whose head stands the city proletariat, and the anti-revolutionary liberal bourgeoisie temporarily in power, is absolutely inevitable. You can, of course,—and the liberal bourgeois and mountain socialist of the philistine type are heartily busy about it—pile up many pitiful words on the subject of the immense advantages of national unity over class split. But nobody has yet succeeded with such incantations in removing social contradictions and stopping the natural development of a revolutionary struggle."

"Already at this moment, immediately, the revolutionary proletariat ought to oppose its revolutionary institutions, the soviets of workers', soldiers' and peasants' deputies, to the executive institutions of the Provisional Government. In this struggle the proletariat, uniting around itself the rising popular masses, ought to make its direct goal the conquest of power. Only a revolutionary workers' government will have the will and ability, even during the preparation for a Constituent Assembly, to carry out a radical democratic clean-up throughout the country, reconstruct the army from top to bottom, convert it into a revolutionary militia and demonstrate in action to the lower ranks of the peasants that their salvation lies only in supporting a revolutionary workers' régime."

MARCH 7:

"While the clique of Nicholas II held the power, dynastic and reactionary aristocratic interests had the last word in foreign policy. For just this reason in Berlin and Vienna they were continually hoping for a separate peace with Russia. But now the interests of naked imperialism are inscribed on the governmental banners. 'The tzar's government is no more,' the Guchkovs and Miliukovs are telling the people, 'Now you must pour out your blood for the all-national interests.' But by national interests the Russian imperialists mean the getting back of Poland, the conquest of Galicia, Constantinople, Armenia, Persia. In other words, Russia now takes her place in the joint ranks of imperialism with other European states, and first of all with her allies, England and France."

"The proletariat of Russia cannot possibly reconcile the transition from a dynastic aristocratic imperialism to a purely bourgeois régime with this butchery. The international struggle against the world butchery and imperialism is now our task more than ever before."

"The imperialist boast of Miliukov—to crush Germany, Austria-Hungary and Turkey—now plays perfectly into the hands of the Hohenzollerns and Hapsburgs. Miliukov will now play the rôle of a garden scarecrow in their hands. Before the new imperialistic-liberal government undertakes reforms in the army, it will help the Hohenzollerns raise the patriotic spirit and restore

473

the 'national unity' of the German people, now cracking in all its seams. If the German proletariat should get the right to think that the whole Russian people, and among them the chief force of the revolution—the Russian proletariat—stands behind its new bourgeois government, that would be a terrible blow to our colleagues, the revolutionary socialists of Germany."

"It is the straight duty of the revolutionary proletariat of Russia to show that behind the evil imperialist will of the liberal bourgeoisie there is no strength, for it has no support in the worker masses. The Russian revolution ought to reveal its authentic face before the whole world—that is, its irreconcilable hostility not only to the dynastic aristocratic reaction, but to liberal imperialism."

MARCH 8:

"Under the banner 'Salvation of the Country' the liberal bourgeois is trying to keep the revolutionary leadership of the people in his hands, and with this aim is dragging after him on a towline not only the Trudovik Kerensky, but evidently also Cheidze, representative of the opportunist elements of the social democracy."

"The agrarian question will drive a deep wedge into the present aristocratic bourgeois social-patriotic bloc. Kerensky will have to choose between the 'liberal,' the 3rd of June [1] men, who want to steal the whole revolution for capitalist goals, and the revolutionary proletariat, which will unfold to its full width the program of agrarian revolution—that is, confiscation in behalf of the people of the tzarist, landlord, appenage, monastery and church lands. What personal choice Kerensky makes will make no difference. . . . It is another matter with the peasant masses, the rural lower ranks. To bring them over to the side of the proletariat is the most urgent unpostponable task."

"It would be a crime to try to accomplish this task (the bringing over of the peasantry) by adapting our policy to the national-patriotic limitedness of the village: the Russian worker would commit suicide if he paid for his union with the peasant at the price of a breaking of his ties with the European proletariat. But there is no political need for this; we have a more powerful weapon in our hands: whereas the present Provisional Government

[1] Members of the Duma which issued from the state overturn of June 3, 1907.

474

and the ministry of Lvov, Guchkov, Miliukov, Kerensky,[1] are compelled—in the name of a preservation of their unity—to sidestep the agrarian question, we can and must present it in its full stature before the peasant masses of Russia.

" 'Since agrarian reform is impossible, we are for the imperialist war,' said the Russian bourgeoisie after the experience of 1905-07.

" 'Turn your back to the imperialist war, opposing to it the agrarian revolution!' we will say to the peasant masses, referring to the experience of 1914-17.

"This same question, the land question, will play an immense rôle in uniting the proletarian cadres of the army with its peasant depths. 'The land of the landlords, and not Constantinople!', the soldier proletarian will say to the soldier peasant, explaining to him whom and what the imperialist war is serving. And upon the success of our agitation and struggle against the war—above all among the workers, and in the second place among the peasant and soldier masses—will depend the answer to the question how soon the liberal imperialist government can be replaced by a revolutionary workers' government resting directly upon the proletariat, and the rural lower ranks adhering to it."

"The Rodziankos, Guchkovs, Miliukovs will bend all their efforts to get a Constituent Assembly in their image. The strongest trump in their hand will be the slogan of the common national war against an external enemy. They will now talk, of course, about the necessity of defending the 'conquests of the revolution' against destruction by the Hohenzollerns. And the social patriots will join the song."

" 'If we had something to defend!' we will say. The first thing is to insure the revolution against the domestic enemy. We must, without waiting for the Constituent Assembly, sweep out the monarchic and feudal rubbish to the last corner. We must teach the Russian peasant not to trust the promises of Rodzianko and the patriotic lies of Miliukov. We must unite the peasant millions against the liberal imperialists under the banner of agrarian revolution and the republic. Only a revolutionary government relying on the proletariat, which will remove the Guchkovs and Miliukovs from power, can carry out this work to the full. This workers' government will bring into play all the instruments of state power in order to raise to their feet, educate, and unite

[1] By Provisional Government the American press meant Provisional Committee of the Duma.

the most backward and dark depths of the toiling masses of the city and village."

" 'And if the German proletariat does not rise? What shall we do then?' "

"That is, you assume that the Russian revolution can go by without affecting Germany—even in case our revolution puts a workers' government in power? But surely that is utterly improbable."

" 'Yes, but suppose it happens?' " . . .

"If the improbable should happen, if the conservative social-patriotic organization should prevent the German working class from rising against its ruling classes in the coming epoch, then of course the Russian working class would defend its revolution with arms in its hands. The revolutionary workers' government would wage war against the Hohenzollerns, summoning the brother proletariat of Germany to rise against the common enemy. In exactly the same way the German proletariat, if in the coming epoch it came to power, would not only have the 'right,' but would be obliged, to wage war against Guchkov and Miliukov in order to help the Russian worker settle accounts with his imperialist enemy. In both these situations the war conducted by a proletarian government would be only an armed revolution. It would be a question not of the 'defense of the government,' but of the defense of the revolution, and its transplantation into other countries."

It is hardly necessary to demonstrate that in the above extended excerpts from popular articles to be read by workers, the same view of the development of the revolution is expounded as that which found its expression in Lenin's *Theses of April 4.*

*

IN connection with the crisis which the Bolshevik Party went through in the first two months of the February revolution, it is not superfluous to adduce here a quotation from an article written by the author of this book in 1909 for the Polish journal of Rosa Luxemburg:

"If the Mensheviks, starting from the abstraction 'Our revolution is a bourgeois revolution,' arrive at the idea of adapting the whole tactic of the proletariat to the conduct of the liberal bourgeoisie, even to the point of a conquest by it of the state power, then the Bolsheviks, starting from an equally bare abstraction 'a democratic and not a socialist dictatorship,' will arrive at the idea of a bourgeois democratic self-limitation of the proletariat in whose hands the governmental power will be found. To be sure, the difference between them on this question is very considerable: while the anti-revolutionary sides of Menshevism are expressed in their full strength even now, the anti-revolutionary traits of Bolshevism threaten a great danger only in the case of a revolutionary victory."

After 1923 those words were widely used by the epigones in their struggle against "Trotskyism." As a matter of fact they give—eight years before the event—a perfectly accurate characterization of the conduct of the present epigones in the case of a revolutionary victory.

The party issued from the April crisis with honor, having settled accounts with the "anti-revolutionary traits" of its right flank. For this reason the author in 1922 supplemented the passage quoted above with the following remark:

"This, as is well known, did not happen, because under the leadership of Lenin, Bolshevism carried out (not without inner struggle) its intellectual rearmament upon this all-important question in the spring of 1917—that is, before the conquest of power."

Lenin, in April 1917, in his struggle with the opportunist tendencies of the dominant layer of the Bolsheviks, wrote:

"The Bolshevik slogans and ideas *in general* are completely confirmed, but *concretely* things have shaped themselves *otherwise* than anybody (no matter who) could have expected—more originally, uniquely, variously. To ignore, to forget this fact would mean to be like those 'old Bolsheviks' who have more than once already played a pitiful rôle in the history of our party, meaninglessly repeating a formula *learned by rote* instead of *studying* the unique living reality. Whoever talks *now* only of a 'revolutionary-democratic dictatorship of the proletariat and peasantry' is lagging behind life. He has by that very fact *gone over* actually to the bourgeoisie against the proletarian class struggle. Him we must put away in the archives of 'Bolshevik' pre-revolutionary curiosities (you might call them the archives of the 'old Bolsheviks')."

477

APPENDIX III

(To the Chapter The Soviet Congress and the June Demonstration)

TO Professor A. Kaun, The University of California.

You ask me how correctly Sukhanov describes my meeting in May 1917 with the editors of *Novy Zhizn*, a newspaper nominally directed by Maxim Gorky. In order that what follows may be understood, I must say a few words as to the general character of the seven-volume *Notes of the Revolution* by Sukhanov. With all the faults of that work (wordiness, impressionism, political shortsightedness) which make the reading of it at times unbearable, it is impossible not to recognize the conscientiousness of the author which renders his *Notes* a valuable source for the historian. Jurists know, however, that the conscientiousness of a witness by no means guarantees the reliability of his testimony. It is necessary to take into consideration his level of development, his vision, hearing, memory, his mood at the moment of the event, etc. Sukhanov is an impressionist of the intellectual type, and like the majority of such people lacks the ability to understand the political psychology of men of a different mold. Notwithstanding the fact that he himself in 1917 stood in the left wing of the Compromise camp, and so in close neighborhood to the Bolsheviks, he was and remained, with his Hamlet temperament, the very opposite of a Bolshevik. There lives always in him a feeling of hostile revulsion from integrated people, people who know firmly what they want and where they are going. All of this brings it about that Sukhanov in his *Notes* quite conscientiously piles up mistake after mistake so soon as he tries to understand the springs of action of the Bolsheviks, or reveal their motivation behind the scenes. At times it seems as though he consciously confuses simple and clear questions. In reality he is organically incapable, at least in politics, of finding the shortest distance between two points.

Sukhanov wastes no little strength in the effort to contrast my line with Lenin's. Being very sensitive to the moods of the *couloir* and the gossip of intellectual circles—in which, by the way, lies one of the merits of the *Notes*, which contain much material for characterizing the psychology of the liberal, radical, and socialistic upper circles—

Sukhanov naturally nourished a hope that disagreements would arise between Lenin and Trotsky—the more so that this must lighten somewhat the unenviable fate of *Novy Zhizn*, standing between the Social Patriots and the Bolsheviks. In his *Notes* Sukhanov is still living in the atmosphere of those unrealized hopes under the form of political recollections and *ex post facto* guesses. Peculiarities of personality, temperament, style, he tries to interpret as a political line.

In connection with the abandoned Bolshevik manifestation of June 10, and more especially the armed demonstration of the July days, Sukhanov tries throughout many pages to demonstrate that Lenin was directly striving in those days for a seizure of power by way of conspiracy and insurrection, while Trotsky by contrast was striving for the real power of the soviets in the person of the then dominant parties, that is, the Social Revolutionaries and Mensheviks. There is not a shadow of foundation for all this.

At the first congress of the soviets on June 4, Tseretelli during his speech remarked in passing: "In Russia at the present moment there is not one political party which would say, Give us the power in our hands." At that moment a voice was heard from the benches: "There is!" Lenin did not like to interrupt orators, and did not like to be interrupted. Only serious considerations could have impelled him to abandon on that occasion his customary restraint. According to Tseretelli's logic, when the nation gets into a tangle of enormous difficulty, the first thing to do is to try to slip the power to others. In this lay the cleverness of the Russian Compromisers who after the February uprising slipped the power to the liberals. To a not very attractive fear of responsibility, Tseretelli was giving the color of political disinterestedness and extraordinary farsightedness. To a revolutionist who believes in the mission of his party such cowardly swanking is absolutely intolerable. A revolutionary party which is capable in difficult conditions of turning away from the power, deserves only contempt.

In a speech at that same session Lenin explained his reply from the benches: "The Citizen Minister of Posts and Telegraph (Tseretelli) said that there is no political party in Russia which would express its readiness to take upon itself the whole power. I answer there is. No party can decline to do that, and our party does not decline. It is ready at any minute to take the whole power. (Applause and laughter.) You may laugh all you want to, but if the Citizen Minister puts this question to us he will get the proper answer." It would seem as though Lenin's thought is transparent through and through.

At the same congress of the soviets, speaking after the Minister of Agriculture, Peshekhonov, I expressed myself as follows: "I do not belong to the same party with him (Peshekhonov) but if they told me that a ministry was to be formed out of twelve Peshekhonovs, I should say that this was an immense step forward."

I do not think that at that time, amid those events, my words about a ministry of Peshekhonovs could be understood as an antithesis to Lenin's readiness to take the power. Sukhanov appears as an *ex post facto* theoretician of this pretended antithesis. Interpreting the Bolshevik preparation of the demonstration of June 10 in favor of the power of the soviets as a preparation for the seizure of power, Sukhanov writes: "Lenin two or three days before the 'manifestation' publicly stated that he was ready to take the power in his hands. But Trotsky said at the same time that he would like to see twelve Peshekhonovs in power. That is the difference. But nevertheless I assume that Trotsky was drawn into the affair of June 10. . . . Lenin was not then inclined to enter a decisive engagement without the dubious 'Mezhdurayonets.'[1] For Trotsky was to him a kind of monumental partner in a monumental game, and in his own party after Lenin himself there was nothing—for a long, long, long distance."

This whole passage is full of contradictions. According to Sukhanov, Lenin would seem to have been really intending what Tseretelli accused him of: "An immediate seizure of power by the proletarian minority." A proof of such Blanquism Sukhanov sees, if you can believe it, in those words of Lenin about the readiness of the Bolsheviks to take the power in spite of all difficulties. But if Lenin had really intended on June 10 to seize the power by way of a conspiracy, he would hardly have forewarned his enemies of this at a plenary session of the soviets on June 4. It should hardly be necessary to recall that from the first day of his arrival in Petrograd, Lenin had been telling the party that the Bolsheviks could assume the task of overthrowing the Provisional Government only after winning a majority in the soviets. In the April days Lenin decisively opposed those Bolsheviks who advanced the slogan "Down with the Provisional Government" as the task of the day. Lenin's reply of June 4 had only one meaning: We,

---

[1] Sukhanov calls me a "dubious Mezhdurayonets" (member of the interdistrict organization of united social democrats), evidently meaning by this that in reality I was a Bolshevik. That is in any case the truth. I remained in the interdistrict organization only in order to bring it into the Bolshevik Party, a thing which was accomplished in August.

the Bolsheviks, are ready to take the power even today if the workers and soldiers give us their confidence; in this we are distinguished from the Compromisers who, possessing the confidence of the workers and soldiers, dare not take the power.

Sukhanov contrasts Trotsky with Lenin as a realist with a Blanquist. "Without accepting Lenin, one could fully agree to Trotsky's presentation of the question." At the same time Sukhanov announces that: "Trotsky was drawn into the affair of June 10"—that is, to the conspiracy for the seizure of power. Having discovered two lines where there were not two, Sukhanov cannot deny himself the pleasure of afterward uniting these two lines in one in order to be able to convict me of adventurism. This is a unique and somewhat platonic revenge for the disappointed hope of the left intelligentsia for a split between Lenin and Trotsky.

On the placards which had been prepared by the Bolsheviks for the canceled demonstration of June 10, and which were afterward carried by the demonstrators of June 18, a central place was occupied by the slogan: "Down with the Ten Minister-Capitalists!" Sukhanov, in the quality of æsthete, admires the simple expressiveness of this slogan, but in his quality of statesman he reveals an incomprehension of its meaning. In the government besides the "ten Minister-Capitalists" there were also six Minister-Compromisers. The Bolshevik placards had nothing to say of them. On the contrary, according to the sense of the slogan, the Minister-Capitalists were to be replaced by Minister-Socialists, representatives of the Soviet majority. It was exactly this sense of the Bolshevik placards that I expressed before the Soviet Congress: Break your bloc with the liberals, remove the bourgeois ministers and replace them with your Peshekhonovs. In proposing to the Soviet majority to take the power, the Bolsheviks did not, of course, bind themselves in the least as to their attitude to these Peshekhonovs; on the contrary, they made no secret of the fact that within the frame of the Soviet democracy they would wage an implacable struggle—for a majority in the soviets and for the power.

But all this is after all mere A-B-C. Only the above-mentioned traits of Sukhanov—not so much as a person but as a type—can explain how this participant and observer of events could get so hopelessly mixed up upon so serious and at the same time so simple a question.

In the light of this analysis of a political episode it is easy to understand the false light which Sukhanov throws upon my meeting which interests you with the editors of *Novy Zhizn*. The moral of my en-

481

counter with the circle of Maxim Gorky is expressed by Sukhanov in the concluding phrase which he puts in my mouth: "Now I see that nothing remains for me but to found a paper together with Lenin." The inference is that only my inability to reach an agreement with Gorky and Sukhanov—that is, with people whom I never regarded as either men of politics or revolutionists—compelled me to find my way to Lenin. It is only necessary to formulate this idea in order to demonstrate its absurdity.

Incidentally, how characteristic of Sukhanov is the phrase, "found a paper together with Lenin"—as though the tasks of a revolutionary policy reduced themselves to the founding of a newspaper. For anybody with a minimum of creative imagination, it ought to be clear that I could not so think or so define my tasks.

In order to explain my visit to the newspaper circle of Gorky, it is necessary to remember that I arrived in Petrograd at the beginning of May, something over two months after the revolution, a month after the arrival of Lenin. During this time many things had adjusted and defined themselves. I had to have a direct, and so to say empirical, orientation, not only in the fundamental forces of the revolution, in the moods of the workers and soldiers, but also in all the groupings and political shadings of "educated" society. The visit to the editors of *Novy Zhizn* was for me a small political reconnoiter executed with a view to finding out the forces of attraction and repulsion possessed by this "left" group, the chances of splitting off certain elements, etc. A short conversation convinced me of the complete hopelessness of this circle of literary wiseacres, for whom revolution reduced itself to the problem of the leading editorial. And, besides that, since they were accusing the Bolsheviks of self-isolation, laying the blame for this upon Lenin and his April Theses, I undoubtedly must have told them that with all their speeches they had only once more demonstrated to me that Lenin was completely right in isolating the party from them, or rather isolating them from the party. This conclusion, which I had to emphasize with special energy for the sake of its effect upon Riazanov and Lunacharsky, who participated in the conversation, and who were opposed to a union with Lenin, evidently supplied the occasion for Sukhanov's version.

＊

It goes without saying that you are completely right in assuming that I would in no case have agreed in the autumn of 1917 to speak about a Gorky jubilee from the tribune of the Petrograd Soviet. Sukhanov did well that time at least in renouncing one of his fantastic ideas: to induce me on the eve of the October insurrection to take part in a celebration of Gorky who stood on the other side of the barricades.

VOLUME TWO

The Attempted Counter-Revolution

INTRODUCTION TO VOLUMES TWO AND THREE

RUSSIA was so late in accomplishing her bourgeois revolution that she found herself compelled to turn it into a proletarian revolution. Or in other words: Russia was so far behind the other countries that she was compelled, at least in certain spheres, to out-strip them. That seems inconsistent, but history is full of such paradoxes. Capitalist England was so far in advance of other countries, that she had to trail behind them. Pedants think that the dialectic is an idle play of the mind. In reality it only reproduces the process of evolution, which lives and moves by way of contradictions.

The first volume of this work should have explained why that historically belated democratic regime which replaced tzarism proved wholly unviable. The present volumes are devoted to the coming to power of the Bolsheviks. Here too the fundamental thing is the narrative. In the facts themselves the reader ought to find sufficient support for the inferences.

By this the author does not mean to say that he has avoided sociological generalizations. History would have no value if it taught us nothing. The mighty design of the Russian revolution, the consecutiveness of its stages, the inexorable pressure of the masses, the finishedness of political groupings, the succinctness of slogans, all this wonderfully promotes the understanding of revolution in general, and therewith of human society. For we may consider it proven by the whole course of history that society, torn as it is by inner contradictions, conclusively reveals in a revolution not only its anatomy, but also its "soul."

In a more immediate manner the present work should pro-

i

mote an understanding of the character of the Soviet Union. The timeliness of our theme lies not only in that the October revolution took place before the eyes of a generation still living—although that of course has no small significance—but in the fact that the regime which issued from the revolution still lives and develops, and is confronting humanity with ever new riddles. Throughout the whole world the question of the soviet country is never lost sight of for a moment. However, it is impossible to understand any existent thing without a preliminary examination of its origin. For large-scale political appraisals an historic perspective is essential.

The eight months of the revolution, February to October 1917, have required three volumes. The critics, as a general rule, have not accused us of prolixity. The scale of the work is explained rather by our approach to the material. You can present a photograph of a hand on one page, but it requires a volume to present the results of a microscopic investigation of its tissues. The author has no illusion as to the fullness or finishedness of his investigation. But nevertheless in many cases he was obliged to employ methods closer to the miscroscope than the camera.

At times, when it seemed to us that we were abusing the patience of the reader, we generously crossed out the testimony of some witness, the confession of a participant or some secondary episode, but we afterward not infrequently restored much that had been crossed out. In this struggle for details we were guided by a desire to reveal as concretely as possible the very process of the revolution. In particular it was impossible not to try to make the most of the opportunity to paint history from the life.

Thousands and thousands of books are thrown on the market every year presenting some new variant of the personal romance, some tale of the vacillations of the melancholic or the career of the ambitious. The heroine of Proust requires several finely-wrought pages in order to feel that she does not feel anything. It would seem that one might, at least with equal justice, demand attention to a series of collective historic dramas which lifted hundreds of millions of human beings out of non-existence, transforming the character of nations and intruding forever into the life of all mankind.

The accuracy of our references and quotations in the first volume no one has so far called in question: that would indeed be difficult. Our opponents confine themselves for the most part to reflections upon the topic of how personal prejudice *may* reveal itself in an artificial and one-sided selection of facts and texts. These observations, although irrefutable in themselves, say nothing about the given work, and still less about its scientific methods. Moreover we take the liberty to insist firmly that the coefficient of subjectivism is defined, limited, and tested not so much by the temperament of the historian, as by the nature of his method.

The purely psychological school, which looks upon the tissue of events as an interweaving of the free activities of separate individuals or their groupings, offers, even with the best intentions on the part of the investigator, a colossal scope to caprice. The materialist method disciplines the historian, compelling him to take his departure from the weighty facts of the social structure. For us the fundamental forces of the historic process are classes; political parties rest upon them; ideas and slogans emerge as the small change of objective interests. The whole course of the investigation proceeds from the objective to the subjective, from the social to the individual, from the fundamental to the incidental. This sets a rigid limit to the personal whims of the author.

When a mining engineer finds magnetic ore in an uninvestigated region by drilling, it is always possible to assume that this was a happy accident: the construction of a mine is hardly to be recommended. But when the same engineer, on the basis, let us say, of the deviation of a magnetic needle, comes to the conclusion that a vein of ore lies concealed in the earth, and subsequently actually strikes ore at various different points in the region, then the most cavilling sceptic will not venture to talk about accidents. What convinces is the system which unites the general with the particular.

The proof of scientific objectivism is not to be sought in the eyes of the historian or the tones of his voice, but in the inner logic of the narrative itself. If episodes, testimonies, figures, quotations, fall in with the general pointing of the needle of his social analysis, then the reader has a most weighty guarantee of the scientific solidity of his conclusions. To be more concrete: the present author has been true to objectivism in the degree that his book actually reveals the inevitability of the October revolution and the causes of its victory.

The reader already knows that in a revolution we look first of all for the direct interference of the masses in the destinies of society. We seek to uncover behind the events changes in the collective consciousness. We reject wholesale references to the "spontaneity" of the movement, references which in most cases explain nothing and teach nobody. Revolutions take place according to certain laws. This does not mean that the masses in action are aware of the laws of revolution, but it does mean that the changes in mass consciousness are not accidental, but are subject to an objective necessity which is capable of theoretic explanation, and thus makes both prophecy and leadership possible.

Certain official soviet historians, surprising as it may seem, have attempted to criticize our conception as idealistic. Professor Pokrovsky, for example, has insisted that we underestimate the objective factors of the revolution. "Between February and October there occurred a colossal economic collapse." "During this time the peasantry . . . rose against the Provisional Government." It is in these "objective shifts," says Pokrovsky, and not in fickle psychic processes, that one should see the motive force of the revolution. Thanks to a praiseworthy incisiveness of formulation, Pokrovsky exposes to perfection the worthlessness of that vulgarly economic interpretation of history which is frequently given out for Marxism.

The radical turns which take place in the course of a revolution are as a matter-of-fact evoked, not by those episodic economic disturbances which arise during the events themselves, but by fundamental changes which have accumulated in the very foundations of society throughout the whole preceding epoch. The fact that on the eve of the overthrow of the monarchy, as also between February and October, the economic collapse was steadily deepening, nourishing and whipping up the discontent of the masses—that fact is indubitable and has never lacked our attention. But it would be the crudest mistake to assume that the second revolution was accomplished eight months after the first owing to the fact that the bread ration was lowered during that period from one-and-a-half to three-quarters of a pound. In the years immediately following the October revolution the food situation of the masses continued steadily to grow worse. Nevertheless the hopes of the counter-revolutionary politicians for a new overturn were defeated every time. This circumstance can seem puzzling only to one who looks upon the insurrection of the masses as "spontaneous"—that is, as a herd-mutiny artificially made use of by leaders. In reality the mere existence of privations is not enough to cause an insurrection; if it were, the masses would be always in revolt. It is necessary that the bankruptcy of the social regime, being conclusively revealed, should make these privations intolerable, and that new conditions and new ideas should open the prospect of a revolutionary way out. Then in the cause of the great aims conceived by them, those same masses will prove capable of enduring doubled and tripled privations.

The reference to the revolt of the peasantry as a second "objective factor" shows a still more obvious misunderstanding. For the proletariat the peasant war was of course an objective circumstance—insofar as the activity of one class does in general become an external stimulus to the consciousness of another. But the direct cause of the peasant revolt itself lay in changes in the consciousness of the villages; a discovery of the character of these changes makes the content of one chapter of this book. Let us not forget that revolutions are accomplished through people, although they be nameless. Materialism does not ignore the feeling, thinking and acting man, but explains him. What else is the task of the historian? [1]

Certain critics from the democratic camp, inclined to oper-

[1] News of the death of M. N. Pokrovsky, with whom we have had to do battle more than once in the course of these two volumes, arrived after our work was finished. Having come over to Marxism from the liberal camp when already a finished scholar, Pokrovsky enriched the most recent historic literature with precious works and beginnings. But nonetheless he never fully mastered the method of dialectic materialism. It is a matter of simple justice to add that Pokrovsky was a man not only of high gifts and exceptional erudition, but also of deep loyalty to the cause which he served.

ate with the help of indirect evidence, have looked upon the "ironic" attitude of the author to the compromise leaders as the expression of an undue subjectivism vitiating the scientific character of his exposition. We venture to regard this criterion as unconvincing. Spinoza's principle, "not to weep or laugh, but to understand" gives warning against inappropriate laughter and untimely tears. It does not deprive a man, even though he be a historian, of the right to his share of tears and laughter when justified by a correct understanding of the material itself. That purely individualistic irony which spreads out like a smoke of indifference over the whole effort and intention of mankind, is the worst form of snobbism. It rings false alike in artistic creations and works of history. But there is an irony deep laid in the very relations of life. It is the duty of the historian as of the artist to bring it to the surface.

A failure of correspondence between subjective and objective is, generally speaking, the fountain-source of the comic, as also the tragic, in both life and art. The sphere of politics less than any other is exempted from the action of this law. People and parties are heroic or comic not in themselves but in their relation to circumstances. When the French revolution entered its decisive stage the most eminent of Girondists became pitiful and ludicrous beside the rank-and-file Jacobin. Jean-Marie Rolland, a respected figure as factory inspector of Lyons, looks like a living caricature against the background of 1792. The Jacobins, on the contrary, measure up to the events. They may evoke hostility, hatred, horror—but not irony.

The heroine of Dickens who tried to hold back the tide with a broom is an acknowledged comic image because of the fatal lack of correspondence between means and end. If we assert that this person symbolizes the policies of the compromise parties in the revolution, it may seem an extravagant exaggeration. And yet Tseretelli, the actual inspirator of the dual-power regime, confessed to Nabokov, one of the liberal leaders, after the October revolution: "Everything we did at that time was a vain effort to hold back a destructive elemental flood with a handful of insignificant chips." Those words sound like spiteful satire, but they are the truest words spoken by the Compromisers about themselves. To renounce irony in depicting "revolutionists" who tried to hold back a revolution with chips, would be to plunder reality and betray objectivism for the benefit of pedants.

Peter Struvé, a monarchist from among the former Marxists, wrote as an emigré: "Only Bolshevism was logical about revolution and true to its essence, and therefore in the revolution it conquered." Miliukov, the leader of liberalism, made approximately the same statement: "They knew where they were going, and they went in the direction which they had chosen once for all, toward a goal which came nearer and nearer with every new, unsuccessful experiment of compromisism." And finally, one of the white emigrés not so well known, trying in his own way to understand the revolution, has expressed himself thus: "Only iron people could take this road . . . only people who were revolutionists by their very 'profession' and had no fear of calling into life the all-devouring spirit of riot and revolt." You may say of the Bolsheviks with still more justice what was said above about the Jacobins. They were adequate to the epoch and its tasks; curses in plenty resounded in their direction, but irony would not stick to them—it had nothing to catch hold of.

In the introduction to the first volume it was explained why the author deemed it suitable to speak of himself as a participant of the events in the third person, and not the first. This literary form, preserved also in the second and third volumes, does not in itself of course offer a defense against subjectivism, but at least it does not make subjectivism necessary. Indeed it reminds one of the obligation to avoid it.

On many occasions we hesitated long whether to quote this or that remark of a contemporary, characterizing the rôle of the author in the flow of events. It would have been easy to renounce any such quotation, were nothing greater involved than the rules of correct tone in polite society. The author of this book was president of the Petrograd Soviet after the Bolsheviks won a majority there, and he was afterward president of the Military Revolutionary Committee which organized the October uprising. These facts he neither wishes nor is able to erase from history. The faction now ruling in the Soviet Union has of late years dedicated many articles, and no few books, to the author of this work, setting themselves the task of proving that his activity was steadily directed against the interests of the revolution. The question why the Bolshevik party placed so stubborn an "enemy" during the most critical years in the most responsible posts remains unanswered. To pass these retrospective quarrels in complete silence would be to renounce to some extent the task of establishing the actual course of events. And to what end? A pretense of disinterestedness is needful only to him whose aim is slyly to convey to his readers conclusions which do not flow from the facts. We prefer to call things by their whole name as it is found in the dictionary.

We will not conceal the fact that for us the question here is not only about the past. Just as the enemy in attacking a man's prestige are striking at his program, so his own struggle for a definite program obliges a man to restore his actual position in the events. As for those who are incapable of seeing anything but personal vanity in a man's struggle for great causes and for his place under the banner, we may be sorry for them but we will not undertake to convince them. In any case we have taken measures to see to it that "personal" questions should not occupy a greater place in this book than that to which they can justly lay claim.

Certain of the friends of the Soviet Union—a phrase which often means friends of the present Soviet powers and that only so long as they remain powers—have reproached the author for his critical attitude to the Bolshevik party or its individual leaders. Nobody, however, has made the attempt to refute or correct the picture given of the condition of the party during the events. For the information of these "friends" who consider themselves called to defend against us the rôle of the Bolsheviks in the October revolution, we give warning that our book teaches not how to love a victorious revolution after the event in the person of the bureaucracy it has brought forward, but only how a revolution is prepared, how it develops, and how it conquers. A party is not for us a machine whose sinlessness is to be defended by state measures of repression, but a complicated organism which like all living things develops in contradictions. The uncovering of these contradictions—among them the waverings and mistakes of the general staff—does not in our view weaken in the slightest degree the significance of that gigantic historic task which the Bolshevik party was the first in history to take upon its shoulders.

L. TROTSKY

Prinkipo
May 13, 1932

P.S. The critics have already paid their tribute to Max Eastman's translation. He has brought to his work not only a creative gift of style, but also the carefulness of a friend. I subscribe with warm gratitude to the unanimous voice of the critics.

L. T.

The Attempted Counter-Revolution

Chapter I

THE "JULY DAYS": PREPARATION AND BEGINNING

IN 1915, the war cost Russia 10 billion rubles; in 1916, 19 billion; during the first half of 1917, 10½ billion; by the beginning of 1918, the national debt would have amounted to 60 billion—would have almost equalled, that is, the entire wealth of the country, estimated at 70 billion. The Central Executive Committee was preparing an appeal for a war loan, under the sugary name of "Liberty Loan," while the government was arriving at the not very complicated conclusion that without an immense new foreign loan, it not only could not pay for its foreign orders, but could not even handle its domestic obligations. The liability side of the trade balance was continually on the rise. The Entente was evidently getting ready to leave the ruble wholly to its fate. On the very day when the appeal for a Liberty Loan filled the first page of the Soviet *Izvestia*, the government *Vyestnik* announced a sharp drop in the value of the ruble. The printing presses could no longer keep up with the tempo of inflation. For the old respectable bank notes, about which there still clung a glamour of their former buying power, they were getting ready to substitute those red bottle-labels which came to be known as "kerenkies." Both the bourgeois and the worker, each in his own way, embodied in that name a slight note of disgust.

In words the government had adopted a program of state regulation of industry, and had even established towards the end of June some lumbering institutions for this purpose. But the word and deed of the February régime, like the spirit and flesh of the pious Christian, were in a continual state of conflict. These appropriately hand-picked regulative institutions were more concerned to protect the capitalist from the caprices of a shaky and tottering state power, than to curb the interests of private persons. The administrative and technical personnel of industry was

3

becoming stratified; the upper layers, frightened by the levelling tendencies of the workers, were going over decisively to the side of the capitalist. The workers had acquired an attitude of disgust toward the war orders by which the disintegrating factories had been guaranteed for a year or two in advance. But the capitalists also were losing their taste for a production which promised more trouble than profits. The deliberate closing-down of the factories from above was now becoming systematic. Metal production was cut down 40 per cent; the textile industry, 20 per cent. The supply of all the necessities of life was inadequate. Prices were rising at a pace with inflation and the decline of industry. The workers were aspiring towards a control of that administrative-commercial mechanism which in concealment from them decides their destinies. The Minister of Labor, Skobelev, was preaching to the workers in wordy manifestoes the inadvisability of their interference in the administration of the factories. On June 24, *Izvestia* told about a new proposal for the closing of a series of plants. Similar news was arriving from the provinces. Railroad transport was stricken even more heavily than industry. Half of the locomotives were in need of capital repairs; the greater part of the rolling stock was at the front; fuel was lacking. The Ministry of Communications was in a continual state of struggle with the railroad workers and clerks. The supply of foodstuffs was steadily on the decrease. In Petrograd, the flour reserve was adequate for ten or fifteen days; in other centers, for little longer. With the semi-paralysis of rolling stock and the impending threat of a railroad strike, this meant a continual danger of famine. The future contained no glimmer of hope. This was not what the workers had expected from the revolution.

Things were still worse, if that is possible, in the sphere of politics. Indecisiveness is the worst possible condition in the life of governments, nations, classes—as also of individuals. A revolution is the most ruthless of all methods of solving historic problems. To introduce evasiveness into a revolution is the most destructive policy imaginable. The party of revolution dare not waver—no more than a surgeon dare who has plunged a knife into a sick body. However, that double régime—or régime of duplicity—which issued from the February overturn was indecisiveness organized. Everything was going against the government. Its qualified friends were becoming opponents; its opponents, enemies; its enemies were taking arms. The counter-revolution was mobilizing quite in the open—inspired by the central committee of the Kadet party, the political staff of all those who had something to lose. The Head Committee of the League of Officers at General Headquarters in Moghiliev, representing about a hundred thousand discontented commanders, and the Council of the Union of Cossack troops in Petrograd, were the two military levers of the counter-revolution. The State Duma, in spite of the decision of the June congress of the soviets, had resolved to continue its "private conferences." Its Provisional Committee supplied a legal covering for the counter-revolutionary work, which was broadly financed by the banks and by the embassies of the Entente. The Compromisers were threatened with dangers both right and left. Glancing uneasily in these two directions, the government secretly resolved to make a disbursement for the organization of a public intelligence service—that is, a secret political police. At about this same time, in the middle of June, the government designated September 17 as the date for elections to the Constituent Assembly. The liberal press, in spite of the participation of Kadets in the ministry, waged a stubborn campaign against this officially designated date—in which nobody believed and which nobody seriously defended. The very image of the Constituent Assembly, so bright in the first days of March, had dissolved and grown dim. Everything was going against the government, even its own thin-blooded good intentions. Only on the 30th of June did it muster the courage to dismiss those aristocratic guardians over the villages, the *zemsky nachalniks*,[1] whose very name had been hateful to the whole country ever since the day of their establishment by Alexander III. And this enforced and belated partial reform only stamped the Provisional Government with a brand of contemptible cowardice. The nobility were by this time recovering from their fright. The landed proprietors were uniting and bringing pressure to bear. Toward the end of June, the Provisional Committee

---

[1] Appointed officials having both administrative and judicial power over the local peasant population.

5

of the Duma addressed to the government a demand that decisive measures be taken to protect the landlords from peasants incited by the "criminal element." On the first of July there met in Moscow an All-Russian Congress of Landed Proprietors, containing an overwhelming majority of nobles. The government wriggled and tried to hypnotize with words, now the muzhiks, now the landlords.

Worst of all, however, was the situation at the front. The offensive against the enemy, which had also become Kerensky's decisive play in a domestic struggle, was dying in convulsions. The soldiers did not want to fight. The diplomats of Prince Lvov were afraid to look the diplomats of the Entente in the eyes. They needed a loan to the point of desperation. In order to make a show of firmness, the condemned and impotent government waged an offensive against Finland, carrying it through, as it did all of its very dirtiest work, by the hands of the socialists. At the same time a conflict had arisen with the Ukraine and was moving towards an open break.

Those days were far away when Albert Thomas sang hymns to the luminous revolution and to Kerensky. At the beginning of July the French ambassador, Paléologue, who smelled too strongly of the aromas of the Rasputin salons, was replaced by the "radical" Noulens. The journalist, Claude Anet, gave the new ambassador an introductory lecture on Petrograd. Opposite the French embassy—he told him—across the Neva, spreads the Vyborg district. "This is a district of big factories which belongs wholly to the Bolsheviks. Lenin and Trotsky reign there as masters." In that same district are located the barracks of the Machine Gun Regiment, numbering about 10,000 men and over 1,000 machine guns. Neither the Social Revolutionaries nor the Mensheviks have access to the barracks of that regiment. The remaining regiments are either Bolshevik or neutral. "If Lenin and Trotsky want to take Petrograd, what will stop them?" Noulens listened with astonishment. "How can the government tolerate such a situation?" "But what can it do?" answered the journalist. "You must understand that the government has no power but a moral one, and even that seems to me very weak. . . ."

Finding no channel, the aroused energy of the masses spent

itself in self-dependent activities, guerrilla manifestations, sporadic seizures. The workers, soldiers and peasants were trying to solve in a partial way those problems which the power created by them had refused to solve. More than anything else, indecisiveness in their leaders exhausts the nerves of the masses. Fruitless waiting impels them to more and more insistent knockings at that door which will not open to them, or to actual outbreaks of despair. Already in the days of the congress of soviets, when the provincials could hardly withhold the hands of their leaders stretched out against Petrograd, the workers and soldiers had plenty of opportunity to find out what was the feeling and attitude toward them of the soviet leaders. Tseretelli, following Kerensky, had become not only an alien, but a hated figure to the majority of the Petrograd workers and soldiers. On the fringes of the revolution there was a growing influence of the anarchists, whose chief rôle so far had been played in the self-constituted revolutionary committee in the summer home of Durnovo. But even the more disciplined layers of the workers —even broad circles of the party—were beginning to lose patience or at least listen to those who had lost it. The manifestation of June 18 had revealed to everybody that the government was without support. "Why don't they get busy up there?" the soldiers and workers would ask, having in mind not only the compromise leaders but also the governing bodies of the Bolsheviks.

Under inflation prices the struggle for wages was exciting the workers and getting on their nerves. During June this question became especially sharp in the giant Putilov factory, where 36,000 men worked. On June 21 a strike of skilled workers broke out in certain parts of the factory. The fruitlessness of these scattered outbreaks was only too clear to the party. On the next day a meeting of representatives of the principal workers' organizations, led by the Bolsheviks, and of 70 factories, announced that "the cause of the Putilov workers is the cause of the whole Petrograd proletariat," but appealed to the Putilov men to "restrain their legitimate indignation." The strike was postponed. But the following 12 days brought no change. The factory masses were seething, seeking an outlet. Every plant had its conflict, and all these conflicts tended upward toward the government. A report of the trade union of the Locomotive Brigade to the Minister of Communications reads: "For the last time we announce: patience has its limit; we simply cannot live in such conditions. . . ." That was a complaint not only against want and hunger, but against duplicity, characterlessness, false dealing. The report protests with especial rage against the "endless exhorting of us to the duties of a citizen and to self-restraint in starvation."

The March transfer of power by the Executive Committee to the Provisional Government had been made on the condition that the revolutionary troops should not be removed from the capital. But those days were far in the past. The garrison had moved to the left, the ruling soviet circles to the right. The struggle with the garrison had never disappeared from the order of the day. Although no whole units were transferred from the capital, nevertheless the more revolutionary—under the pretext of strategic necessities—were systematically weakened by a pumping-out of replacement companies. Rumors from the front of the disbandment of more and more units for disobedience, for refusal to carry out military orders, were continually arriving at the capital. Two Siberian divisions—and were not the Siberian sharp-shooters long considered the finest?—had to be disbanded by military force. In a case of mass disobedience in the Fifth Army only—that nearest the capital—87 officers and 12,725 soldiers were arraigned. The Petrograd garrison—accumulator of discontent from the front, the village, the workers' districts, and the barracks—was in a continual ferment. Bearded men in their forties were demanding with hysterical insistence that they be sent home for work in the fields. The regiments distributed through the Vyborg district—the 1st Machine Gun, the 1st Grenadier, the Moscow, the 180th Infantry, and others—were continually washed by the hot springs of the proletarian suburb. Thousands of workers were passing the barracks, among them no small number of the tireless agitators of Bolshevism. Under those dirty and dilapidated walls impromptu meetings were being held almost continuously. On the 22nd of June, before the patriotic manifestations called out by the offensive had died out, an auto-

8

mobile of the Executive Committee incautiously drove through the Sampsonevsky Prospect, carrying the placard: "Forward for Kerensky!" The Moscow Regiment stopped the agitators, tore up the placard, and turned over the patriotic automobile to the Machine Gun Regiment.

In general the soldiers were more impatient than the workers —both because they were directly threatened with a transfer to the front, and because it was much harder for them to understand considerations of political strategy. Moreover, each one had his rifle; and ever since February the soldier had been inclined to overestimate the independent power of a rifle. An old worker-Bolshevik, Lizdin, told later how the soldiers of the 180th Reserve Regiment said to him: "What are they doing there, fast asleep in Kshesinskaia's Palace? Come on, let's kick out Kerensky!" At meetings of the regiments, resolutions would be adopted continually, proclaiming the necessity of taking final action against the government. Delegations from individual factories would come to a regiment with the query: Will the soldiers go into the streets? The machine-gunners sent representatives to the other units of the garrison with an appeal to rise against the prolongation of the war. The more impatient of these delegates added: The Pavlov and Moscow regiments and forty thousand Putilov men are coming out "tomorrow." Official admonitions from the Executive Committee had no effect. The danger was growing every minute that Petrograd, lacking the support of the front and the provinces, would be broken down bit by bit. On the 21st of June, Lenin appealed in *Pravda* to the Petrograd workers and soldiers to wait until events should bring over the heavy reserves to the side of Petrograd. "We understand your bitterness, we understand the excitement of the Petersburg workers, but we say to them: Comrades, an immediate attack would be inexpedient." On the next day a private conference of leading Bolsheviks—standing, apparently, "to the left" of Lenin—came to the conclusion that in spite of the mood of the soldier and worker masses, they must not give battle: "Better wait until the ruling parties have disgraced themselves completely with their offensive, and then the game is ours." Thus reports the district organizer, Latsis, one of the most impatient in those days. The Central Committee was oftener and oftener compelled to send agitators to the troops and the factories to restrain them from untimely action. With an embarrassed shake of the head, the Vyborg Bolsheviks would complain to their friends: "We have to play the part of the fire hose." Appeals to come into the street did not cease, however, for a single day. Some of them were obviously provocative in character. The Military Organization of the Bolsheviks felt compelled to address the soldiers and workers with an appeal: "Do not trust any summons to go into the street in the name of the Military Organization. The Military Organization is not summoning you to action." And then, even more insistently: "Demand of any agitator or orator who summons you to come out in the name of the Military Organization credentials signed by the president and secretary."

On the famous Yakorny Square in Kronstadt, where the anarchists were more and more confidently lifting their voices, one ultimatum was drawn up after another. On the 23rd of June, delegates from Yakorny Square, acting over the head of the Kronstadt soviet, demanded from the Ministry of Justice the liberation of a group of Petrograd anarchists, threatening, in case their demand was not granted, that the sailors would march on the prison. Upon the following day, representatives from Oranienbaum informed the Ministry of Justice that their garrison was as much disturbed about the arrests in the summer home of Durnovo as Kronstadt, and that they were "already cleaning the machine guns." The bourgeois press caught these threats on the wing, and shook them under the very noses of their compromisist allies. On June 26, delegates from the Grenadier Guard Regiment came from the front to their reserve battalion with the announcement: "The regiment is against the Provisional Government and demands the transfer of power to the soviets, it declines the offensive begun by Kerensky, and expresses an apprehension lest the Executive Committee has gone over along with the minister-socialists to the side of the Bourjui." The organ of the Executive Committee published a reproachful account of this visit.

Not only Kronstadt was boiling like a kettle, but also the whole Baltic fleet with its principal base in Helsingfors. The head boss of the Bolsheviks in the fleet was undoubtedly Antonov-

Ovseënko, who years ago as a young officer had taken part in the Sebastopol insurrection of 1905. A Menshevik during the reaction years, an emigrant-internationalist during the war, a colleague of Trotsky on *Nashe Slovo*, in Paris, he joined the Bolsheviks after his return from abroad. Politically shaky, but personally courageous—impulsive and disorderly, but capable of initiative and improvisation—Antonov-Ovseënko, although still little known in those days, was to play by no means the smallest rôle in the future events of the revolution. "We in the Helsingfors committee of the Party," he relates in his memoirs, "understood the necessity of restraint and serious preparation. We had directions to that effect, moreover, from the Central Committee. But we saw the utter inevitability of an explosion, and were looking with alarm towards Petersburg." And in Petersburg the elements of an explosion were piling up day by day. The 2nd Machine Gun Regiment, which was less advanced than the first, adopted a resolution demanding the transfer of power to the Soviet. The 3rd Infantry Regiment refused to send out fourteen replacement companies. Meetings in the barracks were acquiring a more and more stormy character. A meeting of the Grenadier Regiment on July 1st was signalized by the arrest of the president of the committee, and by the obstructive heckling of the Menshevik orators: Down with the offensive! Down with Kerensky! At the focus of the garrison stood the machine gun men. It was they who opened the sluices for the July flood.

We have already met with the name of the 1st Machine Gun Regiment in the events of the first month of the revolution. Arriving shortly after the overturn, having marched from Oranienbaum to Petrograd upon its own initiative "for the defense of the revolution," this regiment immediately ran into the opposition of the Executive Committee, which adopted a resolution: to send the regiment back with thanks to Oranienbaum. The machine-gunners flatly refused to leave the capital: "Counter-revolutionists might attack the Soviet and restore the old régime." The Executive Committee surrendered, and several thousand machine-gunners remained in Petrograd along with their machine guns. They took up their quarters in the House of the People, and wondered what their further destiny was to be. They had among

11

them, however, a good many Petrograd workers, and therefore by no accident the Bolshevik Committee took upon itself the care of these machine-gunners. Through its intercession they were assured provisions from Peter and Paul fortress. A friendship began. It soon became indestructible. On the 21st of June, the machine-gunners introduced at a mass meeting a resolution: "In the future detachments shall be sent to the front only when the war has a revolutionary character." On the 2nd of July, the regiment called a farewell meeting in the House of the People for the "last" replacement company to depart for the front. The speakers were Lunacharsky and Trotsky. The authorities tried subsequently to attribute unusual significance to this accidental fact. Responses were made in the name of the regiment by the soldier, Zhilin, and the old Bolshevik non-commissioned officer, Lashevich. The mood was exalted. They denounced Kerensky and swore fealty to the revolution—but nobody made any practical proposal for the immediate future. However, during those last days the city persisted in expecting something to happen. The "July Days" were casting their shadow before them. "Everywhere," Sukhanov remembers, "in all corners, in the Soviet, in the Mariinsky Palace, in people's apartments, on the public squares and boulevards, in the barracks, in the factories, they were talking about some sort of manifestation to be expected, if not today, tomorrow. . . . Nobody knew exactly who was going to manifest what, or where, but the city felt itself to be upon the verge of some sort of explosion." And the explosion did actually come. The stimulus was given from above—from the ruling circles.

On the same day when Trotsky and Lunacharsky were speaking to the machine gun men about the bankruptcy of the coalition, four Kadet ministers exploded the coalition by withdrawing from the government. They chose as pretext an agreement which their compromisist colleagues had concluded with the Ukraine, an agreement unacceptable to their imperial ambitions. The real cause of this demonstrative break lay in the fact that the Compromisers had been dilatory about bridling the masses. The moment chosen was suggested by the collapse of the offensive —not yet officially acknowledged, but no longer a matter of doubt to the well-informed. These Liberals considered it ex-

12

pedient to leave their left allies face to face with defeat, and with the Bolsheviks. The rumor of the resignation of the Kadets immediately spread through the capital, and generalized all the existing conflicts politically in one slogan—or rather, one cry to heaven: "Let us have an end of this coalition rigmarole!" The soldiers and workers considered that all other questions—that of wages, of the price of bread, and of whether it is necessary to die at the front for nobody knows what—depended upon the question who was to rule the country in the future, the bourgeoisie or their own Soviet. In these expectations there was a certain element of illusion—in so far, at least, as the masses hoped with a change of power to achieve an immediate solution of all sore problems. But in the last analysis they were right: the question of power determined the direction of the revolution as a whole, and that means that it decided the fate of everyone in particular. To imagine that the Kadets may not have foreseen the effect of this act of open sabotage of the Soviet would be decidedly to underestimate Miliukov. The leader of liberalism was obviously trying to drag the Compromisers into a difficult situation from which they could make a way out only with bayonets. In those days Miliukov firmly believed that the situation could be saved with a bold blood-letting.

On the morning of July 3, several thousand machine-gunners, after breaking up a meeting of the company and regimental committees of their regiment, elected a chairman of their own and demanded immediate consideration of the question of an armed manifestation. The meeting was a storm from the first moment. The problem of the front intercrossed with the crisis in the government. The chairman of the meeting, a Bolshevik, Golovin, tried to apply the brakes, proposing that they have a preliminary talk with other units and with the Military Organization. But every suggestion of delay set the soldiers on edge. There appeared at this meeting the anarchist, Bleichman, a small but colorful figure on the background of 1917, with a very modest equipment of ideas but a certain feeling for the masses —sincere in his limited and ever inflammable intelligence—his shirt open at the breast and curly hair flying out on all sides. Bleichman was greeted at such meetings with a certain amount

13

of semi-ironical sympathy. The workers, it is true, treated him somewhat coolly, a little impatiently—especially the metal-workers. But the soldiers smiled delightedly at his speeches, nudging each other with their elbows and egging the orator on with pithy comments. They plainly liked his eccentric looks, his unreasoning decisiveness, and his Jewish-American accent sharp as vinegar. By the end of June, Bleichman was swimming in all these impromptu meetings like a fish in a river. His opinion he had always with him: *It is necessary to come out with arms in our hands.* Organization? "The street will organize us." The task? "To overthrow the Provisional Government just as it overthrew the tsar although no party was then demanding it." These speeches perfectly met the feelings of the machine-gunners at that moment—and not theirs alone. Many of the Bolsheviks did not conceal their satisfaction when the lower ranks pressed forward against their official admonition. The progressive workers remembered that in February their leaders had been ready to beat a retreat just on the eve of the victory; that in March the eight hour day had been won by action from below; that in April Miliukov had been thrown out by regiments who went into the street on their own initiative. A recollection of these facts augmented the tense and impatient mood of the masses.

The Military Organization of the Bolsheviks, being promptly informed that a meeting of the machine-gunners was at the boiling point, sent over one agitator after another. Soon came Nevsky himself, the leader of the Military Organization, a man respected by the soldiers. They seemed to listen to him. But the mood of that endless meeting changed with its ingredients. "It was an immense surprise to us," relates Podvoisky, another leader of the Military Organization, "when at seven o'clock in the evening a horseman galloped up to inform us that . . . the machine-gunners had again resolved to come out." In place of the old regimental committee they had elected a provisional revolutionary committee consisting of two men from each company under the presidency of ensign Semashko. Specially appointed delegates were already making the rounds of the shops and regiments with an appeal for support. The machine-gunners had not forgotten, either, to send their men to Kronstadt. In this way, one step

14

below the official organizations, and partly under their protection, new temporary relations were established between the more restive regiments and the factories. The masses had no intention of breaking with the Soviet; on the contrary, they wanted the Soviet to seize the power. Still less did the masses intend to break with the Bolshevik party. But they did feel that the party was irresolute. They wanted to get their shoulder under it—shake a fist at the Executive Committee, give the Bolsheviks a little shove. Thus impromptu systems of representation were created, new knots were tied, new centers of activity formed—not permanently, but for the given situation. Changes in circumstance and mood were taking place so fast and sharply, that even such extremely flexible organizations as the soviets inevitably lagged behind, and the masses were compelled at every new turn to create auxiliary organs for the demands of the moment. In the course of these improvisations accidental and not always reliable elements would often spring into prominence. The anarchists poured oil on the fire. But so did some of the new and impatient Bolsheviks. Provocateurs also undoubtedly mixed in—perhaps also German agents, but surest of all the agents of the 100 per cent Russian secret police. How can one analyze the complicated web of a mass movement into its separate threads? The general character of the event emerges at least with complete clarity. Petrograd was feeling its strength, was straining at the leash, not glancing round at either the provinces or the front, and even the Bolshevik party was no longer able to hold it back. Only experience could teach them.

In calling the factories and regiments into the street, the delegates of the machine-gunners did not forget to add that the manifestation was to be armed. Yes, and how could it be otherwise? You wouldn't present yourself unarmed to the blows of an enemy? Moreover—and this perhaps was the chief thing—we must show our force, and a soldier without weapons is not a force. Upon this point all the regiments and all the factories were of one mind: if we do go out, we must go with plenty of lead. The machine-gunners lost no time: having started a big job, they intended to push it through as fast as possible. The report of a Court of Inquiry subsequently characterized the activities of

15

ensign Semashko, one of the principal leaders of the regiment in these words: "He demanded automobiles from the factories, armed them with machine guns, sent them to the Tauride Palace and other points, designating the route, personally led out his regiment from the barracks into the town, rode out to the reserve battalion of the Moscow Regiment to persuade it to come out, in which he was successful, promised the soldiers of the Machine Gun Regiment support from the regiments of the Military Organization, kept in continual touch with this organization, quartered in the house of Kshesinskaia, and with the leader of the Bolsheviks, Lenin, despatched sentries for the protection of the Military Organization. . . ." The reference to Lenin here is inserted only to fill out the picture. Lenin was not in Petrograd either on that day or the days preceding. Since the 29th of June he had been ill in a bungalow in Finland. But for the rest, the compressed language of the military court official conveys not at all badly the feverish preparations of the machine-gunners. In the yard of the barracks a no less feverish work was going on. They were giving out rifles to the soldiers who did not possess them, giving bombs to some, installing three machine guns with operators on each motor truck supplied by the factories. The regiment was to go into the street in full military array.

And just about the same thing was going on in the factories. Delegates would arrive from the machine-gunners, or from a neighboring factory, and summon the workers into the street. It would seem as though they had been waiting for the delegates. Work would stop instantly. A worker of the Renaud Factory tells this story: "After dinner a number of machine gun men came running with the request that we give them some motor trucks. In spite of the protest of our group (the Bolsheviks), we had to give up the cars. . . . They promptly loaded the trucks with 'Maxims' (machine guns) and drove down the Nevsky. At this point we could no longer restrain our workers . . . They all, just as they were, in overalls, rushed straight outdoors from the benches . . ." The protests of the factory Bolsheviks were not always, we may assume, very insistent. The longest struggle took place at the Putilov Factory. At about two in the afternoon a rumour went round that a delegation had come from the machine

16

gun unit, and was calling a meeting. About ten thousand men assembled. To shouts of encouragement, the machine-gunners told how they had received an order to go to the front on the 4th of July, but they had decided "to go not to the German front, against the German proletariat, but against their own capitalist ministers." Feeling ran high. "Come on, let's get moving!" cried the workers. The secretary of the factory committee, a Bolshevik, objected, suggesting that they ask instructions from the party. Protests from all sides: "Down with it! Again you want to postpone things. We can't live that way any longer . . ." Towards six o'clock came representatives from the Executive Committee, but they succeeded still less with the workers. The meeting continued, the everlasting nervous obstinate meeting of innumerable masses seeking a way out and unwilling to be told that there is none. It was proposed that they send a delegation to the Executive Committee—still another delay, but, as before, the meeting did not disperse. About this time a group of workers and soldiers brought news that the Vyborg Side was already on its way to the Tauride Palace. To hold them back longer was impossible. They decided to go. A Putilov worker, Efimov, ran to the district committee of the party to ask: "What shall we do?" The answer he got was: "We will not join the manifestation, but we can't leave the workers to their fate. We must go along with them." At that moment appeared a member of the committee, Chudin, with the word that the workers were going out in all the districts, and that it was up to the party men to "maintain order." In this way the Bolsheviks were caught up by the movement and dragged into it, looking around the while for some justification for an action which flatly contravened the official decision of the party.

By seven o'clock the industrial life of the capital was at a complete standstill. Factory after factory came out, lined up and armed its detachment of the Red Guard. "Amid an innumerable mass of workers," relates the Vyborg Worker, Metelev, "hundreds of young Red Guards were working away loading their rifles. Others were piling cartridges into the cartridge-chambers, tightening up their belts, tying on their knapsacks or cartridge boxes, adjusting their bayonets. And the workers with-

17

out arms were helping the Red Guards get ready . . ." Samsonevsky Prospect, the chief artery of the Vyborg Side, was packed full of people. To the right and left of it stood solid columns of workers. In the middle of the Prospect marched the Machine Gun Regiment, the spinal column of the procession. At the head of each company went an automobile truck with its Maxims. After the Machine Gun Regiment came the workers. Covering the manifestation as a rear guard, came detachments of the Moscow Regiment. Over every detachment streamed a banner: "All Power to the Soviets!" The funeral procession in March and the First of May demonstration were probably more numerous, but the July procession was incomparably more eager, more threatening, and—more homogeneous in its composition. "Under the red banners marched only workers and soldiers," writes one of the participants. "The cockades of the officials, the shiny buttons of students, the hats of 'lady sympathizers' were not to be seen. All that belonged to four months ago, to February. In today's movement there was none of that. Today only the common slaves of capital were marching." As before, automobiles flew through the streets in all directions full of armed workers and soldiers—delegates, agitators, reconnoiterers, telephone men, and detachments for calling out workers and regiments. They all held their bayonets advanced. The bristling motor trucks completed a picture of the February days, electrifying some, terrorizing others. The Kadet Nabokov writes: "The same insane, dumb, beastlike faces which we all remember from the February days"—that is, the days of that very revolution which the liberals had officially pronounced glorious and bloodless. By nine o'clock seven regiments were already moving toward the Tauride Palace. They were joined on the way by columns from the factories and by new military detachments. The movement of the Machine Gun Regiment developed a colossal power of contagion. The "July days" had begun.

Meetings were held on the march. Shots rang out. According to a worker, Korotkov, "they dragged out of a cellar on the Liteiny a machine gun and an officer whom they killed on the spot." All conceivable rumours ran ahead of the demonstration. Fears rayed out from it on all sides like beams of light. What imaginable thing was not reported over the telephones from the frightened central districts? It was said that about eight o'clock in the evening an armed automobile dashed up to the Warsaw station seeking Kerensky who had left that very day for the front, intending to arrest him, but that the train had gone and the arrest did not occur. That episode was subsequently repeated more than once as proving a conspiracy. Just who was in the automobile and who discovered its mysterious intentions, has nevertheless remained unknown. On that evening automobiles with armed men were careering in all directions—doubtless, therefore, in the vicinity of the Warsaw station. Strong words were to be heard about Kerensky in many places. This evidently served as a basis for the myth—if it was not indeed simply manufactured out of whole cloth.

Izvestia sketched the following outline of the events of July 3rd: "At five o'clock in the afternoon there came out, armed, the First Machine Gun, a part of the Moscow, a part of the Grenadier, and a part of the Pavlovsky Regiments. They were joined by crowds of workers . . . By eight o'clock in the evening, separate parts of regiments began to pour towards the Palace of Kshesinskaia, armed to the teeth and with red banners and placards demanding the transfer of power to the soviets. Speeches were made from the balcony . . . At ten-thirty a meeting was held on the square in front of the Tauride Palace . . . The troops elected a deputation to the All-Russian Central Executive Committee which presented in their name the following demands: Removal of the ten bourgeois ministers, all power to the soviets, cessation of the offensive, confiscation of the printing plants of the bourgeois press, the land to be state property, state control of production." Aside from certain prunings—"parts of regiments" instead of regiments, "crowds of workers" instead of entire factories—you may say that the official report of Tseretelli and Dan does not distort the general picture of what happened. In particular it correctly notes the two focal points of the demonstration: the private residence of Kshesinskaia and the Tauride Palace. Both spiritually and physically the movement revolved around those two antagonistic centers: It came to the house of Kshesinskaia for instructions, leadership, inspirational

19

speeches; to the Tauride Palace it came to present demands and even to threaten a little with its power.

At three o'clock in the afternoon, two delegates from the machine-gunners came to an all-city conference of the Bolsheviks, sitting that day in the house of Kshesinskaia, with the information that their regiment had decided to come out. Nobody had expected this, and nobody wanted it. Tomsky declared: "The regiments which have come out have acted in an uncomradely manner, not having invited the Central Committee of our party to consider the question of a manifestation. The Central Committee proposes to the conference: in the first place, to issue an appeal in order to hold back the masses; in the second, to prepare an address to the Executive Committee urging them to take the power in their hands. It is impossible to talk of a manifestation at this moment unless we want a new revolution." Tomsky, an old worker-Bolshevik who had certified his loyalty to the party with years at hard labor—famous subsequently as leader of the trade unions—was in general more inclined by character to restrain the masses from action than summon them to it. But on this occasion he was merely carrying out the thought of Lenin: "It is impossible to talk of a manifestation at this moment unless we want a new revolution." Even the attempt at a peaceful demonstration on June 10th had been denounced by the Compromisers as a conspiracy. An overwhelming majority of the conference was at one with Tomsky. We must at all costs postpone the final conflict. The offensive at the front is holding the whole country at high tension. Its failure is inevitable—as also the determination of the government to throw all the responsibility for the defeat upon the Bolsheviks. We must give the Compromisers time to ruin themselves completely. Volodarsky answered the machine-gunners in the name of the conference to the effect that the regiment must submit to the decisions of the party. The machine-gunners departed with a protest. At four o'clock the Central Committee confirmed the decision of the conference. Its members dispersed to the districts and factories to restrain the masses from going out. Appeals to the same effect were sent to *Pravda* to be printed on the front page the following morning. Stalin was appointed to bring the decision to the attention of the joint session of the Executive Committees. There remains, therefore, no doubt whatever as to the intention of the Bolsheviks. Their Central Committee addressed an appeal to the workers and soldiers: "Unknown persons . . . are summoning you into the streets under arms," and that proves that the summons does not come from any one of the soviet parties . . . Thus the central committees—both of the party and the Soviet—proposed, but the masses disposed.

At eight o'clock in the evening, the Machine Gun Regiment, and soon after it the Moscow Regiment, came up to the palace of Kshesinskaia. Popular Bolsheviks—Nevsky, Lashevich, Podvoisky—speaking from the balcony, tried to send the regiments home. They were answered from below: *Doloi! Doloi!* Such cries the Bolshevik balcony had never yet heard from the soldiers; it was an alarming sign. Behind the regiments the factories began to march up: "All Power to the Soviets!" "Down with the ten minister capitalists!" Those had been the banners of June 18th, but now they were hedged with bayonets. The demonstration had become a mighty fact. What was to be done? Could the Bolsheviks possibly stand aside? The members of the Petrograd committee, together with the delegates to the conference and representatives from the regiments and factories, passed a resolution: to reconsider the question, to end all fruitless attempts to restrain the masses and guide the developing movement in such a way that the governmental crisis may be decided in the interests of the people; with this goal, to appeal to the soldiers and workers to go peacefully to the Tauride Palace, elect delegates, and through them present their demands to the Executive Committee. The members of the Central Committee who were present sanctioned this change of tactics. This new decision, announced from the balcony, was met with welcoming shouts and with singing of the Marseillaise. The movement had been legalized by the party. The machine-gunners could heave a sigh of relief. A part of the regiment immediately went to the Peter and Paul fortress to influence its garrison, and in case of necessity protect from its blows the Palace of Kshesinskaia, which was separated from the fortress only by the narrow Kronverksky canal.

The principal ranks of the demonstration moved out into the

Nevsky, the artery of the bourgeoisie, bureaucracy and officers, as though into a foreign country. From the sidewalks, windows, balconies, thousands of eyes looked out with no good wishes. Regiment pressed upon factory, factory upon regiment. Fresh masses arrived continually. All the banners, in gold letters on red, cried out with one voice: "All Power to the Soviets!" The procession brimmed the Nevsky and poured like a river at the flood to the Tauride Palace. The placards "Down with the war!" provoke the bitterest hostility from the officers—among them many war-invalids. Waving their arms and straining their voices, students, college girls, officials, endeavor to persuade the soldiers that German agents behind them are aiming to let Wilhelm's troops into Petrograd to strangle freedom. To these orators their own conclusions seem irrefutable. "They are deceived by spies," say the officials, pointing at the workers, and the workers' answer is a surly growl. "Led astray by fanatics!" say the more indulgent. "Ignorant elements," others agree. But the workers have their own way of measuring things. They did not learn from German spies those ideas which have brought them into the streets today. The demonstrators impolitely push aside their importunate tutors, and move forward. This drives the patriots of the Nevsky out of their heads. Shock groups, led for the most part by war-cripples and Cavaliers of St. George, fall upon individual sections of the demonstration, trying to snatch away the banners. Clashes occur here and there. The atmosphere grows hot. Shots ring out. One, and then another. From a window? From the Anichkin Palace? The pavement answers with a volley in the air, aimed nowhere. In a short time the whole street is in confusion. At about midnight—relates a worker from the "Vulcan" Factory—as the Grenadier Regiment was passing through the Nevsky in the vicinity of the Public Library, somebody opened fire on them from somewhere, and the shooting continued several minutes. A panic followed. The workers began to scatter into the side streets. The soldiers lay down under fire—they had learned that in the war school. That midnight scene on the Nevsky, with Grenadier Guards lying down on the pavement, was a fantastic spectacle. Neither Pushkin nor Gogol, singers of the Nevsky, ever imagined it thus. Moreover, there was reality in this fantasia: dead and wounded men stayed there on the pavement.

✻

THE TAURIDE was living a life of its own in those days. In view of the resignation of the Kadets, both Executive Committees, the worker-soldier's and the peasant's, had met in joint session to consider a discourse of Tseretelli on how to pour out the coalition bath without the baby. The secret of this operation would undoubtedly have been discovered in the long run, if the restless suburbs had not intervened. A telephone communication about the manifestation under preparation by the Machine Gun Regiment produced frowns of anger and vexation on the faces of the leaders. Can it be that the soldiers and workers will not wait until our newspapers bring them salvation in the form of a resolution? Oblique glances were cast in the direction of the Bolsheviks. But for them too, this time, the demonstration was a surprise. Kamenev, and other representatives of the party who happened to be present, even agreed at the end of the day's session to go to the factories and barracks and attempt to restrain the masses from going out. This gesture was afterward interpreted by the Compromisers as a military trick. The Executive Committee as usual hastily adopted a proclamation declaring any manifestation an act of treachery to the revolution. But even so, how were they going to deal with the governmental crisis? A way out was found: they would leave the mutilated cabinet as it was, postponing the whole question until the provincial members of the Executive Committee could be summoned. To drag things out, to gain time for your own vacillations—is not that the most ingenious of all political policies?

Only in their struggle against the masses did the Compromisers consider it unwise to lose time. The official apparatus was immediately set in motion to prepare arms against the "insurrection" —for so they named the demonstration from the very beginning. The leaders searched everywhere for armed forces to defend the government and the Executive Committee. Over the signature of

23

Cheidze and other members of the Praesidium, demands were sent to various military institutions to send to the Tauride Palace armored cars, three-inch guns and shells. At the same time almost every regiment received orders to send armed detachments for the defense of the palace. But they did not stop there. Their bureau telegraphed an order that same day to the front—to the Fifth Army, stationed nearest the capital—to "send to Petrograd a cavalry division, a brigade of infantry, and armored cars." The Menshevik, Voitinsky, to whom was allotted the task of protecting the Executive Committee, let the whole thing out later in his retrospective survey: "The entire day of July 3rd was spent in getting together troops to fortify the Tauride Palace. . . . Our problem was to bring in at least a few companies. . . . At one time we had absolutely no forces. Six men stood at the doors of the Tauride Palace without power to hold back the crowd . . ." And again: "On the first day of the demonstration we had at our disposal only a hundred men—we had no other forces. We sent out commissars to all the regiments with a request to give us soldiers to form a patrol . . . But each regiment looked to the next to see what it was going to do. We were compelled at whatever cost to put a stop to this outrage, and we summoned troops from the front." It would be difficult, even with malice aforethought, to devise a more vicious satire upon the Compromisers. Hundreds of thousands of demonstrators were demanding the transfer of power to the soviets. Cheidze, standing at the head of the soviet system and thus the logical candidate for premier, was hunting for armed forces to employ against the demonstrators. This colossal movement in favor of power to the democracy, was denounced by the democratic leaders as an attack upon the democracy by an armed gang.

In the Tauride Palace at that same time the workers' section of the Soviet was meeting after a long intermission. In the course of the last two months this section had so far changed its composition, as a result of by-elections in the factories, that the Executive Committee had well-grounded fears of a predominance of Bolsheviks. The artificially delayed meeting of the section— finally called a few days before by the Compromisers themselves —accidentally coincided with the armed demonstration. In this the newspapers saw the hand of the Bolsheviks. Zinoviev in a speech to the section convincingly developed the thought that the Compromisers, being allies of the bourgeoisie, were unable and unwilling to struggle against the counter-revolution, since that word meant to them only individual manifestations of Black Hundred hooliganism; it did not mean what it was—a political union of the possessing classes for the purpose of strangling the soviets as centers of the resistance of the toiling masses. His speech hit the mark. The Mensheviks, finding themselves for the first time in a minority on soviet soil, proposed that no decision should be arrived at, and that they should disperse to the districts to preserve order. But it was already too late! The news that armed workers and machine-gunners were approaching the Tauride Palace produced a mighty excitement in the hall. Kamenev ascended the tribune: "We did not summon the manifestation," he said. "The popular masses themselves came into the street . . . But once the masses have come out, our place is among them. . . . Our present task is to give the movement an organized character." Kamenev concluded with a proposal that they elect a commission of twenty-five men for the leadership of the movement. Trotsky seconded the motion. Cheidze feared a Bolshevik commission, and vainly insisted that the question be turned over to the Executive Committee. The debate became fiercer. Convinced finally that all together they constituted only a third of the assembly, the Mensheviks and Social Revolutionaries left the hall. This was becoming a favorite tactic with the democrats; they began to boycott the soviets from the moment they lost the majority there. A resolution summoning the Executive Committee to take the power was adopted in the absence of the opposition by 276 votes. Elections were immediately held for the fifteen members of the commission. Ten places were left for the minority— and these ten would remain unoccupied. This fact of the election of a Bolshevik commission signified both to friends and enemies that the workers' section of the Petrograd soviet would henceforth become a Bolshevik base. A vast step forward! In April the influence of the Bolsheviks had extended to approximately a third of the Petrograd workers; in the Soviet of those days they occupied a wholly insignificant sector. Now, at the beginning of

July, the Bolsheviks were sending to the workers' section about two-thirds of its members. That meant that among the masses their influence had become decisive.

Through the streets leading to the Tauride Palace there is flowing a steady column of working men and women and soldiers, with banners, songs and bands playing. The light artillery comes along, its commander reporting amid rapture that all the batteries of his division are at one with the workers. The thoroughfares and square near the Tauride are filled with people. All are trying to crowd in around the tribune at the chief entrance to the palace. Cheidze comes out to the demonstrators with the gloomy look of a man who has been unnecessarily torn from his work. The popular soviet president is met with an unfriendly silence. In a tired and hoarse voice Cheidze repeats those commonplaces which have long puckered his mouth. Voitinsky, who comes out to help him, is no better received. "Trotsky, however"—according to the account of Miliukov, "having announced that the moment was now come when the power should go over to the soviets, was met with loud applause. . . ." This sentence of Miliukov's is purposely ambiguous. None of the Bolsheviks declared that "the moment was come." A machinist from the small Duflon factory on the Petrograd side said later about that meeting under the wall of the Tauride Palace: "I remember the speech of Trotsky, who said that it was not yet time to seize the power in our hands." The machinist reports the essence of the speech more correctly than the professor of history. From the lips of the Bolshevik orators the demonstrators learned of the victory just won in the Workers' Section, and that fact gave them almost as palpable a satisfaction as would an entrance upon the epoch of soviet power.

The joint session of the Executive Committees met again a little before midnight. (Just then the grenadiers were lying down on the Nevsky.) On a motion from Dan, it was resolved that only those could remain at the meeting who should bind themselves in advance to defend and carry out its decisions. This was a new note! From a workers' and soldiers' parliament, which was what the Mensheviks had declared the Soviet to be, they were trying to convert it into an administrative organ of the compromise majority. After they have become a minority—and this is only two months away—the Compromisers will passionately defend the principle of democracy in the soviet. Today, however—as indeed at all decisive moments in social life—democracy is held in reserve. A number of Mezhrayontsi [1] left the hall with a protest. The Bolsheviks were not there; they were in the Palace of Kshesinskaia getting ready for tomorrow. During the further course of the meeting the Mezhrayontsi and the Bolsheviks appeared in the hall with the announcement that no one could take from them the mandate given them by their electors. The majority greeted this announcement with silence, and Dan's resolution was quietly dropped into oblivion. The session dragged out like a death agony. In tired voices the Compromisers kept on assuring each other that they were right. Tseretelli, in his character of Postmaster General, entered a complaint against his employees: "I just now learned of the strike of the postal and telegraph workers. . . . As to their political demands, their slogans are the same: All Power to the Soviets!"

Delegates from the demonstrators, now surrounding the Tauride Palace on all sides, demanded admission to the meeting. They were admitted with alarm and hostility. The delegates, however, sincerely believed that this time the Compromisers could not help coming to meet them. Had not today's issues of the Menshevik and Social Revolutionary papers, wrought up over the resignation of the Kadets, themselves exposed the intrigues and sabotage of their bourgeois allies? Moreover the workers' section had come out in favor of a soviet government. What else was there to wait for? But their fervent appeals, in which hope still mingled with indignation, dropped impotent and inappropriate into the stagnant atmosphere of that parliament of compromise. The leaders had but one thought: how quickest to get rid of their uninvited guests. To suggest that they withdraw to the gallery, to drive them back into the street to the demonstrators, would be indiscreet. In the gallery machine gun men were listening with amazement to the evolving debate, which had only one goal—to gain time. The Compromisers were waiting for

[1] Members of the "Inter-district" organization to which the author at that time belonged. Trans.

reliable regiments. "A revolutionary people is in the streets," cried Dan, "but that people is engaged in a counter-revolutionary work." Dan was supported by Abramovich, one of the leaders of the Jewish Bund, a conservative pedant whose every instinct had been outraged by the revolution. "We are witnesses to a conspiracy," he asserts, in defiance of the obvious, and he proposes to the Bolsheviks that they openly announce that "this is their work." Tseretelli deepens the discussion: "To go out into the streets with the demand, 'All Power to the Soviets'—is that to support the soviets? If the soviets so desired, the power could pass to them. There is no obstacle anywhere to the will of the soviets. . . . Such a manifestation is not along the road of revolution, but of counter-revolution." These considerations the workers' delegates could not possibly understand. It seemed to them that the high-up leaders were a little bit out of their heads. The meeting at last resolved once more, by all votes except 11, that an armed manifestation would be a stab in the back at the revolutionary army, etc., etc. The meeting adjourned at five o'clock in the morning.

The masses were gradually gathered back into their districts. Armed automobiles traveled all night, uniting regiments, factories and district centers. As in the last days of February, the masses spent the night casting the balance of the day's struggle. But now they did this with the aid of a complicated system of organizations—factory, party and regimental—which conferred continually. In the districts it was considered self-evident that the movement could not stop half way. The Executive Committee had postponed the decision about the power. The masses regarded that as wavering. The conclusion was clear: we must bring more pressure to bear. A night session of Bolsheviks and Mezhrayontsi, meeting in the Tauride Palace simultaneously with the Executive Committees, also cast the balance of the day and tried to foretell what the morrow would bring. Reports from the districts testified that today's demonstration had merely set the masses in motion, presenting to their minds nakedly for the first time the question of power. Tomorrow the factories and regiments would go after the answer, and no force in the world could hold them in the suburbs. The debate was not about whether to summon the masses to a seizure of power—as enemies later asserted—but about whether to try to call off the demonstration the next morning or to stand at the head of it.

Late in the night, or rather at about three o'clock in the morning, the Putilov factory approached the Tauride Palace—a mass of eighty thousand workers, many with wives and children. The procession had started at eleven o'clock in the evening, and other belated factories had joined it on the road. In spite of the late hour, there was such a mass of people at the Narva Gate as to suggest that nobody stayed home that night in the whole district. The women had exclaimed: "Everybody must go—we will watch the houses." At a signal from the belfry of the Church of the Savior shots had rattled out as though from a machine gun. From below a volley was fired at the belfry. "Near Gostiny Dvor a company of junkers and students fell upon the demonstrators and tried to tear away their placards. The workers resisted. The crowd piled up. Somebody fired a shot. The writer of these lines got his head broken, his sides and chest badly mashed by tramping feet." These are the words of the worker Efimov, already known to us. Passing across the whole town, silent now, the Putilov men finally arrived at the Tauride Palace. Thanks to the insistent efforts of Riazanov, closely associated at that time with the trade unions, a delegation was admitted to the Executive Committee. The throng of workers, hungry and dead-tired, scattered about on the street and in the garden, a majority immediately stretching themselves out, thinking to wait there for an answer. The entire Putilov factory lying there on the ground at three o'clock in the morning around the Tauride Palace, where the democratic leaders were waiting for the arrival of troops from the front—that is one of the most startling pictures offered by the revolution on this summit of the pass between February and October. Twelve years before no small numbers of these same workers had participated in the January procession to the Winter Palace with ikons and religious standards. Ages had passed since that Sunday afternoon; other ages will pass during the next four months.

The sombre image of these Putilov workers lying down in the courtyard hung over the conference of Bolshevik leaders and organizers as they debated about the next day's plans. Tomorrow the Putilovtsi will refuse to work—yes, and what work would they be good for after the night's vigil? Zinoviev was summoned to the telephone. Raskolnikov had rung up from Kronstadt to say that tomorrow early in the morning the garrison of the fortress would start for Petrograd and nobody and nothing could stop it. The young midshipman was holding on in suspense at the other end of the wire: Would the central committee order him to break with the soviets, and ruin himself in their eyes? To the picture of the Putilov factory as a gypsy camp was thus joined the no less suggestive picture of the sailors' island getting ready in those sleepless hours of the night to support workers' and soldiers' Petrograd. No, the situation was too clear. There was no more room for wavering. Trotsky inquired for the last time: Can we, nevertheless, try to make it an unarmed demonstration? No, there can be no question of that. One squad of Junkers can scatter tens of thousands of unarmed workers like a flock of sheep. The soldiers and the workers, too, will regard that proposal as a trap. The answer was categorical and convincing. All unanimously decided to summon the masses in the name of the party to prolong the demonstration on the next day. Zinoviev hastened to relieve the mind of Raskolnikov, languishing at the other end of the telephone. An address to the workers and soldiers was immediately drawn up: Into the streets! The afternoon's summons from the Central Committee to stop the demonstration, was torn from the presses—but too late to replace it with a new text. A white page in *Pravda* the next morning will be deadly evidence against the Bolsheviks: Evidently getting frightened at the last moment, they withdrew the appeal for an insurrection; or maybe, just the opposite—maybe they renounced an earlier appeal for a peaceful demonstration in order to go in for insurrection. Meanwhile the real decision of the Bolsheviks was issued on a separate leaflet. It summoned the workers and soldiers "by way of a peaceful and organized demonstration to bring their will to the attention of the Executive Committees now in session." No, that was not a summons to insurrection.

CHAPTER II

THE "JULY DAYS": CULMINATION AND ROUT

FROM that moment the direct leadership of the movement passed conclusively into the hands of the Petrograd committee of the party, whose chief force as an agitator was Volodarsky. The task of mobilizing the garrison was assigned to the Military Organization. The direction of this organization ever since March had been in the hands of two old Bolsheviks to whom the organization was to owe much in its further development. Podvoisky was a sharply outlined and unique figure in the ranks of Bolshevism, with traits of the Russian revolutionary of the old type—from the theological seminaries—a man of great although undisciplined energy, with a creative imagination which, it must be confessed, often went to the length of fantasy. The word "Podvoiskyism" subsequently acquired on the lips of Lenin a friendly-ironical and admonitory flavor. But the weaker sides of this ebullient nature were to show themselves chiefly after the conquest of power, when an abundance of opportunities and means gave too many stimuli to the extravagant energy of Podvoisky and his passion for decorative undertakings. In the conditions of the revolutionary struggle for power, his optimistic decisiveness of character, his self-abnegation, his tirelessness, made him an irreplaceable leader of the awakening soldiers. Nevsky, a university instructor in the past, of more prosaic mould than Podvoisky, but no less devoted to the party, in no sense an organizer, and only by an unlucky accident made soviet Minister of Communications a year later, attached the soldiers to him by his simplicity, sociability, and attentive kindness. Around these leaders stood a group of close assistants, soldiers and young officers, some of whom in the future were to play no small rôle. On the night of July 4th the Military Organization suddenly came forward to the center of the stage. Under Podvoisky, who easily mastered the functions of command, an impromptu general staff was formed. Brief appeals and instructions were issued to all the troops of the garrison. In order to protect the demonstration from attack, armored cars were to be placed at the bridges leading from the suburbs to the capital and at the central crossings of the chief streets. The machine-gunners had already, during that night, established their own sentries at the Peter and Paul fortress. The garrisons of Oranienbaum, Peterhoff, Krasnoe Selo and other points near the capital, were informed of tomorrow's demonstration by telephone and special messenger. The general political leadership, of course, remained in the hands of the Central Committee of the party.

The machine-gunners returned to their barracks at dawn, tired and, in spite of the July weather, shivering. A night rain had soaked the Putilov men also to the skin. The demonstrators did not assemble until eleven o'clock in the morning. The military sections got there still later. Today the 1st Machine Gun Regiment was on the street to the last man. But it will no longer play the rôle of initiator as it did yesterday. The factories have moved into the front rank. Moreover, those plants have been drawn into the movement which yesterday stood aside. Where the leaders wavered or resisted, younger workers had compelled the member-on-duty of the factory committee to blow the whistle as a signal to stop work. In the Baltic factory, where Mensheviks and Social Revolutionaries dominated, about four out of five thousand workers came out. In the Skorokhod shoe factory, long considered a stronghold of the Social Revolutionaries, the mood had so sharply changed that an old deputy from that factory, a Social Revolutionary, did not dare show his face for several days. All the factories struck and held meetings. They elected leaders for the demonstration and delegates to present their demands to the Executive Committee. Again hundreds of thousands moved in radii toward the Tauride Palace, and again tens of thousands turned aside on their way there to the Palace of Kshesinskaia. Today's movement was more impressive and organized than yesterday's: the guiding hand of the party was evident. But the feeling too was hotter today. The soldiers and workers were out for a solution of the crisis. The government was in despair, for on this second day of the demonstration its im-

potence was even more obvious than on the first. The Executive
Committee was waiting for loyal troops, and getting reports
from all sides that hostile troops were moving on the capital.
From Kronstadt, from New Peterhoff, from Krasnoe Selo, from
the Krasnaia Gorka fort, from all the nearby centers, by land
and sea, soldiers and sailors were marching in with music, with
weapons, and, worst of all, with Bolshevik standards. A number
of regiments were bringing their officers with them, just as in the
February days, pretending to be acting under their command.

"The sitting of the government was not over," relates Miliukov, "when news came from the staff that there was shooting
on the Nevsky. It was decided to transfer the sitting to staff-
headquarters. Here were Prince Lvov, Tseretelli, Minister of
Justice Pereverzev, and two assistants from the Ministry of War.
There was one moment when the situation of the government
seemed hopeless. The Preobrazhentsi,[1] the Semenovtsi,[1] and the
Izmailovtsi,[1] who had not joined the Bolsheviks, announced to the
government that they would remain 'neutral.' On Palace Square,
for the defense of headquarters, there were to be found only war-
invalids and a few hundred Cossacks." General Polovtsev published on the morning of July 4th an announcement that he was
going to cleanse Petrograd of armed hordes. The inhabitants were
strictly advised to lock their doors and not go into the streets
except in case of absolute necessity. This threatening order fell
flat. The commander of all the troops of the district was able
to bring out against the demonstrators only petty detachments
of Cossacks and junkers. In the course of the day they caused
some meaningless shootings and some bloody clashes. An ensign
of the First Don Regiment guarding the Winter Palace reported
subsequently to a commission of inquiry: "We were ordered to
disarm small groups of people who passed by, no matter who
they were, and also armed automobiles. To carry out this
order, we would run out of the palace on foot from time to time
and disarm people . . ." The ingenuous tale of the Cossack ensign correctly portrays the correlation of forces, and gives a
picture of the struggle. The "mutinous" troops came out of the
barracks in companies and battalions, taking possession of the

---

[1] Members of the regiments named Preobrazhensky, etc. Trans.

streets and squares. The government troops acted from ambush, or made raids in small detachments—that is, they functioned exactly as insurrectionary bands are supposed to. This exchange of rôles is explained by the fact that almost the whole armed force of the government was hostile to it—or at the best, neutral. The government was living by the authorization of the Executive Committee; the power of the Executive Committee derived in turn from the hopes of the masses that it might at last come to its senses and take the power.

The demonstration attained its highest point with the appearance on the Petrograd arena of the Kronstadt sailors. Delegates from the machine-gunners had been working the day before in the garrison of the naval fortress. A meeting had assembled in Yakorny Square, unexpectedly to the local organization, on the initiative of some anarchists from Petrograd. The orators had appealed to the sailors to come to the help of Petrograd. Roshal, a medical student, one of the young heroes of Kronstadt and a favorite on Yakorny Square, had tried to make a speech counselling moderation. Thousands of voices cut him off. Roshal, accustomed to a different welcome, had been compelled to leave the tribune. Not until night did it become known that in Petrograd the Bolsheviks were calling the masses into the streets. That settled the matter. The Left Social Revolutionaries—and in Kronstadt there could be no right ones—announced that they intended to take part in the demonstration. These people belonged to the same party with Kerensky, who at that very moment was at the front collecting troops to put down the demonstration. The mood at that night's session of the Kronstadt organization was such that even the timid commissar of the Provisional Government, Parchevsky, voted for the march on Petrograd. A plan was drawn up; transports were mobilized. For the necessities of this political siege, two and a half tons of arms and ammunition were given out from the stores. Crowded on tugs and passenger steamers, about 10,000 armed sailors, soldiers and workers came into the narrows of the Neva at twelve o'clock noon. Disembarking on both sides of the river, they formed a procession with bands playing and with rifles slung over their shoulders. Behind the detachments of sailors and soldiers came columns of workers from the Petrograd and Vassilievsky Island districts, interspersed with companies of the Red Guard flanked by armored cars and with innumerable standards and banners rising above them.

The Palace of Kshesinskaia was but two steps away. A little lank man, black as tar, Sverdlov—one of the basic organizers of the party elected to the Central Committee in the April conference—was standing on the balcony and in a businesslike manner, as always, shouting down instructions in his powerful bass voice: "Head of the procession, advance—close up ranks—rear ranks come closer." The demonstrators were greeted from the balcony by Lunacharsky, a man always easily infected by the moods of those around him, imposing in appearance and voice, eloquent in a declamatory way—none too reliable, but often irreplaceable. He was stormily applauded from below. But most of all the demonstrators wanted to hear Lenin himself. He had been summoned that morning, by the way, from his temporary Finland refuge. And the sailors so insisted on having their will, that in spite of ill health Lenin could not beg off. An irresistible wave of ecstasy, a genuine Kronstadt wave, greeted the leader's appearance on the balcony. Impatiently—and as always with some embarrassment—awaiting the end of the greeting, Lenin began speaking before the voices died down. His speech, which the hostile press for weeks after growled over and tore to pieces in every possible manner, consisted of a few simple phrases: a greeting to the demonstrators; an expression of confidence that the slogan, "All Power to the Soviets," would conquer in the end, an appeal for firmness and self-restraint. With renewed shouts the procession marched away to the music of the band.

Between this holiday introduction and the next stage of the proceedings, when blood began to flow, a curious episode intruded. The leaders of the Kronstadt Left Social Revolutionaries noticed only after they arrived on Mars Field a colossal standard of the Central Committee of the Bolsheviks which had appeared at the head of the procession after the stop at the Palace of Kshesinskaia. Burning with party rivalry, they demanded its removal. The Bolsheviks refused. The Social Revolutionaries then announced that they would withdraw entirely. However, none of the sailors or soldiers followed the leaders. The whole policy

35

THE ATTEMPTED COUNTER-REVOLUTION

of the Left Social Revolutionaries consisted of such capricious waverings, now comic and now tragic.

At the corner of the Nevsky and Liteiny, the rear guard of the demonstration was suddenly fired on, and several people were wounded. A more cruel fire occurred on the corner of the Liteiny and Panteleimonov Street. The leader of the Kronstadt men, Raskolnikov, tells how "like a sharp pain to the demonstrators was their uncertainty where the enemy was, from what side he was shooting." The soldiers seized their rifles. Disorderly firing began in all directions. Several were killed and wounded. Only with great difficulty was order restored in the ranks. The procession again moved forward with music, but not a trace was left of its holiday spirit. "There seemed to be a hidden enemy everywhere. Rifles no longer rested peacefully on the left shoulder, but were held ready for action."

There were no few bloody encounters on that day in different parts of the town. A certain number of them were doubtless due to misunderstanding, confusion, stray shots, panic. Such tragic accidents are one of the inevitable overhead expenses of a revolution—itself one of the overhead expenses of historic progress. But an element of bloody provocation was also indubitable in the July events. It was manifest in those very days, and was subsequently confirmed. Says Podvoisky: "When the demonstrating soldiers began to pass through the Nevsky and the surrounding sections, inhabited for the most part by the bourgeoisie, ominous indications of a clash began to appear: strange shots were fired, nobody knew whence or by whom . . . The columns were seized at first with confusion, and then the least steady and self-restrained began to open an irregular fire." In the official *Izvestia,* the Menshevik, Kantorovich, described the firing upon one of the workers' columns in the following words: "A crowd of sixty thousand workers from many factories was marching along Sadovaia Street. As they were passing by a church, a bell tolled in the steeple and as though at a signal both rifle and machine gun fire was opened from the roofs of the houses. When the crowd of workers dashed to the other side of the street, shots came also from the roofs opposite." In those attics and roofs, where in February Protopopov's "Pharaohs" had posted themselves with machine guns, members of the officers' organizations were now at work. They were attempting—and not without success—by firing on the demonstrators to spread panic and produce clashes between the different military units participating. When the houses from which shots came were searched, machine gun nests were found, and sometimes also the gunners.

The chief instigators of the bloodshed, however, were the government troops—powerless to put down the movement, but adequate for purposes of provocation. At about eight o'clock in the evening, when the demonstration was in full swing, two Cossack squadrons with flying artillery rode up as a guard for the Tauride Palace. On the way they stubbornly refused to enter into conversation with the demonstrators—in itself a bad sign. These Cossacks seized armored automobiles wherever they could and disarmed individual small groups. Cossack weapons on streets occupied by workers and soldiers seemed an intolerable challenge. Everything pointed to a clash. Near the Liteiny Bridge the Cossacks drew near to a compact mass of the enemy, who had here, on the road to the Tauride, succeeded in throwing up some sort of barrier. There was a moment of ominous silence broken by shots from neighboring houses. Then the fight began. "The Cossacks used up cartridges by the box," writes the worker, Metelev. "The workers and soldiers, scattering to shelter, or simply lying down on the sidewalk under fire, replied in the same fashion." The soldiers' fire compelled the Cossacks to retreat. Having fought their way through to the quay along the Neva, they fired three volleys from cannon—the cannon shots are also remarked upon by *Izvestia*—but under the long-range rifle fire they retired in the direction of the Tauride Palace. Running into another workers' column the Cossacks received a decisive blow. Abandoning their cannon, horses, rifles, they sought shelter in the entrances of bourgeois houses, or dispersed altogether.

That encounter on Liteiny, an actual small battle, was the biggest military episode of the July days, and stories about it are to be found in the recollections of many demonstrators. Bursin, a worker of the Ericcson factory which came out with the machine-gunners, tells how upon meeting them "the Cossacks immediately opened fire with their rifles." "Many workers were left lying

37

dead, and it was here that I was struck by a bullet, which passed through one leg and stopped in the other. . . . As a memento of the July days I have my crutch and my useless leg. . . ." In the encounter on the Liteiny seven Cossacks were killed, and nineteen wounded or knocked out by shell explosions. Among the demonstrators six were killed, and about twenty wounded. Here and there lay the dead bodies of horses.

We have an interesting testimony from the opposing camp. That same ensign, Averin, who in the morning had made guerrilla attacks on the regular troops of the mutineers, writes as follows: "At eight o'clock in the evening we received an order from General Polovtsev to go out in two companies with two field-guns to the Tauride Palace. . . . We got as far as the Liteiny Bridge, upon which I saw armed workers, soldiers and sailors. . . . With my advance detachment I approached them and asked them to surrender their weapons, but my request was not granted, and the whole gang turned and ran across the bridge to the Vyborg side. I had not yet started after them, when a small-sized soldier without shoulder straps turned round and fired at me, but missed. That shot served as a signal, and an irregular rifle fire was opened on us from all sides. The crowd sent up a shout: 'The Cossacks are shooting us.' And that was the fact: the Cossacks slid from their horses and began to shoot. They even attempted to open fire with cannon, but the soldiers let go such a hurricane of rifle fire that the Cossacks were compelled to retreat and scatter through the town." It is not at all impossible that some soldier shot at the ensign; a Cossack officer could better expect a bullet than a greeting from that July crowd. But it is easier to believe the abundant testimony to the fact that the first shots came not from the streets, but from ambush. A rank-and-file Cossack from the same squadron as the ensign has testified with conviction that the Cossacks were shot at from the direction of the District Court, and afterward from other houses in Samursky Alley and on the Liteiny. In the official organ of the Soviet, it was related that the Cossacks, before arriving at the Liteiny Bridge, were fired on with machine guns from a stone house. The worker, Metelev, asserts that when the soldiers searched that house they found in the apartment of a general who lived there a store of fire-arms,

THE "JULY DAYS": CULMINATION AND ROUT

including two machine guns with cartridges. There is nothing unlikely in that. By hook or crook quantities of all kinds of weapons had been accumulated in the hands of the commanding staff during the war period. And the temptation to sprinkle that "rabble" with a hail of lead from above must have been great. To be sure, shots did fall among the Cossacks, but there was a conviction among the July crowds that counter-revolutionists were consciously shooting at the government troops in order to incite them to ruthless action. Officers who only yesterday possessed unlimited powers, recognize no limits to trickery and cruelty when the civil war comes. Petrograd was swarming with secret and semi-secret officer organizations enjoying lofty protection and generous support. In a confidential report made by the Menshevik, Lieber, almost a month before the July Days, it was asserted that the officer-conspirators were in touch with Buchanan. Yes, and how could the diplomats of the Entente help trying to promote the speedy establishment of a strong power in Russia?

In all excesses the Liberals and Compromisers would see the hand of "Anarcho-Bolsheviks" and German agents. The workers and soldiers, on the other hand, confidently laid the responsibility for the July clashes and victims upon patriotic provocateurs. Which side was right? The judgment of the masses is of course not infallible. But it is a crude mistake to imagine that the mass is blind and credulous. Where it is touched to the quick, it gathers facts and conjectures with a thousand eyes and ears, tests rumors by its own experience, selects some and rejects others. Where versions touching a mass movement are contradictory, those appropriated by the mass itself are nearest to the truth. It is for this reason that international sycophants of the type of Hippolyte Taine, who in studying great popular movements ignore the voices of the street, and spend their time carefully collecting and sifting the empty gossip produced in drawing-rooms by moods of isolation and fear, are so useless to science.

The demonstrators again besieged the Tauride Palace and demanded their answer. At the moment the Kronstadt men arrived, some group or other brought Chernov out to them. Sensing the mood of the crowd, the word-loving minister pronounced upon this one occasion a very brief speech. Sliding over the crisis in the problem of power, he referred scornfully to the Kadets who had withdrawn from the government. "Good riddance!" he cried. Shouts interrupted him: "Then why didn't you say so before?" Miliukov even relates how "a husky worker, shaking his fist in the face of the minister, shouted furiously: 'Take the power, you son-of-a-bitch, when they give it to you.'" Even though nothing more than an anecdote, this expresses with crude accuracy the essence of the July situation. Chernov's answers have no interest; in any case, they did not win him the hearts of the Kronstadters. . . . In just two or three minutes someone ran into the hall where the Executive Committee was sitting, and yelled that the sailors had arrested Chernov and were going to end him. With indescribable excitement the Executive Committee delegated several of its prominent members, exclusively internationalists and Bolsheviks, to rescue the minister. Chernov testified subsequently before a government commission that as he was descending from the tribune he noticed in the entrance behind the columns a hostile movement of several people. "They surrounded me and would not let me through to the door. . . . A suspicious-looking person in command of the sailors who were holding me back, kept pointing to an automobile standing near. . . . At that moment Trotsky, emerging from the Tauride Palace, came up and mounting on the front of the automobile in which I found myself, made a short speech." Proposing that Chernov be released, Trotsky asked all those opposed to raise their hands. "Not one hand was raised. The group which had conducted me to the automobile then stepped aside with a disgruntled look. Trotsky, as I remember, said: 'Citizen Chernov, nobody is hindering you from going back.' . . . The general picture of this whole episode leaves no doubt in my mind that there was here a planned attempt of dark elements, acting over the heads of the general mass of the workers and soldiers, to call me out and arrest me."

A week before his own arrest Trotsky stated at a joint session of the Executive Committees, "These facts are going into history and we will try to establish them as they were. . . . I saw that a bunch of thugs was standing around the entrance. I said

40

to Lunacharsky and Riazanov that those were *okhranniki* [1] and they were trying to break into the Tauride Palace (Lunacharsky from his seat: 'That's correct.') . . . I would know them, I said, in a crowd of ten thousand." In his testimony of July 24th, Trotsky, already in solitary confinement in Kresty Prison, wrote: "I was first minded to ride out of the crowd in the automobile along with Chernov and those who wanted to arrest him, in order to avoid conflict and panic in the crowd. But Midshipman Raskolnikov, running up in extreme excitement, called to me: 'That is impossible. . . . If you ride away with Chernov, they will say tomorrow that the Kronstadters arrested him. Chernov must be freed immediately.' As soon as the trumpeter had summoned the crowd to silence, and given me a chance to make a short speech, which ended with the question: 'Those here in favor of violence, raise their hands,' Chernov found it possible to go back immediately into the palace without hindrance." The testimony of these two witnesses, who were at the same time the chief participants in the adventure, exhausts the factual side of it. But that did not in the least hinder the press hostile to the Bolsheviks from presenting the Chernov incident, together with the "attempt" at an arrest of Kerensky, as the most convincing of proofs that an armed insurrection had been organized by the Bolsheviks. There was no lack of allusion also, especially in oral agitation, to the fact that Trotsky had directed the arrest of Chernov. That version even arrived at the Tauride Palace. Chernov himself, who described the circumstances of his half-hour arrest with sufficient accuracy in a secret document addressed to a Commission of Inquiry, nevertheless refrained from making any public statement, in order not to hinder his party from creating indignation against the Bolsheviks. Moreover Chernov was a member of the government which put Trotsky in prison. The Compromisers, to be sure, might have remarked that a gang of dark conspirators would never have ventured upon so insolent a plot as to arrest a minister in the middle of a crowd in broad daylight, had they not hoped that the hostility of the mass to the "victim" would be a sufficient protection. Such indeed to a certain degree it was.

[1] Agents of the tsarist secret police.

Nobody around the automobile made of his own accord the slightest attempt to liberate Chernov. If to supplement this, somebody had somewhere arrested Kerensky, of course neither the workers nor soldiers would have grieved about that either. In this sense the moral sympathy of the masses for actual and imaginary attempts against the socialist ministers did exist and give support to the accusations against the Kronstadters. But the Compromisers were hindered from drawing this candid conclusion by their worry about the relics of their democratic prestige. While fencing themselves off with hostility from the demonstrators, they continued nevertheless to be heads of the system of workers', soldiers' and peasants' soviets in the besieged Tauride Palace.

At eight o'clock in the evening, General Polovtsev revived the hopes of the Executive Committee by telephone: two Cossack squadrons with flying artillery are on the way to the Tauride Palace. At last! But this time, too, their expectations were disappointed. Telephone calls in all directions only deepened their panic: the Cossacks had disappeared as though by evaporation, and their horses, saddles and flying artillery with them. Miliukov writes that towards evening there appeared "the first results of the governmental appeal to the troops." Thus, he adds, the 176th regiment was said to be hastening to the Tauride Palace. This remark, which sounds so accurate, is curiously characteristic of those *qui pro quo's* which inevitably arise in the first period of a civil war when the two camps are still only beginning to divide. A regiment did actually arrive at the Tauride Palace in campaign array: knapsacks and folded coats on their backs, canteens and kettles at their belts. The soldiers had got wet through on the way and were tired; they had come from Krasnoe Selo. It was, too, the 176th regiment. But they had no intention whatever of rescuing the government. Affiliated with the Mezhrayontsi, this regiment had come out under the leadership of two soldier-Bolsheviks, Levinson and Medvediev, to win the power for the soviets. It was immediately reported to the leaders of the Executive Committee, sitting so-to-speak on pins and needles, that a regiment in campaign array had arrived from a distance with its officers, and was settling down to a well-earned rest beneath the windows of the palace. Dan, dressed in the uniform of a mili-

tary physician, went to the commander with the request that he
supply sentries for the defense of the palace. The sentries were
soon actually supplied. Dan, we may imagine, communicated
this fact with satisfaction to the praesidium, and from that
source it arrived in the newspapers. Sukhanov in his "Notes"
makes fun of the submissiveness with which a Bolshevik regiment fulfilled the directions of a Menshevik leader—a further
proof, he thinks, of the "absurdity" of the July demonstration.
In reality the matter was both simpler and more complex. Having
received the request for sentries, the commander of the regiment
turned to an assistant commandant on duty in the palace, the
young lieutenant, Prigorovsky. By good or bad luck Prigorovsky
was a Bolshevik, a member of the Mezhrayonny organization,
and he immediately turned for advice to Trotsky, who was occupying a point of observation with a small group of Bolsheviks
in one of the side rooms of the palace. It goes without saying that
Prigorovsky was advised to post the sentries immediately: far
better to have friends than enemies at the entrances and exits of
the palace! Thus it happened that the 176th regiment, having
come out for a demonstration against the government, defended
the government against demonstrators. If it had really been a
question of insurrection, Lieutenant Prigorovsky with four
soldiers at his back could easily have arrested the whole Executive
Committee. But nobody thought of arresting anybody. The
soldiers of the Bolshevik regiment conscientiously fulfilled their
duty as sentries.

After the Cossack squadrons, who were the sole obstacle on the
road to the Tauride Palace, had been swept away, it seemed to
many demonstrators that victory was assured. In reality the
chief obstacle was sitting in the very palace itself. At the joint
session of the Executive Committees, which had begun at six
o'clock in the evening, there were present 90 representatives from
54 shops and factories. The five orators, who were given the floor
by agreement, began by protesting against the denunciation of
the demonstrators as counter-revolutionists in the manifestoes
of the Executive Committee. "You see what is written on our
standards," said one. "Such are the decisions adopted by the workers. . . . We demand the resignation of the ten minister-

capitalists. We have confidence in the Soviet, but not in those in whom the Soviet has confidence. . . . We demand that the land be seized immediately, that control of industry be established immediately. We demand a struggle against the famine which threatens us. . . ." Another added: "This is not a meeting, but a fully organized manifestation. We demand the transfer of the land to the peasants. We demand an annulment of the orders directed against the revolutionary army. . . . At this time when the Kadets have refused to work with you, we ask you with whom further you want to dicker. We demand that the power pass to the soviets." The propaganda slogans of the manifestation of June 18th had now become an armed ultimatum of the masses. But the Compromisers were still bound with too heavy chains to the chariot of the possessing classes. Power to the soviets? But that means first of all a bold policy of peace, a break with the Allies, a break with our own bourgeoisie, complete isolation, and in the course of a few weeks, ruin. No! A responsible democracy will not enter on the path of adventurism! "The present circumstances," said Tseretelli, "make it impossible in the Petrograd atmosphere to carry out any new decisions whatever." It remains, therefore, "to recognize the government with the staff it has left . . . to call an extraordinary session of the soviets in two weeks . . . in a place where it may be able to work without interference, best of all in Moscow."

But the course of the meeting was continually interrupted. The Putilovtsi were knocking at the door of the palace: they came up only towards evening, tired, irritated, in extreme excitement. "Tseretelli—we want Tseretelli!" This mass, thirty thousand strong, sends its representatives into the palace, somebody shouting after them that if Tseretelli won't come out of his own accord they must bring him out. It is a long way from threat to action, but nevertheless the thing is taking a rough turn, and the Bolsheviks hasten to interfere. Zinoviev subsequently reported: "Our comrades proposed that I should go out to the Putilov men . . . a sea of heads such as I never saw before. Tens of thousands of men were solidly packed together. The cries of 'Tseretelli' continued. . . . I began: 'In place of Tseretelli, it is I who have come out to you.' Laughter. That changed the mood. I was able to make quite a long speech. . . . And in conclusion I appealed to that audience to disperse peacefully at once, keeping perfect order, and under no circumstances permitting anyone to provoke them to any aggressive action. The assembled workers applauded stormily, formed in ranks, and began to disperse." This episode offers the best possible illustration of the keen discontent of the masses, their lack of any plan of attack, and the actual rôle of the Bolshevik party in the July events.

During the moments when Zinoviev was exchanging views with the Putilovtsi outdoors, a large group of their delegates, some of them with rifles, burst stormily into the hall where the Executive Committees were in session. The members of the Committees jumped up from their seats. "Some of them did not reveal a sufficient courage and self-restraint," says Sukhanov, who has left a vivid description of this dramatic moment. One of the workers, "a classic sansculotte in cap and short blue blouse without belt, with a rifle in his hand," jumped up on the speaker's tribune, trembling with excitement and wrath: " 'Comrades! How long are we workers going to stand for this treachery? You are making bargains with the bourgeoisie and the landlords. . . . Here we are, thirty thousand Putilovtsi. . . . We are going to have our will!' Cheidze, before whose nose the rifle was dancing, showed great presence of mind. Calmly leaning down from his elevation, he thrust into the quivering hand of the worker a printed manifesto: 'Here, comrade, take this, please, and I ask you to read it. It says here what the Putilov comrades should do. . . .' " In the manifesto it said nothing at all except that the demonstrators ought to go home, as otherwise they would be traitors to the revolution. And what else, indeed, was there left for the Mensheviks to say?

In the agitation under the walls of the Tauride Palace—as everywhere in the agitational whirlwind of that period—a great place was occupied by Zinoviev, an orator of extraordinary power. His high tenor voice would surprise you at first, but afterward win you with its unique music. Zinoviev was a born agitator. He knew how to infect himself with the mood of the masses, excite himself with their emotions, and find for their thoughts and feelings a somewhat prolix, perhaps, but very gripping expression. En-

emies used to call Zinoviev the greatest demagogue among the
Bolsheviks. This was their usual way of paying tribute to his
strongest trait—his ability to penetrate the heart of the demos
and play upon its strings. It is impossible to deny, however, that
being merely an agitator, and neither a theoretician nor a revolutionary strategist, Zinoviev, when he was not restrained by an
external discipline, easily slid down the path of demagoguism—
speaking not in the philistine, but in the scientific sense of that
word. That is, he showed an inclination to sacrifice enduring
interests to the success of the moment. Zinoviev's agitatorial
quick scent made him an extraordinarily valuable counsellor
whenever it was a question of estimating political conjunctures—
but nothing deeper than that. At meetings of the party he was
able to conquer, convince, bewitch, whenever he came with a
prepared political idea, tested in mass meetings and, so-to-speak,
saturated with the hopes and hates of the workers and soldiers.
On the other hand, Zinoviev was able in a hostile meeting—even
in the Executive Committee of those days—to give to the most
extreme and explosive thoughts an enveloping and insinuating
form, making his way into the minds of those who had met him
with a preconceived distrust. In order to achieve these invaluable
results, he had to have something more than a consciousness that
he was right; he had to have a tranquillizing certainty that he was
to be relieved of the political responsibility by a reliable and
strong hand. Lenin gave him this certainty. Armed with a prepared strategic formula containing the very essence of a question, Zinoviev would adroitly and astutely supplement it with
fresh exclamations, protests, demands, just now caught up by
him on the street, in the factory or the barrack. In those moments
he was an ideal mechanism of transmission between Lenin and
the masses—sometimes between the masses and Lenin. Zinoviev
always followed his teacher except in a very few cases. But the
hour of disagreement was just that hour when the fate of the
party, of the class, of the country, was to be decided. The agitator
of the revolution lacked revolutionary character. When it was
a question of conquering minds and hearts Zinoviev remained a
tireless fighter, but he suddenly lost his fighting confidence when

46

he came face to face with the necessity of action. Here he drew back from the masses—from Lenin too—responded only to voices of indecision, caught up every doubt, saw nothing but obstacles. And then his insinuating, almost feminine voice, losing its conviction, would expose his inner weakness. Under the walls of the Tauride Palace in the July days, Zinoviev was extraordinarily active, ingenious and strong. He raised the excitement of the masses to its highest note—not in order to summon them to decisive action, but, on the contrary, in order to restrain them. This corresponded to the moment and to the policy of the party. Zinoviev was wholly in his element.

The battle on the Liteiny produced a sharp break in the development of the demonstration. Nobody was now watching the procession from window or balcony. The more well-to-do part of the public, besieging the railroad stations, were leaving town. The struggle in the streets turned into a scattered skirmishing without definite aim. During the night there were hand-to-hand fights between demonstrators and patriots, unsystematic disarmings, transfers of rifles from one hand to another. Groups of soldiers from the dispersed regiments functioned helter-skelter. "Shady elements and provocateurs, attaching themselves to the soldiers, incited them to anarchistic activities," adds Podvoisky. On a hunt for those who had shot from the roofs, groups of sailors and soldiers carried out searches in the cellars. Here and there, under the pretext of a search, plunderings would occur. On the other side deeds of a pogrom character were perpetrated. Merchants furiously attacked the workers in those parts of the town where they felt strong, and ruthlessly beat them up. Says Afanassiev, a worker from the New Lessner factory: "With cries of 'Beat the Yids and Bolsheviks! Drown them!' the crowd attacked us and gave it to us good." One of the victims died in the hospital. Afanassiev himself was dragged by sailors, bruised and bloody, from the Ekaterininsky Canal.

Skirmishes, victims, fruitlessness of the struggle, and indefiniteness of practical aim—that describes the movement. The Central Committee of the Bolsheviks passed a resolution: to call on the workers and soldiers to end the demonstration. This time that appeal, which was immediately brought to the attention of the Executive Committee, met hardly any opposition at all in the lower ranks. The masses ebbed back into the suburbs, and they cherished no intention of renewing the struggle on the following day. They felt that the problem of "Power to the Soviets" was considerably more complicated than had appeared.

The siege of the Tauride Palace was conclusively raised. The nearby streets stood empty. But the vigil of the Executive Committees continued, with intermissions, with long-drawn-out speeches, meaningless and fruitless. Only afterwards did it become clear that the Compromisers were waiting for something. In neighboring rooms the delegates of the factories and regiments were still languishing. "It was already long after midnight," relates Metelev, "and we were still waiting for a 'decision'. . . . Irritated with weariness and hunger, we were wandering through the Alexandrovsky hall. . . . At four o'clock in the morning on the 5th of July our waiting came to an end. . . . Through the open doors of the chief entrance to the palace burst in a noisy crowd of officers and soldiers." The whole building was filled with the brassy sounds of the Marseillaise. The trampling of feet and the thunder of the band at that hour before the dawn, caused an extraordinary excitement in the session hall. The deputies leapt from their seats. A new danger? But Dan was in the tribune. . . . "Comrades," he shouted, "don't get excited. There is no danger. Those are regiments loyal to the revolution that have arrived." Yes, the reliable troops had arrived at last. They occupied the corridors, viciously fell upon the few workers still remaining in the palace, grabbed the weapons of those having them, arrested them and led them away. Lieutenant Kuchin, a well-known Menshevik, ascended the tribune in field uniform. The chairman, Dan, received him with open arms to the triumphal notes of the band. Choking with delight, and scorching the Lefts with their triumphant glances, the Compromisers seized each other by the hand, opened their mouths wide, and poured out their enthusiasm in the notes of the Marseillaise. "A classic picture of the beginning of a counter-revolution," angrily muttered Martov, who knew how to see and understand many things. The political meaning of this scene—recorded by Sukhanov—will become still more

48

clear if you remember that Martov belonged to the same party with Dan for whom it represented the highest triumph of the revolution.

Only now, as they observed the joy of the majority bubbling like a fountain, did the Left Wing of the Soviet begin to understand in a downright way how isolated was this highest organ of the official democracy when the genuine democracy came into the streets. For thirty-six hours these people had been alternately disappearing behind the scenes, running to a telephone booth to get in touch with headquarters or with Kerensky at the front, to demand troops, to appeal, to urge, to beseech, to dispatch agitators and ever more agitators, and again to come back and wait. The danger was past, but the fear retained its momentum. The tramping steps of the "loyal" at five o'clock in the morning therefore sounded to their ears like a symphony of liberation. At last from the tribune came frank speeches about the lucky putting down of an armed revolt, and about the necessity of settling with the Bolsheviks this time for good. That detachment which entered the Tauride Palace had not come from the front, however, as many in the heat of the moment thought. It had been hand-picked from the Petrograd garrison—chiefly from the three most backward guard battalions, the Preobrazhensky, the Semenovsky and the Izmailovsky. On the 3rd of June these regiments had declared themselves neutral, and vain efforts had been made to capture them with the authority of the government and the Executive Committee. The soldiers sat gloomily in their barracks waiting. Only in the afternoon of July 4th did the authorities at last discover an effective means of influencing them. They showed the Preobrazhentsi documents demonstrating as plain as $2 + 2 = 4$ that Lenin was a German spy. That moved them. The news flew round the regiments. Officers, members of the regimental committee, agitators of the Executive Committee, were active everywhere. The mood of the neutral battalions changed. By dawn, when there was no longer any need of them, it became possible to assemble them and lead them through the deserted streets to the empty Tauride Palace. The Marseillaise was played that night by the band of the Izmailovsky Regiment—the same reactionary regiment to which on December 3, 1905 had been intrusted the task of arresting the first Petrograd Soviet of Workers' Deputies, in session with Trotsky in the chair. The blind director of the historic drama achieves striking theatrical effects at every step without striving after them; he simply gives a loose rein to the logic of events.

*

WHEN the streets had been cleansed of the masses, the young government of the revolution stretched out its gouty limbs. Workers' representatives were arrested, weapons were seized, one district of the town was cut off from another. At about six o'clock in the morning an automobile stopped in front of the editorial office of *Pravda*.[1] It was loaded with junkers and soldiers with a machine gun which was immediately set up at the window. After the departure of these uninvited guests the office was a picture of destruction: desk drawers smashed open, the floor heaped with torn-up manuscripts, the telephones ripped loose. The sentries and employees of the office had been beaten up and arrested. A still more violent attack was made on the printing plant for whose purchase the workers had been collecting money during the last three months. The rotary presses were destroyed, monotypes ruined, linotype machines smashed to pieces. The Bolsheviks were wrong, it seems, when they accused the Kerensky government of lacking energy!

"Generally speaking, the streets had now become normal," writes Sukhanov. "There were almost no crowds or street meetings; almost all the stores were open." In the morning the summons of the Bolsheviks to stop the demonstration—the last product of the destroyed printing plant—was distributed. Cossacks and junkers were arresting sailors, soldiers and workers on the streets, and sending them to jail or to the guardhouses. In the stores and on the sidewalks the talk was of German money. They arrested everybody who made a peep in defense of the Bolsheviks. "It was no longer possible to declare Lenin an honest man—they would take you to the police station." Sukhanov as always appears as an attentive observer of what is happening on the streets of

[1] Official organ of the Bolshevik party.

the bourgeoisie, the intelligentsia, the burghers. But things looked different in the workers' districts. The factories and shops were still closed. The mood was vigilant. Rumors went round that troops had arrived from the front. The streets of the Vyborg section were filled with groups discussing what to do in case of attack. "The Red Guards and the factory youth in general," says Metelev, "were getting ready to penetrate the Peter and Paul fortress and support the detachment besieged there, concealing hand grenades in their pockets, in their shoes, under their coats. They crossed the river in row-boats and partly by the bridges." The typesetter, Smirnov, from the Kolomensky district, remembers: "I saw a tugboat with naval cadets coming down the Neva from Duderhoff and Oranienbaum. Toward two o'clock the situation cleared up in the bad sense . . . I saw how the sailors one by one were returning to Kronstadt along the back streets. . . . The story was being spread that all Bolsheviks were German spies. A vile hue and cry was raised. . . ." The historian, Miliukov, sums it all up with satisfaction: "The mood and personnel of the public on the streets had completely changed. By evening Petrograd was entirely tranquil."

So long as the troops from the front had not arrived, Petrograd headquarters, with the political co-operation of the Compromisers, continued to disguise its intentions. In the afternoon some members of the Executive Committee, with Lieber at their head, came to the Palace of Kshesinskaia for a conference with the Bolshevik leaders. That visit alone testified to a very peaceable feeling. According to the agreement then arrived at, the Bolsheviks were to induce the sailors to return to Kronstadt, to withdraw the machine gun company from Peter and Paul fortress, and to remove the patrols and armored cars from their positions. The government, on its part, promised not to permit any pogroms or repressions against the Bolsheviks, and to liberate all arrested persons except those who had engaged in criminal activities.

But the agreement did not last long. As the rumors spread about German money and the approach of troops from the front, more and more detachments and small groups were discovered in the garrison mindful of their loyalty to the government and to Kerensky. They sent delegates to the Tauride Palace or to the district staff. Finally echelons from the front actually began to arrive. The mood in compromise spheres grew fiercer and fiercer from hour to hour. The troops from the front had arrived all ready to snatch the capital with bloody hands from the agents of the Kaiser. Now that it was clear the troops were not needed, it became necessary to justify sending for them. To avoid falling under suspicion themselves, the Compromisers tried with all their might to show the commanders that Mensheviks and Social Revolutionaries belong to the same camp with them, and that Bolsheviks are a common enemy. When Kamenev tried to remind the members of the praesidium of the Executive Committee about the agreement arrived at a few hours before, Lieber answered in the tone of an iron-hearted statesman: "The correlation of forces has now changed." Lieber had learned from the popular speeches of Lassalle that cannon is an important part of a constitution. A delegation of Kronstadters headed by Raskolnikov was several times summoned before the military commission of the Executive Committee, where the demands, increasing from hour to hour, at last resolved themselves into an ultimatum from Lieber: that they should agree at once to the disarming of the Kronstadt men. "Departing from the session of the military commission," related Raskolnikov, "we renewed our conferences with Trotsky and Kamenev. Lyev Davidovich (Trotsky) advised us immediately and secretly to send the Kronstadters home. A decision was adopted to send comrades around the barracks to warn the Kronstadters that they were going to be forcibly disarmed." A majority of the Kronstadters got away in time. Only a few detachments remained in the house of Kshesinskaia and the Peter and Paul fortress.

With the knowledge and consent of the minister-socialists, Prince Lvov had already on July 4 given General Polovtsev a written order to "arrest the Bolsheviks occupying the house of Kshesinskaia, clear out the house, and occupy it with troops." At this time, after the destruction of the editorial office and printing plant, the question of the fate of the central headquarters of the Bolsheviks became a very vital one. It was necessary to put the residence in a state of defense. The Military Organization appointed Raskolnikov commander of the building. He took his

duties in a broad way—in a Kronstadt way—sent requisitions for
cannon and even ordered a small warship to enter the mouth of
the Neva. Raskolnikov subsequently explained this step in the
following manner: "These military preparations were of course
made on my part not merely with a view to self-defense, since
there was a smell in the air not only of powder but of pogroms.
. . . I also thought—and not, I believe, without foundation—
that one good warship in the mouth of the Neva would be enough
to considerably shake the resolution of the Provisional Government." All this is rather indefinite and none too serious. We may
rather assume that at five o'clock in the afternoon of July 5th the
leaders of the Military Organization, including Raskolnikov, had
not yet estimated the extent of the changes in the situation, and
hence at that moment, when the armed demonstration was compelled to beat a hasty retreat in order not to turn into an armed
insurrection imposed by the enemy, some of the military leaders
made certain accidental and not well thought-out steps forward.
The young Kronstadt leaders did in this first action over-reach
themselves. But can you make a revolution without the help of
people who over-reach themselves? Indeed, does not a certain
percentage of light-mindedness enter as a constituent part into
all great human deeds? This time it came to nothing more than
instructions, and these moreover were soon annulled by Raskolnikov himself. During this time more and more alarming news
was pouring into the place. One man had seen in the windows of
a house on the opposite shore of the Neva machine guns aimed at
the Palace of Kshesinskaia; another had observed a column of
armored automobiles traveling in the same direction; a third
brought news of the approach of a detachment of Cossacks. Two
members of the Military Organization were sent to the commander of the district to negotiate. Polovtsev assured the emissaries that the raid on *Pravda* had been made without his knowledge, and that no repressions were in preparation against the
Military Organization. In reality he was only awaiting sufficient
reinforcements from the front.

During this time, while Kronstadt was retreating, the Baltic
Fleet as a whole was still only getting ready to advance. The
principal part of the fleet was in the Finland waters, with a total

of about 70,000 sailors. An army corps was also located in Finland, and ten thousand Russian workers were in the port factories of Helsingfors. That was a good-sized fist of the revolution. The pressure of the sailors and soldiers was so irresistible that even the Helsingfors committee of the Social Revolutionaries had come out against the Coalition, and in consequence all the soviet bodies of the fleet and army in Finland had unanimously demanded that the Executive Committee take the power. In support of their demand the Baltic men were ready at any moment to move into the mouth of the Neva. They were restrained, however, by the fear of weakening the naval line of defense, and making it easy for the German fleet to attack Kronstadt and Petrograd.

But here something completely unexpected occurred. The Central Committee of the Baltic Fleet—the so-called Centrobalt—called on the 4th of July an extraordinary session of the ship committees at which the president, Dybenko, read two secret orders just received by the fleet commander and signed by the assistant minister of the navy Dudarev. The first obliged the Admiral Verderevsky to send four destroyers to Petrograd to prevent by force the landing of sailors from the side of Kronstadt; the second demanded of the commander of the fleet that he should not on any pretext permit the departure of ships from Helsingfors to Kronstadt, not hesitating to sink disobedient ships with submarines. Finding himself between two fires, and worried most of all about his own head, the admiral anticipated events by turning over the telegram to the Centrobalt with the announcement that he would not carry out the orders even if countersigned by the Centrobalt. The reading of the telegram startled the sailors. To be sure, they had been ready on any pretext to abuse Kerensky and the Compromisers in no kind-hearted terms. But up to now this had been in their eyes an intra-soviet struggle. A majority in the Executive Committee belonged to the same parties as the majority in the Regional Committee of Finland which had just come out for a soviet government. It seemed clear enough that neither Mensheviks nor Social Revolutionaries could possibly approve the sinking of ships which had come out for the power of the Executive Committee. How could

an old naval officer like Dudarev get mixed up in a family quarrel
of the soviets, turning it into a naval battle? Only yesterday the
big battleships had been officially regarded as the bulwark of the
revolution—and this in contrast to the backward destroyers and
submarines, which had hardly been touched by revolutionary
propaganda. Could it be that the government now seriously intended to sink the battleships with the help of the submarines?

These facts simply could not find their way into the stubborn skulls of the sailors. That order which justifiably seemed
to them to belong to the realm of nightmare was nevertheless a
legitimate July harvest of the March sowing. Already in April
the Mensheviks and Social Revolutionaries had begun to appeal
to the provinces against Petrograd, to the soldiers against the
workers, to the cavalry against the machine-gunners. They had
given the troops representative privileges in the soviets above the
factories; they had favored the small and scattered enterprises as
against the giants of the metal industry. Themselves representing
the past, they had sought support in backwardness of all kinds.
With the ground slipping under their feet, they were now inciting the rear guard against the advance guard. Politics has its
own logic, especially in times of revolution. Pressed from all sides,
the Compromisers had found themselves obliged to direct Admiral Verderevsky to sink the more advanced battleships. Unfortunately for the Compromisers, the backward ones upon
whom they were relying were more and more striving to catch
up to those in advance. The submarine command was no less indignant at Dudarev's orders than the commanders of the battleships.

The men at the head of Centrobalt were not at all of the
Hamlet type. They lost no time in passing a resolution, together
with the members of the ship committees, to send immediately
to Petrograd the squadron destroyer *Orpheus*, designated for the
sinking of the Kronstadters, in the first place to get information as to what was happening there, and in the second "to
arrest the Assistant-Minister of the Navy, Dudarev." However
unexpected this decision may seem, it nevertheless clearly reveals
to what an extent the Baltic sailors were still inclined to regard
the Compromisers as a private opponent in contrast to any old

Dudarev whom they considered a public enemy. The *Orpheus* entered the mouth of the Neva twenty-four hours after the ten thousand armed Kronstadters had moored their vessels there. But "the correlation of forces had changed." For a whole day the crew was not permitted to disembark. Only in the evening a delegation consisting of sixty-seven sailors from the Centrobalt and the ship's crews was admitted to the joint session of the Executive Committees, then engaged in casting up the first balance of the July Days. The victors were luxuriating in their new victory. The spokesman, Voitinsky, was complacently describing the hours of weakness and humiliation, in order the more sharply to depict the triumph which followed. "The first unit which came to our help," he said, "was the armored cars. We firmly intended in case of violence from the side of the armed gang to open fire. . . . Seeing the extent of the danger threatening the revolution we issued an order to certain units (on the front) to entrain and come to the capital. . . ." A majority of that high assembly were breathing out hatred for the Bolsheviks, and especially for the sailors. It was in this atmosphere that the Baltic delegates arrived armed with an order for the arrest of Dudarev. With a wild yelp, a pounding of fists on tables, and a stamping of feet, the victors greeted the reading of the resolution of the Baltic fleet. Arrest Dudarev? Why, this gallant captain of the first rank was only fulfilling his sacred duty to the revolution, which they, the sailors, the rebels, the counter-revolutionists, were stabbing in the back! In a special resolution the joint session solemnly declared its solidarity with Dudarev. The sailors looked at the orators and at each other with startled eyes. Only at this moment did they begin to understand what had been taking place before their eyes. The next day the whole delegation was arrested, and completed its political education in jail! Immediately after that, the president of the Centrobalt, the non-commissioned naval officer Dybenko, who had followed them up, was arrested, and after him also Admiral Verderevsky who had been summoned to the capital to explain matters.

On the morning of the 6th the workers went back to work. Only the troops summoned from the front were now demonstrating in the streets. Agents of the Intelligence Service were examining passports and making arrests right and left. A young worker, Voinov, who was distributing the "Pravda Leaflet," published in place of the destroyed Bolshevik paper, was killed in the streets by a gang—perhaps composed of these same intelligence men. The Black Hundred elements were acquiring a taste for the putting down of revolts. Plundering, violence, and in some places shooting continued in different parts of the city. In the course of the day echelon after echelon arrived from the front—the Cavalier Division, the Don Cossack regiment, the Uhlan division, the Izborsky, the Malorossisky, the Dragoon regiment, and others. "The Cossack divisions, arriving in great numbers," writes Gorky's paper, "were in a very aggressive mood." Machine gun fire was opened on the newly arrived Izborsky regiment in two parts of the city. In both cases the machine guns were found in an attic; those guilty were not discovered. In other places, too, the arriving troops were shot at. The deliberate madness of this shooting deeply disturbed the workers. It was clear that experienced provocateurs were greeting the soldiers with lead with a view to anti-Bolshevik inoculation. The workers were eager to explain this to the arriving soldiers, but they were denied access to them. For the first time since the February days the junker or the officer stood between the worker and soldier.

The Compromisers joyfully welcomed the arriving regiments. At a meeting of representatives of the troops, in the presence of a great number of officers and junkers, our friend Voitinsky unctuously explained: "Now along Milliony Street troops and armored cars are traveling towards Palace Square to place themselves at the disposal of General Polovtsev, and this is our real strength upon which we rely." To act as a political covering, four socialist assistants were appointed to the commander of the district: Avksentiev and Gotz from the Executive Committee, Skobelev and Chernov from the Provisional Government. But that did not save the commander. Kerensky subsequently boasted to the White Guards that on returning from the front in the July Days, he had discharged General Polovtsev for "irresolution."

Now at last it was possible to solve the so long postponed problem: to clean up that wasp's nest of Bolsheviks in the house

of Kshesinskaia. In social life in general, and particularly in a
time of revolution, secondary facts which act upon the imagination sometimes acquire through their symbolic meaning an
enormous significance. Thus a disproportionately large place in
the struggle against the Bolsheviks was occupied by the question
of the "seizure" by Lenin of the Palace of Kshesinskaia, a court
ballerina famous not so much for her art as for her relations with
the male representatives of the Romanov dynasty. Her private
palace was the fruit of these relations—the foundation of which
was laid down, it seems, by Nicholas II when still heir to the
throne. Before the war, people gossiped with a tinge of envious
respectfulness about this den of luxury, spurs, and diamonds
located opposite the Winter Palace. But in wartime they more
frequently remarked: "Stolen goods." The soldiers expressed
themselves even more accurately. Arriving at a critical age, the
ballerina took up a career in patriotism. The outspoken Rodzianko
has this to say on that subject: "The high commander-in-chief
(the Grand Duke Nikolai Nikolaievich) remarked that he was
aware of the participation and influence in artillery matters of
the ballerina, Kshesinskaia, through whom various firms had received orders." It is no wonder if after the revolution the abandoned Palace of Kshesinskaia failed to awaken benevolent feelings among the people. In those times when the revolution was
making an insatiable demand for quarters, the government never
dared lay its hands on a single private residence. To requisition
the peasants' horses for the war—that is one thing; to requisition
vacant palaces for the revolution—that is quite another. But the
masses of the people saw it otherwise.

On a search for suitable quarters, a reserve armored-car division had run into the residence of Kshesinskaia in the first days
of March, and occupied it: the ballerina had an excellent garage.
The division gladly turned over the upper story of the building
to the Petrograd committee of the Bolsheviks. The friendship
of the Bolsheviks with this armored-car division supplemented
their friendship with the machine-gunners. The occupation of the
palace, which occurred a few weeks before the arrival of Lenin,
passed almost unnoticed at first. The indignation against the
usurpers grew with the growth of the influence of the Bolsheviks.

The wild stories in the newspapers about how Lenin was occupying the boudoir of the ballerina, and how all the decorations of the palace had been shattered to pieces and torn up, were mere lies. Lenin lived in the modest apartment of his sister. The ballerina's furnishings were put away by the commandant of the building and kept under seal. Sukhanov, who visited the palace at the time of Lenin's arrival, has left an interesting description of the quarters. "The chambers of the famous ballerina had a rather strange and inappropriate look; the exquisite ceilings and walls did not harmonize at all with the unpretentious furnishings, the primitive tables, chairs, and benches set casually about according to the demands of business. In general there was very little furniture. Kshesinskaia's movable property had been put away somewhere. . . ." Discreetly avoiding the question of the armored-car division, the press represented Lenin as guilty of an armed seizure of the house from the hands of a defenseless devotee of art. This theme was developed in leading editorials and feuilletons. Tattered workers and soldiers among those velvets and silks and beautiful rugs! All the drawing-rooms of the capital shuddered with moral indignation. As once the Girondists held the Jacobins responsible for the September murders, the disappearance of mattresses in the barracks, and the campaign for an agrarian law, so now the Kadets and democrats accused the Bolsheviks of undermining the pillars of human morality and hawking and spitting on the polished floors of the Palace of Kshesinskaia. The dynastic ballerina became a symbol of culture trampled under the hoofs of barbarism. This apotheosis gave wings to the lady herself, and she complained to the court. The court decided that the Bolsheviks should be removed from the premises. But that was not quite so easy to do. "The armored cars on duty in the courtyard looked sufficiently imposing," remembers Zalezhsky, then a member of the Petrograd committee. Moreover the Machine Gun Regiment, and other units too, were ready in case of need to back up the armored cars. On May 25, the bureau of the Executive Committee, upon a complaint from the ballerina's lawyer, recognized that "the interests of the revolution demand submission to the decisions of the court." Beyond this platonic aphorism, however, the Compromisers did not venture—to the extreme distress of the ballerina, who was not by nature inclined to platonism.

The Central Committee, the Petrograd committee, and the Military Organization, continued to work in the palace side by side. "A continuous mass of people crowded into the house of Kshesinskaia," says Raskolnikov. "Some would come on business to this or that secretariat, others to the literature department, others to the editorial offices of the soldiers' *Pravda,* others to some meeting or other. Meetings took place very often, sometimes continually—either in the spacious wide hall below, or in the room upstairs with a long table which had evidently been the dining-room of the ballerina." From the palace balcony, above which waved the impressive banner of the Central Committee, orators carried on a continuous mass meeting, not only by day but by night. Often out of the darkness some military detachment would approach the building, or some crowd of workers with a demand for an orator. Accidental groups of citizens would also stop before the balcony, their curiosity aroused by some uproar in the newspapers. During the critical days hostile manifestations would draw near to the building for a time, demanding the arrest of Lenin and the driving out of the Bolsheviks. Under the streams of people flowing past the palace one felt the seething depths of the revolution. The house of Kshesinskaia reached its apogee in the July days. "The chief headquarters of the movement," says Miliukov, "was not the Tauride Palace, but Lenin's citadel, the house of Kshesinskaia with its classic balcony." The putting down of the demonstration led fatally to the break-up of this staff headquarters of the Bolsheviks.

At three o'clock in the morning there advanced against the house of Kshesinskaia and the Peter and Paul fortress—separated from each other by a strip of water—the reserve battalion of the Petrograd regiment, a machine gun detachment, a company of Semenovtsi, a company of Preobrazhentsi, the training squad of the Volynsky regiment, two cannon, and a detachment of eight armored cars. At seven o'clock in the morning an assistant of the commander of the district, the Social Revolutionary Kuzmin, demanded that the house be vacated. Not wishing to surrender their weapons, the Kronstadters, of whom there remained only a hundred and twenty in the palace, dashed across to the Peter and Paul fortress. When the government troops occupied the house, they found nobody there but a few employees. There then remained the problem of the Peter and Paul fortress. Young Red Guards, as we remember, had gone over from the Vyborg district in order in case of need to help the sailors. "On the fortress walls," one of them relates, "stood a number of cannon, evidently set up by the sailors in case anything should happen. . . . It began to look like bloody doings." But diplomatic negotiations settled the problem peacefully. At the direction of the Central Committee, Stalin proposed to the compromise leaders to adopt joint measures for the bloodless termination of the action of the Kronstadt men. In company with the Menshevik, Bogdanov, he had no difficulty in persuading the sailors to accept Lieber's ultimatum of the day before. When the government armored cars approached the fortress, a deputation came out of its gates announcing that the garrison would submit to the Executive Committee. The weapons given up by the sailors and soldiers were carried away in trucks. The disarmed sailors were sent to the barges for return to Kronstadt. The surrender of the fortress may be considered the concluding episode of the July movement. A bicycle brigade from the front occupied the house of Kshesinskaia and the Peter and Paul fortress. This brigade in its turn, will go over on the eve of the October revolution, to the Bolsheviks.

CHAPTER III

COULD THE BOLSHEVIKS HAVE SEIZED THE POWER IN JULY?

THE demonstration forbidden by the government and the Executive Committee had been a colossal one. On the second day not less than five hundred thousand people participated. Sukhanov, who cannot find words strong enough for the "blood and filth" of the July Days, nevertheless writes: "Political results aside, it was impossible not to look with admiration upon that amazing movement of the popular masses. Even while deeming it fatal, one could not but feel a rapture in its gigantic spontaneous scope." According to the reckonings of the Commission of Inquiry, 29 men were killed and 114 wounded—about an equal number on each side.

That the movement had begun from below, irrespective of the Bolsheviks—to a certain extent against their will—was at first recognized even by the Compromisers. But on the night of July 3, and yet more on the following day, official opinion began to change. The movement was declared an insurrection, the Bolsheviks its organizers. "Under the slogan, 'All Power to the Soviets,'" writes Stankevich, a man close to Kerensky, "there occurred an organized insurrection of the Bolsheviks against the majority of the soviets, consisting at that time of the defensist parties." This charge of organizing an insurrection was something more than a method of political struggle. During the month of June those people had well convinced themselves of the strong influence of the Bolsheviks on the masses, and they now simply refused to believe that a movement of workers and soldiers could have surged up over the heads of the Bolsheviks. Trotsky tried to explain the situation at a session of the Executive Committee: "They accuse us of creating the mood of the masses; that is wrong, we only tried to formulate it." In books published by their enemies after the October revolution, particularly in Sukhanov, you will find it asserted that the Bolsheviks covered up their actual aim only in consequence of the defeat of the July insurrection, hiding behind the spontaneous movement of the masses. But could one possibly conceal, like a buried treasure, the plans of an armed insurrection which drew into its whirlpool hundreds of thousands of people? Were not the Bolsheviks compelled in October to summon the masses quite openly to insurrection, and to make preparations for it before the eyes of all? If no one discovered such a plan in July, it is only because there was none. The entry of the machine-gunners and Kronstadters into the Peter and Paul fortress with the consent of its permanent garrison—upon which "seizure" the Compromisers especially insist—was not at all an act of armed insurrection. That building situated on an island—a prison rather than a military post—might perhaps serve as a refuge for men in retreat, but it offers nothing whatever to attacking forces. In making their way to the Tauride Palace the demonstrators passed calmly by the most important government buildings—to occupy which the Putilov detachment of the Red Guard would have been an adequate force. They took possession of the Peter and Paul fortress exactly as they took possession of the streets, the sentry posts, the public squares. An additional motive was its nearness to the Palace of Kshesinskaia to whose aid it could have come in case of need.

The Bolsheviks made every effort to reduce the July movement to a demonstration. But did it not, nevertheless, by the very logic of things transcend these limits? This political question is harder to answer than the criminal indictment. Appraising the July Days immediately after they occurred, Lenin wrote: "An anti-government demonstration—that would be the most formally accurate description of the events. But the point is that this was no ordinary demonstration. It was something considerably more than a demonstration and less than a revolution." When the masses once get hold of some idea, they want to realize it. Although trusting the Bolshevik party, the workers, and still more the soldiers, had not yet acquired a conviction that they ought to come out only upon the summons of the party and under its leadership. The experiences of February and April had taught them rather the opposite. When Lenin said in May that the workers and

63

peasants were a hundred times more revolutionary than the party, he undoubtedly generalized this February and April experience. But the masses had also generalized the experience in their own way. They were saying to themselves: "Even the Bolsheviks are dawdling and holding us back." The demonstrators were entirely ready in the July Days to liquidate the official government if that should seem necessary in the course of business. In case of resistance from the bourgeoisie they were ready to employ arms. To that extent there was an element of armed insurrection. If, in spite of this, it was not carried through even to the middle—to say nothing of the end—that is because the Compromisers confused the whole picture.

In the first volume of this work we described in detail the paradox of the February régime. The petty bourgeois democrats, Mensheviks and Social Revolutionaries received the power from the hands of the revolutionary people. They had not set themselves the task of winning it. They had not conquered the power. They were put in possession of it against their will. Against the will of the masses, they tried to hand over this power to the imperialist bourgeoisie. The people did not trust the Liberals, but they trusted the Compromisers. The Compromisers, however, did not trust themselves. And in this they were in a way right. Even in turning over the whole power to the bourgeoisie, the democrats had continued to be somebody. But once they had seized the power in their own hands, they would have become nothing at all. From the democrats the power would almost automatically have slid into the hands of the Bolsheviks. This was inevitable, for it was involved in the organic insignificance of the Russian democracy.

The July demonstrators wanted to turn over the power to the soviets, but for this the soviets had to agree to take it. Even in the capital, however, where a majority of the workers and the active elements of the garrison were already for the Bolsheviks, a majority in the Soviet—owing to that law of inertia which applies to every representative system—still belonged to those petty bourgeois parties who regarded an attempt against the power of the bourgeoisie as an attempt against themselves. The workers and soldiers felt clearly enough the contrast between their moods and the policy of the Soviet—that is, between their today and their yesterday. In coming out for a government of the soviets, they by no means gave their confidence to the compromisist majority in those soviets. But they did not know how to settle with this majority. To overthrow it by violence would have meant to dissolve the soviets instead of giving them the power. Before they could find the path to a change of the personal composition of the soviets, the workers and soldiers tried to subject the soviets to their will by the method of direct action.

In a proclamation of the two Executive Committees on the subject of the July Days, the Compromisers indignantly appealed to the workers and soldiers against the demonstrators, who, they alleged, had "attempted by force of arms to impose their will upon your elected representatives." As though the demonstrators and the electors were not merely two names for the same workers and soldiers! As though electors have not a right to impose their will upon those they have elected! And as though this will consisted of anything else but the demand that they should fulfill their duty—namely, get possession of the power in the interests of the people! The masses concentrated around the Tauride Palace were shouting into the ears of the Executive Committee the very same phrase which that nameless worker had thrust up at Chernov with his horny fist: "Take the power when they give it to you!" In answer the Compromisers sent for the Cossacks. These gentlemen of the democracy preferred a civil war against the people to a bloodless transfer of power into their own hands. It was the White Guards who fired the first shots, but the political atmosphere of the civil war was created by the Mensheviks and Social Revolutionaries.

Running into this armed resistance from the very institution to which they wished to turn over the power, the workers and soldiers lost a clear sense of their goal. From their mighty mass movement the political axis had been torn out. The July campaign was thus reduced to a demonstration partially carried out with the instruments of armed insurrection. Or, it would be equally true to say: It was a semi-insurrection, directed toward goals which did not permit other methods than those proper to a demonstration.

Although declining the power, the Compromisers had not wholly given it over to the Liberals. This was both because they feared them—the petty bourgeois always fears the big bourgeois—and because they feared for them. A pure Kadet ministry would have been immediately overthrown by the masses. Moreover, as Miliukov rightly points out, "In struggling against independent armed actions, the Executive Committee of the Soviet was fortifying its own right, proclaimed in the tumultuous days of the 20th and 21st of April, to deploy at its own discretion the armed forces of the Petrograd garrison." The Compromisers were continuing to steal the power from under their own pillows. In order to offer armed resistance to those who had written on their banners "All Power to the Soviets," the Soviet was obliged actually to concentrate the power in its hands.

The Executive Committee went even farther in the July Days: it formally proclaimed its sovereignty. "If the revolutionary democracy deemed necessary a transfer of all power into the hands of the soviets," says their resolution of July 4, "the decision of that question could belong only to a plenary session of the Executive Committees." While declaring the demonstration in favor of the soviet power a counter-revolutionary insurrection, the Executive Committee thus at the same time constituted itself the supreme power, and decided the fate of the government.

When at dawn on the 5th of July the "loyal troops" entered the Tauride Palace, their commander reported that his detachment submitted to the Executive Committee wholly and without reserve. Not a word about the government! But the rebels also wanted to submit to the Executive Committee in the character of a sovereign power. In surrendering the Peter and Paul fortress, the garrison considered it sufficient to announce their submission to the Executive Committee. Nobody demanded a submission to the official authority. The troops summoned from the front also placed themselves wholly at the disposal of the Executive Committee. Why, in that case, was there any shedding of blood?

If this conflict had taken place toward the end of the Middle Ages, both sides in slaughtering each other would have cited the same text from the Bible. Formalist historians would afterwards have come to the conclusion that they were fighting about the

correct interpretation of texts. The craftsmen and illiterate peasants of the Middle Ages had a strange passion, as is well known,
for allowing themselves to be killed in the cause of philological
subtleties in the Revelations of Saint John, just as the Russian Separatists submitted to extermination in order to decide the question whether one should cross himself with two fingers or three.
In reality there lies hidden under such symbolic formulae—in the
Middle Ages no less than now—a conflict of life interests which
we must learn to uncover. The very same verse of the Evangelist
meant serfdom for some, freedom for others.

But there is a far more fresh and modern analogy. In the June
days of 1848 in France, the same shout went up on both sides of
the barricades: "Long live the Republic!" To the petty bourgeois
idealist, therefore, the June fight has seemed a misunderstanding
caused by the inattention of one side, the hot-headedness of the
other. In reality the bourgeoisie wanted a republic for themselves,
the workers a republic for everybody. Political slogans serve
oftener to disguise interests than to call them by name.

In spite of the paradoxical character of the February régime
—scribbled all over to boot with Marxian and Narodnik hieroglyphics by the Compromisers—the actual inter-relation of
classes is easy enough to see. It is only necessary to keep in view the
twofold nature of the compromise parties. The educated petty
bourgeois oriented himself upon the workers and peasants, but
hobnobbed with the titled landlords and owners of sugar factories. While forming a part of the soviet system, through which
the demands of the lower classes found their way up to the official
state, the Executive Committee served at the same time as a political screen for the bourgeoisie. The possessing classes "submitted"
to the Executive Committee so long as it pushed the power over
to their side. The masses submitted to the Executive Committee,
in so far as they hoped it might become an instrument of the rule
of workers and peasants. Contradictory class tendencies were intersecting in the Tauride Palace and they both covered themselves
with the name of the Executive Committee—the one through unconscious trustfulness, the other with cold-blooded calculation.
The struggle was about nothing more or less than the question
who was to rule the country, the bourgeoisie or the proletariat?

But if the Compromisers did not want to take the power, and the bourgeoisie did not have the strength to take it, maybe the Bolsheviks could have seized the helm in July? In the course of those two critical days the power in Petrograd completely dropped from the hands of the governmental institutions. The Executive Committee then felt for the first time its own complete impotence. In such circumstances it would have been easy enough for the Bolsheviks to seize the power. They could have seized the power, too, at certain individual points in the provinces. That being the case, was the Bolshevik party right in refraining from an insurrection? Might they not, fortifying themselves in the capital and in certain industrial districts, have subsequently extended their rule to the whole country? That is an important question. Nothing gave more help to the triumph of imperialism and reaction in Europe at the end of the war than those few months of Kerenskyism, exhausting revolutionary Russia and immeasurably damaging her moral authority in the eyes of the warring armies and of the toiling masses of Europe who had been hopefully awaiting some new word from the revolution. To shorten the birth pains of the proletarian revolution by four months would have been an immense gain. The Bolsheviks would have received the country in a less exhausted condition; the authority of the revolution in Europe would have been less undermined. This would not only have given the soviets an immense predominance in conducting the negotiations with Germany, but would have exerted a mighty influence on the fortunes of war and peace in Europe. The prospect was only too enticing!

But nevertheless the leadership of the party was completely right in not taking the road of armed insurrection. It is not enough to seize the power—you have to hold it. When in October the Bolsheviks did decide that their hour had struck, the most difficult days came after the seizure of power. It requires the highest tension of the forces of the working class to sustain the innumerable attacks of an enemy. In July even the Petrograd workers did not yet possess that preparedness for infinite struggle. Although able to seize the power, they nevertheless offered it to the Executive Committee. The proletariat of the capital, although inclining toward the Bolsheviks in its overwhelming majority, had still not broken the February umbilical cord attaching it to the Compromisers. Many still cherished the illusion that everything could be obtained by words and demonstrations—that by frightening the Mensheviks and Social Revolutionaries you could get them to carry out a common policy with the Bolsheviks. Even the advanced sections of the class had no clear idea by which roads it was possible to arrive at the power. Lenin wrote soon after: "The real mistake of our party on the 3rd and 4th of July, as events now reveal, was only this . . . that the party still considered possible a peaceful development of the political transformation by way of a change of policy on the part of the soviets. In reality the Mensheviks and Social Revolutionaries had already tangled and bound themselves up by compromisism with the bourgeoisie, and the bourgeoisie had become so counterrevolutionary, that there was no longer any use talking about a peaceful development."

If the proletariat was not politically homogeneous and not sufficiently resolute, still less so was the peasant army. By its conduct on the 3rd and 4th of July the garrison made it wholly possible for the Bolsheviks to seize the power, but nevertheless there were neutral units which by the evening of the 4th were decisively inclining to the side of the patriotic party. By July 5, the neutral regiments had taken their stand with the Executive Committee, and the regiments tending towards Bolshevism were striving to assume a color of neutrality. It was this, far more than the belated arrival of troops from the front, that gave a free hand to the authorities. If the Bolsheviks in the heat of the moment had seized the power on the evening of July 4th, the Petrograd garrison would not itself have held it, and would have hindered the workers from defending it against the inevitable blow from without.

The situation looked still less favorable in the active army. The struggle for peace and land had made the army extremely hospitable, especially since the June offensive, to the slogans of the Bolsheviks, but the so-called "spontaneous" Bolshevism of the soldier was not in the least identified in his consciousness with a definite party, with its Central Committee, or its leaders. The soldiers' letters of those times clearly depict this condition of the army. "Remember, Messers Ministers, and all you chief leaders," writes the crooked hand of a soldier from the front, "we don't understand very well about parties, only that the future and the past are not far off. The Tzar sent you to Siberia and sat you in jail, and we will sit you on our bayonets." In these lines an extreme bitterness against those higher up who are deceiving the soldiers, is united with a recognition of the soldiers' own helplessness. "We don't understand very well about parties." The army mutinied continually against the war and the officers, making use of slogans from the Bolshevik dictionary. But it was far from ready to raise an insurrection in order to give the power to the Bolshevik party. For the subduing of Petrograd the government picked out reliable detachments from the troops nearest the capital without encountering active resistance from other detachments, and it transported the echelons without resistance from the railroad workers. The discontented, rebellious, easily excitable army was still formless politically. It still contained too few compact Bolshevik nuclei capable of giving a single direction to the thought and activity of the crumbly soldier mass.

On the other hand the Compromisers, in order to turn the front against Petrograd and the peasant rear, made successful use of that poisoned weapon which in March the reaction had so carefully tried to bring to bear against the Soviet. The Social Revolutionaries and Mensheviks said to the soldiers on the front: The Petrograd garrison, under the influence of the Bolsheviks, is refusing to send replacements; the workers do not want to work for the necessities of the front; if the peasant listens to the Bolsheviks and seizes the land now, nothing will be left for the men at the front. The soldiers needed some supplementary experience before they would understand for whom the government was saving the land, whether for the peasants at the front or the landlords.

Between Petrograd and the active army stood the provinces. Their reaction to the July events serves in itself as a very important *a posteriori* criterion for deciding the question whether the Bolsheviks were right in refraining from a direct struggle for power in July. Even in Moscow the pulse of the revolution was incomparably weaker than in Petrograd. In the session of the

Moscow committee of the Bolsheviks stormy debates arose. Individuals belonging to the extreme left wing of the party—such, for example, as Bubnov—proposed that they occupy the Post Office, the telegraph and telephone stations, the editorial offices of Russkoe Slovo—that is, that they take the road of insurrection. The committee, very moderate in its general spirit, decisively rejected these proposals, considering that the Moscow masses were not in the least ready for such action. It was nevertheless decided to hold a demonstration in spite of the veto of the Soviet. A considerable crowd of workers marched to Skobelevsky Square with the same slogans as in Petrograd, but with far from the same enthusiasm. The garrison reacted by no means unanimously; individual units joined the procession, but only one of them came fully armed. The artillery soldier, Davidovsky, who subsequently took a serious part in the October struggles, testifies in his memoirs that Moscow was not prepared for the July Days, and that the leaders of the demonstration were left with a bad taste in their mouths by its unsuccess.

In Ivanovo-Voznesensk, the textile capital where the soviet was already under the leadership of the Bolsheviks, news came of the events in Petrograd, accompanied by a rumor that the Provisional Government had fallen. At a night session of the Executive Committee it was resolved, as a preliminary measure, to establish control over the telephone and telegraph. Work was stopped in the factories on July 6. Forty thousand took part in the demonstration, many of them armed. When it was learned that the Petrograd demonstration had not led to victory, the Ivanovo-Voznesensk soviet hastily beat a retreat.

In Riga, under influence of the news from Petrograd, a clash occurred on the night of July 6 between Lettish sharpshooters inclined towards Bolshevism and the "Battalion of Death," the patriotic battalion being compelled to retire. The Riga soviet adopted on that same night a resolution in favor of a government of the soviets. Two days later a similar resolution was adopted in Ekaterinburg, the capital of the Urals. The fact that this slogan of Soviet Power, which had been advanced in the early months only in the name of the party, became henceforward the program of individual local soviets indubitably meant a gigantic step for-

71

ward. But from resolutions in favor of a Soviet Power to insurrection under the banner of the Bolsheviks, there was still a considerable road to travel.

In certain parts of the country the Petrograd events served as a stimulus to set off acute conflicts of a private character. In Nizhni-Novgorod, where some soldiers on furlough had long been resisting their entrainment for the front, junkers sent from Moscow to enforce orders aroused the indignation of two local regiments by their violence. Shooting followed, and men were killed and wounded. The junkers surrendered and were disarmed. The authorities disappeared. A punitive expedition set out from Moscow with three kinds of troops. At its head was the commander of the Moscow district, the impulsive Colonel Verkhovsky—a future War Minister of Kerensky—and the president of the Moscow soviet, the old Menshevik Khinchuk, a man of no military temper, the future head of the cooperatives, and afterward soviet ambassador in Berlin. However, they found nobody to subdue, as a committee elected by the mutinous soldiers had fully restored order by the time they arrived.

In Kiev, during approximately the same hours of the same night, and on the same ground—refusal to go to the front—soldiers of the regiment named after the Hetman Polubotko mutinied to the number of five thousand, seized a store of weapons, occupied the fortress and the district headquarters, and arrested the commander and the head of the militia. The panic in the city lasted several hours, until by the combined efforts of the military authorities, a committee of social organizations, and the institutions of the central Ukrainian Rada, the arrestees were liberated and the greater part of the mutinous troops disarmed.

In far away Krasnoyarsk the Bolsheviks, thanks to the mood of the garrison, felt so strong that, in spite of the wave of reaction already gathering in the country, they held a demonstration on July 9, in which eight to ten thousand people took part, a majority of them soldiers. A detachment of 400 soldiers with artillery was moved against Krasnoyarsk from Irkutsk, led by the district military commander, the Social Revolutionary, Krakovetsky. During the two days of conferences and negotiations necessitated by the two-power régime, the punitive detachment became so

demoralized by the soldiers' agitation that the commissar hastened to send them back to Irkutsk. But Krasnoyarsk was upon
the whole an exception.

In a majority of the provinces and county seats, the situation
was incomparably less favorable. In Samara, for instance, the
local Bolshevik organization, upon receiving news of the fights in
the capital, "awaited the signal for action, although there was almost nobody they could count on." One of the local members of
the party says: "The workers had begun to sympathize with the
Bolsheviks" but it was impossible to hope that they would go into
a fight; it was still less possible to count on the soldiers. As for the
Bolshevik organizations: "They were altogether weak; we were a
mere handful. In the soviet of workers deputies there were a few
Bolsheviks, but in the soldiers' soviet there was, it seems, not a
single one; and moreover the soviet consisted almost exclusively
of officers." The principal cause of this weak and unfavorable reaction of the country lay in the fact that the provinces, having
received the February revolution from the hands of Petrograd
without a struggle, were far slower than the capital in digesting
new facts and ideas. An additional period was necessary before
the vanguard could draw up to its own position the heavy reserves.

Thus the state of the popular consciousness—decisive factor
in a revolutionary policy—made impossible the seizure of power
by the Bolsheviks in July. At the same time the offensive on the
front impelled the party to oppose the demonstration. The collapse of the offensive was absolutely inevitable. As a fact it had
already begun, but the country did not yet know it. The danger
was that if the party were incautious, the government might lay
the blame upon the Bolsheviks for the consequences of its own
madness. The offensive must be given time to exhaust itself. The
Bolsheviks had no doubt that the break in the mood of the masses
would be very abrupt when it came. Then it would be clear what
should be undertaken. Their reckoning was absolutely right.
Events, however, have their own logic which takes no account of
political reckonings, and this time events came down cruelly on
the heads of the Bolsheviks.

The failure of the offensive became catastrophic on the 6th of

July, when the Germans broke through the Russian troops on a front twelve versts [1] long and to a depth of ten versts. The breach became known in the capital on July 7, at the very height of the punitive and repressive activities. Many months later, when passions ought to have quieted down a little, or at least become a little more sensible, Stankevich—not one of the most vicious enemies of Bolshevism—was nevertheless still writing about the "mysterious sequence of events" to be observed in the breach at Tarnopol following just after the July Days in Petrograd. Those people did not see, or did not want to see, the real sequence of events—the fact that a hopeless offensive begun under the whip of the Entente could not but lead to military catastrophe and, simultaneously therewith, to an outbreak of indignation in the masses deceived in their hopes of the revolution. But what difference does it make what the real concatenation of events was? The temptation to link up the Petrograd manifestation with the misfortune at the front was too strong. The patriotic press not only did not conceal the reverses, but exaggerated them with all its might, not hesitating even to reveal military secrets—printing the names of divisions and regiments and indicating their position. "Beginning on July 8," Miliukov confesses, "the newspapers began purposely to print outspoken telegrams from the front which struck Russian society like a clap of thunder." And that was their purpose—to shock, to frighten, to deafen, in order the more easily to link up the Bolsheviks with the Germans.

Provocation undoubtedly played a certain rôle in the events at the front as well as on the streets of Petrograd. After the February revolution the government had thrown over into the active army a large number of former gendarmes and policemen. None of them of course wanted to fight. They were more afraid of the Russian soldiers than of the Germans. In order to get their past forgotten, they would simulate the most extreme moods of the army, incite the soldiers against the officers, come out loudest of all against discipline, and often openly give themselves out for Bolsheviks. Bound naturally together as accomplices, they created a kind of special Brotherhood of Cowardice and Villainy. Through them would penetrate and quickly spread through the

[1] A verst is very nearly ⅔ of a mile.

army the most fantastic rumors, in which ultra-revolutionism was combined with Black Hundredism. In critical hours these creatures would give the first signals for panic. The press more than once referred to this demoralizing work of the police and gendarmes. No less frequent references of this kind are to be found in the secret documents of the army itself. But the high command remained silent, preferring to identify the Black Hundred provocateurs with the Bolsheviks. And now, after the collapse of the offensive, this method was legalized, and the Menshevik papers endeavored not to fall behind the dirtiest sheets of the chauvinists. With shouts about "Anarcho-Bolsheviks" and German agents, and about former gendarmes, they succeeded for a time in drowning out the question of the general condition of the army and of the policy of peace. "Our deep breach on the Lenin front," Prince Lvov openly boasted, "has incomparably more importance for Russia in my firm opinion than the breach made by the Germans on the southwestern front. . . ." The respected head of the government was like Rodzianko, the Lord Chamberlain, in that he did not know when to keep still.

If it had been possible to restrain the masses from demonstrating on July 3–4, the demonstration would inevitably have broken out as a result of the Tarnopol breach. However, a delay even of a few days would have brought important changes in the political situation. The movement would have assumed at once a broader scope, taking in not only the provinces but also, to a considerable degree, the front. The government would have been exposed politically, and would have found it incomparably more difficult to lay the blame upon "traitors" in the rear. The situation of the Bolshevik party would have been more advantageous in every respect. However, even in that case the thing could not have been carried to the point of an immediate conquest of power. Only this much, indeed, can be confidently affirmed: If the July movement had broken out a week later, the reaction would not have come off so victorious. It was just that "mysterious sequence" of the date of the demonstration and the date of the breach which counted heavily against the Bolsheviks. The wave of indignation and despair rolling back from the front fell in with the wave of shattered hopes radiating from Petrograd. The lesson received by the masses in the capital was too severe for anyone to think of an immediate renewal of the struggle. Moreover the bitter feelings caused by the meaningless defeat sought expression, and the patriots succeeded to a certain extent in directing it against the Bolsheviks.

In April, June, and July, the principal actors were the same: the Liberals, the Compromisers and the Bolsheviks. At all these stages the masses were trying to crowd the bourgeoisie out of the government. But the difference in the political consequences of mass interference in the several cases was enormous. It was the bourgeoisie who suffered in consequence of the "April days." The annexation policy was condemned—in words at least; the Kadet party was humiliated; the portfolio of foreign affairs was taken from it. In June the movement came to nothing. A gesture was made against the Bolsheviks, but the blow was not struck. In July the Bolshevik party was accused of treason, shattered, deprived of food and drink. Whereas in April Miliukov had been forced out of the government, in July Lenin was forced underground.

What was the cause of this sharp change occurring in a period of ten weeks? It is quite obvious that in the ruling circles a serious shift had occurred to the side of the liberal bourgeoisie. However, in that same period—April to July—the mood of the masses had sharply shifted to the side of the Bolsheviks. These two opposing processes developed in close dependence one upon the other. The more the workers and soldiers closed up around the Bolsheviks, the more resolutely were the Compromisers compelled to support the bourgeoisie. In April the leaders of the Executive Committee, worrying about their own influence, could still come one step to meet the masses and throw Miliukov overboard—supplying him, to be sure, with a reliable life-belt. In July the Compromisers joined the bourgeoisie and the officers in raiding the Bolsheviks. The change in the correlation of forces was thus caused this time, too, by a shift of the least stable of political forces, the petty bourgeois democracy—its abrupt movement to the side of the bourgeois counter-revolution.

But if this is so, were the Bolsheviks right in joining the demonstration and assuming responsibility for it? On July 3, Tomsky expounded the thought of Lenin: "It is impossible to talk of a

76

manifestation at this moment unless we want a new revolution." In that case how could the party a few hours later stand at the head of an armed demonstration without summoning the masses to a new revolution? Doctrinaires will see inconsistency here—or still worse, political light-mindedness. Sukhanov, for instance, sees the matter in this way, and incorporates in his "Notes" no few ironical references to the vacillation of the Bolshevik leadership. The masses take part in events, however, not at the bidding of doctrinaires, but at whatever time this flows inevitably from their own political development. The Bolshevik leadership understood that only a new revolution could change the political situation, but the workers and soldiers did not yet understand this. The Bolshevik leadership saw clearly that the heavy reserves—the front and the provinces—needed time to make their own inferences from the adventure of the offensive. But the advanced ranks were rushing into the street under the influence of that same adventure. They combined a most radical understanding of the task with illusions as to its methods. The warnings of the Bolsheviks were ineffective. The Petrograd workers and soldiers had to test the situation with their own experience. And their armed demonstration was such a test. But the test might, against the will of the masses, have turned into a general battle and by the same token into a decisive defeat. In such a situation the party dared not stand aside. To wash one's hands in the water of strategical morals would have meant simply to betray the workers and soldiers to their enemies. The party of the masses was compelled to stand on the same ground on which the masses stood, in order, while not in the least sharing their illusions, to help them make the necessary inferences with the least possible loss. Trotsky answered in the press the innumerable critics of those days: "We do not consider it necessary to justify ourselves before anybody for not having stood aside waiting while General Polovtsev 'conversed' with the demonstrators. In any case our participation could not possibly have increased the number of victims, nor converted a chaotic armed manifestation into a political insurrection."

A prototype of the July Days is to be found in all the old revolutions—with various, but generally speaking unfavorable, and frequently catastrophic, results. This stage is involved in the inner mechanics of a bourgeois revolution, inasmuch as that class which sacrifices most for the success of the revolution and hopes the most from it, receives the least of all. The natural law of the process is perfectly clear. The possessing class which is brought to power by the revolution is inclined to think that with this the revolution has accomplished its mission, and is therefore most of all concerned to demonstrate its reliability to the forces of reaction. This "revolutionary" bourgeoisie provokes the indignation of the popular masses by those same measures with which it strives to win the good will of the classes it has overthrown. The disappointment of the masses follows very quickly; it follows even before their vanguard has cooled off after the revolutionary struggle. The people imagine that with a new blow they can carry through, or correct, that which they did not accomplish decisively enough before. Hence the impulse to a new revolution, a revolution without preparation, without program, without estimation of the reserves, without calculation of consequences. On the other hand those bourgeois layers which have arrived at the power are in a way only waiting for a stormy outbreak from below, in order to make the attempt decisively to settle accounts with the people. Such is the social and psychological basis of that supplementary semi-revolution, which has more than once in history become the starting-point of a victorious counter-revolution.

On July 17, 1791, on the Champs de Mars, Lafayette fired on a peaceful demonstration of republicans attempting to bring a petition to the National Assembly which was engaged in screening the treachery of the monarchical power, just as the Russian Compromisers one hundred and twenty-six years later were screening the treachery of the Liberals. The royalist bourgeoisie hoped with a timely bath of blood to settle accounts with the party of the revolution forever. The republican leaders, still not feeling strong enough for victory, declined the battle—and that was entirely reasonable. They even hastened to separate themselves from the petitioners—and that was, to say the least, unworthy and a mistaken policy. The régime of the bourgeois terror compelled the Jacobins to quiet down for several months. Robespierre took shelter with the carpenter Duplay. Desmoulins went into hiding. Danton spent several weeks in England. But the royalist provocation nevertheless failed: the settlement on the Champ de Mars did not prevent the republican movement from going on to victory. The great French revolution thus had its "July Days"—both in the political and the calendar sense of the word.

Fifty-seven years later in France, the "July Days" came in June and were incomparably more colossal and tragic. The so-called "June Days" of 1848 grew irresistibly out of the February overturn. The French bourgeoisie had proclaimed in the hour of its victory "the right to labor"—just as in 1789 it announced a great many admirable things, just as in 1914 it swore that it was now waging its last war. Out of that vainglorious "right to labor" arose those pitiful national sweatshops where a hundred thousand workers, after winning the power for their bosses, got a wage of twenty-three sous a day. Only a few weeks later the republican bourgeoisie, generous of phrase but stingy of money, could find no words insulting enough for these "spongers" living on a national starvation dole. In the abundance of those February promises and the cold-bloodedness of the pre-June provocations, the national traits of the French bourgeoisie find admirable expression. But even without provocation, the Parisian worker with the February weapons still in his hands could not help reacting to the contrast between gorgeous program and miserable reality—that intolerable contrast every day gnawing at his stomach and his conscience. With what cool and barely concealed calculation did Cavaignac before the eyes of the whole dominant society, permit an insurrection to develop in order the better to drown it in blood! No less than 12,000 workers were slaughtered by the republican bourgeoisie, no less than 20,000 were imprisoned, in order to divest the remainder of their faith in that "right to labor" which the bourgeoisie had proclaimed. Without plan, without program, without leadership, the movement of the June days of 1848 was like a mighty and unrestrainable reflex action of the proletariat. Deprived of their most elementary necessities and insulted in their highest hopes, the insurrectionary workers were not only put down but slandered. The left democrat, Flaucon, a follower of Ledru-Rollin, a predecessor of Tseretelli, assured the National Assembly that the insurrectionaries had been bribed by monarchists and foreign governments. The Compromisers of 1848 did not even have to have a war atmosphere in order to discover English and Russian gold in the pockets of the rebels. It was in this way that the democrats laid down the road to Bonapartism.

The gigantic outbreak of the Commune bore the same relation to the September overturn of 1870, as the June Days to the February revolution of 1848. That March uprising of the Parisian proletariat was least of all a matter of strategic calculation. It resulted from a tragic combination of circumstances, supplemented by one of those acts of provocation in which the French bourgeoisie is so inventive when fear puts the spurs to its spiteful will. Against the plans of the ruling clique, which wished above all to disarm the people, the workers wanted to defend that Paris which they had first tried to make their own. The National Guard had given them an armed organization—one very close to the soviet type— and it had given them political leadership in the person of its Central Committee. In consequence of unfavorable objective conditions and political mistakes, Paris became opposed to France— misunderstood, not supported, in part actually betrayed by the provinces—and fell into the hands of the enraged men of Versailles with Bismarck and Moltke behind their backs. The depraved and beaten officers of Napoleon III proved indispensable hangmen in the service of the gentle Marianne, whom the Prussians in heavy boots had just freed from the embraces of a false Bonaparte. In the Paris Commune the reflex protest of the proletariat against the deceitfulness of a bourgeois revolution first rose to the height of proletarian revolution—but rose only to fall immediately.

Spartacus Week in January 1919 in Berlin belonged to the same type of intermediate, semi-revolution as the July Days in Petrograd. Owing to the prevailing position of the proletariat in the German nation, especially in its industry, the November revolution automatically transferred the state sovereignty to the Workers' and Soldiers' Soviet. But the proletariat was politically identical with the Social Democracy, which in turn identified itself with the bourgeois régime. The independent party occupied in the German revolution the place which in Russia belonged to the Social Revolutionaries and Mensheviks. The thing lacking was a Bolshevik party.

Every day after the 9th of November gave the German workers a vivid feeling as though of something slipping from their hands, being withdrawn, sliding through their fingers. The desire to keep what they had won, to fortify themselves, to put up a resistance, was growing from day to day. And this defensive tendency lay at the bottom of the January fights of 1919. Spartacus Week began, not in the manner of a strategy calculated by the party, but in the manner of a pressure from the indignant lower ranks. It developed around a question of third-rate importance, that of retaining the office of chief-of-police, although it was in its tendencies the beginning of a new revolution. Both organizations participating in the leadership, the Spartacus League and the Left Independents, were taken unawares; they went farther than they intended and at the same time did not go through to the end. The Spartacus men were still too weak for independent leadership. The Left Independents balked at those methods which could alone have brought them to the goal, vascillated, and played with the insurrection, combining it with diplomatic negotiations.

In number of victims the January defeat falls far below the colossal figures of the "June Days" in France. However, the political importance of a defeat is not measured only by the statistics of killed and executed. It is enough that the young communist party was physically beheaded, and the Independent Party demonstrated that by the very essence of its methods it was incapable of leading the proletariat to victory. From a larger point of view the "July Days" repeated themselves in Germany in several different editions: the January week of 1919, the March days of 1921, the October retreat of 1923. The whole subsequent history of Germany derives from those events. The unachieved revolution was switched over into Fascism.

At the present moment, while these lines are being written—early in May 1931—the bloodless, peaceful, glorious (the list of these adjectives is always the same) revolution in Spain, is preparing before our eyes its "June Days"—if you go by the French calendar—its "July Days" by the Russian. The Provisional Government in Madrid, bathing in phrases—a good part of them apparently translated from the Russian language—is promising broad measures against unemployment and land-hunger, but dares not touch a single one of the old social sores. The coalition socialists are helping the republicans sabotage the tasks of the revolution. Is it hard to foresee the feverish growth of indignation among workers and peasants? The incompatible movements of the mass revolution on the one hand, and the policy of the new ruling classes on the other—that is the source of an irreconcilable conflict, which as it develops will either bury the first, the April, revolution, or lead to a second.

*

ALTHOUGH the underlying mass of Russian Bolsheviks felt in July, 1917, that beyond certain limits it was still impossible to go, still there was no complete homogeneity of mood. Many workers and soldiers were at times inclined to estimate the developing movement as a decisive action. Metelev, in his memoirs written five years later, expresses himself about the meaning of the events in the following words: "In that insurrection our chief mistake was that we proposed to the compromisist Executive Committee to seize the power. . . . We ought not to have proposed, but to have seized the power ourselves. Our second mistake may be considered to be this, that we spent almost two days marching in the streets, instead of immediately occupying all the institutions, palaces, banks, railroad stations, telegraph offices, arresting the whole Provisional Government," etc., etc. As applied to an insurrection those words would be unanswerable, but to convert the July movement into an insurrection would have meant almost certainly to bury the revolution.

The anarchists in summoning the masses to battle referred to the fact that "the February revolution also took place without the leadership of a party." But the February revolution had its prepared tasks laid down by the struggle of whole generations, and above the February revolution stood an oppositional liberal society and a patriotic democracy ready to receive the power. The July movement, on the contrary, would have had to lay down a wholly new historic road-bed. The whole of bourgeois society, the soviet democracy included, were implacably hostile to it. This basic difference between the conditions of a bourgeois and a workers' revolution, the anarchists did not see, or did not understand.

Had the Bolshevik party, stubbornly clinging to a doctrinaire appraisal of the July movement as "untimely," turned its back on the masses, the semi-insurrection would inevitably have fallen under the scattered and uncoordinated leadership of anarchists, of adventurers, of accidental expressers of the indignation of the masses, and would have expired in bloody and bootless convulsions. On the other hand, if the party, after taking its place at the head of the machine-gunners and Putilov men, had renounced its own appraisal of the situation as a whole, and glided down the road to a decisive fight, the insurrection would indubitably have taken a bold scope. The workers and soldiers under the leadership of the Bolsheviks would have conquered the power—but only to prepare the subsequent shipwreck of the revolution. The question of power on a national scale would not have been decided, as it was in February, by a victory in Petrograd. The provinces would not have caught up to the capital. The front would not have understood or accepted the revolution. The railroads and the telegraphs would have served the Compromisers against the Bolsheviks. Kerensky and headquarters would have created a government for the front and the provinces. Petrograd would have been blockaded. Disintegration would have begun within its walls. The government would have been able to send considerable masses of soldiers against Petrograd. The insurrection would have ended, in those circumstances, with the tragedy of a Petrograd Commune.

At the July forking of historic roads, the interference of the Bolshevik party eliminated both fatally dangerous variants— both that in the likeness of the June Days of 1848, and that of the Paris Commune of 1871. Thanks to the party's taking its place boldly at the head of the movement, it was able to stop the masses at the moment when the demonstration began to turn into an armed test of strength. The blow struck at the masses and the party in July was very considerable, but it was not a decisive blow. The victims were counted by tens and not by tens of thousands. The working class issued from the trial, not headless and not bled to death. It fully preserved its fighting cadres, and these cadres had learned much.

During the February overturn all the many preceding years' work of the Bolsheviks came to fruition, and progressive workers educated by the party found their place in the struggle, but there was still no direct leadership from the party. In the April events the slogans of the party manifested their dynamic force, but the movement itself developed independently. In June the enormous influence of the party revealed itself, but the masses were still functioning within the limits of a demonstration officially summoned by the enemy. Only in July did the Bolshevik Party, feeling the pressure of the masses, come out into the street against all the other parties, and not only with its slogans, but with its organized leadership, determine the fundamental character of the movement. The value of a close-knit vanguard was first fully manifested in the July Days, when the party—at great cost—defended the proletariat from defeat, and safeguarded its own future revolution.

"As a technical trial," wrote Miliukov, speaking of the significance of the July Days to the Bolsheviks, "the experience was for them undoubtedly of extraordinary value. It showed them with what elements they had to deal, how to organize these elements, and finally what resistance could be put up by the government, the Soviet and the military units. . . . It was evident that when the time came for repeating the experiment, they would carry it out more systematically and consciously." Those words correctly evaluate the significance of the July experiment for the further development of the policy of the Bolsheviks. But before making use of these July lessons, the party had to go through some heavy weeks, during which it seemed to the shortsighted enemy that the power of Bolshevism was conclusively broken.

84

CHAPTER IV

THE MONTH OF THE GREAT SLANDER

DURING that night of July 4, when the two hundred members of both Executive Committees, the worker-soldiers' and the peasants', were sitting around between fruitless sessions, a mysterious rumor arrived among them. Material had been discovered connecting Lenin with the German general staff; tomorrow the newspapers would publish the documents. The gloomy Augurs of the praesidium, crossing the hall on their way to one of those endless conferences behind the scenes, responded unwillingly and evasively even to questions from their nearest friends. The Tauride Palace, already almost abandoned by the outside public, was bewildered. "Lenin in the service of the German staff?" Amazement, alarm, malicious pleasure, drew the delegates together in excited groups. "It goes without saying," says Sukhanov, who was very hostile to the Bolsheviks in the July Days, "that not one person really connected with the revolution doubted for an instant that these rumors were all nonsense." But those with a revolutionary past constituted an insignificant minority among the members of the Executive Committee. March revolutionists, accidental elements caught up by the first wave, predominated even in the ruling soviet institutions. Among those provincials—town-clerks, shopkeepers, heads of villages—deputies were to be found with a definitely Black Hundred odor. These people immediately began to feel at home: Just what was to be expected! They had known it all along!

Alarmed by this unforeseen and too abrupt turn of events, the leaders sparred for time. Cheidze and Tseretelli suggested to the newspapers by telephone that they refrain from printing the sensational exposure as "unverified." The editors did not dare ignore this "request" from the Tauride Palace—except one of them. The small yellow sheet published by one of the sons of Suvorin, the powerful publisher of *Novoe Vremya,* served up to

85

its readers the next morning an official-sounding document about Lenin's receiving directions and money from the German government. The censorship was thus broken, and within a day the whole press was full of this sensation. Thus began the most incredible episode of a year rich in events: The leaders of a revolutionary party, whose lives for decades had been passed in a struggle against rulers, both crowned and uncrowned, found themselves portrayed before the country and the whole world as hired agents of the Hohenzollern. On a scale hitherto unheard of, this slander was sown in the thick of the popular masses, a vast majority of whom had heard of the Bolshevik leaders for the first time only after the February revolution. Mud-slinging here became a political factor of primary importance. This makes necessary an attentive examination of its mechanism.

The primary source of this sensational document was the testimony of a certain Ermolenko. The image of this hero is sufficiently delineated by the official records: In the period from the Japanese War to 1913, he was an agent of the Intelligence Service; in 1913, for reasons not established, he was discharged from service with the title of ensign from the ranks; in 1914 he was called to service in the army, gallantly permitted himself to be captured, and became a police spy among the war prisoners. The régime of a concentration camp was not to this spy's taste, however, and "at the insistence of his friends," so he testifies, he took service with the Germans—needless to say, with patriotic aims. Here a new chapter opened in his life. On April 25 this ensign from the ranks was "thrown over the Russian front" by the German military authorities for the purpose of dynamiting bridges, reporting military secrets, struggling for the independence of the Ukraine, and agitating for a separate peace. The German officers, Captains Shiditsky and Liebers, in contracting with Ermolenko for these services, informed him in passing, without any practical necessity and evidently merely in order to keep up his spirits, that besides the ensign himself, Lenin would be working in Russia in the same direction. That was the foundation of the whole affair.

Who—or what—suggested to Ermolenko his testimony about Lenin? Not the German officers, in any case. A simple juxtaposition of dates and facts will introduce us into the intellectual workshop of the ensign. On April 4 Lenin issued his famous theses, constituting a declaration of war against the February régime. On April 20–21 occurred the armed demonstration against a continuance of the war. The attack upon Lenin at that time became a veritable hurricane. On the 25th Ermolenko was "thrown over" the front, and during the first half of May was getting in contact with the Intelligence Service at headquarters. Ambiguous newspaper articles demonstrating that the policy of Lenin was advantageous to the Kaiser gave birth to the idea that Lenin was a German agent. Officers and commissars at the front, struggling with the irrepressible "Bolshevism" of the soldiers, were still less ceremonious in their forms of expression when the talk was about Lenin. Ermolenko promptly plunged into these waters. Whether he himself thought up the dragged-in remark about Lenin, whether it was suggested to him by some outside person, or whether it was cooperatively manufactured by Ermolenko and the officials of the Intelligence Service, has no great significance. The demand for slanders against the Bolsheviks had reached such intensity that a supply could not fail to turn up. The chief of the headquarters staff, General Denikin, future generalissimo of the White Guards in the civil war—himself not very much higher in his outlook than the agents of the tzarist secret service—attributed, or pretended to attribute, great importance to the testimony of Ermolenko, and turned it over to the War Minister on May 16 with an appropriate letter. Kerensky, we may assume, exchanged opinions with Tseretelli or Cheidze, who could hardly have failed to put a curb on his righteous indignation. That evidently explains why the thing went no further. Kerensky wrote later that, although Ermolenko had testified to a connection of Lenin with the German staff, he did so "not with sufficient credibility." The report of Ermolenko-Denikin thus remained for a month and a half under a bushel. The Intelligence Service dismissed Ermolenko as superfluous, and the ensign wandered off to the Far East to drink away the money he had received from two sources.

The events of the July Days, however, revealing the danger of Bolshevism in its full stature, called to mind the exposures of

Ermolenko. He was hastily summoned from Blagoveshchensk, but owing to a sheer lack of imagination he could not, in spite of all cluckings and jerkings of the reins, add one word to his original testimony. By that time, however, the Department of Justice and the Intelligence Service were working under full steam. Inquiries about possible criminal connections of the Bolsheviks were addressed to politicians, generals, gendarmes, merchants, innumerable people of any and every profession. The respectable tzarist secret police conducted themselves in this investigation with considerably more discretion than the brand-new representatives of democratic justice. "Such evidence," wrote a former chief of the Petrograd secret police, the venerable general Globachev, "as that Lenin worked in Russia to her injury and on German money, was not, at least during my period of service, in the possession of the secret police." Another secret police officer, Yakubov, chief of the intelligence department of the Petrograd military district, testified: "I know nothing of a connection between Lenin and his followers and the German general staff, but I also know nothing of the resources upon which Lenin worked." Thus from the institutions of the tzarist spy system, which had kept watch of Bolshevism from its very inception, nothing useful could be squeezed out.

However, when people seek long, especially if they are armed with power, they find something in the end. A certain Z. Burstein, a merchant by official calling, opened the eyes of the Provisional Government to a "German espionage organization in Stockholm, headed by Parvus,"—a well-known German social democrat of Russian origin. According to the testimony of Burstein, Lenin was in contact with this organization through the Polish revolutionists, Ganetsky and Kozlovsky. Kerensky wrote later: "Some extraordinarily serious data—unfortunately not of a legal, but merely of a secret police character—were to receive absolutely unquestionable confirmation with the arrival in Russia of Ganetsky, who had been arrested on the border, and were to be converted into authentic juridical material against the Bolshevik staff." Kerensky knew in advance into what this material would be converted!

The testimony of the merchant, Burstein, concerned the trade operations of Ganetsky and Kozlovsky between Petrograd and Stockholm. This wartime commerce, which evidently had recourse at times to a code correspondence, had no relation to politics. The Bolshevik party had no relation to this commerce. Lenin and Trotsky had publicly denounced Parvus, who combined good commerce with bad politics, and in printed words had appealed to the Russian revolutionists to break off all relations with him. But who was there in the swirlpool of events who had time to look into all this? An espionage organization in Stockholm—that sounded plain enough. And so the light unsuccessfully ignited by the hand of ensign Ermolenko, flared up from another direction. To be sure, here too they ran into a difficulty. The head of the Intelligence Service of the general staff, Prince Turkestanov, to the query of an investigator into the especially important affair of Alexandrov, had answered, "Z. Burstein is a person not deserving the slightest confidence. Burstein is an unscrupulous type of business man, who will not stop at any kind of undertaking." But could Burstein's bad reputation stand in the way of an attempt to besmirch the reputation of Lenin? No, Kerensky did not hesitate to recognize the testimony of Burstein as "extraordinarily serious." Henceforth the investigation was off on the Stockholm scent. The exposures of a spy who had been in the service of two general staffs, and an unscrupulous business man, "not deserving the slightest confidence," lay at the foundation of that utterly fantastic accusation against a revolutionary party which a nation of 160 million were about to raise to the supreme power.

But how did it happen that the materials of a preliminary investigation appeared in print, and moreover just at the moment when the shattered offensive of Kerensky was becoming a catastrophe, and the July demonstration in Petrograd was revealing the irresistible growth of the Bolsheviks? One of the initiators of this business, the attorney general, Bessarabov, later frankly described in the press how, when it became clear that the Provisional Government in Petrograd was wholly without reliable armed forces, it was decided in the district headquarters to try to create a psychological change in the regiments by means of some strong medicine. "The substance of the documents was communicated to representatives of the Preobrazhensky regiment

nearest to headquarters; those present observed what an overwhelming impression the communication made. From that moment it was clear what a powerful weapon was in the hands of
the government." After this successful experimental test, these
conspirators from the Department of Justice, the Intelligence
Service and the General Staff hastened to make known their dis-
coveries to the Minister of Justice. Pereverzev answered that no
official communication could be issued, but that by the members
of the Provisional Government who were present "no obstacle
would be put in the way of a private initiative." The names of
the juridical and staff officials were rightly judged inapposite to
the best interests of the business: in order to get the sensational
slander into circulation a "political figure" was needed. By the
method of private initiative the conspirators had no difficulty in
finding exactly the personage they needed. A former revolutionist, a member of the second Duma, a shrieking orator and a
passionate lover of intrigue, Alexinsky had once stood on the extreme left flank of the Bolsheviks. Lenin had been a hopeless opportunist in his eyes. In the years of reaction Alexinsky had created a special ultra-left group, which he had continued to lead
from abroad until the war, at the beginning of which he took an
ultra-patriotic position and straightway made a specialty of accusing all and everybody of being in the service of the Kaiser.
Along this line he developed an extensive espionage business in
Paris in company with Russian and French patriots of the same
type. The Paris Association of Foreign Journalists—that is, the
correspondents of Allied and neutral countries, a very patriotic
and by no means austere body—found it necessary in a special
resolution to declare Alexinsky "a dishonest slanderer" and expel
him from its midst. Arriving in Petrograd with this attestation
after the February revolution, Alexinsky made an attempt, in the
character of a former Left, to get into the Executive Committee.
In spite of all their tolerance, the Mensheviks and Social Revolutionaries by a resolution of April 11 shut the door in his face,
suggesting that he make an attempt to re-establish his honor.
That was easy to propose! Having decided that he was better
fitted to besmirch others than rehabilitate himself, Alexinsky got
into connection with the Intelligence Service, and laid hold of a

national field of operation for his instinct for intrigue. By the second half of July he had already begun to include Mensheviks, too, in the widening circle of his slanders. A leader of the latter party, Dan, abandoning the policy of watchful waiting, printed in the official soviet *Izvestia* (June 22) a letter of protest: "It is time to put an end to the doings of a man officially denounced as a dishonest slanderer." Is it not clear that Themis, inspired by Ermolenko and Burstein, could find no better intermediary between herself and public opinion than Alexinsky? It was his signature which adorned the documents of the exposure.

Behind the scenes the minister-socialists protested against the handing over of these documents to the press, as also did two of the bourgeois ministers, Nekrasov and Tereshchenko. On the day of their publication, June 5, Pereverzev, with whom the government had already been willing to part, found himself obliged to resign. The Mensheviks passed the hint that this was their victory. Kerensky subsequently asserted that the minister had been removed for being too hasty with the exposure, thus hindering the course of the investigation. In any case, Pereverzev, with his departure, if not with his presence in the government, gave satisfaction to everybody.

On that same day Zinoviev appeared at a sitting of the bureau of the Executive Committee, and in the name of the Central Committee of the Bolsheviks demanded that immediate measures be taken to exonerate Lenin and to prevent possible consequences of the slander. The bureau could not refuse to appoint a commission of inquiry. Sukhanov writes: "The commission itself understood that what needed investigation was not the question of Lenin's selling out Russia, but only of the sources of the slander." But the commission ran into the jealous competition of the Institutions of Justice and the Intelligence Service, which had every reason not to desire outside interference in their trade. To be sure, the soviet bodies had not up to that time had any difficulty in getting the better of the governmental bodies when they found it necessary. But the July Days had produced a serious shift of power to the right, and moreover the soviet commission was in no hurry to fulfill a task obviously in conflict with the political interests of those who had intrusted it. The more serious of the compromise leaders—that is, properly speaking, only the Mensheviks—were concerned to establish a formal disconnection with the slander, but nothing more. In all cases where it was impossible to avoid making some direct answer, they would in a few words clear themselves of guilt. But they did not extend a finger to ward off the poisoned sword poised over the head of the Bolsheviks. A popular image of their policy was once provided by the Roman pro-consul, Pilate. Yes, and could they behave otherwise without betraying themselves? It was only the slander against Lenin that in the July Days turned away a part of the garrison from the Bolsheviks. If the Compromisers had made a fight against the slander, it is easy to imagine that the battalion of the Izmailovstsi would have stopped singing the Marseillaise in honor of the Executive Committee and gone back to their barracks, if not to the Palace of Kshesinskaia.

In line with the general policy of the Mensheviks, the Minister of the Interior, Tseretelli, who took the responsibility for the arrest of Bolsheviks soon to follow, did indeed, under pressure from the Bolshevik faction, announce at a meeting of the Executive Committee that he personally did not suspect the Bolshevik leaders of espionage, but that he did accuse them of conspiracy and armed insurrection. On July 13, Lieber, in introducing a resolution which in essence outlawed the Bolshevik party, deemed it necessary to remark: "I myself consider that the accusations directed against Lenin and Zinoviev have no foundation." Such declarations were met by all in gloomy silence: to the Bolsheviks they seemed dishonorably evasive, to the patriots, superfluous or unprofitable.

Speaking on the 17th at a joint session of the two Executive Committees, Trotsky said: "An intolerable atmosphere has been created, in which you as well as we are choking. They are throwing dirty accusations at Lenin and Zinoviev. (Voice: 'That is true.' Uproar. Trotsky continues.) There are in this hall, it appears, people who sympathize with these accusations. There are people here who have only sneaked into the revolution. (Uproar. The president's bell long tries to restore order.) . . . Lenin has fought thirty years for the revolution. I have fought twenty years against the oppression of the people. And we cannot but cherish a hatred for German militarism. . . . A suspicion against us in that direction could be expressed only by those who do not know what a revolutionist is. I have been sentenced by a German court to eight months' imprisonment for my struggle against German militarism. . . . This everybody knows. Let nobody in this hall say that we are hirelings of Germany, for that is not the voice of convinced revolutionists but the voice of scoundrels. (Applause)" Thus the episode was reported in the anti-Bolshevik publications of the day. The Bolshevik publications were already closed. It is necessary to explain, however, that the applause came from a small left sector. A part of the deputies bellowed with hatred. The majority were silent. No one, however, even of the direct agents of Kerensky, ascended the tribune to support the official version of the accusation, or even indirectly to defend it.

In Moscow, where the struggle between Bolsheviks and Compromisers had in general assumed a milder character—only to become so much the more cruel in October—a joint session of the two soviets, the workers' and soldiers', passed a resolution on July 10th to "publish and paste up a manifesto in which it shall be declared that the accusation of espionage against the Bolshevik faction is a slander and a plot of the counter-revolution." The Petrograd soviet, more directly dependent upon governmental combinations, took no steps whatever, awaiting the conclusions of a Commission of Inquiry which had not even met.

On July 5, Lenin, in a conversation with Trotsky, raised the question: "Aren't they getting ready to shoot us all?" Only such an intention could explain the official stamp placed upon that monstrous slander. Lenin considered the enemy capable of carrying through to the end the scheme they had thought up, and decided not to fall into their hands. On the evening of the 6th, Kerensky arrived from the front all stuffed full of the suggestions of the generals, and demanded decisive measures against the Bolsheviks. At about two o'clock at night the government resolved to bring to trial all the leaders of the "armed insurrection," and to disband the regiments which had taken part in the mutiny. The military detachment sent to the apartment of Lenin for purposes of search and arrest had to content itself with search, for the occupant had already left home. Lenin still remained in

Petrograd, but hid in a worker's apartment, demanding that the
soviet Inquiry Commission hear him and Zinoviev in conditions
precluding the danger of attack from the counter-revolution. In
a declaration sent to the Commission, Lenin and Zinoviev wrote:
"This morning (Friday, July 7) it was communicated to
Kamenev from the Duma that the commission was to go at 12
o'clock to an apartment agreed upon. We are writing these lines
at 6:30 in the evening of July 7, and we remark that up to now
the Commission has not appeared or given the slightest sign of its
existence. . . . The responsibility for the delay of the inquiry
does not rest upon us." The disinclination of the soviet commission to begin the promised investigation finally convinced Lenin
that the Compromisers were washing their hands of the case, and
leaving it to the mercies of the White Guards. The officers and
junkers, who had by that time broken up the party printing
plant, were now beating up and arresting in the streets everyone
who protested against the charge of espionage against the Bolsheviks. Lenin therefore finally decided to go into hiding—not from
the investigation, but from possible attempts upon his life.

On the 15th, Lenin and Zinoviev explained in the Kronstadt
Bolshevik paper, which the authorities had not dared to shut
down, why they did not consider it possible to hand themselves
over to the authorities: "From a letter of the former Minister of
Justice, Pereverzev, printed on Sunday in the newspaper *Novoe
Vremya*, it has become perfectly clear that the 'case' of the spy
activities of Lenin and others was a perfectly deliberate frame-up
by the party of counter-revolution. Pereverzev quite openly
acknowledges that he put in circulation unverified accusations in
order to arouse the rage (his verbatim expression) of the soldiers
against our party. This is the confession of yesterday's Minister
of Justice! . . . There is no guarantee of justice in Russia at this
moment. To turn oneself over to the authorities would mean to
put oneself in the hands of the Miliukovs, Alexinskies, Pere-
verzevs, in the hands of infuriated counter-revolutionists for
whom the whole accusation against us is a mere episode in a civil
war." In order to explain at this day the meaning of the phrase
"episode in a civil war," it is sufficient to remember the fate of

Karl Liebnekcht and Rosa Luxemburg. Lenin knew how to see ahead.

While agitators of the hostile camp were telling a thousand stories—Lenin is on a destroyer, Lenin has fled to Germany in a submarine, etc.—the majority of the Executive Committee hastily condemned Lenin for avoiding an investigation. Ignoring the political essence of the accusation, and the pogrom situation in which, and for the sake of which, it was launched, the Compromisers came out as champions of pure justice. This was the least inexpedient position of all those remaining open to them. A resolution of the Executive Committee on July 13 not only declared the conduct of Lenin and Zinoviev "absolutely unpermissible," but also demanded of the Bolshevik faction "an immediate, categorical and clear condemnation" of its leaders. The faction unanimously rejected the demands of the Executive Committee. However in the Bolshevik ranks—at least in the upper circles— there were waverings on the subject of Lenin's avoiding an investigation. And among even the most extreme Left Compromisers Lenin's disappearance caused downright indignation—an indignation not always hypocritical, either, as we see in the example of Sukhanov. The slanderous character of the material supplied by the secret police had not been subject to the slightest doubt in his mind, as we know, from the beginning. "The nonsensical accusation went up like smoke," he wrote. "It had no confirmation, and people simply stopped believing it." But it remained a mystery for Sukhanov how Lenin could decide to avoid an inquiry. "That was something wholly special, unexampled, incomprehensible. Any other mortal would have demanded a court and an investigation, no matter how unfavorable the circumstances." Yes, any other mortal. But no other mortal could have become an object of such raging hatred to the ruling classes. Lenin was not any other mortal, and did not for one moment forget the responsibility which rested on him. He knew how to draw all the inferences from a situation, and he knew how in the name of those tasks to which he had consecrated his life, to ignore the oscillations of "public opinion." Quixotism was just as foreign to him as posing.

In company with Zinoviev Lenin passed a number of weeks in the environs of Petrograd in a forest near Sestroretsk. They had to spend the nights and find shelter from rain in a haystack. Disguised as a fireman Lenin then crossed the Finland border on a locomotive, and concealed himself in the apartment of a Helsingfors police chief, a former Petrograd worker. Afterward he moved nearer the Russian border, to Vyborg. From the end of September he lived secretly in Petrograd. And on the day of the insurrection he appeared, after an almost four months' absence, in the open arena.

July became a month of shameless, unbridled and triumphant slander. By August the slander had already begun to exhaust itself. Just a month after the attack was let loose, Tseretelli, ever true to himself, deemed it necessary to repeat at a session of the Executive Committee: "On the day after the arrests I gave an oral answer to the questions of the Bolsheviks, and I said: 'The leaders of the Bolsheviks, under indictment for inciting to insurrection on July 3–5, I do not suspect of connection with the German staff.' " To say less than that would have been impossible; to say more would have been inexpedient. The press of the compromise parties went no farther than these words of Tseretelli, and since this press was at the same time bitterly denouncing the Bolsheviks as auxiliaries of German militarism, the voice of the compromisist papers merged politically with the outcry of all the rest of the press, which was speaking of the Bolsheviks not as "Auxiliaries" of Ludendorff but as his hired agents. The highest notes in this chorus were sung by the Kadets. *Russkie Vedomosti,* the paper of the liberal Moscow professors, printed a communication to the effect that in a search in the editorial offices of *Pravda* a German letter had been found in which a Baron from Gaparanda "welcomes the activities of the Bolsheviks and foresees what legitimate rejoicing this will cause in Berlin." The German Baron on the Finland border well knew what letters were needed by the Russian patriots. The press of cultivated society, defending itself against Bolshevik barbarism, was filled with such communications.

Did the professors and lawyers believe their own words? To admit this, at least in regard to the leaders in the capital, would

96

be to think far too little of their political intelligence. Even if not considerations of principle, or of psychological possibility, mere business considerations alone ought to have revealed to them the vacuity of these accusations—and first of all financial considerations. The German government could obviously have helped the Bolsheviks, not with ideas, but with money. But money was just what the Bolsheviks did not have. The center of the party abroad during the war was struggling with cruel need; a hundred francs was a big sum; the central organ was appearing once a month, or once in two months, and Lenin was carefully counting the lines in order not to exceed his budget. The expenses of the Petrograd organization during the war years amounted to a few thousand rubles, which went mostly to the printing of illegal leaflets. In two and a half years only 300,000 copies of these leaflets were distributed in Petrograd. After the revolution the inflow of members and of means increased, of course, remarkably. The workers were wonderfully ready to tax themselves for the Soviet and for the soviet parties. "Contributions, all kinds of dues, collections and deductions in behalf of the Soviet," reported the lawyer Bramson, a Trudovik, at the first congress of the soviets, "began on the very first day after our revolution broke out. . . . You could see the extraordinarily touching spectacle of an uninterrupted pilgrimage to us in the Tauride Palace from early morning to late at night bringing these contributions." As time went on, the workers were still more ready to make these deductions in behalf of the Bolsheviks. However, in spite of the swift growth of the party and of money receipts, *Pravda* was, in physical proportions, the smallest of all the party papers. Soon after his arrival in Russia Lenin wrote to Radek in Stockholm: "Write articles for *Pravda* about foreign politics—extremely short and in the spirit of *Pravda* (there is very, very little space—we are trying hard to enlarge it)." In spite of the Spartan régime of economy instituted by Lenin, the party was always in need. The disbursement of two or three thousand war-time rubles in behalf of some local organization would mean always a serious problem for the Central Committee. In order to send papers to the front, it became necessary again and again to take up special collections among the workers. And even so, the Bolshevik papers arrived in the trenches in incomparably fewer number than the papers of the Compromisers and Liberals. Complaints about this were continual. "We are living only on the rumor of your papers," wrote the soldiers. In April a city conference of the party appealed to the workers of Petrograd to collect in three days the 75,000 rubles lacking for the purchase of a printing plant. The sum was more than covered, and the party finally acquired its own printing press—the same one which the junkers shattered to the ground in July. The influence of the Bolshevik slogans spread like a fire in the steppes, but the material instruments of their propaganda remained exceedingly scant. The personal lives of the Bolsheviks gave still less occasion for slander. What then remained? Nothing, in the last analysis, but Lenin's trip through Germany. But that very fact, advanced oftenest of all before inexperienced audiences as proof of Lenin's friendship with the German government, in reality proved the opposite. An agent would have traveled through the hostile territory concealed and without the slightest danger. Only a revolutionist confident of himself to the last degree would have dared openly to transgress the laws of patriotism in wartime.

The Ministry of Justice, however, did not hesitate to carry out its unpleasant task. It had not for nothing inherited employees trained during the final period of the autocracy, when the murder of liberal deputies by Black Hundred agents known by name to the whole country would remain systematically undiscovered, while a Jewish salesman in Kiev would be accused of using the blood of a Christian boy. Over the signature of the investigator in the exceptionally important affair of Alexandrov, and that of the Attorney General, Karinsky, a decree was published on the 21st of July, indicting on a charge of state treason Lenin, Zinoviev, Kollontai and a number of other people, among them the German social democrat Helfand-Parvus. The same articles of the Criminal Code, 51, 100 and 108, were afterwards invoked in indicting Trotsky and Lunacharsky, arrested by military detachments on the 23rd of July. According to the text of the decree, the leaders of the Bolsheviks "being Russian citizens, did, according to a preliminary agreement between themselves and other parties, with the aim of aiding other states engaged in hostile activities within the borders of Russia, enter into an agreement with the agents of the said governments to co-operate in the disorganization of the Russian army and rear for the purpose of weakening the fighting power of the army. For which purpose, with monies received by them from these states, they did organize a propaganda among the population and troops, summoning them to an immediate refusal of military activity against the enemy, and they did also with the same ends in view, during the period from the 3rd to the 5th of July, 1917, organize in Petrograd an armed insurrection." Although every educated person in those days, at least in the capital, knew in what circumstances Trotsky had come from New York through Christiania and Stockholm to Petrograd, the Court of Inquiry charged him also with having traveled through Germany. The Department of Justice evidently desired to leave no doubt as to the solidity of the materials which had been placed at its disposition by the Intelligence Service.

The latter institution has nowhere been a propagator of good morals. But in Russia the Intelligence Service was the very sewer of the Rasputin régime. The scum of the military officers, the police, the gendarmerie, together with discharged agents of the secret police, formed the cadres of that foul, stupid and all-powerful institution. Colonels, captains and ensigns who were useless for military deeds took under their supervision all branches of the social and governmental life, establishing throughout the country a system of spy feudalism. "The situation became absolutely catastrophic," complains a former director of police, Kurlov, "when the notorious Intelligence Service began to take part in the affairs of civil administration." Kurlov himself has no little dirty business to his credit—among other things an indirect participation in the murder of the Prime Minister, Stolypin. Nevertheless the activities of the Intelligence Service made even his experienced imagination shudder. During the time when "the struggle with enemy espionage . . . was being carried on very weakly," he writes, notoriously framed-up cases would frequently come down upon the heads of completely innocent people with the aim of naked blackmail. Kurlov ran into one such case: "To my horror," he says, "[I] heard the pseudonym of a secret agent known to me in my former service with the police department as having been expelled for blackmail." One of the provincial heads of the Intelligence Service, a certain Ustinov, a notary before the war, describes the morals of this service in his memoirs in practically the same terms as those used by Kurlov: "In search of something to do, the agents themselves would manufacture material."

It is still more instructive to verify the intellectual level of the institution by the example of this very accuser. "Russia went to ruin," writes Ustinov, speaking of the February revolution, "the victim of a revolution created by German agents on German money." The attitude of the patriotic notary to the Bolsheviks needs no further explanation. "The reports of the Intelligence Service as to the former activities of Lenin, as to his connection with the German staff, as to his receipt of German gold, are convincing enough to hang him immediately." Kerensky did not do this, it would seem, only because he was himself a traitor. "Especially astonishing, and even downright exasperating, was the leadership of a good-for-nothing lawyer among the Yids, Sashka Kerensky." Ustinov testifies that Kerensky "was well-known as a provocateur who betrayed his comrades." The French general, Anselm, as was found out later, abandoned Odessa in March, 1919, not under pressure from the Bolsheviks, but because he received an immense bribe. From the Bolsheviks? No. "The Bolsheviks had nothing to do with it," said Ustinov. "Here the Free Masons were at work." Such was that world.

Soon after the February revolution this institution, consisting of sharpers, falsificators and blackmailers, was put in charge of a patriotic Social Revolutionary, Mironov, who had arrived from abroad and whom an assistant minister, Demianov, a "people's socialist," characterized in the following words: "Mironov creates a good impression externally. . . . But I shall not be surprised if I learn that this is not a wholly normal person. It is quite possible to believe he is not: a normal person would hardly have agreed to stand at the head of an institution which ought to have been simply disbanded and its walls washed with sublimate." As a result of that administrative mix-up caused by the revolution, the Intelligence Service came under the supervision of the Minister of Justice, Pereverzev, a man of incredible light-mindedness and complete indifference to the means he employed. The same Demianov says in his memoirs that his minister "enjoyed almost no prestige at all in the Soviet." Under the protection of Mironov and Pereverzev, the Intelligence men, frightened at first by the revolution, soon came to themselves and accommodated their old activities to the new political situation. In June even the left wing of the governmental press began to publish information about blackmail and other crimes committed by the highest ranks of the Intelligence Service, even including two chiefs of the institution, Shukin and Broy, first assistants of the miserable Mironov. A week before the July crisis the Executive Committee, under pressure from the Bolsheviks, had addressed a demand to the government for an immediate inspection of the Intelligence Service with the participation of soviet representatives. The intelligence men thus had their own departmental reasons—or rather reasons of livelihood—for striking at the Bolsheviks as quickly and as hard as possible. Prince Lvov had signed a timely law giving the Intelligence Service the right to hold an arrestee under lock and key for three months.

The character of the accusation, and of the accusers, inevitably gives rise to the question, how could people of normal mould believe, or even pretend to believe, in this notorious lie which was inept from beginning to end. The success of the Intelligence Service would in truth have been unthinkable, except for the general atmosphere created by war, defeat, ruin, revolution, and the embitterment of the social struggle. Since the autumn of 1914 nothing had gone well with the ruling classes of Russia. The ground was crumbling under their feet. Everything was falling from their hands. Misfortunes were coming down on them from all directions. How could they help seeking a scapegoat? The former Attorney General, Zavadsky, remembers that "entirely healthy people were inclined in the alarming years of the war to suspect treachery where it apparently, and even indubitably, was not to be found. The majority of the cases of this kind prosecuted while I was attorney general, were fanciful." These cases were initiated, not only by spiteful agents, but by ordinary philistines who had lost their heads. But often, too, the war psychosis united with the pre-revolutionary political fever to produce even more freakish fruits. The Liberals, in common with the unsuccessful generals, sought everywhere and in everybody for the hand of the Germans. The court camarilla had been considered Germanified. The whole clique of Rasputin had been believed, or at least declared by the Liberals, to be under instructions from Potsdam. The tzarina had been widely and openly accused of espionage. She had been held responsible even in court circles for the sinking by Germans of the vessel in which General Kitchener was coming to Russia. The Rights, it goes without saying, were not slow to pay back the debt. Zavadsky relates how the Assistant Minister of the Interior, Beletsky, attempted early in 1916 to bring a charge against the national-liberal industrialist, Guchkov, accusing him of "activities bordering upon state treason in wartime." In exposing the performances of Beletsky, Kurlov, also a former Assistant Minister of the Interior, in his turn put the question to Miliukov: "For what honorable work in behalf of the fatherland did he (Miliukov) receive two hundred thousand rubles of 'Finland' money, transferred to him by mail in the name of the janitor of his house?" The quotation marks around "Finland" are supposed to show that it was really a question of German money. But nevertheless Miliukov had a well-earned reputation for Germanophobia! In governmental circles it was generally considered as proven that all the opposition parties were operating with German money. In August 1915, when disturbances were expected in connection with the dissolution of the Duma, the naval minister, Grigorovich, considered to be almost a Liberal, said at a session of the government: "The Germans are conducting a reinforced propaganda and showering the anti-government organizations with money." The Octobrists and Kadets, although indignant at these insinuations, nevertheless never thought of fending them off in a leftward direction. On the subject of a semi-patriotic speech of the Menshevik, Cheidze, at the beginning of the war, the president of the Duma, Rodzianko, wrote: "Subsequent events proved the closeness of Cheidze to German circles." You will wait in vain for the slightest shadow of such proof!

In his "History of the Second Russian Revolution," Miliukov

says: "The rôle of the 'dark sources' in the revolution of February 27 is wholly unclear, but judging by all that followed it is difficult to deny it." Peter Struve, a former Marxist and now a reactionary Slavophile of German origin, expresses himself more decisively: "When the Russian revolution, planned and created by Germany, succeeded, Russia had to all intents and purposes withdrawn from the war." Like Miliukov, Struve is here speaking not of the October, but of the February Revolution. On the subject of the famous "Order No. 1," the Magna Charta of soldiers' liberties drawn up by the delegates of the Petrograd garrison, Rodzianko wrote: "I have not the slightest doubt of the German origin of Order No. 1." The chief of one of the divisions, General Barkovsky, told Rodzianko that "Order No. 1 was supplied to his troops in enormous quantities from the German trenches." When he became war minister, Guchkov, whom they had tried to indict for state treason under the tzar, hastened to switch this accusation to the left. The April orders of Guchkov to the army read: "Persons who hate Russia, and are undoubtedly in the service of our enemies, have penetrated into the active army with the persistence characteristic of our enemies, and evidently in fulfilment of their demands are preaching the necessity of ending the war as soon as possible." On the subject of the April manifestation, which was directed against an imperialist policy, Miliukov writes: "The task of removing both ministers (Miliukov and Guchkov) was directly imposed by Germany," and the workers got 15 rubles a day from the Bolsheviks for taking part in the demonstration. With this key of German gold the liberal historian unlocks all those enigmas against which he bumped his head as a politician.

The patriotic socialists who baited the Bolsheviks as involuntary allies, if not agents, of the German ruling circles, were themselves under the same accusation from the right. We have seen what Rodzianko said about Cheidze. He did not even spare Kerensky himself. "It was he, undoubtedly, who through secret sympathy for the Bolsheviks, but perhaps also because of other considerations, impelled the Provisional Government" to admit the Bolsheviks into Russia. "Other considerations" can mean nothing but a partiality for German gold. In his curious memoirs, which have been translated into foreign languages, the General of Gendarmes, Spiridovich, remarking upon the abundance of Jews in the ruling circles of the Social Revolutionaries, adds: "Among them Russian names also glimmered, such as the future Rural Minister, the German spy, Victor Chernov." And it was by no means only this gendarme who suspected the leader of the Social Revolutionary party. After the July pogrom of the Bolsheviks, the Kadets lost no time in raising a hue and cry against the Minister of Agriculture, Chernov, a man suspected of connections with Berlin; and the unhappy patriot had to resign temporarily in order to exonerate himself. Speaking in the autumn of 1917 on the instructions given by the patriotic Executive Committee to the Menshevik, Skobelev, for his participation in an international socialist conference, Miliukov, in the tribune of the Pre-parliament, demonstrated by means of a meticulous syntactical analysis of its text, the obvious "German origin" of the document. The style of the instructions, as indeed of all the compromisist literature, was as a fact bad. The belated democracy, without ideas, without will, glancing round affrightedly on all sides, piled up qualification after qualification in its writings, until they sounded like a bad translation from a foreign language—just as the democracy itself was, indeed, the shadow of a foreign past. Ludendorff, however, is not in the least to blame for that.

The journey of Lenin through Germany offered inexhaustible possibilities for chauvinist demagoguism. But as though to demonstrate beyond a doubt the purely instrumental rôle of patriotism in their policies, the bourgeois press, after having at first met Lenin with a hypocritical good-will, started their licentious attack upon his "Germanophilism" only after his social program had become clear. "Land, bread, and peace"—those slogans he could only have brought from Germany. At that time there were still no revelations of Ermolenko.

After Trotsky and several other emigrants, returning from America, had been arrested by the military authorities of King George in the latitude of Halifax, the British ambassador in Petrograd gave to the press an official communication in a quite inimitable Anglo-Russian language: "Those Russian citizens on the steamer Christianiafiord were detained in Halifax because it was communicated to the British government that they had connections with a plan subsidized by the German government to overthrow the Russian Provisional Government. . . ." Buchanan's communication was dated April 14: at that time neither Burstein nor Ermolenko had appeared upon the horizon. Miliukov, in his capacity of Minister of Foreign Affairs, found himself obliged, however, to request the British government through the Russian ambassador, Nabokov, to liberate Trotsky and permit him to come to Russia. "Knowing of Trotsky's activities in America," writes Nabokov, "the British government was perplexed: 'Is this ill-will or blindness?' The Englishmen shrugged their shoulders, understood the danger, gave us warning." Lloyd George however was compelled to yield. In answer to a question put by Trotsky to the British Ambassador in the Petrograd press, Buchanan took back in some embarrassment his first explanation, and this time announced: "My government detained the group of emigrants in Halifax only for the purpose of, and until, the establishment of their identity by the Russian government. . . . That is the whole story of the detaining of the Russian emigrants." Buchanan was not only a gentleman, but also a diplomat.

At a conference of members of the State Duma early in June, Miliukov, having been pushed out of the government by the April demonstration, demanded the arrest of Lenin and Trotsky, unequivocally hinting at their connections with Germany. On the following day at the congress of the soviets, Trotsky declared: "Until Miliukov confirms or withdraws this accusation, he wears the brand of a dishonest slanderer." Miliukov answered in the newspaper *Rech* that he was "in truth dissatisfied that Messrs. Lenin and Trotsky are at liberty," but that he had motivated the demand for their arrest "not on the ground that they are agents of Germany, but that they have sufficiently violated the criminal code." Miliukov was a diplomat without being a gentleman. The necessity of arresting Lenin and Trotsky had been perfectly clear to him before the revelations of Ermolenko; the juridical dressings of the arrest were a mere question of technique. The leader of the Liberals had been playing with the sharp blade of this accusation long before it was set in motion in a "juridical" form.

The rôle of the myth of German gold becomes most obvious of all in a colorful episode described by the general administrator of the Provisional Government, the Kadet Nabokov (not to be confused with the Russian ambassador in London mentioned above). In one of the sittings of the government, Miliukov, speaking on some other question, remarked: "It is no secret to anybody that German money played its rôle among the factors promoting the revolution. . . ." That was quite in the character of Miliukov, although the formula was obviously softened. "Kerensky," according to Nabokov's report, "went into a rage. He seized his portfolio and slamming it down on the table, cried out: 'Since Miliukov has dared in my presence to slander the sacred cause of the great Russian Revolution, I do not wish to remain here another minute.'" That is wholly in the character of Kerensky although his gestures were perhaps a little exaggerated. A Russian proverb advises us not to spit in the well from which we may have to drink. When he was offended by the October Revolution, Kerensky could think of nothing better to use against it than this myth of German gold. That which in Miliukov's mouth had been a "slander against a sacred cause" became for Kerensky in the mouth of Burstein the sacred cause of slandering the Bolsheviks.

The unbroken chain of suspicions of Germanophilism and espionage, extending from the tzarina, Rasputin and the court circles, through the ministry, the staffs, the Duma, the liberal newspapers, to Kerensky and a number of the Soviet leaders, strikes one most of all by its monotony. The political enemy seem to have firmly resolved not to overwork their imaginations: they simply switched the same old accusations about from one point to another, the movement being predominantly from right to left. The July slander against the Bolsheviks least of all fell down out of a clear sky. It was the natural fruit of panic and hate, the last link in a shameful chain, the transfer of a stereotyped slanderous formula to its new and final object, permitting a reconciliation of the accusers and the accused of yesterday. All the insults of the ruling group, all their fears, all their bitterness, were now directed against that party which stood at the extreme left and incarnated most completely the unconquerable force of the revo-

lution. Was it in actual fact possible for the possessing classes to
surrender their place to the Bolsheviks without having made a
last desperate effort to trample them in the blood and filth? That
tangle of slander, well snarled up from long usage, was inevitably
fated to come down on the heads of the Bolsheviks. The revelations of the retired ensign from the Intelligence Service were only
a materialization of the ravings of possessing classes who found
themselves in a blind alley. For that reason the slander acquired
such frightful force.

The idea of German agentry was not in itself, to be sure, mere
raving. The German espionage in Russia was incomparably better
organized than the Russian in Germany. It is sufficient to recall
the fact that the War Minister, Sukhomlinov, was arrested even
under the old régime as the trusted man of Berlin. It is also
indubitable that German agents inserted themselves not only
into the court and Black Hundred circles, but also among the
Lefts. The Austrian and German governments had flirted from
the first days of the war with separatist tendencies, beginning
among the Ukrainian and Caucasian emigrants. It is interesting
that Ermolenko, recruited in April 1917, was sent over to struggle
for the secession of the Ukraine. As early as 1914, both Lenin and
Trotsky in Switzerland had demanded in print a break with those
revolutionists who were getting caught on the hook of Austro-
German militarism. Early in 1917 Trotsky repeated this printed
warning to the left German social democrats, the followers of
Liebknecht, with whom agents of the British embassy were trying to establish connections. But in flirting with separatists in order to weaken Russia and frighten the tzar, the German government was far from the thought of overthrowing tzarism. The
best evidence of this is a proclamation scattered in the Russian
trenches after the February revolution, and read on March 11 at a
session of the Petrograd soviet. "At the beginning the English
joined hands with your tzar; now they have turned against him
because he would not agree to their self-interested demands. They
have overthrown your tzar, given to you by God. Why has this
happened? Because he understood and divulged the faults and
crafty schemes of the English." Both the form and contents of
this document give internal guarantee of its genuineness. Just

as you cannot imitate a Prussian lieutenant, so you cannot imitate his historic philosophy. Hoffmann, a Prussian lieutenant with a general's rank, imagined that the Russian revolution was thought up and its foundations laid in England. In that, however, there is less absurdity than in the theory of Miliukov and Struve, for Potsdam continued to the end to hope for a separate peace with Tzarskoe Selo, while in London they feared more than anything else a separate peace between them. Only when the impossibility of restoring the tzar became wholly obvious, did the German staff transfer its hopes to the disintegrating power of the revolutionary process. Even in the matter of Lenin's trip through Germany, the initiative came not from German circles but from Lenin himself —in its very first form, indeed, from the Menshevik, Martov. The German staff only consented to it, and that probably not without hesitation. Ludendorff said to himself: Perhaps relief will come from that side.

During the July events the Bolsheviks themselves sought for an alien and criminal hand in certain unexpected excesses that were obviously provoked with malice aforethought. Trotsky wrote in those days: "What rôle has been played in this by counter-revolutionary provocation and German agents? It is difficult at present to pronounce definitely upon this question. . . . We must await the results of an authentic investigation. . . . But even now it is possible to say with certainty that the results of such an investigation will throw a clear light upon the work of Black Hundred gangs, and upon the underground rôle played by gold, German, English or 100 per cent Russian, or indeed all three of them. But no judicial investigation will change the political meaning of the events. The worker and soldier masses of Petrograd were not, and could not have been, bought. They are not in the service of Wilhelm, or Buchanan, or Miliukov. . . . The movement was prepared by the war, by oncoming hunger, by the reaction lifting its head, by the headlessness of the government, by the adventurist offensive, by the political distrust and revolutionary alarm of the workers and soldiers. . . ." All the material in the archives, the documents and memoirs, which have become public since the war and the two revolutions, prove beyond a doubt that the partiality of German agents for the revolutionary processes in Russia did not for one moment rise out of the military-police sphere into the sphere of big politics. Is there, by the way, any need of insisting upon this, after the revolution in Germany itself? How pitiful and impotent did these supposedly all-powerful Hohenzollern agents turn out to be in the autumn of 1918 in the face of the German workers and soldiers! "The calculation of our enemy in sending Lenin to Russia was absolutely right," says Miliukov. Ludendorff himself quite otherwise estimates the results of the undertaking: "I could not suppose" so he justifies himself, speaking of the Russian revolution, "that it would become the tomb of our own might." This merely means that of the two strategists, Ludendorff who permitted Lenin to go, and Lenin who accepted his permission, Lenin saw farther and better.

"The enemy propaganda and Bolshevism" complains Ludendorff in his memoirs, "were seeking one and the same goal within the boundaries of the German state. England gave opium to China, our enemies gave us revolution. . . ." Ludendorff attributes to the Entente the same thing of which Miliukov and Kerensky were accusing Germany. Thus cruelly does the insulted reason of history avenge itself! But Ludendorff did not stop there. In February 1931, he informed the world that behind the back of the Bolsheviks stood international and especially Jewish finance capital, united in the struggle against tzarist Russia and imperialist Germany. "Trotsky arrived in Petrograd from America through Sweden, provided with great supplies of the money of international capitalists. Other moneys were supplied to the Bolsheviks by the Jew, Solmsen, from Germany." (*Ludendorff's Volkswarte*, February 15, 1931). However the testimonies of Ludendorff and Ermolenko may disagree, they coincide in one point: a part of the money did actually come from Germany—not from Ludendorff, it is true, but from his mortal enemy, Solmsen. Only this testimony was lacking to provide an esthetic finish to the whole question.

But not Ludendorff, nor yet Miliukov, nor Kerensky, invented this device, although they first made a broad use of it. "Solmsen" has many predecessors in history, both as Jew and as German agent. Count Fersen, a Swedish ambassador in France during the great revolution, a passionate partisan of the monarchical power of the king, and more especially of the queen, more than once sent to his government in Stockholm such communications as the following: "The Jew, Efraim, an emissary of Herr Herzberg in Berlin, (the Prussian Minister of Foreign Affairs) is supplying them (the Jacobins) with money; not long ago he received another 600,000 livres." The moderate newspaper, *Les Revolutions de Paris* made the supposition that during the republican revolution "emissaries of the European diplomats, such as for instance the Jew Efraim, an agent of the Prussian king, made their way into the volatile and fickle crowd. . . ." The same Fersen reported: "The Jacobins would have perished, but for the help of the rabble bribed by them." If the Bolsheviks paid daily wages to the participants in that demonstration, they only followed the example of the Jacobins, and moreover the money for bribing the "rabble" came in both cases from a source in Berlin. This similarity in the action of revolutionists in the twentieth and eighteenth centuries would be striking, were it not outweighed by a more striking similarity in the slanders peddled by their enemies. But we need not limit ourselves to the Jacobins. The history of all revolutions and civil wars invariably testifies that a threatened or an overthrown ruling class is disposed to find the cause of its misfortunes, not in itself, but in foreign agents and emissaries. Not only Miliukov in his character as a learned historian, but even Kerensky in his character as a superficial reader of history, must be aware of this. However, in their character as politicians they were victims of their own counter-revolutionary functions.

Under these theories about the revolutionary rôle of foreign agents, as under all typical mass-misunderstandings, there lies an indirect historical foundation. Consciously or unconsciously, every nation at the critical period of its existence makes especially broad and bold borrowings from the treasury of other peoples. Not infrequently, moreover, a leading rôle in the progressive movement is played by people living on the border or emigrants returning to the homeland. The new ideas and institutions thus appear to the conservative strata first of all as alien, as foreign inventions. The village against the city, the backwoods against the capital, the petty bourgeois against the worker—they all defend themselves under the guise of a national force resisting foreign influence. Miliukov portrayed the Bolshevik movement as "German" for the same reason in the last analysis that the Russian muzhik has for a hundred years regarded as a German any man dressed up in city clothes. The difference is that the muzhik was making an honest mistake.

In 1918—that is, after the October Revolution—a press bureau of the American government triumphantly published a collection of documents connecting the Bolsheviks with the Germans. This crude forgery, which would not stand up under a breath of criticism, was believed in by many educated and perspicacious people, until it was discovered that the originals of the documents supposed to have been drawn up in different countries were all written on the same machine. The forgers did not stand on ceremony with their customers: they were obviously confident that the political demand for exposures of the Bolsheviks would outweigh the voice of criticism. And they made no mistake, for they were well paid for the documents. However, the American government, separated by an ocean from the scene of the struggle, was only secondarily interested in this matter.

But why after all is political slander as such so poor and monotonous? Because the social mind is economical and conservative. It does not expend more efforts than are necessary for its goal. It prefers to borrow the old, when not compelled to create the new. But even when so compelled, it combines with it elements of the old. Each successive religion has created no new mythology, but has merely repersonified the superstitions of the past. In the same manner philosophical systems are created, and doctrines of law and morals. Separate individuals, even those possessed of genius, develop in the same inharmonious way as the society which nourishes them. A bold imagination lives in the same skull with a slavish adherence to trite images. Audacious flights reconcile themselves with crude prejudices. Shakespeare nourished his creative genius upon subjects handed down from the deep ages. Pascal used the theory of probability to demonstrate the existence of God. Newton discovered the law of gravitation and believed in the Apocalypse. After Marconi had established a wireless station in the residence of the pope, the vicar of Christ distributed his mystic blessing by radio. In ordinary times these contradictions do not rise above a condition of drowsiness, but in times of catastrophe they acquire explosive force. When it comes to a threat against their material interests, the educated classes set in motion all the prejudices and confusion which humanity is dragging in its wagon-train behind it. Can we too much blame the lords of old Russia, if they built the mythology of their fall out of indiscriminate borrowings from those classes which were overthrown before them? To be sure, the circumstance that Kerensky resurrects the tale of Ermolenko in his memoirs many years after the event, is, to say the least, superfluous.

The slander of those years of war and revolution was striking, we remarked, in its monotony. However, it does contain a variation. From the piling up of quantity we get a new quality. The struggle of the other parties among themselves was almost like a family spat in comparison with their common baiting of the Bolsheviks. In conflict with one another they were, so to speak, only getting in training for a further conflict, a decisive one. Even in employing against each other the sharpened accusation of German connections, they never carried the thing through to the limit. July presents a different picture. In the assault upon the Bolsheviks all the ruling forces, the government, the courts, the Intelligence Service, the staffs, the officialdom, the municipalities, the parties of the soviet majority, their press, their orators, constituted one colossal unit. The very disagreements among them, like the different tone qualities of the instruments in an orchestra, only strengthened the general effect. An inept invention of two contemptible creatures was elevated to the height of a factor in history. The slanders poured down like Niagara. If you take into consideration the setting—the war and the revolution—and the character of the accused—revolutionary leaders of millions who were conducting their party to the sovereign power—you can say without exaggeration that July 1917 was the month of the most gigantic slander in world history.

CHAPTER V

THE COUNTER-REVOLUTION LIFTS ITS HEAD

DURING the first two months, when the power belonged formally to the government of Guchkov and Miliukov, it was as a fact wholly in the hands of the Soviet. During the following two months the Soviet grew weaker. A part of its influence upon the masses went over to the Bolsheviks; a part of its power the minister-socialists took with them into their portfolios in the Coalition Government. From the outset of preparations for the offensive there began an automatic increase of the influence of the commanding staff, the organs of finance capital and the Kadet party. Before shedding the blood of the soldiers, the Executive Committee carried out a substantial transfusion of its own blood into the arteries of the bourgeoisie. Behind the scenes the threads of all this were held in the hands of the embassies and governments of the Entente.

At an inter-allied conference in London the western friends "forgot" to invite the Russian ambassador. Only after he had reminded them of his existence, did they send him an invitation— it was about ten minutes before the opening of the session—and moreover there was no place for him at the table, and he had to crowd in between the Frenchmen. This mockery of the ambassador of the Provisional Government and the demonstrative exit of the Kadets from the government—both events happening on the 2nd of July—had the same purpose: to bring the Compromisers to their knees. The armed demonstration, bursting out just after this, had an especially exasperating effect upon the soviet leaders, because having been struck this double blow, they were at the time directing all their attention in exactly the other direction. Once it had become necessary to take up a bloody task in alliance with the Entente, it would be hard after all to find better intermediaries than the Kadets. Chaikovsky, one of the oldest revolutionists, who had become metamorphosed after long years abroad into a moderate British Liberal, moralized as follows: "Money is necessary for war, and the Allies will not give money to socialists." The Compromisers were embarrassed by this argument, but fully understood the force of it.

The correlation of forces had obviously changed to the disadvantage of the people, but nobody was able to say how much: The appetites of the bourgeoisie, at least, had grown considerably more than their opportunities. In this uncertainty lay the source of the conflict, for the strength of class forces is tested in action, and all the events of a revolution reduce themselves to these repeated trials of force. However great may have been the shift of power from left to right, in any case it very little affected the Provisional Government which remained a vacant space. The people who in those critical July Days were interested in the ministry of Prince Lvov could be counted on the fingers of one hand. General Krymov, the same one who once had a conversation with Guckhov about overthrowing Nicholas II—we will soon meet this general for the last time—sent the prince a telegram concluding with the urgent demand: "It is time to pass from words to deeds." The advice sounded funny, and merely further emphasized the impotence of the government.

"At the beginning of July," subsequently wrote the Liberal, Nabokov, "there was one short moment when the authority of the government seemed again to lift its head; that was after the putting down of the first Bolshevik uprising. But the Provisional Government was unable to make use of this opportunity, and let slip the favorable conditions of the moment. It was never repeated." Other representatives of the right camp have expressed themselves to the same effect. In reality, in the July Days as in all other critical moments, the constituent parts of the coalition were pursuing different goals. The Compromisers would have been perfectly ready to permit a final wiping out of the Bolsheviks, had it not been obvious that after settling with the Bolsheviks, the officers, Cossacks, Cavaliers of St. George and shock battalions would have cleaned up the Compromisers themselves. The Kadets wanted to carry through, and sweep away not only the Bolsheviks but the soviets also. However, it was no accident that at all acute moments the Kadets found themselves outside the government. In the last analysis what pushed them out was the pressure of the masses, irresistible in spite of the buffer provided by the Compromisers. Even if they had succeeded in seizing the power, the Liberals could not have held it. Subsequent events conclusively proved this. The idea of a lost opportunity in July is a retrospective illusion. At any rate, the July victory did not strengthen the government, but on the contrary opened a prolonged period of crisis which was formally resolved only on the 24th of July, and was in essence an introduction to the four months' death agony of the February régime.

The Compromisers were torn between the necessity of reviving their half-friendship with the bourgeoisie, and the need of softening the hostility of the masses. Tacking became for them a form of existence. Their zigzags became a feverish tossing to and fro, but the fundamental line kept swinging sharply to the right. On the 7th of July, a whole series of repressive measures was decreed by the government. But at the same session, and so to speak by stealth, taking advantage of the absence of the "old man"—that is, the Kadets—the minister-socialists proposed to the government that it undertake to carry out the program of the June congress of the soviets. This, however, straightway led to a further disintegration of the government. The great landlord and former president of the land union, Prince Lvov, accused the government of "undermining" with its agrarian policy "the popular sense of right." The landlords were worried not only lest they be deprived of their hereditary possessions, but lest the Compromisers "attempt to place the Constituent Assembly before the fact of a decision already arrived at." All the pillars of the monarchist reaction now became flaming partisans of pure democracy! The government decided that Kerensky should occupy the position of Minister-President, retaining also the portfolios of war and navy. To Tseretelli as the new Minister of the Interior fell the task of responding in the Executive Committee to questions about the arrest of the Bolsheviks. A protesting question was raised by Martov, and Tseretelli unceremoniously answered his old party comrade that he would rather deal with Lenin than Martov: with the former he knew what to do, but with the latter his hands were tied. . . . "I take upon myself the responsibility for these arrests": the minister threw this challenge into the tensely attentive hall.

In dealing blows to the left, the Compromisers would justify themselves by citing a danger to the right. "Russia is threatened with a military dictatorship," declared Dan at the session of July 9th. "We are obliged to snatch the bayonet from the hand of the military dictator. And this we can do only by declaring the Provisional Government a Committee of Public Safety. We must give it unlimited powers, so that it may root out to the bottom anarchy on the left and counter-revolution on the right. . . ." As though in the hands of a government fighting against workers and soldiers and peasants there could be any other bayonet but the bayonet of counter-revolution! By 253 votes with 47 abstaining, the joint session adopted the following resolutions: "1. The country and the revolution are in danger. 2. The Provisional Government is a government of the Salvation of the Revolution. 3. It is endowed with unlimited powers." The resolution resounded as loud as an empty barrel. The Bolsheviks present at the session abstained from the voting, which testifies to an indubitable disconcertedness among the heads of the party at that time.

Mass movements, even when shattered, never fail to leave their traces. The place of the titled nobleman at the head of the government was now occupied by a radical lawyer. The Ministry of the Interior was occupied by a former hard-labor convict. The plebeian transformation of the government was at hand. Kerensky, Tseretelli, Chernov, Skobelev, leaders of the Executive Committee, now determined the physiognomy of the government. Was not this a realization of the slogan of the June Days, "Down with the ten minister-capitalists"? No, this was only an exposure of its inadequacy. The minister-democrats took the power only in order to bring back the minister-capitalists. *La Coalition est morte, vive la coalition!*

The comedy is now put on—the solemnly shameful comedy of the disarming of the machine-gunners on Palace Square. A series of regiments are disbanded, the soldiers are sent in small detachments to fill up the ranks at the front. Forty-year-old men are brought to submission, and herded into the trenches. They are all agitators against the régime of Kerenskyism. There are tens of thousands of them, and in the autumn they will accomplish a great work in the trenches. At the same time the workers are disarmed, although with less success. Under pressure from the generals—we shall see in a minute what forms it took—the death penalty is reintroduced at the front. But on the same day, the 12th of July, a decree is published limiting the sales of land. That belated half-measure, adopted under the axe of the muzhik, provokes mockery from the left and a grinding of teeth on the right. While forbidding all processions in the streets—a threat to the left—Tseretelli warns of the prevalence of unlegalized arrests—an attempt to pull up the reins on the Right. In removing the commander-in-chief of the forces of the Petrograd district, Kerensky explains to the Left that this is because he broke up the workers' organizations, to the Right that it is because he was not decisive enough.

The Cossacks became the veritable heroes of bourgeois Petrograd. "There were occasions," relates the Cossack officer, Grekov, "when upon the entrance into a public place, a restaurant for example, of someone in a Cossack uniform, all would stand up and greet the newcomer with applause." The theaters, the moving-picture houses, the public gardens, instituted a series of benefit evenings for the wounded Cossacks and the families of the slain. The bureau of the Executive Committee found itself compelled to elect a commission, with Cheidze at the head, to participate in the organization of a public funeral for the "warriors fallen while fulfilling their revolutionary duty in the days of July 3–5." The Compromisers had to drink the cup of humiliation to the dregs. The ceremonial began with a liturgy in the Isaakievsky Cathedral. The pall-bearers were Rodzianko, Miliukov, Prince Lvov, Kerensky, and they marched in procession to the burial-place in the Alexandro-Nevsky Monastery. On the line of march the militia were not to be seen; order was preserved by the Cossacks. The day of the funeral was the day of their complete dominion of Petrograd. The workers and soldiers slain by the Cossacks, own brothers of the February martyrs, were buried secretly, as were the martyrs of January 9th under tzarism.

The Kronstadt Executive Committee was ordered by the government, under threat of a blockade of the island, to put

Raskolnikov, Roshal and ensign Remnev at the disposal of the Court of Inquiry. At Helsingfors, Left Social-Revolutionaries were for the first time arrested along with Bolsheviks. The retired Prince Lvov complained in the newspapers that "the soviets are beneath the level of state morals and have not yet cleansed themselves of Leninists—those agents of the Germans. . . ." It became a matter of honor with the Compromisers to demonstrate their state morals. On July 13th the Executive Committees in joint session adopted a resolution introduced by Dan: "Any person indicted by the courts is deprived of membership in the Executive Committees until sentence is pronounced." This placed the Bolsheviks in fact beyond the law. Kerensky shut down the whole Bolshevik press. In the provinces the land committees were arrested. *Izvestia* sobbed impotently: "Only a few days ago we witnessed a debauch of anarchy on the streets of Petrograd. Today on the same streets there is an unrestrained flow of counter-revolutionary Black Hundred speeches."

After the disbandment of the more revolutionary regiments and the disarming of the workers, the resultant of the composition of forces moved still farther to the right. A considerable part of the real power was now clearly in the hands of the military chiefs, the industrial and banking and Kadet groups. The rest of it remained as before in the hands of the soviets. The dual power was still there, but now no longer the legalized, contactual or coalitional dual power of the preceding two months, but the explosive dual power of a clique—of two cliques, the bourgeois-military and the compromisist, who feared, but at the same time needed each other. What remained to be done? To resurrect the Coalition. "After the insurrection of July 3–5," says Miliukov quite justly, "the idea of a Coalition not only did not disappear, but acquired for the time being more force and importance than it had possessed before."

The Provisional Committee of the state Duma unexpectedly came to life at this time and adopted a drastic resolution against the Government of Salvation. That was the last straw. All the ministers handed their portfolios to Kerensky, thereby making him the focus of the national sovereignty. In the further development of the February revolution, as also in the personal fate of

Kerensky, that moment acquired an important significance. In the chaos of groupings, resignations and appointments, something in the nature of an immovable point had been designated around which everything else revolved. The resignation of the ministers served only as an introduction to negotiations with the Kadets and industrialists. The Kadets laid down their conditions: responsibility of the members of the government "exclusively to their own conscience"; complete unity with the Allies; restoration of discipline in the army; no social reforms until the Constituent Assembly. A point not written down was the demand that the elections to the Constituent Assembly be postponed. This was called a "non-party and national program." A similar program was advanced by the representatives of trade and industry, whom the Compromisers had tried vainly to set against the Kadets. The Executive Committee again confirmed its resolution endowing the Government of Salvation with "unlimited powers." That meant agreeing to the government's independence of the soviets. On the same day Tseretelli as Minister of the Interior sent out instructions for the taking of "swift and decisive measures putting an end to all illegal activities in the matter of land relations." The Minister of Food Supply, Peshekhonov, likewise demanded an end of all "violent and criminal manifestations against the landlords." The Government of the Salvation of the Revolution recommended itself above all as a government of the salvation of the landlord's property. But not that alone. An industrial magnate, the engineer Palchinsky, in his three-fold calling as director of the Ministry of Trade and Industry, plenipotentiary administrator of fuel and metal, and head of the Commission on Defense, was conducting an energetic campaign for syndicated capital. The Menshevik economist, Cherevanin, complained in the economic department of the Soviet that the noble undertakings of the democracy were going to smash against the sabotage of Palchinsky. The Minister of Agriculture, Chernov, to whose shoulders the Kadets had shifted the accusation of German connections, felt obliged "for purposes of rehabilitation" to resign. On June 18, the government, in which socialists predominated, issued a decree dissolving the unsubmissive Finnish Seim [1] with its

---

[1] Parliament.

socialist majority. In a solemn note to the Allies on the third anniversary of the World War, the government not only repeated the ritual oath of loyalty, but also reported the happy putting down of an insurrection caused by agents of the enemy. A priceless documentary record of bootlicking! At the same time a fierce law was promulgated against transgressions of discipline on the railroads. After the government had thus demonstrated its statesmanly maturity, Kerensky finally made up his mind to answer the ultimatum of the Kadet party. His answer was to the effect that the demands presented by it "could not serve as an obstacle to its participation in the Provisional Government." This veiled capitulation was, however, not enough for the Liberals. They had to bring the Compromisers to their knees. The central committee of the Kadet party declared that the governmental declaration issued after the break-up of the coalition on July 8— a collection of democratic commonplaces—was unacceptable to them, and broke off the negotiations.

It was a concentrated attack. The Kadets were acting in close union, not only with the industrialists and Allied diplomats, but also with the army generals. The head committee of the League of Officers at headquarters functioned under the *de facto* leadership of the Kadet party. Through the high commanding staff the Kadets brought pressure against the Compromisers on their most sensitive side. On July 8th the commander-in-chief of the southwestern front, General Kornilov, gave orders to open fire upon retreating soldiers with machine-guns and artillery. Supported by the commissar of the front, Savinkov—former head of a terrorist organization of Social Revolutionaries—Kornilov had before this demanded the introduction of the death penalty at the front, threatening otherwise to resign the command. A secret telegram had immediately appeared in the press. Kornilov was trying to get publicity for himself. The supreme commander-in-chief, Brussilov, more cautious and evasive, wrote to Kerensky in pedagogical tone: "The lessons of the great French Revolution, partially forgotten by us, nevertheless forcibly call themselves to mind. . . ." These lessons lay in the fact that the French Revolutionists, after vainly trying to reorganize the army "upon humane principles" afterward adopted the death penalty and "their triumphal banners filled half the world." This was all that the general had learned from the book of revolution. On July 12, the government restored the death penalty "in war time for certain major crimes committed by men on military duty." However, the commander-in-chief of the northern front, General Klembovsky, wrote three days later: "Experience has shown that those military units in which there have been many replacements have become utterly incapable of fighting. An army cannot be healthy if the source of its replacements is rotten." This rotten source of replacements was the Russian people.

On the 16th of July, Kerensky called a conference of the older military chiefs at headquarters with the participation of Tereshchenko and Savinkov. Kornilov was absent. The recoil on his front was in full swing, and came to a stand only several days later when the Germans themselves called a halt on the old state frontier. The names of the conferees, Brussilov, Alexeiev, Ruszky, Klembovsky, Denikin, Romanovsky, sounded like the last echo of an epoch that was disappearing in the abyss. For four months these high generals had been regarding themselves as half-dead. They now came to life and, considering the minister-president an incarnation of the revolution which had so vexed them, spitefully pinched and slapped him with impunity.

According to headquarters' figures, the army on the south-western front had lost between June 18 and July 6, 56,000 men. An insignificant sacrifice measured by the scale of the war! But two revolutions, the February and the October, cost a great deal less. What had the Liberals and Compromisers got out of the offensive besides death, destruction and disaster? The social earthquakes of 1917 changed the aspect of one-sixth of the earth's surface and opened new possibilities before humanity. The cruelties and horrors of revolution—which we have no desire either to soften or deny—do not fall from the sky. They are inseparable from the whole process of historic development.

Brussilov made a report on the results of the offensive begun a month before: "Complete failure." Its cause lay in the fact that "the officers, from the company commander to the commander-in-chief, have no power." How and why they lost it, he did not say. As for future operations: "We cannot get ready for them

before spring." While insisting like the rest upon repressive measures, Klembovsky expressed a doubt whether they could be real.
"The death penalty? But is it possible to put to death whole divisions? Court-martials? But in that case half of the army would
be in Siberia. . . ." The chief of the general staff reported: "Five
regiments of the Petrograd garrison disbanded; the instigators
court-martialled. . . . In all about 90,000 men will be transferred from Petrograd." This news was received with satisfaction.
It did not occur to anybody to ponder the consequences of an
evacuation of the Petrograd garrison.

As to the committees, said Alexeiev, "they must be abolished.
. . . Military history extending over thousands of years has
created its laws. We tried to violate these laws, and we have had
a fiasco." This man confused the laws of history with the rules
of the drill-master. "People followed the old banners as sacred
things and went to their deaths," boasted Ruszky. "But to what
have the red banners brought us? To the surrender of armies in
whole corps." The decrepit general had forgotten that he himself
in August 1915 reported to the Council of Ministers: "The contemporary demands of military technique are beyond our powers;
in any case we cannot keep up with the Germans." Klembovsky
insisted with spiteful pleasure that the army had not really been
ruined by Bolsheviks, but by "other persons" who had introduced
a good-for-nothing military code, "persons who do not understand the life and conditions of existence of an army." This was
a direct slap at Kerensky. Denikin came down on the ministers
more decisively: "You have trampled them in the mud, our
glorious war banners, and you will lift them again if you have
a conscience. . . ." And Kerensky? Suspected of lacking a conscience, he humbly thanked the military boor for his "frankly
and justly expressed opinion." And as for the declaration of rights
of the soldier: "If I had been minister when it was drawn up, the
declaration would not have been issued. Who first put down the
Siberian sharp-shooters? Who first shed blood to bring the disobedient into line? My appointee! My commissar!" the Minister
of Foreign Affairs, Tereshchenko, ingratiated himself with this
consoling observation: "Our offensive even though unsuccessful
has increased the confidence in us of the Allies." The confidence

122

of the Allies! Was it not for this that the earth rotated upon its axis?

"At the present time the officers are the sole bulwark of freedom and the revolution," declaimed Klembovsky. "The officer is not a bourgeois," explained Brussilov, "he is the most real proletarian." General Ruszky added: "Generals also are proletarian." To abolish the committees, restore power to the old chiefs, drive politics—and that means revolution—out of the army: such was the program of these proletarians with a general's rank. And Kerensky did not object to the program itself; he was only troubled about the date. "As for the proposed measures," he said, "I think that even General Denikin would not insist upon their immediate introduction. . . ." Those generals were mere drab mediocrities, but they could hardly have failed to say to themselves: "That's the kind of language to use with these fellows!"

As a result of the conference there was a change in the high command. The compliant and flexible Brussilov who had replaced the cautious bureaucrat Alexeiev, the latter having opposed the offensive, was now removed, and General Kornilov named in his place. The change was variously motivated: to the Kadets they promised that Kornilov would establish iron discipline; they assured the Compromisers that Kornilov was a friend of the committees and commissars; Savinkov himself vouched for his republican sentiments. In answer to his high appointment the general sent a new ultimatum to the government: He, Kornilov, would accept the appointment only on the following conditions: "Responsibility only to his own conscience and the people; no interference in the appointment of the high-commanding staff; restoration of the death penalty at the rear." The first point created difficulties. Kerensky had started the business of "answering to his own conscience and the people," and this particular business does not tolerate competitors. Kornilov's telegram was published in the most widely circulated liberal papers. The cautious politicians of the reaction puckered their noses. Kornilov's ultimatum was merely the ultimatum of the Kadet party translated into the forthright language of a Cossack general. But Kornilov's calculations were right: The exorbitant demands and impudent tone of his ultimatum delighted all the enemies of the revolution, and above all the regular officers. Kerensky took fright and wanted to remove Kornilov forthwith, but found no support in his government. In the end, upon the advice of his backers, Kornilov agreed to concede in an oral statement that by responsibility to the people he meant responsibility to the Provisional Government. For the rest, the ultimatum was accepted with some slight qualifications. Kornilov became commander-in-chief. At the same time the military engineer, Filonenko, was appointed as his commissar, and the former commissar of the southwestern front, Savinkov, was made general administrator of the War Ministry. The one was an accidental figure, a parvenu, the other a man with a big revolutionary past—both of them pure adventurers, ready for anything. Filonenko at least was ready for anything, and Savinkov was ready for much. Their close connection with Kornilov, promoters of the swift career of the general, played its rôle as we shall see in the further development of events.

The Compromisers were surrendering all along the line. Tseretelli asserted: "The Coalition is a union of salvation." In spite of the formal split, negotiations were in full swing behind the scenes. In order to hasten the solution, Kerensky, in obvious agreement with the Kadets, resorted to a purely histrionic measure—a measure, that is to say, wholly in the spirit of his general policy, but at the same time useful to his goal. He resigned and left town, abandoning the Compromisers to their own desperation. Miliukov says on this theme: "By his demonstrative departure he proved to his enemies, rivals and adherents that, however they might look upon his personal qualities, he was indispensable at the present moment simply because of the political position he occupied between the two warring camps." He won the game by giving it away. The Compromisers threw themselves upon "Comrade Kerensky" with suppressed curses and public prayers. Both sides, the Kadets and the socialists, easily persuaded the headless ministry to abolish itself, empowering Kerensky to form the government anew and at his sole personal discretion.

In order to drive out of their wits the already frightened members of the Executive Committees, the latest news was handed to them of the deteriorating situation at the front. The Germans were driving the Russian troops, the Liberals were driving Kerensky, Kerensky was driving the Compromisers. The Menshevik and Social Revolutionary factions were in session all night on July 24. Wearied out with their own helplessness, the Executive Committees, by a majority of 147 votes against 46, with 42 abstaining —unprecedented opposition!—finally ratified the turning over of unconditional and unlimited powers to Kerensky. At the Kadet ·Congress, sitting simultaneously, voices were raised for the overthrow of Kerensky, but Miliukov curbed this impatience, suggesting that they limit themselves for the present to bringing pressure to bear. This does not mean that Miliukov had any illusions about Kerensky, but he saw in him a point of application for the power of the possessing classes. Once having freed the government from the soviets, it would be no labor to free it from Kerensky.

In those days the gods of the Coalition remained athirst. The decree demanding the arrest of Lenin had preceded the formation of the transitional government of July 7. Now some firm act was needed to signalize the resurrection of the Coalition. Already on the 13th of July there had appeared in Maxim Gorky's paper —the Bolshevik press no longer existing—an open letter from Trotsky to the Provisional Government which read: "You can have no logical foundation for excepting me from the implications of the decree under which Lenin, Zinoviev and Kamenev are liable to arrest. So far as concerns the political side of the question, you can have no reason to doubt that I am as implacable an enemy of the general policy of the Provisional Government as the above-named comrades." On the night when the new ministry was created, Trotsky and Lunacharsky were arrested in Petrograd, and ensign Krylenko, the future Bolshevik commander-in-chief, on the front.

The new government, having got born into the world after a three-day crisis, had the appearance of a runt. It consisted of second and third-rate figures selected on the basis of a choice between evils. The Vice-President turned out to be the engineer Nekrasov, a left Kadet who on February 27 had proposed that they put down the revolution by turning over the power to one of the tzarist generals. A writer without party and without personality, Prokopovich, a man who had been dwelling on the borderland between Kadets and Mensheviks, became Minister of Trade and Industry. A former attorney general, afterward a radical lawyer, Zarudny, son of a "liberal" minister of Alexander II, was called to the Ministry of Justice. The president of the Executive Committee of the peasant soviet, Avksentiev, received the portfolio of the Interior. The Menshevik, Skobelev, remained Minister of Labor, and the People's Socialist, Peshekhonov, became Minister of Provisions. The Liberals supplied equally secondary figures, men who played a leading rôle neither before nor after their appointment. Chernov somewhat unexpectedly returned to his post as Minister of Agriculture. In the four days between his resignation and this new appointment he had had time to rehabilitate himself. Miliukov in his "History" dispassionately remarks that the nature of the relation between Chernov and the German authorities "remained unexplained." "It is possible," he adds, "that the testimony of the Russian Intelligence Service and the suspicions of Kerensky, Tereshchenko and others went a little too far in this matter." The reappointment of Chernov to the post of Minister of Agriculture was nothing more than a tribute paid to the prestige of the ruling party of the Social Revolutionaries—in which, by the way, Chernov was steadily losing influence. Finally, Tseretelli had the foresight to remain outside the ministry. In May he had thought that he would be useful to the revolution in the staff of the government; now he intended to be useful to the government in the staff of the Soviet. From this time on Tseretelli actually fulfilled the duties of a commissar of the bourgeoisie in the system of the soviets. "If the interests of the country should be transgressed by the Coalition," he said at a session of the Petrograd soviet, "our duty would be to withdraw our comrades from the government." It was no longer a question then—as Dan had not long ago vouchsafed—of crowding out the Liberals after using them up; it was a question of retiring in good season upon finding out that you had been used up. Tseretelli was preparing a complete surrender of power to the bourgeoisie.

In the first Coalition, formed on May 6, the socialists had been in the minority, but they were in fact masters of the situation.

In the ministry of July 24, the socialists were in a majority, but they were mere shadows of the Liberals. "With a slight nominal predominance of socialists," writes Miliukov, "the actual predominance in the cabinet unquestionably belonged to the convinced partisans of bourgeois democracy." It would be more accurate to say bourgeois property. In the matter of democracy the thing was much less definite. In the same spirit, although with an unexpected motivation, Minister Peshekhonov compared the July with the May Coalition: At that time, he said, the bourgeoisie needed support from the left; now when counter-revolution threatens it needs support from the right. "The more forces we attract from the right, the fewer will remain of those who wish to make an attack upon the government." This suggests a superb rule for political strategy: In order to raise the siege of a fortress, the best method is to open the gates from the inside. That was the formula of the new Coalition.

The reaction was on the offensive, the democracy in retreat. Classes and groups which had retired in fright during the first days of the revolution began to lift their heads. Interest which yesterday had lain concealed, today came into the open. Merchants and speculators demanded the extermination of the Bolsheviks and—freedom of trade. They raised their voice against all restrictions upon trade whatsoever, even those which had been introduced under tzarism. The food commissions which had tried to struggle with speculation were declared to blame for the lack of the necessities of life. From the commissions, hatred was transferred to the soviets. The Menshevik economist Grohman has reported that the campaign of the merchants "became especially strong after the events of July 3–4." The soviets were held responsible for the defeat, the high cost of living and nocturnal burglaries.

Alarmed by monarchist intrigues and fearing some answering explosion from the left, the government on August 7 sent Nicholas Romanov and his family to Tobolsk. On the following day the new Bolshevik paper, *Worker and Soldier,* was suppressed. News was arriving from all sides of the mass arrests of the soldier committees. The Bolsheviks were able to assemble their congress at the end of July only semi-legally. Army congresses were forbidden. Congresses were now held by all who had been sitting at home: landlords, merchants, industrialists, Cossack chiefs, the clergy, the Cavaliers of St. George. Their voices sounded alike, distinguished only in the degree of boldness. The indubitable, although not always open, conductor of the symphony was the Kadet party.

At a Congress of Trade and Industry which early in August assembled about three hundred representatives of the most important industrial and stock-exchange organizations, the opening speech was made by the textile king, Riabushinsky, and he did not hide his light under a bushel. "The Provisional Government," he said, "possesses only the shadow of power. . . . Actually a gang of political charlatans are in control. . . . The government is concentrating on taxes, imposing them primarily and cruelly upon the merchant and industrial class. . . . Is it expedient to give to the spendthrifts? Would it not be better in the name of the salvation of the fatherland to appoint a guardian over the spendthrifts?" And then a concluding threat: "The bony hand of hunger and national destitution will seize by the throat the friends of the people!" That phrase about the bony hand of hunger, generalizing the policy of lock-outs, entered from that time forth into the political dictionary of the revolution. It cost the capitalists dear.

There was held in Petrograd a congress of commissars of the provinces. These agents of the Provisional Government, who were supposed to stand like a wall around it, virtually united against it, and under the leadership of their Kadet nucleus took in hand the unhappy Minister of the Interior, Avksentiev. "You can't sit down between two chairs: a government ought to govern and not be a puppet." The Compromisers defended themselves and protested half-heartedly, fearing lest Bolsheviks overhear their quarrel with their ally. Avksentiev walked out of the congress as though he had got burnt.

The Social Revolutionary and Menshevik press gradually began to adopt the language of injury and complaint. Unexpected revelations began to appear on its pages. On August 6, the Social Revolutionary paper *Dyelo Naroda*, published a letter from a group of left junkers, mailed by them while on the road to the front. They were "surprised by the rôle being played by the junkers. . . . Systematic striking of people in the face, participation in punitive expeditions characterized by executions without trial or investigation at a mere order from the battalion commander. . . . Embittered soldiers have begun to snipe isolated junkers from hiding-places. . . ." Thus looked the business of restoring health to the army.

The reaction was on the offensive, the government in retreat. On August 7, the most popular Black Hundred agents, partisans of the Rasputin circles and of Jewish pogroms, were liberated from prison. The Bolsheviks remained in the Kresty Prison, where a hunger strike of arrested soldiers and sailors was impending. The workers' section of the Petrograd soviet sent greetings on that day to Trotsky, Lunacharsky, Kollontay and other prisoners.

The industrialists, the commissars of the provinces, the Cossack congress in Novocherkassk, the patriotic press, the generals, the liberals, everybody, thought it would be impossible to hold the elections for the Constituent Assembly in September—best of all to postpone them to the end of the war. To this, however, the government would not agree. A compromise was found. The convocation of the Constituent Assembly was deferred to the 28th of November. The Kadets accepted this postponement, although not without grumblings. They were firmly counting on certain decisive events happening during the three remaining months, which would shift the whole question of the Constituent Assembly to a different level. These hopes were being more and more openly connected with the name of Kornilov.

The réclame surrounding the figure of this new "chief" henceforth occupied the center of the bourgeois policy. A biography of the "First People's Commander-in-chief" was distributed in enormous quantities with the active co-operation of headquarters. When Savinkov, speaking as general administrator of the War Ministry, would say to the journalists, "We assume, etc."—his "we" did not mean Savinkov and Kerensky, but Savinkov and Kornilov. The noise surrounding the name of Kornilov put Kerensky on his guard. Rumors were spreading more and more persistently about a conspiracy centering in the League of Officers at headquarters. Personal meetings between the heads of the government and the chiefs of the army in the first days of August only fanned the fires of their mutual antipathy. "Does that lightweight elocutionist think he can give orders to me?" Kornilov doubtless said to himself. "Does that dull and ignorant Cossack expect to save Russia?" Kerensky could not but think. And they were both right in their way. Kornilov's program, which included the militarisation of the factories and railroads, the extension of the death penalty to the rear, and the subordination of the Petrograd military district and therewith the garrison of the capital to headquarters, became known in those days to the compromisist circles. Behind this official program another program—unexpressed but no less actual—could easily be guessed at. The left press sounded the alarm. The Executive Committee advanced a new candidate for commander-in-chief in the person of General Cheremissov. There was open talk of the impending retirement of Kornilov. The reaction became alarmed.

On the 6th of August, the council of the Union of Twelve Cossack Armies—the Don, the Kuban, the Tver, etc.—passed a resolution, not without help from Savinkov, to bring it "loudly and forcibly" to the attention of the government and the people that they would not be responsible for the behavior of Cossack troops at the front or rear in case of the removal of the "hero-chief," General Kornilov. A conference of the League of Cavaliers of St. George even more forcibly threatened the government. If Kornilov was removed the League would immediately issue "a war-cry to all the Knights of St. George, summoning them to united action with the Cossacks." Not one of the generals protested against this active insubordination, and the press of the existing order printed with delight this resolution which contained the threat of civil war. The head committee of the League of Officers of the Army and Fleet sent out telegrams in which it placed all its hopes in "our dear leader, General Kornilov," and summoned "all honest people" to express their confidence in him. A conference of "Public Men" of the right camp, sitting in Moscow during those days, sent Kornilov a telegram in which it joined its voice with those of the officers, the Georgian Cavaliers and the Cossacks: "All thinking Russia looks with hope and confidence to you." It would be impossible to speak more clearly. The conference was attended by industrialists and bankers like Riabushinsky and Tretiakov, generals Alexeiev and Brussilov, representatives of the clergy, professors, and leaders of the Kadet party with Miliukov at their head. In the character of a smoke screen, representatives were present from a semi-fictitious "peasant union," designed to give the Kadets some support among the peasant leaders. In the president's chair loomed the monumental figure of Rodzianko, offering public thanks to the delegation of a Cossack regiment for putting down the Bolsheviks. The candidacy of Kornilov for the rôle of savior of the country was thus openly advanced by the most authoritative representatives of the possessing and educated classes of Russia.

After these preparations the high commander-in-chief appeared for a second time at the War Ministry for negotiations as to his program for the salvation of the country. "Upon his arrival in Petrograd," says his chief of staff, General Lukomsky, describing this visit of Kornilov, "he went to the Winter Palace escorted by Tekintsi [1] with two machine guns. These machine guns were taken from the automobile after General Kornilov entered the Winter Palace, and the Tekintsi stood guard at the palace gate in order in case of need to come to the aid of the commander-in-chief." It was assumed that the commander-in-chief might require military aid against the Minister-President. The machine guns of the Tekintsi were machine guns of the bourgeoisie aimed at the Compromisers who kept getting under their feet. Such was the position of this government of salvation so independent of the soviets!

Shortly after Kornilov's visit a member of the Provisional Government, Kokoshkin, announced to Kerensky that the Kadets would resign "if Kornilov's program is not accepted today." Although without the machine guns, the Kadets were now talking to the government in the same ultimative language as Kornilov. And that was a help. The Provisional Government hastened to examine the report of the supreme commander, and to recognize in principle the possibility of adopting the measures proposed by him, "including the restoration of the death penalty at the rear."

In this mobilization of the forces of reaction there was nat-

[1] Caucasian native cavalry.

urally included the All-Russian Council of Churches, which had for its official aim to complete the emancipation of the orthodox church from bureaucratic activities, but whose real aim was to protect it from the revolution. With the overthrow of the monarchy the church had been deprived of its official head. Its relation to the state, which had been its defense and protector from time immemorial, was now left hanging in the air. To be sure, the Holy Synod, in an epistle of March 9, had hastened to extend its blessing to the accomplished revolution and summon the people to "place their trust in the Provisional Government." However, the future contained a menace. The government had kept silent on the church question as on all others. The clergy were completely at a loss. Occasionally from some far-off region—from the city of Verny on the borders of China—a telegram would come from a local cleric assuring Prince Lvov that his policy fully corresponded to the Testament of the Evangelists. Although thus tuning in on the revolution, the church had not dared to interfere in events. This was plainest of all at the front, where the influence of the clergy had evaporated along with the discipline of fear. Denikin acknowledges this: "Whereas the officers' corps did for a long time fight for its military authority and power to command, the voice of the pastors was silent from the first days of the revolution and their every participation in the life of the soldiers came to an end." The congresses of the clergy at headquarters and in the staffs of the army went by without leaving a trace.

The Council of Churches, although primarily a caste affair of the clergy itself, and especially of its upper tiers, nevertheless did not remain confined within the limits of the church bureaucracy. Liberal society tried with might and main to get hold of it. The Kadet party, having found no political roots among the people, fancied that a reformed church might serve as a transmitting mechanism between it and the masses. In the preparations for the meeting of the Council, an active rôle was played side by side with princes of the church, and even ahead of them, by temporal politicians of various tints, such as Prince Troubetskoy, Count Olsufiev, Rodzianko, Samarin, and by liberal professors and writers. The Kadet party tried in vain to create around the Council an atmosphere of church reform, stepping softly the while, lest some incautious motion might shake down the whole rotting structure. Not a word was said about the separation of church and state, either among the clergy or among the temporal reformers. The princes of the church were naturally inclined to weaken the control of the state over their inner affairs, but at the same time they desired that in the future the state should not only guarantee their privileged situation, their lands and income, but also continue to carry the lion's share of their expenses. In their turn the liberal bourgeoisie were willing to guarantee to the orthodox church a continuance of its dominant position, but on the condition that it learn to serve the interests of the ruling class among the masses in the new style.

But just here the chief difficulties began. Denikin himself remarks with sorrow that the Russian revolution "did not create one single popular religious movement worth remarking upon." It would be truer to say that in proportion as new layers of the people were drawn into the revolution, they almost automatically turned their backs on the church, even where they had formerly been attached to it. In the country individual priests may still have had some personal influence, dependent upon their behavior in regard to the land question; in the cities it occurred to nobody, either among the workers or the petty bourgeoisie, to turn to the clergy for the solution of any problem raised by the revolution. The preparations for the Council of Churches were met with complete indifference by the people. The interests and passions of the masses were finding their expression in socialist slogans, not in theological texts. Belated Russia enacted her history in an abridged edition: she found herself obliged to step over, not only the epoch of the reformation, but that of bourgeois parliamentarism as well.

Although planned for in the months of the flood-tide of the revolution, the Church Council took place during the weeks of its ebb. This still further thickened its reactionary coloring. The constitution of the Council, the circle of problems it touched upon, even the ceremony of its opening—all testified to radical changes in the attitude of the different classes toward the church. At the divine services in the Uspensky Cathedral, side by side with Rodzianko and the Kadets, sat Kerensky and Avksentiev. The burgomaster of Moscow, the Social Revolutionary Rudner, said in his speech of greeting: "So long as the Russian people shall live, the Christian faith will burn in its soul." Only yesterday those people had considered themselves the direct descendants of the prophet of the Russian Enlightenment, Chernishevsky.

The Council distributed printed appeals in all directions, prayed for a strong government, denounced the Bolsheviks, and adjured the workers in concert with the Minister of Labor, Skobelev: "Laborers, do your work, sparing no efforts, and subject your own needs to the welfare of the fatherland." But the Council gave its more special attention to the land question. The metropolitans and bishops were no less frightened and embittered than the landlords by the scope of the peasant movement; fear for the church and monastery lands had seized hold of their souls more firmly than the question of the democratization of the parish. With threats of the wrath of God and excommunication from the church, the epistles of the Council demanded "an immediate restoration to the churches, monasteries, parishes, and private proprietors, of the land, forests and harvests of which they have been robbed." Here it is appropriate to recall the voice crying in the wilderness! The Council dragged along from week to week, and arrived at the high point of its labors—the re-establishment of patriarchism [1] abolished by Peter two hundred years before—only after the October revolution.

At the end of July the government decided to call a State Conference of all classes and social institutions of the country to meet in Moscow August 13. Membership in the conference was to be determined by the government itself. In direct contradiction to the results of all democratic elections which had taken place in the country without a single exception, the government took care to make sure in advance that the conference should contain an equal number of representatives from the possessing classes and the people. Only by means of this artificial

---

[1] Before Peter the Great the heads of the church had called themselves patriarchs and had their own court, their own administration—were in effect a second order of tzars. He abolished this title and reduced the church to a department in his own administration. Trans.

equilibrium could the government of the salvation of the revolution still hope to save itself. This national congress did not possess any definite rights. To quote Miliukov: "The conference . . . received at the most a merely advisory voice." The possessing classes wished to give the people an example of self-abnegation, in order afterward the more surely to seize the power as a whole. Officially the goal of the conference was "a rapprochement between the state power and all the organized forces of the country." The press talked about the necessity of solidarity, reconciliation, encouragement and of raising everybody's spirits. In other words, they did not wish to say, and others were incapable of saying, for just what purpose the conference had been called. Here again, giving things their true names became the task of the Bolsheviks.

CHAPTER VI

KERENSKY AND KORNILOV

(Elements of Bonapartism in the Russian Revolution)

A GOOD deal has been written to the effect that subsequent misfortunes, including the advent of the Bolsheviks, might have been avoided if instead of Kerensky a man of clear head and strong character had stood at the helm of the government. It is indubitable that Kerensky possessed neither of these attributes. But the question is, why did certain well-defined social classes find themselves obliged to lift up just this man, Kerensky, upon their shoulders?

As though to freshen our historic memory, events in Spain are now again showing us how a revolution, washing away the customary political boundary lines, surrounds everybody and everything during its first days with a rosy mist. At this stage even its enemies try to tint themselves with its color. This mimicry expresses a semi-instinctive desire of the conservative classes to accommodate themselves to the changes impending, so as to suffer from them as little as possible. This solidarity of the nation, founded upon loose phrases, makes of compromisism an indispensable political function. Petty bourgeois idealists, overlooking class distinctions, thinking in stereotyped phrases, not knowing what they want, and wishing well to everybody, are at this stage the sole conceivable leaders of the majority. If Kerensky had possessed clear thoughts and a strong will, he would have been completely unfit for his historic rôle. This is not a retrospective estimate. The Bolsheviks so judged the matter in the heat of the events. "An attorney for the defense in political cases, a Social Revolutionary who became leader of the Trudoviks, a radical without any socialist schooling whatever, Kerensky has expressed more completely than anyone else the first epoch of the revolution, its 'national' formlessness, the idealism of its hopes and expectations": thus wrote the author of these lines while locked up in Kerensky's prison after the July Days. "Kerensky made speeches about land and freedom, about law and order, about peace among nations, about the defense of the fatherland, the heroism of Liebknecht, about how the Russian revolution ought to astonish the world with its magnanimity—waving the while a little red silk handkerchief. The everyday man who was just beginning to wake up politically listened to these speeches with rapture: it seemed to him that he himself was speaking from the tribune. The army greeted Kerensky as their savior from Guchkov. The peasants heard about him as a Trudovik, as a muzhik's deputy. The Liberals were won over by the extreme moderateness of idea under his formless radicalism of phrase. . . ."

But the period of universal and indiscriminate embraces does not last long. The class struggle dies down at the beginning of a revolution only to come to life afterward in the form of civil war. In the faery-like rise of compromisism is contained the seed of its inevitable fall. The official French journalist, Claude Anet, explained Kerensky's swift loss of popularity by a lack of tact which impelled the socialist politician to actions "little harmonizing" with his rôle. "He frequents the imperial loges, he lives in the Winter Palace or at Tsarskoe Selo, he sleeps in the bed of Russian emperors. A little too much vanity and vanity a little too noticeable—that is shocking in a country which is the simplest in the world." Tact implies, in the small as well as the great, an understanding of the situation and of one's place in it. Of this understanding Kerensky had not a trace. Lifted up by the trustful masses, he was completely alien to them, did not understand, and was not the least interested in, the question of how the revolution looked to them and what inferences they were drawing from it. The masses expected bold action from him, but he demanded from the masses that they should not interfere with his magnanimity and eloquence. Once when Kerensky was paying a theatrical visit to the arrested family of the tzar, the soldiers on duty around the palace said to their commandant: "We sleep on boards, we have bad food, but Nicholashka even after he is arrested has meat to throw in the pail." Those were not "magnanimous" words, but they expressed what the soldiers were feeling.

Breaking free of their age-old chains, the people were transgressing at every step those boundaries which educated leaders wanted to lay down for them. Towards the end of April Kerensky voiced a lament upon this subject: "Can it be that the Russian Free State is a state of slaves in revolt? . . . I regret that I did not die two months ago. I should have died with the great dream," etc. etc. With this bad rhetoric he hoped to exert an influence on the workers, soldiers, sailors, and peasants. Admiral Kolchak related subsequently before a soviet tribunal how in May the radical War Minister made the rounds of the Black Sea Fleet in order to reconcile the sailors with their officers. It seemed to the orator after each speech that the goal had been attained: "There, you see, admiral, everything is fixed. . . ." But nothing at all was fixed. The disintegration of the fleet was only beginning.

As time went on Kerensky's affectations, insolence, and braggadoccio more and more keenly offended the masses. During his journey around the front he once cried out irascibly to his adjutant in the railroad car—perhaps on purpose to be heard by a general: "Kick all those damned committees to hell!" Arriving on a visit to the Baltic fleet, Kerensky ordered the Sailors' Central Committee to appear before him on the admiral's warship. The Centrobalt, being a soviet body, was not under the war ministry and considered the order offensive. The president of the committee, the sailor Dybenko, answered: "If Kerensky wants to talk to the Centrobalt, let him come to us." Wasn't that an intolerable act of impudence! On the vessels where Kerensky did enter into conversation with the sailors, it went no better— especially on the warship *Republic* whose mood was Bolshevik. Here they questioned the minister on the following points: Why had he voted for war in the State Duma? Why had he put his signature to the imperialist note of Miliukov on the 21st of April? Why had he given the tzarist senators a pension of six thousand rubles a year? Kerensky refused to answer these "crafty" questions put to him by "foes." The crew dryly declared the minister's explanations "unsatisfactory." In a silence like the tomb Kerensky withdrew from the ship. "Slaves in revolt!" muttered the radical lawyer, grinding his teeth. But the sailors were experiencing an emotion of pride: "Yes, we were slaves and we have revolted!"

Kerensky's high-handed treatment of democratic social opinion called out at every step semi-conflicts with the soviet leaders, who were traveling the same road but with more of a disposition to look round at the masses. Already on the 8th of March, the Executive Committee, frightened by protests from below, had warned Kerensky of the impossibility of liberating arrested policemen. A few days later the Compromisers found themselves obliged to protest against the plan of the Minister of Justice to export the tzar's family to England. Again in two or three weeks, the Executive Committee raised the general question of a "regulation of their relations" with Kerensky, but those relations never were and never could be regulated. The same difficulties arose about his party relations. At a Social Revolutionary congress early in June, Kerensky was voted down in the elections to the party central committee, receiving 135 votes out of 270. And how the leaders did squirm in their effort to explain, both to right and left, that "many did not vote for Comrade Kerensky because he is already overloaded with work." The fact is that, while the staff and departmental Social Revolutionaries adored Kerensky as the source of all good things, the old Social Revolutionaries bound up with the masses regarded him without confidence and without respect. But neither the Executive Committee nor the Social Revolutionary party could get along without Kerensky: He was necessary to them as the connecting link of the coalition.

In the Soviet bloc the leading rôle belonged to the Mensheviks. They invented the decisions—that is, the methods by which to avoid doing anything. But in the state apparatus the Narodniks clearly outbalanced the Mensheviks—a fact which was most obviously expressed in the dominating position of Kerensky. Half Kadet and half Social Revolutionary, Kerensky was not a representative of the soviets in the government, like Tseretelli or Chernov, but a living tie between the bourgeoisie and the democracy. Tseretelli and Chernov formed one side of the Coalition. Kerensky was a personal incarnation of the Coalition itself. Tseretelli complained of the predominance in Kerensky of "personal motives," not understanding that these were inseparable

139

from his political function. Tseretelli himself as Minister of the Interior issued a circular to the effect that the commissars of the provinces ought to rely upon all the "living forces" of their locality—that is, upon the bourgeoisie and upon the soviets—and carry out the policies of the Provisional Government without surrendering to "party influences." That ideal commissar, rising above all hostile classes and parties in order to find his whole duty in himself and in a circular—that is Kerensky on a provincial or a county scale. As a crown to this system there was needed one independent all-Russian commissar in the Winter Palace. Without Kerensky compromisism would have been like a church steeple without a cross.

The history of Kerensky's rise is full of lessons. He became Minister of Justice thanks to the February revolution which he feared. The April demonstration of "slaves in revolt" made him Minister of War and Marine. The July struggle, caused by "German agents," put him at the head of the government. At the beginning of September a movement of the masses will make this head of the government supreme commander-in-chief as well. The dialectic of the compromise régime, and its malicious irony, lie in the fact that the masses had to lift Kerensky to the very highest height before they could topple him over.

While contemptuously drawing away his skirts from the people who had given him power, Kerensky the more thirstily grabbed after any sign of encouragement from educated society. In the very first days of the revolution the leader of the Moscow Kadets, Doctor Kishkin, said, upon returning from Petrograd: "If it were not for Kerensky, we should not have what we have. His name will be written in golden letters on the tablets of history." The praise of these Liberals became one of the most important political criteria for Kerensky, but he could not, and did not wish to, lay his popularity in a simple way at the feet of the bourgeoisie. On the contrary, he more and more acquired a taste for seeing all classes at his own feet. "The thought of setting off and balancing against each other the government of the bourgeoisie and the democracy," testifies Miliukov, "was not foreign to Kerensky from the very beginning of the revolution." This course was the natural outcome of his whole life's journey, which had run be-

140

tween the functions of a liberal lawyer and the underground circles. While respectfully assuring Buchanan that "the Soviet will die a natural death," Kerensky was frightening his bourgeois colleagues at every step with the wrath of the Soviet. And on those frequent occasions when the leaders of the Executive Committee disagreed with Kerensky, he dismayed them by mentioning the most horrible of catastrophes, the resignation of the Liberals.

When Kerensky reiterated that he did not wish to be the Marat of the Russian revolution, that meant that he would refuse to take severe measures against the reaction, but not so against "anarchy." Generally speaking, by the way, that is the moral of the opponents of violence in politics: they renounce violence when it comes to introducing changes in what already exists, but in defense of the existing order they will not stop at the most ruthless acts.

In the period of preparation for the offensive, Kerensky became the especially beloved figure of the possessing classes. Tereshchenko kept telling each and everybody how highly our Allies esteem "the labors of Kerensky." The Kadet paper, *Rech*, while severe with the Compromisers, continually emphasized its favorable attitude to the War Minister. Rodzianko himself recognized that "this young man . . . is reborn each day with redoubled strength for creative labor and the welfare of the fatherland." With such remarks the Liberals were, of course, deliberately flattering Kerensky, but also they could not help seeing that in the essence he was working for them. "Imagine how it would have been," remarked Lenin, "if Guchkov had attempted to issue orders for an offensive, to disband regiments, to arrest soldiers, to forbid congresses, to shout 'thou' at the soldiers, to call the soldiers 'cowards' etc. But Kerensky could permit himself this 'luxury'—only, it is true, until he had squandered that incredibly quick-melting confidence which the people had placed to his credit. . . ."

The offensive, while elevating Kerensky's reputation in the ranks of the bourgeoisie, completely undermined his popularity with the people. The collapse of the offensive was in essence a collapse of Kerensky in both camps. But the striking thing is that exactly this two-sided loss of standing rendered him henceforth "irreplaceable." As to the rôle of Kerensky in creating the second Coalition, Miliukov expresses himself thus: "the only possible man." Not, alas: "the only man needed." This leading liberal politician, be it remarked, never took Kerensky any too seriously, and broad circles of the bourgeoisie were more and more inclined to lay the blame on him for all the blows of fate. "The impatience of patriotically inclined groups" impelled them, according to Miliukov, to search for a strong man. At one time Admiral Kolchak was suggested for this rôle. Moreover, this installing of a strong man at the helm was "thought of in different terms from those of negotiation and compromise." That we may easily believe. "Hopes of democracy, of the will of the people, of the Constituent Assembly," writes Stankevich of the Kadet party, "were already thrown overboard. The municipal elections throughout all Russia had given an overwhelming majority to the socialists . . . and there were beginning to be convulsive reachings out for a power which should not persuade but only command." More accurately speaking, a power which should take the revolution by the throat.

*

IN the biography of Kornilov, and in his personal attributes, it is easy to distinguish the traits which justified his candidacy for the post of national savior. General Martynov, who had been Kornilov's superior in peace time, and in war time had shared his captivity in an Austrian fortress, characterizes Kornilov as follows: "Distinguished by a sustained love of work and great self-confidence, he was in his intellectual faculties an ordinary and mediocre man, not possessed of any broad outlook." Martynov places to the credit of Kornilov two traits: personal bravery and disinterestedness. In those circles where most people were thieving and worrying about their own skin, these qualities were striking. Of strategic ability—above all the ability to estimate a situation as a whole, both in its material and moral elements—Kornilov hadn't a trace. "Moreover he lacked organizing ability," says Martynov, "and with his violent temper and lack of equilibrium was little fitted for planned activity." Brussilov, who observed the entire military activity of his subordinate during the World War, spoke of him with supreme contempt: "The chief of a bold guerrilla band and nothing more. . . ." The official legend created around the Kornilov division was dictated by the demand of patriotic social opinion for some bright spot on the dark background of events. "The forty-eighth division," writes Martynov, "was destroyed thanks to the abominable administration . . . of Kornilov himself, who . . . did not know how to organize a retreat, and worst of all kept continually changing his mind and losing time. . . ." At the last moment Kornilov abandoned to their fate the division he had led into a trap, and tried himself to escape capture. However, after four days and nights of wandering the unlucky general surrendered to the Austrians, and he only escaped some time later. "Upon his return to Russia Kornilov, in conversing with various newspaper correspondents, touched up the story of his escape with bright colors supplied by his own imagination." We need not pause upon the prosaic corrections which well-informed witnesses have introduced into his legend. It is evident that from that moment on Kornilov began to acquire a taste for newspaper réclame.

Before the revolution Kornilov had been a monarchist of the Black Hundred tint. In captivity when reading the papers, he would frequently remark that "he would gladly hang all those Guchkovs and Miliukovs." But political ideas occupied him, as is usual with people of his mould, only insofar as they directly affected his own person. After the February revolution Kornilov found it easy to declare himself a republican. "He was very little acquainted," according to the report of Martynov, "with the interlacing interests of the different strata of Russian society, knew nothing either of party groups or of individual political leaders." Mensheviks, Social Revolutionaries, and Bolsheviks constituted for him one hostile mass which hindered the officers from commanding, the landlord from enjoying his estate, the merchant from trading, and the factory owner from producing goods.

Already on the 2nd of March, the committee of the State Duma laid hold upon General Kornilov, and over the signature of Rodzianko demanded of headquarters that this "valiant hero known to all Russia" be appointed commander-in-chief of the troops of the Petrograd district. The tzar, who had already ceased to be a tzar, wrote on Rodzianko's telegram: "Carry out." Thus the revolutionary capital acquired its first red general. In a report of the Executive Committee dated March 10, this phrase is applied to Kornilov: "A general of the old stripe who wants to put an end to the revolution." In those early days, however, the general tried to put his best foot forward, and even carried out without grumbling the ritual of arresting the tzarina. That was placed to his credit. In the memoirs of Colonel Kobylinsky, however—the commander of Tzarskoe Selo appointed by him—it becomes known that Kornilov was here playing a double game. After his presentation to the tzarina, Kobylinsky guardedly relates: "Kornilov said to me: 'Colonel, leave us alone. Go and stand outside the door.' I went out. After about five minutes Kornilov called me. I entered. The Empress extended her hand. . . ." It is clear that Kornilov had recommended the colonel as a friend. Later on we shall hear of the embraces exchanged between the tzar and his "jailer" Kobylinsky. As an administrator Kornilov in his new position proved unspeakably bad. "His closest associates in Petrograd," writes Stankevich, "continually complained of his incapacity to do the work or to direct it." Kornilov lingered in the capital, however, only a short time. In the April days he attempted, not without a hint from Miliukov, to inaugurate the first blood-letting of the revolution, but ran into the opposition of the Executive Committee, resigned, was given command of an army, and afterward of the southwestern front. Without waiting for the legal introduction of the death penalty, Kornilov here gave orders to shoot deserters and set up their corpses on the road with an inscription, threatened the peasants with severe penalties for violating the proprietory rights of landlords, created shock battalions, and on every appropriate occasion shook his fist at Petrograd. This immediately surrounded his name with a halo in the eyes of the officers and the possessing classes. But many of Kerensky's commissars, too, would say to themselves: there is no hope left but in Kornilov. In a few weeks this gallant general with a mournful experience as commander of a division, became the supreme commander-in-chief of those disintegrating armies of millions which the Entente was trying to make wage a war to complete victory.

It made Kornilov's head swim. His narrow horizon and political ignorance rendered him an easy prey for seekers of adventure. While wilfully defending his personal prerogative, this "man with a lion's heart and the brain of a sheep," as Kornilov was described by General Alexeiev, and after him by Verkhovsky, submitted very easily to personal influences, if only they fell in with the voice of his ambition. Miliukov, who was friendly to Kornilov, remarks in him a "childish trust in people who knew how to flatter him." The closest inspirer of the supreme commander was a certain Zavoiko, who followed the modest calling of orderly—an obscure figure from among the former landlords, an oil speculator, an adventurer, who especially impressed Kornilov with his pen. Zavoiko did indeed have the brisk style of the swindler who will stop at nothing. This orderly became Kornilov's press agent, author of the "People's Biography," drawer-up of reports, ultimatums, and all those documents for which there was needed—in the words of the general—"a strong artistic style." To Zavoiko was added another seeker of adventure, Alladin, a former deputy of the first Duma, who had spent some years abroad, who never removed an English pipe from his mouth, and therefore considered himself a specialist upon international affairs. These two men stood at Kornilov's right hand, keeping him in touch with the centers of the counter-revolution. His left flank was covered by Savinkov and Filonenko, who employed every means to hold up the general's exaggerated opinion of himself, and at the same time keep him from taking any premature step which might make him impossible in the eyes of the democracy. "To him came the honest and the dishonest, the sincere and the intriguing, political leaders, and military leaders, and adventurers," writes the unctuous General Denikin, "and all with one voice cried: Save us!" It would be difficult to determine the exact proportion of the honest and the dishonest. At any rate Kornilov seriously considered himself called to "save," and thus became a direct rival of Kerensky.

*

145

THE rivals quite sincerely hated each other. "Kerensky," according to Martynov, "assumed a high-and-mighty tone in his relations with the older generals. A humble hard worker like Alexeiev, or the diplomatically-inclined Brussilov, could permit this treatment. But such tactics would not go down with the self-complacent and touchy Kornilov, who . . . for his part looked down upon the lawyer, Kerensky." The weaker of the two was prepared to yield, and did make serious advances. At least Kornilov told Denikin towards the end of July that a proposal had come to him from governmental circles to enter the ministry. "No sir! Those gentlemen are too bound up with the soviets. . . . I said to them: give me the power and then I will make a decisive fight."

The ground was quaking under Kerensky's feet like a peat bog. He sought a way out, as always, in the sphere of verbal improvisations: call meetings, announce, proclaim! His personal success on the 21st of July, when he had risen above the hostile camps of the democracy and the bourgeoisie in the character of the irreplaceable, suggested to Kerensky the idea of a state conference in Moscow. That which had taken place in a closed chamber of the Winter Palace would now be brought out in the open. Let the country see with its own eyes that everything will go to pieces if Kerensky does not take in his hands the reins and the whip.

According to the official list, the State Conference was to include "representatives of political, social, democratic, national, commercial, industrial, and co-operative organizations, leaders of the institutions of the democracy, the higher representatives of the army, scientific institutions, universities, and members of the four State Dumas." About 1500 conferees were indicated, but more than 2500 assembled—the number having been enlarged wholly in the interests of the right wing. The Moscow Journal of the Social Revolutionaries wrote reproachfully about its own government: "As against 150 representatives of labor, there are 120 representatives of trade and industry; against 100 peasant deputies, 100 representatives of the landlords have been invited; against 100 representatives of the Soviet, there will be 300 members of the State Duma. . . ." This official paper of

Kerensky's party expressed a doubt as to whether such a conference would be able to give the government "that support which it seeks."

The Compromisers went to the Conference gritting their teeth: We must make an honest effort, they were saying to each other, to come to an agreement. But how about the Bolsheviks? We must at whatever cost prevent them from interfering in this dialogue between the democracy and the possessing classes. By a special resolution of the Executive Committee, party factions were deprived of the right to take the floor without the consent of the praesidium. The Bolsheviks decided to make a declaration in the name of the party and walk out of the conference. The praesidium, watchful of their every movement, demanded that they abandon this criminal plan. Then the Bolsheviks unhesitatingly handed back their cards of admission. They were preparing another and more significant answer: Proletarian Moscow was to speak its word.

Almost from the first days of the revolution the partisans of law and order had on all possible occasions contrasted the peaceful "country" against tumultuous Petrograd. The convocation of the Constituent Assembly in Moscow had been one of the slogans of the bourgeoisie. The National-Liberal "Marxist," Potressov, had sent curses to Petrograd for imagining itself to be "a new Paris." As though the Girondists had not threatened the old Paris with thunder and lightning—had not proposed that it reduce its rôle to $\frac{1}{83}$ of what it was! A provincial Menshevik said in June at the congress of soviets: "Some sort of place like Novocherkassk far better reflects the conditions of life in Russia than Petrograd." In the essence of the matter the Compromisers like the bourgeoisie were seeking support, not in the actual moods of "the country," but in consoling illusions which they themselves created. Now, when it came time to feel the actual political pulse of Moscow, a cruel disappointment awaited the initiators of the conference.

Those counter-revolutionary conferences which had followed each other in Moscow from the first days of August, beginning with a congress of landlords and ending with the Church Council, had not only mobilized the possessing circles, but had also brought the workers and soldiers to their feet. The threats of Riabushinsky, the appeals of Rodzianko, the fraternization of Kadets with Cossack generals—all this had taken place before the eyes of the lower ranks in Moscow. All this had been interpreted by Bolshevik agitators hot on the trail of the news-stories. But the danger of a counter-revolution had now taken a palpable, even a personal form. A wave of indignation ran through the shops and factories. "If the soviets are powerless," wrote the Moscow Bolshevik paper, "the workers must unite round their own living organizations." In the first rank of these organizations were named the trade-unions, a majority of them already under Bolshevik leadership. The mood of the factories was so hostile to the State Conference that the idea of a general strike, suggested from below, was adopted almost without opposition at a meeting of representatives of all the Moscow nuclei of the Bolshevik organization. The trade-unions had taken the initiative. The Moscow soviet by a majority of 364 against 304 voted against the strike. But since at the caucus of their factions the Menshevik and Social Revolutionary workers had voted for the strike, and were now merely submitting to party discipline, this decision of a soviet elected long ago, adopted moreover against the will of its actual majority, was far from stopping the Moscow workers. A meeting of the officers of 41 trade unions passed a resolution to call a one-day strike of protest. The district soviets, a majority of them, came out on the side of the party and the trade-unions. The factories here advanced a demand for re-elections to the Moscow soviet, which was not only lagging behind the masses, but coming into sharp conflict with them. In the Zamoskvoretsky district soviet, which met jointly with the factory committees, a demand for the recall of those deputies who had "gone against the will of the working-class" received 175 votes against 4, with 19 abstaining!

The night before the strike was, nevertheless, a bad night for the Moscow Bolsheviks. The country was indeed following in the steps of Petrograd, but lagging behind. The July demonstration had been unsuccessful in Moscow: a majority, not only of the garrison, but also of the workers had feared to go into the streets against the voice of the Soviet. How would it be this time? Morning brought the answer. The counter-efforts of the Compromisers did not prevent the strike from becoming a powerful demonstration of hostility to the Coalition and the government. Two days before, the newspaper of the Moscow industrialists had confidently declared: "Let the Petrograd government come soon to Moscow. Let them listen to the voice of the holy places, the bells and sacred towers of the Kremlin. . . ." Today the voice of the sacred places was drowned—by an ominous stillness.

A member of the Moscow committee of the Bolsheviks, Piatnitsky, subsequently wrote: "The strike came off magnificently. There were no lights, no tramcars; the factories and shops were closed and the railroad yards and stations; even the waiters in the restaurants had gone on strike." Miliukov adds a sharp light to this picture: "The delegates coming to the Conference . . . could not ride on the tramways, nor lunch in the restaurants." This permitted them, as the liberal historian acknowledges, the better to estimate the strength of the Bolsheviks, who had not been admitted to the Conference. The *Izvestia* of the Moscow soviet adequately described the significance of this manifestation of August 12th: "In spite of the resolutions of the soviets . . . the masses followed the Bolsheviks." 400,000 workers went on strike in Moscow and the suburbs upon the summons of a party which for five weeks had been under continual blows, and whose leaders were still in hiding or in prison. The new Petrograd organ of the party, *The Proletarian,* managed before it was shut down to put a question to the Compromisers: "From Petrograd you went to Moscow—where will you go from there?"

Even the masters of the situation must have put this question to themselves. In Kiev, Kostroma, Tzaritzyn, similar one-day strikes of protest occurred, general or partial. The agitation covered the whole country. Everywhere, in the remotest corners, the Bolsheviks gave warning that the State Conference bore the "clearly marked imprint of a counter-revolutionary conspiracy." By the end of August the meaning of this formula was disclosed before the eyes of the whole people.

The delegates to the Conference, as well as bourgeois Moscow, expected a coming-out of the masses with arms, expected clashes, battles, "August days." But for the workers to go into the street, would have meant for them to offer themselves to the blows of the Cavaliers of St. George, the officer detachments, junkers, individual cavalry units, burning with the desire to take revenge for the strike. To summon the garrison to the street would have introduced a split, and lightened the task of the counter-revolution which stood ready with its hand on the trigger. The party did not summon them to the street, and the workers themselves, guided by a correct strategic sense, avoided any open encounter. The one-day strike perfectly corresponded to the situation. It could not be hid under a bushel, as was the declaration of the Bolsheviks at the Conference. When the city was plunged in darkness, all Russia saw the hand of the Bolsheviks at the switchboard. No, Petrograd was not isolated. "In Moscow, upon whose patriarchal humbleness so many had set their hopes, the workers' districts suddenly showed their teeth." Thus Sukhanov describes the significance of that day. In the absence of the Bolsheviks, but under the sign of the unfleshed teeth of the proletarian revolution, the Coalition conferees had to take their seats.

Moscow wits were saying that Kerensky had come there "to be crowned." But the next day Kornilov arrived from headquarters with the same purpose, and was met by innumerable delegates—among them those from the Church Council. The Tekintsi leapt from the approaching train in their bright red long coats, with their naked curved swords, and drew up in two files on the platform. Ecstatic ladies sprinkled the hero with flowers as he reviewed this body-guard and the deputations. The Kadet, Rodichev, concluded his speech of greeting with the cry: "Save Russia, and a grateful people will reward you!" Patriotic sobbings were heard. Morozova, a millionaire merchant's wife, went down on her knees. Officers carried Kornilov out to the people on their shoulders. While the commander-in-chief was reviewing the Cavaliers of St. George, the cadets, the officers' schools, and the Cossack squadron drawn up on the square before the station, Kerensky, in his character as rival and Minister of War, was reviewing a parade of the troops of the Moscow garrison. From the station Kornilov took his way—in the steps of the tzars—to the Ivarsky shrine, where a service was held in the presence of his escort of Mussulmen Tekintsi in their gigantic fur hats. "This circumstance," writes the Cossack officer Grekov, "disposed believing Moscow still more favorably to Kornilov." The counter-revolution was meanwhile trying to capture the street. Kornilov's biography, together with his portrait, was generously scattered from automobiles. The walls were covered with posters summoning the people to the aid of the hero. Like a sovereign, Kornilov received in his private car statesmen, industrialists, financiers. Representatives of the banks made reports to him about the financial condition of the country. The Octobrist Shidlovsky significantly writes: "The only one of all the members of the Duma to visit Kornilov in his train was Miliukov, who had a conversation with him, the matter of which is unknown to me." We shall hear later from Miliukov as much about this conversation as he himself thinks it necessary to relate.

During this time the preparations for a military insurrection were in full swing. Several days before the conference Kornilov had given orders, under pretext of going to the help of Riga, to prepare four cavalry divisions for a movement on Petrograd. The Orenburg Cossack regiment had been sent by headquarters to Moscow "to preserve order," but at Kerensky's command it had been held up on the way. In his subsequent testimony before an Inquiry Commission on the Kornilov affair, Kerensky said: "We were informed that during the Moscow conference a dictatorship would be declared." Thus in those triumphant days of national unity, the War Minister and the commander-in-chief were engaged in strategic counter-maneuvers. So far as possible, however, decorum was observed. The relations between the two camps oscillated between officially friendly assurances and civil war.

In Petrograd, notwithstanding the self-restraint of the masses—the July experience having left its lesson—rumors kept coming down from above, from the staffs and editorial offices, furiously insisting upon an impending insurrection of the Bolsheviks. The Petrograd organizations of the party warned the masses in an open manifesto against possible provocatory appeals upon the part of the enemy. The Moscow soviet meanwhile took its own measures. A secret revolutionary committee was formed, consisting of six people, two from each of the soviet parties, including the Bolsheviks. A secret order was issued forbidding the formation of cordons of Cavaliers of St. George, officers, and junkers, along the line of march of Kornilov. The Bolsheviks, who had been forbidden entry into the barracks since the July Days, were now freely admitted: without them it was impossible to win over the soldiers. While in the open arena the Mensheviks and Social Revolutionaries were negotiating with the bourgeoisie for the creation of a strong power against the masses led by the Bolsheviks, behind the scenes these same Mensheviks and Social Revolutionaries in co-operation with the Bolsheviks, whom they would not admit to the conference, were preparing the masses for a struggle against the conspiracy of the bourgeoisie. Although yesterday they had opposed the protest strike, today they were summoning the workers and soldiers to prepare for a struggle. The contemptuous indignation of the masses did not prevent them from responding to the summons with a fighting eagerness which frightened the Compromisers more than it pleased them. This arrant duplicity, almost amounting to an open treachery in two directions, would have been incomprehensible if the Compromisers had still been consciously carrying out their policy; as a matter of fact they were merely suffering its consequences.

Big events were clearly in the air. But apparently nobody had settled upon the days of the Conference for an overturn. At any rate no confirmation of the rumors to which Kerensky subsequently referred has been found either in documents, or in the compromisist literature, or in the memoirs of the Right Wing. It was still merely a matter of getting ready. According to Miliukov —and his testimony coincides with the further development of events—Kornilov himself had already before the Conference chosen the date for his action: August 27. This date of course was known to but few. The half-informed, however, as always in such circumstances, kept advancing the day of the great event, and rumors forerunning it poured in upon the authorities from all sides. It seemed from moment to moment as though the blow would fall.

Indeed, the very mood of excitement among the bourgeois and officer circles in Moscow might have led, if not to an attempted overturn, at least to counter-revolutionary manifestations designed as a test of power. Still more probable would have been an attempt to create out of the members of the Conference some sort of center for the salvation of the fatherland in competi-

tion with the soviets. The right press had spoken openly of this.
But things did not even go that far: the masses prevented it.
Even if perhaps some had cherished the thought of hastening the
decisive hour, the strike compelled them to pause and say to themselves: We cannot catch the revolution unawares; the workers
and soldiers are on their guard; we must postpone action. Even
that universal popular procession to the Ivarsky shrine which had
been planned by the priests and Liberals in agreement with
Kornilov, was called off.

As soon as it became clear that there was no immediate danger,
the Social Revolutionaries and Mensheviks hastened to pretend
that nothing special had happened. They even refused to continue admitting Bolsheviks into the barracks, although the barracks insistently continued to demand Bolshevik orators. "The
Moor has done his duty," Tseretelli and Dan and Khinchuk,
president of the Moscow soviet, must have said to each other with
a foxy smile. But the Bolsheviks had not the slightest intention of
falling into the position of the Moor. They were still only intending to carry their work through to the end.

*

EVERY class society has need of unity in the governmental will.
The dual power is in its essence a régime of social crisis signifying
an utter dividedness of the nation. It contains within itself potential or actual civil war. Nobody any longer wanted the dual
power. On the contrary, all were searching for a strong, single-
minded, "iron" government. The July government of Kerensky
had been endowed with unlimited powers. The design had been
by common consent to establish above the democracy and the
bourgeoisie, who were paralyzing each other, a "real" sovereign
power. This idea of a master of destiny rising above all classes, is
nothing but Bonapartism. If you stick two forks into a cork
symmetrically, it will, under very great oscillations from side to
side, keep its balance even on a pin point: that is the mechanical
model of the Bonapartist superarbiter. The degree of solidity of
such a power, setting aside international conditions, is determined
by the stability of equilibrium of the two antagonistic classes

within the country. In the middle of May at a session of the Petersburg soviet, Trotsky had defined Kerensky as "the mathematical center of Russian Bonapartism." The immateriality of this description shows that it was not a question of personality but of function. At the beginning of July, as you will remember, all the ministers, acting upon instructions from their parties, had resigned in order to permit Kerensky to form a government. On the 21st of July this experiment was repeated in a more demonstrative form. The two hostile camps invoked Kerensky, each seeing in him a part of itself, and both swearing fealty to him. Trotsky wrote while in prison: "Led by politicians who are afraid of their own shadow, the Soviet did not dare take the power. The Kadet party, representing all the propertied cliques, could not yet seize the power. It remained to find a great conciliator, a mediator, a court of arbitration."

In a manifesto to the people issued by Kerensky in his own name, he declared: "I, as head of the government . . . consider that I have no right to hesitate if the changes (in the structure of the government) . . . increase my responsibility in the matters of supreme administration." That is the unadulterated phraseology of Bonapartism. But nevertheless, although supported from both right and left, it never got beyond phraseology. What is the reason for this?

In order that the Little Corsican might lift himself above a young bourgeois nation, it was necessary that the revolution should already have accomplished its fundamental task—the transfer of land to the peasants—and that a victorious army should have been created on the new social foundation. In the 18th century a revolution had no farther to go: it could only from that point recoil and go backward. In this recoil, however, its fundamental conquests were in danger. They must be defended at any cost. The deepening but still very immature antagonism between the bourgeoisie and the proletariat kept the nation, shaken as it was to its foundations, in a state of extreme tension. A national "judge" was in those conditions indispensable. Napoleon guaranteed to the big bourgeois the possibility to get rich, to the peasants their pieces of land, to the sons of peasants and the hoboes a chance for looting in the wars. The judge held a sword in his hand and himself also fulfilled the duties of bailiff. The Bonapartism of the first Bonaparte was solidly founded.

The revolution of 1848 did not give the peasants the land, and could not do so. That was not a great revolution, replacing one social régime with another, but a political re-shuffle within the framework of the same social régime. Napoleon III did not have under him a victorious army. The two chief elements of classical Bonapartism were thus lacking. But there were other favorable conditions, and no less real. The proletariat, which had been maturing for half a century, showed its threatening force in June, but was incapable of seizing the power. The bourgeoisie feared the proletariat and its own bloody victory over them. The peasant proprietors feared the June insurrection, and wanted the state to protect them from those who wished to divide the land. And finally a powerful industrial boom, extending with slight moments of lull over two decades, had opened before the bourgeoisie unheard of sources of wealth. These conditions proved sufficient for an epigone Bonapartism.

In the policies of Bismarck, who also stood "above classes," there were, as has been often pointed out, indubitable Bonapartist elements, although disguised by legitimism. The stability of the Bismarck régime was guaranteed by the fact that, having arisen after an impotent revolution, it offered a solution, or a half-solution, of such a mighty national problem as the unification of Germany. It brought victory in three wars, indemnities, and a mighty up-growth of capitalism. That was enough to last several decades.

The misfortune of the Russian candidates for Bonaparte lay not at all in their dissimilarity to the first Napoleon, or even to Bismarck. History knows how to make use of substitutes. But they were confronted by a great revolution which had not yet solved its problems or exhausted its force. The bourgeoisie was trying to compel the peasant, still without land, to fight for the estates of the landlords. The war had given nothing but defeats. There was not the shadow of an industrial boom; on the contrary the breakdown of industry was producing ever new devastations.

If the proletariat had retreated, it was only to close up its ranks. The peasantry were only drawing back for their last assault upon the lords. The oppressed nationalities were assuming the offensive against a Russifying despotism. In search of peace, the army was coming closer and closer to the workers and their party. The lower ranks were uniting, the upper weakening. There was no equilibrium. The revolution was still full-blooded. No wonder Bonapartism proved anemic.

Marx and Engels compared the rôle of a Bonapartist régime in the struggle between the bourgeoisie and the proletariat, with the rôle of the old absolute monarchy in the struggle between the feudal lords and the bourgeoisie. Traits of similarity are indubitable, but they stop just where the social content of the power begins to appear. The rôle of court of arbitration between the elements of the old and the new society was possible at a certain period owing to the fact that the two exploiting régimes both needed defense against the exploited. But between feudal lords and peasant serfs no "impartial" mediation was possible. While reconciling the interests of the landlords to those of a youthful capitalism, the tzarist autocracy functioned in relation to the peasants, not as a mediator, but as an authorized representative of the exploiting classes.

Similarly Bonapartism was not a court of arbitration between the proletariat and the bourgeoisie. It was in reality the most concentrated dominion of the bourgeoisie over the proletariat. Having climbed up with his boots on the neck of the people, whatever Bonaparte happened to come along could not fail to adopt a policy of protection of property, rent and profits. The peculiarities of a régime do not go beyond its means of defense. The watchman does not now stand at the gate, but sits on the roof of the house, yet his function is the same. The independence of Bonapartism is to an enormous degree external, decorative, a matter of show. Its appropriate symbol was the mantle of the emperor.

While skilfully exploiting the fear of the bourgeoisie before the workers, Bismarck remained in all his political and social reforms the unchanging plenipotentiary of the possessing classes, whom he never betrayed. Nevertheless, the growing pressure of the proletariat indubitably permitted him to rise above the

Junkerdom, and the capitalists in the quality of a weighty bureaucratic arbiter: that was his essential function.

The soviet régime permits a very considerable independence of the government in relation to proletariat and peasantry, and consequently a "mediation" between them insofar as their interests, although giving rise to debates and conflicts, remain fundamentally reconcilable. But it would not be easy to find an "impartial" court of arbitration between the soviet state and a bourgeois state, at least so far as concerns the fundamental interests of each. On the international arena the Soviet Union is prevented from adhering to the League of Nations by those same social causes which within the national borders make impossible anything but a pretended "impartiality" of any government in the struggle between bourgeoisie and proletariat.

While lacking the force of Bonapartism, Kerenskyism had all its vices. It lifted itself above the nation only to demoralize the nation with its own impotence. Whereas in words the leaders of the bourgeoisie and the democracy promised to "obey" Kerensky, in reality Kerensky, the omnipotent arbiter, obeyed Miliukov—and more especially Buchanan. Kerensky waged the imperialist war, protected the landlord's property from attack, and postponed social reforms to happier days. If his government was weak, this was for the same reason that the bourgeoisie in general could not get its people into power. However, with all the insignificance of the "government of salvation" its conservatively capitalistic character grew manifestly with the growth of its "independence."

Their understanding that the régime of Kerensky was the inevitable form of bourgeois rulership for the given period, did not prevent the bourgeois politicians from being extremely dissatisfied with Kerensky, nor from preparing to get rid of him as quickly as possible. There was no disagreement among the possessing classes that the national arbiter put forward by the petty bourgeois democracy must be opposed by a figure from their own ranks. But why Kornilov, exactly? Because the candidate for Bonaparte must correspond to the character of the Russian bourgeoisie. He must be backward, isolated from the people, ungifted, and on the decline. In an army which had seen almost nothing but humiliating defeats, it was not easy to find a popular general. Kornilov was arrived at by a process of elimination of other candidates still less suitable.

Thus the Compromisers and Liberals could neither seriously unite in a coalition, nor agree upon a single candidate for savior. They were prevented from doing so by the uncompleted tasks of the revolution. The Liberals did not trust the democrats, the democrats did not trust the Liberals. Kerensky, it is true, opened his arms wide to the bourgeoisie, but Kornilov made it clearly understood that at the first opportunity he would twist the neck of the democracy. The clash between Kornilov and Kerensky, inevitably resulting from the preceding development, was a translation of the contradictions of the dual power into the explosive language of personal ambition.

Just as in the midst of the Petrograd proletariat and garrison there was formed, toward the beginning of July, an impatient wing dissatisfied with the too cautious policy of the Bolsheviks, so among the possessing classes there accumulated, towards the beginning of August, an impatience of the watchful-waiting policy of the Kadet leaders. This mood expressed itself, for example, at the Kadet congress, where demands were voiced for the overthrow of Kerensky. A still keener political impatience was to be seen outside the framework of the Kadet party—in the military staffs where they lived in continual dread of the soldiers, in the banks where they were drowning in the waters of inflation, in the manors of the landlords where the roofs were burning over the heads of the nobility. "Long live Kornilov!" became a slogan of hope, of despair, and of thirst for revenge.

While agreeing throughout to the program of Kornilov, Kerensky quarreled about the date: "We cannot do everything at once." While recognizing the necessity of getting rid of Kerensky, Miliukov answered his impatient followers: "It is still, I suggest, a little too soon." Just as out of the eagerness of the Petrograd masses arose the semi-insurrection of July, so out of the impatience of the property owners arose the Kornilov insurrection of August. And just as the Bolsheviks found themselves obliged to take the side of an armed insurrection, in order if possible to guarantee its success, and in any case to prevent its extermination, so the Kadets found themselves obliged, for like purposes, to take part in the Kornilov insurrection. Within these limits, there is an astonishing symmetry in the two situations. But inside this symmetrical framework there is a complete contrast of goals, methods and results. It will develop fully in the course of the coming events.

CHAPTER VII

THE STATE CONFERENCE IN MOSCOW

IF a symbol is a concentrated image, then a revolution is the master-builder of symbols, for it presents all phenomena and all relations in concentrated form. The trouble is that the symbolism of a revolution is too grandiose; it fits in badly with the creative work of individuals. For this reason artistic reproductions of the greatest mass dramas of humanity are so poor.

The Moscow State Conference ended in the failure assured in advance. It created nothing and decided nothing. However, it has left to the historian an invaluable impression of the revolution —although a negative impression, one in which light appears as shadow, weakness parades as strength, greed as disinterestedness, treachery as the highest valor. The mightiest party of the revolution, which in only ten weeks was to arrive at the power, was left outside the walls of the Conference as a magnitude not worth noticing. At the same time the "party of evolutionary socialism," unknown to anybody, was taken seriously. Kerensky stepped forth as the incarnation of force and will. The Coalition, wholly exhausted in the past, was spoken of as a means of future salvation. Kornilov, hated by the soldier millions, was greeted as the beloved leader of the army and the people. Monarchists and Black Hundred men registered their love for the Constituent Assembly. All those who were about to retire from the political arena behaved as though they had agreed for one last time to play their best rôles on the stage of a theater. They were all eager to shout with all their might: Here is what we wanted to be! Here is what we would have been, if they had not prevented us! What prevented them was the workers, the soldiers, the peasants, the oppressed nationalities. Tens of millions of "slaves in revolt" prevented them from demonstrating their loyalty to the revolution. In Moscow where they had gone for shelter a strike fol-

lowed on their heels. Harried by "dark elements," by "ignorance," by "demagoguism," these two and a half thousand people,
having crowded into a theater, tacitly agreed together not to
violate the histrionic illusion. Not a word was spoken about the
strike. They tried never to mention the Bolsheviks by name.
Plekhanov recalled "the unhappy memory of Lenin" just in passing, and as though he were talking of an enemy completely
routed. The impression thus bore the character of a negative to
the last detail: in this kingdom of half-buried shades, giving
themselves out for "the living forces of the nation," the authentic
people's leader could not possibly figure otherwise than as a
political cadaver.

"The brilliant auditorium," writes Sukhanov, "was quite
sharply divided into two halves: to the right sat the bourgeoisie,
to the left the democracy. In the orchestra and loges to the right
many uniforms of generals were to be seen, and to the left ensigns
and soldiers. Opposite the stage in the former imperial loge were
seated the higher diplomatic representatives of the Allied and
friendly powers. . . . Our group, the extreme Left, occupied a
small corner of the orchestra." The extreme Left, in the absence
of the Bolsheviks, were the followers of Martov.

Towards four o'clock Kerensky appeared on the stage accompanied by two young officers, a soldier and a sailor, symbolizing
the power of the revolutionary government. They stood stock
still as though rooted in the ground behind the back of the
Minister-President. In order not to irritate the Right Wing with
the word republic—so it was agreed in advance—Kerensky
greeted "the representatives of the Russian land" in the name of
the government of the "Russian state." "The general tone
of the speech," writes our liberal historian, "instead of
being one of dignity and confidence, was, as a result of the influence of recent days . . . one of badly concealed fright, which
the orator seemed to be trying to suppress within himself by
adopting the high notes of a threat." Without directly naming
the Bolsheviks, Kerensky began with a fist-shake in their direction. Any new attempts against the government "will be put
down with blood and iron." Both wings of the conference joined
in a stormy applause. Then a supplementary threat in the direc-

161

tion of Kornilov, who had not yet arrived: "Whatever ultimatums no matter who may present to me, I will know how to subdue him to the will of the supreme power, and to me, its supreme head." Although this evoked ecstatical applause, the applause came only from the left half of the Conference. Kerensky kept coming back again and again to himself as the "supreme head": he had need of that thought. "To you here who have come from the front, to you say I, your War Minister and supreme leader . . . there is no will and no power in the army higher than the will and power of the Provisional Government." The democrats were in rapture at these blank cartridges. They believed that in this way they could avoid the resort to lead.

"All the best forces of the people and the army," affirms the head of the government, "associated the triumph of the Russian revolution with the triumph of our arms on the front, but our hopes have been trampled in the mud and our faith spat upon." Such is his lyrical summing up of the June offensive. He himself, Kerensky, intends in any case to wage the war to complete victory. Speaking of the danger of a peace at the expense of Russia's interests—that course having been suggested in the peace proposals of the Pope on August 4—Kerensky pays a tribute of praise to the noble loyalty of our Allies. To which he adds: "And I, in the name of the mighty Russian people, say only one thing: We have expected nothing else and we can expect nothing else." An ovation addressed to the loges of the Allied diplomats brings all to their feet except a few internationalists and those solitary Bolsheviks who have come as delegates from the trade unions. From the officers' loge somebody shouts: "Martov, get up!" Martov, to his honor be it said, had the force not to offer homage to the disinterestedness of the Entente.

To the oppressed nationalities of Russia striving to rebuild their destiny, Kerensky offers a Sunday school lesson interwoven with threats. "When languishing and dying in the chains of the tzarist autocracy"—thus he boasts of chains that others have worn—"we poured out our blood in the name of the welfare of all the peoples." Out of a feeling of gratitude, he suggests to the oppressed nationalities, they ought now to endure a régime which deprives them of rights.

162

Where lies the way out? "Do you not feel it in you, this mighty flame? . . . Do you not feel within you the strength and the will to discipline, self-sacrifice and labor? . . . Do you not offer here a spectacle of the united strength of the nation?" These words were pronounced on the day of the Moscow strike, and during the hours of the mysterious movements of Kornilov's cavalry. "We will destroy our souls, but we will save the state." That was all the government of the revolution had to offer the people.

"Many provincials," writes Miliukov, "saw Kerensky in this hall for the first time, and they went out half disappointed and half indignant. Before them had stood a young man with a tortured pale face, and a pose like an actor speaking his lines. . . . This man seemed to be trying to frighten somebody and create upon all an impression of power and force of will in the old style. In reality he evoked only a feeling of pity."

The speeches of the other members of the government exposed not so much a personal bankruptcy, as the bankruptcy of the compromise system. The grand idea which the Minister of the Interior, Avksentiev, submitted to the judgment of the country, was the institution of "travelling commissars." The Minister of Industry advised the capitalists to content themselves with a modest profit. The Minister of Finance promised to lower the direct tax upon the possessing classes by increasing indirect taxation. The Right Wing was incautious enough to greet these words with a stormy applause, in which Tseretelli afterward, with some embarrassment, pointed out a lack of eagerness for self-sacrifice. The Minister of Agriculture, Chernov, had been told to keep still entirely, in order not to irritate the Allies on the right with the specter of land expropriation. In the interests of national unity it had been decided to pretend that the agrarian question did not exist. The Compromisers had no objection. The authentic voice of the muzhik never once sounded from the tribune. Nevertheless in those very weeks of August the agrarian movement was billowing throughout the whole country, getting ready to break loose in autumn in the form of an unconquerable peasant war.

After a day's intermission—a day passed in reconnoitering and mobilizing of forces on both sides—the session of the 14th opened in an atmosphere of extreme tension. When Kornilov appeared in his loge, the right half of the Conference gave him a stormy ovation, the left remained seated almost as a body. Cries of "get up!" from the officers' loges were followed with coarse abuse. When the government appeared, the left section gave Kerensky a prolonged ovation, in which, as Miliukov testifies, "the right just as demonstratively refused to participate, remaining in their seats." In those hostile clashing waves of applause were heard the close approaching battles of the civil war. Meanwhile upon the stage representatives of both halves of the divided hall continued to sit with the title of government; and the president, who had secretly taken military measures against the commander-in-chief, did not for a moment forget to incarnate in his figure "the unity of the Russian people." In pursuance of this rôle, Kerensky announced: "I propose to all that in the person of the supreme commander-in-chief who is present here, we should all greet our army, courageously dying for freedom and the fatherland." On the subject of that army he had said at the first session: "Our hopes have been trampled in the mud, and our faith spat upon." But never mind! A saving phrase had been found. The hall rose and stormily applauded Kornilov and Kerensky. The unity of the nation was once more preserved!

The ruling classes, whom historic necessity had seized by the throat, resorted to the method of historic masquerade. It evidently seemed to them that if they could once more stand before the people in all their transformations, this would make them more significant and stronger. In the character of experts on the national conscience, they brought out on the stage all the representatives of all the four state Dumas. Their mutual disagreements, once so sharp, had disappeared. All the parties of the bourgeoisie now united without difficulty upon the "extra-party and extra-class program" of those public men who a few days back had sent a telegram of greeting to Kornilov. In the name of the first Duma—of the year 1906!—the Kadet Nabokov renounced "the very intimation of the possibility of a separate peace." This did not prevent the liberal politician from subsequently relating in his memoirs how he, and with him many of the leading Kadets, saw in a separate peace the only way to salvation. In the same way representatives of the other tzarist Dumas demanded of the revolution first of all a tribute of blood.

"General! you have the floor!" The session has now arrived at its critical moment. What will the high commander-in-chief have to say, after Kerensky has insistently but vainly urged him to limit himself to a mere outline of the military situation? Miliukov writes as an eye-witness: "The short, stumpy but strong figure of a man with Kalmuck features, appeared up the stage, darting sharp piercing glances from his small black eyes in which there was a vicious glint. The hall rocked with applause. All leapt to their feet with the exception of . . . the soldiers." Shouts of indignation mingled with abuse were addressed from the right to the delegates who did not stand: "You roughnecks, get up!" From the delegates not standing the answer comes back: "Serfs!" The uproar turns into a storm. Kerensky demands that they all quietly listen to the "first soldier of the Provisional Government." In the sharp, fragmentary, imperious tone appropriate to a general who intends to save the country, Kornilov read a manuscript written for him by the adventurer Zavoiko at the dictation of the adventurer Filonenko. But the program proffered in the manuscript was considerably more moderate than the design to which it formed an introduction. Kornilov did not hesitate to paint the condition of the army and the situation at the front in the blackest colors, and with an obvious intent to cause fright. The central point in his speech was a military prognosis: "The enemy is already knocking at the gates of Riga, and if the instability of our army does not make it possible to restrain him on the shores of the Gulf of Riga, then the road to Petrograd is open." Here Kornilov hauls off and deals a blow to the government: "By a whole series of legislative measures introduced after the revolution by people strange to the spirit and understanding of an army, the army has been converted into a crazy mob trembling only for its own life." The inference is obvious: There is no hope for Riga, and the commander-in-chief openly and challengingly says so before the whole world, as though inviting the Germans to seize the defenseless city. And Petrograd? Kornilov's thought was this: If I am empowered to carry out my program, Petrograd may still be saved, but hurry up! The Moscow

Bolshevik paper wrote: "What is this, a warning or a threat? The Tarnopol defeat made Kornilov commander-in-chief, the surrender of Riga might make him dictator." That suggestion accorded far more accurately with the designs of the conspirators than could have been guessed by the most suspicious Bolshevik.

The Church Council, having participated in the gorgeous welcome of Kornilov, now sent to the support of the commander-in-chief one of its most reactionary members, the Archbishop Platon. "You have just seen the deadly picture of our army," says this representative of the living forces, "and I have come here in order from this platform to say to Russia: Do not be troubled, dear one. Have no fear, my own one. . . . If a miracle is necessary for the salvation of Russia, then in answer to the prayers of his church, God will accomplish this miracle. . . ." For the protection of the church lands, however, the orthodox prelates preferred some good Cossack troops. The point of the speech was not there, though. The Archbishop complained that in the speeches of the members of the government, he "had not once heard even by a slip of the tongue the word *God*." Just as Kornilov had accused the revolutionary government of demoralizing the army, so Platon accused "those who now stand at the head of our God-loving people" of criminal unbelief. These churchmen who had been squirming in the dust at the feet of Rasputin were now bold enough publicly to confess the revolutionary government.

A declaration of the 12th Cossack Army was read by General Kaledin, whose name was persistently mentioned during this period among the strongest of those in the military party. "Kaledin," to quote one of his eulogists, "not desiring and not knowing how to please the mob, broke with General Brussilov on this ground, and as not adaptable to the spirit of the times was retired from the command." Returning to the Don at the beginning of May, the Cossack general had soon been elected ataman of the Don army, and so to him as chief of the oldest and strongest of the Cossack armies was allotted the task of presenting the program of the privileged Cossack upper circles. Rejecting the accusation of counter-revolutionism, his declaration ungraciously reminded the minister-socialists how at the moment of danger they had come to the Cossacks for help against the Bolsheviks.

166

The gloomy general unexpectedly won the hearts of the democrats by pronouncing in a thunderous voice the word which
Kerensky had not dared to speak out loud: *Republic*. The majority of the hall, and with special zeal the minister Chernov, applauded this Cossack general, who was quite seriously demanding
of the republic that which the autocracy was no longer able to
give. Napoleon predicted that Europe would become either Cossack or republican. Kaledin agreed to see Russia republican on
condition that she should not cease to be Cossack. Having read
the words: "There should be no place for defeatists in the government," the ungrateful general roughly and impudently
turned in the direction of the unlucky Chernov. The report of
the liberal press remarks: "All eyes were fixed upon Chernov,
whose head was bowed low over the table." Being unretained by
any political position, Kaledin developed to the full the military
program of the reaction: abolish the committees, restore power
to the commanders, equalize the front and the rear, reconsider
the rights of the soldiers—that is, reduce them to nothing. (Applause from the Right was here mingled with protests and even
whistling from the Left.) The Constituent Assembly "in the
interest of tranquil and deliberative labors" should be convoked
in Moscow. This speech, prepared in advance of the Conference,
was read by Kaledin the next day after a general strike which
made his phrase about "tranquil" labors in Moscow sound like a
joke. The speech of the Cossack republican finally raised the
temperature of the hall to the boiling point, and prompted Kerensky to show his authority: "It is unbecoming for anybody in
the present assembly to address demands to the government."
But in that case why had he summoned the conference? Purishkevich, a popular member of the Black Hundreds, shouted from
his seat: "We are in the position of supers to the government!"
Two months before, this organizer of pogroms had not dared
show his face.

The official declaration of the democracy, an endless document which tried to answer all questions and answered none, was
read by the president of the Executive Committee, Cheidze, who
received a warm greeting from the Left. Their cries of "Long
live the leader of the Russian revolution!" must have embar-

rassed this modest Caucasian, who was the last man in the world to imagine himself a leader. In a tone of self-justification the democracy announced that it "had not striven after the power, and had not desired a monopoly for itself." It was prepared to support any power capable of preserving the interests of the country and the revolution. But you must not abolish the soviets: they alone have saved the country from anarchy. You must not destroy the soldiers' committees: only they can guarantee the continuation of the war. The privileged classes must in some things act in the interests of the whole people. However, the interests of the landlords must be protected from forcible seizures. The solution of nationality questions must be postponed to the Constituent Assembly. It is necessary, on the other hand, to carry out the more urgent reforms. Of an active policy of peace, the declaration said not a word. In general the document seemed to have been especially designed to provoke the indignation of the masses without giving satisfaction to the bourgeoisie.

In an evasive and colorless speech, the representative of the peasants' Executive Committee reminded his auditors of the slogan "Land and Freedom," under which "our best fighters have died." An account in a Moscow paper records an episode omitted from the official stenographic report: "The whole hall rises and gives a stormy ovation to the prisoners of Schlüsselburg who are seated in a loge." Astonishing grimace of the revolution! "The whole hall" does honor to those few of the former political hard-labor convicts whom the monarchy of Alexeiev, Kornilov, Kaledin, Archbishop Platon, Rodzianko, Guchkov, and in essence also Miliukov, had not succeeded in strangling to death in its prisons. These hangmen, or colleagues of hangmen, wanted to decorate themselves with the martyr's aureole of their own victims!

Fifteen years before that, the leaders of the right half of this hall were celebrating the two hundredth anniversary of the capture of Schlüsselburg fortress by Peter the First. *Iskra,* the journal of the revolutionary wing of the social democracy, wrote during those days: "What indignation awakens in the breast at the thought of this patriotic celebration on that accursed island

168

which has been the place of execution of Minakov, Myshkin, Rogachev, Stromberg, Ulianov, Generalov, Ossipanov, Chevyrev; Andryushkin; within sight of those stone cages in which Klimenko strangled himself with a rope, Grachevsky soaked himself with kerosene and set fire to his body, Sophia Ginsburg stabbed herself with a pair of scissors; under the walls within which Shchedrin, Yuvachev, Konashevich, Pokhitonov, Ignatius Ivanov, Aronchik and Tikhonovich sank into the black night of madness, and scores of others died of exhaustion, scurvy and tuberculosis. Abandon yourself, then, to your patriotic bacchanal for today you are still the lords in Schlüsselburg!" The motto of *Iskra* was a sentence from the letter of a Dekabrist hard-labor convict to Pushkin: "The spark will kindle a flame." The flame had been kindled. It had reduced to ashes the monarchy and its Schlüsselburg hard-labor prison, and now today in the hall of this State Conference yesterday's jail-keepers were offering an ovation to the victims torn from their clutches by the revolution. But most paradoxical of all was the fact that the jailers and their prisoners had actually united together in a feeling of common hatred for the Bolsheviks—for Lenin, the former chief-editor of *Iskra*, for Trotsky, the author of the above-quoted lines, for the rebelling workers and the unsubmissive soldiers who now filled the prisons of the republic.

The National-Liberal, Guchkov, president of the third Duma, who in his day had refused to admit the left deputies into the Committees of Defense, and for this was named by the Compromisers first War Minister of the revolution, made the most interesting speech—a speech, however, in which irony struggled vainly with despair: "But why then . . ." he said, alluding to the words of Kerensky, "why have the representatives of the government come to us with 'mortal alarm' and 'in mortal terror' with a sort of morbid, I would even say, hysterical, cry of despair? And why does this alarm, this terror and this cry, why do they find in our souls a kindred piercing pain as of the anguish of those about to die?" In the name of those who had lorded, commanded, and pardoned, and punished, the great Moscow merchant publicly confesses to a feeling as of "the anguish of those about to die." "This government," he said, "is the shadow of a power." Guchkov was right. But he himself, too, the former partner of Stolypin, was but a shadow of himself.

On the very day of the opening of the conference, there appeared in Gorky's paper an account of how Rodzianko had got rich by supplying worthless wood for rifle-stocks. This untimely revelation—due to Karakhan, the future soviet diplomat, then still unknown to anybody—did not prevent the Lord Chamberlain from speaking at the conference with dignity in defense of the patriotic program of the manufacturers of military supplies. All misfortunes, he said, flowed from the fact that the Provisional Government did not go hand in hand with the state Duma, "the sole, legal and absolutely all-national popular representative assembly in Russia." That seemed a little too much. There was laughter on the left. There were shouts: "The third of June!" There had been a time when that date, the third of June, 1907, the day of the trampling underfoot of the constitution they had granted, burned like the brand of a galley-slave on the brow of the monarchy and the party supporting it. Now it was only a pale memory. But Rodzianko himself, too, with his thundering bass, ponderous and portentous, seemed as he stood on the tribune rather a living monument of the past than a political figure.

As against attacks from within, the government brought forward some encouragements received a long time ago from without. Kerensky read a telegram of greeting from the American president, Wilson, promising "every material and moral support to the government of Russia for success in the common cause uniting both peoples and in which they are pursuing no selfish aims." The renewed applause addressed to the diplomatic loge could not drown the alarm caused in the right half of the assembly by this telegram from Washington. Praise for their disinterestedness had too often meant to the Russian imperialists the prescription of a starvation diet.

In the name of the compromisist democracy, Tseretelli, its acknowledged leader, defended the soviets and the army committees, as one defends for honor's sake a lost cause. "We cannot yet remove these scaffoldings, when the temple of free revolutionary Russia is not yet completely built." After the revolution "the popular masses had trusted nobody in the essence of the matter, but themselves"; only the efforts of the compromisist soviets had made it possible for the possessing classes to stay on top at all, even though at first deprived of their comforts. Tseretelli placed it to the special credit of the soviets that they "had handed over all state functions to the Coalition Government." Did this sacrifice, he asked, have to be "wrested from the democracy by force?" The orator was like the commander of a fortress who boasts publicly that he has surrendered the position entrusted to him without a struggle. . . . And in the July days—"Who then came forward in defense of the country against anarchy?" A voice resounded on the right: "The Cossacks and junkers." Those short words cut like the blow of a whip through the flow of democratic commonplaces. The bourgeois wing of the conference perfectly understood the rescuing services done them by the Compromisers; but gratitude is not a political feeling. The bourgeoisie had promptly drawn their conclusion from the services rendered them by the democracy. It was this: The chapter of the Social Revolutionaries and Mensheviks is at an end, the Cossack and junker chapter is next in order.

Tseretelli approached the problem of power with special caution. During the recent months elections had been held to the city dumas, in part also to the zemstvos, on a basis of universal franchise—and what had happened? The representatives of these democratic, self-governing bodies had turned up at the State Conference in the left group, side by side with the soviets, under the leadership of those same parties, the Social Revolutionaries and Mensheviks. If the Kadets intend to insist upon their demand: to abolish all dependence of the government upon the democracy, then what will be the use of the Constituent Assembly? Tseretelli only just suggested the contours of this argument, for carried to its conclusion it would have condemned the policy of coalition with the Kadets as standing in contradiction even with formal democracy. They are accusing the revolution of overdoing its speeches about peace, he said, but do not the possessing classes understand that the slogan of peace is now the sole means by which the war can be continued? The bourgeoisie

understood this all right. They merely wished to take this means
of continuing the war, along with the power, into *their own*
hands. Tseretelli concluded with a hymn of praise to the Coalition. In that divided assembly which saw no way out of its
problems, his compromisist commonplaces awakened for the last
time a ray of hope. But Tseretelli, too, was already in essence a
phantom of himself.

The democracy was answered in the name of the right half
of the hall by Miliukov, the hopelessly sober representative of
those classes for whom history had made a sober policy impossible. In his "History" the leader of liberalism has expressly set
forth his own speech at the State Conference. "Miliukov made
. . . a brief factual survey of the mistakes of the 'revolutionary
democracy' and summarized them: . . . Capitulation on the
question of 'democratization of the army,' involving the retirement of Guchkov; capitulation on the question of a 'Zimmerwaldist' foreign policy, involving the retirement of the Minister
of Foreign Affairs (Miliukov); capitulation before the utopian
demands of the working class, involving the retirement of Konovalov (Minister of Commerce and Industry); capitulation before the extreme demands of the national minorities, involving
the retirement of the rest of the Kadets. The fifth capitulation—
before the tendency of the masses to direct action in the agrarian
problem . . . had caused the retirement of the first president
of the Provisional Government, Prince Lvov." That was no bad
history of the case. When it came to suggesting a cure, however,
Miliukov's wisdom did not go beyond police measures: We must
strangle the Bolsheviks. "Confronted by obvious facts," he reproached the Compromisers, "these more moderate groups have
been compelled to admit that there are criminals and traitors
among the Bolsheviks. But they have not yet acknowledged that
the very fundamental idea uniting these partisans of anarcho-
syndicalist militant action is criminal (applause)."

The extremely submissive Chernov still seemed to be the link
uniting the Coalition with the revolution. Almost all the orators
of the Right Wing, Kaledin, the Kadet Maklakov, the Kadet
Astrov, aimed a blow at Chernov, who had been ordered in ad-

172

vance to keep still, and whom no one undertook to defend. Miliukov for his part called to mind the fact that the Minister of Agriculture "had himself been at Zimmerwald and Kienthal, and had there introduced the most extreme resolutions." That was a blow straight to the jaw. Before becoming a minister—the minister of an imperialist war—Chernov had actually placed his signature under certain documents of the Zimmerwald Left— that is, of the faction of Lenin.

Miliukov did not conceal from the Conference the fact that from the very beginning he had been opposed to the Coalition, considering that it would be "not stronger but weaker than the government which issued from the revolution"—that is, the government of Guchkov and Miliukov. And now he "greatly fears that the present staff of executives . . . cannot guarantee the safety of persons and property." But however that may be, he, Miliukov, promises to support the government, "voluntarily and without any argument." The treachery of this magnanimous promise will become adequately clear in two weeks. At the moment his speech did not evoke any enthusiasm nor occasion any stormy protest. The orator was both greeted and dismissed with a rather dry applause.

The second speech of Tseretelli reduced itself to promises, asseverations, clamor: Don't you understand that it is all for you—soviets, committees, democratic programs, slogans of pacifism—all this is a protection for you? "Who is more capable of setting in motion the troops of the Russian revolutionary state, the war-minister Guchkov, or the war-minister Kerensky?" Tseretelli was here repeating the words of Lenin almost verbatim, although the leader of compromise regarded as a service what the leader of revolution had branded as treachery. The orator even apologized for his excessive mildness in relation to the Bolsheviks: "I tell you that the revolution was inexperienced in the struggle with anarchy on the left (stormy applause from the right)." But after it had "received its first lessons" the revolution corrected its mistake: "An exceptional law has already been passed." During those very hours Moscow was in the secret control of a committee of six—two Mensheviks, two Social Revolutionaries, two Bolsheviks—defending it against a seizure of power by those to whom the Compromisers were giving this promise to shatter the Bolsheviks.

The high point of the last day was the speech of General Alexeiev, in whose authority the mediocrity of the old military chancelleries stood incarnate. To the wild enthusiasm of the Right, this former chief-of-staff of Nicholas II and organizer of defeats for the Russian army, talked about those destructive characters "in whose pockets is to be heard the melodious clink of German marks." For the restoration of the army, discipline is necessary; for discipline, the authority of the commanders is necessary; and for this again, discipline is necessary. "Call discipline 'iron,' call it 'conscious,' call it 'genuine' . . . at bottom these three kinds of discipline are one and the same." For Alexeiev all history was comprised in the domestic service regulations. "Is it so difficult, gentlemen, to sacrifice some imaginary advantage— the existence of these organizations (laughter on the left) for a certain period of time? (uproar and shouts on the left)." The general urged them to give the disarmed revolution into his keeping, not forever—oh, God save us, no—but only "for a certain period of time!" Upon the conclusion of the war he promised to return the goods undamaged. But Alexeiev concluded with an aphorism that was not bad: "We need measures and not half-measures." These words were a blow at the declaration of Cheidze, the Provisional Government, the Coalition, the whole February régime. Measures and not half-measures! To that the Bolsheviks heartily subscribed.

General Alexeiev's speech was immediately offset by the delegates of the Petrograd and Moscow left officers, who spoke in support of "our supreme chief, the Minister of War." After him Lieutenant Kuchin, an old Menshevik, spokesman of the "representatives of the front at the State Conference" spoke in the name of the soldier millions, who, however, would scarcely have recognized themselves in the mirror of compromisism. "We have all read the interview of General Lukomsky, printed in all the papers, where he says that if the Allies do not help us, Riga will be surrendered. . . ." Why did the high commanding staff which has heretofore always concealed its failures and defeats, consider it necessary to lay on these black colors? Cries of "For shame!" from the left were aimed at Kornilov, who had expressed the same thought at the conference the day before. Kuchin here touched the possessing classes on their sorest point. The upper circles of the bourgeoisie, the commanding staff, the whole right half of the hall, were saturated with defeatist tendencies in all three spheres, economic, political and military. The motto of these respectable and cool-blooded patriots had become: the worse it gets the better! But the compromisist orator hastened to abandon a theme which would have mined the ground under his own feet. "Whether we shall save the army or not, we do not know," said Kuchin. "But if we fail, the commanding staff will not save it either. . . ." "It will!" cried a voice from the officers' seats. Kuchin: "No, it won't!" A burst of applause from the left. Thus the commanders and the committees, upon whose pretended solidarity the whole program of the restoration of the army was based, shouted their hostility across the hall—and thus likewise the two halves of the Conference, which was supposed to constitute the foundation of "an honest coalition." These clashes were merely a weak, smothered, parliamentarized echo of those contradictions which were convulsing the country. Obeying their Bonapartist stage directions, the orators from left and right followed each other alternately, balancing each other off as well as possible. If the hierarchs of the orthodox Church Council supported Kornilov, then the evangelical Christian parsons sided with the Provisional Government. The delegates of the zemstvos and the city dumas made speeches in pairs—one from the majority adhering to the declaration of Cheidze, the other from the minority supporting the declaration of the State Duma.

The representatives of the oppressed nationalities one after another assured the government of their patriotism, but beseeched it to deceive them no longer: In the localities we have the same officials, the same laws, the same oppression. "You must not delay—no people is able to live upon mere promises." Revolutionary Russia must show that she is "mother and not stepmother of all her peoples." These timid reproaches and humble adjurations found hardly a sympathetic response even from the left side of the hall. The spirit of an imperialist war is least of all compatible with an honest policy upon the question of nationalities.

"Up to the present time the nationalities from beyond the Caucasus have not made a single separative move," announced the Menshevik, Chenkeli, in the name of the Georgians, "and they will not make one in the future." This promise, which was roundly applauded, was soon to prove false: from the moment of the October revolution Chenkeli became one of the leaders of separatism. There was no contradiction here, however: the patriotism of democrats does not extend beyond the framework of the bourgeois régime.

Meanwhile certain more tragic specters of the past are taking their place upon the stage; the war cripples are going to lift their voices. They too are not unanimous. The handless, the legless, the blind, have also their aristocracy and their plebs. In the name of the "immense and mighty League of the Cavaliers of St. George, in the name of its 128 departments in all parts of Russia," a crippled officer, outraged in his patriotic feelings, supports Kornilov (applause from the right). The All-Russian League of Crippled Warriors adheres through the voice of its delegate to the declaration of Cheidze (applause from the left).

The Executive Committee of the recently organized union of railroad workers—destined under the abbreviated name of Vikzhel to play an important rôle—joins its voice to the declaration of the Compromisers. The president of the Vikzhel, a moderate democrat and an extreme patriot, paints a vivid picture of counter-revolutionary intrigue among the railroad lines: malicious attacks upon the workers, mass discharges, arbitrary violations of the eight-hour day, arrests and indictments. Underground forces, he says, directed from hidden but influential centers, are clearly trying to provoke the hungry railroad workers to a fight. The enemy remains undiscovered. "The Intelligence Service is dreaming, and the prosecuting attorney's inspectors are fast asleep." And this most moderate of the moderates concludes his speech with a threat: "If the Hydra of counter-revolution lifts its head, we will go out and we will choke him with our own hands."

176

Here one of the railroad magnates immediately takes the floor with counter accusations: "The clear spring of the revolution has been poisoned." Why? "Because the idealistic aims of the revolution have been replaced by material aims (applause from the right)." In a similar spirit the Kadet landlord, Rodichev, denounces the workers for having appropriated from France "the shameful slogan: get rich!" The Bolsheviks will soon give extraordinary success to the formula of Rodichev, although not quite of the kind which the orator hoped for. Professor Ozerov, a man of pure science and a delegate from the agricultural banks, exclaims: "The soldier in the trenches ought to be thinking of war, not of dividing the land." This is not surprising: a confiscation of privately owned land would mean a confiscation of bank capital. On the first of January, 1915, the debts of the private land owners amounted to more than 3¼ billion rubles.

On the right spokesmen took the floor from the high staffs, from the industrial league, from chambers of commerce and banks, from the society of horse breeders, and other organizations comprising hundreds of eminent people. On the left spokesmen appeared for the soviets, the army committees, the trade unions, the democratic municipalities, and the cooperatives behind which in the distant background stood nameless millions and tens of millions. In normal times the advantage would have been with the short arm of the lever. "It is impossible to deny," preached Tseretelli, "especially at such a moment, the great relative weight and significance of those who are strong through the possession of property." But the whole point was that this weight was becoming more and more impossible to weigh. Just as weight is not an inner attribute of individual objects, but an inter-relation between them, so social weight is not a natural property of people, but only that class attribute which other classes are compelled to recognize in them. The revolution, however, had come right up to the point where it was refusing to recognize this most fundamental "attribute" of the ruling classes. It was for this reason that the position of the eminent minority on the short arm of the lever was becoming so uncomfortable. The Compromisers were trying with might and main to preserve the equilibrium, but they also were already without power: the masses were too irresistibly pressing down on the long arm. How cautious were the great agrarians, bankers, industrialists about coming out in the defense of their interests! Did they indeed defend them at all? Almost not at all. They spoke for the rights of idealism, the interests of culture, the prerogatives of a future Constituent Assembly. The leader of the heavy industries, Von Ditmar, even concluded his speech with a hymn in honor of "liberty, equality, fraternity." Where were the metallic baritones of profits, the hoarse bass of land rents—where were they hiding? Only the over-sweet tenor melodies of disinterestedness filled the hall. But listen for a moment: how much spleen and vinegar under all this syrup! How unexpectedly these lyric roulades break into a spiteful falsetto! The president of the All-Russian Chamber of Agriculture, Kapatsinsky, standing with all his heart for the coming agrarian reform, does not forget to thank "our pure Tseretelli" for his circular in defense of law against anarchy. But the land committees? They will straightway turn over the power to the muzhik! To this "dark, semi-illiterate man, crazy with joy that they have at last given him the land, it is proposed to turn over the inauguration of justice in the country!" If in their struggle with this dark muzhik, the landlords happen to be defending property, it is not for their own sakes— Oh no!—but only in order afterwards to lay it upon the altar of freedom.

The social symbolism would now seem to have been completed. But here Kerensky is blessed with a happy inspiration. He proposes that they give the floor to one more group—"a group out of Russian history—namely Breshko-Breshkovskaia, Kropotkin and Plekhanov." Russian Narodnikism, Russian anarchism, and Russian social democratism take the floor in the person of the older generation—anarchism and Marxism in the person of their most eminent founders.

Kropotkin asked only to join his voice "to those voices which are summoning the whole Russian people to break once for all with Zimmerwaldism." The apostle of non-government promptly gave his adherence to the right wing of the Conference. A defeat threatens us, he cried, not only with the loss of vast territories and the payment of indemnities: "You must know, comrades, that there is something worse than all this—that is the psychology of a defeated nation." This ancient internationalist prefers to see the psychology of a defeated nation on the other side of the border. While recalling how a conquered France had humbled herself before the Russian tzars, he did not foresee how a conquering France would humble herself before American bankers. He exclaimed: "Are we going to live through the same thing? Not by any means!" He was applauded by the entire hall. And then what rainbow prospects, he said, are opened by the war: "All are beginning to understand that we must build a new life on new socialist principles. . . . Lloyd George is making speeches imbued with the socialist spirit. . . . In England, in France and in Italy, there is forming a new comprehension of life, imbued with socialism—unfortunately state socialism." If Lloyd George and Poincaré have not yet "unfortunately" renounced the state principle, at least Kropotkin has come over to it frankly enough. "I think," he said, "that we will not be depriving the Constituent Assembly of any of its rights—I fully recognize that to it belongs the sovereign decision upon such questions—if we, the Council of the Russian land, loudly express our desire that Russia should be declared a republic." Kropotkin insisted upon a confederative republic: "We need a federation such as they have in the United States." That is what Bakunin's federation of free communes had come down to! "Let us promise each other at last," adjured Kropotkin in conclusion, "that we will no longer be divided into the left and right halves of this theater. . . . We all have one fatherland, and for her we ought all to stand together, or to lie down together if need be, both Lefts and Rights." Landlords, industrialists, generals, Cavaliers of St. George, all those who did not recognize Zimmerwald, extended to the apostle of anarchism a well-earned ovation.

The principles of liberalism can have a real existence only in conjunction with a police system. Anarchism is an attempt to cleanse liberalism of the police. But just as pure oxygen is impossible to breathe, so liberalism without the police-principle means the death of society. Being a shadow-caricature of liberalism, anarchism as a whole has shared its fate. Having killed liberalism, the development of class contradictions has also killed anarchism. Like every sect which founds its teaching not upon the actual development of human society, but upon the reduction to absurdity of one of its features, anarchism explodes like a soap bubble at that moment when the social contradictions arrive at the point of war or revolution. Anarchism as represented by Kropotkin was about the most spectral of all the specters at the State Conference.

In Spain, the classic country of Bakuninism, the anarcho-syndicalist and so-called "specific," or pure anarchists, in abstaining from politics, are really repeating the policy of the Russian Mensheviks. These bombastic deniers of the state respectfully bow down to force the moment it changes its skin. Having warned the proletariat against the temptations of power, they self-sacrificingly support the power of the "left" bourgeoisie. Cursing the gangrene of parliamentarism, they secretly hand their followers the election ballot of the vulgar republican. No matter how the Spanish revolution develops, it will at least put an end to anarchism once for all.

Plekhanov, who was greeted by the whole conference with stormy applause—the lefts were honoring their old leader, the rights their new ally—represented that early Russian Marxism whose outlook had in the course of the decades become fixed within the boundaries of political freedom. For the Bolsheviks the revolution had only begun, for Plekhanov it was already finished. Advising the industrialists to "seek a rapprochement with the working class," Plekhanov suggested to the democrats: "It is absolutely necessary for you to come to an agreement with the representatives of the commercial and industrial class." As a horrible example Plekhanov introduced the "unhappy memory of Lenin," who had fallen to such a level that he was summoning the proletariat to "an immediate seizure of political power." It was just for this warning against a struggle for power that the Conference had need of Plekhanov, who had abandoned the last item of the armor of a revolutionist upon the threshold of the revolution.

On the evening of the day that the delegates from "Russian history" spoke, Kerensky gave the floor to a representative of the Chamber of Agriculture and the Union of Horse Breeders, also a Kropotkin, another member of the old princely family which had, if you believe their genealogical tree, a better right than the Romanovs to the Russian throne. "I'm not a Socialist," said this feudal aristocrat, "though I have a respect for genuine socialism. But when I see seizures, robberies and violence I am obliged to say . . . the government ought to compel people who are attaching themselves to socialism to withdraw from the task of reconstructing the country." This second Kropotkin, obviously aiming his shot at Chernov, had no objection to such socialists as Lloyd George or Poincaré. Along with his family-opposite, the anarchist, this monarchist Kropotkin condemned Zimmerwald, the class struggle and the land seizures—alas, he had been in the habit of calling them "anarchy"—and also demanded union and victory. Unfortunately the records do not state whether the two Kropotkins applauded each other.

In this conference, corroded with hatred, they talked so much about unity that unity simply had to materialize at least for one second in the inevitable symbolic handshake. The Menshevik paper tells of this incident in rapturous words: "During the speech of Bublikov an incident occurred which made a deep impression upon all the members of the Conference . . . 'Yesterday,' said Bublikov, 'a noble leader of the revolution, Tseretelli, extended his hand to the business world, and I want him to know that that hand is not left hanging in the air. . . .' " When Bublikov stopped speaking Tseretelli came up and shook hands with him. Stormy ovations.

How many ovations! A little too many. A week before the scene just described, this same Bublikov, a big railroad magnate, attending a congress of industrialists, had bellowed against the soviet leaders: "Away with the dishonest, the ignorant, all those who have driven us toward destruction!" and his words were still echoing in the atmosphere of Moscow. The old Marxist, Riazanov, who attended the conference as a trade union delegate, very appropriately recalled the kiss of the prelate of Lyon, Lamourette— "That kiss which was exchanged by two parts of the National Assembly—not the workers and the bourgeoisie, but two parts of the bourgeoisie—and you know that the struggle never burst out more furiously than just after that kiss." Miliukov acknowledges with unaccustomed frankness that this union was, upon the side of the industrialists, "not sincere, but practically necessary for a class which would have too much to lose. The celebrated handshake of Bublikov was just such a reconciliation, with mental reservations."

Did the majority of the members of the conference believe in the force of handshakes and political kisses? Did they believe in themselves? Their feelings were contradictory, like their plans. To be sure, in certain individual speeches, especially from the provinces, there was still to be heard the crackle of the first raptures, hopes, illusions. But in a conference where the left half was disappointed and demoralized, and the right enraged, these echoes of the March days sounded like the correspondence of a betrothed couple made public in their divorce trial. Having already departed into the kingdom of shades, these politicians were saving with spectral measures a spectral régime. A deathly cold breath of hopelessness hung over this assembly of "living forces," this final parade of the doomed.

Towards the very end of the conference an incident occurred revealing the deep split even in that group which was considered the model of unity and loyalty to the state, the Cossacks. Nagaiev, a young Cossack officer in the soviet delegation, declared that the working Cossacks were not with Kaledin. The Cossacks at the front, he said, do not trust the Cossack leaders. That was true, and touched the conference upon its sorest point. The newspaper accounts here report the stormiest of all the scenes at the conference. The Left ecstatically applauded Nagaiev and shouts were heard: "Hurrah for the revolutionary Cossacks!" Indignant protests from the Right: "You will answer for this!" A voice from the officers' benches: "German marks!" In spite of the inevitability of these words as the last argument of patriotism, they produced an effect like an exploding bomb. The hall was filled with a perfectly hellish noise. The soviet delegates jumped from their seats, threatening the officers' benches with their fists. There were cries of "Provocateurs!" The president's bell clanged continually. "Another moment and it seemed as though a fight would begin."

After all that had taken place Kerensky declared in his concluding speech: "I believe and I even know . . . that we have

182

achieved a better understanding of each other, that we have achieved a greater respect for each other. . . ." Never before had the duplicity of the February régime risen to such disgusting and futile heights of falsity. Himself unable to sustain this tone, the orator suddenly burst out in the midst of his concluding phrases into a wail of threat and despair. As Miliukov describes it: "With a broken voice which fell from a hysterical shriek to a tragic whisper, Kerensky threatened an imaginary enemy, intently searching for him throughout the hall with inflamed eyes. . . ." Miliukov really knew better than anybody else that this enemy was not imaginary. "Today citizens of the Russian land, I will no longer dream. . . . May my heart become a stone. . . ." Thus Kerensky raged— "Let all those flowers and dreams of humanity dry up. (A woman's voice from the gallery: 'You cannot do that. Your heart will not permit you.') I throw far away the key of my heart, beloved people. I will think only of the state."

The hall was stupefied, and this time both halves of it. The social symbol of the State Conference wound up with an insufferable monologue from a melodrama. That woman's voice raised in defense of the flowers of the heart sounded like a cry for help, like an S. O. S. from the peaceful, sunny, bloodless February revolution. The curtain came down at last upon the State Conference.

CHAPTER VIII

KERENSKY'S PLOT

THE Moscow Conference damaged the position of the government by revealing, as Miliukov correctly states, "that the country was divided into two camps between which there could be no essential reconciliation or agreement." The Conference raised the spirits of the bourgeoisie and sharpened their impatience. In the other hand it gave a new impulse to the movement of the masses. The Moscow strike opened a period of accelerated regrouping to leftward of the workers and soldiers. Henceforth the Bolsheviks grew unconquerably. Among the masses, only the Left Social Revolutionaries, and to some extent the Left Mensheviks, held their own. The Petrograd organization of the Mensheviks signalized its political shift leftward by excluding Tseretelli from the list of candidates for the city duma. On the 16th of August, a Petrograd conference of the Social Revolutionaries demanded, by 22 votes against 1, the dissolution of the League of Officers at headquarters, and other decisive measures against the counter-revolution. On August 18, the Petrograd Soviet, over the objection of its president, Cheidze, placed upon the order of the day the question of abolishing the death penalty. Before the voting, Tseretelli put this challenging question: "If as a consequence of your resolution, the death penalty is not abolished, then will you bring the crowd into the street and demand the overthrow of the government?" "Yes," shouted the Bolsheviks in answer. "Yes, we will call out the crowd, and we will try our best to overthrow the government." "You have lifted your heads high these days," said Tseretelli. The Bolsheviks had lifted their heads together with the masses. The Compromisers had lowered their heads as the heads of the masses were lifted. The demand for an abolition of the death penalty was adopted by all votes—about 900—against 4. Those four were Tseretelli, Cheidze, Dan, Lieber! Four days later, at a joint session of

184

Mensheviks and groups surrounding them, where upon fundamental questions a resolution of Tseretelli was adopted in opposition to that of Martov, the demand for an immediate abolition of the death penalty was passed without debate. Tseretelli, no longer able to resist the pressure, remained silent.

This thickening political atmosphere was pierced by events at the front. On the 19th of August, the Germans broke through the Russian line near Ikskul. On the 21st, they occupied Riga. This fulfillment of Kornilov's prediction became, as though by previous agreement, the signal for a political attack of the bourgeoisie. The press multiplied tenfold its campaign against "workers who will not work" and "soldiers who will not fight." The revolution had to answer for everything: it had surrendered Riga; it was getting ready to surrender Petrograd. The slandering of the army—just as furious as two and a half months ago—had now not a shadow of justification. In June the soldiers had actually refused to take the offensive: they had not wanted to stir up the front, to break the passivity of the Germans, to renew the fight. But before Riga the initiative was taken by the enemy, and the soldiers behaved quite differently. It was, moreover, the most thoroughly propagandized part of the 12th army which proved least subject to panic.

The commander of the army, General Parsky, boasted, and not without foundation, that the retreat was accomplished "in model formation," and could not even be compared to the retreats from Galicia and East Prussia. Commissar Voitinsky reported: "Our troops have carried out the tasks allotted to them in the region of the breach honorably and irreproachably, but they are not in a condition long to sustain the attack of the enemy, and are retreating slowly, a step at a time, suffering enormous losses. I consider it necessary to mention the extraordinary valor of the Lettish sharpshooters, the remnant of whom, in spite of complete exhaustion, has been sent again into the battle. . . ." Still more enthusiastic was the report of the president of the army committee, the Menshevik Kuchin: "The spirit of the soldiers was astonishing. According to the testimony of members of the committee and officers, their staunchness was something never before seen." Another representative of the same army reported a few days later at a session of the bureau of the Executive Committee: "In the center of the point of attack was a Lettish brigade consisting almost exclusively of Bolsheviks. . . . Receiving orders to advance, the brigade went forward with red banners and bands playing and fought with extraordinary courage." Stankevich wrote later to the same effect, although more restrainedly: "Even in the army headquarters which contained people notoriously ready to lay the blame upon the soldiers, they could not tell me one single concrete instance of non-fulfillment, not only of fighting orders, but of any orders whatever." The landing force of marines engaged in the Moonsund operation, as appears in the official documents, also showed noticeable fortitude. A part was played in determining the mood of the soldiers, especially the Lettish sharpshooters and Baltic sailors, by the fact that it was a question this time of the direct defense of two centers of the revolution, Riga and Petrograd. The more advanced troops had already got hold of the Bolshevik idea that "to stick your bayonets in the ground does not settle the question of the war," that the struggle for peace was inseparable from the struggle for power, for a new revolution.

Even if certain individual commissars, frightened by the attack of the generals, exaggerated the staunchness of the army, the fact remains that the soldiers and sailors obeyed orders and died. They could not do more. But nevertheless in the essence of the matter there was no defense. Incredible as it may seem, the twelfth army was caught wholly unprepared. Everything was lacking: men, arms, military supplies, gas masks. The communications were unspeakably bad. Attacks were delayed because Japanese cartridges had been supplied for Russian rifles. Yet this was no incidental sector of the front. The significance of the loss of Riga had been no secret to the high command. How then explain the extraordinarily miserable condition of the defense forces and supplies of the twelfth army? "The Bolsheviks," writes Stankevich, "had already begun to spread rumors that the city was surrendered to the Germans on purpose, because the officers wanted to get rid of that nest and nursery of Bolshevism. These rumors could not but win belief in the army, which knew that

essentially there had been no defense or resistance." The fact is
that as early as December 1916, Generals Ruzsky and Brussilov
had complained that Riga was "the misfortune of the Northern
front," that it was "a nest of propaganda," which could only be
dealt with by the method of executions. To send the Riga workers and soldiers to the training school of a German military occupation, must have been the secret dream of many generals of
the northern front. Nobody imagined of course that the
commander-in-chief had given an order for the surrender of
Riga. But all the commanders had read the speech of Kornilov
and the interview of his chief-of-staff, Lukomsky. This made an
order entirely unnecessary. The commander-in-chief of the
northern front, General Klembovsky, belonged to the inside
clique of conspirators, and was consequently awaiting the surrender of Riga as a signal for the beginning of the movement to
save the country. Moreover, even in normal conditions these
Russian generals had a preference for surrender and retreat. On
this occasion, when they were relieved of responsibility in advance
by headquarters, and their political interests impelled them along
the road of defeatism, they did not even make the attempt at a
defense. Whether this or that general added some damaging action
to the passive sabotage of the defense, is a secondary question and
in its essence hard to solve. It would be naïve to imagine, however, that the generals restrained themselves from lending what
help they could to destiny in those cases where their traitorous
activities would remain unpunished.

The American journalist, John Reed, who knew how to see and
hear, and who has left an immortal book of chronicler's notes of
the days of the October Revolution, testifies without hesitation
that a considerable part of the possessing classes of Russia preferred a German victory to the triumph of the revolution, and
did not hesitate to say so openly. "One evening I spent at the
house of a Moscow merchant," says Reed, among other examples.
"During tea we asked eleven people at the table whether they
preferred 'Wilhelm or the Bolsheviks.' The vote was ten to one
for Wilhelm." The same American writer conversed with officers
on the northern front, who "frankly preferred a military defeat
to working with the soldiers' committees."

To sustain the political accusation made by the Bolsheviks—and not only by them—it is wholly sufficient that the surrender of Riga entered into the plans of the conspirators and occupied a definite place in the calendar of their conspiracy. This was quite clearly evident between the lines of the Moscow speech of Kornilov. Subsequent events illumined that aspect of the matter completely. But we have also a piece of direct testimony, to which, in the given instance, the personality of the witness imparts an irreproachable authority. Miliukov in his "History" says: "In Moscow, Kornilov indicated in his speech that moment beyond which he did not wish to postpone decisive steps for the 'salvation of the country from ruin and the army from collapse.' That moment was the fall of Riga predicted by him. This event in his opinion would evoke . . . a flood of patriotic excitement. . . . As Kornilov told me personally at a meeting in Moscow on the 13th of August, he did not wish to let pass this opportunity. And the moment of open conflict with the government of Kerensky was completely determined in his mind even to the point of settling in advance upon the date, August 27." Could one possibly speak more clearly? In order to carry out the march on Petrograd, Kornilov had need of the surrender of Riga several days before the date settled upon. To strengthen the Riga position, to take serious measures of defense, would have meant to destroy the plan of another campaign immeasurably more important for Kornilov. If Paris is worth a mass, then Riga is a small price to pay for power.

During the week which passed between the surrender of Riga and the insurrection of Kornilov, headquarters became the central reservoir of slander against the army. The communications from the Russian staff printed in the Russian press found immediate echo in the press of the Entente. The Russian patriotic papers in their turn enthusiastically reprinted the taunts and abuse addressed to the Russian army by *The Times, Le Temps* and *Le Matin.* The soldiers' front quivered with resentment, indignation and disgust. The commissars and committees, even the compromisist and patriotic ones, felt injured to the quick. Protests poured in from all sides. Especially sharp was the letter of the executive committee of the Rumanian front, the Odessa military district, and the Black Sea fleet—the so-called Rumcherod—which demanded that the Executive Committee "establish before all Russia the valor and devoted bravery of the soldiers who are dying by the thousands every day in cruel battles for the defense of revolutionary Russia. . . ." Under the influence of these protests from below, the compromisist leaders abandoned their passivity. "It seems as if there exists no filth which the bourgeois papers will not fling at the revolutionary army," wrote *Izvestia* of its allies in a political bloc. But nothing had any effect. This slandering of the army was a necessary part of the conspiracy which had its center in headquarters.

Immediately after the abandonment of Riga, Kornilov gave order by telegram to shoot a few soldiers on the road before the eyes of others as an example. Commissar Voitinsky and General Parsky reported that in their opinion the conduct of the soldiers did not at all justify such measures. Kornilov, beside himself, declared at a meeting of committee representatives at headquarters that he would court-martial Voitinsky and Parsky for giving untrue reports of the situation in the army—which meant, as Stankevich explains, "for not laying the blame on the soldiers." To complete the picture, it is necessary to add that on the same day Kornilov ordered the army staffs to supply a list of Bolshevik officers to the head committee of the League of Officers—that is, to the counter-revolutionary organization headed by the Kadet Novosiltsev which was the chief center of the plot. Such was this supreme commander-in-chief, "the first soldier of the revolution!"

Having made up its mind to lift a tiny corner of the curtain, *Izvestia* wrote: "Some mysterious clique extraordinarily close to the high commanding circles is doing a monstrous work of provocation. . . ." Under the phrase "mysterious clique" they were alluding to Kornilov and his staff. The heat lightnings of the advancing civil war began to cast a new illumination not only upon today's, but upon yesterday's doings. Under the head of self-defense, the Compromisers began to uncover suspicious activities of the commanding staff during the June offensive. There appeared in the press more and more details of the malicious slandering by the staffs of divisions and regiments. "Russia has

THE ATTEMPTED COUNTER-REVOLUTION

the right to demand," wrote *Izvestia,* "that the whole truth be laid bare to her about our July retreat." Those words were eagerly read by soldiers, sailors, workers—especially by those who, under the pretense that they had been guilty of the catastrophe at the front, were still keeping the prisons full. Two days later *Izvestia* felt compelled to declare more openly that: "Headquarters with its communiqués is playing a definite political game against the Provisional Government and the revolutionary democracy." The government is portrayed in these lines as an innocent victim of the designs of headquarters, but it would seem as though the government had every opportunity to pull up on the generals. If it did not do so, that was because it did not want to.

In the above-mentioned protest against treacherous baitings of the soldiers, Rumcherod spoke with especial indignation of the fact that "the communiqués from headquarters . . . while emphasizing the gallantry of the officers seem deliberately to belittle the devotion of the soldiers to the defense of the revolution." The protest of Rumcherod appeared in the press of August 22, and the next day a special order of Kerensky was published devoted to the laudation of the officers, who "from the first days of the revolution have had to endure a diminution of their rights," and undeserved insults on the part of soldier masses "concealing their cowardice under idealistic slogans." At a time when his closest assistants, Stankevich, Voitinsky and others, were protesting against the taunting of soldiers, Kerensky demonstratively associated himself with this business, crowning it with a provocatory order from the War Minister and Head of the Government. Kerensky subsequently acknowledged that as early as the end of July he had in his hands "accurate information" as to an officers' plot grouped around headquarters. "The head committee of the League of Officers," to quote Kerensky, "appointed active conspirators from its midst, and its members were agents of the conspiracy in various localities. They gave to the legal actions of the League the necessary tone." That is perfectly correct. We need only add that "the necessary tone" was a tone of slander against the army, the committees, and the revolution—that is, the very tone of Kerensky's order of August 23.

How shall we explain this riddle? That Kerensky had no con-

190

sistent and thought-out policy is absolutely indubitable. But he must needs have been altogether out of his senses, in order with knowledge of an officer's plot to put his head under the knife of the plotters and at the same time to help them disguise themselves. The explanation of the conduct of Kerensky, incomprehensible at first glance, is in reality very simple: he was himself at that time a party to the plot against the baffled régime of the February revolution.

When the time came for revelations, Kerensky himself testified that from the Cossack circles, from officers, and from bourgeois politicians, proposals of a personal dictatorship had come to him more than once. "But they fell upon unfertile soil. . . ." The position of Kerensky was at any rate, then, such that the leaders of counter-revolution were able without risk to exchange opinions with him about a coup d'état. "The first conversations on the subject of a dictatorship, taking the form of a slight feeling out of the ground," began—according to Denikin —at the beginning of June, that is, during the preparations for the offensive. Kerensky not infrequently participated in these conversations, and in such cases it was assumed as a matter of course, especially by Kerensky himself, that he would occupy the center of the dictatorship. Sukhanov rightly says of Kerensky: "He was a Kornilovist—only on the condition that he himself should stand at the head of the Kornilovists." During the collapse of the offensive, Kerensky promised Kornilov and the other generals far more than he could fulfil. "During his journeys on the front," relates General Lukomsky, "Kerensky would often pump up his courage and discuss with his companions the question of creating a firm power, of forming a directory, or of turning over the power to a dictator." In conformity with his character, Kerensky would introduce into these conversations an element of formlessness, a slovenly, dilettante element. The generals, on the other hand, would incline towards military precision.

These casual participations of Kerensky in the conversations of the generals gave a certain legalization to the idea of a military dictatorship, a thing which, out of cautiousness before the not yet strangled revolution, they most often called by the name of "directory." What rôle historic recollections about the government of France after the Thermidor played here, it would be difficult to say. But aside from questions of mere verbal disguise, the directory presented in the first place this indubitable advantage, that it permitted a subordination of personal ambitions. In a directory, places ought to be found not only for Kerensky and Kornilov, but also for Savinkov, even for Filonenko —in general, for people of "iron will," as the candidates themselves expressed it. Each of them cherished in his own mind the thought of passing over afterward from the collective to the single dictatorship.

For a conspiratorial bargain with headquarters Kerensky therefore did not have to make any abrupt change: it was sufficient to develop and continue what he had already begun. He assumed, moreover, that he could give to the conspiracy of the generals a suitable direction, bringing it down not only on the heads of the Bolsheviks, but also, within certain limits, upon his allies and tiresome guardians, the Compromisers. Kerensky maneuvered in such a way that, without exposing the conspirators completely, he could adequately frighten them and involve them in his own design. In this he went to the very limit beyond which the head of a government would become an illegal conspirator. "Kerensky needed an energetic pressure upon him from the right, from the capitalist cliques, the Allied embassies, and especially from headquarters," wrote Trotsky early in September, "in order to enable him to get his own hands absolutely free. Kerensky wanted to use the revolt of the generals in order to reinforce his own dictatorship."

The State Conference was the critical moment. Carrying home from Moscow, along with the illusion of unlimited opportunities, a humiliating sense of his personal failure, Kerensky finally decided to cast away all hesitations and show himself to *them* in his full stature. But whom did he mean by "them"? Everybody—but above all the Bolsheviks, who had placed the mine of a general strike under his gorgeous national tableau. In doing this he would also settle matters once for all with the Rights, with all those Guchkovs and Miliukovs who would not take him seriously, who made fun of his gestures and considered his power the shadow of a power. And finally he would give a good reprimand to "them," the compromisist tutors, the hateful Tseretelli who kept correcting and instructing him, Kerensky, the chosen of the nation, even at the State Conference. Kerensky firmly and finally decided to show the whole world that he was by no means a "hysteric," a "juggler," a "ballerina," as the Guard and Cossack officers were more and more openly calling him, but a man of iron who had closed tight the doors of his heart and thrown the key in the ocean in spite of the prayers of the beautiful unknown in the loge at the theater.

Stankevich remarked in Kerensky in those days, "a desire to speak some new word answering the universal alarm and con-sternation of the country. Kerensky . . . decided to introduce disciplinary punishments into the army; probably he was also ready to propose other decisive measures to the government." Stankevich knew only that part of his chief's intentions which the latter deemed it timely to communicate to him. In reality the designs of Kerensky at that time already went considerably further. He had decided at one blow to cut the ground under the feet of Kornilov by carrying out the latter's program, and thus binding the bourgeoisie to himself. Guchkov had been un-able to move the troops to an offensive; he, Kerensky, had done it. Kornilov would not be able to carry out the program of Kornilov; he, Kerensky, could. The Moscow strike had reminded him, it is true, that there would be obstacles on this road, but the July Days had shown that it was possible to overcome them. Now again it was only necessary to carry the job through to the end, not permitting the friends on the left to get hold of your coat-tails. First of all it was necessary to change completely the Petrograd garrison: the revolutionary regiments must be re-placed by "healthy" detachments, who would not be always glancing round at the soviets. There would be no chance to talk of this plan with the Executive Committee. And why indeed should that be necessary? The government had been recognized as independent and crowned under that banner in Moscow. To be sure, the Compromisers understood independence only in a formal sense, as a means of pacifying the Liberals. But he, Keren-sky, would convert the formal into the material. Not for nothing had he declared in Moscow that he was neither with the Rights nor the Lefts, and that therein lay his strength. Now he would prove this in action!

After the conference Kerensky's line and the line of the Executive Committee had continued to diverge: the Compromisers were afraid of the masses, Kerensky of the possessing classes. The popular masses were demanding the abolition of the death penalty at the front; Kornilov, the Kadets, the embassies of the Entente, were demanding its introduction at the rear.

On August 19, Kornilov telegraphed the Minister-President: "I insistently assert the necessity of subordinating to me the Petrograd district." Headquarters was openly stretching its hand toward the capital. On August 24, the Executive Committee summoned the courage to demand vocally that the government put an end to "counter-revolutionary methods," and undertake "without delay and with all energy" the realization of the democratic transformation. This was a new language. Kerensky was compelled to choose between accommodating himself to a democratic platform, which with all its meagerness might lead to a split with the Liberals and generals, and the program of Kornilov which would inexorably lead to a conflict with the soviets. Kerensky decided to extend his hand to Kornilov, to the Kadets, to the Entente. He wanted to avoid an open conflict on the right at any cost.

It is true that on August 21, the grand dukes Mikhail Alexandrovich and Pavel Alexandrovich were put under house arrest, and a few other persons at the same time placed under observation. But there was nothing serious in all that, and Kerensky was compelled to liberate the arrestees immediately. "It seems," he said in subsequent testimony on the Kornilov affair, "that we had been consciously led off on a false scent." To this it is only necessary to add—"with our own co-operation." It was perfectly clear that for serious conspirators—that is, for the whole right wing of the Moscow Conference—it was not at all a question of restoring monarchy, but of establishing the dictatorship of the bourgeoisie over the people. It was in this sense that Kornilov and all his colleagues rejected, not without indignation, the charge of "counter-revolutionary"—that is, monarchist—designs. To be sure, there were former officials, aides-de-camp, ladies-in-waiting,

Black Hundred courtiers, witch-doctors, monks, ballerinas, whispering here and there in the back yards. That was a thing of no consequence whatever. The victory of the bourgeoisie could come only in the form of a military dictatorship. The question of monarchy could rise only at some future stage, and then too on the basis of a bourgeois counter-revolution, not of Rasputin's ladies-in-waiting.

For the given period the real thing was the struggle of the bourgeoisie against the people under the banner of Kornilov. Seeking an alliance with this camp, Kerensky was all the more willing to screen himself from the suspicions of the Left with a fictitious arrest of grand dukes. The trick was so obvious that the Moscow Bolshevik paper wrote at the time: "To arrest a pair of brainless puppets from the Romanov family and leave at liberty . . . the military clique of the army commanders with Kornilov at the head—that is to deceive the people. . . ." The Bolsheviks were hated for this, too, that they saw everything, and talked out loud about it. Kerensky's inspiration and guide in those critical days had come to be Savinkov—a mighty seeker of adventures, a revolutionist of the sporting type, one who had acquired a scorn for the masses in the school of the individual terror, a man of talent and will—qualities which had not, however, prevented him from becoming for a number of years an instrument in the hands of the famous provocateur, Azef—a sceptic and a cynic, who believed, not without foundation, that he had a right to look down upon Kerensky, and while holding his right hand to his vizor respectfully to lead him by the nose with his left. Savinkov imposed himself upon Kerensky as a man of action, and upon Kornilov as a genuine revolutionist with a historic name. Miliukov has a curious story of the first meeting between the commissar and the general, as told by Savinkov. "General," said Savinkov, "I know that if conditions arise in which you ought to shoot me, you will shoot me." After a prolonged pause he added: "But if conditions arise in which I have to shoot you, I will do that too." Savinkov was fond of literature, knew Corneille and Hugo, and was inclined to the lofty genre. Kornilov intended to get rid of the revolution without regard to the formulae of pseudo-classicism and romanticism, but the general, too, was not a stranger to the charm of a "strong artistic style." The words of the former terrorist must have tickled pleasantly the heroic principle buried in the breast of the former member of the Black Hundreds.

In one of the later newspaper articles, obviously inspired and perhaps also written by Savinkov, his own plans were quite lucidly explained: "While still a commissar . . ." says the article, "Savinkov came to the conclusion that the Provisional Government was incapable of getting the country out of its difficult situation. Here other forces must be brought into play. However, all the work in that direction could be done only under the banner of the Provisional Government, and in particular of Kerensky. It would have to be a revolutionary dictatorship established by an iron hand. That iron hand Savinkov saw in General Kornilov." Kerensky as a "revolutionary" screen, Kornilov as an iron hand. As to the rôle of the third party, the article has nothing to say, but there is no doubt that Savinkov, in reconciling the commander-in-chief with the prime minister, had some thought of crowding them both out. At one time this unspoken thought came so close to the surface that Kerensky, just on the eve of the Conference and against the protest of Kornilov, compelled Savinkov to resign. However, like everything else that happened in that sphere, the resignation was not conclusive. "On the 17th of August it was announced," testified Filonenko, "that Savinkov and I would keep our posts, and that the Minister-President had accepted in principle the program expounded in the report presented by General Kornilov, Savinkov and me." Savinkov, to whom Kerensky on August 17, "gave orders to draft a law for measures to be adopted in the rear," created to this end a commission under the presidency of General Apushkin. Although seriously fearing Savinkov, Kerensky definitely decided to use him for his own great plan, and not only kept his place for him in the war ministry but gave him one in the ministry of the navy to boot. That meant, according to Miliukov, that for the government "the time had come to take some definite measures even at the risk of *bringing the Bolsheviks into the street*." Savinkov on this subject "frankly stated that with two regiments it would be easy to put down a Bolshevik revolt and break up the Bolshevik organizations."

Both Kerensky and Savinkov perfectly understood, especially after the Moscow Conference, that the compromisist soviets would in no case accept the program of Kornilov. The Petrograd soviet, having only yesterday demanded the abolition of the death penalty at the front, would rise with redoubled strength against the extension of the death penalty to the rear. The danger, therefore, was that the movement against the coup d'état planned by Kerensky might be led, not by the Bolsheviks, but by the soviets. However, we must not stop for that of course: it is a question of saving the country!

"On the 22nd of August," writes Kerensky, "Savinkov went to headquarters at my direction in order, among other things (!) to demand of General Kornilov that he place a cavalry corps at the disposal of the government." Savinkov himself, when it came his turn to justify himself before public opinion, described his mission in the following terms: "To get from General Kornilov a cavalry corps for the actual inauguration of martial law in Petrograd and for the defense of the Provisional Government against any attempt whatever, in particular (!) an attempt of the Bolsheviks who . . . according to information received from a foreign intelligence service, were again preparing an attack in connection with a German siege and an insurrection in Finland. . . ." The fantastic information of the Intelligence Service was used simply to cover the fact that the government itself, in the words of Miliukov, was assuming the "risk of bringing the Bolsheviks into the street." That is, it was ready to provoke an insurrection. And since the publication of the decree establishing a military dictatorship was designated for the last days of August, Savinkov accommodated to that date the anticipated insurrection.

On the 25th of August, the Bolshevik organ *Proletarian* was suppressed without any external motive. *The Worker*, which came out in its place, declared that its predecessor had been "closed the day after it had summoned the workers and soldiers, in connection with the breach on the Riga front, to self-restraint and tranquil-

ity. Whose hand is taking such care that the workers shall not
know that the party is warning them against provocation?" That
question was directly to the point. The fate of the Bolshevik press
was in the hands of Savinkov. The suppression of the paper gave
him two advantages: it irritated the masses and it prevented the
party from protecting them against a provocation which came
this time from governmental high places.

According to the minutes of headquarters—perhaps a little
polished up, but in general fully corresponding to the situation
and the persons involved—Savinkov informed Kornilov: "Your
demands, Lavr Georgievich, will be satisfied in a few days. But
the government fears that in connection with this, serious complications may arise in Petrograd. . . . The publication of your
demands will be a signal for a coming-out of the Bolsheviks.
. . . It is not known what attitude the soviets will take to the
new law. The latter may also oppose the government. . . .
Hence I request you to give an order that the third cavalry corps
be sent to Petrograd toward the end of August and placed at
the disposition of the Provisional Government. In case the members of the soviets as well as the Bolsheviks come out, we shall
have to take action against them." Kerensky's emissary added
that the action would have to be very decisive and ruthless—to
which Kornilov answered that he "understands no other kind of
action." Afterward, when it became necessary to justify himself, Savinkov added, ". . . if at the moment of the insurrection
of the Bolsheviks, the soviets should be Bolshevik. . . ." But that
is too crude a trick. The decree announcing the coup d'état of
Kerensky was to come out in three or four days. It was thus not
a question of some future soviets, but of those in existence at
the end of August. In order that there should be no misunderstanding, and the Bolsheviks should not come out "before the
proper moment" the following sequence of actions was agreed
upon: First concentrate a cavalry corps in Petrograd, then declare the capital under martial law, and only after that publish
the new laws which were to provoke a Bolshevik insurrection. In
the minutes of headquarters this plan is written down in black
and white. "In order that the Provisional Government shall know

exactly when to declare the Petrograd military district under martial law and when to publish the new law, it is necessary that General Kornilov shall keep him (Savinkov) accurately informed by telegraph of the time when the corps will approach Petrograd."

The conspiring generals understood, says Stankevich, "that Savinkov and Kerensky . . . wanted to carry out some sort of coup d'état with the help of the staff. Only this was needed. They hastily agreed about all demands and conditions. . . ." Stankevich, who was loyal to Kerensky, makes the reservation that at headquarters, they "mistakenly associated" Kerensky with Savinkov. But how could these two be dissociated, once Savinkov had arrived with precisely formulated instructions from Kerensky? Kerensky himself writes: "On the 25th of August, Savinkov returns from headquarters and reports to me that the troops to be at the disposition of the Provisional Government will be sent according to instructions." The evening of the 26th was designated for the adoption by the government of the law on measures for the rear, which was to be the prologue for decisive action by the cavalry corps. Everything was ready—it remained only to press the button.

The events, the documents, the testimony of the participants, and finally the confession of Kerensky himself, unanimously bear witness that the Minister-President, without the knowledge of a part of his own government, behind the back of the soviets which had given him the power, in secrecy from the party of which he considered himself a member, had entered into agreement with the highest generals of the army for a radical change in the state régime with the help of armed forces. In the language of the criminal law this kind of activity has a perfectly definite name— at least in those cases where the undertaking does not come off victorious. The contradiction between the "democratic" character of Kerensky's policy and his plan of saving the government with the help of the sword, can seem insoluble only to a superficial view. In reality the cavalry plan flowed inevitably from the compromisist policy. In explaining the law of this process it is possible to abstract to a considerable extent, not only from the personality of Kerensky, but even from the peculiarities of the national milieu. It is a question of the objective logic of compromisism in the conditions of revolution.

Friedrich Ebert, the people's plenipotentiary of Germany, a compromisist and a democrat, not only acted under the guidance of the Hohenzollern generals behind the back of his own party, but also at the beginning of December 1918 became a direct participant in a military plot having as its goal the arrest of the highest soviet body, and the declaration of Ebert himself as President of the Republic. It is no accident that Kerensky subsequently declared Ebert the ideal statesman.

When all their schemes—those of Kerensky, Savinkov, Kornilov—had gone to smash, Kerensky, to whom fell the none too easy work of obliterating the tracks, testified as follows: "After the Moscow Conference it was clear to me that the next attempt against the government would be from the right and not the left." It is not to be doubted that Kerensky feared headquarters, and feared that sympathy with which the bourgeoisie surrounded the military conspirators; but the point is that Kerensky thought it necessary to struggle against headquarters, not with a cavalry corps, but by carrying out in his own name the program of Kornilov. The double-faced accomplice of the Prime Minister was not merely fulfilling an ordinary mission—for that a telegram in code from the Winter Palace to Moghiliev would have been enough. No, he went as an intermediary to reconcile Kornilov with Kerensky, to bring their plans, that is, into agreement, and thus guarantee that the coup d'état should proceed so far as possible legally. It was as though Kerensky said through Savinkov: "Go ahead, but within the limits of *my* scheme. You will thus avoid risk and get almost everything you want." Savinkov on his own part added the hint: "*Do not go prematurely* beyond the limits of Kerensky's plan." Such was that peculiar equation with three unknown quantities. Only in this way is it possible to understand Kerensky's appealing to headquarters through Savinkov for a cavalry corps. The conspirators were addressed by a highly placed conspirator, preserving his legality, and himself aspiring to stand at the head of the conspiracy.

Among the directions given to Savinkov, only one seemed a

measure actually directed against the conspirators on the right: it concerned the head committee of the League of Officers, whose dissolution had been demanded by a Petrograd conference of Kerensky's party. But here a remarkable thing is the very formulation of the order: ". . . *in so far as possible* to dissolve the League of Officers." Still more remarkable is the fact that Savinkov not only did not find any such possibility at all, but did not seek it. The question was simply buried as untimely. The very order had been given merely to have something on paper for justification before the Lefts. The words "so far as possible" meant that the order was not to be carried out. As though to emphasize the decorative character of this order, it was placed first on the list.

Attempting at least to weaken a little the deadly meaning of the fact that, in expectation of a blow from the right, he had removed the revolutionary regiments from the capital, and simultaneously appealed to Kornilov for "reliable" troops, Kerensky later referred to the three sacramental conditions with which he had surrounded the summoning of the cavalry corps. Thus his agreement to subordinate to Kornilov the Petrograd military district Kerensky had conditioned upon the separation of the capital and its immediate suburbs from the district, so that the government would not be wholly in the hands of headquarters. For as Kerensky expressed himself among his own friends: "We here would be eaten up." This condition merely shows that in his dream of subordinating the generals to his own designs, Kerensky had no weapon in his hands but impotent chicanery. Kerensky's desire not to be eaten alive can be credited without demonstration. The two other conditions amounted to nothing more: Kornilov was not to include in the expeditionary corps the so-called "Savage Division" consisting of Caucasian mountaineers, and was not to put General Krymov in command of the corps. So far as concerned defending the interests of the democracy, that really meant swallowing the camel and choking on the gnat. But so far as concerned disguising a blow at the revolution, Kerensky's conditions were incomparably more purposeful. To send against the Petrograd workers Caucasian mountaineers who did not speak Russian would have been too imprudent; even the tzar in his day never made up his mind to that! The inconvenience of appointing General Krymov, about whom the Executive Committee possessed some rather definite information, Savinkov convincingly explained at headquarters on the ground of their common interest: "It would be undesirable," he said, "in case of disturbances in Petrograd that these disturbances should be put down by General Krymov. Public opinion might perhaps connect with his name motives by which he is not guided. . . ." Finally, the very fact that the head of the government, in summoning a military detachment to the capital, anticipated events with that strange request: not to send the Savage Division and not to appoint Krymov, convicts Kerensky as clearly as he could be convicted of possessing advance knowledge, not only of the general scheme of the conspiracy, but also of the constituent units of the punitive expedition, and the candidates for its more important executive positions.

Moreover, no matter how things had stood in these secondary points, it was perfectly obvious that a cavalry corps of Kornilov could not be of any use in defending "the democracy." On the contrary, Kerensky could not possibly doubt that of all the units in the army this corps would be the most reliable weapon *against* the revolution. To be sure it might have been well to have a detachment in Petrograd personally loyal to Kerensky, who was elevating himself above the Rights and Lefts. However, as the whole further course of events demonstrates, no such troops existed in nature. For the struggle against the revolution there was nobody but Kornilov men, and to them Kerensky had recourse.

These military preparations only supplemented the political ones. The general course of the Provisional Government during the not quite two weeks separating the Moscow Conference from the insurrection of Kornilov, would have been enough in itself essentially to prove that Kerensky was getting ready, not for a struggle against the Right, but for a united front with the Right against the people. Ignoring the protests of the Executive Committee against this counter-revolutionary policy, the government on August 26 took a bold step to meet the landlords with its unexpected decree doubling the price of grain. The hatefulness of this measure—which was introduced, moreover, upon the spoken demand of Rodzianko,—put the government almost in the position of consciously provoking the hungry masses. Kerensky was clearly trying to win over the extreme right flank of the Moscow Conference with an immense bribe. "I am yours!" he hastened to cry to the landlords on the eve of a cavalry assault upon what was left of the February revolution.

Kerensky's testimony before the commission of inquiry named by himself, was disgraceful. Although appearing in the character of a witness, the head of the government really felt himself to be the chief of the accused, and moreover, one caught red-handed. The experienced judiciary officials, who excellently well understood the mechanics of the events, pretended to take seriously the explanations of the head of the government, but all other mortals —among them the members of Kerensky's own party—quite frankly asked themselves how one and the same cavalry corps might be useful both for accomplishing a coup d'état and for preventing it. It was just a little too reckless on the part of the "Social Revolutionary" to bring into the capital a force which had been composed for the purpose of strangling it. The Trojans, to be sure, did once bring a hostile detachment into the walls of their city, but they were at least ignorant of what was inside the belly of the wooden horse. And even so an ancient historian disputes the story of the poet: in the opinion of Pausanius, you can believe Homer only if you consider the Trojans to have been "stupid men not possessed of a glimmer of reason." What would the old man have said of the testimony of Kerensky?

CHAPTER IX

KORNILOV'S INSURRECTION

AS early as the beginning of August, Kornilov had ordered the transfer of the Savage Division and the Third Cavalry Corps from the southwestern front to the sector of the railroad triangle, Nevel-Novosokolniki-Velikie Luki, the most advantageous base for an attack on Petrograd—this under the guise of reserves for the defense of Riga. At the same time the commander-in-chief had concentrated one Cossack division in the region between Vyborg and Byeloöstrov. This fist thrust into the very face of the capital—from Byeloöstrov to Petrograd is only thirty kilometers!—was given out as a preparation of reserves for possible operations in Finland. Thus even before the Moscow Conference four cavalry divisions had been moved into position for the attack on Petrograd, and these were the divisions considered most useful against Bolsheviks. Of the Caucasian division it was customary in Kornilov's circle to remark: "Those mountaineers don't care whom they slaughter." The strategic plan was simple. The three divisions coming from the south were to be transported by railroad to Tzarskoe Selo, Gatchina, and Krasnoe Selo, in order from those points *"upon receiving* information of disorders beginning in Petrograd, *and not later* than the morning of September 1" to advance on foot for the occupation of the southern part of the capital on the left bank of the Neva. The division quartered in Finland was at the same time to occupy the northern part of the capital.

Through the mediation of the League of Officers Kornilov had got in touch with Petrograd patriotic societies who had at their disposal, according to their own words, 2000 men excellently armed but requiring experienced officers to lead them. Kornilov promised to supply commanders from the front under the pretext of leave-of-absence. In order to keep watch of the mood of the Petrograd workers and soldiers and the activity of revolutionists, a secret intelligence service was formed, at the head of which stood a colonel of the Savage Division, Heiman. The affair was conducted within the framework of military regulations. The conspiracy made use of the headquarters' apparatus.

The Moscow Conference merely fortified Kornilov in his plans. Miliukov, to be sure, according to his own story, recommended a delay on the ground that Kerensky still enjoyed a certain popularity in the provinces. But this kind of advice could have no influence upon the impatient general. The question after all was not about Kerensky, but about the soviets. Moreover, Miliukov was not a man of action, but a civilian, and still worse a professor. Bankers, industrialists, Cossack generals were urging him on. The metropolitans had given him their blessing. Orderly Zavoiko offered to guarantee his success. Telegrams of greeting were coming from all sides. The Allied embassies took an active part in the mobilization of the counter-revolutionary forces. Sir Buchanan held in his hands many of the threads of the plot. The military attachés of the Allies at headquarters assured him of their most cordial sympathies. "The British attaché in particular," testifies Deniken, "did this in a touching form." Behind the embassies stood their governments. In a telegram of August 23, a commissar of the Provisional Government abroad, Svatikov, reported from Paris that in a farewell reception the Foreign Minister Ribot had "inquired with extraordinary eagerness who among those around Kerensky was a man of force and energy." And President Poincaré had "asked many questions . . . about Kornilov." All this was known at headquarters. Kornilov saw no reason to postpone and wait. On or about the 20th, two cavalry divisions were advanced further in the direction of Petrograd. On the day Riga fell, four officers from each regiment of the army were summoned to headquarters, about 4000 in all, "for the study of English bomb-throwing." To the most reliable of these officers it was immediately explained that the matter in view was to put down "Bolshevik Petrograd" once for all. On the same day an order was given from headquarters to supply two of the cavalry divisions with several boxes of hand grenades: they would be the most useful in street fighting. "It was agreed," writes the chief-of-staff, Lukomsky, "that everything should be ready by the 26th of August."

As the troops of Kornilov approached Petrograd an inside organization "was to come out in Petrograd, occupy Smolny Institute and try to arrest the Bolshevik chiefs." To be sure in Smolny Institute the Bolshevik chiefs appeared only at meetings, whereas continually present there was the Executive Committee which had appointed the ministers, and continued to number Kerensky among its vice-presidents. But in a great cause it is not possible or necessary to observe the fine points of things. Kornilov at least did not bother about them. "It is time," he said to Lukomsky, "to hang the German agents and spies, Lenin first of all, and disperse the Soviet of Workers' and Peasants' Deputies —yes, and disperse it so it will never get together again."

Kornilov firmly intended to give the command of the operations to Krymov, who in his own circles enjoyed the reputation of a bold and resolute general. "Krymov was at that time happy and full of the joy of life," says Denikin, "and looked with confidence into the future." At headquarters they looked with confidence upon Krymov. "I am convinced," said Kornilov, "that he will not hesitate, if need arises, to hang the whole membership of the Soviet of Workers' and Soldiers' Deputies." The choice of this general, so happy and full of the joy of life, was consequently most appropriate.

At the height of these labors, which drew attention from the German front, Savinkov arrived at headquarters in order to dot the i's of an old agreement, and introduce some secondary changes into it. Savinkov named the same date for the blow against the common enemy as that which Kornilov had long ago designated for his action against Kerensky: the semi-anniversary of the revolution. In spite of the fact that the conspiracy had split into two halves, both sides were trying to operate with the common elements of the plan—Kornilov for the purpose of camouflage, Kerensky in order to support his own illusions. The proposal of Savinkov played perfectly into the hands of headquarters: the government had presented its head, and Savinkov was ready to slip the noose. The generals at headquarters rubbed their hands: "He's biting!" they exclaimed like happy fishermen. Kornilov was quite ready to make the proposed concessions, which cost him nothing. What difference will the non-subordination of the Petrograd garrison to headquarters make, once the Kornilov troops have entered the capital? Having agreed to the other two conditions, Kornilov immediately violated them: the Savage Division was placed in the vanguard and Krymov at the head of the whole operation. Kornilov did not consider it necessary to choke on the gnats.

The Bolsheviks debated the fundamental problems of their policy openly: a mass party cannot do otherwise. The government and headquarters could not but know that the Bolsheviks were restraining the masses, and not summoning them to action. But as the wish is father to the thought, so political needs become the basis for a prognosis. All the ruling classes were talking about an impending insurrection because they were in desperate need of one. The date of the insurrection would approach or recede a few days from time to time. In the War Ministry—that is, in the office of Savinkov—according to the press, the impending insurrection was regarded "very seriously." *Rech* stated that the Bolshevik faction of the Petrograd soviet was assuming the responsibility for the attack. Miliukov was to such an extent involved in this matter of the pretended insurrection of the Bolsheviks in his character of politician, that he has considered it a matter of honor to support the tale in his character of historian. "In subsequently published documents of the Intelligence Service," he writes, "new assignments of German money for Trotsky's enterprise relate to exactly this period." The learned historian, together with the Russian Intelligence Service, forgets that Trotsky—whom the German staff for the convenience of the Russian patriots was kind enough to mention by name—was "exactly at this period," from the 23rd of July to the 4th of September, locked up in prison. The fact that the earth's axis is merely an imaginary line does not of course prevent the earth from rotating on its axis. In like manner the Kornilov operations rotated round an imaginary insurrection of the Bolsheviks as round its own axis. That was amply sufficient for the period of preparation. But for the denouement something a little more substantial was needed.

One of the leading military conspirators, the officer Vinberg, revealing in his interesting notes what was going on behind the scenes in this business, wholly confirms the assertion of the Bolsheviks that a vast work of military provocation was in progress. Even Miliukov is obliged, under the whip of facts and documents, to admit that "the suspicions of the extreme left circles were correct: agitation in the factories was undoubtedly one of the tasks which the officers' organizations were supposed to fulfill." But even this did not help: "The Bolsheviks," complains the same historian, decided "not to be put upon," and the masses did not intend to go out without the Bolsheviks. However, even this obstacle had been taken into consideration in the plan, and paralyzed as it were in advance. The "republican center," as the leading body of the conspirators in Petrograd was called, decided simply to replace the Bolsheviks. The business of imitating a revolutionary insurrection was assigned to the Cossack colonel, Dutov. In January 1918, Dutov, to a question from his political friends: "What was to have happened on the 28th of August, 1917?" answered as follows (the quotation is verbatim): "Between the 28th of August and the 2nd of September I was to take action in the form of a Bolshevik insurrection." Everything had been foreseen. This plan had not been labored over by the officers of the general staff for nothing.

Kerensky, on his side, after the return of Savinkov from Moghiliev, was inclined to think that all misunderstandings had been removed, and that headquarters was entirely drawn into his plan. "There were times," writes Stankevich, "when all those active not only believed they were all acting in the same direction, but that they had a like conception of the very methods of action." Those happy moments did not last long. An accident occurred, which like all historic accidents opened the sluice-gates of necessity. To Kerensky came the Octobrist, Lvov, a member of the first Provisional Government—that same Lvov who as the expansive Procuror of the Holy Synod had reported that this institution was filled with "idiots and scoundrels." Fate had allotted to Lvov the task of discovering that under the appearance of a single plan there were in reality two plans, one of which was directed in a hostile manner against the other.

In his character as an unemployed but word-loving politician, Lvov had taken part in endless conversations about the transformation of the government and the salvation of the country—now at headquarters, now in the Winter Palace. This time he appeared with a proposal that he be permitted to mediate in the transformation of the cabinet along national lines, incidentally frightening Kerensky in a friendly manner with the thunders and lightnings of a discontented headquarters. The disturbed Minister-President decided to make use of Lvov in order to test the loyalty of the staff—and at the same time, apparently, that of his accomplice, Savinkov. Kerensky expressed his sympathy for the plan of a dictatorship—in which he was not hypocritical—and encouraged Lvov to undertake further mediations —in which there was military trickery.

When Lvov again arrived at headquarters, weighed down now with the credentials of Kerensky, the generals looked upon his mission as a proof that the government was ripe for capitulation. Only yesterday Kerensky through Savinkov had promised to carry out the program of Kornilov if defended by a corps of Cossacks; today Kerensky was already proposing to the staff a co-operative transformation of the government. "It is time to put a knee in his stomach," the generals justly decided. Kornilov accordingly explained to Lvov that since the forthcoming insurrection of the Bolsheviks has as its aim "the overthrow of the Provisional Government, peace with Germany, and the surrender to her by the Bolsheviks of the Baltic fleet," there remains no other way out but "the immediate transfer of power by the Provisional Government into the hands of the supreme commander-in-chief." To this Kornilov added: ". . . no matter who he may be"—but he had no idea of surrendering his place to anybody. His position had been fortified in advance by the oath of the Cavaliers of St. George, the League of Officers and the Council of the Cossack army. In order to make sure of the "safety" of Kerensky and Savinkov from the hands of the Bolsheviks, Kornilov urgently requested them to come to headquarters and place themselves under his personal protection. The orderly, Zavoiko, gave Lvov an unequivocal hint as to just what this protection would consist of.

Returning to Moscow, Lvov fervently urged Kerensky, as a "friend," to agree to the proposal of Kornilov "in order to save the lives of the members of the Provisional Government, and above all his own life." Kerensky could not but understand at last that his political playing with the idea of dictatorship was taking a serious turn, and might end most unfortunately for him. Having decided to act, he first of all summoned Kornilov to the wire in order to verify the facts: Had Lvov correctly conveyed his message? Kerensky put his questions, not only in his own name, but in the name of Lvov, although the latter was not present during the conversation. "Such an action," remarks Martynov, "appropriate for a detective, was of course improper for the head of a government." Kerensky spoke of his arrival at headquarters the next day as a thing already decided upon. This whole dialogue on the direct wire seems incredible. The democratic head of the government and the "republican" general converse about yielding the power the one to the other, as though they were discussing a berth in a sleeping car!

Miliukov is entirely right when he sees in the demand of Kornilov that the power be transferred to him, merely "a continuation of all those conversations openly begun long ago about a dictatorship, a re-organization of the government, etc." But Miliukov goes too far when he tries upon this basis to present the thing as though there had been in essence no conspiracy at headquarters. It is indubitable that Kornilov could not have presented his demand through Lvov, if he had not formerly been in a conspiracy with Kerensky. But this does not alter the fact that with one conspiracy—the common one—Kornilov was covering up another—his own private one. At the same time that Kerensky and Savinkov were intending to clean up the Bolsheviks, and in part the soviets, Kornilov was intending also to clean up the Provisional Government. It was just this that Kerensky did not want.

For several hours on the evening of the 26th headquarters was actually in a position to believe that the government was going to capitulate without a struggle. But that does not mean that there was no conspiracy; it merely means that the conspiracy seemed about to succeed. A victorious conspiracy always finds ways of legalizing itself. "I saw General Kornilov after this conversation," says Troubetskoy, a diplomat who represented the Ministry of Foreign Affairs at headquarters. "A sigh of relief lifted his breast, and to my question, 'This means that the government is coming to meet you all along the line?' he answered: 'Yes.' " Kornilov was mistaken. It was at that very moment that the government, in the person of Kerensky, had stopped coming to meet him.

Then headquarters has its own plans? Then it is not a question of dictatorship in general, but of a Kornilov dictatorship? To him, to Kerensky, they are offering as if in mockery the post of Minister of Justice? Kornilov had actually been so imprudent as to make this suggestion through Lvov. Confusing himself with the revolution, Kerensky shouted out to the Minister of Finance, Nekrasov: "I won't hand over the revolution to them!" And the disinterested friend, Lvov, was immediately arrested and spent a sleepless night in the Winter Palace with two sentries at his feet, listening through the wall with a grinding of his teeth to "the triumphant Kerensky in the next room, the room of Alexander III, happy at the successful progress of his affairs and endlessly singing a roulade from an opera." During those hours Kerensky experienced an extraordinary afflux of energy.

Petrograd in those days was living in a two-fold state of alarm. The political tension, purposely exaggerated by the press, contained the material of an explosion. The fall of Riga had brought the front nearer. The question of evacuating the capital, raised by the events of the war long before the fall of the monarchy, now came up with new force. Well-to-do people were leaving town. The flight of the bourgeoisie was caused far more by fear of a new insurrection than by the advance of the enemy. On August 26th the Central Committee of the Bolsheviks repeated its warning: "A provocational agitation is being carried on by unknown persons supposedly in the name of our party." The leading organs of the Petrograd soviet, the trade unions, and the shop and factory committees, announced on the same day that not one workers' organization, and not one political party, was calling for any kind of demonstration. Nevertheless rumors of an overthrow of the government to occur on the fol-

211

lowing day did not cease for one minute. "In government circles," stated the press, "they are talking of a unanimously adopted decision that all attempted manifestations shall be put down." And measures had been taken to call out the manifestation before putting it down.

In the morning papers of the 27th there was not only no news of the insurrectionary intensions of headquarters, but, on the contrary, an interview with Savinkov declared that "General Kornilov enjoys the absolute confidence of the Provisional Government." On the whole the semi-anniversary began in unusual tranquillity. The workers and soldiers avoided anything which might look like a demonstration; the bourgeoisie, fearing disorders, stayed at home; the streets stood empty; the tomb of the February martyrs on Mars Field seemed abandoned.

On the morning of that long-expected day which was to bring the salvation of the country, the supreme commander-in-chief received a telegraphic command from the Minister-President: to turn over his duties to the chief-of-staff, and come immediately to Petrograd. This was a totally unexpected turn of affairs. The general understood—to quote his own words—that "here a double game was being played." He might have said with more truth that his own double game had been discovered. Kornilov decided not to surrender. Savinkov's urgings over the direct wire made no difference. "Finding myself compelled to act openly"—with this manifesto the commander-in-chief appealed to the people—"I, General Kornilov, declare that the Provisional Government, under pressure from the Bolshevik majority of the soviets, is acting in full accord with the plans of the German general staff, and simultaneously with the impending descent of hostile forces upon the Riga coastline is murdering the army and unsettling the country from within." Not wishing to surrender the power to the enemy, he, Kornilov "prefers to die upon the field of honor and battle." Of the author of this manifesto Miliukov subsequently wrote, with a tinge of admiration: "resolute, scornful of juridical refinements, and accustomed to go directly toward the goal which he has once decided is right." A commander-in-chief who withdraws troops from the enemy front in order to overthrow his own government certainly cannot be accused of a partiality for "juridical refinements."

Kerensky removed Kornilov upon his sole personal authority. The Provisional Government had by that time ceased to exist. On the evening of the 26th the ministers had resigned—an act which, by a happy conjuncture of events, corresponded to the desires of all sides. Several days before the break between headquarters and the government, General Lukomsky had already suggested to Lvov through Alladin, that "it would not be a bad idea to warn the Kadets that they should withdraw from the government before the 27th of August, so as to place the government in a difficult situation and themselves avoid any unpleasantness." The Kadets did not fail to take cognizance of this suggestion. On the other side, Kerensky himself announced to the government that he considered it possible to struggle with the revolt of Kornilov "only on condition that the whole power be conferred upon him personally." The rest of the ministers, it seemed, were only waiting for some such happy occasion to take their turn at resigning. Thus the Coalition received one more test. "The ministers from the Kadet Party," writes Miliukov, "announced that they would resign for the given moment, without prejudicing the question of their future participation in the Provisional Government." True to their traditions, the Kadets wanted to stay on the side-lines until the struggle was over, so that their decision might be guided by its outcome. They had no doubt that the Compromisers would keep their seats inviolable for them. Having thus relieved themselves of responsibility, the Kadets, along with all the other retired ministers, took part thereafter in a series of conferences of the government, conferences of a "private character." The two camps who were preparing for a civil war grouped themselves, in a "private" manner, around the head of the government, who was endowed with all possible authorizations but no real power.

Upon a telegram from Kerensky received at headquarters reading, "Hold up all echelons moving towards Petrograd and its districts, and return them to their last stopping-point," Kornilov wrote: "Do not carry out this order. Move the troops towards Petrograd." The military insurrection was thus firmly set in motion. This must be understood literally: three cavalry divisions, in railroad echelons, were advancing on the capital.

Kerensky's order to the soldiers of Petrograd read: "General Kornilov, having announced his patriotism and loyalty to the people . . . has withdrawn regiments from the front . . . and . . . sent them against Petrograd." Kerensky wisely omitted to remark that the regiments were withdrawn from the front, not only with his knowledge, but at his direct command, in order to clean up that same garrison before whom he was now disclosing the treachery of Kornilov. The rebellious commander of course was not slow with his answer. "The traitors are not among us," his telegram reads, "but there in Petrograd, where for German money, with the criminal connivance of the government, they have been selling Russia." Thus the slander set in motion against the Bolsheviks found ever new roads.

That exalted nocturnal mood in which the President of the Council of Retired Ministers was singing arias from the opera, very quickly passed. The struggle with Kornilov, whatever turn it took, threatened dire consequences. "On the first night of the revolt of headquarters," writes Kerensky, "in the soldier and worker circles of Petrograd a persistent rumor went round associating Savinkov with the movement of General Kornilov." The rumor named Kerensky in the next breath after Savinkov, and the rumor was not wrong. Extremely dangerous revelations were to be feared in the future.

"Late at night on the 26th of August," relates Kerensky, "the general administrator of the War Ministry entered my office in a great state of excitement. 'Mr. Minister,' Savinkov addressed me, standing at attention, 'I ask you to arrest me immediately as an accomplice of General Kornilov. If, however, you trust me, I ask you to give me the opportunity to demonstrate to the people in action that I have nothing in common with the revoltees . . .' " "In answer to this announcement," continued Kerensky, "I immediately appointed Savinkov temporary governor-general of Petersburg, endowing him with ample authority for the defense of Petersburg from the troops of General Kornilov." Not content with that, at the request of Savinkov, Kerensky appointed Filonenko his assistant. The business of revolting and the business of putting down the revolt were thus concentrated within the narrow circle of the "directory."

This so hasty naming of Savinkov governor-general was dictated to Kerensky by his struggle for political self-preservation. If Kerensky had betrayed Savinkov to the soviets, Savinkov would have immediately betrayed Kerensky. On the other hand, having received from Kerensky—not without blackmail—the possibility of legalizing himself by an overt participation in the actions against Kornilov, Savinkov was bound to do his best to exonerate Kerensky. The "governor-general" was needed not so much for the struggle against counter-revolution, as for covering up the tracks of the conspiracy. The friendly labors of the accomplices in this direction began immediately.

"At four o'clock on the morning of August 28th," testifies Savinkov, "I returned to the Winter Palace, summoned by Kerensky, and there found General Alexeiev and Tereshchenko. We all four agreed that the ultimatum of Lvov had been nothing more than a misunderstanding." The rôle of mediator in this early-morning conference belonged to the new governor-general. Miliukov was directing it all from behind the scenes. During the course of the day he will come out openly upon the stage. Alexeiev, although he had called Kornilov a sheep's brain, belonged to the same camp with him. The conspirators and their seconds made a last attempt to declare the whole business a "misunderstanding"—that is, to join hands in deceiving public opinion, in order to save what they could of the common plan. The Savage Division, General Krymov, the Cossack echelons, the refusal of Kornilov to retire, the march on the capital—all these things were the mere details of a "misunderstanding"! Frightened by the ominous tangle of circumstances, Kerensky was no longer shouting: "I will not hand over the revolution to them!" Immediately after the conference with Alexeiev he went to the journalists' room in the Winter Palace and demanded that they withdraw from the papers his manifesto declaring Kornilov a traitor. When in answer the journalists had made it clear that this was a physical impossibility, Kerensky exclaimed: "That's too bad." This miserable episode, described in the newspapers of the following day, illumines with marvelous clarity the figure of

the now hopelessly entangled super-arbiter of the nation. Kerensky had so perfectly embodied in himself both the democracy
and the bourgeoisie, that he had now turned out to be at the
same time the supreme incarnation of governmental power and
a criminal conspirator against it.

By the morning of the 28th, the split between the government
and the commander-in-chief had become an accomplished fact
before the eyes of the whole country. The stock exchange immediately took a hand in the matter. Whereas it had reacted to the
Moscow speech of Kornilov threatening the surrender of Riga
with a fall in the value of Russian stocks, it reacted to the news
of an open insurrection of the general with a rise of all values.
With this annihilating appraisal of the February régime, the
stock exchange gave unerring expression to the moods and hopes
of the possessing classes who had no doubt of Kornilov's victory.

The chief-of-staff, Lukomsky, whom Kerensky the day before had ordered to take upon himself the temporary command,
answered: "I do not consider it possible to take the command
from General Kornilov, for that will be followed by an explosion in the army which will ruin Russia." With the exception
of the commander-in-chief in the Caucasus, who after some delay
declared his loyalty to the Provisional Government, the rest of
the commanders in various tones of voice supported the demands of Kornilov. Inspired by the Kadets, the head committee
of the League of Officers sent out a telegram to all the staffs of the
army and fleet: "The Provisional Government, which has already more than once demonstrated to us its political incapacity,
has now dishonored its name with acts of provocation and can
no longer remain at the head of Russia . . ." That same Lukomsky was the respected president of the League of Officers. At
headquarters they said to General Krasnov, appointed to command the Third Cavalry Corps: "Nobody will defend Kerensky.
This is only a promenade. Everything is ready."

A fair idea of the optimistic calculations of the leaders and
backers of the plot is conveyed by the code telegram of the afore-
mentioned Prince Troubetskoy to the Ministry of Foreign Affairs:
"Soberly estimating the situation," he writes, "it must be acknowledged that the whole commanding staff, an overwhelming

majority of the officers, and the best of the rank-and-file elements of the army, are for Kornilov. On his side at the rear stand all the Cossacks, a majority of the military schools, and also the best fighting units. To these physical forces it is necessary to add . . . the moral sympathy of all the non-socialist layers of the population, and in the lower orders . . . an indifference which will submit to the least blow of the whip. There is no doubt that an enormous number of the March socialists will come quickly over to the side" of Kornilov in case of his victory. Troubetskoy here expressed not only the hopes of headquarters, but also the attitude of the Allied missions. In the Kornilov detachments advancing to the conquest of Petrograd, there were English armored cars with English operatives—and these we may assume constituted the most reliable units. The head of the English military mission in Russia, General Knox, reproached the American Colonel Robbins, for not supporting Kornilov: "I am not interested in the government of Kerensky," said the British General, "it is too weak. What is wanted is a strong dictatorship. What is wanted is the Cossacks. This people needs the whip! A dictatorship—that is just what it needs." All these voices from different quarters arrived at the Winter Palace, and had an alarming effect upon its inhabitants. The success of Kornilov seemed inevitable. Minister Nekrassov informed his friends that the game was completely up, and it remained only to die an honorable death. "Several eminent members of the Soviet," affirms Miliukov, "foreseeing their fate in case of Kornilov's victory, had already made haste to supply themselves with foreign passports."

From hour to hour came the messages, one more threatening than the other, of the approach of Kornilov's troops. The bourgeois press seized them hungrily, expanded them, piled them up, creating an atmosphere of panic. At 12:30 noon on August 28th: "The troops sent by General Kornilov have concentrated themselves in the vicinity of Luga." At 2:30 in the afternoon; "Nine new trains containing the troops of Kornilov have passed through the station Oredezh. In the forward train is a railroad engineering battalion." At 3:00 P. M.: "The Luga garrison has surrendered to the troops of General Kornilov and turned over all its weapons. The station and all the government buildings of Luga are occupied by the troops of Kornilov." At 6:00 in the evening: "Two echelons of Kornilov's army have broken through from Narva and are within half a verst of Gatchina. Two more echelons are on the road to Gatchina." At two o'clock in the morning of the 29th: "A battle has begun at the Antropshino Station (33 kilometers from Petrograd) between government troops and the troops of Kornilov. Killed and wounded on both sides." By nightfall comes the news that Kaledin has threatened to cut off Petrograd and Moscow from the grain-growing south of Russia. "Headquarters," "commanders-in-chief at the front," "British mission," "officers," "echelons," "railroad battalions," "cossacks," "Kaledin"—all these words sounded in the Malachite Hall of the Winter Palace like the trumpets of the Last Judgment.

Kerensky himself acknowledges this in a somewhat softened form: "August 28th was the day of the greatest wavering," he writes, "the greatest doubt as to the strength of the enemy, Kornilov, the greatest nervousness among the democracy." It is not difficult to imagine what lies behind those words. The head of the government was torn by speculations, not only as to which of the two camps was stronger, but as to which was personally the less dangerous to him. "We are neither with you on the right, nor with you on the left"—those words had seemed effective on the stage of the Moscow theater. Translated into the language of a civil war on the point of explosion, they meant that the Kerensky group might appear superfluous both to right and left. "We were all as though numb with despair," writes Stankevich, "seeing this drama unfold to the destruction of everything. The degree of our numbness may be judged by the fact that even after the split between headquarters and the government was before the eyes of the whole people, attempts were made to find some sort of reconciliation. . . ."

"A thought of mediation . . . was in these circumstances spontaneously born," says Miliukov, who himself preferred to function in the capacity of mediator. On the evening of the 28th he appeared at the Winter Palace "to advise Kerensky to renounce the strictly formal viewpoint of the violation of law." The liberal leader, who understood that it is necessary to distinguish the kernel of a nut from the shell, was at that moment a most suitable person for the task of loyal intermediary. On the 13th of August, Miliukov had learned directly from Kornilov that he had set the 27th as the date for the revolt. On the following day, the 14th, Miliukov had demanded in his speech at the Conference that "the immediate adoption of the measures designated by the supreme commander-in-chief should not serve as a pretext for suspicions, verbal threats, or even removals from office." Up to the 27th Kornilov was to remain above suspicion! At the same time Miliukov promised Kerensky his support—"voluntarily and without any argument." That would have been a good time to remember the hangman's noose which also, as they say, "supports without argument." Kerensky upon his side acknowledges that Miliukov, appearing with his proposal of mediation, "chose a very comfortable moment to demonstrate to me that the real power was on the side of Kornilov." The conversation ended so successfully that in conclusion Miliukov called the attention of his political friends to General Alexeiev as a successor to Kerensky against whom Kornilov would offer no objection. Alexeiev magnanimously gave his consent.

And after Miliukov came a greater than he. Late in the evening the British Ambassador Buchanan handed to the Minister of Foreign Affairs a declaration in which the representatives of the Allied Powers unanimously offered their good services "in the interests of humanity and the desire to avoid irrevocable misfortune." This official mediation between the government and the general in revolt was nothing less than support and insurance to the revolt. In reply, Tereshchenko expressed, in the name of the Provisional Government, "extreme astonishment" at the revolt of Kornilov, a greater part of whose program had been adopted by the government. In a state of loneliness and prostration, Kerensky could think of nothing better to do than to call one more of those everlasting conferences with his retired ministers. In the midst of this wholly disinterested business of killing time, some especially alarming news arrived as to the approach of the enemy's echelons. Nekrasov voiced an apprehension that "in a few hours Kornilov's troops will probably be in Petrograd." The former ministers began to guess "how in those circumstances the governmental power would have to be formed." The thought of a directory again swam to the surface. The idea of including General Alexeiev in the staff of the "directory" found sympathy both right and left. The Kadet Kokoshkin thought that Alexeiev ought to be placed at the head of the government. According to some accounts, the proposal to tender the power to some other was made by Kerensky himself, with a direct reference to his conversation with Miliukov. Nobody objected. The candidacy of Alexeiev reconciled them all. Miliukov's plan seemed very, very near to realization. But just here—as is proper at the moment of highest tension—resounds a dramatic knock on the door. In the next room a deputation is waiting from the "Committee of Struggle against the Counter-Revolution." It was a most timely arrival. One of the most dangerous nests of counter-revolution was this pitiful, cowardly and treacherous conference of Kornilovists, intermediaries, and capitulators in the hall of the Winter Palace.

This new soviet body— The Committee of Struggle against Counter-Revolution—had been created at a joint session of both Executive Committees, the worker-soldiers' and the peasants'. It was created on the evening of the 27th, and consisted of specially delegated representatives of the three soviet parties from both executive committees, from the trade union center, and from the Petrograd soviet. This creation *ad hoc* of a fighting committee was in essence a recognition of the fact that the governing soviet bodies were themselves conscious of their decrepit condition, and their need of a transfusion of fresh blood for the purposes of revolutionary action.

Finding themselves compelled to seek the support of the masses against the rebellious general, the Compromisers hastened to push their left shoulder forward. They immediately forgot all their speeches about how all questions of principle should be postponed to the Constituent Assembly. The Mensheviks announced that they would press the government for an immediate declaration of a democratic republic, a dissolution of the State Duma, and the introduction of agrarian reform. It was for this reason that the word "republic" first appeared in the announcement of the government about the treason of the commander-in-chief.

On the question of power, the Executive Committees considered it necessary for the time being to leave the government in its former shape—replacing the retired Kadets with democratic elements—and for a final solution of the problem to summon in the near future a congress of all those organizations which had united in Moscow on the platform of Cheidze. After midnight negotiations it became known, however, that Kerensky resolutely rejected the idea of a democratic control of the government. Feeling that the ground was slipping under him both to left and right, he was holding out with all his might for the idea of a "directory," in which there was still room for his not yet dead dreams of a strong power. After renewed fruitless and wearisome debates in Smolny, it was decided to appeal again to the irreplaceable and one and only Kerensky, with the request that he agree to the preliminary project of the Executive Committees. At seven-thirty in the morning Tseretelli returned with the information that Kerensky would make no concession, that he demanded "un-conditional" support, but that he agreed to employ "all the powers of the state" in the struggle against the counter-revolution. Wearied out with their night's vigil, the Executive Committees surrendered at last to that idea of a "directory" which was as empty as a knot-hole.

Kerensky's solemn promise to throw "all the powers of the state" into the struggle with Kornilov did not, as we already know, prevent him from carrying on those negotiations with Miliukov, Alexeiev, and the retired ministers, about a peaceful surrender to headquarters—negotiations which were interrupted by a midnight knock on the door. Several days later the Menshevik, Bogdanov, one of the members of the Committee of Defense, made a report to the Petrograd soviet in cautious but un-equivocal words about the treachery of Kerensky. "When the Provisional Government was wavering, and it was not clear how the Kornilov adventure would end, intermediaries appeared, such as Miliukov and General Alexeiev . . ." But the committee of defense interfered and "with all energy" demanded an open struggle. "Under our influence," continued Bogdanov, "the government stopped all negotiations and refused to entertain any proposition from Kornilov. . . ."

After the head of the government, yesterday's conspirator against the left camp, had become today its political captive, the

Kadet ministers who had resigned on the 26th only in a preliminary and hesitating fashion, announced that they would conclusively withdraw from the government, since they did not wish
to share the responsibility for Kerensky's action in putting down
so patriotic, so loyal, and so nation-saving a rebellion. The retired
ministers, the counsellors, the friends—one after another they all
left the Winter Palace. It was, according to Kerensky himself, "a
mass abandonment of a place known to be condemned to destruction." There was one night, August 28–9, when Kerensky
was actually walking about almost in "complete solitude" in the
Winter Palace. The opera bravuras were no longer running in his
head. "A responsibility lay upon me in those anguishingly long
days and nights that was really super-human." This was in the
main a responsibility for the fate of Kerensky himself: everything else had already been accomplished over his head and without any attention being paid to him.

CHAPTER X

THE BOURGEOISIE MEASURES STRENGTH WITH THE DEMOCRACY

ON the 28th of August, while fright was shaking the Winter Palace like a fever, the commander of the Savage Division, Prince Bagration, informed Kornilov by telegraph that "the natives would fulfil their duty to the fatherland and at the command of their supreme hero . . . would shed the last drop of their blood." Only a few hours later the division came to a halt; and on the 31st of August a special deputation, with the same Bagration at the head, assured Kerensky that the division would submit absolutely to the Provisional Government. All this happened not only without a battle, but without the firing of a single shot. To say nothing of its last, the division did not shed even its first drop of blood. The soldiers of Kornilov never even made the attempt to employ weapons to force their way to Petrograd. The officers did not dare give them the command. The government troops were nowhere obliged to resort to force in stopping the onslaught of the Kornilov army. The conspiracy disintegrated, crumbled, evaporated in the air.

In order to understand this, it is only necessary to look closely at the powers which had come in conflict. First of all we must notice—and this will not be an unexpected discovery—that the staff of the conspiracy was the same old tzarist staff, composed of clerical people without brains, incapable of thinking out in advance two or three moves in the vast game they had undertaken. Notwithstanding the fact that Kornilov had set the day of the insurrection several weeks in advance, nothing whatever had been foreseen or properly reckoned upon. The purely military preparation of the uprising was carried out in an inept, slovenly and light-headed manner. Complicated changes in the organization and commanding staff were undertaken on the eve of the action—just on the run. The Savage Division, which was to deal the first blow at the revolution, consisted all told of 1,350 fighters, and they were short 600 rifles, 1,000 lances and 500 sabers. Five days before the beginning of active fighting, Kornilov gave an order for the transformation of the division into a corps. This measure, which any schoolbook would condemn, was obviously considered necessary in order to attract the officers with higher pay. "A telegram stating that the lacking weapons would be supplied at Pskov," writes Martynov, "was received by Bagration only on August 31st after the complete collapse of the whole enterprise." The sending of instructors from the front to Petrograd was also taken up at headquarters only at the very last moment. The officers accepting the commission were liberally supplied with money and private cars, but the patriotic heroes were in no great hurry, it seems, to save the fatherland. Two days later railroad communications between headquarters and the capital were cut off, and the majority of the heroes had not yet arrived at the place of their proposed deeds.

The capital, however, had its own organization of Kornilovists numbering about 2,000. The conspirators here were divided into groups according to the special tasks allotted to them; seizure of armored automobiles; arrest and murder of the more eminent members of the Soviet; arrest of the Provisional Government; capture of the more important public institutions. Vinberg, the president of the League of Military Duty, known to us above, says: "By the time Krymov's troops arrived, the principal forces of the revolution were supposed to have already been broken, annihilated, or rendered harmless, so that Krymov's task would be merely to restore order in the town." At Moghiliev, to be sure, they considered this program exaggerated, and relied upon Krymov for most of the work, but headquarters did also expect very serious help from the detachments of the Republican Center. As it turned out, however, the Petrograd conspirators never showed themselves for an instant, never lifted a voice, never moved a finger; it was quite as though they did not exist in the world. Vinberg explains this mystery rather simply. It seems that the superintendent of the Intelligence Service, Colonel Heiman, spent the decisive hours in a roadhouse somewhere outside of town, while Colonel Sidorin, whose duty it was, under the immediate command of Kornilov, to co-ordinate the activities of all the patriotic societies of the capital, and Colonel Duceme-tière, the head of the military department, "had disappeared without a trace and could not be found anywhere." The Cossack colonel Dutov, who was supposed to take action "in the guise of" Bolsheviks, subsequently complained: "I ran . . . and called people to come into the streets, but nobody followed me." The sums of money set aside for organization were, according to Vin-berg, appropriated by the principal participants and squandered on dinner parties. Colonel Sidorin, according to Denikin's asser-tion, "fled to Finland, taking with him the last remnants of the treasury of the organization, something around a hundred or a hundred and fifty thousand rubles." Lvov, whom we last saw under arrest in the Winter Palace, subsequently told about one of the secret contributors who was to deliver to some officers a considerable sum of money, but upon arriving at the designated place found the conspirators in such a state of inebriation that he could not deliver the goods. Vinberg himself thinks that if it had not been for these truly vexatious "accidents," the plan might have been crowned with complete success. But the question re-mains: Why was a patriotic enterprise entered into and sur-rounded, for the most part, by drunkards, spendthrifts and traitors? Is it not because every historic task mobilizes the cadres that are adequate to it?

As regards personnel the conspiracy was in a bad case, be-ginning from the very top. "General Kornilov," according to the right Kadet, Izgoyev, "was the most popular general . . . among the peaceful population, but not among the soldiers, at least not among those in the rear whom I had an opportunity to ob-serve." By peaceful population, Izgoyev means the people of the Nevsky Prospect. To the popular masses, both front and rear, Kornilov was alien, hostile, hateful.

The general appointed to command the Third Cavalry Corps, Krasnov, a monarchist who soon after tried to become a vassal of Wilhelm II, expressed his surprise that "Kornilov conceived such a great undertaking, but himself remained at Moghiliev in a palace surrounded by Turkomen and shock troops, as though he did not believe in his own success." To a question from the

French journalist, Claude Anet, why Kornilov himself did not go to Petrograd at the decisive moment, the chief of the conspiracy answered: "I was sick. I had a serious attack of malaria, and was not in possession of my usual energy."

There were too many of these unfortunate accidents: it is always so when a thing is condemned to failure in advance. The moods of the conspirators oscillated between drunken toploftiness, when the ocean only came up to their knees, and complete prostration before the first real obstacle. The difficulty was not Kornilov's malaria, but a far deeper, more fatal, and incurable disease paralyzing the will of the possessing classes.

The Kadets have seriously denied any counter-revolutionary intentions upon the part of Kornilov, understanding by that the restoration of the Romanov monarchy. As though that were the matter in question! The "republicanism" of Kornilov did not in the least prevent the monarchist Lukomsky from going hand in hand with him, nor did it prevent the president of the Union of Russian People, the Black Hundreds, Rimsky-Korsakov, from telegraphing Kornilov on the day of the uprising: "I heartily pray God to help you save Russia. I put myself absolutely at your disposal." The Black Hundred partisans of tzarism would not stop for a cheap little thing like a republican flag. They understood that Kornilov's program was to be found in himself, in his past, in the Cossack stripes on his trousers, in his connections and sources of financial support, and above all in his unlimited readiness to cut the throat of the revolution.

Designating himself in his manifestos as "the son of a peasant" Kornilov based the plan of his uprising wholly upon the Cossacks and the mountaineers. There was not a single infantry detachment among the troops deployed against Petrograd. The general had no access to the muzhik and did not even try to discover any. There was at headquarters, to be sure, an agrarian reformer, some sort of "professor," who was ready to promise every soldier a fantastic number of dessiatins of land, but the manifesto prepared upon this theme was not even issued. The generals were restrained from agrarian demagoguism by a well-justified dread of frightening and repelling the landlords.

A Moghiliev peasant Tadeush, who closely observed the environs of the staff in those days, testifies that among the soldiers and in the villages nobody believed in the manifestos of the general. "He wants the power," they said, "and not a word about the land and not a word about ending the war." Upon life-and-death questions, the masses had somehow or other learned to find their way during the six months of revolution. Kornilov was offering the people war and a defense of the privileges of generals and the property of landlords. He could give them nothing more, and they expected nothing else from him. In his inability to rely upon the peasant infantry—evident in advance to the conspirators themselves—to say nothing of relying upon the workers, is expressed the socially outcast position of Kornilov's clique.

The picture of political forces traced by the headquarters' diplomat, Prince Trubetskoy, was correct in many things, but mistaken in one. Of that indifference of the people which made them ready "to submit to the least blow of the whip," there was not a trace. On the contrary, the masses were as if only awaiting a blow of the whip in order to show what sources of energy and self-sacrifice were to be found in their depths. This mistake in estimating the mood of the masses brought all their other calculations to the dust.

The conspiracy was conducted by those circles who were not accustomed to know how to do anything without the lower ranks, without labor forces, without cannon-fodder, without orderlies, servants, clerks, chauffeurs, messengers, cooks, laundresses, switchmen, telegraphers, stablemen, cab drivers. But all these little human bolts and links, unnoticeable, innumerable, necessary, were for the Soviet and against Kornilov. The revolution was omnipresent. It penetrated everywhere, coiling itself around the conspiracy. It had everywhere its eye, its ear, its hand.

The ideal of military education is that the soldier should act when unseen by the officer exactly as before his eyes. But the Russian soldiers and sailors of 1917, without carrying out official orders even before the eyes of the commanders, would eagerly catch on the fly the commands of the revolution, or still oftener fulfil them on their own initiative before they arrived. The innumerable servants of the revolution, its agents, its intelligence men, its fighters, had no need either of spurs or of supervision.

Formally the liquidation of the conspiracy was in the hands of the government, and the Executive Committee co-operated. In reality the struggle was carried on within totally different channels. While Kerensky, bending under the weight of a "more than human responsibility," was measuring the floors of the Winter Palace in solitude, the Committee of Defense, also called the Military Revolutionary Committee, was taking action on a vast scale. Early in the morning instructions were sent by telegram to the railroad workers, and postal and telegraph clerks, and soldiers. "All movements of troops"—so Dan reported on the same day—"are to be carried out at the direction of the Provisional Government when countersigned by the committee of People's Defense." Qualifications aside, this meant: The Committee of Defense deploys the troops under the firm name of Provisional Government. At the same time steps were taken for the destruction of Kornilovist nests in Petrograd itself. Searches and arrests were carried out in the military schools and officers' organizations. The hand of the Committee was felt everywhere. There was little or no interest in the governor-general.

The lower soviet organizations in their turn did not await any summons from above. The principal effort was concentrated in the workers' districts. During the hours of greatest vacillation in the government, and of wearisome negotiations between the Executive Committee and Kerensky, the district soviets were drawing more closely together and passing resolutions: to declare the inter-district conferences continuous; to place their representatives in the staff organized by the Executive Committee; to form a workers' militia; to establish the control of the district soviets over the government commissars; to organize flying brigades for the detention of counter-revolutionary agitators. In the total, these resolutions meant an appropriation not only of very considerable governmental functions, but also of the functions of the Petrograd Soviet. The logic of the situation compelled the soviet institutions to draw in their skirts and make room for the lower ranks. The entrance of the Petrograd districts into the arena of the struggle instantly changed both its scope and its direction. Again the inexhaustible vitality of the soviet form of organization was revealed. Although paralyzed above by the leadership of the Compromisers, the soviets were reborn again from below at the critical moment under pressure from the masses.

To the Bolshevik leaders of the districts, Kornilov's uprising had not been in the least unexpected. They had foreseen and forewarned, and they were the first to appear at their posts. At the joint session of the Executive Committees, on August 27, Sokolnikov announced that the Bolshevik party had taken all measures available to it in order to inform the people of the danger and prepare for defense; the Bolsheviks announced their readiness to co-ordinate their military work with the organs of the Executive Committee. At a night session of the Military Organization of the Bolsheviks, participated in by delegates of numerous military detachments, it was decided to demand the arrest of all conspirators, to arm the workers, to supply them with soldier instructors, to guarantee the defense of the capital from below, and at the same time to prepare for the creation of a revolutionary government of workers and soldiers. The Military Organization held meetings throughout the garrison; the soldiers were urged to remain under arms in order to come out at the first alarm.

"Notwithstanding the fact that they were in a minority," writes Sukhanov, "it was quite clear that in the Military Revolutionary Committee the leadership belonged to the Bolsheviks." He explains this as follows: "If the committee wanted to act seriously, it was compelled to act in a revolutionary manner," and for revolutionary action "only the Bolsheviks had genuine resources," for the masses were with them. Intensity in the struggle has everywhere and always brought forth the more active and bolder elements. This automatic selection inevitably elevated the Bolsheviks, strengthened their influence, concentrated the initiative in their hands, giving them *de facto* leadership even in those organizations where they were in a minority. The nearer you came to the district, to the factory, to the barrack, the more complete and indubitable was the leadership of the Bolsheviks.

All the nuclei of the party were on their toes. The big factories organized a system of guard duty by Bolsheviks. In the district committees of the party representatives of small plants were put on duty. A tie was formed from below, from the shop, leading through the districts, to the Central Committee of the party.

Under direct pressure from the Bolsheviks and the organizations led by them, the Committee of Defense recognized the desirability of arming individual groups of workers for the defense of the workers' quarters, the shops and factories. It was only this sanction that the masses lacked. In the districts, according to the workers' press, there immediately appeared "whole queues of people eager to join the ranks of the Red Guard." Drilling began in marksmanship and the handling of weapons. Experienced soldiers were brought in as teachers. By the 29th, Guards had been formed in almost all the districts. The Red Guard announced its readiness to put in the field a force of 40,000 rifles. The unarmed workers formed companies for trench-digging, sheet-metal fortification, barbed-wire fencing. The new governor-general Palchinsky who replaced Savinkov,—Kerensky could not keep his accomplice longer than three days—was compelled to recognize in a special announcement that when the need arose for the work of sappers in the defense of the capital "thousands of workers . . . by their irreplaceable, personal labor achieved in the course of a few hours a colossal task which without their help would have required several days." This did not prevent Palchinsky, following the example of Savinkov, from suppressing the Bolshevik paper, the sole paper which the workers considered their own.

The giant Putilov factory became the center of resistance in the Peterhoff district. Here fighting companies were hastily formed; the work of the factory continued day and night; there was a sorting out of new cannon for the formation of proletarian artillery divisions. The worker, Minichev, says: "In those days we worked sixteen hours a day . . . We got together about 100 cannon."

The newly formed Vikzhel received a prompt baptism of war. The railroad workers had a special reason to dread the victory of Kornilov, who had incorporated in his program the inauguration of martial law on the railroads. And here, too, the lower ranks far outdistanced their leaders. The railroad workers tore up and barricaded the tracks in order to hold back Kornilov's army. War experiences came in handy. Measures were also taken to isolate the center of the conspiracy, Moghiliev, preventing movements both towards and away from headquarters. The postal and telegraph clerks began to hold up and send to the Committee telegrams and orders from headquarters, or copies of them. The generals had been accustomed during the years of war to think of transport and communications as technical questions. They found out now that these were political questions.

The trade unions, least of all inclined toward political neutrality, did not await any special invitation before occupying military positions. The railroad workers' union armed its members, and sent them along the lines for inspection, and for tearing up railroads, guarding bridges, etc. The workers in their enthusiasm and resolution pushed ahead of the more bureaucratic and moderate Vikzhel. The metal workers' union put its innumerable office workers at the disposal of the Committee of Defense, and also a large sum of money for expenses. The chauffeurs' union put in charge of the committee its technical and transportation facilities. The printers' union arranged in a few hours for the issue of Monday's papers, so as to keep the population in touch with events, and at the same time availed themselves of the most effective of all possible means of controlling the press. The rebel general had stamped his foot, and legions rose up from the ground—but they were the legions of the enemy.

All around Petrograd, in the neighboring garrisons, in the great railroad stations, in the fleet, work was going on night and day. They were inspecting their own ranks, arming the workers, sending out detachments as patrols along the tracks, establishing communications with neighboring points, and with Smolny. The task of the Committee of Defense was not so much to keep watch over and summon the workers, as merely to register and direct them. Its plans were always anticipated. The defense against the rebellion of the generals turned into a popular round-up of the conspirators.

In Helsingfors a general congress of all the soviet organizations created a revolutionary committee which sent its commissars to the offices of the governor-general, the commandant, the Intelligence Service, and other important institutions.

Thenceforth no order was valid without its signature. The telegraphs and telephones were taken under control. The official representatives of a Cossack regiment quartered in Helsingfors, chiefly officers, tried to declare themselves neutral: they were secret Kornilovists. On the second day, a rank-and-file cossack appeared before the Committee with the announcement that the whole regiment was against Kornilov. Cossack representatives were for the first time introduced into the soviet. In this case as in others a sharp conflict of classes was pushing the officers to the right and the rank-and-file to the left.

The Kronstadt soviet, which had completely recovered from the July wounds, sent a telegraphic declaration: "The Kronstadt garrison is ready as one man at the first word from the Executive Committee to come to the defense of the revolution." The Kronstadters did not know in those days to what extent the defense of the revolution meant the defense of themselves against annihilation: at that time they could still only guess this.

Soon after the July Days it had been decided by the Provisional Government to vacate the Kronstadt fortress as a nest of Bolshevism. This measure, adopted in agreement with Kornilov, was officially explained as due to "strategic motives." Sensing some dirty work, the sailors had resisted. "The legend of treachery at headquarters"—wrote Kerensky after he himself had accused Kornilov of treachery—"was so deeply rooted in Kronstadt that every attempt to remove the artillery evoked actual ferocity from the crowd there." The task of devising a way to liquidate Kronstadt was laid by the government upon Kornilov. Kornilov devised a way: immediately after the conquest of the city Krymov was to despatch a brigade with artillery to Oranienbaum and, under threat of bombardment from the shores, demand that the Kronstadt garrison disarm the fortress and transfer themselves to the mainland, where the sailors were to undergo mass executions. But while Krymov was entering upon his task of saving the government, the government found itself obliged to ask the Kronstadters to save it from Krymov.

232

The Executive Committee sent telephonegrams to Kronstadt and Vyborg asking for the despatch of considerable detachments of troops to Petrograd. On the morning of the 29th, the troops began to arrive. These were chiefly Bolshevik units. In order that the summons of the Executive Committee should become operative, it had to be confirmed by the central committee of the Bolsheviks. A little earlier, at midday of the 28th, upon an order from Kerensky which sounded very much like a humble request, sailors from the cruiser *Aurora* had undertaken the defense of the Winter Palace. A part of the same crew were still imprisoned in Kresty for participation in the July demonstration. During their hours off duty the sailors came to the prison for a visit with the imprisoned Kronstadters, and with Trotsky, Raskolnikov and others. "Isn't it time to arrest the government?" asked the visitors. "No, not yet," was the answer. "Use Kerensky as a gun-rest to shoot Kornilov. Afterward we will settle with Kerensky." In June and July these sailors had not been inclined to pay much attention to revolutionary strategy, but they had learned much in a short two months. They raised this question of the arrest of the government rather to test themselves and clear their own consciences. They themselves were beginning to grasp the inexorable consecutiveness of events. In the first half of July, beaten, condemned, slandered; at the end of August, the trusted defenders of the Winter Palace against Kornilovists; at the end of October, they will be shooting at the Winter Palace with the guns of the *Aurora*.

But although the sailors were willing to postpone for a certain time a general settlement with the February régime, they did not want to endure for one unnecessary day the Kornilovist officers hanging over their heads. The commanding staff which had been imposed upon them by the government since the July Days was almost solidly on the side of the conspirators. The Kronstadt soviet immediately removed the government commander of the fortress and installed their own. The Compromisers had now ceased to shout about the secession of the Kronstadt republic. However the thing did not everywhere stop at mere removals from office: it came to bloody encounters in several places.

"It began in Vyborg," says Sukhanov, "with the beating to

233

death of generals and officers by a sailor-soldier crowd infuriated and panic-stricken." No, these crowds were not infuriated, and it would not be possible to speak in this instance of panic. On the morning of the 29th, Centroflot sent a telegram to the commandant at Vyborg, General Oranovsky, for communication to the garrison, informing them of the mutiny at headquarters. The commandant held up the telegram for a whole day, and to questions about what was happening, answered that he had received no information. In the course of a search instituted by the sailors the telegram was found. Thus caught in the act, the general declared himself a partisan of Kornilov. The sailors shot the commandant and along with him two other officers who had declared themselves of the same party. From the officers of the Baltic fleet the sailors required a signed declaration of loyalty to the revolution, and when four officers of the ship-of-the-line *Petropavlovsk* refused to sign, declaring themselves Kornilovists, they were by resolution of the crew immediately shot.

A mortal danger was hanging over the soldiers and sailors; a bloody purgation not only of Petrograd and Kronstadt, but of all the garrisons of the country, was impending. From the conduct of their suddenly emboldened officers,—from their tones, their side glances—the soldiers and sailors could plainly foresee their own fate in case of a victory of headquarters. In those localities where the atmosphere was especially hot, they hastened to cut off the road of the enemy, forestalling the purgation intended by the officers with their own sailors' and soldiers' purgation. Civil war, as is well known, has its laws, and they have never been considered identical with the laws of humane conduct.

Cheidze immediately sent a telegram to Vyborg and Helsingfors condemning lynch law as "a mortal blow against the revolution." Kerensky on his part telegraphed to Helsingfors: "I demand an immediate end of disgusting acts of violence." If you seek the political responsibility for these individual cases of lynch law—not forgetting that revolution as a whole is a taking of the law into one's own hands—in the given case the responsibility rests wholly on the government and the Compromisers, who at a moment of danger would run for help to the revolutionary masses, in order afterward to turn them over again to the counter-revolutionary officers.

As during the State Conference in Moscow, when he was expecting an uprising from moment to moment, so now after the break with headquarters, Kerensky turned to the Bolsheviks with a request "to influence the soldiers to come to the defense of the revolution." In summoning the Bolshevik sailors to the defense of the Winter Palace, however, Kerensky did not set free their comrades, the July prisoners. Sukhanov writes on this theme: "The situation with Alexeiev whispering to Kerensky and Trotsky in prison was absolutely intolerable." It is not hard to imagine the excitement which prevailed in the crowded prisons. "We were boiling with indignation," relates midshipman Raskolnikov, "against the Provisional Government which in such days of alarm . . . continued to let revolutionists like Trotsky rot in Kresty . . . 'What cowards, what cowards they are,' said Trotsky as some of us were circling around together on our walk. 'They ought immediately to declare Kornilov an outlaw, so that any soldier devoted to the revolution might feel that he had a right to put an end to him.' "

The entrance of Kornilov's troops into Petrograd would have meant first of all the extermination of the arrested Bolsheviks. In his order to General Bagration, who was to enter the capital with the vanguard, Krymov did not forget this special command: "Place a guard in prisons and houses of detention, in no case let out the people now under restraint." This was a concerted program, inspired by Miliukov ever since the April days: "In no case let them out." There was not a single meeting in Petrograd in those days which did not pass resolutions demanding the release of the July prisoners. Delegation after delegation came to the Executive Committee, which in turn sent its leaders for negotiations to the Winter Palace. In vain! The stubbornness of Kerensky on this question is the more remarkable since during the first day and a half or two days he considered the position of the government hopeless, and was therefore condemning himself to the rôle of the old-time jailkeeper—holding the Bolsheviks so that the generals could hang them.

It is no wonder that the masses led by the Bolsheviks in fighting against Kornilov did not place a moment of trust in Kerensky. For them it was not a case of defending the government, but of defending the revolution. So much the more resolute and devoted was their struggle. The resistance to the rebels grew out of the very road beds, out of the stones, out of the air. The railroad workers of the Luga station, where Krymov arrived, stubbornly refused to move the troop trains, alluding to a lack of locomotives. The Cossack echelons also found themselves immediately surrounded by armed soldiers from the Luga garrison, 20,000 strong. There was no military encounter, but there was something far more dangerous: contact, social exchange, inter-penetration. The Luga soviet had had time to print the government announcement retiring Kornilov, and this document was now widely distributed among the echelons. The officers tried to persuade the Cossacks not to believe the agitators, but this very necessity of persuasion was a bad sign.

On receiving Kornilov's order to advance, Krymov demanded under threat of bayonets that the locomotives be ready in half an hour. The threat seemed effective: the locomotives, although with some delays, were supplied; but even so, it was impossible to move, since the road out was damaged and so crowded with cars that it would take a good twenty-four hours to clear it. To get free of demoralizing propaganda, Krymov on the evening of the 28th, removed his troops several versts from Luga. But the agitators immediately turned up in the villages. These were soldiers, workers, railroad men—there was no refuge from them. They went everywhere. The Cossacks began even to hold meetings. Thus stormed with propaganda and cursing his impotence, Krymov waited in vain for Bagration. The railroad workers were holding up the echelon of the Savage Division, which also in the coming hours was to undergo a most alarming moral attack.

No matter how spineless and even cowardly the compromisist democracy was in itself, those mass forces upon which it again partly relied in its struggle against Kornilov, opened before it inexhaustible resources for action. The Social Revolutionaries and Mensheviks did not see it as their task to conquer the forces of Kornilov in open struggle, but to bring the forces over to their

236

own side. That was right. Against "compromisism" along that line, it goes without saying, the Bolsheviks had no objection. On the contrary that was their own fundamental method. The Bolsheviks only demanded that behind the agitators and parliamentaries armed workers and soldiers should stand ready. For this moral mode of action upon the Kornilov regiments, an unlimited choice of ways and means was suddenly discovered. Thus a Mussulman delegation was sent to meet the Savage Division on the staff of which were included native potentates who had immediately made themselves known, beginning with the grandson of the famous Shamil who heroically defended the Caucasus against tzarism. The mountaineers would not permit their officers to arrest the delegation: that was a violation of the ancient customs of hospitality. Negotiations were opened and soon became the beginning of the end. The Kornilov commanders, in order to explain the whole campaign, had kept referring to a rebellion of German agents supposed to have begun in Petrograd. The delegates, arriving directly from the capital, not only disproved the fact of a rebellion, but also demonstrated with documents in their hands that Krymov was a rebel and was leading his troops against the government. What could the officers of Kornilov reply to that?

On the staff car of the Savage Division the soldiers stuck up a red flag with the inscription: "Land and freedom." The staff commander ordered them to take down the flags—"merely to avoid confusing it with a railroad signal," as the lieutenant-colonel politely explained. The staff soldiers were not satisfied with this cowardly explanation, and arrested the lieutenant-colonel. Were they not mistaken at headquarters when they said that the Caucasian mountaineers did not care whom they slaughtered?

The next morning a colonel arrived at Krymov's headquarters from Kornilov with an order to concentrate his corps, advance swiftly on Petrograd, and "unexpectedly" occupy it. At headquarters they were obviously still trying to shut their eyes to the facts. Krymov replied that the different units of the corps were scattered on various railroads and in some places were detraining; that he had at his disposition only eight Cossack squadrons; that the railroads were damaged, overloaded, barricaded, and that it was possible to move farther only on foot; and that finally there could be no talk of an unexpected occupation of Petrograd, now that the workers and soldiers had been placed under arms in the capital and its environs. The affair was still further complicated by the fact that the possibility was hopelessly past of carrying out the operation "unexpectedly" even to the troops of Krymov himself. Sensing something unpropitious, they had demanded explanations. It had become necessary to inform them of the conflict between Kornilov and Kerensky—that is, to place soldiers' meetings officially on the order of the day.

An order issued by Krymov at just that moment read: "This evening I received from the headquarters of the commander-in-chief and from Petrograd information that rebellions have begun in Petrograd . . ." This deceit was designed to justify an already quite open campaign against the government. An order of Kornilov himself on the 29th of August, had read: "The intelligence service from Holland reports: (a) In a few days a simultaneous attack upon the whole front is to begin, with the aim of routing and putting to flight our disintegrating army; (b) An insurrection is under preparation in Finland; (c) Explosions are to be expected of bridges on the Dnieper and the Volga; (d) An insurrection of Bolsheviks is being organized in Petrograd." This was that same "information" to which Savinkov had already referred on the 23rd. Holland is mentioned here merely to distract attention. According to all evidence the document was fabricated in the French war mission or with its participation.

Kerensky on the same day telegraphed Krymov: "There is complete tranquillity in Petrograd. No demonstrations are expected. Your corps is not needed." The demonstrations were to have been evoked by the military edicts of Kerensky himself. Since it had been necessary to postpone this governmental act of provocation, Kerensky was entirely justified in concluding that "no demonstrations are expected."

Seeing no way out, Krymov made an awkward attempt to advance upon Petrograd with his eight Cossack squadrons. This was little but a gesture to clear his own conscience, and nothing of course came of it. Meeting a force on patrol duty a few versts from Luga, Krymov turned back without even trying to give battle. On the theme of this single and completely fictitious "operation," Krasnov, the commander of the Third Cavalry Corps, wrote later: "We should have struck Petrograd with a force of eighty-six cavalry and Cossack squadrons, and we struck with one brigade and eight weak squadrons, half of them without officers. Instead of striking with our fist, we struck with our little finger. It pained the finger, and those we struck at were insensible of the blow." In the essence of the matter there was no blow even from a finger. Nobody felt any pain at all.

The railroad workers in those days did their duty. In a mysterious way echelons would find themselves moving on the wrong roads. Regiments would arrive in the wrong division, artillery would be sent up a blind alley, staffs would get out of communication with their units. All the big stations had their own soviets, their railroad workers' and their military committees. The telegraphers kept them informed of all events, all movements, all changes. The telegraphers also held up the orders of Kornilov. Information unfavorable to the Kornilovists was immediately multiplied, distributed, pasted up, passed from mouth to mouth. The machinists, the switchmen, the oilers, became agitators. It was in this atmosphere that the Kornilov echelons advanced—or what was worse, stood still. The commanding staff, soon sensing the hopelessness of the situation, obviously did not hasten to move forward, and with their passivity promoted the work of the counter-conspirators of the transport system. Parts of the army of Krymov were in this way scattered about in the stations, sidings, and branch lines, of eight different railroads. If you follow on the map the fate of the Kornilov echelons, you get the impression that the conspirators were playing at blind man's buff on the railroad lines.

"Almost everywhere," says General Krasnov, writing his observations made on the night of August 30, "we saw one and the same picture. On the tracks or in the cars, or in the saddles of their black or bay horses, who would turn from time to time to gaze at them, dragoons would be sitting or standing, and in the midst of them some lively personality in a soldier's long coat." The name of this "lively personality" soon became legion. From the direction of Petrograd innumerable delegations continued to arrive from regiments sent out to oppose the Kornilovists. Before fighting they wanted to talk things over. The revolutionary troops were confidently hopeful that the thing could be settled without fighting. This hope was confirmed: the Cossacks readily came to meet them. The communication squad of the corps would seize locomotives, and send the delegates along all railroad lines. The situation would be explained to every echelon. Meetings were continuous and at them all the cry was being raised: "They have deceived us!"

"Not only the chiefs of divisions," says Krasnov, "but even the commanders of regiments did not know exactly where their squadrons and companies were. The absence of food and forage naturally irritated everybody still more. The men . . . seeing all this meaningless confusion which had been created around them, began to arrest their chiefs and officers." A delegation from the Soviet which had organized its own headquarters reported: "Fraternization is going on rapidly . . . We are fully confident that the conflict may be considered liquidated. Delegations are coming from all sides . . ." Committees took the place of the officers in directing the units. A soviet of deputies of the corps was very soon created, and from its staff a delegation of forty men was appointed to go to the Provisional Government. The Cossacks began to announce out loud that they were only waiting an order from Petrograd to arrest Krymov and the other officers.

Stankevich paints a picture of what he found on the road when he set out on the 30th with Voitinsky in the direction of Pskov. In Petrograd, he says, they had thought Tzarskoe was occupied by Kornilovists; there was nobody there at all. "In Gatchina, nobody . . . On the road to Luga, nobody. In Luga, peace and quiet . . . We arrived at the village where the staff of the corps was supposed to be located . . . empty . . . We learned that early in the morning the Cossacks had left their positions and gone away in the direction opposite to Petrograd." The insurrection had rolled back, crumbled to pieces, been sucked up by the earth.

But in the Winter Palace they were still dreading the enemy. Kerensky made an attempt to enter into conversation with the commanding staff of the rebels. That course seemed to him more hopeful than the "anarchist" initiative of the lower ranks. He sent delegates to Krymov, and "in the name of the salvation of Russia," invited him to come to Petrograd, guaranteeing him safety on his word of honor. Pressed upon all sides, and having completely lost his head, the general hastened, of course, to accept the invitation. On his heels came a deputation from the Cossacks.

The fronts did not support headquarters. Only the South-western made a somewhat serious attempt. Denikin's staff had adopted preparatory measures in good season. The unreliable guards at the staff were replaced by Cossacks. The printing presses were seized on the night of the 27th. The staff tried to play the rôle of self-confident master of the situation, and even forbade the committee of the front to use the telegraph. But the illusion did not last more than a few hours. Delegates from various units began to come to the committee with offers of support. Armored cars appeared, machine guns, field artillery. The committee immediately asserted its control of the activity of the staff, leaving it the initiative only in operations against the enemy. By three o'clock on the 28th the power on the Southwestern front was wholly in the hands of the committee. "Never again," wept Denikin, "did the future of the country seem so dark, our impotence so grievous and humiliating."

On the other fronts the thing passed off less dramatically: the commander-in-chief had only to look around in order to sense a torrent of friendly feeling going out to the commissars of the Provisional Government. By the morning of the 29th, telegrams had arrived at the Winter Palace with expressions of loyalty from General Sherbachev, on the Rumanian front, Valuyev on the Western, and Przevalsky on the Caucasian. On the Northern front, where the commander-in-chief was an open Kornilovist, Klembovsky, Stankevich named a certain Savitsky as his deputy. "Savitsky, little known to anybody until then, and appointed by telegram at the moment of the conflict," writes Stankevich himself, "could appeal with confidence to any bunch of soldiers— infantry, Cossacks, orderlies and even junkers—with any order whatever, even if it were a question of arresting the commander-in-chief, and the order would be promptly carried out." Klembovsky was replaced, without further difficulties, by General Bonch-Bruevich, who through the mediation of his brother, a well-known Bolshevik, became afterward one of the first to enter the service of the Bolshevik government.

Things went a little better with the southern pillar of the military party, the ataman of the Don Cossacks, Kaledin. They were saying in Petrograd that Kaledin was mobilizing the Cossack army and that echelons from the front were marching to join him on the Don. Meanwhile the ataman, according to one of his biographers, "was riding from village to village, far from the railroad . . . peacefully conversing with villagers." Kaledin actually did conduct himself more cautiously than was imagined in revolutionary circles. He chose the moment of open revolt, the date of which had been made known to him in advance, for making a "peaceful" round of the villages, in order that during the critical days he might be beyond control by telegraph or otherwise, and at the same time might be feeling out the mood of the Cossacks. On the 27th he telegraphed his deputy, Bogayevsky: "It is necessary to support Kornilov with all means and forces." However, his conversations with the villagers were demonstrating at just that moment that properly speaking there were no means or forces: those Cossack wheat-growers would not think of rising in defense of Kornilov. When the collapse of the uprising became evident, the so-called "troop ring"[1] of the Don decided to refrain from expressing its opinion "until the real correlation of forces has become clear." Thanks to these maneuvers, the chiefs of the Don Cossacks succeeded in making a timely jump to the sidelines.

In Petrograd, in Moscow, on the Don, at the front, along the course followed by the echelons, here, there and everywhere, Kornilov had had his sympathizers, partisans, friends. Their number seemed enormous to judge by telegrams, speeches of greeting, newspaper articles. But strange to say, now when the hour had come to reveal themselves, they had disappeared. In many cases the cause did not lie in personal cowardice. There were plenty of brave men among the Kornilov officers. But their bravery could find no point of application. From the moment the masses got

[1] The Cossacks' name for their elective assembly.

242

into motion the solitary individual had no access to events. Not only the weighty industrialists, bankers, professors, engineers, but also students and even fighting officers, found themselves pushed away, thrown aside, elbowed out. They watched the events developing before them as though from a balcony. Along with General Denikin they had nothing left to do but curse their humiliating and appalling impotence.

On the 30th of August, the Executive Committee sent to all soviets the joyous news that "there is complete demoralization in the troops of Kornilov." They forgot for the moment that Kornilov had chosen for his undertaking the most patriotic units, those with the best fighting morale, those most protected from the influence of the Bolsheviks. The process of demoralization consisted in the fact that the soldiers had decisively ceased to trust their officers, discovering them to be enemies. The struggle for the revolution against Kornilov meant a deepening of the demoralization of the army. That is exactly the thing of which they were accusing the Bolsheviks.

The generals had finally got an opportunity to verify the force of resistance possessed by that revolution which had seemed to them so crumbly and helpless, so accidentally victorious over the old régime. Ever since the February days, on every possible occasion, the gallant formula of soldier-braggadoccio had been repeated: "Give me one strong detachment and I will show them." The experience of General Khabalov and General Ivanov at the end of February had taught nothing to these warriors of loud mouth. The same song was frequently sung too by civilian strategists. The Octobrist Shidlovsky asserted that if in February there had appeared in the capital "a military detachment, not especially large but united by discipline and fighting spirit, the February revolution would have been put down in a few days." The notorious railway magnate, Bublikov, wrote: "One disciplined division from the front would have been enough to crush the insurrection to the bottom." Several officers who participated in the events assured Denikin that "one firm battalion under a commander who knew what he wanted, could have changed the whole situation from top to bottom." During the days of Guchkov's war ministry, General Krymov came to him from the front and offered to "clean up Petrograd with one division—of course not without bloodshed." The thing was not put through merely because "Guchkov did not consent." And finally Savinkov, preparing in the interests of a future directory his own particular "August 27th," asserted that two regiments would be amply sufficient to make dust and ashes of the Bolsheviks. Now fate had offered to all these gentlemen, in the person of the "happy" general "full of the joy of life," an ample opportunity to verify the truth of their heroic calculations. Without having struck a single blow, with bowed head, shamed and humiliated, Krymov arrived at the Winter Palace. Kerensky did not let pass the opportunity to play out a melodramatic scene with him—a scene in which his chief effects were guaranteed their success in advance. Returning from the prime-minister to the war office, Krymov ended his life with a revolver shot. Thus turned out his attempt to put down the revolution "not without bloodshed."

In the Winter Palace they breathed more freely, having concluded that a matter so pregnant with difficulties was ending favorably. And they decided to return as soon as possible to the order of the day—that is to a continuation of the business which had been interrupted. Kerensky appointed himself commander-in-chief. From the standpoint of preserving his political ties with the old generals, he could hardly have found a more suitable figure. As chief of the headquarters staff he selected Alexeiev, who two days ago had barely missed landing in the position of Prime Minister. After hesitating and conferring with his friends, the general, not without a contemptuous grimace, accepted the appointment—with the aim, as he explained to his own people, of liquidating the conflict in a peaceful manner. The former chief-of-staff of the supreme commander-in-chief, Nicholas Romanov, thus arrived at the same position under Kerensky. That was something to wonder at! "Only Alexeiev, thanks to his closeness to headquarters and his enormous influence in high military circles" —so Kerensky subsequently tried to explain his wonderful appointment—"could successfully carry out the task of peacefully transferring the command from the hands of Kornilov to new hands." Exactly the opposite was true. The appointment of Alexeiev—that is, one of their own men—could only inspire the conspirators to further resistance, had there remained the slightest possibility of it. In reality Alexeiev was brought forward by Kerensky after the failure of the insurrection for the same reason that Savinkov had been summoned at the beginning of it: it was necessary at any cost to keep open a bridge to the right. The new commander-in-chief considered a restoration of friendship with the generals now especially needful. After the disturbance it will be necessary to inaugurate a firm order, and accordingly a doubly strong power is needed.

At headquarters nothing was now left of that optimism which had reigned two days before. The conspirators were looking for a way to retreat. A telegram sent to Kerensky stated that Kornilov "in view of the strategic situation" was disposed to surrender the command peacefully, provided he was assured that "a strong government will be formed." This large ultimatum the capitulator followed up with a small one: he, Kornilov, considered it "upon the whole impermissible to arrest the generals and other persons most indispensable to the army." The delighted Kerensky immediately took a step to meet his enemy, announcing by radio that the orders of General Kornilov in the sphere of military operations were obligatory upon all. Kornilov himself wrote to Krymov on the same day: "An episode has occurred— the only one of its kind in the history of the world: a commander-in-chief accused of treason and betrayal of the fatherland, and arraigned for this crime before the courts, has received an order to continue commanding the armies . . ." This new manifestation of the good-for-nothingness of Kerensky immediately raised the hopes of the conspirators, who still dreaded to sell themselves too cheap. In spite of the telegram sent a few hours earlier about the impermissibility of inner conflict "at this terrible moment," Kornilov, half-way restored to his rights, sent two men to Kaledin with a request "to bring pressure to bear" and at the same time suggested to Krymov: "If circumstances permit, act independently in the spirit of my instructions to you." The spirit of those instructions was: Overthrow the government and hang the members of the Soviet.

General Alexeiev, the new chief-of-staff, departed for the seizure of headquarters. At the Winter Palace they still took this operation seriously. In reality Kornilov had had at his immediate disposition: a battalion of St. George, the "Kornilovist" infantry regiment, and a Tekinsky cavalry regiment. The St. George battalion had gone over to the government at the very beginning, the Kornilovist and Tekinsky regiments were still counted loyal, but part of them had split off. Headquarters had no artillery at all. In these circumstances there could be no talk of resistance. Alexeiev began his mission by paying ceremonial visits to Kornilov and Lukomsky—visits during which we can only imagine both sides unanimously squandering the soldierly vocabulary on the subject of Kerensky, the new commander-in-chief. It was clear to Kornilov, as also to Alexeiev, that the salvation of the country must in any case be postponed for a certain period of time.

But while at headquarters peace without victors or vanquished was being so happily concluded, the atmosphere in Petrograd was getting extraordinarily hot, and in the Winter Palace they were impatiently awaiting some reassuring news from Moghiliev which might be offered to the people. They kept nudging Alexeiev with inquiries. Colonel Baranovsky, one of Kerensky's trusted men, complained over the direct wire: "The soviets are raging, the atmosphere can be discharged only by a demonstration of power, and the arrest of Kornilov and others . . ." This did not at all correspond to the intentions of Alexeiev. "I remark with deep regret," answers the general, "that my fear lest at present we have fallen completely into the tenacious paws of the Soviet has become an indubitable fact." By the familiar pronoun "we" is implied the group of Kerensky, in which Alexeiev, in order to soften the sting, conditionally includes himself. Colonel Baranovsky replies in the same tone: "God grant that we shall get out of the tenacious paws of the Soviet into which we have fallen." Hardly had the masses saved Kerensky from the paws of Kornilov, when the leader of the democracy hastened to get into agreement with Alexeiev against the masses: "We shall get out of the tenacious paws of the Soviet." Alexeiev was nevertheless compelled to submit to necessity, and carry out the ritual of arresting the principal conspirators. Kornilov offered no objection to sitting quietly under house arrest four days after he had announced to the people: "I prefer death to my removal from the post of commander-in-chief." The Extraordinary Commission of Inquiry, when it arrived at Moghiliev, also arrested the Vice-Minister of Communications, several officers of the general staff, the unarrived diplomat Alladin, and also the whole personnel of the head committee of the League of Officers.

During the first hours after the victory the Compromisers gesticulated ferociously. Even Avksentiev gave out flashes of lightning. For three whole days the rebels had left the front without any command! "Death to the traitors!" cried the members of the Executive Committee. Avksentiev welcomed these voices: Yes, the death penalty was introduced at the demand of Kornilov and his followers—"so much the more decisively will it be applied to them." Stormy and prolonged applause.

The Moscow Church Council which had two weeks ago bowed its head before Kornilov as the restorer of the death penalty, now beseeched the government by telegraph "in the name of God and the Christlike love of the neighbor to preserve the life of the erring general." Other levers also were brought into operation. But the government had no idea at all of making a bloody settlement. When a delegation from the Savage Division came to Kerensky in the Winter Palace, and one of the soldiers in answer to some general phrases of the new commander, said that "the traitor commanders ought to be ruthlessly punished," Kerensky interrupted him with the words: "Your business now is to obey your commander and we ourselves will do all that is necessary." Apparently this man thought that the masses ought to appear on the scene when he stamped with his left foot, and disappear again when he stamped with his right.

"We ourselves will do all that is necessary." But all that they did seemed to the masses unnecessary, if not indeed suspicious and disastrous. The masses were not wrong. The upper circles were most of all occupied with restoring that very situation out of which the Kornilov campaign had arisen. "After the first few questions put by the members of the Inquiry Commission," relates Lukomsky, "it became clear that they were all in the highest degree friendly toward us." They were in essence accomplices and accessories. The military prosecutor Shablovsky gave the accused a consultation on the question how to evade justice. The organizations of the front sent protests. "The generals and their accomplices are not being held as criminals before the state and the people . . . The rebels have complete freedom of communication with the outside world." Lukomsky confirms this: "The staff of the commander-in-chief kept us informed about all matters of interest to us." The indignant soldiers more than once felt an impulse to try the generals in their own courts, and the arrestees were saved from summary execution only by a counter-revolutionary Polish division sent to Bykhov where they were detained.

On the 12th of September, General Alexeiev wrote to Miliukov from headquarters a letter which reflected the legitimate indignation of the conspirators at the conduct of the big bourgeoisie, which had first pushed them on, but after the defeat left them to their fate. "You are to a certain degree aware"—wrote the general, not without poison in his pen—"that certain circles of our society not only knew about it all, not only sympathized intellectually, but even to the extent that they were able helped Kornilov . . ." In the name of the League of Officers Alexeiev demanded of Vyshnegradsky, Putilov and other big capitalists, who had turned their backs to the vanquished, that they should collect 300,000 rubles for the benefit of "the hungry families of those with whom they had been united by common ideas and preparations . . ." The letter ended in an open threat: "If the honest press does not immediately begin an energetic explanation of the situation . . . General Kornilov will be compelled to make a broad exposure before the court of all the preparatory activities, all conversations with persons and circles, the parts they played, etc." As to the practical results of this tearful ultimatum, Denikin reports: "Only towards the end of October did they bring to Kornilov from Moscow about 40,000 rubles." Miliukov during this period was in a general way absent from the political arena. According to the official Kadet version he had "gone to the Crimea for a rest." After all these violent agitations the liberal leader was, to be sure, in need of rest.

The comedy of the Inquiry Commission dragged along until the Bolshevik insurrection, after which Kornilov and his accomplices were not only set free, but supplied by Kerensky's headquarters with all necessary documents. These escaped generals laid the foundation of the civil war. In the name of the sacred aims which had united Kornilov with the liberal Miliukov and the Black Hundredist, Rimsky-Korsakov, hundreds of thousands of people were buried, the south and east of Russia were pillaged and laid waste, the industry of the country was almost completely destroyed, and the Red Terror imposed upon the revolution. Kornilov, after successfully emerging from Kerensky's courts of justice, soon fell on the civil war front from a Bolshevik shell. Kaledin's fate was not very different. The "troop ring" of the Don demanded, not only a revocation of the order for Kaledin's arrest, but also his restoration to the position of ataman. And here too Kerensky did not miss the opportunity to go back on himself. Skobelev was sent to Novocherkassk to apologize to the troop ring. The democratic minister was subjected to refined mockeries conducted by Kaledin himself. The triumph of the Cossack general was not, however, long-lasting. Pressed from all sides by the Bolshevik revolution breaking out on the Don, Kaledin in a few months ended his own life. The banner of Kornilov then passed into the hands of General Denikin and Admiral Kolchak, with whose names the principal period of the civil war is associated. But all that has to do with 1918 and the years that followed.

CHAPTER XI

THE MASSES UNDER ATTACK

THE immediate causes of the events of a revolution are changes in the state-of-mind of the conflicting classes. The material relations of society merely define the channel within which these processes take place. Changes in the collective consciousness have naturally a semi-concealed character. Only when they have attained a certain degree of intensity do the new moods and ideas break to the surface in the form of mass activities which establish a new, although again very unstable, social equilibrium. The development of a revolution lays bare at each new stage the problem of power, but only to disguise it again immediately afterward—until the hour of a new exposure. A counter-revolution has the same dynamic, except that the picture is reeled off in the opposite direction.

What goes on in the governmental and soviet upper circles is by no means without effect upon the course of events. But it is impossible to understand the real significance of a political party or find your way among the maneuvers of the leaders, without searching out the deep molecular processes in the mind of the mass. In July the workers and soldiers were defeated, but in October with an unconquerable onslaught they seized the power. What happened in their heads during those four months? How did they live through the blows rained upon them from above? With what ideas and feelings did they meet the open attempt at a seizure of power by the bourgeoisie? Here the reader will find it necessary to go back to the July defeat. It is often necessary to step back a few paces in order to make a good leap. And before us is the October leap.

In the official soviet histories the opinion has become established, and been converted into a kind of rubber-stamp, that the July attack upon the party—the combination of repression and slander—went by almost without leaving a trace upon the workers' organizations. That is utterly untrue. The decline in the ranks of the party and the ebbing away of workers and soldiers did not, to be sure, last very long—not longer than a few weeks. The revival began so quickly—and what is more important, so boisterously—that it more than half wiped out the memory of the days of persecution and decline. Victories always throw a new light upon the defeats which led up to them. But in proportion as the minutes of local party organizations begin to be published, the picture emerges more and more sharply of a July decline of the revolution—a thing which was felt in those days the more painfully in proportion as the preceding upward swing had been uninterrupted.

Every defeat, resulting as it does from a definite correlation of forces, changes that correlation in its turn to the disadvantage of the vanquished, for the victor gains in self-confidence and the vanquished loses faith in himself. Moreover this or that estimate of one's own forces constitutes an extremely important element in the objective correlation of forces. A direct defeat was experienced by the workers and soldiers of Petrograd, who in their urge forward had come up against the confusedness and contradictions in their own aims, on the one hand, and on the other, the backwardness of the provinces and the front. It was in the capital, therefore, that the consequences of the defeat revealed themselves first and most sharply. The assertion is also untrue, however—although as frequently to be found in the official literature—that for the provinces the July defeat passed almost unnoticed. This is both theoretically improbable, and refuted by the testimony of facts and documents. Whenever great questions arose, the whole country involuntarily and always looked toward Petrograd. The defeat of the workers and soldiers of the capital was therefore bound to produce an enormous impression, and especially upon the more advanced layers of the provinces. Fright, disappointment, apathy, flowed down differently in different parts of the country, but they were to be observed everywhere.

The lowered pressure of the revolution expressed itself first of all in an extraordinary weakening of the resistance of the masses to the enemy. While the troops brought into Petrograd were carrying out official punitive activities in the way of disarming

251

soldiers and workers, semi-volunteer gangs under their protection were attacking with impunity the workers' organizations. After the raid on the editorial rooms of *Pravda* and the printing plant of the Bolsheviks, the headquarters of the metal workers' union was raided. The next blow fell upon the district soviets. Even the Compromisers were not spared. On the 10th, one of the institutions of the party led by the Minister of the Interior, Tseretelli, was attacked. It required no small amount of self-abnegation on the part of Dan to write on the subject of the arriving soldiers: "Instead of the ruin of the revolution, we are now witnessing its new triumph." This triumph went so far that—in the words of the Menshevik, Prushitsky—passers-by on the streets, if they happened to look like workers or be suspected of Bolshevism, were in danger at any moment of cruel beatings. Could there be a more unmistakable symptom of a sharp change in the whole situation?

A member of the Petrograd committee of the Bolsheviks, Latsis—subsequently a well-known member of the "Cheka"—wrote in his diary: "July 9. All our printing plants in the city are destroyed. Nobody dares print our papers and leaflets. We are compelled to set up an underground press. The Vyborg district has become an asylum for all. Here have come both the Petrograd committee and the persecuted members of the Central Committee. In the watchman's room of the Renaud factory there is a conference of the committee with Lenin. The question is raised of a general strike. A division occurs in the committee. I stand for calling the strike. Lenin, after explaining the situation, moves that we abandon it . . . June 12. The counter-revolution is victorious. The soviets are without power. The junkers, running wild, have begun to raid the Mensheviks too. In some sections of the party there is a loss of confidence. The influx of members has stopped. . . . But there is not as yet a flight from our ranks." After the July Days "there was a strong Social Revolutionary influence in the Petersburg factories," writes the worker, Sisko. The isolation of the Bolsheviks automatically increased the weight and self-confidence of the Compromisers. On July 16, a delegate from Vassillievsky Ostrov reported at a Bolshevik city conference that the mood in his district was "in general" hearty, with the exception of a few factories. "In the Baltic factories the Social Revolutionaries and Mensheviks are crowding us out." Here the thing went very far: the factory committee decreed that the Bolsheviks attend the funeral of the slain Cossacks, and this they did. . . . The official loss of membership of the party was, to be sure, insignificant. In the whole district, out of four thousand members not more than a hundred openly withdrew. But a far greater number in those first days quietly stood apart. "The July Days," a worker, Minichev, subsequently remembered, "showed us that in our ranks too there were people who, fearing for their own skin, 'chewed up' their party cards, and denied all connection with the party." "But there were not many of them . . ." he adds reassuringly. "The July events," writes Shliapnikov, "and the whole accompanying campaign of violence and slander against our organization interrupted that growth of our influence which by the beginning of July had reached enormous proportions. . . . The very party became semi-illegal, and had to wage a defensive struggle, relying in the main upon the trade unions and the shop and factory committees."

The charge that the Bolsheviks were in the service of Germany could not but create an impression even upon the Petrograd workers—at least upon a considerable number of them. Those who had been wavering, drew off. Those who were about to join, wavered. Even of those who had already joined, a considerable number withdrew. Together with the Bolsheviks a large part had been played in the July demonstrations by workers belonging to the Social Revolutionaries and Mensheviks. After the blow they were the first to jump back under the banners of their own parties. It now seemed to them that in violating party discipline they had really made a mistake. Broad layers of non-party workers, traveling companions of the party, also stepped away from it under the influence of that officially proclaimed and juridically embellished slander.

In this changed political atmosphere the repressive blows produced a redoubled effect. Olga Ravich, one of the old and active workers of the party, a member of the Petrograd committee, subsequently stated in a report: "The July Days brought such a break-up of the organization that for the first three weeks afterward there could be no talk of any kind of activities." Ravich here has in view, for the most part, public activities of the party. For a long time it was impossible to arrange for the issue of the party paper; there were no printing plants which would agree to serve the Bolsheviks. The resistance here did not always come from the owners, either. In one printing plant the workers threatened to stop work if Bolshevik papers were printed, and the proprietor tore up a contract already concluded. For a certain period of time Petrograd was supplied by the Kronstadt paper.

The extreme Left Wing upon the open arena during those weeks was the group called "Menshevik-Internationalists." The workers eagerly listened to the speeches of Martov, whose fighting instinct woke up in this period of retreat when it was not necessary to lay out new roads for the revolution, but only to fight for what remained of its conquests. Martov's courage was the courage of pessimism. He said at a session of the Executive Committee: "It seems as though they had put a full stop to the revolution. . . . If it has got so that . . . there is no place in the Russian revolution for the voice of the peasantry and the workers, then let us make our exit honorably. Let us accept this challenge not with silent renunciation, but with honest fighting." This proposal to make their exit with honest fighting, Martov made to those party comrades of his, such as Dan and Tseretelli, who regarded the victory of the generals and Cossacks over the workers and soldiers as a victory of the revolution over anarchy. On a background of unrestrained Bolshevik-baiting and continuous belly-crawling by the Compromisers before Cossack trouser-stripes, the conduct of Martov raised him high during those weeks in the eyes of the workers.

The July crisis struck an especially damaging blow at the Petrograd garrison. The soldiers were far behind the workers politically. The soldiers' section of the Soviet remained a bulwark of compromisism after the workers had gone over to the Bolsheviks. This is not in the least contradicted by the fact that the soldiers showed a remarkable readiness to get out their guns. In demonstrations they would play a far more aggressive rôle than the workers, but under blows they would retreat much farther. The wave of hostility against Bolshevism swept up very high in the Petrograd garrison. "After the defeat," says the former soldier, Mitrevich, "I did not show up in my regiment, as I might have been killed there before the squall passed." It was exactly in those more revolutionary regiments which had marched in the front rank in the July Days, and therefore received the most furious blows, that the influence of the party fell lowest. It fell so low that even three months later it was impossible to revive the organization. It was as though these units had been morally disintegrated by too strong a shock. The Military Organization was compelled to draw in very decidedly. "After the July defeat," writes a former soldier, Minichev, "not only in the upper circles of our party, but also in some of the district committees, the comrades were none too friendly toward the Military Organization." In Kronstadt the party lost about 250 members. The mood of the garrison of this Bolshevik fortress declined vastly. The reaction also spread to Helsingfors. Avksentiev, Bunakov, and the lawyer, Sokolov, went up there to bring the Bolshevik ships to repentance. They achieved certain results. By arresting the leading Bolsheviks, by playing up the official slander, by threats, they succeeded in getting a declaration of loyalty even from the Bolshevik battleship, *Petropavlovsk*. Their demand for the surrender of the "instigators" was rejected, however, by all the ships.

It was not greatly different in Moscow. "The attacks of the bourgeois press," remembers Piatnitsky, "produced a panic even in certain members of the Moscow committee." The organization weakened numerically after the July Days. "I will never forget," writes the Moscow worker, Ratekhin, "one mortally hard moment. A plenary session was assembling (of the Zamoskvoretsky district soviet). . . . I saw there were none too many of our comrade Bolsheviks. . . . Steklov, one of the energetic comrades, came right up close to me and, barely enunciating the words, asked: 'Is it true they brought Lenin and Zinoviev in a sealed train? Is it true they are working on German money . . . ?' My heart sank with pain when I heard those questions. Another comrade came up—Konstantinov: 'Where is Lenin? He has beat it, they say. . . . What will happen now?' And so it went." This living picture introduces us correctly to the experience of the advanced workers of that time. "The appearance of the documents published by Alexinsky," writes the Moscow artillerist, Davidovsky, "produced a terrible confusion in the brigade. Even our battery, the most Bolshevik, wavered under the blow of this cowardly lie. . . . It seemed as though we had lost all faith."

"After the July Days," writes V. Yakovleva, at that time a member of the Central Committee and a leader of the work in the extensive Moscow region, "all the reports from the localities described with one voice not only a sharp decline in the mood of the masses, but even a definite hostility to our party. In a good number of cases our speakers were beaten up. The membership fell off rapidly, and several organizations, especially in the southern provinces, even ceased to exist entirely." By the middle of August no noticeable change for the better had taken place. Work was going on among the masses to sustain the influence of the party, but no growth of the organization was observable. In Riazan and Tambov provinces, no new bonds were established, no new Bolshevik nuclei arose. In general, these were the domains of the Social Revolutionaries and Mensheviks.

Evreinov, who directed the work in proletarian Kineshma, remembers what a difficult situation arose after the July events, when at a grand conference of all social organizations the question was put of expelling the Bolsheviks from the soviets. The efflux from the party in some cases reached such a scale that only after a new registration of members could the organization begin to live a proper life. In Tula, thanks to a preliminary serious selection of workers, the organization did not experience a loss of members, but its solidarity with the masses weakened. In Nizhni-Novgorod, after the punitive campaign under the leadership of Colonel Verkhovsky and the Menshevik Khinchuk, a sharp decline set in: at the elections to the city duma the party carried only four deputies. In Kaluga the Bolshevik faction took under consideration the possibility of its being expelled from the soviets. At certain points in the Moscow region the Bolsheviks were obliged to withdraw not only from the soviets, but also from the trade unions.

In Saratov, where the Bolsheviks had kept up very peaceful relations with the Compromisers, and even at the end of June were intending to nominate common candidates with them for the city duma, the soldiers were to such a point incited against the Bolsheviks after the July storm that they would break into campaign meetings, tear the Bolshevik bulletins from people's hands, and beat up their agitators. "It became difficult," writes Lebedev, "to speak at election meetings. They would often yell at us: 'German spies! Provocateurs!' " Among the Saratov Bolsheviks the faint-hearted were numerous: "Many announced their resignation, others went into hiding."

In Kiev, which had long been famous as a Black Hundred center, the baiting of Bolsheviks took on an especially unbridled character, soon even including Mensheviks and Social Revolutionaries. The decline of the revolutionary movement was here felt especially. At the elections to the local duma the Bolsheviks received only 6 per cent of the votes. At a city conference the speakers complained that apathy and inactivity were to be felt everywhere. The party paper was compelled to abandon daily for weekly publication.

The disbandment and transfer of the more revolutionary regiments must in itself not only have lowered the political level of the garrisons, but also grievously affected the local workers, who had felt firmer when friendly troops were standing behind their backs. Thus the removal from Tver of the 57th regiment abruptly changed the political situation both among the soldiers and the workers. Even among the trade unions the influence of the Bolsheviks became negligible. This was still more evident in Tiflis, where the Mensheviks, working hand in hand with the staff, replaced the Bolshevik units with wholly colorless regiments.

At certain points, owing to the constitution of the garrison, the level of the local workers, and other causes accidentally intervening, the political reaction took a paradoxical form. In Yaroslavl, for example, the Bolsheviks were almost completely crowded out of the workers' soviet in July, but kept their predominant influence in the soviet of soldiers' deputies. In certain individual localities, moreover, the July events did seem to pass without effect, not stopping the growth of the party. So far as we can judge, this occurred in those cases where an arrival upon the revolutionary arena of new backward strata coincided with the general retreat. Thus in certain textile districts a considerable influx of women workers into the organization was to be observed in July. But these cases do not alter the general fact of the decline.

The indubitable and even exaggerated acuteness of this reaction to a partial defeat, was in some sense a payment made by the workers, and yet more the soldiers, for their too smooth, too rapid, too uninterrupted flow to the Bolsheviks during the preceding months. This sharp turn in the mood of the masses produced an automatic, and moreover an unerring, selection within the cadres of the party. Those who did not tremble in those days could be relied on absolutely in what was to come. They constituted a nucleus in the shops, in the factories, in the districts. On the eve of October in making appointments and allotting tasks, the organizers would glance round many a time calling to mind who bore himself how in the July Days.

On the front, where all relations are more naked, the July reaction was especially fierce. The staff made use of the events chiefly in order to create special units of "Duty to the Free Fatherland." Each regiment would organize its own shock companies. "I often saw these shock companies," Denikin relates, "and they were always tense and gloomy. The attitude of the rest of the regiment to them was aloof or even hostile." The soldiers rightly saw in these "Divisions of Duty" the nuclei of a Praetorian guard. "The reaction went fast," relates the Social Revolutionary, Degtyarev, who subsequently joined the Bolsheviks. He is speaking of the backward Rumanian front: "Many soldiers were arrested as deserters. The officers lifted their chins and began to ignore the army committees. In some places the officers tried to restore the salute." The commissars carried out a purgation of the army. "Almost every division," writes Stankevich, "had its Bolshevik with his name better known in the army than that of the chief of the division. . . . We gradually removed one celebrity after another." The unsubmissive units were disarmed simultaneously throughout the entire front. In this operation the commanders and commissars relied upon the Cossacks and upon those special companies so hateful to the soldiers.

On the day Riga fell, a conference of the commissars of the Northern front with representatives of the army organizations, declared necessary a more systematic application of severe measures of repression. Some soldiers were shot for fraternizing with the Germans. Many of the commissars, pumping up their nerve with hazy recollections of the French revolution, tried to show the iron fist. They did not understand that the Jacobin commissars were relying upon the lower ranks; they were not sparing the aristocrats and the bourgeoisie; only the authority of a plebeian ruthlessness nerved them to the introduction of severe discipline in the army. These commissars of Kerensky had no popular support under them, no moral halo about their heads. In the eyes of the soldiers they were agents of the bourgeoisie, cattle-drivers of the Entente, and nothing more. They could frighten the army for a time—this indeed to a certain extent they actually did— but they were powerless to resurrect it.

It was reported in the bureau of the Executive Committee in Petrograd at the beginning of August that a favorable change had occurred in the mood of the army, that drilling activities were getting under way. But on the other hand, an increasing tyranny was observable, increasing acts of despotism and oppression. The question of the officers was becoming especially critical. "They were completely isolated, and formed a closed organization of their own." Other testimony bears out the fact that externally a greater order was being established at the front—the soldiers had ceased to rebel about petty and accidental things—but their dissatisfaction with the situation as a whole was only the more intense. In the cautious and diplomatic speech of the Menshevik, Kuchin, at the State Conference, an alarmed warning could be heard underneath the note of reassurance. "There is an indubitable tranquillity," he said, "but there is also something else. There is a feeling of something like disappoinment, and of this feeling also we are extremely afraid. . . ." The temporary victory over the Bolsheviks had been first of all a victory over the new hopes of the soldiers, over their faith in a better future. The masses had become more cautious, they had acquired a certain amount of discipline. But the gulf between the rulers and the soldiers had deepened. What and whom will it swallow up tomorrow?

The July reaction established a kind of decisive water-shed between the February and October revolutions. The workers, the garrisons at the rear, the front—in part even, as will appear later, the peasantry—recoiled and jumped back as though from a blow in the solar plexus. The blow was in reality psychological rather than physical, but it was no less real for that. During the first four months all the mass processes had moved in one direction—to the left. Bolshevism had grown, strengthened, and become bold. But now the movement had run into a stone wall. In reality it had only become clear that further progress along the road of the February revolution was impossible. Many thought that the revolution in general had exhausted itself. The February revolution had indeed exhausted itself to the bottom. This inner crisis in the mass consciousness, combining with the slanders and measures of repression, caused confusion and retreat—in some cases panic. The enemy grew bolder. In the masses themselves all the backward and dubious elements rose to the surface, those impatient of disturbances and deprivations. These receding waves in the flood of the revolution developed an overwhelming force. It seemed as though they were obeying the fundamental laws of social hydrodynamics. You cannot conquer such a wave head on —it is necessary to give way to it, not let it swamp you. Hold out until the wave of reaction has exhausted itself, preparing in the meantime points of support for a new advance.

Observing certain individual regiments which on July 3rd had marched under Bolshevik banners and a week later were calling down awful punishments upon the agents of the Kaiser, educated sceptics might have exulted, it would seem, in a complete victory: Such are your masses, such is their stability and comprehension! But that is a cheap scepticism. If the masses really did change their feelings and thoughts under the influence of accidental circumstances, then that mighty obedience to natural law which characterizes the development of great revolutions would be inexplicable. The deeper the popular millions are caught up by a revolution, and the more regular therefore is its development, the more confidently can you predict the sequence of its further stages. Only in doing this you must remember that the political development of the masses proceeds not in a direct line, but in a complicated curve. And is not this, after all, the essential movement of every material process? Objective conditions were powerfully impelling the workers, soldiers and peasants

toward the banners of the Bolsheviks, but the masses were entering upon this path in a state of struggle with their own past, with
their yesterday's beliefs, and partly also with their beliefs of
today. At a difficult turn, at a moment of failure and disappointment, the old prejudices not yet burnt out would flare up, and
the enemy would naturally seize upon these as upon an anchor
of salvation. Everything about the Bolsheviks which was unclear, unusual, puzzling—the novelty of their thoughts, their
audacity, their contempt for all old and new authorities—all this
now suddenly acquired one simple explanation, convincing in
its very absurdity: They are German spies! In advancing this
accusation against the Bolsheviks, the enemy were really staking
their game upon the enslaved past of the people, upon the relics
among them of darkness, barbarism, superstition. And it was no
fatuous game to play. That gigantic patriotic lie remained
throughout July and August a political factor of primary importance, playing its accompaniment to all the questions of the
day. The ripples of slander spread out over the whole country,
carried by the Kadet press, swallowing up the provinces, the
frontiers, penetrating even into the remotest backwoods. At the
end of July the Ivanovo-Voznesensk organization of the Bolsheviks was still demanding a more energetic campaign against
slander. The question of the relative weight of slander in a political struggle in civilized society still awaits its sociologist.

And yet the reaction among the workers and soldiers, although
nervous and impetuous, was neither deep nor lasting. The more
advanced factories in Petrograd began to recover in the very next
days after the raids. They protested against arrests and slanders,
they came knocking on the doors of the Executive Committee;
they restored their lines of communication. At the Sestroretsk
arms factory, which had been stormed and disarmed, the workers
soon had the helm again in their hands: a general meeting on July
20 resolved that the workers must be paid for the days of the
demonstration, and that the pay should be used entirely in supplying literature to the front. The open agitational work of the Bolsheviks in Petrograd began again, according to the testimony of
Olga Ravich, between the 20th and 30th of July. At meetings
comprising no more than 200 or 300 people, three men began to

appear in different parts of the city: Slutsky, later killed by the Whites in the Crimea, Volodarsky, killed by the Social Revolutionaries in Petrograd, and Yefdokimov, a Petrograd metal worker, one of the ablest orators of the revolution. In August the educational work of the party acquired a broader scope. According to the notes of Raskolnikov, Trotsky, when arrested on the 23rd of July, gave those in prison the following picture of the situation in the city: "The Mensheviks and Social Revolutionaries are continuing their insane baiting of the Bolsheviks. The arrests of our comrades continue, but there is no gloom in party circles On the contrary, everybody is looking to the future with hope, calculating that the repressions will only strengthen the popularity of the party. . . . In the workers' districts no loss of spirit is to be observed." And it is true that a meeting of the workers of 27 plants in the Peterhoff district passed soon after that a resolution of protest against the irresponsible government and its counter-revolutionary policy. The proletarian districts were fast coming to life.

During those very days when up on top, in the Winter Palace or the Tauride, they were creating new Coalitions, tearing them up, and then pasting them together again—in those same days, and even hours, of the 21st and 22nd of July, a gigantic event was taking place in Petrograd, an event hardly noticed in the official sphere, but which signified the formation of another, more solid coalition—a coalition of the Petrograd workers with the soldiers of the active army. Delegates from the front had begun to arrive in the capital with protests from their regiments against the strangling of the revolution at the front. For some days these delegates had been knocking in vain at the doors of the Executive Committee. The Committee did not admit them. It turned them away and recoiled from them. Meanwhile new delegates had been arriving, and following the same course. All these repulsed soldiers would run into each other in the corridors and reception rooms, would complain, abuse the Committee, and then seek some common way out. In this they would be helped by the Bolsheviks. The delegates would decide to exchange thoughts with the workers of the capital, with the soldiers and sailors. And these would meet them with open arms, give them shelter and feed them. At a conference which nobody summoned from above but which grew up spontaneously from below, representatives were present from 29 regiments at the front, from 90 Petrograd factories, from the Kronstadt sailors, and from the surrounding garrisons. At the focus of the conference stood the trench delegates— among them a number of young officers. The Petersburg workers listened to the men from the front eagerly, trying not to let fall a word of their own. The latter told how the offensive and its consequences had devoured the revolution. Those gray soldiers— not in any sense agitators—painted in unstudied words the workaday life of the front. The details were disturbing—they demonstrated so nakedly how everything was crawling back to the old, hateful, pre-revolutionary régime. The contrast between the hopes of yesterday and today's reality struck home to every man there and brought them all to one mood. Although Social Revolutionaries obviously predominated among the men from the front, a drastic Bolshevik resolution was passed almost unanimously: only three men abstained from the voting. That resolution will not remain a dead letter. The dispersing delegates will tell the truth about how the compromise leaders repulsed them, and how the workers received them. And the trenches will believe their delegates. These men would not deceive them.

In the Petrograd garrison itself the beginning of a break was evident toward the end of the month—especially evident after those meetings participated in by delegates from the front. Of course the more heavily stricken regiments could not so soon recover from their apathy. But on the other hand in those units which had preserved longest the patriotic attitude, submitting to discipline throughout the first months of the revolution, the influence of the party was noticeably growing. The Military Organization, which had suffered especially from the persecution, began to get on its feet. As always after a defeat, they looked unfavorably in party circles on the leaders of the military work, laying up against them both actual and imaginary mistakes and deviations. The Central Committee drew the Military Organization closer under its wing, established a more direct control over it through Sverdlov and Dzerzhinsky, and the work got under way again, more slowly than before but more reliably.

By the end of July the position of the Bolsheviks in the Petrograd factories was already restored. The workers were united under the same banners, but they were now different workers, more mature—that is, more cautious but at the same time more resolute. "We have a colossal, an unlimited influence in the factories," reported Volodarsky to a congress of the Bolsheviks on July 27. "The party work is carried out chiefly by the workers themselves. . . . The organization has grown from below, and we have every reason to believe therefore that it will not disintegrate." The Union of Youth had at that time 50,000 members, and was coming continually more and more under the influence of the Bolsheviks. On August 7 the workers' section of the Soviet adopted a resolution demanding the abolition of the death penalty. In sign of protest against the State Conference, the Putilov workers set aside a day's wages for the workers' press. At a conference of factory and shop committees, a resolution was passed unanimously declaring the Moscow Conference "an attempt to organize the counter-revolutionary forces."

Kronstadt was healing its wounds. On July 20, a meeting in Yakorny Square demanded the transfer of power to the soviets, the sending of the Cossacks to the front together with the gendarmes and police, the abolition of the death penalty, the admission of Kronstadt delegates to Tsarskoe Selo to make sure that Nicholas II was adequately guarded, the disbandment of the battalions of death, the confiscation of the bourgeois newspapers, etc. At about the same time the new admiral, Tyrkov, on taking command of the fortress had ordered the red flags lowered on military vessels and the Andreievsky flag raised; the officers and a part of the soldiers had put on chevrons. The Kronstadters protested against this. A government commission to investigate the events of July 3–5 was compelled to return from Kronstadt without results: it was met with hisses, protests and even threats.

A shift was occurring throughout the whole fleet. "At the end of July and the beginning of August," writes one of the Finland leaders, Zalezhsky, "it was clearly felt that the outside reaction had not only not broken the revolutionary strength of Helsingfors, but on the contrary there was to be observed here a sharp shift to the left and a broad growth of sympathy for the

Bolsheviks." The sailors had been to a considerable degree the instigators of the July movement, acting over the head of, and to an extent against the will of the party, which they suspected of moderation and almost of compromisism. The experience of the armed demonstration had shown them that the question of power is not so easily solved. Semi-anarchistic moods had now given place to a confidence in the party. Upon this theme the report of a Helsingfors delegate at the end of July is very interesting: "On the small vessels the influence of the Social Revolutionaries prevails, but on the big battleships, cruisers and destroyers, all the sailors are either Bolsheviks or Bolshevik sympathizers. This was (even before) the attitude of the sailors on the *Petropavlovsk* and the *Republic*, but since July 3–5 there have come over to us the *Gangut*, the *Sebastopol*, the *Rurik*, the *Andrei Pervozvanny*, the *Diana*, the *Gromoboi*, and the *India*. Thus we have in our hands a colossal fighting force. . . . The events of July 3–5 taught the sailors many things, showing them that a mere state of mind is not sufficient for the attainment of a goal."

Although lagging behind Petrograd, Moscow was traveling the same road. "The fumes began gradually to clear up," relates the artillerist Davidovsy. "The soldier masses began to come to themselves, and we again took the offensive all along the line. That lie which stopped for a time the leftward movement of the masses afterward only reinforced their rush to us." Under blows the friendship between factory and barrack had grown closer. A Moscow worker, Strelkov, tells about the close relation gradually established between the Michaelson factory and a neighboring regiment. The workers' and soldiers' committees often decided at joint sessions the practical life-questions of both factory and regiment. The workers arranged cultural and educational evenings for the soldiers, bought them the Bolshevik papers, and gave them help in all kinds of ways. "If somebody was disciplined," says Strelkov, "they would come immediately to us to complain. During the street meetings, if a Michaelson man was insulted anywhere, it was enough for one soldier to hear of it, and they would come running in whole groups to protect him. And there were many insults in those days; they baited us with talk of German gold, treason and the whole vile compromisist lie."

The Moscow conference of factory and shop committees at the end of July opened on a moderate note, but swung strongly to the left during the week of its labors, and towards the end adopted a resolution quite obviously tinged with Bolshevism. In those same days a Moscow delegate, Podbelsky, reported to a party conference: "Six district soviets out of ten are in our hands. . . . Under the present organized slanderous attacks only the worker mass which firmly supports Bolshevism is saving us." At the beginning of August, in elections at the Moscow factories Bolsheviks were already getting elected in place of Mensheviks and Social Revolutionaries. The growth of the party's influence became boisterously evident in the general strike on the eve of the Conference. The official Moscow *Izvestia* wrote: "It is time to understand at last that the Bolsheviks are not an irresponsible group, but one of the divisions of the organized revolutionary democracy, and that broad masses stand behind them, not always disciplined perhaps, but nevertheless devotedly loyal to the revolution."

The July weakening of the position of the proletariat gave courage to the industrialists. A conference of thirteen of the most important business organizations, including the banks, formed a Committee for the Defense of Industry, which took upon itself the leadership of the lockouts and of the whole political offensive against the revolution. The workers put up a resistance. A wave of big strikes and other conflicts swept over the whole country. While the more experienced ranks of the proletariat moved cautiously, the new and fresh layers went the more resolutely into the fight. The metal workers were waiting and getting ready, but the textile workers and the workers of the rubber, leather and paper industries were rushing into the arena. The most backward and submissive strata of the laboring population were beginning to rise. Kiev was disturbed by a riotous strike of the nightwatchmen and janitors. Making the rounds of the houses, the strikers put out lights, removed keys from elevators, opened street doors, etc., etc. Every conflict, no matter upon what theme it arose, showed a tendency to spread to the whole given branch of industry and become a struggle about principles. With the support of labor throughout the whole country, the leatherworkers of Moscow started in August a long and stubborn fight for the right of the factory committees to employ and discharge men. In many instances, especially in the provinces, the strikes were very dramatic, going even to the point of arrests by the strikers of the managers and executives. The government preached self-restraint to the workers, formed a coalition with the capitalists, sent the Cossacks to the Don basin, and doubled the prices of bread and of military supplies. While raising the indignation of the workers to white heat, this policy did not satisfy the capitalists. "The commissars of labor in the localities," complains Auerbach, one of the captains of heavy industry, "had not yet seen the light which had come to Skobelev. . . . In the ministry itself . . . they did not trust their own provincial agents. . . . They would summon representatives of the workers to Petrograd and in the Marble Palace scold them and try to persuade and reconcile them with the industrialists and engineers." But all this came to nothing: "The laboring masses were by this time steadily falling under the influence of the more resolute leaders and those unashamed in their demagoguism."

Economic defeatism became the chief weapon of the industrialists against the dual power in the factories. At a conference of factory and shop committees during the first half of August, the sabotage policy of the industrialists aiming at a disorganization and stoppage of production was exposed in detail. Aside from financial machinations, there was a general resort to the concealment of raw materials, the closing of tool and repair shops, etc. An illuminating testimony as to the sabotage of the capitalists is given by John Reed, who had access as an American correspondent to the most heterogeneous circles, having credentials from the diplomatic agents of the Entente, and who listened to frank confessions from the Russian bourgeois politicians. "The secretary of the Petrograd branch of the Kadet Party," writes Reed, "told me that the breakdown of the country's economic life was part of a campaign to discredit the revolution. An Allied diplomat, whose name I promised not to mention, confirmed this from his own knowledge. I know of certain coal mines near Kharkov which were fired and flooded by the owners, of textile factories at Moscow whose engineers put the machinery out of order when they left, of railroad officials caught by the workers in the act of crippling the locomotives." Such was the cruel economic reality. It corresponded not to the compromisist illusions, not to the politics of the Coalition, but to the preparation of the Kornilov uprising.

At the front the sacred union got along about as badly as at the rear. Arrests of individual Bolsheviks, complains Stankevich, did not settle the question. "Criminality was in the air; its contours were not sharply defined because the whole mass was infected with it." If the soldiers had become more restrained, it was only because they had learned to a certain extent to discipline their hatred; when the dams broke their feelings were only the more clearly revealed. One of the companies of the Dubensky regiment, when ordered to disband for refusing to recognize a newly appointed company commander, induced several other companies and finally the whole regiment to mutiny, and when the regiment commander made an attempt to restore order by force of arms, they killed him with the butts of their rifles. That happened on July 31. If it did not go so far as that in other regiments, the commanding staffs nevertheless felt inwardly that it might do so at any moment.

In the middle of August, General Sherbachev reported to headquarters: "The mood of the infantry, with the exception of the battalions of death, is very unstable. Sometimes in the course of a few days the attitude of certain infantry units will swing sharply to its diametric opposite." Many of the commissars were beginning to understand that the July methods would solve nothing. On August 22, the commissar Yamandt reported: "The practice of military revolutionary court-martial on the western front is causing a dreadful disaccord between the commanding staff and the mass of the population, discrediting the very idea of these courts. . . ." The Kornilov program of salvation had already, before the revolt of headquarters, been sufficiently tried out, and had led into the same blind alley.

What the possessing classes feared most of all was the specter of a disintegration of the Cossacks. Here the last bulwark threatened to give way. In February the Cossack regiments in Petrograd had surrendered the monarchy without resistance. In their own country, to be sure, in Novocherkassk, the Cossack authorities had tried to conceal the telegram about the revolution, and had car-

ried out with the usual solemnity the March 1st mass in memory
of Alexander II. But in the long run the Cossacks were willing
to get along without the tzar, and had even managed to dig up
republican traditions in their own past. But farther than this
they would not go. From the beginning the Cossacks refused to
send their deputies to the Petrograd soviet in order not to put
themselves on a level with the workers and soldiers; and they
formed a soviet of the Cossack armies which brought together
all the twelve Cossackdoms in the person of their rear commanders.
The bourgeoisie tried, and not without success, to base upon the
Cossacks their plans against the workers and peasants.

The political rôle of these Cossacks was determined by their
special situation in the state. The Cossacks had from long ago
been a unique privileged caste of a lower order. The Cossacks paid
no taxes and enjoyed a considerably larger land allotment than
the peasant. In the three neighboring territories, Don, Kuban
and Tver, the Cossack population of 3 million owned 23 million
dessiatins of land, while the 4.3 million peasants in the same territories owned only 6 million dessiatins. The Cossacks owned on
the average, that is, five times as much *per capita* as the peasants.
Among the Cossacks themselves the land was divided, to be sure,
very unequally. They had here their landlords and Kulaks, even
more powerful than in the North; they had also their poor. Every
Cossack was obliged to present himself at the demand of the
state on his own horse and with his own equipment. The rich
Cossacks more than covered this expense with their freedom from
taxes; but the lower ranks were bowed down under the burden
of this liability to service. These fundamental data sufficiently
explain the self-contradictory position of the Cossackdom as a
whole. In its lower strata it came in close contact with the peasantry; in its upper, with the landlords. At the same time the
upper and lower strata were united by a consciousness of their
special situation, their position as a chosen people, and were accustomed to look down not only upon the worker but also upon
the peasant. This was what made the middle Cossack so useful
for putting down revolts.

During the years of the war, when the younger generations
were at the front, the old men, carrying conservative traditions

and closely bound up with their officers, became the bosses. Under
the pretext of a resurrection of Cossack democracy, the Cossack
landlords during the first months of the revolution summoned the
so-called "troop rings" which elected atamans—presidents of a
kind—and under them "troop governments." The official commissars and soviets of the non-Cossack population had no power
in the Cossack territories, for the Cossacks were stronger, richer
and better armed. The Social Revolutionaries tried to form common soviets of peasant and Cossack deputies, but the Cossacks
would not consent, since they feared, rightly enough, that an
agrarian revolution would take away a part of their land. It was
no empty phrase that Chernov let fall as Minister of Agriculture:
"It will be necessary for the Cossacks to make a little room on
their lands." Still more important was the fact that the local
peasants and infantry soldiers were themselves oftener and oftener
addressing such remarks as this to the Cossacks: "We will get
at your land, you have bossed things long enough." That was the
aspect of affairs at the rear, in the Cossack villages—partly also
in the Petrograd garrison, the political focus. And that explains
the conduct of the Cossack regiments in the July demonstration.

On the front the situation was essentially different. In the
summer of 1917 there were 162 regiments in the active Cossack
army, and 171 separate squadrons. Torn away from their village
connections, the Cossacks at the front shared the experiences of
the war with the whole army, and they passed through, although
somewhat belatedly, the same evolution as the infantry—lost
faith in the victory, became embittered at the insane confusion,
grumbled against the command, got to longing for peace and
for home. As many as 45 regiments and 65 squadrons were gradually drawn away for police duty at the front and in the rear! The
Cossacks had again been turned into gendarmes. The soldiers,
workers and peasants grumbled against them, reminding them
of their hangman's work in 1905. Many of the Cossacks, who had
begun to enjoy a pride in their conduct in February, began to
feel a gnawing at the heart. The Cossack began to curse his whip,
and would often refuse to include a whip in his equipment. There
were not many deserters, though, among the Don and Kuban
Cossacks; they were afraid of their old men in the village. In

general the Cossack units remained considerably longer in control of the officers than the infantry.

From the Don and the Kuban news came to the front that the Cossack chiefs, along with the old men, had set up their own government without asking the Cossacks at the front. This awakened sleeping social antagonisms: "We will show them when we get home," the men at the front would say. The Cossack general, Krasnov, one of the leaders of the counter-revolution on the Don, has vividly described how the strong Cossack units at the front were gradually torn asunder: "Meetings began to be held and they would pass the wildest resolutions. . . . The Cossacks stopped cleaning and feeding their horses regularly. There was no thought of any kind of serious occupation. The Cossacks decorated themselves with crimson bands, decked themselves out with red ribbon, and would not hear of any kind of respect for their officers." Before finally arriving at this condition, however, the Cossack had long hesitated, scratching his head and wondering which way to turn. At a critical moment, therefore, it was not easy to guess how this or that Cossack unit would behave.

On August 8 the troop ring on the Don formed a bloc with the Kadets for the elections to the Constituent Assembly. News of this immediately reached the army. "Among the Cossacks," writes the Cossack officer Yanov, "this bloc was greeted very adversely. The Kadet Party had no roots in the army." As a matter-of-fact the army hated the Kadets, identifying them with everything that was strangling the popular masses. "The old folks have sold you out to the Kadets," the soldiers would tease them. "We will show them!" the Cossacks would reply. On the Southwestern front the Cossack units passed a special resolution declaring the Kadets "the sworn enemies and enslavers of the working people," and demanded the expulsion from their troop ring of all those who dared to enter an agreement with the Kadets.

Kornilov, himself a Cossack, counted strongly on the help of the Cossacks, especially those of the Don, and filled out with Cossack units the division designated for his *coup d'état*. But the Cossacks never stirred in behalf of this "son of a peasant." The villagers were ready to defend their land in their own territory ferociously enough, but they had no desire to get mixed up in somebody else's quarrel. The Third Cavalary Corps also failed to justify the hopes placed in it. Although unfriendly to fraternization with the Germans, on the Petrograd front the Cossacks willingly came to meet the soldiers and sailors. It was this fraternization which broke up Kornilov's plan without bloodshed. In this way the last prop of the Old Russia, the Cossacks, weakened and crumbled away.

During this same time and far beyond the border of Russia, on French territory, an experiment in the "resurrection" of the Russian armies was carried out on a laboratory scale—beyond the reach of the Bolsheviks and therefore the more convincing. During the summer and autumn despatches appeared in the Russian press, but remained almost unnoticed in the whirlwind of events, telling of armed revolts among the Russian troops in France. As early as January 1917—that is, before the revolution—the soldiers of the two Russian brigades in France, to quote the officer Lissovsky, "were firmly convinced that they had all been sold to the French in exchange for ammunition." The soldiers were not so badly mistaken, either. For their Allied masters they had not the "slightest sympathy," and in their own officers not the slightest confidence. The news of the revolution found these exported brigades politically prepared, so to speak, yet nevertheless, it took them unawares. An explanation of the revolution was not to be expected from the officers—the officers were the more at a loss, the higher they were—but democratic patriots from among the emigrants appeared in the camps. "It was observed more than once," writes Lissovsky, "that certain of the diplomats and officers of the guard regiments . . . would obligingly draw up chairs for the former emigrants." Elective institutions were formed among the regiments, and at the head of the committee would soon arrive a Lettish soldier. Here, too, then, they had their "foreign elements." The first regiment, formed in Moscow and consisting almost wholly of workers, clerks and salesmen—proletarian and semi-proletarian elements in general—had first stepped on French soil a year before, and during the winter had fought well on the fields of Champagne. But "the disease of demoralization struck this same regiment first." The second regiment, which had

272

in its ranks a large percentage of peasants, remained longer tranquil. The second brigade, which consisted almost exclusively of Siberian peasants, seemed wholly reliable. Very soon after the February revolution the first brigade broke discipline. It did not want to fight either for Alsace or for Lorraine; it did not want to die for beautiful France. It wanted to try living in the New Russia. The brigade was withdrawn to the rear, and quartered in the center of France, in Camp La Courtine. "Amid quiet bourgeois villages," relates Lissovsky, "about ten thousand mutinous Russian soldiers, armed, having no officers, and absolutely refusing to submit to anybody, lived in this vast camp an entirely unique and special kind of life." Here Kornilov had an extraordinary opportunity to apply his methods for restoring the army, with the co-operation of his warm sympathizers, Poincaré and Ribot. The commander-in-chief telegraphed a command that the soldiers be brought "into submission," and sent to Salonika. But the rebels would not surrender. On the 1st of September heavy artillery was brought up, and placards posted within the camp quoting the threatening telegram of Kornilov. But just here a new complication thrust itself into the course of events. News appeared in the French papers that Kornilov himself had been declared a traitor and a counter-revolutionist. The mutinous soldiers firmly decided that there was no reason why they should die in Salonika—especially at the command of a traitor-general. These workers and peasants who had been sold for ammunition decided to stand up for themselves. They refused to hold conversations with anybody whatever from the outside. From then on not one single soldier ever left the camp.

The second Russian brigade was brought into action against the first. The artillery occupied positions on the nearby mountain slopes, the infantry, employing all the rules of engineering science, dug trenches and approaches to La Courtine. The surroundings were strongly occupied by Alpine sharpshooters, to make sure that no single Frenchman should enter the theater of war of the two Russian brigades. Thus the military authorities of France set the stage on their territory for a Russian civil war, prudently surrounding it with a hedge of bayonets. This was merely a re-

273

hearsal. Later on the French ruling classes organized a civil war on the territory of Russia herself, surrounding it with the barbed ring of the blockade.

"A regular methodical bombardment of the camp began." Several hundred soldiers came out of the camp, agreeing to surrender. They were received, and the artillery fire immediately began again. This lasted for four days and four nights. The La Courtine men surrendered in detachments. On the 6th of September, there remained about two hundred men who had decided not to give themselves up alive. At their head stood a Ukrainian, Globa, a Baptist, a fanatic: in Russia they would have called him a Bolshevik. Under cover of artillery, machine gun and rifle fire, combining in one general roar, the place was actually stormed. In the end the rebels were subdued. The number of victims is unknown. Law and order was in any case re-established. But in just a few weeks the second brigade which had bombarded the first was seized with the same disease.

The Russian soldiers had carried this dreadful infection with them across the sea in their canvas knapsacks, in the linings of their coats, in the secret places of their hearts. This dramatic episode at La Courtine is significant; it was a kind of consciously arranged ideal experiment, almost as though under a bell-glass, for testing out those inner processes in the Russian army, the foundation for which had been laid by the whole past history of the country.

Chapter XII

THE RISING TIDE

THE strong weapon of slander proved a two-edged one. If the Bolsheviks are German spies, why does the news come chiefly from sources most hateful to the people? Why is it the Kadet press, which has always attributed to the workers and soldiers the lowest possible motives, that is loudest and clearest of all in accusing the Bolsheviks? Why does that reactionary overseer or engineer who has been crouching in a corner since the insurrection, now suddenly jump out and begin to curse the Bolsheviks? Why have the most reactionary officers begun to swagger in their regiments? And why in accusing "Lenin & Co." do they shake their fists in the very faces of the soldiers, as though *they* were the traitors?

Every factory had its Bolsheviks. "Do I look like a German spy, boys, eh?" a fitter would ask, or a cabinet-maker, whose whole life history was known to the workers. At times even the Compromisers, in their struggle against the assault of the counter-revolution, would go farther than they planned and unintentionally smooth the path for the Bolsheviks. The soldier Pireiko tells how at a soldiers' meeting an army physician Markovich, a follower of Plekhanov, refuted the accusation of espionage against Lenin, in order the more effectively to attack his political views as inconsistent and ruinous. In vain! "If Lenin is intelligent and not a spy, not a traitor, and wants to make peace, then we are for him," said the soldiers after the meeting.

After the temporary halt in its growth Bolshevism again began confidently spreading its wings. "The compensation is coming fast," wrote Trotsky in the middle of August. "Driven, persecuted, slandered, our party has never grown so swiftly as in recent days. And this process will not be long in running from the capital into the provinces, from the cities into the villages and the army. . . . All the toiling masses of the country will

275

have learned, when new trials come, to unite their fate with the fate of our party."

As before, Petrograd took the lead. It seemed as though an almighty broom was busy in the factories, sweeping the influence of the Compromisers out of every last nook and cranny. "The last fortresses of defensism are falling . . ." said the Bolshevik paper. "Was it so long ago that the defensist gentlemen were the sole bosses in the giant Obukhovsky factory? . . . Now they don't dare show their faces in that factory." About 550,000 votes were cast in the elections for the Petrograd city duma on August 20, considerably less than in the July elections for the district dumas. After losing upwards of 375,000, the Social Revolutionaries still got over 200,000 votes, or 37 per cent of the whole number. The Kadets got a fifth of the whole number. "A pitiful 23,000 votes," writes Sukhanov, "were cast for our Menshevik ballot." Unexpectedly to everybody, the Bolsheviks got almost 200,000 votes or about one third of the whole number.

At a regional conference of trade unions which took place in the Urals in the middle of August, uniting 150,000 workers, resolutions of a Bolshevik character were carried upon all questions. In Kiev at a conference of the factory and shop committees on the 20th of August, the Bolshevik resolution was carried by a majority of 161 votes against 35, with 13 abstaining. At the democratic elections for the city duma of Ivonovo-Voznesensk which coincided exactly with the Kornilov revolt, the Bolsheviks got 58 seats out of 102, the Social Revolutionaries 24, the Mensheviks 4. In Kronstadt a Bolshevik, Brekman, was elected president of the soviet, and a Bolshevik, Pokrovsky, burgomaster. It was far from being so obvious everywhere, and in some places there was a decline. But during August Bolshevism was growing almost throughout the whole breadth of the land.

The revolt of Kornilov gave a powerful impetus to the radicalization of the masses. Slutsky has recalled upon this theme a word of Marx: a revolution needs from time to time the whip of the counter-revolution. The danger had awakened not only energy, but penetration. The collective thought was working at a higher tension. There was no lack of data from which to draw conclusions. A Coalition had been declared necessary for the defense of the revolution, and meanwhile the ally in the Coalition had turned up on the side of the counter-revolution. The Moscow Conference had been declared a review of the national unity. Only the Central Committee of the Bolsheviks had given warning: "The Conference . . . will inevitably turn into the instrument of a counter-revolutionary conspiracy." Events had verified this. And now Kerensky was declaring: "The Moscow Conference . . . this was a prologue to the 27th of August . . . Here was carried out an estimate of forces . . . Here the future dictator, Kornilov, was first introduced to Russia. . . ." As though Kerensky had not been the initiator, organizer and president of this conference, and as though it were not he who had introduced Kornilov as "the first soldier" of the revolution. As though it had not been the Provisional Government which armed Kornilov with the death penalty against the soldier, and as though the warnings of the Bolsheviks had not been denounced as demagoguism.

The Petrograd garrison remembered, moreover, that two days before the uprising of Kornilov, the Bolsheviks had voiced the suspicion at a meeting of the soldiers' section that the progressive regiments were being removed from the capital with counter-revolutionary aims. To this the representatives of the Mensheviks and Social Revolutionaries had replied with a threatening demand: Do not venture upon a discussion of the military orders of General Kornilov. A resolution had been introduced and carried in that spirit. "The Bolsheviks, it seems, were not talking through their hats!" That is what the non-party worker and soldier must be saying to himself now.

If the conspiring generals were guilty, according to the belated accusation of the Compromisers themselves, not only of surrendering Riga but also of the July breach, then why bait the Bolsheviks and execute the soldiers? If military provocateurs attempted to bring the workers and soldiers into the streets on the 27th of August, did they not play their rôle also in the bloody encounters of July 4? Moreover, what is the position of Kerensky in all this history? Against whom did he summon the Third Cavalry Corps? Why did he name Savinkov Governor-

277

general, and Filonenko his assistant? And who is this Filonenko, this candidate for the directory? An unexpected answer came from the armored-car division: Filonenko, who had served with them as a lieutenant, had inflicted the worst kinds of taunts and humiliations upon the soldiers. Where did this shady performer, Zavoiko, come from? What, in general, does this selection of swindlers for the highest positions signify?

The facts were simple, remembered by many, accessible to all, irrefutable and deadly. The echelons of the Savage Division, the torn-up rails, the mutual accusations between the Winter Palace and headquarters, the testimonies of Savinkov and Kerensky— all spoke for themselves. What an irrefutable indictment of the Compromisers and their régime! The meaning of the baiting of Bolsheviks had become utterly clear: it had been an indispensable element in the preparation for a *coup d'état*. The workers and soldiers, as they began to see all this, were seized with a sharp feeling of shame. Lenin is in hiding, then, merely because they have vilely slandered him. The others are in jail, then, to please the Kadets, the generals, the bankers, the diplomats of the Entente. The Bolsheviks, then, are not office-seekers, and they are hated up above exactly because they do not want to join that stock company which they call a Coalition! This was the understanding arrived at by the hard workers, by the simple people, by the oppressed. And out of these moods, together with a feeling of guilt before the Bolsheviks, grew an unconquerable loyalty to the party and confidence in its leaders.

The old soldiers, the standing elements of the army, the artillery men, the staff of non-commissioned officers, resisted up to the very last days, with all their power. They did not want to set a cross against all their fighting labors, their sacrifices, their deeds of heroism: can it be that all that was squandered for nothing? But when the last prop was knocked out from under them, they turned sharply—left about face!—to the Bolsheviks. Now they had utterly come over to the revolution, their non-commissioned officer chevrons, their soldier wills tempered in battle, their bulging jaw muscles, and all. They had got fooled on the war, but this time they would carry the thing through to the end.

In the reports of local authorities, both military and civil, Bolshevism had become in these days a synonym for every kind of mass activity, every decisive demand, every resistance against exploitation, every forward motion—in a word, it had become another name for revolution. Does that mean that all these things *are* Bolshevism? the strikers would ask themselves—and the protesting sailors, and the dissatisfied soldiers' wives, and the muzhiks in revolt. The masses were, so to speak, compelled from above to identify their intimate thoughts and demands with the slogans of Bolshevism. Thus the revolution turned to its own uses a weapon directed against it. In history not only does the reasonable become nonsensical, but also, when the course of evolution requires it, the nonsensical becomes reasonable.

The change in the political atmosphere revealed itself very clearly in the joint session of the Executive Committees of August 30, when delegates from Kronstadt demanded that they receive seats in that high body. Could it be possible that, where these unbridled Kronstadters had been subjected only to condemnations and excommunications, their representatives were now to take seats? But how refuse them? Only yesterday the Kronstadt sailors and soldiers had come to the defense of Petrograd. Sailors from the *Aurora* were even now guarding the Winter Palace. After whispering among themselves, the leaders offered the Kronstadters four seats with a voice but not a vote. The concession was accepted dryly, without expressions of gratitude.

"After the attempt of Kornilov," relates Chinenov, a soldier of the Moscow garrison, "all the troops acquired a Bolshevik color. . . . All were struck by the way in which the statement (of the Bolsheviks) came true . . . that General Kornilov would soon be at the gates of Petrograd." Mitrevich, a soldier of the armored-car division, recalls the heroic legends which passed from mouth to mouth after the victory over the rebellious generals: "They were nothing but stories of bravery and of great deeds, and of how—well, if there is such bravery, we can fight the whole world. Here the Bolsheviks came into their own."

Antonov-Ovseënko, liberated from prison on the day of the Kornilov campaign, went immediately to Helsingfors. "An immense change had occurred in the masses," he says. At the re-

gional congress of the Finland soviets the Right Social Revolutionaries were in a tiny minority; the Bolsheviks, in coalition with
the Left Social Revolutionaries, had taken the lead. As president
of the regional committee of the soviet they elected Smilga, who
in spite of his extreme youth was a member of the Central Committee of the Bolsheviks—a man with a strong urge leftward, and
who had already in the April Days revealed an inclination to shake
down the Provisional Government. As president of the Helsingfors soviet, which rested upon the garrison and the Russian workers, they elected Scheineman, a Bolshevik, the future director of
the Soviet State Bank—a man of cautious and bureaucratic
mould, but who at that time was marching abreast with the other
leaders. The Provisional Government had forbidden the Finlanders to convoke the Seim, dissolved by it. The regional committee
suggested that the Seim assemble, and volunteered to defend it.
The committee refused to fulfil the orders of the Provisional Government withdrawing various military units from Finland. Essentially the Bolsheviks had here already established a dictatorship of the soviets in Finland.

The Bolshevik paper in Kiev stated on the 19th of September:
"In the election for the soviets twelve comrades were elected
from the arsenal—all Bolsheviks. All the Menshevik candidates
were defeated. The same thing is happening in a whole series of
other plants." Similar despatches are to be found from now on
every day in the pages of the workers' press. The hostile press tried

in vain to minimize or hush up the growth of Bolshevism. The masses, leaping forward, seemed to be trying to make up for the time lost in their former waverings, hesitations, and temporary retreats. There was a universal, obstinate and unrestrainable flood tide.

A member of the Central Committee of the Bolsheviks, Barbara Yakovleva, from whom we learned in July and August about the extreme weakening of the Bolsheviks in the whole Moscow region, now testifies to an abrupt change. "During the second half of September," she reports to the conference, "the workers of the regional bureau made the rounds of the region. . . . Their impressions were absolutely identical: everywhere, in all the provinces, the process was under way of general Bolshevization of the masses, and everyone observed likewise that the villages were demanding Bolsheviks. . . ." In those localities where after the July Days the organizations of the party had disintegrated they were now reborn and were growing rapidly. In the districts into which Bolsheviks had not been admitted, party nuclei were now spontaneously arising. Even in the backward provinces of Tambovsk and Riazan—in those bulwarks of the Social Revolutionaries and Mensheviks, which formerly in making their rounds the Bolsheviks had passed by through sheer hopelessness—a veritable revolution was now occurring: the influence of the Bolsheviks was growing by leaps and bounds, and the compromisist organizations were dissolving.

The reports of the delegates to the Bolshevik conference of the Moscow region, a month after the Kornilov uprising and a month before the insurrection of the Bolsheviks, are filled with confidence and enthusiasm. In Nizhni-Novgorod, after a two months' decline, the party is again living a full life. Social Revolutionary workers are coming over to the Bolsheviks by the hundreds. In Tver a broad party work has developed only since the Kornilov days. The Compromisers are going to pieces; nobody listens to them; they are being chased out. In Vladimir province the Bolsheviks have grown so strong that at a provincial congress of the soviets only five Mensheviks are to be found and only three Social Revolutionaries. In Ivanovo-Voznesensk, the Russian Manchester, the whole work in the soviets, the duma, and the zemstvo has been turned over to the Bolsheviks as the semi-sovereign masters.

The organizations of the party are growing, but its force of attraction is growing incomparably faster. The lack of correspondence between the technical resources of the Bolsheviks and their relative political weight finds its expression in the small number of members of the party compared to the colossal growth of its influence. Events are sweeping the masses so powerfully and swiftly into their whirlpool, that the workers and soldiers have no time to organize themselves in a party. They have no time even to understand the necessity of any special party organization. They drink up the Bolshevik slogans just as naturally as they breathe the air. That the party is a complicated laboratory in which these slogans have been worked out on the basis of collective experience, is still not clear to their minds. There are over twenty million people represented in the soviets. The party, which had on the very eve of the October revolution only 240,000 members, was more and more confidently leading these millions, through the medium of the trade unions, the factory and shop committees, and the soviets.

Throughout this vast country, shaken to its depths and with an inexhaustible variety of local conditions and political levels of development, some sort of elections were going on every day— to the dumas, the zemstvos, the soviets, the factory and shop committees, the trade unions, the army or land committees. And throughout all these elections there appears like a red thread one unchanging fact: the growth of the Bolsheviks. The elections to the district dumas of Moscow astonished the country especially with the sharp change they indicated in the mood of the masses. The "great" party of the Social Revolutionaries retained at the end of September only 54,000 of the 375,000 votes it had counted in June. The Mensheviks had fallen from 76,000 to 16,000. The Kadets kept 101,000, having lost only 8,000. The Bolsheviks, on the other hand, had risen from 75,000 to 198,000. Whereas in June the Social Revolutionaries had 58 per cent of the votes, in September the Bolsheviks had approximately 52 per cent. The garrison voted 90 per cent for the Bolsheviks; in some detachments over 95 per cent. In the shops of the heavy artillery,

the Bolsheviks got 2,286 out of 2,347 votes. A considerable lowering of the number of voters was due to the fact that many
small town people, who in the vapor of their first illusions had
joined the Compromisers, fell back soon after into political non-
existence. The Mensheviks were melting away completely; the
Social Revolutionaries received half as many votes as the Kadets;
the Kadets received half as many as the Bolsheviks. Those September votes for the Bolsheviks were won in a bitter struggle
with all the other parties. They were strong votes. They were
to be relied on. The wiping out of intermediate groups, the significant stability of the bourgeois camp, the gigantic growth of
the most hated and persecuted proletarian party—these were
unmistakable symptoms of a revolutionary crisis. "Yes, the Bolsheviks worked zealously and unceasingly," writes Sukhanov,
who himself belonged to the shattered party of the Mensheviks.
"They were among the masses, in the factories, every day and
all the time. . . . They became the party of the masses because
they were always there, guiding both in great things and small
the whole life of the factories and barracks. The masses lived and
breathed together with the Bolsheviks. They were wholly in the
hands of the party of Lenin and Trotsky."

On the front the political picture was more variegated. There
were regiments and divisions which had never yet heard or seen
a Bolshevik. Many of them were sincerely astounded when they
were themselves accused of Bolshevism. On the other hand, divisions were to be found which took their own anarchistic moods,
mingled with a dash of Black Hundredism, for pure Bolshevism.
The mood of the front was leveling out in one direction, but in
that colossal political flood which took the trenches for its channels there occurred many whirlpools and backwashes, and there
was no little turgidity.

In September the Bolsheviks broke through the cordon and got
access to the front, from which they had been cut off in dead
earnest for the last two months. Even now the official veto was
not removed. The compromisist committees did everything to
keep the Bolsheviks out of their units; but all efforts were vain.
The soldiers had heard so much about their own "Bolshevism"
that they were all, without exception, dying to see and hear a

live Bolshevik. The formal obstacles, delays, and complications thought up by the committee men were wiped away by the insistence of the soldiers as soon as the news came that a Bolshevik had arrived. The old revolutionist, Efgenia Bosh, who did a great work in the Ukraine, has left brilliant memoirs of her bold excursions into the primitive soldier jungle. The frightened warnings of her friends, both sincere and insincere, were everywhere refuted. In those divisions which had been described as bitterly hostile to the Bolsheviks, the orator, approaching her theme very cautiously, would soon find out that the listeners were with her. "There was no coughing, or hawking, or nose-blowing—those first indications of boredom in a soldier audience; the silence and order were complete." The meetings would end in stormy ovations in honor of that bold agitator. In general, the whole journey of Efgenia Bosh along the front was a kind of triumphal procession. Less heroic, less effective, but essentially the same, was the experience of agitators of less distinguished caliber.

New ideas, or ideas convincing in a new way, new slogans, new generalizations, were bursting into the stagnant life of the trenches. The millions of soldier brains were grinding over the events, casting the balance of their political experience. "Dear comrade-workers and soldiers," writes a soldier at the front to the editor of the party paper, "do not give free rein to that bad letter K which has sold the whole world into bloody slaughter. That includes the first murderer, Kolka (Nicholas II), Kerensky, Kornilov, Kaledin, the Kadets, all of them on one letter K. The Kossacks are also dangerous for us . . . Sidor Nikolaiev." Do not look for superstition here: this is merely a method of political mnemonics.

The insurrection, starting at headquarters, could not but shock every fiber of the soldiers' being. That external discipline, the effort to restore which had cost so many victims, was again going to pieces on all sides. The military commissar of the western front, Zhdanov, reported: "The general mood is nervous . . . suspicious of officers, waiting; refusal to obey orders is explained on the ground that they are Kornilov orders, and should not be obeyed." Stankevich, who replaced Filonenko in the position of head commissar, writes to the same effect: "The soldier

masses . . . felt themselves surrounded on all sides by treason. . . . Anyone who tried to dissuade them from this seemed
also a traitor."

For the ranking officers the collapse of Kornilov's adventure
meant the collapse of their last hope. Even before that, the self-
confidence of the commanding staff had been none too brilliant.
We observed during the last days of August the military conspirators in Petrograd, drunk, boastful and weak-willed. The officers now felt utterly despised and rejected. "That hatred, that
baiting," writes one of them, "that complete inactivity, and
eternal expecting of arrest and shameful death, drove the officers into the roadhouses, the private dining rooms, the hotels.
. . . In this drunken vapor the officers were drowned." In contrast to this, the soldiers and sailors were more sober than ever
before. They were caught up by a new hope.

"The Bolsheviks," according to Stankevich, "lifted up their
heads, and felt themselves to be complete masters in the army.
The lower committees began to turn into Bolshevik nuclei. Every
election in the army showed an amazing Bolshevik growth. And
moreover it is impossible to ignore the fact that the best and
most tightly disciplined army, not only on the Northern front
but perhaps on the whole Russian front, the Fifth Army, was the
first to elect a Bolshevik army committee."

The fleet was still more clearly, concisely and colorfully going
Bolshevik. On September 8, the Baltic sailors raised the battle-
flags on all ships as an expression of their readiness to fight for
the transfer of power to the proletariat and peasantry. The fleet
demanded an immediate armistice on all fronts, the transfer of
land to the peasant committees, and the establishment of workers'
control of production. Three days later the central committee
of the Black Sea Fleet, less advanced and more moderate, supported the Baltic sailors, adopting the slogan of Power to the
Soviets. The same slogan was adopted in the middle of September
by 23 Siberian and Lettish infantry regiments of the Twelfth
Army. Other divisions followed steadily. The demand for Power
to the Soviets never again disappeared from the order of the day
in the army or the fleet.

"The sailors' meetings," says Stankevich, "nine-tenths of

them, consisted of Bolsheviks only." The new head commissar happened to be defending the Provisional Government before the sailors at Reval. He felt the futility of the attempt from the very first words. At the mere word "government" the audience drew together with hostility: "A wave of indignation, hatred and distrust instantly seized the whole crowd. It was clear, strong, passionate, irresistible, and poured out in one unanimous shout: *Down with it!*" We cannot withhold a word of praise to this story-teller who does not forget to see beauty in the attack of a crowd mortally hostile to him.

The question of peace, driven underground for these two months, now emerges with tenfold strength. At a meeting of the Petersburg Soviet, the officer Dubassov, arriving from the front, declares: "Whatever you may say here, the soldiers will not fight any more." Voices reply: "Even the Bolsheviks don't say that!" But the officer, not a Bolshevik, comes back: "I tell you what I know, and what the soldiers directed me to tell you." Another man from the front, a gloomy soldier in a long coat soaked with the filth and stink of the trenches, declared to the Petrograd Soviet in those same September days that the soldiers needed peace, any kind of peace, even "some sort of an indecent peace." Those harsh soldier words gave the soviet a fright. That is how far things had gone then! The soldiers at the front were not little children. They excellently understood that with the present "war map," the peace could only be an oppressor's peace. And for this understanding of his, the trench delegate purposely chose the crudest words possible, expressing the whole force of his disgust for a Hohenzollern peace. But with this very nakedness of his mind the soldier compelled his hearers to understand that there was no other road, that the war had unwound the spirit of the army, that an immediate peace was necessary no matter what it cost. The bourgeois press seized the words of the trench orator with malicious joy, attributing them to the Bolsheviks. That phrase about an indecent peace was henceforward continually to the fore as an extreme expression of the savagery and depravity of the people!

*

As A general rule the Compromisers were not at all inclined, like the political dilettant Stankevich, to admire the beauties of that rising tide which threatened to wash them off the revolutionary arena. They learned from day to day with amazement and horror that they no longer possessed any power of resistance. As a matter of fact, under the confidence of the masses in the Compromisers there had lain concealed from the first hours of the revolution a misunderstanding—historically inevitable but not long-lasting. Only a few months had been required to clear it up. The Compromisers had been compelled to talk with the workers and soldiers in a wholly different language from that which they employed in the Executive Committee, and still more in the Winter Palace. The responsible leaders of the Social Revolutionaries and Mensheviks, were more and more afraid as weeks passed, to come out into the open square. Agitators of the second and third rank would go out, and they would accommodate themselves to the social radicalism of the people with the help of equivocal phrases. Or else they would become sincerely infected with the mood of the factories, mines and barracks, would begin to speak their language, and soon break away from their own parties.

The sailor Khovrin tells in his memoirs how the seamen who considered themselves Social Revolutionaries would in reality defend the Bolshevik platform. This was to be observed everywhere. The people knew what they wanted, but they did not know how to call it by name. That "misunderstanding" which belonged to the inner essence of the February revolution had a universal popular mass character—especially in the villages, where it lasted longer than in the cities. Only experience could introduce order into this chaos. Events, little and great, were tirelessly shaking up the mass parties, bringing their membership into correspondence with their policy and not their sign-boards.

An excellent example of this *qui pro quo* between the Compromisers and the masses, is to be seen in an oath taken at the beginning of July by 2,000 Donetz miners, kneeling with uncovered heads in the presence of a crowd of 5,000 people and with its participation. "We swear by our children, by God, by

287

the heaven and earth, and by all things that we hold sacred in the world, that we will never relinquish the freedom bought with blood on the 28th of February, 1917; believing in the Social Revolutionaries and the Mensheviks, we swear we will never listen to the Leninists, for they, the Bolshevik-Leninists, are leading Russia to ruin with their agitation, whereas the Social Revolutionaries and Mensheviks united in a single union, say: The land to the people, land without indemnities; the capitalist structure must fall after the war and in place of capitalism there must be a socialist structure. . . . We give our oath to march forward under the lead of these parties, not stopping even at death." This oath of the miners directed against the Bolsheviks in reality led straight to the Bolshevik revolution. The February shell and the October kernel appear in this naïve and fervent picture so clearly as in a way to exhaust the whole problem of the Permanent Revolution.

By September the Donetz miners, without betraying either themselves or their oath, had already turned their backs on the Compromisers. The most backward ranks of the Ural miners had done the same thing. A member of the Executive Committee, the Social Revolutionary Ozhegov, a representative of the Urals, paid a visit early in August to his Izhevsky factory. "I was dreadfully shocked," he writes in his sorrowful report, "by the sharp changes which had taken place in my absence. That organization of the Social Revolutionary Party which, both for its numbers (8,000 members), and its activities, was known throughout the whole Ural region . . . had been disintegrated and reduced to 500 people, thanks to irresponsible agitators."

The report of Ozhegov did not bring any unexpected news to the Executive Committee: the same picture was to be seen in Petrograd. If after the July raids the Social Revolutionaries temporarily leapt to the front in the factories, and even in some places increased their influence, their subsequent decline was only the more headlong. "To be sure, Kerensky's government conquered at the time," wrote the Social Revolutionary V. Zenzinov later, "the Bolshevik demonstrators were scattered, and the chiefs of the Bolsheviks arrested, but that was a Pyrrhic victory." That is quite true: like King Pyrrhus the Compromisers won a victory

288

at the price of their army. "Whereas earlier, before July 3–5," writes the Petrograd worker, Skorinko, "the Mensheviks and Social Revolutionaries had been able in some places to appear before the workers without the risk of being whistled down, at present they had no such guarantee. . . ." In general they had no guarantees left.

The Social Revolutionary Party had not only lost its influence, but had also changed its social constituency. The revolutionary workers had already either gone over to the Bolsheviks or, in taking flight, were going through an inner crisis. On the other hand, the sons of shopkeepers, kulaks and petty officials who had been hiding in the factories during the war, had had time to find out that the perfect place for them was the Social Revolutionary party. In September, however, even they were afraid to call themselves Social Revolutionaries any longer—at least in Petrograd. The workers, the soldiers, and in some provinces already even the peasants, had abandoned that party. There remained in it only the conservative, bureaucratic and philistine strata.

When the masses, awakened by the revolution, gave their confidence to the Social Revolutionaries and Mensheviks, both these parties were tireless in praising the lofty intelligence of the people. When those same masses, having passed through the school of events, began to turn sharply toward the Bolsheviks, the Compromisers laid the blame for their own collapse upon the ignorance of the people. But the masses would not agree that they had become more ignorant. On the contrary it seemed to them that they now understood what they had not understood before.

The Social Revolutionary party, as it withered and weakened, also began to split along a social seam, in this process throwing its members over into hostile camps. In the fields and villages there remained those Social Revolutionaries who, side by side with the Bolsheviks and usually under their leadership, had defended themselves against the blows dealt out by Social Revolutionaries in the government. The sharpening struggle between the two wings brought to life an intermediate group. Under the leadership of Chernov, this group tried to preserve a unity between the persecutors and the persecuted, became tangled up, arrived in hopeless and often ludicrous contradictions, and still further compromised the party. In order to make it possible for them to appear at mass meetings, the Social Revolutionary orators were compelled insistently to recommend themselves as "Lefts," as internationalists, having nothing in common with the clique of "March Social Revolutionaries." After the July Days the Left Social Revolutionaries came out in open opposition—still not breaking formally with the party, but belatedly catching up the arguments and slogans of the Bolsheviks. On the 21st of September, Trotsky, not without a hidden pedagogical intention, declared at a session of the Petrograd Soviet that it was becoming "easier and easier for the Bolsheviks to come to an understanding with the Left Social Revolutionaries." In the end these people split off in the form of an independent party, to inscribe in the book of revolution one of its most fantastic pages. This was the last flare-up of self-sufficient intellectual radicalism, and a few months after October there remained nothing of it but a small heap of ashes.

There was a deep differentiation also among the Mensheviks. Their Petrograd organization came into sharp conflict with their central committee. Their central nucleus, led by Tseretelli, having no peasant reserve such as the Social Revolutionaries possessed, melted even more rapidly than they did. Intermediate social democratic groups, who adhered to neither of the two principal camps, were still trying to unite the Bolsheviks with the Mensheviks: they were still nourishing the illusions of March, when even Stalin had thought desirable a union with Tseretelli, and had believed that "we will live down petty disagreements within the party." In the latter part of August there occurred a fusion of the Mensheviks with these advocates of union. At their joint session the right wing had a decided preponderance, and the resolution of Tseretelli favoring war and a coalition with the bourgeoisie got 117 votes against 79. Tseretelli's victory in the party hastened the defeat of the party in the working class. The Petrograd organization of worker-Mensheviks, extremely few in number, followed Martov, pushing him along, irritated by his indecisiveness and getting ready to go over to the Bolsheviks. In the middle of September the organization of the Vassilie Island district joined the Bolshevik party almost as a unit. That hastened the agitation in other districts and in the provinces. The leaders of the different trends of Menshevism furiously accused each other in joint sessions of destroying the party. Gorky's paper, belonging to the left flank of the Mensheviks, stated at the end of September that the Petrograd organization of the party, which had a little while ago numbered about 10,000 members, "had practically ceased to exist. . . . The last all-city conference was unable to meet for lack of a quorum."

Plekhanov was attacking the Mensheviks from the right. "Tseretelli and his friends," he said, "without themselves knowing or desiring it, have been preparing the road for Lenin." The political condition of Tseretelli himself in the days of the September tide, is clearly depicted in the memoirs of the Kadet, Nabokov: "The most characteristic quality of his mood at that time was fright at the rising tide of Bolshevism. I remember how he spoke to me in a heart to heart conversation about the possibility of a seizure of power by the Bolsheviks. 'Of course,' he said, 'they will not hold out more than two or three weeks, but only think what destruction that will mean. This we must avoid at any cost.' In his voice was a note of genuine, panic-stricken alarm. . . ." Tseretelli was experiencing before October those same moods which had been familiar to Nabokov in the February days.

*

The soviets were the arena in which the Bolsheviks functioned side by side with the Social Revolutionaries and Mensheviks, although in continual conflict with them. The change in the relative power of the soviet parties did not, to be sure, immediately, but only with unavoidable laggings and artificial postponements, find its expression in the make-up of the soviets and their social functioning.

Many of the provincial soviets had already, before the July Days, become organs of power. It was so in Ivanovo-Voznesensk, Lugansk, Tzaritzyn, Kherson, Tomsk, Vladivostok—if not formally, at least in fact, and if not continually at least sporadically. The Krasnoyarsk Soviet quite independently introduced a system of cards for the purchase of objects of personal consumption. The compromisist soviet in Saratov was compelled to interfere in economic conflicts, to arrest manufacturers, confiscate the tramway belonging to Belgians, introduce workers' control, and organize production in the abandoned factories. In the Urals, where ever since 1905 the Bolsheviks had enjoyed a predominant political influence, the soviets frequently instituted courts of justice for the trial of citizens, created their own militia in several factories, paying for its equipment out of the factory cash-box, organized a workers' inspection which assembled raw materials and fuel for the factories, superintended the sale of manufactured goods and established a wage scale. In certain districts of the Urals the soviets took the land from the landlords and put it under social cultivation. At the Simsk metal works, the soviets organized a regional factory administration which took charge of the whole administration, the cash-box, the bookkeeping, and the sales department. By this act the nationalization of the Simsk metal district was roughly accomplished. "As early as July," writes V. Eltsin, from whom we borrow these data, "not only was everything in the Ural factories in the hands of the Bolsheviks, but the Bolsheviks were already giving object lessons in the solution of political, economic and agrarian problems." These lessons were primitive—they were not reduced to a system, not illumined by a theory—but in many respects they anticipated the future roads to be traveled.

The July Days hit the soviets far harder than the party or the trade unions, for the struggle then was primarily for the life and death of the soviets. The party and the trade unions would retain their significance both in a "peaceful" period and during the difficult times of reaction. Their tasks and methods would change, but not their basic functions. The soviets, however, could survive only on the basis of a revolutionary situation, and would disappear along with it. Uniting the majority of the working class, they brought it face to face with a problem which rises above the needs of all private persons, groups and guilds, above the wage problem, the problem of reforms and improvements in general—the problem, that is, of a conquest of power. But the slogan "All Power to the Soviets" seemed shattered along with the July demonstration of the workers and soldiers. That defeat which weakened the Bolsheviks in the soviets, weakened the soviets in the state incomparably more. "The government of salvation" meant the resurrection of an independent bureaucracy. The renunciation of power by the soviets meant their humiliation before the commissars, their enfeeblement, their fading away.

The decline in the significance of the Executive Committee found a vivid external expression: the government suggested to the Compromisers that they evacuate the Tauride Palace on the ground that it required repairs in preparation for the Constituent Assembly. During the first half of July the building of Smolny, where formerly the daughters of the nobility had been educated, was set apart for the soviets. The bourgeois press now wrote about the giving over to the soviets of the house of the "white doves," in the same tone in which they had formerly talked of the seizure of the Palace of Kshesinskaia by the Bolsheviks. Various revolutionary organizations, among them the trade unions which were occupying requisitioned buildings, were subjected to attack at the same time on the ground of the housing problem. It was no other but a question of crowding the workers' revolution out of the too extensive quarters seized by it within bourgeois society. The Kadet press knew no limit to its indignation—somewhat belated to be sure,—over the vandalism of the people, their trampling upon the rights of private and state property. But toward the end of July an unexpected fact was laid bare through the medium of the typographical workers. The parties grouped around the notorious Committee of the State Duma had long ago, it appeared, appropriated to their needs the opulent state printing plant, its despatching facilities and its franking privileges. The agitational brochures of the Kadet party were not only being printed free, but freely distributed by the ton, and moreover with preferential rights, throughout the whole country. The Executive Committee, placed under the necessity of examining this charge, was obliged to confirm it. The Kadet party, to be sure, only found a new theme for indignation: Could you, indeed, for a moment place in the same category the seizure of government buildings for destructive purposes, and the use of the properties of the state for the defense of its greatest treasures? In a word, if we gentlemen have somewhat light-fingeredly robbed the state, it is only in its own interest. But this argument did not seem convincing to all. The building trades stubbornly believed that they had more right to a building for their union than the Kadets had to the government printing office. This disagreement was not accidental: it was leading straight to the second revolution. The Kadets were compelled, in any case, to bite their tongues a little.

One of the instructors sent out during the second half of August by the Executive Committee, having made the rounds of the soviets in the south of Russia, where the Bolsheviks were considerably weaker than in the north, made this report of his disturbing observations: "The political moods are noticeably changing. . . . In the upper circles of the masses a revolutionary mood is growing, as a result of the shift in the policy of the Provisional Government. . . . In the masses a weariness and indifference to the revolution is to be felt. There is a noticeable coolness toward the soviets. . . . The functions of the soviets are decreasing little by little. . . ." That the masses were getting tired of the vacillations of their democratic intermediaries is beyond a doubt, but it was not to the revolution, but to the Social Revolutionaries and Mensheviks, that they were growing cold. This situation was especially unbearable in those localities where the power was, in spite of all programs, actually concentrated in the hands of the compromisist soviets. Utterly entangled in the capitulation of the Executive Committee before the bureaucracy, the leaders no longer dared make any use of their power, and merely compromised the soviets in the eyes of the masses. A considerable part of the ordinary everyday work, moreover, had passed over from the soviets to the democratic municipalities—a still greater part to the trade unions and factory and shop committees. Less and less clear became the answer to the question: Will the soviets survive? And what will their future be?

During the first months of their existence, the soviets, far outstripping all other organizations, had taken upon themselves the task of creating trade unions, factory committees, clubs, and played a leading part in their work. But once they got on their own feet, these workers' organizations came more and more under the leadership of the Bolsheviks. "The factory and shop committees," wrote Trotsky in August, "are not created out of temporary meetings. The masses elect to these committees those who at home in the everyday life of the factory have demonstrated their firmness, their business-like character, and their devotion to the interests of the workers. And these same factory committees . . . in their overwhelming majority consist of Bolsheviks." There could no longer be any talk of a guardianship over the factory committees and trade unions exercised by the compromisist soviets. On the contrary, there was a bitter struggle between them. In those problems which touched the masses to the quick, the soviets were proving less and less capable of standing up against the trade unions and factory committees. Thus, for instance, the Moscow unions carried out a general strike in opposition to the decision of the soviets. In a less clear form similar conflicts were taking place everywhere, and it was not the soviets which usually came off victorious.

Driven up a blind alley by their own policy, the Compromisers found themselves obliged to "think up" incidental occupations for the soviets, to switch them over into the cultural field—in the essence of the matter, to entertain them. In vain. The soviets were created to conduct a struggle for power; for other tasks, other more appropriate organizations existed. "The entire work of our soviet, running in the Menshevik and Social Revolutionary channel," writes the Saratov Bolshevik, Antonov, "lost all meaning. . . . At a meeting of the Executive Committee we would yawn from boredom till it became indecent. The Social Revolutionary-Menshevik talking-mill was empty and trivial."

The sickly soviets were becoming less and less able to serve as a support to their Petrograd center. The correspondence between Smolny and the localities was going into a decline: there was nothing to write about, nothing to propose; no prospects remained, and no tasks. This isolation from the masses took the very palpable form of a financial crisis. The compromisist soviets in the provinces were themselves without means, and therefore could not offer support to their staff in Smolny; and the left soviets demonstratively refused financial support to an Executive Committee which had dishonored itself by participating in the work of the counter-revolution.

This process of fading out of the soviets was crossed, however, by processes of another and partly opposite character. Far-off frontiers, backward counties, and inaccessible corners were waking up and creating their own soviets, and these would manifest a revolutionary freshness until they fell under the demoralizing influence of the center, or under the repressions of the government. The total number of soviets was growing rapidly. At the end of August, the secretariat of the Executive Committee counted as many as 600 soviets, behind which stood 23 million electors. The official soviet system had been raised up over a human ocean which was billowing powerfully and driving its waves leftward.

The political revival of the soviets, which coincided with their Bolshevization, began from the bottom. In Petrograd the first voice to be lifted was that of the district locals. On July 21, a delegation from an inter-district conference of the soviets presented to the Executive Committee a list of demands: dissolve the State Duma, confirm the inviolability of the army organizations by a decree of the government, restore the left press, stop the disarming of workers, put an end to mass arrests, bridle the right press, bring to an end the disbandment of regiments and the death penalty at the front. A lowering of the political demands here, in comparison with the July demonstration, is quite obvious; but this was only a first step toward convalescence. In cutting down the slogans, the districts were trying to broaden their base. The leaders of the Executive Committee diplomatically welcomed the "sensitiveness" of the district soviets, but confined their response to the assertion that all misfortunes had resulted from the July insurrection. The two sides parted politely but coolly.

Upon this program of the district soviets a significant campaign was opened. *Izvestia* printed from day to day resolutions of soviets, trade unions, factories, battleships, army units, demanding the dissolution of the State Duma, an end of repressions against the Bolsheviks and indulgences to the counter-revolution. Upon this general background, certain more radical voices were heard. On the 22nd of July the soviet of Moscow Province, considerably in advance of the soviet of Moscow itself, passed a resolution in favor of the transfer of power to the soviets. On July 26 the Ivanovo-Voznesensk soviet "branded with contempt" the method of struggle employed against the party of the Bolsheviks, and sent a greeting to Lenin, "the glorious leader of the revolutionary proletariat." Elections held at the end of July and during the first half of August at many points in the country brought about as a general rule a strengthening of the Bolshevik factions in the soviets. In Kronstadt, raided and made notorious throughout Russia, the new soviet contained 100 Bolsheviks, 75 Left Social Revolutionaries, 12 Menshevik-Internationalists, 7 anarchists, and over 90 non-party men of whom not one dared openly acknowledge his sympathy for the Compromisers. At a regional congress of the soviets of the Urals, opening on August 18, there were 86 Bolsheviks, 40 Social Revolutionaries, 23 Mensheviks. Tzaritzyn became an object of special hatred to the bourgeois press, for here not only had the soviet become Bolshevik, but the leader of the local Bolsheviks, Minin, was elected burgomaster. Kerensky sent a punitive expedition against Tzaritzyn, a city which was a red rag to the Don Cossack ataman Kaledin—without any serious pretext and with the sole aim of destroying a revolutionary nest. In Petrograd, Moscow, and all the industrial districts, more and more hands were being raised every day for the Bolshevik proposals.

The events at the end of August subjected the soviets to a test. Under the shadow of danger an inner regrouping took place very swiftly; it took place everywhere, and with comparatively little debate. In the provinces as in Petrograd, the Bolsheviks—stepchildren of the official soviet system—were advanced to the front rank. But also in the staff of the Compromise party, the "March" socialists, the politicians of ministerial and official waiting-rooms, were temporarily crowded back by more militant elements tempered in the underground movement. For this new grouping of forces a new organizational form was needed. The leadership of the revolutionary defense was nowhere concentrated in the hands of the executive committees. They were of little use in the form in which Kornilov's insurrection found them for fighting action. Everywhere there were formed special committees of defense, revolutionary committees, staffs. They relied upon the soviets, made reports to them, but represented a new selection of elements, a new method of action corresponding to the revolutionary nature of the task.

The Moscow soviet created—as in the days of the State Conference—a fighting group of six, which alone should have the right to deploy armed forces and make arrests. The regional congress of Kiev, which met at the end of August, advised its local soviets not to hesitate to replace unreliable representatives of the power, both military and civil, and take measures for the immediate arrest of counter-revolutionists and the arming of the workers. In Vyatka the soviet committee assumed extraordinary rights, including the disposition of the armed forces. In Tzaritzyn the whole power went over to the soviet staff. In Nizhni-Novgorod the revolutionary committee established its sentries at the post and telegraph offices. The Krasnoyarsk soviet concentrated both the civil and military power in its hands.

With various qualifications—at times substantial—this same picture was reproduced almost everywhere. And it was by no means a mere imitation of Petrograd. The mass constitution of the soviets gave the character of a general law to their inner evolution, making them all react in like manner to any great event. While the two parts of the coalition were divided by a civil war front, the soviets had actually gathered around themselves all the living forces of the nation. Running into this wall the offensive of the generals had crumbled into dust. A more instructive lesson could not possibly be demanded. "In spite of all efforts of the authorities to crowd out the soviets and deprive them of power," says the declaration of the Bolsheviks on this theme, "the soviets manifested during the putting down of the Kornilov revolt the irrepressible . . . might and initiative of the popular mass. . . . After this new experience, which nothing will ever drive out of the consciousness of the workers, soldiers and peasants, the cry raised at the very beginning of the revolution by our party—'All Power to the Soviets!'—has become the voice of the whole revolutionary country."

The city dumas, which had made an effort to compete with the soviets, died down in the days of danger and vanished. The

Petrograd duma humbly sent its delegation to the Soviet "for an explanation of the general situation and the establishment of contact." It would seem as though the soviets, elected by a part of the city's population, should have had less power and influence than the dumas, elected by the whole population. But the dialectic of the revolutionary process has demonstrated that in certain historic conditions the part is incomparably greater than the whole. As in the government, so in the duma, the Compromisers formed a bloc with the Kadets against the Bolsheviks, and that bloc paralyzed the duma as it had the government. The soviet, on the other hand, proved the natural form of defensive co-operation between the Compromisers and the Bolsheviks against the attack of the bourgeoisie.

After the Kornilov days a new chapter opened for the soviets. Although the Compromisers still retained a considerable number of bad spots, especially in the garrison, the Petrograd soviet showed such a sharp career in the direction of the Bolsheviks as to astonish both camps—both Right and Left. On the night of September 1, while still under the presidency of Cheidze, the Soviet voted for a government of workers and peasants. The rank-and-file members of the compromisist factions almost solidly supported the resolution of the Bolsheviks. The rival proposal of Tseretelli got only about 15 votes. The compromisist praesidium could not believe their eyes. The Right demanded a roll call, and this dragged on until three o'clock in the morning. To avoid openly voting against their parties, many of the delegates went home. But even so, and in spite of all methods of pressure, the resolution of the Bolsheviks received in the final vote 279 votes against 115. That was a big fact. That was the beginning of the end. The praesidium, stunned, announced that they would resign.

On September 2nd at a joint session of the Russian soviet institutions of Finland, a resolution was adopted by 700 votes against 13, with 36 abstaining, favoring a government of soviets. On the 5th, the Moscow soviet followed in the steps of the Petrograd. By 355 votes against 254, it not only expressed its want of confidence in the Provisional Government, declaring it a weapon of counter-revolution, but also condemned the coalition policy of the Executive Committee. The praesidium, headed by Khinchuk, announced they would resign. A congress of the soviets of central Siberia, meeting at Krasnoyarsk on September 5, followed the Bolshevik leadership throughout. On the 8th, the Bolshevik resolution was adopted in the Kiev soviet of workers' deputies by a majority of 130 against 66—although there were only 95 deputies in the official Bolshevik faction. At the Finland congress of the soviets which met on the 10th, 150,000 sailors, soldiers and Russian workers were represented by 69 Bolsheviks, 48 Left Social Revolutionaries, and a few non-party men. The soviet of peasants' deputies of Petrograd Province elected the Bolshevik, Sergeiev, as delegate to the Democratic Conference. Here again it was revealed that in those cases where the party is able through the mediation of workers or soldiers to get into immediate contact with the villages, the peasantry eagerly flock to its banner.

The dominance of the Bolshevik party in the Petrograd Soviet was dramatically certified at the historic session of September 9. All the factions had diligently rounded up their members: "It is a question of the fate of the soviets." About 1,000 workers' and soldiers' deputies assembled. Had the vote of September 1st been a mere episode caused by the accidental constitution of the session, or did it mean a complete change in the policy of the Soviet? Thus the question was posed. Fearing lest they could not assemble a majority against the praesidium, of which all the compromise leaders were members—Cheidze, Tseretelli, Chernov, Gotz, Dan, Skobelev—the Bolshevik faction made a motion that the praesidium be elected on a proportional basis. This proposal, which would obscure to a certain degree the sharpness of the conflict about principles, and was on this account roundly condemned by Lenin, had this tactical advantage, that it made sure of the support of the wavering elements. But Tseretelli rejected the compromise. The praesidium wants to know, he said, whether the Soviet has actually changed its direction: "We cannot carry out the tactics of the Bolsheviks." The resolution introduced by the Right declared that the vote of September 1st did not correspond to the political line of the Soviet, and that the Soviet had confidence, as before, in its praesidium. There was nothing left for the Bolsheviks to do but accept the challenge, and that they did

with great willingness. Trotsky, appearing for the first time after
his liberation from prison and warmly welcomed by a considerable
part of the assembly—both sides were inwardly measuring the
applause: is it a majority or not?—demanded an explanation before the vote: Is Kerensky, as before, a member of the praesidium?
The praesidium, after hesitating a moment, answered in the affirmative—thus, although already weighed down with sins, tying
another millstone around its neck. "We had firmly believed,"
said Trotsky, ". . . that Kerensky would not be allowed to sit
in the praesidium. We were mistaken. The ghost of Kerensky now
sits between Dan and Cheidze. . . . When they propose to you
to sanction the political line of the praesidium, do not forget that
you will be sanctioning the policies of Kerensky." The meeting
proceeded in the utmost imaginable tension. Order was preserved
by the desire of each and every person there not to permit an
explosion. They all wanted to count as soon as possible the numbers of their friends and enemies. All understood that they were
deciding the question of power—of the war—of the fate of the
revolution. It was decided to vote by the method of withdrawing
from the room. Those should go out who accepted the resignation
of the praesidium: it is easier for a minority to go out than a
majority. In every corner of the hall an impassioned although
whispered agitation now began. The old praesidium or the new?
The Coalition or the Soviet Power? A large crowd of people seemed
to be drifting towards the door—too large, in the opinion of the
praesidium. The Bolshevik leaders, on their part, estimated that
they would lack about 100 votes of the majority. "And that will
be doing excellently well," they comforted themselves in advance. But the workers and soldiers kept on drifting and drifting
toward the door. There was a hushed rumble of voices—brief
explosions of loud argument. From one side a voice shouted out:
"Kornilovists!" From the other: "July heroes!" The procedure
lasted about an hour. The arms of an unseen scale were oscillating. The praesidium, hardly able to contain its excitement, remained throughout the whole hour upon the platform. At last
the result was counted and weighed: For the praesidium and the
Coalition, 414 votes; against, 519; abstaining, 67! The new majority applauded like a storm, ecstatically, furiously. It had a right

to. The victory had been well paid for. A good part of the road lay behind.

Still bewildered by the blow, with long faces, the overthrown leaders withdraw from the platform. Tseretelli cannot refrain from one last dreadful prophecy. "We withdraw from this tribune," he cries, turning halfway round as he moves, "in the consciousness that for half a year we have held worthily and held high the banner of the revolution. This banner has now passed into your hands. We can only express the wish that you may be able to hold it in the same way for half as long!" Tseretelli was cruelly mistaken about his dates as about everything.

The Petrograd Soviet, the parent of all the other soviets, henceforth stood under the leadership of the Bolsheviks, who had been only yesterday "an insignificant little bunch of demagogues." Trotsky, from the tribune, reminded the praesidium that the charge against the Bolsheviks of being in the service of the German staff had not been withdrawn. "Let the Miliukovs and Guchkovs tell the story of their lives day by day. They dare not do it. But we are ready any day to give an account of our activities. We have nothing to hide from the Russian people. . . ." The Petrograd soviet in a special resolution "branded with contempt the authors, distributors and promoters of the slander."

The Bolsheviks now entered upon their inheritance. It proved at once colossal and extraordinarily slender. The Executive Committee had in good season taken away from the Petrograd Soviet the two newspapers established by it, all the administrative offices, all funds and all technical equipment, including the typewriters and inkwells. The innumerable automobiles which had been at the disposal of the Soviet since the February days had every last one of them been transferred into the keeping of the compromisist Olympus. The new leaders had nothing—no treasury, no newspapers, no secretarial apparatus, no means of locomotion, no pen and no pencil. Nothing but the blank walls and—the burning confidence of the workers and soldiers. That, however, proved sufficient.

After this fundamental break in the policy of the Soviet, the ranks of the Compromisers began to melt even more rapidly. On the 11th of September, when Dan defended the Coalition before

302

the Petrograd Soviet and Trotsky spoke for a soviet government, the Coalition was rejected by all votes against 10, with 7 abstaining! On the same day the Moscow soviet by a unanimous vote condemned the repressions against the Bolsheviks. The Compromisers soon found themselves pushed away into a narrow sector on the right, such as that which the Bolsheviks had occupied on the left at the beginning of the revolution. But with what a difference! The Bolsheviks had always been stronger among the masses than in the soviets. The Compromisers, on the contrary, still had a larger place in the soviets than among the masses. The Bolsheviks in their period of weakness had a future. The Compromisers had nothing left but a past—and one of which they had no reason to be proud.

Together with its change of course the Petrograd Soviet changed its external aspect. The compromise leaders completely disappeared from the horizon, digging themselves in in the Executive Committee. In the Soviet they were displaced by stars of the second and third magnitude. With the disappearance of Tseretelli, Chernov, Avksteniev, Skobelev, the friends and admirers of these democratic ministers also ceased to appear—the radical-minded officers and ladies, the semi-socialistic writers, the people of culture and celebrity. The Soviet became more homogeneous—grayer, darker, more serious.

Chapter XIII

THE BOLSHEVIKS AND THE SOVIETS

UPON a close examination, the means and implements of the Bolshevik agitation seem not only completely out of proportion to the political influence of Bolshevism, but simply amazing in their insignificance. Up to the July days the party had 41 publications counting weeklies and monthlies, with a total circulation, counting everything, of 320,000. After the July raids the circulation dwindled by half. At the end of August the central organ of the Party was printing 50,000 copies. In the days when the party was winning over the Petrograd and Moscow soviets, the cash in the treasury of the Central Committee amounted to only 30,000 paper rubles.

The intelligentsia hardly came into the Bolshevik party at all. A broad layer of so-called "old Bolsheviks," from among the students who had associated themselves with the revolution of 1905, had since turned into extraordinarily successful engineers, physicians, government officials, and they now unceremoniously showed the party the hostile aspect of their backs. Even in Petrograd there was felt at every step a lack of journalists, speakers, agitators; and the provinces were wholly deprived of what few they had had. "There are no leaders; there are no politically literate people who can explain to the masses what the Bolsheviks want!" —this cry came from hundreds of remote corners, and especially from the front. In the villages there were almost no Bolshevik nuclei at all. Postal communications were in complete disorder. The local organizations, left to their own devices, would occasionally reproach the Central Committee—and not without foundation—that it was concerning itself only with Petrograd.

How was it that with this weak apparatus and this negligible circulation of the party press, the ideas and slogans of Bolshevism were able to take possession of the people? The explanation is very simple: those slogans which correspond to the keen demands

of a class and an epoch create thousands of channels for themselves. A red-hot revolutionary medium is a high conductor of
ideas. The Bolshevik papers were read aloud, were read all to
pieces. The most important articles were learned by heart, recited,
copied, and wherever possible reprinted. "Our staff printing
plant," says the soldier, Pereiko, "performed a great service for
the revolution. How many individual articles from *Pravda* were
reprinted by us, and how many small brochures, very close and
comprehensible to the soldiers! And all these were swiftly distributed along the front with the help of air mails, bicycles and
motorcycles. . . ." At the same time the bourgeois press, although supplied to the front free of cost in millions of copies,
hardly found a reader. The heavy bales remained unopened. This
boycott of the "patriotic" press at times assumed a demonstrative
form. Representatives of the 18th Siberian division passed a resolution asking the bourgeois parties to stop sending literature, inasmuch as it was "fruitlessly used to boil the hot water for tea."
The Bolshevik press was very differently employed. Hence the co-
efficient of its useful—or if you prefer, harmful—effectiveness
was incomparably higher.

The usual explanation of the success of Bolshevism reduced
itself to a remark upon "the simplicity of its slogans," which
fell in with the desires of the masses. In this there is a certain element of truth. The wholeness of the Bolshevik policy was due to
the fact that, in contrast to the "democratic parties," the Bolsheviks were free from unexpressed or semi-expressed gospels reducing themselves in the last analysis to a defense of private property. However, that distinction alone does not exhaust the matter.
While on the right the "democracy" was competing with the
Bolsheviks, on the left too there were the anarchists, the Maximalists, the Left Social Revolutionaries, trying to crowd them
out. But these groups too—none of them ever emerged from its
impotent state. What distinguished Bolshevism was that it subordinated the subjective goal, the defense of the interests of the
popular masses, to the laws of revolution as an objectively conditioned process. The scientific discovery of these laws, and first of
all those which govern the movement of popular masses, constituted the basis of the Bolshevik strategy. The toilers are guided

in their struggle not only by their demands, not only by their needs, but by their life experiences. Bolshevism had absolutely no taint of any aristocratic scorn for the independent experience of the masses. On the contrary, the Bolsheviks took this for their point of departure and built upon it. That was one of their great points of superiority.

Revolutions are always verbose, and the Bolsheviks did not escape from this law. But whereas the agitation of the Mensheviks and Social Revolutionaries was scattered, self-contradictory and oftenest of all evasive, the agitation of the Bolsheviks was distinguished by its concentrated and well thought-out character. The Compromisers talked themselves out of difficulties; the Bolsheviks went to meet them. A continual analysis of the objective situation, a testing of slogans upon facts, a serious attitude to the enemy even when he was none too serious, gave special strength and power of conviction to the Bolshevik agitation.

The party press did not exaggerate success, did not distort the correlation of forces, did not try to win by shouting. The school of Lenin was a school of revolutionary realism. The data supplied by the Bolshevik press of 1917 are proving, in the light of historic criticism and the documents of the epoch, incomparably more correct than the data supplied by all the other newspapers. This correctness was a result of the revolutionary strength of the Bolsheviks, but at the same time it reinforced their strength. The renunciation of this tradition has subsequently become one of the most malignant features of epigonism.

"We are not charlatans," said Lenin immediately after his arrival. "We must base ourselves only upon the consciousness of the masses. Even if it is necessary to remain in a minority, be it so. . . . We must not be afraid to be a minority. . . . We will carry on the work of criticism in order to free the masses from deceit. . . . Our line will prove right. All the oppressed will come to us. . . . They have no other way out." Here we have the Bolshevik policy, comprehensible from beginning to end as the direct opposite of demagoguism and adventurism.

Lenin is in hiding. He is intently watching the papers, reading as always between the lines, or catching in personal conversations —not very frequent—the echo of ideas not thought out, intentions not expressed. The masses are on the ebb. Martov, while defending the Bolsheviks from slander, is at the same time indulging in mournful irony at the expense of a party which has been so "crafty" as to defeat itself. Lenin guesses—and direct rumors of this will soon reach him—that even some of the Bolsheviks, too, are not free from a note of repentance, that the impressionable Lunacharsky is not alone. Lenin writes about the whimpering of the petty bourgeois, and about the "renegadism" of those Bolsheviks who show a disposition to respond to this whimpering. The Bolsheviks in the districts and in the provinces catch up with approval these austere words. They are again and more solidly convinced: "The old man" is not losing his head. His will is firm. He will not surrender to any accidental mood.

A member of the central committee of the Bolsheviks—perhaps Sverdlov—writes to a province: "We are temporarily without newspapers. . . . The organization is not broken up. . . . The congress is not postponed." Lenin, so far as his enforced isolation permits, attentively follows the preparation for the party congress, and designates its fundamental problem: to plan the further offensive. The congress was described in advance as a joint congress, since it was to bring about the inclusion in the Bolshevik party of certain autonomous revolutionary groups. Chief among these was the Petrograd inter-district organization to which belonged Trotsky, Joffé, Uritsky, Riazanov, Lunacharsky, Pokrovsky, Manuilsky, Karakhan, Urenev, and several other revolutionists known in the past, or still only coming to be known.

On July 2, on the very eve of the demonstration, a conference had been held of the Mezhrayontsi [the above-mentioned inter-district organization—Trans.] representing about 4,000 workers. "The majority," writes Sukhanov, who was present in the gallery, "were workers and soldiers unknown to me. . . . A feverish work had been carried on and its success was palpable to us all. There was only one difficulty: What is the difference between you and the Bolsheviks, and why are you not with them?" In order to hasten that fusion which certain individual leaders of the organization were trying to postpone, Trotsky published in *Pravda* the following statement: "There are in my opinion at

307

the present time no differences either in principle or tactics between the inter-district and the Bolshevik organizations. Accordingly there are no motives which justify the separate existence of these organizations."

The joint congress opened on July 26—in essence the 6th congress of the Bolshevik party—and it conducted its meetings semi-legally, concealing itself alternately in two different workers' districts. There were 175 delegates, 157 with a vote, representing 112 organizations, comprising 176,750 members. In Petrograd there were 41,000 members: 36,000 in the Bolshevik organization, 4,000 Mezhrayontsi, and about 1,000 in the Military Organization. In the central industrial regions, of which Moscow is the focus, the party had 42,000 members; in the Urals 25,000; in the Donetz Basin about 15,000. In the Caucasus, big Bolshevik organizations were to be found in Baku, Grozny, and Tiflis. The first two were almost wholly composed of workers; in Tiflis the soldiers predominated.

The personnel of the congress embodied the pre-revolutionary past of the party. Out of 171 delegates who filled out a questionnaire, 110 had spent 245 years in prison, 10 delegates had spent 41 years at hard labor, 24 had spent 73 years in penal settlements, 55 delegates had been in exile 127 years; 27 had been abroad for 89 years; 150 had been arrested 549 times.

"At that congress," as Piatnitsky, one of the present secretaries of the Communist International, later remembered, "neither Lenin, nor Trotsky, nor Zinoviev, nor Kamenev was present. . . . Although the question of the party program was withdrawn from the agenda, nevertheless the congress went off well and in a businesslike way without the leaders of the party. . . ." At the basis of the work lay the theses of Lenin. Bukharin and Stalin made the principal reports. The report of Stalin is a good measure of the distance traveled by the speaker himself, along with all the cadres of the party, in the four months since Lenin's arrival. With theoretical diffidence, but political decisiveness, Stalin tries to name over those features which define "the deep character of a socialist workers' revolution." The unanimity of this conference in comparison with the April one is noticeable at once.

On the subject of elections to the Central Committee, the report of the congress reads: "The names of the four members of the Central Committee receiving the most votes are read aloud: Lenin—133 votes out of 134. Zinoviev 132, Kamenev 131, and Trotsky 131. Besides these four, the following members were elected to the Central Committee: Nogin, Kollantai, Stalin, Sverdlov, Rykov, Bukharin, Artem, Joffé, Uritsky, Miliutin, Lomov." The membership of this Central Committee should be well noted. Under its leadership the October Revolution is to be achieved.

Martov greeted the congress with a letter in which he again expressed his deep indignation against the campaign of slander, but on fundamental problems remained standing upon the threshold of action. "We must not substitute for the conquest of power by a majority of the revolutionary democracy, the conquest of power in a struggle with that majority and against it. . . ." By "a majority of the revolutionary democracy" Martov meant, as before, the official soviet representation which had no longer any ground under its feet. "Martov is bound up with the social patriots, not only by an empty factional tradition," wrote Trotsky at that time, "but by a profoundly opportunistic attitude to the social revolution as to a far-off goal which cannot determine our approach to the problems of today. That of itself separates him from us."

Only a small number of Left Mensheviks, headed by Larin, decisively came over to the Bolsheviks during this period. Urenev, future soviet diplomat, making the report to the conference on the subject of fusion with these Internationalists, came to the conclusion that it was necessary to fuse with "a minority of the minority of the Mensheviks. . . ." A copious flow of former Mensheviks into the party began only after the October revolution. Adhering not to the proletarian insurrection, but to the power which issued from it, the Mensheviks here revealed the fundamental quality of opportunism—submission to the existing powers. Lenin, always extremely sensitive to the question of the ingredients of the party, soon came forward with the demand that 99 per cent of the Mensheviks who had joined after the October revolution be expelled. He was far from attaining that goal. Subsequently the doors were opened wide to Mensheviks and Social Revolutionaries, and former Compromisers have become one of the bulwarks of the Stalinist party régime. But all that has to do with later times.

Sverdlov, the practical organizer of the congress, reported: "Trotsky had already before the congress joined the editorial staff of our paper, but his imprisonment prevented his actual participation." It was only at this July congress that Trotsky formally joined the Bolshevik party. The balance was here struck to years of disagreement and factional struggle. Trotsky came to Lenin as to a teacher whose power and significance he understood later than many others, but perhaps more fully than they. Raskolnikov, who was in close contact with Trotsky from the time of his arrival from Canada, and afterward passed several weeks side by side with him in prison, has written in his memoirs: "Trotsky's attitude to Vladimir Ilych (Lenin) was one of enormous esteem. He placed him higher than any contemporary he had met with, either in Russia or abroad. In the tone in which Trotsky spoke of Lenin you felt the devotion of a disciple. In those times Lenin had behind him thirty years' service to the proletariat, and Trotsky twenty. The echoes of their disagreements during the pre-war period were completely gone. No difference existed between the tactical line of Lenin and Trotsky. Their rapprochement, already noticeable during the war, was completely and unquestionably determined, from the moment of the return of Lyev Davidovich (Trotsky) to Russia. After his very first speeches all of us old Leninists felt that he was ours." To this we may add that the mere number of votes cast for Trotsky in electing him to the Central Committee proves that even at the very moment of his entrance into the party, nobody in Bolshevik circles looked upon him as an outsider.

Invisibly present at the congress, Lenin introduced into its work a spirit of responsibility and audacity. The founder and teacher of this party could not endure slovenliness, either in theory or in practical politics. He knew that an incorrect economic formula, like an inattentive political observation, takes cruel vengeance in the hour of action. In defending his fastidiously attentive attitude to every party text, even the secondary ones, Lenin said more than once: "This is not a trivial detail. We must

310

have accuracy. Our agitators will learn this and not go astray. . . ." "We have a good party," he would add, having in view just this serious, meticulous attitude of the rank-and-file agitator upon the question what to say and how to say it.

The audacity of the Bolshevik slogans more than once produced a fantastic impression. Lenin's April theses were greeted in this way. In reality the fantastic thing in a revolutionary epoch is near-sightedness. Realism at such times is unthinkable without a policy of long aim. It is not enough to say that anything fantastic was wholly alien to Bolshevism. The fact is that the party of Lenin was the sole party of political realism in the revolution.

In June and early July the worker Bolsheviks complained more than once that they were often compelled to play the rôle of fire hose in relation to the masses—and this, too, not always successfully. July brought, along with its defeat, a lesson dearly paid for. The masses became far more attentive to the warnings of the party, more understanding of its tactical calculations. The July congress of the party ratified those warnings. "The proletariat must not yield to the provocations of the bourgeoisie, who at the present time would be only too glad to incite us to a premature battle." The whole of August, and especially the latter half, was marked by continual warnings from the party to the workers and soldiers: Do not go into the street. The Bolshevik leaders themselves often joked about the similarity of their warnings to the political *leit-motif* of the German social democracy, which has invariably restrained the masses from every serious struggle by referring to the danger of provocateurs and the necessity of accumulating strength. In reality the similarity was imaginary. The Bolsheviks well understood that strength is accumulated in struggle and not in passive evasion of it. The study of reality was for Lenin only a theoretical reconnoitre in the interests of action. In appraising a situation he always conceived his party in its very center as an active force. He viewed with especial hostility—or more accurately, disgust—that Austro-Marxism of Otto Bauer, Hilferding and others for whom theoretical analysis consists merely of the learned commentaries of passivity. Prudence is a brake and not a motive force. Nobody ever made a journey on brakes, and nobody every created any-

thing out of prudence. But the Bolsheviks knew well, just the
same, that a struggle demands a calculation of forces—that one
must be prudent to win the right to be bold.

The resolution of the 6th Congress, in giving its warning
against premature conflicts, at the same time pointed out that the
battle must be joined at that moment "when the all-national crisis
and the deep movement of the masses have created a favorable
condition for the coming over of the city and country poor to
the side of the workers." At the tempo of the revolution, this was
a question not of decades, nor of years, but of a few months.

In placing upon the order of the day the task of explaining
to the masses the necessity of getting ready for an armed insurrection, the congress decided at the same time to withdraw the
central slogan of the preceding period: transfer of power to the
soviets. The one thing was bound up with the other. Lenin had
opened the way to this change of slogan with his articles, letters
and personal conversations.

The transfer of power to the soviets meant, in its immediate
sense, a transfer of power to the Compromisers. That might have
been accomplished peacefully, by way of a simple dismissal of
the bourgeois government, which had survived only on the good
will of the Compromisers and the relics of the confidence in them
of the masses. The dictatorship of the workers and soldiers had
been a fact ever since the 27th of February. But the workers and
soldiers were not to the point necessary aware of that fact. They
had confided the power to the Compromisers, who in their turn
had passed it over to the bourgeoisie. The calculations of the
Bolsheviks on a peaceful development of the revolution rested,
not on the hope that the bourgeoisie would voluntarily turn over
the power to the workers and soldiers, but that the workers and
soldiers would in good season prevent the Compromisers from
surrendering the power to the bourgeoisie.

The concentration of the power in the soviets under a régime
of soviet democracy, would have opened before the Bolsheviks a
complete opportunity to become a majority in the soviet, and
consequently to create a government on the basis of their program. For this end an armed insurrection would have been unnecessary. The interchange of power between parties could have

been accomplished peacefully. All the efforts of the party from April to July had been directed towards making possible a peaceful development of the revolution through the soviet. "Patiently explain"—that had been the key to the Bolshevik policy.

The July Days had radically changed the situation. From the soviets the power had gone over into the hands of a military clique in close contact with the Kadets and the embassies, a clique which only tolerated Kerensky temporarily in the character of a democratic trademark. If the Executive Committee should now have decided to introduce a resolution transferring the power into its own hands, the result would have been wholly different from three days before. A Cossack regiment with men from the military schools would probably have entered the Tauride Palace and attempted to arrest the "usurpers." The slogan "Power to the Soviets" from now on meant armed insurrection against the government and those military cliques which stood behind it. But to raise an insurrection in the cause of "Power to the Soviets" when the soviets did not want the power, was obvious nonsense.

On the other hand, it had become doubtful from this point on—some even considered it improbable—whether the Bolsheviks could win a majority in those powerless soviets by means of peaceful elections. Having associated themselves with the July raids upon workers and peasants, the Mensheviks and Social Revolutionaries would of course continue to furnish a screen for acts of violence against the Bolsheviks. Remaining compromisist, the soviets would turn into a spineless opposition under a counter-revolutionary government, and then soon come to an end altogether.

Under these circumstances there could no longer be any talk of a peaceful transfer of power to the proletariat. For the Bolshevik party this meant: We must prepare for an armed insurrection. Under what slogan? Under the candid slogan of the conquest of power by the proletariat and the peasant poor. We must present the revolutionary task in its naked form. We must liberate the class essence of the thing from its equivocal soviet form. This was not a renunciation of the soviets as such. After winning the power, the proletariat would have to organize the state upon the soviet type. But those would be other soviets, fulfilling a historic

313

work directly opposite to the defensive function of the compromisist soviets.

"The slogan of the transfer of power to the soviets," wrote Lenin, under the first volleys of slander and attack, "would now sound like quixotism or like a joke. That slogan, taken objectively, would be a deceiving of the people—a suggesting to them of the illusion that it would be now enough for the soviets to desire to take the power or pass a resolution to that effect, in order to receive the power. As though there were in the Soviet a party which had not disgraced itself by helping the hangman! As though we could make what has been as though it had not been."

Renounce the demand for a transfer of power to the soviets? At the first blush this idea shocked the party—or rather it shocked the agitatorial cadres, who for the preceding three months had so much lived with this popular slogan, that they had almost come to identify it with the whole content of the revolution. A discussion began in the party circles. Many eminent party workers, such as Manuilsky, Urenev and others, argued that withdrawing the slogan "Power to the Soviets" would create a danger of isolating the proletariat from the peasantry. This argument substituted institutions for classes. The fetishism of organizational forms— strange as it may seem at a first glance—is an especially common disease among revolutionary circles. "Insofar as we remain within the membership of these soviets," wrote Trotsky, ". . . we will try to bring it about that the soviets, reflecting the past days of the revolution, may be able to raise themselves to the height of the future task. But no matter how important is the question of the rôle and fate of the soviets, it is for us wholly subordinate to the question of the struggle of the proletariat and the semi-proletarian masses of the city, the army and the country, for political power, for a revolutionary dictatorship."

The question, what mass organizations were to serve the party for leadership in the insurrection, did not permit an *a priori*, much less a categorical, answer. The instruments of the insurrection might have been the factory committees and trade unions, already under the leadership of the Bolsheviks, and at the same time in individual cases certain soviets that had broken free from the yoke of the Compromisers. Lenin, for example, said to Ordzhonikidze:

"We must swing over the center of gravity to the factory and shop committees. The factory and shop committees must become the organs of insurrection."

After the masses had come into conflict with the soviets in July, finding them at first passive opponents and then active enemies, this change of slogan found in their consciousness a prepared soil. Just here lay the everlasting preoccupation of Lenin: to express with the utmost simplicity that which on the one hand flowed from the objective conditions, and on the other formulated the subjective experience of the masses. It is not to Tseretelli's soviets that we must now offer the power—so the advanced workers and soldiers felt. We must now take it in our own hands.

The Moscow strike demonstration against the State Conference not only came about against the will of the soviets, but did not put forward the demand for a soviet power. The masses had succeeded in learning the lesson offered by events and interpreted by Lenin. At the same time the Moscow Bolsheviks did not for a moment hesitate to occupy fighting positions as soon as a danger arose that the counter-revolution would attempt to strangle the compromisist soviets. The Bolshevik policy always united revolutionary implacableness with the greatest flexibility, and in just this combination lay the whole secret of its power.

Events in the theater of the war soon subjected the policy of the party, so far as concerns its internationalism, to a very severe test. After the fall of Riga the question of the fate of Petrograd touched the workers and soldiers to the quick. At a meeting of the factory and shop committees in Smolny, the Menshevik Mazurenko, an officer who had recently taken the lead in disarming the Petrograd workers, made a speech about the danger threatening Petrograd, and raised practical questions concerning defense. "What are you trying to say to us," cried one of the Bolshevik orators. "Our leaders are in prison and you ask us to take up questions connected with the defense of the capital?" As industrial workers, as citizens of a bourgeois republic, the proletarians of the Vyborg district had no intention of sabotaging the defense of the revolutionary capital, but as Bolsheviks, as members of the party, they did not for a minute intend to share with the ruling groups the responsibility before the Russian peo-

ple and the people of other countries for the war. Fearing that
defensive moods would turn into a defensist policy, Lenin wrote:
"We will become defensists only after the transfer of power to the
proletariat. . . . Neither the capture of Riga nor the capture of
Petersburg will make us defensists. Up to that moment we are
for the proletarian revolution. We are against the war. We are
not defensists." "The fall of Riga," wrote Trotsky from prison,
"is a cruel blow. The fall of Petersburg would be a misfortune.
But the fall of the international policy of the Russian proletariat
would be ruinous."

Was this the doctrinairism of fanatics? During the very days
while Bolshevik sharp-shooters and sailors were dying under the
walls of Riga, the government was withdrawing troops for the
purpose of raiding the Bolsheviks, and the supreme commander-
in-chief was making ready to wage war on the government. For
this policy, whether at the front or rear, whether for defense or
offense, the Bolsheviks could not and would not bear a shadow of
responsibility. Had they behaved otherwise, they would not have
been Bolsheviks.

Kerensky and Kornilov were two variants of one and the same
danger. But those two variants, the one chronic and the other
acute, came into conflict with each other towards the end of
August. It was necessary to ward off the acute danger first, in
order afterwards to settle with the chronic one. The Bolsheviks
not only entered the committee of defense, although condemned
there to the position of a small minority, but they announced that
in the struggle with Kornilov they were prepared to form a "military-technical union" even with the directory. On this theme
Sukhanov writes: "The Bolsheviks revealed extraordinary tact
and political wisdom. . . . To be sure, in entering a compromise not proper to their natures, they were pursuing certain aims
of their own not foreseen by their allies. But so much the greater
was their wisdom in this matter." There was nothing whatever
"not proper" to the nature of Bolshevism in this policy: on the
contrary, nothing could correspond better to the whole character of the party. The Bolsheviks were revolutionists of the deed
and not the gesture, of the essence and not the form. Their policy was determined by the real grouping of forces, and not by

sympathies and antipathies. When taunted by the Social Revolutionaries and Mensheviks, Lenin wrote: "It would be the profoundest mistake to imagine that the revolutionary proletariat is capable, so to speak, out of 'vengeance' upon the Social Revolutionaries and Mensheviks for the support they have given to anti-Bolshevik raids, to shootings at the front, and the disarming of workers, of refusing to 'support' them against the counterrevolution."

Support them technically, but not politically. Lenin gave a decisive warning against political support in one of his letters to the Central Committee: "We ought not even now to support the government of Kerensky. That would be unprincipled. You ask: But mustn't we fight Kornilov? Of course, yes. But that is not the same thing. There is a limit here. Some of the Bolsheviks are crossing it, slipping into 'compromisism,' getting carried away by the flood of events."

Lenin knew how to catch the finest shadings of a political mood from afar. On the 29th of August at a session of the Kiev city duma, one of the local Bolshevik leaders, G. Piatakov, declared: "In this dangerous moment we must forget all the old accounts . . . and unite with all revolutionary parties which stand for a decisive struggle against counter-revolution. I summon you to unity, etc." This was that false political tone against which Lenin gave his warning. "To forget the old accounts" would have meant to open new credits for the candidates in bankruptcy. "We will fight, we are fighting against Kornilov," wrote Lenin, "but we are not supporting Kerensky, but exposing his weakness. This is a different thing. . . . We must struggle ruthlessly against phrases . . . about supporting the Provisional Government, etc., etc., precisely as mere phrases." The workers had no illusions about the nature of their bloc with the Winter Palace. "In fighting Kornilov the proletariat will fight not for the dictatorship of Kerensky, but for all the conquests of the revolution." Thus spoke factory after factory—in Petrograd, in Moscow, in the provinces. Without making the slightest political concession to the Compromisers, without confusing either organizations or banners, the Bolsheviks were ready as always to harmonize their action with that of opponent and enemy, if this made it possible to deal a blow at another enemy more dangerous at the given moment.

In the struggle against Kornilov, the Bolsheviks were pursuing their own "special aims." Sukhanov hints that they had already at that time set themselves the task of converting the committee of defense into an instrument of proletarian revolution. It is indubitable that the revolutionary committees of the Kornilov days became to a certain extent the prototype of those organs which subsequently led the proletarian insurrection. But Sukhanov nevertheless attributes too much foresight to the Bolsheviks, when he thinks they saw this organizational factor in advance. The "special aims" of the Bolsheviks were to shatter the counter-revolution, tear away the Compromisers from the Kadets if possible, unite the largest masses possible under their own leadership, arm as many revolutionary workers as they could. Of these aims the Bolsheviks made no secret. The persecuted party saved the government which had repressed and slandered it, but it saved the government from military destruction only in order the more surely to destroy it politically.

The last days of August brought another abrupt shift in the correlation of forces, but this time from right to left. The masses once called into the fight had no difficulty in re-establishing the soviets in the position which they had occupied before the July crisis. Henceforth the fate of the soviets was in their own hands. The power could be seized by them without a struggle. For this the Compromisers had only to ratify the situation which had already been created in reality. The whole question was, did they want to do this? The Compromisers now declared with heat that a coalition with the Kadets was no longer thinkable. If that was so, then it had been unthinkable at any time. The renunciation of a coalition, however, could mean nothing but the transfer of power to the Compromisers.

Lenin immediately seized the essence of the new situation, and made the necessary inferences from it. On the 3rd of September he wrote an admirable article, "On Compromises." The rôle of the soviets has again changed, he declared: At the beginning of July they were organs of struggle against the proletariat. At the end of August they have become organs of struggle against the

318

bourgeoisie. The soviets have again got the troops in their control. History again half-opens the possibility for a peaceful development of the revolution. That is an extraordinarily rare and precious possibility. We must make an attempt to achieve it. In passing Lenin made fun of those phrasemakers who reject all compromises whatever: the problem is "throughout all compromises insofar as they are inevitable" to carry out your own aims and fulfil your own tasks. "The compromise upon our part," he said, "will be a return to our pre-July demand: All power to the soviets, a government of Social Revolutionaries and Mensheviks responsible to the soviets. Now and now only, perhaps only in the course of a few days, or one or two weeks, such a government might be created and fortified in a wholly peaceful manner." That short date was meant to characterize the acuteness of the whole situation: the Compromisers had only days in which to make their choice between the bourgeoisie and the proletariat.

The Compromisers recoiled hastily from Lenin's proposal as from a wily trap. In reality there was not the slightest hint of wiliness in Lenin's proposal. Confident that his party was destined to stand at the head of the people, Lenin made a frank attempt to soften the struggle, weakening the resistance of the enemy against the inevitable.

Lenin's bold changes of policy, always resulting from changes in the situation itself, and invariably preserving the unity of his strategic design, constitute an invaluable text-book of revolutionary strategy. This proposal of compromise was significant first of all as an object lesson to the Bolshevik party itself. It demonstrated that in spite of their experience with Kornilov, there was no longer a possibility of the Compromisers' turning down the road of revolution. The Bolshevik party now conclusively felt itself to be the sole party of revolution.

The Compromisers refused to play the part of a transmitting mechanism carrying the power from the bourgeoisie to the proletariat, as they had in March carried the power from the proletariat to the bourgeoisie. By virtue of this fact, the slogan "Power to the Soviets" was again suspended. However, not for long: In the next few days the Bolsheviks got a majority in the Petrograd Soviet, and afterward in a number of others. The phrase

"Power to the soviets" was not, therefore, again removed from the order of the day, but received a new meaning: All power to the *Bolshevik* soviets. In this form the slogan had decisively ceased to be a slogan of peaceful development. The party was launched on the road of armed insurrection through the soviets and in the name of the soviets.

In order to understand the further course of events, it is necessary to raise the question: In what manner did the compromisist soviets regain at the beginning of September the power which they had squandered in July? Throughout the resolutions of the Sixth Congress of the Bolshevik party there runs the assertion that, as a result of the July events, the dual power has been liquidated and replaced by a dictatorship of the bourgeoisie. The most recent soviet historians have copied this idea from book to book, without even trying to revalue it in the light of the events which followed. Moreover it has never occurred to them to ask: If in July the power went over wholly into the hands of a military clique, why was this same military clique compelled in August to resort to an insurrection? Those who have power do not choose the risky path of conspiracy, only those who want to get it.

The formula of the Sixth Congress was, to say the least, inaccurate. Once we designate as a dual power that régime in which an essentially fictitious power lies in the hands of the official government and the real power in the hands of the Soviet, then there is no reason to assert that the dual power is liquidated from the moment when a part of the real power passes over from the Soviet to the bourgeoisie. From the point of view of the military problems of the moment it was permissible, and indeed necessary, to overestimate the concentration of power in the hands of the counter-revolution. Politics is not a mathematical science. Practically, it would have been incomparably more dangerous to minimize the significance of the change, than to magnify it. But a historical analysis has no need of those exaggerations proper to agitation.

Simplifying the thought of Lenin, Stalin said at the congress: "The situation is clear. Nobody talks now of the dual power. If the soviets formerly represented a real power, they are now merely instruments of the union of the masses, possessing no power." Some of the delegates replied to the effect that the reaction had triumphed in July, but that the counter-revolution was not victorious. Stalin answered with a surprising aphorism: "During a revolution there is no reaction." As a matter of fact a revolution triumphs only through a series of intermittent reactions. It always makes a step back for every two steps forward. Reaction is to counter-revolution as reform is to revolution. We may call *victories of the reaction* those changes in the régime which bring it in the direction of the demands of the counter-revolutionary class, without, however, altering the possessor of power; but a *victory of the counter-revolution* is unthinkable without the transfer of power to a different class. This decisive transfer of power did not occur in July.

"If the July insurrection was a semi-insurrection, then to a certain degree the victory of the counter-revolution was a semi-victory." Thus wrote Bukharin a few months ago—correctly enough, but without drawing the necessary inferences from his words. A semi-victory could not give the power to the bourgeoisie. The dual power was reconstructed, transformed, but it did not disappear. In the factories it was impossible as before to do anything against the will of the workers; the peasants retained enough power to prevent the landlord from enjoying his property rights; the commanders felt no confidence before the soldiers. But what is the power if it is not the material possibility to dispose of property rights and the military force? On August 13 Trotsky wrote in regard to the shifts which had occurred: "It was not merely that alongside the government stood the soviets, fulfilling a whole series of governmental functions. . . . The essence of the thing was that behind the soviets and behind the government stood two different régimes relying upon different classes. . . . The régime of the capitalist republic imposed from above, and the régime of the workers' democracy taking form below, paralyzed each other."

It is absolutely indubitable that the Executive Committee had lost the lion's share of its importance. But it would be a mistake to imagine that the bourgeoisie had received all that the compromise leaders had lost. These leaders had lost not only to the right, but also to the left—not only to the benefit of the military cliques, but also to the benefit of the factory and regimental committees. The power was decentralized, scattered—in part concealed underground together with that weapon which the worker hid away after the July defeat. The dual power had ceased to be "peaceful," contactual, regulated. It had become more concealed, more decentralized, more antithetic and explosive. At the end of August this concealed dual power again became active. We shall see what significance this fact acquired in October.

CHAPTER XIV

THE LAST COALITION

TRUE to its tradition, not to survive a single serious shock,
the Provisional Government went to pieces, as we remember, on the night of August 26. The Kadets withdrew in
order to make it easier for Kornilov. The socialists withdrew in
order to make it easier for Kerensky. Thus began a new governmental crisis. First of all arose the problem of Kerensky himself.
The head of the government had turned out to be an accomplice
in the conspiracy. The indignation against him was so great that
at the mention of his name the compromise leaders would occasionally even resort to the vocabulary of the Bolsheviks. Chernov,
who had recently jumped out of the ministerial train while
traveling at full speed, wrote in the central organ of his party
about "this general mix-up in which you can't make out where
Kornilov ends and where Filonenko and Savinkov begin, where
Savinkov ends and where begins the Provisional Government as
such." The hint was sufficiently clear. "The Provisional Government as such"—that was of course Kerensky, who belonged to
the same party as Chernov.

But having relieved their feelings with strong words, the
Compromisers decided that they could not get along without
Kerensky. Although they would not let Kerensky grant an amnesty to Kornilov, they themselves promptly granted one to
Kerensky. By way of compensation he agreed to make concessions on the question of the form of the Russian government.
Only yesterday it had been maintained that a Constituent Assembly alone could decide this question. Now the juridical difficulty suddenly disappeared. In the declaration of the government, the removal of Kornilov was explained by the necessity of
"saving the fatherland, freedom and the republican régime."
This purely verbal, and moreover belated, donation to the Left
did not, of course, in the least strengthen the authority of the

323

government—especially since Kornilov too had declared himself a republican.

On August 30 Kerensky was compelled to discharge Savinkov, who a few days later would even be expelled from the all-embracing party of the Social Revolutionaries. But a political equivalent of Savinkov was immediately appointed to the post of Governor-General—Palchinsky, who began by closing the Bolshevik paper. The Executive Committee protested. *Izvestia* called this act a "crude provocation." Palchinsky had to be removed in three more days. How little Kerensky intended to change the course of his policy at large, is demonstrated by the fact that as early as the 31st he had formed a new government with the participation of Kadets. Even the Social Revolutionaries would not go that far: they threatened to recall their representatives. It was Tseretelli who found a new recipe for the power: "Preserve the idea of the Coalition, but remove all those elements which hang like a millstone upon the government." "The idea of Coalition has been strengthened," sang Skobelev in chorus, "but there can be no place in the government for that party which was connected with the conspiracy of Kornilov." Kerensky would not agree to this limitation, and in his way he was right.

A Coalition with the bourgeoisie which excluded the ruling bourgeois party was obviously absurd. This was pointed out at a joint session of the Executive Committees by Kamenev, who in his characteristic tone of admonition drew the conclusions from the recent events. "You want to start us off on the still more dangerous road of Coalition with irresponsible groups. But you have forgotten about that coalition sealed and ratified by the ominous events of these past days—the coalition between the revolutionary proletariat, the peasantry, and the revolutionary army." The Bolshevik orator recalled the words spoken by Trotsky on May 26, in defending the Kronstadt sailors against the accusation of Tseretelli: "When a counter-revolutionary general tries to throw a noose around the neck of the revolution, the Kadets will soap the rope, and the Kronstadt sailors will come to fight and die with us." This recollection hit the mark. To the bombast about a "united democracy" and about an "honest coalition," Kamenev answered: "The unity of the democracy depends upon whether or not you enter into coalition with the Vyborg district. . . . Any other coalition is dishonest." The speech of Kamenev made an indubitable impression, registered by Sukhanov in these words: "Kamenev spoke very intelligently and tactfully." But it did not go beyond making an impression. The courses of the two sides were predetermined.

From the beginning the break between the Compromisers and the Kadets had been merely a matter of show. The liberal Kornilovists themselves understood that it behooved them to stay in the shadow for a few days. Behind the scenes it was therefore decided—in obvious agreement with the Kadets—to create a government standing to such a degree above all the real forces of the nation, that its temporary character could be a matter of doubt to nobody. Besides Kerensky, the directory of five members included the Minister of Foreign Affairs, Tereshchenko, who had already become irreplaceable thanks to his connections with the diplomats of the Entente; the commander of the Moscow military district, Verkhovsky, who was hastily promoted for this purpose from colonel to general; Admiral Verderevsky, who was for this purpose hastily let out of prison; and finally, the dubious Menshevik, Nikitin, whom his own party soon after acknowledged to be sufficiently ripe for expulsion from its ranks.

Having conquered Kornilov with the hands of others, Kerensky had only one concern, it would seem, and that was to carry out Kornilov's program. Kornilov had wished to unite the power of the commander-in-chief with the power at the head of the government. Kerensky accomplished this. Kornilov had intended to screen a personal dictatorship behind a directory of five members. Kerensky carried out this plan. Chernov, whose resignation had been demanded by the bourgeoisie, Kerensky put out of the Winter Palace. General Alexeiev, the hero of the Kadet party and its candidate for Minister-President, he named chief of the headquarters staff—that is, *de facto* head of the army. In his order to the army and fleet, Kerensky demanded a cessation of political struggle among the troops—that is, a restoration of the original situation. Lenin from his hiding-place described this situation in the upper circles with the extreme simplicity characteristic of him: "Kerensky is a Kornilovist who has accidentally quarreled

325

with Kornilov, and continues in intimate union with the other Kornilovists." There was only one drawback: the victory over the counter-revolution had been far more sweeping than was demanded by the personal plans of Kerensky.

The directory hastened to let out of prison the former War Minister, Guchkov, who was considered one of the instigators of the conspiracy. In general, the Department of Justice did not raise a hand against the Kadet instigators. In these circumstances it became more and more difficult to keep the Bolsheviks under lock and key. The government found a way out: without withdrawing the indictment, it would release the Bolsheviks on bail. The Petrograd soviet and trade unions took upon themselves "the honor of furnishing bail for the esteemed leader of the revolutionary proletariat," and on the 4th of September Trotsky was set free under the modest—indeed essentially fictitious—bail of 3,000 rubles. In his "History of the Russian Disturbance" General Denikin writes with unction: "On the 1st of September General Kornilov was arrested, and on the 4th of September Bronstein-Trotsky was set free by the same Provisional Government. Those two dates ought to remain in the memory of Russia." The liberation of Bolsheviks under bond continued during the next few days. Those liberated from prison wasted no time. The masses were waiting and calling. The party needed men.

On the day of Trotsky's liberation, Kerensky issued an order in which, recognizing that the Military Committee had given "very substantial help to the governmental power," he commanded this committee to cease from any further activity. Even *Izvestia* conceded that the author of this order revealed a rather feeble understanding of the situation. An inter-district conference of the soviets in Petrograd adopted a resolution: "Not to dissolve the revolutionary organizations of struggle with the counter-revolution." The pressure from below was so strong that the compromisist Military Revolutionary Committee decided not to accede to the order of Kerensky, and summoned its local branches "in view of the continued alarming situation to work with their former energy and restraint." Kerensky took this in silence. There was nothing else for him to do.

The omnipotent head of the Directory was compelled to ob-

serve at every step that the situation had altered, that the opposition had grown, and that it was necessary to make some change
—at least in words. On September 7, Verkhovsky announced in
the press that the program for the revival of the army prepared
before the Kornilov rebellion must be set aside for the time being,
since "in the present psychological condition of the army it would
only bring about its further demoralization." In token of the
beginning of a new era, the War Minister appeared before the
Executive Committee. Let them have no fear, he announced,
General Alexeiev is going, and along with him everybody who
had any connection whatever with the Kornilov insurrection.
Healthy principles must be inoculated into the army, he went on,
"not with whips and machine guns, but by way of the suggestion
of right, justice and firm discipline." That sounded quite like the
spring days of the revolution. But it was September outdoors, and
the autumn was coming. Alexeiev was actually removed after a
few days, and his place taken by General Dukhonin. The superiority of this general lay in the fact that nobody knew him.

In return for these concessions the Minister of War and Marine demanded immediate help from the Executive Committee:
the officers are standing under the sword of Damocles; it is worst
of all in the Baltic Fleet; you must pacify the sailors. After long
debate it was decided, as usual, to send a delegation to the fleet.
The Compromisers insisted, moreover, that the delegation should
include Bolsheviks, and above all Trotsky: only upon this condition, they said, could the delegation be sure of success. Trotsky
announced: "We decisively reject the form of co-operation with
the government which Tseretelli defends. . . . The government
is conducting a policy false to the bottom, against the interests of
the people, and uncontrolled by them. But when this policy runs
into a bag's end or produces a catastrophe, then they want to impose upon the revolutionary organizations the hard labor of
smoothing out the inevitable consequences. . . . One of the
tasks of this delegation, as you formulate it, is to hunt out in the
staff of the garrison the "dark forces"—that is, provocateurs and
spies. . . . Have you forgotten then that I myself am indicted
under Article 108? . . . In the struggle against lynch-law we
will travel our own road. . . . Not hand in hand with the At-

torney General and the Intelligence Service, but as a revolutionary party which is persuading, organizing, and educating."

The convocation of a "Democratic Conference" had been decided upon in the days of the Kornilov insurrection. Its functions were: to reveal the strength of the democracy, to instill respect for it among its enemies, both right and left, and finally—by no means the least of its tasks—to bridle the too eager Kerensky. The Compromisers seriously intended to subject the government to some sort of improvised representative institution until the convocation of the Constituent Assembly. The bourgeoisie took a hostile attitude in advance, looking upon this Conference as an attempt to fortify the position which the democracy had regained through the victory over Kornilov. "This device of Tseretelli," writes Miliukov in his history, "was in essence a complete capitulation before the plans of Lenin and Trotsky." Exactly the contrary: Tseretelli's device was aimed to paralyze the struggle of the Bolsheviks for a soviet government. The Democratic Conference was set over against the Congress of the Soviets. The Compromisers were creating a new base for themselves, trying to strangle the soviets by an artificial combination of all kinds of organizations. The democrats apportioned the votes at their own discretion, guiding themselves by one thought only: to guarantee themselves an indubitable majority. The higher-up organizations were vastly better represented than the lower. The organs of self-government, among them the undemocratic zemstvos, enormously outbalanced the soviets. The Cooperators [1] appeared in the rôle of masters of destiny.

Having up to this time occupied no place in politics, the Cooperators were first pushed forward into the political arena during the days of that Moscow conference, and from then on they began to appear no otherwise than as the representatives of their 20 million members—or, to put it more simply, of some half the population of Russia. The cooperatives sent their roots down into the village through its upper strata, through those who approved of a "just" expropriation of the nobility on condition that their own landed property, often very considerable, should receive not only defense but augmentation. The leaders of the

---

[1] Official personnel of the cooperatives.

328

cooperatives were recruited from the liberal-Narodnik and partly the liberal-Marxist intelligentsia, which formed a natural bridge between the Kadets and the Compromisers. To the Bolsheviks the Cooperators took the same attitude of hatred which the Kulak takes to an unsubmissive hired man. The Compromisers eagerly seized upon the Cooperators, after the latter had thrown off the mask of neutrality, in order to strengthen themselves against the Bolsheviks. Lenin mercilessly denounced these chefs of the democratic kitchen. "Ten convinced soldiers or workers from a backward factory are worth a thousand times more than a hundred of these hand-picked . . . delegates." Trotsky argued in the Petrograd Soviet that the officials of the cooperatives as little expressed the political will of the peasants as a physician the political will of his patients, or a Post Office clerk the views of those who send and receive letters. "The Cooperators have to be good organizers, merchants, bookkeepers, but for the defense of their class rights the peasants, like the workers, trust the soviets." This did not prevent the Cooperators from receiving 150 seats and, along with the unreformed zemstvos and all sorts of other organizations dragged in by the hair, completely dislocating the representation of the masses.

The Petrograd Soviet included Lenin and Zinoviev in the list of its delegates to the Conference. The government issued an order for the arrest of both delegates at the entrance to the theater building, but not in the actual hall of the Conference. Such was, evidently, the agreement arrived at between the Compromisers and Kerensky. But the matter went no farther than a political demonstration on the part of the Soviet: neither Lenin nor Zinoviev intended to appear at the Conference. Lenin considered that the Bolsheviks had no business there at all.

The Democratic Conference opened on the 14th of September, exactly a month after the State Conference, in the auditorium of the Alexandrinsky Theatre. The credentials of 1,775 representatives were accepted; about 1,200 were present at the opening. The Bolsheviks of course were in the minority, but in spite of all the tricks of the elective method, they constituted a very considerable group, which upon certain questions gathered around itself more than a third of the whole assembly.

Would it be suitable for a strong government to appear before a mere "private" conference of this sort? That question became a matter of enormous indecision in the Winter Palace, and of reflected excitements in the Alexandrinsky. In the long run the head of the government decided to show himself to the democracy. "He was met with applause," says Shliapnikov, describing the arrival of Kerensky, "and went over to the praesidium to shake hands with those sitting at the table. We (the Bolsheviks) were sitting not far from each other, and when it came our turn, we glanced at each other and agreed not to extend our hands. A theatrical gesture across the table—I drew back from the hand offered me, and Kerensky with his hand extended, not meeting ours, passed along the table!" The head of the government got a like greeting on the opposite wing from the Kornilovists—and besides the Bolsheviks and the Kornilovists there were now no real forces left.

Being compelled by the whole situation to offer an explanation on the subject of his rôle in the conspiracy, Kerensky once again relied too much upon improvisation.

"I knew what they wanted," he let fall. "Before they went to Kornilov they came to me and suggested that I take the same course." Cries on the left: "Who came? Who suggested?" Frightened by the echo of his own words, Kerensky closed up. But the political background of the plot had already been revealed to the most naïve. The Ukrainian Compromiser Porsh reported to the rada[1] in Kiev upon his return: "Kerensky did not succeed in proving his non-participation in the Kornilov uprising." But the head of the government dealt himself another no less heavy blow in his speech, when in answer to those phrases that everybody was sick of—"In the moment of danger all will come forward and give an account of themselves," etc., somebody shouted: "And the death penalty?" The orator, losing his equilibrium, cried out, to the complete surprise of everybody probably including himself: "Wait a little. When one single death penalty has been signed by me, the supreme commander-in-chief, then I will permit you to curse me." A soldier came right up to the edge of the platform and shouted at close quarters. "You are

[1] Parliament.

330

the calamity of the country!" So that is what it had come to! He, Kerensky, had been ready to forget the high place which he occupied, and talk things over with the conference as a man. "But not all here understand a man." Therefore he would speak in the language of authority: "Anyone who dares . . ." Alas, that had been heard before in Moscow, and Kornilov nevertheless had dared.

"If the death penalty was necessary," asked Trotsky in his speech, "then how does he, Kerensky, dare say that he will not make use of it? And if he considers it possible to give his promise to the democracy not to apply the death penalty, then . . . its restoration becomes an act of light-mindedness transcending the limits of criminality." The whole assembly agreed to that—some silently, some with an uproar. "With that confession Kerensky seriously discredited both himself and the Provisional Government," says his colleague and admirer, the Assistant Minister of Justice, Demianov.

Not one of the ministers was able to report anything that the government had done besides solving the problem of how to exist. Economic measures? Not one could be named. Peace policy? "I do not know," said the former Minister of Justice, Zarudny—more frank than the others—"whether the Provisional Government has done anything in this regard. I have not seen it." Zarudny complained perplexedly that "the whole power has arrived in the hands of a man" at whose nod ministers come and go. Tseretelli incautiously took up this theme: "Let the democracy upbraid itself, if on the heights its representative has got a little dizzy." But it was Tseretelli who most fully incarnated all those traits of the democracy which had given rise to Bonapartist tendencies in the government. "Why does Kerensky occupy the place which he occupies today?" retorted Trotsky. "A place was opened for Kerensky by the weakness and irresolution of the democracy. . . . I have not heard a single speaker here who would take upon himself the unenviable honor of defending the directory or its president. . . ." After an outbreak of protests the speaker continued: "I am sorry to say that the point of view which now finds such a stormy expression in the hall has not found any deliberated expression from this tribune. Not one speaker has come out here

331

and said to us: 'Why are you arguing about the past of the Coalition? Why are you worrying about the future? We have Kerensky and that is enough. . . .' " But the Bolshevik presentation of the question almost automatically united Tseretelli with Zarudny, and united them both with Kerensky. Of this Miliukov has pointedly written: Zarudny could complain of the arbitrary power of Kerensky; Tseretelli could throw out a hint that the government was getting dizzy—"those were mere words"— But when Trotsky stated that nobody in the conference would undertake the open defense of Kerensky "the assembly immediately felt that this was spoken by a common enemy."

The power was spoken of by these people who embodied it no otherwise than as a burden and a misfortune. A struggle for power? Minister Peshekhonov instructed the delegates: "The power has now become a thing from which everybody is trying to protect himself." Was this true? Kornilov had not tried to protect himself. But that quite fresh lesson was already half forgotten. Tseretelli stormed at the Bolsheviks because they did not take the power themselves, but were pushing the soviets toward the power. Others took up the thought of Tseretelli. Yes, the Bolsheviks ought to take the power!—murmured the praesidium, as they sat around the table. Avksentiev turned to Shliapnikov who sat near him: "Take the power, the masses will follow you." Answering his neighbor in the same tone, Shliapnikov suggested that they first lay the power on the table of the praesidium. These semi-ironical challenges to the Bolsheviks, issued both through speeches in the tribune and conversations in the couloir, were partly taunts and partly reconnoiters. What are these people going to do next, now that they have come to the head of the Petrograd, the Moscow, and many of the provincial soviets? Can it be that they will really dare seize the power? This could hardly be believed. Ten days before the challenging speech of Tseretelli, Rech had declared that the best way to get rid of Bolshevism for many years would be to turn the country over to its leaders. "But those sorry heroes of the day are themselves far from desirous of seizing the whole power. . . . Practically their position cannot be taken seriously from any standpoint." This proud conclusion was, to say the least, a little hasty.

An immense advantage of the Bolsheviks—and one up to this time, it seems to me, not adequately appreciated—was the fact that they excellently understood their enemies, that they completely saw through them. They were aided in this by the materialistic method, the Leninist school of clarity and simplicity, and the keen vigilance proper to people who have decided to carry a struggle through to the end. On the other hand, the Liberals and Compromisers invented Bolsheviks to suit themselves and the demands of the moment. It could not have been otherwise. Those parties for whom evolution has left no future never prove capable of looking reality in the face—just as a hopeless invalid dares not look in the face of his disease.

However, although they did not believe in the insurrection of the Bolsheviks, the Compromisers feared it. This was best of all expressed by Kerensky. "Make no mistake," he cried out suddenly in the midst of his speech. "Do not think that when the Bolsheviks bait me, the forces of the democracy are not there to support me. Do not think that I am hanging in the air. Remember that if you start something, the railroads will stop. There will be no transmission of dispatches . . ." A part of the hall applauded, a part kept an embarrassed silence. The Bolshevik section laughed outright. It is a poor dictatorship which is compelled to argue that it is not hanging in the air!

To these ironical challenges, accusations of cowardice, and clumsy threats, the Bolsheviks made answer in their Declaration: "In struggling for the power in order to realize its program, our party has never desired and does not desire to seize the power against the organized will of the majority of the toiling masses of the country." That meant: We will take the power as the party of the soviet majority. Those words about "the organized will of the toiling masses" referred to the coming Congress of Soviets. "Only such decisions and proposals of the present Conference . . . can find their way to realization" said the Declaration, "as are recognized by the All-Russian Congress of Soviets. . . ."

During the reading of the Bolshevik Declaration by Trotsky, its mention of the necessity of immediately arming the workers evoked persistent cries from the benches of the majority: "What for? What for?" Here was that same note of alarm and provocation. What for? "In order to create a real bulwark against the counter-revolution," answered the orator. But not only for that: "I say to you in the name of our party and the proletarian masses adhering to it that the armed workers . . . will defend the country of the revolution against the armies of imperialism with a heroism such as Russian history has never known. . . ." Tseretelli characterized this promise, which sharply divided the hall, as an empty phrase. The history of the Red Army subsequently refuted him.

Those hot moments when the compromise chiefs had renounced their coalition with the Kadets were now far behind: without the Kadets a coalition had proved impossible. Surely you wouldn't ask us to take the power ourselves! "We might have seized the power on the 27th of February," meditated Skobelev, "but . . . we employed all our influence in helping the bourgeois elements recover from their confusion . . . and come into the power." Why then had these gentlemen prevented the Kornilovists, as they recovered from their confusion, from taking the power? A purely bourgeois government, explained Tseretelli, is still impossible: that would cause a civil war. It was necessary to break Kornilov in order that with his adventure he should not prevent the bourgeoisie from coming to power through a series of stages. "Now when the revolutionary democracy has proven victorious, the moment is especially favorable for a coalition."

The political philosophy of the cooperatives was expressed by their leader, Berkenheim: "Whether we want it or not, the bourgeoisie is the class to whom the power will belong." The old revolutionary Narodnik, Minor, beseeched the conference to adopt a unanimous decision in favor of coalition. Otherwise "there is no use deceiving ourselves. Otherwise we will slaughter. . . ." "Whom?" cried the Left benches. "We will slaughter each other," concluded Minor in an ominous silence. But in reality what made a governmental bloc necessary according to the views of the Kadets, was the struggle against the "anarchist hooliganism" of the Bolsheviks. "That really constitutes the essence of the idea of the coalition," as Miliukov quite frankly explained. While Minor was hoping that a coalition would make it possible for the Compromisers and the Bolsheviks not to slaughter each other, Miliukov, on the contrary, was firmly calculating that the coalition would make it possible for the joint forces of the Compromisers and the Kadets to slaughter the Bolsheviks.

During the debate about a coalition, Riazanov read an editorial from *Rech* of August 29 which Miliukov had withdrawn at the last moment, leaving a blank space in the paper: "Yes, we do not fear to state that General Kornilov was pursuing those same objects which we consider necessary for the salvation of the fatherland." The reading made a sensation. "They will save it all right!" somebody shouted on the left. But the Kadets found their defenders: After all, the editorial had not been printed! Moreover, not all the Kadets had stood for Kornilov, and we must learn to distinguish the sinners from the saints.

"They say that we must not accuse the whole Kadet Party of participation in the Kornilov insurrection," Trotsky answered. "Znamensky has said to us Bolsheviks here and not for the first time: 'You protested when we held your whole party responsible for the movement of July 3–5; do not repeat the same mistake; do not hold all the Kadets responsible for the insurrection of Kornilov.' But in my opinion there is a slight inaccuracy in this comparison. When they accused the Bolsheviks of calling out the movement of July 3–5, it was not a question of inviting them into the ministry, but of inviting them into the jails. Zarudny (the Minister of Justice) will not, I trust, deny this difference. We say now too: If you want to drag the Kadets to prison for the Kornilov movement, don't do this wholesale, but inspect each individual Kadet from all sides (Laughter; voice: 'Bravo!'). When it is a question of introducing the Kadet Party into the ministry, then the decisive thing is not the circumstance that this or that Kadet was in contact with Kornilov behind the scenes— not that Maklakov stood at the telegraph apparatus while Savinkov conducted his negotiations with Kornilov—not that Rodichev went to the Don and conducted political negotiations with Kaledin—not *that* is the essence of the thing; the essence of it is that the *whole* bourgeois press either openly welcomed Kornilov or cautiously kept mum awaiting his victory. . . . That is why I tell you that you have no partners for a coalition!" The next day a representative from Helsingfors and Sveaborg, the sailor Shishkin, spoke more briefly and suggestively on the same theme: "A Coalition Ministry will have neither confidence nor support among the sailors of the Baltic Fleet and the garrison of Finland. . . . Against the creation of a Coalition Ministry the sailors have raised their battle flag!" Arguments from reason had been ineffective. The sailor Shishkin advanced the argument of the naval guns. He was heartily supported by other sailors doing sentry duty at the entrance to the hall. Bukharin subsequently related how "the sailors posted by Kerensky to defend the Democratic Conference against us, the Bolsheviks, turned to Trotsky and asked him, shaking their bayonets: 'How soon can we get to work with these things?'" That was merely a repetition of the question asked by the sailors of the *Aurora* at the interview in Kresty prison. But now the moment was drawing near.

If we disregard fine shades, it is easy to distinguish three groupings in the Democratic Conference: an extensive but very unstable center which does not dare seize the power, agrees to a coalition, but does not want the Kadets; a weak Right Wing which stands unconditionally for Kerensky and a coalition with the bourgeoisie; a Left Wing, twice as strong, which stands for a government of the soviets or a socialist government. At a caucus of the soviet delegates to the Democratic Conference, Trotsky spoke for the transfer of power to the soviets, Martov for a homogeneous socialist ministry. The first formula got 86 votes, the second 97. Formally only about one-half of the workers' and soldiers' soviets were at that moment in control of the Bolsheviks; the other half were wavering between the Bolsheviks and the Compromisers. But the Bolsheviks spoke in the name of the powerful soviets of the more industrial and cultural centers of the country. In the soviets they were immeasurably stronger than at the Conference, and in the proletariat and army immeasurably stronger than in the soviets. The backward soviets were, moreover, rapidly drawing up to the advanced ones.

At the Democratic Conference 766 deputies against 688 voted for a coalition, with 38 abstaining. The two camps were almost equal! An amendment excluding the Kadets from the coalition got a majority: 595 against 493, with 72 abstaining. But the re-

336

moval of the Kadets made a coalition entirely purposeless. For that
reason the resolution as a whole was voted down by a majority of
813—that is, a bloc of the extreme wings, the resolute partisans
and implacable enemies of the coalition, against the center, which
had melted to 133 votes, with 80 abstaining. That was the most
united of all the votes, but it was just as meaningless as the idea
of a coalition without the Kadets which it rejected.

"Upon the basic question . . ." as Miliukov just observes,
"the Conference thus remained without an opinion and without a
formula."

What remained for the leaders to do? To trample on the will
of "the democracy" which had rejected their own will. A
praesidium was assembled consisting of representatives of separate parties and groups to re-decide a question which had already
been decided by a plenary session. The result: 50 votes for a
coalition, 60 against. Now it would seem that the thing was clear?
The question whether the government should be responsible to the
Democratic Conference as a permanent body, was unanimously
decided in the affirmative by this same enlarged praesidium. 56
hands against 48 with 10 abstaining were raised in favor of filling
out the body with representatives of the bourgeoisie. Kerensky
then appeared and announced that he would refuse to participate
in a homogeneous government. After that the only thing left to
do was to send the unhappy Conference home, and replace it with
institutions in which the partisans of unconditional coalition
would be in the majority. To attain this desired consummation it
was only necessary to understand the rules of arithmetic. In the
name of the praesidium Tseretelli introduced a resolution in the
Conference to the effect that this representative body had been
summoned "to co-operate in the creation of a government," and
that the government would have to "sanction this body." The
dream of putting a bridle on Kerensky was thus filed in the
archives. Having been filled out with the necessary proportion of
bourgeois representatives, the future Council of the Republic, or
Pre-Parliament, would have as its task the sanctioning of a coalition government with the Kadets. The resolution of Tseretelli
meant the exact opposite of what the conference wanted, and
what the praesidium had just now resolved upon, but the general

breakdown, decay and demoralization were so great that the assembly adopted the slightly disguised capitulation presented to it by 829 votes against 106, with 69 abstaining. "And so for the moment you have conquered, Messrs. Compromisers and Kadets," wrote the Bolshevik paper. "Play your game. Make your new experiment. It will be your last—we will vouch for that."

"The Democratic Conference," says Stankevich, "astonished even its own initiators with its extraordinary looseness of thought." In the compromise parties—"complete confusion"; on the Right, in the bourgeois circles—"a noise of muttering, slanders conveyed in a whisper, a slow corroding of the last remnants of governmental authority . . . ; and only on the Left, a consolidation of moods and forces." This was spoken by an opponent. This is the testimony of an enemy who will again be shooting at the Bolsheviks in October. This Petrograd parade of the democracy proved to be for the Compromisers what the Moscow parade of national unity had been for Kerensky—a public confession of bankruptcy, a review of political prostration. Whereas the State Conference gave an impetus to the insurrection of Kornilov, the Democratic Conference finally cleared the road for the Bolshevik insurrection.

Before dispersing, the Conference appointed from its members a permanent body composed of 15 per cent of the membership of each of its groups—in all, about 350 delegates. The institutions of the possessing classes were to receive in addition to this 120 seats. The government in its own name added 20 seats for the Cossacks. All these together were to constitute a Council of the Republic, or Pre-Parliament, which was to represent the nation until the Constituent Assembly.

What attitude to adopt toward the Council of the Republic immediately became for the Bolsheviks an acute tactical problem. Should they enter it or not? The boycott of parliamentary institutions on the part of anarchists and semi-anarchists is dictated by a desire not to submit their weakness to a test on the part of the masses, thus preserving their right to an inactive hauteur which makes no difference to anybody. A revolutionary party can turn its back to a parliament only if it has set itself the immediate task of overthrowing the existing régime. During the years between the two revolutions, Lenin had gone with great profundity into this problem of revolutionary parliamentarism.

Even a parliament based on the most limited franchise may become, and has more than once in history become, an expression of the actual correlation of classes. Such were, for example, the State Dumas after the defeated revolution of 1905–7. To boycott such parliaments is to boycott the actual correlation of forces, instead of trying to change it to the advantage of the revolution. But the Pre-Parliament of Tseretelli and Kerensky did not correspond in the slightest degree to the correlation of forces. It was created by the impotence and trickery of the upper circles—by their mystic faith in institutions, their fetishism of forms, their hope of subjecting to this fetishism an incomparably more powerful enemy and therewith disciplining him.

In order to compel the revolution, hunching its shoulders and bending its back, to pass submissively under the yoke of the Pre-Parliament, it was first necessary to shatter the revolution, or in any case to inflict upon it a serious defeat. In reality, however, it was only three weeks ago that the vanguard of the bourgeoisie had suffered a defeat. The revolution had experienced an influx of forces. It had taken for its goal not a bourgeois republic, but a republic of workers and peasants. It had no reason for crawling under the yoke of the Pre-Parliament when it was steadily broadening its power in the soviets.

On the 20th of September, the Central Committee of the Bolsheviks called a party conference consisting of the Bolshevik delegates to the Democratic Conference, the members of the Central Committee itself, and of the Petrograd committee. As spokesman for the Central Committee, Trotsky proposed the slogan of boycotting the Pre-Parliament. The proposal was met with decisive resistance by some (Kamenev, Rykov, Riazanov) and with sympathy by others (Sverdlov, Joffé, Stalin). The Central Committee, having divided in two on the debated question, had found itself compelled, in conflict with the constitution and traditions of the party, to submit the question to the decision of the conference. Two spokesmen, Trotsky and Rykov, took the floor as champions of the opposing views. It might seem, and for the majority it did seem, that this hot debate was purely tactical in char-

339

acter. In reality the quarrel revived the April disagreements and initiated the disagreements of October. The question was whether the party should accommodate its tasks to the development of a bourgeois republic, or should really set itself the goal of conquering the power. By a majority of 77 votes against 50, this party conference rejected the slogan of boycott. On September 22nd, Riazanov had the satisfaction of announcing at the Democratic Conference in the name of the party that the Bolsheviks would send their representatives to the Pre-Parliament, in order "in this new fortress of compromisism to expose all attempts at a new coalition with the bourgeoisie." That sounded very radical, but it really meant substituting a policy of oppositional exposure for a policy of revolutionary action.

Lenin's April theses had been appropriated by the whole party; but upon every big question that arose, the March attitudes would swim out from under them. And these attitudes were very strong in the upper layers of the party, which in many parts of the country had only just now divided from the Mensheviks. Lenin was able to take his part in this argument only after the event. On the 23rd of September he wrote: "We must boycott the Pre-Parliament. We must go out into the soviets of workers, soldiers, and peasants' deputies, go out into the trade unions, go out in general to the masses. We must summon them to the struggle. We must give them a correct and clear slogan: To drive out the Bonapartist gang of Kerensky with its fake Pre-Parliament. . . . The Mensheviks and Social Revolutionaries even after the Kornilov events refused to accept our offer of compromise. . . . Ruthless struggle against them! Ruthless expulsion of them from all revolutionary organizations! . . . Trotsky was for the boycott. Bravo, Comrade Trotsky! Boycottism was defeated in the faction of the Bolsheviks who attended the Democratic Conference. Long live the boycott!"

The deeper down this question went into the party, the more decisively did the correlation of forces change in favor of the boycott. Almost all the local organizations formed into majorities and minorities. In the Kiev committee, for example, the advocates of boycott, Efgenia Bosh at their head, were a weak minority. But only a few days later at a general city conference, a resolution in favor of boycotting the Pre-Parliament was adopted by an over-whelming majority. "There is no use wasting time," the resolution declared, "in chattering and spreading illusions." Thus the party promptly corrected its leaders.

During this time Kerensky, having abandoned all languid pretenses at democracy, was trying with all his might to show the Kadets that he had a firm hand. On September 18 he issued an un-expected order dissolving the central committee of the fleet. The sailors answered: "The order dissolving the Centroflot, being un-lawful, is to be considered inoperative, and its immediate annul-ment is demanded." The Executive Committee intervened, and supplied Kerensky with a formal pretext for annulling his de-cision after three days. In Tashkent the soviet, which had a Social Revolutionary majority, seized the power and removed the old officials. Kerensky sent the general designated to put down Tash-kent a telegram: "No negotiations whatever with the rebels. . . . The most decisive measures are necessary." The troops occupied the city, and arrested the representatives of the soviet power. A general strike occurred immediately with forty trade unions par-ticipating. For a week no papers were published, and the garrison was in a ferment. Thus in pursuit of a phantom law and order, the government was sowing bureaucratic anarchy.

On the day the Conference adopted its decision against a coalition with the Kadets, the central committee of the Kadet party had proposed to Konovalov and Kishkin that they accept Kerensky's offer of a place in the ministry. The move, it is said, was directed by Buchanan. That, however, you need not take too literally. If Buchanan was not himself the director, his shadow was: a government acceptable to the Allies had to be born. The Moscow industrialists and brokers had got their backs up. They had raised their price, and presented an ultimatum. The Demo-cratic Conference passed off in voting, imagining that its votes had a real significance. In reality the question had been decided in the Winter Palace at a joint session of the fragments of the gov-ernment with the representatives of the coalition parties. The Kadets had sent here their most frank Kornilovists. All joined in persuading each other of the necessity of unity. Tseretelli, that inexhaustible layer-down of commonplaces, discovered that the chief obstacle to an agreement "has consisted up to this point in mutual distrust. . . . This distrust ought to be removed." The Minister of Foreign Affairs, Tereshchenko, figured up and reported that out of the 197 days' existence of the revolutionary government, 56 days had been occupied in crises. How the remaining days had been occupied he did not state.

Even before the Democratic Conference in direct conflict with its own intentions had swallowed Tseretelli's resolution, the correspondents of the English and American papers had cabled home that a Coalition with the Kadets was assured, and had confidently given the names of the new ministers. On its part, the Moscow Council of Public Men, with our old friend Rodzianko in the chair, sent congratulations to its member Tretiakov who had been invited to enter the government. On the 9th of August these same gentlemen had sent Kornilov a telegram: "In this threatening hour of severe trial all thinking Russia looks to you with hope and faith."

Kerensky graciously consented to the existence of the Pre-Parliament on condition that "it be recognized that the organization of the power and the appointment of the staff of the government belong to the Provisional Government only." This humiliating condition was dictated by the Kadets. The bourgeoisie could not, of course, fail to understand that the membership of a Constituent Assembly would be far less favorable to it than the membership of the Pre-Parliament. "The elections for the Constituent Assembly"—to quote Miliukov—"can only give the most accidental and perhaps pernicious results." If in spite of this, the Kadet party—which had not long ago tried to subject the government to the tzarist Duma—absolutely refused legislative rights to the Pre-Parliament, this could only mean that it had not given up hope of quashing the Constituent Assembly.

"Either Kornilov or Lenin": thus Miliukov defined the alternative. Lenin on his part wrote: "Either a Soviet government or Kornilovism. There is no middle course." To this extent Miliukov and Lenin coincided in their appraisal of the situation—and not accidentally. In contrast to the heroes of the compromise phrase, these two were serious representatives of the basic classes of society. According to Miliukov the Moscow State Con-

342

ference had already made it clearly obvious that "the country is dividing into two camps, between which there can be no essential conciliation or agreement." But where there can be no agreement between two social camps, the issue is decided by civil war.

However, neither the Kadets nor the Bolsheviks withdrew the slogan of the Constituent Assembly. It was needful to the Kadets as the last court of appeal against immediate social reform, against the soviets, against the revolution. That shadow which democracy cast before it in the form of the Constituent Assembly, was employed by the bourgeoisie in opposition to the living democracy. The bourgeoisie could openly reject the Constituent Assembly only after they had crushed the Bolsheviks. They were far from that. At the given stage the Kadets were trying to assure the government's independence of those organizations bound up with the masses, in order afterward the more surely and completely to subject the government to themselves.

But the Bolsheviks also, although finding no way out on the road of formal democracy, had not yet renounced the idea of the Constituent Assembly. Moreover, they could not do this without abandoning revolutionary realism. Whether the future course of events would create the conditions for a complete victory of the proletariat, could not with absolute certainty be foreseen. Exactly as the Bolsheviks defended the compromisist soviets and the democratic municipalities against Kornilov, so they were ready to defend the Constituent Assembly against the attempts of the bourgeoisie.

The thirty day crisis ended at last in the creation of a new government. The chief rôle, after Kerensky, was to be played by the very rich Moscow industrialist, Konovalov, who at the beginning of the revolution had financed Gorky's paper, had thereafter become a member of the first coalition government, had resigned in protest after the first congress of the soviets, entered the Kadet party when it was ripe for the Kornilov events, and now returned into the government in the capacity of Vice-President and Minister of Commerce and Industry. Along with Konovalov, ministerial posts were occupied by Tretiakov, the president of the Moscow stock exchange committee, and Smirnov, president of the Moscow Military Industrial Committee. The sugar manufacturer from Kiev, Tereshchenko, remained Minister of Foreign Affairs. The other ministers—among them the Socialists—had no traits of identification, but were wholly prepared to sing in tune. The Entente could be the more satisfied with the government in that the old diplomatic official, Nabokov, remained ambassador in London; the Kadet Maklakov, an ally of Kornilov and Savinkov, went as an ambassador to Paris; and to Berne, the "progressive" Efremov. The struggle for a democratic peace was thus placed in reliable hands. The Declaration of the new government was a spiteful parody of the Moscow Declaration of the democracy. The meaning of the Coalition lay, however, not in its program of transformations, but in its attempt to carry through the business of the July days: to behead the revolution by shattering the Bolsheviks. But here *Rabochy Put,* one of the reincarnations of *Pravda,* impudently reminded the partners: "You have forgotten that the Bolsheviks are now the Soviets of Workers' and Soldiers' Deputies." This reminder touched a sore point. As Miliukov recognizes: "The fatal question presented itself: Is it not now too late to declare war on the Bolsheviks?"

And indeed it actually was too late. On the day the new government was formed, with six bourgeois and ten semi-socialist ministers, the Petrograd Soviet completed the formation of a new Executive Committee, consisting of thirteen Bolsheviks, six Social Revolutionaries and three Mensheviks. The Soviet greeted the governmental coalition with a resolution introduced by its new president, Trotsky. "The new government . . . will go into the history of the revolution as the civil war government. . . . The news of the formation of the government will be met by the whole revolutionary democracy with one answer: Resign! Relying upon this unanimous voice of the authentic democracy, the All-Russian Congress of Soviets will create a genuinely revolutionary government." The enemy tried to see in this resolution a mere ritual vote of non-confidence. In reality it was a program of revolution. Exactly a month was required for its realization.

The curve of industry continued sharply downward. The government, the Central Executive Committee, and soon the newly created Pre-Parliament, registered the facts and symptoms of decline as arguments against anarchy, the Bolsheviks, and the revolution. But they had not themselves the ghost of an industrial plan. A body constituted by the government for the regulation of industry did not take one single serious step. The capitalists were shutting down the factories; the movement of the railroads was decreasing through lack of coal; electric power stations were dying down in the cities; the press was wailing about a catastrophe; prices were rising; the workers were striking, layer after layer, in spite of the warnings of parties, soviets, and trade unions. Only those layers of the working class did not enter the strike conflict, which were already consciously moving towards a revolution. The most peaceful city of all, perhaps, was Petrograd.

The government, with its inattention to the masses, its light-minded indifference to their needs, its impudent phrase-mongering in answer to protests and cries of despair, was raising up everybody against it. It seemed as though the government were deliberately seeking a conflict. The railroad workers and clerks almost since the February revolution had been demanding a raise. Commission had followed commission, nobody had made an answer, and this was getting on the nerves of the railroad workers. The Compromisers had pacified them; the Vikzhel had held them back. But on the 24th of September the explosion came. Only then did the government wake up to the situation. Some sort of concessions were made to the railroad workers, and on September 27th the strike, which had already seized a large section of the railroads, was called off.

August and September were months of swift deterioration in the food situation. Already in the Kornilov days the bread ration had been cut down in Moscow and Petrograd to half a pound a day. In Moscow county they began to give out no more than two pounds a week. The Volga, the South, the Front, and the immediate rear—all parts of the country were experiencing a sharp food crisis. In the textile district near Moscow a number of factories had already begun to starve in the literal sense of the word. The working-men and women of the Smirnov factory—whose owner was in those very days invited as State Auditor into the new coalition ministry—held a demonstration in the neighboring town of Orekhov-Zuyev with placards reading: "We are starving", "Our children are starving", "Whoever is not for us is against us." The workers of Orekhov and the soldiers of the local military hospital divided their scanty rations with the demonstrators. That was another coalition rising against the Coalition Government.

The newspapers were every day recording new centers of conflict and rebellion. Workers, soldiers and the town petty bourgeoisie were protesting. Soldiers' wives were demanding increased subventions, living quarters, wood for the winter. Black Hundred agitation was trying to find fuel in the hunger of the masses. The Moscow Kadet paper *Russkie Vedomosti,* which in the old times united Liberalism with Narodnikism, now looked with hatred and disgust upon the authentic *narod*—the people. "A broad wave of disorders has swept through all Russia," wrote the liberal professors. "The spontaneousness and meaninglessness of these pogroms . . . more than anything else, makes it difficult to struggle with them. . . ." Resort to measures of repression, to the aid of armed forces? But it is exactly the armed forces, in the shape of soldiers from the local garrison, that play the chief part in these pogroms. The crowd comes into the streets and begins to feel itself master of the situation.

The Saratov district attorney reported to the Minister of Justice Maliantovich, who in the epoch of the first revolution had counted himself a Bolshevik: "The chief evil against which we have no power to fight is the soldiers. Lynch-law, arbitrary arrests and searches, requisitions of every kind—all these things are carried out in the majority of cases either exclusively by the soldiers, or with their immediate participation." In Saratov itself, in the county seats, in the villages, there is "a complete absence on all sides of assistance to the Department of Justice." The district attorney's offices have no time even to register the crimes which a whole people are committing.

The Bolsheviks had no illusions about the difficulties which would fall upon them along with the power. "In advancing the slogan 'All power to the soviets,'" said the new president of the Petrograd Soviet, "we know that it will not heal all sores in a minute. We need a power created in the image of the executive of the trade unions, which will give the strikers all that it can, which

346

will conceal nothing, and when it cannot give, will openly acknowledge the fact. . . ."

One of the first sittings of the government was devoted to the problem of "anarchy" in the localities, especially in the villages. Once more it was declared necessary "not to stop at the most decisive measures." In passing, the government discovered that the cause of the failure of the struggle against disorders lay in the "inadequate popularity" of the government commissars among the masses of the peasant population. In order to help out, it was decided to organize immediately in all provinces affected by disorders "special committees of the Provisional Government." Henceforth the peasantry were expected to meet punitive detachments with shouts of welcome.

Inexorable historic forces were dragging the rulers down. Nobody seriously believed in the success of the new government. Kerensky's isolation was beyond mending. The ruling classes could not forget his betrayal of Kornilov. "Those who were ready to fight against the Bolsheviks," writes the Cossack officer Kakliugin, "did not want to do it in the name of, or in defense of, the power of the Provisional Government." Although hanging on to the power, Kerensky himself feared to make any use of it. The growing force of the opposition paralyzed his will to the last fibre. He evaded any decisions whatever, and avoided the Winter Palace where the situation compelled him to act. Almost immediately after the formation of the new government he slipped the presidency to Konovalov, and himself went to headquarters where there was the least possible need of him. He came back to Petrograd only to open the Pre-Parliament. Although urged to remain by his ministers, he nevertheless returned to the front on the 14th. Kerensky was running away from a fate which followed at his heels.

Konovalov, the closest colleague of Kerensky and his Vice-President, got into a state of despair, according to Nabokov, over Kerensky's instability and the complete impossibility of relying upon his word. But the mood of the other members of the cabinet differed little from that of their chief. The ministers kept looking round and listening in alarm, waiting, jotting down little notes of evasion, occupying themselves with trifles. The Minister of Justice, Maliantovich, was dreadfully troubled, according to Nabokov, over the fact that the senators would not admit into their body the new colleague Sokolov, who wore a black business suit. "What do you think must be done?" asked Maliantovich with alarm. According to the ritual established by Kerensky, and carefully observed, the ministers addressed each other, not by the first and middle name as simple mortals do, but by the title of their position—"Mr. Minister of this or that"—as the representatives of a strong power are supposed to. The memoirs of the members sound like a satire. Kerensky himself subsequently wrote about his own war minister: "That was the most unfortunate of all my appointments. Verkhovsky introduced something indescribably comic into his activities." But the misfortune was that a tint of the involuntary comic lay over the whole activity of the Provisional Government. These people did not know what to do or where to turn. They did not govern, they played at government as little boys play soldier, though far more amusingly.

Speaking as an eye-witness, Miliukov has depicted in very definite strokes the condition of the head of the government at this period: "Having lost the ground under his feet, the further he went the more Kerensky revealed all the signs of that pathological condition of spirit which may be called in medical language 'psychic neurasthenia.' It had long been known to a close circle of his friends that from periods of extreme failure of energy in the morning, Kerensky would pass over in the latter half of the day into a condition of extreme excitement under the influence of the drugs he was taking." Miliukov explains the special influence of the Kadet minister, Kishkin, a psychiatrist by profession, on the ground of his skillful handling of the patient. These testimonies we leave entirely upon the responsibility of the liberal historian, who had, to be sure, every possibility of knowing the truth, but was far from choosing truth as his supreme criterion.

The testimony of a man as near to Kerensky as Stankevich confirms, if not the psychiatric, at least the psychological, characterization given by Miliukov. "Kerensky gave me the impression," writes Stankevich, "of a kind of emptiness in the whole situation, and a strange unprecedented tranquillity. He had around him his invariable 'little aides-de-camp,' but there was no longer the continual crowd surrounding him, neither delegations nor lime-lights. . . . There appeared strange periods of a kind of leisure, and I got the rare opportunity to converse with him for whole hours, during which he would manifest a strange unhurriedness."

Every new transformation of the government was accomplished in the name of a strong power, and each new ministry would open on a major key, only to fall in a very few days into nervous prostration. It would then only wait for an external impetus in order to fall apart. The impetus would be given each time by a movement of the masses. The transformations of the government, if you penetrate below the deceiving exterior, moved in every case in a direction opposite to that of the mass movement. The passage from one government to another would be accompanied by a crisis becoming every time more long drawn out and morbid in its character. Each new crisis squandered a part of the governmental power, enfeebled the revolution, demoralized the ruling groups. The Executive Committee of the first two months could do anything—even summon the bourgeoisie to a nominal power. In the next two months the Provisional Government together with the Executive Committee could still do much—even start an offensive on the front. The third government, together with the enfeebled Executive Committee, was able to begin the destruction of the Bolsheviks, but powerless to carry it through. The fourth government, arising after the longest crisis of all, was incapable of doing anything. Hardly born, it began to die and sat waiting with wide open eyes for the undertaker.

VOLUME THREE

The Triumph of the Soviets

CHAPTER I

THE PEASANTRY BEFORE OCTOBER

CIVILIZATION has made the peasantry its pack animal. The bourgeoisie in the long run only changed the form of the pack. Barely tolerated on the threshold of the national life, the peasant stands essentially outside the threshold of science. The historian is ordinarily as little interested in him as the dramatic critic is in those gray figures who shift the scenery, carrying the heavens and earth on their backs, and scrub the dressing-rooms of the actors. The part played by the peasantry in past revolutions remains hardly cleared up to this day.

"The French bourgeoisie began by liberating the peasantry," wrote Marx in 1848. "With the help of the peasantry they conquered Europe. The Prussian bourgeoisie was so blinded by its own narrow and close-by interests that it lost even this ally, and turned it into a weapon in the hands of the feudal counter-revolution." In this contrast what relates to the German bourgeoisie is true; but the assertion that "the French bourgeoisie began by liberating the peasantry" is an echo of that official French legend which exercised an influence in its day even upon Marx. In reality the bourgeoisie, in the proper sense of the term, opposed the peasant revolution with all the power it had. Even from the rural instructions of 1789 the local leaders of the Third Estate threw out, under the guise of editing, the keenest and most bold demands. The famous decision of August 4th, adopted by the National Assembly amid the glow of rural conflagrations, long remained a pathetic formula without content. The peasants who would not reconcile themselves to this deceit were adjured by the Constituent Assembly to "return to the fulfillment of their duties and have the proper respect for [feudal!] property." The civil guard tried more than once to put down the peasantry in the country. But the city workers, taking the side of those in revolt, met the bourgeois punitive expeditions with stones and broken tile.

3

Throughout five years the French peasantry rose at every critical moment of the revolution, preventing a deal between the feudal and bourgeois property-holders. The Parisian Sansculottes, pouring out their blood for the republic, liberated the peasant from his feudal chains. The French republic of 1792 marked a new social régime—in contradistinction to the German republic of 1918, or the Spanish republic of 1931, which mean only the old régime minus the dynasty. At the bottom of this difference it is not hard to find the agrarian question.

The French peasant did not think directly of a republic; he wanted to throw off the landlord. The Parisian republicans ordinarily forgot all about the country. But it was only the peasant pressure upon the landlord which guaranteed the creation of a republic, clearing the feudal rubbish out of its road. A republic with a nobility is not a republic. This was excellently understood by the old man Machiavelli, who in his Florentine exile 400 years before the presidency of Ebert, between hunting thrushes and playing at tric-trac with the butcher, generalized the experience of democratic revolutions. "Whoever wants to found a republic in a country where there are many nobles, can only do this if to begin with he exterminates them all." The Russian muzhiks were essentially of the same opinion, and they revealed this openly without any "Machiavellianism."

While Petrograd and Moscow played the main rôle in the movement of the workers and soldiers, the first place in the peasant movement must be accorded to the backward Great Russian agricultural center, and the middle region of the Volga. Here the relics of serfdom had especially deep roots; the nobles' proprietorship in the land was most parasitic in character; the differentiation of the peasantry was far behind and the poverty of the village thus more nakedly revealed. Bursting out in this region as early as March, the movement had been immediately adorned with acts of terror. Through the efforts of the dominant parties it was soon switched, however, into the channel of compromise politics.

In the industrially backward Ukraine, agriculture, carried on for export, had acquired a far more progressive and consequently more capitalistic character. Here the stratification of the

4

peasantry had gone considerably farther than in Great Russia. The struggle for national liberation moreover inevitably delayed, at least for the time being, other forms of social struggle. But the variation in regional, and even national, conditions expressed itself in the long run only in a difference of dates. By autumn the territory of the peasant struggle had become almost the whole country. Out of the 624 counties constituting old Russia, 482, or 77 per cent, were involved in the movement. And omitting the borderlands, distinguished by special agrarian conditions—the northern district, the Transcaucasus, the region of the steppes, and Siberia—out of 481 counties, 439, or 91 per cent, were drawn into the peasant revolt.

The methods of struggle differ according to whether it is a question of plowed land, forest, pasture, of rentals or of hired labor. The struggle changed its forms and methods, too, at various stages of the revolution. But in general the movement of the villages passed, with inevitable delay, through the same two great stages as the movement of the cities. In the first stage the peasants were still accommodating themselves to the new régime, and trying to solve their problems by means of the new institutions. Even here, however, it was more a matter of form than substance. The Moscow liberal newspaper—tinted before the revolution with a Narodnik hue—expressed with admirable directness the state of mind of the landlord circles in the summer of 1917. "The muzhik is glancing round, he is not doing anything yet, but look in his eyes—his eyes will tell you that all the land lying around him is his land." A perfect key to this "peaceful" policy of the peasantry, is a telegram sent in April by one of the Tombov villages to the Provisional Government: "We desire to keep the peace in the interests of the freedom won. But for this reason, forbid the sale of the landlords' land until the Constituent Assembly. Otherwise we will shed blood, but we will not let anyone else plow the land."

The muzhik found it easy to maintain a tone of respectful threat, because in bringing his pressure to bear against historic rights he hardly had to come into direct conflict with the state at all. Organs of the governmental power were lacking in the localities. The village committees controlled the militia, the courts

5

were disorganized, the local commissars were powerless. "We elected you," the peasants would shout at them, "and we will kick you out."

During the summer the peasants, developing the struggle of the preceding months, came nearer and nearer to civil war, and their left wing even stepped over its threshold. According to a report of the landed proprietors of the Taganrog district, the peasants on their own initiative seized the hay crop, took possession of the land, hindered the plowing, named arbitrary rental prices, and removed proprietors and overseers. According to a report of the Nizhegorod commissar, violent activities and seizures of land and forest in his province were multiplying. The county commissars were afraid of seeming to the peasants like defenders of the big landlords. The rural militia were not to be relied on. "There have been cases when officers of the militia took part in violence together with the mob." In Schlüsselburg county a local committee prevented the landlords from cutting their own forest. The thought of the peasants was simple: No Constituent Assembly can resurrect the trees that are cut down. The commissar of the Ministry of the Court complains of the seizure of hay: We have had to buy hay for the court horses! In Kursk province the peasants divided among themselves the fertilized fallow land of Tereshchenko. The proprietor was Minister of Foreign Affairs. The peasants declared to Schneider, a horse breeder of Orlov province, that they would not only cut the clover on his estate, but him too they might "send into the army." The village committee directed the overseer of Rodzianko's estate to surrender the hay to the peasants: "If you don't listen to this land committee, you'll get treated different, you'll get arrested. . . ." Signed and sealed.

From all corners of the country complaints and wails poured in—from victims, from local authorities, from noble-minded observers. The telegrams of the land-owners constitute a most brilliant refutation of the crude theory of class struggle. These titled nobles, lords of the latifundia, spiritual and temporal rulers, are worrying exclusively about the public weal. Their enemy is not the peasants, but the Bolsheviks—sometimes the anarchists. Their

6

own property engages the landlord's interest solely from the point
of view of the welfare of the fatherland. Three hundred members
of the Kadet Party in Chernigov province declare that the peasants, incited by Bolsheviks, are removing the war prisoners from
work and themselves independently reaping the harvest. As a result, they cry, we are threatened with "inability to pay the taxes."
The very meaning of existence for these liberal landlords lay in
supporting the national treasury! The Podolsk branch of the
State Bank complains of the arbitrary actions of village committees, "whose presidents are often Austrian prisoners." Here it
is injured patriotism that speaks. In Vladimir province, in the
manor of a registrar of deeds, Odintsov, the peasants took away
building materials that had been "made ready for philanthropic
institutions." Public officials live only for the love of mankind!
A bishop from Podolsk reports the arbitrary seizure of a forest
belonging to the house of the Archbishop. The procurator complains of the seizure of meadowlands from the Alexandro-
Nevsky Monastery. The Mother Superior of the Kizliarsk Convent calls down thunder and lightning upon the members of the
local committee: They are interfering in the affairs of the convent, confiscating rentals for their own use, "inciting the nuns
against their superiors." In all these cases the spiritual interests of
the church are directly affected. Count Tolstoi, one of the sons of
Leo Tolstoi, reports in the name of the League of Agriculturists
of Ufimsk province that the transfer of land to the local committees "without waiting for a decision of the Constituent Assembly . . . is causing an outburst of dissatisfaction . . .
among the peasant proprietors, of whom there are more than
200,000 in the province." The hereditary lord is troubled exclusively about his lesser brothers. Senator Belgardt, a proprietor
of Tver province, is ready to reconcile himself to cuttings in the
forest, but is grieved and offended that the peasants "will not
submit to the bourgeois government." A Tombov landlord,
Veliaminov, demands the rescue of two estates which "are serving
the needs of the army." By accident these two estates happened
to belong to him. For the philosophy of idealism these landlord
telegrams of 1917 are verily a treasure. A materialist will rather

7

see in them a display of the various models of cynicism. He will add perhaps that great revolutions deprive the property-holders even of the privilege of dignified hypocrisy.

The appeals of the victims to the county and provincial authorities, to the Minister of the Interior, to the President of the Council of Ministers, brought as a general rule no result. From whom then shall we ask aid? From Rodzianko, president of the State Duma! Between the July Days and the Kornilov insurrection, the Lord Chamberlain again felt himself an influential figure: much was done at a ring from his telephone.

The functionaries of the Ministry of the Interior send out circulars to the localities about bringing the guilty to trial. The brusque landlords of Samara telegraph in answer: "Circulars without the signature of the socialist minister have no force." The function of socialism is thus revealed. Tseretelli is compelled to overcome his bashfulness. On the 18th of July he sends out a wordy instruction about taking "swift and decisive measures." Like the landlords themselves, Tseretelli worries solely about the army and the state. It seems to the peasants, however, that Tseretelli is protecting the landlords.

There came a sudden change in the government's method of pacifying the peasants. Up to July the prevailing method had been talking them out of it. If military detachments were also sent into the localities, it was only in the capacity of a guard for the government orator. After the victory over the Petrograd workers and soldiers, however, cavalry troops—now without vocal persuaders—put themselves directly at the disposal of the landlords. In Kazan province, one of the most tumultuous, they succeeded—to quote the young historian, Yugov—"only by means of arrests, by bringing armed troops into the villages, and even by reviving the custom of flogging . . . in reducing the peasants to submission." In other places, too, these measures of repression were not without effect. The number of damaged landlord properties fell somewhat in July: from 516 to 503. In August the government achieved still further successes: the number of unsatisfactory counties fell from 325 to 288—that is, 11 per cent; the number of properties involved in the movement was even reduced 33 per cent.

Certain districts, heretofore the most restless, now quiet down or retire to second place. On the other hand, districts which were reliable yesterday now come into the struggle. Only a month ago the Penza commissar was painting a consoling picture: "The country is busy reaping the harvest. . . . Preparations are under way for the elections to the village zemstvos. The period of governmental crisis passed quietly. The formation of the new government was greeted with great satisfaction." In August there is not a trace left of this idyll. "Mass depredations upon orchards and the cutting down of forests. . . . To quell the disorders, we have had to resort to armed force."

In its general character the summer movement still belongs to the "peaceful" period. However, unmistakable, although indeed weak, symptoms of radicalization are already to be observed. Whereas in the first four months cases of direct attack upon the landlords' manors decreased, from July on they begin to increase. Investigators have established in general the following classification of the July conflicts, arranged in a diminishing order starting with the most numerous: Seizure of meadows, of crops, of food-stuffs and fodder, of plowed fields, of implements; conflict over the conditions of employment; destruction of manors. In August the order is as follows: Seizure of crops, of reserve provisions and fodder, of meadows and hay, of land and forest; agrarian terror.

At the beginning of September Kerensky, in his capacity of commander-in-chief, issued a special order repeating the recent arguments and threats of his predecessor, Kornilov, against "violent activities" on the part of the peasants. A few days later Lenin wrote: "Either . . . all the land to the peasants immediately . . . or the landlords and capitalists . . . will bring things to the point of an endlessly ferocious peasant revolt." During the months following this became a fact.

The number of properties affected by agrarian conflicts in September rose 30 per cent over that in August; in October, 43 per cent over that in September. In September and the first three weeks of October there occurred over a third as many agrarian conflicts as all those recorded since March. Their resoluteness rose, however, incomparably faster than their number. During the

9

first months even direct seizures of various appurtenances wore the aspect of bargains mitigated and camouflaged by the compromisist institutions. Now the legal mask falls away. Every branch of the movement assumes a more audacious character. From various forms and degrees of pressure, the peasants are now passing over to violent seizures of the various parts of the landlord's business, to the extermination of the nests of the gentility, the burning of manors, even the murder of proprietors and overseers.

The struggle for a change in the conditions of rent, which in June exceeded in number of cases the destructive movement, falls in October to one-fortieth the number. Moreover the rent movement itself changes its character, becoming merely another way of driving out the landlord. The veto on buying and selling land and forest gives place to direct seizure. The mass wood-cuttings and mass grazings acquire the character of a deliberate destruction of the landlord's goods. In September 279 cases of open destruction of property are recorded; they now constitute more than one eighth of all the conflicts. Over 42 per cent of all the cases of destruction recorded by the militia between the February and the October revolution occurred in the month of October.

The struggle for the forests was especially bitter. Whole villages were frequently burned to the ground. The timber was strongly guarded and selling at a high price; the muzhik was starving for timber; moreover the time had come to lay up firewood for the winter. Complaints came in from Moscow, Nizhegorod, Petrograd, Orel, and Volyn provinces—from all corners of the country—about the destruction of forests and the seizure of the reserves of corded wood. "The peasants are arbitrarily and ruthlessly cutting down the forest. Two hundred dessiatins of the landlords' forest have been burned by the peasants." "The peasants of Klimovichesky and Cherikovsky counties are destroying the forests and laying waste the winter-wheat. . . ." The forest guards are in flight; the landlords' forests are groaning; the chips are flying throughout the whole country. All that autumn the muzhik's axe was feverishly beating time for the revolution.

In the districts which imported grain the food situation in

10

the villages deteriorated at a faster pace than in the city. Not only food was lacking, but seed. In the exporting regions, in consequence of a redoubled pumping out of food resources, the situation was but little better. The raising of the fixed price of grain hit the poor. In a number of provinces there occurred hunger riots, plundering of granaries, assaults on the institutions of the Food Administration. The population resorted to substitutes for bread. Reports came in of cases of scurvy and typhus, of suicides from despair. Hunger and its advancing shadow made the neighborhood of opulence and luxury especially intolerable. The more destitute strata of the villages moved into the front ranks of the fight.

These waves of bitter feeling raised up no little slime from the bottom. In Kostroma province "a Black Hundred and anti-Jew agitation is observed. Criminality is on the increase. . . . A waning of interest in the political life of the country is noticeable." This latter phrase in the report of the commissar means: The educated classes are turning their back on the revolution. The voice of Black Hundred monarchism suddenly rings out from Podolsk province: The committee of the village of Demidovka does not recognize the Provisional Government and considers the tzar Nikolai Alexandrovich "the most loyal leader of the Russian people. If the Provisional Government does not retire, we will join the Germans." Such bold acknowledgements, however, are unique. The monarchists among the peasants have long ago changed color, following the example of the landlords. In places—for instance, in that same Podolsk province—military detachments in company with the peasants invade the wine cellars. The commissar reports anarchy. "The villages and the people are perishing; the revolution is perishing." No, the revolution is far from perishing. It is digging itself a deeper channel. The raging waters are nearing their mouth.

On a night about the 8th of September, the peasants of the village Sychevka in Tombov province, going from door to door armed with clubs and pitchforks, called out everybody, small and great, to raid the landlord, Romanov. At a village meeting one group proposed that they take the estate in an orderly fashion, divide the property among the population, and keep the build-

11

ings for cultural purposes. The poor demanded that they burn
the estate, leaving not one stone upon another. The poor were in
the majority. On that same night an ocean of fire swallowed up
the estates of the whole township. Everything inflammable was
burned, even the experimental fields. The breeding cattle were
slaughtered. "They were drunk to madness." The flames jumped
over from township to township. The rustic warriors were now
no longer content with the patriarchal scythe and pitchfork. A
provincial commissar telegraphed: "Peasants and unknown persons armed with revolvers and hand grenades are raiding the
manors in Ranenburg and Riazhsky counties." It was the war
that introduced this high technique into the peasant revolt. The
League of Landowners reported that 24 estates were burned in
three days. "The local authorities were powerless to restore order."
After some delay troops arrived, sent by the district commander.
Martial law was declared, meetings forbidden, the instigators arrested. Ravines were filled with the landlord's possessions and
much of the booty was sunk in the river.

A Penza peasant, Begishev, relates: "In September all rode
out to raid Logvin (he was raided in 1905, too). A troop of
teams and wagons streamed out to his estate and back, hundreds
of muzhiks and wenches began to drive and carry off his cattle,
grain, etc." A detachment called out by the land administration
tried to get back some of the booty, but the muzhiks and wenches
assembled 500 strong in the village, and the detachment dispersed. The soldiers were evidently not at all eager to restore the
trampled rights of the landlord. In Tauride province, beginning
with the last days of September, according to the recollections
of the peasant, Gaponenko, "the peasants began to raid the buildings, drive out the overseers, take the work animals, the machinery, the grain from the granaries. . . . They even tore off
the blinds from the windows, the doors from their frames, the
floors from the rooms, and the zinc roofs, and carried them
away. . . ." "At first they only came on foot, took what they
could and lugged it off," relates Grunko, a peasant from Minsk,
"but afterwards they hitched up the horses, whoever had any,
and carried things away in whole wagon-loads. There was no

room to pass. They just dragged and carried things off, beginning at twelve o'clock noon, for two days and two nights without a stop. In those forty-eight hours they cleaned out everything." The seizure of property, according to a Moscow peasant, Kuzmichev, was justified as follows: "The landlord was ours, we worked for him, and the property he had ought to belong to us alone." Once upon a time the landlords used to say to the serfs: "You are mine and what is yours is mine." Now the peasants were giving their answer: "He was our lord and all his goods are ours."

"In several localities they began to knock up the landlords in the night," remembers another Minsk peasant, Novikov. "Oftener and oftener they would burn the landlord's manor." It came the turn of the estate of the Grand Duke Nikolai Nikolaievich, former commander-in-chief. "When they had taken away all they could get, they began breaking up the stoves, removing the flue-plates, ripping up the floors and planks, and dragging it all home. . . ."

Behind these destructive activities stood the century-old, thousand-year-old strategy of all peasant wars: to raze to the ground the fortified position of the enemy. Leave him no place to cover his head. "The more reasonable ones," remembers a Kursk peasant, Tzygankov, "would say 'We must not burn up the buildings—they will be of use to us for schools and hospitals,' but the majority were the kind that shout out 'We must destroy everything so that in case anything happens our enemy will have no place to hide.'" "The peasants seized all the landlords' property," relates an Orel peasant, Savchenko, "drove the landlords out of the estates, smashed the windows, doors, ceilings and floors of the landlords' houses. . . . The soldiers said 'if you destroy the wolves' nests, you must strangle the wolves too.' Through such threats the biggest and most important landlords hid out, and for that reason there was no murder of landlords."

In the village of Zalessye, in Vitebsk province, they burned barns full of grain and hay in the estate belonging to a Frenchman, Barnard. The muzhiks were the less inclined to investigate questions of nationality, since many of the landlords had transferred their land in a hurry to privileged foreigners. "The French embassy requests that measures be taken. . . ." In the front region in the middle of October it was difficult to take "measures," even in behalf of the French embassy.

The destruction of the great estates near Riazan continued four days. "Even children took part in the looting." The League of Landed Proprietors brought to the attention of the ministers that if measures were not taken "lynch-law, famine and civil war would break out." It is difficult to understand why the landlords were still speaking of civil war in the future tense. At a congress of the cooperatives at the beginning of September, Berkenheim, one of the leaders of the strong trading peasantry, said: "I am convinced that not yet all Russia has become a madhouse, that as yet for the most part only the population of the big cities has gone mad." This self-complacent voice of the solid and conservative part of the peasantry was hopelessly behind the times. It was during that very month that the villages totally broke loose from all the nooses of reason, and the ferocity of their struggle left the "madhouse" of the cities far behind.

In April Lenin had still considered it possible that the patriotic cooperators and the kulaks would drag the main mass of the peasantry after them along the road of compromise with the bourgeoisie and the landlord. For this reason he so tirelessly insisted upon the creation of special soviets of farm hands' deputies, and upon independent organizations of the poorest peasantry. Month by month it became clear, however, that this part of the Bolshevik policy would not take root. Except in the Baltic state there were no soviets of farm hands. The peasant poor also failed to find independent forms of organization. To explain this merely by the backwardness of the farm hands and the poorest strata of the villages, would be to miss the essence of the thing. The chief cause lay in the substance of the historic task itself—a democratic agrarian revolution.

Upon the two principal questions, rent and hired labor, it becomes convincingly clear how the general interests of a struggle against the relics of serfdom cut off the road to an independent policy not only for the poor peasants, but for the hired hands. The peasants rented from the landlords in European Russia 27

14

million dessiatins—about 60 per cent of all the privately owned land—and they paid a yearly rental tribute of 400 million rubles. The struggle against peonage conditions of rent became after the February revolution the chief element of the peasant movement. A smaller, but still very important, place was occupied by the struggle of the rural wage-workers, which brought them in opposition not only to the landlord, but also to the peasant exploiters. The tenant was struggling for an alleviation of the conditions of rent, the worker for an improvement in the conditions of labor. Both of them, each in his own way, started out by recognizing the landlord as property-holder and boss. But as soon as the possibility opened of carrying the thing through to the end—that is, of taking the land and occupying it themselves— the poor peasants ceased to be interested in questions of rent, and the trade union began to lose its attraction for the hired hand. It was these rural workers and poor tenants who by joining the general movement gave its ultimate determination to the peasant war and made it irrevocable.

But the campaign against the landlord did not draw in quite so completely the opposite pole of the village. So long as it did not come to open revolt, the upper circles of the peasantry played a prominent rôle in the movement, at times a leading rôle. In the autumn period, however, the well-to-do muzhiks looked with continually increasing distrust at the spread of the peasant war. They did not know how this would end; they had something to lose; they stood aside. But they did not succeed in holding off entirely: the village would not permit it.

More reserved and hostile than "our own" communal kulaks, were the small land-owners standing outside the commune. In the whole country there were 600,000 homesteads of peasants owning plots up to 50 dessiatins. In many localities they constituted the backbone of the cooperatives, and gravitated, especially in the south, toward the conservative Peasant Union which had already become a bridge toward the Kadets. "The secessionists [1] and rich peasants," according to Guliss, a Minsk peasant, "sup-

[1] Peasants who had left the commune and taken private land under Stolypin's law of November 9th, 1906. Trans.

ported the landlords and tried to appease the peasantry with arguments." In some places, under the influence of local conditions, the struggle within the peasantry assumed a furious character even before the October revolution. The secessionists suffered most cruelly in this struggle. "Almost all their farm buildings were burnt," says Kuzmichev, a Nizhegorod peasant. "Their property was partly annihilated and partly seized by the peasants." The secessionist was "the landlord's servant entrusted with several of the landlord's forest tracts; he was a favorite of the police, the gendarmerie and the rulers." The richest peasants and merchants of several villages of Nizhegorod county disappeared in the autumn and returned to their neighborhoods only after two or three years.

But in most sections of the country the inner relations among the peasantry were far from reaching such bitterness. The kulaks conducted themselves diplomatically, put on the brakes and resisted, but tried not to set themselves too sharply against the "mir." [1] The rank-and-file villager, on his part, jealously watched the kulaks and would not let them unite with the landlords. The struggle between the nobles and the peasantry for influence upon the kulak continued throughout the whole year 1917 in various different forms, from "friendly" pressure to ferocious terrorism.

While the lords of the latifundia were ingratiatingly throwing open to the peasant proprietors the main entrances to the assemblies of the nobility, the small land-owners were demonstratively drawing apart from the nobility in order not to perish with them. In politics this found expression in the fact that the landlords, who had belonged before the revolution to the extreme right party, redecorated themselves now in the tints of liberalism, adopting them from memory as a protective coloration, whereas the peasant proprietors, who had often supported the Kadets in the past, now shifted to the left.

A congress of petty proprietors of Perm province, held in September, emphatically distinguished itself from the Moscow Congress of Landed Proprietors at the head of whom stood "counts, dukes and barons." An owner of 50 dessiatins said: "The

[1] This word, applied to the village as a commune, literally means "the world"—that is, everybody. Trans.

16

Kadets never wore *armyaki* and *lapti* [1] and therefore will never defend our interests." Pushing away from the liberals, the laboring proprietor would look around for such "socialists" as would stand for property rights. One of the delegates came out for the social democracy. "The worker?" he said. "Give him land and he will come to the village and stop spitting blood. The social democrats will not take the land away from us." He was speaking, of course, of the Mensheviks. "We will not give away our land to anybody. Those will easily part with it who easily got it, as for example, the landlord, but the peasant had a hard time getting the land."

In that autumn period the villages were struggling with the kulaks, not throwing them off, but compelling them to adhere to the general movement and defend it against blows from the right. There were even cases where a refusal to participate in a raid was punished by the death of the culprit. The kulak maneuvered while he could, but at the last moment, scratching the back of his head once more, hitched the well-fed horses to the iron-rimmed wagon and went out for his share. It was often the lion's share. "The well-to-do got the most out of it," says the Penza peasant, Begishev, "those who had horses and free men." Savchenko from Orel expressed himself in almost the same words: "The kulaks mostly got the best of it, being well-fed and with something to draw the wood in."

According to the calculations of Vermenichev, to 4,954 agrarian conflicts with landlords between February and October, there were 324 conflicts with the peasant bourgeoisie. An extraordinarily clear correlation! It alone firmly establishes the fact that the peasant movement of 1917 was directed in its social foundations not against capitalism, but against the relics of serfdom. The struggle against kulakism developed later, in 1918, after the conclusive liquidation of the landlord.

This purely democratic character of the peasant movement, which should, it would seem, have given the official democracy an inconquerable power, did in fact completely reveal its rottenness. If you look at the thing from above, the peasants were

---

[1] *Armyak* is a home-made woollen coat, *lapti* are shoes made out of woven strips of bark. Trans.

wholly led by the Social Revolutionaries, elected them, followed them, almost blended with them. At the May congress of peasant soviets, in the elections to the executive committee, Chernov received 810 votes, Kerensky 804, whereas Lenin got only 20 votes all in all. It was not for nothing that Chernov dubbed himself Rural Minister! But it was not for nothing, either, that the strategy of the villages brusquely parted company with Chernov's strategy. Their industrial isolation makes the peasants, so determined in struggle with a concrete landlord, impotent before the general landlord incarnate in the state. Hence the organic need of the muzhiks to rely upon some legendary state as against the real one. In olden times they created pretenders, they united round an imagined Golden Edict of the tzar, or around the legend of a righteous world. After the February revolution they united round the Social Revolutionary banner "Land and Freedom," seeking help in it against the liberal landlord who had become a governmental commissar. The Narodnik program bore the same relation to the real government of Kerensky, as the imagined edict of the tzar to the real autocrat.

In the program of the Social Revolutionaries there was always much that was utopian. They hoped to create socialism on the basis of a petty trade economy. But the foundation of their program was democratically revolutionary: to take the land from the landlord. When confronted with the necessity of carrying out its program, the party got tangled up in a coalition. Not only the landlords rose against the confiscation of the land, but also the Kadet bankers. The banks had loaned against real estate no less than four billion rubles. Intending to dicker with the landlords at the Constituent Assembly regarding prices but end things in a friendly manner, the Social Revolutionaries zealously kept the muzhik away from the land. They went to pieces, therefore, not on the utopian character of their socialism, but on their democratic inconsistency. It might have taken years to test out their utopianism. Their betrayal of agrarian democracy became clear in a few months. Under a government of Social Revolutionaries the peasants had to take the road of insurrection in order to carry out the Social Revolutionary program.

18

In July, when the government was coming down on the villages with measures of repression, the peasants in hot haste ran for defense to those same Social Revolutionaries. From Pontius the young they appealed for protection to Pilate the old. The month of the greatest weakening of the Bolsheviks in the cities was the month of the greatest expansion of the Social Revolutionaries in the country. As usually happens, especially in a revolutionary epoch, the maximum of organizational scope coincided with the beginning of a political decline. Hiding behind Social Revolutionaries from the blows of a Social Revolutionary government, the peasants steadily lost confidence both in the government and the party. Thus the swelling out of the Social Revolutionary organizations in the villages became fatal to this universal party, which was rebelling at the bottom but restoring order at the top.

In Moscow at a meeting of the Military Organization on the 30th of July, a delegate from the front, himself a Social Revolutionary, said: Although the peasants still think themselves Social Revolutionaries, a rift has formed between them and the party. The soldiers confirmed this: Under the influence of Social Revolutionary agitation the peasants are still hostile to the Bolsheviks, but in practice they decide the questions of land and power in a Bolshevik manner. The Bolshevik, Povolzhsky, who worked in the Volga region, testifies that the most respected Social Revolutionaries, those who had taken part in the movement of 1905, were more and more feeling themselves pushed aside: "The muzhiks called them 'old men,' treating them with external deference, but voting in their own way." It was the workers and soldiers who had taught the villages to vote and take action "in their own way." It is impossible to weigh the influence of the revolutionary workers upon the peasantry. It was continuous, molecular, penetrating everywhere, and therefore not capable of calculation. A mutual penetration was made easier by the fact that a considerable number of the industrial plants were situated in rural districts. But even the workers of Petrograd, the most European of the cities, kept up a close connection with their native villages. Unemployment, increasing during the summer months, and the lockouts of the employers, threw back many thousands of workers into the villages. A majority of them became agitators and leaders.

From May to June there were created in Petrograd back-home clubs corresponding to different provinces, counties and even villages. Whole columns in the workers' press were devoted to announcements of back-home club meetings, where reports about journeys to the villages would be heard, instructions drawn up for delegates, and money collected for agitation. Not long before the uprising, these clubs united round a special central bureau under the leadership of the Bolsheviks. This back-home club movement soon spread to Moscow, Tver, and probably to a number of other industrial cities.

However, in the matter of direct influence upon the village the soldiers were still more important. It was only in the artificial conditions of the front or in the city barrack that the young peasants, overcoming to a certain degree their isolation, would come face to face with problems of nation-wide scope. Here too, however, their political dependence made itself felt. While continually falling under the leadership of patriotic and conservative intellectuals and then striving to get free of them, the peasants tried to organize in the army separately from other social groups. The authorities looked unfavorably upon these inclinations, the War Ministry opposed them, the Social Revolutionaries did not welcome them. The soviets of peasants' deputies took but weak root in the army. Even under the most favorable conditions the peasant is unable to convert his overwhelming quantity into a political quality! Only in the big revolutionary centers under the direct influence of the workers did the soviets of peasant soldiers succeed in developing any important work. Thus between April 1917 and January 1, 1918 the peasant soviet in Petrograd sent 1,395 agitators into the villages with special mandates; and about the same number went without mandates. These delegates covered 65 provinces. In Kronstadt back-home clubs were formed among the sailors and soldiers, following the example of the workers, and they supplied their delegates with credentials giving them the "right" to free passage on railroads and steamboats. The private lines accepted these papers without a murmur. Conflicts arose on the government lines.

These official delegates of organizations were after all, however, mere drops in the peasant ocean. An infinitely greater work was accomplished by those hundreds of thousands and millions of soldiers who quit the front and the rear garrisons of their own accord with the strong slogans of mass-meeting speeches ringing in their ears. Those who had sat silent at the front became garrulous at home in the villages. They found no lack of greedy listeners. "Among the peasantry surrounding Moscow," says Muralov, one of the Moscow Bolsheviks, "there was a tremendous swing to the left. . . . The villages and towns of Moscow province were swarming with deserters from the front. They were visited also by city proletarians who had not yet cut off their connections with the country." The dreamy and backward villages of Kaluga province, according to the peasant Naumchenkov —"were waked up by soldiers coming home from the front for various reasons during June and July." The Nizhegorod commissar reports that "all the lawbreaking and lawlessness is connected with the appearance within the boundaries of the province of deserters, soldiers on furlough, or delegates from the regimental committees." The overseer of the properties of Princess Bariatinsky of Zolotonoshzky county complains in August of the arbitrary acts of the land committee whose president is a Kronstadt sailor, Gatran. "Soldiers and sailors on furlough," reports the commissar of Bugulminsk county, "are carrying on an agitation with a view to creating anarchy and a pogrom state of mind." "In Mglinsk county, in the village of Bielogosh, an arriving sailor on his own authority forbade the preparation and export of firewood and railroad ties from the forest." And when it was not the soldiers who began the struggle, it was they who finished it. In Nizhegorod county the muzhiks harried a convent, cut the meadow grass, broke down the fences, and bothered the nuns. The mother superior refused to give in, and the militia would carry off the muzhiks and punish them. "So the thing dragged along," writes the peasant Arbekov, "until the soldiers arrived. The buddies immediately took the bull by the horns. . . ." The convent was cleaned out. In Moghiliev province, according to the peasant Bobkov, "the soldiers home from the front were the first leaders in the committee, and directed the expulsion of the land-lords."

The men from the front introduced into the business the heavy determination of people accustomed to handle their fellow-men with rifle and bayonet. Even the soldiers' wives caught this fighting mood from their husbands. Says the Penza peasant, Begi-shev: "In September there was a strong movement of soldiers' wives who spoke at meetings in favor of the raids." The same thing was observed in other provinces. In the cities, too, the sol-diers' wives were often the leaven in the lump.

Those cases in which soldiers took the lead in peasant disor-ders constituted in March, according to Vermenichev's calcula-tions, 1 per cent, in April 8 per cent, in September 12 per cent, and in October 17 per cent. These figures cannot pretend to be accurate, but they show the general tendency unmistakably. The dying leadership of the Social Revolutionary teachers, town-clerks and functionaries, was giving place to the leadership of soldiers who would stop at nothing.

Parvus, a German Marxian writer prominent in his day, who succeeded in acquiring wealth and losing both his principles and his penetration during the war, has compared the Russian soldiers with the mercenary troopers, robbers and hold-up men of medie-val times. For this it is necessary to shut one's eyes to the fact that in all their lawlessness the Russian soldiers remained merely the executive organ of the greatest agrarian revolution in history.

So long as the movement had not broken completely with legality, the sending of troops into the villages preserved a sym-bolic character. In practice it was almost the Cossacks alone who could be used as punitive troops. "Four hundred Cossacks were sent into Serdobsky county . . . this measure had a tranquiliz-ing effect; the peasants declared that they would await the Con-stituent Assembly," says the liberal paper, *Russkoe Selo,* on the 11th of October. Four hundred Cossacks is certainly an argument in favor of the Constituent Assembly. But there were not enough Cossacks, and moreover they too were uncertain. Meantime the government was oftener and oftener being compelled to "take decisive measures." During the first four months of the revolution Vermenichev counts 17 cases in which armed forces were sent against the peasants; in July and August, 39 cases; in September and October, 105 cases.

To put down the peasantry by armed force was only to pour oil on the fire. In a majority of cases the soldiers went over to the peasants. A county commissar of Podolsk province reports: "The army organizations and even individual units are deciding social and economic questions, are forcing (?) the peasants to carry out seizures and cut the forest, and at times, in certain localities, they themselves take part in the looting. . . . The local military units refuse to join in putting down acts of violence. . . ." Thus the rural revolt loosened the last bolts of the army. There was not the slightest possibility that in the circumstances of a peasant war headed by the workers, the army would permit itself to be thrown against the insurrection in the cities.

From the workers and soldiers the peasants first learned something new—something other than what the Social Revolutionaries had told them—about the Bolsheviks. The slogans of Lenin, and his name, penetrated the villages. The steadily increasing complaints against Bolsheviks were, however, in many cases invented or exaggerated. The landlords hoped in this way to make more sure of getting help. "In Ostrovsky county complete anarchy reigns, a consequence of Bolshevik propaganda." From Ufa province comes the news: "A member of a village committee, Vassiliev, is distributing the program of the Bolsheviks and openly declaring that the landlords are to be hanged." In seeking "protection from robbery" the Novgorod landlord, Polonnik, does not forget to add: "The Executive Committees are brimful of Bolsheviks." That means that they are unfavorable to the landlord. "In August," remembers a Simbirsk peasant, Zumorin, "workers began to make the rounds of the villages, agitating for the Bolshevik party and telling about its program." An investigator of Sebezh county tells about the arrival from Petrograd of a weaver Tatiana Mikhailova, 26 years old, who "called on the people of her village to overthrow the Provisional Government, and praised the tactics of Lenin." In Smolensk province towards the end of August, according to the peasant Kotov, "We began to

23

interest ourselves in Lenin, began to listen to the voice of Lenin. . . ." In the village zemstvo, however, they were still electing an immense majority of Social Revolutionaries.

The Bolshevik party was trying to get closer to the peasant. On the 10th of September Nevsky demanded that the Petrograd committee undertake the publication of a peasant newspaper: "We must fix things so that we shall not have the experience of the French Commune, where the peasantry did not understand Paris and Paris did not understand the peasantry." The newspaper, *Byednotá*, soon came out. But even so, the purely party work among the peasants remained insignificant. The strength of the Bolshevik party lay not in technical resources, not in machinery, but in a correct policy. As air currents carry seeds, the whirlwinds of the revolution scattered the ideas of Lenin.

"By September," remembers a Tver peasant, Vorobiev, "not only the soldiers, but the poor peasants themselves were oftener and more boldly beginning to come out at meetings in defense of the Bolsheviks. . . ." This is confirmed by the Simbirsk peasant, Zumorin: "Among the poor and some of the middle peasants the name of Lenin was on everybody's lips; the talk was only of Lenin." A Novgorod peasant, Grigoriev, tells how a Social Revolutionary in the village called the Bolsheviks "usurpers" and "traitors" and how the muzhiks thundered: "Down with the dog! Pound him with rock! Don't tell us any more fairy stories. Where is the land? That's enough from you! Give us the Bolsheviks!" It is possible, by the way, that this episode—and there were many like it—derives from the post-October period. Facts stand strong in a peasant's memory but his chronology is weak.

The soldier Chinenov, who came back to his home in Orel province with a trunkful of Bolshevik literature, had not been welcomed by the home village. It's probably German gold, they said. But in October "the village nucleus has 700 members and many rifles, and always comes out in defense of the soviet power." The Bolshevik Vrachev tells how the peasants of the purely agricultural province of Voronezh "woke up from the effects of the Social Revolutionary fumes, and began to take an interest in our party. Thanks to which we already had a number of village and township locals and subscribers to our papers, and received many good fellows in the tiny headquarters of our committee." In Smolensk province, according to the recollections of Ivanov, "Bolsheviks were very rare in the villages. There were very few of them in the counties. There were no Bolshevik papers. Leaflets were very rarely given out. . . . And nevertheless the nearer it came to October, the more the villages swung over to the Bolsheviks."

"In those counties where there was a Bolshevik influence in the soviet before October," writes Ivanov again, "the element of raids upon landlords' estates either did not appear, or appeared only to a small extent." In this respect, however, it was not the same everywhere. "The Bolshevik demand for the transfer of land to the peasants," says, for example, Tadeush, "was taken up with extraordinary rapidity by the mass of the peasants of Moghiliev county, who laid waste the estates, in some cases burning them, and seized the harvests and the forest." In essence there is no contradiction between these two testimonies. The general agitation of the Bolsheviks undoubtedly nourished the civil war in the country. But wherever the Bolsheviks had succeeded in putting down firm roots, they naturally tried, without weakening the assault of the peasants, to regulate its forms and decrease the amount of destruction.

The land question did not stand alone. The peasant suffered especially during the last period of the war, both as seller and buyer. Grain was taken from him at a fixed price, and the products of industry were becoming more and more unattainable. The problem of economic correlation between the country and the city, destined subsequently under the name of the "scissors" to become the central problem of soviet economy, was already showing its threatening face. The Bolsheviks were saying to the peasants: The soviets must seize the power, give you the land, end the war, demobilize industry, establish workers' control of production, and regulate the price relations between industrial and agricultural products. However summary this answer may have been, it did indicate the road. "The partition wall between us and the peasantry," said Trotsky on the 10th of October at a conference of factory committees, "is the little counsellors of Avksentiev. We must break through this wall. We must explain to the village that all the attempts of the worker to help the peasant by supplying the village with agricultural implements will give no result until workers' control of organized production is established." The conference issued a manifesto to the peasants in this sense.

The Petrograd workers created at the factories in those days special commissions which would assemble metals, damaged parts, and fragments for the use of a special center called "Worker To Peasant." This scrap-iron was used for making the simplest agricultural implements and reserve parts. That first planned entry of the workers into the process of production—still tiny in scope and with agitational aims prevailing over economic—nevertheless opened out a prospect for the near future. Frightened at this entrance of the Bolsheviks into the forbidden sphere of the village, the peasant Executive Committee made an attempt to get hold of the new enterprise. But the decrepit Compromisers were no longer in any condition to compete with the Bolsheviks on the city arena when the ground was already slipping from under their feet in the villages.

The echoes of the Bolshevik agitation "so aroused the peasant poor," writes Vorobiev, the Tver peasant, "that we may definitely say: If October had not come in October it would have come in November." This colorful description of the political strength of Bolshevism does not contradict the fact of its organizational weakness. Only through such striking disproportions does a revolution make its way. It is for this very reason, to tell the truth, that its movement cannot be forced into the framework of formal democracy. To accomplish the agrarian revolution, whether in October or November, the peasantry had no other course but to make use of the unravelling web of that same Social Revolutionary party. Its left elements were hastily and unsystematically forming a group under the pressure of the peasant revolt—following the Bolsheviks and competing with them. During the coming months the political shift of the peasantry will take place chiefly under the glossy banner of the Left Social Revolutionaries. This ephemeral party will become a reflected and unstable form of rural Bolshevism, a temporary bridge from the peasant war to the proletarian revolution.

The agrarian revolution had to have its own local institutions. How did they look? There existed several types of organization in the village: state institutions such as the executive committee of the township, the land and food committees; social institutions like the soviets; purely political institutions like the parties; and finally organs of self-government exemplified in the town zemstvos. The peasant soviets had as yet developed only on a province, or to some extent a county scale. There were few town soviets. The town zemstvos had been slow to take root. The land and executive committees, on the other hand, although state organs in design, became—strange as it may seem at a first glance —the organs of the peasant revolution.

The head land committee, consisting of governmental functionaries, landlords, professors, scientific agriculturists, Social Revolutionary politicians and an admixture of dubious peasants, became in essence the main brake of the agrarian revolution. The province committees never ceased to be the conducting wires of the governmental policy. The county committees oscillated between the peasants and the men higher up. The town committees, however—elected by the peasants and working right there before the eyes of the village—became the instruments of the agrarian movement. The circumstance that the members of these committees usually registered as Social Revolutionaries made no difference. They kept step with the peasant's hut and not the lord's manor. The peasants especially treasured the state character of their land committees, seeing in this a sort of patent-right to civil war.

"The peasants say that they recognize nothing but the town committee," complains one of the chiefs of militia in Saransky county as early as May. "All the county and city committees, they say, work for the landlords." According to a Nizhegorod commissar, "the attempts of certain town committees to oppose the independent action of the peasants almost always ends in failure and brings about a change of membership of the committee." According to Denissov, a peasant from Pskov, "the committees were always on the side of the peasants' movement against the landlord because the most revolutionary part of the peasantry and soldiers from the front were elected to them."

The county, and more especially the province committees were led by the functionary "intelligentsia," which was trying to keep up peaceful relations with the landlord. "The peasants saw," writes the Moscow peasant, Yurkov, "that this was the same coat only inside out, the same power but with another name." "An effort is under way," reports the Kurksk commissar, ". . . to get new elections to the county committees, which are invariably carrying out the directions of the Provisional Government." It was very hard, however, for the peasants to get into the county committees. The Social Revolutionaries kept hold of the political ties between the villages and townships, and the peasants were thus compelled to act through a party whose chief mission consisted of turning the old coat inside out.

The coolness of the peasantry toward the March soviets, astonishing at first glance, had as a matter of fact very deep causes. The soviet was not a special organization like the land committee, but a universal organ of the revolution. Now in the sphere of general politics the peasant cannot take a step without leadership. The only question is, where is it to come from. The provincial and county peasant soviets were created on the initiative, and to a considerable extent at the expense, of the cooperatives, not as organs of a peasant revolution but as organs of a conservative guardianship over the peasants. The villagers tolerated these Right Social Revolutionary soviets standing above them as a shield against the authorities. But at home, among themselves, they preferred the land committees.

In order to prevent the village from shutting itself up in a circle of "purely peasant interests," the government made haste to create democratic zemstvos. That alone was enough to put the muzhik on his guard. It was frequently necessary to enforce the elections. "There were cases of lawlessness," reports the Penza commissar, "resulting in a break-up of the elections." In Minsk province the peasants arrested the president of the electoral commission of the town, Prince Drutskoi-Liubetskoi, accusing him of tampering with the lists. It was not easy for the muzhiks to come to an agreement with him about the democratic solution of their age-old quarrel. The county commissar of Bugulminsk reported: "The elections to the town zemstvos throughout the county have not gone quite according to plan. . . . The members of the electorate are exclusively peasants. There is a noticeable estrangement from the local intelligentsia, especially from the land-owners." In this form the zemstvo was but little different from the committee. "The attitude of the peasant masses toward the intelligentsia, and especially the land-owners," complains the Minsk county commissar, "is adverse." We read in a Moghiliev newspaper of September 23rd: "Cultural work in the county is accompanied with a certain risk, unless one categorically promises to co-operate toward the immediate transfer of all the land to the peasants." Where agreement and even intercourse between the fundamental classes of the population becomes impossible, the ground for democratic institutions disappears. The still-birth of the town zemstvos unmistakably foretold the collapse of the Constituent Assembly.

"The local peasantry," reports the Nizhegorod commissar, "have got a fixed opinion that all civil laws have lost their force, and that all legal relations ought now to be regulated by peasant organizations." Getting control of the militia in certain localities, the town committees would issue local laws, establish rents, regulate wages, put their own overseers on estates, take over the land, the crops, the woods, the forests, the tools, take the machinery away from the landlords, and carry out searches and arrests. The voice of centuries and the fresh experience of the revolution both said to the muzhik that the question of land is a question of power. The agrarian revolution needed the organs of a peasant dictatorship. The muzhik did not yet know this latin word, but the muzhik knew what he wanted. That "anarchy" of which the landlords, liberal commissars, and compromise politicians complained, was in reality the first stage of the revolutionary dictatorship in the village.

The necessity of creating special, purely peasant organs of land revolution in the localities had been defended by Lenin during the events of 1905–6. "The peasant revolutionary committees," he argued at the party congress in Stockholm, "present the sole road along which the peasant movement can travel." The muzhiks had not read Lenin, but Lenin knew how to read the minds of the muzhiks.

29

The villages changed their attitude to the soviets only in the fall, when the soviets themselves changed their political course. The Bolshevik and Left Social Revolutionary soviets in the county or provincial city now no longer held back the peasants, but on the contrary pushed them forward. Whereas during the first months the villages had looked to the compromisist soviets for a legal covering, only to come later into hostile conflict with them, now they first began to find in the revolutionary soviets a real leadership. The Saratov peasants wrote in September: "The power throughout all Russia ought to go . . . to the Soviets of Workers, Peasants and Soldiers' Deputies. That will be safer." Only in the fall did the peasantry begin to join their land program to the slogan of Power to the Soviets. But here too they did not know by whom or how these soviets were to be led.

Agrarian disturbances in Russia had their great tradition, their simple but clear program, their local martyrs and heroes. The colossal experience of 1905 had not passed without leaving its trace in the villages. And to this we must add the work of the sectarian ideas which had taken hold of millions of peasants. "I knew many peasants," writes a well-informed author, "who accepted . . . the October revolution as the direct realization of their religious hopes." Of all the peasant revolts known to history the movement of the Russian peasantry in 1917 was undoubtedly in the highest degree fertilized by political ideas. If nevertheless it proved incapable of creating an independent leadership and taking the power in its own hands, the causes of this are to be found in the organic nature of an isolated, petty and routine industry. While sucking all the juice out of the muzhik, his economic position did not give him in return the ability to generalize.

The political freedom of a peasant means in practice the ability to choose between different city parties. But even this choice is not made *a priori*. The peasantry pushed the Bolsheviks toward power with their revolt. But only after conquering the power could the Bolsheviks win over the peasantry, converting their agrarian revolution into the laws of a workers' state.

A group of investigators under the guidance of Yakovlev have made an extremely valuable classification of material, characterizing the evolution of the agrarian movement from February to October. Designating the number of disorganized actions in each month as 100, these investigators have estimated that there were in April 33 organized conflicts, in June 86, in July 120. July was the moment of highest success of the Social Revolutionary organizations in the country. In August for one hundred disorganized conflicts there were only 62 organized, and in October 14. From these figures—wonderfully instructive although of qualified significance—Yakovlev draws a totally unexpected conclusion. "Whereas up to August," he says, "the movement had grown steadily more organized; in the fall it acquired a more and more 'spontaneous' [1] character." Another investigator, Vermenichev, arrives at the same formula: "The lowering of the figure of organized movements in the period of the pre-October waves, testifies to the spontaneousness of the movements of those months." If the spontaneous is contrasted to the conscious, as blindness to eyesight—and this is the only scientific contrast—then we must come to the conclusion that the consciousness of the peasant movement increased up to August, and then began to fall rapidly enough to disappear completely at the moment of the October insurrection. But this our investigators obviously did not wish to say. Taking a somewhat reflective attitude to the question, it is not difficult to understand, for example, that the peasant elections to the Constituent Assembly, in spite of their externally "organized" character, were incomparably more "spontaneous"—that is, thoughtless, sheeplike, blind —than the "disorganized" peasant campaigns against the landlord, where each peasant knew quite well what he wanted.

In the autumn crisis the peasants did not abandon conscious action for spontaneousness, but abandoned compromisist leadership for the civil war. The decline in organization was really a superficial feature: the compromisist organization fell away, but what it left was by no means a vacant space. The peasants came out on the new road under the direct leadership of the most revolutionary elements, the soldiers, sailors and workers. In entering

[1] The Russian word translated "spontaneous" means literally *elemental,* and is commonly contrasted in revolutionary literature to class-conscious movements led by an organization with a theory and program. Trans.

upon decisive activities the peasants would quite often call a mass-meeting, and even take pains that the resolution adopted should be signed by all those living in the same village. "In the autumn period of the peasant movement with its raiding forms," writes a third investigator, Shestakov, "what oftenest appears upon the scene is the 'old peasant assembly. . . .' By means of the assembly the peasants divide the appropriated goods, through the assembly they conduct negotiations with the landlord and overseers, with the county commissars and with punitive expeditions of all kinds."

The question why the town committees, which have led the peasants right up to the civil war, now disappear from the scene, finds no direct answer in these materials. But the explanation comes of itself. A revolution very quickly wears out its organs and implements. Owing to the mere fact that the land committees had been conducting semi-peaceful activities, they were bound to seem of little use for direct assaults. And this general cause is supplemented by particular ones no less weighty. In taking the road of open war with the landlord, the peasants knew too well what awaited them in case of defeat. A number of the land committees even without that were under Kerensky's lock and key. To scatter the responsibility became a tactical need. The "mir" offered the most expedient form for this. The customary mutual mistrust of the peasants undoubtedly worked in the same direction. It was a question now of the direct seizure and division of the landlord's goods; each wanted to take part in this himself, not entrusting his rights to anybody. Thus the highest tension of the struggle led to a temporary retirement of the representative organs in favor of primitive peasant democracy in the form of the assembly and the communal decree.

This crude mistake in defining the character of the peasant movement may seem especially surprising from the pen of Bolshevik investigators. But we must not forget that these are Bolsheviks of the new mould. The bureaucratization of thought has inevitably led to an overvaluing of those forms of organization which were imposed upon the peasants from above, an undervaluing of those which the peasants themselves assumed. The educated functionary, following the liberal professor, looks upon

social processes from the point of view of administration. In his
position as People's Commissar of Agriculture, Yakovlev subsequently showed the same summary bureaucratic mode of approach
to the peasantry, but in an infinitely broader and more responsible
sphere—that namely of introducing "complete collectivization."
Theoretic superficiality takes a cruel revenge when it comes to
practical action on a large scale!

But we are still a good thirteen years before the mistakes of
complete collectivization. It is now only a question of the expropriation of the landed estates. One hundred thirty-four thousand landlords are still trembling for their 18 million dessiatins.
Most threatened is the situation of those on the summit, the 30,000
lords of old Russia who own 70 million dessiatins—over 2,000 on
the average per person. A lord, Boborykin, writes to the Chamberlain, Rodzianko: "I am a landlord, and somehow it won't fit into
my head that I am to be deprived of my land, and that, too, for
a most improbable purpose—for an experimental test of socialistic teachings." But it is the task of revolution to accomplish just
those things which will not fit into the heads of the ruling class.

The more farsighted landlords cannot help realizing, however, that they will not be able to keep their estates. They are no
longer even trying to. The sooner we get rid of our land, they
are saying, the better. The Constituent Assembly presents itself
to them primarily as a vast clearing-house where the state will
recompense them not only for the land, but also for their
anxieties.

The peasant land-owners adhered to this program of theirs
on the left. They were not unwilling to have an end of the para-
sitical nobility, but they were afraid of unsettling the conception
of landed property. The state is rich enough, they declared at
their meetings, to pay the landlords something like 12 billion
rubles. In their quality of "peasants" they were counting on being
able to make use of these noble estates, once they had been paid
for by the people, on favorable terms.

The proprietors understood that the extent of the indemnity
was a political magnitude to be determined by the correlation of
forces at the moment of payment. Up to the end of August there
remained a hope that the Constituent Assembly, convoked *à la*

Kornilov, would follow a line of agrarian reform midway between Rodzianko and Miliukov. The collapse of Kornilov meant that the possessing classes had lost the game.

During September and October the possessing classes were awaiting the outcome as a hopelessly sick man awaits death. Autumn with the muzhiks is the time for politics. The fields are mowed, illusions are scattered, patience is exhausted. Time to finish things up! The movement now overflows its banks, invades all districts, wipes out local peculiarities, draws in all the strata of the villages, washes away all considerations of law and prudence, becomes aggressive, fierce, furious, a raging thing, arms itself with steel and fire, revolvers and hand-grenades, demolishes and burns up the manorial dwellings, drives out the landlords, cleanses the earth and in some places waters it with blood.

Gone are the nests of the gentility celebrated by Pushkin, Turgeniev and Tolstoi. The old Russia has gone up in smoke. The liberal press is a collection of groans and outcries about the destruction of English gardens, of paintings from the brushes of serfs, of patrimonial libraries, the parthenons of Tombov, the riding horses, the ancient engravings, the breeding bulls. Bourgeois historians have tried to put the responsibility upon the Bolsheviks for the "vandalism" of the peasant's mode of settling accounts with the "culture" of his lords. In reality the Russian muzhik was completing a business entered upon many centuries before the Bolsheviks appeared in the world. He was fulfilling his progressive historic task with the only means at his disposal. With revolutionary barbarism he was wiping out the barbarism of the middle ages. Moreover, neither he himself, nor his grandfather, nor his great grandfather before him ever saw any mercy or indulgence!

When the feudal landlords got the best of the Jacquerie four and a half centuries before the liberation of the French peasants, a pious monk wrote in his chronicle: "They did so much evil to the country that there was no need of the coming of the English to destroy the kingdom; these never could have done what was done by the nobles of France." Only the bourgeoisie—in May 1871—proved able to exceed the French nobles in ferocity. The Russian peasants—thanks to the leadership of the workers, and the Russian workers—thanks to the support of the peasants,

avoided learning this twofold lesson from the defenders of culture and humanity.

The inter-relations between the fundamental classes of Russia
at large were reproduced in the village. Just as the workers and
soldiers went into a fight with the monarchy contrary to the
plans of the bourgeoisie, so the peasant poor rose boldest of all
against the landlord, not heeding the warnings of the kulak. Just
as the Compromisers believed that the revolution would stand
firmly on its feet only from the moment it was recognized by
Miliukov, so the middle peasants, glancing round to right and
left, imagined that the signature of the kulak would legitimize
the seizures. And finally, somewhat as the bourgeoisie, although
hostile to the revolution, did not hesitate to appropriate the power,
so the kulaks, after resisting the raids, did not refuse to enjoy their
fruits. The power did not remain long in the hands of the bourgeoisie, nor the landlord's chattels in the hands of the kulaks—
for like reasons.

The strength of the agrarian-democratic and essentially bourgeois revolution was manifested in the fact that it overcame for
a time the class contradictions of the village: the farm hand helped
the kulak in raiding the landlord. The 17th, 18th and 19th
centuries of Russian history climbed up on the shoulders of the
20th, and bent it to the ground. The weakness of this belated
bourgeois revolution was manifested in the fact that the peasant
war did not urge the bourgeois revolutionists forward, but threw
them back conclusively into the camp of reaction. Tseretelli, the
hard-labor convict of yesterday, defended the estates of the landlords against anarchy! The peasant revolution, thus rejected by
the bourgeoisie, joined hands with the industrial proletariat. In
this way the 20th century not only got free of those past centuries hanging upon it, but climbed up on their shoulders to a
new historic level. In order that the peasant might clear and fence
his land, the worker had to stand at the head of the state: that is
the simplest formula for the October revolution.

CHAPTER II

THE PROBLEM OF NATIONALITIES

LANGUAGE is the most important instrument of human communication, and consequently of industry. It becomes national together with the triumph of commodity exchange which integrates nations. Upon this foundation the national state is erected as the most convenient, profitable and normal arena for the play of capitalist relations. In Western Europe the epoch of the formation of bourgeois nations, if you leave out the struggle of the Netherlands for independence and the fate of the island country, England, began with the great French revolution, and was essentially completed approximately one hundred years later with the formation of the German Empire.

But during that period when in Europe the national state could no longer contain the productive forces and was overgrown into the imperialist state, in the East—in Persia, the Balkans, China, India—the era of national democratic revolutions, taking its impetus from the Russian revolution of 1905, was only just beginning. The Balkan war of 1912 marked the completion of the forming of national states in southeastern Europe. The subsequent imperialist war completed incidentally the unfinished work of the national revolutions in Europe leading as it did to the dismemberment of Austria-Hungary, the establishment of an independent Poland, and of independent border states cut from the empire of the tzars.

Russia was formed not as a national state, but as a state made up of nationalities. This corresponded to its belated character. On a foundation of extensive agriculture and home industry commercial capital developed not deeply, not by transforming production, but broadly, by increasing the radius of its operation. The trader, the landlord and the government official advanced from the center toward the periphery, following the peasant settlers who, in search of fresh lands and freedom from imposts, were penetrating new territory inhabited by still more backward tribes. The expansion of the state was in its foundation an expansion of agriculture, which with all its primitiveness showed a certain superiority to that of the nomads in the south and east. The bureaucratic-caste state which formed itself upon this enormous and continually broadening basis, became sufficiently strong to subjugate certain nations in the west, possessed of a higher culture but unable because of their small numbers or condition of inner crisis to defend their independence (Poland, Lithuania, the Baltic states, Finland).

To the seventy million Great Russians constituting the main mass of the country, there were gradually added about ninety million "outlanders" sharply divided into two groups: the western peoples excelling Russia in their culture, and the eastern standing on a lower level. Thus was created an empire of whose population the ruling nationality constituted only 43 per cent. The remaining 57 per cent were nationalities of various degrees of culture and subjection, including Ukrainians 17 per cent, Poles 6 per cent, white Russians $4\frac{1}{2}$ per cent.

The greedy demands of the state and the meagerness of the peasant foundation under the ruling classes gave rise to the most bitter forms of exploitation. National oppression in Russia was incomparably rougher than in the neighboring states not only on its western but even on its eastern borders. The vast numbers of these nationalities deprived of rights, and the sharpness of their deprivation, gave to the national problem in tzarist Russia a gigantic explosive force.

Whereas in nationally homogeneous states the bourgeois revolutions developed powerful centripetal tendencies, rallying to the idea of overcoming particularism, as in France, or overcoming national disunion, as in Italy and Germany—in nationally heterogeneous states on the contrary, such as Turkey, Russia, Austria-Hungary, the belated bourgeois revolution released centrifugal forces. In spite of the apparent contrariness of these processes when expressed in mechanical terms, their historic function was the same. In both cases it was a question of using the national unity as a fundamental industrial reservoir. Germany had for this purpose to be united, Austria-Hungary to be divided.

37

Lenin early learned the inevitability of this development of centrifugal national movements in Russia, and for many years stubbornly fought—most particularly against Rosa Luxemburg —for that famous paragraph 9 of the old party program which formulated the right of nations to self-determination—that is, to complete separation as states. In this the Bolshevik party did not by any means undertake an evangel of separation. It merely assumed an obligation to struggle implacably against every form of national oppression, including the forcible retention of this or that nationality within the boundaries of the general state. Only in this way could the Russian proletariat gradually win the confidence of the oppressed nationalities.

But that was only one side of the matter. The policy of Bolshevism in the national sphere had also another side, apparently contradictory to the first but in reality supplementing it. Within the framework of the party, and of the workers' organizations in general, Bolshevism insisted upon a rigid centralism, implacably warring against every taint of nationalism which might set the workers one against the other or disunite them. While flatly refusing to the bourgeois states the right to impose compulsory citizenship, or even a state language, upon a national minority, Bolshevism at the same time made it a verily sacred task to unite as closely as possible, by means of voluntary class discipline, the workers of different nationalities. Thus it flatly rejected the national-federation principle in building the party. A revolutionary organization is not the prototype of the future state, but merely the instrument for its creation. An instrument ought to be adapted to fashioning the product; it ought not to include the product. Thus a centralized organization can guarantee the success of a revolutionary struggle—even where the task is to destroy the centralized oppression of nationalities.

For the oppressed nations of Russia the overthrow of the monarchy inevitably meant also their own national revolution. In this matter, however, we observe the same thing as in all other departments of the February régime: the official democracy, held in leash by its political dependence upon an imperialist bourgeoisie, was totally incapable of breaking the old fetters. Holding inviolable its right to settle the fate of all other nations, it continued jealously to guard those sources of wealth, power and influence which had given the Great Russian bourgeoisie its dominant position. The compromisist democracy merely translated the traditions of the tzarist national policy into the language of libertarian rhetoric: it was now a question of defending the unity of the revolution. But the ruling coalition had also another more pointed argument: wartime expediency. This meant that the aspirations of individual nationalities toward freedom must be portrayed as the work of the Austro-German General Staff. Here too the Kadets played first violin and the Compromisers second.

The new government could not, of course, leave absolutely untouched that disgusting legal tangle, the complicated medieval mockeries of the outlanders. But it did hope and endeavor to stop at a mere annulment of the exceptional laws against individual nations—that is, to establish a bare equality of all parts of the population before the Great Russian state bureaucracy.

This formal equality gave most of all to the Jews, for the laws limiting their rights had reached the number of 650. Moreover, being city dwellers and the most scattered of all the nationalities, the Jews could make no claim either to state independence or even territorial autonomy. As to the project of a so-called "national-cultural autonomy" which should unite the Jews throughout the whole country around schools and other institutions, this reactionary utopia, borrowed by various Jewish groups from the Austrian theoretician, Otto Bauer, melted in those first days of freedom like wax under the sun's rays.

But a revolution is a revolution for the very reason that it is not satisfied either with doles or deferred payments. The abolition of the more shameful national limitations established a formal equality of citizens regardless of their nationality, but this revealed only the more sharply the unequal position of the nationalities as such, leaving the major part of them in the position of step-children or foster-children of the Great Russian state.

The proclamation of equal rights meant nothing to the Finns especially, for they did not desire equality with the Russians but independence of Russia. It gave nothing to the Ukrainians, for their rights had been equal before, they having been forcibly proclaimed to be Russian. It changed nothing in the situation of the Letts and Esthonians, oppressed by the German landlord's manor and the Russo-German city. It did not lighten in the least the fate of the backward peoples and tribes of Central Asia, who had been held down to the rock bottom not by juridical limitations, but by economic and cultural ball and chain. All these questions the Liberal-Compromisist coalition refused even to bring up. The democratic state remained the same old state of the Great Russian functionary, who did not intend to yield his place to anybody.

The deeper the revolution sank among the masses in the borderlands, the more clear it became that the Russian state language was there the language of the possessing classes. The régime of formal democracy, with its freedom of press and assemblage, made the backward and oppressed nationalities only the more painfully aware to what extent they were deprived of the most elementary means of cultural development: their own schools, their own courts, their own officials. References to a future Constituent Assembly only irritated them. They knew well enough that the same party would dominate that assembly which had created the Provisional Government, and was continuing to defend the tradition of Russification, making clear with its jealous greed that line beyond which the ruling classes would not go.

Finland became from the first a thorn in the flesh of the February régime. Thanks to the bitterness of the agrarian problem, in Finland a problem of "torpars"—that is, small enslaved tenants —the industrial workers, although comprising only 14 per cent of the population, carried the rural population with them. The Finnish Seim was the only parliament in the world where the social-democrats got a majority: 103 seats out of 200. Having by their law of June 5 declared the Seim a sovereign power except on questions of war and foreign policy, the Finnish social-democrats appealed for support "to the comrade party of Russia." But their appeal, as it turned out, was sent quite to the wrong address. The Provisional Government stepped aside at first, permitting the "comrade party" to act. An advisory delegation headed by Cheidze went to Helsingfors and returned empty-handed. Then the socialist ministers of Petrograd—Kerensky,

Chernov, Skobelev, Tseretelli—decided to dissolve by force the socialist government at Helsingfors. The chief of the headquarters staff, the monarchist Lukomsky, gave warning to the civil authorities and the population of Finland that in case of any action against the Russian army "their cities, and Helsingfors, first of all, would be laid waste." After this preparation, the Government issued a solemn manifesto—a plagiarism from the monarchy even in its literary style—dissolving the Seim. And on the first day of the offensive they placed Russian soldiers withdrawn from the front at the doors of the Finnish parliament. Thus the revolutionary masses of Russia—making their way to October—got a good lesson on the qualified place occupied by the principles of democracy in a struggle of class forces.

Confronted by this unbridled nationalism of the ruling classes, the revolutionary troops in Finland adopted a worthy attitude. A regional congress of the soviets held in Helsingfors early in September announced: "If the Finnish democracy finds it advisable to renew the sessions of the Seim, any attempt to hinder this will be regarded by the soviet congress as a counter-revolutionary act." That was a direct offer of military help. But the Finnish democracy, in which compromisist tendencies predominated, was not ready to take the road of insurrection. New elections, held under the threat of a new dissolution, gave a majority of 180 out of 200 to those bourgeois parties in agreement with whom the government had dissolved the Seim.

But here domestic questions come to the front, questions which in this Switzerland of the North, a land of granite mountains and greedy proprietors, would lead inexorably to civil war. The Finnish bourgeoisie was half openly preparing its military cadres. Secret nuclei of the Red Guard were forming at the same time. The bourgeoisie turned to Sweden and Germany for weapons and instructors. The workers found support in the Russian troops. Meanwhile in bourgeois circles—yesterday still inclined to agreement with Petrograd—a movement was developing for complete separation from Russia. Their leading newspaper, *Khuvudstatsbladet*, wrote: "The Russian people is possessed by an anarchist frenzy. . . . Ought we not in these circumstances . . . to separate ourselves as far as possible from that chaos?" The

Provisional Government found itself obliged to make concessions without awaiting the Constituent Assembly. On the 23rd of October a decree was adopted recognizing "in principle" the independence of Finland except in military and foreign affairs. But "independence" given by the hand of Kerensky was not worth much: it was now only two days before his fall.

A second and far more gigantic thorn in the flesh was the Ukraine. Early in June, Kerensky forbade the holding of a Ukrainian soldier-congress convoked by the Rada. The Ukrainians did not submit. In order to save the face of his government Kerensky legalized the congress *ex post facto,* sending a declamatory telegram which the assembled deputies greeted with disrespectful laughter. This bitter lesson did not prevent Kerensky from forbidding three weeks later a military congress of the Mussulmans in Moscow. The democratic government seemed anxious to make it plain to the discontented nations: you will get only what you grab.

In its first "universal" issued on June 10th, the Rada, accusing Petrograd of opposing national independence, declared: "Henceforth we will build our own life." The Kadets denounced the Ukrainian leaders as German agents; the Compromisers addressed them with sentimental admonitions; the Provisional Government sent a delegation to Kiev. In the heated atmosphere of the Ukraine, Kerensky, Tseretelli and Tereschenko felt obliged to take a few steps to meet the Rada. But after the July raids on workers and soldiers, the Government veered right on the Ukrainian question also. On August 5, the Rada by an overwhelming majority accused the government, "imbued with the imperialist tendencies of the Russian bourgeoisie," of having broken the agreement of July 3rd. "When the time came for the government to redeem its pledge," declared the head of the Ukrainian government, Vinnichenko, "it turned out that the Provisional Government . . . is a petty cheat, who hopes to get rid of a great historic problem by swindling." This unequivocal language conveys an adequate idea of the authority of the government even in those circles which ought politically to be rather close to it. For in the long run the Ukrainian Compromiser, Vinnichenko, was distinguished from Kerensky only as a mediocre novelist from a mediocre lawyer.

It is true that in September the government did finally issue a decree recognizing for all the nationalities of Russia—within limits to be designated by the Constituent Assembly—the "right of self-determination." But this wholly unguaranteed and inwardly contradictory promise for the future—extremely vague in everything but its limitations—inspired no confidence in anybody. The doings of the Provisional Government were already crying out too loudly against it.

On September 2nd the Senate—that same body which refused to admit new members without the old uniform—decided to deny publication to the instructions issued to the Ukrainian General Secretariat—that is, to the Ministerial Cabinet in Kiev— and confirmed by the Government. Justification: no law provides for this Secretariat, and it is impossible to issue instructions to an illegal institution. The lofty jurists did not conceal the fact, either, that the very agreement entered into between the government and the Rada was a usurpation of the rights of the Constituent Assembly—these tzarist senators having now become the most inflexible partisans of pure democracy. In this show of courage the oppositionists from the Right were risking nothing at all: they knew that their opposition was quite after the heart of the ruling classes. Although the Russian bourgeoisie had swallowed a certain amount of independence for Finland—united to Russia as she was by weak economic ties—it could not possibly agree to an "autonomy" of Ukrainian grain, Donetz coal, and the ores of Krivorog.

On October 19, Kerensky sent a telegraphic order to the General Secretary of the Ukraine "to come promptly to Petrograd for personal explanations" in regard to a criminal agitation started there in favor of a Ukrainian Constituent Assembly. At the same time the District Attorney of Kiev was directed to begin an investigation of the Rada. But these threats gave as little fright to the Ukraine as the acts of grace had given joy to Finland.

The Ukrainian Compromisers were at this time feeling infinitely more secure than their elder cousins in Petrograd. Aside

43

from the auspicious atmosphere surrounding their struggle for national rights, the comparative stability of the petty bourgeois parties in the Ukraine—as also in a number of other oppressed nations—had economic and social roots describable in one word, *backwardness*. In spite of the swift industrial development of the Donetz and Krivorog Basins, the Ukraine as a whole continued to lag behind Great Russia. The Ukrainian proletariat was less homogeneous, less tempered. The Bolshevik party was weak both in numbers and quality, had been slow in breaking away from the Mensheviks, and was poorly versed in the political, and especially the national situation. Even in the industrial eastern parts of the Ukraine, a regional conference of the soviets as late as the middle of October showed a slight compromisist majority!

The Ukrainian bourgeoisie was comparatively still weaker. One of the causes of the social instability of the Russian bourgeoisie taken as a whole lay, we remember, in the fact that its more powerful section consisted of foreigners not even dwelling in Russia. In the borderlands this fact was supplemented by another no less significant: their own domestic bourgeoisie did not belong to the same nation as the principal mass of the people.

The population of the cities in these borderlands was completely different in its national ingredients from the population of the country. In the Ukraine and White Russia the landlord, capitalist, lawyer, journalist, was a Great Russian, a Pole, a Jew, a foreigner; the rural population was wholly Ukrainian and White Russian. In the Baltic states the cities were havens of the German, Russian and Jewish bourgeoisie; the country was altogether Lettish and Esthonian. In the cities of Georgia, a Russian and Armenian population predominated, as also in Turkish Azerbaidjan, being separated from the fundamental mass of the people not only by their level of life and culture, but also by language, as are the English in India. Being indebted for the protection of their possessions and income to the bureaucratic machine, and being closely bound up with the ruling classes of all other countries, the landlords, industrialists and merchants in these borderlands grouped around themselves a narrow circle of Russian functionaries, clerks, teachers, physicians, lawyers, journalists, and to some extent workers also, converting the cities into centers of Russification and colonization.

It was possible to ignore the villages so long as they remained silent. When they began, however, more and more impatiently to lift their voices, the city resisted and stubbornly continued to resist, defending its privileged position. The functionary, the merchant, the lawyer, soon learned to disguise his struggle to retain the commanding heights of industry and culture under the form of a top-lofty condemnation of an increasing "chauvinism." The desire of a ruling nation to maintain the *status quo* frequently dresses up as a superiority to "nationalism," just as the desire of a victorious nation to hang on to its booty easily takes the form of pacifism. Thus MacDonald in the face of Ghandi feels as though he were an internationalist. Thus too the gravitation of the Austrians toward Germany appears to Poincaré an offense against French pacifism.

"People living in the cities of the Ukraine"—so wrote a delegation of the Rada to the Provisional Government in May— "see before them the Russified streets of these cities . . . and completely forget that these cities are only little islets in the sea of the whole Ukrainian people." When Rosa Luxemburg, in her posthumous polemic against the program of the October revolution, asserted that Ukrainian nationalism, having been formerly a mere "amusement" of the commonplace petty bourgeois intelligentsia, had been artificially raised up by the yeast of the Bolshevik formula of self-determination, she fell, notwithstanding her luminous mind, into a very serious historic error. The Ukrainian peasantry had not made national demands in the past for the reason that the Ukrainian peasantry had not in general risen to the height of political being. The chief service of the February revolution—perhaps its only service, but one amply sufficient—lay exactly in this, that it gave the oppressed classes and nations of Russia at last an opportunity to speak out. This political awakening of the peasantry could not have taken place otherwise, however, than through their own native language—with all the consequences ensuing in regard to schools, courts, self-administration. To oppose this would have been to try to drive the peasants back into non-existence.

The difference in nationality between the cities and the villages was painfully felt also in the soviets, they being predominantly city organizations. Under the leadership of the compromise parties the soviets would frequently ignore the national interests of the basic population. This was one cause of the weakness of the soviets in the Ukraine. The soviets of Riga and Reval forgot about the interests of the Letts and the Esthonians. The compromisist soviet in Baku scorned the interests of the basic Turcoman population. Under a false banner of internationalism the soviets would frequently wage a struggle against the defensive nationalism of the Ukrainians or Mussulmans, supplying a screen for the oppressive Russifying movement of the cities. A little time after, under the rule of the Bolsheviks, the soviets of these borderlands began to speak the language of the villages.

Their general economic and cultural primitiveness did not permit the Siberian outlanders—kept down as they were both by nature and exploitation—to rise even to that level where national aspirations begin. Vodka, taxes and compulsory orthodoxy were here from time immemorial the principal instruments of statehood. That disease which the Italians called the French evil, and the French, the Neapolitan, was called "Russian" by the Siberian peoples. That shows from what sources came the seeds of civilization. The February revolution did not reach that far. The hunters and reindeer breeders of the polar wastes must still wait long for their dawn.

The peoples and tribes along the Volga, in the northern Caucasus, in Central Asia—awakened for the first time out of their pre-historic existence by the February revolution—had as yet neither national bourgeoisie nor national proletariat. Above the peasant or shepherd mass a thin layer had detached itself from among their upper strata, constituting an intelligentsia. Not yet rising to a program of national self-administration, the struggle here was about matters like having their own alphabet, their own teachers—even at times their own priests. In these ways the most oppressed were being compelled to learn in bitter experience that the educated masters of the state would not voluntarily permit them to rise in the world. The most backward of the backward were thus compelled to seek the most revolutionary class as an

46

ally. Through the left elements of their young intelligentsia the Votiaks, the Chuvashes, the Zyrians, the tribes of Daghestan and Turkestan, began to find their way toward the Bolsheviks.

The fate of the colonial possessions, especially in central Asia, would change together with the industrial evolution of the center, passing from direct and open robbery, including trade robbery, to those more disguised methods which converted the Asiatic peasants into suppliers of industrial raw material, chiefly cotton. Hierarchically organized exploitation, combining the barbarity of capitalism with the barbarity of patriarchal life, successfully held down the Asiatic peoples in extreme national abasement. And here the February régime left everything as it was.

The best lands, seized under tzarism from the Bashkirs, Buriats, Kirghiz, and other nomadic tribes, had continued in the possession of the landlords and wealthy Russian peasants scattered about in colonizing oases among the native population. The awakening of a national spirit of independence here meant first of all a struggle against these colonizers, who had created an artificial stripe system of land-ownership and condemned the nomads to hunger and gradual extinction. The colonizers, on their side, furiously defended the unity of Russia—that is, the sanctity of their grabbings—against the "separatism" of the Asiatics. The hatred of the colonizers for the native movements assumed zoological forms in the Transbaikal. Pogroms of the Buriats were in full swing under the leadership of March Social Revolutionaries recruited from village clerks and non-commissioned officers returning from the front.

In their anxiety to preserve the old order as long as possible, all the exploiters and violators in the colonized regions appealed henceforth to the sovereign rights of the Constituent Assembly. This phraseology was supplied them by the Provisional Government, which had found here its surest bulwark. On the other hand, the privileged upper circles of the oppressed peoples were also calling more and more often on the name of the Constituent Assembly. Even the Mussulman clergy who would lift above the awakening mountain peoples and the tribes of the northern Caucasus the green banner of the Shariat whenever a pressure from below made their position difficult, were now postponing the question "until the Constituent Assembly." This became the slogan of conservatism, of reaction, of special interest and privilege all over the country. To appeal to the Constituent Assembly meant to postpone and gain time. Postponement meant: assemble your forces and strangle the revolution.

The leadership fell into the hands of the clergy or feudal gentry, however, only at first, only among the backward peoples—almost only among the Mussulmans. In general, the national movement in the villages was headed as a matter of course by rural teachers, village clerks, functionaries and officers of low rank, and, to some extent, merchants. Alongside the Russian or Russianized intelligentsia, composed of the more respectable and well provided elements, there was formed in the borderland cities another layer, a younger layer, closely bound up with its village origin and lacking access to the banquet of capital, and this layer naturally took upon itself the task of representing politically the national, and in part also the social interests of the basic peasant mass.

Although hostilely disposed to the Russian Compromisers along the line of this national aspiration, these borderland Compromisers belonged to the same fundamental type, and even for the most part went by the same name. The Ukrainian Social Revolutionaries and social democrats, the Georgian and Lettish Mensheviks, the Lithuanian "Trudoviks," tried like their Great Russian namesakes to confine the revolution within the framework of the bourgeois régime. But the extreme weakness of the native bourgeoisie here compelled the Mensheviks and Social Revolutionaries, instead of entering a coalition, to take the state power into their own hands. Compelled to go farther on agrarian and labor questions than the central government, these borderland compromisers had also the great advantage of being able to appear before the army and the country as opponents of the coalitional Provisional Government. All this was sufficient, if not to create different destinies for the Russian Compromisers and those of the borderlands, at least to give a different tempo to their rise and fall.

The Georgian social democrats not only led after them the pauper peasantry of Little Georgia, but also laid claim—and that

48

not without success—to lead the movement of the "revolutionary democracy" for all Russia. During the first months of the revolution the heads of the Georgian intelligentsia regarded Georgia not as a national fatherland, but as a Gironde—a blessed southern province called to provide leaders for the whole country. At the Moscow State Conference one of the prominent Georgian Mensheviks, Chenkeli, boasted that the Georgians had always said even under tzarism, in fair weather and foul: "A single fatherland, Russia." "What shall we say of the Georgian nation?" cried this same Chenkeli a month later at the Democratic Conference. "It is wholly at the service of the Great Russian revolution." And it is quite true that the Georgian Compromisers, like the Jewish, were always "at the service" of the great Russian bureaucracy when it was necessary to moderate, or put brakes on the national claims of individual regions.

This continued only so long, however, as the Georgian social democrats still hoped to confine the revolution within the framework of bourgeois democracy. In proportion as the danger appeared of a victory of the masses led by Bolshevism, the Georgian social democrats relaxed their ties with the Russian Compromisers and united closely with the reactionary elements of Georgia itself. The moment the soviets were victorious, these Georgian partisans of a single Russia became the trumpeters of separation, and showed to the other peoples of Transcaucasia the yellow fangs of their chauvinism.

This inevitable national disguise of social contradictions—less developed in the borderlands, anyway, as a general rule—adequately explains why the October revolution was destined to meet more opposition in most of the oppressed nations than in Central Russia. But, on the other hand, the conflict of nationalities by its very nature cruelly shook the February régime and created sufficiently favorable surroundings for the revolution in the center.

In these circumstances the national antagonisms whenever they coincided with class contradictions became especially hot. The age-old hostility between the Lettish peasants and the German barons impelled many thousands of laboring Letts to volunteer at the outbreak of the war. The sharp-shooting regiments of

Lettish farm hands and peasants were among the best troops at the front. As early as May, however, they had already come out for a soviet government. Their nationalism was only the outer shell of an immature Bolshevism. A like process took place in Esthonia.

In White Russia, with its Polish or Polized landlords, its Jewish population in the cities and small towns, and its Russian officials, the twice and thrice oppressed peasantry had some time before October, under the influence of the nearby front, poured its national and social indignation into the channel of Bolshevism. In the elections for the Constituent Assembly the overwhelming mass of White Russians would cast its vote for the Bolsheviks.

All these processes in which an awakened national dignity was linked up with social indignation, now holding it back, now pushing it forward, found an extremely sharp expression in the army. Here there was a veritable fever for creating national regiments, and these were at one time patronized, at another tolerated, at still another persecuted by the central government, according to their attitude to the war and the Bolsheviks. But in general they kept growing more and more hostile to Petrograd.

Lenin kept a firm hand on the "national" pulse of the revolution. In a famous article, "The Crisis Is Ripe," written toward the end of September, he insistently pointed out that the National curia of the Democratic Conference "had stood second in the matter of radicalism, yielding only to the trade unions, and standing higher than the soviet curia in its percentage of votes against the Coalition (40 out of 55)." This meant that the oppressed peoples were no longer hoping for any benefit from the Great Russian bourgeoisie. They were more and more trying to get their rights by independent action, a bite at a time and in the form of revolutionary seizures.

In an October congress of the Buriats in far off Verkhneyudinsk, a speaker declared that "the February revolution introduced nothing new" in the position of the outlander. His summing up of the situation made it seem necessary, if not yet to take the side of the Bolsheviks, at least to observe an attitude of more and more friendly neutrality toward them.

An all-Ukrainian soldier-congress which met during the very days of the Petrograd insurrection, adopted a resolution to struggle against the transfer of power to the Ukrainian Soviet, but at the same time refused to regard the insurrection of the Great Russian Bolsheviks as an "anti-democratic action," and promised to take all measures to prevent the soldiers being sent to put down the insurrection. This equivocation which perfectly characterizes the petty bourgeois stage of the national struggle, facilitated that revolution of the proletariat which intended to put an end to all equivocations.

On the other hand the bourgeois circles in the borderlands, which had heretofore invariably and always gravitated toward the central power, now launched into a separatism which in many cases no longer had a shred of national foundation. The Baltic bourgeoisie, which only yesterday had been following in a state of hurrah-patriotism the German barons, the first bulwark of the Romanovs, took its stand in the struggle against Bolshevik Russia and its own masses, under the banner of separatism. Still more curious phenomena appeared along this road. On the 20th of October the foundations were laid for a new state formation, "The Southeastern Union of Cossack Troops, Caucasian Mountaineers and Free Peoples of the Steppes." Here the leaders of the Don, Kuban, Tyer and Astrakhan Cossacks, the chief bulwark of imperial centralism, were transformed in the course of a few months into passionate defenders of the federal principle, and united on this ground with the leaders of the Mussulman mountaineers and steppe-dwellers. The boundaries of the federative structure were to serve as a barrier against the Bolshevik danger coming from the north. However, before creating the principal drill ground for the civil war against the Bolsheviks, this counter-revolutionary separatism went directly against the ruling coalition, demoralizing and weakening it.

Thus the national problem, along with all others, showed the Provisional Government a Medusa's head on which every hair of the March and April hopes had changed into a snake of hate and indignation.

A Further Note on the Problem of Nationalities

The Bolshevik party did not by any means immediately after the February revolution adopt that attitude on the national question which in the long run guaranteed its victory. This was true not only in the borderlands, with their weak and inexperienced party organizations, but also in the Petrograd center. During the war the party had so weakened, the theoretical and political level of its cadres had become so lowered, that on the national question too its official leaders took an extremely confused and half-way position until the arrival of Lenin.

To be sure, following their tradition, the Bolsheviks defended the right of a nation to self-determination. But the Mensheviks also subscribed to this formula in words. The text of the two programs remained identical. It was the question of power which was decisive. And the temporary leaders of the party proved wholly incapable of understanding the irreconcilable antagonism between the Bolshevik slogans on the national, as well as the agrarian, question, and the preservation of a bourgeois-imperialistic régime, even though disguised in democratic forms.

The democratic position found its most crass expression from the pen of Stalin. On March 25th, in an article dealing with a government decree on the abolition of national limitations, Stalin tried to formulate the national question on a historic scale. "The social basis of national oppression," he writes, "the power inspiring it, is a decaying land aristocracy." The fact that national oppression developed unprecedentedly during the epoch of capitalism, and found its most barbaric expression in colonial policies, seems to be beyond the ken of the democratic author. "In England," he continues, "where the landed aristocracy shares the power with the bourgeoisie, where the unlimited power of this aristocracy long ago ceased to exist, national oppression is milder, less inhumane —leaving out of account, of course, the circumstance that during the course of the war, when the power had gone over into the hands of the landlords (!), national oppression was considerably strengthened (persecution of Ireland and India)." Those guilty of oppressing Ireland and India are the landlords, who—evidently in the person of Lloyd George— have seized the power thanks to the war. ". . . In Switzerland and North America," continues Stalin, "where there is no landlordism and never has been (!), where the power is undivided in the hands of the bourgeoisie, nationalities have developed freely. National oppression, generally speaking, finds no place. . . ." The author completely forgets

52

the Negro, Indian, immigrant and colonial problems in the United States.

From this hopelessly provincial analysis, which comes only to a confused contrasting of feudalism with democracy, purely liberal political inferences are drawn. "To remove the feudal aristocracy from the political scene, to snatch the power from it—that is exactly the same thing as to put an end to national oppression, to create the actual conditions necessary for national freedom. Insofar as the Russian revolution has conquered," writes Stalin, "it has actually created these conditions. . . ." We have here perhaps a more principled apology for the imperialistic "democracy" than all that has been written on this theme by the Mensheviks. Just as in foreign policy Stalin, along with Kamenev, hoped to achieve a democratic peace by means of a division of labor with the Provisional Government, so in domestic policy he found in the democracy of Prince Lvov the "actual conditions" of national freedom.

As a matter of fact the fall of the monarchy first fully exposed the fact that not only the reactionary landlords, but also the whole liberal bourgeoisie, and following after it the whole petty bourgeois democracy, along with the patriotic upper crust of the working class, was implacably hostile to a genuine equality of national rights—that is to say, an abolition of the privileges of the dominant nation. Their whole program came down to a business of mitigation, of cultural sugar-coating, of democratic concealment of the Great Russian ascendancy.

At the April conference, in defending Lenin's resolution on the national question, Stalin formally starts from the thesis that "national oppression is that system . . . those measures which are adopted by the imperialistic circles." But he straightway and inevitably gets off the track and goes back to his March position. "The more democratic a country, the weaker its national oppression and vice versa." Such is the speaker's own summary, and not the one he borrowed from Lenin. The fact that democratic England is oppressing feudal and caste-ridden India escapes, as before, from his limited field of vision. In distinction from Russia, where "an old land aristocracy" has dominated—continues Stalin—"in England and Austria-Hungary the national oppression has never taken the form of pogroms." As though a land aristocracy "never" dominated in England, and as though it does not dominate to this day in Hungary! The combined character of historic development which unites "democracy" with the strangling of weak nations, had remained for Stalin a sealed book.

That Russia took form as a state made up of nationalities, is the result of her historic belatedness. But belatedness is a complex conception inevitably contradictory. The backward country does not follow in the tracks of the advanced, keeping the same distance. In an epoch of world-wide economy the backward nations, becoming involved under pressure from the advanced in the general chain of development, skip over whole series of intermediate stages. Moreover the absence of firmly established social forms and traditions makes the backward country—at least within certain limits—extremely hospitable to the last word in international technique and international thought. Backwardness does not, however, for this reason cease to be backwardness. The whole development gets a contradictory and combined character. A predominance of historic extremes is proper to the social structure of a belated nation—predominance of the backward peasants and the advanced proletarians over the intermediate formations of the bourgeoisie. The tasks of one class are shouldered off upon another. In the national sphere also, the uprooting of medieval remnants falls to the lot of the proletariat.

Nothing so clearly characterizes the historic belatedness of Russia when considered as a European country, as the fact that in the twentieth century she had to liquidate compulsory land rent and the pale—those twin barbarisms, serfdom and the Ghetto. But in performing these tasks Russia, exactly because of her belated development, made use of new and utterly modern classes, parties, programs. To make an end of the ideas and methods of Rasputin, she required the ideas and methods of Marx.

Political practice remained, of course, far more primitive than political theory. For things are harder to change than ideas. But theory nevertheless only carried the demands of practical action clear through. In order to achieve liberation and a cultural lift, the oppressed nationalities were compelled to link their fate with that of the working class. And for this they had to free themselves from the leadership of their own bourgeois and petty bourgeois parties—they had to make a long spurt forward, that is, on the road of historic development.

This subordination of the national movements to the fundamental process of the revolution, the struggle of the proletariat for power, was not accomplished at once, but in several stages—and moreover differently in different regions. The Ukrainian, White Russian and Tartar workers, peasants, and soldiers who were hostile to Kerensky, the war and Russification, became thereby, in spite of their compromisist leadership, allies of the proletarian insurrection. From being an objective support of the Bolsheviks, they became obliged at a farther stage to go over consciously also to the Bolshevik road. In Finland, Latvia and Esthonia, and more weakly in the Ukraine, the stratification of the national movement had taken such sharp forms by October, that only the

interference of foreign troops could prevent the success of the proletarian revolution. In the Asiatic East, where the national awakening
was taking place in more primitive forms, it could only by degrees and
with a considerable lag come under the leadership of the proletariat—
only, indeed, after the proletariat had conquered the power. If you take
this complicated and contradictory process as a whole, the conclusion
is obvious: the national current, like the agrarian, was pouring into the
channel of the October revolution.

The irrevocable and irresistible going over of the masses from the
most rudimentary tasks of political, agrarian and national emancipation and abolition of serfdom to the slogan of proletarian rulership, resulted not from "demagogic" agitation, not from preconceived schemes,
not from the theory of Permanent Revolution, as the Liberals and Compromisers thought, but from the social structure of Russia and the conditions of the world-wide situation. The theory of Permanent Revolution only formulated the combined process of this development.

It is a question here not of Russia alone. This subordination of belated national revolutions to the revolution of the proletariat follows a
law which is valid throughout the world. Whereas in the nineteenth
century the fundamental problem of wars and revolutions was still
to guarantee a national market to the productive forces, the problem
of our century is to free the productive forces from the national
boundaries which have become iron fetters upon them. In the broad
historic sense the national revolutions of the East are only stages of the
world revolution of the proletariat, just as the national movements of
Russia became stepping stones to the soviet dictatorship.

Lenin appraised with admirable profundity the revolutionary force
inherent in the development of the oppressed nationalities, both in
tzarist Russia and throughout the world. That hypocritical "pacifism,"
which "condemns" in the same way the war of Japan against China
aiming at her enslavement, and the war of China against Japan in the
cause of her liberation, got nothing but scorn from Lenin. For him a
war of national liberation, in contrast to wars of imperialistic oppression, was merely another form of the national revolution which in its
turn enters as a necessary link in the liberating struggle of the international working class.

This appraisal of national wars and revolutions does not by any means
imply, however, that the bourgeoisie of the colonial and semi-colonial
nations have a revolutionary mission. On the contrary, this bourgeoisie
of backward countries from the days of its milk teeth grows up as an
agentry of foreign capital, and notwithstanding its envious hatred of
foreign capital, always does and always will in every decisive situation

turn up in the same camp with it. Chinese compradorism is the classic form of the colonial bourgeoisie, and the Kuomintang is the classic party of compradorism. The upper circles of the petty bourgeoisie, including the intelligentsia, may take an active and occasionally a very noisy part in the national struggles, but they are totally incapable of playing an independent rôle. Only the working class standing at the head of the nation can carry either a national or an agrarian revolution clear through.

The fatal mistake of the Epigones, and above all Stalin, lies in this, that from Lenin's teaching about the progressive historic significance of the struggle of oppressed nations they have inferred a revolutionary mission of the bourgeoisie of the colonial countries. A failure to understand the permanent character of revolution in an imperialist epoch; a pedantic schematization of the course of development; a chopping up of the living and combined process into dead stages imagined to be necessarily separated in time—all these errors have brought Stalin to a vulgar idealization of democracy or a "democratic dictatorship," a thing which can be nothing in reality but either an imperialist dictatorship or a dictatorship of the proletariat. Step by step Stalin's groups have proceeded along this road to a complete break with the position of Lenin on the national question, and to their catastrophic policy in China.

In August 1927, in conflict with the Opposition (Trotsky, Rakovsky, and others) Stalin said at a plenary session of the Central Committee of the Bolsheviks: "A revolution in imperialist countries is one thing; there the bourgeoisie . . . is counter-revolutionary at all stages of the revolution. . . . A revolution in colonial and dependent countries is something else . . . ; there the national bourgeoisie can at a given stage and a given date support the revolutionary movement of their country against imperialism."

With side remarks and softenings due only to his lack of confidence in himself, Stalin here transfers to the colonial bourgeoisie those same traits with which he was adorning the Russian bourgeoisie in March. Obedient to its deeply organic nature Stalin's opportunism finds its way as though impelled by some law of gravitation, through whatever channels always in the same direction. The choice of theoretic arguments becomes here a purely accidental matter.

From this transfer of his March appraisal of the Provisional Government to the "national" government of China resulted Stalin's three-year cooperation with the Kuomintang, a policy which led up to one of the most shocking facts of modern history. In the capacity of loyal armor-bearer, the Bolshevism of the Epigones accompanied the Chinese bourgeoisie right up to April 11, 1927, the day of its bloody massacre of the Shanghai proletariat. "The fundamental mistake of the Opposition"—thus Stalin tried to justify his comradeship in arms with Chang Kai Shek—"lies in the fact that it identifies the revolution of 1905 in Russia—in an imperialist country oppressing other peoples, with the revolution in China, an oppressed country. . . ." It is astonishing even in Stalin that he has never thought of viewing the revolution in Russia, not from the standpoint of the nation "oppressing other peoples," but from the standpoint of the experience of these same "other peoples" of Russia who have suffered no less oppression than the Chinese.

In that gigantic field of experience represented by Russia in the course of her three revolutions, you can find every variant of national and class struggle except one: that in which the bourgeoisie of any oppressed nation played a liberating rôle in relation to its own people. At every stage of its development every borderland bourgeoisie, no matter in what colors it might dance, was invariably dependent upon the central banks, trusts, and commercial institutions which were in essence the agents of all Russian capital. They subjected the bourgeoisie to the Russifying movement, and subjected to the bourgeoisie broad circles of the liberal and democratic intelligentsia. The more "mature" a borderland bourgeoisie might be, the more closely was it bound up with the general state machine. Taken as a whole, the bourgeoisie of the oppressed nation played the same rôle in relation to the ruling bourgeoisie that the latter played in relation to international finance capital. The complex hierarchy of antagonisms and dependencies did not remove for one single day the fundamental solidarity of the three in the struggle against the insurrectionary masses.

In the period of counter-revolution (1907–17), when the leadership of the national movements was in the hands of the native bourgeoisie, they were even more candid than the Russian liberals in seeking a working agreement with the Russian monarchy. The Polish, Baltic, Tartar, Ukrainian, Jewish bourgeoisie vied with each other in the display of imperialist patriotism. After the February revolution they hid behind the backs of the Kadets—or, like the Kadets, behind the backs of their own national Compromisers. The bourgeoisie of the border nations entered the road of separatism in the autumn of 1917, not in a struggle against national oppression, but in a struggle against the advancing proletarian revolution. In the sum total the bourgeoisie of the oppressed nations manifested no less hostility to the revolution than the Great Russian bourgeoisie.

This gigantic historic lesson of three revolutions has left not a trace, however, in the minds of many of those who took part in the events—notably in the mind of Stalin. The compromisist—that is, petty bourgeois—conception of the correlation of classes within colonial nations, that conception which killed the Chinese revolution of 1925–27, has even been introduced by the Epigones into the program of the Communist International, converting this program in that section into a mere trap for the oppressed peoples of the East.

IN ORDER to understand the real character of Lenin's policy on the national question, it is a good idea—following the method of contrasts —to compare it with the policy of the Austrian social democrats. Bolshevism based itself upon the assumption of an outbreak of national revolutions continuing for decades to come, and instructed the advanced workers in this spirit. The Austrian social democracy, on the contrary, submissively accommodated itself to the policy of the ruling classes; it defended the compulsory co-citizenship of ten nations in the Austro-Hungarian monarchy, and at the same time, being absolutely incapable of achieving a revolutionary union of the workers of these different nationalities, fenced them off in the party and in the trade unions with vertical partitions. Karl Renner, an educated Hapsburg functionary, was never tired of probing the inkwells of Austro-Marxism in search of some means of rejuvenating the rule of the Hapsburgs—until one day he found himself the bereaved theoretician of the Austro-Hungarian monarchy. When the Central Empires were crushed, the Hapsburg dynasty again tried to raise the banner of a federation of autonomous nations under its sceptre. The official program of the Austrian social democracy, based as it was upon the assumption of a peaceful development within the frame-work of the monarchy, now became in one second the program of the monarchy itself, covered with the bloody filth of its four years of war. But that rusty hoop which had bound ten nations together flew to pieces. Austria-Hungary fell apart as a result of internal centrifugal tendencies reinforced by the surgery of Versailles. New states were formed, and the old ones reconstructed. The Austrian Germans hung over an abyss. Their problem was no longer to preserve their dominance over other nations, but to avoid falling themselves under a foreign yoke. And Otto Bauer, representing the "left" wing of the Austrian social democracy, considered this a suitable moment to bring forward the formula of national self-determination. That program which during the preceding decades should have inspired the struggle of the proletariat against the Hapsburgs and the ruling bourgeoisie, was now brought in as an instrument of self-preservation for the nation which had dominated yesterday, but today was in danger from the side of the liberated Slavic peoples. Just as the reformist program of the Austrian social democracy had become in the wink of an eye the straw at which a drowning monarchy tried to grab, so the formula of self-determination, emasculated by these Austro-Marxists, was now to become the anchor of salvation for the German bourgeoisie.

On October 3, 1918, when the matter no longer depended on them in the slightest degree, the social democratic deputies of the reichsrath magnanimously "recognized" the right of the peoples of the former empire to self-determination. On October 4th, the bourgeois parties also adopted the program of self-determination. Having thus outstripped the Austro-German imperialists by one day, the social democrats immediately resumed their waiting policy, it being still uncertain what turn things would take and what Wilson was going to say. Only on the 13th of October, when the conclusive collapse of the army and the monarchy had created—in the words of Otto Bauer—"the revolutionary situation for which our national program was designed," did the Austro-Marxists raise the question of self-determination in a practical form. In very truth they had now nothing to lose. "With the collapse of its rulership over other nations," explains Bauer quite frankly, "the German national bourgeoisie considered at an end that historic mission in whose cause it had voluntarily suffered a separation from the German fatherland." Thus the new program was put in circulation not because it was needful to the oppressed, but because it had ceased to be dangerous to the oppressors. The possessing classes, driven into a tight place historically, had found themselves obliged to recognize the national revolution juridically, and Austro-Marxism found this an appropriate moment to legitimize it theoretically. This was a mature revolution, they said, timely, historically prepared—it is all over anyway. The spirit of the social democracy is here before us as though in the palm of the hand!

It was quite otherwise with the social revolution, which could not hope for any recognition from the possessing classes. This had to be postponed, compromised, robbed of glory. Since the empire had split up along the weakest, that is the national, seams, Otto Bauer drew the following conclusion as to the character of the revolution: "It was by no means a social, but a national revolution." In reality the movement had had from the very beginning a deep social-revolutionary content. Its "purely national" character is fairly well illustrated by the fact that the possessing classes of Austria openly invited the Entente to take prisoner the whole army. The German bourgeoisie beseeched the Italian general to seize Vienna with Italian troops!

This vulgar and pedantic separation of national form from social content in the revolutionary process, as though they constituted two independent historic stages—we see here how closely Otto Bauer approaches Stalin!—had an extremely utilitarian destination. Its purpose was to justify the collaboration of the social democracy with the bourgeoisie in its struggle against the danger of social revolution.

If you adopt the formula of Marx that revolution is the locomotive of history, then Austro-Marxism occupies the position of the brake. Even after the actual collapse of the monarchy, the social democracy, called to participate in the government, was still unable to make up its mind to a rupture with the old Hapsburg ministry. The "national" revolution limited itself to reinforcing the old ministers with state secretaries. Only after October 9th, when the German revolution had thrown out the Hohenzollerns, did the Austrian social democrats propose to the State Council that they proclaim a republic, frightening their bourgeois partners into it with the movement of the masses at which they were already themselves quaking to the marrow of their bones. "The Christian Socialists," says Otto Bauer with imprudent irony, "who on the 9th and 10th of November were still on the side of the monarchy, decided on November 11th to cease their resistance. . . ." For two whole days the social democrats were in advance of this party of the Black Hundred Monarchy! All the heroic legends of humanity grow pale before this revolutionary audacity.

Against its will the Austrian social democracy took its place automatically from the beginning of the revolution at the head of the nation, just as had the Russian Mensheviks and Social Revolutionaries. Like them too it feared above all things its own power. In the coalition government the social democrats tried to occupy just as small a place as possible. Otto Bauer explains this as follows: "The fact that the social democrats at first demanded only a modest participation in the government corresponded primarily to the purely national character of the revolution." The question of power was decided by those people not on a basis of the real correlation of forces, the might of the revolutionary movement, the bankruptcy of the ruling classes, the political influence of the party, but by a pedantic little label "purely national revolution" pasted by some wiseacre classifiers upon the actual course of events.

Karl Renner waited out the storm in the position of head secretary of the State Council. The other social democratic leaders converted themselves into assistants of the bourgeois ministers. In other words, the social democrats hid under the office tables. The masses, however, were not satisfied to feed on the national shell of that nut whose social meat the Austro-Marxists were saving up for the bourgeoisie. The workers and soldiers shoved out the bourgeois ministers and compelled the social democrats to come out of hiding. The irreplaceable theoretician, Otto Bauer, explains this also: "Only the events of the following days, driving the national revolution over to the side of social revolution, increased our weight in the government." To translate this into intelligible language: under the assault of the masses, the social democrats were compelled to crawl out from under the tables.

But this did not change their function for a moment. They took the power, but only to start a war against romanticism and adventurism, with which titles these sycophants now designated that same social revolution which had "increased their weight in the government." If these Austro-Marxists successfully fulfilled in 1918 their historic mission as guardian angels protecting the Vienna Kreditanstalt from the revolutionary romanticism of the proletariat, it is only because they met no obstacle from the side of a genuine revolutionary party.

The two states composed of nationalities, Russia and Austria-Hungary, have with their most recent fate set a seal upon the difference between Bolshevism and Austro-Marxism. Throughout a decade and a half Lenin, in implacable conflict with all shades of Great Russian chauvinism, preached the right of all oppressed nations to cut away from the empire of the tzars. The Bolsheviks were accused of aspiring toward the dismemberment of Russia, but this bold revolutionary formulation of the national problem won for the Bolshevik party the indestructible confidence of the small and oppressed peoples of tzarist Russia. In April 1917 Lenin said: "If the Ukrainians see that we have a soviet republic they will not cut away, but if we have a Miliukov republic they will." In this he proved right. History has provided an incomparable checkup of the two policies on the national question. Whereas Austria-Hungary, whose proletariat was educated in the spirit of a cowardly halfway policy, went all to pieces under a formidable shake-up, and moreover the initiative in this process was taken in the main by the national sections of the social democratic party, in Russia on the ruins of tzarism a new state composed of nationalities has been formed, and has been closely welded together both economically and politically by the Bolshevik party.

Whatever may be the further destiny of the Soviet Union—and it is still far from a quiet haven—the national policy of Lenin will find its place among the eternal treasures of mankind.

CHAPTER III

WITHDRAWAL FROM THE PRE-PARLIAMENT AND STRUGGLE FOR THE SOVIET CONGRESS

E VERY additional day of war was disintegrating the front, weakening the government, damaging the international position of the country. At the beginning of October the German fleets, both naval and air, developed active operations in the Gulf of Finland. The Baltic sailors fought courageously trying to protect the road to Petrograd. But they, more clearly and profoundly than any other unit of the front, understood the deep contradiction in their position as vanguards of a revolution and involuntary participants in an imperialist war, and through the radio stations on their ships they sent out a cry to the four corners of the horizon for international revolutionary help. "Attacked by superior German forces our fleet will go down in unequal battle. Not one of our ships will decline the fight. The slandered and maligned fleet will do its duty . . . but not at the command of a miserable Russian Bonaparte, ruling by the long-suffering patience of the revolution . . . not in the name of the treaties of our rulers with the Allies, binding in chains the hands of Russian freedom. . . ." No, but in the name of the defense of the approaches to the hearth-fire of the revolution, Petrograd. "In the hour when the waves of the Baltic are stained with the blood of our brothers, while the waters are closing over their bodies, we raise our voice: . . . Oppressed people of the whole world! Lift the banner of revolt!"

These words about battles and victims were not empty. The squadron had lost the ship *Slava* and retired after fighting. The Germans had captured the Moon-sund Archipelago. One more black page in the book of the war had been turned. The government decided to use this new military blow as a pretext for moving the capital. This old idea swam out at every suitable opportunity. It was not that the ruling circles had any particular affection for Moscow, but they hated Petrograd. The monarchist reaction, the liberals, the democracy—all strove in turn to demote the capital, to bring it to its knees, to beat it down. The most extreme patriots were now hating Petrograd with a far more bitter hatred than they felt for Berlin.

The question of evacuating the capital was taken up as a thing to be accomplished in extraordinary haste. Only two weeks were allotted for the transfer of the government together with the Pre-Parliament. It was also decided to evacuate in the briefest possible time the factories working for the defense. The Central Executive Committee as a "private institution" would have to look out for itself.

The Kadet instigators of the plan understood that a mere transfer of the government would not settle their problem, but they counted on afterward capturing the seat of revolutionary infection with hunger, disease and exhaustion. An internal blockade of Petrograd was already in full swing. The factories were being deprived of orders; the supply of fuel had been cut down three-quarters; the ministry of provisions was holding up cattle on their way to the capital; freight movements on the Mariinsky Railroad System had been stopped.

The warlike Rodzianko, president of that State Duma which the government had at last dissolved at the beginning of October, spoke quite frankly in the liberal Moscow newspaper *Utro Rossii* about the military danger threatening the capital. "I say to myself, God help her, God help Petrograd. . . . A fear was expressed in Petersburg lest the central institutions (that is the soviets, etc.) will be destroyed. To this I answered that I would be very glad if those institutions were destroyed, for they have brought nothing whatever but evil to Russia." To be sure, with the capture of Petrograd the Baltic fleet also would have been destroyed, but against that too Rodzianko had no complaint: "The ships there are completely depraved." Thanks to the fact that the Lord Chamberlain could not keep his tongue behind his teeth, the people had this chance to find out the most intimate thoughts of noble and bourgeois Russia.

The Russian chargé d'affaires reported from London that the British naval headquarters, in spite of all urgings, did not consider it possible to relieve the situation of its Ally in the Baltic. It was not the Bolsheviks alone who interpreted this answer to mean that the Allies, in common with the patriotic upper circles of Russia herself, looked only for benefits to the common cause from a German blow at Petrograd. The workers and soldiers had no doubt —especially after Rodzianko's confession—that the government was consciously getting ready to send them to school to Ludendorff and Hoffmann.

On the 6th of October the soldiers' section adopted with a unanimity hitherto unknown the resolution introduced by Trotsky: "If the Provisional Government is incapable of defending Petrograd, it must either make peace or give place to another government." The workers were no less irreconcilable. They considered Petrograd their fortress. Their revolutionary hopes were bound up with her. They did not intend to surrender Petrograd. Frightened by the military danger, the evacuation, the indignation of the soldiers and workers, the excitement of the whole population, the Compromisers, on their side, sounded an alarm: We must not abandon Petrograd to the caprice of fate. Convinced that an attempted evacuation would meet resistance from all sides, the government began to draw back: We were not troubled so much, you know, about our own safety as about the question of a meeting-place for the future Constituent Assembly. But this position, too, they could not maintain. In less than a week the government was compelled to announce that it not only intended to remain in the Winter Palace itself, but proposed as before to convoke the Constituent Assembly in the Tauride Palace. This announcement changed nothing in the military and political situation. But it revealed once more the political power of Petrograd, which considered itself called to put an end to the government of Kerensky, and would not let that government escape from its walls. It was only the Bolsheviks who subsequently dared transfer the capital to Moscow. They carried this out without the slightest difficulty because for them it was really a strategic move. They could not have any political reason for flying from Petrograd.

That contrite declaration about the defense of the capital was made by the government upon the demand of the compromisist majority of a commission of the Council of the Russian Republic or "Pre-Parliament." This wonderful institution had at last succeeded in getting born. Plekhanov, who loved jokes and knew how to make them, disrespectfully named this impotent and ephemeral Council of the Republic "the little house on chicken's feet." [1] Politically this definition is not at all inaccurate. It is only necessary to add that, for a little house the Pre-Parliament put up a pretty good front: the magnificent Mariinsky Palace, which had formerly sheltered the State Council of Ministers, was placed at its disposal. The contrast between this elegant palace and Smolny Institute, run-down and saturated with soldier smells, made a great impression upon Sukhanov: "Amid all this magnificence," he confesses, "one wanted to rest, to forget about labor and struggle, about hunger and war, about ruin and anarchy, about the country and the revolution." But there was very little time left for rest and forgetfulness.

The so-called "democratic" majority of the Pre-Parliament consisted of 308 men: 120 Social Revolutionaries, among them about 20 Lefts, 60 Mensheviks of various shades, 66 Bolsheviks; after that came the Cooperators, the delegates of the peasant executive committee, etc. The possessing classes were accorded 156 seats, of which the Kadets occupied almost half. Together with the Cooperators, the Cossacks, and the rather conservative members of Kerensky's Executive Committee, the Right Wing on a number of questions came near being a majority. The distribution of seats in that comfortable little house on chicken's feet was thus in flagrant contradiction to all decisive expressions of the will of the people that had been made either in city or country. Moreover, in opposition to the dull gray representation to be found in the soviets and elsewhere, the Mariinsky Palace assembled within its walls the "flower of the nation." Inasmuch as the members of the Pre-Parliament did not depend upon the accidents of elective competition, upon local influences and provincial preferences, each social group and each party sent its most eminent leaders. The personnel was, to quote Sukhanov, "extraordinarily brilliant." When the Pre-Parliament assembled for its first session, a weight was lifted, says Miliukov, from the hearts of many sceptics: "It will be fine if the Constituent Assembly is no worse

[1] The allusion is to a Russian fairy-story. Trans.

65

than this." The flower of the nation looked upon itself in the palace mirrors with great satisfaction and neglected to notice that it was incapable of bearing fruit.

In opening this Council of the Republic on October 7, Kerensky did not forego the opportunity to remark that although the government possessed "all the fullness of power," it was nevertheless ready to listen to "any genuinely valuable suggestion." Although absolute, that is to say, the government had not ceased to be cultivated. In the præsidium, which consisted of five members with Avksentiev as president, one place was offered to the Bolsheviks: It remained unoccupied. The directors of this pitiful and unhappy comedy felt sick at heart. The entire interest of its gray opening on a gray rainy day was centered upon the forthcoming action of the Bolsheviks. In the couloirs of the Mariinsky Palace, according to Sukhanov, a "sensational rumor" was in the air: "Trotsky has won by a majority of two or three votes . . . and the Bolsheviks are going to withdraw at once from the Pre-Parliament." In reality the decision to withdraw demonstratively from the Mariinsky Palace was adopted on the 5th at a meeting of the Bolshevik faction by all votes except one. So great had been the shift leftward during the preceding two weeks! Only Kamenev remained true to his original position—or rather he alone dared defend it. In a special declaration addressed to the Central Committee, Kamenev candidly described the course adopted as "very dangerous for the party." The doubt about the intentions of the Bolsheviks caused a certain anxiety in the Pre-Parliament. It was not so much a breakdown of the régime that they feared, as a "scandal" before the eyes of the Allied diplomats, whom the majority had just greeted with an appropriate volley of patriotic applause. Sukhanov relates how they despatched an official personage—Avksentiev himself—to the Bolsheviks to inquire in advance: What is going to happen? "A mere nothing," answered Trotsky, "a mere nothing, a little shot from a pistol." After the opening of the session, upon the basis of rules of order taken over from the State Duma, Trotsky was offered ten minutes for a special announcement in the name of the Bolshevik faction. A tense silence reigned in the hall. The declaration began by stating that the government was at present just as irresponsible as it had been before the Democratic Conference, which was supposed to have been convoked for the curbing of Kerensky, and that the representatives of the possessing classes were present in this provisional council in numbers to which they had not the slightest right. If the bourgeoisie were really preparing for a Constituent Assembly to meet in a month and a half, their leaders would have no reason to defend so fiercely at the present time the irresponsibility of the government even to this doctored representation. "The essence of it all is that the bourgeois classes have decided to quash the Constituent Assembly." The blow was well aimed, and the Right Wing protested the more noisily. Without departing from the text of the declaration the speaker denounced the industrial, agrarian and food policy. It would be impossible to adopt any other policy, even if you set yourself the conscious aim of impelling the masses to insurrection. "The idea of surrendering the revolutionary capital to the German troops . . . we accept as a natural link in a general policy designed to promote . . . a counter-revolutionary conspiracy." The protest here turned into a storm. Cries about Berlin, about German gold, about the sealed train—and on this general background, like pieces of broken bottle in the mud, foul-mouthed abuse. Nothing like it was ever heard during the most passionate conflicts in Smolny, dirty and run-down and spat all over by soldiers as it was. "We only have to get into the good society of Mariinsky Palace," writes Sukhanov, "in order to revive at once that atmosphere of the low-class saloon which prevailed in the State Duma with its restricted franchise."

Picking his way through these explosions of hatred alternating with moments of hush, the speaker concluded: "No, the Bolshevik faction announce that with this government of treason to the people and with this Council of counter-revolutionary connivance we have nothing whatever in common. . . . In withdrawing from the provisional council we summon the workers, soldiers and peasants of all Russia to be on their guard, and to be courageous. Petrograd is in danger! The revolution is in danger! The people are in danger! . . . We address ourselves to the people. All power to the soviets!" As the orator descended from the tribune the few score of Bolsheviks left the hall accompanied by curses. After their moment of alarm the majority heaved a happy sigh of relief. Only the Bolsheviks went out. The flower of the nation remained at their posts. The Left Wing of the Compromisers bent a little under a blow not directed, it seemed, at themselves. "We, the nearest neighbors of the Bolsheviks," confesses Sukhanov, "sat there completely appalled by all that had happened." These immaculate Knights of the word were sensing the fact that the time for words had passed.

The Minister of Foreign Affairs, Tereshchenko, informed the Russian ambassadors about the opening of the Pre-Parliament in a secret telegram: "The first session passed off uneventfully with the exception of a scandal created by the Bolsheviks." The historic break between the proletariat and the state mechanism of the bourgeoisie was conceived by those people as a mere "scandal." The bourgeois press did not miss the opportunity to goad the government by references to the resoluteness of the Bolsheviks: The honorable ministers will only then lead the country out of anarchy when they "acquire as much resolution and will to action as is to be found in Comrade Trotsky." As though it were a question of resolution and the will of individual people and not of the historic destiny of classes! And as though the sorting out of people and characters goes on independently of historic tasks. "They spoke and acted," wrote Miliukov on the subject of the Bolshevik withdrawal from the Pre-Parliament, "like people feeling a power behind them, knowing that the morrow belonged to them."

The loss of the Moon-sund Islands, the growing danger to Petrograd, and the withdrawal of the Bolsheviks from the Pre-Parliament into the street, compelled the Compromisers to take thought for the further development of the war. After a three-day discussion participated in by the Minister of War and Navy, and the commissars and delegates of the army organizations, the Central Executive Committee came at last to a saving decision: "To insist that representatives of the Russian democracy be admitted to the Paris Conference of the Allies." After renewed efforts they named Skobelev as delegate. Detailed instructions were drawn up: Peace without annexations or indemnities; neutralization of straits and canals, including the Suez and Panama

Canals—the Compromisers had a wider outlook geographically
than politically; abolition of secret diplomacy; gradual disarmament. The Central Executive Committee explained that the
aim of its delegate in the Paris Conference was "to bring pressure
to bear upon the Allies." Pressure of Skobelev upon France, Great
Britain and the United States! The Kadet paper put a poisonous
question: "What will Skobelev do if the Allies unceremoniously
reject his conditions? Will he threaten them with another appeal
to the people of the whole world?" The Compromisers, alas, had
long been blushing for that old appeal of theirs.

While intending to force upon the United States the neutralization of the Panama Canal, the Central Executive Committee
proved incapable in actual fact of bringing pressure to bear even
upon the Winter Palace. On the 12th, Kerensky sent Lloyd George
a voluminous letter full of gentle reproaches, sorrowful complaints, and fervent promises. The front, he said, is "in better
condition than it was last spring." Of course the defeatist
propaganda—thus the Russian premier complains to a Britisher
against the Russian Bolsheviks—has hindered the carrying out of
all the plans indicated. But there can be no talk of peace. The
government knows only one question: "How to continue the
war!" It goes without saying that as an earnest of his patriotism
Kerensky begged for credits.

Having got rid of the Bolsheviks, the Pre-Parliament also lost
no time in taking up the war. On the 10th the debate opened on
improving the fighting capacity of the army. The dialogue, which
occupied three weary sessions, developed according to one invariable scheme. We must convince the army that it is fighting
for peace and democracy, said the Left. We must not convince
but compel, answered the Right. You have nothing to compel
with; in order to compel you must first at least partially convince, answered the Compromisers. In the matter of convincing
the Bolsheviks are stronger than you, answered the Kadets. Both
sides were right. But a drowning man is also right when he lets
out a yell before going down.

On the 18th came that decisive hour which in the nature of
things nothing in the world could alter. The formula of the
Social Revolutionaries got 95 votes against 127, with 50 abstain-

ing. The formula of the Right got 135 votes against 139. Astonishing! There was no majority! Throughout the hall, according to the newspaper accounts, there was general movement and confusion. In spite of its unity of aim, the flower of the nation proved incapable of adopting even a platonic decision upon the most urgent question of the national life. This was no accident. The same thing was being repeated day by day in the commissions and in the plenary sessions upon all other questions. The fragments of opinion could not be put together. All the groups were living on illusive shadings of political thought: thought itself was absent. Maybe it had gone out into the street with the Bolsheviks? . . . The blind alley of the Pre-Parliament was the blind alley of the whole régime.

To reconvince the army was difficult, but to compel it was also impossible. To a new shout from Kerensky at the Baltic fleet, which had just been through a battle and lost victims, a congress of the sailors addressed to the Central Executive Committee a demand that they remove from the staff of the Provisional Government "a person who is disgracing and destroying the great revolution with his shameless political chantage." It was the first time Kerensky had heard such language from the sailors. The Regional Committee of the Army, Fleet and Russian Workers in Finland, functioning as a sovereign power, held up the government freight. Kerensky threatened the soviet commissars with arrest. The answer was: The Regional Committee tranquilly accepts the challenge of the Provisional Government. Kerensky made no reply. In essence the Baltic fleet was already in a state of insurrection. On the land front, things had not yet gone so far, but they were traveling in the same direction. The food situation was rapidly deteriorating throughout October. The commander-in-chief of the northern front reported that hunger "is the chief cause of the moral disintegration of the army." At the same time that the compromisist upper circles on the front were continuing to assert—to be sure, now only behind the backs of the soldiers —that the fighting capacity of the army was improving, the lower ranks, regiment after regiment, were putting forth demands for a publication of the secret treaties and an immediate offer of peace. The commissar of the western front, Zhdanov, reported during the first days of October: "The mood is extremely alarming, taken in connection with the nearness of cold weather and the deterioration of the food . . . The Bolsheviks are scoring a definite success."

The governmental institutions at the front were hanging in the air. The commissar of the Second Army reported that the military courts could not function because the soldier-witnesses refused to appear and testify. "The mutual relations between the commanding staff and the soldiers is embittered. The officers are blamed for dragging out the war." The hostility of the soldiers to the government and the commanding staff had long ago been transferred also to the army committees, which had not been renewed since the beginning of the revolution. Over the heads of the committees the regiments were sending delegates to Petrograd, to the Soviet, to complain of the intolerable situation in the trenches, where they lived without bread, without clothing, without faith in the war. On the Rumanian front, where the Bolsheviks were very weak, whole regiments were refusing to shoot. "In two or three weeks the soldiers themselves will declare an armistice and lay down their arms." The delegates from one of the divisions reported: "With the coming of the first snow the soldiers have decided to go home." The delegates of the 133rd army corps made this threat at a plenary session of the Petrograd Soviet: "If there is not a real struggle for peace, the soldiers themselves will take the power and declare an armistice." The commissar of the Second Army reported to the War Minister: "There is no little talk to the effect that with the arrival of cold weather they will abandon their position."

Fraternizing, which had almost stopped since the July days, began again and grew rapidly. Instances not only of the arrest of officers by the soldiers, but of the murder of the more hateful began to multiply. These things were done almost publicly, before the eyes of the soldiers. Nobody interfered: the majority did not want to, the small minority did not dare. The murderer always succeeded in hiding: he was drowned and lost in the soldier mass. One of the generals wrote: "We convulsively grasp at this or that, we pray for some sort of miracle, but the majority of us understand that there is already no hope of salvation."

71

Mixing cunning with stupidity, the patriotic papers continued to write about a continuation of the war, about an offensive and about victory. The generals shook their heads; some of them equivocally joined in. "Only completely crazy people," wrote Baron Budberg, the commander of a corps near Dvinsk, on the 7th of October, "could dream about an offensive at the present time." The very next day he was compelled to write in the same diary: "Startled and appalled to receive orders for an offensive not later than October 20th." Headquarters, believing in nothing and shrugging its shoulders at everything, was drawing up plans for a new operation. There were not a few generals who saw the last hope of salvation in a repetition on a grand scale of Kornilov's experiment with Riga: Drag the army into battle and try to bring down a defeat on the head of the revolution.

On the initiative of War Minister Verkhovsky it was decided to transfer the oldest classes into the reserve. The railroad groaned under the burden of these returning soldiers. In the overloaded cars the springs broke and the floors fell through. This did not improve the mood of those left behind. "The trenches are breaking down," writes Budberg. "The communication trenches are flooded; there is refuse and excrement everywhere . . . The soldiers flatly refuse to work at cleaning up the trenches . . . It is dreadful to think where this will lead when spring comes and all this begins to rot and decompose." In a state of embittered inaction the soldiers refused in droves even to undergo preventive inoculation. This too became a form of struggle against the war.

After vain efforts to raise the fighting capacity of the army by decreasing its numbers, Verkhovsky suddenly came to the conclusion that only peace could save the country. At a private conference with the Kadet leaders, whom this young and naïve minister imagined he could bring over to his side, Verkhovsky drew a picture of the material and spiritual collapse of the army: "Any attempt to prolong the war can only bring on a catastrophe." The Kadets could not understand this. But while the others remained silent Miliukov scornfully shrugged his shoulders: "The honor of Russia," "loyalty to the Allies" . . . Not believing in one of these words, the leader of the bourgeoisie was stubbornly striving to bury the revolution under the ruins and piles of corpses that would be left by the war. Verkhovsky revealed a certain amount of political audacity. Without informing or warning the government, he appeared on the 20th before the commission of the Pre-Parliament and announced the necessity of an immediate peace with or without the consent of the Allies. He was furiously attacked by all those who agreed with him in private conversations. The patriotic press wrote that the war minister "had jumped on the footboard of Comrade Trotsky's chariot." Burtsev hinted at the presence of German gold. Verkhovsky was sent away on a vacation. In heart to heart conversations the patriots were saying: In essence he is right. Budberg had to speak cautiously even in his diary: "From the point of view of keeping our word," he wrote, "the proposal of course is tricky. But from the standpoint of the egoistic interests of Russia, it is perhaps the only one which offers hope of a saving way out." Incidentally the baron confessed his envy of the German generals to whom "fate has given the good luck to be the authors of victories." He did not foresee that the turn of the German generals would come next. Those people never foresaw anything, even the cleverest of them. The Bolsheviks foresaw much and that was their strength.

The withdrawal from the Pre-Parliament in the eyes of the people burned the last bridges uniting the party of insurrection with official society. With renewed energy—for the nearness of the goal redoubles one's strength—the Bolsheviks carried on their agitation, an agitation called demagogism by the enemy because it brought out into the public square what they themselves were hiding in the chancellories and private offices. The convincingness of this tireless evangel grew out of the fact that the Bolsheviks understood the course of the objective development, subjected their policy to it, were not afraid of the masses, and inconquerably believed in their own truth and their victory. The people never tired of hearing them. The masses felt a need to stand close together. Each wanted to test himself through others, and all tensely and attentively kept observing how one and the same thought would develop in their various minds with its different shades and features. Unnumbered crowds of people stood about the circuses and other big buildings where the more popular

Bolsheviks would address them with the last arguments and the last appeals.

The number of leading agitators had greatly decreased by October. First of all Lenin was lacking—both as an agitator and still more as an immediate day-to-day inspiration. His simple and deep generalizations which could so lastingly insert themselves into the consciousness of the masses, his clear sayings caught up from the people and handed back to them, were sadly missed. The first-class agitator Zinoviev was lacking. Having hidden from prosecution under an indictment for "insurrection" in July, he decisively turned against the October insurrection, and thus for the whole critical period withdrew from the field of action. Kamenev, the irreplaceable propagandist, the experienced political instructor of the party, condemned the policy of insurrection, did not believe in the victory, saw catastrophes ahead and gloomily retired into the shadows. Sverdlov, by nature an organizer rather than an agitator, appeared often at mass meetings and his even, powerful and tireless bass voice inspired tranquil confidence. Stalin was neither agitator nor orator. He never appeared as a spokesman at party conferences. But did he appear so much as once in the mass meetings of the revolution? In the documents and memoirs no record of it has been preserved.

A brilliant agitation was conducted by Volodarsky, Lashevich, Kollontai, Chudnovsky, and after them by scores of agitators of lesser caliber. People listened with interest and sympathy—and the mature also with a certain condescension—to Lunacharsky, a skilled orator who knew how to present fact and generalization and pathos and joke, but who did not pretend to lead anybody. He himself needed to be led. In proportion as the revolution approached, Lunacharsky faded rapidly and lost his colorful effects.

Sukhanov says of the president of the Petrograd Soviet: [1] "Tearing himself from the work in revolutionary headquarters he would fly from the Obukhovsky factory to the Trubocheny, from the Putilov to the Baltic shipyards, from the Riding Academy to the barracks, and seemed to be speaking simultaneously in all places. Every Petersburg worker and soldier knew him and heard him personally. His influence—both in the masses and in

[1] Trotsky. Trans.

74

headquarters—was overwhelming. He was the central figure of those days, and the chief hero of this remarkable page of history."

But incomparably more effective in that last period before the insurrection was the molecular agitation carried on by nameless workers, sailors, soldiers, winning converts one by one, breaking down the last doubts, overcoming the last hesitations. Those months of feverish political life had created innumerable cadres in the lower ranks, had educated hundreds and thousands of rough diamonds, who were accustomed to look on politics from below and not above, and for that very reason estimated facts and people with a keenness not always accessible to orators of the academic type. The Petersburg workers stood in the front rank —hereditary proletarians who had produced a race of agitators and organizers of extraordinary revolutionary temper and high political culture, independent in thought, word and action. Carpenters, fitters, blacksmiths, teachers of the unions and factories, each already had around him his school, his pupils, the future builders of the Republic of Soviets. The Baltic sailors, close comrades in arms of the Petersburg workers—to a considerable extent issued from their midst—put forward a brigade of agitators who took by storm the backward regiments, the county towns, the villages of the muzhiks. A generalizing formula tossed out in the *Cirque Moderne* by one of the revolutionary leaders would take flesh and blood in hundreds of thinking heads, and so make the rounds of the whole country.

From the Baltic states, from Poland and Lithuania, thousands of revolutionary workers and soldiers had been evacuated during the retreat of the Russian armies, coming with the industrial enterprises or one by one. All these became agitators against the war and those guilty of it. The Lettish Bolsheviks, torn away from their home soil and wholeheartedly standing on the soil of the revolution, convinced, stubborn, resolute, were carrying on day by day and all day long a mining operation in all parts of the country. Their angular faces, harsh accent, and often their broken Russian phrases, gave special expressiveness to an unceasing summons to insurrection.

The mass would no longer endure in its midst the wavering, the dubious, the neutral. It was striving to get hold of everybody, to attract, to convince, to conquer. The factories joined with the regiments in sending delegates to the front. The trenches got into connection with the workers and peasants nearby in the rear. In the towns along the front there was an endless series of meetings, conferences, consultations in which the soldiers and sailors would bring their activity into accord with that of the workers and peasants. It was in this manner that the backward White Russian front was won over to Bolshevism.

In places where the local party leadership was irresolute and disposed to wait, as for example in Kiev, Voronezh, and many other points, the masses not unfrequently fell into a passive condition. To justify their policy, the leaders would point to this mood of depression which they themselves had created. On the other hand: "The more resolute and bold was his summons to insurrection," writes Povolzhsky, one of the Kazan agitators, "the more trustful and hearty would be the attitude of the soldier mass toward the speaker."

The factories and regiments of Petrograd and Moscow were now more insistently knocking at the wooden gates of the villages. The workers would join together in sending delegates into their native provinces. The regiments would pass resolutions summoning the peasants to support the Bolsheviks. The workers in factories within the cities would make pilgrimages to the surrounding villages, distributing newspapers and laying the foundations of Bolshevik nuclei. From these rounds they would come back bringing in the pupils of their eyes a reflection from the flames of the peasant war.

Bolshevism took possession of the country. The Bolsheviks became an inconquerable power. The people were with them. The city dumas of Kronstadt, Tzaritzyn, Kostroma, Shuia, elected on a universal franchise, were wholly in the hands of the Bolsheviks. The Bolsheviks received 52 per cent of the votes at an election to the district dumas of Moscow. In far-off and tranquil Tomsk, as also in the wholly non-industrial Samara, the Bolsheviks dominated in the duma. Out of four members of the Schlüsselberg county zemstvo, three were Bolsheviks. In the Ligovsky county zemstvo, the Bolsheviks got 50 per cent of the votes. It was not so favorable everywhere, but everywhere it was changing in the same direction. The relative weight of the Bolshevik party was on the rapid rise.

The Bolshevization of the masses revealed itself far more clearly, however, in the class organizations. The trade unions in the capital comprised over a half million workers. The Mensheviks themselves, who still had the administration of certain unions, felt that they were a relic of past days. No matter what parts of the proletariat might form an organization, and no matter what its immediate aim might be, it would inevitably arrive at Bolshevik conclusions. And this was no accident: The trade unions, the factory committees, the economic and cultural assemblies of the working class, both permanent and transitory, were compelled by the whole situation, upon every private problem which might arise, to raise one and the same question: Who is the master of the house?

The workers of the artillery factories, being called together in conference to regulate their relations with the administration, decided that they could best regulate them through a soviet government. This was no longer a mere formula, but a program of economic salvation. As they approached the power the workers also approached more and more concretely the problems of industry. The artillery conference even established a special center for the study of methods of transition from munition factories to peaceful production.

The Moscow conference of factory and shop committees declared that the local soviet should in the future decide all strike conflicts by decree, on its own authority open the plants shut down by the lockouts, and by sending its own delegates to Siberia and the Donetz Basin guarantee coal and grain to the factories. The Petrograd conference of factory and shop committees devoted its attention to the agrarian question, and upon a report by Trotsky drew up a manifesto to the peasants: The proletariat feels itself to be not only a special class, but also the leader of the people.

The All-Russian conference of factory and shop committees, meeting during the second half of October, raised the question of workers' control to the position of a national problem: "The workers are more interested than the owners in the correct and uninterrupted operation of the plants." Workers' control "is in the interest of the whole country and ought to be supported by the revolutionary peasantry and the revolutionary army." This resolution, opening the door to a new economic order, was adopted by the representatives of all the industrial enterprises of Russia with only five votes opposing and nine abstaining from the vote. The few individual abstainers were old Mensheviks no longer able to follow their own party, but still lacking courage to raise their hands openly for the Bolshevik revolution. Tomorrow they will do it.

The democratic municipal governments, only recently created, were dying away along with the organs of the governmental power. The most important tasks, such as guaranteeing water, light, fuel and food to the cities, were all falling more and more upon the soviets and other workers' organizations. The factory committee of the lighting station of Petrograd was rushing about the city and the surroundings hunting up at one time coal, at another grease for the turbines, and getting them both through committees of other plants acting in opposition to their owners and the administration.

No, the government of the soviets was not a chimera, an arbitrary construction, an invention of party theoreticians. It grew up irresistibly from below, from the breakdown of industry, the impotence of the possessors, the needs of the masses. The soviets had in actual fact become a government. For the workers, soldiers and peasants there remained no other road. No time left to argue and speculate about a soviet government: it had to be realized.

At the first congress of the soviets, in June, it had been decided to call the congress every three months. The Central Executive Committee, however, had not only failed to call the second conference on time, but had shown a disposition not to call it at all, in order to avoid confronting a hostile majority. The chief task of the Democratic Conference had been to crowd out the soviets, replacing them with organs of the "democracy." But that had not been so easy. The soviets did not intend to make way for anybody.

On September 21, at the close of the Democratic Conference,

the Petrograd Soviet raised its voice for the prompt calling of a congress of the soviets. A resolution in this sense was adopted upon the report of Trotsky and a guest from Moscow, Bukharin, formally based on the necessity of getting ready for "a new wave of counter-revolution." Their plan for a defensive which should lay down the road to the coming offensive relied upon the soviets as the sole organizations capable of making the struggle. The resolution demanded that the soviets strengthen their position among the masses. Where the *de facto* power is already in their hands, they are in no case to let it slip. The revolutionary committees created in the Kornilov days must remain ready for action. "In order to unite and coordinate the action of all the soviets in their struggle with the advancing danger, and in order to decide problems of organization of the revolutionary power, the immediate calling of a congress of the soviets is necessary." Thus a resolution on self-defense brings us right up to the necessity of overthrowing the government. The agitation will be conducted on this political key-note from now straight on to the moment of insurrection.

The delegates from the soviets to the Democratic Conference raised the question of a Soviet Congress before the Central Executive Committee the next day. The Bolsheviks demanded that the congress be called within two weeks, and proposed, or rather threatened, to create for this purpose a special body resting on the Petersburg and Moscow soviets. In reality they preferred to have the Congress called by the old Central Executive Committee. This would obviate quarrels about the juridical rights of the congress, and make it possible to overthrow the Compromisers with their own cooperation. The semi-camouflaged threat of the Bolsheviks was effective. Not yet risking a break with soviet legality, the leaders of the Central Executive Committee declared that they would entrust to nobody the fulfillment of their duties. The Congress was called for October 20—within less than a month.

The provincial delegates had no more than departed, however, when the leaders of the Central Executive Committee suddenly opened their eyes to the fact that the Congress would be untimely—it would withdraw local party workers from the electoral campaign, and thus do harm to the Constituent Assembly. Their real fear was that the Congress would prove a mighty pretender to the power, but about this they kept a diplomatic silence. On the 26th of September Dan made haste to introduce into the bureau of the Central Executive Committee, without bothering about the necessary preparation, a proposal to postpone the congress.

With the elementary principles of democracy these patent medicine democrats were least of all concerned. They had just got through quashing the resolution of a Democratic Conference, which they themselves had summoned, rejecting a coalition with the Kadets. And now they revealed their sovereign contempt for the soviets, beginning with the Petrograd Soviet upon whose shoulders they had been lifted into their seats. After all, how could they, without abandoning their league with the bourgeoisie, pay any attention to the hopes and demands of those tens of millions of workers, soldiers, and peasants who stood for the soviets?

Trotsky answered the proposal of Dan by stating that the Congress would be called just the same, if not constitutionally, then by revolutionary means. The usually so submissive bureau refused this time to follow along the road of a soviet *coup d'état*. But this little defeat was far from compelling the conspirators to lay down their arms. On the contrary it seemed to egg them on. Dan found an influential support in the military section of the Central Executive Committee, which decided to "query" the organizations of the front as to whether a congress should be called or not—that is, whether they should carry out a decision twice adopted by the highest soviet body. In the interval the compromise press opened a campaign against the congress. In this the Social Revolutionaries were particularly furious. "Shall a congress be summoned or not?" wrote *Dyelo Naroda*. "It can have nothing to say in solution of the question of power . . . The government of Kerensky will not submit in any case." To what will it not submit? asked Lenin. "To the power of the soviets, to the power of the workers and peasants, which *Dyelo Naroda*, in order to keep up with the pogrom-makers and anti-semites, the monarchists and Kadets, calls the power of Trotsky and Lenin."

The peasant Executive Committee, in its turn, declared the calling of the Congress "dangerous and undesirable." A confusion of ill-will thus prevailed in the soviet upper-circles. Delegates of the compromise parties traveling over the country mobilized the local organizations against a Congress which had been officially called by the supreme soviet body. The official organ of the Central Executive Committee printed from day to day resolutions against the Congress adopted at the bidding of the leading Compromisers, inspired entirely by the old March ghosts—wearing, to be sure, very imposing names. *Izvestia* buried the soviets in a leading article, declaring them temporary barricades which should be removed as soon as the Constituent Assembly crowns the "edifice of the new structure."

The Bolsheviks least of all were caught napping by this agitation against the Congress. On the 24th of September the Central Committee of the party, without banking upon any action by the Central Executive Committee, had decided to set in motion from below, through the local soviets and organizations of the front, a campaign for the congress. The Bolsheviks delegated Sverdlov to sit in the Central Executive Committee's official commission on the calling—or rather the sabotage—of the congress. Under his leadership the local organizations of the party were mobilized, and through them also the soviets. On the 27th all the revolutionary institutions of Reval demanded that the Pre-Parliament be immediately dissolved, and a conference of the soviets for the formation of a government immediately called; they moreover solemnly promised to support it "with all the forces and instrumentalities to be found in the fortress." Many local soviets, beginning with the districts of Moscow, proposed that the function of summoning the congress be withdrawn from the hands of the disloyal Central Executive Committee. Against the resolutions of the army committees opposing the Congress demands for its convocation flowed in from battalions, regiments, corps and local garrisons. "The Congress of Soviets must seize the power and stop at nothing," says a mass meeting of soldiers in Kyshtin in the Urals. The soldiers of Novgorod province summoned the peasants to take part in the Congress, and pay no attention to the resolution of the peasants' Executive Committee.

Provincial soviets, county soviets—these, too, in the farthest corners of the country—factories, mines, regiments, dreadnoughts, destroyers, war hospitals, meetings, an automobile detachment in Petrograd, an ambulance squad in Moscow—all were demanding the removal of the government and the transfer of power to the soviets.

Not content with this agitational campaign, the Bolsheviks created an important organizational base by calling a congress of the soviets of the northern region consisting of 150 delegates from 23 points. That was a well-calculated blow! The Central Executive Committee under the leadership of its great masters in small affairs declared this northern congress a private conference. The handful of Menshevik delegates refused to take part in the work of the congress, remaining only "for purposes of information." As though that could diminish by a tittle the significance of a congress in which were represented the soviets of Petrograd and its suburbs, Moscow, Kronstadt, Helsingfors, and Reval—that is to say, both capitals, the naval fortresses, the Baltic fleet and the garrisons surrounding Petrograd. The congress, opened by Antonov—to whom a military tint was being intentionally given—took place under the presidency of Ensign Krylenko, the best agitator of the party at the front, the future Bolshevik commander-in-chief. At the center of the political report, made by Trotsky, stood the question of the new attempt of the government to remove the revolutionary regiments from Petrograd: The congress will not permit "the disarming of Petrograd and strangling of the Soviet." The question of the Petrograd garrison is an element in the fundamental problem of power. "The whole people is voting for the Bolsheviks; the people are trusting us and authorizing us to seize the power." The resolution proposed by Trotsky read: "The hour has come when the question of the central government . . . can be decided only by a resolute and unanimous coming-out of all the soviets." This almost undisguised summons to insurrection was adopted by all votes with three abstaining.

Lashevich urged the other soviets to follow Petrograd's example and get control of the local garrisons. The Lettish delegate, Peterson, promised forty thousand Lettish sharp-shooters for the defense of the congress of soviets. This announcement of Peterson, rapturously greeted, was no empty phrase. Only a few days later the soviet of the Lettish regiments announced: "Only a popular insurrection . . . will make possible the transfer of power to the soviets." On the 13th the radio stations of the warships broadcast throughout the whole country the summons of the northern congress to prepare for an All-Russian Congress of Soviets. "Soldiers, sailors, peasants, workers! It is your duty to overcome all obstacles . . ."

The Central Committee of the party suggested to the Bolshevik delegates of the northern congress that in view of the approaching congress of the soviets they should not leave Petrograd. Individual delegates, at the direction of a bureau elected by the congress, went to the army organizations and the local soviets to make reports—in other words, to prepare the province for insurrection. The Central Executive Committee saw a powerful apparatus grown up beside itself, resting upon Petrograd and Moscow, conversing with the country through the radio stations on the dreadnoughts, and ready at any moment to replace the decrepit supreme soviet organ in the matter of summoning the congress. Petty organizational tricks could be of no help to the Compromisers here.

This struggle for and against the congress gave the last impulse in the localities to the Bolshevization of the soviets. In a number of backward provinces, Smolensk for example, the Bolsheviks, either alone or together with the Left Social Revolutionaries, got their first majority only during this campaign for the congress or during the election of delegates to it. Even in the Siberian congress of the soviets the Bolsheviks succeeded in the middle of October in creating with the Left Social Revolutionaries a permanent majority which easily placed its imprint upon the local soviets. On the 15th the soviet of Kiev, by 159 votes against 28, with 3 abstaining, recognized the coming Congress of Soviets as "the sovereign organ of power." On the 16th the Congress of soviets of the northwestern region at Minsk—that is, in the center of the western front—declared the calling of the Congress unpostponable. On the 18th the Petrograd Soviet held elections for the coming Congress: 443 votes were cast for the Bolshevik list (Trotsky, Kamenev, Volodarsky, Yurenev and Lashevich); for the Social Revolutionaries 162—these all Left Social Revolutionaries, tending toward the Bolsheviks; for the Mensheviks 44. Under the presidency of Krestinsky a Congress of the soviets of the Urals, where 80 out of the 110 delegates were Bolsheviks, demanded in the name of 223,900 organized workers and soldiers that the Congress of Soviets be called at the appointed date. On the same day, the 19th, an All-Russian conference of factory and shop committees, the most direct and indubitable representation of the proletariat in the whole country, came out for an immediate transfer of power to the soviets. On the 20th Ivanovo-Voznesensk declared all the soviets of the province to be "in a state of open and ruthless struggle against the Provisional Government," and summoned them to solve independently the industrial and administrative problems of their localities. Against this resolution, which meant the overthrow of local governmental authorities, only one voice was raised, with one abstaining. On the 22nd, the Bolshevik press published a new list of 56 organizations demanding a transfer of power to the soviets. These were all composed of the authentic masses of the people, and to a considerable degree armed masses.

This all-powerful muster-roll of the detachments of the coming revolution did not prevent Dan from reporting to the bureau of the Central Executive Committee that out of 917 existing soviet organizations, only 50 had responded with an agreement to send delegates, and these had done so "without any enthusiasm." It is easy enough to understand that those few soviets who still considered it necessary to report their feelings to the Central Executive Committee regarded the congress without enthusiasm. An overwhelming majority of the local soviets and the army committees had simply ignored the Central Executive Committee altogether.

Although they had exposed and compromised themselves with these efforts to sabotage the congress, the Compromisers did not dare carry the work through to the end. When it became utterly obvious that they could not avoid a congress, they made an abrupt about-face and summoned all the local organizations to elect delegates to the congress in order not to give the Bolsheviks a majority. Having waked up to the situation too late, however, the Central Executive Committee found itself obliged only two or three days before the appointed date to postpone the Congress to October 25.

Thanks to this last maneuver of the Compromisers, the February régime, and bourgeois society along with it, received an unexpected period of grace—from which, however, it was no longer capable of deriving any substantial benefits. The Bolsheviks, moreover, employed these five supplementary days to great advantage. The enemy acknowledged this later on. "The postponement of the coming-out," says Miliukov, "was made use of by the Bolsheviks, first of all to reinforce their position among the Petersburg workers and soldiers. Trotsky appeared at meetings in the various units of the Petrograd garrison. The mood created by him is exemplified in the fact that in the Semenovsky regiment the members of the Executive Committee appearing after him, Skobelev and Gotz, were not allowed to speak."

This turning of the Semenovsky regiment, whose name had been written in letters of ill omen in the history of the revolution, had a kind of symbolic significance. In December, 1905, it was the Semenovtsi who did the chief work of crushing the insurrection in Moscow. The commander of the regiment, General Min, gave the order: "Take no prisoners." On the Moscow-Golutvino railroad section the Semenovtsi shot 150 workers and clerks. General Min, flattered by the tzar for his heroic deed, was killed in the autumn of 1906 by a Social Revolutionary woman, Konopliannikova. Tangled up in these old traditions the Semenovsky regiment had held its ground longer than the majority of the units of the guard. Its reputation for "reliability" was so strong, that in spite of the doleful failure of Skobelev and Gotz, the government stubbornly continued to count upon the Semenovtsi right up to the day of the insurrection and even after it.

The question of the congress of the soviets remained the central political question throughout the five weeks dividing the Democratic Conference from the October insurrection. At the Conference itself the declaration of the Bolsheviks had proclaimed the coming congress of the soviets the sovereign organ of the country. "Only such decisions and proposals of the present Conference . . . can find their way to realization as are ratified by the All-Russian Congress of Workers, Peasants, and Soldiers Deputies." The resolution favoring a boycott of the Pre-Parliament, supported by one-half of the members of the Central Committee against the other half, declared: "We place the question of our parties' participation in the Pre-Parliament in direct dependence upon those measures which the All-Russian Congress of Soviets shall take to create a revolutionary government." This appeal to the Congress of Soviets runs through all the Bolshevik documents of this period almost without exception.

With the peasant war kindling, the national movements growing bitter, the breakdown going deeper, the front disintegrating, the government unravelling, the soviets were becoming the sole support of the creative forces. Every question turned into a question about the power, and the problem of power led straight to the Congress of Soviets. This Congress must give the answer to all questions, among them the question of the Constituent Assembly.

Not one party had yet withdrawn the slogan of the Constituent Assembly, and this included the Bolsheviks. But almost unnoticeably in the course of the events of the revolution, this chief democratic slogan, which had for a decade and a half tinged with its color the heroic struggle of the masses, had grown pale and faded out, had somehow been ground between millstones, had become an empty shell, a form naked of content, a tradition and not a prospect. There was nothing mysterious in this process. The development of the revolution had reached the point of a direct battle for power between the two basic classes of society, the bourgeoisie and the proletariat. A Constituent Assembly could give nothing either to the one or the other. The petty bourgeoisie of the town and country could play only an auxiliary and secondary rôle in this conflict. They were in any case incapable of seizing the power themselves. If the preceding months had proved anything, they had proved that. Nevertheless in a Constituent Assembly the petty bourgeoisie might still win—and they actually did win as it turned out—a majority. And to what end? Only to the end of not knowing what to do with it. This reveals the bankruptcy of formal democracy in a deep historic crisis. It reveals the strength of tradition, however, that even on the eve of the last battle neither camp had yet renounced the name of the Constituent Assembly. But as a matter of fact the bourgeoisie had appealed from the Constituent Assembly to Kornilov, and the Bolsheviks to the Congress of Soviets.

It may be confidently assumed that rather wide sections of the people, and even certain small strata of the Bolshevik party, nourished certain constitutional illusions of their own in regard to the Congress of Soviets—that is, they associated with it the idea of an automatic and painless transfer of power from the hands of the Coalition to the hands of the Soviet. In reality it would be necessary to take the power by force; it was impossible to do this by voting. Only an armed insurrection could decide the question.

However, of all the illusions which accompany as an inevitable premise every great popular movement, even the most realistic, this illusion of a soviet "parliamentarism" was in all the combined circumstances the least dangerous. The soviets were in reality struggling for the power; they were continually more and more relying upon armed force; they were becoming governments in the localities; they were winning their own congress in a fight. Thus there remained but little place for constitutional illusions, and what few survived were washed away in the process of the struggle.

In coordinating the revolutionary efforts of the workers and soldiers of the whole country, giving them a single goal, giving them unity of aim and a single date for action, the slogan of the Soviet Congress at the same time made it possible to screen the semi-conspirative, semi-public preparation of an insurrection with continual appeals to the legal representation of the workers, soldiers and peasants. Having thus promoted the assembling of forces for the revolution, the Congress of Soviets was afterward to sanction its results and give the new government a form irreproachable in the eyes of the people.

Chapter IV

THE MILITARY-REVOLUTIONARY COMMITTEE

IN spite of the change of mood beginning toward the end of July, the Social Revolutionaries and Mensheviks dominated the reorganized Petrograd garrison all through August. The proletariat was disarmed; the Red Guard had kept only a few thousand rifles. In those circumstances, notwithstanding the fact that the masses were again coming over to the Bolsheviks, an insurrection might end in cruel defeat.

The situation steadily changed, however, through September. After the revolt of the generals the Compromisers swiftly lost their following in the garrison. Distrust of the Bolsheviks was replaced by sympathy, or at the worst by a watchful neutrality. But the sympathy was not active. The garrison remained in a political sense extremely shaky and—as muzhiks are—suspicious. Aren't the Bolsheviks going to deceive us? Will they really give us peace and land? The majority of the soldiers still had no idea of fighting for these aims under the banner of the Bolsheviks. And since there remained in the garrison an almost completely unabsorbed minority hostile to the Bolsheviks—five or six thousand junkers, three Cossack regiments, a bicycle battalion and an armored car division—the outcome of a conflict in September seemed doubtful. To help things along, however, the course of events brought one more object lesson in which the fate of the Petrograd soldiers was shown to be inseparably bound up with the fate of the revolution and the Bolsheviks.

The right to control bodies of armed men is a fundamental right of the state power. The first Provisional Government, wished upon the people by the Executive Committee, gave an obligation not to disarm and not to remove from Petrograd those military units which had taken part in the February overturn. This was the formal beginning of a military dualism inseparable in essence from the double sovereignty. The major political disturbances of the succeeding months—the April demonstration, the July Days, the preparation of the Kornilov insurrection and its liquidation—each one inevitably ran into the question of the subordination of the Petrograd garrison. But conflicts between the government and the Compromisers upon this theme were, after all, a family matter, and ended amicably. With the Bolshevization of the garrison things took a different turn. The soldiers themselves now began to recall that obligation given by the government to the Executive Committee in March and treacherously broken by them. On September 8th the soldiers' section of the Soviet put forward a demand that the regiments transferred to the front in connection with the July events be returned to Petrograd. This while the members of the Coalition were tearing their hair about how to get rid of the remaining regiments.

In a number of provincial cities things stood about the same way as in the capital. During July and August the local garrisons underwent a patriotic reconstruction; during August and September the reconstructed garrisons underwent a process of Bolshevization. It was then necessary to begin over from the beginning—that is, once more undertake transfers and reconstructions. In preparing its blow against Petrograd the government began with the provinces. Its political motives were carefully concealed under pretexts of strategy. On September 27th a joint session of the soviets of Reval—that of the city and the fortress— adopted on the question of transfers the following resolution: To consider a re-grouping of forces admissible only when agreed to in advance by the corresponding soviets. The leaders of the Vladimir soviet inquired of Moscow whether they should obey an order of Kerensky transferring the whole garrison. The Moscow regional bureau of the Bolsheviks observed that "orders of this kind are becoming systematic in relation to the revolutionary-minded garrisons." Before surrendering all its rights, the Provisional Government was trying to get hold of the fundamental right of every government—the right to dispose of armed bodies of men.

The reorganization of the Petrograd garrison was becoming all the more urgent because the coming Congress of Soviets was destined to carry to a decision one way or other the struggle for power. The bourgeois press, led by the Kadet organ *Rech,* was asserting every morning that we must not "let the Bolsheviks choose the moment for a declaration of civil war." That meant: We must strike a timely blow at the Bolsheviks. The attempt at a preliminary change of the correlation of forces in the garrison flowed inevitably from this premise. Arguments from strategic considerations looked sufficiently impressive after the fall of Riga and the loss of the Moon-sund Islands. District headquarters issued an order for the reorganization of the Petrograd units in preparation for an offensive. At the same time, upon the initiative of the Compromisers, the matter was brought up in the soldiers' section of the Soviet. Here the plan of the enemy was not bad: presenting a peremptory strategic demand to the Soviet, to snatch their military support from under the feet of the Bolsheviks, or in case the Soviet resisted, to provoke a sharp conflict between the Petrograd garrison and the front, which was in need of supplementary forces and replacements.

The leaders of the Soviet, quite well aware of the trap which had been set for them, made up their minds to feel out the ground carefully before taking any irrevocable step. A flat refusal to fulfil the order was possible only if they were sure that the motives of the refusal would be correctly understood by the front. Otherwise it might be more advantageous to carry out, by agreement with the trenches, a replacement of certain units of the garrison with revolutionary units from the front which were in need of rest. It was in this latter sense, as we have shown above, that the Reval soviet had already spoken.

The soldiers approached the question more brusquely. Take the offensive at the front now, in the middle of autumn? Reconcile themselves to a new winter campaign? No, they simply had no room in their heads for that idea. The patriotic press immediately opened fire on the garrison: the Petrograd regiments, grown fat in idleness, are betraying the front. The workers took the side of the soldiers. The Putilov men were the first to protest against the transfer of the regiments. From that time on the question was never absent from the order of the day either in barrack or factory. This drew together the two sections of the Soviet. The regiments began to support most heartily the demand that the workers be armed.

Attempting to kindle the patriotism of the masses by threatening the loss of Petrograd, the Compromisers introduced into the Soviet on October 9 a motion to create a "Committee of Revolutionary Defense," whose task should be to take part in the defense of the capital with the active cooperation of the workers. While refusing to assume responsibility for "the so-called strategy of the Provisional Government and in particular the removal of troops from Petrograd" the Soviet nevertheless had made no haste to express itself upon the substance of the order removing the soldiers, but had decided to test its motives and the facts upon which it was based. The Mensheviks had raised a protest: It is not permissible to interfere in the operative orders of the commanding staff. But it was only a month and a half since they had talked the same way about the conspiratorial orders of Kornilov, and they were reminded of this. In order to test the question whether the removal of the troops was dictated by military or political considerations, a competent body was needed. To the extreme surprise of the Compromisers the Bolsheviks accepted the idea of a "Committee of Defense." This committee should be the one to gather all data relating to the defense of the capital. That was an important step. Having snatched this dangerous weapon from the hands of the enemy, the Soviet remained in a position to turn the decision about removing the troops this way or that according to circumstances—but in any case against the government and the Compromisers.

The Bolsheviks quite naturally seized upon this Menshevik project of a military committee, for there had been conversations often enough in their own ranks about the necessity of creating in good season an authoritative Soviet committee to lead the coming insurrection. In the Military Organization of the party they had even drawn up plans for such a body. The one difficulty they had not yet got over was that of reconciling an instrument of insurrection with an elective and openly functioning Soviet, upon whose benches, moreover, sat representatives of the hostile parties. The patriotic proposal of the Mensheviks, therefore, came up most appropriately, and came up just in time to assist in the creation of a revolutionary headquarters—a body soon to be re-named "Military Revolutionary Committee" and to become the chief lever of the revolution.

Two years after the events described above, the author of this book wrote in an article dedicated to the October revolution: "As soon as the order for the removal of the troops was com-municated by Headquarters to the Executive Committee of the Petrograd soviet . . . it became clear that this question in its further development would have decisive political significance." The idea of an insurrection began to take form from that mo-ment. It was no longer necessary to invent a Soviet body. The real aim of the future committee was unequivocally brought out when in the same session Trotsky concluded his report on the withdrawal of the Bolsheviks from the Pre-Parliament with the exclamation: "Long live the direct and open struggle for a revolutionary power throughout the country!" That was a translation into the language of soviet legality of the slogan: "Long live the armed insurrec-tion!"

On the very next day, the 10th, the Central Committee of the Bolsheviks, adopted in secret session the resolution of Lenin presenting armed insurrection as the practical task of the com-ing days. From that moment the party assumed a clear and im-perative fighting formation. The Committee of Defense was in-cluded in its plans for a direct struggle for power.

The government and its allies surrounded the garrison with concentric circles. On the 11th the commander of the Northern front, General Cheremissov, reported to the War Minister a de-mand of the army committees that the tired-out front units be replaced by Petersburg units from the rear. In this instance Headquarters was merely a transmitting mechanism between the Compromisers in the army committees and their Petrograd leaders, who were striving to create a broad cover for the plans of Kerensky. The Coalition press accompanied this encircling opera-tion with a symphony of patriotic ravings. Daily meetings of the regiments and factories demonstrated, however, that this music of the ruling spheres was not making the slightest impression upon the lower ranks. On the 12th, a mass meeting of the work-ers of one of the most revolutionary factories of the capital (the

Old Parviainen) made the following answer to the attacks of the bourgeoisie: "We declare that we will go into the street when we deem it advisable. We are not afraid of the approaching struggle, and we confidently believe that we will come off victorious."

In creating a commission to draw up regulations for the "Committee of Defense," the Executive Committee of the Petrograd Soviet designated for the future military body such tasks as the following: to get in touch with the Northern front and with the headquarters of the Petrograd district, with Centrobalt and the regional soviet of Finland, in order to ascertain the military situation and take the necessary measures: to take a census of the personal composition of the garrison of Petrograd and its environs, also of the ammunition and military supplies; to take measures for the preservation of discipline in the soldier and worker masses. The formulæ were all-inclusive and at the same time ambiguous: they almost all balanced on a fine line between defense of the capital and armed insurrection. However, these two tasks, heretofore mutually exclusive, were now in actual fact growing into one. Having seized the power, the Soviet would be compelled to undertake the military defense of Petrograd. The element of defense-camouflage was not therefore violently dragged in, but flowed to some extent from the conditions preceding the insurrection.

With this same purpose of camouflage a Social Revolutionary and not a Bolshevik was placed at the head of the commission on the "Committee of Defense." This was a young and modest intendant, Lazimir, one of those Left Social Revolutionaries who were already traveling with the Bolsheviks before the insurrection—although, to be sure, not always foreseeing whither the course would lead. Lazimir's preliminary rough draft was edited by Trotsky in two directions: the practical plans relating to the conquest of the garrison were more sharply defined, the general revolutionary goal was still more glazed over. As ratified by the Executive Committee against the protest of two Mensheviks, the draft included in the staff of the Military Revolutionary Committee the præsidiums of the Soviet and of the soldiers' section, representatives of the fleet, of the regional committee of Finland, of the railroad unions, of the factory committees, the trade unions,

93

the party military organizations, the Red Guard, etc. The organizational basis was the same as in many other cases, but the personal composition of the committee was determined by its new tasks. It was assumed that the organizations would send representatives familiar with military affairs or standing near to the garrison. The character of an organ should be conditioned by its function.

Another new formation of this period was no less important. Under the direction of the Military Revolutionary Committee there was created a Permanent Conference of the Garrison. The soldiers' section represented the garrison politically, the deputies being elected under the party symbols. The Garrison Conference, however, was to consist of the regimental committees which guided the daily lives of their units and thus constituted a more immediate practical "guild" representation. The analogy between the regimental and the factory committees is obvious. Through the mediation of the workers' section of the Soviet the Bolsheviks were able upon big political questions to rely confidently upon the workers. But in order to become masters in the factories it had been necessary to carry the factory and shop committees. The composition of the soldiers' section guaranteed to the Bolsheviks the political sympathy of the majority of the garrison. But in order to get the practical disposal of the military units it was necessary to rely directly on the regimental committees. This explains why in the period preceding the insurrection the Garrison Conference naturally crowded out the Soldiers' section and moved to the center of the stage. The more prominent deputies in the section were also, by the way, members of the Conference.

In an article written not long before these days—"The Crisis is Ripe"—Lenin had reproachfully asked: "What has the party done in the matter of ascertaining the attitude of the troops, etc. . . ?" Notwithstanding the devoted work of the Military Organization Lenin's reproach was just. A strictly military examination of the forces and materials was difficult for the party to achieve: the habit of mind was lacking and the approach. This situation changed the moment the Garrison Conference came on the scene. Henceforth a living panorama of the garrison—not

only of the capital but also of the military ring surrounding it—
passed before the eyes of the leaders.

On the 12th the Executive Committee took up the regulations
drafted by Lazimir's commission. In spite of the session's being
secret the debate was carried on to a certain extent in equivocal
language. "Here they said one thing and meant another," writes
Sukhanov not unjustly. The regulations provided for the establishment under the Committee of departments of defense, supplies, communications, intelligence, etc.: this was a headquarters
or counter-quarters. They declared it to be the aim of the Conference to raise the fighting capacity of the garrison: that was
entirely true, but a fighting capacity may be applied in different
ways. The Mensheviks observed with helpless indignation that
an idea advanced by them for patriotic purposes was being converted into a screen for the preparation of an insurrection. The
camouflage was by no means impenetrable—everybody understood what the talk was about—but at the same time it could not
be broken through. Had not the Compromisers themselves behaved in exactly the same way in the past, grouping the garrison
around themselves at critical moments and creating sovereign
bodies parallel with those of the government? The Bolsheviks
were merely following the traditions, so to speak, of the dual
power. But they were bringing a new content into these old forms.
What had formerly served the purpose of compromise was now
leading to civil war. The Mensheviks demanded that it be placed
in the record that they were against the undertaking as a whole.
This platonic request was granted.

On the next day the question of the Military Revolutionary
Committee and the Garrison Conference was taken up by the
soldiers' section, which only a little while before had constituted
the lifeguard of the Compromisers. The chief place in this very
significant session was rightly occupied by the president of the
Centrobalt, the sailor Dybenko, a black-bearded giant, a man
who never had to look in his pocket for a word. The speech of
this Helsingfors guest crashed into the stagnant atmosphere of
the garrison like a keen and fresh sea wind. Dybenko told about
the final break of the fleet with the government and their new

attitudes to the command. Before the latest naval operations began, he said, the admiral addressed a question to the Congress of Sailors then sitting: Will they carry out military orders? We answered: "We will—under supervision from our side. But . . . if we see that the fleet is threatened with destruction, the commanding staff will be the first to hang from the mast head." To the Petrograd garrison this was a new language. Even in the fleet it had come into use only in the last few days. It was the language of insurrection. The little group of Mensheviks grumbled distractedly in a corner. The præsidium looked out with some alarm upon that compact mass of gray soldier coats. Not one protesting voice from their ranks! Eyes burned like coals in their excited faces. A spirit of daring was in the air.

In conclusion, stimulated by the universal sympathy, Dybenko confidently exclaimed: "They talk about the need of bringing out the Petrograd garrison for the defense of the approaches to Petrograd and of Reval in particular. Don't believe a word of it. We will defend Reval ourselves. Stay here and defend the interests of the revolution . . . When we need your support we will say so ourselves, and I am confident that you will support us." This challenge, which exactly matched the mood of the soldiers, called out a veritable whirlwind of sincere enthusiasm in which the protests of a few individual Mensheviks were completely drowned. The question of removing the regiments was settled from that moment.

The regulations proposed by Lazimir were adopted by a majority of 283 votes against 1, with 23 abstaining. These figures, unexpected even to the Bolsheviks, gave a measure of the pressure of the revolutionary masses. The vote meant that the soldiers' section had openly and officially transferred the administration of the garrison from headquarters to the Military Revolutionary Committee. The coming days would show that this was no mere gesture.

On that same day the Executive Committee of the Petrograd Soviet made public the creation under its supervision of a special department of the Red Guard. The matter of arming the workers, neglected under the Compromisers and even obstructed by them, had become one of the most important tasks of the Bolshevik Soviet. The suspicious attitude of the soldiers toward the Red Guard was already far in the past. On the contrary, almost all the resolutions of the regiments contained a demand for the arming of the workers. From now on the Red Guard and the garrison stand side by side. Soon they will be still more closely united by a common submission to the Military Revolutionary Committee.

The government was worried. On the morning of the 14th, a conference of the ministers in Kerensky's office ratified the measures undertaken by headquarters against the "coming-out" under preparation. The rulers were guessing: Will it stop this time at an armed demonstration or will it go to the point of insurrection? The commander of the district said to the representatives of the press: "In any case we are ready." Those doomed to death not infrequently experience an afflux of life force just before the end.

At a joint session of the Executive Committees, Dan, imitating the June intonations of Tseretelli, who had now taken refuge in the Caucasus, demanded of the Bolsheviks an answer to the question: Do they intend to come out, and if they do, when? From the answer of Riazanov, the Menshevik Bogdanov drew the not unjustified conclusion that the Bolsheviks were preparing an insurrection and would stand at the head of it. The Menshevik paper wrote: "And the Bolsheviks are evidently relying in their plans for a coming 'seizure of power' on the garrison's staying here." But in this remark the phrase "seizure of power" was in quotation marks. The Compromisers still did not seriously believe in the danger. They did not fear the victory of the Bolsheviks so much as the triumph of the counter-revolution in consequence of new civil war conflicts.

Having undertaken to arm the workers, the Soviet had to find its way to the weapons. This did not happen all at once. Here too each practical step forward was suggested by the masses. It was only necessary to listen attentively to their suggestions. Four years after the event, Trotsky, in an evening devoted to recollections of the October revolution, told the following story: "When a delegation from the workers came to me and said they needed weapons, I answered: 'But the arsenals, you see, are not in our hands.' They answered: 'We have been to the Sestroretsk Arms Factory.' 'Well, and what about it?' 'They said that if the Soviet ordered they would deliver.' I gave an order for five thousand rifles, and they got them the same day. That was a first experiment." The hostile press immediately raised a cry against this delivery of weapons by a government factory upon the order of a person indicted for state treason and only released from prison on bail. The government kept still, but the highest organ of the democracy came forward with a strict command. Weapons were to be given to nobody without its permission—the permission of the Central Executive Committee of the Soviets. It might seem that on the question of delivering weapons Dan and Gotz were as little in a position to forbid, as Trotsky to permit or give orders. The factories and arsenals were supposed to be under government administration. But ignoring the official authorities at all serious moments had become a tradition with the Central Executive Committee, and had permanently entered into the customs of the government itself, corresponding as it did to the nature of things. The violation of tradition and custom, came however from another direction. Having ceased to distinguish the thunderings of the Central Executive Committee from the lightnings of Kerensky, the workers and soldiers ignored them both.

It was more convenient to demand the transfer of the Petrograd regiments in the name of the front than in the name of the chancelleries at the rear. For these reasons Kerensky placed the Petrograd garrison under the commander-in-chief of the Northern front, Cheremissov. While excluding the capital in its military aspect from his own administration as the head of the government, Kerensky took comfort in the thought that he would subject it to himself as commander-in-chief of the army. In his turn General Cheremissov, who was going to have a very hard nut to crack, sought help from the commissars and committee-men. With their common labors a plan of future activities was drawn up. On the 7th the headquarters at the front, together with the army organizations, was to summon representatives of the Petrograd Soviet to Pskov in order in the presence of the trenches to present them with a brusque demand.

There was nothing for the Petrograd Soviet to do but accept the challenge. The delegation of a score or so appointed at the session of the 16th—about half members of the Soviet and half representatives of the regiments—was headed by the president of the Workers' Section, Feodorov, and leaders of the Soldiers' Section and the Military Organization of the Bolsheviks—Lashevich, Sadovsky, Mekhonoshin, Dashkevich and others. A few Left Social Revolutionaries and Menshevik-Internationalists, included in the delegation, promised to defend the policy of the Soviet. At a conference of the delegates held before their departure the draft of a declaration proposed by Sverdlov was adopted.

The same session of the Soviet took up the regulations of the Military Revolutionary Committee. This institution had barely come into existence when it assumed in the eyes of the enemy an aspect growing every day more hateful. "The Bolsheviks make no answer," cried an orator of the opposition, "to the direct question: Are they preparing an attack? This is either cowardice or lack of confidence in their forces." The meeting greeted this remark with hearty laughter: the representative of the government party was demanding that the party of insurrection open the secrets of its heart to him. The new committee, continued the orator, is nothing else but "a revolutionary headquarters for the seizure of power." They, the Mensheviks, would not enter it. "How many are there of you?" cried a voice from the benches: there were indeed only a few Mensheviks in the Soviet, fifty altogether. But nevertheless it seemed authoritatively known to them that "the masses are not in favor of coming out." In his reply Trotsky did not deny that the Bolsheviks were preparing for a seizure of power: "We make no secret of that." But at present, he said, that is not the question. The government has demanded the removal of the revolutionary troops from Petrograd and to that "we have to answer yes or no." The regulations drafted by Lazimir were adopted by an overwhelming majority. The president proposed to the Military Revolutionary Committee to begin work on the following day. Thus one more forward step was taken.

The commander of the district, Polkovnikov, had that day once more reported to the government that an action was under preparation by the Bolsheviks. The report was couched in bold language: the garrison as a whole is on the side of the government; the officers' schools have received an order to be ready. In an appeal to the population Polkovnikov promised in case of necessity to adopt "the most extreme measures." The burgomaster, Schreider, a Social Revolutionary, added a prayer on his part that "no disorders shall be instigated so that we may avoid actual famine in the capital." Threatening and adjuring, making bold and making timid, the press meanwhile was rising to a higher and higher note.

To impress the imagination of delegates from the Petrograd Soviet, a military-theatrical setting was arranged for the reception in Pskov. In the office of headquarters around tables covered with imposing maps stood notable generals, high commissars, with Voitinsky at their head, and representatives of the army committees. The chiefs of the departments read reports of the military situation on land and sea. All the reports came to one and the same conclusion: It is necessary to call out the Petrograd garrison immediately for the defense of the approaches to the capital. The commissars and committee-men indignantly refuted all suspicions in regard to hidden political motives: the whole operation, they declared, has been dictated by strategic necessity. The delegates had no direct proofs to the contrary: in this kind of business evidence does not grow on every bush. But the whole situation was a refutation. The front had no lack of men. What it lacked was willingness to fight. The mood of the Petrograd garrison was by no means such as to reinforce a front so shaken. Moreover the lessons of the Kornilov days were still in the memories of all. Thoroughly convinced of their correctness, the delegation easily resisted the assault of headquarters, and returned to Petrograd more unanimous than when they had left.

Those direct proofs which the participants at that time lacked are now at the disposal of the historian. The secret military correspondence proves that it was not the front which had demanded the Petrograd regiments, but that Kerensky had imposed them upon the front. To a telegram from his War Minister, the commander-in-chief of the Northern front answered on the direct wire: "Secret. 17. X. The initiative for sending the troops

of the Petrograd garrison to the front was yours and not mine.
. . . When it became clear that the troops of the Petrograd garrison did not want to go to the front, that is, that they are not
capable of fighting, I then in a private conversation with your
officer-representative said that . . . we have already plenty of
such troops at the front; but in view of the desire expressed by
you to send them to the front I did not refuse them and I do
not refuse them now, if you, as before, consider their transfer
from Petrograd necessary." The semi-bellicose tone of this telegram is explained by the fact that Cheremissov, a general with a
taste for high politics, having been considered "red" while in
the tzar's army, and having afterward become, according to
Miliukov's expression, "the favorite of the revolutionary democracy," had evidently come to the conclusion that it would
be better to draw apart in good season from the government and
its conflict with the Bolsheviks. The conduct of Cheremissov
during the days of the revolution wholly confirms this assumption.

The struggle about the garrison interwove with the struggle
about the Soviet Congress. Only four or five days remained before the date originally designated. The "coming-out" was expected in connection with the Congress. It was assumed that as
in the July Days the movement would develop on the type of an
armed mass demonstration with street fighting. The right Menshevik Potressov, obviously relying upon data supplied by the
Intelligence Service, or by the French War Mission—always bold
in the manufacture of forged documents—expounded in the
bourgeois press the plan of a Bolshevik action which was to take
place on the night of October 17. The ingenious authors of the
plan did not forget to foretell that at one of the gates of the city
the Bolsheviks were to pick up the "dark elements." The soldiers
of the Guard regiments were as good at laughing as the gods of
Homer. The white pillars and chandeliers of Smolny shook with
uproarious volleys when Potressov's article was read at a meeting of the Soviet. But the all-wise government, unable as ever
to see what was taking place before its eyes, took serious fright
at this awkward forgery, and hastily assembled at two o'clock
in the morning in order to hold off these "dark elements." After

renewed conferences between Kerensky and the military authorities the necessary measures were taken. The guards of the Winter Palace and the State Bank were reinforced; two training schools were called in from Oranienbaum, and even an armored train from the Rumanian front. "At the last moment," writes Miliukov, "the Bolsheviks revoked their preparations. Why they did this is not clear." Even several years after the event the learned historian still prefers to believe an invention which contained its own refutation.

The authorities directed the militia to investigate the environs of the city to see if they could find signs of any preparation for a coming-out. The reports of the militia were a combination of live observations with police stupidity. In the Alexandro-Nevsky section, which contains a number of big factories, the investigators found complete tranquillity. In the Vyborg district the necessity of overthrowing the government was being openly preached, but "externally" all was quiet. In the Vassilie-Ostrov district the mood was high, but here too "external" signs of an action were not to be observed. On the Narva side a redoubled agitation in favor of action was going on, but it was impossible to get an answer from anybody to the question, just when. Either the day and hour were being kept strictly secret, or they were really unknown to anybody. Decision: to reinforce the patrols in the suburbs and have the commissars of the militia inspect the sentry posts more frequently.

Certain correspondence in the Moscow liberal press is not a bad supplement to the reports of the militia: "In the suburbs, at the Petersburg factories, Nevsky, Obukhovsky and Putilov, Bolshevik agitation in favor of a coming-out is in progress everywhere. The workers are in a state to start moving at any moment. During recent days there has been observed in Petrograd an unheard of influx of deserters. . . . At the Warsaw station you can't get through because of the soldiers with their suspicious looks, their burning eyes in excited faces. . . . There is information of the presence in Petrograd of whole gangs of thieves who have caught the smell of their prey. The dark forces are being organized, and the dens and lunchrooms are brim full of them. . . ." Philistine fright and police rumor here interweave with a certain amount of austere fact. In approaching its climax the revolutionary crisis stirred up the social deeps to the very bottom. Deserters and robber-gangs and the dens of iniquity did actually all rise at the rumble of the approaching earthquake. The leaders of society gazed with physical horror at the unleashed forces of their own régime, at its ulcers and vices. The revolution had not created but only uncovered them.

At the headquarters of a corps in Dvinsk in those days, Baron Budberg, a man already known to us, a bilious reactionary, but not wanting a gift of observation and his own kind of penetration, wrote: "The Kadets, the Kadetoids, the Octobrists, and the many-colored revolutionists of the ancient and of the March formation, feel their end approaching and chirp and chatter on all sides, reminding one of the Mussulman who tried to stop an eclipse of the moon with a rattle."

The Garrison Conference was first called together on the 18th. The telephonogram sent to the military units told them to refrain from actions on their own initiative, and fulfil only those orders of headquarters which should be countersigned by the Soldiers' Section. In this the Soviet was making a decisive and open attempt to take control of the garrison. The telephonogram was in essence nothing else than a summons to overthrow the existing authorities. But it could be interpreted, if one wished, as a peaceful act of replacing the Compromisers with Bolsheviks in the mechanic of the dual power. Practically this came to the same thing, but the more flexible interpretation left room for illusions. The præsidium of the Central Executive Committee, considering itself the master of Smolny, made an attempt to stop the despatch of the telephonogram. It only compromised itself once more. The assembly of representatives of the regimental and company committees of Petrograd and the environs occurred at the designated hour, and turned out to be extraordinarily large.

Thanks to the atmosphere created by the enemy, the reports of the participants in this Garrison Conference automatically concentrated upon the question of the prospective "coming-out." There occurred a significant muster-roll, upon which the leaders would scarcely have ventured upon their own initiative. Those against the action were the military school in Peterhof and the

Ninth Cavalry Regiment. The squadrons of the cavalry of the Guard were inclined to neutrality. The military school in Oranienbaum would submit only to the commands of the Central Executive Committee. That exhausted the hostile or neutral voices. Those declaring their readiness to come out at a word from the Petrograd Soviet were the following: the Egersky, the Moscow, the Volynsky, the Pavlovsky, the Keksgolmsky, the Semenovsky, the Izmailovsky, the first sharpshooters and the third reserve regiments, the second Baltic crew, the electro-technical battalion and the artillery division of the Guard; the grenadier regiment would come out only at the summons of the Congress of Soviets. That was enough. The less important units followed the lead of the majority. The representatives of the Central Executive Committee, who had not long ago justly considered the Petrograd garrison the source of their power, were now almost unanimously denied the floor. In a state of impotent exasperation they left the "unauthorized" assembly, which immediately thereafter at the suggestion of the president declared: No orders are valid without the countersign of the Soviet.

That which had been preparing in the minds of the garrison during the last months, and especially weeks, was now crystallizing. The government turned out more insignificant than it had been possible to think. While the town was buzzing with rumors of a coming-out and of bloody battles, the Conference of Regimental Committees, showing an overwhelming predominance of Bolsheviks, made both demonstrations and mass battles essentially unnecessary. The garrison was confidently advancing to the revolution, seeing it not as an insurrection, but as a realization of the irrefutable right of the Soviet to decide the fate of the country. This movement had incomparable power, but at the same time a certain heaviness. The party was obliged to attune its activity with some skill to the political stride of the regiments, a majority of whom were awaiting a summons from the Petersburg Soviet, but some from the Congress of Soviets.

In order to ward off the danger of even a temporary interference with the development of the offensive, it was necessary to answer one question which was disturbing not only enemies but friends: Will not an insurrection spontaneously break out almost any day? In the tramways, on the streets, in the stores, there was no talk but of an expected coming-out. On the Palace Square, in front of the Winter Palace and the General Staff, long queues of officers were offering the government their services and receiving revolvers in exchange: in the hours of danger neither the revolvers nor their owners will put in one second's appearance. The leading editorials in all the current papers were devoted to the question of the insurrection. Gorky demanded of the Bolsheviks that unless they were the "helpless playthings of the enraged multitude," they should refute these rumors. This alarm of uncertainty penetrated even the workers' sections, and still more the regiments. To them, too, it began to seem as though a coming-out were being prepared without them. And by whom? Why was Smolny silent? The self-contradictory situation of the Soviet as a public parliament and at the same time a revolutionary headquarters, created great difficulties in those last moments. It became impossible to remain longer silent.

"During the last days," declared Trotsky at the end of an evening's session of the Soviet, "the press has been full of communications, rumors, articles about an impending action. . . . The decisions of the Petrograd Soviet are published and made known to everybody. The Soviet is an elective institution, and . . . cannot have a decision which would not be known to the workers and soldiers. . . . I declare in the name of the Soviet that no armed actions have been settled upon by us, but if the Soviet in the course of events should be obliged to set the date for a coming-out the workers and soldiers would come out to the last man at its summons. They say that I signed an order for five thousand rifles. . . . Yes, I signed it. . . . The Soviet will continue to organize and arm the workers' guard." The delegates understood: the battle was near, but without them and over their heads the signal would not be given.

However, besides a reassuring explanation, the masses had to have a clear revolutionary prospective. For this purpose the speaker united the two questions—removal of the garrison and coming Congress of Soviets. "We are in conflict with the government upon a question which may become extremely sharp. . . . We will not permit them . . . to strip Petrograd of its revolutionary garrison." This conflict is in its turn subordinate to another that approaches. "It is known to the bourgeoisie that the Petrograd Soviet is going to propose to the Congress of Soviets that they seize the power. . . . And foreseeing an inevitable battle, the bourgeois classes are trying to disarm Petrograd." The political set-up of the revolution was first given in this speech with complete definition: We expect to seize the power, we need the garrison, and we will not give it up. "At the first attempt of the counter-revolution to break up the Congress, we will answer with a counter-attack which will be ruthless, and which we will carry through to the end." Here, too, the announcement of a decisive political offensive was made under the formulæ of military defense.

Sukhanov, who turned up at this meeting with a hopeless plan to draw the Soviet into a celebration of Gorky's fiftieth anniversary, subsequently made an apt comment on the revolutionary knot which was tied there. For Smolny, he said, the question of the garrison is a question of insurrection; for the soldiers it is a question of their own fate. "It would be difficult to imagine a more fortunate starting point for the policy of those days." This did not prevent Sukhanov from considering the policy of the Bolsheviks as a whole ruinous. Along with Gorky and thousands of radical intellectuals he feared above all things that so-called "enraged multitude" which was with admirable deliberation developing its offensive from day to day.

The Soviet was sufficiently powerful to announce openly its program of state revolution and even set the date. At the same time—right up to the date set by itself for the complete victory—the Soviet was powerless in thousands of great and small questions. Kerensky, politically already reduced to a zero, was still giving out decrees in the Winter Palace. Lenin, the inspirer of this incomparable movement of the masses, was hiding underground, and the Minister of Justice, Maliantovich, had renewed in those days his instructions to the district attorney to bring about Lenin's arrest. Even in Smolny, on its own territory, the all-powerful Petrograd Soviet seemed to be living only by grace of the authorities. The administration of the building, of the cash-box, of the despatching room, the automobiles, the telephones—

106

all was still in the hands of the Central Executive Committee which itself only hung on by the mere thread of an abstract right of succession.

Sukhanov tells how after the meeting he came out in the thick of night on Smolny Square, in black darkness with rain coming down in sheets. The whole crowd of delegates were hopelessly milling around a couple of smoking and stinking automobiles which had been assigned to the Bolshevik Soviet from the opulent garages of the Central Executive Committee. "The president, Trotsky, was also about to approach the automobile," relates this omnipresent observer. "But after stopping and looking on for a minute he chuckled and, splashing through the puddles, disappeared in the darkness." On the platform of the tramcar Sukhanov ran into some unknown small-sized fellow of modest appearance with a black goatee. The unknown tried to console Sukhanov in all the discomforts of the long journey. Who is that? asked Sukhanov of his Bolshevik companion. "An old party worker, Sverdlov." In less than two weeks this small man with a little black goatee will be president of the Central Executive Committee, the supreme governing power of the Soviet Republic. It may be that Sverdlov consoled his traveling companion out of a feeling of gratitude: Eight days before that in the apartment of Sukhanov—to be sure, without his knowledge—had occurred that meeting of the Bolshevik Central Committee which placed the armed insurrection on the order of the day.

The next morning the Central Executive Committee made an attempt to turn back the wheel of events. The præsidium convoked a "lawful" assembly of the garrison, drawing into it also those backward committees which should long ago have been re-elected, and which had not been present the day before. This supplementary test of the garrison, while also giving something new, still more clearly confirmed yesterday's picture. This time those opposed to the coming-out were: a majority of the committees of the troops quartered in the Peter and Paul Fortress, and the committees of the armored car division. They both announced their submission to the Central Executive Committee. This information was not to be ignored.

Situated on an island washed by the Neva and its canal, between the center of the city and two outlying districts, this fortress dominates the nearby bridges, and protects—or, if you will, lays bare—from the side of the river the approaches to the Winter Palace where the government had its seat. Although deprived of military significance in large scale operations, the fortress can speak a weighty word in a street fight. Moreover—and this, perhaps, is more important—the well-stocked Kronverksky Arsenal adjoins the fortress. The workers were in need of rifles—yes, and the more revolutionary regiments too were almost disarmed. The importance of armored cars in a street battle needs no explanation. On the side of the government they might cause many fruitless sacrifices; on the side of the insurrection they would shorten the road to victory. In the approaching days the Bolsheviks would have to give special attention to the fortress and the armored car division. For the rest, the correlation of forces at this new conference turned out to be the same as on the preceding day. The attempt of the Central Executive Committee to carry its own very cautious resolution was coldly repulsed by an overwhelming majority. Not having been summoned by the Petrograd Soviet, it was noted, the conference does not consider itself empowered to adopt decisions. The compromise leaders had themselves begged for this supplementary slap in the face.

Finding the approach to the regiments barricaded below, the Central Executive Committee tried to get hold of the garrison from above. By agreement with the staff, they appointed Captain Malevsky, a Social Revolutionary, chief commissar for the whole district, and announced their willingness to recognize the commissars of the Soviet on condition that they submit to the chief commissar. This attempt to get astride of the Bolshevik garrison through the instrumentality of a captain unknown to anybody was obviously hopeless. Having rejected it, the Soviet broke off the negotiations.

The insurrection laid bare by Potressov had not occurred. The enemy now confidently named another date: the 20th of October. On that day, as we know, the Congress of Soviets was originally to have opened, and the insurrection followed that Congress like its own shadow. To be sure, the Congress had already postponed its opening five days. Never mind: the object had moved, but the shadow remained. This time, too, all necessary measures were taken by the government to prevent a "coming-out." Reinforced sentry guards were placed in the suburbs; Cossack patrols rode through the workers' districts all night long; cavalry reserves were concealed at various points throughout the city; the militia was made ready for action and half of its members did continual duty in the commissariats. Armored cars, light artillery and machine guns were set up near the Winter Palace. The approaches to the Palace were guarded by patrols.

Once more the insurrection which no one was preparing, and for which no one had issued a call, did not take place. The day went by more peacefully than many others; work in the shops and factories never ceased. *Izvestia,* edited by Dan, crowed about this victory over the Bolsheviks: "Their adventuring with armed demonstrations in Petrograd is about over." The Bolsheviks have been crushed by the mere indignation of the united democracy: "They are already surrendering." One might literally think that the enemy had lost their heads and were deliberately trying with untimely frights and still less timely trumpetings of victory to lead "public opinion" astray, and conceal the actual plans of the Bolsheviks.

The decision to create a Military Revolutionary Committee, first introduced on the 9th, was passed at a plenary session of the Soviet only a week later. The Soviet is not a party; its machinery is heavy. Four days more were required to form the Committee. Those ten days, however, did not go for nothing: the conquest of the garrison was in full swing, the Conference of Regimental Committees had demonstrated its viability, the arming of the workers was going forward. And thus the Military Revolutionary Committee, although it went to work only on the 20th, five days before the insurrection, found ready to its hands a sufficiently well organized dominion. Being boycotted by the Compromisers, the staff of the Committee contained only Bolsheviks and Left Social Revolutionaries: that eased and simplified the task. Of the Social Revolutionaries only Lazimir did any work, and he was even placed at the head of the bureau in order to emphasize the fact that the Committee was a Soviet and not a party institution. In essence, however, the Committee, whose president was Trotsky, and its chief workers Podvoisky, Antonov-Ovseënko, Lashevich, Sadovsky, and Mekhonoshin, relied exclusively upon Bolsheviks. The committee hardly met once in plenary session with delegates present from all the institutions listed in its regulations. The work was carried on through the bureau under the guidance of the president, with Sverdlov brought in upon all important matters. And that was the general staff of the insurrection.

The bulletin of the Committee thus modestly registers its first steps: commissars were appointed in the combatant units of the garrison and in certain institutions and store houses "for observation and leadership." This meant that, having won the garrison politically, the Soviet was now getting organizational control of it. The dominant rôle in selecting these commissars was played by the Military Organization of the Bolsheviks. Among its Petrograd members, approximately a thousand, there was no small number of resolute soldiers and young officers utterly devoted to the revolution, and who had since the July Days been tempered in the prisons of Kerensky. The commissars recruited from its midst found in the troops of the garrison a soil well prepared. The garrison considered them its own and submitted to their orders with complete willingness.

The initiative in getting possession of institutions came in most cases from below. The workers and clerical employees of the arsenal adjoining the Peter and Paul Fortress themselves raised the question of the necessity of establishing control over the giving out of arms. A commissar sent there succeeded in stopping a supplemental arming of the junkers, held back 10,000 rifles on their way to the Don region, and smaller assignments to a number of suspicious organizations and persons. This control was soon extended to other arsenals and even to private dealers in weapons. It was only necessary to appeal to the committee of the soldiers, workers or clerical employees of the given institution or store, and the resistance of the administration would be immediately broken. Weapons were given out henceforth only upon the order of the commissars.

The typographical workers, through their union, called the attention of the Committee to an increase of Black Hundred leaflets and brochures. It was decided that in all suspicious cases the printers' union should come for instructions to the Military Revolutionary Committee. This control through the typographical workers was the most effective of all possible forms of control over the printed agitation of the counter-revolution.

Not satisfied with its formal denial of the rumor of an insurrection, the Soviet openly designated Sunday the 22nd as the day for a peaceful review of its forces—not, however, in the form of street processions, but of meetings in the factories, barracks, and all the major institutions of Petrograd. With the obvious aim of provoking bloody interference, some mysterious worshippers set the same day for a church procession through the streets of the capital. Their summons, issued in the name of some unknown Cossacks, invited the citizens to take part in a religious procession "in memory of the delivery of Moscow from the enemy in 1812." This historical pretext was none too genuine, but over and above this the organizations proposed to the Almighty to hand down a blessing upon the Cossack arms "standing guard against the enemies of the Russian land," a proposal which clearly related to the year 1917.

There was no reason to fear a serious counter-revolutionary manifestation. The clergy had no power among the Petrograd masses; they could raise up against the Soviet under church banners only pitiful remnants of the Black Hundred gangs. But with the cooperation of the experienced provocateurs of the Intelligence Service and of Cossack officers, bloody encounters were not impossible. As a measure of prevention the Military Revolutionary Committee undertook in the first place to strengthen its influence upon the Cossack regiments; a stricter régime was also introduced in the building occupied by the revolutionary staff. "It was no longer easy to get into Smolny," writes John Reed. "The pass system was changed every few hours; for spies continually sneaked through." At a meeting of the Garrison Conference on the 21st devoted to a discussion of the "Soviet Day" to follow, the spokesman proposed a series of measures for the prevention of possible street clashes. The fourth Cossack regiment, which stood farthest to the Left, announced through its delegates that it would not take part in the religious procession. The fourteenth Cossack regiment announced that it would struggle with all its power against the attempts of the counter-revolution, but at the same time that it considered a coming-out for the seizure of power "untimely." Of the three Cossack regiments only one was absent—the Uralsky—the most backward regiment, one brought into Petrograd in July for the crushing of the Bolsheviks.

Upon the proposal of Trotsky, the Conference adopted three short resolutions: (1) "The garrison of Petrograd and its environs promises the Military Revolutionary Committee full support in all its steps . . ."; (2) October 22nd is to be a day devoted to a peaceful review of forces. . . . The garrison appeals to the Cossacks: . . . "We invite you to our meetings tomorrow. You are welcome, brother Cossacks!"; (3) "The All-Russian Congress of Soviets must take the power in its hands and guarantee to the people peace, land and bread." The garrison solemnly promises to place all its forces at the disposal of the Soviet Congress. "Rely upon us, authorized representatives of the soldiers, workers and peasants. We are all at our posts ready to conquer or die." Hundreds of hands were raised for this resolution which sealed the program of the insurrection. Fifty-seven men abstained. These were the "neutrals"—that is, the wavering enemy. Not one hand was raised against the resolution. The noose around the neck of the February régime was being drawn in a reliable knot.

In the course of the day it became known that the mysterious instigators of the religious procession had given up their demonstration "at the suggestion of the commander-in-chief of the district." This serious moral success, an excellent measure of the social pressure of the Garrison Conference, permitted a confident prediction that on the following day the enemy, generally speaking, would not venture to poke their heads into the street.

The Military Revolutionary Committee appointed three commissars to the district headquarters—Sadovsky, Mekhonoshin and Lazimir. Orders of the commander were to become effective only when countersigned by one of these three. At a telephone call from Smolny the staff sent an automobile for the delegation—the customs of the dual power were still in effect—but contrary to expectations this extreme politeness of the staff did not imply a readiness to make concessions.

After listening to the declaration of Sadovsky, Polkovnikov stated that he did not recognize any commissars and had no need of any guardianship. To a hint from the delegation that along that road headquarters might meet with resistance from the side of the troops, Polkovnikov dryly answered that the garrison was in his hands and its submission was assured. "His assurance was sincere," writes Mekhonoshin in his memoirs. "We felt no affectation in it." For the return trip to Smolny the delegates did not receive an official automobile.

A special session of the Conference, to which Trotsky and Sverdlov were summoned, adopted a decision: To consider the break with headquarters an accomplished fact, and make it the starting point for a further offensive. The first condition of success: The districts must be kept in touch with all stages and episodes of the struggle. The enemy must not be allowed to catch the masses unaware. Through the district soviets and committees of the party the information was sent into all parts of the town. The regiments were immediately informed of what had happened. The instructions were confirmed: Carry out only those orders which are countersigned by the commissars. It was also suggested that they send out only the most reliable soldiers for patrol duty.

But headquarters also decided to take measures. Spurred on evidently by his compromisist allies, Polkovnikov called together at one o'clock in the afternoon his own conference of the garrison, with representatives of the Central Executive Committee present. Anticipating this move of the enemy, the Military Revolutionary Committee called an emergency conference of the regimental committees at eleven o'clock, and here it was decided to formulate the break with headquarters. The appeal to the troops of Petrograd and the environs drawn up at this meeting speaks the language of a declaration of war. "Having broken with the organized garrison of the capital, headquarters is a direct instrument of the counter-revolutionary forces." The Military Revolutionary Committee disclaims all responsibility for the activities of headquarters, and standing at the head of the garrison takes upon itself "the defense of revolutionary order against counter-revolutionary attempts."

That was a decisive step on the road to insurrection. Or was it perhaps only the next conflict in the mechanics of that dual power which is so full of conflicts? Headquarters, at any rate, tried for its own consolation so to interpret it—after conferring with the representatives of those units which had not received in good season the summons of the Military Revolutionary Committee. A delegation sent from Smolny under the leadership of the Bolshevik ensign, Dashkevich, briefly made known to headquarters the resolution of the Garrison Conference. The few representatives of the troops present reaffirmed their loyalty to the Soviet, but refused to make a decision and dispersed. "After a prolonged exchange of opinions"—the press so quoted the words of headquarters—"no definite decision was adopted; it was thought necessary to await a solution of the conflict between the Central Executive Committee and the Petrograd Soviet." Headquarters thus conceived its downfall as a quarrel between two soviet institutions as to which one should control its activities. That policy of voluntary blindness had this advantage, that it relieved them of the necessity of declaring war on Smolny, for which act the rulers lacked adequate forces. Thus the revolutionary conflict, already on the point of breaking out, was once more, with the help of the governmental organs, confined within the legal framework of the dual power. Fearing to look reality in the face, headquarters the more loyally cooperated in camouflaging the insurrection. But was not this light-minded conduct of the powers only a camouflage for their own actual purpose? Did not headquarters intend, under cover of this bureaucratic naiveté, to deal an unexpected blow at the Military Revolutionary Committee? Such an attempt upon the part of the distraught and demoralized organs of the Provisional Government was considered highly improbable in Smolny. The Military Revolutionary Committee, however, took the most simple measures of precaution: in the nearby barracks companies were kept under arms night and day, ready at the first signal of alarm to come to the aid of Smolny.

In spite of the calling-off of the religious procession, the bourgeois press foretold bloodshed on Sunday. The compromisist paper announced in its morning edition: "Today the authorities expect a coming-out with better probability than on the 20th."

Thus for the third time in one week—the 17th, the 20th, the 22nd—this naughty boy had deceived the people with a false cry of "wolf!" The fourth time, if we can believe the old fable, the boy will fall into the wolf's jaws. The Bolshevik press, in summoning the masses to attend meetings, spoke of a peaceful appraisal of revolutionary forces on the eve of the Congress of Soviets. This fully answered the plan of the Military Revolutionary Committee: to carry out a gigantic review without clashes, without employing weapons, even without showing them. They wanted to show the masses their own numbers, their strength, their resolution. They wanted with unanimous numbers to compel the enemy to hide, to keep out of sight, to stay indoors. By exposing the impotence of the bourgeoisie beside their own masses, they wanted to erase from the consciousness of the workers and soldiers the last hindering recollections of the July Days—to bring it about that having seen themselves the masses should say: Nothing and nobody can any longer oppose us.

"The frightened population," wrote Miliukov five years later, "remained at home or stood aside." It was the bourgeoisie that remained at home, and they really had been frightened by their own press. All the rest of the population thronged out to meetings from early morning to night—young and old, men and women, boys and girls, mothers with children in their arms. No meetings like this had been seen before throughout the revolution. All Petrograd, with the exception of its upper strata, was one solid meeting. In those auditoriums, continually packed to the doors, the audiences would be entirely renewed in the course of a few hours. Fresh and ever fresh waves of workers, soldiers and sailors would roll up to the buildings and flood them full. The petty bourgeoisie of the town bestirred themselves, too, aroused by these waves and by those warnings which were supposed to frighten them. Tens of thousands brimmed that immense building known as the House of the People. They filled all the theaters, filled the auditoriums of the theaters, their smoke-rooms, buffets, and foyers—filled them with a solid and excited and at the same time disciplined mass. From iron columns and upstairs windows human heads, legs and arms were hanging in garlands and clusters. There was that electric tension in the air which forbodes a coming discharge. Down with Kerensky! Down with the war! Power to the Soviets! None of the Compromisers any longer dared appear before these red hot crowds with arguments or warnings. The Bolsheviks had the floor. All the oratorical forces of the party, including delegates to the Congress who were beginning to arrive from the provinces, were brought into action. Occasionally Left Social Revolutionaries spoke—in some places anarchists—but they both tried as little as possible to distinguish themselves from Bolsheviks.

The people of the slums, of the attics and basements, stood still by the hour in threadbare coat or gray uniform, with caps or heavy shawls still on their heads, the mud of the streets soaked through their shoes, an autumn cough catching at their throat. They stood there packed shoulder to shoulder, and crowding ever closer to make room for more, to make room for all, listening tirelessly, hungrily, passionately, demandingly, fearing lest they miss a word of what it is so necessary to understand, to assimilate, and to do. It had seemed as though during the months past, the weeks —at least during the very last days—all the words had been spoken. But no! Today at least those words have a different sound. The masses are experiencing them in a new way, not as a gospel but as an obligation to act. The experience of the revolution, the war, the heavy struggle of a whole bitter lifetime, rose from the deeps of memory in each of those poverty-driven men and women, expressing itself in simple and imperious thoughts: This way we can go no farther, we must break a road into the future.

Everyone who took part in the events here described has subsequently turned his eyes back to that simple and wonderful day so clearly shining out against the background of the revolution—vivid enough even without that. The image of that inspired human flood—inspired, and yet in its unconquerable power restrained—is chiseled forever in the memory of those who saw it. "The day of the Petrograd Soviet," writes the Left Social Revolutionary, Mstislavsky, "was celebrated at innumerable meetings with enormous enthusiasm." The Bolshevik, Testkovsky, who spoke at two factories of the Vassilie-Ostrov district, says: "We spoke frankly to the masses of the coming seizure of power by us, and heard nothing but words of encouragement." "Around me," says Sukhanov, describing a meeting in the House of the People, "there was a mood very near to ecstasy . . . Trotsky had formulated some brief general resolution. . . . Those in favor . . . Thousands and thousands raised their hands as one man. I looked at the lifted hands and burning eyes of men, women, boys, workers, soldiers, peasants, and of typically petty bourgeois characters too. . . . Trotsky continued to speak. The multitude continued to hold their hands in the air. Trotsky chiseled out each word: Let this vote of yours be your oath. . . . The multitude held their hands high. They agreed. They took the oath." The Bolshevik Popov tells of a rapturous oath sworn by the masses: "To rush out at the first word from the Soviet." Mstislavsky tells of an electrified crowd taking an oath of loyalty to the soviets. The same scene was to be observed on a smaller scale in all parts of the city from center to suburbs. Hundreds of thousands of people, at one and the same hour, lifted their hands and took a vow to carry the struggle through to the end. The daily meetings of the Soviet, the soldiers' section, the Garrison Conference, the factory and shop committees, had given inner solidarity to a big group of leaders; separate mass meetings had united the factories and regiments; but that day, the 22nd of October, welded in one gigantic caldron and under high temperature the authentic popular masses. The masses saw themselves and their leaders; the leaders saw and listened to the masses. Each side was satisfied with the other. The leaders were convinced: We can postpone no longer! The masses said to themselves: This time the thing will be done!

The success of this Sunday's review of forces by the Bolsheviks shattered the self-confidence of Polkovnikov and his high command. By agreement with the government and the Central Executive Committee, headquarters made an attempt to come to terms with Smolny. Why not after all re-establish the good old friendly customs of contact and compromise? The Military Revolutionary Committee did not refuse to send emissaries for an exchange of opinion: A better opportunity for reconnoitering could hardly be wished. "The negotiations were brief," remembers Sadovsky. "The representatives of headquarters agreed in advance to all the conditions put forth by the Soviet . . . in exchange for which the order of the Military Revolutionary Committee for October 22 was to be annulled." This referred to the document declaring headquarters an instrument of the counter-revolutionary forces. The very same emissaries whom Polkovnikov had so discourteously sent home two days ago now demanded, and received in their hands for the purposes of their report to Smolny, the rough draft of an agreement signed by headquarters. On Saturday these conditions of semi-honorable capitulation would have been accepted. Today, on Monday, they were already too late. Headquarters awaited an answer which never came.

The Military Revolutionary Committee addressed to the population of Petrograd a proclamation explaining the appointment of commissars in the military units and the most important points of the capital and its environs. "The commissars as representatives of the Soviet are inviolable. Opposition to the commissars is opposition to the Soviet of Workers' and Soldiers' Deputies." The citizens were invited in case of disturbances to appeal to the nearest commissar to call out armed forces. That was the language of sovereignty. But still the Committee did not give the signal for open insurrection. Sukhanov asks: "Is Smolny acting stupidly, or is it playing with the Winter Palace like a cat with a mouse, trying to provoke an attack?" Neither the one nor the other. The Committee is crowding out the government with the pressure of the masses, with the weight of the garrison. It is taking all that it can without a battle. It is advancing its positions without firing, integrating and reinforcing its army on the march. It is measuring with its own pressure the resisting power of the enemy, not taking its eyes off him for a second. Each new step forward changes the disposition of forces to the advantage of Smolny. The workers and the garrison are growing up to the insurrection. Who is to be first to issue the call to arms, will become known in the course of this offensive, this crowding out. It is now only a question of hours. If at the last moment the government finds the courage, or the despair, to give the signal for battle, responsibility for this will lie upon the Winter Palace. But the initiative just the same will have been taken by Smolny. Its declaration of October 23 had meant the overthrow of the power before the government itself was overthrown. The Military Revolutionary

Committee was tying up the arms and legs of the enemy régime before striking him on the head. It was possible to apply this tactic of "peaceful penetration," to break the bones of the enemy legally and hypnotically paralyze the remnants of his will, only because of the indubitable superiority of forces on the side of the Committee and because they were increasing hour by hour.

The Committee had been studying from day to day the map of the garrison wide open before it. It knew the temperature of each regiment, and followed every shift in the views and sympathies of the barracks. A surprise from that side was impossible. There remained, however, some dark shadows on the map. An attempt must be made to eradicate, or at least decrease, them. It had become clear on the 19th that the majority of the committees of the Peter and Paul Fortress were unfavorably, or at least dubiously, disposed. Now when the whole garrison is for the Committee and the fortress is caught in a ring, at least politically, it is time to take decisive measures for its conquest. Corporal Blagonravov, the commissar appointed to the fortress, had met resistance. The governmental commandant of the fortress had refused to recognize this Bolshevik guardianship; there were even rumors of his boasting that he would arrest the young guardian. It was necessary to do something and do it quick. Antonov offered to take a reliable battalion of the Pavlovsky regiment into the fortress and disarm the hostile units. But that was a too drastic operation, one which might be used by the officers to cause bloodshed and break the unity of the garrison. Was it really necessary to adopt such extreme measures? Says Antonov in his memoirs: "Trotsky was called in to consider this question . . . Trotsky was then playing the decisive rôle. The advice he gave us was a product of his revolutionary intuition: that we capture the fortress from within. 'It cannot be that the troops there are not sympathetic,' he said. And he was right. Trotsky and Lashevich went to a meeting in the fortress." The results of this enterprise, which seemed risky, were awaited in Smolny with the greatest excitement. Trotsky subsequently wrote: "On the 23rd I went to the fortress at about two o'clock in the afternoon. A meeting was in progress in the court. The orators of the Right Wing were in the highest degree cautious and evasive. . . .

119

The soldiers listened to us and they came with us." On the third floor of Smolny they drew a deep breath when the telephone brought this joyful news: The garrison of Peter and Paul has solemnly promised to take orders henceforth only from the Military Revolutionary Committee.

That change in the mood of the fortress troops was not of course the result of one or two speeches. It had been well prepared in the past. The soldiers turned out to be far to the left of their committees. It was only the cracked shell of the old discipline that held out a little longer behind the fortress walls than in the city barracks. One tap was enough to shatter it.

Blagonravov could now confidently establish himself in the fortress, organize his little headquarters, and set up communications with the Bolshevik soviet of the adjoining district and the committees of the nearest barracks. Meanwhile delegations from the factories and military units were coming up to see what they could do about getting weapons. An indescribable liveliness now prevailed in the fortress. "The telephone rang continually bringing news of our new successes at assemblies and mass meetings." Occasionally an unfamiliar voice would announce the arrival at some railroad station of punitive detachments from the front. Immediate investigation would reveal that this was an invention put in circulation by the enemy.

That day the evening session of the Soviet was distinguished by the exceptional number present and the exalted mood. The occupation of Peter and Paul and the conquest of the Kronversky arsenal containing 100,000 rifles—this was no small guarantee of success. The spokesman for the Military Revolutionary Committee was Antonov. He drew a picture of the crowding out of the governmental organs step by step by the agents of the Military Revolutionary Committee. These agents, he said, are being received everywhere as natural authorities; they are obeyed not through fear but through principle. "From all sides come demands for the appointment of commissars." The backward units are hurrying to catch up to the advanced. The Preobrazhensky, which in July had been the first to fall for the slander about German gold, had now issued through its commissar Chudnovsky a violent protest against the rumor that the Preobrazhentsi are for the government. The very idea is regarded as a malicious insult! . . . To be sure, the customary patrol duties are still being carried out, relates Antonov, but this is done with the consent of the Committee. Orders of headquarters for the delivery of weapons and automobiles are not being carried out. Headquarters thus had ample opportunity to find out who is the master of the capital.

To a question: "Does the committee know about the movement of government troops from the front and the surrounding districts, and what measures have been taken against this?" the spokesman answered: "Cavalry units were sent from the Rumanian front, but they have been held up at Pskov; the 17th Infantry Division, finding out on the road where and why they had been sent, refused to go; in Venden two regiments successfully resisted the attempt to send them against Petrograd; we have as yet no news about the Cossacks and junkers supposed to have been sent from Kiev, or the shock troops summoned from Tzarskoe-Selo. They do not dare, and they will not dare, lay hands on the Military Revolutionary Committee." Those words sounded pretty good in the white hall of Smolny. As Antonov read his report, one had the impression that the headquarters of the insurrection was working with wide open doors. As a matter of fact Smolny had almost nothing to hide. The political set-up of the revolution was so favorable that frankness itself became a kind of camouflage: Surely this isn't the way they make an insurrection? That word "insurrection," however, was not spoken by any one of the leaders. This was not wholly a formal measure of caution, for the term did not fit the actual situation. It was being left to the government of Kerensky, as you might say, to insurrect. In the account in *Izvestia* it does say that Trotsky at the session of the 23rd first acknowledged that the aim of the Military Revolutionary Committee was a seizure of power. It is unquestionably true that the original attitude, when the task of the Committee had been declared to be a testing out of the strategic arguments of Cheremissov, had long been abandoned. The transfer of the regiments was indeed all but forgotten. But on the 23rd the talk was still not about insurrection, but about the "defense" of the coming Congress of Soviets—with armed forces if necessary. It was still in this spirit that the resolution was adopted on the report of Antonov.

How were these events estimated in the governmental upper circles? On the night of the 22nd, in communicating to the chief of the headquarters staff, Dukhonin, the news of the attempt of the Military Revolutionary Committee to get the regiments away from the command, Kerensky added: "I think we can easily handle this." His own departure for headquarters was delayed, he said, not at all through fear of any sort of an insurrection: "That matter could be regulated without me, since everything is organized." To his anxious ministers Kerensky reassuringly declared that he personally, unlike them, was very glad of the coming attack since it would give him the opportunity to "settle once for all with the Bolsheviks." "I would be ready to offer a prayer," says the head of the government to the Kadet Nabokov, a frequent guest at the Winter Palace, "that such an attack may occur." "But are you sure that you will be able to handle them?" "I have more forces than I need. They will be stamped out for good."

In their subsequent ridicule of this optimistic light-mindedness of Kerensky, the Kadets have evidently been a little forgetful. In reality Kerensky was looking at those events through their own eyes. On the 21st, Miliukov's paper wrote that if the Bolsheviks, corroded as they are with a profound inner crisis, dare to come out, they will be put down instantly and without difficulty. Another Kadet paper added: "A storm is coming, but it will perhaps clear the air." Dan testifies that in the couloirs of the Pre-Parliament the Kadets and those grouped around them were talking aloud of their wish that the Bolsheviks might come out as soon as possible: "In an open battle they will be beaten to the last man." Prominent Kadets said to John Reed: After being defeated in an insurrection, the Bolsheviks won't dare lift their heads at the Constituent Assembly.

During the 22nd and 23rd Kerensky took counsel, now with the leaders of the Central Executive Committee, now with headquarters: Would it not be advisable to arrest the Military Revolutionary Committee? The Compromisers did not advise it: they themselves would try to regulate the question about commissars.

Polkovnikov also thought it would hardly be worth while to hasten with the arrests: the military forces in case of need are "more than adequate." Kerensky listened to Polkovnikov, but still more to his friends, the Compromisers. He was confidently calculating that in case of danger the Central Executive Committee, in spite of all family misunderstandings, would come to his aid in time. It was so in July and in August. Why should it not continue so?

But now it is no longer July and no longer August. It is October. Cold and raw Baltic winds from the direction of Kronstadt are blowing through the squares and along the quays of Petrograd. Junkers in long coats to their heels are patrolling the streets, drowning their anxiety in songs of triumph. The mounted police are riding up and down, prancing, their revolvers in brand-new holsters. No. The power still looks imposing enough! Or is this perhaps an optical illusion? At a corner of the Nevsky, John Reed, an American with naïve and intelligent eyes in his head, buys a brochure of Lenin's entitled "Will the Bolsheviks Be Able To Hold the State Power?", paying for it with one of those postage stamps which are now circulating in place of money.

Chapter V

LENIN SUMMONS TO INSURRECTION

BESIDES the factories, barracks, villages, the front and the soviets, the revolution had another laboratory: the brain of Lenin. Driven underground, Lenin was obliged for a hundred and eleven days—from July 6 to October 25—to cut down his meetings even with members of the Central Committee. Without any immediate intercourse with the masses, and deprived of contacts with any organizations, he concentrated his thought the more resolutely upon the fundamental problems of the revolution, reducing them—as was both his rule and the necessity of his nature—to the key problems of Marxism.

The chief argument of the democrats, even the most leftward, against seizing the power, was that the toilers were incapable of mastering the machinery of state. Opportunist elements even within the Bolshevik party cherished the same fears. "The machinery of state!" Every petty bourgeois is brought up in adoration of this mystic principle elevated above people and above classes. And the educated philistine carries in his marrow the same awe that his father did, or his uncle, the shopkeeper or well-off peasant, before these all-powerful institutions where questions of war and peace are decided, where commercial patents are given out, whence issue the whips of the taxes, where they punish and once in a while also pardon, where they legitimize marriages and births, where death itself has to stand in line respectfully awaiting recognition. The machinery of state! Removing in imagination not only his hat but his shoes too, the petty bourgeois comes tip-toeing into the temple of the idol on stocking feet—it matters not what his name is, Kerensky, Laval, MacDonald or Hilferding—that is the way he comes when personal good-luck or the force of circumstances makes him a minister. Such gracious condescension he can answer only with a humble submission before the "machinery of state." The Russian radical

124

intelligentsia, who had never dared crawl into the seats of power even during the revolution except behind the backs of titled landlords and big business men, gazed with fright and indignation upon the Bolsheviks. Those street agitators, those demagogues, think that they can master the machinery of state!

After the Soviet, confronted by the spineless impotence of the official democracy, had saved the revolution in the struggle against Kornilov, Lenin wrote: "Let those of little faith learn from this example. Shame on those who say, 'We have no machine with which to replace that old one which gravitates inexorably to the defense of the bourgeoisie.' For we have a machine. And that is the soviets. Do not fear the initiative and independence of the masses. Trust the revolutionary organizations of the masses, and you will see in all spheres of the state life that same power, majesty and inconquerable will of the workers and peasants, which they have shown in their solidarity and enthusiasm against Kornilovism."

During the first months of his underground life Lenin wrote a book *The State and Revolution*, the principal material for which he had collected abroad during the war. With the same painstaking care which he dedicated to thinking out the practical problems of the day, he here examines the theoretic problems of the state. He cannot do otherwise: for him theory is in actual fact a guide to action. In this work Lenin has not for a minute proposed to introduce any new word into political theory. On the contrary, he gives his work an extraordinarily modest aspect, emphasizing his position as a disciple. His task, he says, is to revive the genuine "teaching of Marxism about the state."

With its meticulous selection of quotations, its detailed polemical interpretations, the book might seem pedantic—to actual pedants, incapable of feeling under the analysis of texts the mighty pulsation of the mind and will. By a mere re-establishment of the class theory of the state on a new and higher historical foundation, Lenin gives to the ideas of Marx a new concreteness and therewith a new significance. But this work on the state derives its immeasurable importance above all from the fact that it constituted the scientific introduction to the greatest revolution in history. This "commentator" of Marx was preparing his party for the revolutionary conquest of a sixth part of the habitable surface of the earth.

If the state could simply re-accommodate itself to the demands of a new historic régime, revolutions would never have arisen. As a fact, however, the bourgeoisie itself has never yet come to power except by way of revolution. Now it is the workers' turn. Upon this question, too, Lenin restored to Marxism its significance as the theoretic weapon of the proletarian revolution.

You say the workers cannot master the machinery of state? But it is not a question—Lenin teaches—of getting possession of the old machine and using it for new aims: that is a reactionary utopia. The selection of personages in the old machine, their education, their mutual relations, are all in conflict with the historic task of the proletariat. After seizing the power our task is not to re-educate the old machine, but to shatter it to fragments. And with what replace it? With the soviets. From being leaders of the revolutionary masses, instruments of education, the soviets will become organs of the new state order.

In the whirlpool of the revolution this work will find few readers; it will be published, indeed, only after the seizure of power. Lenin is working over the problem of the state primarily for the sake of his own inner confidence and for the future. One of his continual concerns was to preserve the succession of ideas. In July he writes to Kamenev: "*Entre nous*. If they bump me off, I ask you to publish my little note-book *Marxism on the State* (stranded in Stockholm). Bound in a blue cover. All the quotations are collected from Marx and Engels, likewise from Kautsky against Pannekoek. There is a whole series of notes and comments. Formulate it. I think you could publish it with a week's work. I think it important, for it is not only Plekhanov and Kautsky who got off the track. My conditions: all this to be absolutely *entre nous*." The revolutionary leader, persecuted as the agent of a hostile state and figuring on the possibility of attempted assassination by his enemies, concerns himself with the publication of a "blue" note-book with quotations from Marx and Engels. That was to be his secret last will and testament. The phrase "bump me off" [1] was to serve as an antidote against that pathos

---

[1] Ukokoshit.

126

which he hated, for the commission is pathetic in its very essence.

But while awaiting this blow in the back, Lenin himself was getting ready to deliver a frontal blow. While he was putting in order, between reading the papers and writing letters of instruction, his precious note-book—procured at last from Stockholm—life did not stand still. The hour was approaching when the question of the state was to be decided in practical action.

While still in Switzerland immediately after the overthrow of the monarchy Lenin wrote: "We are not Blanquists, not advocates of the seizure of power by a minority. . . ." This same thought he developed on his arrival in Russia: "We are now in a minority—the masses do not trust us yet. We know how to wait. . . . They will swing to our side, and after explaining the correlation of forces we will then say to them: Our day is come." The question of the conquest of power was presented during those first months as a question of winning a majority in the soviets.

After the July raids Lenin declared: "The power can be seized henceforth only by an armed insurrection; we must obviously rely in this operation not upon the soviets, demoralized by the Compromisers, but on the factory committees; the soviets as organs of power will have to be created anew after the victory." As a matter of fact, only two months after that the Bolsheviks had won over the soviets from the Compromisers. The nature of Lenin's mistake on this question is highly characteristic of his strategic genius: for the boldest designs he based his calculations upon the least favorable premises. Thus in coming to Russia through Germany in April he counted on going straight to prison from the station. Thus on July 5 he was saying: "They will probably shoot us all." And thus now he was figuring: the Compromisers will not let us get a majority in the soviets.

"There is no man more faint-hearted than I am, when I am working out a military plan," wrote Napoleon to General Berthier. "I exaggerate all dangers and all possible misfortunes. . . . When my decision is taken everything is forgotten except what can assure its success." Except for the pose involved in the inappropriate word faint-hearted, the essence of this thought applies perfectly to Lenin. In deciding a problem of strategy he began by clothing the enemy with his own resolution and far-sightedness. The tactical mistakes of Lenin were for the most part by-products of his strategic power. In the present instance, indeed, it is hardly appropriate to use the word mistake. When a diagnostician arrives at the definition of a disease by a method of successive eliminations, his hypothetical assumptions, beginning with the worst possible, are not mistakes but methods of analysis. As soon as the Bolsheviks had got control of the soviets of the two capitals, Lenin said: "Our day is come." In April and July he had applied the brakes; in August he was preparing theoretically the new step; from the middle of September he was hurrying and urging on with all his power. The danger now lay not in acting too soon, but in lagging. "In this matter it is now impossible to be premature."

In his articles and letters addressed to the Central Committee, Lenin analyzes the situation, always emphasizing first of all the international conditions. The symptoms and the facts of an awakening European proletariat are for him, on the background of the war, irrefutable proof that the direct threat against the Russian revolution from the side of foreign imperialism will steadily diminish. The arrest of the socialists in Italy, and still more the insurrections in the German fleet, made him announce a supreme change in the whole world situation: "We stand in the vestibule of the world-wide proletarian revolution."

The epigone historians have preferred to hush up this starting point of Lenin's thought—both because Lenin's calculation has been refuted by events, and because according to the most recent theories the Russian Revolution ought to be sufficient unto itself in all circumstances. As a matter of fact Lenin's appraisal of the international situation was anything but illusory. The symptoms which he observed through the screen of the military censorship of all countries did actually portend the approach of a revolutionary storm. Within a year it shook the old building of the Central Empires to its very foundation. But also in the victor countries, England and France—to say nothing of Italy—it long deprived the ruling classes of their freedom of action. Against a strong, conservative, self-confident capitalistic Europe, the proletarian revolution in Russia, isolated and not yet fortified, could not have held out even for a few months. But that Europe no longer existed. The revolution in the west did not, to be sure, put the proletariat into power—the reformists succeeded in saving the bourgeois régime—but nevertheless it proved powerful enough to defend the Soviet Republic in the first and most dangerous period of its life.

Lenin's deep internationalism was not expressed solely in the fact that he always gave first place to his appraisal of the international situation. He regarded the very conquest of power in Russia primarily as the impetus for a European revolution, a thing which, as he often repeated, was to have incomparably more importance for the fate of humanity than the revolution in backward Russia. With what sarcasm he lashed those Bolsheviks who did not understand their international duty. "Let us adopt a resolution of sympathy for the German insurrectionists," he mocks, "and reject the insurrection in Russia. That will be a genuinely reasonable internationalism!"

In the days of the Democratic Conference, Lenin wrote to the Central Committee: "Having got a majority in the soviets of both capitals . . . the Bolsheviks can and should seize the state power in their hands. . . ." The fact that a majority of the peasant delegates of the stacked Democratic Conference voted against a coalition with the Kadets, had for him decisive significance: The muzhik who does not want a union with the bourgeoisie has nothing left but to support the Bolsheviks. "The people are tired of the wavering of the Mensheviks and Social Revolutionaries. Only our victory in the capitals will bring the peasants over to us." The task of the party is: "To place upon the order of the day armed insurrection in Petersburg and Moscow, conquest of power, overthrow of the government. . . ." Up to that time nobody had so imperiously and nakedly set the task of insurrection.

Lenin very studiously followed all the elections and votings in the country, carefully assembling those figures which would throw light on the actual correlation of forces. The semi-anarchistic indifference to electoral statistics got nothing but contempt from him. At the same time Lenin never identified the indexes of parliamentarism with the actual correlation of forces. He always introduced a correction in favor of direct action. "The strength of a revolutionary proletariat," he explained, "from the point of view of its action upon the masses and drawing them into the struggle, is infinitely greater in an extra-parliamentary than a parliamentary struggle. This is a very important observation when it comes to the question of civil war."

Lenin with his sharp eye was the first to notice that the agrarian movement had gone into a decisive phase, and he immediately drew all the conclusions from this. The muzhik, like the soldier, will wait no longer. "In the face of such a fact as the peasant insurrection," writes Lenin at the end of September, "all other political symptoms, even if they were in conflict with this ripening of an all-national crisis, would have absolutely no significance at all." The agrarian question is the foundation of the revolution. A victory of the government over the peasant revolt would be the "funeral of the revolution. . . ." We cannot hope for more favorable conditions. The hour of action is at hand. "The crisis is ripe. The whole future of the international workers' revolution for socialism is at stake. The crisis is ripe."

Lenin summons to insurrection. In each simple, prosaic, sometimes angular line, you feel the highest tensity of passion. "The revolution is done for," he writes early in October to the Petrograd party conference, "if the government of Kerensky is not overthrown by proletarians and soldiers in the near future. . . . We must mobilize all forces in order to impress upon the workers and soldiers the unconditional necessity of a desperate, last, resolute struggle to overthrow the government of Kerensky."

Lenin had said more than once that the masses are to the left of the party. He knew that the party was to the left of its own upper layer of "old Bolsheviks." He was too well acquainted with the inner groupings and moods in the Central Committee to expect from it any hazardous steps whatever. On the other hand he greatly feared excessive caution, Fabianism, a letting slip of one of those historic situations which are decades in preparation. Lenin did not trust the Central Committee—without Lenin. In that lies the key to his letters from underground. And Lenin was not so wrong in his mistrust.

Being compelled in a majority of cases to express himself after a decision had already been reached in Petrograd, Lenin was continually criticizing the policy of the Central Committee from the left. His opposition developed with the question of insurrection as a background. But it was not limited to that. Lenin thought that the Central Committee was giving too much attention to the compromisist Executive Committee, the Democratic Conference, parliamentary doings in the upper soviet circles in general. He sharply opposed the proposal of the Bolsheviks for a coalition præsidium in the Petrograd Soviet. He branded as "shameful" the decision to participate in the Pre-Parliament. He was indignant at the list of Bolshevik candidates for the Constituent Assembly published at the end of September. Too many intellectuals, not enough workers. "To jam up the Constituent Assembly with orators and litterateurs will mean to travel the worn-out road of opportunism and chauvinism. This is unworthy of the Third International." Moreover there are too many new names among the candidates, members of the party not tried out in the struggle! Here Lenin considers it necessary to make an exception: "It goes without saying that . . . nobody would quarrel with such a candidacy for example as that of L. D. Trotsky, for in the first place Trotsky took an internationalist position immediately upon his arrival; in the second place, he fought for amalgamation among the Mezhrayontsi; in the third place, in the difficult July Days he stood at the height of the task and proved a devoted champion of the party of the revolutionary proletariat. It is clear that this cannot be said of a majority of the yesterday's party members who have been introduced into this list. . . ."

It might seem as though the April Days had returned—Lenin again in opposition to the Central Committee. The questions stand differently, but the general spirit of his opposition is the same: the Central Committee is too passive, too responsive to social opinion among the intellectual circles, too compromisist in its attitude to the Compromisers. And above all, too indifferent, fatalistic, not attacking à la Bolshevik the problem of the armed insurrection.

It is time to pass from words to deeds: "Our party has now at the Democratic Conference practically its own congress, and this congress has got to decide (whether it wants to or not) the fate of the revolution." Only one decision is thinkable: Armed overthrow. In this first letter on insurrection Lenin makes another exception: "It is not a question of 'the day' of the insurrection, nor 'the moment' in a narrow sense. This can be decided only by the general voice of those who are in contact with the workers and soldiers, with the masses." But only two or three days later (letters in those days were commonly not dated—for conspirative reasons, not through forgetfulness) Lenin, obviously impressed by the decomposition of the Democratic Conference, insists upon immediate action and forthwith advances a practical plan.

"We ought at once to solidify the Bolshevik faction at the Conference, not striving after numbers. . . . We ought to draw up a short declaration of the Bolsheviks. . . . We ought to move our whole faction to the factories and barracks. At the same time without losing a minute we ought to organize a staff of insurrectionary detachments, deploy our forces, move the loyal regiments into the most important positions, surround the Alexandrinka (the theater where the Democratic Conference was sitting), occupy Peter and Paul, arrest the General Staff and the government, send against the junkers and the Savage Division those detachments which are ready to die fighting, but not let the enemy advance to the center of the city; we ought to mobilize the armed workers, summon them to a desperate, final battle, occupy the telegraph and telephone stations at once, install our insurrectionary staff at the central telephone station, placing in contact with it by telephone all the factories, all the regiments, all the chief points of armed struggle, etc." The question of date is no longer placed in dependence upon the "general voice of those who are in contact with the masses." Lenin proposed an immediate act: To leave the Alexandrinsky theater with an ultimatum and return there at the head of the armed masses. A crushing blow is to be struck not only against the government, but also, simultaneously, against the highest organ of the Compromisers.

"Lenin who in private letters was demanding the arrest of the Democratic Conference,"—such is the accusation of Sukhanov —"in the press, as we know, proposed a 'compromise': Let the Mensheviks and Social Revolutionaries take over the whole power and then see what the Soviet Congress says. . . . The same idea was insistently defended by Trotsky at the Democratic Conference and around it." Sukhanov sees a double game where there was not the slightest hint of it. Lenin proposed an agreement to the Compromisers immediately after the victory over Kornilov—during the first days of September. The Compromisers passed it up with a shrug of their shoulders. They were engaged in converting the Democratic Conference into a screen for a new coalition with the Kadets against the Bolsheviks. With that the possibility of an agreement fell away absolutely. The question of power could henceforth be decided only in open struggle. Sukhanov mixes up two stages, one of which preceded the other by two weeks and politically conditioned it.

But although the insurrection flowed inexorably from the new coalition, nevertheless the sharpness of Lenin's change of front took even the heads of his own party by surprise. To unite the Bolshevik faction at the Conference on the basis of his letter, even without "striving after numbers" was clearly impossible. The mood of the faction was such that it rejected by seventy votes against fifty the proposal to boycott the Pre-Parliament—the first step, that is, on the road to insurrection. In the Central Committee itself Lenin's plan found no support whatever. Four years later at an evening of reminiscences, Bukharin with characteristic exaggerations and witticisms, gave a true account of that episode. "The letter (of Lenin) was written with extraordinary force and threatened us with all sorts of punishments. We all gasped. Nobody had yet posed the question so abruptly. . . . At first all were bewildered. Afterwards, having talked it over, we made a decision. Perhaps that was the sole case in the history of our party when the Central Committee unanimously decided to burn a letter of Lenin. . . . Although we believed unconditionally that in Petersburg and Moscow we should succeed in seizing the power, we assumed that in the provinces we could not yet hold out, that having seized the power and dispersed the Democratic Conference we could not fortify ourselves in the rest of Russia."

The burning of several copies of this dangerous letter, owing to conspirative considerations, was as a matter of fact not unanimously resolved upon, but by six votes against four with six abstaining. One copy, luckily for history, was preserved. But it is true, as Bukharin relates, that all the members of the Central Committee, although for different motives, rejected the proposal. Some opposed an insurrection in general; others thought that the moment of the conference was the least advantageous of all; others simply vacillated and adopted a waiting attitude.

Having run into this direct resistance, Lenin entered into a sort of conspiracy with Smilga, who was also in Finland and as President of the Regional Committee of the Soviets held a tolerable amount of real power in his hands. Smilga stood in 1917 on the extreme left wing of the party and already in July had been inclined to carry the struggle through to the end. At turning points in his policy Lenin always found somebody to rely on. On September 27 Lenin wrote Smilga a voluminous letter: ". . . What are we doing? Only passing resolutions? We are losing time, we are setting 'dates' (October 20—Congress of Soviets—Isn't it ridiculous to postpone this way? Isn't it ridiculous to rely on that?). The Bolsheviks are not carrying on a systematic work of preparing their armed forces for the overthrow of Kerensky. . . . We must agitate in the party for a serious attitude toward armed insurrection. . . . And further, as to your rôle . . . : To create a secret committee of the most loyal military men, talk the thing over on all sides with them, collect (and yourself verify) the most accurate information about the make-up and position of the troops in and around Petrograd, about the transportation of Finland troops to Petrograd, about the movements of the fleet, etc." Lenin demanded "a systematic propaganda among the Cossacks located here in Finland. . . . We must study all information about the attitude of the Cossacks and organize a sending of agitatorial detachments from our best forces of sailors and soldiers of Finland." And finally: "For a correct preparation of minds we must immediately put into circulation a slogan of this kind: The power must immediately pass to the Petrograd Soviet which will hand it over to the Congress of Soviets. For why endure three more weeks of war and of Kornilovist preparations by Kerensky?"

In this letter we have a new plan of insurrection: A secret committee of the more important military men in Helsingfors as a fighting staff, the Russian troops quartered in Finland as fighting forces. "It seems that the only ones we can fully control and who will play a serious military rôle are the Finland troops and the Baltic Fleet." Thus we see that Lenin counted on dealing the chief blow against the government from outside Petrograd. At the same time a "correct preparation of minds" is necessary, so that an overthrow of the government by military forces from Finland shall not fall unexpectedly upon the Petrograd Soviet, which until the Congress of Soviets was to be the inheritor of power.

This new draft of a plan, like the preceding one, was not realized. But it did not go by without effect. The agitation among the Cossack divisions soon gave results: we have heard about this from Dybenko. The participation of Baltic sailors in the chief blow against the government also entered into the plan later adopted. But that was not the chief thing: With his extremely sharp posing of the question Lenin permitted nobody to evade or maneuver. What seemed untimely as a direct tactical proposal became expedient as a test of attitudes in the Central Committee, a support to the resolute against the wavering, a supplementary push to the left.

With all the means at his disposal in his underground isolation Lenin was trying to make the cadres of the party feel the acuteness of the situation and the strength of the mass pressure. He summoned individual Bolsheviks to his hiding-place, put them through partisan cross questionings, tested out the words and deeds of the leaders, used indirect ways to get his slogans into the party—deep down in it—in order to compel the Central Committee to act in the face of necessity and carry the thing through.

A day after his letter to Smilga Lenin wrote the above quoted document *The Crisis is Ripe*, concluding it with something in the nature of a declaration of war against the Central Committee. "We must . . . acknowledge the truth that there is in the Central Committee and the upper circles of the party a tendency or an opinion in favor of waiting for the Congress of Soviets, against the immediate seizure of power, against immediate insurrection." This tendency we must overcome at any cost. "Conquer Kerensky first and then summon the Congress." To lose time waiting for the Congress of Soviets is "complete idiotism or else complete treachery. . . ." There remain more than twelve days until the Congress designated for the 20th: "Weeks and even days are now deciding everything." To postpone the show-down means a cowardly renunciation of insurrection, since during the Congress a seizure of power will become impossible: "They will get together the Cossacks for the day of that stupidly 'appointed' insurrection."

The mere tone of the letter shows how ruinous the Fabianism of the Petrograd leadership seemed to Lenin. But this time he is not satisfied with furious criticism; by way of protest he resigns from the Central Committee. He gives his reasons: the Central Committee has made no response since the beginning of the Conference to his insistence in regard to the seizure of power; the editorial board of the party organ (Stalin) is printing his articles with intentional delays, omitting from them his indication of such "flagrant mistakes of the Bolsheviks as their shameful decision to participate in the Pre-Parliament," etc. This procedure Lenin does not consider it possible to conceal from the party: "I am compelled to request permission to withdraw from the Central Committee, which I hereby do, and leave myself freedom of agitation in the lower ranks of the party and at the party congress."

The documents do not show what further formal action was taken in this matter. Lenin in any case did not withdraw from the Central Committee. By announcing his resignation, an act which could not possibly be with him the fruit of momentary irritation, Lenin obviously wanted to make it possible to free himself in case of need from the internal discipline of the Central Committee. He could be quite sure that as in April a direct appeal to the lower ranks would assure him the victory. But the road of open mutiny against the Central Committee required the preparation of a special session; it required time; and time was just what was lacking. Keeping this announcement of his resignation in reserve, but not withdrawing completely beyond the limits of party legality, Lenin now continued with greater freedom to develop his offensive along internal lines. His letter to the Central Committee he not only sent to the Petrograd and Moscow committees, but he also saw to it that copies fell into the hands of the more reliable party workers of the district locals. Early in October—and now over the heads of the Central Committee—Lenin wrote directly to the Petrograd and the Moscow committees: "The Bolsheviks have no right to await the Congress of Soviets. They ought to seize the power *right now*. . . . Delay is a crime. Waiting for the Congress of Soviets is a childish toying with formalities, a shameful toying with formalities, betrayal of the revolution." From the standpoint of hierarchical attitudes towards action, Lenin was by no means beyond reproach, but the question here was of something bigger than considerations of formal discipline.

One of the members of the Vyborg District Committee, Sveshnikov, remembers: "Ilych from underground was writing and writing untiringly, and Nadyezhda Constantinovna (Krupskaia) often read these manuscripts to us in the district committee. . . . The burning words of the leader would redouble our strength. . . . I remember as though it were yesterday the bending figure of Nadyezhda Constantinovna in one of the rooms of the district administration, where the typists were working, carefully comparing the copy with the original, and right alongside stood Uncle and Gene demanding a copy each." "Uncle" and "Gene" were old conspirative pseudonyms for two leaders of the district. "Not long ago," relates the district worker, Naumov, "we got a letter from Ilych for delivery to the Central Committee. . . . We read the letter and gasped. It seems that Lenin had long ago put before the Central Committee the question of insurrection. We raised a row. We began to bring pressure on them." It was just this that was needed.

In the first days of October Lenin appealed to a Petrograd party conference to speak a firm word in favor of insurrection. Upon his initiative the conference "insistently requests the Central Committee to take all measures for the leadership of the inevitable insurrection of the workers, soldiers and peasants." In this phrase alone there are two kinds of camouflage, juridical and diplomatic: It speaks of the leadership of an "inevitable insurrection" instead of the direct preparation of insurrection, in order not to place trump cards in the hands of the district attorney; and it "requests the Central Committee"—it does not demand, and it does not protest—this in obvious deference to the prestige of the highest institution of the party. But in another resolution, also written by Lenin, the speech is more frank: "In the upper circles of the party a wavering is to be observed, a sort of dread of the struggle for power, an inclination to replace this struggle with resolutions, protests, and conferences." This is already almost a direct pitting of the party against the Central Committee. Lenin did not decide lightly upon such steps. But it was a question of the fate of the revolution, and all other considerations fell away.

On October 8, Lenin addressed the Bolshevik delegates of the forthcoming Northern Regional Congress: "We must not await the All-Russian Congress of Soviets which the Central Executive Committee is able to postpone even to November. We must not delay and let Kerensky bring in more Kornilov troops." That Regional Conference, at which Finland, the fleet and Reval were represented, should take the initiative in "an immediate move on Petrograd." The direct summons to immediate insurrection was this time addressed to the representatives of scores of soviets. The summons came from Lenin personally. There was no party decision; the higher institutions of the party had not yet expressed themselves.

It required a mighty confidence in the proletariat, in the party, but also a very serious mistrust of the Central Committee, in order over its head, upon his own personal responsibility, from underground, and by means of a few small sheets of note-paper minutely inscribed, to raise an agitation for an armed revolution, for an armed overthrow of the government. How could it happen that Lenin, whom we have seen at the beginning of April isolated among the leaders of his own party, found himself again solitary in the same group in September and early October? This cannot be understood if you believe the unintelligent legend which portrays the history of Bolshevism as an emanation of the pure revolutionary idea. In reality Bolshevism developed in a definite social milieu undergoing its heterogeneous influences and among them the influence of a petty bourgeois environment and of cultural backwardness. To each new situation the party adapted itself only by way of an inner crisis.

In order that the sharp pre-October struggle in the Bolshevik upper circles may come before us in a true light, it is necessary again to look back at those processes in the party of which we spoke in the first volume. This is the more necessary since exactly at this present time the faction of Stalin is making unheard of efforts, and that too on an international scale, to wipe out of historic memory every recollection of how the October revolution was in reality prepared and achieved.

In the years before the war the Bolsheviks had described themselves in the legal press as "consistent democrats." This pseudonym was not accidentally chosen. The slogans of revolutionary democracy, Bolshevism and Bolshevism alone carried through to its logical conclusion. But in its prognosis of the revolution it did not go beyond this. The war, however, inseparably binding up the bourgeois democrats with imperialism, proved conclusively that the program of "consistent democracy" could be no otherwise enacted than through a proletarian revolution. Every Bolshevik to whom the war did not make this clear was inevitably destined to be caught unaware by the revolution, and converted into a left fellow-traveler of the bourgeois democracy.

However, a careful study of the materials characterizing the party life during the war and the beginning of the revolution, notwithstanding the extreme and unprecedented scantiness of these materials—and then beginning with 1923 their increasing disingenuousness—reveals more clearly every day the immense intellectual backsliding of the upper stratum of the Bolsheviks during the war when the proper life of the party practically came to an end. The cause of this backsliding is twofold: isolation from the masses and isolation from those abroad—that is primarily from Lenin. The result was a drowning in isolation and provincialism.

Not one of the old Bolsheviks in Russia, left each to himself, formulated throughout the whole war one document which might be looked upon as even the tiniest beacon-light on the road from the Second International to the Third. "The problems of peace, the character of the coming revolution, the rôle of the party in a future Provisional Government, etc."—thus wrote one of the old members of the party, Antonov-Saratovsky, some years ago—"were conceived by us vaguely enough or did not enter into our field of reflection at all." Up to this time there has not been published one article, not one page of a diary, not one letter, in which Stalin, Molotov, or any other of the present leaders, formulated even indirectly, even very hastily, his views upon the perspectives of the war and the revolution. This does not mean, of course, that the "old Bolsheviks" wrote nothing on these questions during the years of the war, of the collapse of the social democracy and the preparation of the Russian revolution. These historic events too insistently demanded an answer; jail and exile, moreover, gave plenty of leisure for meditation and correspondence. But among all that was written on these themes, not one thing has turned up which might even with stretching be interpreted as an approach to the ideas of the October revolution. It is sufficient to remember that the Institute of Party History has been forbidden to print one line from the pen of Stalin during the years 1914–17, and has been compelled to hide carefully the most important documents of March 1917. In the official political biographies of a majority of the present ruling stratum, the years of the war present a vacant space. That is the unadorned truth.

One of the most recent young historians, Bayevsky, specially delegated to demonstrate how the upper circles of the party developed during the war in the direction of proletarian revolution, was unable, in spite of his manifest flexibility of scientific conscience, to squeeze out of the materials anything more than the following meagre statement: "It is impossible to follow the course of this process, but certain documents and memoirs indubitably prove that there were subterranean searchings of the party mind in the direction of the April theses of Lenin. . . ." As though it were a question of subterranean searchings, and not of scientific appraisals and political prognoses!

It was possible to arrive *a priori* at the ideas of the October revolution, not in Siberia, not in Moscow, not even in Petrograd, but only at the crossing of the roads of world history. The tasks of a belated bourgeois revolution had to be seen intercrossing with the perspectives of a world proletarian movement, before it could seem possible to advance a program of proletarian dictatorship for Russia. A higher point of observation was necessary—not a national but an international horizon—to say nothing of a more serious armament than was possessed by the so-called Russian "practicals" of the party.

In their eyes the overthrow of the monarchy was to open the era of a "free" republican Russia, in which they intended, following the example of the western countries, to begin a struggle for socialism. Three old Bolsheviks, Rykov, Skvortzov, and Vegman, "at the direction of the social democrats of the Narym district liberated by the revolution," sent a telegram in March from Tomsk: "We send a greeting to the resurrected *Pravda* which has so successfully prepared the revolutionary cadres for the conquest of political liberty. We express our profound confidence that it will succeed in uniting all around its banner for the further struggle in the name of the national revolution." A whole world-philosophy emerges from this collective telegram. It is separated by an abyss from the April theses of Lenin. The February revolution immediately converted the leading layer of the party, with Kamenev, Rykov and Stalin at their head, into democratic defensists—in motion, moreover, toward the right, in the direction of a rapprochement with the Mensheviks. The future historian of the party, Yaroslavsky, the future head of the Central Control Commission, Ordzhonikidze, and the future president of the Ukrainian Central Executive Committee, Petrovsky, published during March in Yakutsk, in close union with the Mensheviks, a paper called the *Social Democrat,* which stood on the borderland of patriotic reformism and liberalism. In recent years the issues of this publication have been carefully collected and destroyed.

The Petersburg *Pravda* tried at the beginning of the revolution to occupy an internationalist position—to be sure, a very contradictory one for it did not transcend the framework of bourgeois democracy. The authoritative Bolsheviks arriving from exile immediately imparted to the central organ a democratical-patriotic policy. Kalinin, in defending himself on the 30th of May against a charge of opportunism, recalled this fact: "Take *Pravda* for example. At the beginning *Pravda* had one policy. Came Stalin, Muranov, Kamenev, and turned the helm of *Pravda* to the other side."

141

"We must frankly acknowledge," wrote Angarsky, a member of this stratum, when it was still permissible to write such things, "that an enormous number of the old Bolsheviks held fast up to the April party conference to the old Bolshevik views of 1905 as to the character of the revolution of 1917, and that the renunciation of these views, the outgrowing of them, was not so easily accomplished." It would be well to add that those ideas of 1905, having outlived themselves, had ceased in 1917 to be "old Bolshevik views" and had become the ideas of patriotic reformism.

"The April theses of Lenin," says an official historic publication, "just simply had no luck in the Petrograd committee. Only two against thirteen voted for these theses, which created an epoch, and one abstained from the vote." "Lenin's argument seemed too bold even for his most rapturous followers," writes Podvoisky. Lenin's speeches—in the opinion of the Petrograd committee and the Military Organization—"isolated the party of the Bolsheviks, and thus, it goes without saying, damaged the position of the proletariat and the party in the extreme."

"We must say frankly," wrote Molotov some years ago: "The party lacked that clarity and resolution which the revolutionary moment demanded. . . . The agitation and the whole revolutionary party work in general had no firm foundation, since our thoughts had not yet arrived at bold conclusions in regard to the necessity of an immediate struggle for socialism and the socialist revolution." The break began only in the second month of the revolution. "From the time of Lenin's arrival in Russia in April 1917"—so testifies Molotov—"our party felt firm ground under its feet. . . . Up to that moment the party was only weakly and diffidently groping its way."

Stalin at the end of March had spoken in favor of military defense, of conditional support to the Provisional government and the pacifist manifesto of Sukhanov, and of merging with the party of Tseretelli. "This mistaken position," Stalin himself retrospectively acknowledged in 1924, "I then shared with other party comrades, and I renounced it fully only in the middle of April when I adhered to the theses of Lenin. A new orientation was necessary. Lenin gave the party that new orientation in his celebrated April theses."

Kalinin even at the end of April was still standing for a voting bloc with the Mensheviks. At the Petrograd city conference of the party Lenin said: "I am sharply opposed to Kalinin, because a bloc with . . . chauvinists is unthinkable. . . . That is treason to socialism." Kalinin's attitude was not exceptional even in Petrograd. It was said at the conference: "Under the influence of Lenin the amalgamation fumes are dissipating."

In the provinces the resistance to Lenin's theses lasted considerably longer—in a number of provinces almost to October. According to a Kiev worker, Sivtzov, "The ideas set forth in the theses (of Lenin) were not immediately accepted by the whole Kiev Bolshevik organization. A number of comrades, including G. Piatakov, disagreed with the theses . . ." A railroad worker of Kharkov, Morgunov, says: "The old Bolsheviks enjoyed a great influence among all the railroad workers. . . . Many of the old Bolsheviks remained outside of our faction. After the February revolution a number of them registered as Mensheviks by mistake, a thing at which they themselves afterwards laughed, wondering how it could have happened." There is no lack of this and similar testimony.

In spite of all this, the mere mention of a re-arming of the party carried out by Lenin in April, is regarded by the present official historians as blasphemy. These most recent historians have substituted for the historic criterion the criterion of honor to the party uniform. On this theme they are deprived of the right to quote even Stalin himself, who was obliged to acknowledge the great depth of the April change. "The famous April theses of Lenin were necessary," he wrote, "in order that the party should come out with one bold step on a new road." "A new orientation," "a new road"—that means the re-arming of the party. Six years later, however, Yaroslovsky, who ventured in his capacity of historian to recall the fact that Stalin had occupied at the beginning of the revolution "a mistaken position upon fundamental questions" was furiously denounced from all sides. The idol of prestige is the most gluttonous of all monsters!

143

The revolutionary tradition of the party, the pressure of the workers from below, and Lenin's criticism from above, compelled the upper stratum during the months of April and May —employing the words of Stalin—"to come out on a new road." But one would have to be completely ignorant of political psychology to imagine that a mere voting for the theses of Lenin meant an actual and complete renunciation of the "mistaken position on fundamental questions." In reality those crass democratic views, organically fortified during the war, merely accommodated themselves to the new program, remaining in silent opposition to it.

On the 6th of August Kamenev, contrary to the decision of the April conference of the Bolsheviks, spoke in the Executive Committee in favor of participating in the Stockholm conference of the Social Patriots then in preparation. Kamenev's speech met no opposition in the central organ of the party. Lenin wrote a formidable article, which appeared, however, only ten days after Kamenev's speech. The resolute insistence of Lenin himself and other members of the Central Committee was required to induce the editorial staff, headed by Stalin, to publish the protesting article.

A convulsion of doubt went through the party after the July days. The isolation of the proletarian vanguard frightened many leaders, especially in the provinces. During the Kornilov days these frightened ones tried to get in contact with the Compromisers, which again evoked a warning cry from Lenin.

On August 20 Stalin as editor of *Pravda* printed without dissenting comment an article of Zinoviev entitled "What Not to Do," an article directed against the preparation of an insurrection. "We must look the truth in the face: In Petrograd there are now many conditions favorable to the outbreak of an insurrection of the type of the Paris Commune of 1871. . . ." On September 3, Lenin—in another connection and without naming Zinoviev but striking him an indirect blow—wrote: "The reference to the Commune is very superficial and even stupid. For in the first place the Bolsheviks after all have learned something since 1871. They would not fail to seize the banks, they would not renounce the offensive against Versailles, and in these conditions even the

Commune might have succeeded. Moreover the Commune could not immediately offer the people what the Bolsheviks can if they come to power, namely, land to the peasants and an immediate proposal of peace. . . ." This was a nameless but unequivocal warning not only to Zinoviev, but also to the editor of *Pravda*, Stalin.

The question of the Pre-Parliament split the Central Committee in half. The decision of the Bolshevik faction of the Conference in favor of participating in the Pre-Parliament was ratified by many local committees, if not a majority of them. It was so for instance in Kiev. "On the question of . . . entering the Pre-Parliament," says E. Bosh in her memoirs, "the majority of the committee voted for participation and elected Piatakov as its delegate." In many cases—as for example Kamenev, Rykov, Piatakov and others—it is possible to trace a succession of waverings: against the theses of Lenin in April, against the boycott of the Pre-Parliament in September, against the insurrection in October. On the other hand, the next lower stratum of the Bolsheviks, standing nearer to the masses and being more fresh politically, easily accepted the slogan of boycott and compelled the committees, including the Central Committee itself, to make an about-face. Under the influence of letters from Lenin, the city conference of Kiev voted with an overwhelming majority against their committee. Similarly at almost all sharp political turning points Lenin relied upon the lower strata of the party machine against the higher, or on the party mass against the machine as a whole.

In these circumstances the pre-October waverings could least of all catch Lenin unawares. He was armed in advance with a sharp-eyed suspicion, was watching for alarming symptoms, was making the worst possible assumptions; and he considered it more expedient to bring excess pressure than to be indulgent.

It was at the suggestion of Lenin beyond a doubt that the Moscow Regional Bureau adopted at the end of September a bitter resolution against the Central Committee, accusing it of irresolution, wavering and introducing confusion into the ranks of the party, and demanding that it "take a clear and definite course toward insurrection." In the name of the Moscow Bureau,

Lomov on the 3rd of October reported this decision to the Central Committee. The minutes remark: "It was decided not to debate the question." The Central Committee was still continuing to dodge the question what to do. But Lenin's pressure, brought to bear through Moscow, had its result: After two days the Central Committee decided to withdraw from the Pre-Parliament.

That this step meant entering the road of insurrection was clear to the enemies and opponents. "Trotsky in leading his army out of the Pre-Parliament," writes Sukhanov, "was definitely steering a course towards violent revolution." The report of the Petrograd Soviet on withdrawal from the Pre-Parliament ended with the cry: "Long live the direct and open struggle for revolutionary power in the country!" That was October 9th.

On the following day, upon the demand of Lenin, occurred the famous session of the Central Committee where the question of insurrection was flatly posed. From the beginning of that session Lenin placed his further policy in dependence upon its outcome: either through the Central Committee or against it. "O new jest of the merry muse of history!" writes Sukhanov. "That high-up and decisive session was held in my apartment, still on the same Karpovka (32, Apartment 31). But all this was without my knowledge." The wife of the Menshevik, Sukhanov, was a Bolshevik. "That time special measures were taken to assure my sleeping outside the house: at least my wife made carefully sure of my intention, and gave me friendly and impartial advice—not to tire myself out after my work with the long journey home. In any case the lofty assemblage was completely safe from any invasion from me." What was more important, it proved safe from invasions from Kerensky's police.

Twelve of the twenty-one members of the Central Committee were present. Lenin came in wig and spectacles without a beard. The session lasted about ten hours—deep into the night. In the intervals there were tea with bread and sausage for reinforcement. And reinforcement was needed: it was a question of seizing the power in the former empire of the tzars. The session began, as always, with an organizational report from Sverdlov. This time his communication was devoted to the front—and evidently by previous agreement with Lenin, in order to give him support

146

for the necessary inferences. This was quite in accord with Lenin's methods. Representatives of the army of the northern front gave warning through Sverdlov of preparations by the counter-revolutionary command for some sort of "shady plot involving a withdrawal of troops inland"; from Minsk, the headquarters of the western front, it was reported that a new Kornilov insurrection was in preparation; in view of the revolutionary character of the local garrison, headquarters had surrounded the city with Cossack troops. "Some sort of negotiations of a suspicious character are in progress between headquarters and the general staff"; it is quite possible to seize the headquarters in Minsk: the local garrison is ready to disarm the Cossack ring; they are also in a position to send a revolutionary corps from Minsk to Petrograd; the mood on the front is for the Bolsheviks; they will go against Kerensky.—Such was Sverdlov's report. It was not in every part sufficiently definite, but it was entirely encouraging in character.

Lenin immediately took the offensive: "From the beginning of September there has been a kind of indifference to the question of insurrection." References are made to the cooling off and disappointment of the masses. No wonder. "The masses are tired of words and resolutions." We must take the situation as a whole. Events in the city are now taking place against the background of a gigantic peasant movement. The government would require colossal forces in order to quell the agrarian insurrection. "The political situation is thus ready. We must talk of the technical side. That is the whole thing. Meanwhile in the manner of the defensists we are inclined to regard the systematic preparation of insurrection as something in the nature of a political sin." The speaker was obviously restraining himself: He had too much feeling piled up in him. "We must make use of the northern regional congress and the proposal from Minsk in order to start a decisive action."

The northern congress opened exactly on the day of this session of the Central Committee, and was to close in two or three days. The beginning of "decisive action" Lenin presented as the task of the next days. We must not wait. We must not postpone. On the front—as we have heard from Sverdlov—they are preparing an overturn. Will the Congress of Soviets ever be held?

147

We do not know. We must seize the power immediately and not wait for any congresses. "Never to be communicated or reproduced," wrote Trotsky several years later, "was the general spirit of those tense and passionate impromptu speeches, saturated with a desire to instil into the objecting, the wavering, the doubtful, his thought, his will, his confidence, his courage. . . ."

Lenin expected strong resistance, but his fears were soon dispelled. The unanimity with which the Central Committee had rejected the proposal of immediate insurrection in September had been episodic: The left wing had been against the "surrounding of the Alexandrinka" for temporary reasons; the right for reasons of general strategy, although these were not as yet thoroughly thought out. During the three weeks following, there had been a considerable shift to the left in the Central Committee. Ten against two voted for the insurrection. That was a big victory!

Soon after the revolution, at a new stage in the inner party struggle, Lenin recalled during a debate in the Petrograd committee how up to that session of the Central Committee, he "had fears of opportunism from the side of the internationalist fusionists, but these were dissipated. In our party, however, certain members (of the Central Committee) did not agree. This grieved me deeply." Aside from Trotsky, whom Lenin could hardly have had in mind, the only "internationalists" in the Central Committee were Joffé, the future ambassador in Berlin, Uritzky the future head of the Cheka in Petrograd, and Sokolnikov, the future inventor of the Chervonetz. All three took the side of Lenin. His opponents were two old Bolsheviks, closest of all to Lenin in their past work: Zinoviev and Kamenev. It is to them he referred when he said "this grieved me very much." That session of the 10th reduced itself almost entirely to a passionate polemic against Zinoviev and Kamenev. Lenin led the attack, and the rest joined in one after the other.

The resolution, written hastily by Lenin with the gnawed end of a pencil on a sheet of paper from a child's note-book ruled in squares, was very unsymmetrical in architecture, but nevertheless gave firm support to the course towards insurrection. "The Central Committee recognizes that both the international situation of the Russian revolution (the insurrection in the German fleet, as the extreme manifestation of the growth throughout Europe of a world-wide socialist revolution, and also the threat of a peace between the imperialists with the aim of strangling the revolution in Russia)—and the military situation (the indubitable decision of the Russian bourgeoisie and Kerensky and Co. to surrender Petersburg to the Germans)—all this in connection with the peasant insurrection and the swing of popular confidence to our party (the elections in Moscow), and finally the obvious preparation of a second Kornilov attack (the withdrawal of troops from Petersburg, the importation of Cossacks into Petersburg, the surrounding of Minsk with Cossacks, etc.)—all this places armed insurrection on the order of the day. Thus recognizing that the armed insurrection is inevitable and fully ripe, the Central Committee recommends to all organizations of the party that they be guided by this, and from this point of view consider and decide all practical questions (the Congress of Soviets of the Northern Region, the withdrawal of troops from Petersburg, the coming-out of Moscow and Minsk)."

A remarkable thing here as characterizing both the moment and the author is the very order in which the conditions of the insurrection are enumerated. First comes the ripening of the world revolution; the insurrection in Russia is regarded only as the link in a general chain. That was Lenin's invariable starting-point, his major premise: he could not reason otherwise. The task of insurrection he presented directly as the task of the party. The difficult question of bringing its preparation into accord with the soviets is as yet not touched upon. The All-Russian Congress of Soviets does not get a word. To the northern regional congress and the "coming-out of Moscow and Minsk" as points of support for the insurrection was added, upon the insistence of Trotsky, "the withdrawal of troops from Petersburg." This was the sole hint of that plan of insurrection which was subsequently dictated by the course of events in the capital. Nobody proposed any tactical amendments to the resolution, which defined only the strategical starting-point of the insurrection, as against Zinoviev and Kamenev who rejected the very necessity of insurrection.

The very recent attempt of official historians to present this

149

matter as though the whole guiding stratum of the party except Zinoviev and Kamenev stood for the insurrection, goes to pieces when confronted by facts and documents. Aside from the fact that those voting for insurrection were much of the time inclined to push it off into an indefinite future, the open enemies of the insurrection, Zinoviev and Kamenev, were not alone even in the Central Committee. Rykov and Nogin who were absent at the session of the 10th stood wholly upon their point of view, and Miliutin was close to them. "In the upper circles of the party a wavering is to be observed, a sort of dread of the struggle for power"—such is the testimony of Lenin himself. According to Antonov-Saratovsky, Miliutin, arriving in Saratov after the 10th, "told about the letter of Ilych demanding that we 'begin,' about the waverings in the Central Committee, the preliminary 'failure' of Lenin's proposal, about his indignation, and finally about how the course was taken towards insurrection." The Bolshevik, Sadovsky, wrote later about "a certain vagueness and lack of confidence which prevailed at that time. Even among our Central Committee of those days, as is well known, there were debates and conflicts about how to begin and whether to begin at all."

Sadovsky himself was during that period one of the leaders of the military section of the Soviet and the Military Organization of the Bolsheviks. But it was exactly these members of the Military Organization—as appears from numerous memoirs—who were most exceptionally prejudiced in October against the idea of insurrection. The specific character of the organization inclined its leaders to under-estimate the political conditions and over-estimate the technical. On the 16th of October Krylenko reported: "The larger part of the bureau (the Military Organization) think that we should not force the issue practically, but the minority think that we can take the initiative." On the 18th, another prominent member of the Military Organization, Lashevich, said: "Ought we not to seize the power immediately? I think that we ought not to speed up the course of events. . . . There is no guarantee that we will succeed in holding the power. . . . The strategic plan proposed by Lenin limps on all four legs." Antonov-Ovseënko tells about a meeting of the chief military workers with Lenin: "Podvoisky expressed doubt; Nevsky at first seconded him, but then fell into the confident tone of Ilych; I described the situation in Finland. . . . Lenin's confidence and firmness had a fortifying effect upon me and cheered up Nevsky, but Podvoisky remained stubbornly dubious." We must not forget that in all recollections of this kind, the doubts are painted in with water colors and the confidence in heavy oil.

Chudnovsky spoke decisively against the insurrection. The sceptical Manuelsky warningly asserted that "the front is not with us." Tomsky was against the insurrection. Volodarsky supported Zinoviev and Kamenev. Moreover by no means all the opponents of the insurrection spoke openly. At a session of the Petrograd Committee on the 15th, Kalinin said: "The resolution of the Central Committee was one of the best resolutions ever adopted by the Central Committee. . . . We are practically approaching the armed insurrection. But when it will be possible—perhaps a year from now—is unknown." This kind of "agreement" with the Central Committee, although perfectly characteristic of Kalinin, was not peculiar to him. Many adhered to the resolution in order in that way to insure their struggle against the insurrection.

In Moscow least of all was there unanimity among the leaders. The regional bureau supported Lenin. In the Moscow committee there were very considerable hesitations; the prevailing mood was in favor of delay. The provincial committee occupied an indefinite position, but in the regional bureau, according to Yakovleva, they thought that at the decisive moment the provincial committee would swing over to the opponents of insurrection.

Lebedev from Saratov tells how in visiting Moscow not long before the revolution, he took a walk with Rykov, and how the latter, pointing to the stone houses, the rich stores, the business-like excitement about them, complained of the difficulty of the coming task. "Here in the very center of bourgeois Moscow we really seem to be pygmies thinking of moving a mountain."

In every organization of the party, in every one of its provincial committees, there were people of the same mood as Zinoviev and Kamenev. In many committees they were the majority. Even in proletarian Ivanovo-Voznesensk, where the Bolsheviks ruled alone, the disagreement among the ruling circles took an extraordinarily sharp form. In 1925, when memoirs had already accommodated themselves to the demands of the new course, Kisselev, an old worker Bolshevik, wrote: "The workers' part of the party, with the exception of certain individuals, went with Lenin. Against Lenin, however, was a small group of party intellectuals and solitary workers." In public discussion the opponents of insurrection repeated the same arguments as those of Zinoviev and Kamenev. "But in private arguments," writes Kisselev, "the polemic took a more acute and candid form, and here they went so far as to say that 'Lenin is a crazy man; he is pushing the working-class to certain ruin. From this armed insurrection we will get nothing; they will shatter us, exterminate the party and the working-class, and that will postpone the revolution for years and years, etc.' " Such was the attitude of Frunze in particular, a man of great personal courage but not distinguished by a wide outlook.

Even the victory of the insurrection in Petrograd was far from breaking everywhere the inertia of the waiting policy and the direct resistance of the right wing. The wavering of the leaders subsequently almost shipwrecked the insurrection in Moscow. In Kiev, the committee headed by Piatakov, which had been conducting a purely defensive policy, turned over the initiative in the long run—and afterward the power also—to the Rada. "The organization of our party in Voronezh," says Vrachev, "wavered very considerably. The actual overturn in Voronezh . . . was carried out not by a committee of the party, but by its active minority with Moiseiev at the head." In a whole series of provincial cities the Bolsheviks formed in October a bloc with the Compromisers "against the counter-revolution." As though the Compromisers were not at that moment one of its chief supports! Almost everywhere a push was required both from above and below to shatter the last indecisiveness of the local committee, compel it to break with the Compromisers and lead the movement. "The end of October and the beginning of November were verily days of 'the great turmoil' in our party circles. Many quickly surrendered to moods." Thus reports

Shliapnikov, who himself made no small contribution to these waverings.

All those elements which, like the Kharkov Bolsheviks, had found themselves in the Menshevik camp in the beginning of the revolution and afterwards themselves wondered "just how that could have happened," found no place for themselves at all as a general rule in the October Days but merely wavered and waited. These people have now all the more confidently advanced their claims as "old Bolsheviks" in the period of intellectual reaction. In spite of the vast work that has been done in recent years towards concealing these facts, and even without the secret archives which are now inaccessible to the investigator, plenty of testimony has been preserved in the newspapers, memoirs and historic journals of that time, to prove that on the eve of the overturn the official machine even of this most revolutionary party put up a big resistance. Conservatism inevitably finds its seat in a bureaucracy. The machine can fulfil a revolutionary function only so long as it remains an instrument in the service of the party, so long as it remains subordinate to an idea and is controlled by the mass.

The resolution of October 10th became immensely important. It promptly put the genuine advocates of insurrection on the firm ground of party right. In all the party organizations, in all its nuclei, the most resolute elements began to be advanced to the responsible posts. The party organizations, beginning with Petrograd, pulled themselves together, made an inventory of their forces and material resources, strengthened their communications, and gave a more concentrated character to the campaign for an overturn.

But the resolution did not put an end to disagreements in the Central Committee. On the contrary, it only formulated them and brought them to the surface. Zinoviev and Kamenev, who but yesterday had felt surrounded in a certain section of the leading circles by an atmosphere of sympathy, observed with fright how swiftly things were shifting to the left. They decided to lose no more time, and on the very next day distributed a voluminous address to the members of the party. "Before history, before the international proletariat, before the Russian revolution and the Russian working-class," they wrote, "we have no right to stake the whole future at the present moment upon the card of armed insurrection."

Their plan was to enter as a strong opposition party into the Constituent Assembly, which "in its revolutionary work can rely only upon the soviets." Hence their formula: "Constituent Assembly and soviets—that is the combined type of state institution toward which we are traveling." The Constituent Assembly, where the Bolsheviks, it was assumed, would be a minority, and the soviets where the Bolsheviks were a majority—that is, the organ of the bourgeoisie and the organ of the proletariat—were to be "combined" in a peaceful system of dual power. That had not succeeded even under the leadership of the Compromisers. How could it succeed when the soviets were Bolshevik?

"It is a profound historic error," concluded Zinoviev and Kamenev, "to pose the question of the transfer of power to the proletarian party—either now or at any time. No, the party of the proletariat will grow, its program will become clear to broader and broader masses."

This hope for a further unbroken growth of Bolshevism regardless of the actual course of class conflicts, crashed head on against Lenin's leit-motif in those days: "The success of the Russian and world revolution depends upon a two or three days' struggle."

It is hardly necessary to explain that the truth in this dramatic dialogue was wholly on Lenin's side. A revolutionary situation cannot be preserved at will. If the Bolsheviks had not seized the power in October and November, in all probability they would not have seized it at all. Instead of firm leadership the masses would have found among the Bolsheviks that same disparity between word and deed which they were already sick of, and they would have ebbed away in the course of two or three months from this party which had deceived their hopes, just as they had recently ebbed away from the Social Revolutionaries and Mensheviks. A part of the workers would have fallen into indifferentism, another part would have burned up their force in convulsive movements, in anarchistic flare-ups, in guerrilla skirmishes, in a Terror dictated by revenge and despair. The

breathing-spell thus offered would have been used by the bourgeoisie to conclude a separate peace with the Hohenzollern, and
stamp out the revolutionary organizations. Russia would again
have been included in the circle of capitalist states as a semi-
imperialist, semi-colonial country. The proletarian revolution
would have been deferred to an indefinite future. It was his keen
understanding of this prospect that inspired Lenin to that cry
of alarm: "The success of the Russian and world revolution depends upon a two or three days' struggle."

But now, since the 10th of the month, the situation in the
party had radically changed. Lenin was no longer an isolated
"oppositionist" whose proposals were set aside by the Central
Committee. It was the Right Wing that was isolated. Lenin no
longer had to gain the right of free agitation at the price of resigning from the Central Committee. The party legality was on
his side. Zinoviev and Kamenev, on the other hand, circulating
their document attacking a decision adopted by the majority of
the Central Committee, were now the violators of discipline. And
Lenin in a struggle never left unpunished the oversights of his
enemy—even far slighter ones than that!

At the session of the 10th, upon the proposal of Dzerzhinsky,
a political bureau of seven men was elected: Lenin, Trotsky,
Zinoviev, Kamenev, Stalin, Sokolnikov, Bubnov. This new institution, however, turned out completely impracticable. Lenin
and Zinoviev were still in hiding; Zinoviev, moreover, continued
to wage a struggle against the insurrection, and so did Kamenev.
The political bureau in its October membership never once assembled, and it was soon simply forgotten—as were other organizations created *ad hoc* in the whirlpool of events.

No practical plan of insurrection, even tentative, was sketched
out in the session of the 10th. But without introducing the fact
into the resolution, it was agreed that the insurrection should
precede the Congress of Soviets and begin, if possible, not later
than October 15th. Not all eagerly agreed to that date. It was
obviously too short for the take-off planned in Petrograd. But
to insist on a delay would have been to support the Right Wing
and mix the cards. Besides, it is never too late to postpone!

The fact of this preliminary setting of the date at the 15th was first made public in Trotsky's recollections of Lenin in 1924, seven years after the event. The statement was soon disputed by Stalin, and the question has become an acute one in Russian historic literature. As is known, the insurrection actually occurred only on the 25th, and consequently the date originally set was not held to. The epigone historians consider it impossible that there should be a mistake in the policy of the Central Committee, or even a delay in the matter of a date. "It would follow," writes Stalin upon this theme, "that the Central Committee set the date of the insurrection for October 15th and afterwards itself violated (!) this resolution, delaying the date of the insurrection to October 25th. Is this true? No, it is not true." Stalin comes to the conclusion that "Trotsky's memory has betrayed him." In proof of this he cites the resolution of October 10th which did not set any date.

This debated question of the chronology of the insurrection is very important to an understanding of the rhythm of events and demands clarification. That the resolution of the 10th contained no date is quite true. But this general resolution had to do with an insurrection throughout the whole country, and was destined for hundreds and thousands of leading party workers. To include in it the conspirative date of an insurrection to be carried out in the next few days in Petrograd, would have been unreasonable in the extreme. We must remember that out of caution Lenin did not in those days even put a date on his letters. In the given case it was a question of so important, and withal so simple, a decision that none of the participants could have any difficulty in remembering it—especially seeing that it was a question only of a few days. Stalin's reference to the text of the resolution shows thus a complete failure to understand.

We are prepared to concede, however, that the reference of one of the participants to his own memory, especially when his statement is disputed by another participant, is not sufficient for the historic investigator. Luckily the question is decided beyond possible doubt upon another level—that of an analysis of conditions and documents.

The Congress of Soviets was to open on the 20th of October. Between the session of the Central Committee and the date of the Congress, there remained an interval of ten days. The Congress was not to agitate in favor of power to the soviets but seize it. A few hundred delegates all by themselves, however, were powerless to conquer the power; it was necessary to seize it for the Congress and before the Congress. "First conquer Kerensky and then summon the Congress"—that thought had stood in the center of Lenin's whole agitation since the middle of September. All those agreed with it in principle who stood for the seizure of power in general. Consequently the Central Committee could not help setting itself the task of attempting to carry out an insurrection between the 10th and 20th of October. And since it was impossible to foresee how many days the struggle would last, the beginning of the insurrection was set for the 15th. "About the actual date," wrote Trotsky in his recollections of Lenin, "there was, as I remember, almost no dispute. All understood that the date was approximate, and set, as you might say, merely for purposes of orientation, and that it might be advanced or retarded at the dictation of events. But this could be a question of days only, and not more. The necessity of a date, and that too a near one, was completely obvious."

This testimony of political logic essentially exhausts the question. But there is no lack of supplementary proof. Lenin insistently and frequently proposed that the party avail itself of the Northern Regional Congress of the Soviets for the beginning of military activities. The resolution of the Central Committee adopted this idea. But the Regional Congress, which had opened on the 10th, was to close just before the 15th.

At the conference on the 16th, Zinoviev, while insisting upon the revocation of the resolution adopted six days before, made this demand: "We must say to ourselves frankly that in the next five days we will not make an insurrection." He was referring to the five days still remaining before the Congress of Soviets. Kamenev, arguing at the same conference that "the appointing of an insurrection is adventurism," reminded the conference that "it was said before that the action ought to come before the 20th." Nobody objected to this statement and nobody could object. It was the very delay of the insurrection which Kamenev was interpreting as a failure of Lenin's resolution. According to his words "nothing has been done during this week" towards an insurrection. That is obviously an exaggeration. The setting of the date had compelled all to make their plans more strict and hasten the tempo of their work. But it is indubitable that the five day interval indicated at the session of the 10th had turned out too short. The postponement was already a fact. It was only on the 17th that the Central Executive Committee transferred the opening of the Soviet Congress to the 25th. That postponement was as opportune as anything could be.

Lenin, to whom in his isolation all these inner hindrances and frictions inevitably presented themselves in an exaggerated form, was alarmed by the delay, and insisted upon the calling of a new meeting of the Central Committee with representatives from the more important branches of the party work in the capital. It was at this conference, held on the 16th in the outskirts of the city, in Lesnoi, that Zinoviev and Kamenev advanced the arguments quoted above for revoking the old date and against naming a new.

The dispute was reopened with redoubled vigor. Miliutin's opinion was: "We are not ready to strike the first blow. . . . Another prospect arises: Armed conflict. . . . It is growing, its possibility is drawing near. And we ought to be ready for this conflict. But this prospect is a different thing from insurrection." Miliutin occupied that defensive position which was more concisely defended by Zinoviev and Kamenev. Shotman, an old Petrograd worker who lived through the whole history of the party, has asserted that at this city conference, both in the party committee and in the Military Revolutionary Committee, the mood was far less militant than in the Central Committee. "We cannot come out but we ought to get ready." Lenin attacked Miliutin and Shotman for their pessimistic appraisal of the correlation of forces: "It is not a question of a struggle with the army, but a struggle of one part of the army with another. . . . The facts prove that we have the advantage over the enemy. Why cannot the Central Committee begin?"

Trotsky was not present at this meeting. During those same hours he was carrying through the Soviet the resolution on the Military Revolutionary Committee. But the point of view which had firmly crystallized in Smolny during the past days was defended by Krylenko, who had just been conducting hand in hand with Trotsky and Antonov-Ovseënko the Northern Regional Congress of Soviets. Krylenko had no doubt that "the water is boiling hard enough." To take back the resolution in favor of insurrection "would be the greatest possible mistake." He disagreed with Lenin, however, "on the question who shall begin it and how it shall begin?" To set the date of the insurrection definitely now is still inexpedient. "But the question of the removal of the troops is just that fighting issue upon which the struggle is taking place. . . . The attack upon us is thus already a fact, and this we can make use of. . . . It is not necessary to worry about who shall begin, for the thing is already begun." Krylenko was expounding and defending the policy laid down by the Military Revolutionary Committee and the Garrison Conference. It was along this road that the insurrection continued to develop.

Lenin did not respond to the words of Krylenko. The living picture of the last six days in Petrograd had not passed before his eyes. Lenin feared delay. His attention was fixed upon the outright opponents of insurrection. All by-remarks, conditional formulæ, inadequately categorical answers, he was inclined to interpret as an indirect support to Zinoviev and Kamenev, who were opposing him with the determination of people who have burned their bridges behind them. "The week's results," argued Kamenev, "testify that the data for an insurrection are now lacking. We have no machine of insurrection. The enemy's machine is far stronger and has probably grown still greater during this week. . . . Two tactics are in conflict here: the tactic of conspiracy and the tactic of faith in the motive forces of the Russian revolution." Opportunists always believe in those motive forces whenever it becomes necessary to fight.

Lenin replied: "If you consider that an insurrection is right, it is not necessary to argue about conspiracy. If an insurrection is politically inevitable, then we must relate ourselves to insurrection as to an art." It was along this line that the fundamental and really principled dispute in the party took place—the dispute upon whose decision, upon whose resolution one way or the other, depended the fate of the revolution. However, within the general frame of Lenin's formula, which united the majority of the Central Committee, there arose subordinate, but very important, questions: How on the basis of the ripened political situation are we to approach the insurrection? How find a bridge from the politics to the technique of revolution? And how lead the masses along that bridge?

Joffé, who belonged to the left wing, had supported the resolution of the 10th. But he opposed Lenin in one point: "It is not true that the question is now purely technical. Now too the moment of insurrection must be considered from the political point of view." This very last week has shown that for the party, for the Soviet, for the masses, the insurrection has not yet become a mere question of technique. For that very reason we failed to keep to the date set on the 10th.

Lenin's new resolution summoning "all organizations and all workers and soldiers to an all-sided and most vigorous preparation of armed insurrection," was adopted by 20 voices against 2, Zinoviev and Kamenev, with 3 abstaining. The official historians cite these figures as proof of the complete insignificance of the opposition. But they simplify the matter. The shift to the left in the depths of the party was already so strong that the opponents of insurrection, not daring to come out openly, felt it to their interest to remove any barrier of principle between the two camps. If the overthrow, in spite of the date set before, has not been realized by the 16th, can we not bring it about that in the future, too, the thing will be limited to a platonic "course toward insurrection"? That Kalinin was not so utterly alone, was very clearly revealed in that same session. The resolution of Zinoviev to the effect that "any action before a conference with the Bolshevik section of the Congress of Soviets is inadmissible," was rejected by 15 votes against 6, with 3 abstaining. This is where you find the real test of opinions. Some of the "defenders" of the resolution of the Central Committee really wanted to delay the decision until the Congress of Soviets, and until a new conference with the Bolsheviks of the provinces who were in their majority more moderate. Of these "defenders," counting also those abstaining, there were 9 men out of 24—more, that is, than a third.

That, of course, is still a minority, but as a headquarters rather an important one. The hopeless weakness of this headquarters lay in the fact that it had no support in the lower ranks of the party or the working-class.

On the next day Kamenev, in agreement with Zinoviev, gave to Gorky's paper a declaration attacking the decision adopted the night before. "Not only Zinoviev and I, but also a number of practical comrades,"—thus wrote Kamenev—"think that to take the initiative in an armed insurrection at the present moment, with the given correlation of social forces, independently of and several days before the Congress of Soviets, is an inadmissible step ruinous to the proletariat and the revolution. . . . To stake everything . . . on the card of insurrection in the coming days would be an act of despair. And our party is too strong, it has too great a future before it, to take such a step. . . ." Opportunists always feel "too strong" to go into a fight.

Kamenev's letter was a direct declaration of war against the Central Committee, and that too upon a question upon which nobody was joking. The situation immediately became extraordinarily acute. It was complicated by several other personal episodes having a common political source. At a session of the Petrograd Soviet on the 18th, Trotsky, in answer to a question raised by the enemy, declared that the Soviet had not set the date for an insurrection in the coming days, but that if it became necessary to set one, the workers and soldiers would come out as one man. Kamenev, sitting next to Trotsky in the præsidium, immediately arose for a short statement: He wanted to sign his name to Trotsky's every word. That was a cunning ruse. Whereas Trotsky was juridically screening a policy of attack with a speciously defensive formula, Kamenev tried to make use of Trotsky's formula—with which he was in radical disagreement—in order to screen a directly opposite policy.

In order to annul the effect of Kamenev's maneuver, Trotsky said on the same day in a speech to the All-Russian Conference of Factory and Shop Committees: "A civil war is inevitable. We have only to organize it as painlessly as possible. We can achieve this not by wavering and vacillation, but only by a stubborn and courageous struggle for power." All understood that those words about waverings were directed against Zinoviev, Kamenev and their colleagues.

Besides that, Trotsky referred the question of Kamenev's speech in the Soviet to investigation by the next session of the Central Committee. In the interval Kamenev, desiring to free his hands for agitation against the insurrection, resigned from the Central Committee. The question was taken up in his absence. Trotsky insisted that "the situation created is absolutely intolerable," and moved that Kamenev's resignation be accepted.[1]

Sverdlov, supporting Trotsky's motion, read a letter of Lenin branding Zinoviev and Kamenev as strikebreakers for their declaration in Gorky's paper, and demanding their expulsion from the party. "Kamenev's trick at the session of the Petrograd Soviet," writes Lenin, "was something positively vile. He is in complete accord, says he, with Trotsky! But is it hard to understand that Trotsky *could* not, had no right, to say before the enemy any more than he did say? Is it hard to understand that . . . a decision as to the necessity of an armed insurrection, as to the fact that it is fully ripe, as to its all-sided preparation, etc. . . . makes it *necessary* in public speeches to shoulder off not only the blame, but also the initiative, upon the enemy. . . . Kamenev's trick was plain petty cheating. . . ."

When sending his indignant protest through Sverdlov, Lenin could not yet know that Zinoviev, in a letter to the editors of the central organ, had announced that his views "are very far from those which Lenin combats," and that he "subscribes to yesterday's declaration of Trotsky in the Petrograd Soviet."

---

[1] In the minutes of the Central Committee for 1917, published in 1929, it says that Trotsky explained his declaration to the Soviet on the ground that "it was forced by Kamenev." Here there is obviously an erroneous record, or the record was subsequently incorrectly edited. The declaration of Trotsky needed no special explanation; it flowed from the circumstances. By a curious accident the Moscow Regional Committee, which wholly supported Lenin, found itself obliged to publish in the Moscow party paper on the same day, the 18th, a declaration almost verbally identical with the formula of Trotsky: "We are not a conspirative party and we do not set the date for our actions secretly. . . . When we decide to come out, we will say so in our printed organ. . . ." It was impossible to reply otherwise to the direct queries of the enemy. But although the declaration of Trotsky was not, and could not have been, forced by Kamenev, it was consciously compromised by Kamenev's false solidarity and that moreover under circumstances which deprived Trotsky of the possibility of putting the missing dots on the i's.

Lunacharsky, a third opponent of insurrection, came out in the press to the same effect. To complete the malicious confusion, a letter of Zinoviev's printed in the central organ on the very day of the session of the Central Committee, the 20th, was accompanied with a sympathetic remark from the editors: "We in our turn express the hope that with the declaration made by Zinoviev (and also the declaration of Kamenev in the Soviet) the question may be considered settled. The sharpness of tone of Lenin's article does not alter the fact that in fundamentals we remain of one opinion." That was a new blow in the back, and moreover from a direction from which no one was expecting it. At the time when Zinoviev and Kamenev were coming out in a hostile press with open agitation against the decision of the Central Committee in favor of insurrection, the central organ of the party condemns the "sharpness" of Lenin's tone and registers its solidarity with Zinoviev and Kamenev "in fundamentals." As though at that moment there could be a more fundamental question than the question of insurrection! According to the brief minutes, Trotsky declared at the session of the Central Committee: "The letters of Zinoviev and Lunacharsky to the central organ, and also the remark of the editors are intolerable." Sverdlov supported the protest.

The editors at that time were Stalin and Sokolnikov. The minutes read: "Sokolnikov states that he had no part in the declaration of the editors on the subject of Zinoviev's letter, and considers this declaration an error." It thus became known that Stalin personally and alone—against the other member of the editorial board and a majority of the Central Committee—supported Kamenev and Zinoviev at the most critical moment, four days before the beginning of the insurrection, with a sympathetic declaration. The indignation at this was great.

Stalin spoke against the acceptance of Kamenev's resignation, arguing that "our whole situation is self-contradictory." That is, he took upon himself the defense of that confusion which the members of the Central Committee coming out against the insurrection had introduced into people's minds. Kamenev's resignation was accepted by five votes against three. By six votes, again with Stalin opposing, a decision was adopted forbidding Kamenev

163

and Zinoviev to carry on a struggle against the policy of the Central Committee. The minutes read: "Stalin announces that he withdraws from the editorial board." In order not to complicate an already difficult situation, the Central Committee refused to accept Stalin's resignation.

This conduct on the part of Stalin might seem inexplicable in the light of the legend which has been created around him. In reality it fully corresponds to his spiritual mould and his political methods. When faced by great problems Stalin always retreats—not through lack of character as in the case of Kamenev, but through narrowness of horizon and lack of creative imagination. His suspicious caution almost organically compels him at moments of great decision and deep difference of opinion to retire into the shadow, to wait, and if possible to insure himself against both outcomes. Stalin voted with Lenin for the insurrection; Zinoviev and Kamenev were openly fighting against the insurrection. But nevertheless—aside from the "sharpness of tone" of Lenin's criticism "in fundamentals we remain of one opinion." Stalin made this editorial comment by no means through light-mindedness. On the contrary he was carefully weighing the circumstances and the words. But on the 20th of October he did not think it advisable to burn irrevocably his bridge to the camp of the enemies of the uprising.

The testimony of these minutes, which we are compelled to quote not from the original, but from the official text as worked up by Stalin's secretariat, not only demonstrates the actual position of the figures in the Bolshevik Central Committee, but also, in spite of its brevity and dryness, unfolds before us an authentic panorama of the party leadership as it existed in reality, with all its inner contradictions and inevitable personal waverings. Not only history as a whole, but even its very boldest turns, are accomplished by people to whom nothing human is alien. But does this after all lessen the importance of what is accomplished?

If we were to unfold on a screen the most brilliant of Napoleon's victories, the film would show us, side by side with genius, scope, ingenuity, heroism, also the irresolution of individual marshals, the confusion of generals unable to read the map, the stupidity of officers, and the panic of whole detachments, even down to the bowels relaxed with fright. This realistic document would only testify that the army of Napoleon consisted not of the automatons of legend, but of living Frenchmen born and brought up during the break between two epochs. And the picture of human weaknesses would only the more plainly emphasize the grandeur of the whole.

It is easier to theorize about a revolution afterward than absorb it into your flesh and blood before it takes place. The approach of an insurrection has inevitably produced, and always will produce, crises in the insurrectionary parties. This is demonstrated by the experience of the most tempered and revolutionary party that history has up to this time known. It is enough that a few days before the battle Lenin found himself obliged to demand the expulsion from the party of his two closest and most prominent disciples. The recent attempts to reduce this conflict to "accidents" of a personal character have been dictated by a purely churchly idealization of the party's past. Just as Lenin more fully and resolutely than others expressed in the autumn months of 1917 the objective necessity of an insurrection, and the will of the masses to revolution, so Zinoviev and Kamenev more frankly than others incarnated the blocking tendencies of the party, the moods of irresolution, the influence of petty bourgeois connections, and the pressure of the ruling classes.

If all the conferences, debates, personal quarrels, which took place in the upper layer of the Bolshevik party during October alone had been taken down by a stenographer, posterity might convince itself with what intense inner struggle the determination necessary for the overthrow was crystallized among the heads of the party. The stenographic report would show at the same time how much a revolutionary party has need of internal democracy. The will to struggle is not stored up in advance, and is not dictated from above—it has on every occasion to be independently renewed and tempered.

Citing the assertion of the author of this book that "the party is the fundamental instrument of proletarian revolution," Stalin asked in 1924: "How could our revolution conquer if its 'fundamental instrument' was no good?" His irony did not conceal the primitive falsity of this objection. Between the saints as the church

165

paints them and the devils as the candidates for sainthood portray them, there are to be found living people. And it is they who make history. The high temper of the Bolshevik party expressed itself not in an absence of disagreements, waverings, and even quakings, but in the fact that in the most difficult circumstances it gathered itself in good season by means of inner crises, and made good its opportunity to interfere decisively in the course of events. That means that the party as a whole was a quite adequate instrument of revolution.

In practice a reformist party considers unshakeable the foundations of that which it intends to reform. It thus inevitably submits to the ideas and morals of the ruling class. Having risen on the backs of the proletariat, the social democrats became merely a bourgeois party of the second order. Bolshevism created the type of the authentic revolutionist who subordinates to historic goals irreconcilable with contemporary society the conditions of his personal existence, his ideas, and his moral judgments. The necessary distance from bourgeois ideology was kept up in the party by a vigilant irreconcilability, whose inspirer was Lenin. Lenin never tired of working with his lancet, cutting off those bonds which a petty bourgeois environment creates between the party and official social opinion. At the same time Lenin taught the party to create its own social opinion, resting upon the thoughts and feelings of the rising class. Thus by a process of selection and education, and in continual struggle, the Bolshevik party created not only a political but a moral medium of its own, independent of bourgeois social opinion and implacably opposed to it. Only this permitted the Bolsheviks to overcome the waverings in their own ranks and reveal in action that courageous determination without which the October victory would have been impossible.

CHAPTER VI

THE ART OF INSURRECTION

PEOPLE do not make revolution eagerly any more than they do war. There is this difference, however, that in war compulsion plays the decisive rôle, in revolution there is no compulsion except that of circumstances. A revolution takes place only when there is no other way out. And the insurrection, which rises above a revolution like a peak in the mountain chain of its events, can no more be evoked at will than the revolution as a whole. The masses advance and retreat several times before they make up their minds to the final assault.

Conspiracy is ordinarily contrasted to insurrection as the deliberate undertaking of a minority to a spontaneous movement of the majority. And it is true that a victorious insurrection, which can only be the act of a class called to stand at the head of the nation, is widely separated both in method and historic significance from a governmental overturn accomplished by conspirators acting in concealment from the masses.

In every class society there are enough contradictions so that a conspiracy can take root in its cracks. Historic experience proves, however, that a certain degree of social disease is necessary—as in Spain, for instance, or Portugal, or South America—to supply continual nourishment for a régime of conspiracies. A pure conspiracy even when victorious can only replace one clique of the same ruling class by another—or still less, merely alter the governmental personages. Only mass insurrection has ever brought the victory of one social régime over another. Periodical conspiracies are commonly an expression of social stagnation and decay, but popular insurrections on the contrary come usually as a result of some swift growth which has broken down the old equilibrium of the nation. The chronic "revolutions" of the South American republics have nothing in common with the Permanent Revolution; they are in a sense the very opposite thing.

This does not mean, however, that popular insurrection and conspiracy are in all circumstances mutually exclusive. An element of conspiracy almost always enters to some degree into any insurrection. Being historically conditioned by a certain stage in the growth of a revolution, a mass insurrection is never purely spontaneous. Even when it flashes out unexpectedly to a majority of its own participants, it has been fertilized by those ideas in which the insurrectionaries see a way out of the difficulties of existence. But a mass insurrection can be foreseen and prepared. It can be organized in advance. In this case the conspiracy is subordinate to the insurrection, serves it, smoothes its path, hastens its victory. The higher the political level of a revolutionary movement and the more serious its leadership, the greater will be the place occupied by conspiracy in a popular insurrection.

It is very necessary to understand the relations between insurrection and conspiracy, both as they oppose and as they supplement each other. It is especially so, because the very use of the word conspiracy, even in Marxian literature, contains a superficial contradiction due to the fact that it sometimes implies an independent undertaking initiated by the minority, at others a preparation by the minority of a majority insurrection.

History testifies, to be sure, that in certain conditions a popular insurrection can be victorious even without a conspiracy. Arising "spontaneously" out of the universal indignation, the scattered protests, demonstrations, strikes, street fights, an insurrection can draw in a part of the army, paralyze the forces of the enemy, and overthrow the old power. To a certain degree this is what happened in February 1917 in Russia. Approximately the same picture is presented by the development of the German and Austro-Hungarian revolutions of the autumn of 1918. Since in these events there was no party at the head of the insurrectionaries imbued through and through with the interests and aims of the insurrection, its victory had inevitably to transfer the power to those parties which up to the last moment had been opposing it.

To overthrow the old power is one thing; to take the power in one's own hands is another. The bourgeoisie may win the power in a revolution not because it is revolutionary, but because it is

THE ART OF INSURRECTION

bourgeois. It has in its possession property, education, the press, a network of strategic positions, a hierarchy of institutions. Quite otherwise with the proletariat. Deprived in the nature of things of all social advantages, an insurrectionary proletariat can count only on its numbers, its solidarity, its cadres, its official staff.

Just as a blacksmith cannot seize the red hot iron in his naked hand, so the proletariat cannot directly seize the power; it has to have an organization accommodated to this task. The coordination of the mass insurrection with the conspiracy, the subordination of the conspiracy to the insurrection, the organization of the insurrection through the conspiracy, constitutes that complex and responsible department of revolutionary politics which Marx and Engels called "the art of insurrection." It presupposes a correct general leadership of the masses, a flexible orientation in changing conditions, a thought-out plan of attack, cautiousness in technical preparation, and a daring blow.

Historians and politicians usually give the name of *spontaneous insurrection* to a movement of the masses united by a common hostility against the old régime, but not having a clear aim, deliberated methods of struggle, or a leadership consciously showing the way to victory. This spontaneous insurrection is condescendingly recognized by official historians—at least those of democratic temper—as a necessary evil the responsibility for which falls upon the old régime. The real reason for their attitude of indulgence is that "spontaneous" insurrection cannot transcend the framework of the bourgeois régime.

The social democrats take a similar position. They do not reject revolution at large as a social catastrophe, any more than they reject earthquakes, volcanic eruptions, eclipses and epidemics of the plague. What they do reject—calling it "Blanquism," or still worse, Bolshevism—is the conscious preparation of an overturn, the plan, the conspiracy. In other words, the social democrats are ready to sanction—and that only *ex post facto*—those overturns which hand the power to the bourgeoisie, but they implacably condemn those methods which might alone bring the power to the proletariat. Under this pretended objectivism they conceal a policy of defense of the capitalist society.

From his observations and reflections upon the failure of the many insurrections he witnessed or took part in, Auguste Blanqui derived a number of tactical rules which if violated will make the victory of any insurrection extremely difficult, if not impossible. Blanqui demanded these things: a timely creation of correct revolutionary detachments, their centralized command and adequate equipment, a well calculated placement of barricades, their definite construction, and a systematic, not a mere episodic, defense of them. All these rules, deriving from the military problems of the insurrection, must of course change with social conditions and military technique, but in themselves they are not by any means "Blanquism" in the sense that this word approaches the German "putschism," or revolutionary adventurism.

Insurrection is an art, and like all arts it has its laws. The rules of Blanqui were the demands of a military revolutionary realism. Blanqui's mistake lay not in his direct but his inverse theorem. From the fact that tactical weakness condemns an insurrection to defeat, Blanqui inferred that an observance of the rules of insurrectionary tactics would itself guarantee the victory. Only from this point on is it legitimate to contrast Blanquism with Marxism. Conspiracy does not take the place of insurrection. An active minority of the proletariat, no matter how well organized, cannot seize the power regardless of the general conditions of the country. In this point history has condemned Blanquism. But only in this. His affirmative theorem retains all its force. In order to conquer the power, the proletariat needs more than a spontaneous insurrection. It needs a suitable organization, it needs a plan; it needs a conspiracy. Such is the Leninist view of this question.

Engels' criticism of the fetishism of the barricade was based upon the evolution of military technique and of technique in general. The insurrectionary tactic of Blanquism corresponded to the character of the old Paris, the semi-handicraft proletariat, the narrow streets and the military system of Louis Philippe. Blanqui's mistake in principle was to identify revolution with insurrection. His technical mistake was to identify insurrection with the barricade. The Marxian criticism has been directed against both mistakes. Although at one with Blanquism in regarding insurrection as an art, Engels discovered not only the subordinate place occupied by insurrection in a revolution, but also the declining rôle of the barricade in an insurrection. Engels' criticism had nothing in common with a renunciation of the revolutionary methods in favor of pure parliamentarism, as the philistines of the German Social Democracy, in cooperation with the Hohenzollern censorship, attempted in their day to pretend. For Engels the question about barricades remained a question about one of the technical elements of an uprising. The reformists have attempted to infer from his rejection of the decisive importance of the barricade a rejection of revolutionary violence in general. That is about the same as to infer the destruction of militarism from considerations of the probable decline in importance of trenches in future warfare.

The organization by means of which the proletariat can both overthrow the old power and replace it, is the soviets. This afterwards became a matter of historic experience, but was up to the October revolution a theoretical prognosis—resting, to be sure, upon the preliminary experience of 1905. The soviets are organs of preparation of the masses for insurrection, organs of insurrection, and after the victory organs of government.

However, the soviets by themselves do not settle the question. They may serve different goals according to the program and leadership. The soviets receive their program from the party. Whereas the soviets in revolutionary conditions—and apart from revolution they are impossible—comprise the whole class with the exception of its altogether backward, inert or demoralized strata, the revolutionary party represents the brain of the class. The problem of conquering the power can be solved only by a definite combination of party with soviets—or with other mass organizations more or less equivalent to soviets.

When headed by a revolutionary party the soviet consciously and in good season strives towards a conquest of power. Accommodating itself to changes in the political situation and the mood of the masses, it gets ready the military bases of the insurrection, unites the shock troops upon a single scheme of action, works out a plan for the offensive and for the final assault. And this means bringing organized conspiracy into mass insurrection.

The Bolsheviks were compelled more than once, and long before the October revolution, to refute accusations of conspiratism and Blanquism directed against them by their enemies. Moreover, nobody waged a more implacable struggle against the system of pure conspiracy than Lenin. The opportunists of the international social democracy more than once defended the old Social Revolutionary tactic of individual terror directed against the agents of tzarism, when this tactic was ruthlessly criticized by the Bolsheviks with their insistence upon mass insurrection as opposed to the individual adventurism of the intelligentsia. But in refuting all varieties of Blanquism and anarchism, Lenin did not for one moment bow down to any "sacred" spontaneousness of the masses. He thought out before anybody else, and more deeply, the correlation between the objective and subjective factors in a revolution, between the spontaneous movement and the policy of the party, between the popular masses and the progressive class, between the proletariat and its vanguard, between the soviets and the party, between insurrection and conspiracy.

But if it is true that an insurrection cannot be evoked at will, and that nevertheless in order to win it must be organized in advance, then the revolutionary leaders are presented with a task of correct diagnosis. They must feel out the growing insurrection in good season and supplement it with a conspiracy. The interference of the midwife in labor pains—however this image may have been abused—remains the clearest illustration of this conscious intrusion into an elemental process. Herzen once accused his friend Bakunin of invariably in all his revolutionary enterprises taking the second month of pregnancy for the ninth. Herzen himself was rather inclined to deny even in the ninth that pregnancy existed. In February the question of determining the date of birth hardly arose at all, since the insurrection flared up unexpectedly without centralized leadership. But exactly for this reason the power did not go to those who had accomplished the insurrection, but to those who had applied the brakes. It was quite otherwise with the second insurrection. This was consciously prepared by the Bolshevik party. The problem of correctly seizing the moment to give the signal for the attack was thus laid upon the Bolshevik staff.

Moment here is not to be taken too literally as meaning a definite day and hour. Physical births also present a considerable period of uncertainty—their limits interesting not only to the art of the midwife, but also to the casuistics of the Surrogate's Court. Between the moment when an attempt to summon an insurrection must inevitably prove premature and lead to a revolutionary miscarriage, and the moment when a favorable situation must be considered hopelessly missed, there exists a certain period —it may be measured in weeks, and sometimes in a few months— in the course of which an insurrection may be carried out with more or less chance of success. To discriminate this comparatively short period and then choose the definite moment—now in the more accurate sense of the very day and hour—for the last blow, constitutes the most responsible task of the revolutionary leaders. It can with full justice be called the key problem, for it unites the policy of revolution with the technique of insurrection—and it is needless to add that insurrection, like war, is a continuation of politics with other instruments.

Intuition and experience are necessary for revolutionary leadership, just as for all other kinds of creative activity. But much more than that is needed. The art of the magician can also successfully rely upon intuition and experience. Political magic is adequate, however, only for epochs and periods in which routine predominates. An epoch of mighty historic upheavals has no use for witch-doctors. Here experience, even illumined by intuition, is not enough. Here you must have a synthetic doctrine comprehending the interactions of the chief historic forces. Here you must have a materialistic method permitting you to discover, behind the moving shadows of program and slogan, the actual movement of social bodies.

The fundamental premise of a revolution is that the existing social structure has become incapable of solving the urgent problems of development of the nation. A revolution becomes possible, however, only in case the society contains a new class capable of taking the lead in solving the problems presented by history. The process of preparing a revolution consists of making the objective problems involved in the contradictions of industry and of classes find their way into the consciousness of living human masses, change this consciousness and create new correlations of human forces.

The ruling classes, as a result of their practically manifested incapacity to get the country out of its blind alley, lose faith in themselves; the old parties fall to pieces; a bitter struggle of groups and cliques prevails; hopes are placed in miracles or miracle workers. All this constitutes one of the political premises of a revolution, a very important although a passive one.

A bitter hostility to the existing order and a readiness to venture upon the most heroic efforts and sacrifices in order to bring the country out upon an upward road—this is the new political consciousness of the revolutionary class, and constitutes the most important active premise of a revolution.

These two fundamental camps, however—the big property holders and the proletariat—do not exhaust the population of a country. Between them lie broad layers of the petty bourgeoisie, showing all the colors of the economic and political rainbow. The discontent of these intermediate layers, their disappointment with the policy of the ruling class, their impatience and indignation, their readiness to support a bold revolutionary initiative on the part of the proletariat, constitute the third political premise of a revolution. It is partly passive—in that it neutralizes the upper strata of the petty bourgeoisie—but partly also active, for it impels the lower strata directly into the struggle side by side with the workers.

That these premises condition each other is obvious. The more decisively and confidently the proletariat acts, the better will it succeed in bringing after it the intermediate layer, the more isolated will be the ruling class, and the more acute its demoralization. And, on the other hand, a demoralization of the rulers will pour water into the mill of the revolutionary class.

The proletariat can become imbued with the confidence necessary for a governmental overthrow only if a clear prospect opens before it, only if it has had an opportunity to test out in action a correlation of forces which is changing to its advantage, only if it feels above it a far-sighted, firm and confident leadership. This brings us to the last premise—by no means the last in importance —of the conquest of power: the revolutionary party as a tightly welded and tempered vanguard of the class.

Thanks to a favorable combination of historic conditions both domestic and international, the Russian proletariat was headed by a party of extraordinary political clarity and unexampled revolutionary temper. Only this permitted that small and young class to carry out a historic task of unprecedented proportions. It is indeed the general testimony of history—the Paris Commune, the German and Austrian revolutions of 1918, the soviet revolutions in Hungary and Bavaria, the Italian revolution of 1919, the German crisis of 1923, the Chinese revolution of 1925–27, the Spanish revolution of 1931—that up to now the weakest link in the chain of necessary conditions has been the party. The hardest thing of all is for the working-class to create a revolutionary organization capable of rising to the height of its historic task. In the older and more civilized countries powerful forces work toward the weakening and demoralization of the revolutionary vanguard. An important constituent part of this work is the struggle of the social democrats against "Blanquism," by which name they designate the revolutionary essence of Marxism.

Notwithstanding the number of great social and political crises, a coincidence of all the conditions necessary to a victorious and stable proletarian revolution has so far occurred but once in history: in Russia in October 1917. A revolutionary situation is not long-lived. The least stable of the premises of a revolution is the mood of the petty bourgeoisie. At a time of national crisis the petty bourgeoisie follows that class which inspires confidence not only in words but deeds. Although capable of impulsive enthusiasm and even of revolutionary fury, the petty bourgeoisie lacks endurance, easily loses heart under reverses, and passes from elated hope to discouragement. And these sharp and swift changes in the mood of the petty bourgeoisie lend their instability to every revolutionary situation. If the proletarian party is not decisive enough to convert the hopes and expectations of the popular masses into revolutionary action in good season, the flood tide is quickly followed by an ebb: the intermediate strata turn away their eyes from the revolution and seek a savior in the opposing camp. And just as at flood tide the proletariat draws after it the petty bourgeoisie, so during the ebb the petty bourgeoisie draws after it considerable layers of the proletariat. Such is the dialectic of the communist and fascist waves observable in the political evolution of Europe since the war.

Attempting to ground themselves upon the assertion of Marx that no régime withdraws from the stage of history until it has exhausted all its possibilities, the Mensheviks denied the legitimacy of a struggle for proletarian dictatorship in backward Russia where capitalism had far from exhausted itself. This argument contained two mistakes, both fatal. Capitalism is not a national but a world-wide system. The imperialist war and its consequences demonstrated that the capitalist system had exhausted itself on a world scale. The revolution in Russia was a breaking of the weakest link in the system of world-wide capitalism.

But the falsity of this Menshevik conception appears also from a national point of view. From the standpoint of economic abstraction, it is indeed possible to affirm that capitalism in Russia has not exhausted its possibilities. But economic processes do not take place in the ether, but in a concrete historical medium. Capitalism is not an abstraction, but a living system of class relations requiring above all things a state power. That the monarchy, under whose protection Russian capitalism developed, had exhausted its possibilities is not denied even by the Mensheviks. The February revolution tried to build up an intermediate state régime. We have followed its history: in the course of eight months it exhausted itself completely. What sort of state order could in these conditions guarantee the further development of Russian capitalism?

"The bourgeois republic, defended only by socialists of moderate tendencies, finding no longer any support in the masses . . . could not maintain itself. Its whole essence had evaporated. There remained only an external shell." This accurate definition belongs to Miliukov. The fate of this evaporated system was necessarily, according to his words, the same as that of the tzarist monarchy: "Both prepared the ground for a revolution, and on the day of revolution neither could find a single defender."

As early as July and August Miliukov characterized the situation by presenting a choice between two names: Kornilov or Lenin? But Kornilov had now made his experiment and it had ended in a miserable failure. For the régime of Kerensky there was certainly no place left. With all the varieties of mood, says Sukhanov, "the one thing upon which all united was hate for the Kerensky régime." Just as the tzarist monarchy had toward the end become impossible in the eyes of the upper circle of the nobility and even the grand dukes, so the government of Kerensky became odious even to the direct inspiritors of his régime, the "grand dukes" of the compromisist upper crust. In this universal dissatisfaction, this sharp political nerve-tension of all classes, we have one of the symptoms of a ripe revolutionary situation. In the same way every muscle, nerve and fiber of an organism is intolerably tensed just before an abscess bursts.

The resolution of the July congress of the Bolsheviks, while warning the workers against premature encounters, had at the same time pointed out that the battle must be joined "whenever the general national crisis and the deep mass enthusiasm have created conditions favorable to the going over of the poor people of the city and country to the side of the workers." That moment arrived in September and October.

The insurrection was thenceforth able to believe in its success, for it could rely upon a genuine majority of the people. This, of course, is not to be understood in a formal sense. If a referendum could have been taken on the question of insurrection, it would have given extremely contradictory and uncertain results. An inner readiness to support a revolution is far from identical with an ability clearly to formulate the necessity of it. Moreover, the answer would have depended to a vast degree upon the manner in which the question was presented, the institution which conducted the referendum—or, to put it more simply, the class which held the power.

There is a limit to the application of democratic methods. You can inquire of all the passengers as to what type of car they

like to ride in, but it is impossible to question them as to whether
to apply the brakes when the train is at full speed and accident
threatens. If the saving operation is carried out skilfully however, and in time, the approval of the passengers is guaranteed in
advance.

Parliamentary consultations of the people are carried out at a
single moment, whereas during a revolution the different layers
of the population arrive at the same conclusion one after another
and with inevitable, although sometimes very slight, intervals.
At the moment when the advanced detachment is burning with
revolutionary impatience, the backward layers have only begun
to move. In Petrograd and Moscow all the mass organizations were
under the leadership of the Bolsheviks. In Tambov province,
which has over three million population—that is, a little less than
both capitals put together—a Bolshevik faction first appeared in
the soviet only a short time before the October revolution.

The syllogisms of the objective development are far from
coinciding—day by day—with the syllogisms, of the thought
process of the masses. And when a great practical decision becomes
unpostponable, in the course of events, that is the very moment
when a referendum is impossible. The difference in level and mood
of the different layers of the people is overcome in action. The
advance layers bring after them the wavering and isolate the
opposing. The majority is not counted up, but won over. Insurrection comes into being at exactly that moment when direct
action alone offers a way out of the contradictions.

Although lacking the power to draw by themselves the necessary political inferences from their war against the landlords,
the peasants had by the very fact of the agrarian insurrection
already adhered to the insurrection of the cities, had evoked it
and were demanding it. They expressed their will not with the
white ballot, but with the red cock—a more serious referendum.
Within those limits in which the support of the peasantry was
necessary for the establishment of a soviet dictatorship, the support was already at hand. "The dictatorship"—as Lenin answered
the doubters—"would give land to the peasants and all power
to the peasant committees in the localities. How can you in your
right mind doubt that the peasant would support that dictator-

ship?" In order that the soldiers, peasants and oppressed nationalities, floundering in the snow-storm of an elective ballot should recognize the Bolsheviks in action, it was necessary that the Bolsheviks seize the power.

But what correlation of forces was necessary in order that the proletariat should seize the power? "To have at the decisive moment, at the decisive point, an overwhelming superiority of force," wrote Lenin later, interpreting the October revolution, "—this law of military success is also the law of political success, especially in that seething and bitter war of classes which is called revolution. The capitals, or generally speaking, the biggest centers of trade and industry . . . decide to a considerable degree the political fate of the people—that is, of course, on condition that the centers are supported by sufficient local rural forces, although this support need not be immediate." It was in this dynamic sense that Lenin spoke of the majority of the people, and that was the sole real meaning of the concept of majority.

The enemy democrats comforted themselves with the thought that the people following the Bolsheviks were mere raw material, mere historic clay. The potters were still to be these same democrats acting in cooperation with the educated bourgeoisie. "Can't those people see," asked a Menshevik paper, "that the Petrograd proletariat and garrison were never before so isolated from all other social strata?" The misfortune of the proletariat and the garrison was that they were "isolated" from those classes from whom they intended to take the power!

But was it really possible to rely upon the sympathy and support of the dark masses in the provinces and at the front? "Their Bolshevism," wrote Sukhanov scornfully, "was nothing but hatred for the coalition and longing for land and peace." As though that were little! Hatred for the coalition meant a desire to take the power from the bourgeoisie. Longing for land and peace was the colossal program which the peasant and soldier intended to carry out under the leadership of the workers. The insignificance of the democrats, even the most leftward, resulted from this very distrust—the distrust of "educated" sceptics—in those dark masses who grasp a phenomenon wholesale, not bothering about details and nuances. This intellectual, pseudo-aristocratic, squeamish attitude toward the people was foreign to Bolshevism, hostile to its very nature. The Bolsheviks were not lily-handed, literary friends of the masses, not pedants. They were not afraid of those backward strata now for the first time lifting themselves out of the dregs. The Bolsheviks took the people as preceding history had created them, and as they were called to achieve the revolution. The Bolsheviks saw it as their mission to stand at the head of that people. Those against the insurrection were "everybody"—except the Bolsheviks. But the Bolsheviks were the people.

The fundamental political force of the October revolution was the proletariat, and the first place in its ranks was occupied by the workers of Petrograd. In the vanguard of these workers stood the Vyborg district. The plan of the insurrection chose this fundamental proletarian district as the point of departure for its offensive.

Compromisers of all shades, beginning with Martov, attempted after the revolution to portray Bolshevism as a soldier movement. The European social democrats grabbed up this theory with delight. But fundamental historic facts were here ignored: the fact that the proletariat was the first to come over to the Bolsheviks; that the Petrograd workers were showing the road to the workers of all countries; that the garrison and front much longer than the workers remained bulwarks of compromisism; that the Social Revolutionaries and Mensheviks created all kinds of privileges for the soldier at the expense of the worker in the soviet system, struggled against the arming of the workers and incited the soldiers against them; that the break in the troops was brought about only by the influence of workers; that at the decisive moment the leadership of the soldiers was in the hands of the workers; and finally that a year later the social democrats of Germany, following the example of their Russian colleagues, relied on the soldiers in their struggle against the workers.

By autumn the Right Compromisers had ceased even to be able to make speeches in the factories and barracks. But the Lefts were still trying to convince the masses of the madness of insurrection. Martov, who in the struggle against the counter-revolutionary offensive in July had found a path to the minds of the masses, was now again serving a hopeless cause. "We cannot expect"—he himself acknowledged on the 14th of October, at a meeting of the Central Executive Committee—"We cannot expect the Bolsheviks to listen to us." Nevertheless he considered it his duty to "warn the masses." The masses, however, wanted action and not moral admonition. Even where they did patiently listen to their well-known adviser, they "thought their own thoughts as before," as Mstislavsky acknowledges. Sukhanov tells how he made an effort in a drizzling rain to convince the Putilov men that they could fix things up without an insurrection. Impatient voices interrupted him. They would listen for two or three minutes and interrupt again. "After a few attempts I gave it up," he says. "It was no use . . . and the rain was drizzling down on us heavier and heavier." Under that ungracious October sky the poor Left Democrats, even as described in their own writings, look like wet hens.

· The favorite political argument of the "Left" opponents of the revolution—and this even among the Bolsheviks—was a reference to the absence of fighting enthusiasm among the lower ranks. "The mood of the laboring and soldier masses," write Zinoviev and Kamenev on October 11th, "is far from comparable even to the mood which existed before the 3rd of July." This assertion was not unfounded: there was a certain depression in the Petrograd proletariat as a result of waiting too long. They were beginning to feel disappointed even in the Bolsheviks: Can it be that they are going to cheat us too? On October 16th Rakhia, one of the fighting Petrograd Bolsheviks, a Finn by birth, said at a conference of the Central Committee: "Our slogan is evidently already getting a little out of date, for there exists a doubt as to whether we will do the thing for which we are calling." But this weariness of waiting, which looked like listlessness, lasted only up to the first fighting signal.

The first task of every insurrection is to bring the troops over to its side. The chief means of accomplishing this are the general strike, mass processions, street encounters, battles at the barricades. The unique thing about the October revolution, a thing never before observed in so complete a form, was that, thanks to a happy combination of circumstances, the proletarian vanguard had won over the garrison of the capital before the moment of open insurrection. It had not only won them over, but had fortified this conquest through the organization of the Garrison Conference. It is impossible to understand the mechanics of the October revolution without fully realizing that the most important task of the insurrection, and the one most difficult to calculate in advance, was fully accomplished in Petrograd before the beginning of the armed struggle.

This does not mean, however, that insurrection had become superfluous. The overwhelming majority of the garrison was, it is true, on the side of the workers. But a minority was against the workers, against the revolution, against the Bolsheviks. This small minority consisted of the best trained elements in the army: the officers, the junkers, the shock battalions, and perhaps the Cossacks. It was impossible to win these elements politically; they had to be vanquished. The last part of the task of the revolution, that which has gone into history under the name of the October insurrection, was therefore purely military in character. At this final stage rifles, bayonets, machine guns, and perhaps cannon, were to decide. The party of the Bolsheviks led the way on this road.

What were the military forces of the approaching conflict? Boris Sokolov, who directed the military work of the Social Revolutionary party, says that in the period preceding the overturn "in the regiments all the party organizations except those of the Bolsheviks had disintegrated, and conditions were not at all favorable to the organization of new ones. The mood of the soldiers was tending definitely toward the Bolsheviks. But their Bolshevism was passive and they lacked any tendency whatever toward active armed movements." Sokolov does not fail to add: "One or two regiments wholly loyal and capable of fighting would have been enough to hold the whole garrison in obedience." Literally all of them, from the monarchist generals to the "socialistic" intelligentsia, wanted only those "one or two regiments" and they would have put down the proletarian revolution! But it is quite true that the garrison, although deeply hostile to the government in its overwhelming mass, was not capable of fighting even on the side of the Bolsheviks. The cause of this lay in the hostile break between the old military structure of the troops, and their new political structure. The backbone of a fighting unit is its commanding staff. The commanding staffs were against the Bolsheviks. The political backbone of the troops was composed of Bolsheviks. The latter, however, not only did not know how to command, but in the majority of cases hardly knew how to handle a gun. The soldier crowd was not homogeneous. The active fighting elements were, as always, a minority. The majority of the soldiers sympathized with the Bolsheviks, voted for them, elected them, but also expected them to decide things. The elements hostile to the Bolsheviks in the troops were too insignificant to venture upon any initiative whatever. The political condition of the garrison was thus exceptionally favorable for an insurrection. But its fighting weight was not large—that was clear from the beginning.

However, it was not necessary to dismiss the garrison entirely from the military count. A thousand soldiers ready to fight on the side of the revolution were scattered here and there among the more passive mass, and for that very reason more or less drew it after them. Certain individual units, more happily constituted, had preserved their discipline and fighting capacity. Strong revolutionary nuclei were to be found even in the disintegrating regiments. In the Sixth Reserve Battalion, consisting of about 10,000 men, out of five companies, the first invariably distinguished itself, being known as Bolshevik almost from the beginning of the revolution and rising to the heights in the October days. The typical regiments of the garrison did not really exist as regiments; their administrative mechanism had broken down; they were incapable of prolonged military effort; but they were nevertheless a horde of armed men a majority of whom had been under fire. All the units were united by a single sentiment: Overthrow Kerensky as soon as possible, disperse, and go home and institute a new land system. Thus that completely demoralized garrison was to rally once more in the October days, and rattle its weapons suggestively, before completely going to pieces.

What force did the Petersburg workers offer from a military point of view? This raises the question of the Red Guard. It is

183

time to speak of this in greater detail, for the Red Guard is soon to come out on the great arena of history.

Deriving its tradition from 1905, the Workers' Guard was reborn with the February revolution and subsequently shared the vicissitudes of its fate. Kornilov, while Commander of the Petrograd military district, asserted that during the days of the overthrow of the monarchy 30,000 revolvers and 40,000 rifles disappeared from the military stores. Over and above that, a considerable quantity of weapons came into the possession of the people during the disarming of the police and by the hands of friendly regiments. Nobody responded to the demand to restore the weapons. A revolution teaches you to value a rifle. The organized workers, however, had received only a small part of this blessing.

During the first four months the workers were not in any way confronted with the question of insurrection. The democratic régime of the dual power gave the Bolsheviks an opportunity to win a majority in the soviets. Armed companies of workers formed a constituent part of the militia. This was, however, more form than substance. A rifle in the hands of a worker involves a totally different historic principle than the same rifle in the hands of a student.

The possession of rifles by the workers alarmed the possessing classes from the very beginning, since it shifted the correlation of forces sharply to the advantage of the factory. In Petrograd, where the state apparatus supported by the Central Executive Committee was at first an indubitable power, the Workers' Militia was not much of a menace. In the provincial industrial regions, however, a reinforcement of the Workers' Guard would involve a complete change of all relations, not only within the given plant but all around it. Armed workers would remove managers and engineers, and even arrest them. Upon resolutions adopted by a factory meeting the Red Guard would not infrequently receive pay out of the factory exchequer. In the Urals, with their rich tradition of guerrilla fighting in 1905, companies of the Red Guard led by the old veterans established law and order. Armed workers almost unnoticeably dissolved the old government and replaced it with soviet institutions. Sabotage on

184

the part of the property owners and administrators shifted to the
workers the task of protecting the plants—the machines, stores,
reserves of coal and raw materials. Rôles were here interchanged:
the worker would tightly grip his rifle in defense of the factory
in which he saw the source of his power. In this way elements of
a workers' dictatorship were inaugurated in the factories and
districts some time before the proletariat as a whole seized the
state power.

Reflecting as always the fright of the property owners, the
Compromisers tried with all their might to oppose the arming of
the Petrograd workers or reduce it to a minimum. According to
Minichev, all the arms in the possession of the Narva district consisted of "fifteen or twenty rifles and a few revolvers." At that
time robberies and deeds of violence were increasing in the capital. Alarming rumors were spreading everywhere heralding new
disturbances. On the eve of the July demonstration it was generally expected that the district would be set fire to. The workers were hunting for weapons, knocking at all doors and sometimes breaking them in.

The Putilov men brought back a trophy from the demonstration of July 3rd: a machine gun with five cases of cartridge-belt.
"We were happy as children," said Minichev. Certain individual
factories were somewhat better armed. According to Lichkov, the
workers of his factory had 80 rifles and 20 big revolvers. Riches
indeed! Through the Red Guard headquarters they got two
machine guns. They put one in the dining room, one in the
attic. "Our commander," says Lichkov, "was Kocherovsky, and
his first assistants were Tomchak, who was killed by White
Guards in the October days near Tzarskoe Selo, and Efimov, who
was shot by White bands near Hamburg." These scant words
enable us to glance into the factory laboratory where the cadres
of the October revolution and the future Red Army were forming, where the Tomchaks and Efimovs were being chosen out,
tempered, and were learning to command, and with them those
hundreds and thousands of nameless workers who won the power,
loyally defended it from its enemy, and fell subsequently on all
the fields of battle.

The July Days introduced a sudden change in the situation of the Red Guard. The disarming of the workers was now carried out quite openly—not by admonition but by force. However, what the workers gave up as weapons was mostly old rubbish. All the very valuable guns were carefully concealed. Rifles were distributed among the most reliable members of the party. Machine guns smeared with tallow were buried in the ground. Detachments of the Guard closed up shop and went underground, closely adhering to the Bolsheviks.

The business of arming the workers was originally placed in the hands of the factory and district committees of the Party. It was only after the recovery from the July Days that the Military Organization of the Bolsheviks, which had formerly worked only in the garrison and at the front, took up the organization of the Red Guard, providing the workers with military instructors and in some cases with weapons. The prospect of armed insurrection put forward by the party gradually prepared the advanced workers for a new conception of the function of the Red Army. It was no longer a militia of the factories and workers' districts, but the cadres of a future army of insurrection.

During August, fires in the shops and factories multiplied. Every new crisis is preceded by a convulsion of the collective mind, sending forth waves of alarm. The factory and shop committees developed an intense labor of defending the plants from attacks of this kind. Concealed rifles came out into the open. The Kornilov insurrection conclusively legalized the Red Guard. About 25,000 workers were enrolled in companies and armed— by no means fully, to be sure—with rifles, and in part with machine guns. Workers from the Schlüsselberg powder factory delivered on the Neva a bargeful of hand grenades and explosives —against Kornilov! The compromisist Central Executive Committee refused this gift of the Greeks! The Red Guards of the Vyborg side distributed the gift by night throughout the district.

"Drill in the art of handling a rifle," says the worker Skorinko, "formerly carried on in flats and tenements, was now brought out into the light and air, into the parks, the boulevards." "The shops were turned into camps," says another worker, Rakitov. . . . "The worker would stand at his bench with knapsack on his back and rifle beside him." Very soon all those working in the bomb factory except the old Social Revolutionaries and Mensheviks were enrolled in the Guard. After the whistle all would draw up in the court for drill. "Side by side with a bearded worker you would see a boy apprentice, and both of them attentively listening to the instructor. . . ." Thus while the old tzarist army was disintegrating, the foundation of a future Red Army was being laid in the factories.

As soon as the Kornilov danger passed, the Compromisers tried to slow up on the fulfilment of their promises. To the 30,-000 Putilov men, for instance, only 500 rifles were given out. Soon the giving out of weapons stopped altogether. The danger now was not from the right, but the left; protection must be sought not among the proletarians but the junkers.

An absence of immediate practical aims combined with the lack of weapons caused an ebbing of workers from the Red Guard, but this only for a short interval. The foundation cadres had been laid down solidly in every plant; firm bonds had been established between the different companies. These cadres now knew from experience that they had serious reserves which could be brought to their feet in case of danger.

The going over of the Soviet to the Bolsheviks again radically changed the position of the Red Guard. From being persecuted or tolerated, it now became an official instrument of the Soviet already reaching for the power. The workers now often found by themselves a way to weapons, asking only the sanction of the Soviet. From the end of September on, and more especially from the 10th of October, the preparation of an insurrection was openly placed on the order of the day. For a month before the revolution in scores of shops and factories of Petrograd an intense military activity was in progress—chiefly rifle practice. By the middle of October the interest in weapons had risen to a new height. In certain factories almost every last man was enrolled in a company.

The workers were more and more impatiently demanding weapons from the Soviet, but the weapons were infinitely fewer than the hands stretched out for them. "I came to Smolny every day," relates the engineer, Kozmin, "and observed how both be-

187

fore and after the sitting of the Soviet, workers and sailors would come up to Trotsky, offering and demanding weapons for the arming of the workers, making reports as to how and where these weapons were distributed, and putting the question: 'But when does business begin?' The impatience was very great. . . ."

Formally the Red Guard remained non-party. But the nearer the final day came, the more prominent were the Bolsheviks. They constituted the nucleus of every company; they controlled the commanding staff and the communications with other plants and districts. The non-party workers and Left Social Revolutionaries followed the lead of the Bolsheviks.

However, even now, on the eve of the insurrection, the ranks of the Guard were not numerous. On the 16th, Uritzky, a member of the Bolshevik Central Committee, estimated the workers' army of Petrograd at 40,000 bayonets. The figure is probably exaggerated. The resources of weapons remained still very limited. In spite of the impotence of the government it was impossible to seize the arsenals without taking the road of open insurrection.

On the 22nd, there was held an all-city conference of the Red Guard, its hundred delegates representing about twenty thousand fighters. The figure is not to be taken too literally—not all those registered had shown any signs of activity. But at a moment of alarm volunteers would pour into the companies in large numbers. Regulations adopted the next day by the conference defined the Red Guard as "an organization of the armed forces of the proletariat for the struggle against counter-revolution and the defense of the conquests of the revolution." Observe this: that twenty-four hours before the insurrection the task was still defined in terms of defense and not attack.

The basic military unit was the ten; four tens was a squad, three squads, a company; three companies, a battalion. With its commanding staff and special units, a battalion numbered over 500 men. The battalions of a district constituted a division.[1] Big factories like the Putilov had their own divisions. Special technical commands—sappers, bicyclers, telegraphers, machine-gunners and artillery men—were recruited in the corresponding fac-

---

[1] Otryad.

188

tories, and attached to the riflemen—or else acted independently according to the nature of the given task. The entire commanding staff was elective. There was no risk in this: all were volunteers here and knew each other well.

The working women created Red Cross divisions. At the shops manufacturing surgical supplies for the army, lectures were announced on the care of the wounded. "Already in almost all the factories," writes Tatiana Graff, "the working women were regularly on duty as nurses with the necessary first-aid supplies." The organization was extremely poor in money and technical equipment. By degrees, however, the factory committees sent material for hospital bases and ambulances. During the hours of the revolution these weak nuclei swiftly developed. An imposing technical equipment was suddenly found at their disposal. On the 24th the Vyborg district soviet issued the following order: "Immediately requisition all automobiles. . . . Take an inventory of all first-aid supplies, and have nurses on duty in all clinics."

A growing number of non-party workers were now going out for shooting drill and maneuvers. The number of posts requiring patrol duty was increasing. In the factories sentries were on duty night and day. The headquarters of the Red Guard were transferred to more spacious rooms. On the 23rd at a pipe foundry they held an examination of the Red Guard. An attempt of a Menshevik to speak against the insurrection was drowned in a storm of indignation: Enough, enough! The time for argument is passed! The movement was irresistible. It was seizing even the Mensheviks. "They were enrolling in the Red Guard," says Tatiana Graff, "participating in all duties and even developing some initiative." Skorinko tells how on the 23rd, Social Revolutionaries and Mensheviks, old and young, were fraternizing with the Bolsheviks, and how Skorinko himself joyfully embraced his own father who was a worker in the same factory. The worker Peskovoi says that in his armed detachment "there were young workers of sixteen and old men of fifty." The variety of ages gave "good cheer and fighting courage."

The Vyborg side was especially fervent in preparing for battle. Having stolen the keys of the drawbridges, studied out the vulnerable points of the district, and elected their military-revolutionary committee, the factory committees established continuous patrols. Kayurov writes with legitimate pride of the Vyborg men: "They were the first to go to battle with the autocracy, they were the first to institute in their district the eight-hour day, the first to come out with a protest against the ten minister-capitalists, the first to raise a protest on July 7th against the persecution of our party, and they were not the last on the decisive day of October 25th." What is true is true!

The history of the Red Guard is to a considerable extent the history of the dual power. With its inner contradictions and conflicts, the dual power helped the workers to create a considerable armed force even before the insurrection. To cast up the general total of the workers' detachments throughout the country at the moment of insurrection is hardly possible, at least at the present moment. In any case, tens and tens of thousands of armed workers constituted the cadres of the insurrection. The reserves were almost inexhaustible.

The organization of the Red Guard remained, of course, extremely far from complete. Everything was done in haste, in the rough, and not always skilfully. The Red Guard men were in the majority little trained; the communications were badly organized; the supply system was lame; the sanitary corps lagged behind. But the Red Guard, recruited from the most self-sacrificing workers, was burning to carry the job through this time to the end. And that was the decisive thing. The difference between the workers' divisions and the peasant regiments was determined not only by the social ingredients of the two—many of those clumsy soldiers after returning to their villages and dividing the landlords' land will fight desperately against the White Guards, first in guerrilla bands and afterwards in the Red Army. Beside the social difference there existed another more immediate one: Whereas the garrison represented a compulsory assemblage of old soldiers defending themselves against war, the divisions of the Red Guard were newly constructed by individual selection on a new basis and with new aims.

The Military Revolutionary Committee had at its disposal a third kind of armed force: the sailors of the Baltic Fleet. In their social ingredients they are far closer to the workers than

190

the infantry are. There are a good many Petrograd workers among them. The political level of the sailors is incomparably higher than that of the soldiers. In distinction from the none too belligerent reserves who have forgotten all about rifles, these sailors have never stopped actual service.

For active operations it was possible to count firmly upon the armed Bolsheviks, upon the divisions of the Red Guard, upon the advanced group of the sailors, and upon the better preserved regiments. The different elements of this collective army supplemented each other. The numerous garrisons lacked the will to fight. The sailor detachments lacked numbers. The Red Guard lacked skill. The workers together with the sailors contributed energy, daring and enthusiasm. The regiments of the garrison constituted a rather inert reserve, imposing in its numbers and overwhelming in its mass.

In contact as they were from day to day with workers, soldiers and sailors, the Bolsheviks were aware of the deep qualitative difference between the constituent parts of this army they were to lead into battle. The very plan of the insurrection was based to a considerable degree upon a calculation of these differences.

The possessing classes constituted the social force of the other camp. This means that they were its military weakness. These solid people of capital, the press, the pulpit—where and when have they ever fought? They are accustomed to find out by telegraph or telephone the results of the battles which settle their fate. The younger generation, the sons, the students? They were almost all hostile to the October revolution. But a majority of them too stood aside. They stood with their fathers awaiting the outcome of the battle. A number of them afterward joined the officers and junkers—already largely recruited from among the students. The property holders had no popular masses with them. The workers, soldiers, peasants had turned against them. The collapse of the compromise parties meant that the possessing classes were left without an army.

In proportion to the significance of railroads in the life of modern states, a large place was occupied in the political calculations of both camps by the question of the railroad workers. Here the hierarchical constitution of the personnel leaves room for an extraordinary political variegation, creating favorable conditions for the diplomats of the Compromisers. The lately formed Vikzhel had kept a considerably more solid root among the clerks and even among the workers than, for instance, the army committees at the front. In the railroads only a minority followed the Bolsheviks, chiefly workers in the stations and yards. According to the report of Schmidt, one of the Bolshevik leaders of the trade union movement, the railroad workers of the Petrograd and Moscow junctions stood closest of all to the party.

But even among the compromisist mass of clerks and workers there was a sharp shift to the left from the date of the railroad strike at the end of September. Dissatisfaction with the Vikzhel, which had compromised itself by talking and wavering, was more and more evident in the lower ranks. Lenin remarked: "The army of railroad and postal clerks continues in a state of sharp conflict with the government." From the standpoint of the immediate tasks of the insurrection that was almost enough.

Things were less favorable in the post and telegraph service. According to the Bolshevik, Boky, "the men in the Post and Telegraph Offices are mostly Kadets." But here too the lower personnel had taken a hostile attitude toward the upper ranks. There was a group of mail carriers ready at a critical moment to seize the Post Office.

It would have been hopeless in any case to try to change the minds of the railroad and postal clerks with words. If the Bolsheviks should prove indecisive, the advantage would remain with the Kadets and the compromisist upper circles. With a decisive revolutionary leadership the lower ranks must inevitably carry with them the intermediate layers, and isolate the upper circles of the Vikzhel. In revolutionary calculations statistics alone are not enough; the co-efficient of living action is also essential.

The enemies of the insurrection in the ranks of the Bolshevik party itself found, however, sufficient ground for pessimistic conclusions. Zinoviev and Kamenev gave warning against an underestimation of the enemy's forces. "Petrograd will decide, and in

Petrograd the enemy has . . . considerable forces: 5,000 junkers, magnificently armed and knowing how to fight, and then
the army headquarters, and then the shock troops, and then the
Cossacks, and then a considerable part of the garrison, and then
a very considerable quantity of artillery spread out fan-wise
around Petrograd. Moreover the enemy with the help of the Central Executive Committee will almost certainly attempt to bring
troops from the front. . . ." The list sounds imposing, but it
is only a list. If an army as a whole is a copy of society, then
when society openly splits, both armies are copies of the two
warring camps. The army of the possessors contained the worm-
holes of isolation and decay.

The officers crowding the hotels, restaurants and brothels
had been hostile to the government ever since the break between
Kerensky and Kornilov. Their hatred of the Bolsheviks, however, was infinitely more bitter. As a general rule, the monarchist
officers were most active on the side of the government. "Dear
Kornilov and Krymov, in what you failed to do perhaps with
God's help we shall succeed. . . ." Such was the prayer of officer
Sinegub, one of the most valiant defenders of the Winter Palace
on the day of the uprising. But in spite of the vast number of
officers, only single individuals were really ready to fight. The
Kornilov plot had already proven that these completely demoralized officers were not a fighting force.

The junkers were not homogeneous in social make-up, and
there was no unanimity among them. Along with hereditary
fighters, sons and grandsons of officers, there were many accidental elements gathered up under pressure of war-needs even
during the monarchy. The head of an engineering school said
to an officer: "I must die with you. . . . We are nobles, you
know, and cannot think otherwise." These lucky gentlemen,
who did after all succeed in evading a noble death, would speak
of the democratic junkers as low-breeds, as muzhiks "with coarse
stupid faces." This division into the blue blood and the black
penetrated deeply into the junker schools, and it is noticeable
that here too those who came out most zealously in defense of
the republican government were the very ones who most
mourned the loss of the monarchy. The democratic junkers de-

clared that they were not for Kerensky but for the Central Executive Committee. The revolution had first opened the doors of the junker schools to the Jews. And in trying to hold their own with the privileged upper circles, the sons of the Jewish bourgeoisie became extraordinarily warlike against the Bolsheviks. But, alas, this was not enough to save the régime—not even to defend the Winter Palace. The heterogeneousness of these military schools and their complete isolation from the army brought it about that during the critical hours the junkers began to hold meetings. They began to ask questions: How are the Cossacks behaving? Is anybody coming out besides us? Is it worth while anyway to defend the Provisional Government? According to a report of Podvoisky, there were about 120 socialist junkers in the Petrograd military schools at the beginning of October, and of these 42 or 43 were Bolsheviks. "The junkers say that the whole commanding staff of the schools is counter-revolutionary. They are being definitely prepared in case anything happens to put down the insurrection. . . ." The number of socialists, and especially Bolsheviks, was wholly insignificant, but they made it possible for Smolny to know everything of importance that went on among the junkers. In addition to that, the location of the military schools was very disadvantageous. The junkers were sandwiched in among the barracks, and although they spoke scornfully of the soldiers, they looked upon them with a great deal of dread.

The junkers had plenty of ground for caution. Thousands of hostile eyes were watching them from the neighboring barracks and the workers' districts. This observation was the more effective in that every school had its soldier group, neutral in words but in reality inclining toward the insurrection. The school storerooms were in the hands of non-combatant soldiers. "Those scoundrels," writes an officer of the Engineering School, "not satisfied with losing the key to the storeroom so that I had to give orders to break in the door, also removed the breech-locks from the machine guns and hid them somewhere." In these circumstances you could hardly expect miracles of heroism from the junkers.

But would not a Petrograd insurrection be threatened from

without, from the neighboring garrisons? In the last days of its life the monarchy had never ceased to put its hope in that small military ring surrounding the capital. The monarchy had missed its guess, but how would it go this time? To guarantee conditions excluding every possible danger would have been to make the very insurrection unnecessary. After all, its aim was to break down the obstacles which could not be dissolved politically. Everything could not be calculated in advance, but all that could be, was.

Early in October a conference of the soviets of Petrograd province was held in Kronstadt. Delegates from the garrisons of the environs of the capital—Gatchina, Tzarskoe, Krasnoe, Oranienbaum, Kronstadt itself—took the very highest note set by the tuning-fork of the Baltic sailors. Their resolution was adhered to by the deputies of Petrograd province. The muzhiks were veering sharply through the Left Social Revolutionaries toward the Bolsheviks.

At a conference of the Central Committee on the 16th, a party worker in the province, Stepanov, drew a somewhat variegated picture of the state of the forces, but nevertheless with a clear predominance of Bolshevik colors. In Sestroretsk and Kolpino the workers are under arms; their mood is militant. In Novy Peterhoff the work in the regiment has fallen off; the regiment is disorganized. In Krasnoe Selo the 176th regiment is Bolshevik (the same regiment which patrolled the Tauride Palace on July 4th), the 172nd is on the side of the Bolsheviks, "and, besides, there is cavalry there." In Luga the garrison of 30,000, after swinging over to the Bolsheviks, is wavering in part; the soviet is still defensist. In Gdov the regiment is Bolshevik. In Kronstadt the mood has declined; the garrison boiled over during the preceding months; the better part of the sailors are in the active fleet. In Schlüsselburg, within 60 versts of Petrograd, the soviet long ago became the sole power; the workers of the powder factory are ready at any moment to support the capital.

In combination with the results of that Kronstadt conference of soviets, this information about the first line reserves may be considered entirely encouraging. The radiation of the February insurrection had been sufficient to dissolve discipline over a wide

195

area. And it was now possible to look with confidence upon the nearby garrisons, their conditions being adequately known in advance.

The troops of Finland and the northern front were among the second line reserves. Here conditions were still more favorable. The work of Smilga, Antonov, Dybenko had produced invaluable results. Along with the garrison of Helsingfors the fleet had become a sovereign in Finnish territory. The government had no more power there. The two Cossack divisions quartered in Helsingfors—Kornilov had intended them for a blow at Petrograd—had come in close contact with the sailors and were supporting the Bolsheviks, or the Left Social Revolutionaries, who in the Baltic Fleet were becoming less and less distinguishable from Bolsheviks.

Helsingfors was extending its hands to the sailors of the Reval naval base, whose attitude up to that time had been indefinite. The Congress of Soviets of the Northern Region, in which also apparently the Baltic Fleet had taken the initiative, had united the soviets of the garrisons surrounding Petrograd in such a wide circle that it took in Moscow on one side and Archangel on the other. "In this manner," writes Antonov, "the idea was realized of armoring the capital of the revolution against possible attacks from Kerensky's troops." Smilga returned from the Congress to Helsingfors to organize a special detachment of sailors, infantry and artillery to be sent to Petrograd at the first signal. The Finland flank of the Petrograd insurrection was thus protected to the last degree. On this side no blow was to be expected, only strong help. On other portions of the front, too, things were wholly favorable—at least far more favorable than the most optimistic of the Bolsheviks in those days imagined. During October committee elections were held throughout the army, and everywhere they showed a sharp swing to the Bolsheviks. In the corps quartered near Dvinsk the "old reasonable soldiers" were completely snowed under in the elections to the regimental and company committees; their places were taken by "gloomy, gray creatures . . . with angry piercing eyes and wolfish snouts." The same thing happened in other sectors. "Committee elections are in progress everywhere, and everywhere only Bolsheviks and defeatists are elected." The governmental commissars began to avoid making trips to their units. "Their situation is now no better than ours." We are quoting Baron Budberg. Two cavalry regiments of his corps, the Hussar and Ural Cossacks, who remained longest of all in the control of the commanders, and had not refused to put down mutinous units, suddenly changed color and demanded "that they be relieved of the function of punitive troops and gendarmes." The threatening sense of this warning was clear to the Baron and to everybody else. "You can't command a flock of hyenas, jackals and sheep by playing on a violin," he wrote. "The only salvation lies in a mass application of the hot iron. . . ." And here follows the tragic confession: ". . . a thing which we haven't got and is nowhere to be gotten."

If we do not cite similar testimony about other corps and divisions, it is only because their chiefs were not so observant as Budberg, or they did not keep diaries, or these diaries have not yet come to light. But the corps standing near Dvinsk was distinguished in nothing but the trenchant style of its commander from the other corps of the 5th Army, which in its turn was but little in advance of the other armies.

The compromisist committee of the 5th Army, which had long been hanging in the air, continued to send telegraphic threats to Petrograd to the effect that it would restore order in the rear with the bayonet. "All that was mere braggadoccio and hot air," writes Budberg. The committee was actually living its last days. On the 23rd it failed of re-election. The president of the new Bolshevik committee was Doctor Skliansky, a magnificent young organizer who soon developed his talent widely in the work of creating the Red Army, and who died subsequently an accidental death while canoeing on one of the American lakes.

The assistant of the government Commissar of the Northern Front reports to the War Minister on the 22nd of October that the ideas of Bolshevism are making great headway in the army, that the mass wants peace, and that even the artillery which has held out to the very last moment has become "hospitable to defeatist propaganda." This too is no unimportant symptom. "The Provisional Government has no authority"—reports its own direct agent three days before the revolution.

To be sure, the Military Revolutionary Committee did not then know of all these documents. But what it did know was amply sufficient. On the 23rd, representatives of various units at the front filed past the Petrograd Soviet and demanded peace. Otherwise, they answered, they would march to the rear and "destroy all the parasites who want to keep on fighting for another ten years." Seize the power, the front men said to the Soviet, "the trenches will support you."

In the more remote and backward fronts, the southwestern and Rumanian, Bolsheviks were still rare specimens, curiosities. But the mood of the soldiers here was the same as elsewhere. Evgenia Bosh tells how in the 2nd Corps of the Guards, quartered in the vicinity of Zhmerinka, among 60,000 soldiers there was one young communist and two sympathizers. This did not prevent the corps from coming out in support of the insurrection in the October days.

To the very last hour the government circles rested their hope in the Cossacks. But the less blind among the politicians of the right camp understood that here too things were in a very bad way. The Cossack officers were Kornilovists almost to a man. The rank-and-file were tending more and more to the left. In the government they did not understand this, imagining that the coolness of the Cossack regiments to the Winter Palace was caused by injured feelings about Kaledin. In the long run, however, it became clear even to the Minister of Justice, Maliantovich, that "only the Cossack officers" were supporters of Kaledin. The rank-and-file Cossacks, like all the soldiers, were simply going Bolshevik.

Of that front which in the early days of March had kissed the hands and feet of liberal priests, had carried Kadet ministers on its shoulders, got drunk on the speeches of Kerensky, and believed that the Bolsheviks were German agents—of that there was nothing left. Those rosy illusions had been drowned in the mud of the trenches, which the soldiers refused to go on kneading with their leaky boots. "The denouement is approaching," wrote

Budberg on the very day of the Petrograd insurrection, "and there can be no doubt of its outcome. On our front there is not one single unit . . . which would not be in the control of the Bolsheviks."

CHAPTER VII

THE CONQUEST OF THE CAPITAL

ALL is changed and yet all remains as before. The revolution has shaken the country, deepened the split, frightened some, embittered others, but not yet wiped out a thing or replaced it. Imperial St. Petersburg seems drowned in a sleepy lethargy rather than dead. The revolution has stuck little red flags in the hands of the cast-iron monuments of the monarchy. Great red streamers are hanging down the fronts of the government buildings. But the palaces, the ministries, the headquarters, seem to be living a life entirely apart from those red banners, tolerably faded, moreover, by the autumn rains. The two-headed eagles with the scepter of empire have been torn down where possible, but oftener draped or hastily painted over. They seem to be lurking there. All the old Russia is lurking, its jaws set in rage.

The slight figures of the militia-men at the street corners remind one of the revolution that has wiped out the old "Pharaohs," who used to stand there like live monuments. Moreover Russia has now for almost two months been called a republic. And the tzar's family is in Tobolsk. Yes, the February whirlwind has left its traces. But the tzarist generals remain generals, the senators senatorialize, the privy councillors defend their dignity, the Table of Precedence is still in effect. Colored hat-bands and cockades recall the bureaucratic hierarchy; yellow buttons with an eagle still distinguish the student. And yet more important—the landlords are still landlords, no end of the war is in sight, the Allied diplomats are impudently jerking official Russia along on a string.

All remains as before and yet nobody knows himself. The aristocratic quarters feel that they have been moved out into the backyard; the quarters of the liberal bourgeoisie have moved nearer the aristocracy. From being a patriotic myth, the Russian

200

people have become an awful reality. Everything is billowing and shaking under foot. Mysticism flares up with sharpened force in those circles which not long ago were making fun of the superstitions of the monarchy.

Brokers, lawyers, ballerinas are cursing the oncoming eclipse of public morals. Faith in the Constituent Assembly is evaporating day by day. Gorky in his newspaper is prophesying the approaching downfall of culture. The flight from raving and hungry Petrograd to a more peaceful and well-fed province, on the increase ever since the July Days, now becomes a stampede. Respectable families who have not succeeded in getting away from the capital, try in vain to insulate themselves from reality behind stone wall and under iron roof. But the echoes of the storm penetrate on every side: through the market, where everything is getting dear and nothing to be had; through the respectable press, which is turning into one yelp of hatred and fear; through the seething streets where from time to time shootings are to be heard under the windows; and finally through the back entrance, through the servants, who are no longer humbly submissive. It is here that the revolution strikes home to the most sensitive spot. That obstreperousness of the household slaves destroys utterly the stability of the family régime.

Nevertheless the everyday routine defends itself with all its might. School-boys are still studying the old text-books, functionaries drawing up the same useless papers, poets scribbling the verses that nobody reads, nurses telling the fairy-tales about Ivan Tzarevich. The nobility's and merchants' daughters, coming in from the provinces, are studying music or hunting husbands. The same old canon on the wall of the Peter and Paul fortress continues to announce the noon hour. A new ballet is going on in the Mariinsky theater, and the Minister of Foreign Affairs, Tereshchenko, stronger on choreography than diplomacy, finds time, we may assume, to admire the steel toes of the ballerina and thus demonstrate the stability of the régime.

The remnants of the old banquet are still very plentiful and everything can be had for big money. The Guard officers still click their spurs accurately and go after adventures. Wild parties are in progress in the private dining rooms of expensive restaurants. The shutting-off of the electric lights at midnight does not prevent the flourishing of gambling clubs where champagne sparkles by candlelight, where illustrious peculators swindle no less illustrious German spies, where monarchist conspirators call the bets of Semitic smugglers, and where the astronomical figures of the stakes played for indicate both the scale of debauchery and the scale of inflation.

Can it be that a mere tramcar, run-down, dirty, dilatory, draped with clusters of people, leads from this St. Petersburg in its death-agony into the workers' quarters so passionately and tensely alive with a new hope? The blue-and-gold cupola of Smolny Convent announces from afar the headquarters of the insurrection. It is on the edge of the city where the tram-line ends and the Neva describes a sharp turn south, separating the center of the capital from the suburbs. That long gray three-story building, an educative barrack for the daughters of the nobility, is now the stronghold of the soviets. Its long echoing corridors seem to have been made for teaching the laws of perspective. Over the doors of many of the rooms along the corridors little enameled tablets are still preserved: "Teacher's room," "Third Grade," "Fourth Grade," "Grade Supervisor." But alongside the old tablets, or covering them, sheets of paper have been tacked up as best they might, bearing the mysterious hieroglyphics of the revolution: Tz–K P–S–R, S–D Mensheviki, S–D–Bolsheviki, Left S–R, Anarchist–Communists, Despatching Room of the Tz–I–K, etc., etc. The observant John Reed notices a placard on the walls: "Comrades, for the sake of your own health, observe cleanliness." Alas, nobody observes cleanliness, not even nature. October Petrograd is living under a canopy of rain. The streets, long unswept, are dirty. Enormous puddles are standing in the court of Smolny. The mud is carried into the corridors and halls by the soldiers' boots. But nobody is looking down now underfoot. All are looking forward.

Smolny is more and more firmly and imperiously giving commands, for the passionate sympathy of the masses is lifting her up. However, the central leadership grasps directly only the topmost links of that revolutionary system which as a connected whole is destined to achieve the change. The most important

202

processes are taking place below, and somehow of their own accord. The factories and barracks are the chief forges of history in these days and nights. As in February, the Vyborg district focusses the basic forces of the revolution. But it has today a thing it lacked in February—its own powerful organization open and universally recognized. From the dwellings, the factory lunch-rooms, the clubs, the barracks, all threads lead to the house numbered 33 Samsonevsky Prospect, where are located the district Committee of the Bolsheviks, the Vyborg soviet, and the military headquarters. The district militia is fusing with the Red Guard. The district is wholly in the control of the workers. If the government should raid Smolny, the Vyborg district alone could re-establish a center and guarantee the further offensive.

The denouement was approaching close, but the ruling circles thought, or pretended to think, that they had no special cause for anxiety. The British Embassy, which had its own reasons for following events in Petrograd with some attention, received, according to the Russian ambassador in London, reliable information about the coming insurrection. To the anxious inquiries of Buchanan at the inevitable diplomatic luncheon, Tereshchenko replied with warm assurance: "Nothing of the kind" is possible; the government has the reins firmly in hand. The Russian Embassy in London found out about the revolution in Petrograd from the despatches of a British telegraph agency.

The mine owner, Auerbach, paying a visit during those days to the deputy-minister, Palchinsky, inquired in passing—after a conversation about more serious matters—as to the "dark clouds on the political horizon." He received a most reassuring answer: The next storm in a series, and nothing more; it will pass over and all will be clear—"sleep well." Palchinsky himself was going to pass one or two sleepless nights before he got arrested.

The more unceremoniously Kerensky treated the compromise leaders, the less did he doubt that in the hour of danger they would come punctually to his aid. The weaker the Compromisers grew, the more carefully did they surround themselves with an atmosphere of illusion. Exchanging words of mutual encouragement between their Petrograd turrets and their upper-crust organizations in the provinces and the front, the Mensheviks and

203

Social-Revolutionaries created a simulacrum of public opinion, and thus disguising their own impotence, fooled not so much their enemy as themselves.

The cumbersome and good-for-nothing state apparatus, representing a combination of March socialist with tzarist bureaucrat, was perfectly accommodated to the task of self-deception. The half-baked March socialist dreaded to appear to the bureaucrat a not wholly mature statesman. The bureaucrat dreaded lest he show a lack of respect to the new ideas. Thus was created a web of official lies, in which generals, district attorneys, newspaper-men, commissars, aides-de-camp, lied the more, the nearer they stood to the seats of power. The commander of the Petrograd military district made comforting reports, for the reason that Kerensky, faced by an uncomforting reality, had great need of them.

The traditions of the dual power worked in the same direction. Were not the current orders of the military headquarters, when countersigned by the Military Revolutionary Committee, implicitly obeyed? The patrolling squads throughout the city were filled out by the troops of the garrison in the usual order—and we must add, it had been long since the troops had done their patrol duty with such zeal as now. Discontent among the masses? But "slaves in revolt" are always discontented. Only the scum of the garrison and the workers' districts will take part in mutinous attempts. The soldiers' sections are against headquarters? But the Military department of the Central Executive Committee is for Kerensky. The whole organized democracy, with the exception of the Bolsheviks, supports the government. Thus the rosy March nimbus had turned into a gray vapor, hiding the actual traits of things.

It was only after the break between Smolny and headquarters that the government tried to adopt a more serious attitude toward the situation. There is of course no immediate danger, they said, but this time we must avail ourselves of the opportunity to put an end to the Bolsheviks. Besides, the bourgeois Allies were bringing every pressure to bear on the Winter Palace. On the night of the 24th the government summoned up its courage and passed a resolution: to institute legal proceedings against the Military

Revolutionary Committee; to shut down the Bolshevik papers advocating insurrection; to summon reliable military detachments from the environs and from the front. The proposal to arrest the Military Revolutionary Committee as a body, although adopted in principle, was postponed in execution. For so large an undertaking, they decided, it was necessary to secure in advance the support of the Pre-Parliament.

The rumor of the government's decision spread immediately through the town. In the building of the main headquarters alongside the Winter Palace, the soldiers of the Pavlovsky regiment, one of the most reliable units of the Military Revolutionary Committee, were on sentry duty during the night of the 24th. Conversations went on in their presence about summoning the junkers, about lifting the bridges, about arrests. All that the Pavlovtsi managed to hear and remember they immediately passed on to Smolny. Those in the revolutionary center did not always know how to make use of the communications of this self-constituted Intelligence Service. But it fulfilled an invaluable function. The workers and soldiers of the whole city were made aware of the intentions of the enemy, and reinforced in their readiness to resist.

Early in the morning the authorities began their preparations for aggressive action. The military schools of the capital were ordered to make ready for battle. The cruiser *Aurora* moored in the Neva, its crew favorable to the Bolsheviks, was ordered to put out and join the rest of the fleet. Military detachments were called in from neighboring points: a battalion of shock troops from Tzarskoe Selo, the junkers from Oranienbaum, the artillery from Pavlovsk. The headquarters of the northern front was asked to send reliable troops to the capital immediately. In the way of direct measures of military precaution, the following orders were given: to increase the guard of the Winter Palace; to raise the bridges over the Neva; to have all automobiles inspected by the junkers; to cut Smolny out of the telephone system. The Minister of Justice, Maliantovich, gave an order for the immediate arrest of those Bolsheviks released under bail who had again brought themselves to attention by anti-governmental activity. This blow was aimed primarily at Trotsky. The fickle-ness of the times is well illustrated by the fact that Maliantovich —as also his predecessor, Zarudny—had been Trotsky's defense counsel in the trial of the St. Petersburg Soviet of 1905. Then too it had been a question of the leadership of the Soviet. The indictments were identical in the two cases, except that the former defenders when they became accusers added the little point about German gold.

Headquarters developed a particularly feverish activity in the sphere of typography. Document followed document. No coming-out will be permitted; the guilty will be held strictly responsible; detachments of the garrison not to leave their barracks without orders from headquarters; "All commissars of the Petrograd Soviet to be removed"; their illegal activities to be investigated "with a view to court martial." In these formidable orders it was not indicated who was to carry them out or how. Under threat of personal liability the commander demanded that owners of automobiles place them at the disposal of headquarters "with a view of preventing unlawful seizures," but nobody moved a finger in response.

The Central Executive Committee was also prolific of warnings and forbiddings. And the peasant executive committee, the city duma, the central committees of the Mensheviks and Social-Revolutionaries followed in its steps. All these institutions were sufficiently rich in literary resources. In the proclamations which plastered the walls and fences, the talk was invariably about a handful of lunatics, about the danger of bloody encounters, about the inevitability of counter-revolution.

At five-thirty in the morning a government commissar with a detachment of junkers showed up at the Bolshevik printing-plant, and after manning the exits, presented an order of headquarters for the immediate suppression of the central organ and the soldiers' paper.—What? Headquarters? Does that still exist? No orders are recognized here without the sanction of the Military Revolutionary Committee. But that did not help. The stereotypes were smashed, the building sealed. The government had scored its first success.

A worker and a working-girl from the Bolshevik printing-plant ran panting to Smolny and there found Podvoisky and

Trotsky. If the Committee would give them a guard against the junkers, the workers would bring out the paper. A form was soon found for the first answer to the government offensive. An order was issued to the Litovsky regiment to send a company immediately to the defense of the workers' press. The messengers from the printing-plant insisted that the Sixth Battalion of sappers be also ordered out: these were near neighbors and loyal friends. Telephonograms were immediately sent to the two addresses. The Litovtsi and the sappers came out without delay. The seals were torn from the building, the moulds again poured, and the work went on. With a few hours' delay the newspaper suppressed by the government came out under protection of the troops of a committee which was itself liable to arrest. That was insurrection. That is how it developed.

During this same time the cruiser *Aurora* had addressed a question to Smolny: Shall we go to sea or remain in the Neva? The very same sailors who had guarded the Winter Palace against Kornilov in August were now burning to settle accounts with Kerensky. The government order was promptly countermanded by the Committee and the crew received Order No. 1218: "In case of an attack on the Petrograd garrison by the counter-revolutionary forces, the cruiser *Aurora* is to protect herself with tugs, steam-boats, and cutters." The cruiser enthusiastically carried out this order, for which it had only been waiting.

These two acts of resistance, suggested by workers and sailors, and carried out, thanks to the sympathy of the garrison, with complete impunity, became political events of capital importance. The last remnants of the fetishism of authority crumbled to dust. "It became instantly clear," says one of the participants, "that the job was done!" If not yet done, it was at least proving much simpler than anyone had imagined yesterday.

An attempt to suppress the papers, a resolution to prosecute the Military Revolutionary Committee, an order removing commissars, the cutting-out of Smolny's telephones—these pin-pricks were just sufficient to convict the government of preparing a counter-revolutionary *coup d'état*. Although an insurrection can win only on the offensive, it develops better, the more it looks like self-defense. A piece of official sealing-wax on the door of the Bolshevik editorial-rooms—as a military measure that is not much. But what a superb signal for battle! Telephonograms to all districts and units of the garrison announced the event: "The enemy of the people took the offensive during the night. The Military Revolutionary Committee is leading the resistance to the assault of the conspirators." The conspirators—these were the institutions of the official government. From the pen of revolutionary conspirators this term came as a surprise, but it wholly corresponded to the situation and to the feelings of the masses. Crowded out of all its positions, compelled to undertake a belated defense, incapable of mobilizing the necessary forces, or even finding out whether it had such forces, the government had developed a scattered, unthought-out, uncoordinated action, which in the eyes of the masses inevitably looked like a malevolent attempt. The Committee's telephonograms gave the command: "Make the regiment ready for battle and await further orders." That was the voice of a sovereign power. The commissars of the Committee, themselves liable to removal by the government, continued with redoubled confidence to remove those whom they thought it necessary to remove.

The *Aurora* in the Neva meant not only an excellent fighting unit in the service of the insurrection, but a radio-station ready for use. Invaluable advantage! The sailor Kurkov has remembered: "We got word from Trotsky to broadcast . . . that the counter-revolution had taken the offensive." Here too the defensive formulation concealed a summons to insurrection addressed to the whole country. The garrisons guarding the approaches to Petrograd were ordered by radio from the *Aurora* to hold up the counter-revolutionary echelons, and in case admonitions were inadequate to employ force. All revolutionary organizations were placed under obligation "to sit continually, accumulating all possible information as to the plans and activities of the conspirators." There was no lack of proclamations on the part of the Committee also, as you see. In its proclamations, however, the word was not divorced from the deed, but was a comment on it.

Somewhat belatedly the Military Revolutionary Committee

undertook a more serious fortification of Smolny. In leaving the building at three o'clock on the night of the 24th, John Reed noticed machine guns at the entrances and strong patrols guarding the gates and the adjacent street corners. The patrols had been reinforced the day before by a company of the Litovsky regiment and a company of machine-gunners with twenty-four machine guns. During the day the guard increased continually. "In the Smolny region," writes Shliapnikov, "I saw a familiar picture, reminding me of the first days of the February revolution around the Tauride Palace." The same multitude of soldiers, workers and weapons of all kinds. Innumerable cords of firewood had been piled up in the court—a perfect cover against rifle-fire. Motor trucks were bringing up foodstuffs and munitions. "All Smolny," says Raskolnikov, "was converted into an armed camp. Cannon were in position out in front of the columns. Machine guns alongside them. . . . Almost on every step those same 'maxims,' looking like toy-cannon. And through all the corridors . . . the swift, loud, happy tramp of workers, soldiers, sailors and agitators." Sukhanov, accusing the organizers of the insurrection—not without foundation—of insufficient military precaution, writes: "Only now, in the afternoon and evening of the 24th, did they begin to bring up armed detachments of Red Guards and soldiers to Smolny to defend the headquarters of the insurrection. . . . By the evening of the 24th the defense of Smolny began to look like something."

This matter is not without importance. In Smolny, whence the compromisist Executive Committee had managed to steal away to the headquarters of the government staff, there were now concentrated the heads of all the revolutionary organizations led by the Bolsheviks. Here assembled on that day the all-important meeting of the Central Committee of the Bolsheviks to take the final decision before striking the blow. Eleven members were present. Lenin had not yet turned up from his refuge in the Vyborg district. Zinoviev also was absent from the session. According to the temperamental expression of Dzerzhinsky, he was "hiding and taking no part in the party work." Kamenev, on the other hand, although sharing the views of Zinoviev, was very active in the headquarters of the insurrection. Stalin was not present at the session. Generally speaking he did not appear at Smolny, spending his time in the editorial office of the central organ. The session, as always, was held under the chairmanship of Sverdlov. The official minutes of the session are scant, but they indicate everything essential. For characterizing the leading participants in the revolution, and the distribution of functions among them, they are irreplaceable.

It was a question of taking full possession of Petrograd in the next twenty-four hours. That meant to seize those political and technical institutions which were still in the hands of the government. The Congress of Soviets must hold its session under the soviet power. The practical measures of the nocturnal assault had been worked out, or were being worked out, by the Military Revolutionary Committee and the Military Organizations of the Bolsheviks. The Central Committee was to underline the final points.

First of all a proposal of Kamenev was adopted: "Today no member of the Central Committee can leave Smolny without a special resolution." It was decided over and above that, to keep on duty here members of the Petrograd Committee of the party. The minutes read further: "Trotsky proposes that they place at the disposal of the Military Revolutionary Committee two members of the Central Committee for the purpose of establishing communications with the postal and telegraph workers and the railroad workers; a third member to keep the Provisional Government under observation." It was resolved to delegate Dzerzhinsky to the postal and telegraph workers, Bubnov to the railroad workers. At first, and obviously at Sverdlov's suggestion, it was proposed to allot the watch over the Provisional Government to Podvoisky. The minutes read: "Objections to Podvoisky; Sverdlov is appointed." Miliutin, who passed as an economist, was appointed to organize the supply of food for the period of the insurrection. Negotiations with the Left Social-Revolutionaries were entrusted to Kamenev, who had the reputation of a skilful although too yielding parliamentary. "Yielding," of course only from a Bolshevik criterion. "Trotsky proposes"—we read further—"that a reserve headquarters be established in the Peter and Paul fortress, and that one member of the Central Committee be sent there for that purpose." It was resolved: "To appoint Lashevich and Blagonravov for general observation; to commission Sverdlov to keep in continual touch with the fortress." Further: "to supply all members of the Central Committee with passes to the fortress."

Along party lines all threads were held in the hands of Sverdlov, who knew the cadres of the party as no one else did. He kept Smolny in touch with the party apparatus, supplied the Military Revolutionary Committee with the necessary workers, and was summoned into the Committee for counsel at all critical moments. Since the Committee had a too broad, and to some extent fluid, membership, the more conspirative undertakings were carried out through the heads of the Military Organization of the Bolsheviks, or through Sverdlov, who was the unofficial but all the more real "general secretary" of the October insurrection.

The Bolshevik delegates arriving in those days for the Soviet Congress would come first into the hands of Sverdlov, and would not be left for one unnecessary hour without something to do. On the 24th there were already two or three hundred provincial delegates in Petrograd, and the majority of them were included one way or another in the mechanics of the insurrection. At two o'clock in the afternoon, they assembled at a caucus in Smolny to hear a report from the Central Committee of the party. There were waverers among them who like Zinoviev and Kamenev preferred a waiting policy; there were also newcomers who were merely not sufficiently reliable. There could be no talk of expounding before this caucus the whole plan of the insurrection. Whatever is said at a large meeting inevitably gets abroad. It was still impossible even to throw off the defensive envelope of the attack without creating confusion in the minds of certain units of the garrison. But it was necessary to make the delegates understand that a decisive struggle had already begun, and that it would remain only for the Congress to crown it.

Referring to recent articles of Lenin, Trotsky demonstrated that "a conspiracy does not contradict the principles of Marxism," if objective relations make an insurrection possible and inevitable. "The physical barrier on the road to power must be

211

overcome by a blow. . . ." However, up till now the policy of
the Military Revolutionary Committee has not gone beyond the
policy of self-defense. Of course this self-defense must be understood in a sufficiently broad sense. To assure the publication of
the Bolshevik press with the help of armed forces, or to retain
the *Aurora* in the waters of the Neva—"Comrades, is that not
self-defense?—It is defense!" If the government intends to arrest us, we have machine guns on the roof of Smolny in preparation for such an event. "That also, comrades, is a measure of defense." But how about the Provisional Government? says one of
the written questions. What if Kerensky tries not to submit to
the Congress of Soviets? The spokesman replied: If Kerensky
should attempt not to submit to the Congress of Soviets, then
the resistance of the Government would have created "not a
political but a police question." That was in essence almost exactly what happened.

At that moment Trotsky was called out to consult with a
deputation just arrived from the city duma. In the capital, to
be sure, it was still quiet, but alarming rumors were on foot. The
mayor put these questions: Does the Soviet intend to make an
insurrection, and how about keeping order in the city? And what
will become of the duma itself if it does not recognize the revolution? These respected gentlemen wanted to know too much. The
answer was: The question of power is to be decided by the
Congress of Soviets. Whether this will lead to an armed struggle
"depends not so much upon the soviets as upon those who, in
conflict with the unanimous will of the people, are retaining the
state power in their hands." If the Congress declines the power,
the Petrograd Soviet will submit. But the government itself is
obviously seeking a conflict. Orders have been issued for the arrest of the Military Revolutionary Committee. The workers and
soldiers can only reply with ruthless resistance. What about looting and violence from criminal gangs? An order of the Committee issued today reads: "At the first attempt of criminal elements to bring about disturbances, looting, knifing or shooting
on the streets of Petrograd, the criminals will be wiped off the
face of the earth." As to the city duma, it will be possible in
case of a conflict to employ constitutional methods—dissolution

and a new election. The delegation went away dissatisfied. But what had they as a matter of fact expected?

That official visit of the City Fathers to the camp of the rebels was only too candid a demonstration of the impotence of the ruling groups. "Remember, comrades," said Trotsky upon returning to the Bolshevik caucus, "that a few weeks ago when we won the majority, we were only a trade-name—without a printing press, without a treasury, without departments—and now the city duma sends a deputation to the arrested Military Revolutionary Committee" for information as to the destiny of the city and the state.

The Peter and Paul fortress, won over politically only yesterday, is today completely taken possession of by the Military Revolutionary Committee. The machine gun crew, the most revolutionary unit, is being brought into fighting trim. A mighty work of cleaning the Colt machine guns is in progress—there are eighty of them. Machine guns are set up on the fortress wall to command the quay and the Troitsky bridge. The sentry guard at the gates is reinforced. Patrols are sent out into the surrounding districts. But in the heat of these morning hours it suddenly becomes known that within the fortress itself the situation is not assured. The uncertainty lies in a bicycle battalion. Recruited, like the cavalry, from well-to-do and rich peasants, the bicycle men, coming from the intermediate city layers, constituted a most conservative part of the army. A theme for idealistic psychologists: Let a man find himself, in distinction from others, on top of two wheels with a chain—at least in a poor country like Russia—and his vanity begins to swell out like his tires. In America it takes an automobile to produce this effect.

Brought in from the front to put down the July movement, the bicycle battalion had zealously stormed the Palace of Kshesinskaia, and afterward been installed in Peter and Paul as one of the most reliable detachments. It was learned that at yesterday's meeting which settled the fate of the fortress, the bicycle men had not been present. The old discipline still held in the battalion to such an extent that the officers had succeeded in keeping the soldiers from going into the fortress court. Counting on these bicycle men, the commandant of the fortress held

213

his chin high, frequently got into telephone connection with Kerensky's headquarters, and even professed to be about to arrest the Bolshevik commissar. The situation must not be left indefinite for an extra minute. Upon an order from Smolny, Blagonravov confronts the enemy: the colonel is subjected to house arrest, the telephones are removed from all officers' apartments. The government staff calls up excitedly to know why the commandant is silent, and in general what is going on in the fortress. Blagonravov respectfully reports over the telephone that the fortress henceforward fulfills only the orders of the Military Revolutionary Committee, with which it behooves the government in the future to get in connection.

All the troops of the fortress garrison accepted the arrest of the commandant with complete satisfaction, but the bicycle men bore themselves evasively. What lay concealed behind their sulky silence: a hidden hostility or the last waverings? "We decided to hold a special meeting for the bicycle men," writes Blagonravov, "and invite our best agitational forces, and above all Trotsky, who had enormous authority and influence over the soldier masses." At four o'clock in the afternoon the whole battalion met in the neighboring building of the Cirque Moderne. As governmental opponent, Quartermaster-General Poradelov, considered to be a Social-Revolutionary, took the floor. His objections were so cautious as to seem equivocal; and so much the more destructive was the attack of the Committee's representatives. This supplementary oratorical battle for the Peter and Paul fortress ended as might have been foreseen: by all voices except thirty the battalion supported the resolution of Trotsky. One more of the potential bloody conflicts was settled before the fighting and without bloodshed. That was the October insurrection. Such was its style.

It was now possible to rely upon the fortress with tranquil confidence. Weapons were given out from the arsenal without hindrance. At Smolny, in the Factory and Shop Committee room, delegates from the plants stood in line to get orders for rifles. The capital had seen many queues during the war years— now it saw rifle-queues for the first time. Trucks from all the districts of the city were driving up to the arsenal. "You would hardly have recognized the Peter and Paul fortress," writes the worker Skorinko. "Its renowned silence was broken by the chugging automobiles, shouts, and the creak of wagons. There was a special bustle in the storehouses. . . . Here too they led by us the first prisoners, officers and junkers."

The meeting in the Cirque Moderne had another result. The bicycle men who had been guarding the Winter Palace since July withdrew, announcing that they would no longer consent to protect the government. That was a heavy blow. The bicycle men had to be replaced by junkers. The military support of the government was more and more reducing itself to the officers' schools—a thing which not only narrowed it extremely, but also conclusively revealed its social constitution.

The workers of the Putilov wharf—and not they alone— were insistently urging Smolny to disarm the junkers. If this measure had been taken after careful preparation, in cooperation with the non-combatant units of the schools, on the night of the 25th, the capture of the Winter Palace would have offered no difficulties whatever. If the junkers had been disarmed even on the night of the 26th, after the capture of the Winter Palace, there would have been no attempted counter-insurrection on the 29th of October. But the leaders were still in many directions revealing a "magnanimous spirit"—in reality an excess of optimistic confidence—and did not always listen attentively enough to the sober voice of the lower ranks. In this Lenin's absence, too, was felt. The masses had to correct these omissions and mistakes, with unnecessary losses on both sides. In a serious struggle there is no worse cruelty than to be magnanimous at an inopportune time.

At an afternoon session of the Pre-Parliament, Kerensky sings his swan song. During recent days, he says, the population of Russia, and especially of the capital, has been in a constant state of alarm. "Calls for insurrection appear daily in the Bolshevik papers." The orator quotes the articles of the wanted state criminal, Vladimir Ulianov Lenin. The quotations are brilliant and irrefutably prove that the above-named individual is inciting to insurrection. And when? At a moment when the government is just taking up the question of transferring the land to the peasant committees, and of measures to bring the war to an end. The authorities have so far made no haste to put down the conspirators, wishing to give them the opportunity to correct their own mistakes. "That is just what is wrong!" comes from the section where Miliukov is leader. But Kerensky is unabashed. "I prefer in general," he says, "that a government should act more slowly, and thus more correctly, and at the necessary moment more decisively." From those lips the words have a strange sound! At any rate: "All days of grace are now past"; the Bolsheviks have not only not repented, but they have called out two companies, and are independently distributing weapons and cartridges. This time the government intends to put an end to the lawlessness of the rabble. "I choose my words deliberately: rabble." This insult to the people is greeted on the right with loud applause. He, Kerensky, has already given orders, he says, for the necessary arrests. "Special attention must be given to the speeches of the President of the Soviet, Bronstein-Trotsky." And be it known that the government has more than adequate forces; telegrams are coming in continually from the front demanding decisive measures against the Bolsheviks. At this point Konovalov hands the speaker the telephonogram from the Military Revolutionary Committee to the troops of the garrison, instructing them to "make the regiment ready for battle and await further orders." After reading the document Kerensky solemnly concludes: "In the language of the law and of judicial authority that is called a state of insurrection." Miliukov bears witness: "Kerensky pronounced these words in the complacent tone of a lawyer who has at last succeeded in getting evidence against his opponent." "Those groups and parties who have dared to lift their hands against the state," he concludes, "are liable to immediate, decisive and permanent liquidation." The entire hall, except the extreme Left, demonstratively applauded. The speech ended with a demand: that this very day, in this session, an answer be given to the question, "Can the government fulfil its duty with confidence in the support of this lofty assemblage?" Without awaiting the vote, Kerensky returned to headquarters—confident, according to his own account, that an hour would not pass before he would receive the needed decision. For what purpose it was needed remains unknown.

However, it turned out otherwise. From two to six o'clock the Mariinsky Palace was busy with factional and inter-factional conferences, striving to work out a formula. The conferees did not understand that they were working out a formula for their own funeral. Not one of the compromisist groups had the courage to identify itself with the government. Dan said: "We Mensheviks are ready to defend the Provisional Government with the last drop of our blood; but let the government make it possible for the democracy to unite around it." Towards evening the left faction of the Pre-Parliament, worn out with the search for a solution, united on a formula borrowed by Dan from Martov, a formula which laid the responsibility for insurrection not only on the Bolsheviks, but also on the government, and demanded immediate transfer of the land to the Land Committees, intercession with the Allies in favor of peace negotiations, etc. Thus the apostles of moderation tried at the last moment to counterfeit those slogans which only yesterday they had been denouncing as demagogy and adventurism. Unqualified support to the government was promised by the Kadets and Cossacks—that is, by those two groups who intended to throw Kerensky over at the very first opportunity—but they were a minority. The support of the Pre-Parliament could have added little to the government, but Miliukov is right: this refusal of support robbed the government of the last remnants of its authority. Had not the government itself only a few weeks before determined the composition of the Pre-Parliament?

While they were seeking a salvation formula in the Mariinsky Palace, the Petrograd Soviet was assembling in Smolny for purposes of information. The spokesman considered it necessary to remind the Soviet that the Military Revolutionary Committee had arisen "not as an instrument of insurrection, but on the basis of revolutionary self-defense." The Committee had not permitted Kerensky to remove the revolutionary troops from Petrograd, and it had taken under its protection the workers' press. "Was this insurrection?" The *Aurora* stands today where she stood

217

last night. "Is this insurrection?" We have today a semi-government, in which the people do not believe, and which does not believe in itself, because it is inwardly dead. This semi-government is awaiting that swish of the historic broom that will clear the space for an authentic government of the revolutionary people. Tomorrow the Congress of Soviets will open. It is the duty of the garrison and the workers to put all their forces at the disposal of the Congress. "If, however, the government attempts to employ the twenty-four hours remaining to it in plunging a knife into the back of the revolution, then we declare once more: The vanguard of the revolution will answer blow with blow and iron with steel." This open threat was at the same time a political screen for the forthcoming night attack. In conclusion Trotsky informed the meeting that the Left Social-Revolutionary faction of the Pre-Parliament, after today's speech from Kerensky and a mouse-riot among the compromise factions, had sent a delegation to Smolny to express its readiness to enter officially into the staff of the Military Revolutionary Committee. In this shift of the Left Social Revolutionaries the Soviet joyfully welcomed a reflection of deeper processes: the widening scope of the peasant war and the successful progress of the Petrograd insurrection.

Commenting on this speech of the President of the Petrograd Soviet, Miliukov writes: "Probably this was Trotsky's original plan—having prepared for battle, to confront the government with the 'unanimous will of the people' as expressed in the Congress of Soviets, and thus give the new power the appearance of a legal origin. But the government proved weaker than he expected, and the power fell into his hands of its own accord before the Congress had time to assemble and express itself." What is true here, is that the weakness of the government exceeded all expectations. But from the beginning the plan had been to seize the power before the Congress opened. Miliukov recognizes this, by the way, in a different connection. "The actual intentions of the leaders of the revolution," he says, "went much farther than these official announcements of Trotsky. The Congress of Soviets was to be placed before a *fait accompli.*"

The purely military plan consisted originally of guaranteeing

a united action of the Baltic sailors and the armed Vyborg workers. The sailors were to come by railroad and detrain at the Finland station, which is in the Vyborg district, and then from this
base by way of a further assimilation of the Red Guard and units
of the garrison, the insurrection was to spread to other districts
of the city, and having seized the bridges, to advance into the
center for the final blow. This scheme—naturally deriving from
the circumstances, and formulated, it seems, by Antonov—was
drawn up on the assumption that the enemy would be able to
put up a considerable resistance. It was just this premise that
soon fell away. It was unnecessary to start from a limited base,
because the government proved open to attack wherever the insurrectionists found it necessary to strike a blow.

The strategic plan underwent changes in the matter of dates
also, and that in two directions: the insurrection began earlier
and ended later than had been indicated. The morning attacks
of the government called out by way of self-defense an immediate resistance from the Military Revolutionary Committee. The
impotence of the authorities, thus revealed, impelled Smolny during the same day to offensive actions—preserving, to be sure, a
half-way, semi-disguised and preparatory character. The main
blow as before was prepared, during the night: in that sense the
plan held good. It was transgressed, however, in the process of
fulfillment—but now in an opposite direction. It had been proposed to occupy during the night all the commanding summits,
and first of all the Winter Palace where the central power had
taken refuge. But time-calculations are even more difficult in insurrection than in regular war. The leaders were many hours
late with the concentration of forces, and the operations against
the palace, not even begun during the night, formed a special
chapter of the revolution ending only on the night of the 26th
—that is, a whole twenty-four hours late. The most brilliant
victories are not achieved without duds.

After Kerensky's speech at the Pre-Parliament the authorities
tried to broaden their offensive. The railroad stations were occupied by detachments of junkers. Pickets were posted at the
big street-crossings and ordered to requisition the private automobiles not turned over to headquarters. By three o'clock in the

afternoon the bridges were raised, except for the Dvortsovy which remained open under heavy guard for the movement of the junkers. This measure, adopted by the monarchy at all critical moments and for the last time in the February days, was dictated by fear of the workers' districts. The raising of the bridges was received by the population as an official announcement of the beginning of the insurrection. The headquarters of the districts concerned immediately answered this military act of the government in their own way by sending armed detachments to the bridges. Smolny had only to develop their initiative. This struggle for the bridges assumed the character of a test for both sides. Parties of armed workers and soldiers brought pressure to bear on the junkers and Cossacks, now persuading and now threatening. The guard finally yielded without hazarding a straight-out fight. Some of the bridges were raised and lowered several times.

The *Aurora* received a direct order from the Military Revolutionary Committee: "With all means at your command restore movement on the Nikolaevsky Bridge." The commander of the cruiser at first refused to carry out the order, but after a symbolic arrest of himself and all his officers obediently brought the ship to the bridge. Cordons of sailors spread out along both quays. By the time the *Aurora* had dropped anchor before the bridge, relates Korkov, the tracks of the junkers were already cold. The sailors themselves lowered the bridge and posted guards. Only Dvortsovy bridge remained several hours in the hands of the government patrols.

Notwithstanding the manifest failure of its first experiments, individual branches of the government tried to deal further blows. A detachment of militia appeared in the evening at a big private printing-plant to suppress the newspaper of the Petrograd Soviet, *Worker and Soldier*. Twelve hours before, the workers of the Bolshevik press had run for help in a like case to Smolny. Now there was no need of it. The printers, together with two sailors who happened by, immediately captured the automobile loaded with papers; a number of the militia joined them on the spot; the inspector of militia fled. The captured paper was successfully delivered at Smolny. The Military Revolutionary Committee sent two squads of the Preobrazhentzi to protect the publication. The frightened administration thereupon turned over the management of the printing-plant to the soviet of worker-overseers.

The legal authorities did not even think of penetrating Smolny to make arrests: it was too obvious that this would be the signal for a civil war in which the defeat of the Government was assured in advance. There was made, however, as a kind of administrative convulsion, an attempt to arrest Lenin in the Vyborg district, where, generally speaking, the authorities were afraid even to look in. Late in the evening a certain colonel with a dozen junkers accidentally entered a workers' club instead of the Bolshevik editorial rooms located in the same house. The brave boys had for some reason imagined that Lenin would be waiting for them in the editorial rooms. The club immediately informed the district headquarters of the Red Guard. While the colonel was wandering around from one story to another, arriving once even among the Mensheviks, a detachment of Red Guards, rushing up, arrested him along with his junkers, and brought them to the headquarters of the Vyborg district, and thence to the Peter and Paul fortress. Thus the loudly proclaimed campaign against the Bolsheviks, meeting insuperable difficulties at every step, turned into disconnected jumps and small anecdotes, evaporated, and came to nothing.

During this time the Military Revolutionary Committee was working day and night. Its commissars were on continual duty in the military units. The population was notified in special proclamations where to turn in case of counter-revolutionary attempts or pogroms: "Help will be given on the instant." A suggestive visit to the telephone exchange from the commissar of the Keksgolmsky regiment proved sufficient to get Smolny switched back into the system. Telephone communications, the swiftest of all, gave confidence and regularity to the developing operations.

Continuing to plant its own commissars in those institutions which had not yet come under its control, the Military Revolutionary Committee kept broadening and reinforcing its bases for the coming offensive. Dzerzhinsky that afternoon handed the old revolutionist Pestkovsky a sheet of paper in the form of credentials appointing him to the office of commissar of the central telegraph station. But how shall I get possession of the telegraph station?—asked the new commissar in some surprise. The Keksgolmsky regiment is supplying sentries there and it is on our side! Pestkovsky needed no further illumination. Two Keksgolmtzi, standing by the commutator with rifles, proved sufficient to attain a compromise with the hostile telegraph officials, among whom were no Bolsheviks.

At nine o'clock in the evening another commissar of the Military Revolutionary Committee, Stark, with a small detachment of sailors under the command of the former emigré Savin, also a seaman, occupied the government news agency and therewith decided not only the fate of that institution, but also to a certain degree his own fate: Stark became the first Sòviet director of the agency, before being appointed Soviet ambassador to Afganistan.

Were these two modest operations acts of insurrection, or were they only episodes in the two-power system—transferred, to be sure, from the compromisist to the Bolshevik rails? The question may perhaps reasonably be regarded as casuistic, but for the purpose of camouflaging an insurrection it had a certain importance. The fact is that even the intrusion of armed sailors into the building of the news agency had still a sort of half-way character: it was not yet a question of seizing the institution, but only of establishing a censorship over despatches. Thus right up to the evening of the 24th, the umbilical cord of "legality" was not conclusively severed. The movement was still disguising itself with the remnants of the two-power tradition.

In working out the plans of the insurrection, Smolny rested great hopes on the Baltic sailors as a fighting detachment combining proletarian resolution with strict military training. The arrival of the sailors in Petrograd had been dated in advance to coincide with the Congress of Soviets. To call the Baltic sailors in earlier would have meant to take openly the road of insurrection. Out of this arose a difficulty which subsequently turned into a delay.

During the afternoon of the 24th, two delegates from the Kronstadt soviet, the Bolshevik Flerovsky and the anarchist Yarchuk, who was keeping step with the Bolsheviks, arrived in

Smolny for the Congress. In one of the rooms of Smolny they ran into Chudnovsky, who had just returned from the front, and who, alluding to the mood of the soldiers, spoke against insurrection in the near future. "At the height of the argument," relates Flerovsky, "Trotsky came into the room. . . . Calling me aside, he advised me to return immediately to Kronstadt: 'Events are maturing so fast that everyone must be at his post. . . .' In this curt order I felt keenly the discipline of the advancing insurrection." The argument was cut short. The impressionable and hot-headed Chudnovsky laid aside his doubts in order to take part in drawing up the plans of the fight. On the heels of Flerovsky and Yarchuk went a telephonogram: "The armed forces of Kronstadt are to come out at dawn for the defense of the Congress of Soviets."

Through Sverdlov the Military Revolutionary Committee sent a telegram that night to Helsingfors, to Smilga, the president of the regional Committee of the Soviets: "Send regulations." That meant: Send immediately 1500 chosen Baltic sailors armed to the teeth. Although the sailors could reach Petrograd only during the next day, there was no reason to postpone military action; the internal forces were adequate. Yes, and a postponement was impossible. Operations had already begun. If reinforcements should come from the front to help the government, then the sailors would arrive in time to deal them a blow in the flank or rear.

The tactical plans for the conquest of the capital were worked out chiefly by the staff of the Military Organization of the Bolsheviks. Officers of the general staff would have found many faults in them, but military academicians do not customarily take part in the preparation of a revolutionary insurrection. The essentials at any rate were taken care of. The city was divided into military divisions, each subordinate to the nearest headquarters. At the most important points companies of the Red Guard were concentrated in coordination with the neighboring military units, where companies on duty were awake and ready. The goal of each separate operation, and the forces for it, were indicated in advance. All those taking part in the insurrection from top to bottom—in this lay its power, in this also at times its Achilles' heel—were imbued with absolute confidence that the victory was going to be won without casualities.

The main operation began at two o'clock in the morning. Small military parties, usually with a nucleus of armed workers or sailors under the leadership of commissars, occupied simultaneously, or in regular order, the railroad stations, the lighting plant, the munition and food stores, the waterworks, Dvortsovy bridge, the Telephone Exchange, the State Bank, the big printing-plants. The Telegraph Station and the Post Office were completely taken over. Reliable guards were placed everywhere.

Meagre and colorless is the record of the episodes of that October night. It is like a police report. All the participants were shaking with a nervous fever. There was no time to observe and record and no one to do it. The information flowing in at headquarters was not always jotted down, and if so it was done carelessly. Notes got lost. Subsequent recollections were dry and not always accurate, since they came for the most part from accidental people. Those workers, sailors, and soldiers who really inspired and lead the operation took their places soon after at the head of the first detachments of the Red Army, and the majority laid down their lives in the various theaters of the civil war. In the attempt to determine the sequence of separate episodes, the investigator runs into a vast confusion, which is still more complicated by the accounts in the newspapers. At times it seems as though it was easier to capture Petrograd in the autumn of 1917 than to recount the process fourteen years later.

To the first company of the sapper battalion, the strongest and most revolutionary, was given the task of seizing the nearby Nikolaevsky railroad station. In less than a quarter of an hour the station was occupied by strong guards without a blow. The government squad simply evaporated in the darkness. The keenly cold night was full of mysterious movements and suspicious sounds. Suppressing a sharp alarm in their hearts, the soldiers would conscientiously stop all passers-by, on foot or in vehicles, meticulously inspecting their documents. They did not always know what to do. They hesitated—most often let them go. But confidence increased with every hour. About six in the morning the sappers held up two truckloads of junkers—about sixty men —disarmed them, and sent them to Smolny.

That same sapper battalion was directed to send fifty men to guard the food warehouses, twenty-one to guard the Power Station, etc. Order followed order, now from Smolny, now from the district. Nobody offered a murmur of objection. According to the report of the commissar, the orders were carried out "immediately and exactly." The movement of the soldiers acquired a precision long unseen. However rickety and crumbly that garrison was—good only for scrap-iron in a military sense—on that night the old soldierly drill re-awoke, and for one last moment tensed every nerve and muscle in the service of the new goal.

Commissar Uralov received two authorizations: one, to occupy the printing-plant of the reactionary paper *Russkaia Volia*, founded by Protopopov a little while before he became the last Minister of the Interior of Nikolas II; the other, to get a troop of soldiers from the Semenov Guard Regiment which the government for old times' sake was still considering its own. The Semenovtsi were needed for the occupation of a printing-plant. The printing-plant was needed to issue the Bolshevik paper in large format and with a big circulation. The soldiers had already lain down to sleep. The commissar briefly told them the object of his visit. "I hadn't stopped talking when a shout of 'Hurrah!' went up on all sides. The soldiers were jumping out of their bunks and crowding around me in a close circle." A truck loaded with Semenovtsi approached the printing-plant. The workers of the night-shift quickly assembled in the rotary-press room. The commissar explained why he had come. "And here as in the barracks the workers answered with shouts of 'Hurrah! Long live the Soviets!' " The job was done. In much the same manner the other institutions were seized. It was not necessary to employ force, for there was no resistance. The insurrectionary masses lifted their elbows and pushed out the lords of yesterday.

The commander of the district reported that night to general headquarters and the headquarters of the northern front over the military wire: "The situation in Petrograd is frightful. There are no street demonstrations or disorders, but a regulated seizure

of institutions, railroad stations, also arrests, is in progress. . . .
The junkers' patrols are surrendering without resistance . . .
We have no guarantee that there will not be an attempt to seize
the Provisional Government." Polkovnikov was right: they had
no guarantee of that.

In military circles the rumor was going round that agents of
the Military Revolutionary Committee had stolen from the desk
of the Petrograd commandant the password for the sentries of
the garrison. That was not at all improbable. The insurrection
had many friends among the lower personnel of all institutions.
Nevertheless this tale about stealing the password is apparently
a legend which arose in the hostile camp to explain the too humiliating ease with which the Bolshevik patrols got possession of
the city.

An order was sent out through the garrison from Smolny
during the night: Officers not recognizing the authority of the
Military Revolutionary Committee to be arrested. The commanders of many regiments fled of their own accord, and passed
some nervous days in hiding. In other units the officers were removed or arrested. Everywhere special revolutionary committees
or staffs were formed and functioned hand in hand with the
commissars. That this improvised command did not stand very
high in a military sense, goes without saying. Nevertheless it
was reliable, and the question here was decided primarily in the
political court.

It is necessary to add, however, that with all their lack of
experience the staffs of certain units developed a considerable
military initiative. The committee of the Pavlovsky regiment sent
scouts into the Petrograd district headquarters to find out what
was going on there. The chemical reserve battalion kept careful
watch of its restless neighbors, the junkers of the Pavlovsky and
Vladimirsky schools, and the students of the cadet corps. The
chemical men from time to time disarmed junkers in the street
and thus kept them cowed. Getting into connection with the
soldier personnel of the Pavlovsky school, the staff of the chemical battalion saw to it that the keys to the weapons were in the
hands of the soldiers.

It is difficult to determine the number of forces directly engaged in this nocturnal seizure of the capital—and this not only because nobody counted them or noted them down, but also because of the character of the operations. Reserves of the second and third order almost merged with the garrison as a whole. But it was only occasionally necessary to have recourse to the reserves. A few thousand Red Guards, two or three thousand sailors—tomorrow with the arrivals from Kronstadt and Helsingfors there will be about treble the number—a score of infantry companies: such were the forces of the first and second order with whose aid the insurrectionists occupied the governmental high points of the capital.

At 3:20 in the morning the chief of the political administration of the War Ministry, the Menshevik Sher, sent the following information by direct wire to the Caucasus: "A meeting of the Central Executive Committee together with the delegates to the Congress of Soviets is in progress with an overwhelming majority of Bolsheviks. Trotsky has received an ovation. He has announced that he hopes for a bloodless victory of the insurrection, since the power is in their hands. The Bolsheviks have begun active operations. They have seized the Nikolaevsky bridge and posted armored cars there. The Pavlovsky regiment has posted pickets on Milliony street near the Winter Palace, is stopping everybody, arresting them, and sending them to Smolny Institute. They have arrested Minister Kartashev and the general administrator of the Provisional Government, Halperin. The Baltic railroad station is also in the hands of the Bolsheviks. If the front does not intervene, the government will be unable to resist with the forces on hand."

The joint session of the Executive Committees about which Lieutenant Sher's communication speaks, opened in Smolny after midnight in unusual circumstances. Delegates to the Congress of Soviets brimmed the hall in the capacity of invited guests. Reinforced guards occupied the entrances and corridors. Trench-coats, rifles, machine guns filled the windows. The members of the Executive Committees were drowned in this many-headed and hostile mass of provincials. The high organ of the "democracy" looked already like a captive of the insurrection. The familiar figure of the president, Cheidze, was absent. The invariable spokesman, Tseretelli, was absent. Both of them, frightened by the turn of events, had surrendered their responsible posts, and abandoning Petrograd, left for their Georgian homeland. Dan remained as leader of the compromise bloc. He lacked the sly good humor of Cheidze, and likewise the moving eloquence of Tseretelli. But he excelled them both in obstinate short-sightedness. Alone in the president's chair the Social Revolutionary, Gotz, opened the session. Dan took the floor amid an utter silence which seemed to Sukhanov languid—to John Reed "almost threatening." The spokesman's hobby was a new resolution of the Pre-Parliament, which had tried to oppose the insurrection with the dying echo of its own slogans. "It will be too late if you do not take account of this decision," cried Dan, trying to frighten the Bolsheviks with the inevitable hunger and the degeneration of the masses. "Never before has the counter-revolution been so strong as at the given moment," he said—that is, on the night before October 25th, 1917. The frightened petty-bourgeois confronted by great events sees nothing but dangers and obstacles. His sole recourse is the pathos of alarm. "In the factories and barracks the Black Hundred press is enjoying a far more considerable success than the socialist press." Lunatics are leading the revolution to ruin just as in 1905 "when this same Trotsky stood at the head of the Petrograd Soviet." But no, he cried, the Central Executive Committee will not permit an insurrection. "Only over its dead body will the hostile camps cross their bayonets." Shouts from the benches: "Yes, it's been dead a long time!" The entire hall felt the appropriateness of that exclamation. Over the corpse of Compromisism the bayonets of the bourgeoisie and the proletariat had already crossed. The voice of the orator is drowned in a hostile uproar, his pounding on the table is futile, his appeals do not move, his threats do not frighten. Too late! Too late!

Yes, it is an insurrection! Replying in the name of the Military Revolutionary Committee, the Bolshevik Party, the Petrograd workers and soldiers, Trotsky now throws off the last qualification. Yes, the masses are with us, and we are leading them to the assault! "If you do not weaken there will be no civil war, for the enemy is already capitulating, and you can assume the place

THE CONQUEST OF THE CAPITAL

of master of the Russian land which of right belongs to you."
The astounded members of the Central Executive Committee
found no strength even to protest. Up to now the defensive
phraseology of Smolny had kept up in them, in spite of all the
facts, a glimmering spark of hope. Now that too was extin-
guished. In those hours of deep night the insurrection lifted its
head high.

That session so rich in episodes closed at four o'clock in the
morning. The Bolshevik speakers would appear in the tribune
only to return immediately to the Military Revolutionary Committee, where from all corners of the city news uniformly favorable was pouring in. The patrols in the streets were doing their
work, the government institutions were being occupied one after
the other; the enemy was offering no resistance anywhere.

It had been assumed that the central Telephone Exchange
would be especially well fortified, but at seven in the morning it
was taken without a fight by a company from the Keksgozmsky
regiment. The insurrectionists could now not only rest easy
about their own communications, but control the telephone connections of the enemy. The apparatus of the Winter Palace and
of central headquarters was promptly cut out.

Almost simultaneously with the seizure of the Telephone Exchange a detachment of sailors from the marine guard, about
forty strong, seized the building of the State Bank on the Ekaterininsky Canal. The bank clerk, Ralzevich recalls that the sailors
"worked with expedition," immediately placing sentries at each
telephone to cut off possible help from outside. The occupation
of the building was accomplished "without any resistance, in
spite of the presence of a squad from the Semenovsky regiment."
The seizure of the bank had to some extent a symbolic importance. The cadres of the party had been brought up on the
Marxian criticism of the Paris Commune of 1871, whose leaders, as is well known, did not venture to lay hands on the State
Bank. "No, we will not make that mistake," many Bolsheviks
had been saying to themselves long before October 25th. News
of the seizure of the most sacred institution of the bourgeois state
swiftly spread through the disticts, raising a warm wave of joy.

In the early morning hours the Warsaw railroad station was

229

occupied, also the printing-plant of the "Stock Exchange News," and Dvortsovy bridge under Kerensky's very windows. A commissar of the Committee presented the soldier patrol from the Volinsky regiment in Kresty prison with a resolution demanding the liberation of a number of prisoners according to the lists of the Soviet. The prison administration tried in vain to get instructions from the Minister of Justice: he was too busy. The liberated Bolsheviks, among them the young Kronstadt leader, Roshal, immediately received military appointments.

In the morning, a party of junkers who had left the Winter Palace in a truck in search of provisions, and been held up by the sappers at Nikolaevsky station, were brought to Smolny. Podvoisky relates the following: "Trotsky told them that they were free on condition that they give a promise not to take further action against the Soviet power, and that they might go back to their school and get to work. The youngsters, who had been expecting a bloody end, were unspeakably surprised at this." To what extent their immediate liberation was wise, remains in doubt. The victory was not yet finally achieved. The junkers were the chief force of the enemy. On the other hand with the wavering moods in the military schools, it was important to prove by example that a surrender to the mercy of the victor would not threaten the junkers with punishment. The arguments in both directions seemed about equal.

From the War Ministry, not yet occupied by the insurrectionists, General Levitsky sent word by direct wire to General Dukhonin at headquarters: "The troops of the Petrograd garrison . . . have gone over to the Bolsheviks. The sailors and a light-armed cruiser have come from Kronstadt. They have lowered the raised bridges. The whole town is covered with sentry guards from the garrison. But there has been no coming-out. (!) The Telephone Exchange is in the hands of the garrison. The troops in the Winter Palace are defending it only in a formal sense, since they have decided not to come out actively. The general impression is that the Provisional Government finds itself in the capital of a hostile state which has finished mobilization but not yet begun active operations." Invaluable military and political testimony! To be sure, the General anticipates events when he says the sailors have arrived from Kronstadt: they will arrive a few hours later. The bridge was really let down by the crew of the *Aurora*. The hope expressed in conclusion that the Bolsheviks "having long been actually in a position to get rid of us . . . will not dare come into conflict with the opinion of the army at the front," is rather naïve. However, these illusions about the front were about all that the rear generals had left, or the rear democrats either. At any rate that image of the Provisional Government finding itself in the capital of a hostile state will go into the history of the revolution forever as the best possible explanation of the October event.

Meetings were continuous in Smolny. Agitators, organizers, leaders of factories, regiments, districts, would appear for an hour or two, sometimes for a few minutes, to get news, to check up on their own activities and return to their posts. Before room 18, the quarters of the Bolshevik faction of the Soviet, there was an indescribable jam. Tired to death, those arriving would often fall asleep right in the assembly hall, leaning their unbearably heavy heads against a white column, or against the walls in the corridors, with both arms around their rifles—or sometimes they would simply stretch out in piles on the dirty wet floor. Lashevich was receiving the military commissars and giving them their last instructions. In the quarters of the Military Revolutionary Committee on the third floor, reports coming in from all sides would be converted into orders. Here beat the heart of the insurrection.

The district centers reproduced the picture of Smolny on a smaller scale. In the Vyborg district opposite the headquarters of the Red Guard on Samsonevsky Prospect a whole camp was created: the street was jammed full of wagons, passenger-cars and trucks. The institutions of the district were swarming with armed workers. The soviet, the duma, the trade unions, the factory and shop-committees—everything in this district—were serving the cause of the insurrection. In the factories and barracks and various institutions the same thing was happening in a smaller way as throughout the whole capital: they were crowding out some and electing others, breaking the last threads of the old ties, strengthening the new. The backward ones were adopting resolutions of submission to the Military Revolutionary Committee. The Mensheviks and Social Revolutionaries timidly shrank aside along with the factory administrations and the commanding staff of the troops. At continuous meetings fresh information was given out, fighting confidence kept up and ties reinforced. The human masses were crystallizing along new axes; a revolution was achieving itself.

Step by step we have tried to follow in this book the development of the October insurrection: the sharpening discontent of the worker masses, the coming over of the soviets to the Bolshevik banners, the indignation of the army, the campaign of the peasants against the landlords, the flood-tide of the national movement, the growing fear and distraction of the possessing and ruling classes, and finally the struggle for the insurrection within the Bolshevik party. The final act of the revolution seems, after all this, too brief, too dry, too business-like—somehow out of correspondence with the historic scope of the events. The reader experiences a kind of disappointment. He is like a mountain climber, who, thinking the main difficulties are still ahead, suddenly discovers that he is already on the summit or almost there. Where is the insurrection? There is no picture of the insurrection. The events do not form themselves into a picture. A series of small operations, calculated and prepared in advance, remain separated one from another both in space and time. A unity of thought and aim unites them, but they do not fuse in the struggle itself. There is no action of great masses. There are no dramatic encounters with the troops. There is nothing of all that which imaginations brought up upon the facts of history associate with the idea of insurrection.

The general character of the revolution in the capital subsequently moved Masaryk, among may others, to write: "The October revolution . . . was anything but a popular mass movement. That revolution was the act of leaders working from above and behind the scenes." As a matter of fact it was the most popular mass-insurrection in all history. The workers had no need to come out into the public square in order to fuse together: they were already politically and morally one single whole without that. The soldiers were even forbidden to leave their barracks without permission: upon that point the order of the Military Revolutionary Committee fell in with the order of Polkovnikov. But those invisible masses were marching more than ever before in step with the events. The factories and barracks never lost connection for a minute with the district headquarters, nor the districts with Smolny. The Red Guard detachments felt at their back the support of the factories. The soldier squad returning to the barracks found the new shifts ready. Only with heavy reserves behind them could revolutionary detachments go about their work with such confidence. The scattered government patrols, in contrast, being convinced in advance of their own isolation, renounced the very idea of resistance. The bourgeois classes had expected barricades, flaming conflagrations, looting, rivers of blood. In reality a silence reigned more terrible than all the thunders of the world. The social ground shifted noiselessly like a revolving stage, bringing forward the popular masses, carrying away to limbo the rulers of yesterday.

As early as ten o'clock on the morning of the 25th, Smolny considered it possible to broadcast through the capital and throughout the whole country a triumphant announcement: "The Provisional Government is overthrown. The state power has passed into the hands of the Military Revolutionary Committee." In a certain sense this declaration was very premature. The government still existed, at least within the territory of the Winter Palace. Headquarters existed; the provinces had not expressed themselves; the Congress of Soviets had not yet opened. But the leaders of an insurrection are not historians; in order to prepare events for the historians they have to anticipate them. In the capital the Military Revolutionary Committee was already complete master of the situation. There could be no doubt of the sanction of the Congress. The provinces were awaiting Petrograd's initiative. In order to get complete possession of the power it was necessary to act as a power. In a proclamation to the military organizations of the front and rear, the Committee urged the soldiers to watch vigilantly over the conduct of the commanding staff, to arrest officers not adhering to the revolution, and not to stop at the use of force in case of attempts to throw hostile divisions against Petrograd.

233

The chief commissar of headquarters, Stankevich, having arrived the night before from the front and not wishing to remain wholly inactive, placed himself at the head of a half company of military engineering students in the morning, and undertook to clean the Bolsheviks out of the Telephone Exchange. It was in this way that the junkers first found out who had possession of the telephone connections. "There is a model of energy for you," exclaimed officer Sinegub, grinding his teeth. "But where did they get such leadership?" The sailors occupying the telephone building could easily have shot down the junkers through the windows. But the insurrectionists were striving with all their might to avoid bloodshed, and Stankevich had given strict orders not to open fire lest the junkers be accused of shooting at the people. The commanding officer thought to himself: "Once order is restored, who will dare to peep?" and concluded his meditations with an exclamation: "Damned clowns!" This is a good formula for the attitude of the officers to the government. On his own initiative Sinegub sent to the Winter Palace for hand grenades and sticks of pyroxyle. In the interval a monarchist lieutenant got into an argument at the gates of the Exchange with a Bolshevik ensign. Like the heroes of Homer they exchanged mighty epithets before the battle. Finding themselves between two fires—for the time only wordy ones—the telephone girls gave free rein to their nerves. The sailors let them go home. "What's this? Women? . . ." They fled with hysterical screams through the gates. "The deserted Morskaia," relates Sinegub, "was suddenly enlivened with running and jumping skirts and hats." The sailors managed somehow to handle the work of the switchboard. An armored car from the Reds soon entered the court of the Exchange, doing no damage to the frightened junkers. They on their side seized two trucks and barricaded the gates of the Exchange from the outside. A second armored car appeared from the direction of the Nevsky, and then a third. It all came down to maneuvers and attempts to frighten each other. The struggle for the Exchange was decided without pyroxyle: Stankevich raised the siege after negotiating a free passage for his junkers.

Weapons in general are still serving merely as an external sign of power: they are not being brought into action. On the road to the Winter Palace a half company of junkers runs into a crew of sailors with rifles cocked. The enemies only measure each other with their eyes. Neither side wants to fight: the one through consciousness of strength, the other of weakness. But where chance offers, the insurrectionists—especially the workers—promptly disarm the enemy. A second half-company of those same engineering junkers was surrounded by Red Guards and soldiers, disarmed by them with the help of armored cars, and taken prisoner. Even here, however, there was no conflict; the junkers did not put up a fight. "Thus ended," says the initiator of it— "the sole attempt, so far as I know, at active resistance to the Bolsheviks." Stankevich has in mind, of course, operations outside the Winter Palace region.

By noon the streets around the Mariinsky Palace were occupied by troops of the Military Revolutionary Committee. Members of the Pre-Parliament were just assembling for a meeting. The præsidium made an attempt to get the latest news; their hearts sank when they learned that the telephones of the palace had been cut out. The Council of Elders went into session to decide what to do. The deputies murmured meanwhile in the corners. Avksentiev offered consolation: Kerensky has gone to the front, and will be back soon and fix everything. An armored car drew up at the entrance. Soldiers of the Litovsky and Keksgolmsky regiments and sailors of the Marine Guard entered the building, formed in line on the staircase, and occupied the first hall. The commander of the detachment suggested to the deputies that they leave the palace at once. "The impression created was appalling," testifies Nabokov. The members of the Pre-Parliament decided to disperse, "temporarily suspending their activities." Forty-eight Right Wing members voted against submitting to violence, quite evidently knowing they would be in a minority. The deputies peacefully descended the magnificent stairway between two rows of rifles. An eye-witness testifies: "in all this there was no attempt at dramatics." "Ordinary, meaningless, obtuse, malicious physiognomies," writes the liberal patriot, Nabokov, of these Russian soldiers and sailors. Down below at the entrance the soldiers inspected their papers and let them all through. "A sorting of members and some arrests had been expected," writes Miliukov, himself let out with the others. "But the revolutionary headquarters had other things to worry about." It was not only that. The revolutionary staff had little experience. The instructions read: Arrest members of the government if found. But none were found. The members of the Pre-Parliament were freely released, among them some who soon became organizers of the civil war.

This parliamentary hybrid, which ended its existence twelve hours in advance of the Provisional Government, had lived in the world for eighteen days. That was the interval between the withdrawal of the Bolsheviks from the Mariinsky Palace to the street and the entry of the armed street forces into the Mariinsky Palace. . . . Of all the parodies of popular representation in which history is so rich, this Council of the Russian Republic was perhaps the most absurd.

After leaving the unlucky building, the Octobrist Shidlovsky went strolling through the town to see the fights—for these gentlemen believed that the people were going to rise in their defense. But no fighting was to be seen. Instead, according to Shidlovsky, the public in the streets—the select crowd, that is, along the Nevsky Prospect—were to the last man laughing. "Have you heard about it? The Bolsheviks have seized the power. Well, that won't last more than three days. Ha ha ha!" Shidlovsky decided to remain in the capital "during the period which social rumor designated for the rule of the Bolsheviks."

The Nevsky public had begun to laugh, it may be remarked, only towards evening. In the morning such a mood of alarm had prevailed that hardly anybody in the bourgeois districts dared go into the streets at all. At about nine o'clock a journalist Knizhnik, ran out on Kamenoöstrovsky Prospect in search of newspapers, but could find no stands. In a little group of citizens he learned that the Bolsheviks had occupied the telephone, the telegraph, and the Bank during the night. A soldier patrol listened to them and asked them not to make so much noise. "But even without that everybody was unusually subdued." Armed detachments of workers were going by. The tramcars moved as usual—that is, slowly. "The scarcity of passers-by oppressed me," writes Knizhnik about the Nevsky. Food could be had in the restaurants, but for the most part in back rooms. At noon the canon from the walls of Peter and Paul, now safely occupied by the Bolsheviks, thundered out neither louder nor more gently than usual. The walls and fences were pasted over with proclamations warning against insurrection, but other proclamations were already making their way, announcing the victory of the insurrection. There was no time yet to paste them up; they were tossed out from automobiles. Just off the press, these handbills smelled of fresh inks as though of the events themselves.

Companies of the Red Guard had emerged from their districts. The worker with a rifle, the bayonet above hat or cap, the rifle-belt over a civilian coat—that is the essential image of the 25th of October. Cautiously and still diffidently, the armed worker was bringing order into the capital conquered by him.

The tranquillity of the street instilled tranquillity in the heart. The philistines began to dribble down from their houses. Towards evening they felt even less anxious than during the preceding days. Business, to be sure, had come to an end in the governmental and social institutions, but many stores remained open. Others were closed rather through excessive caution than necessity. Can this be insurrection? Is an insurrection like this? The February sentries have merely been replaced by those of October.

By evening the Nevsky was even fuller than usual of that public which was giving the Bolsheviks three days of life. The soldiers of the Pavlovsky regiment, although their patrols were reinforced by armored cars and even anti-aircraft guns, had already ceased to inspire fear. To be sure something serious was going on around the Winter Palace and they would not let you through there, but still an insurrection could not very well all be concentrated on Winter Palace square. An American journalist saw old men in rich fur coats shake their gloved fists at the Pavlovtsi, and handsomely dressed women scream abuse in their faces. "The soldiers argued feebly with embarrassed grins." They were obviously at a loss on that elegant Nevsky, not yet converted into the "Prospect of the Twenty-Fifth of October."

Claude Anet, the official French journalist in Petrograd, was sincerely surprised that these absurd Russians should make a revolution not at all as he had read about it in the old books. "The city is quiet." He calls up his friends on the telephone, receives visitors, and at noon leaves the house. The soldiers who block his road on Molka Street march in perfect order "as under the old régime." There are innumerable patrols on Milliony Street. There is no shooting anywhere. The immense square of the Winter Palace at this noon hour is still almost empty. There are patrols on Morskaia and Nevsky. The soldiers carry themselves in military style, and are dressed irreproachably. At first glance it seems certain that these are government troops. On Mariinsky Square, whence Anet intends to make his way into the Pre-Parliament, he is stopped by soldiers and sailors. "Mighty polite, I assure you." Two streets leading up to the palace are barricaded with automobiles and wagons—here, too, an armored car. These are all under Smolny. The Military Revolutionary Committee has sent out patrols through the town, posted sentries, dissolved the Pre-Parliament, taken command of the capital, and established therein a state of order "unseen since the revolution began." In the evening the janitress informs her French lodger that telephone numbers have been sent over from soviet headquarters, by which at any moment he can summon military help in case of attack, suspicious search parties, etc. "As a fact they never guarded us better."

At 2:35 in the afternoon—the foreign journalists looked at their watches, the Russians were too busy—an emergency session of the Petrograd Soviet was opened with a report by Trotsky, who in the name of the Military Revolutionary Committee announced that the Provisional Government no longer existed. "They told us that an insurrection would drown the revolution in torrents of blood. . . . We do not know of a single casualty." There is no example in history of a revolutionary movement involving such gigantic masses being so bloodless. "The Winter Palace is not yet taken, but its fate will be settled in the course of the next few minutes." The following twelve hours were to show that this prediction was too optimistic.

Trotsky said: "Troops have been moved against Petrograd from the front; it is necessary at once to send commissars of the soviets to the front, and throughout the country, to make known that the revolution has occurred." Voices from the small right

sector: "You are anticipating the will of the Congress of Soviets."
The speaker answered: "The will of the Congress has been anticipated by the colossal fact of an insurrection of the Petrograd
workers and soldiers. It now remains only to develop our victory."

Lenin, who appeared here publicly for the first time after
emerging from underground, briefly outlined the program of the
revolution: To break up the old governmental apparatus; to create a new system of administration through the soviets; to take
measures for the immediate cessation of war, relying upon revolutionary movements in other countries; to abolish the landlords'
property rights and thus win the confidence of the peasants; to
establish workers' control over production. "The third Russian
revolution," he said, "must in the end lead to the victory of
socialism."

Chapter VIII

THE CAPTURE OF THE WINTER PALACE

KERENSKY was in a great state of excitement when he met Stankevich arriving with his report from the front. He had just returned from a meeting of the Council of the Republic where the insurrection of the Bolsheviks had been conclusively exposed.—Insurrection! Don't you know that we have an armed insurrection?—Stankevich laughed: Why the streets are perfectly quiet; surely that isn't the way a real insurrection ought to look? But anyway we must put an end to these everlasting disturbances.—To this Kerensky heartily agreed; he was only waiting for the resolution of the Pre-parliament.

At nine in the evening the government assembled in the Malachite Chamber of the Winter Palace to work out methods for a "resolute and final liquidation" of the Bolsheviks. Stankevich, returning from the Mariinsky palace, where he had been sent to hurry things up, reported with indignation the passing of the resolution of semi-non-confidence. Even the struggle against insurrection the resolution of the Pre-parliament proposed to entrust not to the government, but to a special committee of public safety. Kerensky hotly announced that under those circumstances "he would not remain a minute longer at the head of the government." The compromise leaders were immediately summoned to the palace by telephone. The possibility of Kerensky's resignation surprised them no less than their resolution had surprised Kerensky. Avksentiev presented their excuses: they had, you know, regarded the resolution "as purely theoretical and accidental, and had not believed it would lead to practical steps." Moreover they now themselves saw that the resolution was "perhaps not quite happily worded." Those people never missed an opportunity to show what they were worth.

This nocturnal conversation of the democratic leaders with the head of the State seems absolutely unbelievable on the back-

240

ground of the developing insurrection. Dan, one of the chief grave-diggers of the February régime, demanded that the government immediately, by night, plaster the town with posters announcing that it had proposed immediate peace negotiations to the Allies. Kerensky reported that the government had no need of such counsels. It is quite possible to believe that the government would have preferred a sharp division; but Dan could not offer that. Kerensky, of course, was attempting to throw the responsibility for the insurrection upon his interlocutors. Dan answered that the government was exaggerating events under the influence of its "reactionary staff." At any rate there was no need of resigning: the disagreeable resolution had been necessary in order to break the mood of the masses. The Bolsheviks will be compelled "not later than tomorrow" to dissolve their headquarters, if the government follows Dan's suggestion. "At that very moment," adds Kerensky with legitimate irony in describing this conversation, "the Red Guard was occupying the government buildings one after another."

This so weighty conference with his Left friends had hardly ended when Kerensky's friends from the Right appeared in the form of a delegation from the Council of the Cossack Troops. The officers pretended that the conduct of the three Cossack regiments in Petrograd depended upon their wills, and presented Kerensky with conditions diametrically opposite to those of Dan: no concessions to the Soviet; this time the settlement with the Bolsheviks must be carried through to the end, and not handled as in July when the Cossacks suffered in vain. Kerensky, himself desiring nothing better, promised everything they asked and apologized to his interlocutors for the fact that up to now owing to considerations of prudence he had not arrested Trotsky, the president of the Soviet of Deputies. The delegates departed, assuring him that the Cossacks would do their duty. An order was issued from headquarters to the Cossack regiment: "In the name of freedom, honor and the glory of the homeland, come to the help of the Central Executive Committee, the Provisional Government, and save Russia from ruin." That bigoted government which had so jealously defended its independence of the Central Executive Committee was compelled to hide humbly behind the

Committee's back at a moment of danger. Beseeching commands were also sent to the military schools in Petrograd and the environs. The railroads were instructed "to dispatch echelons of troops coming toward Petrograd from the front ahead of all other trains, cutting off passenger traffic if necessary."

When the government dispersed at two o'clock in the morning, having done all it could, there remained with Kerensky in the palace only his vice-minister, the liberal Moscow merchant, Konovalov. The commander of the district, Polkovnikov, came to them with a proposal to organize with the help of the loyal soldiers an immediate expedition for the seizure of Smolny. Kerensky accepted this admirable plan without hesitation, but from the words of the commander it was absolutely impossible to make out upon just what forces he was counting. Only now did Kerensky realize, according to his own confession, that the reports of Polkovnikov during the last ten or twelve days about his complete preparedness for the struggle with the Bolsheviks were "based on absolutely nothing." As though Kerensky had no other sources for an appraisal of the political and military situation but the secretarial reports of a mediocre colonel whom he had placed—nobody knows why—at the head of the district. During the aggrieved meditations of the head of the government the commissar of the city government, Rogovsky, brought a series of communications: A number of ships from the Baltic fleet have entered the Neva in fighting array; some of them have come as far as the Nikolaevsky Bridge and occupied it; detachments of the insurrectionaries are advancing on Dvortsovy Bridge. Rogovsky called Kerensky's special attention to the circumstance that "the Bolsheviks are carrying out their whole plan in complete order, meeting nowhere the slightest resistance on the part of the government troops." Just what troops were meant by the word "government" was not quite clear, in any case, from the man's report.

Kerensky and Konovalov rushed from the palace to headquarters: "We must not lose another minute," they cried. The impressive red building was brimful of officers. They had come here not on the business of their troops, but to hide from them. "Civilians unknown to anybody were also poking their noses in among this military crowd." A new report from Polkovnikov finally convinced Kerensky that it was impossible to rely upon the commander or his officers. The head of the government decided to gather around his own person "all those loyal to their duty." Remembering that he was the member of a party—as others remember only on their death beds about the church—Kerensky called up the Social Revolutionaries on the telephone and demanded that they send fighting companies immediately. Before this unexpected appeal to the armed forces of the party could give any results, however—supposing it could do so at all—it would inevitably, as Miliukov says, "repel from Kerensky all the Right Wing elements, who even without that were unfriendly enough." Kerensky's isolation, plainly enough exposed already in the Kornilov insurrection, assumed here a more fatal aspect. "The long hours of that night dragged torturingly," says Kerensky, repeating his autobiographic phrase.

Reinforcements arrived from nowhere. The Cossacks held sittings. Representatives of the regiments said that, generally speaking, they might come out—why not?—but for this it was necessary to have machine guns, armored cars, and above all infantry. Kerensky without a thought promised them armored cars which were getting ready to abandon him, and infantry of which he had none. In answer he was told that the regiments would soon decide all questions and "begin to saddle their horses." The fighting forces of the Social Revolutionaries gave no signs of life. Did they indeed still exist? Where in fact was the boundary between the real and the spectral? The officers assembled in headquarters adopted a "more and more challenging" attitude toward the commander-in-chief and head of the government. Kerensky even asserts that there was talk among the officers of arresting him. The headquarters building was, as before, unguarded. Official negotiations were carried on before outsiders in the intervals between excited private conversations. The mood of hopelessness and disintegration soaked through from headquarters into the Winter Palace. The junkers began to get nervous. The armored car crews became excited. There is no support below, there is no head above. In such circumstances can anything but destruction follow?

At five o'clock in the morning Kerensky summoned to headquarters the general director of the War Ministry, Manikovsky. At the Troitsky bridge General Manikovsky was stopped by patrols and taken to the barracks of the Pavlovsky regiment, but there after brief explanation he was set free. The general convinced them, we may assume, that his arrest might upset the whole administrative mechanism and entail damage to the soldiers at the front. At about the same time the automobile of Stankevich was stopped near the Winter Palace, but the regimental committee released him also. "These were insurrectionaries," relates Stankevich, "but they behaved very irresolutely. I telegraphed about it from my house to the Winter Palace, but received tranquilizing assurances that this had been a mistake." The real mistake was the release of Stankevich. In a few hours he will try, as we know, to get the telephone station away from the Bolsheviks.

Kerensky demanded from the headquarters in Moghiliev and from the staff of the northern front at Pskov the immediate dispatch of loyal regiments. Dukhonin assured him over the direct wire that all measures had been taken for the dispatch of troops to Petrograd, and that certain units ought already to be arriving. But the units were not arriving. The Cossacks were still "saddling their horses." The situation in the city was getting worse from hour to hour. When Kerensky and Konovalov returned to the palace to rest a little, a courier handed them an urgent communication: All the palace telephones were cut off; Dvortsovy bridge, under Kerensky's very windows, was occupied by pickets of sailors. The square in front of the Winter Palace remained deserted as before. "Of the Cossacks neither hide nor hair was to be seen." Kerensky again rushed over to headquarters, but here too he got uncomforting news. The junkers had received from the Bolsheviks a demand that they abandon the palace, and were greatly excited. The armored cars had broken order inopportunely exposing the "loss" of certain important units. There was still no news of the echelons from the front. The close approaches to the palace and headquarters were absolutely unguarded. If the Bolsheviks had not yet penetrated this far it was only through lack of information. The building, brimmed with officers since evening, had been rapidly vacated. Everyone was saving himself in his own way. A delegation from the junkers appeared. They were ready to do their duty in the future "only if there is hope of the arrival of some sort of reinforcements." But reinforcements were just exactly what was lacking.

Kerensky hastily summoned his ministers to headquarters. The majority of them had no automobiles. These important instruments of locomotion, which impart a new tempo to modern insurrection, had either been seized by the Bolsheviks or cut off from the ministers by cordons of insurrectionaries. Only Kishkin arrived, and some time later Maliantovich. What should the head of the government do? Go out at once to meet the echelons and bring them forward no matter what the obstacles might be. Nobody could think of anything else.

Kerensky ordered out his "magnificent open touring-car." But here a new factor entered into the chain of events, demonstrating the indestructible solidarity uniting the governments of the Entente in weal and woe. "In what manner I do not know, but the news of my departure had reached the Allied embassies." The representatives of Great Britain and the United States had immediately expressed the desire that with the head of the government in making his get-away from the capital, "there should go an automobile carrying the American flag." Kerensky himself thought the proposal excessive, and was even embarrassed, but accepted it as an expression of the solidarity of the Allies.

The American ambassador, David Francis, gives a different account—not so much like a Christmas story. According to him an automobile containing a Russian officer followed the American automobile to the embassy, and the officer demanded that they turn over the embassy automobile to Kerensky for a journey to the front. Taking counsel together, the officials of the embassy arrived at the conclusion that since the automobile had already been practically "seized"—which was not at all true—there was nothing left but to bow to the force of circumstance. The Russian officer—in spite, they say, of protests from the diplomatic gentlemen—refused to remove the American flag. And no wonder: it was only that colorful bit which made the automobile inviolable. Francis approved the action of the embassy officials, but told them "to say nothing about it to anybody."

By juxtaposing these two testimonies, which intersect with the line of truth at different angles, a sufficiently clear picture can be made to emerge. It was not the Allies, of course, who imposed the automobile upon Kerensky, but he himself who requested it: but since diplomats are obliged to pay a certain homage to the hypocrisy of non-interference in domestic affairs, it was agreed that the automobile had been "seized," and that the embassy had "protested" against the misuse of the flag. After this delicate matter had been arranged, Kerensky took a seat in his own automobile; the American car followed as a reserve. "It is needless to say," says Kerensky further, "that the whole street—both the passers-by and the soldiers—immediately recognized me. I saluted as always, a little carelessly and with an easy smile." Incomparable picture! Carelessly and smiling—thus the February régime passed into the kingdom of shades. At the gates of the city everywhere stood pickets and patrols of armed workers. At sight of the madly flying automobile the Red Guards rushed into the highway, but did not venture to shoot. In general, shootings were still being avoided. Maybe, too, the little American flag held them back. The automobiles successfully rushed on.

And does this mean that there are no troops in Petrograd prepared to defend the Provisional Government? asked the astonished Maliantovich, who had up to that moment dwelt in the realm of the eternal truths of law. I know nothing, Konovalov answered, shrugging his shoulders. It's pretty bad, he added. And what are these troops that are on their way? insisted Maliantovich. A bicycle battalion, it seems. The minister sighed. There were 200,000 soldiers in Petrograd and in the environs. Things were going badly with the régime, if the head of the government had to fly off with an American flag at his back to meet a bicycle battalion.

The ministers would have sighed deeper if they had known that this third bicycle battalion sent from the front had stopped at Peredolskaia and telegraphed the Petrograd soviet to know for just what purpose it was being sent. The Military Revolutionary Committee telegraphed the battalion a brotherly greeting and asked them to send their representatives immediately. The authorities sought and did not find the bicycle men, whose delegates arrived that same day in Smolny.

It had been proposed in the preliminary calculations to occupy the Winter Palace on the night of the 25th, at the same time with the other commanding high points of the capital. A special trio had been formed already as early as the 23rd to take the lead in seizing the palace, Podvoisky and Antonov being the central figures. The engineer Sadovsky, a man in military service, was included as a third, but soon fell away, being preoccupied with the affairs of the garrison. He was replaced by Chudnovsky, who had come with Trotsky in May from the concentration camp in Canada, and had spent three months at the front as a soldier. Lashevich also took an important part in the operations—an old Bolshevik who had done enough service in the army to become a non-commissioned officer. Three years later Sadovsky remembered how Podvoisky and Chudnovsky quarrelled furiously in his little room in Smolny over the map of Petrograd and the best form of action against the palace. It was finally decided to surround the region of the palace with an uninterrupted oval, the longer axis of which should be the quay of the Neva. On the river side the circle should be closed up by the Peter and Paul fortress, the *Aurora*, and other ships summoned from Kronstadt and the navy. In order to prevent or paralyze attempts to strike at the rear with Cossacks and junker detachments, it was decided to establish imposing flank defenses composed of revolutionary detachments.

The plan as a whole was too heavy and complicated for the problem it aimed to solve. The time allotted for preparation proved inadequate. Small incoordinations and omissions came to light at every step, as might be expected. In one place the direction was incorrectly indicated; in another the leader came late, having misread the instructions; in a third they had to wait for a rescuing armored car. To call out the military units, unite them with the Red Guards, occupy the fighting positions, make sure of communications among them all and with headquarters—all this demanded a good many hours more than had been imagined by the leaders quarrelling over their map of Petrograd.

When the Military Revolutionary Committee announced at about ten o'clock in the morning that the government was overthrown, the extent of this delay was not yet clear even to those in direct command of the operation. Podvoisky had promised the fall of the palace "not later than twelve o'clock." Up to that time everything had run so smoothly on the military side that nobody had any reason to question the hour. But at noon it turned out that the besieging force was still not filled out, the Kronstadters had not arrived, and that meanwhile the defense of the palace had been reinforced. This loss of time, as almost always happens, made new delays necessary. Under urgent pressure from the Committee the seizure of the palace was now set for three o'clock—and this time "conclusively." Counting on this new decision, the spokesman of the Military Revolutionary Committee expressed to the afternoon session of the Soviet the hope that the fall of the Winter Palace would be a matter of the next few minutes. But another hour passed and brought no decision. Podvoisky, himself in a state of white heat, asserted over the telephone that by six o'clock the palace would be taken no matter what it cost. His former confidence, however, was lacking. And indeed the hour of six did strike and the dénouement had not begun. Beside themselves with the urgings of Smolny, Podvoisky and Antonov now refused to set any hour at all. That caused serious anxiety. Politically it was considered necessary that at the moment of the opening of the Congress the whole capital should be in the hands of the Military Revolutionary Committee. That was to simplify the task of dealing with the opposition at the Congress, placing them before an accomplished fact. Meanwhile the hour appointed for opening the Congress had arrived, had been postponed, and arrived again, and the Winter Palace was still holding out. Thus the siege of the palace, thanks to its delay, became for no less than twelve hours the central problem of the insurrection.

The main staff of the operation remained in Smolny, where Lashevich held the threads in his hands. The field headquarters was in the Peter and Paul fortress, where Blagonravov was the responsible man. There were three subordinate headquarters, one on the *Aurora,* another in the barracks of the Pavlovsky regiment, another in the barracks of the sailors. In the field of action the leaders were Podvoisky and Antonov—apparently without any clear order of priority.

In the quarters of the general staff a trio was also bending over the map: the commander of the district Colonel Polkovnikov, the chief of his staff General Bagratuni, and General Alexeiev, especially invited in as a high authority. Notwithstanding this so well qualified commanding staff the plans of the defense were incomparably less definite than those of the attack. It is true that the inexperienced marshals of the insurrection did not know how to concentrate their forces rapidly and deal a punctual blow. But the forces were there. The marshals of the defense had cloudy hopes in place of forces: maybe the Cossacks will make up their minds; maybe loyal units will be found in the neighboring garrison; maybe Kerensky will bring troops from the front. The feelings of Polkovnikov are known from his night telegrams to headquarters: he thought that the game was up. Alexeiev, still less inclined to optimism, soon abandoned the rotten ship.

Delegates from the military schools were brought into headquarters for the purpose of keeping in touch, and an attempt was made to raise their spirits with assurances that troops would soon arrive from Gatchina, Tzarskoe and the front. However they did not much believe in these misty promises, and a depressing rumor began to creep through the schools: "There is a panic in headquarters, nobody is doing anything." And it was so. Cossack officers coming to headquarters to propose that they seize the armored cars in the Mikailovsky Riding Academy found Polkovnikov sitting on the window-seat in a condition of complete prostration. Seize the riding academy? "Seize it. I have nobody. I can't do anything alone."

While this languid mobilization of the schools for the defense of the Winter Palace was going on, the ministers assembled at a meeting. The square before the palace and its adjacent streets were still free from insurrectionists. On the corner of Morskaia and Nevsky armed soldiers were holding up passing automobiles and ejecting their passengers. The crowd was making queries: "Are these soldiers of the government or the Military Revolutionary Committee?" The ministers had for this once the full benefit of their own unpopularity. Nobody was interested in them and hardly anybody recognized them on their way. They all assembled except Prokopovich who was accidentally arrested in a cab—and was, by the way, released again during the day.

The old servants still remained in the palace, having seen much and ceased to be surprised, although not yet cured of fright. Strictly trained, dressed in blue with red collars and gold braids, these relics of the old kept up an atmosphere of order and stability in the luxurious building. They alone perhaps on this alarming morning still gave the ministers an illusion of power.

Not before eleven o'clock in the morning, did the government finally decide to place one of its members at the head of the defense. General Iznikovsky had already refused this honor, offered to him by Kerensky at dawn. Another military man in the staff of the government, Admiral Verderevsky, was still less martially inclined. It thus fell to a civilian to captain the defense —the Minister of Public Charities, Kishkin. An order of the senate confirming his appointment was immediately drawn up and signed by all. Those people had plenty of time to occupy themselves with bureaucratic fandangles. Moreover it never occurred to any of them that Kishkin as a member of the Kadet Party was doubly hated by the soldiers both front and rear. Kishkin in turn selected as his assistants Palchinsky and Ruthenberg. An appointee of the capitalists and protector of lockouts, Palchinsky enjoyed the hatred of the workers. The engineer Ruthenberg was an aide-de-camp of Savinkov, and Savinkov even the all-embracing party of the Social Revolutionaries had expelled as a Kornilovist. Polkovnikov, under suspicion of treason, was discharged. In his place they appointed General Bagratuni who differed from him in nothing.

Although the city telephones of the Winter Palace and headquarters had been cut off, the palace remained in connection with the more important institutions by its own wire—particularly with the War Ministry which had a direct wire to headquarters.

Evidently some of the city apparatus also had not been cut out in the hurry of the moment. In a military sense, however, the telephone connections gave nothing to the government, and in a moral sense they damaged rather than improved its situation for they robbed it of its illusions.

From morning on, the leaders of the defense kept demanding local reinforcements while awaiting reinforcements from the front. Certain people in the city tried to help them. A Doctor Feit who took an active part in this, a member of the Central Committee of the Social Revolutionary Party, told some years later at a legal proceeding about the "astonishing lightning-like change in the mood of the military units." You would learn, he said, from the most reliable sources of the readiness of this or that regiment to come to the defense of the government, but as soon as you called the barracks directly on the telephone, one unit after another would flatly refuse. "The result is known to you," said the old Narodnik. "Nobody came out and the Winter Palace was captured." The fact of the matter is that no lightning-like changes in the garrison took place, but the remaining illusions of the governmental parties did crumble to the ground with lightning speed.

The armored cars upon which they were especially counting in the Winter Palace and headquarters, were divided into two groups: Bolsheviks and pacifists. None of them were in favor of the government. On the way to the Winter Palace a half-company of engineering junkers ran into two armored cars which they awaited with a feeling of hope and fear: Are they friends or enemies? It turned out that they were neutral, and had come into the street with the purpose of preventing conflicts between the two sides. Out of the six armored cars in the Winter Palace only one remained to guard the palace property; the other five departed. In proportion as the insurrection succeeded the number of Bolshevik armored cars increased, and the neutral army melted away. Such is the fate of pacifism in any serious struggle.

Noon is approaching. The vast square before the Winter Palace is vacant as before. The government has nobody to fill it with. The troops of the Committee do not occupy it, because they are absorbed in carrying out their too complicated plan. Military units, workers' detachments, armored cars, are still assembling for this wide encirclement. The palace district begins to look like a plague spot which is being encircled far away to avoid direct contact with the infection.

The court of the palace opening on the square is piled up with logs of wood like the court of Smolny. Black three-inch field guns are set up to left and right. Rifles are stacked up in several different places. The small guard of the palace clings close to the building. In the court and the first story, two schools of ensigns from Oranienbaum and Peterhoff are quartered—not the whole schools by any means—and a squad from the Constantinovsky Artillery School with six cannon.

During the afternoon a battalion of junkers from the engineering school arrived, having lost half a company on the road. The picture presented when they arrived could in no wise have increased the fighting spirit of the junkers which, according to Stankevich, was inadequate even before. Inside the palace they found a lack of provisions. Even of this nobody had thought in time. A truckload of bread had been seized, it turned out, by patrols of the Committee. Some of the junkers did sentry duty; the rest lay around inactive, uncertain and hungry. No leadership whatever made itself felt. In the square before the palace, and on the quay on the other side, little groups of apparently peaceful passers-by began to appear, and they would snatch the rifles from the junker sentries, threatening them with revolvers.

"Agitators" also began to appear among the junkers. Had they gotten in from the outside? No, these were still evidently internal troublemakers. They succeeded in starting a ferment among the Oranienbaum and Peterhoff students. The committees of the school called a conference in the White Hall, and demanded that representatives of the government come in and make an explanation. All the ministers came in, with Konovalov at their head. The argument lasted a whole hour. Konovalov was heckled and stopped talking. The Minister of Agriculture, Maslov, made a speech as an old revolutionist. Kishkin explained to the junkers that the government had decided to stand firm as long as possible. According to Stankevich one of the junkers was

252

about to express his readiness to die for the government, but "the obvious coolness of the rest of his comrades held him back." The speech of the other ministers produced actual irritation among the junkers, who interrupted, shouted and even, it seems, whistled. The blue-bloods explained the conduct of the majority of the junkers by their low social origin: "They were all from the plow, half-illiterate, ignorant beasts, cattle . . ."

The meeting in the besieged palace ended nevertheless in conciliation. The junkers, after they had been promised active leadership and correct information about what was happening, agreed to stay. The chief of the engineering school, appointed commander of the defense, ran his pencil over the plan of the palace, writing in the names of the units. The forces on hand were distributed in fighting positions. The majority of the junkers were stationed on the first floor where they could train their guns on Winter Palace Square through the windows. But they were forbidden to fire first. A battalion of the Engineering School was brought out into the court-yard to cover the artillery. Squads were appointed for barricade work. A communication squad was formed with four men from each unit. The artillery squad was directed to defend the gate in case of a breach. Fortifications of fire-wood were laid up in the court and before the gates. Something like order was established. The sentries felt more confident.

A civil war in its first steps, before real armies have been formed and before they are tempered, is a war of naked nerves. As soon as a little activity developed on the side of the junkers, —their clearing of the square with gun fire from behind the barricades—the forces and equipment of the defense were enormously over-estimated in the attacking camp. In spite of the dissatisfaction of the Red Guard and the soldiers, the leaders now decided to postpone the assault until they had concentrated their reserves; they were chiefly awaiting the arrival of the sailors from Kronstadt.

The delay of a few hours thus created brought some small reinforcements to the besieged. After Kerensky's promise of infantry to the Cossack delegation the Council of the Cossack Troops had gone into session, the regimental committees had gone into session, and the general assembly of the regiments had gone into session. Decision: Two squadrons and the machine gun crew of the Uralsky regiment, brought in from the front in July to crush the Bolsheviks, should immediately enter the Winter Palace, the rest not until the promise was actually fulfilled—that is, not until after the arrival of infantry reinforcements. But even with the two squadrons this was not accomplished without argument. The Cossack youth objected. The "old men" even had to lock the young ones up in the stable, where they could not hinder them from equipping themselves for the march. Only at twilight, when they were no longer expected, did these bearded Uraltsi appear in the palace. They were met like saviors. They themselves, however, looked sulky. They were not accustomed to fight about palaces. Yes, and it was not quite clear which side was right.

Sometime later there arrived unexpectedly forty of the Cavaliers of St. George under command of a staff captain on a cork leg. Patriotic cripples acting as the last reserves of democracy. . . . But even so they felt better. Soon came also a shock company of the Woman's Battalion. What encouraged them most of all was that these reinforcements had made their way through without fighting. The cordon of the besieging forces could not, or did not dare, deny them access to the palace. Quite obviously, therefore, the enemy was weak. "Glory be to God, the thing is beginning to pull itself together," said the officers, comforting themselves and the junkers. The new arrivals received their military allotments, replacing those who were tired. However, the Uraltsi glanced with no great approval upon those "wenches" with rifles. Where is the real infantry?

The besiegers were obviously losing time. The Kronstadters were late—not, to be sure, through their own fault. They had been summoned too late. After a tense night of preparation they had begun to embark at dawn. The destroyer *Amur* and the cruiser *Yastreb* had made straight for Petrograd. The old armored cruiser *Zaria Svobodi*, after landing marines at Oranienbaum, where it was proposed to disarm the junkers, was to anchor at the entrance to the Morskoy Canal, in order in case of need to bombard the Baltic railroad. Five thousand sailors and soldiers disembarked early in the morning from the Island of Kotlin in order to embark on the social revolution. In the officers' cabin a solemn silence reigns. These officers are being taken along to fight for a cause which they hate. The commissar of the detachment, the Bolshevik, Flerovsky, announces to them: "We do not count upon your sympathy, but we demand that you be at your posts. . . . We will spare you any unnecessary unpleasantness." He received the brief naval answer: "Aye, Aye, sir!" All took their places. The commander ascended the bridge.

Upon arriving in the Neva a triumphal hurrah: the sailors are greeting their own. A band strikes up on the *Aurora,* anchored in midstream. Antonov addresses the new arrivals with a brief greeting: "There is the Winter Palace. . . . We must take it." In the Kronstadt detachment the most resolute and bold choose themselves out automatically. These sailors in black blouses with rifles and cartridge belts will go all the way. The disembarkation on Konnogvardeisky Boulevard takes but a few moments. Only a military watch remains on the ship.

The forces are now more than adequate on the Nevsky. There are strong outposts on the bridge of the Ekaterininsky Canal and on the bridge of the Moika armored automobiles and Zenith guns aimed at the Winter Palace. On this side of the Moika the workers have set up machine guns behind screens. An armored car is on duty on Morskaia. The Neva and its crossings are in the hands of the attackers. Chudnovsky and ensign Dashkevich are ordered to send troops from the Guard regiments to hold Mars Field. Blagonravov from the fortress, after crossing the bridge, is to get into contact with the troops on Mars Field. The sailors just arrived are to keep in contact with the fortress and the crew of the *Aurora.* After artillery fire the storm is to begin.

At the same time five ships of war arrive from the Baltic battle fleet: a cruiser, two destroyers, and two smaller vessels. "However sure we may have been of winning with the forces on hand," writes Flerovsky, "this gift from the navy raised everybody's spirits." Admiral Verderovsky, looking from the windows of the Malachite Hall, could probably see an imposing mutinous flotilla, dominating not only the palace and the surrounding district but also the principal approaches to Petrograd.

About four o'clock in the afternoon Konovalov summoned to the palace by telephone the political leaders standing close to the government. The besieged ministers had need at least of moral support. Of all those invited only Nabokov appeared. The rest preferred to express their sympathy by telephone. Minister Tretiakov complained against Kerensky and against fate: The head of the ministry has fled leaving his colleagues without defense. But perhaps reinforcements will come? Perhaps. However, why aren't they here? Nabokov expressed his sympathy, glancing stealthily at his watch, and hastened to take his farewell. He got out just in time. Shortly after six the Winter Palace was at last solidly surrounded by the troops of the Military Revolutionary Committee. There was no longer any passage either for reinforcements or for individuals.

From the direction of Konnogvardeisky Boulevard, the Admiralty Quay, Morskaia Street, Nevsky Prospect, Mars Field, Milliony Street and Dvortsovy Quay, the oval of the besiegers thickened and contracted. Imposing cordons extended from the iron fences of the Winter Palace garden, still in the hands of the besieged, from the arch between Palace Square and Morskaia Street, from the canal by the Hermitage, from the corners of the Admiralty, and the Nevsky nearby the palace. Peter and Paul fortress frowned threateningly from the other side of the river. The *Aurora* looked in from the Neva with her six-inch guns. Destroyers steamed back and forth patrolling the river. The insurrection looked at that moment like a military maneuver in the grand style.

On Palace Square, cleared by the junkers three hours before, armored automobiles now appeared and occupied the entrances and exits. Their old patriotic names were still visible on the armor under the new designations painted hastily in red. Under the protection of these steel monsters the attackers felt more and more confident on the square. One of the armored cars approached the main entrance of the palace, disarmed the junkers guarding it, and withdrew unhindered.

In spite of the complete blockade now at last established, the besieged still kept in touch with the outside world by telephone. To be sure, as early as five o'clock a company of the Keksgolmsky regiment had already occupied the War Ministry, through which the Winter Palace had kept in touch with headquarters. But even after that an officer still remained apparently for some hours at the apparatus of the southwestern front, located in an attic chamber of the ministry where the captors never thought of looking. However, as before, this contact was of no help. The answers from the northern front had become more and more evasive. The reinforcements had not turned up. The mysterious bicycle battalion never arrived. Kerensky himself seemed to have disappeared like a diver. The city friends confined themselves to briefer and briefer expressions of sympathy. The ministers were sick at heart. There was nothing to talk about, nothing to hope for. The ministers disagreed with each other and with themselves. Some sat still in a kind of stupor, others automatically paced up and down the floor. Those inclined to generalization looked back into the past, seeking a culprit. He was not hard to find: the democracy! It was the democracy which had sent them into the government, laid a mighty burden on them, and at the moment of danger left them without support. For this once the Kadets were fully at one with the socialists. Yes, the democracy was to blame! To be sure, in forming the Coalition both groups had turned their back on an institution as near to them as the Democratic Conference. Independence of the democracy had indeed been the chief idea of the Coalition. But never mind: what does a democracy exist for, if not to rescue a bourgeois government when it gets into trouble? The Minister of Agriculture Maslov, a Right Social Revolutionary, made a note which he himself described as a dying utterance. He solemnly promised to die with a curse to the democracy upon his lips. His colleagues hastened to communicate this fateful intention to the Duma by telephone. His death, to be sure, remained only a project, but there was no lack of curses right on hand.

Up above near the chambers of the commandant there was a dining room where the court servants served the officer gentlemen a "divine dinner and wine." One could forget unpleasantnesses for a time. The officers figured out seniorities, made envious comparisons, and cursed the new power for its slow promotions. They gave it to Kerensky especially: yesterday at the Pre-Parliament he was vowing to die at his post, and today he beats it out of town dressed up as a sister of mercy. Certain of the officers demonstrated to the members of the government the folly of any further resistance. The energetic Palchinsky declared such officers Bolsheviks, and tried even to arrest them.

The junkers wanted to know what was going to happen next, and demanded from the government explanations which it was not in a position to give. During this new conference between the junkers and the ministers, Kishkin arrived from staff headquarters, bringing an ultimatum signed by Antonov and delivered from the Peter and Paul fortress to the Quartermaster-General, Poravelov, by a bicycle man: Surrender and disarm the garrison of the Winter Palace; otherwise fire will be opened from the guns of the fortress and the ships of war; twenty minutes for reflection. This period had seemed small. Poravelov had managed to extract another ten minutes. The military members of the government, Manikovsky and Verderevsky, approached the matter simply. Since it is impossible to fight, they said, we must think of surrendering—that is, accept the ultimatum. But the civilian ministers remained obstinate. In the end they decided to make no answer to the ultimatum, and to appeal to the city duma as the only legal body existing in the capital. This appeal to the duma was the last attempt to wake up the drowsy conscience of the democracy.

Poradelov, considering it necessary to end the resistance, asked for his discharge: he lacked "confidence in the correctness of the course chosen by the Provisional Government." The hesitations of the officer were put an end to before his resignation could be accepted. In about half an hour a detachment of Red Guards, sailors and soldiers, commanded by an ensign of the Pavlovsky regiment, occupied the staff headquarters without resistance, and arrested the faint-hearted Quartermaster General. This seizure of the headquarters might have been carried out some time before since the building was completely undefended from within. But until the arrival of armored cars on the Square, the besiegers feared a sortie of junkers from the palace which might cut them off.

After the loss of headquarters the Winter Palace felt still more orphaned. From the Malachite Room, whose windows opened on the Neva, and seemed, as it were, to invite a few shells from the *Aurora,* the ministers removed themselves to one of the innumerable apartments of the palace with windows on the court. The lights were put out. Only one lonely lamp burned on the table, its light shut off from the windows by newspapers.

What will happen to the palace if the *Aurora* opens fire? asked the ministers of their naval colleague. It will be a pile of ruins, exclaimed the admiral readily, and not without a feeling of pride in his naval artillery. Verderevsky preferred a surrender, and was not unwilling to frighten these civilians out of their untimely bravery. But the *Aurora* did not shoot. The fortress also remained silent. Maybe the Bolsheviks after all will not dare carry out their threat?

General Bagratuni, appointed in place of the insufficiently steadfast Polkovnikov, considered this the appropriate moment to announce that he refused any longer to occupy the post of commander of the district. At Kishkin's order the general was demoted "as unworthy," and was requested immediately to leave the palace. On emerging from the gates the former commander fell into the hands of the sailors, who took him to the barracks of the Baltic crew. It might have gone badly with the general, but that Podvoisky, making the rounds of his front before the final attack, took the unhappy warrior under his wing.

From the adjacent streets and quays many noticed how the palace which had just been glimmering with hundreds of electric lights was suddenly drowned in darkness. Among these observers were friends of the government. One of the colleagues of Kerensky, Redemeister, has written: "The darkness in which the palace was drowned presented an alarming enigma." The friends did not take any measures toward solving this enigma. We must confess, however, that the possibilities were not great.

Hiding behind their piles of firewood the junkers followed tensely the cordon forming on Palace Square, meeting every movement of the enemy with rifle and machine gun fire. They were answered in kind. Towards night the firing became hotter. The first casualties occurred. The victims, however, were only a few individuals. On the square, on the quays, on Milliony, the besiegers accommodated themselves to the situation, hid behind projections, concealed themselves in hollows, clung along the walls. Among the reserves the soldiers and Red Guards warmed themselves around campfires which they had kindled at nightfall, abusing the leaders for going so slow.

In the palace the junkers were taking up positions in the corridors, on the stairway, at the entrances, and in the court. The outside Sentries clung along the fence and walls. The building would hold thousands, but it held hundreds. The vast quarters behind the sphere of defense seemed dead. Most of the servants had scattered, or were hiding. Many of the officers took refuge in the buffet, where they compelled those servants who had not yet made their getaway to set out continual batteries of wines. This drunken debauch of the officers in the agonizing palace could not remain a secret to the junkers, Cossacks, cripples and women soldiers. The dénouement was preparing not only from without but from within.

An officer of the artillery squad suddenly reported to the commandant of the defense: The junkers have left their weapons in the entrance and are going home, in obedience to orders received from the commandant of the Constantinovsky school. That was a treacherous blow! The commandant tried to object: nobody but he could give orders here. The junkers understood this, but nevertheless preferred to obey the commandant of the school, who in his turn was acting under pressure from the commissar of the Military Revolutionary Committee. A majority of the artillery men, with four of the six guns, abandoned the palace. Held up on the Nevsky by a soldier patrol, they attempted to resist, but a patrol of the Pavlovsky regiment, arriving just in time with an armored car, disarmed them and sent them to its barracks with two of the guns. The other two were set up on the Nevsky and the bridge over the Moika and aimed at the Winter Palace.

The two squadrons of the Uraltsi were waiting in vain for the arrival of their comrades. Savinkov, who was closely associated with the Council of the Cossack Troops, and had even been sent by it as a delegate to the Pre-parliament, attempted with the co-operation of General Alexeiev to get the Cossacks in motion. But the chiefs of the Cossack Council, as Miliukov justly observes "could as little control the Cossack regiment as the staff could the troops of the garrison." Having considered the question from all sides, the Cossack regiment finally announced that they would not come out without infantry, and offered their services to the Military Revolutionary Committee for the purpose of guarding the government property. At the same time the Uralsky regiment decided to send delegates to the Winter Palace to call its two squadrons back to the barracks. This suggestion fell in admirably with the now quite well-defined mood of the Uralsky's "old men." There was nobody but strangers around: junkers—among them a number of Jews—invalid officers—yes, and then these female shock troops. With angry and frowning faces the Cossacks gathered up their saddle bags. No further arguments could move them. Who remained to defend Kerensky? "Yids and wenches . . . but the Russian people has stayed over there with Lenin." It turned out that the Cossacks were in touch with the besiegers, and they got free passes through an exit till then unknown to the defenders. It was about nine o'clock in the evening when the Uraltsi left the palace. Only their machine guns they agreed to leave for the defense of a hopeless cause.

By this same entrance too, coming from the direction of Milliony Street, Bolsheviks had before this got into the palace for the purpose of demoralizing the enemy. Oftener and oftener mysterious figures began to appear in the corridors beside the junkers. It is useless to resist; the insurrectionists have captured the city and the railroad stations; there are no reinforcements; in the palace they "only keep on lying through inertia." . . . What are we to do next? asked the junkers. The government refused to issue any direct commands. The ministers themselves would stand by their old decision; the rest could do as they pleased. That meant free egress from the palace for those who wanted it. The government had neither will nor idea left; the ministers passively awaited their fate. Maliantovich subsequently related: "We wandered through the gigantic mousetrap, meeting occasionally, either all together or in small groups, for brief conversations—condemned people, lonely, abandoned by all. . . . Around us vacancy, within us vacancy, and in this grew up the soulless courage of placid indifference."

Antonov-Ovseёnko had agreed with Blagonravov that after

261

the encirclement of the palace was completed, a red lantern should be raised on the flagpole of the fortress. At this signal the *Aurora* would fire a blank volley in order to frighten the palace. In case the besieged were stubborn, the fortress should begin to bombard the palace with real shells from the light guns. If the palace did not surrender even then, the *Aurora* would open a real fire from its six-inch guns. The object of this gradation was to reduce to a minimum the victims and the damage, supposing they could not be altogether avoided. But the too complicated solution of a simple problem threatened to lead to an opposite result. The difficulty of carrying this plan out is too obvious. They are to start off with a red lantern. It turns out that they have none on hand. They lose time hunting for it, and finally find it. However, it is not so simple to tie a lantern to a flagpole in such a way that it will be visible in all directions. Efforts are renewed and twice renewed with a dubious result, and meanwhile the precious time is slipping away.

The chief difficulty developed, however, in connection with the artillery. According to a report made by Blagonravov the bombardment of the capital had been possible on a moment's notice ever since noon. In reality it was quite otherwise. Since there was no permanent artillery in the fortress, except for that rusty-muzzled cannon which announces the noon hour, it was necessary to lift field guns up to the fortress walls. That part of the program had actually been carried out by noon. But a difficulty arose about finding gunners. It had been known in advance that the artillery company—one of those which had not come out on the side of the Bolsheviks in July—was hardly to be relied on. Only the day before it had meekly guarded a bridge under orders from headquarters. A blow in the back was not to be expected from it, but the company had no intention of going through fire for the soviets. When the time came for action the ensign reported: The guns are rusty; there is no oil in the compressors; it is impossible to shoot. Very likely the guns really were not in shape, but that was not the essence of it. The artillerists were simply dodging the responsibility, and leading the inexperienced commissars by the nose. Antonov dashes up on a cutter in a state of fury. Who is sabotaging the plan? Blagonravov tells him about the lantern, about the oil, about the ensign. They both start to go up to the cannon. Night, darkness, puddles in the court from the recent rains. From the other side of the river comes hot rifle fire and the rattle of machine guns. In the darkness Blagonravov loses the road. Splashing through the puddles, burning with impatience, stumbling and falling in the mud, Antonov blunders after the commissar through the dark court. "Beside one of the weakly glimmering lanterns," relates Blagonravov . . . "Antonov suddenly stopped and peered inquiringly at me over his spectacles, almost touching my face. I read in his eyes a hidden alarm." Antonov had for a second suspected treachery where there was only carelessness.

The position of the guns was finally found. The artillery men were stubborn: Rust . . . compressors . . . oil. Antonov gave orders to bring gunners from the naval polygon and also to fire a signal from the antique cannon which announced the noon hour. But the artillery men were suspiciously long monkeying with the signal cannon. They obviously felt that the commanders too, when not far-off at the telephone but right beside them, had no firm will to resort to heavy artillery. Even under the very clumsiness of this plan for artillery fire the same thought is to be felt lurking: Maybe we can get along without it.

Somebody is rushing through the darkness of the court. As he comes near he stumbles and falls in the mud, swears a little but not angrily, and then joyfully and in a choking voice cries out: "The palace has surrendered and our men are there." Rapturous embraces. How lucky there was a delay! "Just what we thought!" The compressors are immediately forgotten. But why haven't they stopped shooting on the other side of the river? Maybe some individual groups of junkers are stubborn about surrendering. Maybe there is a misunderstanding? The misunderstanding turned out to be good news: not the Winter Palace was captured, but only headquarters. The siege of the palace continued.

By secret agreement with a group of junkers of the Oranienbaum school the irrepressible Chudnovsky gets into the palace for negotiations: this opponent of the insurrection never misses a chance to dash into the firing line. Palchinsky arrests the daredevil, but under pressure from the Oranienbaum students is compelled to release both Chudnovsky and a number of the junkers.

They take away with them a few of the Cavaliers of St. George. The unexpected appearance of these junkers on the square throws the cordons into confusion. But there is no end of joyful shouting, when the besiegers know that these are surrendering troops. However, only a small minority surrenders. The remainder continue to fire from behind their cover. The shooting of the attackers has increased. The bright electric light in the court makes a good mark of the junkers. With difficulty they succeed in putting out the light. Some unseen hand again switches on the light. The junkers shoot at the light, and then find the electrician and make him switch off the current.

The Woman's Battalion suddenly announce their intention to make a sortie. According to their information the clerks in General Headquarters have gone over to Lenin, and after disarming some of the officers have arrested General Alekseiev—the sole man who can save Russia. He must be rescued at any cost. The commandant is powerless to restrain them from this hysterical undertaking. At the moment of their sortie the lights again suddenly flare up in the high electric lanterns on each side of the gate. Seeking an electrician the officer jumps furiously upon the palace servants: in these former lackeys of the tzar he sees agents of revolution. He puts still less trust in the court electrician: "I would have sent you to the next world long ago if I hadn't needed you." In spite of revolver threats, the electrician is powerless to help. His switch-board is disconnected. Sailors have occupied the electric station and are controlling the light. The women soldiers do not stand up under fire and the greater part of them surrender. The commandant of the defense sends a corporal to report to the government that the sortie of the woman's battalion has "led to their destruction," and that the palace is swarming with agitators. The failure of the sortie causes a lull lasting approximately from ten to eleven. The besiegers are busied with the preparation of artillery fire.

The unexpected lull awakens some hopes in the besieged. The ministers again try to encourage their partisans in the city and throughout the country: "The government in full attendance, with the exception of Prokopovich, is at its post. The situation is considered favorable. . . . The palace is under fire, but only rifle fire and without results. It is clear that the enemy is weak." In reality the enemy is all-powerful but cannot make up his mind to use his power. The government sends out through the country communications about the ultimatum, about the *Aurora,* about how it, the government, can only transfer the power to the Constituent Assembly, and how the first assault on the Winter Palace has been repulsed. "Let the army and the people answer!" But just how they are to answer the ministers do not suggest.

Lashevich meantime has sent two sailor gunners to the fortress. To be sure, they are none too experienced, but they are at least Bolsheviks, and quite ready to shoot from rusty guns without oil in the compressors. That is all that is demanded of them. A noise of artillery is more important at the moment than a well-aimed blow. Antonov gives the order to begin. The gradations indicated in advance are completely followed out. "After a signal shot from the fortress," relates Flerovsky, "The *Aurora* thundered out. The boom and flash of blank fire are much bigger than from a loaded gun. The curious onlookers jumped back from the granite parapet of the quay, fell down and crawled away. . . ." Chudnovsky promptly raises the question: How about proposing to the besieged to surrender. Antonov as promptly agrees with him. Again an interruption. Some group of women and junkers are surrendering. Chudnovsky wants to leave them their arms, but Antonov revolts in time against this too beautiful magnanimity. Laying the rifles on the sidewalk the prisoners go out under convoy along Milliony Street.

The palace still holds out. It is time to have an end. The order is given. Firing begins—not frequent and still less effectual. Out of thirty-five shots fired in the course of an hour and a half or two hours, only two hit the mark, and they only injure the plaster. The other shells go high, fortunately not doing any damage in the city. Is lack of skill the real cause? They were shooting across the Neva with a direct aim at a target as impressive as the Winter Palace: that does not demand a great deal of artistry. Would it not be truer to assume that even Lashevich's artillery-men intentionally aimed high in the hope that things would be settled without destruction and death? It is very difficult now to hunt out any trace of the motive which guided the two nameless sailors. They themselves have spoken no word. Have they dissolved in the immeasurable Russian land, or, like so many of the October fighters, did they lay down their heads in the civil wars of the coming months and years?

Shortly after the first shots, Palchinsky brought the ministers a fragment of shell. Admiral Verderevsky recognized the shell as his own—from a naval gun, from the *Aurora*. But they were shooting blank from the cruiser. It had been thus agreed, was thus testified by Flerovsky, and thus reported to the Congress of Soviets later by a sailor. Was the admiral mistaken? Was the sailor mistaken? Who can ascertain the truth about a cannon shot fired in the thick of night from a mutinous ship at a tzar's palace where the last government of the possessing classes is going out like an oilless lamp?

The garrison of the palace was greatly reduced in number. If at the moment of the arrival of the Uraltsi, the cripples and the woman's battalion, it rose to a thousand and a half, or perhaps even two thousand, it was now reduced to a thousand, and perhaps considerably less. Nothing can save the day now but a miracle. And suddenly into the despairing atmosphere of the Winter Palace there bursts—not, to be sure, a miracle, but the news of its approach. Palchinsky announces: They have just telephoned from the City Duma that the citizens are getting ready to march from there for the rescue of the government. "Tell everybody," he gives orders to Sinegub, "that the people are coming." The officer runs up and down stairs and through the corridors with the joyful news. On the way he stumbles upon some drunken officers fighting each other with rapiers—shedding no blood, however. The junkers lift up their heads. Passing from mouth to mouth the news becomes more colorful and impressive. The public men, the merchantry, the people, with the clergy at their head, are marching this way to free the beleaguered palace. The people with the clergy! "That will be strikingly beautiful!" A last remnant of energy flares up: "Hurrah! Long live Russia!" The Oranienbaum junkers, who by that time had quite decided to leave, changed their minds and stayed.

But the people with the clergy come very slowly. The number of agitators in the palace is growing. In a minute the *Aurora* will open fire. There is a whispering in the corridors. And this whisper passes from lip to lip. Suddenly two explosions. Sailors have got into the palace and either thrown or dropped from the gallery two hand grenades, lightly wounding two junkers. The sailors are arrested and the wounded bound up by Kishkin, a physician by profession.

The inner resolution of the workers and sailors is great, but it has not yet become bitter. Lest they call it down on their heads, the besieged, being the incomparably weaker side, dare not deal severely with these agents of the enemy who have penetrated the palace. There are no executions. Uninvited guests now begin to appear no longer one by one, but in groups. The palace is getting more and more like a sieve. When the junkers fall upon these intruders, the latter permit themselves to be disarmed. "What cowardly scoundrels!" says Palchinsky scornfully. No, these men were not cowardly. It required a high courage to make one's way into that palace crowded with officers and junkers. In the labyrinth of an unknown building, in dark corridors, among innumerable doors leading nobody knew where, and threatening nobody knew what, the daredevils had nothing to do but surrender. The number of captives grows. New groups break in. It is no longer quite clear who is surrendering to whom, who is disarming whom. The artillery continues to boom.

With the exception of the district immediately adjoining the Winter Palace, the life of the streets did not cease until late at night. The theaters and moving-picture houses were open. To the respectable and educated strata of the capital it was of no consequence apparently that their government was under fire. Redemeister on the Troitsky Bridge saw quietly approaching pedestrians whom the sailors stopped. "There was nothing unusual to be seen." From acquaintances coming from the direction of the People's House Redemeister learned, to the tune of a cannonade, that Chaliapin had been incomparable in *Don Carlos*. The ministers continued to tramp the floors of their mousetrap.

"It is clear that the attackers are weak"; maybe if we hold out an extra hour reinforcements will still arrive. Late at night Kishkin summoned Assistant-Minister of Finance Khrushchev, also a Kadet, to the telephone, and asked him to tell the leaders of the party that the government needed at least a little bit of help in order to hold out until the morning hours, when Kerensky ought finally to arrive with the troops. "What kind of a party is this," shouts Kishkin indignantly, "that can't send us three hundred armed men!" And he is right. What kind of a party is it? These Kadets who had assembled tens of thousands of votes at the elections in Petrograd, could not put out three hundred fighters at the moment of mortal danger to the bourgeois régime. If the ministers had only thought to hunt up in the palace library the books of the materialist Hobbes, they could have read in his dialogues about civil war that there is no use expecting or demanding courage from store-keepers who have gotten rich, "since they see nothing but their own momentary advantage . . . and completely lose their heads at the mere thought of the possibility of being robbed." But after all Hobbes was hardly to be found in the tzar's library. The ministers, too, were hardly up to the philosophy of history. Kishkin's telephone call was the last ring from the Winter Palace.

Smolny was categorically demanding an end. We must not drag out the siege till morning, keep the city in a tension, rasp the nerves of the Congress, put a question-mark against the whole victory. Lenin sends angry notes. Call follows call from the Military Revolutionary Committee. Podvoisky talks back. It is possible to throw the masses against the palace. Plenty are eager to go. But how many victims will there be, and what will be left of the ministers and the junkers? However, the necessity of carrying the thing through is too imperious. Nothing remains but to make the naval artillery speak. A sailor from Peter and Paul takes a slip of paper to the *Aurora*. Open fire on the palace immediately. Now, it seems, all will be clear. The gunners on the *Aurora* are ready for business, but the leaders still lack resolution. There is a new attempt at evasion. "We decided to wait just another quarter of an hour," writes Flerovsky, "sensing by instinct the possibility of a change of circumstances." By "instinct" here it is necessary to understand a stubborn hope that the thing would be settled by mere demonstrative methods. And this time "instinct" did not deceive. Towards the end of that quarter of an hour a new courier arrived straight from the Winter Palace. The palace is taken!

The palace did not surrender but was taken by storm—this, however, at a moment when the power of resistance of the besieged had already completely evaporated. Hundreds of enemies broke into the corridor—not by the secret entrance this time but through the defended door—and they were taken by the demoralized defenders for the Duma deputation. Even so they were successfully disarmed. A considerable group of junkers got away in the confusion. The rest—at least a number of them—still continued to stand guard. But the barrier of bayonets and rifle fire between the attackers and defenders was finally broken down.

That part of the palace adjoining the Hermitage is already filled with the enemy. The junkers make an attempt to come at them from the rear. In the corridors phantasmagoric meetings and clashes take place. All are armed to the teeth. Lifted hands hold revolvers. Hand-grenades hang from belts. But nobody shoots and nobody throws a grenade. For they and their enemy are so mixed together that they cannot drag themselves apart. Never mind: the fate of the palace is already decided.

Workers, sailors, soldiers are pushing up from outside in chains and groups, flinging the junkers from the barricades, bursting through the court, stumbling into the junkers on the staircase, crowding them back, toppling them over, driving them upstairs. Another wave comes on behind. The square pours into the court. The court pours into the palace, and floods up and down stairways and through corridors. On the befouled parquets, among mattresses and chunks of bread, people, rifles, hand grenades are wallowing. The conquerors find out that Kerensky is not there, and a momentary pang of disappointment interrupts their furious joy. Antonov and Chudnovsky are now in the palace. Where is the government? That is the door—there where the junkers stand frozen in the last pose of resistance. The head sentry rushes to the ministers with a question: Are we commanded to resist to the end? No, no, the ministers do not command that. After all, the palace is taken. There is no need of bloodshed. We must yield to force. The ministers desire to surrender with dignity, and sit at the table in imitation of a session of the government. The commandant has already surrendered the palace, negotiating for the lives of the junkers, against which in any case nobody had made the slightest attempt. As to the fate of the government, Antonov refuses to enter into any negotiations whatever.

The junkers at the last guarded doors were disarmed. The victors burst into the room of the ministers. "In front of the crowd and trying to hold back the onpressing ranks strode a rather small, unimpressive man. His clothes were in disorder, a wide-brimmed hat askew on his head, eyeglasses balanced uncertainly on his nose, but his little eyes gleamed with the joy of victory and spite against the conquered." In these annihilating strokes the conquered have described Antonov. It is not hard to believe that his clothes and his hat were in disorder: It is sufficient to remember the nocturnal journey through the puddles of the Peter and Paul fortress. The joy of victory might also doubtless have been read in his eyes; but hardly any spite against the conquered in those eyes. I announce to you, members of the Provisional Government, that you are under arrest—exclaimed Antonov in the name of the Military Revolutionary Committee. The clock then pointed to 2:10 in the morning of October 26.— The members of the Provisional Government submit to force and surrender in order to avoid bloodshed—answered Konovalov. The most important part of the ritual was thus observed.

Antonov summoned twenty-five armed men, choosing them from the first detachments to break into the palace, and turned over to them the defense of the ministry. After drawing up a minute of the proceeding, the arrestees were led out into the square. In the crowd, which had made its sacrifice of dead and wounded, there was in truth a flare up of spite against the conquered. "Death to them! Shoot them!" Individual soldiers tried to strike the ministers. The Red Guards quieted the intemperate ones: Do not stain the proletarian victory! Armed workers surrounded the prisoners and their convoy in a solid ring. "Forward!" They had not far to go—through Milliony and across the Troitsky Bridge. But the excitement of the crowd made that short journey long and full of danger. Minister Nikitin wrote later very truly that but for the energetic intercession of Antonov the consequences might have been "very serious." To conclude their misadventure, the procession while on the bridge was fired on by accident, and the arrestees and their convoy had to lie down on the pavement. But here too nobody was injured. Somebody was evidently shooting in the air as a warning.

In the narrow quarters of the garrison club of the fortress, lighted with a smoky kerosene lamp because the electricity had refused to function that day, forty or fifty men are crowded. Antonov, in the presence of the commissar of the fortress, calls the roll of the ministers. There are eighteen of them, including the highest assistants. The last formalities are concluded; the prisoners are distributed in the rooms of the historic Trubetskoy Bastion. None of the defenders had been arrested: the officers and junkers were paroled on their word of honor that they would not take any action against the soviet power. Only a few of them kept their word.

Immediately after the capture of the Winter Palace rumors went round in bourgeois circles about the execution of junkers, the raping of the Woman's Battalion, the looting of the riches of the palace. All these fables had long ago been refuted when Miliukov wrote this in his History: "Those of the Woman's Battalion who had not died under fire were seized by the Bolsheviks, subjected during that evening and night to the frightful attentions of the soldiers, to violence and execution." As a matter of fact there were no shootings and, the mood of both sides being what it was at that period, there could not have been any shootings. Still less thinkable were acts of violence, especially within the palace where alongside of various accidental elements from the streets, hundreds of revolutionary workers came in with rifles in their hands.

Attempts at looting were actually made, but it was just these attempts which revealed the discipline of the victors. John Reed, who did not miss one of the dramatic episodes of the revolution, and who entered the palace on the heels of the first cordons, tells how in the basement stores a group of soldiers were prying drawers open with the butts of their guns and dragging out carpets, linen, china, glassware. It is possible that regular robbers were working in the disguise of soldiers, as they did invariably during the last years of the war, concealing their identity in trenchcoats and *papakhi*. The looting had just begun when somebody shouted: "Comrades, keep your hands off, that is the property of the peo-

271

ple." A soldier sat down at a table by the entrance with pen and paper: two Red Guards with revolvers stood behind him. Everyone going out was searched, and every object stolen was taken back and listed. In this way they recovered little statues, bottles of ink, daggers, cakes of soap, ostrich feathers. The junkers were also subjected to a careful search, and their pockets turned out to be full of stolen bric-a-brac. The junkers were abused and threatened by the soldiers, but that was as far as it went. Meanwhile a palace guard was formed with the sailor Prikhodko at the head. Sentries were posted everywhere. The palace was cleared of outsiders. In a few hours Chudnovsky was appointed commandant of the Winter Palace.

But what had become of the people advancing with the clergy at their head to liberate the palace? It is necessary to tell about this heroic attempt, the news of which had for a moment so touched the hearts of the junkers. The city duma was the center of the anti-Bolshevik forces; its building on the Nevsky was boiling like a cauldron. Parties, factions, sub-factions, groups, remnants and mere influential individuals were there discussing this criminal adventure of the Bolsheviks. From time to time they would call up the ministry languishing in the palace, and tell them that under the weight of universal condemnation the insurrection must inevitably expire. Hours were devoted to dissertations on the moral isolation of the Bolsheviks. Meanwhile the artillery began to speak. The minister Prokopovich, arrested in the morning but soon released, complained to the duma with a weeping voice that he had been deprived of the possibility of sharing the fate of his comrades. He aroused warm sympathy, but the expression of this sympathy used up time.

From the general confusion of ideas and speeches a practical plan is at last produced, and wins stormy applause from the whole meeting. The duma must march in a body to the Winter Palace in order to die there, if necessary, with the government. The Social Revolutionaries, Mensheviks and Cooperators are all alike seized with a willingness either to save the ministers or fall by their sides. The Kadets, not generally inclined to risky undertakings, this time decide to lay down their heads with the rest. Some provincials accidentally turning up in the hall, the duma journalists, and one man from the general public, request permission in more or less eloquent language to share the fate of the duma. The permission is granted.

The Bolshevik faction tries to offer a prosaic piece of advice: Why wander through the streets in the dark seeking death? Better call up the ministers and persuade them to surrender before blood is shed. But the democrats are indignant: These agents of insurrection want to tear from our hands not only the power, but our right to a heroic death. Meanwhile the members decided, in the interest of history, to take a vote by roll call. After all, one cannot die too late—even though the death be glorious. Sixty-two members of the duma ratify the decision: yes, they are actually going to die under the ruins of the Winter Palace. To this the fourteen Bolsheviks answer that it is better to conquer with Smolny than to die in the Winter Palace, and immediately set off for the meeting of the Soviet Congress. Only three Menshevik-Internationalists decide to remain within the walls of the duma: they have nowhere to go and nothing to die for.

The members of the duma are just on the point of setting out on their last journey when the telephone rings and news comes that the whole of the Executive Committee of the Peasants' Deputies is coming to join them. Unending applause. Now the picture is complete and clear: The representatives of one hundred million peasants, together with the representatives of all classes of the city population are going out to die at the hands of an insignificant gang of thugs. There is no lack of speeches and applause.

After the arrival of the Peasants' Deputies the column finally sets out along the Nevsky. At the head of the column march the burgomaster, Schreider, and the minister Prokopovich. Among the marchers John Reed noticed the Social Revolutionary, Avksentiev, president of the Peasant Executive Committee, and the Menshevik leaders, Khinchuk and Abramovich, the first of whom was considered Right, the second Left. Prokopovich and Schreider each carried a lantern: it had been so agreed by telephone with the ministers, in order that the junkers should not take friends for enemies. Prokopovich carried besides this an umbrella, as did many others. The clergy were not present. The clergy had been created out of misty fragments of the history of the fatherland by the none too opulent imagination of the junkers. But the people also were absent. Their absence determined the character of the whole scheme. Three or four hundred "representatives" and not one man of those whom they represented! "It was a dark night," remembers the Social Revolutionary, Zenzinov, "and the lights on the Nevsky were not burning. We marched in a regular procession and only our singing of the Marseillaise was to be heard. Cannon shots resounded in the distance. That was the Bolsheviks continuing to bombard the Winter Palace."

At the Ekaterininsky Canal a patrol of armed sailors was stretched out across the Nevsky, blocking the way for this column of the democracy. "We are going forward," declared the condemned, "What can you do to us?" The sailors answered frankly that they would use force: "Go home and leave us alone." Someone of the marchers suggested that they die right there on the spot. But in the decision adopted by a roll call vote in the duma this variant had not been foreseen. The minister Prokopovich clambered up on some sort of elevation and "waving his umbrella"—rains are frequent in the autumn in Petrograd—urged the demonstrators not to lead into temptation those dark and deceived people who might actually resort to arms. "Let us return to the duma and talk over methods of saving the country and the revolution."

This was truly a wise proposal. To be sure, the original plan would then remain unfulfilled. But what can you do with armed ruffians who will not permit the leaders of the democracy to die a heroic death? "They stood around for a while, got chilly and decided to go back," writes Stankevich mournfully. He too was a marcher in this procession. Without the Marseillaise now—on the contrary in a glum silence—the procession moved back along the Nevsky to the duma building. There at last it would surely find "methods of saving the country and the revolution."

With the capture of the Winter Palace the Military Revolutionary Committee came into full possession of the capital. But just as the nails and hair continue to grow on a corpse, so the overthrown government continued to show signs of life through its official press. The "Herald of the Provisional Government," which on the 24th had announced the retirement of the Privy Councillors with right to uniform and pension, had suddenly disappeared on the 25th—an event which, to be sure, nobody noticed. But on the 26th it appeared again as if nothing had happened. On the first page it carried a rubric: "In consequence of the shutting off of the electric current the issue of October 25 did not appear." In all other respects except only the electric current, the governmental life was going on in due order, and the "Herald" of a government now located in the Trubetskoy Bastion announced the appointment of a dozen new senators. In its column of "administrative information" a circular of the Minister of the Interior, Nikitin, advised the commissars of the provinces "not to be influenced by false rumors of events in Petrograd where all is tranquil." The minister was not after all so far wrong. The days of the revolution went by peacefully enough, but for the cannonading, whose effect was only acoustic. But just the same the historian will make no mistake if he says that on October 25th not only was the electric current shut off in the government printing plant, but an important page was turned in the history of mankind.

Chapter IX

THE OCTOBER INSURRECTION

PHYSICAL analogies with revolution come so naturally that some of them have become worn-out metaphors: "Volcanic eruption," "birth of a new society," "boiling point." . . . Under the simple literary image there is concealed here an intuitive grasp of the laws of dialectic—that is, the logic of evolution.

Armed insurrection stands in the same relation to revolution that revolution as a whole does to evolution. It is the critical point when accumulating quantity turns with an explosion into quality. But insurrection itself again is not a homogeneous and indivisible act: it too has its critical points, its inner crises and accelerations.

An extraordinary importance both political and theoretical attaches to that short period immediately preceding the "boiling point"—the eve, that is, of the insurrection. Physics teaches that the steady increase of temperature suddenly comes to a stop; the liquid remains for a time at the same temperature, and boils only after absorbing an additional quantity of heat. Everyday language also comes to our aid here, designating this condition of pseudo-tranquil concentration preceding an explosion as "the lull before the storm."

When an unqualified majority of the workers and soldiers of Petrograd had come over to the Bolsheviks, the boiling temperature, it seemed, was reached. It was then that Lenin proclaimed the necessity of immediate insurrection. But it is striking to observe that something was still lacking to the insurrection. The workers, and especially the soldiers, had to absorb some additional revolutionary energy.

The contradiction between word and deed is unknown to the masses, but the passing over from word to deed—even to a simple strike, and so much the more to insurrection—inevitably calls out inner frictions and molecular regroupings: some move forward, others have to crowd back. Civil war in general is distinguished in its first steps by an extraordinary indecisiveness. Both camps are as though stuck fast in the same national soil; they cannot break away from their own environment with its intermediate groupings and moods of compromise.

The lull before the storm in the lower ranks produced a sudden hesitation among the guiding groups. Those organs and institutions which had been formed in the comparatively tranquil period of preparation—for revolution has like war its peaceful period, its days of calm—proved even in the most tempered party inadequate, or at least not wholly adequate, to the tasks of insurrection. A certain reconstruction and shifting about is unavoidable at the critical moment. Far from all the delegates of the Petrograd Soviet who voted for a soviet government were really imbued with the idea that an armed insurrection had become the task of the day. In order to convert the Soviet into a machine of insurrection, it was necessary with as little disturbance as possible to bring them over to this new course. In the circumstances of a matured crisis this did not require months, or even many weeks. But just in those last days it was most dangerous to fall out of step, to give orders for a jump some days before the Soviet was ready to make it, to bring confusion into one's own ranks, to cut off the party from the Soviet even for 24 hours.

Lenin more than once repeated that the masses are far to the left of the party, just as the party is to the left of the Central Committee. Applied to the revolution as a whole this was perfectly true. But these correlations too have their deep inward oscillations. In April, in June, and especially at the beginning of July, the workers and soldiers were impatiently pushing the party along the path toward decisive action. After the July raids the masses became more cautious. They wanted a revolution as before, and more than before, but having badly burnt themselves once, they feared another failure. Throughout July, August and September, the party was daily holding back the workers and soldiers, whom the Kornilovists on their part were challenging into the streets with all their might. The political experience of those last months had greatly developed the inhibitory centers not only of the leaders, but of the led. The unbroken success of the agitation had nourished in its turn the inertia of the time-biding attitude. A new political orientation was not enough for the masses: they had need of a psychological readjustment. An insurrection takes in broader masses, the more the commands of the revolutionary party fuse with the command of circumstances.

The difficult problem of passing from the political preparation to the actual technique of insurrection arose throughout the whole country in different forms, but in essence it was everywhere the same. Muralov tells how in the Moscow military organization of the Bolsheviks opinion as to the necessity of a seizure of power was unanimous; however "the attempt to decide concretely how this seizure should be carried out remained unresolved." The last connecting link was lacking.

During those days when Petrograd was full of the transfer of the garrison, Moscow was living in an atmosphere of continual strike conflicts. On the initiative of a factory committee the Bolshevik faction of the soviet put forward a plan to settle economic conflicts by means of decrees. The preparatory steps took a good deal of time. Only on the 23rd of October was "Revolutionary Decree No. 1" adopted by the soviet bodies. It provided that: Workers and clerks in factories and shops shall henceforth be employed and discharged only with the consent of the shop committees. This meant that the soviet had begun to function as a state power. The inevitable resistance of the government would, according to the design of the initiators, unite the masses more closely round the soviet and lead to an open conflict. This idea never came to the test because the revolution in Petrograd gave Moscow, together with all the rest of the country, a far more imperative motive for insurrection—the necessity of coming promptly to the support of the newly formed soviet government.

The attacking side is almost always interested in seeming on the defensive. A revolutionary party is interested in legal coverings. The coming Congress of Soviets, although in essence a Soviet of revolution, was nevertheless for the whole popular mass indubitably endowed, if not with the whole sovereignty, at least with a good half of it. It was a question of one of the elements of a dual power making an insurrection against the other. Appealing to the Congress as the source of authority, the Military Revolutionary Committee accused the government in advance of preparing an attempt against the soviets. This accusation flowed logically from the whole situation. Insofar as the government did not intend to capitulate without a fight it could not help getting ready to defend itself. But by this very fact it became liable to the accusation of conspiracy against the highest organ of the workers, soldiers and peasants. In its struggle against the Congress of Soviets which was to overthrow Kerensky, the government lifted its hand against that source of power from which Kerensky had issued.

It would be a serious mistake to regard all this as juridical hair-splitting of no interest to the people. On the contrary, it was in just this form that the fundamental facts of the revolution reflected themselves in the minds of the masses. It was necessary to make full use of this extraordinarily advantageous tie-up. In thus giving a great political goal to the natural disinclination of the soldier to pass from the barracks to the trenches, and in mobilizing the garrison for the defense of the Soviet Congress, the revolutionary leaders did not bind their hands in the slightest degree regarding the date of the insurrection. The choice of the day and hour depended upon the further course of the conflict. The freedom to maneuver belonged to the strongest.

"First conquer Kerensky and then call the Congress," Lenin kept repeating, fearing that insurrection would be replaced with constitutional by-play. Lenin had obviously not yet appreciated the new factor which had intruded into the preparation of the insurrection and changed its whole character, the sharp conflict between the Petrograd garrison and the government. If the Congress of Soviets was to decide the question of power; if the government wanted to dismember the garrison in order to prevent the Congress from becoming the power; if the garrison without awaiting the Congress of Soviets had refused to obey the government, why this meant that in essence the insurrection had begun, and begun without waiting for the Congress, although under cover of its authority. It would have been wrong politically, therefore, to separate the preparation of the insurrection from the preparation for the Congress of Soviets.

279

The peculiarities of the October revolution can best be understood by contrasting it with the February revolution. In making this comparison it is not necessary, as in other cases, to assume conditionally the identity of a whole series of circumstances. They are in reality identical. The scene is Petrograd in both cases: the same arena, the same social groupings, the same proletariat, and the same garrison. The victory in both cases was attained by the going over of a majority of the reserve regiments to the side of the workers. But within the framework of these fundamental traits what an enormous difference! The two Petrograd revolutions, historically completing each other in the course of eight months, seem in their contrasting traits almost predestined to promote an understanding of the nature of insurrection in general.

The February insurrection is called spontaneous. We have introduced in their due place all the necessary limitations to this description. But it is true in any case that in February nobody laid out the road in advance, nobody voted in the factories and barracks on the question of revolution, nobody summoned the masses from above to insurrection. The indignation accumulated for years broke to the surface unexpectedly, to a considerable degree, even to the masses themselves.

It was quite otherwise in October. For eight months the masses had been living an intense political life. They had not only been creating events, but learning to understand their connections. After each action they had critically weighed its results. Soviet parliamentarism had become the daily mechanics of the political life of the people. When they were deciding by a vote questions of strikes, of street manifestations, of the transfer of regiments to the front, could the masses forego an independent decision on the question of insurrection?

From this invaluable and sole substantial conquest of the February revolution there arose, however, new difficulties. It was impossible to summon the masses to battle in the name of the Soviet without raising the question formally in the Soviet—that is, without making the problem of insurrection a subject of public debate, and that too with the participation of representatives of the hostile camp. The necessity of creating a special, and to the extent possible a disguised, soviet organ for the leadership of the insurrection was obvious. But this too demanded democratic procedures, with all their advantages and all their delays. The resolution on the Military Revolutionary Committee adopted on the 9th of October was carried out only on the 20th. But that was not the chief difficulty. To take advantage of the majority in the Soviet and compose the Committee of Bolsheviks alone, would have provoked discontent among the non-party men, to say nothing of the Left Social Revolutionaries and certain groups of anarchists. The Bolsheviks in the Military Revolutionary Committee would submit to the decisions of their party—although not always without resistance—but it was impossible to demand discipline of the non-party men and the Left Social Revolutionaries. To get an *a priori* resolution on insurrection at a definite date from them was not to be thought of. And moreover it was extremely imprudent even to put the question to them. By means of the Military Revolutionary Committee, therefore, it was possible only to draw the masses into insurrection, sharpening the situation from day to day and making the conflict irrevocable.

Would it not have been simpler in that case to summon the insurrection directly in the name of the party? This form of action undoubtedly has weighty advantages. But its disadvantages are hardly less obvious. In those millions upon whom the party legitimately counted it is necessary to distinguish three layers: one which was already with the Bolsheviks on all conditions; another, more numerous, which supported the Bolsheviks insofar as they acted through the soviets; a third which followed the soviets in spite of the fact that they were dominated by Bolsheviks.

These three layers were different not only in political level, but to a considerable degree also in social ingredients. Those standing for the Bolsheviks as a party were above all industrial workers, with the hereditary proletarians of Petrograd in the front rank. Those standing for the Bolsheviks insofar as they had a legal soviet cover, were a majority of the soldiers. Those standing for the soviets, independently and regardless of the fact that an overplus of Bolsheviks dominated them, were the more conservative groups of workers—former Mensheviks and Social Revolutionaries, who dreaded to break away from the rest of the masses—the more

281

conservative parts of the army even including the Cossacks, and the peasants who had freed themselves from the leadership of the Social Revolutionary party and were adhering to its left flank.

It would be an obvious mistake to identify the strength of the Bolshevik party with the strength of the soviets led by it. The latter was much greater than the former. However, without the former it would have been mere impotence. There is nothing mysterious in this. The relations between the party and the Soviet grew out of the disaccord inevitable in a revolutionary epoch between the colossal political influence of Bolshevism and its narrow organizational grasp. A lever correctly applied makes the human arm capable of lifting a weight many times exceeding its living force, but without the living arm the lever is nothing but a dead stick.

At a Moscow regional conference of the Bolsheviks at the end of September, one of the delegates reported: "In Yegorevsk the influence of the Bolsheviks is undivided. . . . But the party organization as such is weak. It is in complete neglect; there is neither regular registration nor membership dues." This disproportion between influence and organization, although not everywhere so marked, was a general phenomenon. Broad masses knew of the Bolshevik slogans and the soviet organization. The two fused completely in their minds in the course of September and October. What the people were waiting for was that the soviets should show them when and how to carry out the program of the Bolsheviks.

The party itself systematically educated the masses in this spirit. In Kiev, when the rumor went round that an insurrection was preparing, the Bolshevik Executive Committee immediately came out with a denial: "No action without the summons of the Soviet must take place. . . . Not a step without the Soviet!" In denying on the 18th of October the rumors of an insurrection alleged to have been appointed for the 22nd, Trotsky said: "The Soviet is an elective institution and . . . cannot make a decision which is unknown to the workers and soldiers. . . ." Repeated daily and reinforced by practical action, such formulae entered into the flesh and blood of the masses.

According to the report of ensign Berzin, at an October military conference of the Bolsheviks in Moscow the delegates were saying: "It is hard to know whether the troops will come out at the summons of the Moscow committee of the Bolsheviks. At the summons of the Soviet they might all come out." Nevertheless even in September the Moscow garrison had voted 90 per cent Bolshevik. At a conference of October 16th in Petrograd, Boky made this report in the name of the party committee: In the Moscow district "they will come out at the summons of the Soviet, but not of the party"; in the Nevsky district "all will follow the Soviet." Volodarsky thereupon summarized the state of mind in Petrograd in the following words: "The general impression is that nobody is eager to go into the streets, but all will appear at the call of the Soviet." Olga Ravich corrected him: "Some say also at the call of the party." At a Petrograd Garrison Conference on the 18th, delegates reported that their regiments were awaiting the summons of the Soviet to come out. Nobody mentioned the party, notwithstanding that the Bolsheviks stood at the head of many units. Thus unity in the barracks could be preserved only by uniting the sympathetic, the wavering, and the semi-hostile under the discipline of the Soviet. The grenadier regiment even declared that it would come out only at the command of the Congress of Soviets. The very fact that agitators and organizers in estimating the state of mind of the masses always alluded to the distinction between the Soviet and the party, shows what great significance this question had from the standpoint of the summons to insurrection.

The chauffeur Mitrevich tells how in a squad of motor-trucks, where they did not succeed in carrying a resolution in favor of insurrection, the Bolsheviks put through a compromise proposal: "We will not come out either for the Bolsheviks or the Mensheviks, but . . . we will carry out without delay all the demands of the Second Congress of Soviets." These Bolsheviks were applying on a small scale to the motor-truck squad the same enveloping tactics which were being applied at large by the Military Revolutionary Committee. Mitrevich is not arguing but telling a story—the more convincing his testimony!

Attempts to lead the insurrection directly through the party nowhere produced results. A highly interesting piece of testimony

283

is preserved regarding the preparation of the uprising in Kineshma, a considerable center of the textile industry. After insurrection in the Moscow region had been placed on the order of the day, the party committee in Kineshma elected a special trio to take an inventory of the military forces and supplies, and prepare for armed insurrection—calling them for some reason "the Directory." "We must say, however," writes one of the members of this directory, "that little appears to have been done by the elected trio. Events took a somewhat different course. . . . The regional strike wholly took possession of us, and when the decisive events came, the organizational center was transferred to the strike committee and the soviet." On the modest provincial scale the same thing was repeated here which occurred in Petrograd.

The party set the soviets in motion, the soviets set in motion the workers, soldiers, and to some extent the peasantry. What was gained in mass was lost in speed. If you represent this conducting apparatus as a system of cog-wheels—a comparison to which Lenin had recourse at another period on another theme—you may say that the impatient attempt to connect the party wheel directly with the gigantic wheel of the masses—omitting the medium-sized wheel of the soviets—would have given rise to the danger of breaking the teeth of the party wheel, and nevertheless not setting sufficiently large masses in motion.

The opposite danger was, however, no less real—the danger of letting slip a favorable situation as a result of inner frictions in the soviet system. Speaking theoretically, the most favorable opportunity for an insurrection reduces itself to such and such a point in time. There can be no thought of practically lighting upon this ideal point. The insurrection may develop with success on the rising curve approaching this ideal culmination—but also on the descending curve, before the correlation of forces has yet radically changed. Instead of a "moment" we have then a section of time measured in weeks, and sometimes months. The Bolsheviks could have seized the power in Petrograd at the beginning of July. But if they had done so they could not have held it. Beginning with the middle of September they could hope not only to seize the power but also to keep hold of it. If the

Bolsheviks had delayed the insurrection beyond the end of October they would probably—although far from surely—have still been able for a certain time to make up for the omission. We may assume conditionally that for a period of three or four months—September to December approximately—the political premises for a revolution were at hand. The thing had ripened but not yet fallen apart. Within these bounds, which are easier to establish after the fact than in the course of action, the party had a certain freedom of choice which gave rise to inevitable and sometimes sharp disagreements of a practical character.

Lenin proposed to raise the insurrection in the days of the Democratic Conference. At the end of September he considered any delay not only dangerous but fatal. "Waiting for the Congress of Soviets," he wrote at the beginning of October, "is a childish toying with formalities—a shameful toying with formalities, betrayal of the revolution." It is not likely, however, that anybody among the Bolshevik leaders was guided in this question by formal considerations. When Zinoviev, for example, demanded a preliminary conference with the Bolshevik faction of the Soviet Congress, he was not seeking a formal sanction, but simply counting on the political support of the provincial delegates against the Central Committee. But the fact is that the dependence of the party on the Soviet—which, in its turn, was appealing to the Congress of Soviets—introduced an element of indefiniteness into the insurrection which greatly and quite justly alarmed Lenin.

The question when to summon the insurrection, was closely bound up with the question who should summon it. The advantages of summoning it in the name of the Soviet were only too clear to Lenin, but he understood sooner than others what difficulties would arise along that road. He could not but fear, especially from a distance, that the hindering elements would prove still stronger in the soviet summits than in the Central Committee, whose policy even without that he considered irresolute. Lenin approached the question who should begin, the Soviet or the party, as a choice between two possible alternatives, but in the first weeks he was decidedly in favor of the independent initiative of the party. In this there was not the shadow of a thought of contrasting the two plans in principle. It was a question of two approaches to an insurrection resting upon one and the same basis, in one and the same situation, for one and the same goal. But nevertheless these were two different approaches.

Lenin's proposal to surround the Alexandrinka and arrest the Democratic Conference flowed from the assumption that the insurrection would be headed not by the soviets, but by the party appealing directly to the factories and barracks. It could not have been otherwise. To carry such a plan through by way of the Soviet was absolutely unthinkable. Lenin was clearly aware that even among the heads of the party his plan would meet resistance; he recommended in advance that they should "not strive after numbers," in the Bolshevik faction of the Conference. With determination up above, the numbers would be guaranteed by the lower ranks. Lenin's bold plan had the indubitable advantages of swiftness and unexpectedness, but it laid the party too bare, incurring the risk that within certain limits it would set itself over against the masses. Even the Petrograd Soviet, taken unawares, might at the first failure lose its still unstable Bolshevik majority.

The resolution of October 10th proposed to the local organizations of the party to decide all questions practically from the point of view of an approaching insurrection. There is not a word in the resolution of the Central Committee about the soviets as organs of the insurrection. At the conference of the 16th, Lenin said: "Facts show that we have the advantage over the enemy. Why cannot the Central Committee begin?" This question on Lenin's lips was by no means rhetorical. It meant: Why lose time accommodating ourselves to the complicated soviet transmission if the Central Committee can give the signal immediately. However, this time the resolution proposed by Lenin concluded with an expression of "confidence that the Central Committee and the Soviet will indicate in good season the favorable moment and expedient methods of action." The mention of the Soviet together with the party, and the more flexible formulation of the question of date, were the result of Lenin's having felt out through the party leaders the resistance of the masses.

The next day in his polemic with Zinoviev and Kamenev,

Lenin summed up as follows the debates of the day before: "All agreed that at the summons of the soviets and for the defense of the soviets the workers will come out as one man." This meant: Even if not all are in agreement with him, Lenin, that you can issue the summons in the name of the party, all are agreed that you can do it in the name of the soviets.

"Who is to seize the power?" writes Lenin on the evening of the 24th. "That is now of no importance. Let the Military Revolutionary Committee take it, or 'some other institution,' which will declare that it will surrender the power only to the genuine representatives of the interests of the people." "Some other institution" enclosed in mysterious quotation-marks—that is a conspirative designation for the Central Committee of the Bolsheviks. Lenin here renews his September proposal that action be taken directly in the name of the Central Committee—this time in case soviet legality should hinder the Military Revolutionary Committee from placing the Congress before the accomplished fact of an overthrow.

Although this whole struggle about dates and methods of insurrection continued for a week, not all those who took part in it were clearly aware of its sense and significance. "Lenin proposed the seizure of power through the soviets whether in Leningrad or Moscow, and not behind the back of the soviets," wrote Stalin in 1924. "For what purpose did Trotsky require this more than strange legend about Lenin?" And again: "The party knows Lenin as the greatest Marxist of our times . . . strange to any tinge of Blanquism." Whereas Trotsky "gives us not the great Lenin, but some sort of a dwarf Blanquist. . . ." Not only a Blanquist but a dwarf! In reality the question in whose name to raise an insurrection, and in the hands of what institution to seize the power, is not in the least predetermined by any doctrine. When the general conditions for a revolution are at hand, insurrection becomes a practical problem of art, a problem which can be solved by various methods. This part of the disagreements in the Central Committee was analogous to the quarrel of the officers of a general staff educated in the same military doctrine and appraising alike the strategic situation, but proposing different ways of solving their most immediate—extraordinarily important, to be sure, but nevertheless particular—problem. To mix in here the question of Marxism and Blanquism is only to reveal a lack of understanding of both.

Professor Pokrovsky denies the very importance of the alternative: Soviet or party. Soldiers are no formalists, he laughs: they did not need a Congress of Soviets in order to overthrow Kerensky. With all its wit such a formulation leaves unexplained the problem: Why create soviets at all if the party is enough? "It is interesting," continues the professor, "that nothing at all came of this aspiration to do everything almost legally, with soviet legality, and the power at the last moment was taken not by the Soviet, but by an obviously 'illegal' organization created *ad hoc*." Pokrovsky here cites the fact that Trotsky was compelled "in the name of the Military Revolutionary Committee," and not the Soviet, to declare the government of Kerensky non-existent. A most unexpected conclusion! The Military Revolutionary Committee was an elected organ of the Soviet. The leading rôle of the Committee in the overturn did not in any sense violate that soviet legality which the professor makes fun of but of which the masses were extremely jealous. The Council of People's Commissars was also created *ad hoc*. But that did not prevent it from becoming and remaining an organ of the soviet power, including Pokrovsky himself in its staff as deputy People's Commissar of Education.

The insurrection was able to remain on the ground of soviet legality, and to a certain degree even within the limits of the tradition of the dual power, thanks mainly to the fact that the Petrograd garrison had almost wholly submitted to the Soviet before the revolution. In numberless memoirs, anniversary articles and early historic essays, this fact, confirmed by manifold documents, was taken as indubitable. "The conflict in Petrograd developed about the question of the fate of the garrison," says the first book about October—a book written upon the basis of fresh recollections by the author of the present work in the intervals between sessions of the Brest Litovsk conference, a book which for several years served the party as a text-book of history. "The fundamental question about which the whole movement in October was built up and organized"—this is the still more definite

expression of Sadovsky, one of the direct organizers of the uprising—"was the question of the transfer of the Petrograd garrison to the northern front." Not one of the closest leaders of the
insurrection then taking part in a collective conversation with
the immediate purpose of reviving and establishing the course of
events, took it into his head to object to this statement of Sadovsky
or correct it. Only after 1924 did it suddenly become known that
Trotsky had overestimated the significance of the peasant garrison to the detriment of the Petrograd workers—a scientific discovery which most happily supplements the accusation that he
underestimated the peasantry. Scores of young historians with
Professor Pokrovsky at their head have explained to us in recent
years the importance of the proletariat in a proletarian revolution,
have waxed indignant that we do not speak of the workers when
we are talking about the soldiers, have arraigned us for analyzing
the real course of events instead of repeating copy-book phrases.
Pokrovsky condenses the results of this criticism in the following
conclusion: "In spite of the fact that Trotsky very well knows
that the armed insurrection was decided upon by the party . . .
and it was perfectly clear that the pretext to be found for the
action was a secondary matter, nevertheless for him the Petrograd
garrison stands at the center of the whole picture . . . as though,
if it hadn't been for that, there would have been no thought of an
insurrection." For our historian the "decision of the party" regarding the insurrection is alone significant, and how the insurrection took place in reality is "a secondary matter." A pretext,
he says, can always be found. Pokrovsky gives the name of pretext to the method by which the troops were won over—to the
solution, that is, of the very problem which summarizes the
fate of every insurrection. The proletarian revolution would undoubtedly have taken place even without the conflict about the
transfer of the garrison—in that the professor is right. But that
would have been a different insurrection and would have demanded a different exposition. We have in view the events which
actually happened.

One of the organizers and afterward a historian of the Red
Guard, Malakhovsky, insists that it was the armed workers in
distinction to the semi-passive garrison which showed initiative,

determination and endurance in the insurrection. "The Red Guard detachments during the October revolution," he writes, "occupied the governmental institutions, the Post Office, the telegraph, and they were in the front rank during the battles, etc. . . ." All that is indubitable. It is not difficult to understand, however, that if the Red Guard was able to simply "occupy" these institutions, that is only because the garrison was at one with them; it supported or at least did not hinder them. This decided the fate of the insurrection.

The very broaching of such a question as who was more important to the insurrection, the soldiers or the workers, shows that we are on so miserably low a theoretic level that there is hardly room for argument. The October revolution was a struggle of the proletariat against the bourgeoisie for power, but the outcome of the struggle was decided in the last analysis by the muzhik. That general schema, which prevailed throughout the country, found its most perfect expression in Petrograd. What here gave the revolution the character of a brief blow with a minimum number of victims, was the combination of a revolutionary conspiracy, a proletarian insurrection, and the struggle of a peasant garrison for self-preservation. The party led the uprising; the principal motive force was the proletariat; the armed detachments of workers were the fist of the insurrection; but the heavy-weight peasant garrison decided the outcome of the struggle.

It is upon just this question that a contrasting of the February with the October revolution is most indispensable. On the eve of the overthrow of the monarchy the garrison represented for both sides a great unknown; the soldiers themselves did not yet know how they would react to an insurrection of the workers. Only a general strike could create the necessary arena for mass encounters of the workers with the soldiers, for the trying-out of the soldiers in action, for the coming over of the soldiers to the side of the workers. In this consisted the dramatic content of the five February days.

On the eve of the overthrow of the Provisional Government the overwhelming majority of the garrison were standing openly on the side of the workers. Nowhere in the whole country was the government so isolated as in its own residence. No wonder it struggled to get away. But in vain: the hostile capital would not let go. With its unsuccessful attempt to push out the revolution-ary regiments the government conclusively destroyed itself.

To explain the passive policy of Kerensky before the uprising solely by his personal qualities, is merely to slide over the surface of things. Kerensky was not alone. There were people in the gov-ernment like Palchinsky not lacking in energy. The leaders of the Executive Committee well knew that the victory of the Bolshe-viks meant political death for them. All of them, however, jointly and singly, turned out to be paralyzed, fell like Kerensky into a kind of heavy half-sleep—that sleep in which, in spite of the danger hanging over him, a man is powerless to lift a hand to save himself.

The fraternization of the workers and soldiers in October did not grow out of open street encounters as in February, but pre-ceded the insurrection. If the Bolsheviks did not now call a gen-eral strike, it was not because they were unable, but because they did not feel the need. The Military Revolutionary Committee before the uprising already felt itself master of the situation; it knew every part of the garrison, its mood, its inner groupings; it was receiving reports every day—not for show, but expressing the actual facts; it could at any time send a plenipotentiary com-missar, a bicycle man with an order, to any regiment; it could summon to its office by telephone the committee of the unit, or give orders to the company on duty. The Military Revolutionary Committee occupied in relation to the troops the position of a governmental headquarters, not the headquarters of conspirators.

To be sure, the commanding summits of the state remained in the hands of the government. But the material foundation was removed from under them. The ministries and the headquarters were hanging over an empty space. The telephones and tele-graph continued to serve the government—so did the State Bank. But the government no longer had the military forces to retain possession of these institutions. It was as though the Winter Palace and Smolny had changed places. The Military Revolutionary Committee had placed the phantom government in such a posi-tion that it could do nothing at all without breaking up the garrison. But every attempt of Kerensky to strike at the troops only hastened his end.

However, the task of the revolution still remained unachieved. The spring and the whole mechanism of the watch were in the hands of the Military Revolutionary Committee, but it lacked the hands and face. And without these details a clock can not fulfil its function. Without the telegraph and telephone, without the bank and headquarters, the Military Revolutionary Committee could not govern. It had almost all the real premises and elements of power, but not the power itself.

In February the workers had thought, not of seizing the banks and the Winter Palace, but of breaking the resistance of the army. They were fighting not for individual commanding summits, but for the soul of the soldier. Once the victory was won in this field, all remaining problems solved themselves. Having surrendered its guard battalions, the monarchy no longer made an attempt to defend either its court or its headquarters.

In October the government of Kerensky, having irrevocably lost the soul of the soldier, still clung to the commanding summits. In its hands the headquarters, the banks, the telephone, were only the façade of power. When they should come into the hands of the soviets, they would guarantee the conquest of complete power. Such was the situation on the eve of the insurrection, and it decided the forms of activity during the last twenty-four hours.

Demonstrations, street fights, barricades—everything comprised in the usual idea of insurrection—were almost entirely absent. The revolution had no need of solving a problem already solved. The seizure of the governmental machine could be carried through according to plan with the help of comparatively small armed detachments guided from a single center. The barracks, the fortress, the storehouses, all those enterprises in which workers and soldiers functioned, could be taken possession of by their own internal forces. But the Winter Palace, the Pre-Parliament, the district headquarters, the ministries, the military schools, could not be captured from within. This was true also of the telephone, the telegraph, the Post Office and the State Bank. The workers in these institutions, although of little weight in the general combination of forces, nevertheless ruled within their four walls, and these were, moreover, strongly guarded with sentries. It was necessary to penetrate these bureaucratic high points from without. Political conquest was here replaced by forcible seizure. But since the preceding crowding-out of the government from its military bases had made resistance almost impossible, this military seizure of the final commanding heights passed off as a general rule without conflicts.

To be sure, the thing was not after all settled without fighting. The Winter Palace had to be taken by storm. But the very fact that the resistance of the government came down to a defense of the Winter Palace, clearly defines the place occupied by October 25th in the whole course of the struggle. The Winter Palace was the last redoubt of a régime politically shattered during its eight months' existence, and conclusively disarmed during the preceding two weeks.

Conspiratorial elements—understanding by this term, plan and centralized leadership—occupied an insignificant place in the February revolution. This resulted from the mere weakness and scatteredness of the revolutionary groups under the press of tzarism and the war. So much the greater was the task laid upon the masses. The insurrectionaries were not human locusts. They had their political experience, their traditions, their slogans, their nameless leaders. But while the scattered elements of leadership in the insurrection proved adequate to overthrow the monarchy, they were far from adequate to give the victors the fruits of their victory.

The tranquillity of the October streets, the absence of crowds and battles, gave the enemy a pretext to talk of the conspiracy of an insignificant minority, of the adventure of a handful of Bolsheviks. This formula was repeated unnumbered times in the days, months, and even years, following the insurrection. It is obviously with a view to mending the reputation of the proletarian revolution that Yaroslavsky writes of the 25th of October: "Thick masses of the Petrograd proletariat summoned by the Military Revolutionary Committee stood under its banners and overflowed the streets of Petrograd." This official historian only forgets to explain for what purpose the Military Revolutionary Committee had summoned these masses to the streets, and just what they did when they got there.

From the combination of its strong and weak points has grown up an official idealization of the February revolution as an all-national revolution, in contrast to the October one which is held to be a conspiracy. But in reality the Bolsheviks could reduce the struggle for power at the last moment to a "conspiracy," not because they were a small minority, but for the opposite reason—because they had behind them in the workers' districts and the barracks an overwhelming majority, consolidated, organized, disciplined.

The October revolution can be correctly understood only if you do not limit your field of vision to its final link. During the last days of February the chess game of insurrection was played out from the first move to the last—that is to the surrender of the enemy. At the end of October the main part of the game was already in the past. And on the day of insurrection it remained to solve only a rather narrow problem: mate in two moves. The period of revolution, therefore, must be considered to extend from the 9th of October, when the conflict about the garrison began, or from the 12th, when the resolution was passed to create a Military Revolutionary Committee. The enveloping maneuver extended over more than two weeks. The more decisive part of it lasted five to six days—from the birth of the Military Revolutionary Committee to the capture of the Winter Palace. During this whole period hundreds of thousands of workers and soldiers took direct action, defensive in form, but aggressive in essence. The final stage, when the insurrectionaries at last threw off the qualifications of the dual power with its dubious legality and defensive phraseology, occupied exactly twenty-four hours: from 2 o'clock on the night of the 25th to 2 o'clock on the night of the 26th. During this period the Military Revolution Committee openly employed arms for the conquest of the city and the capture of the government. In these operations, generally speaking, as many forces took part as were needed to solve the limited problem—hardly more than 25 or 30 thousand at the most.

An Italian author who writes books not only about "The

Eunuchs' Nights," but also about the highest problems of state, visited soviet Moscow in 1929, misunderstood what little he learned at second or tenth hand, and upon this basis has created a book: *Coup d'État: The Technique of Revolution.* The name of this writer, Malaparte, makes it easy to distinguish him from a certain other specialist in state insurrections called Bonaparte.

In contrast to "the strategy of Lenin" which was bound up with the social and political conditions of Russia in 1917, "Trotsky's tactics," according to Malaparte, "were not bound up with the general conditions of the country." To Lenin's opinions about the political premises of a revolution the author makes Trotsky reply: "Your strategy demands too many favorable circumstances: an insurrection needs nothing, it is self-sufficient." It would be hard to imagine a more self-sufficient absurdity. Malaparte many times repeats that it was not the strategy of Lenin that won in October, but the tactics of Trotsky. And these tactics still threaten the tranquillity of the European states. "The strategy of Lenin does not constitute an immediate danger to the governments of Europe. The real, and moreover permanent, danger to them is the tactics of Trotsky." And still more concretely: "Put Poincaré in Kerensky's place, and the Bolsheviks' state revolution of October 1917 would succeed just as well." It would be futile to try to find out what is the use of Lenin's strategy, which depends upon historic conditions, if Trotsky's tactics will solve the same problem in any circumstances. It remains to add that this remarkable book has already appeared in several languages. The statesmen are evidently learning from it how to repulse a state revolution. We wish them all success.

A criticism of the purely military operations of October 25th has not yet been made. What exists in soviet literature upon this theme is not critical, but purely apologetic in character. Compared with the writings of the Epigones, even Sukhanov's criticism, in spite of all its contradictions is favorably distinguished by an attentive attitude to facts.

In judging the organization of the October uprising, Sukhanov has presented in the course of two years two views diametrically opposed to each other. In his work on the February revolution he says: "I will write some day, from personal

295

reminiscences a description of the October revolution, which was carried through like a piece of music played from notes." Yaroslavsky repeats this comment of Sukhanov word for word. "The insurrection in Petrograd," he says, "was well prepared and played through by the party as though from notes." Claude Anet, a hostile and not profound, but nevertheless attentive, observer, speaks even more emphatically: "The state revolution of November 7 permits only ecstatic praise. Not one misstep, not one rift; the government was overthrown before it could say 'ouch!'" On the other hand, in his volume devoted to the October revolution Sukhanov tells how Smolny "stealthily feeling its way, cautiously, and without system" undertook the liquidation of the Provisional Government.

There is exaggeration in both these comments. But from a broader point of view it may be conceded that both appraisals, however they contradict each other, find some support in the facts. The planned character of the October revolution grew chiefly out of objective relations, out of the maturity of the revolution as a whole, the place occupied by Petrograd in the country, the place occupied by the government in Petrograd, out of the whole preceding work of the party, and finally out of the correct political leadership of the revolution. But there remained the problems of military technique. Here there were no few particular failings, and if you join them all together it is possible to create the impression of a job done blindly.

Sukhanov has several times called attention to the military defenselessness of Smolny itself during the last days before the insurrection. It is true that as late as the 23rd the headquarters of the revolution was little better defended than the Winter Palace. The Military Revolutionary Committee assured its inviolability primarily by strengthening its bonds with the garrison, and by thus being able to follow all the military movements of the enemy. More serious measures of a technical military character were undertaken by the Committee approximately twenty-four hours before the government undertook them. Sukhanov feels sure that during the 23rd and the night of the 24th the government, had it shown some initiative, could have captured the Committee. "A good detachment of 500 men," he says, "would have been enough to liquidate Smolny and everybody in it." Possibly. But in the first place, for this the government would have required determination and daring, qualities inconsistent with its nature. In the second place, it would have had to have that "good detachment of 500 men." Where were they to get it? Make it up out of officers? We have observed them towards the end of August in the character of conspirators: they had to be hunted up in the night clubs. The fighting companies of the Compromisers had disintegrated. In the military schools every acute question produced conflicting groups. Things were still worse with the Cossacks. To create a detachment by the method of individual selection from various units would have involved giving oneself away ten times before the thing could be finished.

However, even the existence of such a detachment would still not have settled things. The first shot in the region of Smolny would have resounded in the workers' districts and barracks with a shocking reverberation. Tens of thousands of armed and half-armed men would have run to the help of the threatened center of the revolution at any hour of the day or night. And finally, even the capture of the Military Revolutionary Committee would not have saved the government. Beyond the walls of Smolny there remained Lenin, and in communication with him the Central Committee and the Petrograd committee. There was a second headquarters in the Peter and Paul fortress, a third on the *Aurora,* and each district had its headquarters. The masses would not have been without leadership. And the workers and soldiers in spite of their slowness to move were determined to conquer at any cost.

It is indubitable, however, that supplementary measures of military precaution might and should have been taken some few days earlier. In this respect Sukhanov's criticism is just. The military apparatus of a revolution functions clumsily, with delays and omissions, and the general leadership is too much inclined to put politics in the place of technique. Lenin's eyes were much lacking in Smolny. Others had not yet learned.

Sukhanov is also right in asserting that it would have been infinitely easier to capture the Winter Palace on the night of the 25th, or the morning of that day, than during the second half of it. The palace, and also the neighboring headquarters building, were defended by the usual detachment of junkers: a sudden attack would almost certainly have been successful. Kerensky had got away unhindered that morning in an automobile. This alone proved that there was no serious reconnoitering in progress in regard to the Winter Palace. Here obviously was a bad slip.

The task of keeping watch over the Provisional Government had been laid upon Sverdlov—too late to be sure, on the 24th!—with Lashevich and Blagonravov as assistants. It is doubtful if Sverdlov, exploding in pieces even without that, ever occupied himself with this additional business at all. It is even possible that the very decision, although inscribed in the minutes, was forgotten in the heat of those hours.

In the Military Revolutionary Committee, in spite of everything, the military resources of the government, and particularly the defenses of the Winter Palace, were overestimated. And even had the direct leaders of the siege known the inner forces of the palace, they might still have feared the arrival of reinforcements at the first alarm: junkers, Cossacks, shock-battalions. The plan for capturing the palace was worked out in the style of a large operation. When civil and semi-civil people undertake the solution of a purely military problem, they are always inclined to excessive strategic ingenuities. And along with their superfluous pedantry, they cannot but prove extraordinarily helpless in carrying them out.

The missteps in the capture of the Palace are explained to a certain degree by the personal qualities of the principal leaders. Podvoisky, Antonov-Ovseënko and Chudnovsky, are men of heroic mould. But after all they are far from being men of system and disciplined thought. Podvoisky, having been too impetuous in the July Days, had become far more cautious and even sceptical about immediate prospects. But in fundamentals he remained true to himself. Confronted with any practical task whatever, he inclined organically to break over its bounds, to broaden out the plan, drag in everybody and everything, give a maximum where a minimum was enough. In the element of hyperbole contained in the plan it is easy to see the impress of his spirit. Antonov-Ovseënko was naturally an impulsive optimist, far more apt at improvisation than calculation. As a former petty officer he possessed a certain amount of military information. An emigré during the Great War, he had conducted in the Paris paper *Nashe Slovo* a review of the military situation, and frequently revealed a gift for guessing out strategy. His impressionable amateurism in this field could not, however, counterbalance the excessive flights of Podvoisky. The third of these military chiefs, Chudnovsky, had spent some months as an agitator on an inactive front—that was the whole of his military training. Although gravitating toward the right wing, Chudnovsky was the first to get into the fight and always sought the place where it was hottest. Personal daring and political audacity are not always, as is well known, in perfect equilibrium. Some days after the revolution Chudnovsky was wounded near Petrograd in a skirmish with Kerensky's Cossacks, and some months later he was killed in the Ukraine. It is clear that the talkative and impulsive Chudnovsky could not make up for what was lacking in the other two leaders. No one of them had an eye to detail, if only for the reason that no one of them had ever learned the secrets of the trade. Feeling their own weakness in matters of reconnoitering, communications, maneuvering, these Red martials felt obliged to roll up against the Winter Palace such a superiority of forces as removed the very possibility of practical leadership. An incongruous grandeur of plan is almost equivalent to no plan at all. What has been said does not in the least mean, however, that it would have been possible to find in the staff of the Military Revolutionary Committee, or around it, any more able military leaders. It would certainly have been impossible to find more devoted and selfless ones.

The struggle for the Winter Palace began with the enveloping of the whole district on a wide circle. Owing to the inexperience of the commanders, the interruption of communications, the unskilfulness of the Red Guard detachments, and the listlessness of the regular units, this complicated operation developed at an extraordinarily slow pace. During those same hours when the detachments were gradually filling up their circle and accumulating reserves behind them, companies of junkers, the Cossack squadrons, the Knights of St. George, and the Women's Battalion made their way into the palace. A resisting fist was being formed simultaneously with the attacking ring. You may say that the very problem arose from the too roundabout way in which it was being solved. A bold attack by night or a daring approach by day would hardly have cost more victims than this prolonged operation. The moral effect of the *Aurora's* artillery might at any rate have been tried out twelve or even twenty-four hours sooner than it was. The cruiser stood ready in the Neva, and the sailors were not complaining of any lack of gun-oil. But the leaders of the operation were hoping that the problem could be solved without a battle, were sending parliamentaries, presenting ultimatums and then not living up to their dates. It did not occur to them to examine the artillery in the Peter and Paul fortress in good season for the simple reason that they were counting on getting along without it.

The unpreparedness of the military leadership was still more clearly revealed in Moscow, where the correlation of forces had been considered so favorable that Lenin even insistently advised beginning there: "The victory is sure and there is nobody to fight." In reality it was in Moscow that the insurrection took the form of extended battles lasting with intervals for eight days. "In this hot work," writes Muralov, one of the chief leaders of the Moscow insurrection, "we were not always and in everything firm and determined. Having an overwhelming numerical advantage, ten to one, we dragged the fight out for a whole week . . . owing to a lack of ability to direct fighting masses, to the undiscipline of the latter, and to a complete ignorance of the tactics of the street fight, both on the part of the commanders and on the part of the soldiers." Muralov has a habit of naming things with their real names: no wonder he is now in Siberian exile. But in the present instance in refusing to load off the responsibility upon others Muralov lays upon the military command a lion's share of the blame which belongs to the political leadership— very shaky in Moscow and receptive to the influence of the compromisist circles. We must not lose sight, either, of the fact that the workers of old Moscow, textile and leather workers, were extremely far behind the Petrograd proletariat. In February no insurrection in Moscow had been necessary: the overthrow of the monarchy had rested entirely with Petrograd. In July again Moscow had remained peaceful. This found its expression in October: the workers and soldiers lacked fighting experience.

The technique of insurrection carries through what politics has not accomplished. The gigantic growth of Bolshevism had undoubtedly weakened the attention paid to the military side of things. The passionate reproaches of Lenin were well founded enough. The military leadership proved incomparably weaker than 'the political. Could it indeed have been otherwise? For a number of months still, the new revolutionary government will show extreme awkwardness in all those cases where it is necessary to resort to arms.

Even so, the military authorities of the governmental camp in Petrograd gave a very flattering judgment of the military leadership of the revolution. "The insurrectionaries are preserving order and discipline," stated the War Ministry over the direct wire to headquarters immediately after the fall of the Winter Palace. "There have been no cases at all of destruction or pogroms. On the contrary, patrols of insurrectionists have detained strolling soldiers. . . . The plan of the insurrection was undoubtedly worked out in advance and carried through inflexibly and harmoniously." Not altogether "from the notes" as Sukhanov and Yaroslavsky have written, nor yet altogether "without system," as the former has subsequently affirmed. Moreover, even in the court of the most austere critic success is the best praise.

CHAPTER X

THE CONGRESS OF THE SOVIET DICTATORSHIP

IN Smolny on the 25th of October the most democratic of all parliaments in the world's history was to meet. Who knows—perhaps also the most important.

Having got free of the influence of compromisist intellectuals, the local soviets had sent up for the most part workers and soldiers. The majority of them were people without big names, but who had proved themselves in action and won lasting confidence in their own localities. From the active army it was almost exclusively rank-and-file soldiers who had run the blockade of army committees and headquarters and come here as delegates. A majority of them had begun to live a political life with the revolution. They had been formed by an experience of eight months. They knew little, but knew it well. The outward appearance of the Congress proclaimed its make-up. The officers' chevrons, the eye-glasses and neckties of intellectuals to be seen at the first Congress had almost completely disappeared. A grey color prevailed uninterruptedly, in costumes and in faces. All had worn out their clothes during the war. Many of the city workers had provided themselves with soldiers' coats. The trench delegates were by no means a pretty picture: long unshaven, in old torn trench-coats, with heavy *papakhi* [1] on their disheveled hair, often with cotton sticking out through a hole, with coarse, weather-beaten faces, heavy cracked hands, fingers yellowed with tobacco, buttons torn off, belts hanging loose, and long unoiled boots wrinkled and rusty. The plebeian nation had for the first time sent up an honest representation made in its own image and not retouched.

The statistics of this Congress which assembled during the hours of insurrection are very incomplete. At the moment of opening there were 650 delegates with votes. 390 fell to the lot

[1] Tall fur hats.

of the Bolsheviks—by no means all members of the party, but they were of the flesh and blood of the masses, and the masses had no roads left but the Bolshevik road. Many of the delegates who had brought doubts with them were maturing fast in the red-hot atmosphere of Petrograd.

How completely had the Mensheviks and Social Revolutionaries squandered the political capital of the February revolution! At the June Congress of Soviets the Compromisers had a majority of 600 votes out of the whole number of 832 delegates. Now the Compromisist opposition of all shades made up less than a quarter of the Congress. The Mensheviks, with the national group adhering to them, amounted to only 80 members—about half of them "Lefts." Out of 159 Social Revolutionaries—according to other reports, 190—about three-fifths were Lefts, and moreover the Right continued to melt fast during the very sitting of the Congress. Toward the end the total number of delegates, according to several lists, reached 900. But this figure, while including a number of advisory members, does not on the other hand include all those with votes. The registration was carried on intermittently; documents have been lost; the information about party affiliations was incomplete. In any case the dominant position of the Bolsheviks in the Congress remains indubitable.

A straw-vote taken among the delegates revealed that 505 soviets stood for the transfer of all power to the soviets; 86 for a government of the "democracy"; 55 for a coalition; 21 for a coalition, but without the Kadets. Although eloquent even in this form, these figures give an exaggerated idea of the remains of the Compromisers' influence. Those for democracy and coalition were soviets from the more backward districts and least important points.

From early in the morning of the 25th, caucuses of the factions were held in Smolny. Only those attended the Bolshevik caucus who were free from fighting duties. The opening of the Congress was delayed: the Bolshevik leaders wanted to finish with the Winter Palace first. But the opposing factions, too, were in no hurry. They themselves had to decide what to do, and that was not easy. Hours passed. Sub-factions were disputing within the factions. The split among the Social Revolutionaries took place after a resolution to withdraw from the Congress had been rejected by 92 votes against 60. It was only late in the evening that the Right and Left Social Revolutionaries began to sit in different rooms. At 8 o'clock the Mensheviks demanded a new delay: they had too many opinions. Night came on. The operations at the Winter Palace were dragging out. But it became impossible to wait longer. It was necessary to say some clear word to the aroused and watchful nation.

The revolution had taught the art of filling space. Delegates, guests, guards, jammed into the commencement hall of the noble maidens, making room for more and more. Warnings of the danger of the floor's collapsing had no effect, nor did appeals to smoke a little less. All crowded closer and smoked twice as much. John Reed with difficulty fought his way through the noisy crowd around the doors. The hall was not heated, but the air was heavy and hot.

Jamming the entries and the side exits, sitting on all the window sills, the delegates now patiently await the president's gong. Tseretelli, Cheidze, Chernov—none of them is on the platform. Only leaders of the second rank have come to their funeral. A short man in the uniform of a military doctor opens the session at 10: 40 in the evening in the name of the Executive Committee. The Congress, he says, assembles in such "exceptional circumstances" that he, Dan, obeying the directions of the Central Executive Committee, will refrain from making a political speech. His party friends are now indeed under fire in the Winter Palace "while loyally fulfilling their duty as ministers." The last thing these delegates are expecting is a blessing from the Central Executive Committee. They look up at the platform with hostility. If those people still exist politically, what have they got to do with us and our business?

In the name of the Bolsheviks a Moscow delegate, Avanessov, moves that the praesidium be elected upon a proportional basis: 14 Bolsheviks, 7 Social Revolutionaries, 3 Mensheviks and 1 Internationalist. The Right immediately declines to enter the praesidium. Martov's group sits tight for the time being; it has not decided. Seven votes go over to the Left Social Revolutionaries. The Congress watches these introductory conflicts with a scowl.

Avanessov announces the Bolshevik candidates for the praesidium: Lenin, Trotsky, Zinoviev, Kamenev, Rykov, Nogin, Skliansky, Krylenko, Antonov-Ovseënko, Riazanov, Muranov, Lunacharsky, Kollontai, Stuchka. "The praesidium," writes Sukhanov, "consisted of the principal Bolshevik leaders and six (in reality seven) Left Social Revolutionaries." Zinoviev and Kamenev were included in the praesidium as authoritative party names in spite of their active opposition to the insurrection; Rykov and Nogin as representatives of the Moscow Soviet; Lunacharsky and Kollontai as popular agitators of that period; Riazanov as a representative of the trade unions; Muranov as an old worker-Bolshevik who had carried himself courageously during the trial of the deputies of the State Duma; Stuchka as head of the Lettish organization; Krylenko and Skliansky as representatives of the army; Antonov-Ovseënko as a leader of the Petrograd battles. The absence of Sverdlov's name is obviously explained by the fact that he himself drew up the list, and in the confusion nobody corrected it. It is characteristic of the party morals of the time that the whole headquarters of the opponents of the insurrection turned up in the praesidium: Zinoviev, Kamenev, Nogin, Rykov, Lunacharsky, Riazanov. Of the Left Social Revolutionaries only the little fragile and courageous Spiridonova, who had served long years at hard labor for assassinating the subduer of the Tombovsk peasants, enjoyed an all-Russian renown. The Left Social Revolutionaries had no other "name." The Rights, on the other hand, had now little or nothing but names left.

The Congress greeted its praesidium with enthusiasm. While the factions had been assembling and conferring, Lenin with his make-up still on, in wig and big spectacles, was sitting in the passage-way in the company of two or three Bolsheviks. On the way to a meeting of their faction Dan and Skobelev stopped still opposite the table where the conspirators were sitting, stared at Lenin, and obviously recognized him. Time, then, to take the make-up off. But Lenin was in no hurry to appear publicly. He preferred to look round a little and gather the threads into his hands while remaining behind the scenes. In his recollections of Lenin published in 1924, Trotsky writes: "The first session of the Second Congress of Soviets was sitting in Smolny. Lenin did not appear there. He remained in one of the rooms of Smolny in which, as I remember, there was for some reason no furniture, or almost none. Later somebody spread blankets on the floor and put two cushions on them. Vladimir Ilych and I took a rest there lying side by side. But in just a few minutes I was called: 'Dan is talking and you must answer him.' [1] Returning after my reply, I again lay down beside Vladimir Ilych, who of course had no thought of going to sleep. Was that indeed possible? Every five or ten minutes somebody would run in from the assembly hall to tell us what was going on."

The president's chair is occupied by Kamenev, one of those phlegmatic types designed by nature herself for the office of chairman. There are three questions, he announces, on the order of the day: organizatiton of a government; war and peace; convocation of the Constituent Assembly. An unusual, dull, alarming rumble breaks into the noise of the meeting from outside. This is Peter and Paul Fortress ratifying the order of the day with artillery fire. A high tension current runs through the Congress, which now suddenly feels and realizes what it really is: the convention of a civil war.

Lozovsky, an opponent of the insurrection, demanded a report from the Petrograd Soviet. But the Military Revolutionary Committee was a little behind hand. Replying artillery testified that the report was not ready. The insurrection was in full swing. The Bolshevik leaders were continually withdrawing to the rooms of the Military Revolutionary Committee to receive communications or give orders. Echoes of the fighting would burst up through the assembly like tongues of flame. When votes were taken hands would be raised among bristling bayonets. A blue-grey acrid tobacco smoke hid the beautiful white columns and chandeliers.

The verbal battles of the two camps were extraordinarily impressive against a background of cannon-shots. Martov demanded the floor. The moment when the balance is still oscillating is his

[1] Evidently the name here should be Martov to whom Trotsky did make a reply.

moment—this inventive statesman of eternal waverings. With his hoarse tubercular voice Martov makes instant rejoinder to the metallic voice of the guns: "We must put a stop to military action on both sides. . . . The question of power is beginning to be decided by conspiratorial methods. All the revolutionary parties have been placed before a *fait accompli*. . . . A civil war threatens us with an explosion of counter-revolution. A peaceful solution of the crisis can be obtained by creating a government which will be recognized by the whole democracy." A considerable portion of the congress applauds. Sukhanov remarks ironically: "Evidently many and many a Bolshevik, not having absorbed the spirit of the teachings of Lenin and Trotsky, would have been glad to take just that course." The Left Social Revolutionaries and a group of United Internationalists support the proposal of peace negotiations. The right wing, and perhaps also the close associates of Martov, are confident that the Bolsheviks will reject this proposal. They are wrong. The Bolsheviks send Lunacharsky to the tribune, the most peace-loving, the most velvety of their orators. "The Bolshevik faction," he says, "has absolutely nothing against Martov's proposal." The enemy are astonished. "Lenin and Trotsky in thus giving way a little to their own masses," comments Sukhanov, "are at the same time cutting the ground from under the Right Wing." Martov's proposal is adopted unanimously. "If the Mensheviks and Social Revolutionaries withdraw now," runs the comment in Martov's group, "they will bury themselves." It is possible to hope, therefore, that the congress "will take the correct road of creating a united democratic front." Vain hope! A revolution never moves on diagonals.

The Right Wing immediately violates the just approved initiation of peace negotiations. The Menshevik Kharash, a delegate from the 12th Army with a captain's stars on his shoulders, makes a statement: "These political hypocrites propose that we decide the question of power. Meanwhile it is being decided behind our backs. . . . Those blows at the Winter Palace are driving nails in the coffin of the party which has undertaken such an adventure. . . ." The captain's challenge is answered by the Congress with a grumble of indignation.

Lieutenant Kuchin who had spoken at the State Conference in Moscow in the name of the front, tries here also to wield the authority of the army organizations: "This Congress is untimely and even unauthorized." "In whose name do you speak?" shout the tattered trench-coats, their credentials written all over them in the mud of the trenches. Kuchin carefully enumerates eleven armies. But here this deceives nobody. At the front as at the rear the generals of compromisism are without soldiers. The group from the front, continues the Menshevik lieutenant, "declines to assume any responsibility for the consequences of this adventure." That means a complete break with the revolution. "Henceforth the arena of struggle is transferred to the localities." That means fusion with the counter-revolution against the soviets. And so the conclusion: "The front group . . . withdraws from this congress."

One after another the representatives of the Right mount the tribune. They have lost the parishes and churches, but they still hold the belfries, and they hasten for the last time to pound the cracking bells. These socialists and democrats, having made a compromise by hook and crook with the imperialist bourgeoisie, today flatly refuse to compromise with the people in revolt. Their political calculations are laid bare. The Bolsheviks will collapse in a few days, they are thinking, we must separate ourselves from them as quickly as possible, even help to overthrow them, and thus to the best of our ability insure ourselves and our future.

In the name of the Right Menshevik faction, Khinchuk, a former president of the Moscow soviet and a future soviet ambassador in Berlin, reads a declaration: "The military conspiracy of the Bolsheviks . . . will plunge the country into civil dissension, demolish the Constituent Assembly, threaten us with a military catastrophe, and lead to the triumph of the counter-revolution." The sole way out: "Open negotiations with the Provisional Government for the formation of a power resting on all layers of the democracy." Having learned nothing, these people propose to the Congress to cross off the insurrection and return to Kerensky. Through the uproar, bellowing, and even hissing, the words of the representative of the Right Social Revolutionaries are hardly distinguishable. The declaration of his party announces "the impossibility of work in collaboration" with the Bolsheviks, and declares the very Congress of Soviets, although convoked and opened by the compromisist Central Executive Committee, to be without authority.

This demonstration of the Right Wing does not cow anybody, but causes alarm and irritation. The majority of the delegates are too sick and tired of these bragging and narrow-minded leaders who fed them first with phrases and then with measures of repression. Can it be that the Dans, Khinchuks and Kuchins still expect to instruct and command us? A Lettish soldier, Peterson, with a tubercular flush on his cheeks and burning hatred in his eyes, denounces Kharash and Kuchin as impostors. "The revolution has had enough gab! We want action! The power should be in our hands. Let the impostors leave the congress—the army is through with them!" This voice tense with passion relieves the mind of the Congress, which has received nothing so far but insults. Other front-line soldiers rush to the support of Peterson. "These Kuchins represent the opinions of little gangs who have been sitting in the army committees since April. The army long ago demanded new elections." "Those who live in the trenches are impatiently awaiting the transfer of power to the soviets."

But the Rights still hold the belfries. A representative of the Bund declares that "all that has happened in Petrograd is a misfortune," and invites the delegates to join the members of the duma who have decided to march unarmed to the Winter Palace in order to die with the government." "Gibes were to be heard in the general uproar," writes Sukhanov, "some coarse and some poisonous." The unctuous orator has obviously mistaken his audience. "Enough from you!" "Deserters!" shout the delegates, guests, Red Guards and sentries at the door to the withdrawing delegates. "Join Kornilov!" "Enemies of the people!"

The withdrawal of the Rights did not leave any vacant space. Evidently the rank-and-file delegates had refused to join the officers and junkers for a struggle against the workers and soldiers. Only about 70 delegates—that is, a little more than half of the Right Wing faction—went out. The waverers took their place with the intermediate groups who had decided not to leave the Congress. Whereas before the opening of the Congress the Social Revolutionaries of all tendencies had numbered not over 190 men, during the next few hours the number of Left Social Revolutionaries alone rose to 180. They were joined by all those who had not yet decided to join the Bolsheviks although ready to support them.

The Mensheviks and Social Revolutionaries were quite ready to remain in a Provisional Government or some sort of a Pre-Parliament under any circumstances. Can one after all break with cultured society? But the soviets—that is only the people. The soviets are all right while you can use them to get a compromise with the bourgeoisie, but can one possibly think of tolerating soviets which have suddenly imagined themselves masters of the country? "The Bolsheviks were left alone," wrote the Social Revolutionary, Zenzinov, subsequently, "and from that moment they began to rely only upon crude physical force." Moral Principle undoubtedly slammed the door along with Dan and Gotz. Moral Principle will march in a procession of 300 men with two lanterns to the Winter Palace, only to run into the crude physical force of the Bolsheviks and—back down.

The motion adopted by the Congress in favor of peace negotiations was left hanging in the air. If the Rights had admitted the possibility of compromising with a victorious proletariat, they would have been in no hurry to break with the congress. Martov could not have failed to understand this. Nevertheless he clung to the idea of a compromise—the thing upon which his whole policy always stands or falls. "We must put a stop to the bloodshed . . ." he begins again. "Those are only rumors!" voices call out. "It is not only rumors that we hear," he answers, "If you come to the windows you will hear cannon shots." This is undeniable. When the Congress quiets down, shots are audible without going to the windows.

Martov's declaration, hostile through and through to the Bolsheviks, and lifeless in its arguments, condemns the revolution as "accomplished by the Bolshevik party alone by the method of a purely military plot," and demands that the congress suspend its labors until an agreement has been reached with all the socialist parties. To try to find the resultant of a parallelogram of forces in a revolution is worse than trying to catch your own shadow!

At that moment there appeared in the congress the Bolshevik faction of the city duma, those who had refused to seek a problematic death under the walls of the Winter Palace. They were led by Joffé, subsequently the first soviet ambassador at Berlin. The Congress again crowded up, giving its friends a joyful welcome.

But it was necessary to put up a resistance to Martov. This task fell to Trotsky. "Now since the exodus of the Rights,"—concedes Sukhanov—"his position is as strong as Martov's is weak." The opponents stand side by side in the tribune, hemmed in on all sides by a solid ring of excited delegates. "What has taken place," says Trotsky, "is an insurrection, not a conspiracy. An insurrection of the popular masses needs no justification. We have tempered and hardened the revolutionary energy of the Petersburg workers and soldiers. We have openly forged the will of the masses to insurrection, and not conspiracy. . . . Our insurrection has conquered, and now you propose to us: Renounce your victory; make a compromise. With whom? I ask: With whom ought we to make a compromise? With that pitiful handful who just went out? . . . Haven't we seen them through and through. There is no longer anybody in Russia who is for them. Are the millions of workers and peasants represented in this congress, whom they are ready now as always to turn over for a price to the mercies of the bourgeoisie, are they to enter a compromise with these men? No, a compromise is no good here. To those who have gone out, and to all who make like proposals, we must say, 'You are pitiful isolated individuals; you are bankrupts; your rôle is played out. Go where you belong from now on—into the rubbish-can of history!' "

"Then we will go!"—cries Martov without awaiting the vote of the Congress. "Martov in anger and affectation," regrets Sukhanov, "began to make his way from the tribune towards the door. And I began to gather together my faction for a conference in the form of an emergency session. . . ." It was not wholly a matter of affectation. The Hamlet of democratic socialism, Martov would make a step forward when the revolution fell back as in July; but now when the revolution was ready for a tiger's leap,

Martov would fall back. The withdrawal of the Rights had deprived him of the possibility of parliamentary maneuvering, and that put him instantly out of his element. He hastened to abandon the congress and break with the insurrection. Sukhanov replied as best he could. The faction split almost in half: Martov won by 14 votes against 12.

Trotsky introduced a resolution—an act of indictment against the Compromisers: They prepared the ruinous offensive of June 18th; they supported the government of treason to the people; they screened the deception of the peasants on the land question; they carried out the disarming of the workers; they were responsible for the purposeless dragging out of the war; they permitted the bourgeoisie to deepen the economic ruin of the country; having lost the confidence of the masses, they resisted the calling of a soviet congress; and finally, finding themselves in a minority, they broke with the soviets.

Here again the order of the day is suspended for a declaration. Really the patience of the Bolshevik praesidium has no bounds. The president of the executive committee of the peasant soviet has come to summon the peasants to abandon this "untimely" congress, and go to the Winter Palace "to die with those who were sent there to do our will." This summons to die in the ruins of the Winter Palace is getting pretty tiresome in its monotony. A sailor just arrived from the *Aurora* ironically announces that there *are* no ruins, since they are only firing blanks from the cruiser. "Proceed with your business in peace," he says. The soul of the congress finds rest in this admirable black-bearded sailor, incarnating the simple and imperious will of the insurrection. Martov with his mosaic of thoughts and feelings belongs to another world. That is why he breaks with the congress.

Still another special declaration—this time half friendly. "The Right Social Revolutionaries," says Kamkov "have gone out, but we, the Lefts, have remained." The congress welcomes those who have remained. However, even they consider it necessary to achieve a united revolutionary front, and come out against Trotsky's sharp resolution shutting the doors against a compromise with the moderate democracy.

Here too the Bolsheviks make a concession. Nobody ever saw

them before, it seems, in such a yielding mood. No wonder: they are the masters of the situation and they have no need to insist upon the forms of words. Again Lunacharsky takes the tribune. "The weight of the task which has fallen upon us is not subject to any doubt," he says. A union of all the genuinely revolutionary elements of the democracy is necessary. But have we, the Bolsheviks, taken any steps whatever to repel the other groups? Did we not adopt Martov's proposal unanimously? For this we have been answered with accusations and threats. Is it not obvious that those who have left the Congress "are ceasing even their compromisist work and openly going over to the camp of the Kornilovists?"

The Bolsheviks did not insist upon an immediate vote on Trotsky's resolution. They did not want to hinder the attempts to reach an agreement on a soviet basis. The method of teaching by object-lesson can be successfully applied even to the accompaniment of artillery! As before with the adoption of Martov's proposal, so now the concession to Kamkov only revealed the impotence of these conciliatory labor pains. However, in distinction from the Left Mensheviks, the Left Social Revolutionaries did not quit the Congress: They were feeling too directly the pressure of the villages in revolt.

A mutual feeling-out has taken place. The primary positions have been occupied. There comes a pause in the evolution of the Congress. Shall we adopt the basic decrees and create a soviet government? It is impossible: the old government is still sitting there in the semi-darkness of a chamber in the Winter Palace, the only lamp on the table carefully barricaded with newspapers. Shortly after two o'clock in the morning the praesidium declares a half-hour recess.

The red marshals employed the short delay accorded to them with complete success. A new wind was blowing in the atmosphere of the Congress when its sitting was renewed. Kamenev read from the tribune a telephonogram just received from Antonov. The Winter Palace has been captured by the troops of the Revolutionary Military Committee; with the exception of Kerensky the whole Provisional Government with the dictator Kishkin at its head is under arrest. Although everybody had already learned the news as it passed from mouth to mouth, this official communication crashed in heavier than a cannon salute. The leap over the abyss dividing the revolutionary class from power has been made. Driven out of the Palace of Kshesinskaia in July, the Bolsheviks have now entered the Winter Palace as rulers. There is no other power now in Russia but the power of the soviets. A complex tangle of feelings breaks loose in applause and shouting: triumph, hope, but also anxiety. Then come new and more confident bursts of applause. The deed is done. Even the most favorable correlation of forces contains concealed surprises, but the victory becomes indubitable when the enemy's staff is made prisoner.

Kamenev impressively reads the list of those arrested. The better known names bring hostile or ironic exclamations from the Congress. Especially bitter is the greeting of Tereshchenko who has guided the foreign destinies of Russia. And Kerensky? Kerensky? It has become known that at ten o'clock this morning he was orating without great success to the garrison of Gatchina. "Where he went from there is not exactly known; rumor says to the front."

The fellow-travelers of the revolution feel bad. They foresee that now the stride of the Bolsheviks will become more firm. Somebody from the Left Social Revolutionaries objects to the arrest of the socialist ministers. A representative of the United Internationalists offers a warning—"lest the Minister of Agriculture, Maslov, turn up in the same cell in which he sat under the monarchy." He is answered by Trotsky, who was imprisoned during the ministry of Maslov in the same "Kresty" as under Nicholas: "Political arrest is not a matter of vengeance; it is dictated . . . by considerations of expediency. The government . . . should be indicted and tried, first of all for its indubitable connection with Kornilov. . . . The socialist ministers will be placed only under house arrest." It would have been simpler and more accurate to say that the seizure of the old government was dictated by the demands of the still unfinished struggle. It was a question of the political beheading of the hostile camp, and not of punishment for past sins.

But this parliamentary query as to the arrests was immediately crowded out by another infinitely more important episode. The third Bicycle Battalion sent by Kerensky against Petrograd had come over to the side of the revolutionary people! This too favorable news seemed unbelievable, but that was exactly what had happened. This selected military unit, the first to be chosen out from the whole active army, adhered to the insurrection before ever reaching the capital. If there had been a shade of restraint in its joy at the arrest of the ministers, the Congress was now seized with unalloyed and irrepressible rapture.

The Bolshevik commissar of Tzarskoe Selo together with a delegate from the bicycle battalion ascended the tribune: They had both just arrived to make a report to the Congress: "The garrison of Tzarskoe Selo is defending the approaches to Petrograd." The defensists withdrew from the soviet. "All the work rested upon us alone." Learning of the approach of the bicycle men, the soviet of Tzarskoe Selo prepared to resist, but the alarm happily turned out to be false. "Among the bicycle men are no enemies of the Congress of Soviets." Another battalion will soon arrive at Tzarskoe, and a friendly greeting is already in preparation there. The Congress drinks down this report in great gulps.

The representative of the bicycle men is greeted with a storm, a whirlwind, a cyclone. This Third Battalion, he reports, was suddenly sent from the southwestern front to the north under telegraphic orders "for the defense of Petrograd." The bicycle men advanced "with eyes blindfolded," only confusedly guessing what was up. At Peredolsk they ran into an echelon of the Fifth Bicycle Battalion, also moving on the capital. At a joint meeting held right there at the station, it became clear that "among all the bicyclers there is not one man to be found who would consent to take action against his brothers." It was jointly decided not to submit to the government.

"I tell you concretely," says the bicycle soldier, "we will not give the power to a government at the head of which stand the bourgeoisie and the landlords!" That word "concretely," introduced by the revolution into the everyday language of the people, sounded fine at this meeting!

How many hours was it since they were threatening the congress from that same tribune with punishments from the front? Now the front itself had spoken its "concrete" word. Suppose the army committees do sabotage the congress. Suppose the rank-and-file soldier mass only succeeds in getting its delegates there rather as an exception. Suppose in many regiments and divisions they have not yet learned to distinguish a Bolshevik from a Social Revolutionary. Never mind! The voice from Peredolsk is the authentic, unmistakable, irrefutable voice of the army. From this verdict there is no appeal. The Bolsheviks, and they only, had understood in time that the soldier-cook of the bicycle battalion infinitely better represented the front than all the Kharashes and Kuchins with their wilted credentials. A portentous change occurred here in the mood of the delegates. "They began to feel," writes Sukhanov, "that things were going to go smoothly and well, that the horrors promised on the right would not after all be so terrible, and that the leaders might be correct in everything else too."

The unhappy Mensheviks selected this moment to draw attention to themselves. They had not yet, it seems, withdrawn. They had been considering in their faction what to do. Out of a desire to bring after him the wavering groups, Kapelinsky, who had been appointed to inform the congress of the decision adopted, finally spoke aloud the most candid reason for breaking with the Bolsheviks: "Remember that the troops are riding towards Petrograd; we are threatened with catastrophe." "What! Are you still here?"—the question was shouted from all corners of the hall. "Why, you went out once!" The Mensheviks moved in a tiny group towards the entrance, accompanied by scornful farewells. "We went out," grieves Sukhanov, "completely untying the hands of the Bolsheviks, turning over to them the whole arena of the revolution." It would have made little difference if they had stayed. In any case they went to the bottom. The waves of events closed ruthlessly over their heads.

It was time for the Congress to address a manifesto to the people, but the session continued to consist only of special declarations. Events simply refused to fit into the order of the day. At 5:17 in the morning Krylenko, staggering tired, made his way to the tribune with a telegram in his hand: The Twelfth Army

sends greetings to the Congress and informs it of the creation of
a military revolutionary committee which has undertaken to
stand guard on the northern front. Attempts of the government
to get armed help have broken against the resistance of the army.
The commander-in-chief of the northern front, General Cheremissov, has submitted to the Committee. The commissar of the
Provisional Government, Voitinsky, has resigned, and awaits a
substitute. Delegations from the echelons moved against Petrograd have one after another announced to the Military Revolutionary Committee their solidarity with the Petrograd garrison.
"Pandemonium," says Reed, "men weeping, embracing each
other."

Lunacharsky at last got a chance to read a proclamation addressed to the workers, soldiers and peasants. But this was not
merely a proclamation. By its mere exposition of what had happened and what was proposed, this hastily written document
laid down the foundations of a new state structure. "The authority of the compromisist Central Executive Committee is at an
end. The Provisional Government is deposed. The Congress assumes the power. . . ." The soviet government proposes immediate peace. It will transfer the land to the peasant, democratize
the army, establish control over production, promptly summon
the Constituent Assembly, guarantee the right of the nations of
Russia to self-determination. "The Congress resolves: That all
power in the localities goes over to the soviets." Every phrase as
it is read turns into a salvo of applause. "Soldiers! Be on your
guard! Railroad workers! Stop all echelons sent by Kerensky
against Petrograd! . . . The fate of the revolution and the fate
of the democratic peace is in your hands!"

Hearing the land mentioned, the peasants pricked up their
ears. According to its constitution the Congress represented only
soviets of workers and soldiers; but there were delegates present
from individual peasant soviets. They now demanded that they
be mentioned in the document. They were immediately given a
right to vote. The representative of the Petrograd peasant soviet
signed the proclamation "with both hands and both feet." A
member of Avksentiev's Executive Committee, Berezin, silent
until now, stated that out of 68 peasant soviets replying to a tele-

317

graphic questionnaire, one-half had expressed themselves for a soviet government, the other half for the transfer of power to the Constituent Assembly. If this was the mood of the provincial soviets, half composed of governmental functionaries, could there be any doubt that a future peasant congress would support the soviet power?

While solidifying the rank-and-file delegates, the proclamation frightened and even repelled some of the fellow-travelers by its irrevocableness. Small factions and remnants again filed through the tribune. For the third time a group of Mensheviks, obviously the most leftward now, broke away from the congress. They withdrew, it seems, only in order to be in a position to save the Bolsheviks: "Otherwise you will destroy yourselves and us and the revolution." The president of the Polish Socialist Party, Lapinsky, although he remained at the congress in order to "defend his point of view to the end," gave essential adherence to the declaration of Martov: "The Bolsheviks will not be able to wield the power which they are assuming." The United Jewish Workers Party abstained from the vote—likewise the United Internationalists. How much, though, did all these "uniteds" amount to altogether? The proclamation was adopted by all votes against two, with 12 abstaining! The delegates had hardly strength left to applaud.

The session finally came to an end at about six o'clock. A gray and cold autumn morning was dawning over the city. The hot spots of the campfires were fading out in the gradually lightening streets. The graying faces of the soldiers and the workers with rifles were concentrated and unusual. If there were astrologers in Petrograd, they must have observed portentous signs in the heavens.

The capital awoke under a new power. The everyday people, the functionaries, the intellectuals, cut off from the arena of events, rushed for the papers early to find out to which shore the wave had tossed during the night. But it was not easy to make out what had happened. To be sure, the papers reported the seizure by conspirators of the Winter Palace and the ministers, but only as a passing episode. Kerensky has gone to headquarters; the fate of the government will be decided by the front. Reports

318

of the Soviet Congress reproduce only the declarations of the Right Wing, enumerate those who withdrew, and expose the impotence of those who remained. The political editorials, written before the seizure of the Winter Palace, exude a cloudless optimism.

The rumors of the street do not wholly coincide with the tone of the newspapers. Whatever you say, the ministers are after all locked up in the fortress. Reinforcements from Kerensky are not yet in sight. Functionaries and officers confer anxiously. Journalists and lawyers ring each other up. Editors try to collect their thoughts. The drawing-room oracles say: We must surround the usurpers with a blockade of universal contempt. Storekeepers don't know whether to do business or refrain. The new authorities give orders to do business. The restaurants open; the tramcars move; the banks languish with evil forebodings; the seismograph of the Stock Exchange describes a convulsive curve. Of course the Bolsheviks will not hold out long, but they may do damage before they tumble.

The reactionary French journalist, Claude Anet, wrote on this day: "The victors are singing a song of victory. And quite rightly too. Among all these blabbers they alone acted. . . . Today they are reaping the harvest. Bravo! Fine work." The Mensheviks estimated the situation quite otherwise. "Twenty-four hours have passed since the 'victory' of the Bolsheviks," wrote Dan's paper, "and the historic fates have already begun to take their cruel revenge. . . . Around them is an emptiness created by themselves . . . They are isolated from all . . . The entire clerical and technical machinery refuses to serve them . . . They . . . are sliding at the very moment of their triumph into the abyss."

The liberal and compromisist circles, encouraged by the sabotage of the functionaries and their own light-mindedness, believed strangely in their own impunity. They spoke and wrote of the Bolsheviks in the language of the July Days. "Hirelings of Wilhelm"—"the pockets of the Red Guard full of German marks" —"German officers in command of the insurrection." . . . The new government had to show these people a firm hand before they began to believe in it. The more unbridled papers were detained already on the night of the 26th. Some others were confiscated on the following day. The socialist press for the time being was spared: It was necessary to give the Left Social Revolutionaries, and also some elements of the Bolshevik party, a chance to convince themselves of the groundlessness of the hope for coalition with the official democracy.

The Bolsheviks developed their victory amid sabotage and chaos. A provisional military headquarters, organized during the night, undertook the defense of Petrograd in case of an attack from Kerensky. Military telephone men were sent to the central exchange where a strike had begun. It was proposed to the armies that they create their own military revolutionary committees. Gangs of agitators and organizers, freed by the victory, were sent to the front and to the provinces. The Central organ of the party wrote: "The Petrograd Soviet has acted; it is the turn of the other soviets."

News came during the day which especially disturbed the soldiers. Kornilov had escaped. As a matter of fact, the lofty captive, who had been living in Bykhov, guarded by Tekintsi, loyal to him, and kept in touch with all events by Kerensky's headquarters, decided on the 26th that things were taking a serious turn, and without the slightest hindrance from anybody abandoned his pretended prison. The connections between Kerensky and Kornilov were thus again obviously confirmed in the eyes of the masses. The Military Revolutionary Committee summoned the soldiers and the revolutionary officers by telegram to capture both former commanders-in-chief and deliver them in Petrograd.

As had the Tauride Palace in February, so now Smolny became the focal point for all functions of the capital and the state. Here all the ruling institutions had their seat. Here orders were issued, and hither people came to get them. Hence a demand went out for weapons, and hither came rifles and revolvers confiscated from the enemy. Arrested people were brought in here from all ends of the city. The injured began to flow in seeking justice. The bourgeois public and its frightened cab-drivers made a great yoke-shaped detour to avoid the Smolny region.

The automobile is a far more genuine sign of present-day

sovereignty than the orb and sceptre. Under the régime of dual power the automobiles had been divided between the government, the Central Executive Committee and private owners. Now all confiscated motors were dragged into the camp of the insurrection. The Smolny district looked like a gigantic military garage. The best of automobiles smoked in those days from the low-grade gas. Motorcycles chugged impatiently and threateningly in the semi-darkness. Armored cars shrieked their sirens. Smolny seemed like a factory, a railroad and power station of the revolution.

A steady flood of people poured along the sidewalks of the adjoining streets. Bonfires were burning at the outer and inner gates. By their wavering light armed workers and soldiers were belligerently inspecting passes. A number of armored cars stood shaking with the action of their own motors in the court. Nothing wanted to stop moving, machines or people. At each entrance stood machine guns abundantly supplied with cartridge-belts. The endless, weakly lighted, gloomy corridors echoed with the tramping of feet, with exclamations and shouts. The arriving and departing poured up and down the broad staircase. And this solid human lava would be cut through by impatient and imperative individuals, Smolny workers, couriers, commissars, a mandate or an order lifted high in their hand, a rifle on a cord slung over their shoulder, or a portfolio under their arm.

The Military Revolutionary Committee never stopped working for an instant. It received delegates, couriers, volunteer informers, devoted friends, and scoundrels. It sent commissars to all corners of the town, set innumerable seals upon orders and commands and credentials—all this in the midst of intersecting inquiries, urgent communications, the ringing of telephone bells and the rattle of weapons. People utterly exhausted of their force, long without sleep or eating, unshaven, in dirty linen, with inflamed eyes, would shout in hoarse voices, gesticulate fantastically, and if they did not fall half dead on the floor, it seemed only thanks to the surrounding chaos which whirled them about and carried them away again on its unharnessed wings.

Adventurers, crooks, the worst off-scouring of the old régime, would sniff about and try to get a pass to Smolny. Some of them succeeded. They knew some little secret of administration: Who has the key to the diplomatic correspondence, how to write an order on the treasury, where to get gasoline or a typewriter, and especially where the best court wines are kept. They did not all find their cell or bullet immediately.

Never since the creation of the world have so many orders been issued—by word of mouth, by pencil, by typewriter, by wire, one following after the other—thousands and myriads of orders, not always issued by those having the right, and rarely to those capable of carrying them out. But just here lay the miracle—that in this crazy whirlpool there turned out to be an inner meaning. People managed to understand each other. The most important and necessary things got done. Replacing the old web of administration, the first threads of the new were strung. The revolution grew in strength.

During that day, the Central Committee of the Bolsheviks was at work in Smolny. It was deciding the problem of the new government of Russia. No minutes were kept—or they have not been preserved. Nobody was bothering about future historians, although a lot of trouble was being prepared for them right there. The evening session of the Congress was to create a cabinet of ministers. M-i-n-i-s-t-e-r-s? What a sadly compromised word! It stinks of the high bureaucratic career, the crowning of some parliamentary ambition. It was decided to call the government the Soviet of Peoples Commissars: that at least had a fresher sound. Since the negotiations for a coalition of the "entire democracy" had come to nothing, the question of the party and personal staff of the government was simplified. The Left Social Revolutionaries minced and objected. Having just broken with the party of Kerensky, they themselves hardly knew what they wanted to do. The Central Committee adopted the motion of Lenin as the only thinkable one: to form a government of Bolsheviks only.

Martov knocked at the door of this session in the capacity of intercessor for the arrested socialist ministers. Not so long ago he had been interceding with the socialist ministers for the imprisoned Bolsheviks. The wheel had made quite a sizeable turn. Through one of its members sent out to Martov for negotiations

—most probably Kamenev—the Central Committee confirmed the statement that the socialist ministers would be transferred to house arrest. Apparently they had been forgotten in the rush of business, or perhaps had themselves declined privileges, adhering even in the Trubetzkoy Bastion to the principle of ministerial solidarity.

The Congress opened its session at nine o'clock in the evening. "The picture on the whole was but little different from yesterday —fewer weapons, less of a jam." Sukhanov, now no longer a delegate, was able to find himself a free seat as one of the public. This session was to decide the questions of peace, land and government. Only three questions: end the war, give the land to the people, establish a socialist dictatorship. Kamenev began with a report of the work done by the praesidium during the day: the death penalty at the front introduced by Kerensky abolished; complete freedom of agitation restored; orders given for the liberation of soldiers imprisoned for political convictions, and members of land committees; all the commissars of the Provisional Government removed from office; orders given to arrest and deliver Kerensky and Kornilov. The Congress approved and ratified these measures.

Again some remnants of remnants took the floor, to the impatient disapproval of the hall. One group announced that they were withdrawing "at the moment of the victory of the insurrection and not at the moment of its defeat." Others bragged of the fact that they had decided to remain. A representative of the Donetz miners urged immediate measures to prevent Kaledin from cutting the north off from coal. Some time must pass, however, before the revolution learns to take measures of such scope. Finally it becomes possible to take up the first point on the order of the day.

Lenin, whom the Congress has not yet seen, is given the floor for a report on peace. His appearance in the tribune evokes a tumultuous greeting. The trench delegates gaze with all their eyes at this mysterious being whom they had been taught to hate and whom they have learned without seeing him to love. "Now Lenin, gripping the edges of the reading-stand, let little winking eyes travel over the crowd as he stood there waiting, apparently oblivious to the long-rolling ovation, which lasted several minutes. When it finished, he said simply, 'We shall now proceed to construct the socialist order.' "

The minutes of the Congress are not preserved. The parliamentary stenographers, invited in to record the debates, had abandoned Smolny along with the Mensheviks and Social Revolutionaries. That was one of the first episodes in the campaign of sabotage. The secretarial notes have been lost without a trace in the abyss of events. There remain only the hasty and tendential newspaper reports, written to the tune of the artillery or the grinding of teeth in the political struggle. Lenin's speeches have suffered especially. Owing to his swift delivery and the complicated construction of his sentences, they are not easily recorded even in more favorable conditions. That initial statement which John Reed puts in the mouth of Lenin does not appear in any of the newspaper accounts. But it is wholly in the spirit of the orator. Reed could not have made it up. Just in that way Lenin must surely have begun his speech at the Congress of Soviets—simply, without unction, with inflexible confidence: "We shall now proceed to construct the socialist order."

But for this it was first of all necessary to end the war. From his exile in Switzerland Lenin had thrown out the slogan: Convert the imperialist war into a civil war. Now it was time to convert the victorious civil war into peace. The speaker began immediately by reading the draft of a declaration to be published by the government still to be elected. The text had not been distributed, technical equipment being still very weak. The Congress drank in every word of the document as pronounced.

"The workers' and peasants' government created by the revolution of October 24–25, and resting upon the soviets of workers', soldiers' and peasants' deputies, proposes to all the warring peoples and their governments to open immediate negotiations for a just, democratic peace." Just conditions exclude annexations and indemnities. By annexations is to be understood the forceful accession of alien peoples or the retention of them against their will, either in Europe or in remote lands over the seas. "Herewith the government declares that it by no means considers the above indicated conditions of peace ultimative—

that is, it agrees to examine any other conditions," demanding only the quickest possible opening of negotiations and the absence of any secrecy in their conduct. On its part the soviet government abolishes secret diplomacy and undertakes to publish the secret treaties concluded before October 25, 1917. Everything in these treaties directed toward the accruing of profit and privilege to the Russian landlords and capitalists, and the oppression of other peoples by the Great Russians, "the government declares unconditionally and immediately annulled." In order to enter upon negotiations, it is proposed to conclude an immediate armistice, for not less than three months at least. The workers' and peasants' government addresses its proposals simultaneously to "the governments and peoples of all warring countries . . . especially the conscious workers of the three most advanced countries," England, France and Germany, confident that it is they who will "help us successfully carry through the business of peace and therewith the business of liberating the toilers and the exploited masses of the population from all slavery and all exploitation."

Lenin limited himself to brief comments on the text of the declaration. "We cannot ignore the governments, for then the possibility of concluding peace will be delayed . . . , but we have no right not to appeal at the same time to the people. The people and the governments are everywhere at variance, and we ought to help the people interfere in the matter of war and peace." "We will, of course, defend in all possible ways our program of peace without annexations or indemnities," but we ought not to present our conditions in the form of an ultimatum, as that will make it easier for the governments to refuse to negotiate. We will consider also every other proposal. *"Consider* does not mean that we will accept it."

The manifesto issued by the Compromisers on March 14th proposed to the workers of other countries to overthrow the bankers in the name of peace; however the Compromisers themselves not only did not demand the overthrow of their own bankers, but entered into a league with them. "Now we have overthrown the government of the bankers." That gives us a right to summon the other peoples to do the same. We have every hope of victory. "It must be remembered that we live not in the depths of Africa, but in Europe where everything can become quickly known." The guarantee of victory Lenin sees, as always, in converting the national into an international revolution. "The workers' movement will get the upper hand and lay down the road to peace and socialism."

The Left Social Revolutionaries sent up a representative to present their adherence to the declaration. Its "spirit and meaning are close and understandable to us." The United Internationalists were for the declaration, but only on condition that it be issued by a government of the entire democracy. Lapinsky, speaking for the Polish Left Mensheviks, welcomed "the healthy proletarian realism" of the document. Dzerzhinsky for the social democracy of Poland and Lithuania, Stuchka for the social democracy of Latvia, Kapsukass for the Lithuanian social democracy, adhered to the declaration without qualification. The only objection was offered by the Bolshevik, Eremeev, who demanded that the peace conditions be given the character of an ultimatum—otherwise "they may think that we are weak, that we are afraid."

Lenin decisively, even fiercely, objected to the ultimative presentation of the conditions: In that way, he said, we will only "make it possible for our enemies to conceal the whole truth from the people, to hide the truth behind our irreconcilability." You say that "our not presenting an ultimatum will show our impotence." It is time to have done with bourgeois falsities in politics. "We need not be afraid of telling the truth about our weariness. . . ." The future disagreements of Brest Litovsk gleam out for a moment already in this episode.

Kamenev asked all who were for the proclamation to raise their delegates' cards. "One delegate," writes Reed "dared to raise his hand against, but the sudden sharp outburst around him brought it swiftly down." The appeal to the peoples and governments was adopted unanimously. The deed was done! And it impressed all the participants by its close and immediate magnitude.

Sukhanov, an attentive although also prejudiced observer, noticed more than once at that first session the listlessness of the Congress. Undoubtedly the delegates—like all the people, indeed

326

—were tired of meetings, congresses, speeches, resolutions, tired of the whole business of marking time. They had no confidence that this Congress would be able and know how to carry the thing through to the end. Will not the gigantic size of the task and the insuperable opposition compel them to back down this time too? An influx of confidence had come with the news of the capture of the Winter Palace, and afterward with the coming over of the bicycle men to the insurrection. But both these facts still had to do with the mechanics of insurrection. Only now was its historic meaning becoming clear in action. The victorious insurrection had built under this congress of workers and soldiers an indestructible foundation of power. The delegates were voting this time not for a resolution, not for a proclamation, but for a governmental act of immeasurable significance.

Listen, nations! The revolution offers you peace. It will be accused of violating treaties. But of this it is proud. To break up the leagues of bloody predation is the greatest historic service. The Bolsheviks have dared to do it. They alone have dared. Pride surges up of its own accord. Eyes shine. All are on their feet. No one is smoking now. It seems as though no one breathes. The præsidium, the delegates, the guests, the sentries, join in a hymn of insurrection and brotherhood. "Suddenly, by common impulse,"—the story will soon be told by John Reed, observer and participant, chronicler and poet of the insurrection—"we found ourselves on our feet, mumbling together into the smooth lifting unison of the Internationale. A grizzled old soldier was sobbing like a child. Alexandra Kollontai rapidly winked the tears back. The immense sound rolled through the hall, burst windows and doors and soared into the quiet sky." Did it go altogether into the sky? Did it not go also to the autumn trenches, that hatchwork upon unhappy, crucified Europe, to her devastated cities and villages, to her mothers and wives in mourning? *"Arise ye prisoners of starvation! Arise ye wretched of the earth!"* The words of the song were freed of all qualifications. They fused with the decree of the government, and hence resounded with the force of a direct act. Everyone felt greater and more important in that hour. The heart of the revolution enlarged to the width of the whole world. "We will achieve emancipation. . . ."

The spirit of independence, of initiative, of daring, those joyous feelings of which the oppressed in ordinary conditions are deprived —the revolution had brought them now. ". . . with our own hand!" The omnipotent hand of those millions who had over-thrown the monarchy and the bourgeoisie would now strangle the war. The Red Guard from the Vyborg district, the gray soldier with his scar, the old revolutionist who had served his years at hard labor, the young black-bearded sailor from the *Aurora*—all vowed to carry through to the end this "last and deciding fight." "We will build our own new world!" We will build! In that word eagerly spoken from the heart was included already the future years of the civil war and the coming five-year periods of labor and privation. "Who was nothing shall be all!" All! If the actual-ities of the past have often been turned into song, why shall not a song be turned into the actuality of the future? Those trench-coats no longer seemed the costumes of galley-slaves. The *papakhi* with their holes and torn cotton took a new aspect above those gleaming eyes. "The race of man shall rise again!" Is it possible to believe that it will not rise from the misery and humiliation, the blood and filth of this war?

"The whole praesidium, with Lenin at its head, stood and sang with excited enraptured faces and shining eyes." Thus testi-fies a sceptic, gazing with heavy feelings upon an alien triumph. "How much I wanted to join it," confesses Sukhanov, "to fuse in one feeling and mood with that mass and its leaders! But I could not." The last sound of the anthem died away, but the Congress remained standing, a fused human mass enchanted by the greatness of that which they had experienced. And the eyes of many rested on the short, sturdy figure of the man in the tribune with his extraordinary head, his high cheekbones and simple features, altered now by the shaved beard, and with that gaze of his small, slightly Mongol eyes which looked straight through everything. For four months he had been absent. His very name had almost separated itself from any living image. But no. He was not a myth. There he stood among his own—how many now of "his own"!—holding the sheets of a message of peace to the peoples of the world in his hand. Even those nearest, those who knew well his place in the party, for the first time fully realized what he meant to the revolution, to the people, to the peoples. It was he who had taught them; it was he who had brought them up. Somebody's voice from the depth of the hall shouted a word of greeting to the leader. The hall seemed only to have awaited the signal. Long live Lenin! The anxieties endured, the doubts overcome, pride of initiative, triumph of victory, gigantic hopes —all poured out together in one volcanic eruption of gratitude and rapture. The sceptical observer dryly remarks: "Undoubted enthusiasm of mood . . . They greeted Lenin, shouted hurrah, threw their caps in the air. They sang the Funeral March in memory of the victims of the war—and again applause, shouts, throwing of caps in the air."

What the Congress experienced during those minutes was experienced on the next day, although less compactly, by the whole country. "It must be said," writes Stankevich, in his memoirs, "that the bold gesture of the Bolsheviks, their ability to step over the barbed-wire entanglements which had for four years divided us from the neighboring peoples, created of itself an enormous impression." Baron Budberg expresses himself more crudely but no less succinctly in his diary: "The new government of Comrade Lenin went off with a decree for immediate peace. . . . This was now an act of genius for bringing the soldier masses to his side: I saw this in the mood of several regiments which I made the rounds of today; the telegram of Lenin on an immediate three months' armistice and then peace, created a colossal impression everywhere, and evoked stormy joy. We have now lost the last chance of saving the front." By saving the front which they had ruined, those men had long ceased to mean anything but saving their own social positions.

If the revolution had had the determination to step over the barbed-wire entanglements in March and April, it might still have soldered the army together for a time—provided the army was at the same time reduced to a half or a third its size—and thus created for its foreign policy a position of exceptional force. But the hour of courageous action struck only in October, when to save even a part of the army for even a short period was unthinkable. The new government had to load upon itself the debt, not only for the war of tzarism, but also for the spendthrift light-

329

mindedness of the Provisional Government. In this dreadful, and for all other parties hopeless, situation, only Bolshevism could lead the country out on an open road—having uncovered through the October revolution inexhaustible resources of national energy.

Lenin is again in the tribune—this time with the little sheets of a decree on land. He begins with an indictment of the over-thrown government and the compromisist parties, who by drag-ging out the land question have brought the country to a peasant revolt. "Their talk about pogroms and anarchy in the country rings false with cowardly deceit. Where and when have pogroms and anarchy been caused by reasonable measures?" The draft of the decree has not been multigraphed for distribution. The speaker has the sole rough draft in his hands, and it is written so badly—Sukhanov remembers—"that Lenin stumbles in the reading, gets mixed up, and finally stops entirely. Somebody from the crowd jammed around the tribune comes to his help. Lenin eagerly yields his place and the undecipherable paper." These rough spots did not, however, in the eyes of that plebeian parliament diminish by an iota the grandeur of what was taking place.

The essence of the decree is contained in two lines of the first point: "The landlord's property in the land is annulled imme-diately and without any indemnity whatever. The landlord, ap-panage, monastery and church estates with all their goods and chattels are given in charge of the town land committees and county soviets of peasant deputies until the Constituent Assembly. The confiscated property is placed as a national possession under the protection of the local soviets. The land of the rank-and-file peasants and rank-and-file Cossacks is protected against con-fiscation. The whole decree does not come to more than thirty lines. It smashes the Gordian knot with a hammer. To the funda-mental text certain broader instructions are adjoined, borrowed wholly from the peasants themselves. In *Izvestia of the Peasant Soviet* there had been printed on August 19th a summary of 242 instructions given by the electors to their representatives at the First Congress of Peasant Deputies. Notwithstanding that it was the Social Revolutionaries who prepared these collated instruc-tions, Lenin did not hesitate to attach the document in its entirety to his decree "for guidance in carrying out the great land transformation."

The collated instructions read: "The right to private property in the land is annulled forever." "The right to use the land is accorded to all citizens . . . desiring to cultivate it with their own labor." "Hired labor is not permitted." "The use of the land must be equalized—that is, the land is to be divided among the toilers according to local conditions on the basis of standards either of labor or consumption."

Under a continuation of the bourgeois régime, to say nothing of a coalition with the landlords, these Social Revolutionary instructions remained a lifeless Utopia, where they did not become a conscious lie. Even under the rule of the proletariat, they did not become realizable in all their sections. But the destiny of the instructions radically changed with a change in the attitude toward them of the governmental power. The workers' state gave the peasants a period in which to try out their self-contradictory program in action.

"The peasants want to keep their small properties," wrote Lenin in August, "standardize them on a basis of equality, and periodically re-equalize them. Let them do it. No reasonable socialist will break with the peasant poor on that ground. If the lands are confiscated, that means that the rule of the banks is undermined—if the equipment is confiscated, that means that the rule of capital is undermined. The rest . . . with a transfer of political power to the proletariat . . . will be suggested by practice."

A great many people, and not only enemies but friends, have failed to understand this far-sighted, and to a certain extent pedagogical, approach of the Bolshevik party to the peasantry and its agrarian program. The equal distribution of the land— objected Rosa Luxemburg for example—has nothing in common with socialism. The Bolsheviks, it goes without saying, had no illusion upon this point. On the contrary, the very construction of the decree bears witness to the critical vigilance of the legislator. Whereas the collated instructions say that all the land, both that of the landlords and the peasants, "is converted into national property," the basic decree does not commit itself at

331

all as to the new form of property in the land. Even a none too pedantic jurist would be horrified at the fact that the nationalization of the land, a new social principle of world-historic importance, is inaugurated in the form of a list of instructions adjoined to a basic law. But there was no reactionary slovenliness here. Lenin wanted as little as possible to tie the hands of the party and the soviet power *a priori* in a still unexplored historic realm. Here again he united unexampled audacity with the greatest caution. It still remained to determine in experience how the peasants themselves would understand the conversion of the land into "the property of the whole people." Having made so long a dash forward, it was necessary to fortify the positions also in case a retreat should become necessary. The distribution of the landlord's land among the peasants, while not in itself a guarantee against bourgeois counter-revolution, made impossible in any case a feudal-monarchic restoration.

It would be possible to speak of socialist perspectives only after the establishment and successful preservation of the proletarian power. And this power could preserve itself only by giving determined co-operation to the peasant in carrying out his revolution. If the distribution of the land would strengthen the socialist government politically, it was then wholly justified as an immediate measure. The peasant had to be taken as the revolution found him. Only a new régime could re-educate him—and not at once, but in the course of a generation, with the help of new technique and a new organization of industry. The decree together with the instructions meant that the dictatorship of the proletariat assumed an obligation not only to take an attentive attitude toward the interests of the land laborer, but also to be patient of his illusions as a petty proprietor. It was clear in advance that there would be a number of stages and turning-points in the agrarian revolution. The collated instructions were anything but the last word. They represented merely a starting-point which the workers agreed to occupy while helping the peasants to realize their progressive demands, and warning them against false steps.

"We must not ignore," said Lenin in his speech, "the resolutions of the lower ranks of the people, even though we are not in agreement with them. . . . We must give full freedom to the creative capacity of the popular masses. The essence of the thing is that the peasantry should have full confidence that there are no more landlords in the country, and let the peasants themselves decide all questions and build their own life." Opportunism? No, it was revolutionary realism.

Before even the applause was over, a Right Social Revolutionary, Pianykh, arrived from the Peasants' Executive Committee and took the floor with a furious protest on the subject of the socialist ministers being under arrest. "During the last days," cried the orator pounding the table as though beside himself, "a thing is on foot which has never happened in any revolution. Our comrades, members of the Executive Committee, Maslov and Salazkin, are locked up in prison. We demand their immediate release!" "If one hair falls from their heads . . ." threatened another messenger in a military coat. To the Congress they both seemed like visitors from another world.

At the moment of the insurrection there were about 800 men in prison in Dvinsk, charged with Bolshevism, in Minsk about 6000, in Kiev 535—for the most part soldiers. And how many members of the peasant committees were under lock and key in various parts of the country! Finally a good share of the delegates to this very Congress, beginning with the praesidium, had passed through the prisons of Kerensky since July. No wonder the indignation of the friends of the Provisional Government could not pluck at any heart-strings in this assembly. To complete their bad-luck a certain delegate, unknown to anybody, a peasant from Tver, with long hair and a big sheepskin coat, rose in his place, and having bowed politely to all four points of the compass, adjured the Congress in the name of his electors not to hesitate at arresting Avksentiev's executive committee as a whole: "Those are not peasants' deputies, but Kadets. . . . Their place is in prison." So they stood facing each other, these two figures: The Social Revolutionary Pianykh, experienced parliamentarian, favorite of ministers, hater of Bolsheviks, and the nameless peasant from Tver who had brought Lenin a hearty salute from his electors. Two social strata, two revolutions: Pianykh was speaking in the name of February, the Tver peasant was fighting for October. The Congress gave the delegate in a sheepskin coat a veritable ovation. The emissaries of the Executive Committee went away swearing.

"The resolution of Lenin is greeted by the Social Revolutionary faction as a triumph of their ideas," announces Kalegaev, but in view of the extraordinary importance of the question we must take it up in caucus. A Maximilist, representative of the extreme left wing of the disintegrated Social Revolutionary party, demands an immediate vote: "We ought to give honor to a party which on the very first day and without any blabber brings such a measure to life." Lenin insisted that the intermission should be at any rate as short as possible. "News so important to Russia should be in print by morning. No filibustering!" The decree on land was not only, indeed, the foundation of the new régime, but also a weapon of the revolution, which had still to conquer the country. It is not surprising that Reed records at that moment an imperative shout breaking through the noise of the hall: "Fifteen agitators wanted in room 17 at once! To go to the front!" At one o'clock in the morning a delegate from the Russian troops in Macedonia enters a complaint that the Petersburg governments one after the other have forgotten them. Support for peace and land from the soldiers in Macedonia is assured! Here is a new test of the mood of the army—this time from a far corner of southeastern Europe. And here Kamenev announces: The Tenth Bicycle Battalion, summoned by the government from the front, entered Petrograd this morning, and like its predecessors has adhered to the Congress of Soviets. The warm applause testifies that no amount of these confirmations of its power will seem excessive to the Congress.

After the adoption, unanimously and without debate, of a resolution declaring it an affair of honor of the local soviets not to permit Jewish or any other pogroms on the part of the criminal element, a vote is taken on the draft of the land law. With one vote opposed and eight abstaining, the congress adopts with a new burst of enthusiasm the decree putting an end to serfdom, the very foundation stone of the old Russian culture. Henceforth the agrarian revolution is legalized, and therewith the revolution of the proletariat acquires a mighty basis.

A last problem remains: the creation of a government. Kamenev reads a proposal drawn up by the Central Committee of the Bolsheviks. The management of the various branches of the state life is allotted to commissions who are to carry into action the program announced by the Congress of Soviets "in close union with the mass organizations of working men and women, sailors, soldiers, peasants and clerical employees." The governmental power is concentrated in the hands of a collegium composed of the presidents of these commissions, to be called the Soviet of Peoples Commissars. Control over the activities of the government is vested in the Congress of Soviets and its Central Executive Committee.

Seven members of the Central Committee of the Bolshevik party were nominated to the first Council of Peoples Commissars: Lenin as head of the government, without portfolio; Rykov as Peoples' Commissar of the Interior; Miliutin as head of the Department of Agriculture; Nogin as chief of Commerce and Industry; Trotsky as head of the Department of Foreign Affairs; Lomov of Justice; Stalin, president of a Commission on the Affairs of the Nationalities; Military and naval affairs were allotted to a committee consisting of Antonov-Ovseënko, Krylenko and Dybenko; the head of the Commissariat of Labor is to be Shliapnikov; the chief of the Department of education, Lunacharsky; the heavy and ungrateful task of Minister of Provisions is laid upon Theodorovich; the Posts and Telegraph upon the worker, Glebov; the position of Peoples Commissar of Communications is not yet allotted, the door being left open here for an agreement with the organizations of the railroad workers.

All fifteen candidates, four workers and eleven intellectuals have behind them years of imprisonment, exile and emigrant life. Five of them had been imprisoned even under the régime of the democratic republic. The future prime-minister had only the day before emerged from the democratic underground. Kamenev and Zinoviev did not enter the Council of Peoples Commissars. The former was selected for president of the new Central Executive Committee, the latter for editor of the official organ of the soviets. "As Kamenev read the list of Commissars," writes

Reed, there were "bursts of applause after each name, Lenin's and Trotsky's especially." Sukhanov adds also that of Lunacharsky.

A long speech against the proposed staff of the government was made by a representative of the United Internationalists, Avilov, once a Bolshevik, literateur from Gorky's paper. He conscientiously enumerated the difficulties standing before the revolution in the sphere of domestic and foreign politics. We must "clearly realize . . . whither we are going. . . . Before the new government stand all the old questions: of bread and of peace. If it does not solve these problems it will be overthrown." There is little grain in the country; it is in the hands of the well-to-do peasants; there is nothing to give in exchange for grain; industry is on the decline; fuel and raw material are lacking. To collect the grain by force is a difficult, long and dangerous task. It is necessary, therefore, to create a government which will have the sympathy not only of the poor but also of the well-to-do peasantry. For this a coalition is necessary.

"It will be still harder to obtain peace." The governments of the Entente will not answer the proposal of the congress for an immediate armistice. Even without that the Allied ambassadors are planning to leave. The new government will be isolated; its peace initiative will be left hanging in the air. The popular masses of the warring countries are still far from revolution. The consequences may be two: either extermination of the revolution by the troops of the Hohenzollern or a separate peace. The peace terms in both cases can only be the worst possible for Russia. These difficulties can be met only by "a majority of the people." The unfortunate thing is the split in the democracy: the left half wants to create a purely Bolshevik government in Smolny, and the right half is organizing in the city duma a Committee of Public Safety. To save the revolution it is necessary to form a government from both groups.

A representative of the Left Social Revolutionaries, Karelin, spoke to the same effect. It is impossible to carry out the program adopted without those parties which have withdrawn from the Congress. To be sure "the Bolsheviks are not to blame for their withdrawal." But the program of the congress ought to unite the

336

entire democracy. "We do not want to take the road of isolating the Bolsheviks, for we understand that with the fate of the Bolsheviks is bound up the fate of the whole revolution. Their ruin will be the ruin of the revolution. If they, the Left Social Revolutionaries, have nevertheless declined the invitation to enter the government, their purpose is a good one: to keep their hands free for mediation between the Bolsheviks and the parties which have abandoned the Congress. In such mediations . . . the Left Social Revolutionaries see their principal task at the present moment." The Left Social Revolutionaries will support the work of the new government in solving urgent problems. At the same time they vote against the proposed government.—In a word the young party has got mixed up as badly as it knows how.

"Trotsky rose to defend a government of Bolsheviks only," writes Sukhanov, himself wholly in sympathy with Avilov and having inspired Karelin behind the scenes. "He was very clear, sharp, and in much absolutely right. But he refused to understand in what consisted the center of the argument of his opponents. . . ." The center of the argument consisted of an ideal diagonal. In March they had tried to draw it between the bourgeoisie and the compromisist soviets. Now Sukhanov dreamed of a diagonal between the compromisist democracy and the dictatorship of the proletariat. But revolutions do not develop along diagonals.

"They have tried to frighten us more than once with a possible isolation of the Left Wing," said Trotsky. "Some days back when the question of insurrection was first openly raised, they told us that we were headed for destruction. And in reality if you judged the grouping of forces by the political press, then insurrection threatened us with inevitable ruin. Against us stood not only the counter-revolutionary bands, but also the defensists of all varieties. The Left Social Revolutionaries, only one wing of them, courageously worked with us in the Military Revolutionary Committee. The rest occupied a position of watchful neutrality. And nevertheless even with these unfavorable circumstances and when it seemed that we were abandoned by all, the insurrection triumphed. . . .

"If the real forces were actually against us, how could it

337

happen that we won the victory almost without bloodshed. No, it is not we who are isolated, but the government and the so-called democrats. With their wavering, their compromisism, they have erased themselves from the ranks of the authentic democracy. Our great superiority as a party lies in the fact that we have formed a coalition with the class forces, creating a union of the workers, soldiers and poorest peasants.

"Political groupings disappear, but the fundamental interests of the classes remain. That party conquers which is able to feel out and satisfy the fundamental demands of a class. . . . We pride ourselves upon the coalition of our garrison, chiefly composed of peasants, with the working class. This coalition has been tried by fire. The Petrograd garrison and proletariat went hand in hand into that great struggle which is the classic example in the history of revolutions among all peoples.

"Avilov has spoken of the vast difficulties which stand before us. To remove those difficulties he proposes that we form a coalition. But he makes no attempt to lay bare his formula and tell us what coalition. A coalition of groups, or classes, or simply a coalition of newspapers? . . .

"They tell us the split in the democracy is a misunderstanding. When Kerensky is sending shock troops against us, when with the consent of the Central Executive Committee we are deprived of the telephone at the most critical moment of our struggle with the bourgeoisie, when they deal us blow after blow —is it possible to talk of misunderstanding?

"Avilov says to us: There is little bread, we must have a coalition with the defensists. Do you imagine that this coalition will increase the quantity of bread? The problem of bread is the problem of a program of action. The struggle with economic collapse demands a definite system from below, and not political groupings on top.

"Avilov speaks of a union with the peasantry: But again of what peasantry is he talking? Today and right here, a representative of the peasants of Tver province demanded the arrest of Avksentiev. We must choose between this Tver peasant and Avksentiev who has filled the prisons with members of the peasant committees. A coalition with the kulak elements of the peasantry we firmly reject in the name of a coalition of the working class and the poorer peasant. We are with the Tver peasants against Avksentiev. We are with them to the end and inseparably.

"Whoever now chases the shadow of coalition is totally cutting himself off from life. The Left Social Revolutionaries will lose support among the masses to the extent that they venture to oppose our party. Every group which opposes the party of the proletariat, with whom the village poor have united, cuts himself off from the revolution.

"Openly and before the face of the whole people we raised the banner of insurrection. The political formula of this insurrection was: All power to the soviets—through the Congress of Soviets. They tell us: You did not await the Congress with your uprising. We thought of waiting, but Kerensky would not wait. The counter-revolutionists were not dreaming. We as a party considered this our task: to make it genuinely possible for the Congress of Soviets to seize the power. If the Congress had been surrounded with junkers, how could it have seized the power? In order to achieve this task, a party was needed which would wrench the power from the hands of the counter-revolution and say to you: 'Here is the power and you've got to take it!' (Stormy and prolonged applause.)

"Notwithstanding that the defensists of all shades stopped at nothing in their struggle against us, we did not throw them out. We proposed to the Congress as a whole to take the power. How utterly you distort the perspective, when after all that has happened you talk from this tribune of our irreconcilability. When a party surrounded with a cloud of gunpowder smoke, comes up to them and says, 'Let us take the power together!' they run to the city duma and unite there with open counter-revolutionists! They are traitors to the revolution with whom we will never unite!

"For the struggle for peace, says Avilov, we must have a coalition with the Compromisers. At the same time he acknowledges that the Allies do not want to make peace. . . . The Allied imperialists laughed, says Avilov, at the oleomargarine delegate Skobelev. Nevertheless if you form a block with the oleomargarine democrats, the cause of peace is assured!

339

"There are two roads in the struggle for peace. One road is to oppose to the Allied and enemy governments the moral and material force of revolution. The other is a bloc with Skobelev, which means a bloc with Tereshchenko and complete subjection to Allied imperialism. In our proclamation on peace we address ourselves simultaneously to the governments and the peoples. That is a purely formal symmetry. Of course we do not think to influence the imperialist governments with our proclamations, although as long as they exist we cannot ignore them. We rest all our hope on the possibility that our revolution will unleash the European revolution. If the revolting peoples of Europe do not crush imperialism, then we will be crushed—that is indubitable. Either the Russian revolution will raise the whirlwind of struggle in the west, or the capitalists of all countries will crush our revolution. . . ."

"There is a third road," says a voice from the benches.

"The third road," answers Trotsky, "is the road of the Central Executive Committee—on the one hand sending delegates to the west European workers, and on the other forming a union with the Kishkins and Konovalovs. That is a road of lies and hypocrisy which we will never enter.

"Of course we do not say that only the day of insurrection of the European workers will be the day that the peace treaty is signed. This also is possible: that the bourgeoisie, frightened by an approaching insurrection of the oppressed, will hasten to make peace. The dates are not set. The concrete forms cannot be foretold. It is important and it is necessary to define the method of struggle, a method identical in principle both in foreign and domestic politics. A union of the oppressed here and everywhere —that is our road."

The delegates of the Congress, says John Reed, "greeted him with an immense crusading acclaim, kindling to the daring of it, with the thought of championing mankind." At any rate it could not have entered the mind of any Bolshevik at that time to protest against placing the fate of the Soviet Republic, in an official speech in the name of the Bolshevik party, in direct dependence upon the development of the international revolution.

The dramatic law of this Congress was that each significant

act was concluded, or even interrupted, by a short intermission during which a figure from the other camp would suddenly appear upon the stage and voice a protest, or a threat, or present an ultimatum. A representative of the Vikzhel, the executive committee of the railroad workers' union, now demanded the floor immediately and on the instant. He must needs throw a bomb into the assembly before the vote was taken on the question of power. The speaker—in whose face Reed saw implacable hostility —began with an accusation. His organization, "the strongest in Russia" had not been invited to the Congress. . . . "It was the Central Executive Committee that did not invite you," was shouted at him from all sides. But he continued: And be it known that the original decision of the Vikzhel to support the Congress of Soviets has been revoked. The speaker hastened to read an ultimatum already distributed by telegraph throughout the country: The Vikzhel condemns the seizure of power by one party; the government ought to be responsible before the "entire revolutionary democracy"; until the creation of a democratic government only the Vikzhel will control the railroad lines. The speaker adds that counter-revolutionary troops will not be admitted to Petrograd; but in general the movements of troops will henceforth take place only at the direction of the old Central Executive Committee. In case of repressions directed against the railroad workers, the Vikzhel will deprive Petrograd of food.

The Congress bristled under the blow. The chiefs of the railroad union were trying to converse with the representatives of the people as one government with another! When the workers, soldiers, and peasants take the administration of the state into their hands, the Vikzhel presumes to give commands to the workers, soldiers, and peasants! It wants to change into petty cash the overthrown system of dual power. In thus attempting to rely not upon its numbers, but upon the exceptional significance of railroads in the economy and culture of the country, these democrats of the Vikzhel exposed the whole frailty of the criterion of formal democracy upon the fundamental issues of a social struggle. Truly revolution has a genius for education!

At any rate the moment for this blow was not badly chosen by the Compromisers. The faces of the praesidium were troubled.

Fortunately the Vikzhel was by no means unconditional boss on the railroads. In the local districts the railroad workers were members of the city soviets. Even here at the Congress the ultimatum of the Vikzhel met resistance. "The whole mass of the railroad workers of our district," said the delegate from Tashkent, "have expressed themselves in favor of the transfer of power to the soviets." Another delegate from railroad workers declared the Vikzhel a "political corpse." That doubtless was exaggerated. Relying upon the rather numerous upper layers of railroad clerks, the Vikzhel had preserved more life force than the other higher-up organizations of the Compromisers. But it belonged indubitably to the same type as the army committees or the Central Executive Committee. Its star was swiftly falling. The workers were everywhere distinguishing themselves from the clerical employees; the lower clerks were opposing themselves to the higher. The impudent ultimatum of the Vikzhel would undoubtedly hasten these processes. No, the station masters can't hold back the locomotive of the October revolution!

"There can be no questioning the legal rights of this congress," declared Kamenev with authority. "The quorum of the Congress was established not by us, but by the old Central Executive Committee. . . . The Congress is the highest organ of the worker and soldier masses." A simple return to the order of the day!

The Council of Peoples Commissars was ratified by an overwhelming majority. Avilov's resolution, according to the excessively generous estimate of Sukhanov, got 150 votes, chiefly Left Social Revolutionaries. The Congress then unanimously confirmed the membership of the new Central Executive Committee: out of 101 members—62 Bolsheviks, 29 Left Social Revolutionaries. The Central Executive Committee was to complete itself in the future with representatives of the peasant soviets and the re-elected army organizations. The factions who had abandoned the Congress were granted the right to send their delegates to the Central Executive Committee on the basis of proportional representation.

The agenda of the Congress was completed! The soviet government was created. It had its program. The work could begin.

And there was no lack of it. At 5:15 in the morning Kamenev closed the Constituent Congress of the soviet régime. To the stations! Home! To the front! To the factories and barracks! To the mines and the far-off villages! In the decrees of the Soviet, the delegates will carry the leaven of the proletarian revolution to all corners of the country.

On that morning the central organ of the Bolshevik party, again under the old name *Pravda*, wrote: "They wanted us to take the power alone, so that we alone should have to contend with the terrible difficulties confronting the country. . . . So be it! We take the power alone, relying upon the voice of the country and counting upon the friendly help of the European proletariat. But having taken the power, we will deal with the enemies of revolution and its saboteurs with an iron hand. They dreamed of a dictatorship of Kornilov. . . . We will give them the dictatorship of the proletariat. . . ."

CONCLUSION

A REMARKABLE consecutiveness of stages is to be observed in the development of the Russian revolution—and this for the very reason that it was an authentic popular revolution, setting in motion tens of millions. Events succeeded each other as though obeying laws of gravitation. The correlation of forces was twice verified at every stage: first the masses would demonstrate the might of their assault, then the possessing classes, attempting revenge, would reveal only the more clearly their isolation.

In February the workers and soldiers of Petrograd rose in insurrection—not only against the patriotic will of all the educated classes, but also contrary to the reckonings of the revolutionary organizations. The masses demonstrated that they were inconquerable. Had they themselves been aware of this, they would have become the government. But there was not yet a strong and authoritative revolutionary party at their head. The power fell into the hands of the petty-bourgeois democracy tinted with a protective socialist coloration. The Mensheviks and Social Revolutionaries could make no other use of the confidence of the masses but to summon to the helm the liberal bourgeoisie, who in their turn could only place the power slipped to them by the Compromisers at the service of the interests of the Entente.

In the April days the indignation of the regiments and factories—again without the summons of any party—brought them out on the streets of Petrograd to resist the imperialist policy of the government wished on them by the Compromisers. This armed demonstration attained an appearance of success. Miliukov, the leader of Russian imperialism, was removed from the government. The Compromisers entered the government, superficially as plenipotentiaries of the people, in reality as call-boys of the bourgeoisie.

Without having decided one of the problems which had evoked the revolution, the coalition government violated in June

344

the *de facto* armistice that had been established on the front, throwing the troops into an offensive. By this act the February régime, already characterized by the declining trust of the masses in the Compromisers, dealt itself a fatal blow. The period opened of direct preparation for a second revolution.

At the beginning of July the government, having all the possessing and educated classes behind it, was prosecuting every revolutionary manifestation whatever as treason to the fatherland and aid to the enemy. The official mass organizations—the soviets, the social-patriotic parties—were struggling against a coming-out with all their power. The Bolsheviks for tactical reasons were trying to restrain the workers and soldiers from coming into the streets. Nevertheless the masses came out. The movement proved unrestrainable and universal. The government was nowhere to be seen. The Compromisers hid. The workers and soldiers proved masters of the situation in the capital. Their offensive went to pieces, however, owing to the inadequate readiness of the provinces and the front.

At the end of August all the organs and institutions of the possessing classes stood for a counter-revolutionary overturn: the diplomats of the Entente, the banks, the leagues of landed proprietors and industrialists, the Kadet party, the staffs, the officers, the big press. The organizer of the overturn was no other than the supreme commander-in-chief with the officer-apparatus of an army of millions to rely on. Military detachments specially selected from all fronts were thrown against Petrograd under pretense of strategic considerations and by secret agreement with the head of the government.

In the capital everything, it seemed, was prepared for the success of the enterprise: the workers had been disarmed by the authorities with the help of the Compromisers; the Bolsheviks were under a steady rain of blows; the more revolutionary regiments had been removed from the city; hundreds of specially selected officers were concentrated in shock brigades—with the officer schools and cossack detachments they should constitute an impressive force. And what happened? The plot, patronized it would seem by the gods themselves, barely came in contact with the revolutionary people when it scattered in dust.

345

These two movements, at the beginning of July and the end of August, relate to each other as a theorem and its converse. The July days demonstrated the might of the self-dependent movement of the masses. The August days laid bare the complete impotence of the ruling groups. This correlation signalized the inevitability of a new conflict. The provinces and the front were meanwhile drawing closer to the capital. This predetermined the October victory.

"The ease with which Lenin and Trotsky overthrew the last coalition government of Kerensky," wrote the Kadet, Nabokov, "revealed its inward impotence. The degree of this impotence was an amazement at that time even to well-informed people." Nabokov himself seems hardly aware that it was a question of his impotence, that of his class, of his social structure.

Just as from the armed demonstration of July the curve rises to the October insurrection, so the movement of Kornilov seems a dress-rehearsal of the counter-revolutionary campaign undertaken by Kerensky in the last days of October. The sole military force against the Bolsheviks found at the front by the democratic commander-in-chief after his flight under cover of the little American flag, was that same Third Cavalry Corps which two months before had been designated by Kornilov for the overthrow of Kerensky himself. The commander of the corps was still the Cossack General, Krasnov, militant monarchist placed in this post by Kornilov. A more appropriate commander for the defense of democracy was not to be found.

Moreover nothing was left of the corps but its name. It had been reduced to a few Cossack squadrons, who after an unsuccessful attempt to take the offensive against the Reds near Petrograd, fraternized with the revolutionary sailors and turned Krasnov over to the Bolsheviks. Kerensky was obliged to take flight—both from the Cossacks and the sailors. Thus eight months after the overthrow of the monarchy the workers stood at the head of the country. And they stood firmly.

"Who would believe," wrote one of the Russian generals, Zalessky, expressing his indignation at this, "that the janitor or watchman of the court building would suddenly become Chief Justice of the Court of Appeals? Or the hospital orderly, manager

346

of the hospital; the barber a big functionary; yesterday's ensign, the commander-in-chief; yesterday's lackey or common laborer, burgomaster; yesterday's train oiler, chief of division or station superintendent; yesterday's locksmith, head of the factory?"

"Who would believe it?" They had to believe it. It was impossible not to believe it, when ensigns routed the generals, when burgomasters from the ranks of common labor put down the resistance of yesterday's lords, train oilers regulated transport, and locksmiths as directors revived industry.

The chief task of a political régime, according to an English aphorism, is to put the right people in the right positions. How does the experiment of 1917 look from this point of view? During the first two months Russia was ruled, through right of monarchic succession, by a man inadequately endowed by nature who believed in saints' mummies and submitted to Rasputin. During the next eight months the liberals and democrats attempted from their governmental high places to prove to the people that the revolution had been accomplished in order that all should remain as before. No wonder those people passed over the country like wavering shadows leaving no trace. From the 25th of October the man at the head of Russia was Lenin, the greatest figure in Russian political history. He was surrounded by a staff of assistants who, as their most spiteful enemies acknowledge, knew what they wanted and how to fight for their aims. Which of these three systems, in the given concrete conditions, proved capable of putting the right people in the right positions?

The historic ascent of humanity, taken as a whole, may be summarized as a succession of victories of consciousness over blind forces—in nature, in society, in man himself. Critical and creative thought can boast of its greatest victories up to now in the struggle with nature. The physico-chemical sciences have already reached a point where man is clearly about to become master of matter. But social relations are still forming in the manner of the coral islands. Parliamentarism illumined only the surface of society, and even that with a rather artificial light. In comparison with monarchy and other heirlooms from the cannibals and cave-dwellers, democracy is of course a great conquest, but it leaves the blind play of forces in the social relations of men untouched. It was against this deeper sphere of the unconscious that the October revolution was the first to raise its hand. The soviet system wishes to bring aim and plan into the very basis of society, where up to now only accumulated consequences have reigned.

Enemies are gleeful that fifteen years after the revolution the soviet country is still but little like a kingdom of universal well-being. Such an argument, if not really to be explained as due to a blinding hostility, could only be dictated by an excessive worship of the magic power of socialist methods. Capitalism required a hundred years to elevate science and technique to the heights and plunge humanity into the hell of war and crisis. To socialism its enemies allow only fifteen years to create and furnish a terrestrial paradise. We took no such obligation upon ourselves. We never set these dates. The process of vast transformations must be measured by an adequate scale.

But the misfortunes which have overwhelmed living people? The fire and bloodshed of the civil war? Do the consequences of a revolution justify in general the sacrifices it involves. The question is teleological and therefore fruitless. It would be as well to ask in face of the difficulties and griefs of personal existence: Is it worth while to be born? Melancholy reflections have not so far, however, prevented people from bearing or being born. Even in the present epoch of intolerable misfortune only a small percentage of the population of our planet resorts to suicide. But the people are seeking the way out of their unbearable difficulties in revolution.

Is it not remarkable that those who talk most indignantly about the victims of social revolutions are usually the very ones who, if not directly responsible for the victims of the world war, prepared and glorified them, or at least accepted them? It is our turn to ask: Did the war justify itself? What has it given us? What has it taught?

It will hardly pay now to pause upon the assertions of injured Russian proprietors that the revolution led to the cultural decline of the country. That aristocratic culture overthrown by the October revolution was in the last analysis only a superficial imitation of higher western models. Remaining inaccessible to the Russian people, it added nothing essential to the treasure-store of humanity. The October revolution laid the foundation of a new culture taking everybody into consideration, and for that very reason immediately acquiring international significance. Even supposing for a moment that owing to unfavorable circumstances and hostile blows the soviet régime should be temporarily over-thrown, the inexpugnable impress of the October revolution would nevertheless remain upon the whole future development of mankind.

The language of the civilized nations has clearly marked off two epochs in the development of Russia. Where the aristocratic culture introduced into world parlance such barbarisms as *tzar, pogrom, knout,* October has internationalized such words as *Bolshevik, soviet* and *piatiletka.* This alone justifies the prole-tarian revolution, if you imagine that it needs justification.

THE END

APPENDIX

NOTE:

Besides our historic references on the theory of permanent revolution, we have transferred into this appendix two independent chapters: "Some Legends of the Bureaucracy," and "Socialism in a Separate Country?". The chapter on "legends" is dedicated to the critical restoration of a series of facts and episodes of the October revolution distorted by the epigone historians. One of the incidental aims of this chapter is to make it impossible for lazy minds, instead of working over the factual material, to quiet themselves with the cheap *a priori* conclusion that "the truth is probably somewhere in the middle."

The chapter "Socialism in a Separate Country?" is dedicated to the most important question concerning the ideology and program of the Bolshevik party. The question here historically illumined by us, not only still preserves all its theoretical interest, but has in recent years acquired a first class practical importance.

We have separated these two chapters from the general text, of which they form an integral part, only for the benefit of the reader not accustomed to concern himself with secondary disputes or theoretical problems. If however a tenth, or even a hundredth, of the readers of this book take the trouble to read attentively this appendix, the author will feel abundantly rewarded for the great labor he has performed. It is through thoughtful, work-loving and critical minds that the truth in the long run makes its way to broader circles.

APPENDIX ONE

SOME LEGENDS OF THE BUREAUCRACY

THE conception of the October revolution developed in this book was set forth by the author more than once during the early years of the soviet régime, although to be sure only in its general features. In order to delineate his thought more clearly he sometimes gave it a quantitative expression: the task of the overturn, he wrote, was "three-quarters if not nine-tenths" completed before the 25th of October by the method of "silent" or "dry" insurrection. If you do not give these figures more importance than figures could pretend to in such a matter, the idea itself remains absolutely unquestionable. But since the revaluation of values began, our conception has been bitterly criticized in this particular.

"If on the 9th of October a nine-tenths 'victorious' insurrection was already an accomplished fact," wrote Kamenev, "then how shall we estimate the intellectual capacities of those who were sitting in the Central Committee of the Bolsheviks, and on the 10th of October deciding in heated debates whether to make an insurrection or not, and if so when? What shall we say of the people who assembled on the 16th of October . . . and again and again estimated the chances of an insurrection? . . . Oh yes, it seems that it was already accomplished on the 9th of October 'silently' and 'legally'—so silently indeed that neither the party nor the Central Committee knew about it." This superficially so effective argument, which is canonized in the epigone literature and has politically outlived its author, is in reality an impressive piling up of mistakes.

On the 9th of October the insurrection could not possibly have been a "nine-tenths" accomplished fact, for on that day the question of the transfer of the garrison had just been raised in the Soviet and it was impossible to know how the thing would develop in the future. It was for this reason that on the next day, the 10th, when insisting on the importance of this question of the transfer of the troops, Trotsky had not yet sufficient grounds to demand that the conflict between the garrison and its command form the basis of the whole plan. Only during the next two weeks of stubborn day-by-day work did the chief task of the insurrection—the firm winning over to the peoples' side of the government troops—become "three-quarters if not nine-tenths" accomplished. This was not so on the 10th, nor yet even on the 16th of October, when the Central Committee took up for a second time the question of insurrection and when Krylenko did quite definitely present as a key-note the question of the garrison.

But even if the revolution had been nine-tenths victorious on the 9th—as Kamenev erroneously presents our thought—this fact could have been reliably ascertained, not by guessing, but only by action—that is, by making an insurrection. The "intellectual capacity" of the members of the Central Committee would not, even in that purely hypothetical case, have been in the least compromised by their participation in heated debates on the 10th and 16th of October. However, even supposing that the members of the Central Committee could have unquestionably assured themselves by an *a priori* calculation that the victory was actually nine-tenths won, it would still have remained necessary to accomplish the last tenth, and that would have demanded just as much attention as though it were ten-tenths. How many "almost" won battles and insurrections does history present—battles and insurrections which led to defeat only because they were not pushed through in good season to the complete defeat of the enemy! And finally—Kamenev is ingenious enough to forget this too—the sphere of activity of the Military Revolutionary Committee was Petrograd only. However important the capital may have been, the rest of the country did nevertheless exist. And from this point of view the Central Committee had sufficient ground for carefully weighing the chances of the insurrection, not only on the 10th and the 16th, but also on the 26th—that is, after the victory in Petrograd.

Kamenev, in the argument we are discussing, comes to the defense of Lenin. All the Epigones defend themselves under this imposing pseudonym. How could Lenin, he asks, have fought so passionately for an insurrection, if it was already nine-tenths accomplished! But Lenin himself wrote at the beginning of October: "It is quite possible that right now we might seize the power without an insurrection." In other words, Lenin postulated that the "silent" revolution had already taken place before the 9th of October, and moreover not by nine but by ten-tenths. He understood however, that this optimistic hypothesis could only be verified in action. For that reason Lenin said in the same letter: "If we can not seize the power without an insurrection, then we must make an insurrection immediately." It was this question that was discussed on the 10th and 16th, and on other days.

The recent soviet histories have completely erased from the October revolution the extremely important and instructive chapter about the disagreements between Lenin and the Central Committee—both upon the basic matter of principle in which Lenin was right, and also upon those particular, but very important, questions upon which the Central Committee was right. According to the new doctrine, neither Lenin nor the Central Committee could make a mistake, and consequently there could have been no conflict between them. In those cases where it becomes impossible to deny that there was a disagreement, it is, in obedience to a general prescription, laid at the door of Trotsky.

The facts speak otherwise. Lenin insisted upon raising an insurrection in the days of the Democratic Conference. Not one member of the Central Committee supported him. A week later Lenin proposed to Smilga to organize an insurrectionary headquarters in Finland, and strike a blow at the government from that point with the sailors. Again ten days later he insisted that the Northern Congress become the starting point of an insurrection. Nobody at the Congress supported this proposal. At the end of September Lenin considered the postponement of the insurrection for three weeks, until the Congress of Soviets, fatal. Nevertheless the insurrection, deferred to the eve of the Congress, was accomplished while the Congress was in session. Lenin proposed that the struggle begin in Moscow, assuming that there it would be resolved without a fight. As a matter of fact, the insurrection in Moscow, notwithstanding the preceding victory in Petrograd, lasted eight days and cost many victims.

Lenin was no automaton of infallible decisions. He was "only" a man of genius, and nothing human was alien to him, therein included the capacity to make mistakes. Lenin said this of the attitude of epigones to the great revolutionists: "After their deaths, attempts are made to convert them into harmless ikons, to canonize them, so to speak, to render a certain homage to their names . . ." in order thus the more safely to betray them in action. The present epigones demand that Lenin be acknowledged infallible in order the more easily to extend the same dogma to themselves.[1]

[1] During the Third Congress of the Communist International, in order to soften his blows at certain "ultra-Lefts," Lenin referred to the fact that he himself had made "ultra-Left" mistakes, especially while an emigré, including one during his last "emigration" in Finland in 1917, when he defended a less expedient plan of insurrection than the one actually carried out. This reference to his own mistake was made by Lenin, unless our memory deceives us, also in a letter to the commission of the congress on German affairs. Unfortunately the archives of the Communist International are not accessible to us, and the declaration of Lenin in question has evidently not been published.

What characterized Lenin as a statesman was a combination of bold perspectives with a meticulous estimation of tiny facts and symptoms. Lenin's isolation did not prevent him from defining with incomparable penetration the fundamental stages and turns of the movement, but it deprived him of the possibility of making timely estimates of episodic factors and temporary changes. The political situation was in general so favorable to an insurrection as to admit several different possibilities of victory. If Lenin had been in Petrograd and had carried through at the beginning of October his decision in favor of an immediate insurrection without reference to the Congress of Soviets, he would undoubtedly have given the carrying out of his own plan a political setting which would have reduced its disadvantageous features to a minimum. But it is at least equally probable that he would himself in that case have come round to the plan actually carried out.

We have given in a separate chapter our estimate of the rôle of Lenin in the general strategy of the revolution. To point our idea in regard to Lenin's tactical proposals we will add that without Lenin's pressure, without his urgings, his suggestions, his variant plans, it would have been infinitely more difficult to get over onto the road toward insurrection. Had Lenin been in Smolny during the critical weeks, the general leadership of the insurrection—and that not only in Petrograd but Moscow—would have been on a considerably higher level. But Lenin as an "emigré" could not take the place of Lenin in Smolny.

Lenin himself felt most keenly of all the inadequacy of his tactical orientation. He wrote on September 24th in *Rabochy Put*: "The growth of a new revolution is obviously in progress—we know little unfortunately of the breadth and rapidity of this growth." These words are both a reproach to the party leaders and a complaint of his own lack of information. When recalling in his letter the most important rules of insurrection, Lenin did not forget to add: "This is all approximate of course and merely for illustration." On the 8th of October, Lenin wrote to the Northern Regional Congress of Soviets: "I will try to appear with my advice from the sidelines in case the probable insurrection of the workers and soldiers of Petersburg . . . soon takes place, but it has not yet taken place." Lenin began his polemic against Zinoviev and Kamenev with these words: "A publicist set somewhat aside by the will of destiny from the main line of history constantly incurs the risk of coming in late or being uninformed, especially when his writings are delayed in publication." Here again a complaint against his isolation together with a reproach to the editors who had delayed the printing of those articles which they judged too incisive, or had thrown out the prickliest passages.

A week before the insurrection Lenin wrote in a conspirative letter to the members of the party: "As to the raising of the question of insurrection now, so near to the 20th of October, I cannot judge *from a distance* just how much the thing has been spoiled by the strike-breaking performance (of Zinoviev and Kamenev) in the non-party press." The words "from a distance" are underlined by Lenin himself.

But how does the epigone school explain the disaccord between the tactical proposals of Lenin and the actual course of the insurrection in Petrograd? It gives to the conflict an anonymous and formless character; or it passes by the disagreements altogether, declaring them unworthy of attention; or it tries to refute facts indestructibly established; or it puts the name Trotsky where Lenin was talking about the Central Committee as a whole or the opponents of insurrection within the Central Committee; or, finally, it combines all these methods, not bothering about whether they are mutually consistent or not.

"The conduct of the October insurrection," writes Stalin, "may be considered a model of (Bolshevik) strategy. To transgress this requirement (the correct choice of the moment) leads to a dangerous mistake called 'loss of tempo,' when the party falls behind the course of events or runs ahead, giving rise to a danger of failure. The attempt of one group of the comrades to begin the insurrection with the arrest of the Democratic Conference in August 1917 must be considered an example of this 'loss of tempo,' an example of how not to choose the moment of insurrection." The designation "one group of the comrades" in these lines means Lenin. Nobody but Lenin proposed that the insurrection begin with the arrest of the Democratic Conference, and nobody supported his proposal. Stalin recommends the tactical plan of Lenin as "an example of how not to choose the moment of insurrection." But the anonymous form of his account permits Stalin at the same time to deny flatly that there was any disagreement between Lenin and the Central Committee.

Yaroslavsky has a still simpler way of getting out of the difficulty. "It is not a question of particulars, of course," he writes, "it is not a question whether the insurrection began in Moscow or Petrograd." The thing is that the whole course of events demonstrated "the correctness of Lenin's line, the correctness of the line of our party." This ingenious historian simplifies his task to an extraordinary degree. That October verified the strategy of Lenin, and demonstrated in particular how important had been his April victory over the ruling stratum of "old Bolsheviks," is indubitable. But if in a general way there is no question about where to begin, when to begin, and how to begin, then, to be sure, nothing is left of the episodic disagreements with Lenin—or for that matter of tactics in general.

In John Reed's book there is a story that on the 21st of October the leaders of the Bolsheviks held a "second historic conference" at which, as Reed was told, Lenin said: "The 24th of October is too soon to act. We must have an All-Russian basis for the insurrection, and on the 24th not all the delegates will have come to the Congress. On the other hand, the 26th will be too late to act. . . . We must act on the 25th, the day of the opening of the Congress." Reed was an extraordinarily keen observer, able to transcribe upon the pages of his book the feelings and passions of the deciding days of the revolution. It was for this reason that Lenin in his day desired that the incomparable chronicle of Reed be distributed in millions of copies in all the countries of the world. But work done in the heat of events, notes made in corridors, on the streets, beside campfires, conversations and fragmentary phrases caught on the wing, and that too with the need of a translator—all these things made particular mistakes unavoidable. This story of a session of October 21st is one of the most obvious mistakes in Reed's book. The argument about the need of an "All-Russian soviet foundation" for the insurrection could not possibly belong to Lenin, for Lenin more than once described the running after such a foundation as nothing more or less than "complete idiotism or complete betrayal." Lenin could not have said that the 24th was too early, for ever since the end of September he had considered inadmissible a postponement of the insurrection for one unnecessary day. It might come too late, he said, but "in that matter it is now impossible to be premature." However, aside from these political considerations— decisive enough in themselves—Reed's story is refuted by the simple fact that on the 21st there was no "second historic conference" of any kind. Such a conference could not fail to leave traces in the documents and memories of the other participants. There were only two conferences with Lenin present: on the 10th and the 16th. Reed could not have known this. But the documents since published leave no place for the "historic session" of October 21st. The epigone historians have not hesitated, however, to include the obviously erroneous testimony of Reed in all the official publications. By this means they have achieved a specious calendar-coincidence of Lenin's directives with the actual course of events. To be sure, in doing this the official historians put Lenin in the position of incomprehensibly and hopelessly contradicting himself. But essentially, you must understand, they are not here concerned about Lenin. The epigones have simply converted Lenin into their own historic pseudonym, and are unceremoniously making use of him in order to establish their own infallibility *ex post facto*.

But the official historians go even farther than this in the business of driving facts into the required line of march. Thus Yaroslavsky writes in his history of the party: "At the session of the Central Committee on the 24th of October, the last session before the insurrection, Lenin was present." The officially published minutes, containing a complete list of those present, testify that Lenin was absent. "Lenin and Kamenev were delegated to negotiate with the Left Social Revolutionaries," writes Yaroslavsky. The minutes say that this task was allotted to Kamenev and Berzin. But it ought to be obvious without any minutes that the Central Committee would not have put upon Lenin this secondary "diplomatic" task. That decisive session of the Central Committee took place in the morning. Lenin did not arrive at Smolny until night. A member of the Petrograd committee, Sveshnikov, relates how Lenin "went out somewhere in the evening (of the 24th) leaving a note in his room stating that he had gone at such and such a time. When we learned this we were frightened to death for Ilych." Only "late in the evening" did it become known in the district that Lenin had gone to the Military Revolutionary Committee.

Most surprising of all, however, is the fact that Yaroslavsky ignores a political and human document of first-class importance: a letter to the leaders of the districts written by Lenin during the hours when the open insurrection had already essentially begun. "Comrades! I am writing these lines on the evening of the 24th. . . . With all my power I want to convince the comrades that everything now hangs upon a thread, that questions are now in order which will not be decided by conferences, not by congresses (even though congresses of soviets) but solely by the people, by the mass, by the struggle of the armed masses. It is necessary at any possible cost this very evening, this very night, to arrest the government, disarming (vanquishing if they resist) the junkers etc. . . ." Lenin feared to such an extent the irresolution of the Central Committee, that he was trying at the very last moment to organize a pressure on it from below. "It is necessary," he writes, "that all districts, all regiments, all forces mobilize on the instant and send delegations immediately to the Military Revolutionary Committee, to the Central Committee of the Bolsheviks, with this insistent demand: In no case leave the power in the hands of Kerensky and Co. until the 25th, not in any case,—but settle the thing today without fail, this evening or night." While Lenin was writing these lines, the regiments and districts he was summoning to mobilize for pressure on the Military Revolutionary Committee were already mobilized by the Military Revolutionary Committee for the seizure of the city and the overthrow of the government. From this letter—every line of which quivers with anxiety and passion—it is at least evident that Lenin could not have proposed on the 21st to defer the insurrection until the 25th, nor have been present at the morning session of the 24th when it was decided to take the offensive immediately.

There is in this letter nevertheless a puzzling element. How could it happen that Lenin, in hiding in the Vyborg district, did not know until evening about a decision of such exceptional importance? From the account of Sveshnikov—as also from other sources—it is evident that communications with Lenin were kept up during that day through Stalin. It can only be assumed that, not having appeared at the morning session of the Central Committee, Stalin also did not know until evening of the decision adopted.

The immediate cause of Lenin's alarm may have been the rumors consciously and persistently circulated during that day from Smolny, that until the decision of the Congress of Soviets no decisive steps would be taken. On the evening of that day, at an emergency session of the Petrograd Soviet, Trotsky said, in his report on the activities of the Military Revolutionary Committee: "An armed conflict today or tomorrow is not included in our plan—on the threshold of the All-Russian Congress of Soviets. We think that the Congress will carry out our slogan with greater power and authority. But if the government wants to use that span of life which still remains to it—24, 48 or 72 hours—in order to take the offensive against us, we will answer with a counter-offensive, blow for blow, steel against iron." Such was the leit-motiv of that whole day. These defensive announcements had for their purpose to lull at the last moment before the blow the none too lively vigilance of the enemy. It was in all probability this maneuver which gave Dan his grounds for assuring Kerensky on the night of the 25th that the Bolsheviks had no intention at all of making an immediate insurrection. But on the other hand, Lenin too, if one of these sedative declarations from Smolny happened to reach him, may, in his state of tension and distrust, have taken a military trick for good money.

Ruses form a necessary element of the art of war. It is a bad ruse, however, which may incidentally deceive one's own camp. Had it been a question of summoning masses wholesale into the streets, those words about the next "72 hours" might have proven a fatal act. But on the 24th the uprising no longer had need of any general revolutionary summons. The armed detachments designated for the seizure of the principal points of the capital were under arms and awaiting from their commanders, who were in telephone communication with the nearest revolutionary headquarters, the signal to attack. In these circumstances the double-edged ruse of the revolutionary headquarters was entirely in place.

Whenever the official investigators run into an unpleasant document they change its address. Thus Yakovlev writes: "The Bolsheviks did not surrender to 'constitutional illusions,' but rejected the proposal of Trotsky to accommodate the insurrection necessarily to the Second Congress of Soviets, and seized the power before the opening of the Congress of Soviets." Just what proposal of Trotsky is here spoken of, where and when it was considered, what Bolsheviks rejected it—of this the author has nothing to say, and not accidentally. We should search in vain among the minutes, or among any memoirs whatever, for any indication of a proposal of Trotsky to "accommodate the insurrection necessarily to the Second Congress of Soviets." The ground of this assertion of Yakovlev is a slightly conventionalized misunderstanding long ago explained away by no other than Lenin himself.

As is evident from memoirs published long ago, Trotsky had more than once since the beginning of September pointed out to those opposed to insurrection that appointing the date for the Congress of Soviets was for the Bolsheviks equivalent to appointing the insurrection. This did not mean, of course, that the uprising must not occur except upon the decision of the Congress of Soviets—there could be no talk of such childish formalism. It was a question of the outside date, of the impossibility of deferring it to an indefinite time after the congress. Through whom and in what form these disputes in the Central Committee reached Lenin, is not clear from the documents. An interview with Trotsky, who was too much in view of the enemy, would have been too great a risk for Lenin. In his attitude of caution at that time he may therefore have feared that Trotsky would place his emphasis upon the Congress and not upon the insurrection, or in any case that he would not put up the necessary resistance to the "constitutional illusions" of Zinoviev and Kamenev. Lenin may have been anxious also about the new members of the Central Committee little known to him, the former Mezhrayontsi (or fusionists), Joffé and Uritzky. There is direct evidence of this in a speech of Lenin at a session of the Petrograd committee on November 1st after the victory. "The question was raised at the session (of October 10th) about an offensive. I had fears of opportunism from the side of the internationalist-fusionists, but these were dissipated; in our party, however, (certain old) members (of the Central Committee) did not agree. This grieved me deeply." According to his own words, Lenin became convinced on the 10th that not only Trotsky, but also Joffé and Uritzky, who were under Trotsky's immediate influence, were decisively in favor of insurrection. The question of dates in general was raised for the first time at that session. When, then, and by whom, was "a proposal of Trotsky" not to begin the insurrection without a preliminary decision of the Congress of Soviets rejected? As though with a special view to enlarge still further the radius of confusion, the official investigators, with their references to an apocryphal decision of October 21st, attribute, as we have seen, exactly the same proposal to Lenin.

At this point Stalin bursts into the argument with a new version which refutes Yakovlev, but along with him also much more. It seems, according to Stalin, that the postponement of the insurrection to the day of the Congress,—that is, to the 25th—met no intrinsic objection from Lenin, but the thing was spoiled by the publication in advance of the date of insurrection. Here let us give the floor, however, to Stalin himself: "The mistake of the Petrograd Soviet in openly designating and publishing abroad the date of the insurrection (October 25th) could not be corrected except by an actual insurrection before this legal date of insurrection." This assertion is disarming in its inconsistency. As though in those disputes with Lenin it was a question of choosing between the 24th and 25th of October! As a matter of fact Lenin wrote almost a month before the insurrection: "To wait for the Congress of Soviets is complete idiotism for it means letting weeks pass. But weeks and even days now decide everything." Where, and when, and from which side, did the Soviet publish abroad the date of the insurrection? It is difficult even to invent motives which might induce it to perform so nonsensical an act. In reality it was not the insurrection, but the opening of the Congress of Soviets, which was publicly and in advance set for the 25th, and this was done not by the Petrograd Soviet but by the compromisist Central Executive Committee. From this fact, and not from a pretended indiscretion of the Soviet, certain inferences were to be drawn by the enemy: The Bolsheviks, if they do not intend to retire from the scene, must attempt to seize the power at the moment of the Congress. "It flowed from the logic of things," we wrote subsequently "that we appointed the insurrection for October 25th. The thing was so understood by the whole bourgeois press." Stalin has converted his confused recollection of this "logic of things" into an "indiscreet" publishing abroad of the day of the insurrection. It is thus that history is being written.

362

On the second anniversary of the revolution the author of this book, referring in the sense just explained to the fact that "the October insurrection was, so to speak, appointed in advance for a definite date, for October 25th, and was accomplished upon exactly that date," added: We should seek in vain in history for another example of an insurrection which was accommodated in advance by the course of things to a definite date. That assertion was erroneous: The insurrection of August 10, 1792 was also appointed approximately a week in advance for a definite date, and also not through indiscretion but through the logic of events.

On August 3 the Legislative Assembly resolved that the petitions of the Paris sections demanding the overthrow of the king should be taken up on the 9th. "In thus naming the day of the debate," writes Jaurès, who has observed many things which escape the attention of the old historians, "it also named the day of the insurrection. Danton, the leader of the sections, took a defensive position: "If a new revolution breaks out," he insistently declared, "it will be an answer to the treachery of the government." This handing over of the question by the sections to the consideration of the Legislative Assembly was by no means a "constitutional illusion." It was merely a method of preparing an insurrection, and therewith a legal cover for it. The sections, as is well known, rose in support of their position at the signal of the fire gong with arms in their hands.

The traits of similarity in these two revolutions separated by an interval of 125 years, are by no means accidental. Both insurrections took place, not at the beginning of a revolution, but in its second stage, a fact which made them politically far more conscious and deliberate. In both cases the revolutionary crisis had reached a high stage of maturity; the masses were well aware of the irrevocableness and close approach of the uprising. The demand for unity of action forced them to concentrate their attention upon a definite "legal" date as the focus of the approaching events. The leaders subordinated themselves to this logic of the mass movement. When already in command of the political situation, with the victory already almost in their hands, they adopted what seemed to be a defensive position: Provoking a weakened enemy, they laid upon him in advance the responsibility for the approaching conflict. It is in this way that insurrection takes place at a "date appointed in advance."

These assertions of Stalin, so striking in their inappropriateness— a number of them have been cited in the preceding chapters—show how little he has thought over the events of 1917 in their inner connection, and what summary traces they have left in his memory. How shall we explain this? It is well known that people make history without understanding its laws, just as they digest food without understanding the physiology of digestion. But it would seem that this ought not to apply to political leaders—above all to leaders of a party acting on a program grounded in science. However, it is a fact that many revolutionists, having taken part in a revolution in prominent positions, reveal very soon after an inability to comprehend the inner meaning of the thing which happened with their direct participation. The extraordinarily abundant literature of epigonism gives the impression that these colossal events roll over human brains and crush them as a steam roller would crush arms and legs. To a certain degree this is true; an excessive psychical tension does quickly consume people. Another circumstance, however, is far more important. A victorious revolution radically changes the situation of yesterday's revolutionists. It lulls their scientific curiosity, reconciles them to rubber-stamp phrases, moves them to estimate past days under the influence of the new interests. Thus a web of bureaucratic legend more and more thickly obliterates the real configuration of events.

In 1924 the author of this book, in his work entitled *Lessons of October,* tried to explain why Lenin in leading the party to insurrection was compelled to struggle so violently against the right wing represented by Zinoviev and Kamenev. Stalin objected to this: "Were there disagreements at that time in our party? Yes, there were. But these were exclusively practical in character, notwithstanding the assertions of Trotsky, who is trying to discover a 'right' and 'left' wing of the party . . ." "Trotsky asserts that in the person of Kamenev and Zinoviev we had in October a right wing of our party. . . . How did it happen that the disagreement with Kamenev and Zinoviev lasted only a few days? . . . There was no split and the disagreements lasted only a few days because, and only because, we had in the person of Kamenev and Zinoviev Leninist-Bolsheviks." Did not Stalin in exactly the same way seven years earlier—five days before the insurrection—accuse Lenin of excessive sharpness, and assert that Zinoviev and Kamenev stood upon the common ground of "Bolshevism"? Throughout all Stalin's zig-zags there is a certain thread of consistency, resulting not from a thought-out philosophy but from the general mould of his character. Seven years after the revolution, just as on the eve of the insurrection he conceives the depth of the disagreements in the party in the same vague way.

The touchstone of a revolutionary political leader is the question of the state. In their letter against the insurrection of October 11th, Zinoviev and Kamenev wrote: "With correct tactics we can win a third, yes and more than a third, of the seats in the Constituent Assembly. . . .

The Constituent Assembly plus the Soviet, that is the combined type of state institution toward which we are traveling." The "correct tactics" meant a renunciation of the conquest of power by the proletariat. The "combined type" of state meant a combination of the Constituent Assembly, in which the bourgeois parties would constitute two-thirds, with the soviets, where the party of the proletariat was in command. This type of combined state subsequently formed the basis of Hilferding's idea of including the soviets in the Weimar constitution. General von Linsingen, commandant of the Mark of Brandenburg, in forbidding the formation of soviets on November 7, 1918, on the ground that "institutions of this kind conflict with the existing state order," showed at least a great deal more penetration than the Austro-Marxists and the German Independent Party.

Lenin gave warning in April that the Constituent Assembly would sink into a subordinate place. However, neither he himself nor the party as a whole ever during the year 1917 formally renounced the idea of democratic representation, it being impossible to declare confidently in advance how far the revolution would go. It was assumed that having seized the power, the soviets would succeed soon enough in winning the army and the peasants so that the Constituent Assembly—especially after a broadening of the electorate (Lenin proposed in particular to lower the voting age to 18)—would give a majority to the Bolsheviks, and merely supply a formal sanction to the soviet régime. In this sense Lenin sometimes spoke of a "combined type" of state—that is, of an accommodation of the Constituent Assembly to the soviet dictatorship. The thing actually developed along different lines. In spite of Lenin's insistence, the Central Committee could not make up its mind after the conquest of power to postpone for a few weeks the call for the Constituent Assembly—although without this it was impossible either to broaden the electorate or, what is most important, give the peasants a chance to redefine their relation to the Social Revolutionaries and the Bolsheviks. The Constituent Assembly came into conflict with the Soviet and was dissolved. The hostile camps represented in the Constituent Assembly entered upon a civil war which lasted for years. In the system of soviet dictatorship not even a secondary place was found for democratic representation. The question of the "combined type" was withdrawn in fact. Theoretically, however, it retained all its importance, as was subsequently proven by the experiment of the Independent Party in Germany.

In 1924 when Stalin, obedient to the demands of an inner-party struggle, first attempted to make an independent appraisal of the past, he came to the defense of Zinoviev's "combined state," supporting himself in this with a reference to Lenin. "Trotsky does not understand . . . the peculiarities of Bolshevik tactics when he snorts at the theory of a combination of the Constituent Assembly with the soviets as Hilferdingism," wrote Stalin in his characteristic manner. "Zinoviev, whom Trotsky is ready to turn into a Hilferdingist, wholly and completely shares the point of view of Lenin." This means that seven years after the theoretical and political battles of 1917, Stalin had completely failed to understand that with Zinoviev as with Hilferding it was a question of bringing into accord and reconciling the powers of two classes, the bourgeoisie through the Constituent Assembly and the proletariat through the soviets, whereas with Lenin it was a question of combining two institutions expressing the power of one and the same class, the proletariat. The idea of Zinoviev, as Lenin explained at the time, was opposed to the very foundation of the Marxian teaching about the state. "With the power in the hands of the soviets," wrote Lenin against Zinoviev and Kamenev on October 17th, "the 'combined type' would be accepted by everybody. But to drag in under the title 'combined type' a refusal to transfer the power to the soviets . . . is it possible to find a parliamentary expression for that?" We see, then, that in order to evaluate this idea of Zinoviev, which Stalin declares to be "a peculiarity of Bolshevik tactics" supposedly not understood by Trotsky, Lenin found it difficult even to find a parliamentary expression, although he was not distinguished by an excessive squeamishness in these matters. A little over a year later Lenin wrote, applying the same thought to Germany: "The attempt to combine the dictatorship of the bourgeoisie with the dictatorship of the proletariat is a complete renunciation both of Marxism and of socialism in general." Could Lenin indeed have written otherwise?

The "combined type" of Zinoviev was essentially an attempt to eternalize the dual power—that is, a revival of the experiment completely exhausted by the Mensheviks. And if Stalin in 1924 was still standing on the same ground with Zinoviev on this question, it means that in spite of his adherence to the theses of Lenin, he has nevertheless remained at least half-way true to that philosophy of dual power which he himself developed in his report of March 29, 1917: "The rôles have been divided. The Soviet has in fact taken the initiative in the revolutionary transformation. . . . The Provisional Government has in fact taken the rôle of fortifier of the conquests of the revolutionary people." The mutual relations between the bourgeoisie and the proletariat are here defined as a simple division of labor.

During the last week before the insurrection Stalin was obviously maneuvering between Lenin, Trotsky and Sverdlov, on the one hand, and Kamenev and Zinoviev on the other. That editorial declaration of the 20th which defended the opponents of insurrection against Lenin's blows, could not—especially from the pen of Stalin—have been accidental. In questions of intra-party maneuvering he was a past master. Just as in April, after Lenin's arrival, Stalin cautiously pushed Kamenev forward, and himself waited on the sidelines in silence before again joining battle, so now on the eve of the insurrection he was obviously making ready, in case of possible failure, a retreat along the Kamenev and Zinoviev line. Stalin moved along that road up to the limit beyond which it would have entailed a break with the majority of the Central Committee. That prospect frightened him. At the session of the 21st Stalin repaired his half-destroyed bridge to the left wing of the Central Committee by moving that Lenin prepare the theses upon fundamental questions for the Congress of Soviets and that Trotsky make the political report. Both these motions were unanimously adopted. Having thus insured himself on the left, Stalin at the last moment withdrew into the shadow: he would wait. All the newest historians, beginning with Yaroslavsky, carefully steer around the fact that Stalin was not present at the session of the Central Committee in Smolny on the 24th, and did not take upon himself any function in the organization of the insurrection! Nevertheless this fact, indisputably established by the documents, characterizes better than anything else the political personality of Stalin and his methods.

Since 1924 innumerable efforts have been made to fill up the vacant space representing October in the political biography of Stalin. This has been done by means of two pseudonyms: the "Central Committee" and the "practical center." We shall not understand either the mechanics of the October leadership, or the mechanics of the latest epigone legends, unless we now approach a little more closely the personal staff of the Central Committee of that time.

Lenin, the recognized leader, authoritative for all but, as the facts show, far from a "dictator" in the party, for a period of four months had taken no direct part in the work of the Central Committee, and upon a number of tactical questions was in sharp opposition to it. The most prominent leaders in the old Bolshevik nucleus, standing at a great distance from Lenin but also from those who came after them, were Zinoviev and Kamenev. Zinoviev was in hiding as well as Lenin. Before October Zinoviev and Kamenev had come into determined opposition to Lenin and the majority of the Central Committee. That removed them both from the ranks. Of the old Bolsheviks, Sverdlov had come swiftly to the front, but he was then still a newcomer in the Central Committee. His organizing talent developed fully only later during the years of the construction of the soviet state. Dzerzhinsky, who had recently joined the party, was distinguished by his revolutionary temperament, but made no pretense to independent political authority. Bukharin, Rykov, and Nogin were living in Moscow. Bukharin was considered a gifted but unreliable theoretician. Rykov and Nogin were opponents of the insurrection. Lomov, Bubnov and Miliutin, were hardly counted upon by anybody in deciding big questions; moreover Lomov was working in Moscow, Miliutin was on the road. Joffé and Uritzky had been closely associated in their emigré past with Trotsky, and were working in agreement with him. The young Smilga was working in Finland. This composition and inner situation of the Central Committee sufficiently explains why until Lenin's return to direct leadership the party headquarters did not play and could not play even in the slightest degree the rôle it was to assume subsequently. The minutes show that the most important questions—that about the Congress of Soviets, the garrison, the Military Revolutionary Committee—were not discussed in advance in the Central Committee and did not issue from its initiative, but arose in Smolny out of the practical activity of the Soviet, and were worked over in the circle of soviet leaders—oftenest with the participation of Sverdlov.

Stalin, generally speaking, did not show up in Smolny. The more decisive the pressure of the revolutionary masses became and the greater the scope assumed by events, the more Stalin would keep in the background, the paler would become his political thought, the weaker his initiative. It was so in 1905; it was so in the fall of 1917. The same thing has been repeated subsequently every time great historic questions have arisen on the world arena. When it became clear that the publication of the minutes of the Central Committee for 1917 only laid bare an October gap in the biography of Stalin, the bureaucratic historians created the legend of the "practical center." An explanation of this story—widely popularized during these last years—becomes a necessary element of any critical history of the October revolution.

At the conference of the Central Committee in Lesny on the 16th of October, one of the arguments against forcing the insurrection was to point out that "we have not yet even a center." At Lenin's suggestion the Central Committee decided straightway, at that hasty sitting in a back corner, to make good the lack. The minutes read: "The Central Committee organizes a military revolutionary center consisting of the

368

following members: Sverdlov, Stalin, Bubnov, Uritzky and Dzerzhinsky. This center becomes a constituent part of the revolutionary Soviet committee." This resolution, which everybody had forgotten, was first discovered in the archives in 1924. It began to be quoted as a most important historic document. Thus Yaroslavsky wrote: "This organ (and no other) guided all the organizations which took part in the insurrection (the revolutionary military units, the Red Guard)." Those words "and no other" reveal frankly enough the goal of this whole *ex post facto* construction. But Stalin has written still more frankly: "In the staff of the practical center summoned to lead the insurrection, Trotsky, strangely enough . . . was not included." In order to be in a position to develop this idea, Stalin was compelled to omit the second half of the resolution: "This center becomes a constituent part of the revolutionary Soviet committee." If you bear in mind that the Military Revolutionary Committee was headed by Trotsky, it is not hard to understand why the Central Committee was content with naming the new workers who were to help those already standing in the center of the work. Neither Stalin nor Yarovslavsky has ever explained, moreover, why the "practical center" was first remembered in 1924.

Between the 16th and 20th of October, as we have seen, the insurrection conclusively took the soviet road. The Military Revolutionary Committee from the moment of its birth had the direct leadership not only of the garrison, but of the Red Guard, which from October 13th on was subject to the Petrograd Executive Committee. No place remained for any other directing center. Neither in the minutes of the Central Committee, nor in any other material whatever relating to the second half of October, can you discover the slightest trace of the activity of this supposedly so important institution. Nobody makes a report of its labors; no tasks are allotted to it; its very name is never pronounced by anybody, although its members are present at sessions of the Central Committee, and take part in the decision of questions which ought to come directly within the competence of a "practical center."

Sveshnikov, a member of the Petrograd committee of the party, who was almost continually on communication duty in Smolny during the second half of October, must at least have known where to go for practical directions upon the problems of the insurrection. Here is what he writes: "The Military Revolutionary Committee was born: from the moment of its birth the various elements of the revolutionary activity of the proletariat acquired a guiding center." Kayurov, well known to us from the February days, tells how the Vyborg district tensely awaited the signal from Smolny: "At nightfall (of the 24th) came the answer of the Military Revolutionary Committee—prepare the Red Guard for battle." Kayurov at the moment of starting the open insurrection knew nothing of any other center. One could cite to the same effect the memoirs of Sadovsky, Podvoisky, Antonov, Mekhonoshin, Blagonravov and other direct participants in the uprising. Not one of them remembers that "practical center" which according to Yaroslavsky is supposed to have guided all the organizations. And finally even Yaroslavsky confines himself in his history to a bare statement of the creation of the center: of its activity he has not a word to say. The conclusion follows of itself: A directing center of which those who were directed know nothing, does not exist in the eyes of history.

But still more direct evidence of the fictitiousness of the "practical center" can be adduced. At a session of the Central Committee on the 20th of October, Sverdlov read a declaration of the Military Organization of the Bolsheviks, containing, as is evident from the debate, a demand that the leaders of the Military Organization be brought in when questions of the insurrection were being decided. Joffé moved that this demand be rejected: "Everybody who wants to work can join the revolutionary center under the Soviet." Trotsky offered a milder formulation of Joffé's motion: "All our organizations can join the revolutionary center and there take up in our faction all questions interesting them." The decision, which was adopted in this form, shows that there was but one revolutionary center, that affiliated with the Soviet—that is, the Military Revolutionary Committee. If any other center for leading the insurrection had existed, somebody ought at least to have remembered about its existence. But nobody remembered it—not even Sverdlov, whose name stood first on the staff of the "practical center."

The minutes of October 24th are, if possible, still more instructive upon this point. During the hours immediately preceding the seizure of the city, not only was there no talk of the "practical center" of the insurrection, but the very resolution creating it had so completely passed into oblivion in the whirlwind of the eight days intervening, that, upon a motion of Trotsky, Sverdlov, Dzerzhinsky and Bubnov, were appointed to be "at the disposal of the Military Revolutionary Committee" —those very members of the Central Committee, who, according to the decision of October 16th, should already and without this motion have become a part of the staff of the Military Revolutionary Committee. The possibility of such a misunderstanding is explained by the fact that the Central Committee, having barely emerged from its underground existence, was still in organization and methods far from the all-powerful, all-embracing chancellery of recent years. The main part of the equipment of the Central Committee was carried by Sverdlov in his side-pocket.

In those hot times no few episodic institutions were created during the last moments of a session and immediately drowned in oblivion. At the session of the Central Committee on October 7th there was created "a bureau of information on the struggle with the counter-revolution." That was the cipher-designation of the first organ created for working on the problems of the insurrection. As to its personnel the minutes read: "Three are elected from the Central Committee to the bureau: Trotsky, Sverdlov, Bubnov, and they are directed to create the bureau." Did this first "practical center" of the insurrection exist? Obviously not, since it has left no traces. The political bureau created at the session of the 10th also proved unviable and revealed itself in absolutely nothing: doubtful if it met even once. In order that the Petrograd organization of the party, the direct leader of the work in the districts, should not become separated from the Military Revolutionary Committee, Trotsky, at the suggestion of Lenin, who liked a system of double or triple insurance, was included for the critical week in the highest administrative organ of the Petrograd committee. However, this decision also remained only a paper one: never one session was held with Trotsky present. The so-called "practical center" met the same fate. As an independent institution it was never intended to exist, but it did not exist even as an auxiliary organ.

Of the five men appointed to the staff of the "center," Dzershinsky and Uritzky entered completely into the work of the Military Revolutionary Committee only after the overturn. Sverdlov played an immense rôle in connecting the Military Revolutionary Committee with the party. Stalin took no part at all in the work of the Military Revolutionary Committee and never appeared at its meetings. In the innumerable documents and testimonies of witnesses and participants, as also in the most recent memoirs, Stalin's name is not once to be met with.

In the official compendium of the history of the revolution a special volume is devoted to October, grouping, on the basis of days, all the factual information from newspapers, minutes, archives, memoirs of participants, etc. Notwithstanding that this compendium was published in 1925, when the revision of the past was already in full swing, the index at the back of the book accompanies Stalin's name with only one number, and when we open the book at the corresponding page we find again this same text of the decision of the Central Committee about the "practical center," with the mention of Stalin as one of its five members. We should seek in vain in that volume—crowded as it is with even third class materials—for any information as to just what work Stalin did in October, whether on the stage of the "center" or off it.

To define the political physiognomy of Stalin in one word, he was always a "centrist" in Bolshevism. That is, he tended organically to occupy an intermediate position between Marxism and opportunism. But this was a centrist who feared Lenin. Any fragment of Stalin's orbit up to 1924 can always be explained as a product of two forces: his own centrist character and the revolutionary pressure of Lenin. The worthlessness of centrism should reveal itself most fully under the test of great historic events. "Our situation is self-contradictory," said Stalin on October 20th in justification of Zinoviev and Kamenev. In reality the self-contradictory character of centrism made it impossible for Stalin to occupy any independent position in the revolution. On the other hand, those traits which paralyzed him at the great turning points of history— watchful waiting and empirical maneuvering—must necessarily assure him a genuine ascendency when the mass movement begins to ebb and the functionary comes to the front with his zeal to consolidate what has been attained—that is, primarily to insure his own position against new disturbances. The functionary, ruling in the name of a revolution, has need of revolutionary prestige. In his capacity as an "old Bolshevik," Stalin proved the most suitable incarnation of this prestige imaginable. In crowding out the masses the collective functionary says to them: "It is we who did this for you." He begins to take a free hand not only with the present, but also with the past. The functionary-historian makes over history, repairs biographies, creates reputations. It was necessary to bureaucratize the revolution before Stalin could become its crown.

In the personal destiny of Stalin, which has outstanding interest for a Marxian analysis, we have a new refraction of the law of all revolutions: the development of a régime created by an uprising inevitably passes through periods of ebb and flow measured by years, and in this process the periods of moral reaction bring to the front those figures who by reason of all their fundamental qualities did not play, and could not play, a leading rôle in the times of the revolutionary offensive.

The bureaucratic revision of the history of the party and the revolution is taking place under Stalin's direct supervision. The sign-posts of this work clearly mark off the stages in the development of the soviet machine. On the 6th of November 1918 (new style), Stalin wrote in an anniversary article in *Pravda:* "The inspirer of the revolution from beginning to end was the Central Committee of the party headed by Comrade Lenin. Vladimir Ilych was then living in Petrograd in a conspirative apartment in the Vyborg district. On the evening of October

24th he was summoned to Smolny for the general leadership of the movement. All the work of practical organization of the insurrection was
conducted under the immediate leadership of the president of the Petrograd Soviet, Comrade Trotsky. It is possible to declare with certainty
that the swift passing of the garrison to the side of the Soviet, and the
skilful direction of the work of the Military Revolutionary Committee,
the party owes principally and first of all to Comrade Trotsky. Comrades
Antonov and Podvoisky were Comrade Trotsky's chief assistants."

Neither the author of this book nor, we must imagine, Lenin, who
was recovering from a Social Revolutionary bullet, gave attention in
those days to this retrospective distribution of rôles and merits. The article stood forth in a new light only some years later when it revealed
the fact that Stalin had already, in those difficult autumn months of
1918, been preparing, still with extraordinary caution, a new picture
of the party leadership in October. "The inspirer of the revolution from
beginning to end was the Central Committee of the party headed by
Comrade Lenin." That phrase is a polemic against those who considered
—and quite rightly—that the real inspirer of the insurrection was Lenin,
acting to a considerable degree in conflict with the Central Committee.
At that period Stalin was still unable to conceal his own October waverings otherwise than under the impersonal pseudonym of the Central
Committee. His two following statements—that Lenin was living in a
conspirative apartment in Petrograd, and that he was called to Smolny
on the evening of the 24th for the general leadership of the movement—
were designed to weaken the impression prevailing in the party that the
leader of the insurrection had been Trotsky. The subsequent phrases
dedicated to Trotsky sound in the political acoustics of today like a
panegyric; in reality they were the very least that Stalin could say. They
were what he was compelled to say in order to disguise his polemical
hints. The complex construction and careful defensive coloring of this
"jubilee" article themselves convey no bad impression of the general
opinion prevailing in the party at that time.

In this article, by the way, there is absolutely no mention of the practical center. On the contrary, Stalin categorically asserts that "all the
work of practical organization of the insurrection was conducted under
the immediate leadership of . . . Trotsky." But Trotsky, we recall, was
not a member of the "practical center." We have heard, however, from
Yaroslavsky that it was "this organ (and no other) which guided all the
organizations which took part in the insurrection." The solution of this
self-contradiction is simple: In 1918 the events were still too fresh in
the minds of all, and the attempt to fish up out of the minutes that reso-

373

lution about a "center" which never existed could not have been successful.

In 1924 when much was already forgotten, Stalin explained in the following manner why Trotsky was not a member of the "practical center": "We must say that Trotsky played no special rôle in the October revolution and could not have done so." In that year Stalin flatly declared it to be the task of the historians to destroy "the legend of the special rôle of Trotsky in the October insurrection." How then does Stalin reconcile this new version with his own article of 1918? Very simply: He has forbidden anybody to quote his former article. Historians who try to steer a middle course between the Stalin of 1918 and the Stalin of 1924 are promptly expelled from the party.

There exist however more authoritative testimonies than this first anniversary article of Stalin. In the notes to the official edition of the works of Lenin, under the word *Trotsky* we read: "After the Petersburg Soviet went Bolshevik he was elected its president and in that capacity organized and led the insurrection of October 25th." Thus the "legend of the special rôle" was firmly established in the collected works of Lenin during the life of their author.

In the official reference books you can follow from year to year this process of revising the historic material. Thus in 1925, when the campaign against Trotsky was already in full swing, the official year-book, *The Communist Almanac*, could still write: "In the October revolution Trotsky took the most active and leading part. In October 1917 he was elected president of the Petrograd Revolutionary Committee which organized the armed insurrection." In the edition of 1926, in place of this there occurs a brief neutral remark: "In October 1927 was president of the Leningrad revolutionary committee." Since 1927 the Stalin school has put forward a brand-new story which has been incorporated in all the soviet text-books. Being an opponent of "socialism in one country," Trotsky must have been essentially an opponent of the October revolution, but by good luck there existed the "practical center" which carried the thing through to a happy ending! The ingenious historian has only neglected to explain why the Bolshevik Soviet elected Trotsky president, and why the same Soviet, guided by the party, placed Trotsky at the head of the Military Revolutionary Committee.

Lenin was not credulous—especially in matters which involved the fate of the revolution. You could never set him at rest with verbal assurances. At a distance he was inclined to interpret every symptom in a bad sense. He finally believed that the thing was being rightly conducted when he saw it with his own eyes—that is, when he arrived is

Smolny. Trotsky tells about this in his recollections published in 1924: "I remember the enormous impression it made upon Lenin when he learned that I had called out a company of the Litovsky regiment with a written order to guarantee the publication of our party and soviet papers. . . . Lenin was in rapture, and expressed his feeling in exclamations, laughter, and rubbing of his hands. Afterward he became more silent, reflected a moment and said: 'Well, well—it can be done that way too. Just take the power.' I understood that only at that moment had he finally become reconciled to the fact that we had refused to seize the power by way of a conspirative plot. Up to the last hour he was fearing that the enemy would cut off our road and catch us unaware. Only now . . . did he feel at rest and finally sanction the course which events were taking."

This story too was subsequently disputed. Nevertheless it has indestructible support in the objective situation. On the evening of the 24th Lenin experienced a last gust of alarm, which seized him with such force that he made a belated attempt to mobilize the soldiers and workers for pressure upon Smolny. How violently his mood must have changed when in Smolny a few hours later he found out the actual situation! Is it not obvious that he could not help marking the end of his anxiety, his direct and indirect reproaches addressed to Smolny, at least with a few phrases, a few words? There was no need of complicated explanations. To each of the two meeting face to face in that not altogether ordinary moment, the sources of the misunderstanding were perfectly understandable. And now they were dissolved. No use returning to them. One phrase was enough: "It can be done that way!" That meant: "Maybe I sometimes went too far in urgency and suspicion, but I guess you understand. . . ." Who wouldn't understand! Lenin was not inclined to sentimentality. One phrase from him, "It can be done that way," with a special kind of smile, was plenty enough to set aside the incidental misunderstandings of yesterday and firmly tie the knots of confidence.

Lenin's mood on the 25th reveals itself with utter clarity in the resolution introduced by him through Volodarsky, in which the insurrection is described as "in rare degree bloodless and in rare degree successful." The fact that Lenin took upon himself this appraisal of the insurrection, scanty in words as always with him, but very high in substance, was not an accident. It was just he himself, the author of "advice from the sidelines," whom he considered most free to pay a tribute not only to the heroism of the masses, but to the services of the leaders. It is hardly possible to doubt that Lenin had additional psychological motives for this. He had continually feared the too slow course taken by Smolny, and he hastened now to be the first to recognize its advantages as revealed in action.

From the moment Lenin appeared in Smolny he naturally took his place at the head of all the work, political, organizational, and technical. On the 29th an insurrection of junkers took place in Petrograd. Kerensky was moving against Petrograd at the head of a number of Cossack squadrons. The Military Revolutionary Committee was confronted with a task of defense. Lenin guided this work. In his recollections Trotsky writes: "A swift success is as disarming as a defeat. Never to lose sight of the underlying thread of events; after each success to say to yourself, 'Nothing is yet attained, nothing is yet assured'; five minutes before a decisive victory to carry on with the same vigilance, the same energy and the same high pressure, as five minutes before the beginning of an armed action; five minutes after the victory, and before the first triumphant cries have died away, to say to yourself, 'The conquest is not yet assured, we must not lose a minute'—such was the approach, such was the manner of action, such the method of Lenin, such the organic substance of his political character, his revolutionary spirit."

The above mentioned session of the Petrograd committee on November 1st, where Lenin spoke of his unjustified fears in regard to the Mezhrayontzi, was devoted to the question of a coalition government with the Mensheviks and Social Revolutionaries. The right wing, Zinoviev, Kamenev, Rykov, Lunacharsky, Riazanov, Miliutin and others insisted upon a coalition after the victory. Lenin and Trotsky spoke decisively against any coalition which should extend beyond the frame of the Second Congress of Soviets. "The disagreements," declared Trotsky "were pretty deep before the insurrection—in the Central Committee and wide circles of our party. . . . The same thing was said then as now after the victorious insurrection! We will have, you see, no technical machinery. The colors were laid on thick then in order to frighten us, just as they are now, in order to prevent our making use of the victory." Hand in hand with Lenin, Trotsky waged against the partisans of coalition the same struggle which he had waged before against the opponents of insurrection. Lenin said at that same session: "An accord? I can't talk about it seriously. Trotsky long ago said that a union was impossible. Trotsky understood this, and since that time there has been no better Bolshevik."

Among the more important conditions of an accord the Social Revolutionaries and Mensheviks put forward a demand for the removal from the government of the two figures most hateful to them—"those primarily guilty of the October insurrection, Lenin and Trotsky." The attitude of the Central Committee and the party to this demand was such that Kamenev, the extreme partisan of an accord—personally ready even for this concession—considered it necessary to declare at the session of the Central Executive Committee of November 2nd: "It is proposed to exclude Lenin and Trotsky; that proposal would behead our party, and we do not accept it."

The revolutionary point of view—for insurrection and against coalition with the Compromisers—was called in the workers' districts "the point of view of Lenin and Trotsky." These words, as documents and minutes testify, became an every day expression. At the moment of crisis within the Central Committee a large conference of women workers in Petrograd unanimously adopted a resolution hailing "the policy of the Central Committee of our party, led by Lenin and Trotsky." As early as November 1917 Baron Budberg writes in his diary of "The new duumvirs, Lenin and Trotsky." When in December a group of Social Revolutionaries decided to "cut off the head of the Bolsheviks," "it was clear to them," according to Boris Sokolov, one of the conspirators, that "the most pernicious and important Bolsheviks are Lenin and Trotsky—it is with them we must begin." During the years of the civil war those two names were always spoken inseparably, as though they were one person. Parvus, once a revolutionary Marxist and afterward a malicious enemy of the October revolution, wrote in 1919: "Lenin and Trotsky—that is a collective name for all those who out of idealism have taken the Bolshevik road. . . ." Rosa Luxemburg, who severely criticized the policy of the October revolution, applied her criticism alike to Lenin and Trotsky. She wrote: "Lenin and Trotsky with their friends were the *first* to give an example to the world proletariat. And they still remain the *only* ones who can exclaim with Hutten: *I dared this!*" In October 1918 at the triumphal session of the Central Executive Committee Lenin read a quotation from the foreign bourgeois press. "The Italian workers," he said, "are acting as though they would let nobody but Lenin and Trotsky travel in Italy." Such testimonies are innumerable. They recur as a leit motif throughout the first years of the soviet regime and the Communist International. Participants and observers, friends and enemies, those near and those far away, have tied together the activities of Lenin and Trotsky in the October revolution with so firm a knot that the epigone historians will not succeed either in untying it or chopping it apart.

APPENDIX TWO

SOCIALISM IN A SEPARATE COUNTRY?

"THE industrially more developed country shows the less developed only the image of its own future." This statement of Marx, which takes its departure methodologically not from world economy as a whole but from the single capitalist country as a type, has become less applicable in proportion as capitalist evolution has embraced all countries regardless of their previous fate and industrial level. England in her day revealed the future of France, considerably less of Germany, but not in the least of Russia and not of India. The Russian Mensheviks, however, took this conditional statement of Marx unconditionally. Backward Russia, they said, ought not to rush ahead, but humbly to follow the prepared models. To this kind of "Marxism" the liberals also agreed.

Another no less popular formula of Marx— "No social formation disappears before all the productive forces have developed for which it has room"—takes its departure, on the contrary, not from the country taken separately, but from the sequence of universal social structures (slavery, medievalism, capitalism). The Mensheviks however, taking this statement from the point of view of the single state, drew the conclusion that Russian capitalism has still a long road to travel before it will reach the European or American level. But productive forces do not develop in a vacuum! You cannot talk of the possibilities of a national capitalism, and ignore on the one hand the class-struggle developing out of it, or on the other its dependence upon world conditions. The overthrow of the bourgeoisie by the proletariat grew out of actual Russian capitalism, thereby reducing to nothing its abstract economic possibilities. The structure of industry, and also the character of the class-struggle in Russia were determined to a decisive degree by international conditions. Capitalism had reached a point on the world arena where it ceased to justify its costs of production—understanding these not in the commercial but the sociological sense. Tariffs, militarism, crises, wars, diplomatic conferences and other scourges, swallow up and squander so much creative energy that in spite of all achievements in technique there remains no room for the further growth of prosperity and culture.

378

The superficially paradoxical fact that the first victim to suffer for the sins of the world-system was the bourgeoisie of a backward country, is in reality quite according to the laws of things. Marx had already indicated its explanation for his epoch: "Violent outbursts take place sooner in the extremities of the bourgeois organism than the heart, because here regulation is more possible." Under the monstrous burdens of imperialism that state must necessarily fall first which has not yet accumulated a large national capital, but to which world competition offers no special privileges. The collapse of Russian capitalism was a local avalanche in a universal social formation. "A correct appraisal of our revolution," said Lenin, "is possible only from an international point of view."

We have attributed the October revolution in the last analysis not to the fact of Russia's backwardness, but to the law of combined development. The historical dialectic knows neither naked backwardness nor chemically pure progressiveness. It is all a question of concrete correlations. The present-day history of mankind is full of "parodoxes," not so colossal as the arising of a proletarian dictatorship in a backward country, but of similar historic type. The fact that the students and workers of backward China are eagerly assimilating the doctrine of materialism, while the labor leaders of civilized England believe in the magic potency of churchly incantations, proves beyond a doubt that in certain spheres China has outstripped England. But the contempt of the Chinese workers for the medieval dull-wittedness of Macdonald, does not permit the inference that in her general development China is higher than Great Britain. The economic and cultural superiority of the latter can be expressed in exact figures. The impressiveness of these figures does not however, preclude the possibility that the workers of China may win the power before the workers of Great Britain. A dictatorship of the Chinese proletariat in its turn will be far from entailing the building of socialism within the boundaries of the Great Chinese Wall. Scholastic, pedantically single-track, or too short national criteria are no good in our epoch. World development forced Russia out of her backwardness and her Asiaticness. Outside the web of this development, her further destiny cannot be understood.

The bourgeois revolutions were directed in similar degree against feudal property relations and against the particularism of the provinces. Nationalism stood beside liberalism on their liberating banners. Western humanity long ago wore out such baby-shoes. The productive forces of our time have outgrown not only the bourgeois forms of property, but also the boundaries of national states. Liberalism and nationalism have become in like degree fetters upon world economy. The proletarian revolution is directed both against private property in the means of production and against the national splitting-up of world economy. The struggle of the eastern peoples for independence is included in this world process and will subsequently merge with it. The creation of a national socialist society, if such a goal were in a general way attainable, would mean an extreme reduction of the economic power of men. But for that very reason it is unattainable. Internationalism is not an abstract principle but the expression of an economic fact. Just as liberalism was national, so socialism is international. Starting from the world-wide division of labor, the task of socialism is to carry the international exchange of goods and services to its highest development.

No revolution has ever anywhere wholly coincided with the conceptions of it formed by its participants, nor could it do so. Nevertheless the ideas and aims of those engaged in the struggle form a very important constituent element of a revolution. This is especially true of the October revolution, for never in all the past have the conceptions of a revolution in the minds of revolutionists approached so closely to the actual essence of the events as in 1917.

A work on the October revolution would remain unfinished if it did not answer with all possible historic accuracy the question: how did the party in the very heat of the events represent to itself the further development of the revolution, and what did the party expect from it? This question acquires a greater significance, the more past days become darkened by the play of new interests. Policies are always seeking support in the past, and if they do not get it as a voluntary offering they not infrequently undertake to extract it by force. The present official policy of the Soviet Union rests upon the theory of "socialism in a separate country" as the alleged traditional viewpoint of the Bolshevik party. The younger generations, not only of the Communist International, but indeed of all other parties, are being brought up in the conviction that the soviet power was won in the name of the creation of an independent socialist society in Russia. Historic reality has nothing in common with this myth. Up to 1917 the party never admitted even the idea that the proletarian revolution might be achieved in Russia before it was achieved in the west. For the first time in the April conference, under pressure of circumstances then completely laid bare, the party recognized as its task the seizure of power. Although opening a new chapter in the history of Bolshevism, this recognition had nothing in common with the perspective of an independent socialist society. On the contrary, the Bolsheviks categorically rejected as a caricature the idea imputed to them by the Mensheviks of creating a "peasant socialism" in a backward country. The dictatorship of the proletariat in Russia was for the Bolsheviks a bridge to a revolution in the west. The problem of a socialist transformation of society was proclaimed to be in its very essence international.

Only in 1924 did a change occur upon this fundamental question. It was then first proclaimed that the building of socialism is wholly realizable within the limits of the Soviet Union independently of the evolution of the rest of mankind, if only the imperialists do not overthrow the soviet power by military intervention. This new theory was immediately endowed with retroactive force. If in 1917—declared the Epigones—the party had not believed in the possibility of creating an independent socialist society in Russia, it would have had no right to take the power. In 1926 the Communist International officially condemned the non-acceptance of the theory of socialism in a separate country, extending this condemnation to the whole past, beginning with the year 1905.

Three series of ideas were thenceforth declared hostile to Bolshevism: (1) denial of the possibility of the Soviet Union's maintaining itself for an indefinite length of time in a capitalist environment (problem of military intervention); (2) denial of the possibility of its overcoming with its own power, and within its national boundaries, the contradiction between city and country (problem of economic backwardness and agrarian problem); (3) denial of the possibility of creating a shut-in socialist society (problem of the world-wide division of labor). It will be possible, according to the new school, to defend the inviolability of the Soviet Union even without revolutions in other countries by way of the "neutralization of the bourgeoisie." The collaboration of the peasantry in the sphere of socialist construction must be acknowledged as assured. Dependence upon world economy has been liquidated by the October revolution and the economic successes of the soviets. A refusal to accept these three propositions is "Trotskyism" —a doctrine incompatible with Bolshevism.

The task of the historian here becomes one of ideological restoration. He must dig out the genuine views and aims of the revolutionary party from under subsequent political accumulations. Despite the briefness of the periods succeeding each other, this task is very much like the deciphering of a palimpsest, for the constructions of the epigone school are by no means always superior to those theological ingenuities for whose sake the monks of the seventh and eighth centuries destroyed the parchment and papyrus of the classics.

In general throughout this book we have avoided burdening the text with innumerable quotations, but the present essay, owing to the essence of its task, will have to supply the reader with the genuine texts, and that too on a sufficient scale to exclude the very idea of their having been artificially selected. We must let Bolshevism speak with its own tongue. Under the régime of the Stalin bureaucracy it is deprived of this possibility.

The Bolshevik party was from the day of its birth a party of revolutionary socialism. But it necessarily saw its immediatehistoric task in the overthrow of tzarism and the inauguration of a democratic structure. The principal content of the revolution was to be a democratic solution of the agrarian problem. The socialist revolution was pushed away into a sufficiently remote or at least indefinite, future. It was considered irrefutable that this revolution might take its place practically upon the order of the day only after the victory of the proletariat in the west. This postulate, forged by Russian Marxism in its struggle with Narodnikism and anarchism, was one of the solidest possessions of the party. There followed certain hypothetical considerations: In case the democratic revolution assumes a mighty scope in Russia, it may give a direct impetus to the socialist revolution in the west, and this will enable the Russian proletariat to come to power afterward with a swifter pace. The general historic perspective remained unchanged even in this more favorable version. The course of development was only accelerated and the dates brought near.

It was in the spirit of these views that Lenin wrote in September 1905: "From the democratic revolution we will immediately begin to pass over, and in the exact measure of our strength, the strength of a conscious and organized proletariat, we will begin to pass over to the socialist revolution. We stand for a continuous revolution. We will not stop half-way." This quotation, surprising as it may be, has been employed by Stalin in order to identify the old prognosis of the party with the actual course of events in 1917. It only remains incomprehensible why the cadres of the party were taken unawares by the "April theses" of Lenin.

In reality the struggle of the proletariat for power was to develop—according to the old conception—only after the agrarian problem had been solved within the frame-work of a bourgeois-democratic revolution. The trouble was that the peasantry, satisfied in their land hunger, would have no impulse to support a new revolution. And since the Russian working class, being an obvious minority in the country, would not be able to win the power with its own forces, Lenin quite consistently considered it impossible to talk of a dictatorship of the proletariat in Russia before the victory of the proletariat in the west.

"The complete victory of the present revolution," wrote Lenin in 1905, "will be the end of the democratic overturn and the beginning of a decisive struggle for the socialist revolution. A realization of the demands of the contemporary peasantry, the complete shattering of the reaction, the winning of a democratic republic, will be the complete end of the revolutionism of the bourgeoisie, and even of the petty bourgeoisie.—It will be the beginning of the real struggle of the proletariat for socialism." By petty bourgeoisie is here meant primarily the peasantry.

Under these conditions whence arises the slogan "continuous" revolution? Lenin answered as follows: The Russian revolutionists, standing on the shoulders of a whole series of revolutionary generations in Europe have the right to "dream" that they will succeed in "achieving with a completeness never before seen the whole democratic transformation, all of our minimum program. . . . And if that succeeds— then . . . then the revolutionary conflagration will set fire to Europe. . . . The European worker will rise in his turn and show us 'how it is done'; then the revolutionary rising of Europe will have a retroactive effect upon Russia and the epoch of several revolutionary years will become an epoch of several revolutionary decades." The independent content of the Russian revolution, even in its highest development, does not transcend the boundaries of a bourgeois-democratic revolution. Only a victorious revolution in the west can open the era of the struggle for power even for the Russian proletariat. That conception was fully in force in the party up to April 1917.

If you throw aside episodic accumulations, polemical exaggerations and individual mistakes, the essence of the dispute about the question of permanent revolution from 1905 till 1917 reduces itself, not to the question whether the Russian proletariat after winning the power could build a national socialist society—about this not one Russian Marxist ever uttered a peep until 1924—but to the question whether a bourgeois revolution really capable of solving the agrarian problem was still possible in Russia, or whether for the accomplishment of this work a dictatorship of the proletariat would be needed.

What part of his earlier views did Lenin revise in his April theses? He did not for a moment renounce either the doctrine of the international character of the socialist revolution, or the idea that the transfer to the socialist road could be realized in backward Russia only with the direct co-operation of the west. But Lenin did here for the first time declare that the Russian proletariat, owing to the very backwardness of the national conditions, might come to power before the proletariat of the advanced countries.

The February revolution proved powerless to solve either the agrarian problem or the national problem. The peasantry and the oppressed peoples of Russia in their struggle for democratic goals were obliged to support the October revolution. Only because the Russian petty-bourgeois democracy was unable to carry out that historic work performed by its older sister in the west, did the Russian proletariat gain access to the power before the western proletariat. In 1905, Bolshevism intended only after the achievement of the democratic tasks to pass over to the struggle for a dictatorship of the proletariat. In 1917 the dictatorship of the proletariat grew out of the non-achievement of the democratic tasks.

But the combined character of the Russian revolution did not stop there. The conquest of power by the working class automatically removed the dividing line between "program-minimum" and "program-maximum." Under the dictatorship of the proletariat—but only there! —the growing over of democratic into socialist problems became inevitable, notwithstanding that the workers of Europe had not yet succeeded in showing us "how it is done."

This change of revolutionary order between west and east, with all its importance for the fate of Russia and the whole world, has nevertheless a historically limited import. No matter how far the Russian revolution skipped ahead, its dependence upon the world revolution has not disappeared nor even decreased. The possibility of a growth of democratic into socialist reforms, is directly created by a combination of domestic conditions—chief among them the interrelation of the proletariat and the peasantry. But in the last instance the limits of socialist transformation are determined by the condition of economy and politics on the world arena. No matter how great the national spurt, it does not make possible a jump over the planet.

In its condemnation of "Trotskyism," the Communist International has attacked with special force the opinion that the Russian proletariat, having come to the helm and not meeting support from the west, "will come into hostile conflicts . . . with the broad masses of the peasantry with whose co-operation it came to power. . . ." Even if you consider that the historic experiment has completely refuted this prognosis—formulated by Trotsky in 1905, when not one of his present critics even admitted the idea of a dictatorship of the proletariat in Russia—even in that case, it remains an indisputable fact that this view of the peasantry as an unreliable and treacherous ally was a common property of all Russian Marxists including Lenin. The actual tradition of Bolshevism has nothing in common with the doctrine of a predetermined harmony of interest between workers and peasants. On the contrary the criticism of this petty-bourgeois theory was always a most important element in the long struggle of the Marxists with the Narodniks.

"Once the epoch of democratic revolution in Russia is past," wrote Lenin in 1905, "then it will be ridiculous even to talk of the 'united will' of proletariat and peasantry. . . ." "The peasantry, as a land-owning class will play the same treacherous, unstable rôle in this struggle (for socialism) that the bourgeoisie is now playing in the struggle for democracy. To forget that is to forget socialism, to deceive oneself and others about the genuine interests and tasks of the proletariat."

In working out for his own use in 1905 a scheme of the correlation of classes during the course of the revolution, Lenin characterized in the following words the situation which must be formed after the liquidation of landlord proprietorship: "The proletariat is already struggling to preserve the democratic conquests for the sake of the socialist revolution. This struggle would be almost hopeless for the Russian proletariat alone, and its defeat would be inevitable . . . if the European socialist proletariat did not come to the help of the Russian proletariat. . . . At that stage the liberal bourgeoisie and the well-to-do (plus a part of the middle) peasantry will organize a counter-revolution. The Russian proletariat plus the European proletariat will organize the revolution. In these circumstances the Russian proletariat may win a second victory. The cause is then not lost. The second victory will be the socialist revolution in Europe. The European workers will show us 'how it is done.' "

During approximately the same days Trotsky wrote: "The contradiction in the situation of a workers' government in a backward country with the peasant population an overwhelming majority can find its solution only on an international scale, in the arena of the world revolution of the proletariat." It is these words that Stalin subsequently quoted in order to show "the vast gulf separating the Leninist theory of the dictatorship of the proletariat from the theory of Trotsky." The quotations testify however that, in spite of indubitable differences between the revolutionary conceptions of Lenin and Trotsky at that time, it was exactly upon the question of the "unstable" and "treacherous" rôle of the peasantry that their views already in those far days essentially coincided.

In February 1906 Lenin writes: "We support the peasant movement to the end, but we ought to remember that this is the movement of another class, not that class which can and will achieve the socialist revolution." "The Russian revolution," he declares in April 1906, "has enough forces of its own to conquer. But it has not enough forces to retain the fruit of its victory . . . for in a country with an enormous development of small-scale industry, the small-scale commodity producers, among them the peasants, will inevitably turn against the proletarian when he goes from freedom toward socialism. . . . In order to prevent a restoration, the Russian revolution has need, not of a Russian reserve; it has need of help from outside. Is there such a reserve in the world? There is: the socialist proletariat in the west."

In various combinations but fundamentally without change these thoughts are carried through all the years of the reaction and the war. There is no need to multiply examples. The party's conception of the revolution must have received its most finished and succinct form in the heat of the revolutionary events. If the theoreticians of Bolshevism were before the revolution already inclining towards "socialism in a separate country," this theory would necessarily have come to full bloom in the period of the direct struggle for power. Did it prove so in reality? The year 1917 will give the answer.

When departing for Russia after the February revolution, Lenin wrote in a farewell letter to the Swiss workers: "The Russian proletariat cannot with its own forces victoriously achieve the socialist revolution. But it can . . . improve the situation in which its chief, its reliable ally, the European and American socialist proletariat, will enter the decisive battle."

The resolution of Lenin ratified by the April conference reads: "The proletariat of Russia, taking action in one of the most backward countries of Europe among the masses of a petty-peasant population, cannot set itself the goal of an immediate realization of the socialist transformation." Although in these initial lines firmly clinging to the theoretical tradition of the party, the resolution does however take a decisive step on a new road. It declares: The impossibility of an independent socialist transformation in peasant Russia does not in any case give us the right to renounce the conquest of power, not only for the sake of democratic tasks, but also in the name of "a series of practically ripened steps towards socialism," such as the nationalization of land, control over the banks and so forth. Anti-capitalist measures may receive a further development thanks to the presence of "the objective premises of a socialist revolution . . . in the more highly developed of the advanced countries." This must be our starting point. "To talk only of Russian conditions," explains Lenin in his speech, "is a mistake. . . . What tasks will rise before the Russian proletariat in case the world-wide movement brings us face to face with a social revolution—that is the principal question taken up in this resolution." It is clear that the new point of departure occupied by the party in April 1917, after Lenin had won his victory over the democratic limitedness of the "old Bolsheviks," is as different from the theory of socialism in a separate country as heaven is from earth!

In all organizations of the party whatever, whether in the capital or the provinces, we meet henceforth the same formulation of the question: In the struggle for power we must remember that the further fate of the revolution as a socialist revolution will be determined by the victory of the proletariat of the advanced countries. This formula was opposed by nobody—was, on the contrary, the presupposition of all disputes as a proposition equally acknowledged by all.

At the Petrograd conference of the party on July 16th, Kharitonov, one of those Bolsheviks who had come with Lenin on the "sealed train," declared: "We are saying everywhere that if there is no revolution in the west, our cause will be lost." Kharitonov is not a theoretician; he is an average party agitator. In the minutes of that same conference we read: "Pavlov calls attention to the general proposition advanced by the Bolsheviks that the Russian revolution will flourish only when it shall be supported by the world revolution, which is conceivable only as a socialist revolution." Tens and hundreds of Kharitonovs and Pavlovs were developing the fundamental idea of the April conference. It never came into the head of anybody to oppose or correct them.

The sixth Congress of the party, taking place at the end of July, defined the dictatorship of the proletariat as a conquest of power by the workers and poorest peasants. "Only these classes . . . will in reality promote the growth of the international proletarian revolution, which is to put an end not only to the war but also to capitalist slavery." The speech of Bukharin was built upon the idea that a world-wide socialist revolution is the sole way out of the existing situation. "If the revolution in Russia conquers before a revolution breaks out in the west, we will have to . . . kindle the fire of the world-wide socialist revolution." Stalin too was at that time compelled to pose the question in much the same way: "The moment will come when the workers will rise and unite round them the poor layers of the peasantry, raise the banner of the workers' revolution, and open an era of socialist revolution in the west."

A Moscow regional conference which met at the beginning of August permits us best of all to glance into the laboratory of the party thought. In the principal report, setting forth the decisions of the sixth Congress, Sokolnikov, a member of the Central Committee, said: "It is necessary to explain that the Russian revolution must take the offensive against world imperialism or be destroyed, be strangled by that same imperialism." A number of delegates expressed themselves to the same effect. Vitolin: "We must get ready for a social revolution which will be the stimulus to the development of social revolution in western Europe." Delegate Byelenky: "If you decide the question within national limits, then we have no way out. Sokolnikov has said rightly that the Russian revolution will conquer only as an international revolution. . . . In Russia the conditions are not yet ripe for socialism, but if the revolution begins in Europe then we will follow western Europe." Stukov: "The proposition that the Russian revolution will conquer only as an international revolution cannot be subject to doubt. . . . The socialist revolution is possible only on a general world scale."

All are in agreement upon three fundamental propositions: the workers' state cannot stand unless it overthrows imperialism in the west; in Russia the conditions are not yet ripe for socialism; the problem of socialist revolution is international in essence. If alongside these views, which were to be condemned in seven or eight years as heresy, there had existed in the party other views now recognized as orthodox and traditional, they would certainly have found expression in that Moscow conference, and in the congress of the party which preceded it. But neither the principal speaker nor those who took part in the debate— nor the newspaper reports—suggest by a word the presence in the party of Bolshevik views opposing these "Trotskyist" ones.

At the general city conference in Kiev preceding the party congress, the principal speaker, Gorovitz, said: "The struggle for the salvation of our revolution can be waged only on an international scale. Two prospects lie before us: If the revolution conquers, we will create the transitional state to socialism, if not, we will fall under the power of international imperialism." After the party congress, at the beginning of August, Piatakov said at a new conference in Kiev: "From the very beginning of the revolution we have asserted that the destiny of the Russian proletariat is completely dependent upon the course of the

proletarian revolution in the west. . . . We are thus entering the stage
of permanent revolution." Commenting on Piatakov's report, Gorovitz,
already known to us, declared: "I am in complete accord with Piatakov
in his definition of our revolution as permanent." Piatakov: ". . . The
sole possible salvation for the Russian revolution lies in a world revolution which will lay down the foundation for the social overturn." But
perhaps these two speakers represented a minority? No. Nobody opposed
them upon this fundamental question. In the elections for the Kiev
committee these two received the largest number of votes.

We may, then, consider it fully established that at a general party
conference in April, at the congress of the party in July, and at conferences in Petrograd, Moscow and Kiev, those very views were set forth
and confirmed by the voting, which were later to be declared incompatible with Bolshevism. More than that: not one voice was raised in
the party which might be interpreted as a presentiment of the future
theory of socialism in a separate country, even to the degree that in
the Psalms of King David foretastes have been discovered of the gospel
of Christ.

On the 13th of August, the Central Organ of the party explained:
"Full power to the soviets, although far from as yet meaning 'socialism,' would in any case break the resistance of the bourgeoisie and—
in dependence upon the existing productive forces and the situation in
the west—would guide and transform the economic life in the interests of the toiling masses. Having thrown off the fetters of capitalist
government, the revolution would become permanent—that is, continuous. It would apply the state power, not in order to consolidate
the régime of capitalist exploitation, but in order to overcome it. Its
final success on this road would depend upon the successes of the proletarian revolution in Europe. . . . Such was and remains the sole
real perspective of the further development of the revolution." The
author of this article was Trotsky, who wrote it in Kresty prison. The
editor of the paper that published it was Stalin. The significance of the
quotation is defined already in the mere fact that the term "permanent
revolution" had been used in the Bolshevik party up to 1917 exclusively to designate the point of view of Trotsky. A few years later
Stalin will declare: "Lenin struggled against the theory of permanent
revolution to the end of his days." Stalin himself at any rate did not
struggle: the article appeared without any editorial comment whatever.

Ten days later Trotsky wrote again in the same paper: "Internationalism for us is not an abstract idea . . . , but a directly guiding,
deeply practical principle. A permanent decisive success is unthinkable

for us outside the European revolution." Again Stalin did not object. Moreover two days later he himself repeated it: "Let them know (the workers and soldiers) that only in union with the workers of the west, only after shaking loose the foundations of capitalism in the west, can we count upon the triumph of the revolution in Russia!" By "the triumph of the revolution" is meant not the building of socialism— of that there was still no talk at all—but only the winning and holding of power.

"The bourgeoisie," wrote Lenin in September, "is shouting about the inevitable defeat of the commune in Russia—that is, the defeat of the proletariat if it wins the power." We must not be frightened by these shouts. "Having conquered the power, the proletariat of Russia has every chance of holding it and bringing Russia through to the victorious revolution in the west." The perspective of the revolution is here defined with utter clearness: to hold the power until the beginning of the socialist revolution in Europe. This formula was not hastily thrown out: Lenin repeats it from day to day. He sums up his program article, *Will the Bolsheviks Be Able to Hold the State Power?* in these words: "There is no power on earth which can prevent the Bolsheviks, if they do not let themselves be frightened and succeed in seizing the power, from holding it until the victory of the world-wide socialist revolution."

The right wing of the Bolsheviks demanded a coalition with the Compromisers, citing the fact that the Bolsheviks "alone" could not hold the power. Lenin answered them on November 1st—that is, after the revolution: "They say that we alone will not hold the power, etc. But we are not alone. Before us is all Europe. We must begin." In this dialogue of Lenin with the Right Wing, it becomes especially clear that the idea of the independent creation of a socialist society in Russia never even came into the head of any of the disputants.

John Reed tells how at one of the Petrograd meetings at the Obukhovsky factory a soldier from the Rumanian front shouted: "We will hold on with all our might until the peoples of the whole world rise to help us." This formula did not fall from the sky, and it was not thought up either by the nameless soldier or by Reed. It was grafted into the masses by Bolshevik agitators. The voice of the soldier from the Rumanian front was the voice of the party, the voice of the October revolution.

The "Declaration Of Rights Of The Toilers And The Exploited Peoples"—the fundamental state program introduced in the name of the soviet power into the Constituent Assembly—proclaimed the task of the new structure to be "the establishment of a socialist organisation of society and the victory of socialism in all countries. . . . The soviet power will proceed resolutely along this road until the complete victory of the international workers' insurrection against the yoke of capital." This Leninist "Declaration of Rights," not formally annulled to this day, converted the permanent revolution into a fundamental law of the Soviet Republic.

If Rosa Luxemburg, who in her prison was following with passionate and jealous attention the deeds and words of the Bolsheviks, had caught in them a shadow of national socialism, she would have sounded the alarm at once. In those days she was very sternly—in the essence mistakenly—criticizing the policies of the Bolsheviks. But no. Here is what she wrote about the general line of the party: "The fact that the Bolsheviks in their policy have steered their course entirely towards the world revolution of the proletariat, is precisely the most brilliant testimony to their political far-sightedness, their principled firmness and the bold scope of their policy."

It is just these views, which Lenin was developing from day to day, which were preached in the central organ of the party under Stalin's editorship, which inspired the speeches of agitators great and small, which were repeated by soldiers from far-off sectors of the front, which Rosa Luxemburg considered the highest testimony to the political far-sightedness of the Bolsheviks—it is just these views which the bureaucracy of the Communist International condemned in 1926. "The views of Trotsky and his followers upon the fundamental question of the character and perspectives of our revolution," says a resolution of the Seventh Plenum of the Communist International, "have nothing in common with the views of our party, with Leninism." Thus the Epigones of Bolshevism have done away with their own past.

If anybody really struggled in 1917 against the theory of permanent revolution, it was the Kadets and Compromisers. Miliukov and Dan exposed the "revolutionary illusions of Trotskyism" as the chief cause of the collapse of the revolution of 1905. In his introductory speech at the Democratic Conference, Cheidze scourged the effort "to put out the fire of the capitalist war by converting the revolution into a socialist and world revolution." On the 13th of October, Kerensky said in the Pre-Parliament: "There is now no more dangerous enemy of the revolution, the democracy and all the conquests of freedom, than those who . . . under the guise of deepening the revolution and converting it into a permanent social revolution, are perverting, and it seems have already perverted, the masses." Cheidze and Kerensky were enemies of

391

the permanent revolution for the same reason that they were enemies of the Bolsheviks.

At the second Congress of Soviets, at the moment of the seizure of power, Trotsky said: "If the people of Europe do not rise and crush imperialism, we will be crushed—that is indubitable. Either the Russian revolution will raise the whirlwind of struggle in the west, or the capitalists of all countries will strangle our revolution." "There is a third road"—shouted a voice from the benches. Was this perhaps Stalin's voice? No, it was the voice of a Menshevik. It was some years before Bolsheviks discovered that "third road."

As a result of innumerable repetitions in the international Stalinist press, it is considered in a great variety of political circles almost established that two conceptions lay at the bottom of the Brest-Litovsk disagreements. One had as its point of departure the possibility, not only of holding out, but of building socialism with the inner forces of Russia; the other rested its hope exclusively on an insurrection in Europe. In reality this contrast of views was created some years later, and its author did not take the trouble to bring his invention even into the most superficial accord with the historic documents. To be sure, this would have been no easy task. All the Bolsheviks without a single exception were at one in the Brest period in thinking that if a revolution did not break out in Europe in the very near future, the Soviet Republic was doomed to destruction. Some counted the time in weeks, others in months: nobody counted it in years.

"From the very beginning of the Russian revolution . . . ," wrote Bukharin on January 28, 1918, "the party of the revolutionary proletariat has declared: either the international revolution, unleashed by the revolution in Russia, will strangle the war and capital, or international capital will strangle the Russian revolution." But was not Bukharin, who then headed the advocates of revolutionary war with Germany, attributing the views of his faction to the whole party? However natural such a supposition may be, it is flatly contradicted by the documents.

The minutes of the Central Committee for 1917 and the beginning of 1918—published in 1929—in spite of abridgements and a tendentious editing, offer invaluable testimony upon this question too. "At the session of January 11th, 1918, comrade Sergeiev (Artem) points out that all the orators are agreed upon the fact that our socialist republic is threatened with destruction in the failure of a socialist revolution in the west." Sergeiev stood for the position of Lenin—that is, for signing the peace. Nobody contradicted Sergeiev. All three of the contending groups competed in appealing to one and the same general premise: Without a world revolution we will not pull through.

Stalin, to be sure, introduced a special note into the debate. He based the necessity of signing a separate peace upon the fact that: "There is no revolutionary movement in the west, there are no facts, there is only a potentiality, and we can't figure on potentialities." Although still far from the theory of socialism in a separate country, he nevertheless clearly revealed in these words his organic distrust of the international movement. "We cannot figure on potentialities." Lenin immediately drew aside "in certain parts" from this Stalinist support. "It is true that the revolution in the west has not yet begun," he said. "However, if in view of this we should change our tactics, then we should be traitors to international socialism." If he, Lenin, favored an immediate separate peace, it was not because he did not believe in the revolutionary movement in the west, and still less because he believed in the viability of an isolated Russian revolution: "It is important for us to hold out until the coming of a general socialist revolution, and we can achieve this only by signing the peace." The meaning of the Brest capitulation was summed up for Lenin in the words "breathing spell."

The minutes testify that after this warning from Lenin, Stalin sought an opportunity to correct himself. "Session of February 23d, 1918. Comrade Stalin: . . . We also are staking our play upon a revolution, but you are reckoning in weeks, and (we) in months." Stalin here repeats verbatim the formula of Lenin. The distance between the two wings in the Central Committee on the question of the world revolution, was the distance between weeks and months.

When defending the signing of the Brest peace at the seventh Congress of the Party in March 1918, Lenin said: "It is absolutely true that without a German revolution we will perish. We will perish perhaps not in Petersburg nor in Moscow, but in Vladivostok, or some other remote place whither we will have to retreat . . . , but in any case, under all possible or conceivable eventualities, if the German revolution does not begin, we perish." It is not only a question of Germany, however. "International imperialism . . . which represents a gigantic actual power . . . could in no case and under no conditions live side by side with the Soviet Republic. Here a conflict would be inevitable. Here . . . is the greatest historic problem, . . . the necessity of evoking an international revolution." In the secret decision adopted, we read: "The Congress sees the most reliable guarantee of the consolidation of the socialist revolution which has won the victory in

Russia only in its conversion into an international workers' revolution."

Some days later Lenin made a report to the Congress of Soviets: "World-wide imperialism and the triumphal march of a social revolution cannot live side by side." On April 23d he said at a session of the Moscow soviet: "Our backwardness has pushed us forward, and we shall perish if we cannot hold out until we meet a mighty support on the part of the insurrectionary workers of other countries." "We must retreat (before imperialism) even to the Urals," he writes in May 1918, "for that is the sole chance of winning time for the maturing of the revolution in the west. . . ."

Lenin was clearly aware of the fact that the dragging out of the negotiations at Brest would make harder the conditions of peace, but he put the revolutionary international tasks higher than the "national" ones. On June 28th, 1918, notwithstanding episodic disagreements with Trotsky on the subject of signing the peace, Lenin said at a Moscow conference of Trade-Unions: "When it came to the Brest negotiations, the exposures of Comrade Trotsky came out before the whole world, and did not this policy bring it about that in the enemy-country . . . in war time an enormous revolutionary movement broke out?" A week later in a report of the Council of Peoples Commissars to the fifth Congress of Soviets, he returns to the same question: "We fulfilled our duty before all the peoples . . . through our Brest delegation headed by Comrade Trotsky." A year later Lenin recalled: "In the epoch of the Brest peace . . . the soviet power placed the world dictatorship of the proletariat and the world revolution higher than any national sacrifices, no matter how heavy they might be."

"What meaning," asked Stalin, when time had erased from his memory the never very definite distinctions between ideas— "What meaning can Trotsky's assertion that revolutionary Russia could not stand in the face of a conservative Europe have? It can have only one meaning: Trotsky does not feel the inward might of our revolution."

In reality the whole party was unanimous in the conviction that "before the face of a conservative Europe" the Soviet Republic could not stand. But that was only the reverse side of a conviction that a conservative Europe could not stand before the face of revolutionary Russia. In negative form it expressed an inconquerable faith in the international power of the Russian revolution. And fundamentally the party was not mistaken. Conservative Europe did not at any rate wholly stand. The German revolution, even betrayed as it was by the social democracy, was still strong enough to trim the claws of Ludendorff and Hoffmann. Without this operation the Soviet Republic could hardly have avoided destruction.

But even after the destruction of German militarism, no change was made in the general appraisal of the international situation. "Our efforts will inevitably lead to a world-wide revolution," said Lenin at a session of the Central Executive Committee at the end of July, 1918. "Things stand in such a way that, having gotten out . . . of the war with one alliance, (we) immediately experienced the assault of imperialism from the other side." In August, when civil war was spreading on the Volga with the participation of the Czecho-Slovaks, Lenin said at a meeting in Moscow: "Our revolution began as a universal revolution. . . . The proletarian masses will guarantee the Soviet Republic a victory over the Czecho-Slovaks and the possibility of holding out until the world-wide socialist revolution breaks out." To hold out until the outbreak of revolution in the west—such as before is the formula of the party.

In those same days Lenin wrote to the American workers: "We are in a besieged fortress until other armies of the international socialist revolution come to our aid." He expressed himself still more categorically in November: "The facts of world history have shown that the conversion of our Russian revolution into a socialist revolution was not an adventure but a necessity, for there was no other choice. Anglo-French and American imperialism will inevitably strangle the independence and freedom of Russia unless world-wide socialist revolution, unless world-wide Bolshevism, conquers." To repeat the words of Stalin, Lenin obviously did not feel the "inner might of our revolution."

The first anniversary of the revolution is past. The party has had time to look round. And nevertheless in his report to the eighth Congress of the Party in March 1919, Lenin again declares: "We live not only in a state but in a system of states, and the existence of the Soviet Republic side by side with imperialist states for an extended period is unthinkable. In the end either one or the other will conquer." On the third anniversary, which coincided with the rout of the Whites, Lenin recalled and generalized: "If on that night (the night of the October revolution) someone had told us that in three years . . . this would be our victory, nobody, not even the most cock-sure optimist, would have believed it. We knew then that our victory would be a victory only when our cause should conquer the whole world, for we began our work counting exclusively upon world revolution." More unassailable testimony could not be asked. At the moment of the October revolution "the most cock-sure optimist" not only did not dream of creating national socialism, but did not believe in the possibility of defending the revolution without direct help from outside! "We began our work counting exclusively upon world revolution." In order to guarantee the victory in a three years' fight over legions of enemies, neither the party nor the Red Army had need of the myth of socialism in a separate country.

The world situation took a more favorable form than could have been expected. The masses revealed an extraordinary capacity for sacrifices in the name of the new goals. The leaders skilfully made use of the contradictions of imperialism during the first and most difficult period. As a result the revolution revealed more stability than "the most cock-sure optimist" had anticipated. But even so, the party wholly preserved its former international position.

"If it hadn't been for the war," Lenin explained in January, 1918, "we would have seen a union of the capitalists of the whole world, a consolidation on the basis of the struggle against us." "Why throughout weeks and months . . . after October did we get a chance to pass so easily from triumph to triumph?" he asked at the seventh Congress of the party. "Only because a specially formed international conjuncture temporarily protected us from imperialism." In April Lenin said at a session of the Central Executive Committee: "We got a breathing spell only because the imperialist war still continued in the west, and in the far east imperialist rivalry is raging wider and wider; this alone explains the existence of the Soviet Republic."

This exceptional combination of circumstances could not last forever. "We have now passed from war to peace," said Lenin in 1920. "But we have not forgotten that war will come again. So long as both capitalism and socialism remain, we cannot live in peace. Either the one or the other in the long run will conquer. There will be a funeral chant either for the Soviet Republic or for world capitalism. This is a moratorium in a war."

The transformation of the original "breathing spell" into a prolonged period of unstable equilibrium, was made possible not only by the struggle of capitalist groupings, but also by the international revolutionary movement. As a result of the November revolution in Germany the German troops were compelled to abandon the Ukraine, the Baltic States and Finland. The penetration of the spirit of revolt into the armies of the Entente compelled the French, English and American governments to withdraw their troops from the southern and northern shores of Russia. The proletarian revolution in the west was not victorious, but on its road to victory it protected the soviet state for a number of years.

In July, 1921 Lenin summarized the situation: "We have got a certain equilibrium, although extremely fragile, extremely unstable, nevertheless such an equilibrium that a socialist republic can exist—of course not for long—in a capitalist environment." Thus passing from weeks to months, from months to years, the party only by degrees assimilated the idea that a workers' state might for a certain time—"of course not for long"—peacefully continue to exist in a capitalist environment.

One not unimportant conclusion flows from the above data quite irrefutably: If according to the general conviction of the Bolsheviks the soviet state could not long hold out without a victory of the proletariat in the west, then the program of building socialism in a separate country is excluded practically by that fact alone; the very question is withdrawn, so to speak, in its preliminary consideration.

It would be, however, a complete mistake to assume, as the epigone school has attempted to suggest in recent years, that the sole obstacle seen by the party on the road to a national socialist society, was the capitalist armies. The threat of armed intervention was in reality practically advanced to the front rank, but the war danger itself was merely the most acute expression of the technical and industrial predominance of the capitalist nations. In the last analysis the problem reduced itself to the isolation of the Soviet Republic and to its backwardness.

Socialism is the organization of a planned and harmonious social production for the satisfaction of human wants. Collective ownership of the means of production is not yet socialism, but only its legal premise. The problem of a socialist society cannot be abstracted from the problem of the productive forces, which at the present stage of human development are world-wide in their very essence. The separate state, having become too narrow for capitalism, is so much the less capable of becoming the arena of a finished socialist society. The backwardness of a revolutionary country, moreover, increases for it the danger of being thrown back to capitalism. In rejecting the perspective of an isolated socialist development, the Bolsheviks had in view, not a mechanically isolated problem of intervention, but the whole complex of questions bound up with the international economic basis of socialism.

At the seventh Congress of the Party Lenin said: "If Russia passes now—and she indubitably is passing—from a 'Tilsit Peace' to a national boom . . . then the outcome of this boom is not a transition to the bourgeois state but a transition to the international socialist revolution." Such was the alternative: either an international revolution or a sliding back—to capitalism. There was no place for national socialism. "How many transitional stages there will yet be to socialism, we do not and cannot know. That depends upon when the European socialist revolution begins on a real scale."

In April of the same year, when calling for a re-formation of the ranks for practical work, Lenin wrote: "We can give serious cooperation to the socialist revolution in the west, delayed for a number of reasons, only to the degree that we succeed in solving the organizational problem which stands before us." This first approach to economic construction is immediately included in the international scheme: it is a question of "cooperation to the socialist revolution in the west," and not of creating a self-sufficient socialist kingdom in the east.

On the theme of the coming hunger, Lenin said to the Moscow workers: "In all our agitation we must . . . explain that the misfortune which has fallen upon us is an international misfortune, that there is no way out of it but the international revolution." In order to overcome the famine we must have a revolution of the world proletariat —says Lenin. In order to create a socialist society a revolution in a separate country is enough—answer the Epigones. Such is the scope of the disagreement! Who is right? Let us not forget anyway that, in spite of the successes of industrialization, hunger is not yet conquered to this day.

The Congress of the Councils of People's Economy in December, 1918 formulated the plan of socialist construction in the following words: "The dictatorship of the world-proletariat is becoming historically inevitable. . . . This is determining the development both of the whole world society and of each country in particular. The establishment of the dictatorship of the proletariat and the soviet form of government in other countries will make possible the inauguration of the most close economic relations between countries, an international division of labor in production, and finally the organization of international economic organs of administration." The fact that such a resolution could be adopted by a congress of the state bodies confronted with purely practical problems—coal, fire-wood, sugar-beets—proves better than anything else how inseparably the perspective of the permanent revolution dominated the consciousness of the party during that period.

In the *A B C of Communism*, the party text-book composed by Bukharin and Preobrazhensky, which went through a great many editions, we read: "The Communist revolution can be victorious only as a world revolution. . . . In a situation where the workers have won only in a single country, economic construction becomes very difficult. . . . For the victory of communism the victory of the world revolution is necessary."

In the spirit of these same ideas Bukharin wrote in a popular brochure reprinted many times by the party and translated into foreign languages: "There rises before the Russian proletariat sharply as never before the problem of international revolution. . . . The permanent revolution in Russia grows into a European revolution of the proletariat."

In a well-known book of Stepanov-Skvortzov, entitled *Electrification*, issued under the editorship of Lenin and with an introduction by him, in a chapter which the editor recommends with special enthusiasm to the attention of the reader, it says: "The proletariat of Russia never thought of creating an isolated socialist state. A self-sufficient 'socialist' state is a petty-bourgeois ideal. A certain approach to this is thinkable with an economic and political predominance of the petty-bourgeoisie; in isolation from the outside world it seeks a means of consolidating its economic forms, which are converted by the new technique and the new economy into very unstable forms." These admirable lines, which were undoubtedly gone over by the hand of Lenin, cast a clear beam of light upon the most recent evolution of the Epigones!

In his theses on the national and colonial questions at the second Congress of the Communist International, Lenin defines the general task of socialism, rising above the national stages of the struggle, as "the creation of a united world-wide economy, regulated according to a general plan by the proletariat of all nations, as a whole the tendency towards which is already revealed with complete clarity under capitalism, and undoubtedly will receive further development and full achievement under socialism." In relation to this heritable and progressive tendency, the idea of a socialist society in a separate country is reaction.

The conditions for the arising of a dictatorship of the proletariat and the conditions for the creation of a socialist society are not identical, not of like nature, in certain respects even antagonistic. The circumstance that the Russian proletariat first came to power by no means implies that it will first come to socialism. That contradictory unevenness of development which led to the October revolution, did not disappear with its achievement. It was laid down in the very foundation of the first workers' state.

"The more backward the country which is compelled, as a result of the zigzags of history, to begin the socialist revolution"—said Lenin in March, 1918—"the harder for it will be the transition from the old capitalist to the socialist relations." This idea finds its way through the speeches and articles of Lenin from year to year. "For us it is easy to begin a revolution and harder to continue it," he says in May of the same year. "In the west it is harder to begin a revolution but it will be easier to continue." In December Lenin developed the same thought before a peasant audience, one which finds it hardest of all to transcend national boundaries: "There (in the west) the transition to a socialist economy . . . will go faster and be achieved more easily than with us. . . . In union with the socialist proletariat of the whole world the Russian laboring peasantry . . . will overcome all handicaps." "In comparison with the advanced countries," he repeats in 1919, "it was easier for Russians to begin the great proletarian revolution, but it will be harder for them to continue it, and carry it through to decisive victory in the sense of the complete organization of a socialist society." "For Russia," Lenin again insisted on the 27th of April, 1920, ". . . it was easy to begin the socialist revolution, whereas to continue it and carry it through to the end will be harder for Russia than for the European countries. I had to point out this circumstance at the begining of 1918, and the two years' experience since then have fully confirmed this judgment."

The ages of history live in the form of different levels of culture. Time is needed to overcome the past—not new ages, but decades. "The coming generation, although more developed, will hardly make the complete transition to socialism," said Lenin at a session of the Central Executive Committee on April 29th, 1918. Almost two years later at a congress of Agricultural Communes he named a still more remote date: "We cannot now introduce a socialist order. God grant that in the time of our children, or perhaps our grand-children, it will be established here." The Russian workers took the road earlier than the rest, but they will arrive later at the goal. This is not pessimism, but historic realism.

"We, the proletariat of Russia, are in advance of any England or any Germany in our political structure . . . ," wrote Lenin in May, 1918, "and at the same time behind the most backward of west European states . . . in the degree of our preparation for the material-productive inauguration of socialism." The same thought is expressed by him in the form of a contrast between two states: "Germany and Russia incarnated in 1918 most obviously of all the material realization of the economic productive, socio-industrial conditions of socialism on the one side, and the political conditions on the other." The elements of the future society are split up, so to speak, among different countries. To collect and subordinate them one to another is the task of a series of national revolutions building into a world revolution.

The idea of the self-sufficient character of the soviet economy Lenin laughed out of court in advance: "While our Soviet Russia remains a solitary suburb of the whole capitalist world," he said in December, 1920 at the eighth Congress of Soviets, "during that time to think of our complete economic independence . . . would be an utterly ridiculous fantaseering and utopianism." On the 27th of March, 1922, at the eleventh Congress of the Party, Lenin gave warning: We are confronted with "a test which is being prepared by the Russian and international market, to which we are subordinate, with which we are bound up, from which we cannot break away. This is a serious test, for here they may beat us economically and politically."

This idea of the dependence of socialist economy upon world economy, the Communist International now considers "counter-revolutionary." Socialism cannot depend upon capitalism! The Epigones have been ingenious enough to forget that capitalism, like socialism, rests upon a world-wide division of labor which is to receive its highest development under socialism. Economic construction in an isolated workers' state, however important in itself, will remain abridged, limited, contradictory: it cannot reach the heights of a new harmonious society.

"The authentic rise of a socialist economy in Russia," wrote Trotsky in 1922, "will become possible only after the victory of the proletariat in the most important countries of Europe." These words have become an indictment; nevertheless they expressed in their time the general thought of the party. "The work of construction," said Lenin in 1919, "depends entirely upon how soon the revolution is victorious in the most important countries of Europe. Only after this victory can we seriously undertake the business of construction." Those words express not a lack of confidence in the Russian revolution, but a faith in the nearness of the world revolution. But now also, after the colossal economic successes of the Union, it remains true that the "authentic rise of a socialist economy," is possible only on an international basis.

From the same point of view the party looked upon the problem of the collectivization of agricultural industry. The proletariat cannot create a new society without bringing the peasantry to socialism through a series of transitional stages, the peasantry being a considerable—in a number of countries a predominant—part of the population, and a known majority on the earth as a whole. The solution of this most difficult of all problems depends in the last analysis upon the quantitative and qualitative correlations between industry and agriculture. The peasantry will the more voluntarily and successfully take the road of collectivization, the more generously the town is able to fertilize their economy and their culture.

Does there exist, however, enough industry for the transformation of the country? This problem, too, Lenin carried beyond the national boundaries. "If you take the question on a world scale," he said at the ninth Congress of the Soviets, "such a flourishing large-scale industry as might supply the world with all products, does exist on the earth. . . . We put that at the basis of our calculations." The correlation of industry and agriculture, incomparably less favorable in Russia than in the countries of the west, remains to this day the basis of the economic and political crises which threaten at certain moments the stability of the soviet system.

The policy of so-called "military communism"—as is clear from the above—was not based upon the idea of building a socialist society within the national boundaries. Only the Mensheviks, making fun of the soviet power, attributed such plans to it. For the Bolsheviks the further destinies of the Spartan régime imposed by the ruin and the civil war, stood in direct dependence upon the development of revolution in the west. In January, 1919, at the height of military communism, Lenin said: "We will defend the foundations of our communist food policy, and we will carry them through unshaken to the time of the complete and world-wide victory of communism." Together with the whole party Lenin was mistaken. It became necessary to change the food policy. At present we may consider it established that, even if the socialist revolution in Europe had taken place during the first two or three years after October, a retreat along the line of the New Economic Policy would have been inevitable just the same. But on a retrospective appraisal of the first stage of the dictatorship, it becomes especially clear to what a degree the methods of military communism and its illusions were closely interwoven with the perspective of permanent revolution.

The deep internal crisis at the end of the three years of civil war involved the threat of a direct break between the proletariat and the peasantry, between the party and the proletariat. A radical reconsideration of the methods of the soviet power became necessary. "We have to satisfy economically the middle peasant, and adopt freedom of trade," Lenin explained. "Otherwise it will be impossible to preserve the power of the proletariat in Russia in view of the delay of the international revolution." Was not the transition to the NEP accompanied, however, by a break in principle of the bond between domestic and international problems?

Lenin gave a general estimate of the new stage then opening in his theses for the third Congress of the Communist International: "From the point of view of the world-wide proletarian revolution as a single process, the significance of the epoch Russia is passing through lies in its practical experimental test of the policy in relation to the petty-bourgeois mass of a proletariat holding the state power." His very definition of the frame-work of the New Economic Policy, cleanly removes the question of socialism in one country.

No less instructive are those lines which Lenin wrote for his own use in the days when the new methods of industry were being considered and worked up: "10 to 20 years of correct relations with the peasantry and victory on a world scale is guaranteed (even with the delay of the proletarian revolutions, which are growing)."

The goal is set: to accommodate ourselves to the new, more prolonged period which may be necessary for the maturing of the revolution in the west. In this sense and only this, Lenin expressed his confidence that: "From Russia of the NEP will come a socialist Russia."

It is not enough to say that the idea of international revolution was not here revised; to a certain degree it received a deeper and more distinct expression: "In the countries of developed capitalism," said Lenin at the tenth Congress of the Party, explaining the historic position of the NEP, "there is a class of hired agricultural laborers which has been forming itself in the course of some decades. . . . Where this class is sufficiently developed, the transition from capitalism to socialism is possible. We have emphasized in a whole series of writings, in all our speeches, in all our press, the fact that in Russia the situation is not like this—that in Russia we have a minority of workers in industry and an enormous majority of petty land-owners. In such a country the social revolution could achieve its final success only on two conditions: first, on condition of its timely support by a social revolution in one or several advanced countries. . . . The other condition is an agreement between . . . the proletariat which holds the state power and the majority of the peasant population. . . . Only an agreement with the peasants can save the socialist revolution in Russia until the revolution begins in other countries." All the elements of the problem are here united in one. A union with the peasantry is necessary for the very

403

existence of the soviet power; but it does not replace the international revolution, which can alone create the economic basis of a socialist society.

At that same tenth Congress a special report was made on *The Soviet Republic in a Capitalist Environment,* dictated by the delay of the revolution in the west. Kamenev was put forward as spokesman for the Central Executive Committee. "We never set ourselves the task," he said, as of something unquestioned by all, "to create a communist structure in a single isolated country. We find ourselves, however, in a position where it is necessary to hold the foundation of the communist structure, the foundation of the socialist state, the soviet proletarian republic, surrounded on all sides by capitalist relations. Can we fulfill this task? I think that this question is scholastic. To this question in such a situation no answer should be made. The question stands thus: How in the given relations can we hold the soviet power, and hold it up to that moment when the proletariat in this or that country shall come to our aid?" If the idea of the spokesman, who had undoubtedly more than once gone over his outline with Lenin, was in contradiction with the tradition of Bolshevism, why did the congress not raise a protest? How did it happen that there was not one delegate to point out that on the very basic question of the revolution, Kamenev was developing views having "nothing in common" with the views of Bolshevism? How was it that nobody in the whole party noticed this heresy?

"According to Lenin," Stalin affirms, "the revolution finds its force first of all among the workers and peasants of Russia itself. Trotsky has it that the necessary forces can be found only on the arena of the world revolution of the proletariat." To this manufactured contrast, as to many another, Lenin made his answer in advance: "Not for one minute have we forgotten, nor will we forget," he said on May 14th, 1918 at a session of the Central Executive Committee, "the weakness of the Russian working class in comparison with other detachments of the international proletariat. . . . But we must remain at our post until our ally comes, the international proletariat." On the third anniversary of the October revolution, Lenin confirmed this: "We always staked our play upon an international revolution and this was unconditionally right. . . . We always emphasized the fact that in one country it is impossible to accomplish such a work as a socialist revolution." In February, 1921 Lenin declared at a congress of the workers in the needle trades: "We have always and repeatedly pointed out to the workers that the underlying chief task and basic condition of our

404

victory is the propagation of the revolution at least to several of the more advanced countries." No. Lenin is too much compromised by his stubborn desire to find forces in the world arena: you cannot wash him white!

Just as Trotsky is placed in opposition to Lenin, so Lenin himself is placed in opposition to Marx—and with the same foundation. If Marx assumed that the proletarian revolution would begin in France but be completed only in England, this is explained, according to Stalin, by the fact that Marx did not yet know the law of uneven development. In reality the Marxist prognosis contrasting the country of revolutionary initiative with the country of socialist accomplishment, was based wholly upon the law of uneven development. In any case Lenin himself, who permitted no reticence upon big problems, never and nowhere recorded his disagreement with Marx and Engels in regard to the international character of the revolution. Exactly the opposite! If "things have turned out otherwise than Marx and Engels expected," Lenin said at the third Congress of the Soviets, it is only in relation to the historic sequence of the countries. The course of events has allotted to the Russian proletariat "the honorable rôle of vanguard of the international social revolution, and we now see clearly how the development of the revolution will proceed further; the Russian began—the German, the Frenchmen, the Englishmen will carry it through, and socialism will conquer."

We are further admonished by an argument from the standpoint of state prestige. A denial of the theory of national socialism—according to Stalin—"leads to the uncrowning of our country." This phraseology alone, intolerable to a Marxian ear, gives away the depth of the break with Bolshevik tradition. It was not "uncrowning" that Lenin feared, but national bigotry. "We are one of the revolutionary detachments of the working class," he taught in April, 1918 at a session of the Moscow soviet "advanced to the front not because we are better than others, but precisely because we were one of the most backward countries in the world. . . . We will arrive at complete victory only together with all the workers of other countries, the workers of the whole world."

The appeal to sober self-valuation becomes a leit motif in Lenin's speeches. "The Russian revolution," he says on June 4th, 1918 ". . . was due not to the special merits of the Russian proletariat, but to the course . . . of historic events, and this proletariat was placed temporarily in the first position by the will of history and made for a time the vanguard of the world revolution." "The first rôle occupied by the proletariat of Russia in the world labor movement," said Lenin at ?

405

conference of Factory Committees on July 23d, 1918, "is explained not by the industrial development of the country—just the opposite, by the backwardness of Russia. . . . The Russian proletariat is clearly aware that the necessary condition and fundamental premise of its victory is the united action of the workers of the whole world, or of several countries advanced in capitalist relations." The October revolution was evoked not only by the backwardness of Russia, and this Lenin well understood. But he consciously bent the stick too far in order to straighten it.

At a congress of the Councils of People's Economy—the organs especially called to build socialism—Lenin said on May 26th, 1918: "We do not shut our eyes to the fact that we alone, with our own forces, could not achieve the socialist revolution in one country, even though it were a good deal less backward than Russia." And here, anticipating the future voice of bureaucratic bigotry, he explained: "This cannot cause a drop of pessimism, because the task which we have set ourselves is a task of world-wide historic difficulty."

At the sixth Congress of the Soviets on November 8th, he said: "The complete victory of the socialist revolution is unthinkable in one country, but demands the most active co-operation at least of several advanced countries, among which Russia cannot be numbered . . ." Lenin not only denies Russia the right to her own socialism, but demonstratively gives her a secondary place in the building of socialism by other countries. What a criminal "uncrowning" of our country!

In March, 1919 at a Congress of the Party, Lenin pulls up on the too mettlesome: "We have a practical experience in taking the first steps in the destruction of capitalism in a country with a special relation between proletariat and peasantry. Nothing more. If we swell ourselves out like a frog, and puff and blow, this will be utterly laughable to the whole world. We shall be mere braggarts." Will anybody be offended by this? On the 19th of May, 1921 Lenin exclaimed: "Did any one of the Bolsheviks at any time ever deny that the revolution can conquer in a final form only when it comprises all or at least several of the more advanced countries!" In November, 1920 at a Moscow provincial conference of the party, he again reminded his audience that the Bolsheviks had neither promised nor dreamed of "making over the whole world with the forces of Russia alone. . . . Such madness we never reached, but we always said that our revolution will conquer when the workers of all countries support it."

"We have not," he writes at the beginning of 1922, "completed even the foundation of a socialist economy. This can still be taken back by the hostile forces of a dying capitalism. We must be clearly aware of this, and openly acknowledge it. For there is nothing more dangerous than illusions and turned heads, especially in high places. And there is absolutely nothing 'terrible,' nothing offering a legitimate cause for the slightest discouragement, in recognizing this bitter truth; for we always have taught and repeated this ABC truth of Marxism, that for the victory of socialism the combined efforts of the workers of several advanced countries are necessary."

A little over two years later Stalin will demand a renunciation of Marxism upon this basic question. And upon what ground? On the ground that Marx remained ignorant of the unevenness of evolution— ignorant, that is, of the most elementary law of the dialectic of nature as well as society. But what is to be said of Lenin himself, who according to Stalin is supposed to have first "discovered" this law of unevenness as a result of the experience of imperialism, and who nevertheless stubbornly held fast to the "ABC truth of Marxism?" We should seek in vain for any explanation of this.

"Trotskyism"—according to the indictment and sentence of the Communist International—"derived and continues to derive from the proposition that our revolution in and of itself (!) is not in essence socialistic, that the October revolution is only the signal, impetus and starting-point for a socialist revolution in the west." Nationalistic degeneration here masks itself with pure scholasticism. The October revolution "in and of itself" does not exist. It would have been impossible without the whole preceding history of Europe, and it would be hopeless without its continuation in Europe and the whole world. "The Russian revolution is only one link in the chain of international revolution" (Lenin). Its strength lies exactly where the Epigones see its "uncrowning." Exactly because, and only because, it is not a self-sufficient whole, but a "signal," "impetus," "starting-point," "link"— exactly for that reason does it acquire a socialist character.

"Of course the final victory of socialism in one country is impossible," said Lenin at the third Congress of Soviets in January, 1918, "but something else is possible: a living example, a getting to work somewhere in one country—that is what will set fire to the toiling masses in all countries." In July at a session of the Central Executive Committee: "Our task now is . . . to hold fast . . . this torch of socialism so that it may continue to scatter as many sparks as possible to the increasing conflagration of the social revolution." A month later at a workers' meeting: "The (European) revolution is growing . . .

407

and we must hold the soviet power until it begins. Our mistakes must serve as a lesson to the western proletariat." A few days later at a congress of educational workers: "The Russian revolution is only an example, only a first step in a series of revolutions." In March, 1919 at a Congress of the Party: "The Russian revolution was in essence a dress-rehearsal . . . of the world-wide proletarian revolution." Not a revolution "in and of itself" but a torch, a lesson, an example only, a first step only, only a link! Not an independent performance, but only a dress-rehearsal! What a stubborn and ruthless "uncrowning"!

But Lenin did not stop even here; "If it should happen," he said on November 8th, 1918, "that we were suddenly swept away . . . we would have the right to say, without concealing our mistakes, that we used the period of time that fate gave us wholly for the socialist world revolution." How far this is, both in method of thinking and in political psychology, from the bigoted self-complacence of the Epigones, imagining themselves an eternal belly-button of the earth.

A lie upon a fundamental question, if political interest compels you to cling to it, leads to innumerable resulting mistakes and gradually revises all your thinking. "Our party has no right to deceive the working class," said Stalin at a plenary session of the Executive Committee of the Communist International in 1926. "It ought to say frankly that a lack of confidence in the possibility of building socialism in our country will lead to a renunciation of power, and the passing of our party from the position of a ruling to that of an opposition party." The Communist International has canonized this view in its resolution: "The denial of this possibility (the possibility of a socialist society in a separate country) on the part of the opposition, is nothing but a denial of the premises for a socialist revolution in Russia." The "premises" are not the general condition of world economy, not the inner contradictions of imperialism, not the correlation of classes in Russia, but a guarantee given in advance of the possibility of realizing socialism in a separate country!

To this teleological argument advanced by the Epigones in the autumn of 1926, we may reply with the same considerations with which we answered the Mensheviks in the spring of 1905. "Once the objective development of the class-struggle confronts the proletariat at a certain moment of the revolution with the alternative: either take upon yourself the rights and obligations of state power or surrender your class position—the social democracy will place the conquest of state power on the order of the day. In doing this it will not in the least ignore developmental processes of a deeper kind, processes of growth and concentration of production. But it says: When the logic of the class struggle, resting in the last analysis upon the course of economic development, impels the proletariat towards dictatorship before the bourgeoisie has fulfilled its economic mission . . . this means only that history has put upon the proletariat a task colossal in its difficulty. Perhaps the proletariat will even become exhausted in the struggle and fall under its weight—perhaps. But it cannot refuse these tasks through fear of class degeneration and of plunging the whole country into barbarism." To this we could add nothing at the present time.

"It would be an irreparable mistake," wrote Lenin in May, 1918, "to declare that once the lack of correspondence between our economic and our political forces is recognized, 'it follows' that we should not have seized the power. . . . Only 'people in a glass case' reason that way, forgetting that there will never be a 'correspondence,' that there cannot be, either in the evolution of nature or in the evolution of society, that only by way of a whole series of attempts—each one of which taken separately will be one-sided, will suffer from a certain lack of correspondence—can complete socialism be created out of the revolutionary co-operation of the proletarians of all countries." The difficulties of the international revolution will be overcome not by passive adaptation, not by a renunciation of power, not by a national watching and waiting for the universal insurrection, but by live action, by overcoming contradictions, by the dynamic of struggle and the extending of its radius.

If you take seriously the historic philosophy of the Epigones, the Bolsheviks ought to have known in advance on the eve of October, both that they would hold out against a legion of enemies, and that they would pass over from military communism to the NEP; also that in case of need they would build their own national socialism. In a word before seizing the power, they ought to have cast their accounts accurately, and made sure of a credit balance. What happened in reality was little similar to this pious caricature.

In a report at the party congress in March, 1919 Lenin said: "We often have to grope our way along; this fact becomes most obvious when we try to take in with one glance what we have been through. But that did not unnerve us a bit, even on the 10th of October, 1917, when deciding the question about the seizure of power. We had no doubt that it was up to us, according to Comrade Trotsky's expression, to experiment—to make the trial. We undertook a job which nobody in the world had ever before undertaken on such a scale." And further: "Who could ever make a gigantic revolution, knowing in advance how to carry it through to the end? Where could you get such knowledge?

It cannot be found in books. No such books exist. Our decision could only be born of the experience of the masses."

The Bolsheviks did not seek any assurance that Russia would be able to create a socialist society. They had no need of it. They had no use for it. It contradicted all that they had learned in the school of Marxism. "The tactics of the Bolsheviks," wrote Lenin against Kautsky, "were the only international tactics, for they were based not on the cowardly fear of the world revolution, not on a Philistine lack of confidence in it . . ." The Bolsheviks "contributed the maximum possible in one country to the development, support, stimulus, of revolution in all countries." With such a tactic it was impossible to mark out in advance an infallible line-of-march, and still less possible to guarantee yourself a national victory. But the Bolsheviks knew that danger was an element of revolution, as of war. They went to meet danger with open eyes.

Placing before the world proletariat as an example and a reproach the manner in which the bourgeoisie boldly risks war in the name of its interests, Lenin branded with hatred those socialists who "are afraid to begin the fight until they are 'guaranteed' an easy victory. . . . Boot-lickers of international socialism, lackeys of bourgeois morality who think this way deserve triple contempt." Lenin, as is well known, did not stop to choose his words when he was choking with indignation.

"But what shall we do," Stalin has kept on inquiring, "if the international revolution is destined to be delayed? Is there any light ahead for our revolution? Trotsky does not give any light." The Epigones demand historic privileges for the Russian proletariat: it must have a road-bed laid down for an uninterrupted movement towards socialism, regardless of what happens to the rest of humanity. History, alas, has prepared no such road-bed. "If you look at things from a world-wide historic scale," said Lenin at the seventh Congress of the Party, "there is not the slightest doubt that the ultimate victory of our revolution, if it should remain solitary . . . would be hopeless."

But even in this case it would not have been fruitless. "Even if the imperialists should overthrow the Bolshevik power tomorrow," said Lenin in May, 1919 at a teachers' congress, "we would not regret for one second that we took the power. And not one of the class-conscious workers . . . would regret it, or would doubt that our revolution had nevertheless conquered." For Lenin thought of victory only in terms of an international succession of development in struggle. "The new society . . . is an abstraction which can take living body not otherwise than through a series of differing incomplete concrete attempts to create this or that socialist state." This sharp distinction, and in some sense contrast, between "socialist state" and "new society" offers a key to the innumerable abuses perpetrated by the epigone literature upon the texts of Lenin.

Lenin explained with the utmost simplicity the meaning of the Bolshevik strategy at the end of the fifth year after the conquest of power. "When we began at the time we did the international revolution, we did this not with the conviction that we could anticipate its development, but because a whole series of circumstances impelled us to begin this revolution. Our thought was: Either the international revolution will come to our aid, and in that case our victories are wholly assured, or we will do our modest revolutionary work in the consciousness that in case of defeat we have nevertheless served the cause of the revolution, and our experiment will be of help to other revolutions. It was clear to us that without the support of the international world revolution a victory of the proletarian overturn was impossible. Even before the revolution, and likewise after it, our thought was: immediately, or at any rate very quickly, a revolution will begin in the other countries, in capitalistically more developed countries—or in the contrary case we will have to perish. In spite of this consciousness we did everything to preserve the soviet system in all circumstances and at whatever cost, since we knew that we were working not only for ourselves, but for the international revolution. We knew this, we frequently expressed this conviction before the October revolution, exactly as we did immediately after it and during the conclusion of the Brest-Litovsk Peace. And, generally speaking, this was right." The dates have shifted, the pattern of events has formed itself in many respects unexpectedly, but the fundamental orientation remains unchanged.

What can be added to these words? "We began . . . the international revolution." If a revolution in the west does not begin "immediately, or at any rate very quickly"—assumed the Bolsheviks—"we will have to perish." But in that case too the conquest of power will have been justified: others will learn from the experience of those who perish. "We are working not only for ourselves but for the international revolution." These ideas, saturated through and through with internationalism, Lenin expounded to the Communist International. Did anybody oppose him? Did anybody offer a hint of the possibility of a national socialist society? Nobody. Not one single word!

Five years later, at the seventh Plenum of the Executive Committee of the Communist International, Stalin developed ideas exactly opposite to these. They are already known to us: If there is not "confidence in the possibility of building socialism in our country," then the party must pass over "from the position of a ruling, to that of an opposition party. . . ." We must have a preliminary guarantee of success before taking the power: it is permitted to seek this guarantee only in national conditions; we must have confidence in the possibility of building socialism in peasant Russia; then we can get along quite well without confidence in the victory of the world proletariat. Each of these links in a chain of reasoning slaps in the face the tradition of Bolshevism.

To cover up their break with the past, the Stalin school have tried to make use of certain lines of Lenin, which seem the least unsuitable. An article of 1915 on *The United States of Europe* throws out incidentally the remark that the working class in each separate country ought to win the power and enter upon the socialist construction without waiting for the others. If behind these indisputable lines there lurked a thought about a national socialist society, how could Lenin so fundamentally have forgotten it during the years following, and so stubbornly have contradicted it at every step? But there is no use resorting to oblique inferences when we have direct statements. The program theses drafted by Lenin in the same year, 1915, answer the question accurately and directly: "The task of the proletariat of Russia is to carry through to the end the bourgeois-democratic revolution in Russia, in order to kindle the socialist revolution in Europe. This second task has now come extremely near to the first, but it remains nevertheless a special and a second task, for it is a question of different classes co-operating with the proletariat of Russia. For the first task the collaborator is the petty-bourgeois peasantry of Russia, for the second the proletariat of other countries." No greater clarity could be demanded.

The second attempt to quote Lenin is no better founded. His unfinished article about co-operation says that in the Soviet Republic we have on hand "all that is necessary and enough" in order without new revolutions to accomplish the transition to socialism. Here it is a question, as is perfectly clear from the text, of the political and legal premises of socialism. The author does not forget to remind his readers that the productive and cultural premises are inadequate. In general Lenin repeated this thought many times. "We . . . lack the civilization to make the transition directly to socialism," he wrote in an article of the same period, the beginning of 1923, "although we have the political premises for it." In this case as in all others, Lenin started from the assumption that the proletariat of the west would come to socialism along with the Russian proletariat and ahead of it. The article on co-operation does not contain a hint to the effect that the Soviet Republic might harmoniously and by reformist measures create its own national socialism, instead of taking its place through a process of antagonistic and revolutionary development in the world socialist society. Both quotations, introduced even into the text of the program of the Communist International, were long ago explained in our *Criticism of the Program,* and our opponents have not once attempted to defend their distortions and mistakes. The attempt would be too hopeless.

In March, 1923—in the same last period of his creative work,—Lenin wrote: "We stand . . . at the present moment before the question: shall we succeed in holding out with our petty and very petty peasant production, with our ruined condition, until the west European capitalist countries complete their development to socialism?" We see again: the dates have shifted, the web of events changed, but the international foundation of the policy remains unshaken. That faith in the international revolution—according to Stalin a "distrust in the inner forces of the Russian revolution"—went with the great internationalist to his grave. Only after pinning Lenin down under a mausoleum, were the Epigones able to nationalize his views.

From the world-wide division of labor, from the unevenness of development of different countries, from their mutual economic dependence, from the unevenness of different aspects of culture in the different countries, from the dynamic of the contemporary productive forces, it follows that the socialist structure can be built only by a system of economic spiral, only by taking the inner discords of a separate country out into a whole group of countries, only by a mutual service between different countries, and a mutual supplementation of the different branches of their industry and culture—that is, in the last analysis, only on the world arena.

The old program of the party, adopted in 1903, begins with the words: "The development of exchange has established such close bonds between the peoples of the civilized world that the great liberating movement of the proletariat must become, and long ago has become, international. . . ." The preparation of the proletariat for the coming social revolution is defined as the task of the "international social-democracy." However, "on the road to their common final goal . . . the social-democrats of various countries are obliged to set themselves dissimilar immediate tasks." In Russia the overthrow of tzarism is such a task. The democratic revolution was thus regarded in advance as a national step to an international socialist revolution.

The same conception lies at the bottom of our program adopted by the party after the conquest of power. In a preliminary discussion of the draft of this program at the seventh Congress, Miliutin proposed an editorial correction in the resolution of Lenin: "I propose," he said, "that we insert the words 'international socialist revolution' where it says 'the era of social revolution now begun' . . . I think it is unnecessary to argue this. . . . Our social revolution can conquer only as an international revolution. It cannot conquer in Russia alone, leaving the bourgeois structure in the surrounding countries . . . I propose that this be inserted to avoid misunderstanding." The chairman Sverdlov: "Comrade Lenin accepts this amendment, a vote is therefore unnecessary." A tiny episode of parliamentary technique ("unnecessary to argue" and "a vote is unnecessary,") refutes the false historiography of the Epigones more convincingly perhaps than the most painstaking investigation! The circumstance that Miliutin himself, like Skvortzov-Stepanov whom we quoted above, and like hundreds and thousands of others, soon after condemned his own views under the name of "Trotskyism," makes no change in the facts. Great historic currents are stronger than human back-bones. The flood-tide lifts up and the ebb-tide sweeps away whole political generations. Ideas, on the other hand, are able to live even after the physical and spiritual death of those who carried them. A year later, at the eighth Congress of the Party which ratified the new program, the same question was again illumined in a sharp exchange of retorts between Lenin and Podbelsky. The Moscow delegate protested against the fact that in spite of the October overturn the program still spoke of the social revolution in the future tense, "Podbelsky," says Lenin, "attacks the fact that in one of the paragraphs the program speaks of the *coming* social revolution. . . . His argument is obviously inconsequent, for in our program we are talking about the social revolution on a world scale." Truly the history of the party has not left the Epigones a single unillumined corner to hide in!

In the program of the Communist Youth adopted in 1921, the same question is put forward in an especially popular and simple form. "Russia" says one paragraph, "although possessing enormous natural resources is nevertheless in the matter of industry a backward country in which a petty-bourgeois population predominates. It can come to socialism only through the socialist world revolution, the epoch for the development of which we have now entered." Ratified in its day by the Politburo, with the participation not only of Lenin and Trotsky but also of Stalin, this program was in full force in the autumn of 1926 when the Executive Committee of the Communist International converted the non-acceptance of socialism in a separate country into a mortal sin.

In the two years ensuing, however, the Epigones were compelled to file away in the archives the program documents of the Lenin epoch. Their new document, patched together out of fragments, they called the program of the Communist International. Whereas with Lenin in the "Russian" program the talk is of international revolution, with the Epigones in the international program the talk is of "Russian" socialism.

Just when and how did the break with the past first openly reveal itself? The historic date is easy to indicate, since it coincides with a turning-point in the biography of Stalin. As late as April, 1924, three months after the death of Lenin, Stalin was modestly expounding the traditional views of the party. "To overthrow the power of the bourgeoisie and establish the power of the proletariat in one country," he wrote in his *Problems of Leninism*, "does not mean to guarantee the complete victory of socialism. The chief task of socialism,—the organization of socialist production—lies still ahead. Can this task be accomplished? Is it possible to attain the final victory of socialism in one country, without the combined efforts of the proletarians of several advanced countries. No, it is not. The efforts of one country are enough for the overthrow of the bourgeoisie—this is what the history of our revolution tells us. For the final victory of socialism, for the organization of socialist production, the efforts of one country, especially a peasant country like Russia, are not enough—for this we must have the efforts of the proletarians of several advanced countries." Stalin concludes his exposition of these thoughts with the words "Such in general are the characteristic features of the Leninist theory of the proletarian revolution."

By autumn of the same year, under the influence of the struggle with Trotskyism, it was suddenly discovered that Russia is the very country, in distinction from others, which will be able to build the socialist society with her own forces, if she is not hindered by intervention. In a new edition of the same work, Stalin wrote; "Having consolidated its power, and taking the lead of the peasantry, the proletariat of the victorious country can and must build a socialist society." Can and must! Only in order "fully to guarantee the country against intervention . . . is the victory of the revolution necessary . . . at least in several countries." The proclamation of this new conception, which allots to the world proletariat the rôle of border police, ends with those same words: "Such in general are the characteristic features of the Leninist theory of the proletarian revolution." In the course of one year, Stalin has imputed to Lenin two directly opposite views upon a fundamental problem of socialism.

At a plenary session of the Central Committee in 1927, Trotsky said

415

about these two contradictory opinions of Stalin: "You may say that Stalin made a mistake and afterward corrected himself. But how could he make *such* a mistake upon *such* a question? If it were true that Lenin already in 1915 gave out the theory of building socialism in a separate country (which is utterly untrue), if it were true that subsequently Lenin only reinforced and developed this point of view (which is utterly untrue)—then how, we must ask, could Stalin think up for himself during the life of Lenin, during the last period of his life, that opinion upon this most important question which finds its expression in the Stalinist quotation of 1924? It appears that upon this fundamental question Stalin had always been a Trotskyist, and only after 1924 ceased to be one. It would be well if Stalin could find at least one quotation from his own writings showing that before 1924 he said something about the building of socialism in one country. He will not find it!" This challenge remained unanswered.

We should not, however, exaggerate the actual depth of the change made by Stalin. Just as in the question of war, of our relation to the provisional government, or the national question, so on the general perspectives of the revolution, Stalin had two positions: one independent, organic, not always expressed, or at least never wholly expressed, and the other conditional, phraseological, borrowed from Lenin. Between two people belonging to one and the same party it would be impossible to imagine a deeper gulf than that which separated Stalin from Lenin, both upon fundamental questions of revolutionary conception and in political psychology. Stalin's opportunist character is disguised now by the fact that his power rests upon a victorious proletarian revolution. But we have seen the independent position of Stalin in March, 1917. Having behind him an already accomplished bourgeois revolution, he set the party the task of "putting brakes on the splitting away" of the bourgeoisie—that is, of actually resisting the proletarian revolution. If that revolution was achieved, it is not his fault. But together with all the bureaucracy Stalin has taken his stand upon the basis of accomplished fact. Once there is a dictatorship of the proletariat, there must be socialism too. Turning inside out the argument of the Mensheviks against the proletarian revolution in Russia, Stalin, with his theory of socialism in a separate country, began to barricade himself against international revolution. And since he has never thought any question of principle through to the end, it could not but seem to him that "in essence" he always thought as he thought in the autumn of 1924. And since he moreover never got into contradiction with the prevailing opinion of the party, it could not but seem to him that the party too "in essence" thought as he did.

The initial substitution was unconscious. It was not a question of falsification, but of ideological shedding. But in proportion as the doctrine of national socialism came up against a well-armed criticism, there was need of an organized, and predominantly surgical, interference on the part of the machine. The theory of national socialism was then decreed. It was proven by the method of contraries—by the arrest of those who did not agree with it. At the same time the era was opened of systematic remaking of the party's past. The history of the party was turned into a palimpsest. This destruction of parchments still continues, and moreover with steadily increasing fury.

The decisive factor, however, was not repressions nor falsifications. The triumph of the new views corresponding to the situation and interests of the bureaucracy, has rested upon objective circumstances—temporary but extremely powerful. The possibility has opened before the Soviet Republic of playing both in foreign and domestic politics a far more significant rôle than anybody before the revolution could have estimated. The isolated worker state has not only held its own among a legion of enemies, but has elevated itself economically. This weighty fact has formed the social opinion of the younger generation, who have not yet learned to think historically—that is, to compare and foresee.

The European bourgeoisie got too badly burned in the last war to lightly undertake another. A fear of revolutionary consequences has so far paralyzed the plans of military intervention. But the factor of fear is an unstable one. The threat of a revolution has never yet replaced the revolution itself. A danger which remains long unrealized loses its effect. At the same time the irreconcilable antagonism between the workers' state and the world of imperialism pushes towards the surface. Recent events have been so eloquent that the hope of a "neutralization" of the world bourgeoisie up to the completion of the socialist structure, has been abandoned by the present ruling faction; to a certain degree it has even been converted into its opposite.

The industrial successes attained during these peaceful years are an imperishable demonstration of the incomparable advantages of a planned economy. This fact in no wise contradicts the international character of the revolution: socialism could not be realized in the world arena, were not its elements and its points of support prepared in separate countries. It is no accident that the enemies of the theory of national socialism were the very protagonists of industrialization, of the planning principle, the

Five Year Plan, and collectivization. Rakovsky, and with him thousands of other Bolsheviks, are paying for their fight for a bold industrial initiative with years of exile and prison. But they too, on the other hand, have been the first to rise against an over-estimation of the results attained, against national complacency. On the other hand, the mistrustful and short-sighted "practicals," who formerly thought that the proletariat of backward Russia could not conquer the power, and after the conquest of power denied the possibility of broad industrialization and collectivization, have taken subsequently exactly the opposite position. The successes attained against their own expectations, they have simply multiplied into a whole series of Five Year Plans, substituting the multiplication table for a historic perspective. That is the theory of socialism in a separate country.

In reality the growth of the present soviet economy remains an antagonistic process. In strengthening the workers' state, the economic successes are by no means leading automatically to the creation of a harmonious society. On the contrary, they are preparing a sharpening of the contradictions of an isolated socialist structure on a higher level. Rural Russia needs, as before, a mutual industrial plan with urban Europe. The world-wide division of labor stands over the dictatorship of the proletariat in a separate country, and imperatively dictates its further road. The October revolution did not exclude Russia from the development of the rest of humanity, but on the contrary bound her more closely to it. Russia is not a Ghetto of barbarism, nor yet an arcadia of socialism. It is the most transitional country in our transitional epoch. "The Russian revolution is only one link in the chain of international revolution." The present condition of world economy makes it possible to say without hesitation: Capitalism has come far closer to the proletarian revolution than the Soviet Union to socialism. The fate of the first workers' state is inseparably bound up with the fate of the liberating movement in the west and east. But this large theme demands independent investigation. We hope to return to it.

418

APPENDIX THREE

HISTORIC REFERENCES ON THE THEORY OF "PERMANENT REVOLUTION"

IN the Appendix to the first volume of this history we gave extended excerpts from a series of articles written by us in March 1917 in New York, and from our more recent polemic articles against Professor Pokrovsky. In both cases the matter concerned was an analysis of the moving forces of the Russian, and partly also of the international, revolution. It was upon the basis of this problem that the fundamental principled groupings had crystallized themselves in the Russian revolutionary camp ever since the beginning of the century. In proportion as the revolutionary tide rose, they acquired more and more the character of a strategic program, and then finally a directly tactical character. The years 1903 to 1906 were a period of intensive crystallization of political tendencies in the Russian social democracy. It was at that time that our work, *Summaries and Perspectives* was written. It was written in sections and for different purposes. An imprisonment in December 1905 permitted the author to expound more systematically than before his views on the character of the Russian revolution and its prospects. This collected work appeared as a book in the Russian language in 1906. In order that the excerpts from it given below may take a proper place in the mind of the reader, we must remind him again that in 1904–05 no one of the Russian Marxists defended, or even uttered, the thought of the possibility of building a socialist society in a single country in general, and particularly in Russia. This conception was first expressed in print only twenty years later, in the autumn of 1924. In the period of the first revolution, as also in the years between the two revolutions, the dispute concerned the dynamics of the bourgeois revolution, and not the chances and possibilities of a socialist revolution. All the present partisans of the theory of socialism in one country, without a single exception, were during that period confining the prospects of the Russian revolution to a bourgeois-democratic republic, and until April 1917 they were considering impossible not only the building of national socialism, but also the conquest of power by the proletariat of Russia before the dictatorship of the proletariat should be inaugurated in more advanced countries.

419

By "Trotskyism," in the period from 1905 to 1917, was meant that revolutionary conception according to which the bourgeois revolution in Russia would not be able to solve its problems without placing the proletariat in power. Only in the autumn of 1924 did "Trotskyism" begin to mean the conception according to which the Russian proletariat, having come to power, would not be able to build a national socialist society with its own forces alone.

For the convenience of the reader we shall present the dispute schematically in the form of a dialogue in which the letter T signifies a representative of the "Trotskyist" conception, and the letter S means one of those Russian "practicals" who now stand at the head of the soviet bureaucracy.

1905–1917

T. The Russian revolution cannot solve its democratic problem, above all the agrarian problem, without placing the working class in power.

S. But does not that mean the dictatorship of the proletariat?

T. Unquestionably.

S. In backward Russia? Before it happens in the advanced capitalist countries?

T. Exactly so.

S. But you are ignoring the Russian village—that is, the backward peasantry stuck in the mud of semi-serfdom.

T. On the contrary, it is only the depth of the agrarian problem that opens the immediate prospect of a dictatorship of the proletariat in Russia.

S. You reject, then, the bourgeois revolution?

T. No, I only try to show that its dynamic leads to the dictatorship of the proletariat.

S. But that means that Russia is ripe for the building of socialism?

T. No, it does not. Historic evolution has no such planned and harmonious character. The conquest of power by the proletariat in backward Russia flows inexorably from the correlation of forces in the bourgeois revolution. What further economic prospects will be opened by the dictatorship of the proletariat depends upon the domestic and world conditions under which it is inaugurated. It goes without saying that Russia cannot arrive at socialism independently. But once having opened an era of socialist transformation, she can supply the impetus to a socialist development of Europe and thus arrive at socialism in the wake of the advanced countries.

420

1917–1923

S. We must acknowledge that Trotsky "even before the revolution of 1905 advanced the original and now especially famous theory of Permanent Revolution, asserting that the bourgeois revolution of 1905 would go directly over into a socialist revolution and prove the first of a series of national revolutions." (The quotation is from the notes to the *Complete Works of Lenin,* published during his life.)

1924–1932

S. And so you deny that our revolution can arrive at socialism?

T. I think, as before, that our revolution can and should lead to socialism after having acquired an international character.

S. You do not believe, then, in the inner forces of the Russian revolution?

T. Strange that this did not prevent my foreseeing and preaching the dictatorship of the proletariat when you rejected it as utopian!

S. But you none the less deny the socialist revolution in Russia?

T. Until April 1917 you accused me of rejecting the bourgeois revolution. The secret of your theoretical contradictions lies in the fact that you got way behind the historic process and now you are trying to catch up and pass it. To tell the truth, this also is the secret of your industrial mistakes.

The reader should have always before him these three historic stages in the development of revolutionary conceptions in Russia, if he wishes correctly to judge the actual issues in the present struggle of factions and groups in Russian communism.

EXCERPTS FROM THE ARTICLE OF THE YEAR 1905, "SUMMARIES AND
PERSPECTIVES."

SECTION 4. *Revolution and the Proletariat.*

The proletariat will grow and strengthen together with the growth of capitalism. In this sense the development of capitalism is the development of the proletariat toward dictatorship. But the day and hour when the power will pass to the hands of the working class depends directly not upon the level obtained by the productive forces, but upon relations in the class struggle, upon the international situation, and finally upon a series of subjective factors—traditions, initiatives, preparedness for fighting. . . .

In a country economically more backward the proletariat may come to power sooner than in a country capitalistically advanced. . . .

The idea of some sort of automatic dependence of the proletarian dictatorship upon the technical forces and resources of a country is a prejudice derived from an extremely oversimplified "economic" materialism. Such a view has nothing in common with Marxism.

The Russian revolution, according to our view, will create conditions in which the power may (and with the victory of the revolution must) pass to the proletariat before the politicians of bourgeois liberalism get a chance to develop their statesmanly genius to the full.

Marxism is above all a method of analysis—not analysis of texts but analysis of social relations. Is it true in regard to Russia that the weakness of capitalistic liberalism necessarily means a weakness of the labor movement?

The numbers of the industrial proletariat, their concentration, their culture, their political weight, undoubtedly depend upon the degree of development of capitalist industry. But this dependence is not direct. Between the productive forces of the country and the political force of its classes at each given moment various socio-political factors of national and international character intervene, and they displace, and even completely change the form of, the political expression of economic relations. Notwithstanding that the productive forces of industry in the United States are ten times higher than ours, the political rôle of the Russian proletariat, its influence upon the policy of the country, and the possibility of its coming influence upon world politics, is incomparably higher than the rôle and significance of the American proletariat.

SECTION 5. *The Proletariat in Power and the Peasantry.*

In the event of a decisive victory of the revolution the power will come into the hands of that class which played the leading rôle in the struggle—in other words, into the hands of the proletariat. We add at once as self-evident that this does not exclude the entry into the government of revolutionary representatives of non-proletarian social groups. . . . The whole question is, who will supply the content of the government policy? Who will consolidate in the government a homogeneous majority? It is one thing when representatives of the democratic layers of the people participate in a government which is working-class in its majority. It is another thing when representatives of the proletariat participate, in the character of more or less respected hostages, in a definitely bourgeois-democratic government.

The proletariat cannot perpetuate its power without broadening the base of the revolution. Many strata of the toiling masses, especially in the country, will be first drawn into the revolution and acquire political organization only after the vanguard of the revolution, the city proletariat, stands at the helm of state.

. . . The character of our socio-historic relations, which throws the whole weight of the bourgeois revolution upon the shoulders of the proletariat, will not only create enormous difficulties for the workers' government, but will also, at least in the first period of its existence, give it priceless advantages. This will express itself in the relations between the proletariat and the peasantry.

The Russian revolution does not permit, and for a long time will not permit, the creation of any sort of bourgeois-constitutional order which might solve the most elementary problems of democracy. . . . In consequence of this the fate of the most elementary revolutionary interests of the peasantry—even of the entire peasantry as a caste—is bound up with the fate of the whole revolution—that is, with the fate of the proletariat. The proletariat in power will appear to the peasantry as an emancipator class.

But perhaps the peasantry itself will crowd out the proletariat and occupy its place? That is impossible. All the experience of history protests against this assumption. It shows that the peasantry is completely incapable of playing an *independent* political rôle.

The Russian bourgeoisie will surrender all revolutionary positions to the proletariat. It will have to surrender also the revolutionary leadership of the peasantry. In the situation which will be created by a transfer of power to the proletariat the peasantry will have nothing left to do but adhere to the régime of workers' democracy. Granted even that they will do this with no more consciousness than they have in adhering to the bourgeois régime! But whereas every bourgeois party after winning the votes of the peasants makes haste to use its power in order to rob them and deceive them of all their hopes and faith in promises, and then when worst comes to worst yields its place to another capitalist party, the proletariat, relying upon the peasantry, will bring all its forces into play to raise the cultural level of the village and develop in the peasantry a political consciousness.

SECTION 6. *The Proletarian Régime.*

The proletariat can come to power only while relying upon a national awakening, upon a universal popular inspiration. The proletariat will enter the government as a revolutionary representative of the nation, as the recognized leader of the people in their struggle with absolutism and feudal barbarism. But having come to power, the proletariat will open a new epoch—an epoch of revolutionary legislation, of affirmative politics—and here the preservation of its rôle as recognized spokesman of the nation is by no means guaranteed.

Each day will deepen the policy of the proletariat in power, and more and more define its class character. And therewith the revolutionary bond between the proletariat and the nation will be broken. The class dismemberment of the peasantry will appear in political form. The antagonism between its constituent parts will increase in the same degree that the policy of the workers' government defines itself, and from being a general democratic policy becomes a class policy.

The destruction of feudal serfdom will have the support of the entire peasantry as a burdened caste. . . . But legislative measures in defense of the agricultural proletariat not only will win no such active sympathy from the majority, but will come up against the active resistance of the minority. The proletariat will find itself obliged to carry the class struggle into the country, and thus destroy that community of interests which is undoubtedly to be found in every peasantry, although within comparatively narrow limits. The proletariat will be obliged, in the very earliest moments of its rule, to seek support in opposing the rural poor to the rural rich, the agricultural proletariat to the peasant bourgeoisie.

Once the power is in the hands of a revolutionary government with a socialist majority, at that moment the difference between minimum and maximum program loses both its significance in principle and its directly practical significance. A proletarian government cannot possibly restrain itself within the limits of this distinction.

Entering the government not as impotent hostages but as a ruling power, the representatives of the proletariat will by this very act destroy the boundary between minimum and maximum program. That is, they will place collectivism on the order of the day. At what point the proletariat will be stopped in this direction depends upon the correlation of forces, but not at all upon the original intentions of the party of the proletariat.

That is why there can be no talk of any special form of proletarian dictatorship in a bourgeois revolution, namely a democratic dictatorship of the proletariat (or of the proletariat and the peasantry). The working class cannot guarantee the democratic character of its dictatorship without transgressing the limits of its democratic program. Any illusions on this point would be absolutely ruinous.

Once the party of the proletariat takes the power, it will fight for it to the end. While one means of waging this struggle for the preservation and perpetuation of its power will be agitation and organization, especially in the country, another means will be a collectivist policy. Collectivism will become not only an inevitable inference from the position of the party in power, but also a means of preserving its position while relying upon the proletariat.

*

When the idea was formulated in the socialist press of an uninterrupted revolution, linking up the liquidation of absolutism and of civil serfdom with a socialist revolution, thanks to multiplying social clashes, uprisings of new layers of the masses, unceasing attacks of the proletariat upon the political and economic privileges of the ruling classes, our "progressive" press raised a unanimous howl of indignation.

The more radical representatives of that same democracy . . . not only considered fantastic the very idea of a workers' government in Russia, but also denied the possibility of a socialist revolution in Europe in the coming historic epoch. The necessary "premises" are not yet at hand. Is this true? It is not of course a question of setting the date of a socialist revolution, but of giving it a place in the actual historic perspective. . . .

(Here follows an analysis of the general premises of a socialist economy and the proof that at the present time—the beginning of the 20th century—these premises, if you take the question on a European and world scale, are already at hand.)

. . . Within the closed boundaries of separate states a socialist production could not in any case be introduced—both for economic and political reasons.

Section 8. *A Workers' Government in Russia and Socialism.*

We have shown above that the objective premises of a socialist revolution have already been created by the economic development of the advanced capitalist countries. But what can be said in this respect about Russia? Can we expect that the transfer of power to the Russian proletariat will be the beginning of a transformation of our national economy upon socialist principles?

The Parisian workers, as Marx said, did not demand miracles of the Commune. Now, too, you cannot expect instantaneous miracles of the dictatorship of the proletariat. The state power is not omnipotent. It would be absurd to imagine that the proletariat has only to receive the power and it will replace capitalism by socialism with a few decrees. An economic structure is not a product of the activity of the state. The proletariat can only employ the state power with all its might in order to promote economic evolution in the direction of collectivism, and shorten its road.

The socialization of production begins in those branches which offer the least difficulties. During the first period socialized production will take the form of oases united with private industrial enterprises by the laws of commodity circulation. The broader the field already seized by socialized industry, the more obvious will be its advantages, the solider will the new political régime feel, and the more bold will be the further industrial undertakings of the proletariat. In these undertakings the proletariat will be able to, and will, rely not only upon the national productive forces, but also upon international technique, just as in its revolutionary politics it will rely not only upon the experience of national class relations, but also upon the whole historic experience of the international proletariat.

The proletarian régime will be compelled from the very first to undertake the solution of the agrarian problem, with which is bound up the fate of the immense mass of the population of Russia. In solving this problem, as in solving all others, the proletariat will take as its point of departure the fundamental effort of its economic policy: to conquer as large a field as possible for the organization of socialist industry. And the forms and tempo of this policy in the agrarian problem will have to be determined both by those material resources in the command of the proletariat, and by the necessity of so deploying its activities as not to push possible allies into the ranks of the counter-revolution.

But how far can the socialist policy of the working class go in the industrial conditions of Russia? Only one thing can be said with certainty. It will run into political obstacles long before it comes up against the technical backwardness of the country. Without direct state support from the European proletariat the working class of Russia cannot remain in power and cannot convert its temporary rule into a prolonged socialist dictatorship. . . .

Political "optimism" may take two forms. It may exaggerate its own forces and the advantageous aspects of the revolutionary situation, and set itself tasks whose solution is not permitted by the given correlation of forces. But it may on the other hand optimistically set a bound to its revolutionary tasks beyond which the logic of the situation will inevitably push us.

We may set a bound to all the problems of the revolution by asserting that our revolution is bourgeois in its objective aims, and therefore in its inevitable result, and we may thus shut our eyes to the fact that the chief agent of this bourgeois revolution will be the proletariat, and the proletariat will be pushed toward the power by the whole course of the revolution. . . .

You may lull yourself with the thought that the social conditions of Russia are not yet ripe for a socialist economy, and therewith you may neglect to consider the fact that the proletariat, once in power, will inevitably be compelled by the whole logic of its situation to introduce an economy operated by the state.

The general sociological definition, "bourgeois revolution," does not by any means solve those politico-tactical problems, contradictions and difficulties, which will be put forward by the mechanics of the given bourgeois revolution.

Within the framework of the bourgeois revolution at the end of the 18th century, whose objective task was to establish the rule of capital, a dictatorship of the Sansculottes proved possible. In a revolution at the beginning of the 20th century, which is also bourgeois in its immediate objective tasks, there appears in the near perspective the inevitability, or at the very least the probability, of a political rulership of the proletariat. That this rulership shall not prove a mere passing "episode," as certain realistic philistines hope—the proletariat itself will see to this. But it is not too early now to pose the question: Must this dictatorship of the proletariat inevitably be shattered against the boundaries of the bourgeois revolution? May it not, upon the given world-historic foundations, open before itself the prospect of a victory to be achieved after shattering these limited boundaries?

(Here follows a development of the thought that the Russian revolution may, and in all probability will, unleash a proletarian revolution in the west, which in its turn will guarantee the socialist development of Russia.)

*

It should be added that during the first years of the existence of the Communist International the above-quoted work was officially published in foreign languages as a theoretic interpretation of the October revolution.

CHRONOLOGICAL TABLE

1774

Pugachev Rebellion of Cossacks and peasants.

1825

December— Dekabrist (Decembrist) uprising against tzarism led by liberal officers.

1848

The Communist Manifesto published by Karl Marx and Friedrich Engels—the foundation of revolutionary socialism or communism.

1861

Peasant Reform; abolition of serfdom in Russia.

1864

"The International" (first international organization of socialist workers) established by Marx and others.

1871

The Paris Commune.

1882

Plekhanov publishes first pamphlet introducing Marxian socialism into Russia.

1905

The Revolution of 1905 in Russia. First organization of soviets by Russian workers.

January 9*— "Bloody Sunday"—workers led by Father Gapon and carrying a petition to the tzar, are mowed down by the tzar's troops.

---

* Russian dates are given according to the old calendar. Add 13 days to find the date according to the calendar that is now international.

429

1914

August 1—   World War begins.

Germany declares war against Russia.

November 4— Bolshevik deputies in the State Duma arrested and sent to Siberia.

1915

April—   Russian revolutionary internationalist paper, *Nashe Slovo,* appears in Paris with Trotsky on the editorial staff.

September— International socialist congress in Zimmerwald, Switzerland.

1916

May—   Second Congress of socialist internationalists at Kienthal.

1917

January 9— Street meetings and a printers' strike celebrate the anniversary of "Bloody Sunday."

February 14— The last State Duma assembles.

February 23— Celebration of International Women's Day begins the revolution.

February 24— Two hundred thousand workers on strike in Petrograd.

February 25— General strike in Petrograd. Shootings and arrests of revolutionists.

February 26— Duma dissolved by the tzar. The deputies disperse but decide not to leave town.

Tens of thousands of workers in the streets.

February 27— Mutiny of the Guard regiments.

Formation of the Soviet of Workers' deputies.

Formation of Provisional Committee of the Duma.

February 28— Arrest of the tzar's ministers.

Capture of Schlusselberg Prison.

First issue of *Izvestia*—"The News of the Soviet."

430

March 1—   "Order No. 1" is issued to the soldiers.
Formation of the soldiers' section of the Soviet.
First session of the Moscow Soviet.

March 2—   The tzar abdicates in favor of the Grand Duke Mikhail.
The Provisional Government is formed by the Provisional Committee of the Duma, with the support of
the Soviet and with Kerensky as Minister of Justice.

March 3—   The Grand Duke Mikhail abdicates.
The Provisional Government announces the revolution
to the world by radio.

March 5—   The first issue of *Pravda*, central organ of the Bolshevik Party.

March 6—   The Provisional Government declares amnesty for
political prisoners.

March 8—   The tzar arrested at Moghiliev.

March 14—   Address of the Soviet "to the people of the whole
world" declaring for peace without annexations or indemnities.

March 23—   Funeral of the martyrs of the revolution.

March 29—   All-Russian conference of the soviets.

April 3—   Lenin, Zinoviev and other Bolsheviks arrive from
Switzerland.

April 4—   Lenin's "April Theses" outlining his policy of proletarian revolution.

April 18—   Celebration of the international socialist holiday of
May 1.
Foreign Minister Miliukov sends a note to the Allies
promising war to victory on the old terms.

April 20—   Armed demonstrations of protest against the note of
Miliukov—the "April Days."

April 24—   Beginning of an All-Russian conference of the Bolshevik party.

May 1—   The Petrograd Soviet votes for a coalition government.

May 2—   Miliukov resigns.

May 4—	Trotsky arrives from America, seconding the policies of Lenin.
	An All-Russian Congress of Peasants' Deputies opens in Petrograd.
May 5—	Coalition government is organized with Kerensky as Minister of War.
May 17—	The Kronstadt Soviet declares itself the sole governing power in Kronstadt.
May 25—	All-Russian congress of the Social Revolutionary party.
May 30—	First conference of factory and shop committees opens in Petrograd.
June 3—	First all-Russian congress of soviets.
June 16—	Kerensky orders Russian armies to take the offensive.
June 18—	A demonstration called by the Mensheviks and Social Revolutionaries turns out to be a Bolshevik demonstration.
June 19—	Patriotic demonstration on Nevsky Prospect, carrying portraits of Kerensky.
July 3-5—	"July Days"—semi-insurrection followed by attempted stamping out of Bolshevism in Petrograd.
July 6—	Kerensky offensive collapses as Germans smash Russian lines at Tarnopol on southern front.
July 7—	Socialist Government of Salvation of the Revolution is formed with Kerensky as president.
July 12—	Restoration of the death penalty in the army.
July 16—	Kornilov replaces Brussilov as commander-in-chief of the army.
July 23—	Trotsky and Lunacharsky imprisoned; Lenin in hiding.
July 24—	New Coalition Government with Kadets replaces Government of Salvation of the Revolution.
July 26—	Sixth Congress of the Bolshevik party; fusion with Mezhrayontzi; Central Committee elected which is to lead party through October revolution.

August 12—   State Conference in Moscow provokes general strike of Moscow workers. Conference hails Kornilov, who secretly sets August 27th for counter-revolutionary insurrection.

August 18–
21—   Germans break through northern front, take Riga, threaten Petrograd.

August 26—   Government doubles price of grain. Ministers resign to give Kerensky free hand.

August 27—   Kerensky tries to remove Kornilov, who ignores his orders and begins march on Petrograd. Soviet Committee for Struggle against Counter-Revolution formed.

August 28, 29,
30—   Kornilov coup collapses as workers sabotage his advance and his troops desert.

September 1—   Kornilov arrested at General Headquarters in Moghilev. Bolshevik resolution carries the Petrograd Soviet for the first time.

September 4—   Trotsky freed on bail by Provisional Government.

September 5—   Bolshevik resolution carries Moscow Soviet.

September 9—   Bolshevik majority of the Petrograd Soviet formally ratified. Compromise praesidium resigns.

September 14—   Democratic Conference opens in Petrograd.

September 21—   Democratic Conference closes after electing a Council of the Republic, or pre-parliament. Petrograd Soviet sends out call for All-Russian Soviet Congress on October 20th.

September 24—   Last Coalition Government formed, with Kerensky as president.

October 7—   Bolsheviks withdraw from the Council of the Republic.

October 9—   Petrograd Soviet votes to form the Committee for Revolutionary Defense.

October 10—   Bolshevik Central Committee adopts Lenin's resolution on armed insurrection as an immediate task.

October 13— Petrograd Soldiers' Soviet votes to transfer military authority from Headquarters to the Military Revolutionary Committee. Northern Regional Soviet Congress endorses coming All-Russian Congress and declares for Soviet power.

October 15— Kiev Soviet declares for Soviet power.

October 16— Southwest Regional Soviet Congress at Minsk declares for Soviet power. Meeting of the Bolshevik Central Committee reaffirms Lenin's resolution on the insurrection against the opposition of Zinoviev and Kamenev.

October 17— Rumored Bolshevik uprising fails to materialize. Zinoviev and Kamenev attack insurrectionary policy of Bolshevik Central Committee in the public press. All-Russian Soviet Central Executive Committee postpones All-Russian Soviet Congress from October 20th to October 25th.

October 19— Ural Regional Soviet Congress declares for Soviet power.

October 20— Committee for Revolutionary Defense, known as the Military Revolutionary Committee, begins active preparations for the insurrection.

October 22— Enormous meetings throughout Petrograd as Soviet forces are mobilized for review.

October 23— Peter and Paul Fortress, the last military obstacle of any importance in Petrograd, comes over to the Soviets.

October 24— Provisional Government issues orders to take legal steps against the Military Revolutionary Committee, to suppress the Bolshevik papers, and to bring loyal troops into the capital, orders which were never carried out. Kerensky makes his last speech to the Council of the Republic. Left Social-Revolutionaries indicate willingness to participate in the Military Revolutionary Committee.

October 25— Insurrection begins at 2:00 A. M. Council of the Republic closed by troops at 12:00 noon. Lenin makes his first public appearance at a session of the Petrograd Soviet at 3:00 P. M. Operations against the seat of the Provisional Government at the Winter Palace begin at 9:00 P. M. Second All-Russian Congress of the Soviets opens at the Smolny at 11:00 P. M.

October 26— Winter Palace falls and the Provisional Government is arrested at 2:00 A. M.

October 26 and 27— Second All-Russian Soviet Congress passes decrees on peace and land and sets up the new government of the Council of People's Commissars. Congress adjourns at 5:00 A. M., October 27th.

A SHORT LIST OF PRINCIPAL PERSONS

GENERAL ALEXEIEV— *Monarchist and active counter-revolutionary, commander-in-chief of the armies of the Provisional Government from April 1st to May 22nd.*

ANTONOV-OVSEËNKO— *Bolshevik military leader, active in the 1905 revolution, associated with the Mensheviks during the years of reaction, internationalist during the war, joined the Bolsheviks after his return to Russia, one of the organizers of the October insurrection in Petrograd.*

AVKSENTIEV— *School-teacher and leader of the Social Revolutionary party. President of the Executive Committee of the Peasants' Congress, Minister of the Interior in various coalition governments, President of the Council of the Republic.*

BLAGONRAVOV— *Bolshevik corporal, who was Commissar of Peter and Paul Fortress at the time of the October insurrection.*

GENERAL BRUSSILOV— *Tzarist general who subsequently gave his allegiance to the Soviet Government.*

BUCHANAN— *British Ambassador to Russia during the revolution.*

BUKHARIN— *Bolshevik theoretician and leader, active in Moscow, member of the Central Committee of the Bolshevik party in October.*

CHEIDZE— *Social Democrat (Menshevik), first president of the Petrograd Soviet.*

CHERNOV— *A leader of the Social Revolutionaries standing between the Rights and Lefts, Minister of Agriculture in the Coalition Government.*

437

CHUDNOVSKY— *Bolshevik military leader, returned from America with Trotsky, one of the organizers of the October insurrection.*

DAN— *Menshevik leader, active in the Soviets, member of the All-Russian Soviet Executive Committee until the insurrection.*

GENERAL DENIKIN— *Tzarist general who later commanded anti-Bolshevik forces in southern Russia.*

DYBENKO— *Bolshevik sailor and leader of the Soviet of the Baltic Fleet.*

DZERZHINSKY— *Polish Social Democrat freed from prison by the February revolution, joined the Bolsheviks, later became first president of the Cheka.*

FATHER GAPON— *Priest who led the working people carrying a petition to the tzar on "Bloody Sunday," January 9, 1905.*

PRINCE GOLYTSIN— *A septuagenarian who headed the last tzarist ministry.*

GOREMYKIN— *Premier of Russia immediately before Prince Golytsin.*

GORKY— *The great Russian short-story writer and novelist.*

GOTZ— *Terrorist and leader of the Social Revolutionary party. Member of the All-Russian Soviet Executive Committee until October.*

GUCHKOV— *The first Minister of War and Marine under the Provisional Government, a moderate conservative and imperialist, one of the founders of the Octobrist party.*

GENERAL IVANOV— *Russian commander who tried to bring his forces to Petrograd to crush the February revolution. Eleven years earlier he had subdued an uprising in Kronstadt.*

IZVOLSKY— *Russian Minister of Foreign Affairs (1906-1910) and Ambassador to France (1910-1917).*

JOFFÉ—

Joined the Bolshevik party with the Mezhrayontzi at the July fusion congress, member of the October Central Committee of the Bolshevik party. First Soviet Ambassador to Germany.

GENERAL KALEDIN—

Cossack general and counter-revolutionary leader, elected Ataman of the Don Cossack Army in July, supporter of the Kornilov insurrection.

KAMENEV—

A prominent member of the Central Committee of the Bolshevik party, subsequently a diplomat of the Soviet Government and president of the Council of Labor and Defense.

KERENSKY—

A Trudovik in the Duma—after the revolution a Social Revolutionary, first Minister of Justice, then of War and Marine, and finally "Minister-President" of the Provisional Government, fled from Russia when the Bolsheviks triumphed.

GENERAL KHABALOV—

Tzarist general, military commander of the troops of the Petrograd district during the first days of the revolution.

ADMIRAL KOLCHAK—

Russian naval officer, subsequently leader of anti-Bolshevik forces in Siberia.

KONOVALOV—

Moscow industrialist, Minister of Trade and Industry in the first coalition, resigned after two weeks, joined the Kadet party, Vice-President of the last (September) Coalition Government.

GENERAL KORNILOV—

Russian general who succeeded Khabalov in command of the Petrograd district—subsequently tried to establish a military dictatorship.

GENERAL KRASNOV—

Commander of the Third Cavalry, monarchist leader of the Kornilov march on Petrograd, later active in the counter-revolution.

KRYLENKO— *Bolshevik ensign and leader at the front, commander-in-chief of the armies after the insurrection, later Attorney General of the Soviet Republic.*

KROPOTKIN— *Anarchist leader who became a patriot during the war and an anti-Bolshevik during the revolution.*

LASHEVICH— *Bolshevik noncommissioned officer, prominent military leader in Petrograd.*

LENIN— *Head of the Bolshevik party, leader of the Russian revolution and first head of the Soviet Government.*

LIEBKNECHT— *German Socialist Reichstag Deputy, one of the few who held an internationalist position during the war, imprisoned, later a leader of the Spartacus Bund, killed during the revolution of 1919.*

LOMOV— *Member of the October Central Committee of the Bolshevik party, first People's Commissar of Justice.*

LUNACHARSKY— *Joined the Bolsheviks with the Mezhrayontzi in July, first People's Commissar of Education in the Soviet Government.*

LUXEMBOURG— *Polish Socialist leader, internationalist during the war, imprisoned, leader of the Spartacus Bund, killed on the same day as Liebknecht during the German revolution of 1919.*

PRINCE LVOV— *A Constitutional Democrat (Kadet), first Prime Minister after the February revolution.*

MARTOV— *Theoretician and leader of the Menshevik party, lifelong opponent of Lenin, an internationalist during the war; he tried to play the role of loyal opposition after the October revolution.*

A SHORT LIST OF PRINCIPAL PERSONS

MILIUKOV—
Head of the Kadet party, Minister of Foreign Affairs and actual boss of the Provisional Government.

MILIUTIN—
Economist and member of the October Central Committee of the Bolshevik party, first People's Commissar for Agriculture.

NABAKOV—
Kadet leader, Minister without Portfolio in the Provisional Government, author of memoirs of the Provisional Government.

NOGIN—
Member of the October Central Committee of the Bolshevik party, first People's Commissar of Commerce and Industry.

PALCHINSKY—
Kadet engineer, Minister of Trade and Industry in the Provisional Government, Governor General of Petrograd.

PLEKHANOV—
Veteran Russian Social Democrat, translator of Karl Marx and regarded as the father of Russian Marxism, took a patriotic and conservative position during the World War and the revolution.

PODVOISKY—
Bolshevik military leader, one of the organizers of the Petrograd insurrection.

PROTOPOPOV—
A leader of the Progressive bloc in the last Duma, later broke with it, joined the court camarilla and became Minister of the Interior under the tzar.

RASKOLNIKOV—
Bolshevik leader in the Baltic fleet and at Kronstadt.

GREGORY RASPUTIN—
An illiterate Siberian monk who exercised a great influence over the tzar and the tzarina and was assassinated in December, 1916, by members of the court.

REED—
American revolutionary journalist in Petrograd, later one of the founders of the Communist party of the United States.

441

RODZIANKO— A great land owner, Lord Chamberlain under the tzar and conservative President of the Duma.

RYKOV— Member of the October Central Committee of the Bolshevik party, first People's Commissar of the Interior.

SAVINKOV— Social Revolutionary terrorist during the revolution of 1905 and after, patriot during the war, active in the Kornilov counter-revolutionary conspiracy, led counter-revolutionary uprisings after the October revolution, died in a Soviet prison.

SAZONOV— Minister of Foreign Affairs in Russia after 1910, dismissed by the tzar in 1917.

PRINCE SHERBATOV— Russian Minister of the Interior during the World War.

SKOBELEV— One of the leaders of the Menshevik party, became Minister of Labor in the Coalition Government.

STALIN— A prominent member of the Central Committee of the Bolshevik party, editor with Kamenev of the official organ Pravda until Lenin's arrival in Russia, became general secretary of the party in 1922 and is at present virtual head of the Soviet Government.

STANKEVICH— Compromise Socialist, Political Commissar for the Provisional Government to the Army Supreme Command, author of memoirs of the revolution.

STÜRMER— Premier of Russia during most of 1916.

SUKHANOV— A social democrat belonging to Gorky's group, one of the leaders of the Petrograd Soviet in the early days of the revolution, author of Notes of the Revolution in seven volumes.

SVERDLOV— *Bolshevik since 1903, released from exile by the February revolution, one of the most talented organizers of the Bolshevik party, active in Petrograd, President of the All-Russian Soviet after the October revolution, died in 1919.*

TERESHCHENKO— *Kadet—Minister of Foreign Affairs in the reconstructed Provisional Government following Miliukov's resignation.*

TSERETELLI— *A leader of the Menshevik party and principal leader of the Soviet until the Bolsheviks won a majority.*

URITSKY— *Joined the Bolshevik party in July with the Mezhrayontzi, member of the October Central Committee, assassinated in 1918.*

VERKHOVSKY— *Military Commander of the Moscow District, Minister of War in Kerensky's last coalition government.*

COUNT WITTE— *Russian statesman of the old régime, champion of industrial development, died in 1915.*

GENERAL YUDENICH— *Tzarist general who subsequently led anti-Bolshevik forces in an attempt to capture Petrograd.*

PRINCE YUSSUPOV— *One of the assassins of Rasputin.*

ZINOVIEV— *Prominent member of the Central Committee of the Bolshevik party, came to Russia with Lenin on April 3rd from Switzerland, subsequently first President of the Third (Communist) International.*

PLACES

Alexandrinsky Theater— *Petrograd theater where the Democratic Conference met.*

Cirque Moderne— *Auditorium near Peter and Paul Fortress.*

Gatchina— *Southern suburb of Petrograd, where Kornilov march on the capital expired.*

Helsingfors— *Seaport capital of Finland, about 120 miles west of Petrograd on the Gulf of Finland.*

Kiev— *Capital of the Ukraine, about 600 miles south of Petrograd.*

Krasnoe Selo— *Southern suburb of Petrograd.*

Kronstadt— *An island fortress in the Gulf of Finland guarding Petrograd.*

Kshesinskaia's Palace— *Palace of a former favorite dancer of the tzar, located near Peter and Paul Fortress. Headquarters of the Bolshevik party until the "July Days."*

Mariinsky Palace— *Palace in Petrograd where the ministry of the Provisional Government held its meetings.*

Moghilev— *Small city about 400 miles south of Petrograd where the High Command was established.*

Moonsund Islands— *Strategic naval base in the Baltic, near Riga.*

Nevsky Prospect— *The main avenue of Petrograd.*

Oranienbaum, Peterhof— *Western suburbs of Petrograd, where military academies were located.*

Peter and Paul Fortress— *Formidable prison fortress on an island in Petrograd.*

444

Riga—

Capital of the former tzarist province of Latvia, a Baltic seaport.

Schlusselburg—

Eastern suburb of Petrograd, location of a munitions factory and a prison.

Smolny Institute—

Former school for the daughters of the nobility, occupied by the Soviet when it moved from the Tauride Palace.

Tauride Palace—

Palace in Petrograd in the right wing of which the Duma met. The Soviet was formed and held its meetings during the first months of the revolution in the left wing of the same palace.

Tsarskoe Selo—

A town near Petrograd where one of the tzar's palaces was located.

Vyborg—

The principal industrial district of Petrograd.

Winter Palace—

The tzar's official residence in Petrograd.

A BRIEF GLOSSARY OF UNFAMILIAR TERMS
OR TERMS USED THROUGHOUT THIS
BOOK IN A SPECIAL SENSE

Ataman—. *Elected chief of the Cossacks.*

Blanquism— *A theory of insurrection by a select clique of conspirators, usually contrasted to the Marxian conception of mass insurrection. The name is taken from Louis Auguste Blanqui, French revolutionist, 1805–1881.*

Bonapartism— *In the Marxian sense: a transitional government based on military force during a period when class rule is not secure.*

bourgeoisie— *Used in feudal times to designate city people as opposed to those who lived in the country, this word came to mean the representatives of capital as opposed to the land-owning nobility and to wage labor. Where the land-owning nobility ceases to play a separate class role, the word often means much the same thing as "propertied classes."*

petty bourgeoisie— *Small proprietors, peasants, artisans, and tradesmen—people, broadly speaking, who employ labor but also labor themselves.*

camarilla— *A company of advisers, a clique—the author's name for that small group surrounding the tzar and tzarina and Rasputin who ruled Russia just before the revolution.*

commissar— *Commissioner. In the central government equivalent to minister; but the name was applied also to the representatives of the government in the provinces who replaced the*

447

tzarist governors, and to those special representatives in the various units of the army—"Commissar of the Western Front," "Commissar of General Headquarters," etc.

communal land— *Land owned in common by the peasants of a village.*

The Commune— *The revolutionary regime established by the proletarian uprising in Paris in 1871, when the power was seized and held for seventy-two days.*

compradors— *Native agents of foreign business concerns in China.*

Constituent Assembly— *The assembly elected by universal suffrage which, it was promised, should determine the permanent constitution of the Russian state.*

Convention— *Revolutionary government of France elected by universal suffrage to replace the Legislative Assembly. The Convention lasted from 1792 to 1795, when it was overthrown by the Directory.*

cooperatives— *Consumers' cooperative societies founded by liberals and moderate socialists throughout Russia.*

Cossacks— *Cavalry soldiers who formed a caste and almost a nationality in tzarist Russia, since they enjoyed special privileges (exemption from taxes and land allotments) in return for obligatory military service, and since the land allotments were consigned to special territories.*

dumas— *Municipal elective governing bodies.*

The Duma— *The Russian Parliament, limited in power and based upon a greatly restricted suffrage.*

epigones— *Disciples who corrupt the doctrines of their*

teacher—applied by the author to the present leaders, historians, and theoreticians of the Bolshevik party in Russia.

Frondeurs— *Members of the Fronde, a faction of the French nobility who opposed the government during the minority of Louis XIV, and made war on the Court party. Also a general term for an opposition arising within the ruling nobility, and sometimes also for an opposition arising out of mere "contrariness."*

Georgian— *A native of Georgia, a province in the south-eastern part of European Russia.*

Girondists— *Members of the Gironde, a party in the French Revolution, which expressed the interests of the big bourgeoisie of southern and western France (most of its leaders coming from the Gironde province). They wanted to overthrow the old regime which stood in the way of economic development, but feared the city poor and the peasant masses who could alone overthrow it, and therefore perpetually wavered between the revolution and the counter-revolution, finally going over to the latter.*

Hansa— *The Hanseatic League of northern German commercial cities during the Middle Ages.*

Izvestia— *"The News," official organ of the Soviet. Its full title was "The News of the Soviet."*

Jacobins— *Left wing of the French Convention, composed of petty bourgeois and worker delegates. The Jacobins overthrew the Girondists in 1792-93 and ruled supreme until the execution of the Jacobin leader, Robespierre, in July, 1794.*

Jacquerie— *Name given to a revolt of the French peasants*

in 1358 and since applied to any spontaneous armed peasant uprising.

Junkers——   *Students of the officers' schools.*

kulak——   *"Fist"—nickname for a wealthy peasant.*

Kuomintang——   *Chinese bourgeois nationalist party, led by Chiang Kai-shek.*

Legislative Assembly——   *A predominately monarchist and big bourgeois congress created by the French National Assembly in October, 1791. The Legislative Assembly was forced to dissolve in favor of the revolutionary Convention in 1792.*

mouzhik——   *Nickname for the Russian peasant in general.*

National Assembly——   *The first representative body of the French Revolution. Composed of the delegates to the States General, who were elected by classes, the National Assembly ruled France from 1789 to 1791, when it was superseded by the Legislative Assembly.*

palace revolution——   *Deposition and, if necessary, assassination, of a reigning monarch by members and associates of the court.*

political strike——   *A strike in which workers have a political objective—frequently a protest against some government policy.*

pogrom——   *Raid on and massacre of the Jewish population, and on rare occasions of other minorities.*

Pravda——   *"The truth"—official newspaper of the Bolshevik party, first published in 1912.*

Rada——   *The Ukrainian national congress.*

Seim——   *The Finnish national congress.*

soviet——   *The Russian word for council. It is used in this translation only to designate the councils of workers' and soldiers' (and later also peas-*

ants') deputies. In other cases the Russian word "soviet" is translated "council."

Holy Synod— *The highest governing body of the Greek Orthodox church in Russia.*

Thermidor— *On the 9th of Thermidor (July 27), 1794, Robespierre was deposed and executed, and the revolutionary power came into the hands of opportunists under whom it gradually passed over to the reaction.*

verst— *A Russian measure of distance, about two-thirds of a mile.*

Vikzhel— *Abbreviated name for the Russian Railroad Workers' Union.*

zemstvo— *Provincial and county council, elected on the basis of a franchise limited by a rather high property qualification, and having only economic and cultural functions.*

A LIST OF PARTIES AND POLITICAL GROUPS

ANARCHISTS—

People who thought that the co-operative commonwealth could be introduced by abolishing the political state.

BLACK HUNDREDS—

Popular name for the Union of the Russian People—a league of the most reactionary monarchists and nationalists who employed methods of criminal terror against the revolutionaries and were the chief instigators of pogroms.

BOLSHEVIKS—

Revolutionary Marxist party, who believed that the working class should unite with the poor peasants, taking the lead in a struggle against all bourgeois society, not only for the overthrow of tzarism, but for the inauguration of a labor republic and a socialist state.

THE BUND—

An organization of Russian Jewish workers, led by Lieber, Menshevik in policy.

THE COMPROMISERS—

General name for the leaders of the Menshevik and Social Revolutionary parties in the Soviet, who, although professing socialist principles, compromised with the Kadets upon essential points, voluntarily handing over the power to them.

DEFENSISTS—

Those who believed in prosecuting

the war as a war in defense of the fatherland.

DEKABRISTS—

Participants in the unsuccessful uprising against the tzar Alexander I in December (Dekabr), 1825.

KADETS—

Popular name for the Constitutional Democrats (K.D.'s)—subsequently also called Party of the People's Freedom—the great liberal party favoring a constitutional monarchy or even ultimately a republic, the party of the progressive landlords, middle bourgeoisie and bourgeois intelligentsia, headed by Miliukov, a professor of history.

LEFT MENSHEVIKS—

Extreme left wing of the Mensheviks, led by Larin, joined the Bolsheviks in July.

LEFT SOCIAL REVOLUTIONARIES—

Left wing of the Social Revolutionary party. As a separate party they participated for a brief time in the government set up by the Bolsheviks, but a few months after the October Revolution were organizing anti-Bolshevik uprisings.

MAXIMALISTS—

An extremist tendency which split off from the Social Revolutionaries in the Revolution of 1905.

MENSHEVIKS—

Moderate socialist party claiming allegiance to Karl Marx, but believing that the working class must combine with the liberal bourgeoisie to overthrow tzarism and establish a democratic republic.

454

MENSHEVIK-INTERNATIONALISTS—A group of left Mensheviks led by Martov, closely associated with Maxim Gorky's radical socialist paper *Novaia Zhizn* and on many issues friendly to the Bolsheviks.

MEZHRAYONTZI—The so-called Inter-City Group, an organization of about 4000 workers and revolutionists, including Trotsky, Joffé, Uritsky, Riazanov, Manuilsky, Lunacharsky, etc., which fused with the Bolsheviks at the July Congress.

NARODNIKS—General name for those revolutionists with socialist ideals who, not knowing or accepting the Marxian theory, looked to the peasants rather than the working class to take the lead in overthrowing tzarism and transforming Russia. The name (from *narod*, meaning people) includes the Terrorists who hoped to destroy tzarism and rouse the peasants by the "propaganda of the deed," as well as the mildest of evangelical socialists who hoped to transform Russia by "going to the people.

OCTOBRISTS—A party named for its support of the imperial Manifesto of October, 1905, establishing a Duma—monarchist and imperialist, the party of the big commercial, industrial and land-owning bourgeoisie, headed by Guchkov, a Moscow capitalist.

PROGRESSIVE BLOC—

An alliance of most of the deputies in the Duma during the war, striving for a strong government.

THE REACTION—

The old churchly, tzarist, and aristocratic landlord opposition to democratic progress even of the kind represented by the Kadet party.

SECOND INTERNATIONAL—

Founded in 1889, the Second International embraced all the working class parties. After its political failure during the war, the Third (Communist) International was formed by the left wing of the Second International, in 1919. Both Internationals exist today.

SOCIAL DEMOCRATS—

Party based upon the theories of Karl Marx, which were translated into Russian during the last two decades of the 19th century by Plekhanov. They looked to the development of industrial capitalism and the creation of a revolutionary working class for the overthrow of tzarism and the transformation of Russia into a socialist state. The party split in 1903 into the Mensheviks (minority men) and Bolsheviks (majority men).

SOCIAL PATRIOTS—

Socialists who abandoned the principle of internationalism and other revolutionary principles in the interest of war-time patriotism.

SOCIAL REVOLUTIONARIES—   Peasant socialist party, formed at the beginning of the century from a fusion of several tendencies of the Narodniks. Representing the wavering interests of the small peasant proprietor in the revolution, this party soon split into a group of Left Social Revolutionaries, anarchist in their leanings but participating for a time in the Bolshevik government, and the Right Social Revolutionaries who supported Kerensky.

TRUDOVIKS—   A party composed of cautious Narodnik intellectuals who defended the peasants as against the landlords, but did not venture too far to the left of the Kadets—the party to which Kerensky belonged when in the Duma.

ZIMMERWALDISTS—   Socialists loyal to the principle of internationalism during the war—so named for their adherence to the program of the International Socialist Congress held in Zimmerwald, Switzerland, in 1915.

INDEX *

(Roman numbers I, II, and III are used to indicate Volumes I, II, and III of the History.)

* The indexes at the end of Volumes I, II, and III are by John W. Gassner.

459

Durnovo, I: 30, 441, 456, II: 7, 10, 220.
Dutov, I: 447, II: 208, 225.
"Duty to the Free Fatherland," II: 258.
Dvortsovy bridge, III: 220, 224, 230, 242, 244, (Quay) 256.
Dybenko, II: 54, 56, 138, II: 95, 96, 135, 196, 335.
Dyelo Naroda, II: 128, III: 80.
Dzerzhinsky, I: 138, 145, 327, 328, II: 263, III: 155, 209, 210, 221, 368, 369, 370, 371.

Eastman, Max, II: xv.
Ebert, Friedrich, I: 229, II: 200, III: 4.
Economic Interpretation of Middle Ages, II: 66-67; of 1848 French Revolution, I: 67.
Efimov, I: 398, II: 17.
Efrain, II: 110.
Efremov, II: 344.
Eight Hour Day, I: 240, 241, 242, 243, 244, 314, 357, 358, 420.
Ekaterinburg, in "July Days," II: 71.
Ekaterininsky Canal, III: 274.
Ekaterinoslav, February Revolution, I: 138.
Electrification, III: 399.
Eliava, I: 302.
Eltsin, V., II: 292.
Ems Despatch, I: 346.
Engelhardt, Colonel, I: 182.
Engels, Frederick, I: 213, 272, 275, II: 156, III: 126, 405; criticism of barricade technique, III: 170-171.
Engineering School, III: 194.
England, I: 5, 20, 49, 99, 292, III: 36, 52-53; Puritan revolution, I: 12, 14, 98, 208.
English military mission, II: 217 (supports Kornilov).
Entente, II: 3, 5, 113, 119, 120, 122-123, 344; III: 336; liberals' loyalty to, I: 201-202, 272, 279, 338, 346, 349, 373, 439; refuses visas to revolutionists, I: 292, 293; supports counter revolution, I: 460, II: 39, 205, 219, 341; praised by Kerensky, II: 162; service of compromisers to, III: 344.
Epigones and epigone historians, III: 128, 156, 295, 353-354, 355, 357, 358, 364, 372, 377, 381, 398, 401; mistakes in nationalistic policy, III: 56.
Ermolenko, II: 86, 87, 104, 105, 107, 112.
Espionage, German, II: 107.
Essays on the History of the October Revolution, I: xxii, 301n.
Esthonians, III: 40, 54-55.
Europeanization of Russia, I: 8.
Evert, Adjutant-General, I: 87.

Evreinov, II: 256.

Executive Committee of Peasants' Deputies. (*See* Peasants' Executive Committee.)

Executive Committee of Soviet, I: 158, 216, 232, 244, 265, 291, II: 13, 25, 40, 48, 54, III: 95, 96, 117; compromisism, I: 160, 161, 166, 177, 202, 219, 235, 236, 237-238, 239-240, 241, 242, 246, 249, 276, 277, 278-279, 280, 282, 344, 345-346, 348, 350, 351, 352, 357, 381, 390, 423, 424, 441; II: 3, 7, 8, 11, 17, 20, 21, 28, 43, 45, 51, 67, 68, 113, 117, 118, 124, 125, 296, III: 206, 228-229; control by, I: 159, 165; conditions to Provisional Government, I: 184-185; character, I: 216-218, 234; prevents escape of Nicholas II, I: 236; foils Kornilov, I: 347-348 (*See* Kornilov's insurrection); Resolutions of April 21st, I: 349, 360; create commissars, I: 281-282; economic proposals, I: 415-416; increase and decline of power, II: 66, 68, 124, 293, 321-322, 349; supports offensive, II: 8, 9, 10 (*See* Offensive), III: 68-69; combats July demonstration, II: 23-24, 33, 48-49, 62, 65; hostility to Bolsheviks, II: 56, 59, 85, 93-94, 147, 302; conflicts with Kerensky, II: 194, 202, 341; new Committee, II: 344; opposes Soviet Congress, III: 79-82, 83; unpopularity, III: 81, 84, 98, 104.

Executive Committees, joint session of, II: 26, 27, 220, 221, 233, 279, III: 97, 227-228.

Factories, I: 416-417.

Factory and shop committees, I: 414, 422, 438, 443, II: 314, 315, III: 77-78, 84, 186.

Fascism, III: 176.

February Days. (*See* February Revolution.)

February régime, character of, II: 67, 115, 183, 216, III: 47.

February Revolution, I: 12, 14, 42, II: 18, 74, 82, 84; mutinies and fraternization with workers, I: 79, 83-86, 116, 124, 125, 127, III: 292; strikes and martial law, I: 79-80; retreat of General Ivanov, I: 85; Provisional Government established, 86, 157, 159-160; abdication of Nicholas II, I: 86-88; the "Five Days," I: 101-135; lack of leadership (spontaneous character), I: 118, 142-144, 152, III: 168, 279; in Moscow, I: 137-138; establishment of soviets, I: 158; paradox, I: 168-171; character, I: 315-316; failure and exhaustion, I: 458, 461, II: 260, III: 384; nationalism in, III: 45, 50.

Feit, Doctor, III: 251.

Feodorchenko, I: 21.

Feodorov, I: 343, III: 99.

Fersen, Count, II: 109-110.

Figner, Vera, I: 400.

Filipovsky, I: 232, 348.

Filonenko, I: 257, II: 124, 145, 165, 196, 214, 278, 284, 323.

October Revolution—*Continued*
276-301, 344-349, 375; pretence at self-defense, III: 207-208, 229;
military plan, III: 218-219, 223-225; causes of, III: 232, description of, III: 236-238, 240-275; criticism of Trotsky's view of the,
III: 353; rôle of garrison in, 288-289, 290, 353-354; bureaucratic
legend of, III: 363-364; leadership in, III: 281-285, 291-292, 369.
(*See* Bolsheviks.) (*See* Winter Palace, siege and capture.)
Octobrists, I: 25, 31, 369, II: 102.
Odintsov, III: 7.
Offensive, Provisional Government's, I: 362, 363, 367, 375, 376, 377,
378-380, 381-382, 383-384, 386-387, 442, II: 6, 8-9, 69, III: 345;
sanctioned by soviet congress, I: 438; collapse of, II: 73-74, 121-
122, 162; undermines Kerensky, II: 141-142; disintegration of, III:
70-72, 104-105.
Officers, I: 248, 249, 250, 252-253, 254, 257, 258, 259, 266, 277, II:
224, 258; counter-revolutionary efforts, I: 250-251, 255, 281-282,
346, 374, 376, 383, 432, III: 193, 226, 242-243, 255, 260; con-
trolled by soldiers, I: 276-278; League of, II: 5, 120, 129, 130, 189,
190, 201, 204, 209, 216, 247, 248, 327; soldiers against, II: 234-
235.
Officer's Schools, III: 226, 242, 249. (*See* Junkers.)
O'Grady, I: 362.
Okhranniki. (*See* Secret political police.)
Old Believers, I: 8.
Old Parviainen factory workers, III: 93.
Olminsky, I: 321, 322, 323.
Olsufiev, Count, II: 133.
On Compromises, Lenin's, II: 318-319.
Opposition, Stalin's criticism of the, III: 57.
Oranienbaum, II: 10, 11, 32, 232, III: 102, 254.
Oranovsky, General, II: 234.
Order Number 1, I: 276, 277, 442, II: 103; Number 2, I: 277.
Ordzhonikidze, II: 314, III: 141.
Orekhov-Zuyev, demonstration in, II: 345-346.
Orel province, peasant movement in, III: 10, 13, 17, 24.
Orpheus, sailors of, II: 55, 56.
Ostrov, Vassilievsky, II: 252.
Ostrovsky county, peasant movement in, III: 23.
Outbreaks of the masses, II: 6-7, (*See* "July Days"; and July Demon-
stration).
Ozerov, Professor, II: 177.

Painlevé, I: 380.
Palace Revolution, I: 69-70, 71, (murder of Rasputin) 73-74.

Palace Square, III: 256.

Palchinsky, Minister of Trade & Industry, I: 416-417, II: 119, 230, III: 203, 250, 258, 263, 266, 291.

Pale, the, III: 54.

Paléologue, I: 23, 49, 57, 58, 62, 194, 336, 337, II: 6.

Pannekoek, III: 26.

Parchevsky, II: 34.

Parliamentarism, Soviet, III: 280, 347; Lenin's attitude, III: 119-130; German Socialists, III: 171.

Parsky, General, II: 185, 189.

Parties, rôle of, I: xix.

Parvus, II: 88, 98, III: 22.

Pascal, II: 111.

Paul, Tzar, I: 55.

Pavel, Alexandrovich, Grand Duke, II: 194.

Pavlovsky regiment, III: 205, 226, 227, 237.

Peace, III: 69-70; demand for separate, II: 9, 10, 286, III: 69, 71, 72-73; Manifesto of March 14, III: 325; Declaration, III: 324-325; Lenin on signing of, III: 324-325, 326, 327, 336, 340, 392-393.

Peasant Committee, III: 32.

Peasant Congress, (May, 1917), I: 398-400, 433; Executive Committee, I: 400-401, III: 26, 273, 312.

Peasantry, II: 155; proletarization of, I: 44-46, 47, 48; cooperatives, I: 46-47; effect of war, I: 48-49; organization in army, I: 170; betrayal of, I: 173; historical position, I: 317, 407; influence of soldier, I: 392; radicalism of, I: 396-397; seizure of the land, I: 391, 392, 401-402, 404-405, 408, 426; revolutionary rôle, II: xi; transfer of land to, II: 44; denounced by church, II: 134; indifference to Kornilov, II: 226-227; problem of, III: 332-333, 338-339, 382-383, 385, 402, 403, 422-423, 426; swing to Bolsheviks, III: 195, 282, 317-318, 365, 384; French, III: 3; monarchism among, III: 11; Ukranian, III: 45-46.

Penza province, peasant movement in, III: 9, 11, 22.

Pepelyaev, I: 430, 431, 441.

Peredolskaia, III: 246.

Pereverzev, I: 365, 399, 432, 456, II: 33, 90, 94, 101.

Permanent Conference of the Garrison. (See Garrison Conference.)

Permanent Revolution, theory of, III: 351, 383, 389, 391, 399, 425.

Persia, I: 16.

Pervozvanny, sailors of, II: 265.

Peshekhonov, Minister of Agriculture, I: 480, II: 119, 127, 332.

Pestkovsky, III: 221-222.

Petain, Marshal, I: 362, 380.

Peter I, I: 8, 56, 233.

Skorokhod factory, II: 32.

Skrypnik, I: 303.

Skvortzov, III: 141.

Skvortzov-Stepanov, III: 414.

Slava, warship, III: 62.

Slavophilism, I: 7, 463.

Slutsky, II: 262, 276.

Smidovich, I: 327.

Smilga, I: 443, III: 134, 135, 196, 223, 368.

Smirnov, II: 51, 343; factory, II: 345.

Smolensk province, peasant movement in, III: 23-24, 25; Bolsheviks in, III: 83.

Smolny, II: 292, 293, 295; Bolshevik headquarters, III: 65, 103, 106, 107, 118, 121, 187, 194, 202, 204, 205, 206, 207, 209, 212, 214, 219, 221, 222-223, 225, 226, 227, 230, 231, 242, 247, 248, 302, 303, 306, 320-322, 360.

Social Democracy, Russian, I: 222, 227, 246; German, I: 229, II: 80.

Social Democrat, III: 141.

Social Democrats, Russian, I: 143, 308; German, I: 214; criticism of Bolsheviks by, III: 169, 180.

Socialism, split in, I: 308 (*See* Zimmerwaldists; Zimmerwald left); future of, III: 348.

"Socialism in One Country," III: 374, 380-381; original Bolshevik view on, III: 380-419; 1926 Communist International on, III: 381, 391. (*See* Stalin on Trotsky and Trotskyism.)

Socialists sent to Russia by Allies, I: 336, 362, 363.

Social Revolutionaries, I: 47, 101, 145, III: 18, 19, 24, 31, 48, 80, 204, 206, 232, 330, 331; influence in Soviet, I: 167-168, 197, 251, 399, 405, 436; compromisism of, I: 172, 214, 225, 226, 230, 286, 345, 351, 359, 361, 369, 370, 392, 395, 397, 401; character, I: 222, 317, 320; split in party, I: 397, 398; left wing, I: 401; unpopularity, I: 317, 446; counter-revolutionary activity of, II: 6, 25, 54, 55, 65, 125, 153, 262, 277; disapprove of Kerensky, II: 139, 146-147; opposition to Kornilov, II: 152; increase and decline of power, II: 32, 252-253, 266, 281, 282, 283, 287, 288, 289, 294, 297; split among, II: 289-290; peasants lose confidence in, III: 19, 24, 26, 282; terrorism, III: 172; decline, III: 303, 304.

Society for Slavic Reciprocity, I: 153.

Sokolnikov, II: 229, III: 155, 163, 388.

Sokolov, Boris, I: 189, 203, II: 255, III: 180, 377.

Soldiers. (*See* Army.)

Soldiers, revolutionary activities, II: 227-228, III: 12, 13, 64, 91, 103, 104, 147, 182, 196, 214, 220-221, 225-226, 315-316, 334; swing toward left, II: 8-15, 58, 261, 263, 278, 279-280, 282-283, 300; demand peace, II: 9, 10, 286; demonstration in July, 15-23, 34

A representative selection

OF SIMON AND SCHUSTER PUBLICATIONS

TWELVE AGAINST THE GODS *by* WILLIAM BOLITHO

MEN OF ART *and* MODERN ART *by* THOMAS CRAVEN

THE LIFE OF OUR LORD *by* CHARLES DICKENS

THE ART OF THINKING *by* ABBÉ ERNEST DIMNET

THE STORY OF PHILOSOPHY *by* WILL DURANT

GOD'S ANGRY MAN *by* LEONARD EHRLICH

LITTLE MAN, WHAT NOW? *by* HANS FALLADA

GEORGE GERSHWIN SONG BOOK *by* GEORGE GERSHWIN

BERNARD SHAW *by* FRANK HARRIS

HARD LINES, FREE WHEELING AND HAPPY DAYS *by* OGDEN NASH

NIJINSKY *by* ROMOLA NIJINSKY

MORE POWER TO YOU! *and* THE PSYCHOLOGY OF
HAPPINESS *by* WALTER B. PITKIN

WOLF SOLENT *and* OTHER NOVELS *by* JOHN COWPER POWYS

A PHILOSOPHY OF SOLITUDE *by* JOHN COWPER POWYS

BAMBI, A LIFE IN THE WOODS *by* FELIX SALTEN

THE NOVELS *of* ARTHUR SCHNITZLER

THE UNPOSSESSED *by* TESS SLESINGER

THE FIRST WORLD WAR, A PHOTOGRAPHIC HISTORY
by LAURENCE STALLINGS

LIVING PHILOSOPHIES (SYMPOSIUM) *by* ALBERT EINSTEIN,
WILLIAM RALPH INGE, JAMES TRUSLOW ADAMS, ET AL

THE HISTORY OF THE RUSSIAN REVOLUTION *by* LEON TROTSKY

VAN LOON'S GEOGRAPHY *by* HENDRIK WILLEM VAN LOON

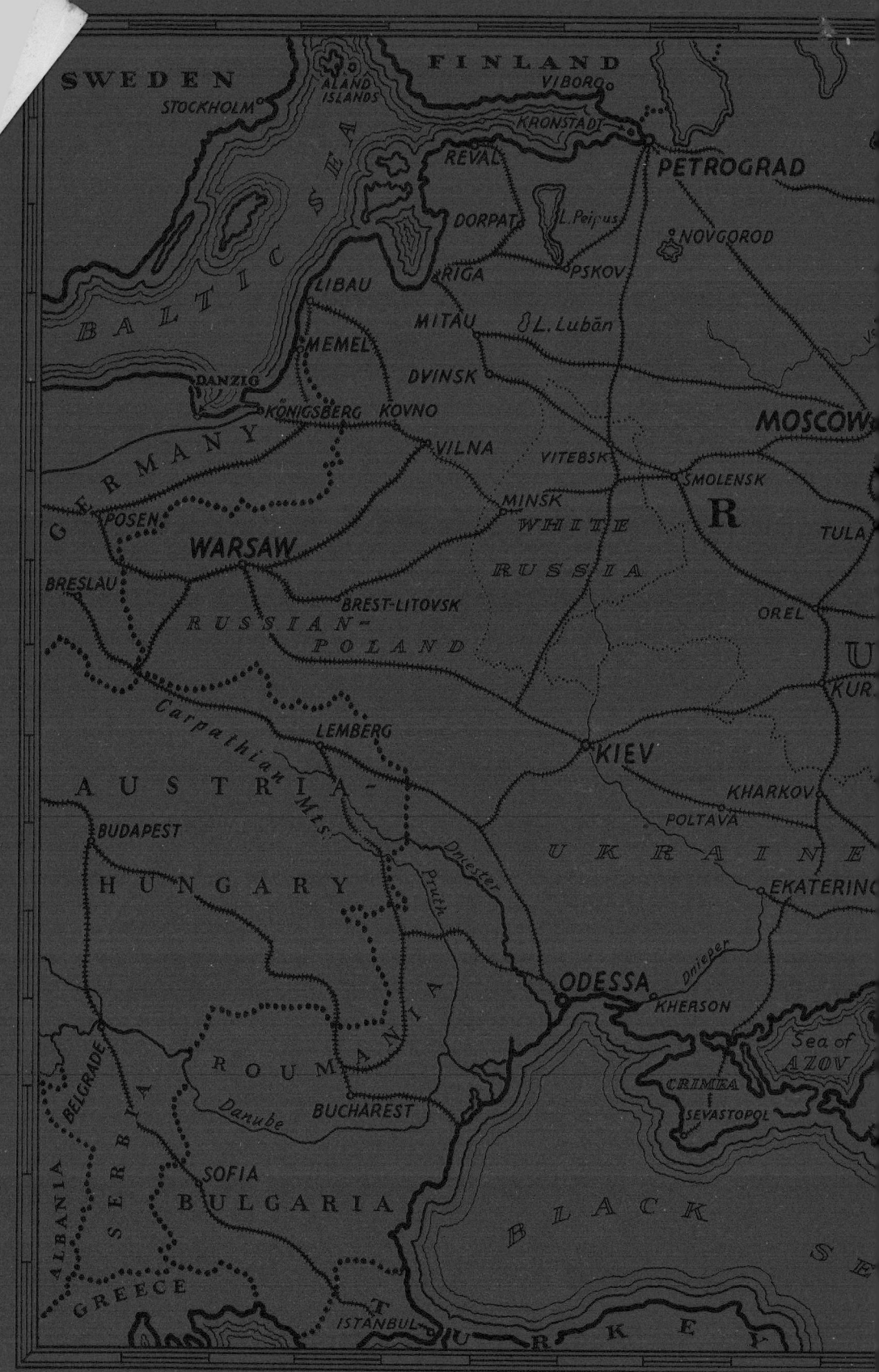